THE OXFORD HANDBOOK OF

CYBERPSYCHOLOGY

T0200120

Alison Attrill-Smith is currently one of the co-ordinators of the Cyberpsychology Research Group, Wolverhampton University, UK. Her expertise lies in understanding online behavior, with an emphasis on researching how we create different versions of our selves online and the role that these self-creations might play in perpetrating online criminal behaviors. Alison was one of the original members of the steering group that led the creation of the British Psychological Society's Cyberpsychology Section, remains a reviewer for many peer-reviewed journals, and has edited a number of books on Cyberpsychology.

Chris Fullwood is a Reader in Cyberpsychology in the Psychology Department at the University of Wolverhampton, UK, where he co-ordinates the CRUW Cyberpsychology Research group. As well as helping to create one of the first masters programmes in Cyberpsychology in the world, he was fundamental in developing the British Psychological Society's Cyberpsychology section, for which he is currently on the committee. His research primarily focuses on self-presentation and identity online, but he also has interests in the use of digital tools (particularly VR) for improving psychological health.

Melanie Keep is a Senior Lecturer in Cyberpsychology and eHealth at University of Sydney, Australia. She has a keen interest in disentangling the psychological processes underpinning online communication, and its impact on health and well-being. Melanie co-ordinates a number of research projects on the bi-directional relationship between digital technologies and health, and leads several eHealth education initiatives.

Daria J. Kuss is a Chartered Psychologist, Chartered Scientist, and Associate Professor in Psychology, Nottingham Trent University, UK. She developed the MSc Cyberpsychology and leads the Cyberpsychology Research Group at NTU. She has published prolifically in peer-reviewed journals and books, and her publications include over 90 peer-reviewed journal articles, three authored books, and over 100 national and international conference presentations, including regular keynote talks. She has an international reputation as an Internet addiction expert.

THE OXFORD HANDBOOK OF

CYBERPSYCHOLOGY

Edited by
ALISON ATTRILL-SMITH,
CHRIS FULLWOOD,
MELANIE KEEP,
and
DARIA J. KUSS

OXFORD
UNIVERSITY PRESS

Great Clarendon Street, Oxford, OX2 6DP,
United Kingdom

Oxford University Press is a department of the University of Oxford.
It furthers the University's objective of excellence in research, scholarship,
and education by publishing worldwide. Oxford is a registered trade mark of
Oxford University Press in the UK and in certain other countries

© Oxford University Press 2019

The moral rights of the authors have been asserted

First published 2019
First published in paperback 2020

Published in the United States of America by Oxford University Press
198 Madison Avenue, New York, NY 10016, United States of America

British Library Cataloguing in Publication Data
Data available

Library of Congress Cataloging in Publication Data
Data available

ISBN 978–0–19–881274–6 (Hbk.)
ISBN 978–0–19–289417–5 (Pbk.)

Acknowledgments

The editors would like to thank all of the authors for their invaluable contributions to this volume. Without them, we would not have such an encompassing volume of the most up-to-date research in the area of cyberpsychology.

Alison would like to thank all of her colleagues who have worked on this volume. She would also like to thank her favorite big person, not-so-little anymore favorite small person and dog for listening to her ramblings and for their ever-present ongoing support.

Chris would like to thank his colleagues and co-authors who have contributed to this volume. I would like to dedicate this book to Dr W., my favorite veterinary surgeon, dancer and platform gamer, but most importantly my best friend. Thank you for helping me to find the 'real' me. I owe you everything.

Melanie also sends a HUGE thank you to her colleagues and co-authors, particularly her co-editors. You have taught me more than you know, and about more than you know. This volume is dedicated to RJK for that moment in New York when your patience and support reoriented my world.

Daria would like to thank everyone involved in this book, her co-editors, authors, and co-authors—you've made it happen! I'd like to dedicate this book to my LB, RBK—thank you for always being there!

TABLE OF CONTENTS

PART III INTERACTION AND INTERACTIVITY

PART IV GROUPS AND COMMUNITIES

PART V SOCIAL MEDIA

PART VI HEALTH AND TECHNOLOGY

PART VII GAMING

PART VIII CYBERCRIME AND CYBERSECURITY

LIST OF CONTRIBUTORS

Sun Joo (Grace) Ahn, University of Georgia, USA

Yair Amichai-Hamburger, Interdisciplinary Center in Herzliya, Israel

Krestina L. Amon, The University of Sydney, Australia

Tiffani Apps, University of Wollongong, Australia

Alison Attrill-Smith, University of Wolverhampton, UK

Maria Bada, University of Oxford, UK

Karley Beckman, University of Wollongong, Australia

Sue Bennett, University of Wollongong, Australia

David P. Brandon, University of Illinois at Urbana-Champaign, USA

Pam Briggs, Northumbria University, UK

Michelle Colder Carras, Radboud University, Nijmegen, Netherlands

Sue Caton, Manchester Metropolitan University, UK

Darren D. Chadwick, University of Wolverhampton, UK

Melanie Chapman, Manchester Metropolitan University, UK

Jenna L. Clark, Duke University, USA

Lindy Clemson, The University of Sydney, Australia

Linda Corrin, Swinburne University of Technology, Australia

Neil S. Coulson, University of Nottingham, UK

Zsolt Demetrovics, Institute of Psychology, Eötvös Loránd University, Hungary

Cody Devyn Weeks, California State University, USA

Michelle Drouin, Department of Psychology, Indiana University-Purdue University, Fort Wayne, USA

Shir Etgar, The Open University of Israel, Israel

Chris Fullwood, University of Wolverhampton, UK

Melanie C. Green, University at Buffalo, USA

Mark D. Griffiths, Nottingham Trent University, UK

Andrea B. Hollingshead, University of Southern California, USA

Thomas J. Holt, Michigan State University, USA

Anna Janssen, The University of Sydney, Australia

Elaine Kasket, Independent Researcher, UK

Linda K. Kaye, Edge Hill University, UK

Melanie Keep, The University of Sydney, Australia

Nenagh Kemp, University of Tasmania, Australia

Young Ji Kim, University of California Santa Barbara, USA

ORSOLYA Király, Eötvös Loránd University, Hungary

Grainne H. Kirwan, Dun Laoghaire Institute of Art, Design, and Technology, Ireland

Rachel Kowert, Independent Scholar, Canada

John H. Krantz, Hanover College, USA

Daria J. Kuss, Nottingham Trent University, UK

Jin Ree Lee, Michigan State University, USA

Joanne Lloyd, University of Wolverhampton, UK

Meryl Lovarini, The University of Sydney, Australia

Jessica McCain, University of Georgia, USA

Brandon T. McDaniel, Illinois State University, USA

Kyle Morrison, University of Georgia, USA

Jason R. C. Nurse, School of Computing, University of Kent, UK

Bradley M. Okdie, The Ohio State University at Newark, USA

Kate O'Loughlin, The University of Sydney, Australia

Lisa J. Orchard, University of Wolverhampton, UK

Angelica B. Ortiz de Gortari, University of Liège, Belgium

Halley Pontes, Nottingham Trent University, UK

Maša Popovac, The University of Buckingham, UK

Thorsten Quandt, University of Münster, Germany

Sally Quinn, University of York, UK

Daniel M. Rempala, Department of Psychology, The University of Hawaii at Manoa, USA

Heyla Selim, University of Sussex, UK/King Saud University, Saudi Arabia

Elizabeth Sillence, Northumbria University, UK

Chris Stiff, Keele University, UK

Kaveri Subrahmanyam, California State University, USA

Bei Yan, University of Southern California, USA

Garry Young, The University of Melbourne, Australia

VOLUME INTRODUCTION

WELCOME to this text on cyberpsychology, the discipline of understanding the psychological processes related to, and underlying, all aspects and features of technologically interconnected human behavior. A truly international book, it is intended as an introduction to many aspects of online behavior that have received theoretical interest over the last twenty years. With its handbook approach, it also outlines current psychological understanding of many newer forms of behavior unique to the Internet. It is important to note that whilst most of the chapters discuss the Internet in a global manner, people use diverse technological devices, ranging from mobile phones (or cell phones if you are not in the UK), to gaming consoles and smart TVs. Therefore, in your reading of this text, bear in mind that whilst we focus on the Internet, human behavior occurs through the interaction of many technologies. You might, at this stage, wonder what the difference is between human computer interaction and cyberpsychology. This book focuses on the latter, namely on the psychology of how people behave in a technologically connected environment. It is important to remain focused on the psychological processes here; from cognition to individual differences, and from developmental features of human behavior to social psychological factors, there are an array of psychological factors that play a role in human behavior, both online and offline. Cyberpsychology, whilst often comparing the two, focuses on understanding online, or digital, behavior, both at the individual and group levels. Such behaviors span the development, maintenance and dissolution of all types of human relationships, to how online activities negatively impact on financial and socioeconomic standing (e.g., gambling and compulsive online shopping behaviors), and from providing support in times of need (e.g., social support groups and specialized forums) to capitalizing on a person's weaknesses to negatively impact on their psychological and physical well-being (e.g., pro-suicide websites). Imagine any facet of human behavior that can be carried out online, and you will likely find a section in this book that covers current thinking and theorizing on that online behavior.

To this end, the Internet most often referred to throughout this text is the infrastructure of connectivity that brings all of these technologies together worldwide. It is the cable network to which we all connect in order to communicate with millions of other computers worldwide. It is not the World Wide Web as we have come to refer to it. The World Wide Web (WWW) is the tool that we use to access information hosted via the Internet. That information is encoded and transmitted via the Internet using codes and languages specifically designed to transmit that information. In order to search the

WWW, you use browsers, such as Google Chrome or Firefox. If you had to hazard a guess as to how many websites there now are worldwide, we wonder how close to the actual figure you would come? Maybe you could use an Internet browser to find the answer to this. While doing so, you might wonder why we are using the upper-case I for the Internet and not writing internet with a lower-case i. The former is the Internet as you have come to know it, whilst a small i for internet denotes a localized network, to which only a limited number of people have access. These are not the focus of this book. We focus on features of human behavior across the WWW. Another feature of the Internet is that it hosts email and other interconnected communications that are based on simple mail transfer protocols (SMTP), such as instant messaging and other file transfer protocols. Now that the technology is out of the way, let's move on to explaining the focus of each of the book sections.

Part I: Introduction and Foundations (edited by Dr Alison Attrill-Smith)

The introductory chapters of this book focus on setting the scene to aid readers' understanding of the psychology of online behavior presented in Parts II–VIII of the book. We begin with a chapter by Professor John Krantz of Hanover College in the USA. John's knowledge of psychology research methods and analyses is second to none, and in this chapter he outlines the main scientific approach to studying online behavior. He considers the different types of data collection that can be applied to cyberpsychology research as well as their advantages and limitations. In doing so, he introduces a number of key terms and ethical considerations that are essential to understanding reports of online behavior that you will come across in most of the remaining book chapters.

Another fundamental component of online behavior is that in order to achieve any task online, a person needs to create an online self. This is the focus of the second chapter in this section, presented by Dr Alison Attrill-Smith of the Cyberpsychology Research Group at the University of Wolverhampton, UK. This chapter explores how different versions of a person's self are created online to achieve diverse goals in the heterogeneous Internet landscape, which consists of lots of different types of websites (e.g., dating, social media, and banking websites). Consideration is given to whether people create different selves to those presented in everyday offline lives and how these are adapted to online behavior to compensate for the absence of the social cues pivotal to offline interactions.

Underlying these self-creations are personality factors and individual differences. The second two chapters of this section therefore revolve around these. In the first, Dr Chris Fullwood, also of the Cyberpsychology Research Group at the University of Wolverhampton, UK, explores how people manage others' impressions of them online through their online self-presentations. Chris considers different theoretical approaches to understanding online self-presentation, and the role of motivations that drive how people are afforded the freedom to experiment with different versions of their self online.

Subsequently, Professor Yair Amichai-Hamburger, the Director of the Research Center for Internet Psychology at the Sammy Ofer School of Communications at the Interdisciplinary Center in Herzliya, Israel, and Dr Shir Etgar, The Research Center for Innovation in Learning Technologies, The Open University of Israel, look at the role of personality in more detail in creating an individually unique psychological environment online. Specifically, Yair and Shir focus on the role of introversion and extroversion as a key dimension underlying online behavior, in both anonymous and identified online environments.

Part II: Technology Across the Lifespan (edited by Dr Melanie Keep)

The chapters in this section build on the foundations established in Part I to consider the role of digital technologies and the Internet across the lifespan. Our current time in history also affords us the opportunity to consider the impact of the Internet and digital tools on how we develop throughout our own lives. This is particularly so in the case of the first chapter on adolescent risk-taking. Professor Kaveri Subrahmanyam, Associate Director of the Children's Digital Media Center@LA and Dr Cody Weeks from California State University, USA, explore how exposure to online risky behaviors, for instance alcohol or drug use, or sexually explicit content, influence the decision to engage in offline risk-taking. The authors also consider how theories of human behavior have led researchers to use technology to reduce adolescent risk-taking.

Outside of our personal lives, the Internet has also shaped our education system. In the second chapter of Part II, Dr Linda Corrin from Swinburne University of Technology, Australia, and her co-authors Dr Tiffani Apps, Dr Karley Beckman, and Professor Sue Bennett from the University of Wollongong, Australia, debunk the myth of the "digital native", that is, that young people who have grown up with digital technology are proficient users of this technology. The authors discuss the implications of this assumption on Higher Education, and explore how university students' experiences of technology are shaped by childhood and adolescence.

From young adulthood, many of us develop romantic relationships and some go onto becoming parents against the backdrop of smartphones, social media, and constant connectivity. Associate Professor Michelle Drouin, leading researcher in relationships and technology at Indiana University-Purdue University, Fort Wayne, USA, and her co-author Dr Brandon T. McDaniel of Illinois State University, Normal, USA, discuss the impact of digital technologies on couple and family relationships, specifically the research on technoference—the interruptions of social interactions by the use of technology. The chapter considers psychological theories of couple relationships and parenting, as well as research on relationship satisfaction and co-parenting quality.

As we mature, and enter into different social, psychological, and biological life stages, technology can be adapted to meet our changing needs. In the final chapter of this section, Dr Meryl Lovarni, Associate Professor Kate O'Loughlin, and Professor Lindy Clemson from the University of Sydney, Australia, explore how the Internet and digital technologies can be used to help us remain independent, socially connected, and healthy as we age. They discuss the role of technology in perpetuating stereotypes of aging, how older adults use technology, evidence for the use of technology for maintaining well-being, and the challenges with implementing systemic changes to policy and infrastructure to enable this.

PART III: INTERACTION AND INTERACTIVITY (EDITED BY DR CHRIS FULLWOOD)

The chapters in this section focus on the manner in which individuals communicate, interact, and develop relationships with others via various forms of digital technology, as well as the consequences to the individual for interacting in an increasingly digital world. The first chapter in this section, authored by Dr Nenagh Kemp, University of Tasmania, Australia, considers the written language of the digital world and how this may be distinct from other more traditional forms of written communication. Within this chapter, Nenagh discusses the different reasons why many individuals may adopt a more casual and abbreviated form of writing, referred to as textese, while online and in their text messages. In addition to providing illustrative examples of various forms of textese, Nenagh evaluates the different methodological approaches which have been used by researchers to collect data from participants who use textese in their communications. Consideration is given to the variety of different factors which have been associated with the amount and types of textese that individuals use. In addition, an important discussion centers on a much debated topic within this literature, namely whether or not using textese is impacting on the development of literacy skills in young people.

In the next chapter in this section, Dr Heyla Selim, University of Sussex, UK/King Saud University, Saudi Arabia, focuses on cultural considerations in online interactions. Within this chapter, Heyla draws on numerous established cultural theories and reflects on how these models might apply to interactions within the cyberspace. Heyla considers how culture might affect one's engagement with the online world, with a special focus on the self-presentation strategies of different cultural groups within social media sites. The chapter considers the important question of whether interacting in the online world is likely to lead to cultural convergence or indeed whether individuals retain aspects of their cultural identity in their online interactions.

Following on from this, Dr Joanne Lloyd, Dr Alison Attrill-Smith, and Dr Chris Fullwood, University of Wolverhampton's Cyberpsychology Research Group, CRUW, UK move on to talk about the development and maintenance of romantic relationships in the online world. Although some thought is given to the numerous ways in which people may begin and maintain romantic relationships online, the primary focus of the chapter is on the ways in which individuals can make use of online sites which have the specific purpose of connecting singles. Consideration is given to the reasons why online dating sites have surged in popularity, as well as the types of individuals who may be more inclined to use them and their motivations for joining these sites. In addition, a discussion is provided around the benefits and drawbacks of seeking love online.

The section concludes with a chapter on the social consequences of online interactions, authored by Dr Melanie C. Green, University of Buffalo, USA and Jenna L. Clark, Center for Advanced Hindsight at Duke University, USA. Whereas the previous three chapters in this section focus on how the introduction of new technology has altered the communication landscape, the concluding chapter considers the broader question of whether interacting in the online space may be thought of as generally harmful or helpful for social connectedness and well-being. Drawing on the Interpersonal Connection Behaviors Framework, the authors argue for the notion that the extent to which individuals may accrue positive outcomes from their online interactions is likely to be related to whether or not those specific interactions serve a relational purpose. Evidence for this assertion is provided through a consideration of research focusing on how online interactions may promote self-disclosure and provide important sources of social support. In addition, the authors provide examples where online interactions may lead to negative consequences, for instance where they arouse social comparison or lead to feelings of loneliness.

PART IV: GROUPS AND COMMUNITIES (EDITED BY DR MELANIE KEEP)

In this section, the social aspect of online interaction is further reinforced through consideration of online groups and communities, and the psychology of participation (or non-participation), the ways in which these communities can facilitate inclusion, and a re-conceptualization of what constitutes an online group or community. The focus shifts from Part III where we consider interactions of individuals and how they navigate the online world, to Part IV where we discuss group dynamics and the social nature of Internet use.

Professor Neil Coulson, leading researcher in online support groups from the University of Nottingham, UK, takes us through the nature and popularity of online support communities, the advantages and disadvantages of these groups, why people engage with online peer support, and the theoretical frameworks for understanding these interactions.

This sets the scene for Dr Darren Chadwick from the Cyberpsychology Research Group at the University of Wolverhampton, UK, and his co-authors Dr Melanie Chapman and Dr Sue Caton from Manchester Metropolitan University, UK. Their chapter focuses on how people with an intellectual disability use the Internet and the benefits of, and barriers to, this engagement with digital technologies. They consider the risks of online participation and the supports required for facilitating digital inclusion of people with an intellectual disability. This chapter shows that whether by choice, or through circumstances or situations beyond their control, some people are not active users of online communities.

Building from that, Dr Maša Popovac from the University of Buckingham, UK, and Dr Chris Fullwood in his third contribution to this handbook, explore the psychology of lurking, of viewing posts and others' contributions to forums, chat rooms, social media and the like, without participating. Their chapter considers the individual and situational factors that affect participation or lurking, and the impact of different levels of participation. Maša and Chris then go into a more detailed discussion of the psychology of lurking within the context of online support groups, and educational settings.

This section closes by taking a step back to reconsider our definitions of online groups and communities. Bei Yan from the University of Southern California, Dr Young Ji Kim from the University of California Santa Barbara, Professor Andrea Hollingshead also from the University of Southern California, and Dr David Brandon from the University of Illinois at Urbana-Champaign, USA, reconceptualize online groups as multidimensional networks that may or may not include a digital agent, such as a robot or algorithm, and that operates within and is influenced by a social context. This chapter challenges us to consider the dynamics of online groups in this new framework, and provides a detailed discussion of how such groups are currently operating within our workplaces and online lives.

Part V: Social Media (edited by Dr Chris Fullwood)

Social media sites like Facebook and Twitter are some of the real success stories of the World Wide Web, and have become incorporated into the everyday routines of the majority of Internet users. For this reason, it is important to not only give social media a special focus in this book, but to also understand how using these sites might impact on the individual and society in both positive and negative ways. The first chapter in this section, authored by Dr Lisa Orchard, University of Wolverhampton's Cyberpsychology Research Group, CRUW, UK , sets the context for the remaining chapters by addressing the question of who uses social media and why? The chapter is underpinned by Uses and Gratifications theory to explain the different motivations that users may have for joining and using various social media platforms. In attempting to understand what specific gratifications may be met by engagement with social media, Lisa discusses how our personalities may drive these specific motivations.

One of the most valued and widespread features of social media sites is their ability to allow users to upload, share, and document images of their life stories. In the next chapter in this section, Dr Melanie Keep, Anna Janssen, and Dr Krestina L. Amon, from the University of Sydney, Australia, consider why photo-sharing via social media sites has become such a popular feature of these sites. Concentrating on three specific social media sites (Facebook, Snapchat, and Instagram), the authors discuss how different personal characteristics, such as personality, are likely to affect the reasons why and the extent and types of images that people share on each site. The chapter concludes with a consideration of how sharing images via social media impacts on one's mental health.

Although we may think of social media sites as primarily serving the function of allowing individuals to build and maintain friendships and family connections, they may also be used to drive social change. In the third chapter in this section, Dr Chris Stiff, University of Keele, UK, focuses on the use of social media sites for cyberactivism. Within the chapter, Chris talks about how the idiosyncratic features of social media sites may be helpful in fostering cyberactivism. Chris draws on numerous models of offline collective action and considers how these might be applied to understanding activism in the online domain. A taxonomy of cyberactivism is introduced and evaluated in the context of how this may explain the antecedents and consequences of engaging in cyberactivism. Finally, the chapter concludes with a deliberation of whether or not cyberactivism genuinely creates meaningful social change in the offline world.

If you were asked to provide an example of a social media site, most of us would likely consider social networking sites like Facebook or Twitter as archetypal examples. Although blogging platforms may not be as popular as they once were, they are still examples of social media sites, but are important to consider separately given that they often serve very different functions to sites like Facebook and Twitter. In the fourth chapter in this section, Dr Bradley M. Okdie, The Ohio State University at Newark, USA, and Daniel M. Rempala, The University of Hawaii at Manoa, USA, discuss trends and motivations for using blogging sites. The chapter focuses on blogging as a tool for self-expression and social connection and examines the many different derivations of blogging services, including microblogging and video-blogging or vlogging.

In the concluding chapter in this section, Dr Sally Quinn, University of York, UK, considers the positive aspects of using social media. This chapter is timely given the predilection for the media to focus on the more negative aspects of using social media, for example how they may be addictive or used by bullies. Within this chapter, Sally introduces a raft of different positive outcomes associated with using social media sites, including increasing connectedness, providing a platform for social support, and how using such sites may increase psychological well-being. Sally also considers which specific groups are likely to reap the most benefits from engagement with social media and a special focus is given to young people's use of these sites.

PART VI: HEALTH AND TECHNOLOGY (EDITED BY DR DARIA J. KUSS)

Technology is now increasingly used for the purpose of health. This section will deal with the ways in which technology use is shaping how we access health information, the possible detrimental impact of excessive use, the use of technology in the context of mourning, as well as how technology may benefit users from a health perspective.

Dr Elizabeth Sillence, Psychology and Communication Technologies (PACT) Lab at the University of Northumbria, and Professor Pamela Briggs, Professor and Chair in Applied Psychology at the University of Northumbria, UK, start off this section with their chapter, "Managing your Health Online: Issues in the Selection, Curation, and Sharing of Digital Health Information". They outline how the shift towards peer-to-peer sharing sites represents a significant change in how online health information is used and perceived, and the challenges that stem from this. These challenges include sharing personal health information and maintaining this vast and complex information resource.

The next chapter introduces "A Psychological Overview of Gaming Disorder", a new psychological disorder, now in the process of being included in the international diagnostic manuals. The chapter is written by Dr Daria J. Kuss and Dr Halley Pontes of the Cyberpsychology Research Group and the International Gaming Research Unit at Nottingham Trent University, UK, and Dr ORSOLYA Király and Professor Zsolt Demetrovics, from the Institute of Psychology, Eötvös Loránd University in Budapest, Hungary. Daria and her team delineate current approaches to clinical and psychometric assessment of Gaming Disorder and the controversies in this new and blossoming research field, with the aim of presenting a balanced view of this emerging mental health problem.

In the subsequent chapter, Dr Elaine Kasket, HCPC-Registered Counselling Psychologist and Independent Researcher, UK, discusses "Mourning and Memorialization on Social Media". Elaine refers to "digital legacies" when considering the digital data left by deceased individuals. The effects are twofold: first, it affects the perception and experience of personhood and mortality. Second, it impacts significant others who mourn and memoralize the deceased person. In Elaine's chapter, she delves into the topic of death in the digital age, and specifically addresses the digital afterlife and the continuing bonds on the social media site Facebook.

In the final chapter in the section on Health and Technology, Dr Mark Griffiths, Distinguished Professor of Behavioural Addictions and Director of the International Gaming Research Unit at Nottingham Trent University, UK, explores "The Therapeutic and Health Benefits of Playing Video Games". Mark looks at the scientific literature base available on the extent to which playing video games can improve health. These benefits include pain management, physiotherapy and occupational therapy, social and communication skills for the learning disabled, psychotherapy, health compliance, stress, anxiety and emotional regulation, and physical activity. Altogether, he concludes that gaming can benefit many individuals, particularly when the gaming targets concrete problems and/or the development of a specific skill.

PART VII: GAMING (EDITED BY DR DARIA J. KUSS)

Gaming is an activity people have engaged in since time immemorial. With the advent of the Internet and digital technologies, networked gaming has gained popularity, with individuals around the world coming together virtually to engage in one of their favorite pastime activities—playing games. This section sees the discussion of gaming in its various forms, including different types of games and the sociodemographics of players, considering how games can lead to behavior change and altered sensory perceptions outside of the game, its psychosocial and moral impact on the individual and the people around them.

Jessica McCain, Kyle Morrison, and Dr Sun Joo (Grace) Ahn, Director of the Games and Virtual Environments Lab at the University of Georgia, USA, start off this section with their chapter "Video Games and Behavior Change". Jessica and her colleagues argue that the role of games goes well beyond entertainment, and that playing games can lead to changes in prosocial and antisocial behavior. In their chapter, the authors consider how virtual cues may lead to behavior alterations, how cognitive and emotional pathways are affected by gaming and may lead to changing behaviors, and how these changes brought about by games may be applied in different contexts, such as within healthcare.

Other than changing how we behave, games can also lead to altered perception. Accordingly Dr Angelica Ortiz de Gortari, Research Fellow at the University of Liège, Belgium, coined the term "Game Transfer Phenomena". This refers to the effects of playing video games on cognition, sensory perception, and human behavior, brought about by the gamer engaging with the game, immersing in the game, and embodying their avatar, whilst using the game's hardware. In her chapter "Game Transfer Phenomena: Origin, Development, and Contributions to the Video Game Research Field", Angelica provides a synopsis on current Game Transfer Phenomena research, paying attention to the characteristics and prevalence of Game Transfer Phenomena, how it impacts the gamer, and the structural characteristics of games that contribute to experiencing it.

In the next chapter, Dr Michelle Colder Carras, Radboud University, Nijmegen, Netherlands, Dr Rachel Kowert, Independent Scholar, Ontario, Canada, and Dr Thorsten Quandt, the University of Münster, Germany, consider the extent to which gaming may have both positive as well as negative effects. Michelle and her team argue that since gaming has become a popular pastime activity, concerns have been raised about possible detrimental effects. In order to shed light on these concerns, the research team conducted a systematic literature review to assess the associations between video gaming and psychological effects. From their results it appears that when there are negative effects, these tend to be temporary and moderate. Additionally, the research assessed also suggests that there are a number of positive psychosocial effects of playing video games, including their use in the healthcare context. To end, Michelle and her team provide suggestions regarding progressing studies to research the associations between gaming and psychosocial effects more thoroughly.

Moving on from there, Dr Garry Young, The University of Melbourne, Australia, considers immoral and taboo behaviors in online games in his chapter "Enacting Immorality within Gamespace: Where Should We Draw the Line and Why?" In his chapter, Garry provides arguments in favor of prohibiting video game content, related to harm, meaningful expression, and player motivation, looking at single-player gamers enacting immoral behaviors against non-player characters.

The final chapter of this section brings together our knowledge and understanding of different types of games and who plays them. In her contribution, Dr Linda K. Kaye, Edge Hill University, UK, introduces "Gaming Classifications and Player Demographics". Linda focuses on how the game's function, content, platform, and context impact upon player demographics, as those aspects are relevant to provide a clear picture of who the players are. To end, Linda outlines a conceptual framework, based on which the aforementioned aspects are affected by gaming domains and play formats. This chapter pulls together important research in the area and offers a comprehensive understanding of gaming in cyber contexts.

PART VIII: CYBERCRIME AND CYBERSECURITY (EDITED BY DR ALISON ATTRILL-SMITH)

In this last section of the book, we consider the darker side of Internet behavior: the side associated with criminal activity and nefarious intent from criminals the world over. It is important to consider these aspects of online behavior, given the exponential rise of online criminality in conjunction with the growth of Internet uptake worldwide. Criminals have found new ways to carry out existing types of crime, but have equally developed entirely new levels and types of crime that prior to the Internet had not existed. In this section, both old and new crimes are explored. Technology is very much considered as a tool to crime, rather than to blame for crime across these four chapters. In the first chapter of this section, Dr Grainne Kirwan from the Dun Laoghaire Institute of Art, Design, and Technology in Ireland outlines the rise in cybercrime concomitant with the spread of Internet and wider technology use. Focusing on defining different types of cybercrime and outlining existing typologies of the groupings of cybercrimes, Grainne goes on to explore the hindrances to reporting many crimes committed online, and to providing an overview of the ways in which our understanding of the psychological factors involved in both perpetrating and falling victim to online crimes can aid our understanding of future prevention of those crimes.

This sets the scene for the following chapter on cybersecurity by Dr Thomas Holt and Jin Ree Lee of the School of Criminal Justice at Michigan State University, USA. In their chapter, they discuss further typologies of cybercrimes and how these can aid our understanding of the prevention and security measures needed to help internationally police the Internet. In doing so, they not only touch upon the more obvious factors associated with cybersecurity, such as moderating and administrating more socially oriented websites, but also explore the role of Internet service providers in protecting their users against online crimes. Interestingly, a brief comparison is offered of both public and non-public police and voluntary organizations that play a role in preventing and reducing Internet crime, as well as catching the criminals when crimes are identified and/or reported. Offering an insight from a more legal than psychological perspective, this chapter provides the reader with an excellent overview of the problems facing a multitude of worldwide agencies in coming together to deal with cybercrime, and highlights why understanding the psychology of crime that uses the international tool that is the Internet is so difficult.

The remaining two chapters in this section focus on crimes against individuals and crimes against groups. Building on the outlines of the previous two chapters, both chapters are led by Dr Jason Nurse from the School of Computing at the University of Kent, UK. In the first, he considers the underlying human factors that play a role in cyber-attacks on individuals. He focuses on a range of cybercrimes, including those more commonly reported in the mass media (e.g., phishing and catfishing), but also considers other less well broadcast crimes, such as denial of service attacks. Jason introduces a new taxonomy that builds on those outlined in the previous chapters, prior to moving on to the second of his chapters, co-authored with Dr Maria Bada from the Global Cyber Security Capacity Centre at the University of Oxford, UK. When we think of cybercrime, we nearly always think of the new and emerging crimes that are perpetrated against individuals, such as revenge pornography and identity theft, or monetary fraud crimes. There is, however, another category of online crimes that is aimed at wider societal groups. These can range from hate crimes based on religion or group identities (e.g., race or sexual orientation) to organized crimes against whole nations. Touching on instances of terrorist activity and hacktivists, Jason and Maria explore crimes from both a perpetrator and victim perspective, using modern examples of group-oriented cybercrimes.

CONCLUDING STATEMENTS

This edition of the *Oxford Handbook of Cyberpsychology* offers you a comprehensive tour of the different psychological processes underpinning the breadth of ways in which we engage with technology across a range of social contexts, and across the lifespan. The discussions from our international experts consider the multiple facets of technology, as a tool used to influence change, or a cause of change in our own behaviors, and share a range of theoretical frameworks and models for understanding cyberpsychology. We are excited to be sharing with you these considered and evidence-based discussions of research into the benefits and limitations of technology in our relationships, development of our own selves, and our health and well-being, and, through this book, connect you to a truly global network of scholars in the field.

PART I

INTRODUCTION AND FOUNDATIONS

CHAPTER 1

CYBERPSYCHOLOGY RESEARCH METHODS

JOHN H. KRANTZ

INTRODUCING RESEARCH METHODS

CYBERPSYCHOLOGY is the study of how humans and computers interact. This volume features much information about this inter-relationship. There are chapters on online behavior (e.g., Chapters 3–5), work behavior (e.g., Chapter 9), school behavior (e.g., Chapter 8), and many others. Reading any of these chapters should prompt an initial question that should always be present as you read: How do we know? Additionally, we should also ask: Are we right? To address these queries, it is vital to understand research methods. Without a sound grasp of these issues, it is impossible to critically engage in any of the other issues around this topic.

The research methods of cyberpsychology exist at a point of intersection of four different levels of concerns: the field is scholarly, it is a science, it is a branch of psychology, and it is its own unique field.

First, cyberpsychology is a scholarly discipline, that is, one of the fields taught at a university or college, and as such, agrees to certain principles of doing research. First, it requires reason from evidence, and a method for collecting evidence to use to form conclusions. Personal opinions, gut feelings, and the like are not to be used. Beyond that, this evidence must be shared with others so that they can critically examine these conclusions. This requirement is true of all scholarly fields. Similar to writing a paper in an English class, sources must be quoted, and a reference section is required.

Second, cyberpsychology is a science, and evidence needs to be collected from observation. The main focus of this chapter is on methods used in what is called empirical observation. Since observations must be repeated to demonstrate their validity, observations must be measured so that they can be compared and evaluated by others. Science has a particular method of showing the general claims of all scholarly disciplines.

Third, cyberpsychology, as the name implies, is a branch of psychology. As such, the field draws on a rich array of research methods and behavioral observational techniques in conducting its research. Thus, many of the methods discussed in this chapter will resemble those seen in other fields of psychology.

Finally, cyberpsychology is its own field and as such the field has adapted all the methods and approaches it has borrowed to meet its particular needs. Most obviously, the research methods must assess how humans interact with computers, and this need influences how data are collected and how studies are constructed. One vital part of research methods includes an intrinsic scientific process: measurement.

The Role of Measurement

Measurement is using a specified procedure to convert an observation to a number. Measurements are all around you. When measuring a fever, the thermometer is placed in your mouth, and after a period of time, will show a number by which you determine if you have a fever or not. You followed a procedure, to some extent determined by the thermometer, and you ended up with a number. Research methods are these specified procedures and they end up with numbers representing observations. These numbers are then reported and used in various analyses to try to determine the outcome of the study. These measurements are the evidence used to reach conclusions in science, in general, and cyberpsychology, more specifically. To be complete, there are methods that generate other sorts of data, called qualitative methods, but there is not room in this chapter to give them adequate coverage.

Important characteristics of any measure is its reliability and validity. Reliability refers to the consistency of the value obtained as you repeat the measurement. Again, using the thermometer example, when checking for a fever, by taking your temperature a few times to make sure the reading is correct, if the values read are very similar, the thermometer is reliable. If they vary from measure to measure, the thermometer is not. The same is true for measures in cyberpsychology. The goal is to get as reliable measures as possible. Validity refers to if the measure actually measures what is says it does. For example, you develop a new social media app that you hope will compete with Facebook as a means of sharing moments with your friends. You create a survey that asks a series of questions that you hope will let you know if your users like the app. However, you phrase the questions awkwardly and the survey let you really know about the persons current mood regardless of the app. This would be an invalid measure. All measures should be determined for the reliability and validity before being used, and while there are many different types of validity, this chapter discusses only a few to do specifically with cyberpsychology.

Common Measures

One of the common measures used in cyberpsychology uses eye movements to track how users view different interfaces and are drawn to different parts of a computer screen (e.g., Surakka, Illi, & Isokoski, 2003). The eye only sees a small part of the world clearly, so our eyes move a lot to make sense of the world around use. This need to move our eyes makes tracking the eye movements very useful in figuring out what parts of a screen a user finds necessary when using a computer. Another set of measures is to track interactions like clicks, mouse movements, and screen touches to track how users interact with a computer (Norman, 2017). Measuring the impact of interacting with computers on broader psychological issues often uses measurements scales like self-esteem or some form of satisfaction. For example, Elphinston and Noller (2011) measured relationship satisfaction as it corresponds to the degree of Facebook intrusion into daily life.

Types of Research Methods

While there are many types of research methods, this chapter focuses on the three basic classes of research methods: observational, correlational (survey), and experimental. Each of these methods provides useful evidence for understanding cyberpsychology. Each method will be discussed in turn, after which, the chapter covers some emerging research techniques: online research methods and the use of devices such as phones for data collection.

Observational Research

Observational Study Example: How do young children just beginning to read interact with a book, specifically, those books with computer technology embedded, and how might these children handle this new more complicated way to start reading? Dünser and Hornecker (2007) devised a study to watch children interact with these books, observing levels of engagement and frustration with the books.

Observational methods are designed to capture behavior in an ongoing fashion. In traditional psychology or ethology, it might be going to a playground and counting acts of aggression on the playground or mating rituals of a species of birds. In cyberpsychology, it might be observing or capturing users' interactions with one or several computer systems.

There are several ways to captures these actions. Users can give verbal statements of what they are doing as they interact with the app and these can be recorded for later evaluation. It is also possible to capture real-time interactions with a computer. For example, users can be given a task to find a particular research article on cyberpsychology. Then they interact with a computer system and the system records what they do, by capturing the mouse clicks and data entry as they proceed through the task. What makes the study observational is less how data is collected, and more that ongoing behavior is recorded as the user interacts with the computer application.

However, several issues and limitations can arise from doing observational research. The biggest issue depends on how the observation is done. Frequently, if people know they are being observed, their behavior often changes—this is known as the Hawthorne Effect (McCambridge, Witton, & Elbourne, 2014). Part of the problem is that the effect of observation is difficult to predict. Many observational studies will try to observe covertly, but that is not always ethically possible. Another issue is observer bias, which calls for establishing clear methods and procedures for recording observations, but that specificity might leave observers unable to record events of interest that happen during the study.

Correlational Designs and Survey Designs

Correlational Study Example: Does greater Facebook use result in girls' increased negative perception of their physical selves. Facebook is an extremely popular social media site that people use frequently and for long periods of time. Meier and Gray (2014) took a sample of middle and high school females and had them complete questionnaires measuring aspects of Facebook use and how they perceive themselves, such as weight dissatisfaction, drive for thinness, thin ideal internalization, appearance comparison, and self-objectification.

In a correlational design, the goal is prediction. The researcher measures two or more variables and then tries to determine if changes in one variable are related to another variable. In the correlational study example, Meier and Gray (2014) developed questionnaires to measure different aspects of Facebook usage. Then they used different questionnaires to measure aspects of girls' self-image, particularly related to their sense of their own body. Each questionnaire is a different variable. This study is not an observational design because the researchers did not directly observe these behaviors. The study is not an experiment because nothing was changed. In the data analysis, the researchers focused on testing if there is a possible predictive relationship between an increase in Facebook and an increase in negative body perception. This is a predictive type of comparison. Here, the researchers determined that Facebook use was not predictive, and rather that it was appearance comparison that was important. If a girl was more involved in comparing others' appearances to their own, then the girl had greater numbers of body perception issues.

External Validity and Random Sampling

When conducting a correlational study, the major concern is the external validity or generalizability of the study. External validity refers to the ability to apply the results to people and situations outside of the study. It is rare that the researcher is only interested in those participants within the study; instead, hopefully the results are applicable beyond this sample. Factors that influence external validity are many and include having valid measures in the study as well as having a sample of participants that are in some way representative of those to which the study will hopefully apply. Let us look at sampling a little more closely.

A correlational study requires participants, but as everyone cannot be tested, researchers must collect a subset, called a sample. The whole group you are interested in is the population, which is not necessarily everyone; rather, it is everyone that is relevant to the study. For example, if the research interest is around issues to do with gaming, the population is gamers. Not everyone games and there are some characteristics of gamers that differ from the population at large. For example, gamers are predominately male and younger than average, although a wide range of ages play these games (Yee, 2006). Or, for an educational game aimed at early school ages, adult participants are not appropriate to the study. Thus, before choosing a sample, the researcher must know and identify the population. For a field like cyberpsychology, this is extremely important as the use and reach of computers is highly variable and depends on many factors.

Next, the researcher needs to collect the sample. The characteristics of this sample are very important, and the sample must, in some way, represent the population. Ideally, the sample should be random. Let me very carefully define this term, so read the definition carefully. A random means that *every member of the population has an equal chance of participating in the study*. Reread that definition a few times until you understand every element of the definition. Often, the word random is used as a synonym for uncontrolled, in the sense that "The sample is random if I did not purposely control who is in the sample." But in rereading the definition, it can been seen that this is not true. If you collect a sample of people for your study from your cyberpsychology class, according to the definition, it can it be a representative sample? It is neither random and only potentially representative of those in your cyberpsychology class. It is also possible to strategically sample and still be random. For example, there can be gender balance in a study and it could still be a random sample as long as the criteria in the definition are met. Sampling to ensure some characteristic, e.g. gender or race, matches the balance of the population, is called stratified sampling, and if it is a random sample, a stratified random sampling.

In practical circumstances, a truly random sample is impossible, so researchers must fall back on a convenience sample, i.e. a sample from a group of potential participants to which the researcher has access. Such a sample is a threat to the external validity of the study to the extent that the sample differs from the population. However, it is often possible that a convenience sample is adequate for your research purposes. Thus, it is vital to describe the sampling procedures so that readers understand how participants are collected (Wilkinson, 1999).

Scale Construction

In many correlational studies, survey instruments are used to collect the data. This method of data collection is sometimes referred to as the survey method. In this method, people are asked a series of questions to which they provide answers. Participants are asked to report their responses in a controlled way. For example, in what is called a Likert (pronounced LIH-kert) scale, the participants are asked to what degree they support a statement by circling the appropriate number:

Seeing photos on Facebook of my friends make me feel less happy.
Agree 1 2 3 4 5 Disagree

This type of question fulfills the need of measurement as the response by the person is recorded as a 1, 2, 3, 4, or 5. There are usually several questions and the responses to all of the questions are usually averaged to give an overall scale response. There are many ways to ask these questions and care must be taken in scale construction. After the scale is developed, the reliability and validity is assessed.

Common ways to test reliability are test–retest, where the scale is taken more than once, and a Chronbach's alpha score calculated which measures the internal consistency of the scale. Reliability usually goes from 0 to 1.0 with a minimum of 0.7 deemed necessary for use of a scale.

Validity is established usually in one of several ways. Scales can be correlated with other measures that seem to measure the same psychological variable or correlated with other types of dependent measures that are supposed to be related, for example. To make this point a bit more concrete, a scale designed to measure depression could be validated by examining if people diagnosed with depression score as more depressed on the scale than those who are not depressed. To read more about reliability and validity, see Cicchetti's (1994) excellent work.

Issues and Limitations

Using questionnaires as a measurement device can be problematic, as our statements about ourselves may not actually relate to our real behavior. In many cases our questionnaire results relate positively to our behavior, but there are many other factors, and the relationship between the two is complicated (Kraus, 1995). One of the biggest limitations is that causal conclusions should not be made from correlational data, however tempting. It is a common statement in research methods that correlation does not imply causation. Prediction is not enough to say that one variable explains the changes in another variable. For example, Messerli (2012) reported a remarkably strong correlation between national per capita chocolate consumption and the per capita number of Nobel prizes one by the country. The correlation was near 0.80 on a scale from −1 to 1 where 0 is no correlation and 1 and −1 are perfect correlations. A correlation of nearly 0.80 is very strong. Researchers in the behavioral sciences would be most excited by this high correlation. So why can we not conclude that chocolate consumption is what we need to improve our societies and win more Nobel prizes? In this correlational study, there are always other variables that the research did not measure, for example, wealth. Wealthier nations are going to have more disposable income to eat chocolate and to also invest in the research that leads to Nobel prizes. Causal conclusions are extremely difficult to make in correlational designs and are instead usually the province of experimental methods.

Experimental Methods

Experimental Study Example: Virtual Reality is growing as a tool and you wonder if it could be used to treat some psychological issues, e.g. smoking. Nicotine is highly addictive, and you are aware that cues to smoking increase cravings. A common treatment in a lab is to repeatedly present pictures of stimuli related to smoking to elicit this nicotine craving where it is not fulfilled. The theory is that, over time, the patient will lose the craving elicited by the pictures through a process called extinction, but the therapy has shown only limited effectiveness. You hypothesize that pictures are just not real enough, and want to test that virtual reality may provide more realistic stimuli due to the nature of the technology. You get two groups of patients: one uses the new VR treatment, and the other group uses the older picture treatment. You have changed something but you must compare it to what used to be. Then you find something to measure, e.g. how much the participant craves a smoke after the two types of presentations (Lee et al., 2003).

Description

The final methodology that will be discussed here is the experimental method. The discussion will get rather technical about what makes an experiment. So, it will be important to remember that an experiment, at its most basic is changing something in the environment and seeing what happens. The core elements of an experiment are manipulation, control, and careful measurement of the outcome. The power of experiments is that, when conducted correctly, new types of statements, causal statements, can be made. We can say that some change in a program or other variable causes a change in how we interact with computers or each other. We will explore how this is possible as we discuss the nature of experiments.

An experiment begins with manipulation. Unlike the other research methods, here the researcher actively intervenes in the situation studied. This manipulation is the changing something referred to above. For example, the researcher might be interested in the best way to interact with an app button, and creates at least two types of buttons: mouse click and touch. The app has been changed, or manipulated. The characteristics being changed by the researcher, e.g. the type of button, is the independent variable.

Now that we have changed something, we need to see what happens. By careful measurement, we measure the outcome of changing the independent variable. What we measure is called the dependent measure. Using the example of button types on an app, we may measure how fast users respond using each type of button. Perhaps, it is found that users respond to touch faster than mouse buttons because they do not have to move them from a certain point. Conversely, we might find that users are faster with mouse buttons because the mouse pointer is always on the screen.

The final key element in an experiment is control. In an experiment, you have at least two different situations: one for each change in the independent variable. But, as the independent variable is changed, everything else in the experiment must remain the same: the experiment is controlled. Control allows causal conclusions. It is worthwhile to examine how control makes causal conclusions possible. In the example of two types of buttons in an app, we hope to find that users respond faster to one type of button. If we control all the elements of the experiment other than the button type, then if we record that users respond faster when using touch buttons, then we can say that using touch buttons caused the faster responses. That is a well-controlled experiment. To see what happens when you don't control other variables, consider an experiment where the touch button is four times the size of the mouse button, we can no longer concluded that the use of touch buttons caused the faster responses. We know from Fitt's Law that people respond faster to larger buttons than smaller buttons (MacKenzie, 1992). Thus, in this poorly controlled study, the results could now be due either to the button size or the way the button was activated. We have a second variable, button size, that could explain our results. We call this accidental variable that changes with our independent variable a confound variable. It is of extreme importance to avoid all confounds. Be on the lookout for confounding variables in all experiments, including those reported in this volume.

Usually we have more than two and often more than one independent variable. How to handle these more complicated situations will be left for more advanced discussions but as you read about experiments in this book you will encounter few experiments with only two levels of one independent variable.

Internal Validity

When we discussed correlational designs we discussed external validity. However, while external validity is often important in experiment as well, *internal* validity is also important. Internal validity refers to having an experiment designed properly so that a causal conclusion can be made. In other words, the confounding variables must be eliminated from the design. In experiments, it is important to maintain internal validity or the particular power of experiments is violated. External validity is often important in experiments as well, but such considerations may become less important when testing theoretical predictions.

One of the main threats to internal validity is the variability both between different people as well as within a single person. For example, in a situation where different participants are subject to different conditions of an experiment, each level (group) of the independent variable contains different people. If the researcher finds differences between the diverse conditions, she must verify if the differences are due to the independent variable and not to the differences between participants—as each group had different people in it. To combat this issue, researchers use random assignment, where each participant has an equal probability of being in any condition of the experiment. Note the difference between random sampling and random assignment. Where random *sampling* focuses on selecting participants from the population, random *assignment* focuses on how these participants, once in the sample, are assigned to the different conditions. The goal of random assignment is to balance out any factors that might influence the outcome of the experiment across the different conditions, thus strengthening the internal validity of the experiment. The goal of random sampling is to draw a sample that matches the desired population, thus strengthening external validity.

Field Experiment

While most experiments are conducted within a laboratory, it is sometimes necessary to conduct experiments in a real-world situation: these are called field experiments. For example, when examining the effectiveness of a new teaching technology, it might be nice to use actual students in an actual class. However, every experiment requires an independent variable, and this experiment would require a group of students that also uses the existing technology. Here, the type of technology used becomes the independent variable. The researcher might look at class grades as the dependent variable to assess effectiveness of the technology.

For example, Deters and Mehl (2013) were interested in the effects (note the causal language here) of making Facebook posts. They were interested in how making posts works in people's actual lives. In a field experiment, external generality is much more important than in most laboratory experiments. Deters and Mehl divided their participants and asked one group to reduce the number of posts that they made; the other groups did not change. The postings were tracked and participants were given measures of loneliness, among others. The independent variable here was the number of posts, normal or reduced, and the dependent variable was the measure of loneliness. The results show that participants felt less lonely when not restricted in making Facebook posts.

Field experiments have to be conducted with great care as, by leaving the laboratory, the researcher gives up a certain amount of control over the situation, and this can result in confounds. Taking the example of new technology use in classrooms, it would be typical to use two different classes. It would be normally not allowable or even ethical to do random assignment between these classes. Students will sign up for classes as they wish; experience indicates that people do not register for classes in a random way. Random assignment means that each participant has an equal chance of being in each condition. If there is a significant conflict with one of the class times, then students do not have an equal chance of being in either condition. Still, the importance of doing the study sometimes outweighs the difficulties, and thus a field experiment is undertaken.

Issues and Limitations

As in all methods, experimental research has its share of issues and limitations. In laboratory studies, the chief concern is external validity, i.e. how much do results from the laboratory have any meaning in the much less controlled real world. Field experiments can alleviate this concern to some extent, but the loss of control in the field can lead to problems in making causal conclusions. Establishing real control in the laboratory, and thus completely eliminating all variation in samples in different conditions, also contributes to limitations in interpreting experiments. There are very good reasons for the variety of research methods as they can help each other lead to better conclusions.

Online Research Methods

Starting in the middle 1990s, not long after the World Wide Web became widely available, researchers started using it as a method for collecting data (Krantz, Ballard, & Scher, 1997; Musch & Reips, 2000; Reips, 1996). The initial studies were more focused on validating the research method, but studies investigating psychological phenomena were conducted soon after (e.g., Birnbaum, 1999). Issues that drew early researchers included increasing sample size, increased statistical power, speed of data collection, geographical diversity, ecological validity, and cost (Musch & Reips, 2000). In a follow-up, after twenty years of Internet research, the reasons for doing research have not greatly changed, but ease of doing the study has arisen as a significant reason people conducting online research (Krantz & Reips, 2017). Validating any research method is important and it is significant that the early studies were focused on validation. There are several research concerns that are unique to online research, including data fraud, participant motivation, multiple entries, and hardware and equipment variation (Krantz & Reips, 2017; Musch & Reips, 2000). When doing an experiment, loss of control of the environment leading to potential confounds is also a serious issue (Krantz & Dalal, 2000). Early studies did find that in many circumstances using the web was a valid way to conduct research (Krantz & Dalal, 2000).

While the web provides opportunities for general psychological research, there are particular opportunities for cyberpsychology. Consider that in order to access the Internet, you are on your computer or some other device, such as a phone, or tablet. Thus, it seems reasonable to examine cyberpsychological issues through the Internet. One study (Keep & Atrill-Smith, 2017) combined both online research methods with the examination of an important issue of the new online world. This study aimed to develop a scale for impression management online, but they also included a preliminary examination of factors that influence our desire for impression management. A couple of findings suggested that as people age, they are more interested in controlling their online impressions, but also that there was no difference in interest in controlling online self-presentation between genders.

Park, Kee, and Valenzuela (2009) examined reasons for college students joining Facebook groups. This study showed some of the advantages of online research methods. Not being limited by physical boundaries, the researchers were able to recruit 1,715 students, and this large number of participants allowed analysis of a greater number of factors than could be done with a smaller sample. While their findings are complex and beyond the scope of this chapter, they did find that fewer people joined groups as the school year progressed, and that people joined predominantly to see information about social events and participation.

However, an experiment by Kramer, Guillory, and Hancock (2014) reveals some of the ethical concerns of which researchers using online research must be aware. Here, without apparent consent, users' Facebook feeds were manipulated to the degree to which people's feeds reflected positive or negative events. They found that if people had a more negative feed, they posted more negatively and if they had a more positive feed they posted more positively. Because they worked with Facebook they got over 600,000 participants. However, the paper has led to a great deal of controversy and even a change in policy at Facebook. None of the participants were given informed consent. This lack of consent did not violate the rules of Facebook, but violates the expectations and ethics of psychological research. The controversy provides a reminder of the need for careful choice of methods when doing research.

Emerging Research Methods

As technology advances, there will be further changes in research methods as researchers take advantage of the new ways to conduct studies. With the advent on new devices connect to the Internet, new methodologies were developed. For example, smartphones introduced large numbers of new possibilities for research. The push notifications allow researchers a methodology for inviting participants to respond throughout the day. In one study (Mikulic, 2016), the researchers combined using the push notifications to gain access and used the rates of push notifications as the independent variable in this field experiment. Different groups were assigned to different levels of push notifications and then the phone use was measured. Interestingly, Mikulic (2016) found that the greater the level of push notification, the greater the level of phone use. However, without clear ethical guidance, psychologists should tread carefully on use of new means of access to participants.

Phones also introduce a large set of new potential dependent measures to go along with new ways of getting access. As researchers find ways to use these devices, new and innovative research in all areas of psychology will be possible

Research Ethics

The chapter concludes with a discussion of research ethics, which determine how we honorably engage in the research enterprise, and include how we treat our research participants, handle our data, and even ascribe credit to various authors. There are several formal statements on research ethics, mostly notably by the APA (American Psychological Association, 2017) in the US and the BPS (British Psychological Society) in the UK, but also by many different funding agencies. Most colleges and universities have committees, often called institutional review boards or ethics committees, which must review all research before it can be conducted.

Review of all the procedures in detail by which studies are reviewed is beyond the scope of this chapter, so only the most important principles focusing on the treatment of participants are discussed here. The fundamental principle behind most ethical codes regarding the treatment of research participants is to remember that they are distinct human beings who must be allowed freedom of choice and not be harmed.

All participants should receive an information statement giving details of what the study is about and what is expected. Participants should be free to make decisions about their participation, and provide informed consent. To make that possible, participants must have a sufficiently detailed description of the study so that they can decide if they want to participate in the study. Rewards are often offered to encourage participation, e.g. research participation credit in an introductory psychology class, or even extra credit. Online studies looking for participants beyond the university frequently offer payments, gift vouchers, or other rewards. However, all rewards must remain modest as they cannot be perceived as coercive. For example, if there is class credit or extra-credit involved, it is expected that the instructor offers a different and equivalent way to gain the same credit that does not require research participation. In addition, participants must be allowed to leave at any time. Interestingly, it is here where online research has an ethical advantage as potential participants feel much freer to leave an online study than an in-lab study (Krantz & Reips, 2017).

Informed consent requirement seems to work for most psychological research, but it is often important to hide the actual hypothesis or even reasons for the study. But is it is ethical to deceive a participant? Without going into detail, the answer is a qualified yes. The deception must be necessary. In other words, it would not be possible to conduct the study without deception, as too much information could potentially influence the study participants. The potential findings should also be more than normally significant. However, participants must be debriefed and have the full study explained as soon as possible, preferably right after participation. It is this requirement for debriefing that limits the use of deception online. Putting two circumstances side by side: participants *must* be debriefed when using deceptions and, because online research participants easily withdraw, there is no guarantee that all participants will make it through to, or even read, the debriefing. As such, the use of deception is very problematic online.

Finally, participants cannot be harmed, and harm does not refer only to physical harm. Some studies of cyberpsychology, such as those examining sensitive issues like cyberstalking, could lead to uncomfortable memories and thoughts. As with deception, it does not mean that such topics cannot be examined, but extra care needs to be taken. Participants must be provided with reference and access to care for any such issues as could arise. In these types of studies, proper informed consent is paramount.

Conclusion

This chapter has introduced and discussed the basics of a variety of research methods. The task of the researcher is to determine the appropriate research method for the question being asked. Whether an observational, correlational, or experimental method is used, it should match the question being asked. Regardless of the method used, each researcher must always ask: are the conclusions justified by the method?

For each type of method, there are better or worse ways to perform the study. It is important to ask if the measures are reliable and valid, if an experiment has any confounds, and if the study emphasizes external validity, has the study good sampling methods and situations to justify those general claims. Furthermore, if the study requires strong internal validity, has the research provided proper controls? If the study was done online, was that the appropriate venue for the study? Finally, has the study been conducted ethically, giving participants informed consent, debriefing if necessary, and treated the participants with appropriate respect?

The key to really understanding a field is to read with a questioning mind. The quality of the methods is what is key to being able to use the results of research in learning more about any field, cyberpsychology included. So, keep this chapter handy as you read and always ask questions.

REFERENCES

American Psychological Association. (2017, January). *Ethical Principles of Psychologists and Code of Conduct.* Retrieved from https://www.apa.org/ethics/code/.

Birnbaum, M. H. (1999). Testing critical properties of decision making on the Internet. *Psychological Science 10*, 399–407.

Cicchetti, D. V. (1994). Guidelines, criteria, and rules of thumb for evaluating normed and standardized assessment instruments in psychology. *Psychological Assessment 6*(4), 284.

Deters, F. G., & Mehl, M. R. (2013). Does posting Facebook status updates increase or decrease loneliness? An online social networking experiment. *Social Psychological and Personality Science 4*(5), 579–586.

Dünser, A., & Hornecker, E. (2007, June). An observational study of children interacting with an augmented story book. In *International Conference on Technologies for E-Learning and Digital Entertainment* (pp. 305–315). Berlin, Heidelberg: Springer.

Elphinston, R. A., & Noller, P. (2011). Time to face it! Facebook intrusion and the implications for romantic jealousy and relationship satisfaction. *Cyberpsychology, Behavior, and Social Networking 14*(11), 631–635.

Keep, M., & Attrill-Smith, A. (2017). Controlling you watching me: Measuring perception control on social media. *Cyberpsychology, Behavior, and Social Networking 20*(9), 561–566.

Kramer, A. D., Guillory, J. E., & Hancock, J. T. (2014). Experimental evidence of massive-scale emotional contagion through social networks. *Proceedings of the National Academy of Sciences 111*(24), 8788–8790.

Krantz, J. H., Ballard, J., & Scher, J. (1997). Comparing the results of laboratory and World Wide Web samples on the determinants of female attractiveness. *Behavior Research Methods, Instruments, and Computers 29*, 264–269.

Krantz, J. H., & Dalal, R. (2000). Validity of Web-based psychological research. In M. H. Birnbaum (Ed.), *Psychological experiments on the Internet* (pp. 35–60). San Diego, CA: Academic Press.

Krantz, J. H., & Reips, U. D. (2017). The state of web-based research: A survey and call for inclusion in curricula. *Behavior Research Methods 49*(5), 1621–1629.

Kraus, S. J. (1995). Attitudes and the prediction of behavior: A meta-analysis of the empirical literature. *Personality and Social Psychology Bulletin 21*(1), 58–75.

Lee, J. H., Ku, J., Kim, K., Kim, B., Kim, I. Y., Yang, B. H., ... Lim, Y. (2003). Experimental application of virtual reality for nicotine craving through cue exposure. *Cyberpsychology & Behavior 6*(3), 275–280.

MacKenzie, I. S. (1992). Fitts' law as a research and design tool in human-computer interaction. *Human-Computer Interaction 7*(1), 91–139.

McCambridge, J., Witton, J., & Elbourne, D. R. (2014). Systematic review of the Hawthorne effect: New concepts are needed to study research participation effects. *Journal of Clinical Epidemiology 67*(3), 267–277.

Meier, E. P., & Gray, J. (2014). Facebook photo activity associated with body image disturbance in adolescent girls. *Cyberpsychology, Behavior, and Social Networking 17*(4), 199–206.

Messerli, F. H. (2012). Chocolate consumption, cognitive function, and Nobel laureates. *New England Journal of Medicine 367*, 1562–1564.

Mikulic, M. (2016). The effects of push vs. pull notifications on overall smartphone usage, frequency of usage and stress levels (Master's dissertation). Uppsala University. Retrieved from http://urn.kb.se/resolve?urn=urn:nbn:se:uu:diva-297091

Musch, J., & Reips, U.-D. (2000). A brief history of Web experimenting. In M. H. Birnbaum (Ed.), *Psychological experiments on the Internet* (pp. 61–88). San Diego, CA: Academic Press.

Norman, K. L. (2017). *Cyberpsychology: An introduction to human-computer interaction*, 2nd ed. Cambridge: Cambridge University Press.

Park, N., Kee, K. F., & Valenzuela, S. (2009). Being immersed in social networking environment: Facebook groups, uses and gratifications, and social outcomes. *Cyberpsychology & Behavior 12*(6), 729–733.

Reips, U.-D. (1996, October). *Experimenting in the World Wide Web*. Paper presented at the 1996 Society for Computer in Psychology conference, Chicago.

Surakka, V., Illi, M., & Isokoski, P. (2003). Voluntary eye movements in human–computer interaction. In J. Hyönä, R. Radach and H. Deubel (Eds.), *The mind's eye: Cognitive and applied aspects of eye movement research* (pp. 473–491). Amsterdam: Elsevier Science.

Wilkinson, L. (1999). Statistical methods in psychology journals: Guidelines and explanations. *American Psychologist 54*(8), 594.

Yee, N. (2006). The demographics, motivations, and derived experiences of users of massively multi-user online graphical environments. *Presence: Teleoperators and Virtual Environments 15*(3), 309–329.

CHAPTER 2

THE ONLINE SELF

ALISON ATTRILL-SMITH

INTRODUCTION

THE "self" is a curious creature. It is you, it is all of the psychological and physiological features that come together to give you a personal identity. It is how you think and feel, and how you interpret, react to, and behave in diverse situations. It is the person you are talking about when you use the pronouns "I" and "we." This list is not exclusive. Many aspects of your daily life will influence how you see, interpret, and present yourself, both offline and online. As this book is about online behavior, the rest of this chapter will refer to the online self—the person you are when perusing the Internet, interacting with others online, or simply observing others in their online activities. That is not to say that we can ignore the offline self entirely. Of course, your offline "you" shapes and influences who you are in your online activities, and vice versa, but there are crossovers, changes, and distinctions between the two. It would be extremely rare for a person to be able to draw a thick black line between who they are online and who they are offline.

Throughout this book, you will read about a whole array of online behaviors and activities, ranging from gaming to dating, from banking and shopping to diverse crimes. One thread that carries through all of these actions is that people need to create online selves to be able to partake in any of the behaviors considered. The sheer fact that you need to enter your details on a website to use it, means that you are sharing information about yourself that enables others to create an image or profile of you. You are putting your "self" online. How people construct their self online is the focus of this chapter, which considers the voluntary online self (information you *choose* to share) and involuntary online self (information you *need* to share in order to complete a goal or task online). It also deliberates some of the advantages and disadvantages to the creation of diverse selves online. There may be differences in how we create ourselves online versus offline based on the time we are afforded to explore how we want to portray ourselves to others online—an advantage we rarely have offline. We can create, edit, and re-edit who we are before we share information about ourselves with others online (Attrill, 2015). There is no need for spontaneous communication; with asynchronous interactions we are in full control of who we want to be online. We might thus suppose that our online selves are reincarnations of the desired or ideal self, or a self that fits the activity in hand. Alternatively, we might consider these online selves to be extensions of already formed offline selves. These notions are explored in more detail as we progress through our consideration of the online self. Chris Fullwood then picks up on some of the concepts and explores them in terms of self-presentation and impression management online in the following chapter.

MULTIPLE SELVES

To set the scene for this exploration, we need to briefly consider the different "selves" in terms of psychological conceptualizations, as these will re-emerge throughout many chapters of this book. You will come across many terms about the self and how this consists of multiple selves. When we use the term "self-concept", it refers to "the individual's belief about himself or herself, including the person's attributes and who and what the self is" (Baumeister, 1999). Higgins (1987) defined one of the most commonly referred to conceptualizations of self: the *actual, ideal,* and *ought* selves. The latter two guide how we interpret and process information about our selves, while the actual self (also called the *real, true,* or *core* self in later theoretical conceptualizations) portrays who we really are in any given situation at a given point in time. The ideal self is the person we really want to be and who we strive to be, whereas the ought self is the person we believe others want us to be. For example, your parents might have wanted you to study psychology; thus, you are a psychology student currently reading this text. You see your ideal self as someone achieving a good grade as a psychology student, and therefore work hard to make that happen. Your actual self might however be more inclined to think that you can wing an important assignment and therefore choose to spend time in the university bar rather than striving to achieve your ideal version of self. These selves do not need to be vastly distinct from one another, and indeed, too much distance between the selves can cause psychological tension and discomfort (Festinger, 1954) to the point of illness. If you have these different selves, you might now be wondering how they reconcile to provide you with a self-identity, a notion of who you are, regardless of whether you are online or offline. When we talk of the *core* self, we assume this is the part of your self-identity that remains unaffected by temporal and situational factors. It guides and influences your behavior but can sometimes be led astray by your ideal or ought selves. Higgins' discrepancy theory will be discussed in more detail later, but it is worth mentioning that Higgins' theory spurned a host of similar distinctions of different types of self that are beyond the scope of this chapter. If you would like to know more about this, you can find overviews in almost any basic social psychology textbook (e.g. Hogg & Vaughan, 2017).

Two notes of distinction before progressing. The first relates to distinguishing the online and offline worlds in which the self is presented. In the early days of the Internet, researchers and lay persons alike often referred to an online world and a "real" world, and the latter has been replaced with the term "offline" world. The self is the self, regardless of whether this is online or offline. Continuing to use the terms real and online worlds negates the effects that online behavior can have offline, and vice versa. You only need to think of the impact that cyberbullying might have on a teenager's offline social life to realize the reality of online behavior.

The second concerns a distinction between human computer interaction (HCI) from this exploration of online self. In HCI, the focus is on the design and usability of technology, and it refers to the interface between people and technology. This chapter instead focuses on how you create your online self, how you act as yourself online, and how you can selectively manipulate and re-edit that self to suit both your and the task's needs and/or demands, as well as those of other users with whom you are interacting (see Attrill, 2015), e.g. people, shops, banks, agencies, discussion groups, review groups, and many more versions of "other" with whom you interact online.

Who Am I Online?

Let us now begin by considering who you think you are online. Who you are online will depend on the theoretical stance you adhere to, diverse research findings, the type of activity you are engaged in, and with whom you are interacting online. In order to complete any online task, you need to create an online self-identity, a cyberself, or a digital self. For the purposes of this chapter, these self terms will be used interchangeably. In some instances, you will be required to share more or less information about yourself (self information). This self will be flexible enough to suit the situational and temporal norms of behavior related to the task in hand, just as it does offline. Offline, you fulfill a number of social roles. As you read this text, you might be a student, a curious wife or husband, a son or daughter, a brother or sister, or you might be a law enforcement officer wanting to understand more about online crime, or a counsellor wanting to explore ways of helping people through online modes of communication. Social roles are not mutually exclusive, with some overlapping elements of your personality, but in any given situation you choose which self to present. If you are a student, for example, you might behave very differently on a Friday night out with your student friends to how you would behave sitting around a restaurant table with your parents and grandparents. Different offline situations create different social norms. Your online self is no different in this respect. If you are an online dater, you might be more brash in dismissing potential dates than you would if you had met them face to face. Your core self might be principally against being rude, but online you can let a bolder you shine through the suspected anonymity of your monitor. You can become a keyboard warrior without revealing your real true self. But what would happen if you continued to do that online? Consider for a moment TV soap operas. Some actors have been in a show for so long that if you were to encounter them out of character, it might be difficult to distinguish between their on-screen character and their "real" self. That is because if we act out a role repeatedly over time, we take on the characteristics of that role. The self is thus malleable and adaptable, and you can, over time change your core self. Thus, whichever "self" you are presenting online can, and does, have both positive and negative consequences offline.

One useful place to begin with understanding who you are online, and how you act out these social roles online, is to play the "I am......" game. Writing twenty "I am" statements about your offline you, you will most definitely write a number of descriptive statements, e.g. I am female, I am British, I am a lecturer. If, however, you were to write down twenty statements beginning with the words "I am" in relation to your online behavior and activities, what would that list look like? I am an online shopper, I am a blogger, I am an online banker, I am on Facebook, I am on Twitter, I am an online gamer, etc. Next, try to group those statements into functional categories. You will likely end up with various categories, for example, that revolve around your functional existence (e.g. financial activities such as shopping or banking) and social activities (e.g. social media and gaming). But how many of your statements relate to activities that you need to do online? For instance, did you write any statement that requires you to tax your vehicle, apply for child tax credits, renew your passport, or check your child's school homework and performance online? In order to execute all of these activities, you need to create versions of your self online. The former are more voluntary and the latter, borne from necessity, are your involuntary online selves. Note, I am talking of selves here, intentionally. These are, however, not separate or distinct from one another, but more fluid and responsive to situational norms. An alternative distinction of these selves is to think of those activities in which you freely engage online as those for which you manage your online self-presentation, whereas involuntary selves are those which engage with the Internet as a tool for completing a desired function or goal. But what does this distinction actually mean?

Leary (1995, p. 2) describes self-presentation as "the process of controlling how one is perceived by other people." When you manipulate how you present your self online, you are also trying to control how others see you in that situation. You then interpret their reactions to your presented self, which, in turn, influences how you present your (possibly edited or changed) self in the future. Alongside this process, some theoretical considerations are necessary to highlight that there is a core self, as already described above, underlying both the voluntary and involuntary online self. This self influences not only how you manipulate and self-present across different online activities, but also how you interpret and respond to others' behavior online. Imagine, for example, that someone posts what they believe to be an innocuous statement on social media. A person who has a negative core self might read that statement as implying harmful intent, whereas a more positive core self could put an entirely different spin on the statement. Both are not as the poster intended! Nonetheless, how you interpret that neutral post will subsequently guide your response to it. Thus, your sense of core self, and the cognitive processes associated with the self, may be difficult to change in the long term, but they will guide those aspects and features of self which you can change across different online activities. The process of online self-creation is therefore just as ongoing and in constant flux as is your offline self with all of its different social roles. This overall process of self-presentation, interpretation, and manipulation comes together to form your sense of online self. While the process of self-presentation is also considered to be one of impression management, you are trying to present a version of your self, with or without conscious awareness, that influences how others see you. The terms impression management and self-presentation have become somewhat synonymous with one another and are consequently used interchangeably in this chapter. However, it could be argued that self-presentation is the act of managing your impression of self to others.

There are a number of reasons as to why we engage in online self-presentation, from having the freedom to explore different selves online (Turkle, 1995) to needing to present a version of self to achieve a certain goal (e.g. Leary, 1995). The former might involve, for example, exploring a more outgoing and expressive version of self online than the offline self, whereas the latter might require a certain style of self-presentation to acquire a new job via a platform such as LinkedIn (http://www.linkedin.com). Another factor of Internet behavior discussed in more detail in other chapters is that the Internet is considered a heterogeneous, ever-changing landscape. In your offline world, you behave differently in diverse situations with various goals. Your online behavior is no different. Offline, you present a different self and behave differently during a first date to how you would behave when at work. Online, you are no different. The self presented on a dating website, for example, will likely be very different to the self you reveal on a professional networking website such as LinkedIn or researchgate (http://www.researchgate.org). Where your goal is one of providing self information that needs to endure for a longer time, or that creates a more positive impression of your self, you may be more truthful and honest in that online self creation than when your goal or online interaction is a brief or short-lived interaction or encounter. Obviously, there will be individual and personal factors that impinge upon how a person presents themselves online. Although online impression management and the role of individual factors is touched upon here, interested readers are referred the next chapter of this volume (see Fullwood, this volume) for a more detailed discussion.

THEORIES OF SELF

In order to understand online self-presentation, it is useful to take a look at some of the theories of self that have been used to explain online impression management. In doing so, it is acknowledged that many people will consciously believe that they do not manipulate who they are online, but are firm in their notion of self being consistent offline and online, regardless of what they are doing and with whom they are interacting. In other words, they believe that they are always presenting a true or real self, regardless of situational or temporal factors. From a psychological perspective, the Internet offers users the opportunity to step outside of these selves, and even to create an entirely fictitious or fantasy self that simply cannot exist offline. Imagine for example, the avatars that people use when gaming online. Although they may don a costume to act out a character when visiting a ComicCon Convention (http://www.mcmcomiccon.com/birmingham/), or take part in offline costume play of an online game, they cannot sensibly exist in that offline environment continuously or for any length of time. A prime example hereof is the game World of Warcraft, a video game that first came to attention in 2004, drew large crowds when acted out offline. Recently, players donned costumes and escaped to a forest in the Czech Republic to partake in an offline construction of a World of Warcraft battle (https://www.news18.com/news/tech/in-pics-real-life-world-of-warcraft-takes-place-in-czech-forest-1734865.html). While this is possible for a brief period of time, imagine turning up to work on a Monday morning wearing the costume of a video game character! Online, however, you can return to this character on a daily basis. It is less sporadic and could potentially become a more integrated part of your daily self. Of course, there are risks around this integration of fantasy selves into one's notion of self that could potentially impinge on daily activities and routines, but its inclusion does illustrate that we cannot assume that the online self will always be identical to the offline self. Sometimes, online selves are used for escapism much in the same way as they are offline; online people may be able to escape for longer periods of time more frequently. But we must ask why people manipulate their self-presentation in this way. Borrowing from long established theories and coupling these with more recently emerging ideas may help answer this question.

Goffman's Theory of Self-Presentation

Over fifty years ago, Goffman (1959) presented a theory of self-presentation that has remained eminent throughout the study of offline selves, and has survived technological advances and adaptations to be even more applicable now than it was of the time of its creation. Goffman suggested that the world is nothing other than a stage on which humans are actors. We are therefore nothing other than actors playing out our roles of everyday life, and it is the arenas in which we stage those roles that are constantly changing. This echoes the earlier outline of the different social roles we embody in our daily lives. When online, we are thus manipulating our self-presentations, working alone or with others, to create, shape, and present impressions of both the self and others in a way that portrays a certain self-image we want others to see. Indeed, Goffman was ahead of his time in stating that the self portrayed via the telephone or in written communication (i.e. letters) was inferior to that presented to another person in face-to-face communication. Online communication in text form via email, instant messenger, or even via the emerging rudimentary social networking sites, often lacked the conveyance of social cues, emotion, and other body language cues of communication. Consider, for example, early bulletin board systems which required single user asynchronous contributions (only one person at a time could contribute to the text-based communications),

Internet Relay Chat, which offered one of the first forms of instant messaging, or online forums. All of these text-based tools helped shape and develop online communication as we now know it, illustrating how capable humans are of adapting, changing, and developing available tools to suit their wants and needs.

With these text-based interactions, which lacked social cues, humans began to develop avatars, abbreviations (LOL, BRB, ROFL), and emoticons. Social cues that could convey the appearance of self as well as momentary feelings and emotions were replaced online with expressions presented in symbols and letters (e.g. [;)], [:( ], [<3], etc.). These have been replaced by fully formed emoticons and miniscule images of almost every conceivable category of items nowadays—e.g. animals, buildings, flags, food types, holidays, etc. If you so desired, you could convey an entire message and emotional self through small images alone. While Goffman's notion of the world as a stage could not be more accurate when considering the ways in which we present ourselves online, many features of his outlined self appeared to stem from futuristic notions or science fiction. For the reader who remembers the 1980's television program Dick Tracy, *Knight Rider*, and David Hasselhoff's character Michael talking to a wrist watch, consider other science fiction predictions that are now a reality—the Apple watch into which you can now talk to communicate rather than tapping on it. We might not yet have a speaking car, but many of us do already speak orders to our dashboards to carry out in transit activities (e.g. make a phone call or find a street). We digress! Humans have forever managed to convey themselves in one form or another, whether it be via face-to-face communication, in text, in images, and in a world filled with technology that is reminiscent of science fiction, people will always find a way to portray the self that they want others to see and experience, and where better to do so than online. The online world offers myriad avenues for self-exploration and self-presentation, be that of an ideal, actual, fictional, ought, or fusion self online.

At this point, you might be asking yourself why people feel inclined to manipulate their online self-presentation. There are many theoretical reasons as to why this might be, but before these are discussed, take a moment to consider your own actions online. Do you ever see images of friends, family, or acquaintances enjoying the perfect lifestyle, with perfect bodies, the perfect house, perfect holidays, and perfect car, etc.? Of course, in order for the Internet to exist, people need to use it and share information, images included, but do you ever take a moment to ask yourself if these portrayals are an actual reflection of life? Also, do they then influence your thinking of how you should be living your life? If this is the case, then rightly or wrongly, others' self-portrayals are influencing how you present your self to others. The next time you look at someone's perfect life as depicted online, think of Turkle's (1995) suggestion of the Internet being a playground, where people can be who they want to be, where they can explore their self identities, and, to some extent, create a completely fake persona if they wish. These ideal life portrayals are possible online due to software and technological advances, e.g. the filters and adaptations available to post perfect images of one's self to Instagram. Recent work in our Cyberpsychology group has highlighted that people tend to manipulate images of themselves when posting to Instagram, but not images of other people. The expectation was that if people scored high on measures that indicate they want to present themselves in a positive light, they might also be inclined to want to make other people look less favorable when posting images of them, but that did not emerge in our data (Attrill-Smith & Shaban, n.d.). Altering self-images in this way raises social pressure for other posters to equally comply, leading to even the most technically challenged of individuals being able to completely alter images of themselves to post online. According to Goffman's theory, people once used written text to attract attention from others. The filtering of Instagram images may reflect the modern equivalent, in that people seek to attract attention by the use of image manipulation to present a perfect image of self to others. After all, Instagram "success" is measured in the amount of likes an image receives and the number of followers a poster has. Although Goffman's theory can help us understand *what* people do when putting themselves online, and illustrates the different selves one might portray across different types of Internet arena, it doesn't offer a great insight into the strategies they might use in doing so.

Arkin's Self-Presentation Strategies

Arkin (1981) suggested two strategies that people use to present the self to achieve the performance outlined by Goffman: acquisitive self-presentation (used to gain others' approval of the depicted self) and protective self-presentation (used to avoid others' disapproval of the self). On an image-sharing platform as Instagram, people may look for approval from others. In online support groups, they may instead be seeking health advice. Whereas the former may promote acquisitive self-presentation, the latter may involve protective self-presentation. Arkin outlines the use of these two steps of self-presentation, which serve to both enhance acceptance of the depicted self, but equally to ensure that a poster can protect themselves against negative feedback or criticism of others. However, both Goffman's and Arkin's theories existed a good few decades before the spread of the Internet as it exists today. Again, there are many factors that influence how people create their online self, not least individual factors, but also what the aims and goals are in portraying their online self. Instagram is a very different online arena to many other forms of online communication. From discussion groups to talking to an online expert via a chatbot, and from online dating to being a member of an online gaming community, it is likely that anyone using the Internet carefully and selectively presents themselves across a diverse and varied Internet landscape in such a way that promotes both a sense of positive self while also protecting the self from others' disapproval.

Having read this chapter thus far, you are now probably wondering how such a fragmented self, consisting of different selves, can exist in psychological harmony online. Firstly, the portrayal here is not of a fragmented self, but of an overall self-concept that consists of many different features of self. It is these features that determine different types of behaviors in different situations and times. The self-concept is actually somewhat stable over time and not as fragmented as this outline would suggest. Secondly, there are countless existing and emerging theories of online self-creation. Reviewing every single theory is beyond the scope of this volume. Thus, the chapter next provides a brief overview of some of the theories that may elucidate why we don't have a fragmented self, and which will hopefully help spark an interest for further reading around this topic.

Self-Discrepancy Theory (SDT)

Built on the notion of people having the three selves outlined above (actual, ideal, and ought selves), Higgins (1987) suggested in his Self-Discrepancy Theory (SDT) that how we perceive ourselves in both our own and others' eyes is pivotal to how we present our self to the world. Depending on the value and weight we give to others' views and social norms, a person will strive to present one of the three selves. If, however, that presentation strays too far from the actual or core self, you would be trying to be someone who you are not. Thus, the cleft between an actual and ideal self, or an actual and ought self, cannot be too great or it will cause psychological tension. This tension can be detrimental and harmful to a person's perceptions of their self. People may engage in some level of comparison with others to gauge how to behave in any given situation (see Tesser, Millar, & Moore, 1988 and their self-evaluation maintenance model of upward and downward comparisons), or to enhance their sense of belonging socially (see Festinger's 1954 social comparison theory), but essentially any self presented other than the core or actual self is a step away from a core or real self; psychological frustrations may result if the ideal or ought self is too far removed from reality. In other words, if you set realistic and achievable goals related to your actual or ought self, there is less likelihood of psychological tension and upset. However, if those ideal or ought selves are so far removed from reality that they cannot be achieved, frustration and psychological discomfort would increase. Hopefully, you are alread the most ideal version of you that you can and want to be, and thus, your ideal and actual selves are in sync—something many endlessly strive for, but few ever achieve. Being at one with your self in this manner is often referred to as having self-concept clarity (Campbell et al., 1996).

Before wondering why very few people achieve self-concept clarity, bear in mind that of importance is your perception of how much your actual self is living up to your expectations of your ideal and ought selves. Your interpretation of what those selves should be is critical in creating or reducing discrepancies between your selves. These perceptions, expectations, and interpretations will, of course, be influenced by your previous experiences of similar situations, or hearsay of what to expect of any given situation. Ultimately, presenting an actual self where possible will help reduce psychological discomfort in a situation where you strive for an ideal or actual self. Moreover, not all selves are based on instant gratification or instant goal attainment. Some behavior goals require a longer time period to achieve than others. For example, you might currently be working on an undergraduate or postgraduate qualification to achieve an ideal version of your self as an accomplished student. It is healthy to have these realistic goals of achieving an ideal self. And in terms of online behavior, as much as offline behavior is governed by social norms, rules, regulations, and laws, any self we present needs to remain within those behavioral boundaries unless we wish to invite unsavory or even illegal consequences of our behavior. When considering online selves, however, it might be the case that the distance between the selves is less prominent than it may be offline, because people don't always have the social reinforcement of the social norms and boundaries that exist offline. Alternatively, we could adopt the view of early reports of the self online, which suggested that online self-presentation as more of an exploration for developing and presenting an ideal self, rather than actual self-presentation (e.g. Turkle, 1995). One of the advantages of this online self-exploration is that versions of self can be acted online that could potentially be transferred to the offline world. For example, in their 2013 study, DeHaan and colleagues reported on 32 lesbian, gay, bisexual, and transgender individuals who were able to explore aspects of their sexuality online, but who often would maintain a low profile in their offline worlds for fear of negative judgment (Mustanski, Newcomb, & Garofalo, 2011). The underlying notion of this line of reasoning is that if an individual pretends to be someone long enough they might eventually "become" that person, along the lines of Arkin's (1981) aforementioned acquisitive self-presentation, and akin to the example of soap opera actors becoming their characters both in and out of role.

Consider for a moment your own online behavior. Are there certain things you do online where you feel you are more *you* than other areas of online behavior? Or, do you filter all of your Instagram photos to present the best possible version of yourself that you believe you could be (ideal self), or, do you filter and amend photos of your self to present someone who you believe others want you to be (ought self)? If you have ever been active on an online dating website, and you like the pictures of a potential dater, do you ever ask yourself if that is really what they look like, only to be hugely disappointed when they turn up to an offline date and it is clear that their images had been altered to present a much better-looking version of them to attract a date? This is SDT in practice online. Now, imagine that when you meet this person offline, you cannot hide your sheer disappoint that s/he does not look as promised by the online photos. Surely, that person returns home from their date with a huge dent to their ego, even more so if they feel that the images they are using reflect their real self. If, however, they admit to themselves that they have altered the images to present a false ideal self, then the reality of the situation and disappointment will have less psychological impact on them than if they believe themselves to be portraying their real self to others online. One feature of this type of online self-creation is that it is flexible, malleable, and constantly changing. It is the individual who chooses which of these selves to use in any given online arena, but this benefit of choice does not translate so readily offline. In the offline world the individual is usually in the moment, and there is no time to edit or re-create the self as easily as can be done online. For example, if you tell a bad joke and experience a tumbleweed silence in a pub, the awkwardness can last for quite a while. In an online environment, however, you probably wouldn't experience the same level of embarrassment as you can suggest that the meaning or pun of the joke was lost in translation. It is worth mentioning though that Schlegel, Vess, and Arndt (2012) proposed that, even online, this level of self-re-creation is not sustainable. They argue that if you have a core or actual self that is well-developed, it will eventually surface, regardless of where you are presenting yourself (offline or online). Specifically, it is the core self that is stable and consistent across time and situations. An individual cannot be in a constant state of self-flux, as it would cause continuous discrepancy and disharmony to the notion of self. Some level of awareness of the core self would guide a person to certain areas of online behavior in the first place. Once there, the individual may decide to slightly or considerably alter the self to comply to the situational norms, presenting an idealized or ought self. The next section considers what role social cues play in online self creation.

Social Information Processing Theory (SIP)

If you meet a person offline for the first time, what cues do you use to form your impression of them? You will likely judge them by their dress sense and level of perceived personal hygiene, as well as by their facial and general body language. All of these factors, and more, are considered to be social cues, i.e. little bits of information gleaned from a person or situation. These cues are then used to interpret and respond in any given situation. Offline these facial expressions and body language convey a wide range of information; someone crossing their arms unwelcomingly can be interpreted as hostility, them throwing open their arms as welcoming, and tears can be shed for both sadness and joy. These emotions, as well as an array of others in between, are instantaneous signals that enable us to interpret and respond to others' behavior in our offline worlds, and which have historically been less available in written forms of online communications. During the infancy of online communication, people needed to create a version of themselves based entirely in written text. However, humans are continuously adapting and using tools to our advantage, and how we use the Internet is no different. According to SIP theory (Walther, 1992), we simply compensate for absent social cues through other online means.

When engaging in online communication, have you ever read an online description of someone and created an image in your own head of what you think they look like? Or has it informed preconceptions of how they might behave? Has that then shaped the way in which you respond to them? This is exactly the premise of SIP theory: your self-identity is shaped and presented based on the world around you. According to McCarthey and Moje (2002), this process of absorbing information around us helps us make sense of the world in which we exist. Offline cues are now increasingly re-created online through means other than the basic emoticons already outlined. Popular on social media sites such as Facebook and Instagram, graphic interchange formats (GIFs) are bitesized, repetitive, bitmap videos that are used to convey an emotion or a reaction to something posted or shared in text format. Use of GIFs, emoticons, and other online substitutes for offline cues could be interpreted as suggesting that humans are adequately able to convey social cues online. However, the assumption here is that people are willing to compensate situational cues in this manner, as well as that people interpret the cues as intended by the original poster thereof, which is not necessarily the case. Information can become lost in translation, and receivers or viewers of that information often misinterpret the intended emotional conveyance. This misinterpretation then shapes the way in which that person presents their self in this situation, through written communication, GIF use, or otherwise. Interpretations of these online compensations are less open to clarification in the first instance and could inadvertently cause an instant unintended behavioral response. We have all done this—have you ever thought about a meeting or phone call you need to make? Before doing so, to organize your own thoughts, you create a script in your own mind of exactly what you will say and imagine the other person's response(s) to your communication. You might, for instance, tell someone that you are breaking up with them romantically. You know exactly how you are going to put it to them and have played it out in your own mind a hundred times. When the time comes, however, they might throw you completely off track with a totally unexpected response. The phone call may not go according to your anticipated plan, and your interpretation of the other person's behavior in that moment will shape how you then proceed with the conversation. Although online behavior is no different, depending upon the mode of communication you use, the instant interpretation and response might be vastly different.

Unlike all other forms of online communication, video communication is the only truly synchronous interaction currently available online. People often use videoconferencing apps such as Skype and FaceTime to stay in touch with people the world over at affordable prices. While it is gaining in popularity, some recent research suggests that people are less comfortable with using synchronous video communication, especially with people outside of immediate family circles (Rai & Attrill, 2014). If we consider the advantage of online communication as enabling individuals to carefully create a version of their self they feel comfortable with online, it stands to reason that video communication would be less preferred, simply because it does not offer the advantage of time lag to carefully creating a self to present to others. Imagine the following three versions of a job interview: face to face, telephone, and videoconferencing. Which do you think would afford you the most flexibility in being able to present the best possible version of you? Different people will accept/reject these modes of interview based on their own individual characteristics. They all have advantages and disadvantages in terms of social information processing. There is evidence to show that people are judged less favorably in video interviews than face to face (e.g. Chapman & Webster, 2001), and less favorably generally via video than face to face (e.g. Fullwood, 2007). In a face-to-face interview, you can use your body language instantly to more or less confidently respond to your interviewer's body language. A brief sideways glance from an interview panel member can convey a lot of information for the interviewee. This is a cue that would be completely absent in a telephone call, where voice intonation and length of pause between questions and answers likely play a role. Subtle cues might not be so easily noticed on a live video interview. Even though video calls are synchronous, it takes a lot of practice to be able to confidently look at the camera while keeping an eye on the little box somewhere on your monitor that shows what's happening at the other end of a conversation. It would appear that although humans have adapted their communication skills in line with technological advances, thus far they have not mastered an entire replication of our offline interactions online. And until they do so, a person's online self may be different or similar to their offline self depending upon the mode of communication and Internet arena in use. These considerations are central to Walther's (1996) initial conceptualizations of his hyperpersonal communication model.

Hyperpersonal Communication Model (HPCM)

Walther put forward his HPCM in 1996, when online communication for the masses was in its infancy, and people were very much restricted to text-based communications. Although his theory has had some modifications over the years, of interest for this chapter is Walther's notion that people use different types of computer-mediated communication (CMC) to create their online self. In particular, asynchronous modes of communication enable people to compensate for the absence of social cues because they have time to think about the self that they are sharing or presenting. Text can be used to embellish and enrich a depiction of self to the online world, creating thoughtful constructions of self that portray the ideal version of self in that moment, or with a particular goal in mind.

Let's return to the example of a job interview. Before getting to the interview stage, you might have to submit a job application via email. Of course, you want your best possible self to shine through in that email, and therefore you would therefore unlikely open the email with "Hey dude...". The recipient will use any cues or information available to them to form an opinion of you; in fact, this begins with your email address, not the email content. Have you ever been embarrassed to share your email address with someone? Online interactions are thus akin to a circular process of self-presentation and image formation; any information conveyed via written text or other modes of communication can, and does, influence how people build an image of a person. It will then also guide their communications and interactions with that person. This response, in turn, influences how that person responds, etc.

Notably, this circular process is not reserved for asynchronous text-based communications. There are some differences between modes of synchronous (real-time) communications that convey more or fewer social cues. Instant messaging, for example, may convey less accurate information about a person than does video communication. Indeed, instant messaging is not really a synchronous communication in this respect. Rather, the respondent can take as little or as long as they like to reply to a message. This length of time, in and of itself, can influence how a message sender will react to the message once received. Many instant messenger services or apps indicate at what time a message was received, and whether it has been read. Moreover, many apps will show that a message recipient is actively typing a response, usually in the form of three dots bouncing up and down. If the reply to you takes quite a while to compose, you might expect a lengthy reply, but it may be only one or two words—maybe just a "yes" or "no". The difference between the send and receive time and the length of the received message is only one of many small factors that come together to aid your impression formation and judgment of another person. Equally, these factors also influence which features of your own self come to the fore to interact in that situation. This is self-creation online in real time. It is you creating you as you interact and communicate with others via the Internet. Even though we may experience an absence of the more traditional offline social cues in these text-based communications, there are ample other cues on which we draw that influence our perceptions and interpretations of others' behavior, which in turn influence how we create our self and our own behavior.

The cues considered thus far will, of course, differ to those employed in synchronous video communication. When Skyping or FaceTiming someone you have instant cues, much in the same way as when you are chatting to them offline—or do you? Do you change your behavior and facial expressions when talking to someone in this manner? There may be subtle differences when video-chatting online to how you would behave offline. You might, for instance, play up or play down certain facets of your body language or behavior in attempts to control others' impressions of you. When doing so, you have an advantage you don't have offline—you can instantly see yourself as others see you because you have that information directly in front of you. This instant self-feedback allows you to amend your self instantly. However, this line of reasoning needs to consider the notion of behavioral intent. Many of the theories outlined thus far suppose that people display intent in their online behaviors, and that any recipient of an online communication is suitably able to detect that intent and respond accordingly. All of these theories assume that 1) we are carefully considering how we present our selves to others, and 2) that we are creating whichever version of the self will best achieve a desired goal. That goal might be to secure a job interview through a very well-written email, or it might be to land a date with a desired other, or it might simply be to make a friend of someone you have interacted with online. Regardless of the goal, it is extremely rare that human beings behave in a non-goal-directed manner. Creating a temporal goal-directed version of your self online is no different.

Uses and Gratifications Theory

When presenting your self online, you may or may not be consciously aware of the goal of that behavior. Goals come in many shapes and forms, and can be overtly behavioral, psychological, cognitive, physical, or emotional, or any combination of these, along with many more facets of human nature. Whatever the goal of your online activity, you will select and present aspects of your self that can be tailored to meet that goal. Katz, Blumler and Gurevitch's (1973) Uses and Gratifications Theory is in line with many other theories that posit all human behavior to be goal-driven. For example, Deci and Ryan (2000) suggest human behavior to be driven by an underlying need for human belonging, while Davis and Kraus (1989) suggest human interaction comes from a desire to fulfill social needs. Which self you are presenting online will not only depend upon the goal you are trying to achieve, but also on which further theory you choose to adhere to. For example, according to McKenna, Green, and Gleason (2002), a person would be more likely to shape their self and engage in online interactions in a way that compensates for their inhibitions in offline social interactions. Whereas this notion presents the use of a distinct self online, a further proposal can be made for people presenting an extended offline self online. Accordingly, if aligning to Valkenburg, Schouten, and Peter's (2005) notion of social enhancement, it could be assumed that one's online self is an extension of their offline self, and that the same crafting and creation of self is present regardless of whether the person is interacting online or offline. Regardless of which of these two proposals (and there are many others available) are explored (or not) beyond this chapter, the inclusion of Uses and Gratifications theory suggests that any form of Internet behavior is likely goal driven, in a way that either consciously or non-consciously aims to fulfill basic human needs and desires. In doing so, online behavior requires a flexible self that can be shaped according to any goals. Our behaviors are, however, not only guided by these internal and external factors. There are many more facets of human behavior that serve to constrain and regulate our online selves. The final section of this chapter investigates two more aspects of human behavior that are often overlooked in considering online selves: moral and social norms, and the unhealthy online self.

Morals and Social Norms

Morals are messages about human behavior that have usually developed culturally over a long period of time. They are different to social norms, which are also culturally developed over time. Whereas social norms are usually constructed based on human social interaction and reflect the boundaries of acceptable social behavior, morals are more a judgment of right or wrong, based on standards of behavior that have been conveyed through fables and myths, and that are often aligned to religious beliefs. A person's core self will likely be developed and shaped through childhood and into adulthood by the moral beliefs and principles to which their families adhere, but the social norms which curtail and constrain behavior are set by the society in which they live. Both morals and social norms shape who a person is in any given situation, regardless of whether this is online or offline. Years ago, with developing technology affording the UK only three TV channels, two of which did not broadcast all day, morality and social norms guided a very different presentation of the self to the masses. As late as the 1970s and 1980s, television, film, and radio were very different to the overflow of modern mass media. Where once a Playboy magazine was half hidden on the newsagent's top shelf, nowadays the Internet can provide similar content, as well as almost anything else the heart desires. For example, Bettie Mae Page was one of the world's first pin up models of the 1950s; she was socially and morally vilified for posing naked. Compare her photos to the abundance of pornography (legal or otherwise) available nowadays at the click of a mouse. In addition to sexual content, racist, homophobic, nationalist, extremist, and many other types of content are available instantaneously, and influence peoples' construction of both their core and other selves. This availability has led some authors to suggest that the western world is losing its sense of morality. Human beings are not just blank canvasses, but are sponges that soak up their surroundings, aspects of the people they interact with, and the nuances of the communications in which they engage. Just think about how your own mood might change in a split second because of something someone says to you online. Selves are constantly shaped through every minute of every day. Seibt and Nørskov (2012) raise questions about the moral self online that have hitherto been largely neglected academically, with most work focusing on social norms. They suggest that an absence of physical and face-to-face interaction online coupled with anonymity leads to individuals presenting multiple different selves online. Offline, most of our moral judgments and behaviors are constrained by social norms of acceptable behavior. Online, these social norms can theoretically be easily avoided through supposedly anonymous online self-presentation to more easily present a judgment that may not be morally reconcilable with a person's core self. Many will remember Peter Steiner's (1993) cartoon from *The New Yorker* of dogs using the Internet, with the caption "On the Internet, nobody knows you're a dog." Absolute anonymity is no longer real online, but, if people perceive themselves to be interacting anonymously online they may dissociate their core self from that behavior to avoid any psychological tension that might arise from the difference in their presented self and core self. In other words, it may be easier to present a different self online—one that is not aligned to the moral and societal norm constraints of offline behavior. There are instances of when this perceived anonymity might be of an advantage to the online self, for example, the exploration of different possible selves outlined by Turkle (1995). It might, however, also be at the root of behaviors online that can be linked to more detrimental constructions of the self online.

THE UNHEALTHY SELF

The final section of this chapter examines the less positive side of online self creation that is unfortunately also gathering pace in light of the supposed reduction in morality and societal norms influencing online behavior. One of the advantages of the Internet is that it opens up a wider playground than people may experience offline in finding like-minded others. As we know from decades of social psychology research, people are drawn to like-minded others (Zajonc, 1968). If that like-mindedness is grounded in positive individual characteristics or group spirit, it is likely to pose little to no threat of harm or negative intent to an individual. If, however, the coming together of people online is motivated by nefarious intent, it can have severely detrimental effects to both the online and offline selves of the user. There exists an array of online spaces that are designed to draw people into a promotion of their negative self, and that reaffirm their skewed negative judgments of their self. Websites that promote eating disorders, suicidal ideations, and acts of self-harm are aimed at reeling in vulnerable individuals. Similarly, online groups and forums that promote idealized political or religious views, and which are aimed at destruction and devastation through terrorist ideations, are all too readily available online to anyone who is seeking a sense of belonging. While people may initially be drawn into such arenas based on ideas or behaviors that cause them to seek out like minded others, others may simply be curious. However, once connected to those others, the continuous positive reinforcement of their ideas and skewed self-perceptions may make it difficult to subsequently extricate themselves from that space. For example, if a person who is extremely underweight finds themselves drawn to a pro-anorexia website, they may see images of other similarly underweight individuals who have received praise and adoration for their look. This will incur in them a sense of acceptability for that body style and reaffirm their positive view of self. They may also interact with other members of the group, who tell them that they look good and provide reinforcement and encouragement that they would unlikely receive offline for their eating behavior. This works both ways, as there are websites available that cater for overeaters, and the notion of big being beautiful. Of importance here is that once a person feels accepted and positively reinforced within such an online environment, the people with whom they interact can become hyperpersonal to the individual (Walther, 1996). That is, the individual may start to neglect offline (and possibly more realistic) relationships that offer healthier interactions and opinions to focus on the online relationships. If someone is being told what they want to hear, they are unlikely to want to remove themselves from that situation and will shun any situation which does not offer that positive reinforcement of their self, or which questions their self. This unhealthy self may then come to over ride any other selves the individual has, online or offline, which could eventually lead to a whole host of negative consequences.

CONCLUSIONS

This very brief outline of a few carefully chosen theories shows that many factors come into play in how we construct the self online. From our current behavioral goals to the mode of communication used, from the ways in which any available social cues are interpreted to their re-creation in some types of online interaction, each shapes both how we perceive and interpret those others, as well as how we subsequently craft and create a self in response. Through words, emoticons, or GIFs, as well as the circular interaction with a single other or multiple groups of others, these are but a few of the facets of human behavior that feed into our online self-creations which have been conceptualized theoretically. In his chapter in this volume, Dr. Chris Fullwood picks up where we leave off and explores further exactly how people manipulate their online self-presentations.

REFERENCES

Arkin, R.M. (1981). Self-presentational styles. In J. T. Tedeschi (Ed.), *Impression management theory and social psychological research* (pp. 311–333). New York: Academic Press.

Attrill, A. (2015). *Cyberpsychology.* Oxford: Oxford University Press.

Attrill-Smith, A., & Shaban, M. (n.d.). Who filters on Instagram? Self-presentation, perception control and self-esteem predictors of Instagram filtering.

Baumeister, R. F. (1999). The nature and structure of the self: An overview. In R. Baumeister (Ed.), *The self in social psychology* (pp. 1–20). Philadelphia, PA: Psychology Press.

Campbell, J., Trapnell, P., Heine, S. J., Katz, I. M., Lavallee, L. R., & Lehman, D. R. (1996). Self-concept clarity: Measurement, personality correlates, and cultural boundaries. *Journal of Personality and Social Psychology 70*, 141–156.

Chapman, D. S., & Webster, J. (2001). Rater correction processes in applicant selection using videoconference technology: The role of attributions. *Journal of Applied Social Psychology 31*(12), 2518–2537.

Davis, M. H., & Kraus, L. A. (1989). Social contact, loneliness, and mass media use: A test of two hypotheses. *Journal of Applied Social Psychology 19*, 1100–1124.

Deci, E. L., & Ryan, R. M. (2000). The "what" and "why" of goal pursuits: Human needs and the self-determination of behaviour. *Psychological Inquiry 11*(4), 227–268.

DeHaan, S., Kuper, L. E., Magee, J. C., Bigelow, L., & Mustanski, B. S. (2013). The interplay between online and offline explorations of identity, relationships, and sex: A mixed-methods study with LGBT youth. *The Journal of Sex Research 50*(5), 421–434.

Festinger, L. (1954). A theory of social comparison processes. *Human Relations 7*(2), 117–140.

Fullwood, C. (2007). The effect of mediation on impression formation: A comparison of face-to-face & video-mediated conditions. *Applied Ergonomics 38*, 267–273.

Goffman, E. (1959). *The presentation of self in everyday life*. Garden City, NY: Doubleday.

Higgins, E. T. (1987). Self-discrepancy: A theory relating self and affect. *Psychological Review 94*, 319–340.

Hogg, M. A., & Vaughan, G. M. (2017). *Social Psychology*. Pearson. UK.

Katz, E., Blumler, J. G., & Gurevitch, M. (1973). Uses and gratifications research. *Public Opinion Quarterly, 37*(4), 509–523.

Leary, M. R. (1995). *Self-presentation, impression management and interpersonal behaviour*. Madison, WI: Brown and Benchmark.

McCarthey, S. J., & Moje, E. B. (2002). Identity matters. *Reading Research Quarterly 37*(2), 228–238.

McKenna, K. Y. A., & Green, A. S., & Gleason, M. E. J. (2002). Relationship formation on the Internet: What's the big attraction? *Journal of Social Issues 58*(1), 9–31.

Mustanski, B., Newcomb, M., & Garofalo, R. (2011). Mental health of lesbian, gay, and bisexual youth: A developmental resiliency perspective. *Journal of Gay and Lesbian Social Services 23*, 204–225.

Rai, R., & Attrill, A. (2014). The effects of synchronous and asynchronous internet communication, personality, and representations of the self on the uptake of online video communication. Poster presented at the 16th International Conference on Human Computer Interaction. 22–27 June, Heraklion, Crete, Greece.

Schlegel, R. J., Vess, M., & Arndt, J. (2012). To discover or to create: Metaphors and the true self. *Journal of Personality 80*, 969–993.

Seibt, J., & Nørskov, M. (2012). "Embodying" the Internet: Towards the moral self via communication robots? *Philosophy and Technology 25*, 285–307.

Steiner, P. (1993, July 5). *On the Internet, nobody knows you're a dog*. Cartoon published in *The New Yorker*.

Tesser, A., Millar, M., & Moore, J. (1988). Some affective consequences of social comparison and reflection processes: The pain and pleasure of being close. *Journal of Personality and Social Psychology 54*(1), 49–61.

Turkle, S. (1995). *Life on the screen: Identity in the age of the Internet*. New York, NY: Simon & Schuster.

Valkenburg, P. M., Schouten, A. P., & Peter, J. (2005). Adolescents' identity experiments on the Internet. *New Media and Society 7*(3), 383–402.

Walther, J. B. (1992). Interpersonal effects in computer-mediated interaction: A relational perspective. *Communication Research 19*, 52–90.

Walther, J. B. (1996). Computer-mediated communication: Impersonal, interpersonal, and hyperpersonal interaction. *Communication Research 23*, 3–43.

Zajonc, R. B. (1968). Attitudinal effects of mere exposure. *Journal of Personality & Social Psychology Monograph Supplement 9*, 1–27.

....

CHAPTER 3

IMPRESSION MANAGEMENT AND SELF-PRESENTATION ONLINE

....

CHRIS FULLWOOD

Introduction

....

A few years ago, while visiting my older brother and his family, two of my nieces (Caitlin and Alyssa) and my nephew (Dylan) sat me down to introduce me to the videos of Stampylonghead. For those who are unfamiliar Stampylonghead, or Stampylongnose as he is also known, is a YouTube gaming broadcaster most recognized for his Minecraft "Let's Play" commentaries. The looks of excitement etched across their faces soon turned to collective disappointment and bewilderment once they slowly came to the realization that I did not share their passion for watching a man with a very high-pitched voice commenting in excruciating detail about his adventures in the world of Minecraft. For me the videos were dull and juvenile, but for them they were a source of wonderment and inspiration. Stampylonghead certainly seems to divide opinion between parents and their offspring, with one mother on Mumsnet (http://www.mumsnet.com) likening his voice and laugh to "fingers down a blackboard" but nonetheless he seems to have hit upon a very successful formula for keeping an army of children glued to his channels, reportedly making him exceptionally wealthy in the process. After seeing his videos, I could have concluded that I was utterly out of touch with youth culture. Instead, I settled with the notion that my nieces and nephew would be equally unlikely to understand my enjoyment for the nostalgia-driven gaming videos of the Angry Video Game Nerd (they would probably guess that a Megadrive was an exceptionally long car journey rather than an old school gaming console). There really is something for everyone on YouTube.

The success story of Stampylonghead and others like him provides perfect illustration for how, with the development of Web 2.0 platforms like YouTube, ordinary people can broadcast themselves to potentially massive worldwide audiences (Krämer & Winter, 2008), even when the content of these broadcasts might appear asinine, peculiar, or niche to many viewers. At the time of writing this chapter Stampylonghead had accrued over eight million subscribers and his main YouTube channel had received over six billion views. Although by no means typical, he is certainly not the only YouTube superstar, and in July 2017 the top ten channels had amassed over 256 million subscribers between them (Fitz-Gerald, 2017), a number approximately equivalent to the population of Indonesia. Incidentally, six of those ten channels involve primarily video gaming content, but many beauty vloggers also attract huge fan bases; for instance as of June 2018, Zoella had over 12 million subscribers. Web 2.0 platforms have transformed Internet users from passive consumers of information to active producers of content, ushering in an era of participation, egalitarianism, and empowerment. While the majority of people will never reach the giddy heights of YouTube stardom, the Internet has indelibly altered the manner in which individuals are able to present themselves to the outside world. The Internet not only provides a potentially global reach for messages and the ability to target specific audiences, but it also enables the ability to craft an image of the self with much more precision than previously possible.

This chapter primarily explores the different ways in which the Internet has impacted on how people present themselves to others. It queries if there are specific features of the cyberspace that afford users more flexible impression management opportunities, if these features encourage more idealized forms of self-presentation, and if certain types of individuals are more likely to take up opportunities to experiment with their self-presentation online. Additionally, it explores if more flexible self-presentation impacts on the manner in which individuals view themselves. Before considering the role that the Internet plays, the chapter begins by providing a theoretical background to understanding the processes involved in managing impressions in order to understand what motivates individuals to partake in self-presentational behavior. It also explores the different ways in which individuals can manufacture images of the self in order to influence how others form impressions of them.

Laying the Foundations: Defining Impression Management and Self-Presentation

During social interactions, we will often find ourselves attempting to influence the opinions of other people. Sometimes this will be a relatively straightforward affair, for example, when the individual is already receptive to our ideas or has an existing positive disposition towards us. On other occasions it might be a much more challenging proposition, for example, when the individual's worldview is very different to our own. Think back to any political debates you may have had with someone whose party affiliation was on the opposite side of the political spectrum to your own. In all probability, you would have found it an enormous challenge to persuade them to change their mind on the issue you were debating. Although in these types of situations we might be attempting to control people's impressions about a variety of different things, for example, ideas, objects or even other people (Chester & Bretherton, 2007), the individual who is attempting to generate, alter, or preserve a specific impression in others is also very much in the spotlight.

An individual's judgment about how credible an argument is will not only hinge on the persuasiveness of the message, but will be influenced by a variety of other peripheral cues, including those relating to the communicator, for example, how attractive, trustworthy, or intelligent the person is perceived to be (Petty & Cacioppo, 1986). As way of illustration, let's say that I had a friend who had never watched an episode of Game of Thrones because she did not consider herself to be fan of the fantasy genre. In trying to convince her that Game of Thrones will enrich her life immeasurably, I might argue that there is much more to the series than simple fantasy, and that political intrigue, captivating heroes, gripping dialogue, clever character development, and plot twists galore were also the order of the day. Whether or not she decides to take my advice will not only depend on my powers of persuasion, but also to some extent on what she thinks about me as an individual. Does she consider me a man of good or poor taste? Am I someone to be trusted on such matters? Do I have a track record for making mostly good or frequently bad recommendations? All of these factors will likely influence whether my persuasion attempts will prove fruitful or fruitless.

Although this might seem like a somewhat flippant example, I hope that it highlights an important point in drawing a parallel between "impression management" and "self-presentation." Although we can manage impressions about a host of different things, we cannot take the individual who is attempting to control those impressions out of the picture. Any attempt to manage impressions, on whatever they might be, invariably communicates some form of information about the self, including attitudes, preferences, or feelings. In endeavoring to convince my friend to watch Game of Thrones, I am not only communicating information about my entertainment preferences, but also, on some level, information about my personality. Indeed, Katz, Blumler, and Gurevitch's (1973) Uses and Gratifications paradigm suggests that people consume different media options in order to gratify specific personal needs (e.g., the need for escapism). Furthermore, personality is important in shaping what these needs may consist of and different personality types have been found to gravitate towards various media options, including preferences for different types of television programs (e.g., see Weaver, 2000).

In evaluating the terms "impression management" and "self-presentation" it is important to consider impression management as representing a "broader and more encompassing term than self-presentation" (Leary & Kowalski, 1990, 34). For instance, Schneider (1981) noted how it was possible for impressions to be managed in other ways than solely through self-presentation, for example other people may react to us on the basis of what a third party has divulged. We may thus think about self-presentation as a subcategory of impression-management which incorporates the controlling of images which are explicitly "self-relevant" (Schlenker, 1980). Self-presentation therefore refers specifically to any form of behavior that is "intended to create, modify, or maintain an impression of *ourselves* in the minds of others" (Brown, 2014, 160), but nevertheless academics have tended to use this term interchangeably with impression management. In spite of the fact that people can manage impressions about almost anything, individuals tend to manage impressions predominantly about the self (Leary & Kowalski, 1990; Rosenberg & Egbert, 2011). This chapter uses the terms impression management and self-presentation interchangeably.

GOFFMAN AND THE "PERFORMED" SELF: A THEORETICAL MODEL OF IMPRESSION MANAGEMENT

One of first scholars to give impression management any serious academic consideration was the Sociologist Irving Goffman (1959) in his ground-breaking work *The presentation of self in everyday life*. Although already outlined to some degree in Attrill-Smith's chapter on "the online self" in this volume, it is fitting to acknowledge and discuss Goffman's theory at this stage in the chapter, given that his ideas have profoundly impacted scholarly consideration of the motivations behind complex self-presentational behaviors within the social context. Goffman developed a metaphorical conceptualization of self-presentation inspired by theatrical performance, arguing that as social "actors" people display different masks to others in social interactions. Concerned with how they may be perceived by others, individuals attempt to impart impressions consistent with their desired goals, and this often involves accentuating positive aspects of the self while suppressing more negative aspects or aligning personal views and ideals with the audience in anticipation of audience judgment. For example, a political candidate will target his or her self-presentation tactics to the segment of the electorate he or she wishes to influence, e.g., Donald Trump's use of Twitter as a "digital PR tool" leading up to his successful campaign for president of the United States. Lee and Lim (2016) note how over half of Trump's tweets were "retweets of or replies to citizens" perhaps demonstrating a deliberate attempt to align himself with the values and beliefs of his core demographic, and almost certainly exploiting economic uncertainty and civil unrest to galvanize his followers.

Taking the metaphor further, Goffman also argued that all people play a wide variety of different parts throughout their lives, and the specific part played will ultimately be determined by the environment and the audience. For example, the types of impression management tactics employed in trying to work up the career ladder would likely be very different from those which would be used in trying to convince someone to continue a friendship after they had been wronged in some way. In the first example, the individual would be more proactive in trying to yield a positive impression, for instance, by using assertive tactics such as ingratiation or self-promotion. The latter example would likely involve more defensive tactics in order to try and repair the damaged impression, for example, by way of apology or making excuses or justifications for hurtful actions (Ellis, West, Ryan, & DeShon, 2002; Lee et al., 1999). Goffman also argued that individuals differ with respect to their levels of self-monitoring, or the extent to which they take cues from their audience and adjust their performance accordingly. Goffman's work therefore disputes the notion of a "true" self. If individuals are able to adapt a performance so malleably to specific situations and audiences, it might challenge the idea that people have a relatively fixed character.

MOTIVATIONS FOR
MANAGING IMPRESSIONS

Any form of impression management necessitates a degree of public self-consciousness, or an awareness that others will view, interpret, and respond to the different ways that people behave (Fenigstein, Scheier, & Buss, 1975). If humans are not able to see themselves through another's eyes, there would be no need to consider and manipulate different aspects of self-presentation to garner a desired response. Impression management is a part of everyday life; it is difficult to envisage any activity which entails social interaction of some description that does not also involve some form of self-presentational behavior (Brown, 2014). Because of the frequency and intensity with which individuals manage the impressions of others, self-presentation plays an important role in influencing how people behave on a day-to-day basis (Chester & Bretherton, 2007). For instance, knowing that people who take care of their appearance tend to be viewed more favorably in society will drive the routines and habits of almost everyone (Brown, 2014; Martin et al., 2000). Of course, there is also a huge degree of variation in terms of how much value we place on what other people think about us. Indeed, in his theory of self-monitoring, Snyder (1987) talks about the distinction between high self-monitors, who are very aware of how they are coming across in social interactions and adapt their behavior on the fly to make good impressions, and low self-monitors, who are generally less concerned with how others might view them. There is also evidence to suggest that high self-monitors are more successful at managing the impressions of others than low self-monitors (e.g., Turnley & Bolino, 2001).

That people differ in how concerned they are about how others might perceive them, suggests that there are likely to be individual differences in how motivated people are to manage the impressions of others. Turnley and Bolino's (2001) findings would also intimate that people might go about forming an image in the minds of others in very different ways. Additionally, there is the expectation that people are more motivated to garner a desired impression in certain contexts over others. There are various situations where impression management concerns would be heightened, and this might be because there would be something important riding on the outcome, e.g., a job interview. The motivation to leave others with a good impression would be intensified here as a successful performance is more likely to result in a job offer, which may, in turn, come with higher levels of job satisfaction, a better salary, etc. (Brown, 2014; Fullwood, 2015). Notwithstanding these more special and somewhat rarer situations, managing impressions of others successfully can help us to get on in life more generally, for example influencing who we become friends with and who will fall in love with us (Brown, 2014).

Therefore, one of the primary motivations for engaging in impression management is to gain personal, material, occupational, or social rewards, or conversely, to avoid "punishments" in these respective domains (Brown, 2014; Leary & Allen, 2011). Returning to Goffman's (1959) self-presentation theory, this also suggests that impression management may have a strategic element, e.g., emphasizing accomplishments in a job interview (accentuation), rather than failures (suppression). However, strategic self-presentation does not necessarily imply deceit. Indeed, Jones (1990) has argued that honesty tends to be the norm in strategic self-presentation, with individuals choosing to selectively disclose information which is in their best interests to convey while neglecting to disclose information which may lead others to judge them less favorably. If there is a level of dishonesty, it is more likely to be deception by omission rather than commission.

Although it might seem logical to assume that the only true motivation for managing impressions of others is to influence them in such a way as to ultimately lead to some form of reward, people may also manage impressions for self-construction or identity management. Through creating impressions of the self in the minds of others, the individual is also simultaneously constructing an identity for him or herself (Brown, 2014; Rosenberg, 1986; Schlenker, 1980). To persuade others that a specific set of characteristics are representative of who we are, we may also concurrently be influencing our own self-perceptions and testing out different identities to see how comfortably they fit with us (Brown, 2014; Rosenberg, 1986). Bem's (1967) self-perception theory, and evidence supporting it (e.g., Laird, 2007), would also infer that we in part learn about who we are from observing and reflecting on our own behaviors in various social contexts. In some instances impression management may help to consolidate a pre-existing self-perception and Swann (1990) has labeled this "self-verification." In other instances, it may help to convince the individual that they possess attributes which are representative of an "ideal" or "possible" self and this has been labeled "self-enhancement" (Swann, 1990). Finally, impression management may also serve the purpose of self-construction. Making specific claims about one's character and attributes may provide the motivation to live up to these representations and work towards self-improvement (Brown, 2014, Goffman, 1959; Schlenker, 1980).

Thus far we have acknowledged that individuals will differ in how much concern they have for managing the impressions of others, that there are a variety of different motivations for engaging in self-presentation, but also that individuals differ in the ways they go about constructing images to influence the impressions of others. Although it might seem on the surface that there should be a direct linear relationship between self-presentation motivation (i.e., how much incentive there is to leave a person with a particular impression) and the different tactics that people might employ to garner those impressions, Leary and Kowalski's (1990) two-component model of impression management implies that they should in fact be viewed as two discrete processes. In other words, just because someone is highly motivated to manage the impressions of others does not necessarily mean that they will make every effort to do so, nor that they will be successful in this endeavor when they do.

Leary and Kowalski's model considers impression management to consists of two distinct components: impression motivation and impression construction, and each are subject to a variety of unique factors. The extent to which individuals are motivated to manage impressions of others will be influenced by the goal-relevance of those impressions, the value of those desired goals, and the discrepancy between one's desired and current image. The different ways that people go about constructing images will be influenced by one's self-concept, desired and undesired identity images, role constraints, the target's values and the individual's current and potential social image. For example, an individual may be highly motivated to leave interviewers with a positive impression because the goal (i.e., being offered the job) relies on successfully persuading the interviewers that he/she possesses certain desirable characteristics. In attempting to achieve this task, the individual may selectively emphasize attributes that he/she believes are consistent with the target's own values (e.g., hard-working, team player) and which are considered to reflect their own desired identity image (this is how I wish the world would see me). In some instances, however, the individual may not feel that they are able to express the image they wish to portray, for example, because they might be constrained by their role. In the job interview scenario, a person may feel that the role of interviewee does not allow them to express themselves in the way they desire, perhaps because wearing a suit is too "formal" and does not give them to the chance to display their individuality.

MOVING IMPRESSION-FORMATION ONLINE: ANONYMITY AND PSEUDOANONYMITY

Now that we have a clearer understanding of the motivations for and processes involved in creating and managing specific impressions in the minds of others, we shall turn our attention to the Internet. The Internet and digital technologies are ubiquitous and are a reality of the everyday lives for most of western society. Whether Internet use involves constructing an online dating profile with the intention of attracting other singletons, sending an email to justify a pay raise, or using social media tools to express opinions and preferences about the world, humans use these forms of technology (often daily) to manage the impressions of others. There are a number of idiosyncratic features of cyberspace that are likely to impact on self-presentation behavior. One of the most debated of these features is the Internet's potential to allow users to interact with others with a perceived anonymity. Although there are many online spaces where users may be expected to make themselves known (for example, on social media sites like Facebook), there are other sites where members may feel that they have more freedom to hide aspects of their identity if desired. For example, many members of discussion boards or online support groups interact with others anonymously (Barak, Boniel-Nissim, & Suler, 2008; Chester & Bretherton, 2007; Fullwood, 2015). However, it is worth noting that no one is ever truly "anonymous" online, because during any online interaction the IP address of the device is being recorded. Although most would not have the technical know-how or inclination to track down an individual from their IP address, with the right level of motivation and knowledge it is technically conceivable to discover the identity of an individual without their revealing any identifying characteristics online (it is technically feasible now for internet users to hide their IP address with the use of VPN (virtual private network) services).

A potential upshot of perceived anonymity is that it creates the conditions in which individuals may feel more at ease with self-disclosing information that they would feel less comfortable revealing face to face. In part, this may be explained by the notion that there could be fewer consequences for the self in making these types of self-disclosures as others cannot link these pieces of information to the "offline" self (McKenna & Bargh, 2000; Valkenburg, Schouten, & Peter, 2005). This may therefore encourage people to be bolder with their self-presentation. A further aspect of anonymity is that it is hypothesized to create a more level playing-field, and this may be advantageous to groups in society who may usually be associated with being less powerful (e.g. minority group members, people with disabilities) by giving them a voice (Christopherson, 2007; Dubrovsky, Kiesler, & Sethna, 1991). This has been coined the "equalization hypothesis" (Dubrovsky et al., 1991) and although it is beyond the scope of this chapter to review this literature in depth, Cromby and Standen (1999) and Chadwick, Fullwood, and Wesson (2013) have discussed how the anonymity of many online spaces can free up people with disabilities to interact with others outside of the dominant disability discourse, without being restricted to the labels that society imposes upon them. In turn this may be a socially liberating experience and help to promote inclusion. However, Chadwick and colleagues (2013) also note that, although non-disclosure of disability can be empowering for individuals, it does little to challenge and change stigma.

A number of scholars have argued that it is unhelpful to conceive of anonymity as a simple anonymous/not-anonymous dichotomy. Indeed, Qian and Scott (2007) discuss the "anonymity continuum" and how the different affordances of technology shape the level of anonymity provided to the user. In other words, one can be more or less anonymous depending on the amount of identifying information (e.g. name, photograph, address) that they disclose. In turn, they highlight an important distinction between the objective aspects of anonymity (e.g., whether the option is given to include a photograph) and subjective aspects (i.e., the extent to which the individual perceives him/herself to be identifiable to others). For example, although someone might reveal identifying information, the disclosure of personal and sensitive information may feel "safe" as other online individuals may be geographically dispersed and unlikely to identify them in the "offline" world (Fullwood, 2015). In this sense, it would imprudent to consider cyberspace as a homogeneous entity as the expectations, norms, and affordances associated with different online spaces around identity disclosure are likely to be extremely diverse.

Scholars like van der Nagel and Frith (2015) have argued for the need to go beyond the "anonymity continuum" to also account for "pseudoanonymity," or instances where individuals adopt false names and identities online. Drawing on the pseudoanonymous practice of individuals posting nude pictures of themselves on subreddit r/gonewild, van der Nagel and Frith argue that embracing pseudonyms permits individuals to explore different identity practices, which would be far less likely to happen on sites (e.g., Facebook) which try to tie users to a single "real" identity. Anonymity and pseudo-anonymity therefore give users a greater degree of freedom to experiment with different types of self-presentation and explore different identities in a space where these investigations can take place with less fear of sustaining damage to one's reputation or offline relationships. This might be particularly beneficial where it involves types of self-presentation which would be viewed more negatively by mainstream society, or where the individual desires for these identity practices to remain very separate from their "offline" self.

WALTHER'S HYPERPERSONAL MODEL OF COMPUTER-MEDIATED COMMUNICATION (CMC)

In addition to many online platforms providing users with opportunities to decide how much identifying information they disclose, there are a variety of other characteristics of cyberspace which may have a bearing on self-presentation behavior. Many of these characteristics are represented in Walther's Hyperpersonal CMC model (Walther, 1996). The basic premise of this model is that users can benefit from many of the features which are unique to different types of CMC platforms. Unlike many of the cues filtered out models which came before it (e.g., Culnan & Markus, 1987)—which focused on how the attenuation or absence of important communication cues (e.g., nonverbal behavior) in CMC may lead to less successful communication and relationship formation/maintenance—the hyperpersonal model focuses on the affordances of technology and how these might benefit self-presentation. First, CMC involves a greater degree of editability than face-to-face communication. Where communication permits spoken language, once a message has been articulated it cannot be retracted; it may only be amended. However, one of the artifacts of text-based CMC is that users normally construct the message in its entirety before sending it, and the message recipient does not have access to the message as it is being constructed. Even in instances where communication is taking place in relative "real time" (e.g., instant messaging services like WhatsApp), users are still afforded the time to reflect on and edit their message before delivery, giving them the opportunity to deliberate more deeply on how they want to appear to others. Additionally, members of many online platforms, e.g., social media sites like Facebook or Instagram, can manage self-presentations predominantly in a visual sense via selectively uploading images, i.e., those that they feel show them in the best possible light or which convey an image of the self which is consistent with how they would like others to see them (Eftekhar et al., 2014; Kramer & Winter, 2008; Siibak, 2009; Van Dijck, 2008). A more prolonged discussion around how people can control aspects of their physical appearance online can be found in Amichai-Hamburger's and Etgar's chapter in this volume on "Personality and Internet Use: The Case of Introversion and Extroversion."

The second affordance discussed by Walther relates to the asynchronous nature of many CMC platforms, in other words, they take place outside of real-time. Email is a good example of an asynchronous mode of communication and although there may be variations between different organizations or groups around (n)etiquette and expectations of an appropriate period of time within which to respond, users are generally not expected to reply instantaneously. Moreover, as the sender does not have access to the receiver's whereabouts and current activities, it cannot be presumed that the recipient is available or able to respond. Like the first feature of editability, having a greater amount of time to formulate the message means that users can cogitate in more detail about the content of the message before sending it. Many email systems also come with spell-checkers built in so users can ensure that their messages are corrected for typos and spelling mistakes.

The third affordance relates to lack of physical proximity to the message recipient. This is considered to be important because unwanted spontaneous communication cues, for example, blushing or shaking, which may reflect negatively on the communicator, are concealed. In line with Goffman's (1959) self-presentation theory, when communicators are less concerned about their bodily conduct "leaking" information which may negatively influence the recipient, they are permitted greater control over accentuating an image they wish to convey while masking an image that they do not wish to. Support for this particular affordance comes from Joinson (2004), who found that individuals with lower self-esteem were more likely to use email as opposed to face-to-face communication where there was a perceived level of risk associated (e.g., asking someone out on a date). Therefore, this feature of cyberspace can provide a means by which those who are shy or socially anxious in particular can communicate and express themselves in ways that would be more difficult offline (Mehdizadeh, 2010). This has been labeled the "poor-get-richer" or social enhancement hypothesis (Zywica & Danowski, 2008).

Walther's final affordance relates to "the reallocation of cognitive resources from environmental scanning and nonverbal management toward message composition" (Walther, 1996, 2541). Specifically, he argued that it is cognitively demanding to attend to the activities of others (e.g., monitoring their feedback and use of nonverbal cues) and other environmental cues, in addition to managing one's own use of nonverbal behavior, to maintain a desirable presence. When these factors are removed from the communication context, e.g., in a text-based interaction taking place outside a co-present environment, cognitive resources which would ordinarily be dedicated to these activities may be reallocated to the lone task of eloquent and coherent expression in CMC. All of these features of CMC are said to benefit self-presentation by affording communicators with the potential to present themselves in a more optimal way; thus, communication may become *hyper*-personal because it exceeds face to face (Walther, 1996; Walther, 2007).

How People Manage Impressions Online

Being online provides a much greater degree of flexibility in terms of managing the impressions of other individuals. Distinctive features of cyberspace, such as editability and asynchronicity, provide opportunities to accentuate positive images of the self which may lead to more favorable judgments by others (Hancock & Dunham, 2001). Moreover, the potential for anonymous interaction may free up more socially anxious individuals to communicate in ways (e.g., more confidently) that would be more diffi-cult for them offline, as they may not be constrained to the same extent by their person-ality (Mehdizadeh, 2010; Valkenburg & Peter, 2009). In addition, theoretically it should also be much easier to construct a fabricated or partially fabricated self-image and to deceive others into accepting the misrepresentation. For example, after the film and TV show of the same name, the term "catfish" describes a person who steals images from other individuals' online profiles (sometimes celebrities, but more often attractive mem-bers of the general public) and tries to pass these off as their own. Despite this potential for the online world to provide many advantages in self-presentation, Fullwood, Quinn, Chen-Wilson, Chadwick, and Reynolds (2015) describe the Internet as a "double-edged sword." Although there are unquestionably abundant opportunities to construct an enhanced self-image while online, CMC may also be characterized as more informal and loosely structured. Thus, CMC does not necessarily need to adhere so rigidly to conventions of grammar, punctuation, and spelling, which might be expected in other forms of written communication (e.g., books, newspapers) (Crystal, 2008). In some areas of cyberspace, e.g., social media, people communicate using more slang and "textspeak," for example, with the use of acronyms (e.g., "LOL" or "laugh out loud"), emojis, or shortenings/contractions (e.g., "ur" instead of "you are") (Drouin, 2011; Farina & Lyddy, 2011; Scott, Sinclair, Short, & Bruce, 2014).

As discussed, self-presentation may be considered to incorporate strategic elements. One way in which individuals can tactically manage the impressions of others online is via selectively disclosing information about themselves (e.g., hobbies, attitudes, interests) which may serve them best for their current purposes (Attrill, 2012). Gosling, Ko, Mannarelli, and Morris (2002) have referred to these types of disclosures which are within direct control as *identity claims*. However, they also argue that people leak unintentional cues via our online behavior, which others will also be likely to judge (e.g., the way language is used), and these are referred to collectively referred to as *behavioral residue*. Although using textspeak might be deemed entirely appropriate in many informal communication contexts, in other instances (e.g., in the online dating arena) others might be making decisions about whether to pursue further communications with another person and the manner in which messages are composed may be influential in guiding these decisions. For example, some people may find a poor use of grammar off-putting (Ellison, Heino, & Gibbs, 2006). Further research suggests that in the context of social media self-presentation, the use of textspeak can lead to more negative impressions of another in terms of judgments of intelligence, competence, and employability (Scott et al., 2014) as well as in the perceptions of personality (i.e., textspeakers are judged as less conscientious and to be less open to new experiences; Fullwood et al., 2015). It is therefore worth acknowledging that although online interactions may offer greater freedom to construct "optimal" self-presentations, the more informal nature of the online medium may also hamper attempts to persuade others to perceive us in the way we would like to be perceived. Moreover, the extent to which perceptions of text-speak are likely to be negative will be influenced by the specific online space in which people are interacting as well as the goals they wish to achieve within those arenas. In the world of online dating, for instance, where individuals are making judgments about the characters and personalities of other online daters in order to decide if they are a desirable mate, the use of textspeak may reflect socially undesirable traits such as carelessness or a lack of imagination or intellect (Fullwood et al., 2015).

Taking these ideas further, there needs to be some recognition of the notion that the Internet is a vast communication landscape with multifarious arenas which are governed by very different sets of social norms, as well as different types of motivations for using them. It is important to acknowledge that the Internet is not a uniform entity and that these factors will have a powerful influence on the types of self-presentation behavior that people employ. Attrill (2012) discusses the idea that people share specific types of information in a goal-directed manner. In her research, she noted how types of self-disclosures (e.g., superficial vs. personal or intimate) differed between various online arenas (e.g., online shopping sites, social networking and instant messaging), and more information around this notion can be found in the chapter by Attrill-Smith in this volume.

Further evidence for this idea comes from online dating research, with findings from numerous studies suggesting that online daters may be more likely to exaggerate and accentuate desirable traits (e.g., see Ellison, Hancock, & Toma, 2012; Hancock, Toma, & Ellison, 2007; Hancock & Toma, 2009). Returning to Leary and Kowalski's (1990) two-component model of impression management, the expectation is that motivation for garnering a desired impression is heightened in an online dating context because of the goal-relevance of making favorable impressions. In other words, the goal (i.e., getting a date) will be very much influenced by the user's impression management behavior (i.e. how one presents oneself on the profile and in direct communications). In these types of instances the individual is likely to be highly motivated to leave others with a very specific impression. Although superficially this might not seem too different from how impressions are managed in equivalent offline romantic contexts, being online does provide more freedom to construct an image with much more flexibility, for example, by choosing images that show the individual in the most attractive light, having more time to contemplate the message, or being able to hide negative nonverbal cues (e.g., nervousness) that might be perceived as unappealing (Fullwood & Attrill-Smith, 2018). As in the offline world, the level of motivation we have to garner a desired impression, as well as the type of impression we wish to leave others with, will be dictated to a large degree by the goal we wish to achieve. In the online dating sphere then, it makes sense that this may be likely to lead to exaggerated self-presentation, particularly in terms of one's appearance, as daters tend to be judged most readily on the way they look (Hancock & Toma, 2009). In other online domains, however, the motivations might be quite different. For example, Sheldon and Bryant (2016) noted how users of Instagram were partly motivated to edit and upload photos because they wanted the community to perceive them as popular or cool.

Predictors of Online Self-Presentation Experimentation

Some of the research covered thus far suggests that the online world affords users opportunities for more selective and experimental self-presentation. However, individuals vary considerably in how much concern they have for the way others perceive them, e.g., Snyder's (1987) distinction between high and low self-monitors. Should we then expect the same degree of variability in the online world with some people presenting more authentic self-presentations while others construct more idealized, exaggerated, experimental or even potentially false self-images? Or should we expect the cyberspace to shape the behavior of everyone more uniformly? Much of the research conducted to address these questions focuses on adolescents, perhaps in part because it is an important stage of human development during which developing a sense of identity becomes a central concern (Brinthaupt & Lipka, 2012). Indeed, adolescents routinely experiment with different ways of behaving and are sensitive to the reactions of their peers in a bid to find an identity with which they are comfortable (Rosenberg, 1986; Coleman, 2012). It has been argued that having access to digital technologies can provide adolescents with a useful "tool" for experimenting with different ways of behaving, due to the different affordances of the medium. In turn, receiving approval from peers (e.g., "likes") can help to validate a particular form of self-presentation which may then be assimilated into one's "offline" identity and help young people strive towards the achievement of "possible" selves (Manago, Graham, Greenfield, & Salimkhan, 2008). For example, Šmahel (2003) notes how over a third of adolescents surveyed went into chat rooms as a gender different to their own in order to explore their own sexual identity.

Fullwood and colleagues (2016) propose that the extent to which adolescents are likely to engage in such "experimental" identity practices may in part be explained by the individual's clarity of self-concept. Self-concept clarity can be defined as the extent to which an individual's view of him/herself is "clearly and confidently defined, internally consistent, and temporally stable" (Campbell et al., 1996, 141). Thus, someone with high self-concept clarity will be more sure of who they are, will behave more consistently across various social contexts, and their perception of themselves will be less likely to alter substantially over time. In their research, Fullwood and colleagues (2016) developed a scale to measure different types of online self-presentation behaviors, including i) ideal self (i.e., the extent to which the person presents idealized self-images online), ii) multiple selves (i.e., the extent to which the individual presents different self-images across multiple platforms), iii) consistent self (i.e., the extent to which the person's self-presentation behavior online is congruent with their offline self-presentations), and iv) online presentation preference (i.e., the extent to which an individual prefers presenting him/herself to others online over offline). Their findings showed that adolescents with lower self-concept clarity were more likely to make multiple online self-presentations, present an idealized self-image online and have a preference for communicating with others online. Additionally, those with higher self-concept clarity reported having a more consistent approach to self-presentations across online and offline communication contexts. Overall, they argue that these findings suggest that adolescents can make use of the online world as a space in which to try out different forms of identity expression in a bid to resolve identity crises and to work towards the discovery of a "true" self.

Numerous additional psychological and individual difference factors have also been identified in the literature to explain people's propensity to engage with different forms of online self-presentational behavior. For instance, Keep and Attrill-Smith (2017) note that older individuals are less motivated to control the impressions of others while online, perhaps because their sense of self is more stable than that of younger individuals. Personality has also been highlighted as an important determinant of online impression management tactics. Research by Seidman (2013) linking online self-presentational behavior to the Big Five markers of personality suggests a number of interesting associations. For example, individuals scoring higher in extraversion (characterized by sociability, assertiveness, and emotional expressiveness) were more likely to present their "actual" self on Facebook. This is consistent with what we know about extraverts, who are generally satisfied with who they are (Cheng & Furnham, 2003) and has been also observed in the online dating arena (e.g., Hall et al., 2010). Individuals who scored higher in conscientiousness (characterized by meticulousness and impulse control) were observed to be less likely to engage in attention-seeking behavior and less likely to reveal hidden and idealized aspects of the self. This suggests that conscientious people are more cautious in their online self-presentation and this is consistent with this trait. Indeed, Hall, Park, Song, and Cody (2010) observed that more conscientious people were less likely to misrepresent themselves on their online dating profiles. Conscientious individuals therefore appear to be concerned with presenting authentic images of the self both on- and offline (Leary & Allen, 2011).

Furthermore, Seidman (2013) found that more agreeable individuals (characterized by altruism and concern for others) were more likely to present an authentic self on Facebook, but less likely to engage in attention-seeking behavior, which makes sense given that agreeable individuals are normally well liked and might be worried about overstepping boundaries and upsetting others. This pattern of behavior has also been observed in online dating profiles, with agreeable people being more likely to represent themselves truthfully (Hall et al., 2010). Finally, those scoring higher in neuroticism (characterized by anxiety and a lack of emotional stability) were more likely to self-disclose generally, disclose emotional information, and present actual, hidden, and idealized self-images. This might suggest a degree of uncertainty in how to present the self online and may reflect a greater degree of social anxiety. Although it is beyond the scope of this chapter to review personality determinants of online self-presentation in depth, Fullwood (2015) discusses a variety of personality dimensions in addition to those already discussed (e.g., narcissism) and their associations with managing impressions in various online spaces. This work also acknowledges the importance of differentiating between various online platforms, i.e. social media sites like Facebook tend to be anchored to an individual's offline networks (which therefore would place restrictions on how far someone may go with self-presentation experiments), while other sites will permit anonymous communication or interactions with strangers, thus self-presentation experimentation on these sites may be more rife (Fullwood, 2015; Zhao et al, 2008). Thus, there is a complex nexus between individual difference factors between the online arena chosen within which to interact and the motivation for choosing it, which combine to determine self-presentation behavior.

IMPACTS OF ONLINE SELF-PRESENTATION ON THE SELF

Research has highlighted the notion that being online allows experimentation with more varied forms of self-presentational behavior. Although there will be individual differences in the extent to which people take up these opportunities, an interesting question arises as to what impact more flexible self-presentation can have on the self. Yee and colleagues' (Yee & Bailenson, 2007; Yee, Bailenson, & Ducheneaut, 2009) classic work on the Proteus effect shows how people tend to adopt the characteristics of their online avatars. For example, people who interact in online worlds with taller avatars have been shown to behave in a more assertive fashion and people who use more attractive avatars have been shown to act more flirtatiously and confidently. Furthermore, this effect has been demonstrated in the lab (Yee & Bailenson, 2007) as well as in more "natural" observational settings (Yee et al., 2009). Additionally, some of the behaviors which were characteristic of these different types of avatars have been shown to spill over into peoples' offline conduct (Yee et al., 2009). In explaining this effect, Yee and colleagues draw on a number of theories. For example, Snyder, Tanke, and Berscheid's (1977) behavioral confirmation theory suggests that humans stereotype people based on physical characteristics, and is a form of cognitive heuristic or mental shortcut. Therefore, people adopt the characteristics they associate with the physical attributes of their avatar. Self-perception theory (Bem, 1967) argues that an individual learns about his or her attitudes and emotions by observing self-behavior in social contexts. Therefore, once the behaviors characteristic of the physical attributes of these avatars have been expressed online, they are assimilated into an individual's self-concept via self-observations of conduct in these environments. These studies also note how interacting anonymously could potentially facilitate this process as it could lead to a loss of self-awareness, making it easier for users to identify with their avatars. Although this research represents somewhat extreme examples of identity manipulation online, the findings are important because they suggest that the person an individual chooses to embody in the online world may actually change the way that person behaves. Moreover, evidence is also coming to light which indicates that these behavioral changes may also affect the way people think about themselves. For example, Fox, Bailenson, and Tricase (2013) noted how participants who adopted sexualized avatars experienced more body-related thoughts compared to participants who embodied non-sexualized avatars.

A further body of evidence has also looked at how presenting the self online might impact on an individual's self-esteem. For example, Kim and Lee (2011) found that positive presentation of the self on Facebook was directly related to subjective well-being. Additionally, Gonzales and Hancock (2011) noted that participants who updated their Facebook profiles during an experiment reported higher levels of self-esteem compared to those participants who did not. They argue that in engaging in selective self-presentation, participants were able to create a more desirable image of the self, which ultimately influenced their self-evaluations and improved their self-esteem. Although one might consider this type of self-enhancement to be primarily positive, more recent research by Fullwood and Attrill-Smith (2018) suggests that constructing a more "optimal" image of the self online could potentially lead to unrealistic expectations around the types of partners that one could feasibly attract on online dating sites. Therefore, although interacting in the online world may help to diminish the gap between one's "actual" and "ideal" self (self-discrepancy theory; Higgins, 1987), the extent to which this translates into long-term changes to the "offline" self is not yet fully understood.

CONCLUSIONS

The research and theory discussed in this chapter posits that there are several unique features of the online world which permit users a greater degree of freedom in how they manage the impressions of others. Some of these features include, but are not limited to, anonymity, editability, and asynchronicity. Having the ability to manufacture images of the self with greater precision, while eliminating many of the social and personal constraints that may be associated with managing impressions offline, should be particularly beneficial to individuals who are shy or socially anxious. If we conceptualize the Internet as a playground for self-experimentation, testing out different forms of self-presentation may also be valuable for individuals (e.g., adolescents) who are less sure of their place in the world and are working towards the discovery of their "true" self. Furthermore, engaging in different identity practices online and having the potential to be freed up from one's "offline" identity has been shown to feed back into the manner in which individuals view themselves. The Proteus effect, and embodying different avatars online, may not only influence one's behavior in the online context and outside of it, but also ultimately the self-perceptions of those users. This ability to take on the form and features of a character that might seemingly be very distinct from the actual "offline" self may be particularly advantageous to individuals who feel that they cannot be who they really desire to be in their "offline" lives (Bargh, McKenna, & Fitzsimmons, 2002). In acknowledging this idea, however, we also need to consider the potential that in only being able to truly be oneself online, this could potentially be very alluring and may be to the detriment of one's offline relationships and life.

This chapter has focused on the more positive aspects of managing impressions online, and has considered how some of the idiosyncratic features of cyberspace may permit people to present a more "optimal" version of the self. Of course, this is not to say that just because the opportunity is there to present oneself in an idealized manner that everyone will necessarily do this. Indeed the Internet is rife with unsavory self-presentational behavior. Managing impressions does not necessitate being pleasant and although most people would like to be perceived in a positive way (Leary & Allen, 2011), there are many others who will present more odious characteristics for very specific reasons, e.g., to gain notoriety or elicit a specific reaction in others. The research considered here, particularly with regards to how online self-presentation experimentation impacts self-perceptions, has usually focused on very short-term changes. Further research is needed to consider the more long-terms impacts of engaging in identity play in the online arena. As these forms of technology are still very new, the field is also in its infancy, and researchers will need to adapt and develop new theories as the technology evolves. For example, although Facebook has dominated the social media landscape for the past decade or so, young people are starting to turn to other social media platforms like Instagram or Snapchat (Smith & Anderson, 2018), and the types of impression management opportunities are likely to be very different, as these sites rely on a much more visual self-presentational style. Finally, future research should also work to coincide with developments in virtual reality and the potential for people to see through the eyes of characters (not even necessarily human ones) that may be enormously distinctive from how an individual perceives himself or herself in the offline world.

References

Attrill, A. (2012). Sharing only parts of me: Selective categorical self-disclosure across Internet arenas. *International Journal of Internet Science, 7*(1), 55–77.

Barak, A., Boniel-Nissim, M., & Suler, J. (2008). Fostering empowerment in online support groups. *Computers in Human Behavior, 24*(5), 1867–1883.

Bargh, J. A., McKenna, K. Y. A., & Fitzsimmons, G. M. (2002). Can you see the Real Me? Activation and expression of the "True Self" on the Internet. *Journal of Social Issues 58*(1), 33–48.

Baumeister, R. F., & Hutton, D. G. (1987). Self-presentation theory: Self-construction and audience pleasing. In B. Mullin & G. R. Goethals (Eds.), *Theories of group behavior* (pp. 71–87). New York: Springer.

Bem, D. J. (1967). Self-perception: An alternative interpretation of cognitive dissonance phenomena. *Psychological Review 74*(3), 183.

Brinthaupt, T. M., & Lipka, R. P. (Eds.). (2012). *Understanding early adolescent self and identity: Applications and interventions.* New York: SUNY Press.

Brown, J. (2014). *The self.* New York: Psychology Press.

Campbell, J. D., Trapnell, P. D., Heine, S. J., Katz, I. M., Lavallee, L. F., & Lehman, D. R. (1996). Self-concept clarity: Measurement, personality correlates, and cultural boundaries. *Journal of Personality and Social Psychology 70*(1), 141.

Chadwick, D., Fullwood, C., & Wesson, C. (2013). Intellectual disability, identity and the Internet. In R. Luppicini (Ed.) *Handbook of research on technoself: Identity in a technological society* (pp. 229–254). Hershey, PA: IGI Global.

Cheng, H., & Furnham, A. (2003). Personality, self-esteem, and demographic predictions of happiness and depression. *Personality and Individual Differences 34*(6), 921–942.

Chester, A., & Bretherton, D. (2007). Impression management and identity online. In A. Joinson, K. McKenna, T. Postmes, & U. Reips (Eds.) *The Oxford handbook of Internet Psychology* (pp. 223–236). Oxford: Oxford University Press.

Christopherson, K. M. (2007). The positive and negative implications of anonymity in Internet social interactions: "On the Internet, nobody knows you're a dog." *Computers in Human Behavior 23*(6), 3038–3056.

Coleman, J. (2012). Introduction: Digital technologies in the lives of young people. *Oxford Review of Education, 38*(1), 1–8.

Cromby, J., & Standen, P. (1999). Cyborgs and stigma: Technology, disability, subjectivity. In A. J. Gordo-Lopez & I. Parker (Eds.), *Cyberpsychology* (pp. 95–112). New York: Routledge.

Crystal, D. (2008). *Txtng: The gr8 db8.* Oxford: Oxford University Press.

Culnan, M. J., & Markus, M. L. (1987). Information technologies. In F. M. Jablin, L. L. Putnam, K. H. Roberts, & L. W. Porter (Eds.), *Handbook of organizational communication: An interdisciplinary perspective* (pp. 420–443). Newbury Park, CA: Sage.

Donath, J. S. (1999). Identity and deception in the virtual community. In M. A. Smith & P. Kollock (Eds.), *Communities in cyberspace* (pp. 29–59). London: Routledge.

Drouin, M. A. (2011). College students' text messaging, use of textese and literacy skills. *Journal of Computer Assisted Learning 27*(1), 67–75.

Dubrovsky, V. J., Kiesler, S., & Sethna, B. N. (1991). The equalization phenomenon: Status effects in computer-mediated and face-to-face decision-making groups. *Human-Computer Interaction 6*(2), 119–146.

Eftekhar, A., Fullwood, C., & Morris, N. (2014). Capturing personality from Facebook photos and photo-related activities: How much exposure do you need? *Computers in Human Behavior 37*, 162–170.

Ellis, A. P., West, B. J., Ryan, A. M., & DeShon, R. P. (2002). The use of impression management tactics in structured interviews: A function of question type? *Journal of Applied Psychology 87*(6), 1200.

Ellison, N., Heino, R., & Gibbs, J. (2006). Managing impressions online: Self-presentation processes in the online dating environment. *Journal of Computer-Mediated Communication 11*(2), 415–441.

Ellison, N. B., Hancock, J. T., & Toma, C. L. (2012). Profile as promise: A framework for conceptualizing veracity in online dating self-presentations. *New Media & Society 14*(1), 45–62.

Farina, F., & Lyddy, F. (2011). The language of text messaging: "Linguistic ruin" or resource? *Irish Psychologist 37*(6), 145–149.

Fenigstein, A., Scheier, M. F., & Buss, A. H. (1975). Public and private self-consciousness: Assessment and theory. *Journal of Consulting and Clinical Psychology 43*(4), 522.

Fitz-Gerald, S. (2017). The ten biggest YouTube channels right now. *Thrillist Entertainment.* Accessed on 22nd August 2017 at https://www.thrillist.com/entertainment/nation/top-youtube-channels-most-popular-youtubers

Fox, J., Bailenson, J. N., & Tricase, L. (2013). The embodiment of sexualized virtual selves: The Proteus effect and experiences of self-objectification via avatars. *Computers in Human Behavior 29*(3), 930–938.

Fullwood, C. (2015). The role of personality in online self-presentation. In A. Attrill (Ed.) *Cyberpsychology* (pp. 9–28). Oxford: Oxford University Press.

Fullwood, C., & Attrill-Smith, A. (2018). Up-dating: Ratings of perceived dating success are better online than offline. *Cyberpsychology, Behavior, and Social Networking 21*(1), 11–15.

Fullwood, C., James, B. M., & Chen-Wilson, C. H. (2016). Self-concept clarity and online self-presentation in adolescents. *Cyberpsychology, Behavior, and Social Networking 19*(12), 716–720.

Fullwood, C., Quinn, S., Chen-Wilson, J., Chadwick, D., & Reynolds, K. (2015). Put on a smiley face: Textspeak and personality perceptions. *Cyberpsychology, Behavior, and Social Networking 18*(3), 147–151.

Goffman, E. (1959). *The presentation of self in everyday life.* Garden City, NY: Anchor Books.

Gonzales, A. L., & Hancock, J. T. (2011). Mirror, mirror on my Facebook wall: Effects of exposure to Facebook on self-esteem. *Cyberpsychology, Behavior, and Social Networking 14*(1–2), 79–83.

Gosling, S. D., Ko, S. J., Mannarelli, T., & Morris, M. E. (2002). A room with a cue: Personality judgments based on offices and bedrooms. *Journal of Personality and Social Psychology 82*(3), 379.

Hall, J. A., Park, N., Song, H., & Cody, M. J. (2010). Strategic misrepresentation in online dating: The effects of gender, self-monitoring, and personality traits. *Journal of Social and Personal Relationships 27*(1), 117–135.

Hancock, J. T., & Dunham, P. J. (2001). Impression formation in computer-mediated communication revisited: An analysis of the breadth and intensity of impressions. *Communication Research 28*(3), 325–347.

Hancock, J. T., & Toma, C. L. (2009). Putting your best face forward: The accuracy of online dating photographs. *Journal of Communication 59*(2), 367–386.

Hancock, J. T., Toma, C., & Ellison, N. (2007). The truth about lying in online dating profiles. In *Proceedings of the SIGCHI conference on Human factors in computing systems* (pp. 449–452). 30 April–3 May, San Jose, CA. New York: ACM.

Higgins, E. T. (1987). Self-discrepancy: A theory relating self and affect. *Psychological Review 94*(3), 319.

Joinson, A. N. (2004). Self-esteem, interpersonal risk, and preference for email and to face-to-face communication. *Cyberpsychology, Behavior and Social Networking 7*(4), 472–478.

Jones, E. E. (1990). *Interpersonal perception.* New York, NY: W. H. Freeman & Co.

Katz, E., Blumler, J. G., & Gurevitch, M. (1973). Uses and gratifications research. *The Public Opinion Quarterly 37*(4), 509–523.

Keep, M., & Attrill-Smith, A. (2017). Controlling you watching me: Measuring perception control on social media. *Cyberpsychology, Behavior, and Social Networking 20*(9), 561–566.

Kim, J., & Lee, J. E. R. (2011). The Facebook paths to happiness: Effects of the number of Facebook friends and self-presentation on subjective well-being. *CyberPsychology, Behavior, and Social Networking 14*(6), 359–364.

Krämer, N. C., & Winter, S. (2008). Impression management 2.0: The relationship of self-esteem, extraversion, self-efficacy, and self-presentation within social networking sites. *Journal of Media Psychology 20*(3), 106–116.

Laird, J. D. (2007). *Feelings: The perception of self.* Oxford: Oxford University Press.

Leary, M. R., & Allen, A. B. (2011). Personality and persona: Personality processes in self-presentation. *Journal of Personality 79*(6), 889–916.

Leary, M. R., & Kowalski, R. M. (1990). Impression management: A literature review and two-component model. *Psychological Bulletin 107*(1), 34–47.

Lee, S. J., Quigley, B. M., Nesler, M. S., Corbett, A. B., & Tedeschi, J. T. (1999). Development of a self-presentation tactics scale. *Personality and Individual Differences, 26*(4), 701–722.

Lee, J., & Lim, Y. S. (2016). Gendered campaign tweets: The cases of Hillary Clinton and Donald Trump. *Public Relations Review 42*(5), 849–855.

Manago, A. M., Graham, M. B., Greenfield, P. M., & Salimkhan, G. (2008). Self-presentation and gender on MySpace. *Journal of Applied Developmental Psychology 29*(6), 446–458.

Martin, K. A., Sinden, A. R., & Fleming, J. C. (2000). Inactivity may be hazardous to your image: The effects of exercise participation on impression formation. *Journal of Sport and Exercise Psychology 22*(4), 283–291.

McKenna, K. Y. A., & Bargh, J. A. (2000). Plan 9 from Cyberspace: The Implications of the Internet for Personality and Social Psychology. *Personality and Social Psychology Review 4*(1), 57–75.

Mehdizadeh, S. (2010). Self-presentation 2.0: Narcissism and self-esteem on Facebook. *Cyberpsychology, Behavior and Social Networking 13*, 357–364.

Petty, R. E., & Cacioppo, J. T. (1986). The elaboration likelihood model of persuasion. *Advances in Experimental Social Psychology 19*, 123–205.

Qian, H., & Scott, C. R. (2007). Anonymity and self-disclosure on weblogs. *Journal of Computer-Mediated Communication 12*(4), 1428–1451.

Rosenberg, M. (1986). *Conceiving the self.* Malabar, FL: R. E. Krieger.

Rosenberg, J., & Egbert, N. (2011). Online impression management: Personality traits and concerns for secondary goals as predictors of self-presentation tactics on Facebook. *Journal of Computer-Mediated Communication 17*, 1–18.

Scott, G. G., Sinclair, J., Short, E., & Bruce, G. (2014). It's not what you say, it's how you say it: Language use on Facebook impacts employability but not attractiveness. *Cyberpsychology, Behavior, and Social Networking 17*(8), 562–566.

Schlenker, B. R. (1980). *Impression management: The self-concept, social identity, and interpersonal relations*. Monterey, CA: Brooks/Cole.

Schneider, D. J. (1981). Tactical self-presentations: Toward a broader conception. In J. T. Tedeschi (Ed.), *Impression management theory and social psychological research* (pp. 23–40). New York: Academic Press.

Seidman, G. (2013). Self-presentation and belonging on Facebook: How personality influences social media use and motivations. *Personality and Individual Differences 54*(3), 402–407.

Sheldon, P., & Bryant, K. (2016). Instagram: Motives for its use and relationship to narcissism and contextual age. *Computers in Human Behavior 58*, 89–97.

Siibak, A. (2009). Constructing the self through the photo selection-visual impression management on social networking websites. *Cyberpsychology: Journal of Psychosocial Research on Cyberspace 3*(1), Article 1 [online].

Šmahel, D. (2003). *Psychologie a internet: děti dospělými, dospělí dětmi* (Vol. 6). Praha: Triton.

Smith, A., & Anderson, M. (2018, March 1). Social media use in 2018. *Pew Research Center: Internet and Technology*. Retrieved from http://www.pewinternet.org/2018/03/01/social-media-use-in-2018/

Snyder, M. (1987). *Public appearances, private realities: The psychology of self-monitoring*. New York, NY: W. H. Freeman & Co.

Snyder, M., Tanke, E. D., & Berscheid, E. (1977). Social perception and interpersonal behavior: On the self-fulfilling nature of social stereotypes. *Journal of Personality and Social Psychology 35*(9), 656.

Swann, Jr., W. B. (1990). To be adored or to be known? The interplay of self-enhancement and self-verification. In E. T. Higgins & R. M. Sorrentino (Eds.), *Handbook of motivation and cognition: Foundations of social behavior*, Vol. 2 (pp. 408–448). New York, NY: Guilford Press.

Turnley, W. H., & Bolino, M. C. (2001). Achieving desired images while avoiding undesired images: Exploring the role of self-monitoring in impression management. *Journal of Applied Psychology 86*(2), 351.

Valkenburg, P. M., & Peter, J. (2009). Social consequences of the Internet for adolescents: A decade of research. *Current Directions in Psychological Science 18*(1), 1–5.

Valkenburg, P. M., Schouten, A. P., & Peter, J. (2005). Adolescents' identity experiments on the internet. *New Media and Society 7*(3), 383–402.

Van Dijck, J. (2008). Digital photography: Communication, identity, memory. *Visual Communication 7*(1), 57–76.

Van der Nagel, E., & Frith, J. (2015). Anonymity, pseudonymity, and the agency of online identity: Examining the social practices of r/Gonewild. *First Monday 20*(3) [online].

Walther, J. B. (1996). Computer-mediated communication: Impersonal, interpersonal, and hyperpersonal interaction. *Communication Research 23*, 3–43.

Walther, J. B. (2007). Selective self-presentation in computer-mediated communication: Hyperpersonal dimensions of technology, language, and cognition. *Computers in Human Behavior 23*(5), 2538–2557.

Weaver, J. B. (2000). Personality and entertainment preferences. In D. Zillermann & P. Vorderer (Eds.), *Media entertainment* (pp. 235–248). Mahwah, NJ: Lawrence Erlbaum & Associates, Inc.

Yee, N., & Bailenson, J. (2007). The Proteus effect: The effect of transformed self-representation on behavior. *Human Communication Research* 33(3), 271–290.

Yee, N., Bailenson, J. N., & Ducheneaut, N. (2009). The Proteus effect: Implications of transformed digital self-representation on online and offline behavior. *Communication Research* 36(2), 285–312.

Zhao, S., Grasmuck, S., & Martin, J. (2008). Identity construction on Facebook: Digital empowerment in anchored relationships. *Computers in Human Behavior* 24, 1816–1836.

Zywica, J., & Danowski, J. (2008). The faces of Facebookers: Investigating social enhancement and social compensation hypotheses; predicting Facebook and offline popularity from sociability and self-esteem, and mapping the meanings of popularity with semantic networks. *Journal of Computer Mediated Communication* 14(1), 1–34.

CHAPTER 4

PERSONALITY AND INTERNET USE: THE CASE OF INTROVERSION AND EXTROVERSION

YAIR AMICHAI-HAMBURGER AND SHIR ETGAR

INTRODUCTION

ONE of the leading definitions of personality suggests that it represents "those characteristics of the person that account for his consistent pattern of behavior" (Pervin, 1993: 3). The key to understanding regularities in the thoughts, feelings, and overt behaviors of people is knowledge of their personality. Whereas most areas of psychology explore specific aspects of human behavior, e.g. perception or memory, the psychology of personality sees the individual as one integrative unit. Amichai-Hamburger (2002) suggested that personality overall is ignored in Internet studies. He suggested that their personality is one of the main reasons as to why people behave differently in the offline than they do when online. Moreover, it helps to provide a major explanation for individual differences found in online patterns of behavior. Since Amichai-Hamburger's complaint back in 2002, many papers have been published in this field that focus on many different theories of personality and demonstrate their importance to the understanding of human behavior online (e.g. Amichai-Hamburger, 2017). This chapter focuses on the theory that has been studied most frequently and in the greatest depth: the interaction between Internet use and extrovert and introvert personalities. To understand this, it is vital to comprehend the unique psychological environment created by the Internet with which the personality of the surfer interacts.

The Unique Components of the Internet Environment

The online environment operates very differently from the offline world (Amichai-Hamburger, 2005, 2008, 2012, 2017; Amichai-Hamburger & Hayat, 2013; Hamburger & Ben-Artzi, 2000; McKenna, Green, & Gleason, 2002). These differences can be encapsulated into seven distinctive factors. Each of which has a psychological effect on the user.

Anonymity

Our offline life is replete with visual cues that frequently lead to social labels and stereotypes. Offline, many of these cues are evident, e.g. race, gender, and dress are social indicators. Online, such visual and social cues are often invisible. On sites such as blogs, chats, or gaming, since much of this interaction is not only anonymous, but also textually based, people can decide how far they wish to expose these types of personal factors (Riordan & Kreuz, 2010). This can actually be beneficial for well-being, since it helps people to feel protected and confident and lead them to feel a greater freedom to express themselves and disclose more personal information (Amichai-Hamburger, 2005; Joinson, 2001). These feelings of security may well enable people to participate in situations online that they would find much harder to join in when offline. Thus, online anonymity can lead individuals to explore aspects of their identity that they would not feel confident to discover offline; moreover, the online environment allows them to validate these newly revealed aspects of themselves (Turkle, 1995). This exploration of their identity may have particular significance to people from stigmatized groups, e.g. LGBTQ. In such cases, anonymity may be crucial as it allows participants safely to investigate their identity, without social stigma, which may lead to greater self-esteem (Amichai-Hamburger & Hayat, 2013). However, people may use Internet anonimity, including social networks, in negative ways, e.g. by using false identities. The ramifications of this lowering of inhibitions as a result of anonymity are complex (Suler, 2004), since it can lead to non-normative behavior and to cyberbullying (e.g. Ševčíková & Šmahel, 2009; Tsikerdekis, 2012).

Control over Physical Appearance

Offline, people are constantly appraised according to their physical appearance and judged differently due to such features as skin color or weight. For example, attractive people are more likely to receive help and be thought to possess superior personality traits (Horai, Naccari, & Fatoullah, 1974; Nisbett & Wilson, 1977; Wilson, 1978). People who do not measure up to perceived beauty standards may well suffer from a negative body image (Annis, Cash, & Hrabosky, 2004; Schwartz & Brownell, 2004; Taleporos & McCabe, 2002), which, in turn, is related to lower self-esteem (McCaulay, Mintz, & Glenn, 1988) and to eating disorders (Cash & Deagle, 1997). Online, people are free to expose as much of their physical appearance as they choose. Even on sites that require a photograph, participants can choose how they wish to represent themselves, e.g. as a baby. For those people who choose to display a standard photograph of themselves, impression management is far easier online. Many people work hard to create and sustain their online impression through photos, even when this is actually directed at people whom they already know and may frequently meet offline (Amichai-Hamburger & Vinitzky, 2010; McAndrew & Jeong, 2012). Such people often work to ensure they upload only their most flattering photos, and often overweight people will choose to display pictures that make them look thinner (Amichai-Hamburger & Hayat, 2013). Another method is to upload carefully chosen photos in which the subjects are happy, good-looking, and participating in hugely enjoyable activities (Amichai-Hamburger & Hayat, 2013). An offshoot of this need for control over one's physical impression is the selfie. A selfie is a self-portrait usually taken using a cell phone with the intention of uploading it to a social network site (Weiser, 2015). One of the motivations for this is the ease with which it is possible to control the content (Mehdizadeh, 2010; Qiu, Lu, Yang, Qu, & Zhu, 2015). In a survey of youth from the US, the UK, and China, it was found that between 96 and 100 percent of the participants take and upload selfies to social network sites, and that due to their own concerns as to how they appear in these photos, all take far more selfies than the number they actually upload to such sites (Katz & Crocker, 2015). Thus, one of the great advantages of the selfie is that protagonists may perform as many attempts as they wish, under their complete control, until the "perfect" photo is achieved. However, there are major risks attached to this behavior, including the possibility of developing an obsessive preoccupation about personal appearance online, and, perhaps unsurprisingly, the use of social network sites is related to higher social comparison in terms of appearance (Chae, 2017). The gap between the number of selfies taken and actual posting may be evidence of this (Katz & Crocker, 2015), as is selfie-editing, which offers "a virtual makeover for online self-presentation" (Chae, 2017).

Greater Control over Interaction

The online world also grants people a far higher degree of control over their social interactions. Offline, they are obliged to keep focused and to give an immediate response to the other side, whereas online the social norms are very different. In the online environment we are not committed immediately to respond to a communication and should a chat reach an uncomfortable topic, it is possible simply to leave. The feeling that an online interaction can be stopped whenever one chooses was found to enhance feelings of security (McKenna, Green, & Gleason, 2002). Since many online interactions are asynchronous, this allows for time to think, rewrite, and revise our comments. This delayed communication gives us a greater sense of control over the interaction (Riva, 2002). Another aspect of control flows from the location in which the interaction takes place. Online, this is wherever we choose, and being able to interact from a secure place can increase the participant's sense of security (Amichai-Hamburger, 2005). Ben-Ze'ev (2004, 2005) examined participants in online versus offline dating situations. His results showed that participants felt less anxious and were more open to disclosure when the interaction was online rather than offline. This was because online, participants felt more secure since they had the ability to finish the interaction whenever they chose.

Control over the interaction may also have some negative outcomes. The ability to control the interaction makes it perceived as slower, more difficult, and less convincing as compared to face-to-face interactions. While evidence suggests that online communication is much more effective for simple tasks, it seems less effective for complicated assignments (An & Frick, 2006), or tasks that require long and collaborative dialogues (Groenke, 2007).

Finding Similar Others

Two of the basic needs in Maslow's (1971) pyramid are the need to belong and the need for appreciation. Tajfel and Turner (1986) suggested that being part of a group that shares one's interests can a have positive influence on self-esteem. People need to feel validated, and sharing interests and goals with others is a way to achieve this validation. It is unsurprising that "belonging" was cited as a leading motivator for using Facebook (Seidman, 2013) and Instagram (Oh, Lee, Kim, Park, & Suh, 2016; Sheldon & Bryant, 2016). This online validation has many benefits, e.g. people from stigmatized groups can find people similar to themselves and thus feel empowered (Cserni and Talmud, 2015). In this way, the Internet may serve as a tool to enrich people's identities (Amichai-Hamburger & Hayat, 2013). Even connecting with familiar others on social network sites was found to result in similar advantages, since bonding online makes connections more powerful (Liu, Ainsworth, & Baumeister, 2016). This may be because people connecting with others online is done on the basis of their similarities, which in some cases could not be exposed offline.

While finding similar others online can be of great benefit, it is also empowering groups such as terror operatives or neo-Nazi cells, which can easily locate and meet up with similar others online. ISIS is an example of a terror organization that has effectively exploited online media to distribute its message (Farewell, 2014).

High Accessibility

It is possible to surf the Internet from almost anywhere, at any time. This process has been made even more convenient due to the advent of smartphones (Adler & Benbunan-Fich, 2012; Amichai- Hamburger, 2009; Ames, 2013), with which we can stay connected constantly. Indeed, in 2013, college students reported that they use smartphones for almost every purpose: learning, working, entertaining, and socializing (Ames, 2013); younger people perceive their smartphones as "everything" in their own lives, and use them constantly (Turner, 2015). People tend to engage with their smartphones even when they are taking part in other activities (David, Kim, Brickman, Ran, & Curtis, 2014). Smartphone apps that are specifically used for communication with others were found to help build and enhance social capital, which in turn leads to a reduction in the feelings of social isolation (Cho, 2015). This may be particularly important to people belonging to stereotyped groups. As mentioned, stereotyped groups receive much social capital from finding similar others on the web (Cserni & Talmud, 2015; McKenna & Bargh, 1998). Now, thanks to their smartphones, these similar others and the feelings of empowerment they promote are constant companions.

However, this ease of accessibility has disadvantages, since permanent online status leads to pressures to multitask, stemming from the need to be available all the time (Ames, 2013; Oulasvirta, Rattenbury, Ma, & Raita, 2012). Evidence suggests that multi-tasking, and especially multitasking using multimedia via a computer or a smartphone, damages attention span and decreases performance (David et al., 2014; Oulasvirta, Tamminen, Roto, & Kuorelahti, 2005; Rosen, Lim, Carrier, & Cheever, 2011). Another psychological price is the fear of missing out (FOMO). This has been defined as a "pervasive apprehension that others might be having rewarding experiences from which one is absent. FOMO is characterized by the desire to stay continually connected with what others are doing" (Przybylski, Murayama, DeHaan, & Gladwell, 2013, p. 1841). This intense feeling that one is missing out on things relates to the need to be highly connected and is positively correlated to engagement in social media activities (Alt, 2015). It can be destructive for the individual, as it is known to lower mood and lessen life satis-faction (Przybylski et al., 2013). In addition, constant accessibility may well come at the expense of time spent in the offline world. A meta-analysis of social network sites showed that greater use of such sites is related to greater feelings of loneliness (Liu & Baumeister, 2016). This suggests that while social network sites might be used instead of offline friendship and activities, their use does not decrease feelings of loneliness.

Fun

The Internet is exciting, interactive, colorful, and enjoyable, and so naturally people want more of it (Wiggins, 2007). The enjoyment we receive from the Internet is largely due to the efforts of web designers to fulfill our needs, so that we wish to remain permanently on their websites (Ehmke & Wilson, 2007). Engaging in fun leisure activities has positive connections for subjective well-being (Kuykendall, Tay, & Ng, 2015; Newman, Tay, & Diener, 2014), and the Internet provides a leisure time that involves entertainment, play, and sociability (Nimrod, 2010). Moreover, the Internet provides a readily available, protected environment where we can find like-minded people, and which meets the needs of participants and allows them to explore many aspects of their identity (Turkle, 1995). While all of this promises an experience of excitement and fun, it can also lead people to prefer the online world over the offline (Amichai-Hamburger & Hayat, 2013) and become addicted to it (Turel & Serenko, 2012; Young, 1998).

Equality

From its earliest stages, the Internet has been deeply rooted in the value of equality. (Amichai-Hamburger, 2008). The Internet is an environment that decreases status symbols, is open to anyone, and is accessible from most places. This promotes feelings of equality, and makes people feel that they are significant and that their opinions count. Anyone can upload their own unique content and every bit of it is valid to someone. From uploading an entry to Wikipedia to playing in a fantasy web game, the Internet allows everyone to express themselves in some way (Amichai-Hamburger & Hayat, 2013). Sometimes, this expression can even upgrade your social status, as happened with the young singer Justin Bieber, who first found fame by uploading his own material to YouTube (Khrabrov & Cybenko, 2010). This kind of success story induces feelings of equality in many people, suggesting that the Internet has the ability to make anyone a star. This emphasis on equality is strongly expressed in the online marketing world, where experiences of ordinary people shared on social network sites are utilized to create positive attitudes, customer engagement, and higher incomes for a product (Le Roux & Maree, 2016).

It is important to note that perceived equality on the Internet is not always real and many surfers feel that their self-esteem is on the line. For example, to reproduce similar reactions among their audience, people feel obligated to produce ever greater amounts of content in order to be "unique" and to generate interest from others. This feeling of obligation frequently leads to inappropriately high levels of disclosure online. These levels need to increase constantly in order to have an effect, since the bar of what is stimulating is continuously being raised. Such self-disclosure online, together with the high use of social networking sites, has been shown to be linked to higher stress levels and to decreased well-being (Bevan, Gomez, & Sparks, 2014; Chen & Lee, 2013).

To summarize, it seems clear that the Internet creates a unique setting that has no equivalent in the offline world. This highly protected environment, which is constantly available, and in which like-minded persons on any topic may be located at ease, affects people in different ways (Amichai-Hamburger, 2008). In some cases, it releases individuals from the "normative persona mask" they wear in their face-to-face interactions. This may well enable them to explore who they are and experiment with different aspects of their identity (Turkle, 1995). It also creates a highly supportive environment which might also help people to reach their deepest level of individuality (McKenna and Bargh, 2000). In other cases, when the group identity offline is very salient, it may enhance the feelings of belonging to a certain group even when the participant is anonymous (Postmes Spears, & Lea, 1998). Some people tend to exploit their anonymity to express different forms of aggression against others on the net

(Malmuth, Linz, & Yao, 2005). Other individuals may feel that the online environment allows them the opportunity to help others on the net (Amichai-Hamburger, 2008), while still determining their limits.

The distinctive psychological environment created by the Internet affects different personality types in different ways. This phenomenon has been found to be especially relevant to the extroversion–introversion personality discussion.

EXTROVERSION–INTROVERSION

Hamburger and Ben-Artzi (2000) pointed out that introverts may well be empowered by the net. The protective environment provided by the Internet can offer people a sort of social compensation for their offline introversion. On the net introverts can reinvent themselves and may even become extroverts. In practical terms this means that socially shy, closed, and withdrawn individuals may undergo a transformation and become highly interactive, open, social beings with a large network of online connections. These outcomes were initially found in regard to introverted women (Hamburger & Ben-Artzi, 2000). The authors suggested that this may be due to the higher self-awareness found among women in general and their ability to receive social support. At the time it is was suggested that as Internet use becomes more widespread, introverted males will also come to realize that the Internet has the potential to respond to their social needs. This approach became known as "the poor get richer" (Amichai-Hamburger, 2002). In other words, that those who are socially poor offline become socially richer online. These findings have been confirmed by other studies. For example, Maldonado, Mora, Garcia, and Edipo (2001) evaluated computer-mediated messages and found that introverted participants send messages with an extroverted tone. Their messages tend to contain more information than those sent by extroverted subjects. It seems that on the Internet, introverts do not act in accordance with their usual behavior patterns, but, due to their reaction to what they perceive as a particularly secure environment, conduct themselves in ways associated with extroverts in offline relationships.

Amichai-Hamburger, Wainapel, and Fox (2002) found that introverts perceive the online world, not the offline world, as their preferred social environment and feel that their relationships on the net are more special than their relationships offline. While these findings gave confirmation to the "poor get richer theory" this model has not been without its critics. For example, Kraut et al. (2002), found that introverts who use the Internet reported higher levels of loneliness, as compared with surfers who are extroverts. Kraut and colleagues explained their results in terms of "the rich get richer" phenomenon. They explained that people who have better social skills and many friends offline will exploit their highly developed social skills and make more friends online, whereas people who are less socially adept and have a poorer social life offline are likely to gain less from their Internet interaction. According to this idea, the Internet is yet another environment in which extroverts demonstrate their dominance over introverts.

Who Actually Gets Richer?

Amichai-Hamburger, Kaplan, and Dorpatcheon (2008) considered whether the "poor get richer" theory and the "rich get richer" theory necessarily contradict one another or whether they are (at least partly) complementary theories. During 2005, when social networks were very new, Amichai-Hamburger and his colleagues studied the relationship between personality and social networks. They found that among social network users, extroverted participants also used other online social services such as chat rooms, forums, or fantasy environments to a greater extent compared with introverts who used them. However, introverts who did not use online social networks were found to exploit the social services available on the Internet more than extroverts who did not use social networks. This led them to suggest that when people's foremost behavior online is using social networks, they are basically duplicating their offline social network on the Internet. In other words, their pattern of social interaction offline is transferred to their behavior online. In this way, such extroverts retain their offline social dominance when they are online. This is consistent with the "rich get richer" theory (Kraut et al., 2002). Conversely, among introverts who do not use social networks, behavior on the Internet will tend to be more explorative, since, as they are freed from any offline persona, they can actually recreate themselves. Such people are therefore more likely to use the Internet as a compensative environment and this, in turn, may lead them to become more socially dominant online as compared with extroverts. This is consistent with the "poor get richer" theory (Hamburger & Ben-Artzi, 2000).

It would seem, then, that two different environments have developed online. The first is one in which people enjoy a high degree of anonymity, which helps them to recreate themselves. They are free to explore different aspects of their identity without the fear of others' retaliation. This may be observed in fantasy games, anonymous chats, and blogs. Conversely, the second environment is one in which users are identified. Here, people do not aim to recreate themselves online but rather to duplicate their offline identity online. This is best demonstrated by behavior on social networks. When we assess how the different online environments apply to people with social inhibitions, it is important to start by examining what at first appears to be two of the greatest extremes found on the Internet: traditional anonymous cyberspace and identified social networks (heavily dominated by Facebook). It is interesting to learn what kind of behavior introverts adopt on social networks. Given the lack of anonymity and thus lowering of perceived levels of safety found there, we may expect them to duplicate their offline behavior. However, the Internet is complex and has a variety of different options through which introverts may compensate themselves. In essence, research found that extroverts have more social interaction on social networks than introverts (Amichai-Hamburger and Vinitzky, 2010). It appears that on social networks introverts do, in fact, transfer their patterns of introverted behavior from the offline into the online world. This is reflected in the size of their social network, which tends to be smaller than that of the extroverts. Interestingly, however, it seems that introverts do invest more effort into building and designing their personal profile on Facebook than do extroverts. Introverts, for example, place more personal information on their

Facebook profiles than extroverts. This may be explained by the fact that extroverts rely on their social skills and so feel less need to promote themselves, whereas introverts tend to feel anxious in real-life interactions and may experience exposure on Facebook as something similar. This demonstrates that, even in the social network environment, introverts find ways to compensate themselves.

Lee, Ahn, and Kim (2014) suggested that extroverts are very dominant on Facebook in terms of self-presentation. They found that extroverts uploaded more photos and updated status more frequently and displayed more friends than did introverted users. In addition, they "like", "share", and write comments more frequently. Interestingly, Gosling, Augustine, Vazire, Holtzman, and Gaddis (2011) found that extroverts are more likely to post photos of others but not of themselves. Seidman (2013) also studied self-presentation and belonging on Facebook, and found that extroverts use Facebook more frequently than introverts to communicate; they feel more comfortable expressing their feelings and inner selves. It is worth noting that Quintelier and Theocharis (2013) found that extroversion is positively related to Facebook political engagement.

Hughes, Rowe, Batey, and Lee (2012) pointed out that not all social networks are the same. While they found a positive association between extroversion and Facebook use, they found a negative association between extroversion and Twitter use. These results suggest that those who are generally more gregarious and sociable will look to use Facebook more often, while less sociable individuals will look to use Twitter. These results may well be a manifestation of the different styles of the two social networks, as Twitter, unlike Facebook, offers greater user anonymity and focuses less on "who you are" and your extant social circles and more on what you think and wish to say (Huberman et al., 2009). These differences in emphasis tend to appeal to different personality types.

ONLINE COMPENSATION FOR INHIBITION

As discussed, it seems that many people with social inhibitions have found creative ways to compensate for these inhibitions, even on social networks. In addition, the Internet contains many other outlets for self-expression, a large number of which may not seem as intrusive as social networks, including, for example, blogs, forums, and fantasy games.

Online Chat

Online chats are instantaneous transmissions of text messages from one sender to many receivers via the Internet. Anonymous chat users tend to value their privacy and are rather introverted. They find the chat environment to be an appropriate forum in which to liberate themselves and develop personal relationships (Anolli Villani, & Riva, 2005). In this case, the anonymous chat can be seen as a forum for introverts to express themselves. Anolli and colleagues (2005) point out that participants to chat rooms appear to be people who need support and approval, which this forum appears to provide.

Blog

A blog, or weblog, is an online diary, usually personal and updated frequently. Bloggers aim to build a community of people around them who comment on their posts and create a dialogue around the topic of the blog. The content of the blog is often expressive and includes links and comments regarding other websites, blogs, news, ideas, photos, poetry, project updates, and stories (Riva, 2002). Blog technology allows a direct uploading of text, photos, and links without the reader needing a high level of technological understanding; the blog can be read at any time and in any situation where there is an Internet connection. Bloggers can allow their readers to post comments after each blog (Huffaker, 2004). Blogs are often written as a series of continuous comments on a specific agenda; this format enables a permanent and continuous information update, provides convenient tools for use, and is offered for free to everyone (Lawson-Borders & Kirk, 2005). In addition, the Blogosphere allows the creation of intimate communities of communication (Ó Baoill, 2004). Herring, Scheidt, Wright, and Bonus (2005) believe that the importance of the blog as an intimate form of self-expression is underestimated. Given our previous knowledge, it may be predicted that the blog format, which allows users to maintain their anonymity, would be an ideal setting for people with social inhibitions as their blogging would allow them to feel totally protected and so enable them to re-create themselves and express themselves freely. In fact, Guadagno, Okdie, and Eno (2007) found that the personality characteristics related to blogging include openness to new experiences and neuroticism, and that, perhaps surprisingly, no relationship was found between introversion and blogging. Although the situation is actually more complex, Guadagno and colleagues (2007) did not actually focus on blogs where authors maintain their anonymity.

The Internet contains many different types of blog, each with varying degrees of anonymity, from those where the user is wholly identified, to others where the blogger is completely anonymous. Guadagno and colleagues (2007) report that as many bloggers provide identifying information, e.g. their name, this type of blog is not a protective environment for the surfer with social inhibitions and may actually produce the reverse effect. Therefore, future studies should examine the relationship between introversion and blogging on unidentified blogs. We predict that such a study would find that introverts see blogging as a protective online activity that helps them to express themselves freely and that a strong link between introversion and anonymous blogging may well exist.

The Fantasy World

In this area of study, fantasy world refers to an online world containing an environment which enables surfers to duplicate a whole range of offline activities. One prominent example is *Secondlife*, where people interact with others through avatars. *Secondlife* declares that it is a place to connect, to shop, to work, to love, and to explore. Alternatively, users may also open their own business and sell to others. From a social point of view, *Secondlife* allows users to find like-minded others, maintain friendships, and develop romantic relationships. This means that for many, *Secondlife* is perceived as an attractive place in which to spend their time.

On entering *Secondlife*, the user must choose an avatar—a graphic body—which will represent them during their stay (Bailenson & Beall, 2006). Creating the avatar includes choosing the gender, body shape, hair, and eye colors. As *Secondlife* is an anonymous environment where people not only can hide their real physical characteristics but also create their desired physical appearance, the inference is that an introvert may feel the inclination to compensate for their introversion when creating their avatar. Dunn and Guadagno (2012) examined how participants in a video game choose to shape the avatar that represents them. They found that introverts—both male and female—and women high in neuroticism are more likely to create exceptionally attractive avatars.

FUTURE RESEARCH

It seems clear that future research would benefit from a stronger focus on the relationship between personality and the seven factors mentioned at the beginning of this chapter. For instance, anonymity, control over physical appearance, and equality seem to relate very strongly to the online experience of introverts. The Internet creates a unique environment where introverts feel empowered and protected. This is particularly true of anonymous online environments where they can recreate themselves (Amichai-Hamburger & Hayat, 2013). Additionally, it is vital to enhance our knowledge of the online experience and how this affects users over the long term. Amichai-Hamburger, Wainapel, and Fox (2002) point out that introverts tend to express their real me online more than in the offline world. The online environment allows them to feel more comfortable revealing intimate aspects of themselves. However, the online persona, i.e. the degree to which people feel comfortable to express themselves online (Bargh, McKenna, & Fitzsimons, 2002) was developed at a stage where most of the users' online experience was anonymous. Today, it is necessary to differentiate between online anonymous environments and online non-anonymous environments, and to develop two distinct concepts of the self, one for anonymous and one for identified environments. It is possible that introverts are more comfortable openly expressing themselves in anonymous online environments, while extroverts feel more comfortable to do so in identified environments.

In addition, it is not clear as to how far our personality develops over time. Some scholars argue that over the long term, personality may well undergo changes across the life stages (Roberts, Walton, & Viechtbauer, 2006). It is therefore vital to run longitudinal research studies in the field of personality and Internet use, which could specifically focus on what happens to personalities of introverts who compensate for their introversion via anonymous online environments. It is possible to hypothesize that, in the long term, this process might lead to a change in their personality type and eventually cause them to express themselves as extroverts offline. This would be a very slow process and move from online environments where the users feel totally protected through to less secure online environments, and all the way to participation in online social networks and offline interaction as self-confidence grows.

The phenomenon of the ease of finding similar others online is also an important topic for future research in relation to introversion and extroversion. Important questions need to be asked. What is the preferred psychological online term for introverts? Do introverts find it more difficult to express themselves when they are surrounded by extroverts? Does this hold true when they are in anonymous environments? What happens with a group of introverts in both the online and the offline worlds?

The high accessibility of the Internet has the potential to enhance introverts' gradual change to more extroverted behavior. This is a very important topic for future study. A related variable to the degree of accessibility of the Internet is the amount of multitasking carried out by an individual. For example, some people restrict themselves to a specific amount of time online, but increasing numbers of people, particularly the young, have integrated the online and offline worlds into their daily lives and continually switch their focus between the two. Even within this large group, however, there will be people who are multitaskers, and those who are not. Thus, when those introverts who behave in (at least some) online environments as extroverts are low in multitasking behavior, it is possible to deduce that their online experience as extroverts is less likely to generalize to the offline, or that it will do so at a slower pace. Conversely, introverts who are high on multitasking and continuously move between the online and the offline worlds may well be more likely to become extroverts.

When it comes to fun, it would be interesting to assess the basic assumption that online fun for introverts is to adapt to an extrovert style. It is possible that not all introverts want to become extroverts, some might be happy to remain as they are. Thus, although they might adopt an extrovert style online, for example in order to function in the virtual team, they may decide not to try to generalize this extroversion from online to offline, particularly if the extroversion experience online was not rewarding psychologically. These ideas need to be examined in future research.

FINAL WORD

The study of personality and Internet use is growing in importance as the Internet takes on an ever-increasing significance in our lives. This chapter focused on a single personality theory in order to illustrate just how imperative it is to study the interaction between personality, Internet, and well-being. It seems clear that many websites are already exploiting their knowledge of our personal characteristics in order to provide us with products and services for us to purchase, rather than to provide for our psychological well-being.

It is extremely important to continue research in this area, especially longitudinal research in order to create a body of knowledge as to what enhances our well-being based on our personality. The hope is that this will lead to a new web design—one which offers users an online experience that will enhance their psychological well-being.

References

Adler, R. F., & Benbunan-Fich, R. (2012). Juggling on a high wire: Multitasking effects on performance. *International Journal of Human-Computer Studies 70*, 156–168.

Alt, D. (2015). College students' academic motivation, media engagement and fear of missing out. *Computers in Human Behavior 49*, 111–119.

Ames, M. G. (2013). Managing mobile multitasking: The culture of iPhones on Stanford campus. In *Proceedings of the 2013 conference on Computer supported cooperative work* (pp. 1487–1498). New York: ACM.

Amichai-Hamburger, Y. (2002). Internet and personality. *Computers in Human Behavior 18*, 1–10.

Amichai-Hamburger, Y. (2005). Personality and Internet. In Y. Amichai-Hamburger (Ed.), *The social net: Understanding human behavior in cyberspace* (pp. 27–55). New York: Oxford University Press.

Amichai-Hamburger, Y. (2008). The contact hypothesis reconsidered: Interacting via internet: Theoretical and practical aspects. In A. Barak (Ed.), *Psychological aspects of cyberspace: Theory, research, applications* (pp. 209–227). Cambridge: Cambridge University Press.

Amichai-Hamburger, Y. (2009). Technology and well-being: Designing the future. In Y. Amichai-Hamburger (Ed.), *Technology and well-being* (pp. 260–278). New York: Cambridge University Press.

Amichai-Hamburger, Y. (2017). *Internet psychology: The basics*. New York: Routledge.

Amichai-Hamburger, Y., & Hayat, Z. (2011). The impact of the Internet on the social lives of users: A representative sample from 13 countries. *Computers in Human Behavior 27*, 585–589.

Amichai-Hamburger, Y., & Hayat, Z. (2013). Personality and the Internet. In Y. Amichai-Hamburger (Ed.), *The social net: Understanding our online behavior* (pp. 1–20). New York: Oxford University Press.

Amichai-Hamburger, Y., & Vinitzky, G. (2010). Social network use and personality. *Computers in Human Behavior 26*, 1289–1295.

Amichai-Hamburger, Y., Kaplan, H., & Dorpatcheon, N. (2008). Click to the past: The impact of extroversion by users of nostalgic website on the use of Internet social services. *Computers in Human Behavior 24*, 1907–1912.

Amichai-Hamburger, Y., Wainapel, G., & Fox, S. (2002). "On the Internet no one knows I'm an introvert": Extroversion, neuroticism and Internet interaction. *Cyberpsychology and Behavior 2*, 125–128.

An, Y. J., & Frick, T. (2006). Student perceptions of asynchronous computer-mediated communication in face-to-face courses. *Journal of Computer-Mediated Communication 11*, 485–499.

Anolli, L., Villani, D., & Riva, G. (2005). Personality of people using chat: An on-line research. *Cyberpsychology & Behavior 8*(1), 89–94.

Annis, N. M., Cash, T. F., & Hrabosky, J. I. (2004). Body image and psychosocial differences among stable average weight, currently overweight, and formerly overweight women: The role of stigmatizing experiences. *Body Image 1*, 155–167.

Bailenson, J. N., & Beall, A. C. (2006). Transformed social interaction: Exploring the digital plasticity of avatars. In R. Schroeder & A. Axelsson (Eds.), *Avatars at work and play: Collaboration and interaction in shared virtual environments* (pp. 1–16). New York: Springer-Verlag.

Bargh, J. A., McKenna, K. Y. A., & Fitzsimons, G. M. (2002). Can you see the real me? Activation and expression of the "True Self" on the Internet. *Journal of Social Issues 58*, 33–48.

Ben-Ze'ev, A. (2005). 'Detattachment': The unique nature of online romantic relationships. In Y. Amichai-Hamburger (Ed.), *The social net: Understanding human behavior in cyberspace* (pp. 115–138). New York: Oxford University Press.

Ben-Ze'ev, B. (2004). *Love online: Emotions on the Internet*. New York: Cambridge University Press.

Bevan, J. L., Gomez, R., & Sparks, L. (2014). Disclosures about important life events on Facebook: Relationships with stress and quality of life. *Computers in Human Behavior 39*, 246–253.

Cash, T. F., & Deagle, E. A. (1997). The nature and extent of body-image disturbances in anorexia nervosa and bulimia nervosa: A meta-analysis. *International Journal of Eating Disorders 22*, 107–126.

Chae, J. (2017). Virtual makeover: Selfie-taking and social media use increase selfie-editing frequency through social comparison. *Computers in Human Behavior 66*, 370–376.

Chen, K., & Lee, K. H. (2013). Sharing, liking, commenting, and distressed? The pathway between Facebook interaction and psychological distress. *Cyberpsychology, Behavior, and Social Networking 16*(10), 728–734.

Cho, J. (2015). Roles of Smartphone app use in improving social capital and reducing social isolation. *Cyberpsychology, Behavior, and Social Networking 18*, 350–355.

Cserni, R. T., & Talmud, I. (2015). To know that you are not alone: The effect of Internet usage on LGBT youth's social capital. *Communication and Information Technologies Annual (Studies in Media and Communications) 9*, 161–182.

David, P., Kim, J. H., Brickman, J. S., Ran, W., & Curtis, C. M. (2014). Mobile phone distraction while studying. *New Media & Society 17*(10), 1661–1679. doi:10.1177/1461444814531692.

Dunn, R. A., & Guadagno, R. E. (2012). My avatar and me? Gender and personality predictors of avatar-self-discrepancy. *Computers in Human Behavior 28*, 97–106.

Ehmke, C., & Wilson, S. (2007). Identifying web usability problems from eyetracking data. In *Proceedings of the 21st British HCI group annual conference on people and computers: HCI…but not as we know it*. Vol. 1. (pp. 119–128). London: British Computer Society.

Farewell, J. (2014). The media strategy of ISIS. *Survival: Global Politics and Strategy 56*(6), 49–55.

Gosling, S. D., Augustine, A. A., Vazire, S., Holtzman, N., & Gaddis, S. (2011). Facebook-related behaviors and observable profile information. *Cyberpsychology, Behavior, and Social Networking 14*, 483–488.

Groenke, S. L. (2007). Collaborative dialogue in a synchronous CMC environment? A look at one beginning English teacher's strategies. *Journal of Computing in Teacher Education 24*, 41–46.

Guadagno, R. E., Okdie, B. M., & Eno, C. A. (2007). Who blogs? Personality predictors of blogging. *Computers in Human Behavior 24*, 1993–2004. doi:10.1016/j.chb.2007.09.001

Hamburger, Y. A., & Ben-Artzi, E. (2000). The relationship between extraversion and neuroticism and the different uses of the Internet. *Computers in Human Behavior 16*, 441–449.

Herring, S. C., Scheidt, L. A., Wright, E., & Bonus, S. (2005). Weblogs as a bridging genre. *Information, Technology, & People 18*, 142–171.

Horai, J., Naccari, N., & Fatoullah, E. (1974). The effects of expertise and physical attractiveness upon opinion agreement and liking. *Sociometry 37*(4), 601–606.

Huberman, B. A., Romero, D. M., & Wu, F. (2009). Social networks that matter: Twitter under the micro-scope. *First Monday 14*(1) [online]. Retrieved from: http://firstmonday.org/ojs/index.php/fm/article/view/2317/2063

Huffaker, D. (2004). The educated blogger: Using weblogs to promote literacy in the classroom. *First Monday 9*(6). Retrieved from: http://www.firstmonday.org/ojs/index.php/fm/article/view/1156

Hughes, D. J., Rowe, M., Batey, M., & Lee, A. (2012). A tale of two sites: Twitter vs. Facebook and the personality predictors social media usage. *Computers in Human Behavior 28*, 561–569.

Joinson, A. (2001). Self-disclosure in computer-mediated communication: The role of self-awareness and visual anonymity. *European Journal Social Psychology 31*, 177–192.

Katz, J. E., & Crocker, E. T. (2015). Selfies and photo messaging as visual conversation: Reports from the United States, United Kingdom and China. *International Journal of Communication 9*, 1861–1872.

Kerkhof, P., Finkenauer, C., & Muusses, L. D. (2011). Relational consequences of compulsive Internet use: A longitudinal study among newlyweds. *Human Communication Research 37*, 147–173.

Khrabrov, A., & Cybenko, G. (2010, August). Discovering influence in communication networks using dynamic graph analysis. In *Social Computing (SocialCom), 2010 IEEE Second International Conference on* (pp. 288–294). IEEE.

Kraut, R., Kiesler, S., Boneva, B., Cummings, J. N., Helgeson, V., & Crawford, A. M. (2002). Internet paradox revisited. *Journal of Social Issues 58*, 49–74.

Kuykendall, L., Tay, L., & Ng, V. (2015). Leisure engagement and subjective well-being: A meta-analysis. *Psychological Bulletin 141*, 364–403.

Lawson-Borders, G., & Kirk, R. (2005). Blogs in campaign communication. *American Behavioral Scientist 49*, 548–559.

Le Roux, I., & Maree, T. (2016). Motivation, engagement, attitudes and buying intent of female Facebook users. *Acta Commercii 16*, a340. doi:10.4102/ac.v16i1.340.

Lee, E., Ahn, J., & Kim, Y. J. (2014). Personality traits and self-presentation at Facebook. *Personality and Individual Differences 69*, 162e167. doi:10.1016/j.paid.2014.05.020

Liu, D., Ainsworth, S. E., & Baumeister, R. F. (2016). A meta-analysis of social networking online and social capital. *Review of General Psychology 20*, 369–391.

Malamuth, N., Linz, D., & Yao, M. (2005). The Internet and aggression: Motivation, disinhibitory and opportunity aspects. In Y. Amichai-Hamburger (Ed.), *The social net: Understanding human behavior in cyberspace* (pp. 163–190). New York: Oxford University Press.

Maldonado, G. J., Mora, M., Garcia, S., & Edipo, P. (2001). Personality, sex and computer communication mediated through the Internet. *Anuario de Psicologia 32*, 51–62.

Maslow, A. (1971). *Farther reaches of human nature*. New York: Viking.

McAndrew, F. T., & Jeong, H. S. (2012). Who does what on Facebook? Age, sex, and relationship status as predictors of Facebook use. *Computers in Human Behavior 28*(6), 2359–2365.

McCaulay, M., Mintz, L., & Glenn, A. A. (1988). Body image, self-esteem, and depression-proneness: Closing the gender gap. *Sex Roles 18*, 381–391.

McKenna, K. Y., & Bargh, J. A. (1998). Coming out in the age of the Internet: Identity "Demarginalization" through virtual group participation. *Journal of Personality and Social Psychology 75*, 681–694.

McKenna, K., & Bargh, J. (2000). Plan 9 from cyber-space: The implications of the Internet for personality and social psychology. *Personality and Social Psychology Review 4*, 57–75.

McKenna, K. Y. A., Green, A. S., & Gleason, M. J. (2002). Relationship formation on the Internet: What's the big attraction? *Journal of Social Issues 58*, 9–32.

Mehdizadeh, S. (2010). Self-presentation 2.0: Narcissism and self-esteem on Facebook. *CyberPsychology, Behavior, and Social Networking 13*, 357–364. doi:10.1089/cyber.2009.0257

Newman, D. B., Tay, L., & Diener, E. (2014). Leisure and subjective well-being: A model of psychological mechanisms as mediating factors. *Journal of Happiness Studies 15*, 555–578.

Nimrod, G. (2010). The fun culture in seniors' online communities. *The Gerontologist 51*, 226–237.

Nisbett, R. E., & Wilson, T. D. (1977). The halo effect: Evidence for unconscious alteration of judgments. *Journal of Personality and Social Psychology 35*, 231–259.

Ó Baoill, A. (2004). Weblogs and the public sphere, In L. J. Gurak, S. Antonijevic, L. Johnson, C. Ratliff and J. Reyman (Eds.), Into the Blogosphere: Rhetoric, community, and culture of Weblogs, URL (consulted March 2006).

Oh, C., Lee, T., Kim, Y., Park, S., & Suh, B. (2016, May). Understanding participatory hashtag practices on Instagram: A case study of weekend hashtag project. In *Proceedings of the 2016 CHI Conference Extended Abstracts on Human Factors in Computing Systems* (pp. 1280–1287). New York: ACM.

Oulasvirta, A., Rattenbury, T., Ma, L., & Raita, E. (2012). Habits make smartphone use more pervasive. *Personal and Ubiquitous Computing 16*(1), 105–114.

Oulasvirta, A., Tamminen, S., Roto, V., & Kuorelahti, J. (2005). Interaction in 4-second bursts: The fragmented nature of attentional resources in mobile HCI. In *Proceedings of the SIGCHI conference on Human factors in computing systems* (pp. 919–928). New York: ACM.

Pervin, L. A. (1993). *Personality: Theory and research.* New York: John Wiley and Sons.

Postmes, T., Spears, R., & Lea, M. (1998). Breaching or building social boundaries? SIDE-effects of computer-mediated communication. *Communication Research 25*, 689–715.

Przybylski, A. K., Murayama, K., DeHaan, C. R., & Gladwell, V. (2013). Motivational, emotional, and behavioral correlates of fear of missing out. *Computers in Human Behavior 29*, 1841–1848.

Qiu, L., Lu, J., Yang, S., Qu, W., & Zhu, T. (2015). What does your selfie say about you? *Computers in Human Behavior 52*, 443–449.

Quintelier, E., & Theocharis, Y. (2013). Online political engagement, Facebook, and personality traits. *Social Science Computer Review 31*, 280–290.

Riordan, M. A., & Kreuz, R. J. (2010). Emotion encoding and interpretation in computer-mediated communication: Reasons for use. *Computers in Human Behavior 26*, 1667–1673.

Riva, G. (2002). The Sociocognitive psychology of computer-mediated communication: The present and future of technology-based interactions. *Cyberpsychology & Behavior 5*(6), 581–598.

Roberts, B. W., Walton, K. E., & Viechtbauer, W. (2006). Patterns of mean-level change in personality traits across the life course: A meta-analysis of longitudinal studies. *Psychological Bulletin 132*, 1–25.

Rosen, L. D., Lim, A. F., Carrier, L. M., & Cheever, N. A. (2011). An empirical examination of the educational impact of text message-induced task switching in the classroom: Educational implications and strategies to enhance learning. *Psicología Educativa 17*, 163–177.

Seidman, G. (2013). Self-presentation and belonging on Facebook: How personality influences social media use and motivations. *Personality and Individual Differences 54*, 402–407.

Ševčíková, A., & Šmahel, D. (2009). Online harassment and cyberbullying in the Czech Republic: Comparison across age groups. *Journal of Psychology 217*, 227–229.

Schwartz, M. B., & Brownell, K. D. (2004). Body image and obesity. *Body Image 1*, 43–56.

Sheldon, P., & Bryant, K. (2016). Instagram: Motives for its use and relationship to narcissism and contextual age. *Computers in Human Behavior 58*, 89–97.

Suler, J. R. (2004). *The Psychology of cyberspace*. Retrieved from: http://www.rider.edu/~suler/psycyber/psycyber.html

Tajfel, H., & Turner, J. (1979). An integrative theory of intergroup conflict. In W. Austin & S. Worchel (Eds.), *The social psychology of intergroup relations* (pp. 33–47). Monterey, CA: Brooks/Cole.

Taleporos, G., & McCabe, M. P. (2002). Body image and physical disability—personal perspectives. *Social Science & Medicine 54*, 971–980.

Tsikerdekis, M. (2012). The choice of complete anonymity versus pseudonymity for aggression online. *eMinds: International Journal on Human-Computer Interaction 2*, 35–57.

Turel, O., & Serenko, A. (2012). The benefits and dangers of enjoyment with social networking websites. *European Journal of Information Systems 21*, 512–528.

Turkle, S. (1995). *Life on the screen: Identity in the age of the Internet*. New York: Simon & Schuster.

Turner, A. (2015). Generation Z: Technology and social interest. *The Journal of Individual Psychology 71*, 103–113.

Weiser, E. B. (2015). #Me: Narcissism and its facets as predictors of selfie-posting frequency. *Personality and Individual Differences 86*, 477e481. doi:10.1016/j.paid.2015.07.007

Wiggins, A. (2007). Information architecture: Data-driven design: Using web analytics to validate heuristics system. *Bulletin of the American Society for Information Science and Technology 33*, 20–24.

Wilson, W. J. (1978). The declining significance of race. *Society 15*, 56–62.

Young, K. S. (1998). Internet addiction: The emergence of a new clinical disorder. *CyberPsychology & Behavior 1*, 237–244.

PART II

TECHNOLOGY ACROSS THE LIFESPAN

CHAPTER 5

ADOLESCENT AND EMERGING ADULT PERCEPTION AND PARTICIPATION IN PROBLEMATIC AND RISKY ONLINE BEHAVIOR

CODY DEVYN WEEKS AND
KAVERI SUBRAHMANYAM

Young People and Social Media

ONLINE environments have become an important setting in young people's lives (Lenhart, Purcell, Smith, & Zickuhr, 2010). As technology has advanced, mobile devices have taken the place of desktop computers and laptops, allowing users to access a variety of online platforms including social media sites such as Facebook, Instagram, and Snapchat, regardless of time or geographic location. This chapter focuses on the risky online content that young people create and consume, and the relation of such content to their beliefs and behaviors.

Adolescence and emerging adulthood have been characterized as a period of self-discovery, exploration, and experimentation (Arnett, 2000), and considerable evidence suggests this is also a stage of life that is synonymous with risky behavior (Coleman & Cater, 2005; NIAA, 2014; Pharo, Sim, Graham, Gross, & Hayne, 2011). Such risky behaviors include increased alcohol consumption (National Institute of Alcohol Abuse and Alcoholism, 2014; Hingson, Zha, & Weitzman, 2009), risky sexual behavior (Center for Disease Control and Prevention, 2017; Galambos & Tilton-Weaver, 1998), or a combination of the two (Mair, Ponicki, & Gruenewald, 2016). Though the legal drinking age is 21 years in the United States, younger people regularly post and are exposed to alcohol content on social networking cites (Moreno et al., 2010). Given that risky behavior increases during adolescence and emerging adulthood, it is vital that we understand the prevalence and role of social media content depicting such behavior in order to leverage youths' social media use to potentially safeguard against and prevent risky behavior.

Research has found that being exposed to risky behavior (including substance use, eating disorders, self-harm behavior, and violence) online is highly correlated with engaging in such risky behavior offline (Branley and Covey, 2017). In addition, higher levels of media use are associated with riskier offline behaviors including alcohol use (Brunborg, Andreas, & Kvaavik, 2017), and adolescent exposure to sexual content online is related to more frequent casual sex relationships (Van Oosten, Peter, & Vandenbosch, 2017).

This chapter focuses on adolescent and emerging adults' social media use and examines the relationship between their potentially negative and risky beliefs and behavior and the online content that they consume and create. It focuses specifically on online exposure to alcohol and sexualized content as well as miscellaneous content that may negatively impact young people. It establishes the theoretical framework used here to explain the role of online content in beliefs and behavior. It then addresses how online contexts can be used for risky networking and communication. Lastly, it evaluates efforts to combat risky online content and to use social media content to combat risky offline behavior.

THEORETICAL FRAMEWORK OF MEDIA RESEARCH

The theoretical framing of this chapter draws from the social norms theory (Perkins & Berkowitz, 1986) and the media cultivation theory (Gerbner & Gross, 1976). The social norms theory has been used widely to understand young adults' risky behavior related to substance use and sex. The media cultivation theory was proposed to account for the influence of television on viewers' attitudes and perceptions. Both of these theories can be valuable in explaining how perception change is related to media consumption and how misperceptions may influence behaviors. The next sections describe the social norms theory, followed by the evidence supporting it, and then do the same for the cultivation theory.

Social Norms Theory

Perkins and Berkowitz proposed the social norms theory of alcohol, which argues that students' perceptions about their peers' alcohol use can help to understand the drinking patterns of undergraduate students (Perkins & Berkowitz, 1986). They documented misperceptions of peer alcohol use, such that there was an expectation that peers were more accepting of use, consuming more alcohol than they actually were, and their expectation was that peers were using alcohol more frequently than they actually were (Perkins & Berkowitz, 1986). According to Perkins and Berkowitz (1986), young adults' misperceptions about peer alcohol acceptance, frequency of use among peers, and exaggerated beliefs about how much alcohol peers are consuming leads to an overall more liberal view of alcohol-related behavior, which can lead to higher rates of alcohol use. This is an example of pluralistic ignorance, which is the idea that one's own private beliefs about a given behavior are unique and dissimilar to the thoughts of society as a whole (Miller & McFarland, 1991). On the contrary, a phenomenon known as false consensus happens when an individual partakes in a behavior that they misperceive is supported and encouraged by the majority of the population (Ross, Greene, & House, 1977). This phenomenon has also been found to extend to the realm of illicit drug use, with those engaging in the behavior overestimating the regularity of the behavior and the average person's acceptance of the behavior (Dunn, Thomas, Swift, & Burns, 2012).

Research on the role of online media and social norms regarding risky behavior have found that misperceptions of both descriptive and injunctive norms are related to engaging in risky behavior (Baumgartner, Valkenburg, & Peter, 2011; Litt & Stock, 2011). Litt and Stock (2011) found that adolescents who viewed posts of peers drinking alcohol on Facebook showed more liberal social norms about alcohol. More specifically, adolescents falsely assumed that peer alcohol use occurred more regularly than it actually did, and were more willing to use alcohol after seeing peers' alcohol posts on Facebook (Litt & Stock, 2011). Besides being influenced by the social media posts of their friends, Elmore, Scull, and Kupersmidt (2017) found the media acted as a "super peer" for adolescents "media related cognitions" and were related to their social norms of alcohol (p. 383). Currently, researchers are actively trying to ascertain whether certain figures/people in social media (celebrities, athletes, Internet personalities, etc.) have greater influence of social media users' norms and their desire to use alcohol.

Similarly, social media posts have been found to influence the perception of normative peer sexuality and to impact risky sexual behavior among young people (Baumgartner, Valkenburg, & Peter, 2011; Young & Jordan, 2013). Furthermore, social norms predicted increased risky sexual behavior online (Baumgartner, Valkenburg, & Peter, 2011). Participants of an online experiment who viewed sexually suggestive Facebook posts reported greater unprotected sex by peers, assumed that peers engaged in inflated numbers of sex with strangers, and self-reported a higher likelihood of partaking in these behaviors compared to participants who viewed less racy photos (Young & Jordan, 2013).

Cultivation Theory

Though initially developed to explain how television consumption was related to views about the prevalence of violence in society (Gerbner & Gross, 1976), cultivation theory is also relevant for explaining the impact of time spent on social media on users' perceptions of a variety of behaviors, including substance use and sexual relationships. Media cultivation theory posits that viewing a given medium over an extended period of time cultivates beliefs about the regularity of given behaviors in society, and that users' resulting views of society will mirror the views displayed in the medium (Gerbner & Gross, 1976; Morgan & Shanahan, 2010). Research suggests that actions and behaviors that are less common in society are over-represented in the media, which cultivates views that these rare occurrences happen more frequently than they actually do (Shrum, Wyer, & O'Guinn, 1998). Thus, increased media consumption may lead to an inaccurate world-view (Gerbner & Gross, 1976).

Media cultivation theory can be used to explain how media content is related to users' perceptions. Yang, Salmon, Pang, and Cheng (2015) utilized cultivation theory to explain perceptions of tobacco use among young people. Their research showed that increased media use was associated with the belief that smoking was more common in society than it actually was, which impacted the likelihood of participants' engaging in tobacco use, when the perceived disapproval of friends was low (Yang, Salmon, Pang, & Cheng, 2015). Thus, when a behavior was perceived as normative and acceptable online, people were more likely to engage in that behavior (Yang, Salmon, Pang, & Cheng, 2015). According to Beullens, Roe, and Van den Bulck (2012), watching music videos may cultivate beliefs about driving under the influence. Consequently, regular music video consumption was positively associated with driving while intoxicated (Beullens, Roe, & Van den Bulck, 2012). Just as with television, increased time spent online might cultivate beliefs that online content reflects real world contexts (Gerbner & Gross, 1976). This is also true for attitudes about sex. In a sample of Kenyan high school students, Miller, Kinnally, Maleche, and Booker (2017) found that increased time spent online was related to more permissive beliefs about sex, suggesting that greater time online may cultivate more liberal beliefs about sexual norms. Such media influences can be especially problematic with regard to unprotected and risky sexual behavior.

SUBSTANCE USE, MEDIA USE, AND YOUNG PEOPLE

As youth are heavy users of social media (Lenhart, 2015; Perrin, 2015), we must evaluate how their beliefs about alcohol and drinking intention is associated with media use. The next section presents the regularity and frequency with which substance use is posted on social media, and then examines empirical research regarding relationship between viewing substance use in social media and changes in the perceptions and/or intentions to use these substances among young people.

Facebook

Facebook is the most popular social media today, with over two billion users (Ingram, 2017). It is also the most popular social media for young people, with 71 percent of teens ages 13–17 having Facebook accounts (Lenhart, 2015). Youth use Facebook to socialize, post, or view friends' posts. Although Facebook is a valuable tool for keeping in touch and communicating with friends and family, alcohol content is commonly found within it (Rodriquez, Litt, Neighbors, & Lewis, 2016). In a content analysis of Belgian college students' Facebook pages, Beullens and Schepers (2013) found that more than 95 percent of profiles had an image that referenced alcohol, roughly 40 percent of profiles had a "text reference to alcohol," and feedback from friends on these posts was overwhelmingly positive (p. 500). Such positive feedback may reinforce the posting and/or use of alcohol. Besides posting, viewing alcohol online is related to use. Boyle, LaBrie, Froidevaux, and Witkovic (2016) reported that viewing alcohol on social networking sites predicted freshman college students' alcohol use six months later, suggesting that merely viewing alcohol content online may be related to alcohol consumption. A content analysis of college students' Facebook posts suggested that alcohol related content comprised about three percent of their posts (Rodriquez et al., 2016). As Facebook is the most used social media platform, even three percent of its content being alcohol-related can have a negative impact, given the size of the audience, number of posts being posted daily, and the fact that 75 percent of users log in daily (Smith & Anderson, 2018). Furthermore, research suggests that time spent using social media is associated with increased alcohol consumption (Brunborg, Andreas, & Kvaavik, 2017; Gutierrez & Cooper, 2016). In addition to elevated alcohol usage, the amount of time spent on social networking sites is positively correlated with the regularity of marijuana use (Gutierrez & Cooper, 2016). This would suggest that there is a relation between social media use and substance use (Gutierrez & Cooper, 2016). With young people exposed to social media posts that reference substance use, social norms regarding the acceptance of use and regularity of use are likely impacted, as well as their intentions to use the substances (Litt & Stock, 2011).

Twitter

Alcohol posts on social media typically have a positive connotation (Cavazos-Rehg, Krauss, Sowles, & Bierut, 2015). Over 400,000 alcohol tweets are posted every day and most of them are pro alcohol consumption. In fact, pro alcohol tweets outnumbered tweets about abstaining from alcohol by a ratio of 10:1 (Cavazos-Rehg et al., 2015). In terms of cultivation theory, the more time someone spent on twitter, the more users will be inundated with alcohol tweets, which likely cultivates their perceptions and behavior of offline alcohol use. Indeed, research by Cabrera-Nguyen and colleagues (2016) found that among emerging adults, viewing of pro-alcohol and marijuana tweets on twitter was positively correlated with self-reported alcohol and marijuana usage. Thus, it appears that viewing pro-substance use tweets may be related to youths' actual substance use (Cabrera-Nguyen et al., 2016). The sheer number of tweets about substance use and the positive connotation of most of these tweets may reinforce misperceived norms, which are related to substance use behavior. Thus, it may be important to limit young people's exposure to pro-substance use content online.

Instagram and Snapchat

Newer social networking sites such as Snapchat and Instagram both have photo and video posting ability, and visual posts about alcohol and other addictive substances are regularly posted on these platforms (Utz, Muscanell, & Khalid, 2015). Boyle, Earle, LaBrie, and Ballou (2017) found that college students identify Instagram as the platform most likely to include posts about alcohol suggesting that alcohol is regularly posted on Instagram and Snapchat. In fact, nearly 50 percent of Snapchat users self-reported posting and sending alcohol related posts via that medium (Utz, Muscanell, & Khalid, 2015).

Like Twitter, pro-substance use content is posted on Instagram (Cavazos-Rehg, Krauss, Sowles, & Bierut, 2016). In a study of marijuana-related posts on Instagram, Cavazos-Rehg and colleagues (2016) found that over a two week period in 2014 more than 400,000 posts that included marijuana-related hashtags were posted. Most of these posts included pictures of marijuana or marijuana accessories, with the majority of these posts being pro-marijuana use (Cavazos-Rehg et al., 2016). Thus, the high number of marijuana posts on Instagram may lead to false or incorrect norms about the regularity of offline use. Using cultivation theory suggests that heavier Instagram users will be more likely to falsely perceive that use and social acceptance online is a mirror of offline realities. In addition, the researchers found that a high proportion of these posts were posted by youth aged 16–24 years of age (Cavazos-Rehg et al., 2016). Therefore, youth are not just consuming substance use content, they are also posting it. These findings could be problematic, and Litt and Stock (2011) found that viewing alcohol posts by similarly aged peers influenced norms and intentions to use alcohol. In addition to the posts of regular Instagram users, marijuana manufacturers are also marketing their products on social media (Cavazos-Rehg et al., 2016). Marketing campaigns of various substances on Instagram can easily be viewed by young people, who may not yet be of age to legally consume the products being marketed.

Online Marketing

With the explosion of social media there has been an increase in alcohol marketing within these platforms (Barry et al., 2016; Hoffman, Pinkleton, Austin, & Reyes-Velázquez, 2014). On most social networking sites, users can easily follow any alcohol brand, see the content posted by its marketing department, as well as like and share their posts, which are actually advertisements. In addition, many companies that market alcohol have not followed self-imposed alcohol regulations, e.g. age restrictions, as researcher-created underage social media profiles have been able to easily access and interact with alcohol-related marketing content (Barry et al., 2016). An important question is whether such aggressive marketing and pro-substance use content on Twitter may impact young people's attitudes and use of substances. A systematic review of alcohol marketing on social media sites concluded that exposure to such marketing campaigns is associated with elevated alcohol consumption and binge drinking (Lobstein, Landon,

Thornton, & Jernigan, 2016). Thus, in addition to concerns about content posted and consumed by youths' peers, we should also consider the impact of the content they consume from alcohol manufacturers (Hoffman et al., 2014; Lobstein et al., 2016). According to Hoffman and colleagues (2014), interacting with alcohol marketing campaigns in social media by college students is positively correlated with alcohol consumption. Research on online social media marketing of alcohol found that the intention for social media users to consume alcohol was related to holding more positive views toward alcohol posts (Alhabash, McAlister, Quilliam, Richards, & Lou, 2015). Furthermore, research has found a direct relationship between alcohol norms and behavior (Litt & Stock, 2011). As a result of the alcohol content that they interact with on social media, young people who perceive alcohol consumption to be more acceptable and to occur at a higher frequency among their peers may also have a stronger urge to drink. In an analysis of 105 of the most popular online alcohol selling websites (seventy-two of which were located in the United States), Williams and Schmidt (2014) found that alcohol prices were significantly cheaper online than offline, and age verification on these websites was lax, encouraging youth to purchase alcohol online whether or not they are of the legal drinking age. It is critical that there be more legislative and law enforcement checks and balances to ensure that alcohol companies follow their self-imposed marketing restrictions and that they are not illegally selling alcohol products to underage youth.

Sex, Media Use, and Young People

As today's young adults have grown up with the Internet (Perrin, 2015) and use it to view and transmit sexualized content (Judge, 2012; Smahel & Subrahmanyam, 2014), it is important to evaluate how such use relates to their beliefs and behaviors particularly problematic ones about sex (Dunn, Thomas, Swift, & Burns, 2012; Van Oosten, Peter, & Boot, 2015; Van Oosten, Peter, & Vandenbosch, 2017). The following section reviews research on the prevalence of sexting, pornography, and revenge porn and also examines the relationship between young people's consumption of sexual content on social media and their beliefs and behaviors.

Sexting (Sex Texts)

Social networking sites and mobile devices may be used to send and receive sexualized content (Judge, 2012; Smahel & Subrahmanyam, 2014). The sending of sexualized content (typically "sexually explicit" pictures) is better known as sexting (Judge, 2012). Benotsch, Snipes, Martin, and Bull (2013) found that sending sext messages is relatively common among emerging adults, with 44 percent of their sample self-reporting as "sexters". A recent study that examined sexting rates in a high school found that "nearly one-fifth of girls and boys" self-reported sending nude pictures of themselves through text messages, and "one-third of girls and half of boys" admitted to receiving such a message (Strassberg, Cann, & Velarde, 2017, p. 19). Sexting is also prevalent among minority populations. In a sample of low-income, predominantly African-American and Latino heterosexual men, 73 percent of males self-reported engaging in sexting, with more than half of the sample both sending and receiving sext messages (Davis, Powell, Gordon, & Kershaw, 2016).

Research suggests that sexting may be related to myriad risky behaviors. According to Champion and Pederson (2015), sexters are more likely to engage in risky sexual behavior. In addition, sending and receiving sext messages among emerging adult men from minority groups was related to a variety of risky sexual behaviors. These behaviors included higher numbers of sexual partners, unprotected sex, and sexual activity under the influence of drugs and alcohol (Davis, Powell, Gordon, & Kershaw, 2016). Likewise, research with adolescents found that sexting was positively associated with offline sexual activity, including vaginal, anal, and oral sex (Rice et al., 2018) and substance use (Ybarra & Mitchell, 2014).

Though typically sent as text messages, social media platforms, particularly newer ones, are becoming a popular method of sending sexually explicit messages (Van Ouytsel, Van Gool, Walrave, Ponnet, & Peeters, 2017). Utz, Muscanell, and Khalid (2015) suggest that social media users preferred Snapchat over Facebook to flirt. Furthermore, focus group research conducted by Van Ouytsel and colleagues (2017) found that young people identified smartphone applications such as Snapchat and Whatsapp as the preferred medium for sexting. In addition, young people preferred these methods of sexting because they perceived them to be safer than other media for sending sensitive photographs (Van Ouytsel et al., 2017). Greater perceived security for sending sext messages via Snapchat may be due to the fact that on this platform, private messages disappear within seconds of the receiver viewing the message (Roesner, Gill, & Kohno, 2014). Thus, the lack of permanence of sexually explicit content may make Snapchat a preferred tool for sending sensitive material. In addition, users are notified if the recipient of a message tries to screenshot or replay the material that they have sent (Roesner, Gill, & Kohno, 2014).

Sexualized Content on Social Media

Posting and consuming sexualized content on social media is common among young people, especially girls (Kapidzic & Herring, 2015). In a content analysis of social media profile pictures, Kapidzic and Herring (2015) found that adolescent girls posed more seductively than adolescent boys, and nearly half of the females in their sample wore revealing clothing in their pictures. An interesting question is whether the consumption of sexualized content on television and social media relates to sexual activity. Vandenbosch, van Oosten, and Peter (2015) found a positive association between adolescents' viewing of sexualized reality television and posting sexual content on social media. However, these results are not unique to television consumption (van Oosten,

Peter, & Vandenbosch, 2017), and similar results have been found for viewing sexual content online. According to van Oosten, Peter, and Vandenbosch (2017), online exposure to sexual content predicted the likelihood of engaging in casual sex among Belgian adolescents. In addition, a longitudinal study suggests that 13–17-year-olds who self-reported being exposed to "sexy self-presentations of others on social networking sites" had a higher likelihood of reporting that they engaged in both oral sex and sexual intercourse six months later (van Oosten, Peter, & Boot, 2015, p. 1086). Similarly, Bobkowski, Shafer, and Ortiz (2016) found that adolescents who self-reported that they consumed higher levels of sexualized content were more likely to present themselves in a sexualized way in an online task that mirrored a social media profile, though extraversion and self-concept also played an important role in online self-expression.

Pornography

Pornography is another form of media content that is regularly accessed by young people, although exposure to pornography might be unintentional in some cases, and Jones, Mitchell, and Finkelhor (2012) found that 23 percent of young people inadvertently access or come in contact with online pornography. Though this may seem high, the number of youth accidently accessing pornography has been gradually declining (Jones, Mitchell, & Finkelhor, 2012). One reason for this may be that young people are far more digitally competent than past generations, given their earlier and substantially greater exposure to digital media.

An important issue is that access to pornography has changed with recent advancements in technology. While accidental exposure to pornography continues to occur, intentional viewing of sexually explicit material is fairly common, and such purposeful viewing of pornography was reported more frequently by male college students (González-Ortega & Orgaz-Baz, 2013). Research suggests that consumption of pornography has been increasing over time. According to Price, Patterson, Regnerus, and Walley (2016), people born after 1980 have consumed more pornography than previous generations. The most parsimonious answer for the increased exposure to pornography is due to its easy accessibility via online contexts. Since people do not have to leave the house and can access pornography in the privacy of their own home, they may feel more at ease to access it.

Research has found that exposure to pornography is related to the commission of both online and offline sexual acts (Van Ouytsel, Ponnet, & Walrave, 2014). According to Van Ouytsel, Ponnet, and Walrave (2014), watching pornography as an adolescent was positively correlated with transmitting sexually explicit messages, including sext messages. Thus, young people who are exposed to sexually explicit media are more likely to engage in and send sexually explicit content of themselves (Van Oosten, Peter, & Boot, 2015). Likewise, Sinković, Štulhofer, and Božić (2013) found that age of exposure to "sexually explicit material" and a high amount of "sexual sensation seeking" predicted riskier sexual behavior among Croatian emerging adults. Thus, it is clear that early exposure to sexually explicit content increases the likelihood of riskier sexual behavior later in life; given the correlation of much of the foregoing research, it is unclear whether preventing early exposure to pornography will be sufficient to limit risky sexual behavior later on in adolescence and emerging adulthood.

Revenge Porn

A newer form of online victimization is revenge porn, which is the "dissemination (without the subject's knowledge or consent) of sexually explicit media, such as digital photographs or videos, that were originally obtained with the subject's consent, typically in the context of an intimate romantic relationship" (Recupero, 2016, p. 324). In addition, websites dedicated to user uploads of revenge porn may ask for personal information about the victim, including their name and hometown (Recupero, 2016). Whether it is a hacker posting nude pictures of famous people online, or Rob Kardashian posting nude pictures of his ex-girlfriend (Black Chyna), revenge porn is occurring, and many of us are witnessing it unintentionally. According to Lenhart, Ybarra, and Price-Feeney (2016), 2 percent of the population have been victims revenge porn, and 4 percent have been threatened by it.

As revenge porn is relatively new, research in this area is scarce. However, early research shows that being a victim of revenge porn is associated with myriad negative psychological outcomes, including PTSD, anxiety, and depression in women (Bates, 2017). This shows that what others post online has offline consequences, especially for individuals who may be the target of such online posts. Given the increasing popularity of revenge porn, government officials and media developers are tasked with strategies for combatting this problem. Fortunately, many states in the US have enacted legislation that holds people accountable for the (revenge porn) content that they post online (Recupero, 2016). In California, it is a misdemeanor crime to transmit and share photographs that were intended to be private (Calvert, 2015). As digital media has made access to pornography and the ability to share pornography easier, vigilance about its potential negative impact on young consumers and victimizers is vital. Please see Kirwan (Chapter 31, this volume), which discusses these topics in greater depth.

MISCELLANEOUS UNHEALTHY
BEHAVIORS ONLINE

Besides online alcohol and sexual content, there are a number of additional online acts, content, and features that could present risks for young people. With adolescents and emerging adults' increased hormone levels, premature neural development, physiological changes, and the difficulties associated with transitioning through developmental stages, we should be especially concerned with what they may be accessing online, how they access it, and its relation to their lives. The next sections discuss how communicating with strangers online (Madden et al., 2013), accessing dangerous online content (Cavazos-Rehg et al., 2017) and new live-streaming features (Dewey, 2016) on social media may negatively relate to young people's perceptions, experiences, and/or online and offline behaviors.

Communicating with Strangers Online/Teen Dating Websites

Social networking sites can be great tools for keeping in touch and communicating with friends online. However, these platforms may also be used by young people to find new friends and network with people who they do not know offline, and more than half of adolescent teenagers have made friends with such strangers (Lenhart, Smith, & Anderson, 2015). The majority of new friendships that start online occur on social networking sites or via online video games (Lenhart, 2015). While many of these friendships may turn out to be healthy, some may turn out to be unhealthy or cause young people to feel uneasy (Madden et al., 2013). According to Madden and colleagues (2013), roughly one out of every six youths is contacted online by someone that they do not know, and who made them feel "scared or uncomfortable" (Madden et al., 2013, p. 12).

Another arena in which young people can communicate with strangers is on teen dating sites (Pujazon-Zazik, Manasse, & Orrell-Valente, 2012). With Internet use and online platforms very popular among young people, meeting potential romantic partners online is not the taboo that it once was. Indeed, Smith and Duggan (2013) note that over 10 percent of Americans have used online dating. Through such sites, teens can divulge their name, age, location, relationship status, and links/user names to their other social media profiles. Teen dating sites also allow users to upload and share photos of themselves. In addition, dating sites such as mylol.com feature an "about me" area, where young people can provide any information that they would like to include, as well as a feature that allows them to communicate how they feel about a potential dating partner by rating their physical attractiveness, and whether they are intriguing, friendly, or sexy. Research on teen dating sites has found that girls were more likely than boys to reference sexual activities (Pujazon-Zazik, Manasse, & Orrell-Valente, 2012).

Recent news stories have also shown that some sexual predators utilize online contexts in order to contact potential youth victims. Although this practice is relatively rare and may be over-represented in the media because of television shows like *To Catch a Predator*, adults looking to have sex with minors do, in fact, utilize online contexts to meet young people for sexual purposes (Wolak, Finkelhor, Mitchell, & Ybarra, 2008). Contrary to popular belief, 95 percent of cases involving statutory rape, in which the victims were seduced online, involved sexual contact that was not forcible (Wolak et al., 2008). In addition, the majority of adults looking for young sex partners online do not hide their identities or sexual intentions (Wolak, Finkelhor, & Mitchell, 2004). It is heartening to note that the number of young people solicited for sex online in the US has been steadily declining since 2000 (Jones, Mitchell, & Finkelhor, 2012). Researchers hypothesize that the possible reasons for this decline is better education, more comfort with technology, and the popularity of social media, which youths can use to communicate with offline friends and acquaintances, and which replace chat rooms where youth often communicated with strangers (Jones, Mitchell, & Finkelhor, 2012; Subrahmanyam & Smahel, 2011).

Negative Impact of Social Media on Relationships

Although social networking sites can be valuable tools for communicating with intimate partners and friends, they may also be negatively associated with youths' relationships (Baker & Carreño, 2016). Adolescents in dating relationships reported that their partners' online communication with members of the opposite sex perpetuated jealousy and disharmony in the relationship (Baker & Carreño, 2016). In addition, focus groups of emerging adults on Snapchat concluded that participants identified the "Best Friend" feature of the app, which identifies the person whom you interact with most, as problematic in the sense that it can create jealousy within relationships (Vaterlaus, Barnett, Roche, & Young, 2016, p. 599). In fact, Snapchat has been found to evoke more jealousy than other social media such as Facebook (Utz, Muscanell, & Khalid, 2015). As visual social media such as Snapchat have become even more popular among young people, problems within intimate relationships may increasingly manifest.

Eating Disorders and Self-Harm Websites

Besides drug and sex risks, young people may access online content that promotes unhealthy lifestyles, including web pages that are pro-anorexia and other eating disorders (Syed-Abdul et al., 2013). Research suggests that Instagram use is positively correlated with "orthorexia nervosa", an eating disorder in which people become overly obsessed with eating healthy foods (Turner & Lefevre, 2017, p. 281). Thus, young people who use more visual social media are more likely to be hyper-concerned about the foods that they are consuming (Turner & Lefevre, 2017). Also, Sherlock and Wagstaff (2018) found that time spent on Instagram was positively correlated with anxiety about their physical appearance. Therefore, time spent on Instagram is related to body image issues. However, Cohen, Newton-John, and Slater (2018) found that Instagram users who were more preoccupied with selfies and how they are presented were associated with "bulimia symptomology" (p. 72). In addition, there are many pro-anorexia social media pages and websites that provide young people susceptible to eating disorders instructions on how to rapidly lose weight, hide their disease from loved ones, as well as other incorrect health information. As such, Syed-Abdul et al. (2013) found that nearly three out of every ten YouTube videos on the topic of anorexia were pro-anorexia in nature. The number of online resources that are pro-anorexia may result in young people's inaccurate perceptions about the regularity of the disorder in society as explained by the social norms theory. In comparison to informative health videos from reputable sources, pro-anorexia videos offered misleading information about the disorder, were "liked" three times more often and commented on twice as much (Syed-Abdul et al., 2013), and this may reinforce risky eating behavior. Therefore, online content on unhealthy eating behavior appears to be preferred in comparison to the more accurate healthy videos that are available online (Syed-Abdul et al., 2013).

Empirical research suggests that social networking sites can be a valuable medium for receiving support from other users during a difficult period (Cavazos-Rehg et al., 2017). However, in some cases, social media interactions and content can fuel unhealthy or self-damaging behavior. Likewise, Cavazos-Rehg et al. (2017) found that conversation and advice on Tumblr about self-harm and depression was mostly supportive, although there were conversations on this platform that promoted unhealthy and self-harming behavior. However, distressed young people may find solace in reaching out for help online (Kendal, Kirk, Elvey, Catchpole, & Pryjmachuk, 2016). Youth who need help can benefit from being a disembodied user in online discussion platforms, and not have to reveal their true identity (Kendal et al., 2016). Consequently, young people may be more comfortable in discussing their problems in online discussion forums in comparison to working through and discussing their problems with offline friends and family (Powell, 2011) and professionals. Thus, online discussion forums can be valuable tools for young people dealing with eating disorders, as they can anonymously receive support, friendship, and guidance without the fear of feeling persecuted or judged (Kendal et al., 2016). At the same time such forums can also serve to normalize problematic and unhealthy behavior and provide incorrect information.

Websites with Racist Content

Recruitment and Susceptibility

Another online avenue that may negatively impact the views of young people are online hate websites (Chau & Xu, 2007; Gerstenfeld, Grant, & Chiang, 2003; McNamee, Peterson, & Peña, 2010). The Internet has become a favored tool of racist groups, with many hate groups migrating online to reach a larger audience more efficiently (Hale, 2012). In previous generations, the concern was that youths would encounter such groups at predetermined demonstrations, or through hate pamphlets. Today's concern is that they may be lured to online hate websites (Hale, 2012). According to Hale (2012), hate websites may include video games or music as a tool to recruit the next batch of young members. Online hate sites may be utilized to recruit new members, spread the ideology and beliefs of the group, and may encourage violence against different races or religions (Chau & Xu, 2007; Gerstenfeld, Grant, & Chiang, 2003). In addition to websites, hate groups are also running blogs that spew their hateful ideology (Chau & Xu, 2007).

According to Chau and Xu (2007), some hate groups use "implicit" and "explicit" hate messages to potentially target and recruit young people for their cause. Such online material may provide justifications for their cause, with the in-group (racist group) being wronged or negatively impacted by the out-group/s that the racist sect is against. It may also elaborate on the need to fight against this threat in a call to arms for the user (McNamee, Peterson, & Peña, 2010) and may influence misperceptions about normative beliefs. In addition, such groups may also tie in religious text as justification for their ideology (McNamee, Peterson, & Peña, 2010).

Cultivation theory is useful in explaining how media content may impact perceptions of ethnic groups. According to Behm-Morawitz and Ta (2014), in a sample of Caucasian college students increased video game play was related to more negative perceptions of African-Americans and Asians. Perhaps video games consistently display inaccurate depictions of minorities that are internalized by the video game user.

Consequences for Victims of Online Hate Sites

Online victimization based on one's race is associated with myriad negative outcomes. According to Tynes, Giang, Williams, and Thompson (2008), being the direct victim of online discrimination is positively associated with depression and anxiety. Besides psychosocial functioning, research suggests that online victimization can also impact motivation. A longitudinal study of African-American and Latino youth (grades 6–12) found that being the victim of online discrimination was positively associated with a decrease in academic motivation (Tynes, Del Toro, & Lozada, 2015). In addition, Tynes et al. (2014) found that time spent online was related to victimization for minority youth. Kirwan discusses online victimization in greater detail (see Chapter 31, this volume).

PRACTICAL CONSIDERATIONS AND FUTURE DIRECTION

While this chapter has covered many circumstances in which social media content and the features of social media present risks to adolescents and emerging adults, online content can be harnessed to positively influence young people (Zabinski, Wilfley, Calfas, Winzelberg, & Taylor, 2004). It is equally important to recognize that social media are not inherently bad. Instead, it is how they are used and perceived that may lead to negative consequences. As discussed, societal perceptions and expectations drive individual beliefs and behaviors, and these social norms are easily manipulated by online social media content (Baumgartner, Valkenburg, & Peter, 2011; Litt & Stock, 2011; Young & Jordan, 2013). Consequently, researchers and social scientists have studied social norms media campaigns, and they have been quite fruitful (Haug et al., 2017; Ridout & Campbell, 2014; Zabinski et al., 2004). Ridout and Campbell (2014) found that correcting the misperceptions of alcohol-drinking college students via Facebook by providing them with information about actual peer behavior lowered the regularity and amount of alcohol that they reported using. In addition, Haug and colleagues (2017) utilized both a texting and online social norms approach to reduce drinking, and were effective in lowering "risky single occasion drinking" (five alcoholic drinks for a male, four alcoholic drinks for a female) in adolescent participants (p. 150). In addition to social norms campaigns to prevent underage and problematic drinking behavior, online social norms campaigns for combatting eating disorders are associated with more positive health outcomes (Zabinski et al., 2004). According to Zabinski and colleagues (2004), online social norms interventions were useful in improving self-esteem and "eating pathology" in comparison to control conditions (p. 917). Similarly, web-based interventions for risky sexual behavior have been found to relate to safer sex practices (Starosta, Cranston, & Earleywine, 2016), such as increased intention to use condoms. In conclusion, with a greater understanding of how perceptions may be distorted by digital media content, and how these misperceptions drive behavior, researchers can leverage social norms media campaigns to target misperceptions and educate young people to try and combat dangerous behaviors related to alcohol, drugs, sex, and other health-related activities.

Summary

This chapter has examined how online functions and content may relate to young people's beliefs and behaviors, and has presented theoretical frameworks that can help to understand this process. More specifically, when people view less common behaviors online it may lead them perceive these behaviors as more normative, and in turn make them more likely to engage in these behaviors (Perkins & Berkowitz, 1986). Consequently, viewing substance use and sexualized content online may lead young people to perceive these acts as acceptable to their peers, as well as to overestimate the actual frequency and regularity of less common acts in everyday life (Baumgartner, Valkenburg, & Peter, 2011; Litt & Stock, 2011). Such misperceptions of risky behaviors are related to an increase in the engagement of various risky acts (Baumgartner, Valkenburg, & Peter, 2011; Litt & Stock, 2011; Young & Jordan, 2013). Besides misperceptions of online content, young people may regularly use online contexts to send, receive, and access sexually explicit content (Champion & Pederson, 2015; Van Oosten, Peter, & Boot, 2015). Engaging in sexual acts online is related to various risky sexual behaviors offline (Sinković, Štulhofer, & Božić, 2013). Besides substance use and sexual content, young people may access websites that reinforce unhealthy behavior (Syed-Abdul et al., 2013). Moreover, pro-anorexia and self-harm websites promote eating disorders and other unhealthy and potentially dangerous behaviors, and provide young people who have serious health problems a platform to not only promote negative eating and harmful behavior, but also to provide instructions and advice to other youth who may be looking to hide these problematic behaviors from their parents and peers (Syed-Abdul et al., 2013). Although this chapter largely focused on the relationship between online media use and problematic behavior among youth, it is important to note that online content and platforms can also be used to combat these less desirable behaviors and to promote healthier lifestyles (Haug et al., 2017; Ridout & Campbell, 2014; Zabinski et al., 2004). Since social media are here to stay, the challenge for researchers, media producers, and policy makers is to better understand their potential for harm, while at the same time leveraging their potential for positive developmental outcomes among youth.

While we have used theories to explain online media effects, each theory makes assumptions. For example, cultivation theory assumes homogeneity in content, where time viewing a given medium is related to misperception of reality. Likewise, social norms theory assumes homogeneity within the user, such that a given content will have similar effects on everyone. To date, a media effects theory that takes individual differences into account has not been proposed. That is, certain people may be inherently more or less vulnerable to online content, based on their offline experiences. The authors of this chapter recommend that future research examines individual user differences when looking at how media impacts beliefs and behaviors.

References

Alhabash, S., McAlister, A. R., Quilliam, E. T., Richards, J. I., & Lou, C. (2015). Alcohol's getting a bit more social: When alcohol marketing messages on Facebook increase young adults' intentions to imbibe. *Mass Communication & Society 18*(3), 350–375.

Arnett, J. J. (2000). Emerging adulthood: A theory of development from the late teens through the twenties. *American Psychologist 55*(5), 469–480.

Baker, C. K., & Carreño, P. K. (2016). Understanding the role of technology in adolescent dating and dating violence. *Journal of Child and Family Studies 25*(1), 308–320.

Barry, A. E., Bates, A. M., Olusanya, O., Vinal, C. E., Martin, E., Peoples, J. E., & Montano, J. R. (2016). Alcohol marketing on Twitter and Instagram: Evidence of directly advertising to youth/adolescents. *Alcohol and Alcoholism 51*(4), 487–492.

Bates, S. (2017). Revenge porn and mental health: A qualitative analysis of the mental health effects of revenge porn on female survivors. *Feminist Criminology 12*(1), 22–42.

Baumgartner, S. E., Valkenburg, P. M., & Peter, J. (2011). The influence of descriptive and injunctive peer norms on adolescents' risky sexual online behavior. *Cyberpsychology, Behavior, and Social Networking 14*(12), 753–758.

Behm-Morawitz, E., & Ta, D. (2014). Cultivating virtual stereotypes? The impact of video game play on racial/ethnic stereotypes. *Howard Journal of Communications 25*(1), 1–15.

Beullens, K., & Schepers, A. (2013). Display of alcohol use on Facebook: A content analysis. *Cyberpsychology, Behavior, and Social Networking 16*(7), 497–503.

Benotsch, E. G., Snipes, D. J., Martin, A. M., & Bull, S. S. (2013). Sexting, substance use, and sexual risk behavior in young adults. *Journal of Adolescent Health 52*(3), 307–313.

Beullens, K., Roe, K., & Van den Bulck, J. (2012). Music video viewing as a marker of driving after the consumption of alcohol. *Substance Use & Misuse 47*(2), 155–165.

Bobkowski, P. S., Shafer, A., & Ortiz, R. R. (2016). Sexual intensity of adolescents' online self-presentations: Joint contribution of identity, media consumption, and extraversion. *Computers in Human Behavior 58*, 64–74.

Boyle, S. C., Earle, A. M., LaBrie, J. W., & Ballou, K. (2017). Facebook dethroned: Revealing the more likely social media destinations for college students' depictions of underage drinking. *Addictive Behaviors 65*, 63–67.

Boyle, S. C., LaBrie, J. W., Froidevaux, N. M., & Witkovic, Y. D. (2016). Different digital paths to the keg? How exposure to peers' alcohol-related social media content influences drinking among male and female first-year college students. *Addictive Behaviors 57*, 21–29.

Branley, D. B., & Covey, J. (2017). Is exposure to online content depicting risky behavior related to viewers' own risky behavior offline? *Computers in Human Behavior 75*, 283–287.

Brunborg, G. S., Andreas, J. B., & Kvaavik, E. (2017). Social media use and episodic heavy drinking among adolescents. *Psychological Reports 120*(3), 475–490.

Cabrera-Nguyen, E. P., Cavazos-Rehg, P., Krauss, M., Bierut, L. J., & Moreno, M. A. (2016). Young adults' exposure to alcohol- and marijuana-related content on Twitter. *Journal of Studies on Alcohol and Drugs 77*(2), 349–353.

Calvert, C. (2015). Revenge porn and freedom of expression: Legislative pushback to an online weapon of emotional and reputational destruction. *Fordham Intellectual Property, Media & Entertainment Law Journal 24*(3), 673–702.

Cavazos-Rehg, P. A., Krauss, M. J., Sowles, S. J., & Bierut, L. J. (2015). "Hey everyone, I'm drunk." An evaluation of drinking-related Twitter chatter. *Journal of Studies on Alcohol and Drugs 76*(4), 635–643.

Cavazos-Rehg, P. A., Krauss, M. J., Sowles, S. J., & Bierut, L. J. (2016). Marijuana-related posts on Instagram. *Prevention Science 17*(6), 710–720.

Cavazos-Rehg, P. A., Krauss, M. J., Sowles, S. J., Connolly, S., Rosas, C., Bharadwaj, M., & . . . Bierut, L. J. (2017). An analysis of depression, self-harm, and suicidal ideation content on Tumblr. *Crisis: The Journal of Crisis Intervention and Suicide Prevention 38*(1), 44–52.

Center for Disease Control and Prevention. (2017). *Sexual risk behaviors: HIV, STD, & teen pregnancy prevention.* Retrieved from https://www.cdc.gov/healthyyouth/sexualbehaviors/

Champion, A. R., & Pedersen, C. L. (2015). Investigating differences between sexters and non-sexters on attitudes, subjective norms, and risky sexual behaviours. *Canadian Journal of Human Sexuality 24*(3), 205–214.

Chau, M., & Xu, J. (2007). Mining communities and their relationships in blogs: A study of online hate groups. *International Journal of Human-Computer Studies 65*(1), 57–70.

Cohen, R., Newton-John, T., & Slater, A. (2018). "Selfie"-objectification: The role of selfies in self-objectification and discorded eating in young women. *Computers in Human Behavior, 79*, 68–74.

Coleman, L. M., & Cater, S. M. (2005). A qualitative study of the relationship between alcohol consumption and risky sex in adolescents. *Archives of Sexual Behavior 34*(6), 649–661.

Davis, M. J., Powell, A., Gordon, D., & Kershaw, T. (2016). I want your sext: Sexting and sexual risk in emerging adult minority men. *AIDS Education and Prevention 28*(2), 138–152.

Dewey, C., (2016, 26 May) The (very) dark side of live streaming that no one seem able to stop. *The Washington Post.* Retrieved from https://www.washingtonpost.com/news/the-intersect/wp/2016/05/26/the-very-dark-side-of-live-streaming-that-no-one-seems-able-to-stop/?utm_term=.19b1390180a4

Dunn, M., Thomas, J. O., Swift, W., & Burns, L. (2012). Elite athletes' estimates of the prevalence of illicit drug use: Evidence for the false consensus effect. *Drug and Alcohol Review 31*(1), 27–32.

Elmore, K. C., Scull, T. M., & Kupersmidt, J. B. (2017). Media as a "super peer": How adolescents interpret media messages predicts their perceptions of alcohol and tobacco use norms. *Journal of Youth and Adolescence 46*(2), 376–387.

Galambos, N. L., & Tilton-Weaver, L. C. (1998). Multiple risk behaviour in adolescents and young adults. *Health Reports 10*(2), 9.

Gerbner, G., & Gross, L. (1976). Living with television: The violence profile. *Journal of Communication 26*(2), 173–199.

Gerstenfeld, P. B., Grant, D. R., & Chiang, C. (2003). Hate online: A content analysis of extremist Internet sites. *Analyses of Social Issues and Public Policy (ASAP) 3*(1), 29–44.

González-Ortega, E., & Orgaz-Baz, B. (2013). Minors' exposure to online pornography: Prevalence, motivations, contents and effects. *Anales de Psicología 29*(2), 319–327.

Gutierrez, K. M., & Cooper, T. V. (2016). The use of social networking sites: A risk factor for using alcohol, marijuana, and synthetic cannabinoids? *Drug and Alcohol Dependence 163*, 247–250.

Hale, W. C. (2012). Extremism on the world wide web: A research review. *Criminal Justice Studies: A Critical Journal of Crime, Law & Society 25*(4), 343–356.

Haug, S., Paz Castro, R., Kowatsch, T., Filler, A., Dey, M., & Schaub, M. P. (2017). Efficacy of a web- and text messaging-based intervention to reduce problem drinking in adolescents: Results of a cluster-randomized controlled trial. *Journal of Consulting and Clinical Psychology 85*(2), 147–159.

Hingson, R. W., Zha, W., & Weitzman, E. R. (2009). Magnitude of and trends in alcohol-related mortality and morbidity among US college students ages 18–24, 1998–2005. *Journal of Studies on Alcohol and Drugs, Supplement*, (16), 12–20.

Hoffman, E. W., Pinkleton, B. E., Austin, E. W., & Reyes-Velázquez, W. (2014). Exploring college students' use of general and alcohol-related social media and their associations with alcohol-related behaviors. *Journal of American College Health 62*(5), 328–335.

Ingram, D. (2017). Facebook hits 2 billion-user mark, doubling in size since 2012. Reuters. Retrieved from https://www.reuters.com/article/us-facebook-users/facebook-hits-2-billion-user-mark-doubling-in-size-since-2012-idUSKBN19I2GG

Jones, L. M., Mitchell, K. J., & Finkelhor, D. (2012). Trends in youth internet victimization: Findings from three youth internet safety surveys 2000–2010. *Journal of Adolescent Health 50*(2), 179–186.

Judge, A. M. (2012). "Sexting" among US adolescents: Psychological and legal perspectives. *Harvard Review of Psychiatry 20*(2), 86–96.

Kapidzic, S., & Herring, S. C. (2015). Race, gender, and self-presentation in teen profile photographs. *New Media & Society 17*(6), 958–976.

Kendal, S., Kirk, S., Elvey, R., Catchpole, R., & Pryjmachuk, S. (2016). How a moderated online discussion forum facilitates support for young people with eating disorders. *Health Expectations 20*(1), 98–111.

Lenhart, A. (2015, 9 April). Teens, social media & technology overview 2015. *Pew Research Center*. Retrieved from http://www.pewinternet.org/2015/04/09/teens-social-media-technology-2015/

Lenhart, A. (2015, 6 August). Teens, technology and friendships. *Pew Research Center*. Retrieved from http://www.pewinternet.org/2015/08/06/teens-technology-and-friendships/

Lenhart, A., Purcell, K., Smith, A., & Zickuhr, K. (2010). Social media & mobile internet use among teens and young adults. Millennials. *Pew Internet & American Life Project*. Retrieved from http://www.pewinternet.org/~/media//Files/Reports/2010/PIP_Social_Media_and_Young_Adults

Lenhart, A., Smith, A., & Anderson, M. (2015, 1 October). Teens, technology and romantic relationships. *Pew Research Center*. Retrieved from http://www.pewinternet.org/2015/10/01/teens-technology-and-romantic-relationships/

Lenhart, A., Ybarra, M., & Price-Feeney, M. (2016). Nonconsensual image sharing: One in 25 Americans has been a victim of "revenge porn". *Data & Society Research Institute*. Retrieved from https://datasociety.net/pubs/oh/Nonconsensual_Image_Sharing_2016.pdf

Litt, D. M., & Stock, M. L. (2011). Adolescent alcohol-related risk cognitions: The roles of social norms and social networking sites. *Psychology of Addictive Behaviors 25*(4), 708–713.

Lobstein, T., Landon, J., Thornton, N., & Jernigan, D. (2016). The commercial use of digital media to market alcohol products: A narrative review. *Addiction 112*(S1), 21–27.

Madden, M., Lenhart, A., Cortesi, S., Gasser, U., Duggan, M., Smith, A., & Beaton, M. (2013). Teens, social media, and privacy. *Pew Research Center 21*, 2–86.

Mair, C., Ponicki, W. R., & Gruenewald, P. J. (2016). Reducing risky sex among college students: Prospects for context-specific interventions. *AIDS and Behavior 20*(Suppl 1), 109–118.

McNamee, L. G., Peterson, B. L., & Peña, J. (2010). A call to educate, participate, invoke and indict: Understanding the communication of online hate groups. *Communication Monographs 77*(2), 257–280.

Miller, A. N., Kinnally, W., Maleche, H., & Booker, N. A. (2017). The relationship between Nairobi adolescents' media use and their sexual beliefs and attitudes. *African Journal of AIDS Research 16*(2), 129–136.

Miller, D. T., & McFarland, C. (1991). When social comparison goes awry: The case of pluralistic ignorance. In J. Suls & T. Wills (Eds.), *Social comparison: Contemporary theory and research* (Chapter 11). Hillsdale, NJ: Lawrence Erlbaum.

Moreno, M. A., Briner, L. R., Williams, A., Brockman, L., Walker, L., & Christakis, D. A. (2010). A content analysis of displayed alcohol references on a social networking web site. *Journal of Adolescent Health 47*(2), 168–175.

Morgan, M., & Shanahan, J. (2010). The state of cultivation. *Journal of Broadcasting & Electronic Media 54*(2), 337–355.

National Institute of Alcohol Abuse and Alcoholism. (2014). Alcohol facts and statistics. Retrieved from https://www.niaaa.nih.gov/alcohol-health/overview-alcohol-consumption/alcohol-facts-and-statistics

Perkins, H. W., & Berkowitz, A. D. (1986). Perceiving the community norms of alcohol use among students: Some research implications for campus alcohol education programming. *International Journal of the Addictions 21*(9–10), 961–976.

Perrin, A. (2015, October 8). Social media usage: 2005–2015: 65 percent of adults now use social networking sites—a nearly tenfold jump in the past decade. *Pew Research Center*. Retrieved from http://www.pewinternet.org/2015/10/08/social-networking-usage-2005-2015/

Pharo, H., Sim, C., Graham, M., Gross, J., & Hayne, H. (2011). Risky business: Executive function, personality, and reckless behavior during adolescence and emerging adulthood. *Behavioral Neuroscience 125*(6), 970–978.

Powell, J. (2011). Young people, self-harm and internet forums: Commentary on online discussion forums for young people who self-harm. *The Psychiatrist 35*(10), 364–368.

Price, J., Patterson, R., Regnerus, M., & Walley, J. (2016). How much more XXX is generation X consuming? Evidence of changing attitudes and behaviors related to pornography since 1973. *Journal of Sex Research 53*(1), 12–20.

Pujazon-Zazik, M. A., Manasse, S. M., & Orrell-Valente, J. K. (2012). Adolescents' self-presentation on a teen dating web site: A risk-content analysis. *Journal of Adolescent Health 50*(5), 517–520.

Recupero, P. R. (2016). New technologies, new problems, new laws. *Journal of the American Academy of Psychiatry and the Law 44*(3), 322–327.

Rice, E., Craddock, J., Hemler, M., Rusow, J., Plant, A., Montoya, J., & Kordic, T. (2018). Associations between sexting behaviors and sexual behaviors among mobile phone-owning teens in Los Angeles. *Child Development 89*(1), 110–117.

Ridout, B., & Campbell, A. (2014). Using Facebook to deliver a social norm intervention to reduce problem drinking at university. *Drug and Alcohol Review 33*(6), 667–673.

Rodriquez, L. M., Litt, D., Neighbors, C., & Lewis, M. A. (2016). I'm a social (network) drinker: Alcohol-related Facebook posts, drinking identity, and alcohol use. *Journal of Social and Clinical Psychology 35*(2), 107–129.

Roesner, F., Gill, B. T., & Kohno, T. (2014). Sex, lies, or kittens? Investigating the use of Snapchat's self-destructing messages. In: N. Christin & R. Safavi-Naini (Eds.), *Financial Cryptography and Data Security. FC 2014* (pp. 64–76). New York, NY: Springer.

Ross, L., Greene, D., & House, P. (1977). The false consensus effect: An egocentric bias in social perception and attribution processes. *Journal of Experimental Social Psychology 13*(3), 279–301.

Sherlock, M., & Wagstaff, D. L. (2018). Exploring the relationship between frequency of Instagram use, exposure to idealized images, and psychological well-being in women. *Psychology of Popular Media Culture* [online]. doi:10.1037/ppm0000182

Shrum, L. J., Wyer, R. J., & O'Guinn, T. C. (1998). The effects of television consumption on social perceptions: The use of priming procedures to investigate psychological processes. *Journal of Consumer Research 24*(4), 447–458.

Sinković, M., Štulhofer, A., & Božić, J. (2013). Revisiting the association between pornography use and risky sexual behaviors: The role of early exposure to pornography and sexual sensation seeking. *Journal of Sex Research 50*(7), 633–641.

Smahel, D., & Subrahmanyam, K. (2014). Sexuality online: A developmental perspective. In A. Grudzinskas Jr., F. Saleh, & A. Judge (Eds.). *Adolescent sexual development, the digital revolution and the law* (pp. 62–88). New York, NY: Oxford University Press.

Smith, A. W., & Anderson, M. (2018). *Social media use in 2018*. Washington, DC: Pew Research Center.

Smith, A. W., & Duggan, M. (2013). *Online dating & relationship*. Washington, DC: Pew Research Center.

Starosta, A. J., Cranston, E., & Earleywine, M. (2016). Safer sex in a digital world: A web-based motivational enhancement intervention to increase condom use among college women. *Journal of American College Health 64*(3), 184–193.

Strassberg, D. S., Cann, D., & Velarde, V. (2017). Sexting by high school students: An exploratory and descriptive study. *Archives of Sexual Behavior 42*(1), 15–21.

Subrahmanyam, K., & Šmahel, D. (2011). *Digital youth: The role of media in development*. New York, NY: Springer Publishing.

Syed-Abdul, S., Fernandez-Luque, L., Jian, W., Li, Y., Crain, S., Hsu, M., & ... Liou, D. (2013). Misleading health-related information promoted through video-based social media: Anorexia on YouTube. *Journal of Medical Internet Research 15*(2), 137–149.

Turner, P. G., & Lefevre, C. E. (2017). Instagram use is linked to increased symptoms of orthorexia nervosa. *Eating and Weight Disorders-Studies on Anorexia, Bulimia and Obesity 22*(2), 277–284.

Tynes, B. M., Del Toro, J., & Lozada, F. T. (2015). An unwelcomed digital visitor in the classroom: The longitudinal impact of online racial discrimination on academic motivation. *School Psychology Review 44*(4), 407–424.

Tynes, B. M., Giang, M. T., Williams, D. R., & Thompson, G. N. (2008). Online racial discrimination and psychological adjustment among adolescents. *Journal of Adolescent Health 43*(6), 565–569.

Tynes, B. M., Rose, C. A., Hiss, S., Umaña-Taylor, A. J., Mitchell, K., & Williams, D. (2014). Virtual environments, online racial discrimination, and adjustment among a diverse, school-based sample of adolescents. *International Journal of Gaming and Computer-Mediated Simulations 6*(3), 1–16.

Utz, S., Muscanell, N., & Khalid, C. (2015). Snapchat elicits more jealousy than Facebook: A comparison of Snapchat and Facebook use. *Cyberpsychology, Behavior, And Social Networking 18*(3), 141–146.

Van Oosten, J. F., Peter, J., & Boot, I. (2015). Exploring associations between exposure to sexy online self-presentations and adolescents' sexual attitudes and behavior. *Journal of Youth and Adolescence 44*(5), 1078–1091.

Van Oosten, J. F., Peter, J., & Vandenbosch, L. (2017). Adolescents' sexual media use and willingness to engage in casual sex: Differential relations and underlying processes. *Human Communication Research 43*(1), 127–147.

Van Ouytsel, J., Ponnet, K., & Walrave, M. (2014). The associations between adolescents' consumption of pornography and music videos and their sexting behavior. *Cyberpsychology, Behavior, and Social Networking 17*(12), 772–778.

Van Ouytsel, J., Van Gool, E., Walrave, M., Ponnet, K., & Peeters, E. (2017). Sexting: Adolescents' perceptions of the applications used for, motives for, and consequences of sexting. *Journal of Youth Studies 20*(4), 446–470.

Vandenbosch, L., van Oosten, J. F., & Peter, J. (2015). The relationship between sexual content on mass media and social media: A longitudinal study. *Cyberpsychology, Behavior, And Social Networking 18*(12), 697–703.

Vaterlaus, J. M., Barnett, K., Roche, C., & Young, J. A. (2016). "Snapchat is more personal": An exploratory study on Snapchat behaviors and young adult interpersonal relationships. *Computers in Human Behavior 62*, 594–601.

Williams, R. S., & Schmidt, A. (2014). The sales and marketing practices of English-language internet alcohol vendors. *Addiction 109*(3), 432–439.

Wolak, J., Finkelhor, D., & Mitchell, K. (2004). Internet-initiated sex crimes against minors: Implications for prevention based on findings from a national study. *Journal of Adolescent Health 35*(5), 424–e11.

Wolak, J., Finkelhor, D., Mitchell, K. J., & Ybarra, M. L. (2008). Online "predators" and their victims: Myths, realities, and implications for prevention and treatment. *American Psychologist 63*(2), 111.

Yang, F., Salmon, C. T., Pang, J. S., & Cheng, W. Y. (2015). Media exposure and smoking intention in adolescents: A moderated mediation analysis from a cultivation perspective. *Journal of Health Psychology 20*(2), 188–197.

Ybarra, M. L., & Mitchell, K. J. (2014). "Sexting" and its relation to sexual activity and sexual risk behavior in a national survey of adolescents. *Journal of Adolescent Health 55*(6), 757–764.

Young, S. D., & Jordan, A. H. (2013). The influence of social networking photos on social norms and sexual health behaviors. *Cyberpsychology, Behavior and Social Networking 16*(4), 243–247.

Zabinski, M. F., Wilfley, D. E., Calfas, K. J., Winzelberg, A. J., & Taylor, C. B. (2004). An interactive psychoeducational intervention for women at risk of developing an eating disorder. *Journal of Consulting and Clinical Psychology 72*(5), 914–919.

CHAPTER 6

THE MYTH OF THE DIGITAL NATIVE AND WHAT IT MEANS FOR HIGHER EDUCATION

LINDA CORRIN, TIFFANI APPS,
KARLEY BECKMAN, AND SUE BENNETT

INTRODUCTION

IN the late 1990s and early 2000s the idea of the "digital native" emerged (Bennett, Maton, & Kervin, 2008). In essence, it was proposed that because young people had grown up surrounded by technology, they had developed sophisticated technology skills superior to the adults around them. This made them "tech savvy" in a way that those from older generations could never be. And because of this difference, young people were dissatisfied with and disengaged from an education system that persisted with old-fashioned approaches to teaching and learning. This argument was used as the basis for calls for revolutionary, transformational change across education systems.

Since then, scholarly critique and empirical research have debunked the notion of the digital native (see Bennett & Corrin, 2017). Critiques have continually called into question the crude characterization of all young people as both highly adept with and avidly interested in digital technologies across the various aspects of their lives as well as the assertions about the implications for education. Research evidence has revealed a much more complex situation. The ways in which young people make use of digital technologies for learning, leisure, socializing, and work are richly diverse and very much dependent on the various contexts in which they engage. These findings reveal that there are indeed young people who are highly engaged with digital technologies, who are using opportunities that technologies provide to create and connect in new ways, and who participate via these technologies in activities and causes that interest them. But not all young people choose to or have the resources available to them to do so. This makes the universality of the digital native label inaccurate and misleading in ways that ignore disparities in social circumstances and discount individual agency.

So what are we to make of the persistence of the notion of digital natives, given the now-substantial body of considered scholarship that has discredited this notion? The idea has had widespread popular appeal, perhaps because is seems to be true, based on anecdotal evidence. When we look around and see young people engaging with their devices and taking up new technologies with seeming ease, the idea that there is something significant occurring seems to align with our observations. Anecdotes are a means by which we make sense of personal experiences and they have been used powerfully in attempts to explain or extrapolate to the wider proposed phenomenon of digital natives. It has been difficult for research evidence and reasoned argument to match the appeal of real-life accounts of digital natives.

Beyond the power of anecdote, however, there are a number of ways to interpret the emergence of and continued interest in the digital native. Generational differences have long been a source of concern in many societies. This is reflected by the labeling and characterization of generations such as the "baby boomers," "Generation X," and the "millennials" (e.g., Howe & Strauss, 2000). The idea of the digital native can be seen as a variation of this familiar theme that pits generations against each other and serves to highlight one of many ways in which young people in general are different to older generations. But these generational stereotypes seldom withstand closer scrutiny, and the digital native stereotype, like others, is ultimately unhelpful in genuinely understanding the needs and interests of young people.

Another possible explanation could be that the notion of the digital native reflects a more general concern about the pace of change in modern life, as well as disquiet about the role of technology in driving social change. Again, this concern is not new. The history and sociology of technology reveal long-held misgivings about the ways in which technology has changed the nature of work, civic engagement, and social interaction well before the twenty-first century. Suggestions that an increased rate of change is further risking our ability to adjust to new technologies may explain recent heightened concerns, but the phenomenon itself is not new. From this perspective, characterizing young people as digital natives aligns with the concerns of many older people that technology is driving rapid change to the ways of life with which they are familiar. Thus, the idea of the digital native may reflect the genuine ambivalence that many feel about the role of technology in their lives and, more broadly, its influence on society.

Questions, too, might be posed about the motivations of those advocating for the existence of digital natives. In the field of educational technology, the vested interests of commercial vendors have led to many exaggerated claims that technology can and will revolutionize education (Buckingham, 2013). Education, for its part, has evolved over time, but much too slowly for some technology advocates. Academic reputations are also built on claims that technology will drive pedagogical innovations that will, in turn, increase student engagement and boost learning outcomes. Skeptics have often been labeled as Luddites in debates where polarized positions, untestable claims, and competing ideologies have, at times, overshadowed the findings of research and scholarship that necessarily lags the introduction of the latest technology.

There is clearly further work needed to discover what is at the heart of the concerns about young people and technology. While this is beyond the scope of this chapter, knowing more about why these questions exist is surely important. At the same time, this uncertainty should not prevent seeking to know more about the role technology plays in young people's lives and consideration of what that means for education. As noted, scholars and researchers have already begun this quest, many doing so in response to the digital native debate. This work provides a strong foundation that enhances our understanding while concurrently suggesting important new avenues to explore.

We argue that while the idea of the digital native has been shown to be, at best, misleading and unhelpful, its persistence in our discourse, particularly about education, signals there is something underlying it that warrants our attention. It continues to invite us to ask important questions about how young people can, do, and could use technology to enhance their learning. This, in turn, raises important questions about teaching and teachers, educational systems and administrations, and institutional provision of technology infrastructure and learning spaces. Such questions continue to offer rich opportunities for research.

We further argue that this research would benefit from a conceptualization of technology use that is underpinned by the notion of practice. A practice perspective allows us to go beyond regarding digital technologies as tools designed for particular uses to focusing on the ways in which individuals and groups adopt and adapt technologies and embed them in socially-constructed activities. These are *technology practices*—a notion that captures a range of possibilities and allows for technologies to be adopted and integrated into existing practices, for technologies to shape and so alter existing practice, and for entirely new practices to emerge. In this conceptualization, technologies are never "value free," but instead carry the values and assumptions of designers and providers. At the same time, it gives possibility for users to adapt or disrupt the intended design or use. In this way, technology use becomes personalized and is both shaped by and shapes our social worlds.

The focus of enquiry then becomes understanding the perspectives and practices of those using technologies, with consideration of the various contexts in which those practices occur. In education, this kind of research uses naturalistic approaches to explore "what is actually taking place when a digital technology meets an educational setting" (Selwyn, 2010, p. 70) rather than studying "state of the art" innovations. Such research complements a well-established and continuing tradition of research into specific pedagogical applications of technology by seeking to understand the nature of technology experiences more broadly. Understanding how students experience technology in their formal education and across their other life contexts is key to understanding how technology might be most effectively integrated, based on the premise that by understanding "what is," we might understand "what could be."

A practice perspective also invites a particular way of considering how technology could best be integrated into education and, specifically, what skills, knowledge, and dispositions young people might need to develop in relation to technology (Bennett, 2014).

Contemporary conceptualizations of digital literacy have evolved significantly from their predecessors, for example, computer literacy, ICT literacy. There is growing recognition that to be digitally literate means much more than having the skills to operate technology. Rather, it means understanding technology's social and political dimensions, as well as making informed choices about how to make use of the various technologies available to achieve desired outcomes effectively. In education, a component of this could be thought of as "academic digital literacy," which would entail an individual understanding how to leverage technology to enable and enhance his or her own learning.

This chapter explores some of these issues in relation to higher education and begins by summarizing what the research tells us about how young adults experience technology, mainly within their formal education, but also extending to other aspects of their lives. It then considers the experiences that have shaped their technology skills, knowledge, and dispositions before they arrive at university or college, with particular attention paid to their experiences at school. Next, it puts forward implications for education before closing by offering some propositions to stimulate further research and practice.

Young People's Experiences with Technology in Higher Education

Not long after the terms "digital natives" and "net generation" emerged in the academic literature and the media, researchers began to evaluate to what extent young people's ownership and use of technologies reflected these generational generalizations. Consistently, large scale studies have demonstrated diverse patterns of engagement with technology and cautioned against reliance on such generalizations as the basis of decisions about the role of technology in university education (Garcia & Qin, 2007; Kennedy et al., 2006; Kvavik, Caruso, & Morgan, 2004). These larger studies were soon followed by smaller, more detailed studies that examined the nuances of young people's technology practices in both academic and everyday life contexts (Corrin, Lockyer, & Bennett, 2010; Jones & Healing, 2010). These studies highlighted that the technology practices of young people varied across academic and non-academic contexts and are not always easily transferable from one context to another.

Research questioning the digital native concept in higher education has continued to evolve. Initial research was concentrated in higher education environments in anglophone countries, including the United Kingdom, Australia, Canada, and the United States. However, evidence of the diversity of young people's technology practices has now emerged from a range of other countries (e.g., France—Wagner & Acier, 2017; Finland—Valtonen et al., 2011; Turkey/Kyrgyzstan—Akçayir, Dundar, & Akçayir, 2016; Singapore/Korea—So, Choi, Lim, & Xiong, 2012). There has also been an increase in studies that focus on particular traits of young people that are associated with the digital native myth. As an example, the recent study by Kirschner and De Bruyckere (2017) supported the findings of previous research (e.g., Judd & Kennedy, 2011) demonstrating young people's lack of capacity to effectively multitask using technology. Taken together, this body of research continues to confirm the diversity of young people's skills, knowledge, and engagement with technologies in higher education and repeatedly provides evidence that undermines claims for the existence of the digital native.

Furthermore, contrary to assumptions about young people's enthusiasm for high levels of technology use for learning, research has found that young people are not necessarily demanding greater levels of technology integration in education environments or radically different ways of teaching with technology. Studies of young people's attitudes to current teaching approaches in higher education found no evidence of a need for substantially different ways of teaching to be used in the classroom (Bekebrede, Warmelink, & Myer, 2011; Ellis, Bliuc, & Goodyear, 2012). A review of digital natives research by Jones and Shao (2011) found that the majority of young people were happy with a moderate use of technology and few were engaging with more advanced technologies in the educational environment, unless specifically directed by teachers. Young people expressed a preference for a clear rationale for the use of technology in learning activities, were dissatisfied with the use of technology simply for novelty's sake, and preferred technology be used as a supplement to, rather than a replacement of, more traditional learning activities (Corrin, Bennett, & Lockyer, 2013). This pragmatic approach is evident in young people's reliance on the recommendation of teachers and course requirements when making decisions about technology adoption (Margaryan, Littlejohn, & Vojt, 2011; Valtonen et al., 2011). Studies have shown that when higher education students are choosing technologies to support their studies they are heavily influenced by the activities, environment, and tools provided by their universities (Ellis et al., 2012; Gros, Garcia, & Escofet, 2012; Margaryan et al., 2011). A study of education students in Singapore and Korea found that, despite the frequency that young people used certain technologies in their everyday lives, they were more heavily influenced by the teaching approaches in their classes in the choice of technology they adopted in the academic environment (So et al., 2012). In short, teachers' guidance was a significant factor in the students' adoption of technologies for academic purposes.

Another assumption of the digital native rhetoric is that young people can readily adopt and adapt technologies from one context of their lives (e.g., everyday life) into another (e.g., academic study), but research shows this is not common. The adoption of technologies in young people's everyday lives are strongly influenced by their personal interests and social priorities (Corrin et al., 2013), and the technology practices used in this context do not always directly translate into an academic context. The lack of transferability of technologies between contexts can also be due to a lack of understanding about which functionalities of the technologies young people use in their everyday life have the potential to be used to support their learning (Valtonen et al., 2011). In the case of social networking, many young people have expressed a preference to keep their personal and educational accounts separate (Ferri & Pozzali, 2012; Prescott, Wilson, & Becket, 2013). However, there was also evidence that some young people had a preference for the integration of technologies across contexts to improve convenience

(Waycott, Bennett, Kennedy, Dalgarno, & Gray, 2010). Such diversity of technological ability, skills, and preferences would seem to indicate a proportion of young people would be well equipped to handle integration, while others would need greater support.

When considering these findings from a practice perspective, it is important to note that while the same tools can often be used across contexts, the required practices to do so can vary markedly. Just because young people make extensive use of a technology in their everyday lives, it does not mean that they have the skills needed to use it effectively in an educational context. For example, some social media technologies assume particular practices of authorship and contribution that are not consistent with academic practices in college or university settings (Dohn, 2009). Young people may need help to understand the capabilities of the technologies they need to use as part of learning activities and how these relate to the academic skills underpinning the task (Corrin et al., 2013). For example, when undertaking a blog activity, young people need to understand the functionality of the blogging platform as well as the reflective writing skills necessary to compose the blog entry. As the array of technologies that young people can encounter in higher education increases, it is important to ensure that adequate time is built into learning activities that allow them to develop an understanding of the technology that will enable more innovative uses to support learning.

A reliance on the assumption that all young people have a high level of digital literacy can result in a lack of support for those who need it. Early discussions of the attributes of digital natives put forward the idea that not only were these young people highly adept at using technology due to their exposure to it from childhood, but that they also have skills far beyond those of their "digital immigrant" teachers. This implies that young people have the skills to be able to tackle any technology given to them without the support of a teacher. However, it is evident from the research that the diversity of young people's technology experiences means that this will not always be the case. This diversity presents a challenge to teachers in supporting young people appropriately and creates a need for innovative ways to provide support to young people to use technology in a way that recognizes that their technology skills, knowledge, and dispositions are likely to vary within cohorts.

Higher education has an important role to play in preparing young people with the knowledge and skills to perform not only within an academic environment, but also in their chosen profession. This includes the digital literacy to function in an increasingly technology-dependent world of work. Yet the manner in which the development of these skills is incorporated into academic programs often remains ad-hoc (Coldwell-Neilson, 2017). A recent study involving 22,000 students across the UK found that only 50 percent felt that university sufficiently prepared them for the workplace in terms of digital skills (Newman & Beetham, 2017). It is clear that there is a need for pedagogic support for young people to develop digital literacy skills not only for the academic environment, but also for the transition to the work environment. There are also deeper questions about the role of higher education in preparing young people to contribute to society beyond preparing them for work, and the kinds of digital literacy needed to support the individual and collective well-being that underpins successful societies.

In sum, research has shown a diversity of attitudes, motivations, and practices in relation to how young people engage with technology in higher education. Within this context the constantly evolving nature of technological innovation provides many opportunities, as well as challenges, for the integration of technology into learning environments. The provision of adequate support for young people to engage with technology as part of their learning is important, as is the broader development of digital literacy, which does not begin only when young people reach higher education. Digital literacy develops as young people participate in different stages of education as well as across life contexts. In order for higher education institutions to respond to and support this continual development of technology practices a better understanding of young people's attitudes, experiences, and practices with technology is needed before they arrive into higher education. The next section explores the influences on technological experiences and practices that young people bring to higher education from the school environment.

SHAPING THESE EXPERIENCES

Young people do not enter higher education in a vacuum. Rather, students arrive at university with 15 years or more of schooling behind them, and a diverse range of everyday life experiences through which they are exposed to varying technology practices and possibilities. This section discusses these histories, paying attention to the structures of schooling and everyday life. It also demonstrates how such an understanding is significant in overcoming socially neutral assumptions that are often entrenched in technology-enhanced learning in higher education.

From a practice perspective, the technology possibilities available to children and young people are shaped by the contexts in which they find themselves. Research shows that children and young people's everyday contexts, particularly the home context, significantly shape their technology practices (Apps, 2015; Beckman, 2015). While access to technology and the Internet in the home is commonplace for many (OECD, 2010), variations in access, such as the kinds of technologies available (e.g., computers, tablets, smartphones), how many devices, and how up to date these technologies are, also shape the way children and young people can use them. Additionally, less obvious contextual factors shape children and young people's technology practices across all ages of schooling from early years to secondary education. These include the culture of technology use by the family (the range of technology practices children and young people experience through observing and participating with their family and others in the home), parents' ideas about how children learn and the place of technologies in the learning process, parents' education levels, the distribution of technologies between family members, and rules and expectations around technology use (Eynon & Malmberg, 2011; Plowman, Stephen, & McPake, 2010; Robinson & Schulz, 2013; Stephen, Stevenson, & Adey, 2013).

From the early years, children are likely to be exposed to a range of digital devices, products and toys at home (Danby et al., 2013). Generally, children may have opportunities to view, read, play, and create with these technologies, as well as engage in role-play about how these devices are used in everyday life (Plowman, 2016). This form of play with technologies, for example, a young child mimicking their parents' use of a smartphone, provides a powerful anecdote that fuels the popular discourse around children's intuitive knowledge and skill with technology. However, these observations tend to overlook role-play as a typical behavior in the early years that allows children to comprehend the social world around them, including both digital and non-digital artifacts, and over-emphasize the intuitive ways that children engage in technologies such as touch screen devices while ignoring their limitations. Furthermore, because children's technology practices are dependent on parents and caregivers, young children's experiences with technologies may be quite varied by the time they begin formal schooling.

As children reach primary school age (5–6 years old) the contexts in which they find themselves broaden. At home, primary children engage with technology mostly for leisure and entertainment, with educational activities allocated a smaller portion of time (Apps, 2015; Selwyn, 2002; Selwyn, Potter, & Cranmer, 2009). Children's technology practice in their everyday lives is varied, and is shaped by personal and contextual factors (Eynon & Malmberg, 2011) as the worlds of primary age children continue to be bound by their homes and families (Hollingworth, Mansaray, Allen, & Rose, 2011). Yet children at this age begin to demonstrate an increased independence and the role of school, teachers, and peers becomes more important. As children transition into adolescence their independence from family increases. This transition is marked by an increase in autonomy, development of identity, and widening of social contexts. While young people's families continue to shape their technology practices, the influence of peers becomes more significant (Eynon & Malmberg, 2012). While the image of a teen glued to a smartphone is synonymous with contemporary understandings of adolescence, research suggests that their technology practices are not universal, but rather more personalized, considered as individual "niches" or "digital habits" (Gurung & Rutledge, 2014, p. 97). For example, many young people use social media, yet their practices in terms of the platforms they choose and the ways in which they use them are diverse (Beckman, 2015).

In educational contexts, beginning with preschool followed by more formal schooling years, children experience a range of technology possibilities, which may be quite different to those experienced at home. Technology practices in preschool settings are characterized by play-based experiences. Such learning tends to be framed by notions of developmental appropriateness in efforts to protect the child. The academic discourse in early childhood education increasingly challenges such views, highlighting the limitations of such a restrictive approach, including underestimation of preschool children's capacity for learning through meaningful interactions with educators (Danby et al., 2013; Plowman & Stephen, 2007); and mitigation of the rich social and cultural practices embedded in technology practice (Bird & Edwards, 2015; Danby et al., 2013). While early learning curriculum and policy acknowledge the importance of digital technology in early childhood education, little is known about the pedagogical use of technologies in this context (Bird & Edwards, 2015). Considering the high degree of variability in children's involvement in early years education (ranging from children who do not attend, to children who attend every day), it is likely that young children's experiences of technology for learning in the early years varies widely.

Technology practices in school settings are underpinned by policy and curriculum, which focuses on the development of digital literacy for future economic participation. This is problematic for two reasons. Firstly, this approach means that digital literacy is operationalized as a discrete set of skills and processes valued in educational contexts for example, searching efficiently, comparing a range of sources, and sorting authoritative from non-authoritative, and relevant from irrelevant, documents (Lankshear & Knobel, 2015; Livingstone, Bober, & Helsper, 2005). Such definitions have been criticized for being overly simplistic. From a practice perspective, focusing solely on skills and measurement sidelines the contextual practices of individuals when engaging with technology (Buckingham, 2008; Livingstone, Mascheroni, Ólafsson, & Haddon, 2014). This means that the context-specific applications of technology may be overlooked, thus limiting opportunities to develop children and young people's digital literacy that may allow them to transfer and adapt skills and knowledge between contexts. Secondly, the focus on economic participation that drives technology practice in schools places emphasis on a narrow range of technological skills and knowledge deemed necessary to be "digitally literate" with flow-on effects to teaching and learning. This is perhaps most clearly demonstrated by the current push to include coding in schools in both Australia and the UK. Such initiatives impose technology practices upon students to "future-proof" them, without being able to clearly explain how these skills and knowledge prepare young people for further study, economic and social participation, and well-being. Additionally, such a preoccupation with the "future" overlooks the richness and diversity of young people's current technology practices and experiences.

Given the strong policy focus on the development of digital literacy in schools for the past fifteen years, the assumption is that digital literacy learning gains would be commonplace. However, school students are far from being the confident, creative, and productive users of new technologies. The digital literacy of children and young people is, in general, of a low level and diverse. Large-scale assessments of school students' technology achievement conducted over the last decade have drawn attention to significant patterns of digital literacy associated with the available economic, social, and cultural capital of young people and their families (ACARA, 2012; OECD, 2015). The persistence of low-level and diverse performance on such assessments raises important questions about current educational practice, at a school and classroom level, including why such inequalities exist and why digital learning gains are not greater, given the significance placed on the development of digital literacy.

In a primary school context, when children engage with technology and the processes of digital literacy for educational purposes, their practice is generally structured, time-tabled, monitored, and restricted to meet educational outcomes, and is predominantly guided by the class teacher. In most models of primary schooling, each year students are taught by one teacher in one classroom, which they experience with one cohort of students. This structure has a significant impact on the technology practices and possibilities available to children at school. A class teacher's technology practices, skills, and knowledge, along with their technological pedagogical knowledge and expertise, frame the way primary students experience technology in the classroom. In practice, this can lead to a discontinuity of experiences with technology throughout primary education, as children progress through a series of classrooms which might run the gamut from very little (or no) technology integration to high levels of integration. This is important for primary students, as teachers' use of and attitude towards technology frames the technology possibilities available to students and therefore is a significant indicator in students' frequency of use and attitudes towards technology (Cotten, Hale, Moroney, O'Neal, & Borch, 2011).

As students move into their secondary education, the structure of schooling changes, characterized by subject-based classes with specialized teachers. Other than subject-specific uses of technology like design or data tools, young people's technology practice at school for learning is characterized by largely routine practices, such as taking notes using word processing tools (Inan, Lowther, Ross, & Strahl, 2010), and often directed by the teacher (Beckman, Bennett, & Lockyer, 2014). In practice, this means that young people's technology practices could be characterized as diverse (based on subjects taken and teachers) and disjointed across subjects (based on the subject area and the teachers' use of and attitude towards technology). Furthermore, an increasingly content-heavy curriculum, especially in the final years of schooling (which often focus on preparation for high-stakes final exams), means there may be little room for the development of young people's digital literacy. Overall, these patterns in the way schooling is structured can limit the opportunities for young people to transfer skills and knowledge between contexts and learn how to adapt these for learning.

In recent years, there has been an increase in the use of mobile technologies in schools with initiatives such as "bring your own device," which offer opportunities to leverage young people's practices with these devices (also used outside of school) into formal learning in the school context. However, the use of mobile devices at school has prompted concerns about how to keep young people focused on their learning at school and how to maintain online safety and avoid cyberbullying. School policy and rules governing the use of technology at school has often resulted in solidifying the boundaries between school and everyday life, thus limiting young people's technology practices at school for learning. This has implications for the range of digital literacies and potential transferability of skills and knowledge outside of formal education to school settings.

Technology practices for learning at school are distinct from young people's everyday life practices with technology. Importantly, the way in which children and young people negotiate the differences between these separate, at times competing, contexts is easier for some than for others. Research shows that those students who experience formal technology practices at home, through shared practices or implicit and explicit family education, come to school with technological skills and knowledge that is already valued. Those students who experience a narrower set of technology practices, confined to leisure and entertainment, or through negotiation with siblings, extended family members, or low-skilled parents, are less familiar with the technological skills and knowledge valued at school (Apps, 2015; Beckman, 2015). Moreover, research illustrates that those children who experience a match of technology culture between home and school demonstrate stronger digital literacy than their peers who experience a mismatch of cultures (Apps, 2015).

This section has explored children and young people's experiences with technologies, both in their everyday lives and in their education, from early childhood to secondary schooling. Children and young people's technology practices are varied, shaped by individual histories, including family background and experiences, peers, personal dispositions, and their schooling. Consequently, the experiences children and young people have with technology throughout formal schooling are also varied and, like many aspects of schooling, advantage some groups more than others. Overall, it highlighted three key issues in shaping children and young people's technology practices in their schooling years: firstly the way technology and digital literacy is conceived in the curriculum has narrowly framed technology practices at school; secondly, how the structure of schooling, the influence of teachers' skills, knowledge, and attitudes towards technology, and perceptions of students skills and knowledge can strongly influence children and young people's technology practices; and finally, how the diversity in children and young people's backgrounds and technology practices in everyday life provides a foundation for all other experiences with technologies. Most importantly, it has highlighted that these variations in technology practices means that some children begin their formal schooling at an advantage, compared to others, based on their prior technology experiences, and these variations can be further amplified through the structure of the curriculum and schooling and technology-based learning experiences that unevenly develop digital literacy.

Implications for Higher Education

This section attends to the implications for higher education. The notion of the digital native as characterizing a generation of young people is not supported by empirical research. This means that we who are engaged in higher education must be vigilant in questioning any assumptions that young people are inherently better equipped with relevant technical skills and knowledge to support their learning, and that they are more readily disposed to adopt new technologies as part of their studies than older students and educators. Incorrect assumptions about younger generations of students will result in complacency about the need to properly develop young people's digital literacy to enable them to effectively engage in study, as well as to prepare them for the future world of work. We also run the risk of failing to recognize the digital literacies that many older adult students possess, as well as those they need to develop. This is a deficit view which may also be mistakenly applied to educators erroneously labeled as recalcitrant or incompetent. The research to date demonstrates a significant diversity in the technology skills, knowledge, and dispositions of young adult students. It is this diversity that educators, institutions, and educational systems need to acknowledge and provide for.

The following sections briefly outline some implications for school education, higher education, institutions, and life-long learning.

Schools have a role to play in preparing students for their digital futures, including higher education. The research to date demonstrates that children and young people's technology practices at school are varied, and thus schools need to do more to cater for a range of digital literacy abilities (OECD, 2010). Part of this is a reframing of digital literacy in the curriculum and a move toward thinking about technology practices, rather than uses of technology for learning. A broader conception of the context-laden technology skills and knowledge may highlight opportunities to transfer skills and knowledge between contexts and support children and young people in learning how to develop and build on their varying skills and knowledge, and, importantly, how to adapt and leverage these in a range of contexts.

The higher education environment provides many opportunities for young people to engage with technologies and develop skills to support technology practices as part of teaching and learning activities. Research has shown that young people are quite discerning when it comes to the use of technology to support learning and therefore teachers need to consider the relevance and role of technology when designing learning activities. Again, it is important to recognize that young people are not always able to easily transition the skills they use when engaging with technology in their everyday lives to the academic context. The provision of time and support for students to develop an understanding of technological tools within the educational context and the associated academic skills necessary to use them is vital to enable innovative uses of technology to support learning.

At an institutional level, the integration of digital technology already has significant ramifications for university and college operations. Technological change is one of four sets of forces placing pressure on traditional teaching and learning practices, together with an increasingly diverse student population, rising expectations of graduates, and the intensification of higher education teaching work (Goodyear, 2015). Institutions need policies and practices that address the inter-relations between the diverse technology practices and preparation of students, the capacity of teaching staff to integrate technology effectively, and the provision of appropriate physical and technical infrastructure. Institutions need simultaneously to build capacity in staff and students, while at the same time providing the overarching vision and support to ensure opportunities are realized and challenges addressed; both will require a deep understanding of student and staff needs and how these can be met.

The need for lifelong learning has gained currency in a world of work characterized by continuous change. Many of us will need to engage in continuous professional development to maintain our currency in the workplace, often as a requirement of professional accreditation. Many others will choose to change careers, possibly multiple times in their working lives. Increased automation of work tasks currently undertaken by humans, coupled with new knowledge flows and networks, all promise to drive further changes to the ways we work. Technologies are instrumental in those changes, and there is every reason to believe that technical skills and knowledge will be even more important in all forms of work, but also critical to engaging in further learning. Higher education is well-positioned to offer forms of study that support professional development and career change, and to do so by using flexible online approaches that can make studying more accessible. As adults continuously re-engage with educational institutions throughout their working lives, the need to update and further develop their digital literacy will only increase. Institutions themselves will need to evolve their own practices to take on new forms of educational delivery as they evolve. There is evidence of a capacity to do this, for example, the way many institutions have adopted massive open online courses (MOOCs) and integrated them into their suite of offerings. Far from representing a threat to higher education, MOOCs have become one of the many ways institutions have adopted and adapted technology to suit their own purposes. Such moves demonstrate that while informal and non-formal learning may be on the rise, the accreditation of learning, a key function of higher education, will still be important in the future.

Conclusion

In higher education, it is now common for young people to be exposed to various technologies and technological practices as part of their learning environment. While this landscape continues to change and evolve as new technological tools emerge, the idea of the digital native has been firmly entrenched in the strategic planning and directions of many higher education institutions. In practice, such generalizations have been used to justify decisions around technology adoption, which tend to influence the pedagogical design decisions of individual teachers. It is within this ever-changing environment that young people are required to adapt and use technology in ways that can support their learning. The constant evolution of new technological tools and related skills contributes to a need for ongoing research to understand how technological practices are changing and what higher education institutions need to do to support this change. Consequently, higher education institutions should not rely on generational generalizations that have been shown not to reflect the true nature of how young people interact with technology in their academic and everyday lives. The following set of propositions can help guide the way forward for researchers, educators, institutions, and policymakers:

- Actively seek to know the students better by acknowledging and exploring the diversity of their technology skills, knowledge, and dispositions without making assumptions based on their age.
- View digital technologies for learning not as "tools" but as sets of practices that are shaped by the social contexts in which they are situated and seek to understand the technical and academic requirements.
- Critically examine and develop ideas about digital literacy, particularly the specific aspects most relevant to successful learning, from the early years through to higher education.

References

ACARA. (2012). "National Assessment Program ICT Literacy: Years 6 and 10 Report 2011." ACARA. Retrieved from http://www.nap.edu.au/verve/_resources/NAP_ICTL_2011_Public_Report_Final.pdf.

Akçayır, M., Dündar, H., & Akçayır, G. (2016). What makes you a digital native? Is it enough to be born after 1980? *Computers in Human Behavior 60*, 435–440.

Apps, T. (2015). *ICT Literacy and the digital divide: Understanding primary students' ICT practices and possibilities* (Doctoral dissertation). University of Wollongong.

Beckman, K. (2015). *Secondary school students' technology practices in their everyday lives and at school* (Doctoral dissertation). University of Wollongong.

Beckman, K., Bennett, S., & Lockyer, L. (2014). Understanding students' use and value of technology for learning. *Learning, Media and Technology 39*(3), 346–367. doi:10.1080/17439 884.2013.878353.

Bekebrede, G., Warmelink, H. J. G., & Myer, I. S. (2011). Reviewing the need for gaming in education to accommodate the net generation. *Computers & Education 57*(2), 1521–1529.

Bennett, S. (2014). Conceptualising technology use as social practice to research student experiences of technology in higher education. In *Proceedings of World Conference on Educational Multimedia, Hypermedia and Telecommunications 2014* (pp. 2567–2572). Chesapeake, VA: AACE.

Bennett, S., & Corrin, L. (2017). From digital natives to student experiences with technology. In M. Khosrow-Pour (Ed.), *Encyclopedia of Information Science and Technology* (pp. 2512–2520). Hershey, PA: IGI Global. doi:10.4018/978-1-5225-2255-3.

Bennett, S., Maton, K., & Kervin, L. (2008). The "digital natives" debate: A critical review of the evidence. *British Journal of Educational Technology 39*(5), 775–786.

Bird, J., and Edwards, S. (2015). Children learning to use technologies through play: A digital play framework. *British Journal of Educational Technology 46*(6), 1149–1160. doi:10.1111/bjet.12191.

Buckingham, D. (2008). Defining digital literacy: What do young people need to know about digital media? In C. Lankshear & M. Knobel (Eds.), *Digital Literacies: Concepts, Policies and Practices* (pp. 73–90). New York: Peter Lang.

Buckingham, D. (2013). *Beyond Technology: Children's Learning in the Age of Digital Culture*. New York: John Wiley & Sons.

Coldwell-Neilson, J. (2017). Assumed digital literacy knowledge by Australian universities: Are students informed? In *Proceedings of the Nineteenth Australasian Computing Education Conference* (pp. 75–80). New York: ACM.

Corrin, L., Bennett, S., & Lockyer, L. (2013). Digital natives: Exploring the diversity of young people's experience with technology, In R. Huang, Kinshuk, & J. M. Spector (Eds.), *Reshaping learning: The frontiers of learning technologies in global context* (pp. 113–138). New York: Springer-Verlag.

Corrin, L., Lockyer, L., & Bennett, S. (2010). Technological diversity: An investigation of students' technology use in everyday life and academic study. *Learning, Media and Technology 35*(4), 387–401.

Cotten, S. R., Hale, T. M., Moroney, M. H., O'Neal, L., & Borch, C. (2011). Using affordable technology to decrease digital inequality: Results from Birmingham's One Laptop Per Child XO Laptop Project. *Information, Communication & Society 14*(4), 424–444. doi:10.1080/136 9118X.2011.559266.

Danby, S., Davidson, C., Theobald, M., Scriven, B., Cobb-Moore, C., Houen, S.,... Thorpe, K. (2013). Talk in activity during young children's use of digital technologies at home. *Australian Journal of Communication 40*(2), 83.

Dohn, N. B. (2009). Web 2.0: Inherent tensions and evident challenges for education. *International journal of computer-supported collaborative learning, 4*(3), 343–363. doi:10.1007/s11412-009-9066-8.

Ellis, R. A., Bliuc, A., & Goodyear, P. (2012). Student experiences of engaged enquiry in pharmacy education: Digital natives or something else? *Higher Education 64*(5), 609–626.

Eynon, R., & Malmberg, L.-E. (2012). Understanding the online information-seeking behaviours of young people: The role of networks of support: Online information-seeking behaviours. *Journal of Computer Assisted Learning 28*(6), 514–529. doi:10.1111/j.1365-2729.2011.00460.x.

Eynon, R., & Malmberg, L.-E. (2011). A typology of young people's Internet use: Implications for education. *Computers & Education 56*(3), 585–595. doi:10.1016/j.compedu.2010.09.020.

Ferri, P., & Pozzali, A. (2012). University students and social media: Reflections from an empirical research. *Journal of Universal Computer Science 18*(3), 377–392.

Garcia, P., & Qin, J. (2007). Identifying the generation gap in higher education. *Innovate 3*(4). Retrieved from http://innovateonline.info/index.php?view=article&id=379.

Goodyear, P. (2015). Teaching as design. *HERDSA Review of Higher Education 2*, 27–50.

Gros, B., Garcia, I., & Escofet, A. (2012). Beyond the net generation debate: A comparison of digital learners in face-to-face and virtual universities. *The International Review of Research in Open and Distance Learning 13*(4), 190–210.

Gurung, B., and Rutledge, D. (2014). Digital learners and the overlapping of their personal and educational digital engagement. *Computers & Education 77*, 91–100. doi:10.1016/j.compedu.2014.04.012.

Hollingworth, S., Mansaray, A., Allen, K., & Rose, A. (2011). Parents' perspectives on technology and children's learning in the home: Parents, social class and the role of the habitus. *Journal of Computer Assisted Learning 27*(4), 347–360. doi:10.1111/j.1365-2729.2011.00431.x.

Howe, N., & Strauss, W. (2000). *Millennials rising: The next great generation.* New York: Vintage.

Inan, F. A., Lowther, D. L., Ross, S. M., & Strahl, D. (2010). Pattern of classroom activities during students' use of computers: Relations between instructional strategies and computer applications. *Teaching and Teacher Education 26*(3), 540–546. doi:10.1016/j.tate.2009.06.017.

Jones, C., & Healing, G. (2010). Networks and locations for student learning. *Learning, Media and Technology 35*(4), 369–385.

Jones, C., & Shao, B. (2011). *The net generation and digital natives: Implications for higher education.* York: Higher Education Academy.

Judd, T., & Kennedy, G. (2011). Measurement and evidence of computer-based task switching and multitasking by "Net Generation" students. *Computers & Education 56*(3), 625–631.

Kennedy, G., Krause, K., Gray, K., Judd, T., Bennett, S., Maton, K.,... Bishop, A. (2006). Questioning the Net Generation: A collaborative project in Australian higher education. In L. Markauskaite, P. Goodyear, & P. Reimann (Eds.), *Annual Conference of the Australasian Society for Computers in Learning in Tertiary Education* (pp. 413–417). Sydney: Sydney University Press.

Kirschner, P. A., & De Bruyckere, P. (2017). The myths of the digital native and the multitasker. *Teaching and Teacher Education 67*, 135–142.

Kvavik, R. B., Caruso, J. B., & Morgan, G. (2004). *ECAR study of students and information technology 2004: Convenience, connection, and control.* Boulder, CO: EDUCAUSE Center for Applied Research.

Lankshear, C., and Knobel, M. (2015). Digital literacy and digital literacies: Policy, pedagogy and research considerations for education. *Nordic Journal of Digital Literacy 9*, 8–20.

Livingstone, S., Bober, M., & Helsper, E. (2005). Internet literacy among children and young people: Findings from the UK Children Go Online Project. OFCOM/ESRC, London, UK.

Livingstone, S., Mascheroni, G., Ólafsson, K., & Haddon, L. (2014). Children's online risks and opportunities: Comparative findings from EU Kids Online and Net Children Go Mobile. Retrieved from http://eprints.lse.ac.uk/60513/1/__lse.ac.uk_storage_LIBRARY_Secondary_libfile_shared_repository_Content_EU%20Kids%20Online_EU%20Kids%20Online-Children%27s%20online%20risks_2014.pdf

Margaryan, A., Littlejohn, A., & Vojt, G. (2011). Are digital natives a myth or reality? University students' use of digital technologies. *Computers & Education 56*(2), 429–440.

Newman, T., & Beetham, H. (2017). *Student digital experience tracker 2017: The voice of 22,000 UK learners.* Bristol: JISC. Retrieved from http://repository.jisc.ac.uk/6662/1/Jiscdigitalstudenttracker2017.pdf

OECD. (2010). *Are the new millennium learners making the grade?* Educational Research and Innovation. OECD Publishing. doi:10.1787/9789264076044-en.

OECD. (2015). *Students, Computers and Learning.* PISA. OECD Publishing. doi:10.1787/9789264239555-en.

Plowman, L. (2016). Learning technology at home and preschool. In N. Rushby & D. W. Surry (Eds.), *The Wiley Handbook of Learning Technology* (pp. 96–112). Chichester: John Wiley & Sons.

Plowman, L., & Stephen, C. (2007). Guided interaction in pre-school settings. *Journal of Computer Assisted Learning 23*(1), 14–26. doi:10.1111/j.1365-2729.2007.00194.x.

Plowman, L., Stephen, C., & McPake, J. (2010). Supporting young children's learning with technology at home and in preschool. *Research Papers in Education 25*(1), 93–113. doi:10.1080/02671520802584061.

Prescott, J., Wilson, S., & Becket, G. (2013). Facebook use in the learning environment: Do students want this? *Learning, Media and Technology 38*(3), 345–350.

Robinson, L., & Schulz, J. (2013). Net time negotiations within the family" *Information, Communication & Society 16*(4), 542–560. doi:10.1080/1369118X.2013.777761.

Selwyn, N. (2002). *Defining the "digital divide": Developing a theoretical understanding of inequalities in the information age.* Cardiff: Cardiff University.

Selwyn, N. (2010). Looking beyond learning: Notes towards the critical study of educational technology. *Journal of Computer Assisted Learning 26*, 65–73.

Selwyn, N., Potter, J., & Cranmer, S. (2009). Primary pupils' use of information and communication technologies at school and home. *British Journal of Educational Technology 40*(5), 919–932. doi:10.1111/j.1467-8535.2008.00876.x.

So, H., Choi, H., Lim, W. Y., & Xiong, Y. (2012). Little experience with ICT: Are they really the Net Generation student-teachers? *Computers & Education 59*(4), 1234–1245.

Stephen, C., Stevenson, O., & Adey, C. (2013). Young children engaging with technologies at home: The influence of family context. *Journal of Early Childhood Research 11*(2), 149–164.

Valtonen, T., Pontinen, S., Kukkonen, J., Dillon, P., Vaisanen, P., & Hacklin, S. (2011). Confronting the technological pedagogical knowledge of Finnish Net Generation student teachers. *Technology, Pedagogy and Education 20*(1), 3–18.

Wagner, V., & Acier, D. (2017). Factor structure evaluation of the French version of the Digital Natives Assessment Scale. *Cyberpsychology, Behavior, and Social Networking 20*(3), 195–201.

Waycott, J., Bennett, S., Kennedy, G., Dalgarno, B., & Gray, K. (2010). Digital divides? Student and staff perceptions of information and communication technologies. *Computers & Education 54*(4), 1202–1211.

CHAPTER 7

TECHNOLOGY INTERFERENCE IN COUPLE AND FAMILY RELATIONSHIPS

MICHELLE DROUIN AND BRANDON T. McDANIEL

INTRODUCTION

THE potential interfering effects of technology in modern culture are omnipresent. Who hasn't seen that family at a restaurant where mom, dad, brother, and sister are all staring at their screens? Scrolling, pressing, responding to the mobile device in their hands, oblivious to the people in front of them. Or maybe it was the park: "Mom…mom…MOM!" the kid shouts, trying to get his mother's attention, as she sits on a bench, attending not to her climbing child, but to the shiny screen in front of her. Or perhaps it was the subway: The couple got on together, sat down beside one another, legs touching, but minds miles apart as they both separately caught up on email or their social media. Alternatively, you may not have to look any further than your own home. You watch TV with your partner—eyes directed towards the TV, eyes directed at the phone, but eyes almost never directed towards each other. You try to finish that last email as your toddler grabs at your leg. You have a conversation with your son, and the ping of your phone makes you shift your attention, for just a moment, from the human being in front of you to the one in cyberspace.

Before the chapter proceeds, it is important to distinguish between *technology use* and *technology interference*. Clearly, there are innumerable benefits of technology use from both a cultural and familial standpoint. From a cultural perspective, technological innovations have been critical to our intellectual advancement in almost every area of study. We can work faster, from remote locations, using equipment that is portable, powerful, and lightweight. I am currently writing this chapter 35,000 feet above the earth, on a laptop that weighs less than one pound, building off the work of my collaborator whom I have met only once in my lifetime. Technology is grand. Meanwhile, within families, technology allows us to make important connections from the comfort of our own homes, and provides a platform for learning, socialization, entertainment, and innovation. As a child of the hard-cover encyclopedia era, I am thrilled to live and work in this generation of technological opportunity. However, technology use sometimes bleeds out into the daily interactions between individuals, and this use can lead to interference or disruption. It is this *technology interference*, the interruption of an activity by attending to a digital device, that is the focus of this chapter. More specifically, the research described in this chapter addresses whether technology is interfering in our lives, and if so, what impact that interference has on our most important relationships.

TECHNOLOGY USE AND RELATIONSHIPS

Mobile technology and Internet usage have become pervasive in our society. According to a global survey in 32 nations that included emerging and developing countries, 44 percent of people reported using the Internet, with highest rates in wealthier nations, such as the United States, where 87 percent of adults reported Internet use (Pew Research Center, 2015a). Moreover, in modern households, multiple people have access to the Internet, often on various devices. Recent statistics report that 90 percent of US households have at least one connected device (e.g., smartphone, computer, or tablet), and the average American family has five such devices (Pew Research Center, 2017). Worldwide, device ownership statistics vary widely, but most people (86 percent) report owning some type of mobile phone, 38 percent have a working computer in their household, and 24 percent report owning a smartphone (Pew Research Center, 2015a). Despite differences in Internet and device penetration, a commonality across countries is that the Internet and mobile phones are used primarily for socializing: in every country surveyed, networking with friends or family emerged as the top online activity (Pew Research Center, 2015a). It is unsurprising, then, that the majority of people (53 percent) considered the Internet to be a "good influence" on personal relationships (Pew Research Center, 2015a).

Although the Internet and mobile technologies can be used to forge and sustain interpersonal relationships (Coyne, Stockdale, Busby, Iverson, & Grant, 2011; Jiang & Hancock, 2013; Papp, Danielewicz, & Cayemberg, 2012), there is a fast-growing body of recent research that explores whether the pervasiveness of mobile technologies can also have an interfering effect in interpersonal communication. According to a Pew Research study (2015c) on mobile etiquette, these interruptions are common. Among the 3,217 US adults they surveyed, 89 percent reported that they had used their cell phones during their most recent social gathering. The activities that they engaged in with their cell phones were varied: checking an email or text message (61 percent), taking a photo or video (58 percent), sending a message (52 percent), and taking a call (52 percent) emerged as the top activities people reported engaging in during these gatherings (Pew Research, 2015c). Regardless of type of mobile phone engagement, a large number of respondents (25 percent) felt that when they personally used their phones during group interactions, it had a negative effect on the interaction (Pew Research, 2015c). Moreover, when asked to consider the interfering effects of cell phones more generally, a much larger percentage acknowledged its potential negative effects. In this case, 82 percent indicated that when people used their phones during a social gathering it hurt the group dynamics or atmosphere at least occasionally (Pew Research, 2015c).

Researchers have used the terms *technoference* (technology interference; McDaniel & Coyne, 2016a) or *phubbing* (phone snubbing; Roberts & David, 2016) to describe the interruptions in relational interaction that can occur when technological device usage intrudes on or interrupts everyday interactions with relationship partners (McDaniel, 2015). Phubbing has been conceptualized by some (e.g., Karadağ et al., 2015) as by-product of a host of obsessive or compulsive uses of technology, and its potential deleterious effects on relationships has been an active area of study for the past few years. Much of this research has focused on couple relationships, either within or outside of family contexts (Czechowsky, 2008; Duran, Kelly, & Rotaru, 2011; Halpern & Katz, 2017; Krasnova, Abramova, Notter, & Baumann, 2016; McDaniel, 2015; McDaniel & Coyne, 2016a; McDaniel & Coyne, 2016b; McDaniel, Galovan, Cravens, & Drouin, 2018; Przybylski & Weinstein, 2012; Roberts & David, 2016; Wang, Xie, Wang, Wang, & Lei, 2017); however, there has also been a recent focus on the effects that technology usage may be having on parents' interactions with their children (McDaniel & Coyne, 2016b; McDaniel & Radesky, 2018a; McDaniel & Radesky, 2018b; Radesky et al., 2016). Overall, these studies have shown that technology use can have an interfering or negative effect on interaction patterns and relationship health. This chapter presents a theoretical background for this work, and details the various findings from these two strains of research, the implications of these findings, and future directions in the study of technology interference in couple and family relationships.

A THEORETICAL BACKGROUND

Propositions that technology may be interfering in relationships are based on some well-regarded and oft-cited theories. Within couples, researchers have sometimes used social exchange theory as a basis for their hypotheses about the potential negative effects of technology use on relationships (e.g., McDaniel et al., 2018). In 1959, Thibault and Kelly proposed the social exchange theory, which posits that exchanges take place between partners, and partners are constantly assessing the value of the relationship—examining the rewards and costs of being in the relationship. These assessments result in either satisfaction or dissatisfaction with one's partner (Sabatelli & Shehan, 1993; Van Lange & Rusbult, 2012). A later addition to this theory was the proposition that equity is also important in relationships. According to equity theory, partners also want to assure that they are putting in similar amounts of effort into the exchange (Stafford & Canary, 1991). When individuals feel that exchanges are equal, and their expectations are met within a relationship, they are more likely to be satisfied (Stafford & Canary, 1991; Turner, 1991; Van Lange & Rusbult, 2012). On the contrary, if either partner recognizes an imbalance in the relationship in terms of investment of resources, negative emotions can arise (Sprecher, 1986). More specifically, if individuals feel they are investing more resources into the relationship than their partner—an *underbenefited* exchange— they may feel a host of negative emotions, including anger, resentment, and hurt (Sprecher, 1986). Similarly, individuals who perceive an *overbenefited* exchange—those who feel that they are devoting fewer resources to the relationship than their partner is to them—can also feel similar negative emotions (Sprecher, 1986). Thus, inequity, generally, is associated with more negative emotions and fewer positive emotions (e.g., trust, respect, commitment). However, among those who are underbenefited in their relationships, these positive and negative emotions are generally stronger in intensity (Sprecher, 1986).

Applied to the context of technology interference in romantic relationships, social exchange theory explains at least some of the negative affect experienced by individuals when their partner chooses to attend to technology instead of them. According to Miller-Ott and Kelly (2015), individuals in romantic relationships expect undivided attention from relationship partners at least some of the time, like during dates or intimate time together. When a partner violates this expectation, an individual might find it rude or annoying, assuming that their partner is more interested in their phone than they are in them (Miller-Ott & Kelly, 2015). Moreover, consistent with expectancy violation theory (EVT; Burgoon, 1978), when their expectations of how their partner should act have been violated, it may cause the individual to assess how positive or negative the violation was and re-evaluate the "reward value" (e.g., status or attractiveness) of their partner. In their recent research with adult focus groups on cell phone usage between romantic partners, Miller-Ott and Kelly (2015) found that when partners used their cell phones during intimate times, expectancies were violated, and most of these violations were perceived as negative. If these findings are considered alongside the social exchange theory, cell phone usage violations (or other such similar technology violations) might be perceived as an increased cost to the relationship, especially when they create conflict (e.g., Miller-Ott, Kelly, & Duran, 2012), or a decreased benefit to the relationship (e.g., less quality time together).

Alternatively, some researchers (e.g., Haplern & Katz, 2017; McDaniel & Coyne, 2016a) have suggested that the theoretical frameworks of symbolic interactionism (Denzin, 1992) or displacement (McCombs, 1972) might better explain the effects of technoference on relationships. Symbolic interactionism is based on the idea that people communicate using symbols, and they infer their relationships and roles with others through their interpretation of these symbols (Denzin, 1992). Thus, every interaction, either face to face or online, serves as a symbol through which individuals can make evaluations about themselves and the relationship. Displacement theory adds a technical dimension to this interpretation, stating that technology use and relationships exist on opposite ends of a spectrum, and time spent on one displaces time spent on the other (McCombs, 1972). Applied to technoference, if an interaction partner is using their phone or constantly checking updates or alerts instead of attending to a conversation, this serves as a symbol to their partner, and when it violates expectations in the relationship—EVT—it can lead to negative affect (Halpern & Katz, 2017; also see McDaniel & Coyne, 2016a). Even within the context of non-romantic relationships (e.g., friendships, acquaintanceships, family relationships), individuals expect that their interaction partners will be attentive and responsive, and violations of this negatively affect conversation quality (Abeele, Antheunis, & Schouten, 2016). Moreover, the sheer use of this technology may displace quality time spent with others; thus, it has been argued that an increase of time spent with technology decreases the opportunity for meaningful interactions with others (Coyne, Padilla-Walker, Fraser, Fellows, & Day 2014; McDaniel & Coyne, 2016a; Valkenburg & Peter, 2009). In this way, technoference might engender higher levels of conflict and lower levels of intimacy (Amichai-Hamburger & Etgar, 2016; McDaniel & Coyne, 2016a).

In sum, there are several theories (e.g., social exchange theory, equity theory, EVT, symbolic interactionism, displacement theory) that might explain how technology might interfere with relationships. Although they each approach the issue from a slightly different angle, a commonality across all of these theoretical perspectives is that individuals may have expectations about interaction partners, the behavior of these interaction partners may evoke feelings (positive and/or negative) in individuals, and partners' behaviors are sometimes evaluated to make assessments about relationship quality. So, whether technology-related interferences occur in the presence of a friend, a relationship partner, or a child, they have the potential to affect the relationship in a profoundly negative way.

TECHNOLOGY INTERFERENCE IN COUPLE RELATIONSHIPS

Mobile technology and the Internet have been lauded for providing effective mediums for the formation and maintenance of intimate relationships. For example, in the case of partners in long-distance relationships, technology is often a critical mechanism for helping them stay connected (Jiang & Hancock, 2013), and even when a partner is near, technology allows partners to connect throughout the day (Coyne et al., 2011). By assisting with relationship maintenance (Papp, Danielewicz, & Cayemberg, 2012), technology may help partners feel more connected, satisfied, and committed (Sidelinger, Avash, Godorhazy, & Tibbles, 2008). However, technology can also create disruptions in couples' interactions. Consider, for example, how an intimate face-to-face conversation might be disrupted if a partner turns his attention to his phone, checking messages, responding to alerts, or taking a phone call. According to the latest research, these interruptions might have deleterious effects on romantic relationships.

It was only recently, between 2014 to 2016, that the terms technoference and phubbing began to surface in research articles and popular media headlines (e.g., McDaniel, 2015; McDaniel & Coyne, 2016a; Holohan, 2014; Roberts & David, 2016). In fact, most of the research on this topic is so new that these terms may still be elusive to the general public. Yet in the past few years there has been a substantial increase in research studies devoted to technology interference in relationships, and most of this research has focused on romantic relationships and the roles of technology in couples' interactions, conflict, and a variety of relationship outcomes and correlates.

In one of the first studies that examined the potential interfering role of technology in relationships, Coyne and colleagues (2011) used a single item measure and found that couples' use of technology to interact with others while with their partner was negatively related to relationship satisfaction. Building on this early research, McDaniel and Coyne (2016a) used structural equation modeling, and found that, in their sample of 143 married/cohabiting women, technology interference in their interactions with partners was positively related to conflict over technology use. In turn, this conflict was related to lower relationship satisfaction, greater levels of depression, and lower life satisfaction (McDaniel & Coyne, 2016a). Soon after, Roberts and David (2016), using items from the McDaniel and Coyne (2016a) measure of technoference, showed that phubbing was quite common: 46.3 percent of adults reported that they had been phubbed by their romantic relationship partner, and 22.6 percent reported that it caused conflict with their partner (Eckert, 2015). Moreover, they found support for a conceptual model that was very similar to the one reported by McDaniel and Coyne (2016a). In other words, those who experienced more partner phubbing also reported more conflict, and this was related (as a sequential mediator) to lower relationship satisfaction and life satisfaction and greater depression. Roberts and David (2016) also examined attachment anxiety as a moderator in their model. They found that partner phubbing increased conflict among individuals with both secure and insecure attachment; however, when partner phubbing was high, those with anxious attachments had higher levels of conflict than those with secure attachments (Roberts and David, 2016). Considered together, McDaniel and Coyne (2016a) and Roberts and David (2016) suggest that greater technology use leads to greater conflict, and this conflict is related to a number of negative relationship correlates.

The findings from these two seminal studies have since been supported through research studies across the globe. Wang and colleagues (2017) found that among their sample of 243 married Chinese adults, phubbing was associated with lower relationship satisfaction. Meanwhile, in a study involving 128 Israeli college students in romantic relationships, Amichai-Hamburger and Etgar (2016) found that a partner's private smartphone multitasking (but not shared multitasking) was negatively related to emotional intimacy. These studies added cross-cultural validation for previous work.

Other, international research extended current understanding in important ways. For example, in a longitudinal study of 717 Chilean adults in relationships, Halpern and Katz (2017) examined the relationship between intimacy, relationship satisfaction, and phubbing using intimacy as a mediator, rather than an outcome variable. Using structural equation modeling, they found that phubbing was a mediator between texting frequency and perceived relationship quality, through phone-related conflicts and lack of intimacy. In other words, when partners texted more often, this was predictive of phubbing behavior, which caused more phone-related conflicts and a lack of intimacy. In turn, this conflict and lack of intimacy was related to lower levels of perceived relationship quality. Moreover, when the longitudinal relationships were examined through cross-lag analysis, texting behavior predicted lower relationship quality, but not the other way around, which lends support to the direction of influence proposed in previous models (e.g., McDaniel & Coyne, 2016a; Roberts & David, 2016).

Additionally, Krasnova and colleagues (2016) examined the emotions experienced by German individuals when their partners used their phones in their presence. Among their 1,276 participants in committed relationships, 62 percent noted negative feelings in response to their partner's phubbing. More specifically, their participants noted a loss of attention, anger, sadness or suffering, and boredom as the negative emotions they experienced when their partner used their cell phones for too long in their presence (Krasnova et al., 2016). Importantly, this study found that a partner's cell phone use predicted relational cohesion, and that jealousy was a mediator in this relationship. This expanded the literature in a critical way, because while McDaniel and Coyne (2016a) and Roberts and David (2016) focused on a relational *behavior* as a mediator between technoference and negative relationship outcomes (i.e., conflict), Krasnova and colleagues (2016) showed that negative *feelings* can be the conduit between technoference and relationship dissatisfaction. Krasnova and colleagues (2016) also examined individuals' behavioral reactions to their partner's phubbing. They found that a sizable minority (27.1 percent) intervened to stop their partner's phubbing behavior, either by asking them to stop using it or taking it away. Another group of participants (22.3 percent) waited for their partner to terminate their cell phone use. Thus, approximately half of their participants were either proactive in getting attention back to them or tolerant and understanding of their partner's behavior. However, there were also a large number of individuals who exited the conversation by getting on their own phones or engaging in another activity (19.9 percent), exhibited no reaction (22.3 percent), or experienced negative emotions from this interaction (7.3 percent). This analysis is an important addition to the literature, as it goes beyond identifying the problem and its various components to providing a framework for the development of solutions. As an example, if individuals learn to navigate these social interactions so that they can effectively communicate their needs to their partner, then the conflict, intimacy, and negative relationship by-products of technoference might be circumvented. In short, this study provides direction for further research into how to support couples experiencing issues related to technoference.

Finally, in a recent study involving both Canadian and American adults, McDaniel and colleagues (2018) examined technoference among married/cohabiting parents, using dyadic, couple-level data to explore whether the models found previously in McDaniel & Coyne (2016a, 2016b) would apply to those in long-term, parenting relationships. Their findings supported and expanded previous models. More specifically,

McDaniel and colleagues (2018) showed that technoference predicted conflict even in long-term, committed relationship contexts, and this conflict was related to lower levels of relationship satisfaction and perceptions of poorer co-parenting quality.

The sum of work on the topic of technology interference in couple relationships paints a rather consistent and somewhat grim picture. When individuals use their cell phones in the presence of their romantic partner, it creates an opportunity for interruptions in the interaction. These interruptions can lead to conflict and lower levels of intimacy, which in turn are related to lower levels of relationship satisfaction. Moreover, this relationship dissatisfaction is related to depression and lower levels of general life satisfaction. However, romantic relationships are not the only contexts within which these interruptions might occur. In fact, technology use might be interfering with and having negative effects on other types of family relationships, including parenting and family relationships. The next section summarizes the findings from this research.

Technology Interference in Parenting and Family Relationships

There are positive effects of technology use in parenting and family relationships. For example, research shows that shared TV viewing and video game playing in families are associated with feeling more connected to family members (Padilla-Walker, Coyne, & Fraser, 2012). Technology can be used to connect family members throughout the day, communicate with or monitor children, coordinate activities, and much more (Coyne et al., 2011; Dworkin, McCann, & McGuire, 2016; Rudi, Dworkin, Walker, & Doty, 2015; Weisskirch, 2009).

Yet the pervasiveness of technology, especially mobile and very immersive technologies such as smartphones, can lead to various forms of interference in family interactions and time spent together (e.g., McDaniel, 2015; McDaniel & Coyne, 2016b). Although much of the work on problematic phone and technology use has focused on implications for individual well-being and couple relationships, parents and children are not immune to the potential impacts of these new technologies and technology habits. Accordingly, a small body of foundational work on parent distraction or use of technology while with their children is beginning to emerge.

As mentions of technoference started emerging in the mainstream media, researchers became interested in parents' and caregivers' feelings about technology or phone use while co-present with their children or family. These studies, based mostly on qualitative interviews and diaries, revealed that some parents use technology as an escape from boredom or the stress of everyday parenting—even pretending to be busy when children or family members need help (Hiniker et al., 2015; Oduor et al., 2016; Radesky et al., 2016). Parents have also reported turning to mobile device use due to notifications, feeling pressure to check and respond to messages, and work expectations (Oduor et al., 2016; Radesky et al., 2016). Overall, this use often makes parents uncomfortable as they know they are multitasking and not giving their children their full attention; they also report that multitasking in this way leads to difficulties in assessing child cues and responding appropriately to child behavior (Radesky et al., 2016).

Several observational studies have examined these processes as they unfold. First, Radesky and colleagues (2014) observed 55 caregivers with their children in a restaurant and found that 73 percent engaged with their phone sometimes and 29 percent showed continuous phone use. The more absorbed the caregiver was in their device, the less conversation took place between the caregiver and child, and some children reacted to the caregiver's absorption by acting out or increasing their bids for attention. Additionally, caregivers' responses to their children were more hostile when caregivers were absorbed in the device. Second, in an observational meal task conducted in a laboratory (completely unrelated to technology use), Radesky et al. (2015) found that 23 percent of the mothers in the study spontaneously used their device, and this led to fewer verbal and nonverbal interactions with their children. Third, Hiniker et al. (2015) observed caregivers with children at playgrounds. They found that 35 percent of caregivers spent 20 percent or more of their time (1 out of every 5 minutes or more) on their phone. Additionally, they found that although most phone use was brief, child bids for the caregiver's attention were much less successful when the caregiver was distracted by their phone as opposed to some other distraction (e.g., conversation with another adult, reading newspaper, etc.). Overall, these studies suggest that parenting quality is directly affected by technology use in terms of decreased responsiveness and perhaps harsher parenting when parents do respond.

More recently, researchers have used cross-sectional survey data to examine how technology might interfere in parent-child relationships. McDaniel and Coyne (2016b) examined mothers' perceptions of technoference—interruptions/intrusions in face-to-face interactions or time spent together with their partner and with their children. They found that 65 percent of mothers reported that technology interrupted their interactions at least sometimes or more often during playtime with the child, and at least 26 percent of mothers reported this happening at least sometimes during mealtimes, bedtimes, and even educational activities. Meanwhile, 58 percent reported technoference due to mobile phones at least sometimes during their co-parenting interactions (parenting interactions while mother, father, and child were all present). Of particular note, greater technoference was associated with perceptions of poorer co-parenting quality. This association between technoference and lower co-parenting quality has also recently been found in a diverse sample of US and Canadian participants (McDaniel et al., 2018), and technoference has also recently been correlated with parental reports of lower parenting quality (McDaniel, Everest, & White, 2018).

The significant relationships between technoference and degraded co-parenting and parenting interactions might be explained by our difficulties with multitasking. It is nearly impossible for individuals to truly multitask (e.g., Ophir, Naas, & Wagner, 2009); instead attention must switch from one task to the next, limiting the attention devoted to each task. Media multitasking while parenting is no exception, and thus, we see parents expressing their struggles to effectively parent while on their device (e.g., Radesky et al., 2016). For parents and co-parents to function at their best, McDaniel & Coyne argue that "parents must be able to coordinate and be in synchrony with one another" (2016b, 437). However, time spent on a device displaces time that should or could have been spent with one's children or family (displacement hypothesis), and hurt feelings and conflict between parents and child(ren) may occur (McDaniel & Coyne, 2016b). As a result, parents may find it even more difficult to be sensitive and respond appropriately to their children.

If parenting quality suffers due to technoference and parental device use, it could lead to worse child behavior. Radesky et al. (2014) observed that children sometimes react negatively to parent device use during mealtimes. Recently, researchers have begun to examine the links between interruptions in parent-child interactions due to technology and child behavior. Utilizing survey data from 170 couples with young children, McDaniel and Radesky (2018a) found that families in which mothers reported more frequent technoference during their time spent with their child also reported that their child exhibited more externalizing symptoms (e.g., acting out, being hyperactive, getting angry) and internalizing symptoms (e.g., whining, sulking, an feeling hurt). Following this same sample, McDaniel and Radesky (2018b) have also found longitudinal links between technoference during parent–child interactions and parent reports of increased child externalizing behavior. Finally, McDaniel and Radesky (2017b) recently reported encountering daily associations between parent problematic phone use (e.g., using their device too much) and child negative behavior, such that on days when parents struggled more with their device use, child behavior also appeared to worsen. McDaniel and Radesky (2017, 2018b) suggest that this deterioration in child behavior could be due to a number of factors, such as children attempting to get parents' attention, children's deteriorating regulatory abilities due to worse parenting quality over time, parents' negatively biased views of child behavior while parents use technology, or parents potentially withdrawing more to technology as an escape from child negative behavior. These patterns have the potential to create dysfunction in parenting, parent-child interactions, or child development, and further research is required.

Relatedly, poor parenting quality due to technoference and parental device use could also lead to potential attachment problems. In turn, attachment has been linked with a variety of child socio-emotional well-being indicators during childhood and later on (e.g., Brumariu & Kerns, 2010; Colonnesi et al., 2011; Fearon et al., 2010). Attachment theory suggests that children rely on a caregiver's sensitivity to form a strong emotional bond with their caregivers (Ainsworth, Blehar, Waters, & Wall, 1978). As suggested earlier by McDaniel and Coyne (2016b), multitasking and technoference have the potential to decrease the quality of all aspects of sensitive parenting. For example, if parents are absorbed in their phones, it is more likely that they will miss or misinterpret a child's needs due to a lack of focused attention. Additionally, absorption with their devices may delay their response or they may respond with anger or frustration over being interrupted by the child. These effects on parenting sensitivity may lead to greater attachment insecurity, as children feel less able to completely trust their caregiver (e.g., Ainsworth et al., 1978), especially if it happens often.

Do children, though, actually experience their parents' device use as negative? Some research suggests that they might. Steiner-Adair and Barker (2013) interviewed 1,000 children ages four to eighteen years about their parents' mobile device use. They found that children often used words such as sad, mad, angry, and lonely when describing these experiences. Overall, many children expressed feeling alienated, dissatisfied, or that their parents were not fully interested in them. Other researchers have examined parents' and children's feelings about phone use during mealtimes, and they found that children expected their parents to be present and a good example of behavior (Hiniker, Schoenebeck, & Kientz, 2016).

It is important to note that parents are not the only players in the parent-child relationship. Parents do have the ultimate responsibility to create a nurturing environment, and most influences on parenting are filtered through the parent's own emotional/psychological state (e.g., Belsky, 1984); however, McDaniel and Radesky (2018b) suggest that, like most development, these processes are transactional and bidirectional in nature. In their study, they found that greater technoference in the parent–child relationship appears to increase child externalizing behavior problems at later time points; yet greater child behavior problems also predict increases in parents' stress levels and the frequency of technoference. In other words, children react to parent distraction with technology, and parents react to children's poor behavior and may withdraw to technology. This can create a dysfunctional circular process in the family (McDaniel & Radesky, 2018b). Although some parents mention turning to phone or technology use as an escape or to calm themselves down during parenting (e.g., Radesky et al., 2016), research suggests that often individuals turn to phone or social media use in the hopes of feeling better, but come away feeling worse (Sagioglou & Greitemeyer, 2014). Moreover, some online interactions appear to be more potentially negative than others. For instance, mothers who make social comparisons while on social media may feel more overloaded and worse about their relationships (Coyne, McDaniel, & Stockdale, 2017).

Overall, research suggests that although technology can facilitate positive outcomes within family contexts, it also provides opportunities for disturbing or interrupting parent–child interactions. Parents seem to be aware that this is happening and may even feel uncomfortable about it, but it still happens. Due to these distractions related to technology, the quality of parenting likely deteriorates, and as these distractions happen more and more often, child development, specifically child behavior and attachment security, may be negatively affected.

SUMMARY AND FUTURE DIRECTIONS

When considering the sum of evidence on the topic of technoference, it is clear that it is both common in modern culture and that it is associated with negative outcomes within both couple and family relationships. Specifically, technoference can spur negative feelings, like anger, loneliness, and sadness, which may motivate those experiencing this interference to confront their interaction partner, ignore their partner, or even disengage. Moreover, this conflict and/or disengagement is related to a host of negative outcomes, including relationship dissatisfaction among couples and externalizing and internalizing behaviors in children.

Although the evidence appears to present a clear picture, this is still a new area of study, and therefore, is not complete. Perhaps there is a file-drawer problem, whereby all of the research suggesting neutral or positive effects has remained unreported. Alternatively, perhaps our measures are not yet sophisticated enough to capture the beneficial aspects of technology interference. It could be possible that when bids for attention from a partner or parent are denied, individuals develop resilience, an appreci- ation for multitasking, or confidence in asserting their needs in a relationship. Or perhaps the reported negative effects may simply be a cohort issue, a reflection of the general sentiment of a non-technological generation. It is possible that as more people who have grown up with technology enter committed relationships and start families, these interactions will not be viewed as problematic or conflict inducing, but rather, they will be viewed as normal interactions in a typical, connected life. As Pew Research (2015c) found, those who are between the ages of eighteen and twenty-nine are far more tolerant of these technological interruptions and view phone use as more acceptable across a wide range of situations (from waiting in line to family dinners). Indeed, all of these various outcomes are *possible*; however, the research to date does not support these suppositions. Instead, there is a rather cohesive picture of the impact of technoference on couple and family relationships, and it is overwhelmingly negative.

According to the theoretical propositions (e.g., Halpern & Katz, 2017), when tech- nology interference occurs during the course of an interaction, it serves as a symbol to the partner not using the device. A simple act—looking down at the phone, swiping an alert, checking a message—may be interpreted as inattention or a preference, even momentarily, for interacting with someone else. This displacement from face-to-face, live interaction towards technology is becoming more and more commonplace (e.g., Pew Research, 2015c), and when individuals interpret this displacement as a violation of their expected interaction sequence, it has the potential to create problems in the relationship (Miller-Ott & Kelly, 2015). Moreover, balances might shift in the social exchange, and the more often these interactions occur, the more likely a partner may feel underbenefited in the relationship (e.g., McDaniel et al., 2018). Clearly, while the problem and the potential pathways through which this problem might cause discord in relationships have been identified, the next step is to ask how these relationship missteps might be addressed.

Perhaps, if the conceptualization of technoference is accepted as the by-product of obsessive or compulsive technology use (Karadağ et al., 2015), then a viable route towards the curbing of technoference would be to address this broader behavior. According to Pew Research (2015b), 46 percent of American adults classify their cell phones as something they cannot live without. Moreover, cell phones facilitate a continuous online presence; in fact, 24 percent of adolescents report being online almost constantly (Lenhart, 2015). The term *nomophobia* has even emerged to describe a fear of being without one's mobile phone (e.g., Argumosa-Villar, Boada-Grau, & Vigil-Colet, 2017; Nagpal & Kaur, 2016), and researchers advocated for the inclusion of nomophobia in the DSM-V (e.g., Bragazzi, & Del Puente, 2014). Perhaps, through addressing problematic mobile phone and Internet use, it is also possible to address the technoference or phubbing that are its consequences. This is a promising direction for future research.

However, when technoference was coined by McDaniel and Coyne (2016a), it was described as the *normative*, everyday beeps and buzzes of mobile phones and other devices that begin to intrude in face-to-face interactions. Developing everyday phone-use boundaries, like turning devices off at certain times, carving out time for uninterrupted face-to-face attention, and informing others of the reasons for technology use at that particular moment, might help reduce technoference or the potential negative effects of technoference (e.g., McDaniel, 2015; McDaniel & Coyne, 2016a, 2016b). Additionally, it might be useful to further explore the line of inquiry began by Krasnova et al. (2016)—examining the reactions of those who experience technoference in their relationships. Krasnova et al. (2016) showed that individuals had different emotional and behavioral reactions to technoference from their romantic partners. There is much room for expansion of this research by exploring the short- and long-term consequences of these various reactions in both couple and family relationships. If some reactions create more positive outcomes than others (e.g., addressing the issue with a partner versus disengaging), then this could serve as a basis for education and therapeutic interventions.

Finally, to address the potential issues that might arise within parent-child relationships specifically, future studies should examine the long-term effects of parental technoference and the effects of responsible media use initiatives on family relationships. Although young adults and older children may be more tolerant of technological interruptions (Pew Research, 2015c), infants and young children still depend on their caregivers for sensitive caregiving, which includes responding appropriately and often immediately to a child's needs (e.g., Ainsworth et al., 1978). When parents are engaged with technology, sensitive parenting can be compromised, which could lead to negative child behavior and attachment/trust issues in relationships throughout the life course (e.g., McDaniel & Radesky, 2018a; McDaniel & Radesky, 2018b; McDaniel & Coyne, 2016b). More longitudinal research with infants and young children is needed to examine whether there are long-term negative consequences of this parental technoference. Moreover, there are a number of reputable child advocacy organizations (e.g., American Academy of Pediatrics, Common Sense Media) that have created family media use guidelines and contract templates that contain suggestions that might help reduce technoference (e.g., restricting time spent on devices, no cell phones at the dinner table). These recommendations are informed by research and are well intentioned, and this kind of instructive outreach is encouraging. However, it is not yet known whether following these guidelines will actually have the intended positive effects on families. Thus, we see this as a critical line of future research. As technology continues to pervade the cultural landscape, it is important to focus on improving and maintaining strong couple and family relationships as individuals continue to adapt to a life bombarded with continual flashes, beeps, and buzzes.

References

AAP Council on Communications and Media. (2016). Media and young minds. *Pediatrics 138*, e20162591. doi:10.1542/peds.2016–2591.

Abeele, M. M. V., Antheunis, M. L., & Schouten, A. P. (2016). The effect of mobile messaging during a conversation on impression formation and interaction quality. *Computers in Human Behavior 62*, 562–569.

Ainsworth, M. D. S., Blehar, M. C., Waters, E., & Wall, S. (1978). *Patterns of attachment: A psychological study of the strange situation.* Hillsdale, NJ: Erlbaum.

Amichai-Hamburger, Y., & Etgar, S. (2016). Intimacy and smartphone multitasking—A new oxymoron? *Psychological Reports 119*, 826–838. doi:10.1177/0033294116662658

Argumosa-Villar, L., Boada-Grau, J., & Vigil-Colet, A. (2017). Exploratory investigation of theoretical predictors of nomophobia using the Mobile Phone Involvement Questionnaire (MPIQ). *Journal of Adolescence 56*, 127–135. doi:10.1016/j.adolescence.2017.02.003

Belsky, J. (1984). The determinants of parenting: A process model. *Child Development 55*(1), 83–96.

Bragazzi, N. L., & Del Puente, G. (2014). A proposal for including nomophobia in the new DSM-V. *Psychology Research and Behavior Management 7*, 155–159.

Brumariu, L. E., & Kerns, K. A. (2010). Parent–child attachment and internalizing symptoms in childhood and adolescence: A review of empirical findings and future directions. *Development and Psychopathology 22*(1), 177–203.

Burgoon, J. K. (1978). A communication model of personal space violations: Explication and an initial test. *Human Communication Research 4*, 129–142. doi:10.111/j.1468–2958.1978.b00603.x

Colonnesi, C., Draijer, E. M., Jan J. M. Stams, G., Van der Bruggen, C. O., Bögels, S. M., & Noom, M. J. (2011). The relation between insecure attachment and child anxiety: A meta-analytic review. *Journal of Clinical Child & Adolescent Psychology 40*, 630–645.

Coyne, S. M., Padilla-Walker, L. M., Fraser, A. M., Fellows, K., & Day, R. D. (2014). Media time = family time: Positive media use in families with adolescents. *Journal of Adolescent Research, 29*, 663–688.

Coyne, S. M., McDaniel, B. T., & Stockdale, L. A. (2017). "Do you dare to compare?" Associations between maternal social comparisons on social networking sites and parenting, mental health, and romantic relationship outcomes. *Computers in Human Behavior 70*, 335–340.

Coyne, S. M., Stockdale, L., Busby, D., Iverson, B., & Grant, D. M. (2011). "I luv u :)!": A descriptive study of the media use of individuals in romantic relationships. *Family Relations 60*, 150–162.

Czechowsky, J. D. (2008). The impact of the Black-Berry on couple relationships. (Unpublished doctoral dissertation). Wilfrid Laurier University. Retrieved from http://scholars.wlu.ca/cgi/viewcontent.cgi?article=2055&context=etd

Denzin, N. K. (1992). *Symbolic interactionism and cultural studies: The politics of interpretation.* Cambridge, MA: Blackwell.

Duran, R. L., Kelly, L., & Rotaru, T. (2011). Mobile phones in romantic relationships and the dialectic of autonomy vs. connection. *Communication Quarterly 59*, 19–36.

Dworkin, J., McCann, E., & McGuire, J. K. (2016). Coparenting in the digital era: Exploring divorced parents' use of technology. In G. Gianesini & S. Lee Blair (Eds.), *Divorce, separation, and remarriage: The transformation of family*, vol. 10 (pp. 279–298). Bingley, UK: Emerald Group Publishing Limited.

Eckert, E. (2015, September 29). "Cellphone use can undermine the bedrock of our happiness – our relationships with our romantic partners," researcher says. *Baylor Media Communications.* Retrieved from http://www.baylor.edu/mediacommunications/news.php ?action=story&story=161554

Fearon, R. P., Bakermans-Kranenburg, M. J., Van IJzendoorn, M. H., Lapsley, A. M., & Roisman, G. I. (2010). The significance of insecure attachment and disorganization in the development of children's externalizing behavior: A meta-analytic study. *Child Development 81*(2), 435–456.

Gold, M. (2015, October 2). "Phubbing" could destroy your relationship, says new study. *Huffington Post.* Retrieved from http://www.huffingtonpost.com/glamour/phubbing-could-destroy-yo_b_8234918.html

Halpern, D., & Katz, J. E. (2017). Texting's consequences for romantic relationships: A cross-lagged analysis highlights its risks. *Computers in Human Behavior 71*, 386–394.

Hiniker, A., Schoenebeck, S. Y., & Kientz, J. A. (2016). Not at the dinner table: Parents' and children's perspectives on family technology rules. In *Proceedings of the 19th ACM Conference on Computer-Supported Cooperative Work & Social Computing* (pp. 1376–1389). 27 February–2 March, San Francisco, CA. New York: ACM.

Hiniker, A., Sobel, K., Suh, H., Sung, Y. C., Lee, C. P., & Kientz, J. A. (2015, April). Texting while Parenting: How Adults Use Mobile Phones while Caring for Children at the Playground. In *Proceedings of the 33rd Annual ACM Conference on Human Factors in Computing Systems* (pp. 727–736). 18–23 April, Seoul, Korea. New York: ACM.

Holohan, M. (2014, December 5). Put down that phone! "Technoference" may be hurting your relationship. *Today.com.* Retrieved from https://www.today.com/health/put-down-smartphone-technoference-can-hurt-your-relationship-1D80339938

Jiang, L. C., & Hancock, J. T. (2013). Absence makes the communication grow fonder: Geographic separation, interpersonal media, and intimacy in dating relationships. *Journal of Communication 63*, 556–577.

Karadağ, E., Tosuntas, S. B., Erzen, E., Duru, P., Bostan, N., Sahin, B. M., … Babadag B. (2015). Determinants of phubbing, which is the sum of many virtual addictions: A structural equation model. *Journal of Behavioral Addictions 4*, 60–74.

Krasnova, H., Abramova, O., Notter, I., & Baumann, A. (2016). Why phubbing is toxic for your relationship: Understanding the role of smartphone jealousy among "Generation Y" users. *Twenty-Fourth European Conference on Information Systems (ECIS)*, İstanbul, Turkey. http://aisel.aisnet.org/ecis2016_rp/109

Lenhart, A. (2015, April). "Teen, social media and technology overview 2015." *Pew Research Center.* Retrieved from http://www.pewinternet.org/2015/04/09/teens-social-media-technology-2015/

McCombs, M. (1972). Mass media in the marketplace. *Journalism Monographs, 24.*

McDaniel, B. T. (2015). "Technoference": Everyday intrusions and interruptions of technology in couple and family relationships. In C. J. Bruess (Ed.), *Family communication in the age of digital and social media* (pp. 228–245). New York: Peter Lang Publishing.

McDaniel, B. T., & Coyne, S. M. (2016a). "Technoference": The interference of technology in couple relationships and implications for women's personal and relational well-being. *Psychology of Popular Media Culture 5*, 85–98. doi:10.1037/ppm0000065

McDaniel, B. T., & Coyne, S. M. (2016b). Technology interference in the parenting of young children: Implications for mothers' perceptions of coparenting. *The Social Science Journal 53*, 435–443. doi:10.1016/j.soscij.2016.04.010

McDaniel, B. T., Everest, J., & White, C. (2018). *Parent distraction with technology and its impact on parenting quality*. Poster presentation: Illinois Council on Family Relations. Normal, IL.

McDaniel, B. T., Galovan, A., Cravens, J., & Drouin, M. (2018). Technoference and implications for mothers' and fathers' couple and coparenting relationship quality. *Computers in Human Behavior 80*, 303–313.

McDaniel, B. T., & Radesky, J. (2017). *"I can't stop thinking about my phone": A daily diary study of parents distracted by technology and child behavior difficulties*. Paper presentation: Society for Research on Child Development. Austin, TX.

McDaniel, B. T., & Radesky, J. (2018a). Technoference: Parent distraction by technology and associations with child behavior problems. *Child Development 89*(1), 100–109. doi:10.1111/cdev.12822

McDaniel, B. T., & Radesky, J. (2018b). Technoference: Parent technology use, stress, and child behavior problems over time. *Pediatric Research* [online]. Available from https://www.nature.com/articles/s41390-018-0052-6

Messman, S. J., Canary, D. J., & Hause, K. S. (2000). Motives to remain platonic, equity, and the use of maintenance strategies in opposite-sex friendships. *Journal of Social and Personal Relationships 17*, 67–94.

Miller-Ott, A., & Kelly, L. (2015). The presence of cell phones in romantic partner face-to-face interactions: An expectancy violation theory approach. *Southern Communication Journal 80*, 253–270. doi:10.1080/1041794X.2015.1055371

Miller-Ott, A. E., & Kelly, L. (2016). Competing discourses and meaning making in talk about romantic partners' cell-phone contact with non-present others. *Communication Studies 67*, 58–76. doi:10.1080/10510974.2015.108887

Miller-Ott, A. E., Kelly, L., & Duran, R. L. (2012). The effects of cell phone usage rules on satisfaction in romantic relationships. *Communication Quarterly 60*(1), 17e34.

Nagpal, S. S., & Kaur, R. (2016). Nomophobia: The problem lies at our fingertips. *Indian Journal of Health & Wellbeing 7*, 1135–1139.

Oduor, E., Neustaedter, C., Odom, W., Tang, A., Moallem, N., Tory, M, & Irani, P. (2016). The Frustrations and Benefits of Mobile Device Usage in the Home when Co-Present with Family Members. In *Proceedings of the 2016 ACM Conference on Designing Interactive Systems* (pp. 1315–1327). 4–8 June, Brisbane, QLD, Australia. New York: ACM.

Ophir, E., Nass, C., & Wagner, A. D. (2009). Cognitive control in media multitaskers. *Proceedings of the National Academy of Sciences 106*(37), 15583–15587.

Padilla-Walker, L. M., Coyne, S. M., & Fraser, A. M. (2012). Getting a high-speed family connection: Associations between family media use and family connection. *Family Relations 61*, 426–440.

Papp, L. M., Danielewicz, J., & Cayemberg, C. (2012). "Are we Facebook official?" Implications of dating partners' Facebook use and profiles for intimate relationship satisfaction. *Cyberpsychology, Behavior, & Social Networking* 15, 85–90.

Pew Research Center (2015a, March 19). Internet seen as positive influence on education but negative influence on morality in emerging and developing nations. Retrieved from http://www.pewglobal.org/2015/03/19/internet-seen-as-positive-influence-on-education-but-negative-influence-on-morality-in-emerging-and-developing-nations/

Pew Research Center (2015b, April 1). "The Smartphone Difference". Retrieved from http://www.pewinternet.org/2015/04/01/us-smartphone-use-in-2015/

Pew Research Center (2015c, August 26). "Americans" views on mobile etiquette. Retrieved from http://www.pewinternet.org/2015/08/26/americans-views-on-mobile-etiquette/

Pew Research Center (2017, May 25). A third of Americans live in a household with three or more smartphones. Retrieved from: http://www.pewresearch.org/fact-tank/2017/05/25/a-third-of-americans-live-in-a-household-with-three-or-more-smartphones/

Przybylski, A. K., & Weinstein, N. (2012). Can you connect with me now? How the presence of mobile communication technology influences face-to-face conversation quality. *Journal of Social and Personal Relationships*, 30, 237–246. doi:10.1177/0265407512453827.

Radesky, J. S., Kistin, C., Eisenberg, S., Gross, J., Block, G., Zuckerman, B., & Silverstein, M. (2016). Parent perspectives on their mobile technology use: The excitement and exhaustion of parenting while connected. *Journal of Developmental & Behavioral Pediatrics* 37(9), 694–701.

Radesky, J. S., Kistin, C. J., Zuckerman, B., Nitzberg, K., Gross, J., Kaplan-Sanoff, M.,...& Silverstein, M. (2014). Patterns of mobile device use by caregivers and children during meals in fast food restaurants. *Pediatrics* 33(4), e843–e849.

Radesky, J., Miller, A. L., Rosenblum, K. L., Appugliese, D., Kaciroti, N., & Lumeng, J. C. (2015). Maternal mobile device use during a structured parent–child interaction task. *Academic Pediatrics* 15(2), 238–244.

Roberts, J. A., & David, M. E. (2016). My life has become a major distraction from my cell phone: Partner phubbing and relationship satisfaction among romantic partners. *Computers in Human Behavior* 54, 134–141. doi:10.1016/j.chb.2015.07.058

Rudi, J., Dworkin, J., Walker, S., & Doty, J. (2015). Parents' use of information and communications technologies for family communication: Differences by age of children. *Information, Communication & Society* 18(1), 78–93.

Sabatelli, R. M., & Shehan, C. L. (1993). Exchange and resource theories. In P. G. Boss, W. J. Doherty, R. LaRossa, W. R. Schumm, & S. K. Steinmetz (Eds.), *Sourcebook of family theories and methods: A contextual approach* (pp. 385–411). New York: Plenum Press.

Sagioglou, C., & Greitemeyer, T. (2014). Facebook's emotional consequences: Why Facebook causes a decrease in mood and why people still use it. *Computers in Human Behavior 35*, 359–363.

Sidelinger, R. J., Ayash, G., Godorhazy, A., & Tibbles, D. (2008). Couples go online: Relational maintenance behaviors and relational characteristics use in dating relationships. *Human Communication*, 11, 341–355.

Sprecher, S. (1986). The relation between inequity and emotions in close relationships. *Social Psychology Bulletin 49*, 309–321.

Stafford, L., & Canary, D. J. (1991). Maintenance strategies and romantic relationship type, gender, and relational characteristics. *Journal of Social and Personal Relationships 8*, 217–242.

Steiner-Adair, C., & Barker, T. H. (2013). *The big disconnect: Protecting childhood and family relationships in the digital age.* New York: HarperCollins.

Turner, J. C. (1991). *Social influence.* Milton Keynes, England: Open University Press and Pacific Grove, CA: Brooks/Cole.

Valkenburg, P. M., & Peter, J. (2009). The effects of instant messaging on the quality of adolescents' existing friendships: A longitudinal study. *Journal of Communication 59*, 79–97.

Van Lange, P. A. M., & Rusbult, C. E. (2012). Interdependence theory. In P. Van Lange, A. Kruglanski, & E. T. Higgins (Eds.), *Handbook of theories of social psychology*, Vol. 2 (pp. 251–272). Thousand Oaks, CA: Sage.

Wang, X., Xie, X., Wang, Y., Wang, P., & Lei, L. (2017). Partner phubbing and depression among married Chinese adults: The roles of relationship satisfaction and relationship length. *Personality and Individual Differences, 110*, 12–17.

Weisskirch, R. S. (2009). Parenting by cell phone: Parental monitoring of adolescents and family relations. *Journal of Youth and Adolescence 38*(8), 1123.

CHAPTER 8

....

OLDER ADULTS AND DIGITAL TECHNOLOGIES

....

MERYL LOVARINI, KATE O'LOUGHLIN,
AND LINDY CLEMSON

INTRODUCTION

....

THE impact of the aging of populations as a global phenomenon is now fully recognized and understood. Increased longevity, improved quality of life, increased spending on healthcare along with advances in preventative and curative interventions, and better social welfare support are generally accepted as factors allowing populations to live to increasingly older ages and for society to accept this as the "normalization" of an aging society (O'Loughlin, Kendig, & Browning, 2017; OECD, 2017; World Health Organization (WHO), 2015). While there is variation in the rate of population aging within and between both developed and developing countries, we do know that all countries are experiencing an unprecedented increase in life expectancy. As noted by the WHO (2015) and HelpAge International (2015 http://www.helpage.org/), for the first time ever it is expected that most people have an expectation of living to 60 years of age and beyond. This is supported by data from the Global AgeWatch Index (HelpAge International, 2015) indicating that by 2050 one in five people across the world will be aged over 60 years.

Along with the aging of populations, other factors at the individual, societal, and structural level have shaped the world we live in, altered our life experiences, and transformed our expectations across the life course. A key factor has been the influence of technology and the increasingly technologized nature of societies (Malinowsky, Kottorp, Patomella, Rosenberg, & Nygård, 2015); other key factors include the unprecedented increase in global mobility (Wilding & Baldassar, 2018), and changes in the traditional family structure through both social change and migration (Baldassar & Merla, 2014; Baldassar, Wilding, Boccagni & Merla, 2017).

This chapter considers the ways in which technology may intersect with aging at the individual and societal level by considering what we know about older people and their use of technology now, particularly digital technology, but also what the possibilities are for technology to assist people as they age in order to remain independent, healthy and socially connected. The chapter is structured around three key themes: 1) an overview of the context of population aging and the social and policy implications, including the focus on aging in place, well-being, and social inclusion; 2) the evolving technological landscape relevant to people as they age, including everyday technology use such as online engagement, and the opportunities and barriers that may need to be considered with older people's use of technology; and 3) the use of technology as it applies to health and aging in place for older people.

THE CONTEXT OF POPULATION AGING

Who are we referring to when we speak of "older" people? Entering older age is usually linked to retirement; that is, the ages at which people leave the paid workforce. In most developed countries this has been between 60 and 65 years for men and 55 and 60 years for women (O'Loughlin, Barrie, & Kendig, 2018). For the purpose of providing a chronological definition of "older people," this chapter uses 65 years as the entry point as that is still considered by many to be the expected retirement age, and for now generally denotes eligibility for retirement and access to forms of retirement income including the age pension.

Most of the demographic and social gerontological research interest in population aging has focused on the post-Second World War baby boom cohorts; that is, those born in the late 1940s through to the mid-1960s. These baby boomers are now entering older age in unprecedented numbers in most developed countries. They are seen as the future older generation and are redefining what aging looks like when compared with earlier generations, particularly through their familiarity with, and use of, technology in both public and private domains. The baby boomers lived through periods of economic prosperity and extensive social change, both of which shaped their attitudes, behaviors, expectations, and social networks, and continues to do so as they enter older age (O'Loughlin, Barrie, & Kendig, 2018; O'Loughlin & Kendig, 2017). While this is a generally accepted definition of baby boomers, there is as much diversity with and between baby boomer cohorts as there will be in any other generation, with clear differences in exposures and experiences across the life course when taking into account factors such as socio-economic status, gender, partnership status, ethnicity, and geographical location.

Current theoretical and policy frameworks applied around aging use positive discourses such as "productive aging," "successful aging," and "aging well" when referring to the need for people to maintain their independence, health, and well-being by remaining physically active and socially engaged (Kendig, 2017; Rowe & Kahn, 2015). Within these frameworks, there is an expectation that older people will age in place; that is, have a choice in where and how they age (Wiles, Leibing, Guberman, Reeve, &

Allen, 2012) and, for most, this means living in the community for as long as possible (Kendig, Gong, Cannon, & Browning, 2017; Faulkner, 2017). This policy approach fosters a sense of identity through independence, autonomy, roles, and relationships and supports the development of age-friendly communities (Kendig, 2017) that facilitate a sense of interaction and social connectedness at the personal and public level. There is an extensive literature on the benefits of remaining active and socially connected in later life (see Windsor, Curtis, & Luszcz, 2016); these benefits are at the individual as well as societal level and recognize the contribution older people continue to make in their retirement (Kendig, 2017).

In today's globally mobile world, people may be aging in place as migrants in another country or in their home country but distant from family members living in other parts of the world (Wilding & Baldassar, 2018). The availability and use of digital technologies, particularly communication technologies such as a mobile phone and Internet access, provide a means of supporting aging in place and facilitating community participation and social connectedness (Neves, Waycott, & Malta, 2018). Increasingly, technology is being used as a means of providing care at a distance for older family members, whether that is within a country or transnationally (Wilding & Baldassar, 2018).

Another major focus of aging-related research is around societal attitudes to aging and the stereotypical views of age and aging portrayed in the media, and also evident in workplaces (O'Loughlin & Kendig, 2017). These stereotypes very often relate to perceptions of the older person's resistance to change, being less capable of taking up new skills, and inflexible in their attitudes and behaviors. One depiction of this stereotypical view of older people is around their assumed limited use of technology, which is often referred to as the "digital divide" that separates younger and older generations (Neves, Waycott, & Malta, 2018).

Are older people technology-resistant? The next section considers the evolving technological landscape relevant to people as they age, including everyday technology, such as remote-control home appliances and smart phones, to the most sophisticated assistive technologies, including robotic devices for health and social care, and the opportunities and barriers that may need to be considered with people's use of technology as they enter and live through older ages. While technology is seen as central to socio-economic and cultural life generally and, more specifically, as a way to address or solve aspects of population aging, it also raises very specific questions regarding access, affordability, and other factors that may influence technology use for adults in later life.

Technology and Aging

Definitions

The McKell Institute (2015) identified the potential for technology to improve the lives of older people. Defining technology can be challenging, and it can encompass both everyday and assistive technologies. Everyday technologies can be defined as electronic, technical, and mechanical artifacts that exist in people's lives at home and in the community (Rosenberg, Kottorp, Winblad, & Nygård, 2009). Assistive technology refers to any device or system aimed at maintaining or improving an individual's function and participation (WHO, 2016a). As technologies advance and become more "mainstream", the lines between commonplace and assistive technologies are becoming more blurred. Technologies can be simple (e.g. pill organizers) through to complex (e.g. smart home technology) and a vast range of technologies is available (http://at-aust.org/ and http://www.eastin.eu/en/searches/products/index). However, technologies are more than devices or systems that support people. The use of technologies can contribute to a sense of self and identity and promote routines and habits that are meaningful (Parks, 2015).

Technology to Support Older People

With populations aging globally, attention is now turning to how technology can support older people to age well. The developing field of "gerontechnology," for example, has been defined as an interdisciplinary field of science for designing technology and environments to promote independent living, social participation, health, comfort, and safety for older people (e.g., http://www.gerontechnology.org/about.html). Given advances in and the use of computer-based, electronic, or "digital" technologies in society more broadly, the use of such technologies by older people is growing in importance.

Digital or computer-based technologies encompass computer hardware, devices, or software applications. Examples include information and communication technologies (ICTs), ambient assisted living systems (AALs), telemedicine and telehealth, assistive robots, and smart home systems (Barnett et al., 2017; Berkowsky, Rikard, & Cotten, 2015). Given their importance, many computer-based technologies have been included in the World Health Organization Priority Assistive Products List (WHO, 2016b).

Digital inclusion has been defined as the ability to make full use of digital technologies for enhancing health, well-being, and quality of life (Thomas et al., 2017). However, despite its importance, there is a gap in digital inclusion between older and younger people, with inclusion further declining with increasing age (Thomas et al., 2017; Berkowsky, Rikard, & Cotten, 2015). With low readiness reported for more complex technologies such as smart homes (Liu, Stroulia, Nikolaidis, Miguel-Cruz, & Rios Rincon, 2016), understanding the use and preferences of older people becomes critical if digital inclusion is to be realized. What, then, is known about older people's use of digital and computer-based technologies?

Digital Technology Use by Older People

A range of studies has explored the use of digital technologies by older people. In the US, current estimates show that 66 percent of Americans aged over 65 years use the Internet compared to 87 percent of adults aged 50–64 years and 97 percent of adults aged 30–49 years (https://www.statista.com/statistics/266587/percentage-of-internet-users-by-age-groups-in-the-us/). However, the use of technologies such as the Internet, home broadband, smartphones, tablets, and social media by older Americans has increased steadily over time (http://www.pewinternet.org/2017/05/17/tech-adoption-climbs-among-older-adults/). Despite this increased use, one-third of older Americans currently do not access the Internet, approximately half do not have broadband services in their home, and technology use is less common among older cohorts such as those aged over 80 years. Similar trends have been reported in Australia and the United Kingdom (https://www.acma.gov.au/theACMA/engage-blogs/engage-blogs/Research-snapshots/Digital-lives-of-older-Australians).

Internet use by older Australians has been estimated at 71 percent, which equates to well over two million people. Drawing on data collected across 2014 and 2015, the Australian Media and Communications Authority (ACMA, 2016) found that 85 percent of older Australian Internet users went online at least once a day, with 50 percent accessing the Internet three or more times a day. Average time online was seven hours a week with most access occurring in the home. Various devices were used to go online, with desktop computers (41 percent), laptops (27 percent), tablets (18 percent), and mobile phones (12 percent) most commonly reported. However, a growth in the use of tablets and mobile phones by older users was also reported. The most common activities included emailing (76 percent), followed by Internet banking (53 percent), paying bills (48 percent), and buying/selling online (40 percent). Older Australians are also using social media, with 43 per ent of Internet users aged 65 and over reporting using of Facebook (88 percent of users), Google+ (16 percent), LinkedIn (12 percent), Pinterest (8 percent), Twitter (4 percent), and Instagram (2 percent). Twenty-three percent of older Australian Internet users are also using communication apps, citing Skype, Facebook Messenger, and Facetime as the most preferred methods. While older Australians do stream video and music, they do so to a much lesser extent than their younger counterparts, with a strong preference for traditional entertainment media such as television and radio.

The findings of a study conducted in the US showed that older people use digital technologies to maintain family and social connections or to access information on health or everyday activities, particularly those aged 65–70 years, with higher education levels, and living with a spouse or partner (Vroman, Arthanet, & Lysack, 2015). Only 15 percent of older Australian Internet users use the Internet to access online government services or health and medical information, with a preference to make contact in person (ACMA, 2016). This finding is concerning given the increasing trend for information and services to be provided online as well as that these older users may benefit the most from such access.

Common reasons for non-use of the Internet among older people include lack of understanding of the benefits of access, little perceived value or interest, and perceptions that the Internet is too difficult and too costly to use. Other factors, such as computer anxiety, self-efficacy, and cognitive abilities can influence technology uptake, although these are factors that may be amenable to intervention and inform the design of supports suited to older users (Czaja, 2017).

When comparing users with non-users, users of technology reported being positive, satisfied with their activities, and more independent, while non-users felt intimidated and anxious about technology (Vroman et al., 2015). Non-users of the Internet aged over 65 in Australia are more likely to be out of employment, have no tertiary qualifications, have a lower income, live in rural areas, and be single (ACMA, 2016). Thus, it has been concluded that "the older population's age, education, attitudes, and personalities influence how they approach ICT" and that what is needed is a "community-centered socio-ecological model to factor in these dispositional characteristics in future ICT training programs" (Vroman, Arthanet, & Lysack et al., 2015, p. 156).

As the use of digital technologies by older people is increasing, so too is the use of such technologies by older people with particular health conditions. For example, in a study conducted in Australia investigating the Internet and eHealth practices of people with mild cognitive impairment or dementia, most participants regularly used mobile phones and computers, with most using email and stating a preference for eHealth interventions targeting cognition and memory (LaMonica et al., 2017).

TECHNOLOGY FOR HEALTH
AND AGING IN PLACE

Potential of Technology

While there is increasing use of the Internet and computer-based technologies generally by older people, research into their use of such systems for improving health, independence, care outcomes, and aging in place is in its infancy. The use of technology in the aged care sector more broadly has been underdeveloped and fragmented, leading to initiatives such as the development of a Technology Roadmap for the aged care sector in Australia (Barnett et al., 2017). Although the potential for technologies to deliver cost savings in home healthcare has been suggested, such technologies and associated services have yet to become fully mainstreamed, with mixed success reported with telecare and telehealth services in the United Kingdom, Scandinavia, and the United States (Berridge, Furseth, Cuthbertson, & Demello, 2014).

The Evidence

General Internet use has been associated with positive impacts on well-being outcomes among older people (Szabo, Allen, Stephens, & Alpass, 2018). While there is some evidence that home-based technologies can improve health outcomes, the evidence is limited by a lack of large, rigorously designed studies with few studies focusing on social connectedness, activities of daily living, leisure, and care support outcomes (Barnett et al., 2017; Czaja, 2018). Although a range of computer-based assistive technologies have been identified (e.g. general information and communication technologies, robotics, telemedicine, sensor technology, medication management applications, video games that may assist older people), the evidence is lacking on their impact on outcomes such as independence, fall risk, chronic disease management, social isolation, depression, well-being, and medication management, as well as their cost-effectiveness (Khosravi & Ghapanchi, 2016). A systematic review of studies investigating the effectiveness of assistive technologies (including digital and computer-based technologies) on the care of older people with dementia was unable to demonstrate a positive difference on outcomes such as independence, prompts and reminders, safety and security, leisure and lifestyle, or communication (Fleming & Sum, 2014).

Two key health issues associated with aging and remaining living independently are the risk of falls and forms of cognitive impairment such as dementia. The application of forms of technology to support people at risk of, or experiencing, these health issues have been considered and there is a significant research literature examining the efficacy of different technologies. A study by Hamm and colleagues (2016) provided a comprehensive review of the literature examining a range of fall technology systems and from this developed a conceptual falls prevention technology framework. They identified a number of challenges in developing technology-based applications for fall prevention, including recognizing the need for new systems that consider and address extrinsic falls risk factors, provide support for an environmental risk assessment process, and enable clients and practitioners to collaborate and engage in a shared decision-making process in any risk assessment and prevention activities.

Ienca and colleagues (2017) carried out a systematic review looking at the application of Intelligent Assistive Technology (IATs) for people with dementia. The purpose of this was to produce a comprehensive index of IATs that could assist people living with dementia. The study identified 539 IATs currently in use, or with potential for use, in dementia care. The findings report that the most common application is in providing support for Activities of Daily Living (n = 148) to assist in maintaining independence to support aging in place, followed by monitoring (n = 100), and physical (n = 88) and cognitive assistance (n = 85). A smaller number of applications address emotional support (n = 15) and aspects of social interaction (n = 64) and engagement (n = 22). The researchers concluded that IAT applications are expanding and provide great potential in dementia care, although there are limitations that need to be examined particularly around clinical effectiveness. At the same time, there needs to be a focus on facilitating successful adoption of IATs in dementia care; this should be done in a way that is most beneficial in meeting the needs of the person with dementia, their family, and carers. Another study (Pinto-Bruno, García-Casal, Csipke, Jenaro-Río, & Franco-Martín, 2017) provided a systematic review of research related to ICTs developed to facilitate social participation and improve quality of life for people with dementia. The six studies included in the review were undertaken across Europe (UK, Netherlands, Finland, Sweden) and included quantitative and qualitative approaches, with one using mixed methods. The findings identified ten interventions used by people with dementia, with the qualitative studies indicating that there are technologies available to foster social participation, but that there are also barriers evident in such technologies being widely accessed or used. The other two studies provided evidence that ICT interventions foster social behaviors more readily than non-technology interventions. The authors concluded that while there are technologies available to support social participation by people with dementia, there is a need for further rigorous research to develop more specific outcome measures.

Holthe and Wulff-Jacobsen's (2016) study of the Norwegian health system's focus on using "welfare technology" as a means to support independent living and quality of life for older adults, as well as reducing costs and increasing the quality of community-based care, identified several factors that need to be taken into account for such an approach to be successful. These include the establishment of an infrastructure for digital communication; any technology introduced must address an identified need and be specific to the individual's situation and context (e.g. dementia); and that health professionals need access to education and training to assess an individual's needs and preferences, and to identify and implement appropriate technology in the care recipient's home.

What Are the Issues?

Equitable access to computer-based technologies and ensuring sufficient knowledge of, and skills in, the use of these devices and services by older people, as well as the people who support them, is critical. For example, it has been shown that older people with chronic diseases are less likely to use the Internet to gain health information (Burns, Jones, Caputi, & Iverson, 2018). Understanding the needs, desires, and preferences of older people becomes a central consideration in this process as research by Malinowsky, Rosenberg, and Nygård (2014) highlighted that older people can have difficulties in adjusting to the ever-changing technology landscape (and in everyday technology use (Hedman, Nygård, Almkvist, & Kottorp, 2015). Additionally, technologies may not always enhance aging in place, which can create difficulties for the older adult and their family and carers. Thus, it is important to explore how technologies can and do support aging in place (Clemson & Laver, 2014).

Reasons why older people may use technology for aging in place include difficulties in independent living, personal beliefs, the influence of social networks, and the physical environment (Peek et al., 2016a). For older people, technology for aging in place can be considered a success if the needs and wishes of older people are prioritized, the technology is acceptable to them and provides benefits (Peek, Wouters, Luijkx, & Vrijhoef, 2016b). Yet how older people use forms of technology to support them to age in place is unclear, with most studies focusing on acceptance and expectations of technology rather than experiences following technology implementation (Peek et al., 2014).

Health professionals or service providers may not consider technologies as a way of facilitating health and aging in place outcomes for their older clients. For example, in a recent review investigating the effectiveness of interventions for older people receiving home care services, none of the included studies incorporated the use of digital or computer-based technologies (Sims-Gould, Tong, Wallis-Mayer, & Ashe, 2017). The findings from a recent scoping review of fourteen studies investigating the use of technology for improving activities of daily living outcomes in older adults with mild dementia found that the rationale underpinning the choice of technology was not clear and there was seemingly little involvement of the older person in technology selection (Patomella, Lovarini, Lindqvist, Kottorp, & Nygård, 2018). It was unclear what the goals of the older participants were or what outcomes were important to them. Tailoring of technologies and interventions to meet the specific needs of the older person was not featured in any of the included studies.

The involvement of families in enhancing technology use by older people has been suggested. As reported by Luijkx and colleagues (2015), adult children may be driven by well-being concerns for their aging parent, thus encouraging the use of specific technologies such as mobile phones or personal alarms, with varying levels of interest, acceptance, and use by the older person. Grandchildren, however, may encourage technology use for more social or entertainment purposes. Despite the potential of families to assist, some older people were ambivalent towards family assistance. Some of the issues identified include having choice in the technology, accepting help, the stigma associated with particular technologies, and challenges in learning new technologies.

Older adults are using e-health and m-health tools as part of formal health promotion programs, but support and motivation is needed. Little is known about how older adults use these tools to monitor and improve their health outside of formal health promotion programs (Kampmeijer, Pavlova, Tambour, Golinowska, & Grorrt, 2016). There are also ethical concerns, particularly in relation to adoption of smart home technologies, and most related to privacy and obtrusiveness, with issues of stigmatization, reliability, and maintenance of such systems as additional factors (Chung, Demiris, & Thompson, 2016).

It has been argued that older people wishing to use digital technologies should be supported and encouraged to do so, but that those who do not should be able to access information and services in the way that suits them (e.g., https://www.ageuk.org.uk/ search/?q=digital+inclusion). However, given the ubiquity of digital technologies, the focus may need to be on how best to support all older people in their use of digital technologies to avoid the possibility of becoming "digitally illiterate", and the negative consequences that may arise from this. For example, a digital coaching system has been suggested as a way of offering personalized services to older people to increase their participation in meaningful activities online (Blusi, Nilsson, & Lindgren, 2018).

So What Is Needed?

There are four key issues that need to be addressed when considering the introduction, application, and efficacy of forms of everyday and assistive technologies in the lives of older adults:

1) An understanding of the concerns and perceived lack of interest that may underpin a continued resistance to the use of technology;

2) Knowledge of the intervention(s) that can facilitate confidence, uptake, and sustained use of different technologies;
3) An understanding of the services and provisions available for training and ongoing support in ways that suit the preferences and capacities of older people;
4) Ensuring that older people have choice, voice, and control over the type, delivery, and provision of technologies to support them to live independently, be socially engaged, and maintain their quality of life.

Governments have recognized that support is needed. Be Connected, an Australia-wide initiative, aims to enhance confidence and skills in the use of digital technologies by all Australians, particularly older Australians (https://beconnected.esafety.gov.au). This initiative provides self-directed online learning resources as well as a network of community partners offering training courses or in-person support. Financial support to access or obtain some digital technologies can be accessed via the government's My Aged Care portal, including those offering specialized support to enhance care outcomes such as telecare services, remote monitoring, or specialized technologies such as communication devices or devices to enhance personal safety. Older people also have taken the initiative to upskill in digital technology use through the formation of organizations such the Australian Seniors Computing Clubs Association (http://www.ascca.org.au/).

WHERE TO FROM HERE?

Although technology continues to develop rapidly, and despite the potential benefits, older people's widespread adoption of technologies, including health-related ones, as a means of remaining independent in their own homes is limited (Kaye, 2017). Researching and evaluating the adoption and sustained use of such technologies presents many challenges. However, as Kaye (2017, p. 56) states, convincing evidence is needed that the "technology solution works, provides an advantage over the status quo and that it is worth spending money on."

Research carried out in the UK investigated the role of technologies in supporting older people to maintain their independence and remain physically and socially active. The Advancing Knowledge of Telecare for Independence and Vitality in Later Life (AKTIVE) project (2011–2014) explored how older people, particularly those at risk of falling or living with a cognitive impairment, could benefit from having access to various types of telecare technology to support them in remaining living in their own home. A particular strength of the project was that it brought together academic researchers in partnership with a company involved in the development and manufacture of health and social care technologies, together with a market research and commercialization company and an advisory board of experts drawn from the UK and Europe (Yeandle, 2013). Drawing on input from key stakeholders including the technology industry, market intelligence, social researchers and, most importantly, older people as end-users, the main aim of the project was to acquire an understanding of user needs; this was done by exploring how older people and their caring networks experienced, valued, responded to, and engaged with, forms of telecare technology. This, in turn, can be used to inform the development of telecare products and services to meet current and future needs. The main findings and conclusions drawn from the project were:

1. Telecare products and services should be seen as tools for living rather than as a clinical intervention;
2. Products and services should provide support and give timely assistance;
3. The aim should be to assist people as they age to live independently and remain socially and physically active for as long as possible; and
4. Older people will reject telecare and other technologies if the equipment and services offered are not appropriate to their needs (Yeandle, 2014).

The SENSE study (2014–2016) was directly linked to the outcomes from the AKTIVE project and included a sample of forty older people with sight and hearing impairments. The study revealed the group's need for a wider range of technologies (everyday and assistive), and how their experiences were affected by prior experience of assistive technologies, and in what ways they contributed to maintaining independence, activity, and relationships (Hamblin, Koivunen, & Yeandle, 2016).

Major international efforts are now underway to further build the evidence base around technologies available and/or needed to support older adults to remain independent and socially engaged through their later life stages. Examples include the UK-led project "Sustainable Care: Connecting People and Systems" (http://circle.group.shef.ac.uk/sustainable-care/) and the US National Institute on Aging initiative "Collaborative Aging (in Place) Research Using Technology", or (CART), a collaboration between the National Institutes of Health, academics, and industry experts to develop and test unobtrusive tools that record and track real-time changes in older adults' health status and activities (https://www.nia.nih.gov/news/nih-initiative-tests-home-technology-help-older-adults-age-place).

Conclusion

This chapter has provided an overview of the available evidence on technology use among older adults (65+ years) in developed countries, and identified aspects of the evolving technological landscape relevant to people as they age, including the use of everyday and assistive technologies. The evidence indicates that different forms of technology are being used across a range of domains to assist people as they age to remain independent, healthy, and socially connected. However, evidence shows that older people are generally slower to engage with digital technologies and to discontinue use with advancing age; this, to some degree, fosters the enduring and often ageist perception of a digital divide or exclusion between younger and older generations.

The use of technologies to better support older people, including those with complex needs, to age well within their community is acknowledged, although the use of technology in the health and social care sector remains underdeveloped and fragmented, limiting the realization of the potential benefits for individuals, service providers, and systems more broadly. There is a clear need for large-scale, rigorously designed studies to expand the evidence base on technologies that can support older people to age in place within their communities. While the technologies exist, the evidence to date is lacking on how these contribute in improving the health outcomes and quality of life of older adults.

From the available evidence, the main themes that emerge as central to the introduction, usefulness, and sustainability of technologies in the lives of older adults are focused on recognizing and addressing what might influence their perceived or actual resistance to technology use, understanding the preferences and capacities of older people, and providing services and supports to facilitate confidence, uptake, and continued use of technologies. Most critically, the focus must be on ensuring that older people have choice, voice, and control over the type, delivery, and provision of technologies to support them to live independently and maintain their quality of life and social connectedness.

References

Australian Media and Communications Authority (ACMA). (2016). Digital lives of older Australians. Retrieved from https://www.acma.gov.au/theACMA/engage-blogs/engage-blogs/Research-snapshots/Digital-lives-of-older-Australians

Baldassar, L., & Merla, L. (2014). *Transnational families, migration and the circulation of care*. New York: Routledge.

Baldassar, L., Wilding, R., Boccagni, P., & Merla, L. (2017). Ageing in place in a mobile world: New media and older people's support networks. *Transnational Social Review 7*(1), 2–9.

Barnett, K., Reynolds, K., Gordon, S., Hobbs, D., Maeder, A., & Sergi, C. (2017). *Developing a technology roadmap for the Australian aged care sector: Literature review*. A Report commissioned by the Aged Care Industry IT Council (ACIITC). Clovelly Park: Medical Device Research Institute, Flinders University.

Berkowsky, R. W., Rikard, R.V., & Cotten, S. R. (2015). Signing off: Predicting discontinued ICT usage among older adults in assisted and independent living. In J. Zhou & G. Salvendy (Eds.), *Human aspects of IT for the aged population: Design for everyday life* (pp. 389–398). Cham: Springer.

Berridge, C., Furseth, P. I., Cuthbertson, R., & Demello, S. (2014). Technology-based innovation for independent living: Policy and innovation in the United Kingdom, Scandinavia, and the United States, *Journal of Aging & Social Policy 26*, 213–228. doi:10.1080/08959420.2014.899177

Blusi, M., Nilsson, I., & Lindgren, H. (2018). Older adults co-creating meaningful individualized social activities online for healthy ageing. *Studies in Health Technology and Informatics 247*, 775–779.

Burns, P., Jones, S. C., Caputi, P., & Iverson, D. (2018). Are older Australians with chronic disease online? *Health Promotion Journal of Australia 29*(1), 72–78. doi:10.1002/hpja.5

Chung, J., Demiris, G., & Thompson, H. J. (2016). Ethical considerations regarding the use of smart home technologies for older adults: An integrative review. *Annual Review of Nursing Research 34*, 155–181. doi:10.1891/0739-6686.34.155

Clemson, L., & Laver, K. (2014). Active ageing and occupational therapy align. *Australian Occupational Therapy Journal 61*, 204–207. doi:10.1111/1440-1630.12125

Czaja, S. J. (2017). The potential role of technology in supporting older adults. *Public Policy & Aging Report 27*(2), 44–48. doi:10.1093/ppar/prx006

Czaja, S. J. (2018). The role of technology in supporting social engagement among older adults. *Public Policy and Aging Report 27*(4), 145–148. doi:10.1093/ppar/prx034

Eurostat (2016). Internet access and use statistics—households and individuals. Retrieved from https://ec.europa.eu/eurostat/statistics-explained/index.php?oldid=379591

Faulkner, D. (2017). Housing and the environments of ageing. In K. O'Loughlin, C. Browning, & H. Kendig (Eds.), *Ageing in Australia: Challenges and opportunities* (pp. 173–191). New York: Springer.

Fleming, R. & Sum, S. (2014). Empirical studies on the effectiveness of assistive technology in the care of people with dementia: A systematic review. *Journal of Assistive Technologies 8*(1), 14–34. doi:10.1108/JAT-09-2012-0021

Hamblin, K., Koivunen, E.-R., & Yeandle, S. (2016). *Keeping in touch with technology? Using telecare and assistive technology to support older people with dual sensory impairment.* Report of study commissioned by SENSE. Centre for International Research on Care, Labour and Equalities (CIRCLE), University of Sheffield. Retrieved from https://www.sheffield.ac.uk/polopoly_fs/1.558815!/file/SENSE-Final-report-WEB.pdf

Hamm, J., Money, A. G., Atwal, A., & Paraskevopoulos, I. (2016). Fall prevention intervention technologies: A conceptual framework and survey of the state of the art. *Journal of Biomedical Informatics 59*, 319–345.

Hedman, A., Nygård, L., Almkvist, O., & Kottorp, A. (2015). Amount and type of technology use over time in older adults with cognitive impairment. *Scandinavian Journal of Occupational Therapy 22*(3), 196–206. doi:10.3109/11038128.2014.982172

HelpAge International. Retrieved from http://www.helpage.org/

Holthe, T. & Wulff-Jacobsen, I. (2016). Matching user needs to technology in dementia care: Experiences with the alma supervisor educational program. *Family Medicine and Primary Care Review 18*(4), 492–496. doi:10.5114/fmpcr.2016.63710

Ienca, M., Fabrice, J., Elger, B., Caon, M., Scoccia Pappagallo, A., Kressig, R.,...Wangmo, T. (2017). Intelligent assistive technology for Alzheimer's disease and other dementias: A systematic review. *Journal of Alzheimer's Disease 56*(4), 1301–1340. doi:10.3233/JAD-161037

Kampmeijer, R., Pavlova, M., Tambour, M., Golinowska, S., & Grorrt, W. (2016). The use of e-health and m-health tools in health promotion and primary prevention among older adults: A systematic literature review. *BMC Health Services Research 16*(Suppl 5), 290. doi:10.1186/s12913-016-1522-3

Kaye, J. (2017). Making pervasive computing technology pervasive for health and wellness in aging. *Public Policy and Aging Report 27*(2), 53–61. doi:10.1093/ppar/prx005

Kendig, H. (2017). Directions and choices on ageing for the future. In K. O'Loughlin, C. Browning, & H. Kendig (Eds.), *Ageing in Australia: Challenges and opportunities* (pp. 263–279). New York: Springer.

Kendig, H., Gong, C., Cannon, L. & Browning, C. (2017). Preferences and predictors of aging in place: Longitudinal evidence from Melbourne, Australia. *Journal of Housing for the Elderly 31*(3), 259–271. doi:10.1080/02763893.2017.1280582

Khosravi, P. & Ghapanchi, A. H. (2016). Investigating the effectiveness of technologies applied to assist seniors: A systematic literature review. *International Journal of Medical Informatics 85*(1), 17–26. doi:10.1016/j.ijmedinf.2015.05.014

LaMonica, H., English, A., Hickie, I., Ip, J., Ireland, C., West, S.,…Naismith, S. (2017). Examining Internet and eHealth practices and preferences: Survey study of Australian older adults with subjective memory complaints, mild cognitive impairment or dementia. *Journal of Medical Internet Research 19*(10), e358. doi:10.2196/jmir.7981

Liu, L. Stroulia, E., Nikolaidis, I., Miguel-Cruz, A., & Rios Rincon, A. (2016). Smart homes and home health monitoring technologies for older adults: A systematic review. *International Journal of Medical Informatics 91*(2016), 44–59. doi:10.1016/j.ijmedinf.2016.04.007

Luijkx, K., Peek, S., & Wouters, E. (2015). "Grandma, you should do it—it's cool": Older adults and the role of family members in their acceptance of technology. *International Journal of Environmental Research and Public Health 12*, 15470–15485. doi:10.3390/ijerph121214999

Malinowsky, C., Kottorp, A., Patomella, A-H., Rosenberg, L., & Nygård, L. (2015). Changes in the technological landscape over time: Relevance and difficulty levels of everyday technologies as perceived by older adults with and without cognitive impairment. *Technology and Disability 27*(3), 91–101. doi:10.3233/TAD-150431

Malinowsky, C., Rosenberg, L., & Nygård, L. (2014). An approach to facilitate healthcare professionals' readiness to support technology use in everyday life for persons with dementia. *Scandinavian Journal of Occupational Therapy 21*(3), 199–209. doi:10.3109/11038128.2013.847119.

McKell Institute (2015). Positive disruption: Healthcare, ageing and participation in the age of technology. Retrieved from https://mckellinstitute.org.au/research/reports/positive-disruption/

Neves, B., Waycott, J., & Malta, S. (2018). Old and afraid of new communication technologies? Reconceptualising and contesting the "age-based digital divide." *Journal of Sociology 54*(2), 236–248. doi:10.1177/1440783318766119

OECD. (2017). *Health at a glance 2017: OECD indicators*. Paris: OECD Publishing.

O'Loughlin, K., Barrie, H., & Kendig, H. (2018). Australia's baby boomers as the future older generation. In T. Klassen, M. Higo, N. Dhirathiti, & T. Devasahayam (Eds.) *Ageing in Asia-Pacific: Interdisciplinary and comparative perspectives* (pp. 237–254). London: Routledge.

O'Loughlin, K. & Kendig, H. (2017). Attitudes to Ageing. In K. O'Loughlin, C. Browning, & H. Kendig (Eds.), *Ageing in Australia: Challenges and opportunities* (pp. 29–45). New York: Springer.

O'Loughlin, K., Kendig, H., & Browning, C. (2017). Introduction. In K. O'Loughlin, C. Browning, & H. Kendig (Eds.), *Ageing in Australia: Challenges and opportunities* (pp. 1–10). New York: Springer.

Parks, J. (2015). Home-based care, technology, and the maintenance of selves. *HEC Forum 27*(2), 127–141. doi:10.1007/s10730-015-9278-4

Patomella, A-H., Lovarini, M., Lindqvist, E., Kottorp, A., & Nygård, L. (2018). Technology use to improve activities of daily living in older persons with mild dementia or mild cognitive impairment: A scoping review. *British Journal of Occupational Therapy* [online]. doi:10.1177/0308022618771533

Peek, S., Luijkx, K., Rijnaard, M., Nieboer, M., van der Voort, C., Aarts, S.,...Wouters, E. (2016a). Older adults' reasons for using technology while aging in place. *Gerontology 62*(2), 226–237. doi:10.1159/000430949

Peek, S., Wouters, E., Luijkx, K., & Vrijhoef, H. (2016b). What it takes to successfully implement technology for aging in place: Focus groups with stakeholders. *Journal of Medical Internet Research 18*(5), e98. doi:10.2196/jmir.5253

Peek, S., Wouters, E., van Hoof, J., Luijkx, K., Boeije, H., & Vrijhoef, H. (2014). Factors influencing acceptance of technology for aging in place: A systematic review. *International Journal of Medical Informatics 83*(4), 235–248. doi:10.1016/j.ijmedinf.2014.01.004

Pinto-Bruno, Á. C., García-Casal, J. A., Csipke, E., Jenaro-Río, C., & Franco-Martín, M. (2017). ICT-based applications to improve social health and social participation in older adults with dementia: A systematic literature review. *Aging & Mental Health 21*(1), 58–65.

Rosenberg, L., Kottorp, A., Winblad, B., & Nygård, L. (2009). Perceived difficulty in everyday technology use among older adults with or without cognitive deficits. *Scandinavian Journal of Occupational Therapy 16*, 216–226.

Rowe, J. W. & Kahn, R. L. (2015). Successful aging 2.0: Conceptual expansions for the 21st century. *The Journals of Gerontology Series B: Psychological Sciences and Social Sciences 70*(4), 593–596. doi:10.1093/geronb/gbv025

Sims-Gould, J., Tong, C., Wallis-Mayer, L., & Ashe, M. (2017). Reablement, reactivation, rehabilitation and restorative interventions with older adults in receipt if home care: A systematic review. *Journal of the American Medical Directors Association 18*(8), 653–663. doi:10.1016/j.jamda.2016.12.070

Szabo, A., Allen, J., Stephens, C., & Alpass, F. (2018). Longitudinal analysis of the relationship between purposes of Internet use and well-being among older adults. *Gerontologist 58*(2) [online]. doi:10.1093/geront/gny036

Thomas, J., Barraket, J., Wilson, C., Ewing, S., MacDonald, T., Tucker, J., & Rennie, E. (2017). *Measuring Australia's digital divide: The Australian digital inclusion index 2017.* Melbourne: RMIT University, doi:10.4225/50/596473db69505

Vroman, K., Arthanet, S., & Lysack, C. (2015). Who over 65 is online? Older adults' disposition toward information communication technology. *Computers in Human Behavior, 43*, 156–166. doi:10.1016/j.chb.2014.10.018

Wiles, J., Leibing, A., Guberman, N., Reeve, J., & Allen, R. E. S. (2012). The meaning of "Ageing in Place" to older people. *The Gerontologist 52*(3), 357–366. doi:10.1093/geront/gnr098

Windsor, T., Curtis, R., & Luszcz, M. (2016). Social engagement in late life. In H. Kendig, P. McDonald, & J. Piggott (Eds.), *Population ageing and Australia's future* (pp185–204). Canberra: ANU Press.

World Health Organization. (2015). *World report on ageing and health.* Retrieved from: http://www.who.int/ageing/events/world-report-2015-launch/en/

World Health Organization. (2016a). *Assistive devices and technologies.* Retrieved from: http://www.who.int/disabilities/technology/en/

World Health Organization. (2016b). *Priority assistive products list.* Retrieved from: http://www.who.int/phi/implementation/assistive_technology/EMP_PHI_2016.01/en/

Wilding, R. & Baldassar, L. (2018). Ageing, migration and new media: The significance of transnational care. *Journal of Sociology 54*(2), 1–10. doi:10.1177/1440783318766168.

Yeandle, S. (2013). Introduction. In *AKTIVE Consortium Research Report, vol.1: The role of telecare in meeting the care needs of older people: Themes, debates and perspectives in the literature on ageing and technology.* Retrieved from http://www.aktive.org.uk/downloads/AKTIVE_Report_Vol_1_16.05.pdf

Yeandle, S. (2014). *AKTIVE: Advancing knowledge of telecare for independence and vitality in later life: A report of the AKTIVE conference.* University of Leeds, 8–9 April 2014. Retrieved from http://www.aktive.org.uk/downloads/HealthKTN%20AKTIVE%20casestudy.pdf

PART III

INTERACTION AND INTERACTIVITY

CHAPTER 9

TEXTESE: LANGUAGE IN THE ONLINE WORLD

NENAGH KEMP

INTRODUCTION

THE reach and importance of digital communication is expanding every year, and with it comes an ever-increasing need to interact via written language. Worldwide, people of all ages communicate via a range of digital methods, including text message, Internet forums, Facebook, Twitter, and email. The written language of online communication does not typically adhere to the conventions of standard written language. Instead, it represents a more casual style, characterized by abbreviations, omissions, and insertions, and is often termed "textese," with reference to its initial popularity in text messages. This chapter explores the rise of textese, its changing nature, and its use by people interacting in the online world.

The earliest widespread use of digital communication was through the use of text messages, because of the relative cheapness and accessibility of mobile (cell) phones. The first text message was sent in 1992, and initial take-up was gradual. However, by 2014 there were nearly as many mobile phone subscriptions as people on the planet (ITU, 2014). Phone ownership rates continue to grow in developing countries (Ericsson, 2015), and text messaging remains the most widely used form of written communication worldwide (Portio, 2015). The small screens and alphanumeric keyboards of earlier models of mobile phones made message composition time-consuming and cumbersome: the multi-press entry method required the user to press each key one to four times to obtain the desired character. For example, pressing the "7" key once would result in a *p*, or four times would result in an *s*. The later adaption of predictive text meant that people could instead press each key just once and then accept or choose from a list of possible words (e.g., 4-6-6-3 could spell *good* or *home*). Furthermore, phone users were constrained by a one hundred and sixty character limit, as well as the fact that each text incurred a charge.

These rather laborious and costly input methods provided a strong incentive for people to keep their messages brief, and to shorten the spelling of the words that they did include. However, the abbreviations common to early text messages were not all invented for this medium: they were drawn from the much earlier, if much less widespread, conventions of computer-mediated communication, or CMC. These conventions together reduced the number of keystrokes, and gave the communication the feel of casual, spoken interaction. Compared to the specialized world of CMC, text messaging was quickly adapted by a much larger and more diverse group of users who enthusiastically embraced the many ways that written language could be changed for digital communication. This chapter uses the term "textism" to describe the individual adapted spelling in the writing style now widely referred to as "textese" (e.g., Drouin & Driver, 2014; Verheijen, 2013; Kemp, Wood, & Waldron, 2014), but a range of other terms also exist, including "textish" (Faulkner & Culwin, 2005), "text speak" (Drouin & Davis, 2009), and "techspeak" (Cingel & Sundar, 2012).

Of course, textese is not confined to text messages. Today, people continue to communicate via both Internet forums and text messages, but also do so through a host of other applications, especially social media sites, which may be accessed via a range of digital devices, including mobile phones, tablets, and full-size computers. None of these media are as physically constrained as the small screens and keyboards of early mobile phones, but textese-style writing is still characteristic of most digital communication.

CATEGORIZING TEXTISMS

Textese has been discussed by many different researchers, who have come up with various ways to categorize the types of changes that people make to standard writing. Most of these schemes share a core set of categories but vary in the detail in which they differentiate them and in the extent to which they recognize certain spellings as constituting types of textisms. For example, most authors have a category for words with abbreviated spellings, but they may also break down abbreviations into finer-grained categories, including shortenings (omission of word-final letters, e.g., *Tues* for *Tuesday*), contractions (omission of word-internal letters, often vowels, e.g., "msg" for message), and clippings (omission of word-final letter, e.g., "comin" for coming). Sound-based spellings have been further differentiated into words deliberately misspelled phonetically (e.g., "skool" for school), as well as words or word sections spelled with a letter, number, or symbol homophone (e.g., "r u" for are you, "gr8" for great, "th@" for that). Most researchers have also noted the use of initialisms and/or acronyms (such as "lol" for laugh(ing) out loud), and many acknowledge the inclusion of spellings that represent accent- or slang-based pronunciations (such as "de" for the, "wanna" for want to), and the widespread use of symbols (such as those representing emoticons (☺), kisses (*xxx*), and hugs (ooo). Some researchers have also counted apparently accidental misspellings (e.g., univresity), and the unconventional use of capitals and punctuation (both omission and overuse, e.g., "im happy, but ARE YOU??!!").

Across the first two decades of the twenty-first century, a number of researchers seem to be converging towards a set of textism categories that evolved from work by Shortis (2001), Thurlow and Brown (2003), and Crystal (2008), which was further elaborated by Plester, Wood, and Joshi (2009), and more recently by Drouin and Driver (2014), Kemp and Grace (2017), and Lyddy, Farina, Hanney, Farrell, and O'Neill (2014). Table 1 presents the set of categories that covers many of the kinds of changes frequently made to standard spelling.

Other researchers have looked in more detail at the use of conventional punctuation (Frehner, 2008; Ling & Baron, 2007) and at variations in how punctuation and capitalization are used in digital writing (e.g., Cingel & Sundar, 2012; Lyddy et al., 2014). In a series of studies examining the representation of grammar in text messages, Wood and colleagues examined the use of punctuation and capitalization in more detail (including which types are most often omitted/reduplicated, and when and where punctuation is

Table 1 Categories of textisms frequently used in analyses of digital messages

Textism category	Definition	Examples
Shortenings	Letters omitted, whether word-final or word-internal	*txt* for *text, Sat* for *Saturday*
Homophones	Letters/numbers used for their pronunciation	*u* for *you, 2night* for *tonight*
Initialisms	Initials of a phrase	*omg* for *Oh my God*
Accent stylizations	Representation of a particular accent/slang term	*wiv* for *with, maybs* for *maybe*
Nonstandard spellings	Apparently deliberate, phonetic respelling of word	*pleez* for *please, thanx* for *thanks*
Spelling errors	Apparently accidental misspelling of word	*shuold* for *should*
Conventional symbols		*@* for *at*
Emoticons	Composed of punctuation marks, or picture "emojis"	:) ☺
Kisses, hugs		*xxx, ooo*
Omitted capitals	From start of sentence or proper nouns	*good morning sarah*
Omitted punctuation	Most often apostrophes, commas, full stops; sometimes replaced with emoticons	*Its on today right* ☹
Extra capitals	Used for emphasis	*SO ANGRY*
Extra punctuation	Usually question and exclamation marks	*Do you like it???!!!*
Extra letters, words	Used for emphasis or expressiveness	*cooooool* for *cool; good good* for *good*

replaced by emoticons/kisses), as well as the omission of grammatical words and word parts (e.g., pronouns, *Going out now*, and grammatical endings, *I am go to school now*) (Kemp et al., 2014; Wood, Kemp, & Waldron, 2014; Wood, Kemp, Waldron, & Hart, 2014).

There is no need for every research group to categorize textisms in the same way: each group will have a different reason for concentrating on the categories that they do, and the range of categories used by message senders seems to be constantly evolving. Nevertheless, the method of categorization can lead to slightly different estimations of the extent to which people use textese. There are some abbreviations that are not unique to the language of digital communication, and researchers therefore disagree on whether they should be counted as textisms, e.g., *Wed* for *Wednesday, wanna* for *want to*, and standard acronyms such as *BBC*. Similarly, researchers are inconsistent in their decisions to count apparently accidental misspellings as textisms. Part of the decision may stem from whether it is important to consider the care that the message writer has taken with their composition. Finally, slightly different estimates of textism use can result from categorizing textisms in terms of the individual words affected, or in terms of the number of changes made. For example, the single word *I'm* written as *im* can be counted as one textism, because it constitutes a single changed word (e.g., Plester et al., 2009) or as two, because it omits both a capital and an apostrophe (e.g., De Jonge & Kemp, 2012).

This chapter focuses on the use of the English language in digital communication, but textese has been observed in virtually all the languages in which people communicate online (e.g., Crystal, 2008; Thurlow & Poff, 2013). At least in messages on older phones, we might see instances of shortenings (e.g., French "l'aniv" for anniversaire, birthday; Malaysian "ank" for anak, child), letter/number homophones (e.g., Italian "c" for ci, us; Spanish "to2" for todos, all; Chinese "555" [the sound of] crying), phonetic spellings (e.g., French "pti" for petit, small; Italian "perke" for perché, why), initialisms (e.g., Chinese "mm" for meimei, younger sister; Italian "tvb" for ti voglio bene, I love you), and accent stylization (e.g., French "moua" for moi, me; German "leida" for leider, unfortunately). Just as in English, the omission of standard punctuation and capitalization, as well as the insertion of extra letters, extra punctuation, and emoticons/emojis, are widespread in worldwide digital communication.

The textism categories discussed so far are reasonably fine-grained, but some research has grouped them into broader categories. For example, Herring and Zelenkauskaite (2009) categorized textisms in Italian text messages according to whether characters were removed from (abbreviations) or added to (insertions) standard writing. The authors used these broader groupings to compare the texting habits of women and men (finding that women used more of both abbreviations and insertions than did men), and concluded that, at the time of the study, abbreviations were more common than insertions. Rosen, Chang, Erwin, Carrier, and Cheever (2010) also created two broader categories to compare textisms that were considered either "linguistic" or "contextual." Linguistic textisms involved changes to the spelling/representation of words (here, shortenings, acronyms, and the omission of capitals and apostrophes), whereas contextual textisms added emotional content to the message (via the insertion of emoticons, special characters—as in *frown*—and the use of capitals for emotional emphasis). Rosen and colleagues used these two broad categories of textisms to examine patterns of association with formal and informal writing in young adults with and without a college education.

Similarly, Grace and Kemp (2015, 2017) divided their textisms into three categories: contractives, expressives, and other. Contractive textisms were those that omit characters, and included shortenings, homophones, omitted apostrophes, initialisms, and conventional symbols. Expressive textisms add emotional or expressive tone to the message by adding characters; specifically, emoticons, kisses and hugs, and extra punctuation, letters, and words. Textisms that did not fit either of these broader categories, and that did not consistently change the number of characters, were grouped separately as "other": omitted or extra capitals, accent stylization, and nonstandard (deliberate) or incorrect (apparently accidental) spelling. As discussed later, the proportions of contractive and expressive textisms seem to be changing over time and seem to be represented differently according to the way that textisms are collected. Thus, categorizing textism types more broadly may provide information that may be overlooked if only the finer-grained categories are considered.

COLLECTING DIGITAL MESSAGES

Researchers examining the language of digital communication must decide how best to collect examples of messages. Until recently, many of these decisions focused on the language of text messages alone, but they apply equally to research on other modalities of digital communication. Accessing personal messages, especially when participants are children, can raise ethical issues, including the understandable desire that people may have to keep their messages and their contact details private. Accordingly, some researchers have instead chosen to ask participants to write messages especially for the study, or to provide estimates about aspects of their messaging behavior. However, in avoiding potential ethical problems, these methods can reduce the ecological validity of the information collected. The methodology chosen thus needs to take into account the age of participants, the resources of the researchers, and the focus of their research questions.

Self-Report

When researchers wish to explore the reasons behind the use of a particular linguistic style, they may hold focus group discussions, or individual structured interviews (e.g., Blair & Fletcher, 2011; Grinter & Eldridge, 2003). Despite the time-consuming nature of these methodologies, they do provide detailed information about people's linguistic decisions that other methods do not. More common is self-report via written survey (e.g., Drouin & Davis, 2009; Rosen et al., 2010). For example, participants are asked to estimate the number of messages they send/receive per day, or how often they use textisms in their messages. Self-report is quick, but it may not be very accurate, especially for children, particularly as the daily number and range of messages continues to increase. Providing a Likert scale can provide more detailed information (e.g., Bodomo, 2010; Drouin & Davis, 2009). However, people might differ in their views of what constitutes "often" or "rarely," and they may also be subject to response bias. For example, university students responding to a university-based researcher may under-report their textism use so as not to be thought of as immature or poor spellers, while children might over-report their textism use to emphasize their tech-savviness or social status.

Kemp and Grace (2017) found that the potential for unreliability in self-report of textism use is high. They asked seven cohorts of first-year undergraduates to rate the extent of their textism use on a three-point scale, and also collected examples of their previously sent text messages. Participants who reported using textisms "most of the time" in fact used the same proportion (19 percent of words written) as those who reported using them "some of the time," which also was not substantially different from the proportion produced by those who reported "never" using textisms at all (13 percent of words written).

Message Translation

Other researchers have asked participants to rewrite individual words or whole messages, for example, "as they normally would in a text message" (e.g., Coe & Oakhill, 2011; Kemp, 2010). This method provides control over the number and type of words being translated, and thus allows the precise counting of textisms and clear comparisons across participants. It also avoids any of the ethical issues of asking for access to participants' own sent messages. However, asking people to translate words and messages in this way could lead them to produce more textisms than they normally would, especially if the researchers have deliberately chosen words that are often written as textisms, and the words are not necessarily representative of those that participants would normally choose.

Message Elicitation

An alternative method is to provide a scenario and then elicit messages by asking participants to write to a friend about that scenario (e.g., Plester et al., 2009; Plester, Lerkkanen, Linjama, Rasku-Puttonen, & Littleton, 2011). Obviously, this does not allow such exact comparisons across messages as does translation, but participants can compose more representative messages. This method thus represents a reasonable compromise between ecological validity and experimenter control.

Naturalistic Messages

The best way to see how people use written language in digital communication is to examine examples of messages that they have sent in real life. Numerous researchers have invited participants to provide a small set of recently sent messages (e.g., Bodomo, 2010; Holtgraves, 2011; Kemp & Grace, 2017). This method has been used successfully for both adults and children, and participants only choose messages that they are comfortable sharing and change any names to pseudonyms. Ideally, these messages are forwarded to a central number for collection, but in order to avoid the potential ethical and financial issues that this method raises, many researchers have instead asked participants to paste, transcribe, or photograph their messages verbatim for later analysis. One drawback is that participants might deliberately choose messages which under- or overestimate their usual textese levels (because of perceived experimenter demands), but generally, the messages collected appear to be reasonably representative of real-life language use in digital communication.

A more resource-intensive, but effective, way to analyze the language of naturalistic messages is to amass a large message database to interrogate. Researchers may make use of publicly available message collections (e.g., Bieswanger, 2007), invite people to contribute to a new collection (e.g., Tagg, 2009), or collect messages as they are sent to a public forum (e.g., Herring & Zelenkauskaite, 2009). Alternatively, researchers may arrange with participants to automatically collect all the messages sent from their device over a given time period (e.g., Tossell et al., 2012; Underwood, Rosen, More, Ehrenreich, & Gentsch, 2012). Of course, not all research groups have the resources to use this method. However, these kinds of large, non-selected databases are likely to provide a more realistic picture of the range of written forms that people use in their digital communication.

THE NATURE OF DIGITAL COMMUNICATION LANGUAGE

The linguistic style of digital messages approximates spoken language more than it does written language (Turner, Abram, Katíc, & Donovan, 2014), and as well as being casual, it often includes the pause fillers, expressions of emotion, and even representations of facial expression that would normally be expected in spoken discourse. However, the extent to which such devices are used seems to vary with a number of factors, including message modality, year, and available technology, and with a number of personal characteristics, such as the message writer's gender, age, and conventional literacy skills. Many of the studies considering textese use across these factors have focused on text messages, but other modalities have been considered as well. Rates of textese use in text messages have varied widely. However, the most common range (in terms of percentage of textisms per message words) in English-speaking adults seems to be about 20 to 25 percent (e.g., Drouin & Davis, 2009; Kemp et al., 2014; Lyddy et al., 2014; Thurlow & Brown, 2003), although some authors have seen textese use closer to 5 to 10 percent of words (e.g., Holtgraves, 2011; Ouellette & Michaud, 2016). In terms of modality differences, young adults have been reported to use more textese in text messages than in instant messages, emails, and social networking messages (Drouin & Davis, 2009; Frehner, 2008; Kemp & Clayton, 2016; Ling & Baron, 2007).

Emoticons

The use of emoticons is a particularly distinctive part of CMC and has received a reasonable amount of attention across writing modalities. The word "emoticon" is a portmanteau of "emotion" and "icon." These expressive faces constructed of punctuation marks and letters, such as [:)] and [:-( ], were introduced as early as 1982 by computer scientist Scott Fahlmann, who saw the need to mark jokes or sarcasm in online communication. In recent years, more advanced technology has instead facilitated the use of "emojis"—pictures of facial expressions and other images that can be inserted into messages. These remain popular in part because interaction via CMC does not easily allow the interpretation of emotional expression or state, and the use of emoticons/emojis can help to clarify these (Aldunate & Gonzalez, 2017). As well as indicating humor or irony, emoticons are used to strengthen expressive linguistic acts (such as greetings and appreciation) and to soften directive acts (such as corrections and requests) (Skovholt, Gronning, & Kankaanranta, 2014).

Increasingly, emoticons are used in place of conventional punctuation, especially in sentence-final position (Kemp et al., 2014), to amplify the apparent emotional intensity of the message to a greater extent than could be achieved even with exaggerated punctuation. For example, Ip's 2002 study of undergraduates showed that the emotional content of instant messages was perceived to be more extreme when written with emoticons than with standard punctuation. Ip also found that exaggerated punctuation (three exclamation marks) did not have this same effect, even when combined with upper-case letters. Positive (happy-face) emoticons influenced the perceived emotional intensity of the instant messages more than negative (sad-face) emoticons. With the increased use of emoticons in phrase-final position, the meaning of conventional punctuation may even attract novel interpretation. Participants rated text message responses as less sincere when they ended in a (conventional) full stop than when this full stop was omitted (Gunraj, Drum-Hewitt, Dashow, Upadhyay, & Klin, 2016). When the exchanges of messages were instead presented as handwritten notes, the perceived "insincerity" of the conventional punctuation mark disappeared. These findings underscore the changing nature of written language in the digital realm and serve as a reminder that one person's interpretation of a message might be quite different from another's, depending on the impressions they take from different elements of the message.

Determinants of Differences
in Textese Use

Differences in the use of textese seem, in a few instances, to stem from differences in spoken language. For example, Shaw (2008) noted that the word "with" was respelled more often as "wit" in the US and "wiv" in the UK on Internet homepages. However, it seems that differences observed between countries with the same language and similar economic conditions (e.g., Australia and Canada) are more likely to reflect differences in the technology used in each country. Grace, Kemp, Martin, and Parrila (2012) found that Australian undergraduates used more textese than Canadian undergraduates in their text messages. The hypothesis that more exposure (in terms of years of experience or messages sent per day) to textese would lead to greater use of textese was not supported. Instead, it seems that the greater use of textese by the Australian students reflected their greater number of previous years with alphanumeric, rather than full qwerty, keyboards, which had encouraged their use of textese abbreviations and respellings.

Textese use also seems to be changing over time, in terms of both extent and type, and this change appears to be in step with the changes in widely available technology. Some of these differences undoubtedly correlate with writers' age: e.g., sending text messages is most popular among teenagers and young adults than other age groups (see Lenhart, 2015), and a range of studies suggest that the use of textese generally tends to diminish with age (e.g., Drouin & Driver, 2014; Kemp & Grace, 2017; Plester, Wood, & Bell, 2008; Wood, Meachem, et al., 2011), regardless of the time of testing (Ling, 2010). The greater use of textese in younger writers might reflect differences in attitudes as people develop as communicators and mature away from perceiving creative respelling as a novelty. Earlier studies of young people's text messaging observed the extensive use of creative respellings such as letter/number homophones (e.g., 2moro), unconventional spellings (e.g., fone), and accent stylization (e.g., anuva) (e.g., Plester et al., 2008, 2009). However, more recent work suggests that these more creative spellings are losing favor. In a study with adolescents, Turner and colleagues (2014) found that the use of number homophones and of vowel-removing contractions (often seen as emblematic of textese) did not appear in the top 50 percent of their participants' textese usage. Sanchez-Moya and Cruz-Moya (2015) found that teenagers used more textese than adults in their instant messages, and although teenagers used stylized spelling, they were most likely to omit non-essential (often grammatical) elements, and to use emoticons in their messages. The changing use of textese across time has been examined more systematically in annual assessments of the use of textese in the naturalistic text messages of Australian first-year psychology students (Grace & Kemp, 2015; Kemp & Grace, 2017). Between 2009 and 2015, the use of textese gradually diminished from about 25 percent of words per message, to about 12 percent over the last few years of data collection. Furthermore, the incidence of contractive textisms (those that reduce the number of characters) has decreased, as has the use of miscellaneous textisms that do not consistently add to, or reduce, word length. The use of expressive textisms (which increases the number of characters and the emotive content of a message) grew at first, but now seems to be declining in line with the overall decrease in textism use. This data collection process is ongoing, and should show whether textese use continues to decline or remains steady at about 12 percent in this population. The use of textese in other modalities has not received detailed study across time, but similar patterns of decline in textese use seem likely as the novelty of this writing style wears off, even with the increasing popularity of smaller, handheld devices for Internet use (rather than desktop or laptop computers).

Textese use seems to vary with the gender of the writer. This conclusion has not been universal: several studies have shown no differences in the use of textese by males and females (De Jonge & Kemp, 2012; Drouin & Driver, 2014). However, most researchers testing this theory have reported gender differences in the extent and nature of textese use. Such differences appear across age groups, with more textisms used by females than males in samples of children (Plester et al., 2009), teenagers (Varnhagen et al., 2010) and adults (Herring & Zelenkauskaite, 2009; Lyddy et al., 2014; Rosen et al., 2010). More detailed analyses have revealed variations in the types of textisms produced. Men seem to use more informal devices than women, such as omitted apostrophes (Squires, 2012), dropped "Gs" (e.g., goin) and swear words (Holtgraves, 2011). In assessments of naturalistic text messages, Kemp and Grace (2017) found that female undergraduates used more textisms overall than males, but that while men used more contractive than expressive textisms, women used contractives and expressives about equally. Most research seems to agree on the greater use by women of emotional and expressive devices, including emoticons (Tossell et al., 2012, Wolf, 2000). A fine-grained examination of undergraduates' text messages by Holtgraves (2011) revealed that women wrote longer messages overall and used significantly more emoticons and expressive lengthening (e.g., hiiiiii) than men, as well as more social words and (personal) pronouns. Similar patterns seem to persist across modalities. In analyses of the tweets of large samples of Twitter users, women use more emoticons, expressive lengthening, (extra) punctuation, and pause fillers than men (Bamman et al., 2014; Rao et al., 2010). These gender differences conform to broader gender differences in language use, with men deliberately diverging from some expected standards of writing (Squires, 2012), and women varying their writing style to communicate expressiveness, friendliness, and social warmth (Herring & Zelenkauskaite, 2009).

TEXTESE AND LITERACY

Relationships between Textese and Literacy in Children

As young people became increasingly enthusiastic users of digital communication, especially via text message, the popular media, parents, and educators began to worry that frequent exposure to textese would have a detrimental effect on their conventional literacy skills. The concern was that children who had already learned to read and write would forget how to spell some words conventionally if they saw too many textese spellings. The danger for younger children just developing their literacy skills was that they would never learn to spell words properly in the first place. Studies by both Burt and Long (2011) and Dixon and Kaminska (1997) showed that, for both adults and children, seeing incorrectly spelled words made it more difficult to then spell those words correctly. However, these empirical studies have focused on words that are relatively difficult to spell in the first place. In general, words that are abbreviated or otherwise re-spelled in digital communication seem to be short, frequently used words that are not often misspelled, such as "you", "are", "message", and "please". In general, it seems unlikely that a child who saw and wrote "u" daily on their phone would eventually forget how to spell "you". However, there is some feasibility to the notion that frequently reading and writing creative or unusual spellings for particular words, or not having to worry about distinctions between words, e.g., to/too, or the use of upper-case letters or apostrophes, might begin to undermine young people's conventional literacy skills.

Here, the research evidence led to a compelling and perhaps counterintuitive conclusion: generally, there exists a *positive* relationship between children's use of textisms and their linguistic skill. Two important early studies revealed that 10- to 12-year-old British children who used a greater number of textisms in a translation task (Plester et al., 2008) and an elicitation task (Plester et al., 2009) scored better on tasks of verbal reasoning, word reading, phonological awareness (the ability to manipulate the sounds of spoken language), and (in one of the two studies) spelling. Similarly, in a sample of 10- to 12-year-old Australian children, Kemp and Bushnell (2011) found positive correlations between faster and more accurate reading aloud of text messages written in textese, and scores on spelling, reading, and non-word reading tasks.

Studies with children who have written and spoken language difficulties have produced slightly different conclusions. Coe and Oakhill (2011) found that poorer readers spent more time on their phones than better readers, but that better readers were faster at reading text messages and used more textese. Veater, Plester, and Wood (2011) looked at the textese use and literacy skills of children with dyslexia (aged 10 to 13 years) compared to children matched for reading age and for chronological age. Although the three participant groups used similar levels of textese overall, the dyslexic group used fewer of the types of textisms that seem to rely on the ability to manipulate language sounds (e.g., phonetic abbreviations, letter/number homophones, accent stylizations), and more initialisms and symbols. Unlike the reading- and chronological age-matched controls, the children with dyslexia did not show a positive correlation between their use of textese and their scores on standard literacy tasks. Durkin, Conti-Ramsden, and Walker (2011) observed that 17-year-olds with Specific Language Impairment (SLI) sent fewer text messages than their typically developing peers and were less likely to reply to a message from the researchers. The replies that they did send were shorter, and included fewer textisms, than those of their peers. Taken together, these findings suggest that young people who are already struggling with some aspects of language might be further challenged by the linguistic and social requirements of digital communication. Not being able to reply as easily, or as creatively, as their friends might result in these students being less often included in digital or real-life conversations and interactions, with potential implications for the development and maintenance of social status and self-esteem. This is an area which requires further research.

Most studies that have considered the links between textese use and literacy skills have been cross-sectional. They have yielded valuable data but have not determined the direction of causality. However, two later studies have shown the possible nature of the relationship. A longitudinal project with British 8- to 12-year-olds examined the relationship between textese use and language skills one year apart. Wood, Meachem, et al. (2011) assessed the children's literacy and language skills, and analyzed their most recent two days' worth of sent text messages at the start of the school year, and again one year later. With stringent analyses controlling for initial age, reading, spelling, verbal IQ, and phonological awareness, the researchers found that initial textese use accounted for growth in spelling skill (although not reading skill) over the course of the year. In contrast, initial reading and spelling skill did not account for growth in textese use. These results suggest that the use of textese contributes to phonological skill, which itself contributes to literacy scores. Wood, Jackson, Hart, Plester, and Wilde (2011) went on to conduct an intervention study to test whether increasing exposure to textese could actually help to improve conventional literacy scores. They worked with 9- to 12-year-olds who did not already own a mobile phone and gave phones to half of the sample to use over the course of ten weeks on weekends and a school break. The group who had received phones showed numerical gains in their reading, spelling, and phonological awareness skills over the ten-week period. The researchers concluded that this had probably been too short a time for major gains to be observed. However, the findings provide strong evidence that children's literacy experienced no harm from exposure to textese, and also showed that their use of textese explained a small but significant amount of variance in their spelling scores. These two studies thus provide clear evidence that at least at the time of the research, reading and producing textisms seemed to boost children's spelling skills, most likely by providing practice in phonological processing. Thus, children who might otherwise not engage in (so much) reading and writing practice would be spending time creating and deciphering textisms. This, in turn, would exercise their ability to manipulate the sound structure of words—an important aspect of literacy skill.

Relationships between Textese and Grammar in Children

One further aspect of literacy examined more recently with respect to textese exposure is grammar, or more specifically, grammatically determined spelling patterns. Such patterns are often ignored in digital communication, and so it is possible that children could never learn to use them correctly, and adolescents and adults may forget how. In English (and other languages), grammar can influence spelling at the level of single or multiple words, and determines several orthographic conventions, and all of these are frequently varied in textese-style spelling. For example, regular English past-tense verbs are spelled with a final -ed, and regular plurals with -s, but phonetic respellings can create textisms such as "I fixt it, thanx". Textisms also include both common (e.g., you're, gonna) and creative combinations of grammatical structures (e.g., shuda for should have). Finally, standard capitalization and punctuation are frequently omitted (e.g., Ling & Baron, 2007; Rosen et al., 2010), or (in the case of punctuation) replaced with emoticons or multiple punctuation marks (De Jonge & Kemp, 2012; Province, Spencer, & Mendel, 2007). Young texters are particularly likely to omit message-final full stops, although not question marks, and to use lower-case "i" for pronominal "I" (even if this means circumventing autocorrection), to assert their own "voice" (Turner et al., 2014). The violation of grammatical conventions in digital communication often seems to represent a deliberate choice, rather than linguistic laziness or ignorance.

Only a handful of studies have considered the potential links between the violation of grammatical conventions in digital communication and children's grammatical and general linguistic ability. Cingel and Sundar (2012) reported a negative correlation between textism use in the sent messages of American children in grades six to eight and their performance on a written grammatical task. However, participants coded their own textism use (which seems unlikely to provide reliable data, especially for the children with the weakest linguistic skills), and the negative relationship was between grammatical skill and general linguistic textisms, rather than the specifically grammar-based ones of capitalization and punctuation. In contrast, three studies by Wood and colleagues failed to identify clear relationships between grammatical violations when texting and children's scores on a range of grammatical and linguistic tasks. Specifically, this research group saw no significant relationship between children's spoken or written grammatical understanding and their tendency to violate grammatical conventions in their sent text messages (Wood, Kemp, Waldron, & Hart, 2014), and in a follow-up study, no significant relationship between their growth in such grammatical understanding over a year and their naturalistic grammatical violations (Wood, Kemp, & Waldron, 2014). Furthermore, there was no clear pattern between children's ability to correct grammatical errors in researcher-provided text messages and the errors that they had themselves made in sent messages (Kemp et al., 2014). Apparently, although the use of textese does not improve the use of grammatical spelling patterns (as it seems to improve spelling more generally), it certainly does not hinder it.

Relationships between Textese and Literacy/Grammar in Adults

The evidence from studies with children is clear: exposure to textese is associated with, and may even improve, literacy skills. However, the evidence from studies with adults for links between textese use and conventional reading and writing scores is mixed. There have been limited findings of a positive relationship in adults: Kemp (2010) found that Australian undergraduates who were quicker at composing text messages to dictation (whether in standard English or textese) had higher spelling and reading scores, and those who made fewer errors in reading aloud messages written in textese had higher reading scores and better awareness of word structure (morphological awareness). Being skilled at analyzing word structure might help with creating and deciphering textisms based on word structure. However, this study was conducted with researcher-provided phones that required multipress entry, but some participants had already begun to use qwerty keyboards. Thus, these results might not be fully representative of adults' naturalistic textese use.

Other studies have found negative correlations: another group of Australian undergraduates translated written text messages into "how they would send them to a friend" (De Jonge & Kemp, 2012). These students showed negative relationships between their use of textese and their scores on tasks of spelling, reading real and nonsense words, and morphological awareness. However, these negative relationships were mostly accounted for by the participants' frequency of sending text messages.

Mixed relationships were observed in a larger study of Australian and Canadian undergraduates (Grace, Kemp, Martin, & Parrila, 2014). Although few correlations reached significance overall, the patterns were different for the two samples: Canadian students showed a negative correlation between textese use and spelling scores, and Australian students, between textese use and both timed reading of nonwords and phonological awareness. In an online study of young Americans, Rosen et al. (2010) reported some significant correlations between self-reported use of textese and the quality of their formal and informal writing, but the direction of these correlations was not consistent as it varied with the type of writing sample and with whether the writers had some or no tertiary education. Finally, other studies have shown no significant correlations at all between adults' use of textese and their conventional literacy scores. In a series of studies with differing designs, Drouin and colleagues showed no significant relations between textese use and scores on spelling, reading, and reading fluency in samples of US undergraduates, whether textese use was self-reported (Drouin, 2011) or taken from sent messages (Drouin & Driver, 2014), and virtually no differences were seen on performance on these tasks by students divided according to whether they reported either using, or never using, textese in their messages (Drain & Davis, 2009). More recently, Ouellette and Michaud (2016) reported few significant correlations between use of textese (in a translation task and in their naturalistic messages) and scores on standardized tests of spelling, reading, and vocabulary. However, these participants used so few textisms that it would have been difficult to find significant relationships in this sample.

The few studies to have considered whether exposure to textese might be related to adults' use of grammar-based spelling patterns have also provided mixed results. Wood and colleagues had university students provide examples of their sent text messages, and also complete grammatical and linguistic tasks. There was one unexpected positive relationship: those who performed better on a task of written grammar made more use of apparently deliberate ungrammatical word forms in their sent messages (such as "you iz", Wood, Kemp, & Waldron, 2014). Undergraduates who enjoy "playing around" with grammatical forms might well be those with the best grammatical understanding. However, there were also some indications that making grammatical violations when composing messages might indicate poorer grammatical skill. Undergraduates who did more poorly on choosing the most grammatically appropriate spelling of nonwords were more likely to make errors of capitalization and punctuation in their own messages (Wood, Kemp, Waldron, & Hart, 2014). Furthermore, young adults who left numerous grammatical errors uncorrected in researcher-provided messages also had the greatest tendency to make grammatical errors when writing text messages (Kemp et al., 2014). Thus, there exists the possibility that young adults who violate grammatical conventions in their digital communication (with the exception of seemingly deliberate, playful violations) might be those with a poorer grasp of conventional grammar.

In sum, the relationship between textese use and conventional literacy skills in adults is far from clear. The difference between this and the positive relationships seen in children can probably be explained by the fact that the adults in the studies published to date would have consolidated their reading and writing skills before they were exposed to textese. Thus, it seems unlikely that their ability to read and spell words would be strongly affected by seeing or creating textisms in their messages. Instead, there is probably a range of additional factors affecting adults' use of textese. Grace and colleagues (2014) suggest that these factors could include the sender's reading and writing skill, but also the technology available on the phone (e.g., whether the phone corrects spelling and punctuation errors), the time pressure under which the message is being composed, the sender's opinion of the importance of writing in a style that suits the recipient versus the perceived importance of writing in standard language. Additionally, experimental attention has generally focused on the building blocks of literacy: single-word reading, spelling, and grammar. There has been much less work on the higher-level skills of the literate individual: the ability to comprehend written language more broadly, to communicate ideas in writing in a cohesive manner, and in a register appropriate for the modality. These variables all deserve further experimental attention.

USING TEXTESE IN THE SOCIAL CONTEXT: REASONS AND RESPONSES

Writers might use textese to save time and effort, but they also use it for social reasons. Young adults, at least, seem to have clear opinions on when it is suitable to use or avoid textese. For example, in a sample of US university students, 75 percent thought it was appropriate to include textese when writing informal emails to friends, but only 6 percent considered it appropriate to do so when writing to a university teacher (Drouin & Davis, 2009). Similarly, Australian students rated the use of textese as more suitable along a continuum—from friends (most suitable) to family members of the same age, to older family members, to strangers (least suitable) (Kemp & Grace, 2017). These ratings are borne out in people's behavior: in a study that considered the extent of textese actually produced in both elicited and naturalistic messages, students used more textisms when writing to their friends than to classroom peers, and more to classroom peers than to university lecturers (Kemp & Clayton, 2016). These findings suggest that, rather than simply peppering all their messages with textese, young people use the more sophisticated strategy of considering their recipient and varying their use of textisms to suit that person and their role.

There is some evidence that young people vary their use of textese not only to suit the recipient, but also to match the recipient's own level of textese. This pattern is congruent with the broader tendencies articulated in the well-known Communication Accommodation Theory (e.g., Giles, 2016): people adjust their accent, vocabulary, writing style, and even gestures to more closely match that of their communicative partner to show affinity for that partner. In line with this theory, Plester and colleagues (2011) found that Finnish and British children modified their use of textese according to the extent to which recipients had used textese themselves. In contrast, an experimental study by Crowe (2014) saw no effects of recipients' use of textese (absent, low, or high) on the level of textese produced by message senders in primary school or high school. It is likely that the reasons for modulating one's use of textese to suit the recipient's use depends on a range of individual and contextual factors, and further work is necessary to determine the important factors in this relationship.

The other side of the self-presentation coin is that message recipients form their own judgments about message senders on the basis of how messages are written. A number of studies have suggested that just such judgments could have important implications in the classroom or workplace. Much of this research has involved asking people to look at digital messages that include or avoid textese, and to rate the writers on various characteristics. Some such studies have been placed in the university context. For example, university instructors were presented with emails written by students making simple requests, some written informally (including textese, but also unconventional grammar and punctuation) and others formally (in standard English) (Stephens, Houser, & Cowan, 2009). The instructors were less likely to grant the requests of the students who had written informal emails, and also rated these informal writers as less likable and less credible than those who had written more formally. Lewandowski and Harrington (2006) asked undergraduates to imagine that they were professors assessing the essays of students who had written an accompanying email using or avoiding textese. The researchers found that the participants rated those who had used textese as having put less effort into their essays. Other research has looked at the impact of standard or more casual written language (including textese) in the workplace context. University students presented with emails from fictitious employees that were written either in standard English or with various spelling and grammatical errors tended to rate the writers of non-standard emails as less polite, less likable, less competent, and less careful (Jessmer & Anderson, 2001), and as less intelligent, less conscientious, and less trustworthy (Vignovic & Thompson, 2010), than the writers of emails in standard English. The inclusion of textese itself has a similarly negative impact on many readers' perceptions. University students who were presented with Facebook posts that contained or avoided textese judged the writers who had used textese as less intelligent and less employable than those who avoided it (Scott, Sinclair, Short, & Bruce, 2014). Whether the use of textese is extensive or more limited seems not to matter: Fullwood, Quinn, Chen-Wilson, Chadwick, and Reynolds (2015) found that participants rated fictitious job applicants as less open, less conscientious, and as lower in self-esteem if they used low or high levels of textese than if they wrote in standard English.

Taken together, these results suggest that people feel less positive about, and less helpful towards, those who use ungrammatical written language, including textese, in contexts traditionally seen as relatively formal—the university and the workplace. This kind of judgment obviously has implications for the way that writers' achievements are perceived, as well as potentially for their progress and success at university or at work. It is clearly important to think about one's use of language, and also one's assumptions about others' use of language, when communicating in the digital realm, in order to avoid potentially long-lasting repercussions from the choice of language style.

CONCLUSIONS

The use of textese arose mainly for reasons of efficiency. However, its popularity has continued not only because it allows messages to be composed more quickly, but also to express the emotion and the "voice" of the message writer. There are many ways in which written language can vary in digital communication and these changes seem to depend on the time and technology of the message, as well as the abilities and opinions of the writer. Different recipients will view the use of textese in different ways, and so it is well worth considering how a message might be judged by the person receiving it, especially as regards academic or workplace recipients. Nevertheless, people's choice to include textese does not usually represent a reduction in their ability to use standard written language, but rather an extra skill—the knowledge of how to vary their written language in a way that suits the modality and the recipient of the communication.

This chapter discussed research conducted over the last decade or two. In earlier studies, especially, the textisms that people used tended to be quite creative, and featured abbreviations and often phonetic respellings. More recently, textisms have been more likely to omit grammatical features and to include representations of expression and emotion, while technology will sometimes automatically correct non-standard spellings. Furthermore, the message writers in previous studies had usually consolidated, or at least started to learn, their written language skills before they had much exposure to textese. Today, children are seeing textese at increasingly young ages, and some adults might engage with written language in the online environment more often than in more standard forms. Thus, the nature of people's knowledge of formal and more casual written language, and its relationship to their literacy and social skills, is likely to be changing over time. It looks as though the use of textese is likely to continue, and ongoing research will be necessary to track its changing nature, and to monitor how the language of digital communication is used by both message senders and message receivers.

References

Aldunate, N., & Gonzalez-Ibanez, R. (2017). An integrated review of emoticons in computer-mediated communication. *Frontiers in Psychology*, *7*, 1–6. doi: 10.3389/fpsyg.2016.02061

Bamman, D., Eisenstein, J., & Schnoebelen, T. (2014). Gender identity and lexical variation in social media. *Journal of Sociolinguistics*, *18*, 135–160. doi: 10.1111/josl.12080

Bieswanger, M. (2007). 2 abbrevi8 or not 2 abbrevi8: A contrastive analysis of different space- and time-saving strategies in English and German text messages. *Texas Linguistics Forum*, *50*. Retrieved May 11, 2018, from http://salsa.ling.utexas.edu/proceedings/2006/Bieswanger.pdf

Blair, B. L., & Fletcher, A. C. (2011). "The only 13-year-old on planet Earth without a cell phone": Meanings of cell phones in early adolescents' everyday lives. *Journal of Adolescent Research*, *26*, 155–177. doi: 10.1177/0743558410371127

Bodomo, A. B. (2010). *Computer-Mediated Communication for Linguistics and Literacy: Technology and Natural Language Education*. Hershey, NY: Information Science Reference. Retrieved from http://www.classjump.com/sideeg/documents/CMC.pdf

Burt, J. S., & Long, J. (2011). Are word representations abstract or instance-based? Effects of spelling inconsistency in orthographic learning. *Canadian Journal of Experimental Psychology*, *65*, 214–228. doi: http://dx.doi.org/10.1037/a0023708

Cingel, D. P., & Sundar, S. S. (2012). Texting, techspeak, and tweens: The relationship between text messaging and English grammar skills. *New Media & Society*, *14*, 1304–1320. doi: 10.1177/1461444812442927

Coe, J. E. L., & Oakhill, J. V. (2011). "text is ez f u no h2 rd": The relation between reading ability and text-messaging behaviour. *Journal of Computer Assisted Learning*, *27*, 4–17. doi: 10.1111/j.1365-2729.2010.00404.x

Crowe, S. M. (2014). *Tutees @ skool: How students and teachers use and respond to the language of digital communication*. (Unpublished honours thesis). University of Tasmania.

Crystal, D. (2008). *Txtng: The gr8 db8*. Oxford: Oxford University Press.

De Jonge, S., & Kemp, N. (2012). Text-message abbreviations and language skills in high school and university students. *Journal of Research in Reading*, *35*, 49–68. doi 10.1111/j.1467-9817.2010.01466.x

Dixon, M., & Kaminska, Z. (1997). Is it misspelled or is it mispelled? The influence of fresh orthographic information on spelling. *Reading and Writing: An Interdisciplinary Journal*, *9*, 483–498. doi: 10.1023/A:1007955314533

Drouin, M. A. (2011). College students' text messaging, use of textese and literacy skills. *Journal of Computer Assisted Learning*, *27*, 67–75. doi: 10.1111/j.1365-2729.2010.00399.x

Drouin, M., & Davis, C. (2009). R u txting? Is the use of text speak hurting your literacy? *Journal of Literacy Research*, *41*, 46–67. doi: 10.1080/10862960802695131

Drouin, M. & Driver, B. (2014). Texting, textese and literacy abilities: A naturalistic study. *Journal of Research in Reading*, *37*, 250–267. doi: 10.1111/j.1467-9817.2012.01532.x

Durkin, K., Conti-Ramsden, G., & Walker, A. J. (2011). Txt lang: Texting, textism use and literacy abilities in adolescents with and without specific language impairment. *Journal of Computer Assisted Learning*, *27*, 49–57. doi: 10.1111/j.1365-2729.2010.00397.x

Ericsson (2015). *Ericsson mobility report*. Retrieved from http://www.ericsson.com/res/docs/2015/ericsson-mobility-report-june-2015.pdf

Faulkner, X., & Culwin, F. (2005). When fingers do the talking: A study of text messaging. *Interacting with Computers, 17*, 167–185. doi: 10.1016/j.intcom.2004.11.002

Frehner, C. (2008). *Email—SMS—MMS: The linguistic creativity of asynchronous discourse in the new media age*. New York, NY: Peter Lang.

Fullwood, C., Quinn, S., Chen-Wilson, J., Chadwick, D., & Reynolds, K. (2015). Put on a smiley face: Textspeak and personality perceptions. *Cyberpsychology, Behaviour, and Social Networking, 18*, 147–151. doi: 10.1089/cyber.2014.0463

Giles, H. (2016). The social origins of CAT. In H. Giles (Ed.), *Communication Accommodation Theory: Negotiating personal relationships and social identities across contexts* (pp. 1–12). Cambridge: Cambridge University Press.

Grace, A., & Kemp, N. (2015). Text messaging language: A comparison of undergraduates' naturalistic textism use in four consecutive cohorts. *Writing Systems Research, 7*(2), 220–234. doi: 10.1080/17586801.2014.898575

Grace, A., Kemp, N., Martin, F. H., & Parrila, R. (2012). Undergraduates' use of text messaging language: Effects of country and collection method. *Writing Systems Research, 4*, 167–184. doi: 10.1080/17586801.2012.712875

Grace, A., Kemp, N., Martin, F. H., & Parrila, R. (2014). Undergraduates' text messaging language and literacy skills. *Reading and Writing: An Interdisciplinary Journal, 27*, 855–873. doi: 0.1007/s11145-013-9471-2

Grinter, R. E., & Eldridge, M. (2003). *Wan2tlk?: Everyday text messaging*. In *Proceedings of ACM Conference on Human Factors in Computing System, CHI 2003* (pp. 441–448). Fort Lauderdale, FL, April 5–10 2003. Retrieved from http://www.cc.gatech.edu/~beki/c24.pdf

Gunraj, D. N., Drum-Hewitt, A. M., Dashow, E. M., Upadhyay, S. S. N., & Klin, C. M. (2016). Texting insincerely: The role of the period in text messaging. *Computers in Human Behaviour, 55*, 1067–1075. doi: 10.1016/j.chb.2015.11.003

Herring, S. C., & Zelenkauskaite, A. (2009). Symbolic capital in a virtual heterosexual market: Abbreviation and insertion in Italian iTV SMS. *Written Communication, 26*, 5–31. doi: 10.1177/0741088308327911

Holtgraves, T. (2011). Text messaging, personality, and the social context. *Journal of Research in Personality, 45*, 92–99. doi: 10.1016/j.jrp.2010.11.015

International Telecommunication Union (ITU) (2014). *ICT facts and figures 2015*. Retrieved from http://www.itu.int/en/ITU-D/Statistics/Pages/stat/default.aspx

Ip, A. (2002). The impact of emoticons on affect interpretation in instant messaging. Retrieved from http://www.amysmile.com/doc/emoticon_paper.pdf

Jessmer, S. L., & Anderson, D. (2001). The effect of politeness and grammar on user perceptions of electronic mail. *North American Journal of Psychology, 3*, 331–346. Retrieved from http://mydba.lagrana.net/articles/09/ART09.pdf

Kemp, N. (2010). Texting vs. txting: Reading and writing text messages, and links with other linguistic skills. *Writing Systems Research, 2*, 53–71. doi: 10.1093/wsr/wsq002

Kemp, N., & Bushnell, C. (2011). Children's text messaging: Abbreviations, input methods and links with literacy. *Journal of Computer Assisted Learning, 27*, 18–27. doi: 10.1111/j.1365-2729.2010.00400.x

Kemp, N., & Clayton, J. (2016). University students vary their use of textese in digital messages to suit the recipient. *Journal of Research in Reading, 40*, S141–S157. doi: 10.1111/1467-9817.12074

Kemp, N., & Grace, A. (2017). Txting across time: Undergraduates' use of "textese" in seven consecutive first-year psychology cohorts. *Writing Systems Research, 9*, 82–98. doi: 10.1080/17586801.2017.1285220

Kemp, N., Wood, C., & Waldron, S. (2014). do i know its wrong: Children's and adults' use of unconventional grammar in text messaging. *Reading and Writing, 27*, 1585–1602. doi: 10.1007/s11145-014-9508-1

Lenhart, A. (2015). *Teens, social media & technology overview 2015*. Pew Research Center. Retrieved from http://www.pewinternet.org/2015/04/09/teens-social-media-technology-2015/

Lewandowski, G., & Harrington, S. (2006). The influence of phonetic abbreviations on evaluation of student performance. *Current Research in Social Psychology, 11*, 215–226. Retrieved from http://www.uiowa.edu/~grpproc/crisp/crisp11_15.pdf

Ling, R. (2010). Texting as a life phase medium. *Journal of Computer-Mediated Communication, 15*, 277–292. doi: 10.1111/j.1083-6101.2010.01520.x

Ling, R., & Baron, N. (2007). Text messaging and IM: Linguistic comparison of American college data. *Journal of Language and Social Psychology, 26*, 291–298. doi: 10.1177/0261927X06303480

Lyddy, F., Farina, F., Hanney, J., Farrell, L., & O'Neill, N. K. (2014). An analysis of language in university students' text messages. *Journal of Computer-Mediated Communication, 19*, 546–561. doi: 10.1111/jcc4.12045

Ouellette, G. & Michaud, M. (2016). Generation Text: Relations among undergraduates' use of text messaging, textese, and language and literacy skills. *Canadian Journal of Behavioural Science, 48*, 217–221. doi: 10.1037/cbs0000046

Plester, B., Lerkkanen, M.-K., Linjama, L. J., Rasku-Puttonen, H., & Littleton, K. (2011). Finnish and UK English pre-teen children's text message language and its relationship with their literacy skills. *Journal of Computer Assisted Learning, 27*, 37–48. doi: 10.1111/j.1365-2729.2010.00402.x

Plester, B., Wood, C., & Bell, V. (2008). Txt msg n school literacy: Does texting and knowledge of text abbreviations adversely affect children's literacy attainment? *Literacy, 42*, 137–144. doi: 10.1111/j.1741-4369.2008.00489.x.

Plester, B., Wood, C., & Joshi, P. (2009). Exploring the relationship between children's knowledge of text message abbreviations and school literacy outcomes. *British Journal of Developmental Psychology, 27*, 145–161. doi: 10.1348/026151008X320507

Portio (2015). *SMS: The language of 6 billion people*. Retrieved from http://www.openmarket.com/wp-content/uploads/2015/10/OpenMarket-Portio-Research-SMS-the-language-of-6-billion-people.pdf

Province, R. R., Spencer, R. J., & Mandell, D. L. (2007). Emotional expression online: Emoticons punctuate website text messages. *Journal of Language and Social Psychology, 26*, 299–307.

Rao, D., Yarowsky, D., Shreevats, A., & Gupta, M. (2010). *Classifying latent user attributes in Twitter*. In *Proceedings of the 2nd International Workshop on Search and Mining User-Generated Contents*. New York: ACM. 37–44. Retrieved from http://dl.acm.org/citation.cfm?id=1871993

Rosen, L. D., Chang, J., Erwin, L., Carrier, L. M., & Cheever, N. A. (2010). The relationship between "textisms" and formal and informal writing among young adults. *Communication Research, 37*, 420–440. Doi 10.1177/0093650210362465

Sanchez-Moya, A. & Cruz-Moya, O. (2015). "Hey there! I am using WhatsApp": A preliminary study of recurrent discursive realisations in a corpus of WhatsApp statuses. *Procedia—Social and Behavioral Sciences, 212*, 52–60. doi: 10.1016/j.sbspro.2015.11.298

Scott, G. G., Sinclair, J., Short, E., & Bruce, G. (2014). It's not what you say, it's how you say it: Language use on Facebook impacts employability but not attractiveness. *Cyberpsychology, Behavior, and Social Networking, 17*(8), 562–566. doi: 10.1089/cyber.2013.0584

Shaw, P. (2008). Spelling, accent and identity in computer-mediated communication. *English Today, 24*, 42–49. doi: 10.1017/S0266078408000199

Shortis, T. (2001). *The language of ICT: Information and communication technology.* London: Routledge.

Skovholt, K., Grønning, A., & Kankaanranta, A. (2014). The communicative functions of emoticons in workplace emails: :-) *Journal of Computer Mediated Communication, 19,* 780–797. doi: 10.1111/jcc4.12063

Squires, L. (2012). Whos punctuating what? Sociolinguistic variation in instant messaging. In A. Jaffe, J. Androutsopoulos, M. Sebba, & S. Johnson (Eds.), *Orthography as social action: Scripts, spelling, identity and power* (pp. 289–323). Berlin: Mouton de Gruyter.

Stephens, K. K., Houser, M. L., & Cowan, R. L. (2009). R U able to meet me: The impact of students' overly casual email messages to instructors. *Communication Education, 58*, 303–326. doi: 10.1080/03634520802582598

Tagg, C. (2009). *A Corpus Linguistics Study of Text Messaging* (Doctoral dissertation). University of Birmingham.

Thurlow, C., & Brown, A. (2003). Generation txt? The sociolinguistics of young people's text-messaging. *Discourse Analysis Online.* Retrieved from http://extra.shu.ac.uk/daol/articles/v1/n1/a3/thurlow2002003.html

Thurlow, C., & Poff, M. (2013). Text messaging. In S. C. Herring, D. Stein, & T. Virtanen (Eds.), *Handbook of the pragmatics of CMC* (pp. 163–190). New York, NY: Mouton de Gruyter.

Tossell, C. C., Kortum, P., Shepard, C., Barg-Walkow, L. H., Rahmati, A., & Zhong, L. (2012). A longitudinal study of emoticon use in text messaging from smartphones. *Computers in Human Behavior, 28*, 659–663. doi: 10.1016/j.chb.2011.11.012

Turner, K. H., Abram, S. S., Katíc, E., & Donovan, M. J. (2014). Demystifying digital: The what and why of the language teens use in digital writing. *Journal of Literacy Research, 46*, 157–193. doi: 10.1177/1086296X14534061

Underwood, M. K., Rosen, L. H., More, D., Ehrenreich, S. E., & Gentsch, J. K. (2012). The BlackBerry Project: Capturing the content of adolescents' text messaging. *Developmental Psychology, 48*, 295–302. http://psycnet.apa.org/doiLanding?doi=10.1037%2Fa0025914

Varnhagen, C. K., McFall, G. P., Pugh, N., Routledge, L., Sumida-MacDonald, H., & Kwong, T. E. (2010). lol: New language and spelling in instant messaging. *Reading and Writing, 23*, 719–733. doi: 10.1007/s11145-009-9181-y

Veater, H. M., Plester, B., & Wood, C. (2011). Use of text message abbreviations and literacy skills in children with dyslexia. *Dyslexia, 17*, 65–71. doi: 10.1002/dys.406

Verheijen, L. (2013). The effects of text messaging and instant messaging on literacy. *Journal of English Studies, 94*(5), 585–602. doi: 10.1080/0013838X.2013.795737

Vignovic, J. A., & Thompson, L. F. (2010). Computer-mediated cross-cultural collaboration: Attributing communication errors to the person versus the situation. *Journal of Applied Psychology, 95*, 265–276. doi: 10.1037/a0018628

Wolf, A. (2000). Emotional expression online: Gender differences in emoticon use. *Cyberpsychology and Behavior, 3*, 827–834.

Wood, C., Jackson, E., Hart, L., Plester, B., & Wilde, L. (2011). The effect of text messaging on 9- and 10-year-old children's reading, spelling and phonological processing skills. *Journal of Computer Assisted Learning, 27*, 28–36. doi: 10.1111/j.1365-2729.2010.00398.x

Wood, C., Kemp, N., & Waldron, S. (2014). Exploring the longitudinal relationships between the use of grammar in text messaging and performance on grammatical tasks. *British Journal of Developmental Psychology, 32*, 415–429. doi 10.1111/bjdp.12049

Wood, C., Kemp, N., Waldron, S., & Hart, L. (2014). Grammatical understanding, literacy and text messaging in school children and undergraduate students: A concurrent analysis. *Computers and Education, 70*, 281–290. doi: 10.1016/j.compedu.2013.09.003

Wood, C., Meachem, S., Bowyer, S., Jackson, E., Tarczynski-Bowles, M. L., & Plester, B. (2011). A longitudinal study of children's text messaging and literacy development. *British Journal of Psychology, 102*, 431–442. doi 10.1111/j.2044-8295.2010.02002.x

CHAPTER 10

CULTURAL CONSIDERATIONS ON ONLINE INTERACTIONS

HEYLA SELIM

INTRODUCTION

OF all the twentieth century's innovations, it is the Internet that now seems the most vital to, and emblematic of, the modern social experience. With more than half the world's population now using a smartphone, and with over 3.77 billion people accessing the Internet in 2017 (Kemp, 2017), we inhabit an era of hyper-connectivity, one in which the lines between real and virtual are regularly redrawn. Today's younger generations, born into this new, digital world—Prensky's (2001) "digital natives"—are arguably encountering a different experience of time and space than their parents and grandparents did, an experience that is no longer exclusive to the West. The Internet has spread across the world, embracing a staggeringly diverse range of cultures within a new digital consciousness.

This chapter explores the uneasy, two-way relationship between this new digital world and the pre-existing cultures we all inhabit. The investigation of culture is still a relatively new area within cyberpsychology. Although recent research has provided some valuable initial insights, these remain outnumbered by our many questions. Not only is this a relatively new area, it is also highly interdisciplinary. Researchers have plucked useful insights from media studies, cultural theory, and linguistics, among others, in order to fully understand the complexities of their subject matter. As such, the current structure of knowledge within this field is broad and varied, with an obvious topicality to the modern world.

The chapter begins with "culture" and introduces several key models that grapple with this multi-faceted concept. It then moves to online social networks (OSNs) and asks what position OSNs hold in everyday life, what psychological motivations drive users online, and how culture affect them all Subsequently, it then explores three strategies of the self: *self-concept*, *self-presentation*, and *self-disclosure*. Each will be explored in regards to the rise of the Internet and, in particular, OSNs. Finally, it offers speculative conclusions. Throughout the chapter some key questions are raised, including if the Internet can facilitate new modes of cultural citizenship, if cultural traditions can be retained in a global digital culture, and will the Internet increase cultural belonging, or erode it? Finally, it asks what the future holds for those cultures in which every citizen has a smartphone in their pocket

DEFINING ONLINE SOCIAL NETWORKS

Due to their prominence in modern social life and the far-reaching psychological consequences of their dominance as communication and self-presentation tools, Online Social Networks (OSNs) have been the subject of much research within cyberpsychology. This chapter, too, focuses on OSNs such as Twitter, Facebook, and Instagram—networks that pervade our lives. For an in-depth discussion of OSNs and motivations for use, see Stiff, this volume.

Facebook's "newsroom" webpage tells us that 1.94 billion active users logged onto the site throughout March 2017, approximately 85.5 percent of whom were located outside the US and Canada (Ingram, 2017). Such numbers indicate that OSNs are providing a common social experience to a hugely diverse international audience: what are the commonalities here? Which psychological needs motivate such diverse groups to engage in online interactions? A sensible place to start in answering such questions is to ask what, exactly, *is* culture?

DEFINING CULTURE

While we all possess an idea of what culture is, it is a concept that has repeatedly proved very difficult to adequately define. Much of this difficulty comes from the fact that culture works on different levels, something that anthropologist Gary P. Ferraro (1990; p. 19) captured well in his definition of "culture" as "everything that people have, think, and do as members of their society." Consider Ferraro's use of the words "have," "think," and "do," implying that we think of culture in three ways: as objects, as attitudes, and as behaviors. For example, many people think of art as culture, perhaps reflecting the most sophisticated elements of a society. Some attitudes may be cultural, for example, one's attitude towards homosexuality might be shaped by one's cultural background. Finally, certain behaviors, such having a mid-day siesta or fasting through Ramadan, may also be symptomatic of one's cultural heritage. Consider, too, how Ferraro describes individuals as "members of their society," thereby positioning culture as a *social* tool with a common, instructive element—something other scholars have also highlighted. Hill (2008; p. 79), for example, sees culture as "a system of values and norms…that when taken together constitute a design for living," while Hofstede (1991; p. 5) also refers to culture as "the collective programming of the mind."

Of course, such definitions can be frustrating, implicitly assuming that culture will seamlessly determine our behavior. While most of us are self-aware enough to know that we are influenced by culture, we also know that we are capable of thinking for ourselves. Ultimately, as Vignoles and colleagues (2016; p. 969) suggest, while culture may provide the guidelines for our behavior, we "individuals within the same system may adopt very different ways of fulfilling these broad "'cultural mandates'". Still, few would deny the impact of culture upon everyday life, and many researchers have proposed various ways of understanding and measuring it. Some of these models have proved untenable and faded from view; others have remained prominent, shaping our thinking around culture for decades.

Major Models of Culture: Hall's High/Low Context Model

Long-term Internet users will know that the web has changed rapidly in the last decade, moving from the Web 1.0 era of rigid, information-giving websites chiefly maintained by experts, into the modern Web 2.0 era, characterized by an endless stream of ever-changing, constantly updated content, much produced by everyday users. Today's websites are interactive and fluid, designed for connection. This functional focus on communication makes an analysis of Edward T. Hall's classic 1976 model of "Low Context" and "High Context" culture particularly topical. In Hall's model, "context" refers to all the external factors shaping communication: the shared history between speaker and listener, the environment in which they are located, the wider social norms limiting the acceptable expressions that speech might take, and so on. High-context cultures tend to be found among groups with close, long-standing relationships; rich, shared histories; deep mutual understandings. Within such groups, information may be communicated indirectly (without being explicitly spoken) because communication tends to contain high levels of contextual cues. For example, speakers may adopt a specific body language, a certain rhetorical device such as irony, or a discursive form such as politeness. All three of these will have a different significance in different cultures and can be used by individuals to communicate implicitly. In Hall and Hall's 1990 study, Japan was found to have the highest levels of context in communication. This is hardly surprising: in Japanese conversation, an individual will rarely say what they think, and instead pursue their point indirectly, through a complex system of strategic politeness. Low-context cultures, in contrast, tend to be characterized by clear and direct communication. As Hall (1976; p. 91) puts it, "the mass of the information is vested in the explicit code"; words are trusted to reflect the true intentions of the speaker. Germany is an oft-cited example of a low-context culture for its insistence on clear, straightforward communication.

Hall's model has faced some criticism. Craig and Douglas (2006) question the model's ability to address today's globalized, multi-cultural world, and Kittler and colleagues (2011) claim the model neglects local differences between smaller groups within larger cultures. Still, the model has value for emphasizing the importance of non-verbal and the culturally specific factors upon communication. To Hall, culture becomes manifest in interaction and all interaction is, to some degree, cultural.

Can Hall's model of culture help us to understand OSN usage? An interesting study addressing this question is Pflug's 2011 exploration of Indian and German chat forums, which found Indian participants much less likely than German participants to talk about themselves in depth online. Allegedly, such findings reflect the high context communication of India and the low context communication of Germany, but how? OSNs, Pflug argues, represent "a lean medium" (p. 133). At the time of Pflug's study, online messenger systems mainly revolved around text; they focused chiefly on words and were not particularly effective at conveying all the other contextual cues that help individuals make their points—body language, tone of voice, and so on. This leanness might be restrictive to members of high-context cultures, for whom the ability to disclose information about themselves is "highly dependent on trust as well as on the availability of social and socio-demographic cues" (p. 133). On the other hand, members of low-context cultures, in which speech tends to be straightforward and direct, will find online self-disclosure easier. Another fascinating insight from the study suggested that Indian participants frequently used emoticons (a small, pictorial representation of a facial expression) in an attempt to counter the "leanness" of online messaging and convey the non-verbal elements of their message that simply cannot be put into words. Take a moment to consider this. Are there any cultural elements of *your* everyday communication that cannot be put into words, or emoticons?

Another key consideration here concerns the opportunities that may be made available to users due to the absence of cultural context on OSNs. For example, Attrill (2015) draws upon Walther's (1996) concept of Hyperpersonal Communication to argue that OSNs afford individuals a unique range of self-presentation opportunities unavailable in their offline lives through the *absence* of cultural context. Such absences can be manipulated, leading to online communication becoming "hyperpersonal", i.e. loaded with *more* importance and consequence to the individual than offline interactions. In such situations, online communication not only is equally important to offline communication but can even exceed it in significance.

Let us look, for example, to the Arabic world, where high levels of conservatism often lead to a strongly enforced and restrictive cultural context regarding communication. Selim, Long, and Vignoles (2016) compared OSN usage among British and Saudi Arabian participants and found that male and female Saudis used OSNs differently, reflecting the unique restrictions both faced in their offline lives. While male participants emphasized the opportunity to talk with females outside of the extended family group as a significant motivation for online interaction, female participants saw OSNs as giving Saudi women a way to voice their views in a way that is simply not possible in offline Saudi society. Supporting these findings, other researchers studying young Arabic Facebook users have also claimed the chance to communicate with the opposite sex as a key motivation (Newsom & Lengel, 2012), while other studies of Saudi females also attest to how OSNs can be used for political purposes (Freedom House, 2012; Worth, 2012). Agarwal, Lim, and Wigand (2012) explored how Saudi women used Twitter to protest for their right to drive, and succeeded in raising considerable awareness of their situation. Due to Saudi Arabia's highly restrictive culture, most of the protestors operated anonymously through unnamed Twitter accounts to avoid reprisal and punishment. Interactions such as these, one would imagine, must be extremely important to the individual and often weighted with more consequence than offline interactions (we know that OSN usage under such restrictive circumstances may gain a new, profound importance due to per-ceived danger and risk, which in turn may lead to an anger and frustration that fuels risk-taking; see Ayanian & Tausch, 2016). For many of these women, their Twitter pro-files revealed little more than their gender and their nationality. What is important to recognize here is that OSNs allow us to manipulate and frame the sending and receiving of information, increasing or decreasing the cultural context surrounding the message, for maximum effect, affording users the opportunity to satisfy motives that may be difficult to achieve in their offline context.

How, *exactly*, can OSNs help individuals overcome such pervasive cultural constraints? What technical features make OSNs so useful in these instances? The answers given by research exploring this question often make reference to the architectural features of OSNs. Most often cited is the "asynchronous" nature computer-mediated communica-tion, which often takes place *outside* of real time, allowing users to craft messages for maximum impact. The physical absence of a communications partner may also restructure the available boundaries surrounding the expression of culturally-relevant information. Identity, too, can be manipulated and reduced online. We can remain anonymous, or interact with strangers in conversations that seemingly have little conse-quence or risk for one's offline life. In political arguments anonymity may allow the culturally unspeakable to be uttered. The difficulty and danger one might feel voicing their political activism in front of their disapproving father or mother is completely different from the danger of voicing views anonymously to several thousand followers on Twitter, as an OSN such as Twitter may help such statements reach audiences of hundreds or even thousands, potentially drawing international support from third parties. In Haslam and Reicher's (2014) model of successful collective resistance, "third-party" support is a key factor for resistance to proceed into meaningful social and cultural change; thus, the ability of OSNs to work across borders should not be underestimated. In such instances OSNs take on an "emancipatory" role (Enzensberger, 1970), freeing users from the constraints of their geography and from the confines of their culture's accepted limits of self-expression. While individual OSN usage is often rooted in cultural influence, individuals can also access, through the Internet, a separate, networked public sphere existing alongside everyday offline communication, a sphere where cultural contexts can be increased or decreased, affording users the "opportunity to experiment with different ways of doing things in an environment where failure is not costly" (Coulson & Barnett, 2015; p. 119).

Major Models of Culture: Hofstede's Various Dimensions Model

In 1965 Geert Hofstede, leading an investigation into the morale of IBM's huge international workforce, began to develop a model of culture revolving around six "dimensions": *Power Distance, Uncertainty Avoidance, Long-term Orientation, Indulgence vs. Restraint, Masculinity vs. Femininity*, and *Individualistic vs. Collectivistic*. Since then, Hofstede's model has grown in stature to become one of the most prominent tools of cross-cultural analysis, remaining in constant use all over the world. Its popularity is unsurprising; it allows researchers to easily operationalize culture, and provides clear, easily presentable results: each country analyzed is ranked "high" or "low" according to the dimension in question, with the resulting mix of dimensions forming a unique cultural character.

While Hofstede's model can seem almost omnipresent at times, it is not without detractors. Woodhouse and Ahn (2008), for example, have asserted that Hofstede's sample (IBM employees) is unrepresentative. Several others have accused the model of lacking nuance, claiming that it neglects local pockets of culture in favor of generalized portrayals of national character—a critique that raises an important point and should be expanded upon here. This chapter includes several studies that explicitly draw on Hofstede's model, often focusing on the individualism-collectivism dimension. This dimension, more than any other, has proved particularly inspirational for research which has tended to classify Western countries as individualistic (prioritizing personal liberty and achievement) and Eastern countries as collectivistic (valuing the needs of the community over the individual). This binary, now a well-established theory, has provided the starting point for many studies. Recently, however, critics have voiced concerns about this, accusing Hofstede's model of propagating an unsustainable conceptual dichotomy. Schwartz (1990) also highlights how certain actions benefit both individuals *and* groups, which suggests that the simple categorization of cultures as individually focused or collectively focused might be unjustifiably reductionist. Protecting the environment, for example, benefits both the individual and the wider society. In a wide-ranging study using participants from 33 countries, Vignoles and colleagues (2016) also found the individualistic West and collectivistic East dichotomy unable to "adequately capture the diverse models of selfhood that prevail in different world regions" (p. 967). It is clearly problematic, in our ever-changing global landscape, to assume that we can talk about a stable or coherent "East" or "West" and a common experience within these categories.

Major Models of Culture: Schwartz's Model of Universal Human Values

While Hall offers us a model of culture-as-communication, and Hofstede offers a model that gleans insights from cultural contrasts, Schwartz's later Theory of Basic Human Values model (1992) might provide what is missing: a more fluid, nuanced model incorporating culture's inevitable overlaps and paradoxes. Schwartz's model revolves around the concept of "values"—relatively stable beliefs, standards, and criteria that guide individual decision making. The model identifies ten "universal values," recognized by all cultures: Self-Direction, Stimulation, Hedonism, Achievement, Power, Security, Conformity, Tradition, Benevolence, and Universalism. These values are linked, ultimately, to the goals we want to achieve as individuals—goals which will be influenced by our larger cultural frameworks. Depending on these goals, we will prioritize one value other another. *Cultural difference*, therefore, emerges from the way in which different societies prioritize each value.

The model strategically arranges these ten values to highlight how pursuing value-driven behavior is rarely entirely separate, but often involves the conflict or compliance between several different value sets (Figure 1). Accordingly, Schwartz places "openness to change" values (hedonism, stimulation, and self-direction) opposite "conservation" values (security, conformity, and tradition), while "self-enhancement" values are contrasted with "self-transcendence" values, illustrating the conflict between actions that emphasize concern for others' welfare, and those that emphasize pursuing one's own advancement. Values arranged adjacently will share similar motivational drives,

FIGURE 1 Theoretical model of relations among motivational value types and two basic bipolar value dimensions.

i.e. tradition and conformity both "share the goal of subordinating the self in favor of socially imposed expectations" (Schwartz 1992; p. 1).

Although Schwartz's model has faced some criticism, primarily around the difficulty of operationalizing the framework, there is immense value in its emphasis on the complex, interdependent play of values upon cultural behavior. In fact, if any of these models give us any insight at all, it is in illustrating the messy interconnectedness of modern culture in our globalized yet fragmented world. We might even say that it is in their failings that these models reveal the most, highlighting the complications—perhaps even the impossibilities—of constructing any overarching model of culture.

OSNs, Culture, and Motivation

Once we have defined culture, we can ask how it influences our drive to engage in online interactions. Luckily, much recent research has asked the same question (e.g. Bonds-Raacke & Raacke, 2010; Brandtzæg and Heim, 2009; Hew, 2011). When reading through these studies from many different nations, three broad motivational drives keep recurring: information, friendship, and connection. In light of such recurrences, it is possible to assume that the same universal human needs drive both online and offline behavior: the human desire to connect with, and know about, others. We should not, however, be too quick to make assumptions—as Kim, Sohn, and Choi (2011; p. 365) warn, "computer-mediated communication does not occur in a cultural void, but depends on a social and cultural milieu wherein individuals acquire the fundamental values and norms that shape their social behaviours". Thus, although we may share broad motivational drives, they may manifest in culturally distinct ways.

In an in-depth analysis of the factors underlying motivations for using OSNs in British and Saudi Arabian participants, Selim et al. (2016) found that, despite some commonalities, the differences between these two cultures remained evident. In a wide-ranging exploration, they investigated who individuals choose to connect with online, and the self-presentation strategies they employ when doing so. British users, from a more relationally mobile cultural context that values openness to change, were motivated to use OSNs to maintain and strengthen pre-existing relationships, targeting their posts at those with whom they have strong ties. Also, British participants were more concerned about maintaining a positive image, a trait characteristic of relationally mobile cultural contexts. Saudi users, from less relationally mobile context, were more likely to target those with whom they had weak ties in order to extend their social circle. Saudi Arabian users, from a highly conservative culture, used Facebook and, particularly, Twitter as a "pressure valve"—a way to let off steam and express themselves in ways simply not available in their restrictive offline culture. That being said, Saudi users also showed heightened awareness of their cultural backgrounds and norms, and were more likely to use pseudonyms, false pictures, and multiple accounts when discussing divisive issues—a clear example of a culturally shaped motivational drive.

Although the drive to express and connect is likely a universal one, the manifestation of such a drive is framed by cultural concerns.

The study highlights other interesting contrasts; UK participants sought self-esteem by sharing their external achievements, while Saudi participants showed more focus upon internal qualities. Against the stereotypical expectations of the UK's individualism and Saudi Arabia's collectivism, UK users were found to be more concerned with belonging, focusing on building and maintaining quality relationships with an in-group. Conversely, Saudi users placed more emphasis on striving for distinctiveness, and were motivated to adopt strategies of self-presentation that leaned heavily on self-promotion, life-streaming (continuously broadcasting one's life on OSNs), and acceptance-seeking— a finding interpreted as the individual seeking distinctiveness within a larger collectivistic, homogenous culture. An interesting implication from this particular insight is that our larger cultural ethos can *negatively* predict how we might act. For example, those from an individualistic culture might feel the negative psychological consequences of a lack of close, long-lasting relationships and thus actively seek out belonging, while those from a collectivistic culture might feel the negative psychological consequences of a lack of distinctiveness, and seek in their actions to address this discrepancy. Such findings testify to the two-way cultural flow evident in so much of the research we will encounter here: we use the Internet as cultural beings in order to *escape* culture. How can a model ever predict these reverse effects?

A further interesting area of research concerns how our motivations can be shaped by technological architecture—the unique layouts and features—of OSNs such as Facebook and Twitter. Fogg and Iizawa (2008), for example, found that structural differences between Facebook and Mixi (a popular Japanese social networking site) reflected the US and Japanese cultures in which they were respectively created, a finding later confirmed by Thomson and Ito (2012), also concerning Facebook and Mixi. A technological structure such as Facebook, designed and created in the US, may therefore more effectively facilitate the expression of motivations common within US culture, such as the self-promotion and networking celebrated within that individualistic nation. Likewise, the design and layout of Mixi might reflect the low relational mobility within Japanese culture, with features prioritizing the respecting and strengthening of existing relationships.

Such technological structuring may also influence how users engage with OSNs. This is a particularly intriguing question, in which some interesting tensions have emerged. Acar and Deguchi (2013) analyzed the Twitter habits of Japanese and US students and, contrary to what we might expect from inhabitants of highly collectivistic culture disapproving of self-promotion, found that Japanese students tweeted *more* self-related posts than US students. How can we explain this? Were the Japanese students responding in kind to a Western-influenced virtual environment? If so, such findings give a glimpse of the possibilities for cultural cross-pollination and cultural convergence that arise from the OSNs status as a "cultural import…an idea or product created in one culture and transported to other cultures" (Brown, Michinov, & Manago, 2017; p. 144). Speaking rather speculatively, can we almost use OSNs as a window through which we can visualize, and experiment with, alternative methods of cultural being?

To speak in such a way—interpreting the Internet as a humanitarian tool eroding cultural differences, creating a global, unified consciousness that should (in theory) lead to global accountability, fostering close relationships between far-flung nations—is to buy into Convergence Theory (Tomlinson, 2007). The "convergence" here refers to a process wherein the traditional relationships defining our lives are reshaped by new and emerging technologies. Thus the rise of the Internet has begun to break down traditional allegiances to community, to nation, and to family. In essence, the community that arises from our geographic placement (i.e. where we physically *are*) has waned, and Jenkins (2004, p. 35) suggests that new forms of community have emerged in its place that are "defined through voluntary, temporary and tactical affiliations...through common intellectual enterprises and emotional investments...held together through the mutual production and reciprocal exchange of knowledge." Those of us who are highly connected are, in a sense, nomadic, i.e. free to opt into or out of online communities that exist not in one geographic location, but stretch across the globe.

Some spectators have predicted that this new paradigm will lead to the eventual obliteration of cultural difference (Lin, 2012). While such claims may seem speculative, there is admittedly something democratic and indiscriminating in the Internet's nature. One can now interact with other individuals from almost anywhere in the world, free from previous temporal and spatial limitations, continually exposed to, and interacting with, other cultures. Such interactions can result in convergence in terms of cultural values by showing us the arbitrary, constructed nature of our own cultural environments, and giving us insights into better, or worse, ways of being (Fenton & Downey, 2003; Gao & Newman, 2005). As ever, such optimistic narratives must inevitably be tempered with realism. The evidence behind convergence theory is thin and ambiguous, chiefly suggesting that while exposure to new cultures may open up possibilities for change, it may equally lead to reaffirmation of a culture's existing value framework. Alternatively, when exposed to new cultural ideas, a culture may selectively "borrow" elements of those ideas and integrate them into their existing cultural frameworks—e.g. Japan, which has borrowed extensively from American culture while retaining a quintessentially Japanese outlook. Such integration does not so much result in convergence but in the creation of new, unique cultural hybrids (Smith, Fischer, Vignoles, & Bond, 2013).

Much like in convergence theory, there are no simple answers here; however, one important point to note concerns the structuring of the research studies mentioned earlier. Notice how participants often admit to actions that, ultimately, are the manifestation of psychological motivations, while saying little about the motivations themselves. To give an example: while my motivation might be to go online and connect with friends, it is likely that a deeper psychological need is really driving this exterior action—perhaps a need for belonging. While studies into motivations offer useful insights, they often only seem to provide half of the picture. To fully understand the psychological consequences of the interplay between the structures of culture and the cultural structuring of technology, we need to look at how both allow us new, meaningful ways of approaching, of being, communicating, and improving the psychological self.

OSNs, Culture, and the Online Self

Today, there is little room left for doubting that OSNs can facilitate the expression of very consequential psychological needs. The Internet does not simply let us share our lives—it now allows us to expand, create, and recreate them. Several scholars have powerfully argued that online interactions are now as consequential to users as offline interactions, so much so that both should be recognized as functioning as important facets of twenty-first century life, influencing and shaping the other (Baym, 2010). Even referring to "online" and "offline" phenomena as two separate realities may now be slightly outdated! To gain a deeper understanding into how such processes of the self can be facilitated through the use of OSNs, we now turn to look at three well-established strategies of self: self-concept, self-presentation, and self-disclosure. Such theories have long served researchers as tools for operationalizing the mind, but with the recent invention of the Internet, many of these theories have gained fascinating new facets.

Online Self-concept and Culture

"Self-concept" refers to an individual's fundamental beliefs about themselves, whether fair or unfair, truthful or misjudged. These beliefs constitute the individual's self-concept (Baumeister, 1999). How we construct our self-concept will be influenced by our culture. In a very influential paper, Markus and Kitayama (1991) proposed a distinction between an independent self-construal (characteristic of Western cultures) and an interdependent self-construal (characteristic of Eastern cultures). While their original aim was to argue against research that comprehended only a single, monogamous construal of the self by highlighting the existence of other means of selfhood, they were only partly successful; as Vignoles and colleagues (2016) contend, the independent/interdependent interpretations proposed in their work were eventually used to support the problematic individualistic/collectivism dichotomy dominant within social psychology literature. While readers familiar with criticisms aimed at other models of cultural variation will know enough to be cautious of the reductionism inherent in *any* major model, Markus and Kitayama's model does offer us a clear place to start thinking about how people in different cultures might vary in their construction of self.

Regarding research exploring self-concept in online contexts, much has focused on how the Internet can give the individual the ability to improve their self-concept. An interesting, and very topical, area of research concerns sexuality. Macintosh and Bryson (2008) have described how LGBT teens might use OSNs to establish contact with their LGBT peers, the Internet here providing a safe sphere in which many young people "come out." Similarly, Hillier, Mitchell, and Ybarra (2012, p. 241) found that young LGBT individuals in the US used certain online sites as "safe spaces to explore their sexuality" without the risk of rejection or disapproval. In such examples, we see online interactions being manipulated to transcend culturally specific restrictions in order to construct a more positive self-construct that can then be transferred into the offline environment.

It is beyond the scope of this chapter to adequately explore the range of problems and difficulties that individuals have experienced in attempting to build a self-concept in a restrictive or hostile culture. If we did have time, however, we would undoubtedly see more examples of the Internet's ability to provide individuals with a degree of affordance and autonomy over the construction of their self-concept. As Leach and Livingstone (2015; p. 616) have powerfully argued, the Internet's ability to provide a voice with which the disadvantaged can repudiate their position and "assert their own view of themselves and the world despite dominant pressures to accept societal messages to the contrary" is a very real and consequential form of "psychological resistance," of huge importance for the self-construction of thousands of individuals now rejecting the narratives of inferiority often imposed upon the oppressed. Furthermore, as the links between disadvantage and culture are often highly complex and hugely consequential, this is something that must necessarily concern us here.

We would be remiss, however, not to mention how such affordances can also be reversed, becoming restrictive. As some individuals can avoid their cultural traditions online, so others can use the Internet in a conservative and reactionary fashion to preserve and reinforce them. For example, we earlier saw evidence of the Internet providing a safe spaces for LGBT teens, yet the independent watchdog Freedom House, in their 2015 *Freedom On The Net* report, noted that 14 of the 65 countries under analysis frequently censored LGBT content "on moral, religious, or other grounds, reflecting the entrenched and often state-endorsed bias against the LGBTI community in some parts of the world" (p. 4). In such environments, seeking online support might entail a level of risk substantial enough to deter LGBT youths from initially undertaking such an activity. Dhoest and Szulc's (2016) study presented examples of diasporic gay men using the Internet to construct a new, more positive perception of self, yet participants in this study recalled others who, having disclosed sensitive information online, often found themselves blackmailed and exploited. Such stories force us to acknowledge the inescapable geographic reality underlying Internet usage: one's computer, one's smartphone, exists *somewhere*, and that *somewhere* has a powerful effect on our online interactions.

Supporting this, research has recently emerged repudiating earlier predictions of a world of online relationships based on choice and personal interest instead of the rather arbitrary fact of one's geographic placement. Instead, new research argues that our online relationships augment or reflect our offline relationships, supplementing and expanding users' existing social and cultural worlds (Vergeer & Pelzer, 2009). Furthermore, users are seen to work to *maintain* consistency between online and offline identities, and expect others to do the same, thereby "creating a self-moderating environment where authentic culture and identities flow between the so-called offline and online worlds" (Thomson & Ito, 2012, p. 4). Thus the online world is not so much a realm of escape and liberation, but a heightened extension of our daily cultural lives.

Such evidence might lead us to reject the emancipatory narratives of convergence theory. Whereas convergence theorists maintain that the Internet should, and will, lead to greater levels of cultural democracy and co-operation through connectivity and interactivity, those who instead follow divergence theory are likely to maintain a more level outlook. They highlight instead the Internet's tendency to fragment and diversify its users (Castells, 1996), to produce sheltered groups of publics whose "echo chamber" news feeds only show them stories they want to read written by journalists with views similar to their own. As every story is slanted or angled for maximum impact, the middle ground of neutral reporting disappears, replaced by stories shot through with political bias. Such a state of affairs allows extremism and radicalism to flourish, often predicated on the "othering" of a foreign group (Sunstein, 2001), while having poten tially fatal consequences for democracy—as Fenton and Downey (2003) argue, a key factor of democracy which is often seen to be missing from OSNs, with their like- and network-based newsfeeds, is the exposure to arguments you did not choose to see. Users stay protected within an endlessly shifting content bubble crafted by personalized algorithms that endlessly provide agreeable content, editing out the objectionable and unpalatable, reflecting our existing personalities back to us (and leading to surprise and even shock when one discovers the extent of opposition to one's own viewpoint—as discovered in 2016 by dismayed "remain" voters in the UK and Hillary Clinton supporters in the US). Divergence theorists dispute any notion of the Internet creating an overarching, global population with a universal, cross-border culture. Instead, it leads to the growth of several distinct, inward-looking groups inhabited by individuals streaming information from sources designed to maintain their pre-existing beliefs through unchallenging and unthreatening content. Such a vision, of course, leads to a conception of the Internet as a tool for reinforcing existing beliefs, not as a tool for new visions and new relationships.

The literature on cultural divergence is rich and vast, and worth exploring; most points produced by convergence theory have been, at some point, disputed by divergence theory. In light of this, we end by advising caution against narratives of emancipation or oppression. OSNs can free us from our cultures just as they can deliver us unto them; OSNs can help to restore our voices and rebuild our self-concepts just as they can perpetuate the conditions that originally silenced us and throw us into psychological disarray. We would, therefore, be wise to view the Internet as Attrill (2015) does, as "a tool that aids the execution of a wide and varied array of human behaviours" driven by the complex set of needs underlying each individual's psychology, and determined by both national and local contexts.

ONLINE SELF-PRESENTATION AND CULTURE

Having considered self-concept, the discussion now explores the vital role others can play in the formation of individual self-concepts. Ultimately, how other people see us influences how we see ourselves. We therefore understandably seek to manage the impressions we make on others through employing strategic methods of "self-presentation" (see Fullwood, this volume, for a discussion of online self-presentation).

There is evidence in existing research to suggest that culture can influence online self-presentation. Lee-Won, Shim, Joo, and Park (2014), exploring self-presentation on Facebook amongst US and South Korean students, found that US college students were more likely to portray a positive self-presentation on Facebook than South Korean students. Such findings further the existing consensus that positive self-presentation is a cultural norm in the individualistic cultures that promote independence and self-expression (e.g. Kim & Sherman, 2007), but is less valued in collectivist cultures that traditionally value self-effacement (Cho, 2010). Expanding their results, Lee-Won and colleagues highlighted a positive correlation between positive self-presentation and an individual's levels of public self-consciousness i.e. being aware of how one is viewed by others, and subsequently acting in accordance with this awareness. South Korean participants, having higher levels of public self-consciousness due to the collectivistic nature of their culture, were more likely to act consistently regarding the norms of their culture and thus rarely engaged in positive self-presentation. This aside, the study yielded a second, more interesting insight concerning the quantity and quality of one's online audience on self-presentation. Findings showed that while South Koreans will engage in strategic and positive self-presentation, this tends to take place in earlier stages of online relationships, when there is not yet much intimacy between the participants; in these early stages, positive self-presentation is deployed in order to form strong and enduring relationships. In contrast, US participants engaged in high levels of positive self-presentation irrespective of the levels of intimacy involved. Although this finding clearly reflects the influence of the larger cultural environment, it also complicates it, suggesting individuals at times adopt culturally uncharacteristic behavior for culturally appropriate aims.

Rui and Stefanone (2013), investigating the effects of cultural identity and audience on online self-presentation, also concluded that our online worlds reflect our offline cultural environments, while highlighting some interesting structural variations. Their study contrasting American and Singaporean Facebook users found that Americans were more likely to frequently present information about themselves via wall posts. Yet interestingly, and surprisingly, Singaporean participants were found to share more online photos. The authors put this down to the different goals that can be achieved through sharing photos, which may be less overtly self-referential, revealing less about the self than a written announcement, and yet are still useful for relationship maintenance purposes. Unsurprisingly, Americans were more active in the management and editing of their online image (untagging themselves from unflattering photos, for example), providing support for previous work by Gudykunst, Yang, and Nishida (1987), which suggests that individualistic cultures produce individuals with higher levels self-awareness more likely to engage in greater impression management.

Perhaps the most interesting insight from Rui and Stefanone's paper concerns the notion of "promiscuous friending," the practice of making online connections with people one has not met in person. Studying promiscuous friends in the US, Rui and Stefanone (2013) found that the primary goal of such behavior is attention seeking and in order to fulfill this goal individuals are often willing to present *negative* images of themselves in order to achieve their goal of gaining attention. A key complication is raised here: constructing a positive public image is not always the goal of self-presentation in all cultures. This, of course, is the sort of nuance we might often miss when operationalizing culture through broad models which, in their search for solid, big, usable results, must necessarily forego subtlety. However, as critics of culture, and critics of research, it is our job to spot such nuances and to consider the consequences of them. For example, a recent study by Brown, Michinov, and Manago (2017) emphasized the importance of local and neighborly cultural variation, hypothesizing that countries with higher levels of cultural individualism would be more comfortable using Facebook as a means of broadcasting messages to large groups of people. From an analysis of the US and France—two individualistic cultures—this hypothesis was largely supported, with findings indicating that the structure of Facebook is somehow reflective of, and facilitative of, the ethos of a highly individualistic US culture and is thus most suited for use by those within such cultures. American students gather expansive social networks and self-present to large audiences more frequently, utilizing the affordances of Facebook to the fullest. Meanwhile, French students may certainly use Facebook, but will still prefer and privilege more intimate methods of communication. The implication here is that while individualistic cultures may have the same *general* approach towards a psychological strategy, the intensity of that approach will vary in each, and such nuances need to be addressed if we are to gain a richer understanding of our world.

ONLINE SELF-DISCLOSURE AND CULTURE

Self-disclosure takes place when we "communicate" information regarding ourselves to others. This information might include our thoughts, our feelings, and our experiences (Posey, Lowry, Roberts, & Ellis, 2010). Generally, self-disclosure is seen as having several beneficial effects on psychological well-being, with a particular emphasis on the role gradual disclosure plays in the formation of relationships. Several scholars have applied social penetration theory to this dynamic: one individual shares information regarding themselves, another responds in kind. As relationships progress, they become more penetrative, with deeper information being disclosed, resulting in strong, trusting relationships (Altman & Taylor, 1973). Throughout this process, each individual will continually evaluate the cost of giving information away against the strength of information received. Based on these evaluations, the individual decides whether to pursue relationships further.

All communication, being inherently cultural, is shaped by the same wider cultural characteristics that determine our other forms of communication. Accordingly, self-disclosure—which is itself a form of communication—will also vary within cultural groups. As Adams, Anderson, and Adonu (2004) claim, people in individualistic cultures, which tend to have high relational mobility, are usually more open to self-disclosure, interpreting it as a means of forming new, intimate relationships; however, although self-disclosure in individualistic cultures tends to be done with greater frequency, the disclosures often have less depth. The reverse can be seen in collectivistic societies where self-disclosure takes place less often, but tends to be deeper (Marshall, 2008). These patterns may be due partly to the relationship structures within the society. Individuals in individualistic societies tend to have many weaker relationships and a focus on gaining social status, whereas individuals in collectivistic societies tend to have deeper, long-standing relationships with less focus on cultivating new bonds. Societies with high relation mobility will often encourage individuals to self-disclose more frequently, as relations in such environments are weak and easily broken as individuals move vertically and horizontally through social spheres. It thus requires effort and investment within relationships to form and maintain them. Alongside the individualism/collectivism dimension, a culture's approach towards uncertainty avoidance has been shown to be influential on its self-disclosure practices. Higher uncertainty avoidance has been shown to correlate with higher levels of secrecy and thus lower levels of self-disclosure (Verderber, Sellnow, & Verderber, 2010). Lower levels of uncertainty avoidance, conversely, are associated with lower levels of secrecy and higher levels of self-disclosure.

While there has been some research questioning how the online environment effects self-disclosure, when it comes to considering the influence of culture on online self-disclosure, we only have a limited amount of research to draw on. Additionally, what research we do have does not support the easy formation of conclusions (Zhao, Grasmuck, & Martin, 2008). To complicate things further, studies by Attrill (2015) and Attrill and Jalil (2011) recognizing the plurality of available online environments emphasize how different online contexts work alongside user motivations to influence the type of self-disclosure likely to take place. Anonymous chat rooms, for example, may better facilitate deeper disclosure than Facebook—anonymity having been shown to encourage higher self-disclosure (McKenna & Bargh, 2000). This huge variety of Internet platforms in which self-disclosure can now take place might make any form of generalizing extremely difficult.

Cho (2010) extended these cultural considerations to OSNs and found that US participants more likely to frequently self-disclose online than Korean participants, who were more likely to infrequently, but deeply, self-disclose. This has been challenged, however, by Posey and colleagues (2010), who found that collectivism *increases* the likelihood of self-disclosure, a conclusion explained with reference to the high levels of reciprocity in collectivistic relationships and collectivistic society: one loses face if one does not return favors and gifts. Thus the *inclination* to reciprocate is higher, and when met with self-disclosure, one may feel more obliged to repay the act with a disclosure of one's own.

Interestingly, Thomson and Ito (2012), analyzing 131 Japanese OSN users of both Facebook and Mixi, found that participants engaged in lower self-disclosure on Mixi than on Facebook. This difference was explained by looking towards the differing views of relational mobility in the original cultures of the platform itself; Mixi reflects Japanese low relational mobility, and Facebook reflects North America's high relational mobility. These results not only indicate that cultural contexts are present in online platforms, but raise important questions of how technology can cross borders, influencing the value structures of different cultures. Both insights testify to the importance of cultural context on questions of online self-disclosure.

The consistent conceptual problems regarding an over-reliance on the individualistic-collectivistic divides should once again be noted. Contrasting cultural contexts at a national level often necessitates that studies use only two or three countries (often one individualistic and the other collectivistic). If such contrasts are to remain valid, countries grouped in the same end of the dichotomy—individualistic cultures, for example—need to be analyzed, their similarity continually proven. If they are not, the validity of such dichotomies is hugely diminished. Such similarity, however, is not always present: comparing OSN usage in two individualistic Western cultures—Germany and America—Wu and Lu (2013) found notable differences between the two, with Germans being significantly less open in their OSN privacy settings than Americans. Quirks like this, stemming the nature of OSNs as cultural exports, will no doubt keep recurring as we move into an ever more shared digital world. What they amount to is an acknowledgment that global cultures are not as firmly bound to time and place as before. In the wake of the Internet, the old dichotomies are crumbling, the cultural boundaries blurring: while individuals, on the whole, might self-disclose as one would expect, one constantly finds recurring exceptions which make any general characterizations increasingly hard to enforce.

CONCLUSION

Much of the research presented in this chapter has argued for culture's ongoing effect on how individuals interact on OSNs. However, there is no easy line of cause and effect; an individual living in an individualistic culture will not *solely* partake in individualistic online behaviors. OSNs do not simply reflect culture—they provide opportunities for users to avert it, to make up for their culture's shortcomings, or to fix their culture's flaws. The pursuit of goals such as these might involve unpredictable behavior at odds with larger cultural mandates. Ultimately, OSNs cannot be seen as parallel, digital components to the offline world, but should instead be viewed as new spheres of tension and conflict, in which highly significant identity work can be undertaken by individuals through strategic communications and self-presentation.

Also vital is the relative newness of OSNs—we still have much to learn about how these shifting and changing technologies are shaping our lives. The chief purpose of this chapter is to demonstrate the need for nuance when considering culture, and to illustrate where such nuance might be lacking. Our existing ways of understanding the world—as a distinct, separate set of cultural states—is no longer tenable. We need new models that allow complexities to emerge, that recognize and celebrate the complicated processes of cultural cross-pollination instigated by the emergence of the Internet technologies.

Before we finish, let us look to the future. In response to a conviction that existing models of culture were not adequately approaching the complexity and variety of cultural selfhood, Vignoles and colleagues (2016) offer a new, seven-dimensional model exploring ways of being independent or interdependent. While they do not contest the claim that the individual's experience of their culture will inform their constructions of self—and that such constructions will be maintained through cultural interaction and practice—they clearly maintain the necessity of considering the variety that can emerge within such processes: "prevailing representations of selfhood may be internalized or resisted by individuals, generating substantial variation in individuals' construals of themselves within any given cultural context. Nevertheless, it suggests that some partial agreement exists within a culture, and that this partial agreement will have meaningful consequences" (p. 17).

Primarily, the model seeks to escape the independent/interdependent dichotomy, emphasizing instead the possibility of simultaneously and productively engaging in behaviors from both ends of this spectrum, thereby collapsing the dichotomy by rendering it invalid. The key understanding is recognizing that in modern, fragmented society, much of our daily activities take place in separate spheres. Our romantic lives, our spiritual lives, our political lives: each has been affected in differing ways by the globalization that has so relentlessly exposed one culture's customs to another. We communicate differently in different places; at work, at home, to our friends, to our parents. Each of the many spheres constituting our world displays distinct cultural influences and tensions. The success of Vignoles and colleagues' model is that it seeks to explore the manifestation of culture in several different dimensions, including (i) being self-reliance vs. dependence on others, (ii) self-containment vs. connection to others, (iii) a desire for difference vs. a desire for similarity, (iv) commitment to others vs. self-interest, (v) consistency vs. variability, (vi) self-direction vs. receptiveness to influence, and (vii) self-expression vs. harmony. Interestingly, while the authors found support for cultural variations within *all seven* dimensions, there was no evidence for an overarching cultural difference in terms of independence vs. interdependence, with participants instead exhibiting different combinations of independence and interdependence in separate spheres. Additionally, some nations thought to be independent displayed remarkable contrasts with other "independent" nations! As we have seen this to be true in offline life, so we can suspect it will be true to online life too. Culture does not dictate. It directs but does not determine, and the scope for subversion is substantial.

Vignoles and colleagues' (2016) model is exciting and thought provoking, and recommended reading for any student entering this new and exciting area of investigation. It leads us, once again, to recognize that we can no longer rely on the analysis of national *character*: the chaotic nature of postmodernity has put paid to that. Better for us, as cultural analysts, to start recognizing the nature of our times, and design our research to be local *and* national, and so to remain open to the pluralities of culture in the digital age.

REFERENCES

Acar, A., & Deguchi, A. (2013). Culture and social media usage: Analysis of Japanese Twitter users. *International Journal of Electronic Commerce Studies* 4(1), 21–32.

Adams, G., Anderson, S. L., & Adonu, J. K. (2004). The cultural grounding of closeness and intimacy. In D. Mashek & A. Aron (Eds.), *Handbook of closeness and intimacy* (pp. 321–339). Mahwah, NJ: Erlbaum.

Agarwal, N., Lim, M., & Wigand, R.T. (2012). Online collective action and the role of social media in mobilizing opinions: A case study on women's right-to-drive campaigns in Saudi Arabia. In C. G. Reddick and S. K. Aikins (Eds.), *Web 2.0 Technologies and democratic governance, public administration and information technology 1* (pp. 99–123) New York: Springer.

Altman, I., & Taylor, D. (1973). *Social penetration theory.* New York: Holt, Rinehart & Winston.

Attrill, A. (2015). *The Manipulation of online self-presentation: Create, edit, re-edit and present.* Basingstoke: Palgrave Macmillan.

Attrill, A., & Jalil, R. (2011). Revealing only the superficial me: Exploring categorical self-disclosure online. *Computers in Human Behavior* 27(5), 1634–1642.

Ayanian, A. H., & Tausch, N. (2016). How risk perception shapes collective action intentions in repressive contexts: A study of Egyptian activists during the 2013 post-coup uprising. *British Journal of Social Psychology* 55(4), 700–721.

Baumeister, R. F. (1999). Self-concept, self-esteem, and identity. In V. J. Derlega, B. A. Winstead, & W. H. Jones (Eds.), *Nelson-Hall series in psychology. Personality: Contemporary theory and research* (pp. 339–375). Chicago: Nelson-Hall.

Baym, N. K. (2010). Communities and networks. *Personal connections in the digital age.* Malden, MA: Polity Press.

Bonds-Raacke, J., & Raacke, J. (2010). MySpace and Facebook: Identifying dimensions of uses and gratifications for friend networking sites. *Individual Differences Research* 8(1), 27–33.

Brandtzæg, P. B., & Heim, J. (2009). Why people use social networking sites. In A. A. Ozok & P. Zaphiris, (Eds.), *Online communities and social computing,* (pp. 143–152). Berlin, Heidelberg: Springer-Verlag.

Brown, G., Michinov, N., & Manago, A. (2017). Private message me s'il vous plait: Preferences for personal and masspersonal communications on Facebook among American and French students. *Computers in Human Behavior 70*, 143–152.

Castells, M. (1996). *The Rise of the network society.* Oxford: Blackwell.

Cho, S. E. (2010). *A cross-cultural comparison of Korean and American social network sites: Exploring cultural differences in social relationships and self-presentation* (Unpublished doctoral dissertation). Rutgers University.

Coulson, M., & Barnett, J. (2015). The presentation of self in otherworldly life. In A. Attrill (Ed.), *Cyberpsychology* (pp. 108–127). Oxford: Oxford University Press.

Craig, C. S., & Douglas, S. P. (2006). Beyond national culture: Implications of cultural dynamics for consumer research. *International Marketing Review* 23(3), 322–342.

Dhoest, A., & Szulc, L. (2016). Navigating online selves: Social, cultural, and material contexts of social media use by diasporic gay men. *Social Media + Society* 2(4), 1–10.

Enzensberger, H. M. (1970). Constituents of a theory of the media. In: N. Wardrip-Fruin & N. Montfort (Eds.), *The New Media Reader* (pp. 261–275). Cambridge, MA: MIT Press.

Fenton, N., & Downey, J. (2003). New media, counter publicity and the public sphere. *New Media & Society* 5(2), 185–202.

Ferraro, G. P. (1990). *The cultural dimension of international business*. Englewood Cliffs, NJ: Prentice Hall.

Fogg, B. J., & Iizawa, D., (2008). Online persuasion in Facebook and Mixi: A cross-cultural comparison. In H. Oinas-Kukkonen, P. Hasle, M. Harjumaa, K. Segerståhl, & P. Øhrstrøm (Eds.), *Persuasive Technology* (pp. 35–46). Berlin, Heidelberg: Springer. https://freedomhouse.org/report/freedom-net/2012/saudi-arabia

Gao, Z., & Newman, C. (2005). Converging cultural values? A comparative study of Chinese and U.S. college students. Paper presented at the Cross-Cultural Research Conference, Puerto Rico, 2004.

Gudykunst, W. B., Yang, S. J. M., & Nishida, T. (1987). Cultural differences in self-consciousness and self-monitoring. *Communication Research 14*(1), 7–34.

Hall, E. T. (1976). *Beyond culture*. New York, NY: Doubleday.

Hall, E. & Hall, M. (1990). *Understanding cultural differences: Germans, French and Americans*. Boston, MA: Intercultural Press.

Haslam, S. A. & Reicher, S. D. (2014). When prisoners take over the prison: A social psychology of resistance. *Personality and Social Psychology Review 16*(2), 154–179.

Hew, K. F. (2011). Students' and teachers' use of Facebook. *Computers in Human Behavior 27*(2), 662–676.

Hill, C. W. L. (2008). *International business: Competing in the global marketplace* (6th ed.). New York, NY: McGraw-Hill/Irwin.

Hillier, L., Mitchell, J. K., & Ybarra, M. L. (2012). The internet as a safety net: Findings from a series of online focus groups with LGB and Non-LGB young people in the United States. *Journal of LGBT Youth 9*(3), 225–246.

Hofstede, G. (1991). *Cultures and organisations: Software of the mind*. London: McGraw-Hill.

Hofstede, G. (2001). *Culture's consequences: Comparing values, behaviors, institutions and organizations across nations*. Thousand Oaks, CA: Sage Publications, Inc.

Ingram, D. (2017, 27 June). *Facebook hits 2 billion-user mark, doubling in size since 2012*. Retrieved from https://uk.reuters.com/article/us-facebook-users/facebook-hits-2-billion-user-mark-doubling-in-size-since-2012-idUKKBN19I2GG

Jenkins, H. (2004). The cultural logic of media convergence. *International Journal of Cultural Studies 7*(33), 33–43.

Kemp, S. (2017, 24 January). *Digital in 2017 Global Overview*. Retrieved from https://wearesocial.com/special-reports/digital-in-2017-global-overview

Kim, H. S., & Sherman, D. K. (2007). Express yourself: Culture and the effect of self-expression on choice. *Journal of Personality and Social Psychology 92*(1), 1–11.

Kim, Y., Sohn, D., & Choi, S. M. (2011). Cultural difference in motivations for using social network sites: A comparative study of American and Korean college students. *Computers in Human Behavior 27*(1), 365–372.

Kittler, M. G., Rygl, D., & Mackinnon, A. (2011). Beyond culture or beyond control? Reviewing the use of Hall's high-/low-context concept. *International Journal of Cross Cultural Management 11*(1), 63–82.

Leach, C. W., & Livingstone, A. G. (2015). Contesting the meaning of intergroup disadvantage: Towards a psychology of resistance. *Journal of Social Issues 71*(3), 614–632.

Lee-Won, R. J., Shim, M., Joo, K. Y., & Park, S. G. (2014). Who puts the best "face" forward on Facebook? Positive self-presentation in online social networking and the role of self-consciousness, actual-to-total Friends ratio, and culture. *Computers in Human Behavior 39*, 413–423.

Lin, C. A. (2012). International advertising theory and methodology in the digital information age. In S. Okazaki (Ed.), *Handbook of research on international advertising* (pp. 279–302), Cheltenham: Edward Elgar Publishing.

Macintosh, L., & Bryson, M. (2008). Youth, MySpace, and the interstitial spaces of becoming and belonging. *Journal of LGBT Youth* 5(1), 133–142.

Markus, H. R., & Kitayama, S. (1991). Culture and the self: Implications for cognition, emotion, and motivation. *Psychological Review 98*(2), 224.

Marshall, T. C. (2008). Cultural differences in intimacy: The influence of gender-role ideology and individualism-collectivism. *Journal of Social and Personal Relationships* 25(1), 143–168.

McKenna, K. Y. A., & Bargh, J. A. (2000). Plan 9 From cyberspace: The implications of the Internet for personality and social psychology. *Personality and Social Psychology Review* 4(1), 57–75.

Newsom, V., & Lengel, L. (2012). Arab women, social media, and the Arab Spring: Applying the framework of digital reflexivity to analyze gender and online activism. *Journal of International Women's Studies* 13(5), 31–45. Retrieved from http://vc.bridgew.edu/jiws/vol13/iss5/5

Pflug, J. (2011). Contextuality and computer-mediated communication: A cross cultural comparison. *Computers in Human Behavior* 27(1), 131–137.

Posey, C., Lowry, P. B., Roberts, T. L., & Ellis, T. S. (2010). Proposing the online community self-disclosure model: The case of working professionals in France and the U.K. who use online communities. *European Journal of Information Systems* 19(2), 181–195.

Prensky, M. (2001). Digital natives, digital immigrants Part 1. *On the Horizon* 9(5), 1–6.

Rui, J. R., & Stefanone, M. A. (2013). Strategic self-presentation online: A cross-cultural study. *Computers in Human Behavior* 29(1), 110–118.

Schwartz, S. H. (1990). Individualism-collectivism critique and proposed refinements. *Journal of Cross-Cultural Psychology* 21(2), 139–157.

Schwartz, S. H. (1992). Universals in the content and structure of values: Theoretical advances and empirical tests in 20 countries. In M. Zanna (Ed.), *Advances in experimental social psychology* (pp. 1–65). New York: Academic Press.

Selim, A. H. (2016). *Why the caged bird sings: Cultural factors underlying the use of Online Social Networks among Saudi Arabian and UK users* (Doctoral thesis). University of Sussex.

Selim, A. H., Long, K. M., & Vignoles, V. L. (2014). Exploring identity motives in Twitter usage in Saudi Arabia and the UK. *Studies in Health Technology and Informatics 199*, 128–132.

Smith, P. B., Fischer, R., Vignoles, V. L., & Bond, M. H. (2013). *Understanding social psychology across cultures: Engaging with others in a changing world.* London: Sage.

Sunstein, C. (2001). *Republic.com.* Princeton, NJ: Princeton University Press.

Tomlinson, J. (2007). Cultural globalization. In G. Ritzer (ed.), *The Blackwell companion to globalization*, 352–366. Malden, MA: Blackwell.

Thomson, R. & Ito, N. (2012). The effect of relational mobility on SNS user behavior: A study of Japanese dual-users of Mixi and Facebook. *The Journal of International Media, Communication, and Tourism Studies 14*, 3–22.

Verderber, K. S., Sellnow, D. D., & Verderber, R. F. (2010). *Communicate!* Boston, MA: Cengage Learning.

Vergeer, M., & Pelzer, B. (2009). Consequences of media and Internet use for offline and online network capital and well-being. A causal model approach. *Journal of Computer-Mediated Communication* 15(1), 189–210.

Vignoles, V. L., Owe, E., Becker, M., Smith, P. B., Easterbrook, M. J., Brown, R., . . . Bond, M. H. (2016). Beyond the "east–west" dichotomy: Global variation in cultural models of selfhood. *Journal of Experimental Psychology: General 145*(8), 966–1000.

Walther, J. B. (1996). Computer-mediated communication: Impersonal, interpersonal, and hyperpersonal Interaction. *Communication Research 23*(1), 3–43.

Woodhouse, A. G., and Ahn, I. (2008) Culture's consequences on experiencing international tourism services and products. In A. G. Woodhouse and D. Martin (Eds.) *Tourism management: Analysis, behaviour and strategy* (pp. 28–62). Oxford: CABI.

Worth, R. F. (2012). Saudis cross social boundaries on Twitter. The New York Times. Retrieved from http://www.nytimes.com/2012/10/21/world/middleeast/saudis-cross-social-boundaries-on-twitter.html?_r=0

Wu, J. & Lu, H. (2013). Cultural and gender differences in self-disclosure on social network sites. In J. Pertley, (Ed.), *Media and public shaming: Drawing the boundaries of disclosure* (pp. 97–113). London: I. B. Tauris & Co. Ltd.

Zhao, S., Grasmuck, S., & Martin, J. (2008). Identity construction on Facebook: Digital empowerment in anchored relationships. *Computers in Human Behavior 24*(5), 1816–1836.

CHAPTER 11

ONLINE ROMANTIC RELATIONSHIPS

JOANNE LLOYD, ALISON ATTRILL-SMITH,
AND CHRIS FULLWOOD

INTRODUCTION

A wide range of interactions and experiences fall under the umbrella of "online romantic relationships" (Attrill, 2015). Perhaps one of the most obvious uses of the Internet for romantic relationships is online dating, where people typically seek connections with potential real-world romantic and/or sexual partners via the Internet (Hamilton, 2016). However, the Internet is also used as a tool to maintain or support existing *offline* romantic relationships, and this can take a number of forms (Hampton, Rawlings, Treger, & Sprecher, 2017). Although less commonplace, some people also have romantic relationships which are conducted solely in the online domain, with no offline component at all (Rabby, 2007).

This chapter begins by providing an overview of how people in existing relationships relate to one another in online spaces, and how they use online technologies in their relationships. It then narrows its focus to online dating and presents a summary of what we know about who does it, how they do it, and why. It then addresses the pros and cons of online dating in detail. Finally, it considers the practical and psychological benefits people can derive from it, and the potential harm that can be experienced when online dating goes wrong.

Existing Romantic Relationships
in Online Spaces

Remote methods have been used for both initiating and maintaining romantic relationships throughout history; Whitty (2007) draws parallels between contemporary "online courting" and the use of telegrams and letters in the past. Romantic relationships developed and nurtured via methods alternative to face-to-face interactions are certainly not a novelty. However, the nature and scope of such interactions have been dramatically influenced by the inception of the Internet (Murray & Campbell, 2015), the increase in its accessibility and affordability, and the growing proportion of the population who use it on a regular basis (Dutton & Blank, 2014). The development of high-speed Internet, increasingly affordable tariffs, and smartphone technology have all contributed to a situation where keeping in touch with people online—at least in economically more developed countries (Crowcroft, Wolisz, & Sathiaseelan, 2015)—is easier than ever before. It is also a particularly rewarding use of technology; using mobile phones for the purpose of social communication has been found to be associated with bonding and self-rated feelings of well-being (Chan, 2015).

People in long-distance relationships are certainly using the Internet as a means of maintaining those existing relationships (Hampton et al., 2017), and researchers are exploring ways in which "non-proximal" romantic couples can use technology to sustain relationships and improve well-being (Craft & Garcia, 2016). However, while people who live far away from one another are particularly frequent users of online tools such as social networking to keep their relationships going, those who live near to one another also make use of these methods to sustain their relationships (Billedo, Kerkhof, & Finkenauer, 2015; Lomanowska & Guitton, 2016).

One of the means of online relationship maintenance is through direct, text-based, two-way communication through various forms of text or instant messaging, or through emails. This is arguably very similar in format to traditional letters, but a key difference is that online text messages have the capacity to be used in a more immediate or "synchronous" way (hence the term "instant messaging"). In line with this, some romantic couples describe appreciating the way that text messages enable them to feel connected, allowing for contact with their partner to be sustained in a more consistent, constant way than even telephone calls or voicemails can afford (Pettigrew, 2009). However, there is some evidence that the nature, rather than the frequency, of messages exchanged between romantic partners is the better measure of their affection for one another, and of their satisfaction with the relationship (Schade, Sandberg, Bean, Busby, & Coyne, 2013), so it is not a simple case of "the more the better."

In contrast to the aforementioned benefits of text messages, research has found that in all kinds of relationships, "richer" communication methods with wider availability of non-verbal cues, e.g. voice or video chat, are generally linked to greater relationship satisfaction (Goodman-Deane, Mieczakowski, Johnson, Goldhaber, & Clarkson, 2016). Methods of online communication that incorporate visual information, such as FaceTime, video messaging, and Skype, are particularly favored by couples in long-distance relationships, compared with those who live close to their partners, as the additional audio and/or visual cues are perceived as facilitating intimacy (Janning, Gao, & Snyder, 2018). Evidently, different formats of online communication offer different benefits, and individual couples will vary in their use of, and preference for, these formats.

Beyond one-to-one online communications between people in a relationship, there has been some interesting research into the ways that individuals in a couple use relatively "public" online spaces within their relationships. For example, there are at least two contrasting ways in which couples use social networking sites (SNSs), as illustrated by a survey of 272 young adult attached Facebook users carried out by Billedo, Kerkhof, and Finkenauer (2015). The first can be summed up as "relational maintenance," i.e. to maintain closeness or keep the relationship going. There are a number of ways in which social networking can do this, e.g. an individual can update their relationship status information to acknowledge their commitment to their partner, post pictures of themselves with the partner, or make affectionate statements about them (Utz & Beukeboom, 2011).

Other online behaviors that are sometimes use in relational maintenance (not necessarily via SNSs) are broadly referred to as "partnered online sexual activities" (Shaughnessy, Fudge, & Byers, 2017). These encompass many forms of two-way online sexual interactions such as exchanging sexual messages or using webcams for erotic purposes. A recent study of 239 university students in Canada found that around three-quarters of those surveyed had engaged in such behaviors in their lifetime, and two-thirds within the last few months (Shaughnessy, Fudge, & Byers, 2017). While this particular study did not specifically enquire about who engaged in the activities with whom ("partnered" simply refers to the fact that they are non-solo activities, and doesn't presume an ongoing romantic partnership), the results do serve to illustrate some of the means by which romantic partners can engage with one another online. Of course, being a convenience sample of students with a relatively young average age means that this study does not present a comprehensive picture of the frequency or popularity of online sexual activities among the general population.

Another way in which SNSs are used by those in pre-existing romantic relationships is for the purpose of "partner surveillance," i.e. keeping an eye on a partner's activities online (Billedo, Kerkhof, & Finkenauer, 2015; Fox & Warber, 2014). This motive is generally much less positive, with use of Facebook for monitoring one's partner being linked with feelings of jealousy (Dainton & Stokes, 2015), and some evidence suggesting that jealousy and surveillance on Facebook are associated with psychological and physical aggression towards the partner in the offline world (Brem, Spiller, & Vandehey, 2015).

ONLINE INFIDELITY AND
EXTRA-DYADIC INTERACTIONS

The themes of surveillance and jealousy lead to the issue of online infidelity, another topic of study within the realm of online relationships (Sahni & Jain, 2018). The term "extra-dyadic interactions" has been coined to describe romantic liaisons with someone outside of a supposedly monogamous relationship, and there is a growing body of research into online extra-dyadic interactions (Martins et al., 2016). There is a certain amount of disagreement between individuals about what constitutes "cheating" when the infidelity is constrained to the online realm, and in general, people judge online infidelities as less serious than physical transgressions involving sexual intimacy (Thompson & O'Sullivan, 2016), although they are nevertheless linked with negative impact on mental health and quality of life (Desai, Jha, Choudhury, & Garg, 2018). The ambiguity over what constitutes infidelity online, and the relative perceived acceptability of it, are thought to contribute to its prevalence (Vossler, 2016), though it is important to remember that traits associated with the individual, rather than just the nature of the Internet, are also key in predicting who engages in online infidelity (Vossler, 2016).

Several forms of online infidelity, which are generally considered more clear-cut examples of "cheating," *do* overlap with the offline, physical world. For example, when people in a (supposedly) monogamous relationship use online dating sites specifically to progress to meeting offline with someone who is not their partner. Weiser et al. (2017) surveyed over 500 Tinder users, and while relatively few confessed to this behavior themselves, most reported knowing someone who had used the dating site to facilitate offline affairs.

It is worth noting at this point that, in recent years, research has begun to explore more diverse forms of online romantic relationships, such as polyamory, or consensual non-monogamy (Manning & Bloedel, 2017), in which multiple partners are openly involved—with the consent of everyone involved. A recent study in the US estimated that around one in five single people had, at some point, had a consensual non-monogamous relationship (Haupert, Gesselman, Moors, Fisher, & Garcia, 2017), so this preference is not as rare as might be imagined. While online daters who subscribe to this relationship model sometimes simply use free-text in their profile description to explain this to prospective partners, there are websites (e.g. the popular mainstream site "OKCupid") which have responded to this demand by adding the functionality for romantically attached polyamorous members to link their profiles to one another, and search for additional parties as a linked unit.

The majority of online dating service users, however, are single people seeking to make a connection with a potential partner (Finkel, Eastwick, Karney, Reis, & Sprecher, 2012), with the goal generally being to progress to meeting for a date offline (Khan & Chaudhry, 2015). The next section discusses the popularity of online dating, and the range of online dating services available.

Popularity of Online Dating

A 2013 random sampling telephone survey of 2,252 US adults found that 11 percent of the population had participated in online dating by using an app or website. This number increased to 38 percent when looking specifically at people who described their relationship status as "single and looking" (Smith & Duggan, 2013). Dating website use, at the time of the survey, was somewhat more common than dating app use, with 11 percent of Internet users (which equates to 9 percent of adults) reporting that they had used a dating website, and 7 percent of mobile phone app users (which equates to 3 percent of adults) reporting that they had used a dating app on their phone (Smith & Duggan, 2013).

In a national survey of over 19,000 Americans who got married between 2005 and 2012, Cacioppo, Cacioppo, Gonzaga, Ogburn, and VanderWeele (2013) found that over a third met online, which fits with the findings of Rosenfeld and Thomas (2012), who report that online dating is becoming as popular as other, more traditional methods of meeting a romantic partner. Attitudes of the general population towards online dating are also becoming more positive, with fewer people considering it to be an act of "desperation," and the majority of people deeming it "a good way to meet people" (Smith & Duggan, 2013). This has led to predictions that, in the coming years, the proportion of the population engaging in online dating will continue to increase; however, researchers have also stressed that it is unlikely that other means of meeting partners will be completely displaced by the Internet (Rosenfeld & Thomas, 2012).

Types of Online Dating

Online dating platforms are many and varied in their user base, format, and features. Some are primarily website based, while others are available only in mobile app format. However, increasingly they are accessible in multiple modalities, so that users can access the same content on a laptop or PC at home, and also on their smartphone while on the go. There has been little research into differences between website and app use, but a recent study comparing Tinder (app) users with users of online dating websites found that age was the main difference, with the app users being younger, on average. They were also more sexually permissive, but the authors attributed this to the age difference, rather than to the app preference per se (Gatter & Hodgkinson, 2016). There is also some evidence that app use may be particularly engaging, at least initially, when online daters migrate from a web-based dating site to an app interface, resulting in more frequent usage and more interactions with other daters (Jung, Bapna, Ramaprasad, & Umyarov, 2018). However, as mentioned, it is not necessarily a dichotomy, and many users interact with the same service via both modalities.

"Location-based real-time dating" (LBRTD) services use location tracking technology to allow users to connect with people in close geographical proximity. One of the first

LBRTD apps, launched in 2009, was Grindr, an app for men seeking men, which is still very popular, with millions of daily users. Subsequent, well-known providers of LBRTD include Tinder and Happn. While they all use location data in order to support inter-actions between daters who are physically near to one another, the exact architecture of LBRTD sites varies. Grindr, for example shows only a set number of users, who are clos-est geographically, at any point in time (Blackwell, Birnholtz, & Abbott, 2015), whereas apps such as OKCupid allow users to use geolocation features based on the immediate location, or set a search area independent of their current location.

While many online dating services do not have a specific target user base, and are used by individuals of all genres and sexual orientations from a wide range of demographic backgrounds (e.g. OKCupid, Match.com, Tinder), there are some that are marketed towards users of a specific sexual orientation (e.g. Grindr), age (e.g. silversingles.co.uk), or domestic situation (e.g. justsingleparents.com). Some sites are aimed at niche mar-kets such as those seeking partners in uniform (uniformdating.com), those with beards or an affinity for them (bristlr.com), and those in search of fellow dog owners (twindog.co), to name but a few.

Online dating services also vary in the nature of the connections they promote. Some are overtly marketed towards people seeking a long-term relationship (e.g. "notforplayers. com") whereas others are aimed at those seeking a "hook-up," a casual sex arrangement, or a short-term relationship (e.g. "fling.com"). As mentioned, there are also sites that target those seeking discrete affairs (e.g. "illicitencounters.com"; see Harrison, 2017 for a discussion of the potential impact of this). Many online dating providers cater to a range of relationship "seriousness" preferences, and users are prompted within their profile information to indicate what type of connection they are seeking. However, some sites and apps evolve a particular reputation through being primarily frequented by "serious" versus "casual" daters over time. Tinder, for example, is not marketed specifically as an app for casual encounters, but even in the scientific literature it has earned the label of "hook-up app" (Sevi, Aral, & Eskenazi, 2017). It is debatable how accurate this assump-tion is, however. Timmermans and De Caluwé (2017a) examined motives for using Tinder, and while casual sex was a motivating factor, it was on average a weaker motive than seeking love. The interesting question of motivations is discussed later in the chapter.

Another variable feature across online dating platforms is the mechanics behind the "matching" process. Tong, Hancock, and Slatcher (2016) summarized three key formats which they refer to as "see-and-screen," "algorithm," and "blended." The "see-and-screen" label refers to systems where the user can view other users at their leisure and identify for themselves those in whom they are interested, using filters of their choosing to per-sonalize their search. Tong and colleagues refer to Match.com and PlentyOfFish.com as well-known examples using this approach. The "algorithm" label refers to systems such as that used by eHarmony.com, where the site or app suggests users with whom a person might be compatible, based on information such as responses to personality question-naires. Finally, the blended format encompasses platforms where the user can both screen other users themselves, and benefit from algorithmic match suggestions, and this approach is used by sites including OKCupid.com (Tong, Hancock, and Slatcher, 2016).

Within and beyond these categories, however, there is yet further differentiation. Some services allow all users to view the profiles of all other members, whereas others restrict views in some way, e.g. to "compatible" users, who match on specific predetermined criteria. Some sites allow unrestricted *viewing* of profiles, but restrict *contact* to those who mutually confirm interest in one another; while others place no restrictions on contact, or allow users to "block" other users under particular conditions. Methods by which users can signal interest in one another also vary by site. Many sites offer relatively passive methods, such as "liking" other members' profiles, or sending virtual "winks," alongside more active methods of sending direct messages. Tong and colleagues (2016) highlight that the nature of the interface within dating sites is important psychologically, as it can influence users' sense of autonomy, and their perceived control over their dating behavior, although interestingly, other researchers have found that more choice does not necessarily lead to better decisions about compatible matches (Wu & Chiou, 2009).

CHARACTERISTICS OF ONLINE DATERS

Perhaps one of the most widely investigated demographic characteristics in relation to online dating is gender. The majority of studies that have explored gender differences have found that males are generally somewhat more likely to use online dating services than females (Abramova, Baumann, Krasnova, & Buxmann, 2016). In a 2016 YouGov poll of UK adults, for example, 22 percent of males reported having used an online dating service, compared with 19 percent of females (Dahlgreen, 2016). Abramova and colleagues suggest that this could be because males tend to have positive opinions about online dating and its effectiveness (see also Madden & Lenhart, 2006), although this could, of course, be a consequence rather than a cause of higher rates of online dating in males. Additionally, it could even simply be that males are more likely to admit to online dating, given their tendency to express more positive attitudes towards it.

In terms of sexuality, Johnson, Vilceanu, and Pontes (2017) analyzed data from the Pew Foundation's 2013 survey of over 2,200 US adults, and found that lesbian, gay, and bisexual individuals were significantly more likely than heterosexual participants to report having used a dating app or website. The authors suggest that the ease of communicating sexual orientation may be one of the reasons why online dating might appeal to LGBT adults (Johnson, Vilceanu, & Pontes, 2017). Rosenfield and Thomas (2012) also reflect on popularity of online dating among gay and lesbian individuals, and apply a market forces metaphor. They postulate that having a comparatively small pool of potential mates is a driving factor. They refer to single, middle-aged heterosexuals as another group of people operating in what they term a "thin market," due to a large proportion potential mates being already partnered by this life-stage, and they reference findings by Lever, Grov, Royce, and Gillespie (2008) that online dating is also popular with this demographic (Rosenfield & Thomas, 2012).

Indeed, a number of studies have found interest in online dating increases rather than declines with age (e.g. Stephure, Boon, MacKinnon, & Deveau, 2009). However, it is not a straightforward linear relationship; it appears to be particularly popular between ages 30–50, with a peak at around age 40 (Valkenburg & Peter, 2007). It is worth noting that the relationship between age and online dating is likely to vary depending on the type of dating being engaged in, and the end goal. A recent study found that use of the dating app Tinder was actually very common amongst a Dutch sample of young "emerging adults," aged 18–30 (Sumter, Vandenbosch, & Ligtenberg, 2017), but rather than being indicative of a concerted strategy to seek a partner, many reported using it as entertainment or for "trendiness."

In terms of personality traits, some studies have found that certain features seem linked with likelihood of engaging in online dating. Timmermans and De Caluwé (2017b) for example, found that single people who used the popular dating app Tinder were, on average, higher on the traits of extraversion and openness to experience, and lower on conscientiousness, than people who didn't use the app. Hance, Blackhart, and Dew (2017) found that people high on rejection sensitivity (i.e. more easily hurt by rejection) were more likely to participate in online dating than those less sensitive to rejection, and this appeared to be because they felt more able to "be themselves" online. This may be because features of the online environment make rejection less aversive; for example, it is easy to imagine that the person doing the rejecting is simply swamped with other messages (Hamilton, 2016). However, it could also be linked to the fact that people tend to think they are more likely to succeed (i.e. less likely to face rejection) in online than offline dating (Fullwood & Attrill-Smith, 2018).

Bearing in mind the vast array of types of online dating services, and the multiple ways in which people use them, it is interesting to consider how particular personality traits vary across different types of online daters. Chan (2017) examined links between an array of personal attributes and attitudes, and people's intentions to use dating sites in the pursuit of romance versus casual sex. While sensation-seeking and use of a smartphone were linked with both romantic and sexual motives for online dating, other characteristics were only associated with one or the other. Trust of people online, for example, was linked to intentions to use online dating for romance, whereas perceptions of social norms regarding use of online dating to find casual sex were linked to intentions to use online dating in that way oneself. In other words, people who felt that seeking casual sex via online dating is *the norm* were more likely to plan on using it in that way themselves.

Sevi, Aral, and Eskenazi (2017) also explored what predicted use of the dating app Tinder for pursuing casual sex, and in a sample of 169 users they found that it was linked to scoring low on a measure of sexual disgust and high on a measure of sociosexuality. As many of the items in the sociosexuality scale refer to positive feelings about casual sexual interactions, this may seem a fairly self-evident connection, but is useful in that it serves to demonstrate that people's everyday attitudes towards sex are played out in the ways in which they use online dating services.

Individuals' aims and objectives when using online dating services differ in more ways than simply whether they are seeking casual sex or a romantic, long-term relationship. The following section summarizes what we know about the motivations for using online dating services, and how these can vary across individuals.

Motivations for Online Dating

Online dating has sometimes been referred to as "relationshopping" (Heino, Ellison, & Gibbs, 2010), and perhaps the most obvious answer to the question of why people engage in it is that they want to secure some kind of relationship or other. But why do people choose to seek a relationship online, in particular? One feature of online dating that appears to attract people is the ability to easily screen potential matches for particular characteristics (Hamilton, 2016). This can facilitate finding someone with particular physical characteristics, but these are, arguably, relatively easy to screen for in offline interactions as well. Where the online environment gives a more pronounced advantage is in allowing users to learn upfront whether a potential partner matches with them on less visible features such as their desire for children (Hitsch, Hortaçsu, & Ariely, 2010), educational level (Skopek, Schulz, & Blossfeld, 2010), or political beliefs (Huber & Malhotra, 2017). While homophily (tendency to be attracted to people who are similar to oneself) is important to many people when selecting a partner (Hamilton, 2016), these types of questions can be difficult to ask a potential partner about in a face-to-face situation. However, in the online dating realm, they are often expected, and even incorporated into standard profile information, so that members need not even explicitly ask them.

Even if an online dater is presented with potential matches who perhaps don't list certain pieces of desired information, it is generally easier to ask awkward or personal questions of others in the online environment. This is linked to the "online disinhibition effect," or the tendency to behave in more uninhibited ways in an online environment than in an offline encounter (Suler, 2004). Of particular relevance here is the benign online disinhibition effect, which relates to the positive side of the phenomenon, whereby features such as invisibility and lack of eye contact encourage people to disclose more personal information online (Lapidot-Lefler & Barak, 2015).

As mentioned in the previous section, there is a distinction between using online dating as a means of embarking on a romantic relationship, and as a means of pursuing casual sexual encounters. Homophily is likely to be less important to individuals using online dating for initiating short-term encounters, if we extrapolate from findings in the offline realm that typical gender differences in the characteristics sought in a (long-term) partner become less pronounced when choosing a short-term mate, and both males and females focus on physical attractiveness (Li et al., 2013). However, it is possible that the expectation of improving one's chances of finding an attractive partner is also one of the motivations for using online dating services. Fullwood and Attrill-Smith (2018) found that people perceive their chances of success in a dating scenario as higher, even when ratings are based on pictures of the same people, when framed in an online versus an off-line meeting context.

While both love and casual sex are, as might be expected, key motivations for the use of online dating services, it is worth noting that there are also a number of motivating factors that are not actually related to relationship initiation per se. Specifically, "validation of self-worth," "thrill of excitement," and "trendiness" all feature as motives for using the Tinder app (Sumter, Vandenbosch, & Ligtenberg, 2017). In Timmermans and De Caluwé's (2017a) examination of motivations for using Tinder, "entertainment" was actually the top reason for use. This finding is likely partially related to the game-like nature of the Tinder app, which is common to many dating apps. This is consistent with findings that dating app users were more likely to be seeking fun or casual sex, compared with dating website users who were more likely to be seeking a relationship (Bryant & Sheldon, 2017).

Certain groups of people, i.e. those who experience obstacles or limitations of some kind in an offline dating scenario, may have additional specific motivations for online dating. Lemke and Weber (2017) explored the online dating behavior of men who have sex with men, and in particular, those whose sexuality is hidden in their offline lives (i.e. who overtly identify as heterosexual to their friends and family). This group of men used dating sites in somewhat different ways to openly homosexual online daters, and avoided "gay venues" offline, but did report engaging in online sexual activities, and used online dating sites to initiate offline meetings. This suggests that anonymity (in terms of separation from one's offline social circle) may be an important motivator for this group of online daters, along with the opportunity to express one's sexuality in a way that is, for whatever reason, difficult in their day-to-day offline world.

Individuals with disabilities may also have specific motivations for online dating. Mazur (2017) describes how online dating affords a relative respite from stigma that may be experienced offline, as people can "be strategic in how they present both themselves and their disabilities" (p. 150). It also gives people the ability to seek romantic connections with people with similar disabilities, if this is desired (Mazur, 2017).

This leads us onto the many and varied potential advantages of online dating, which are covered in more detail in the next section.

PROS OF ONLINE DATING

Perhaps one of the most obvious advantages of using online dating platforms, particularly those which can be accessed on our smartphones, is that it is a more convenient, straightforward, and accessible way to tap into a large network of potential romantic or sexual partners. In contrast to more "traditional" methods of meeting people (e.g. singles nights), online dating services work around the clock and are not bound by space or time. As long as the user has access to an Internet connection, he or she can cultivate and advance relationships with multiple potential partners simultaneously, at any time of the day, from any location, and without the need to don one's glad rags and venture to the nearest drinking establishment. Perpetual connectivity, a priori declarations of "availability," and a swifter process of intimate self-disclosure (Cooper & Sportolari, 1997)—a probable artifact of the online disinhibition effect (Suler, 2004)—are also likely to result in the acceleration of the dating process (Bergström, 2011). In other words, online daters should be able to come to a decision much more quickly about whether a specific online contact is worth pursuing further, for example, deciding if they want to "take it offline." Although to some this might appear shallow and calculated, drawing further comparisons with the "relationshopping" analogy, this approach to finding a partner might be particularly appealing to individuals who lead very busy lives, for example, because of work or family commitments (Henry-Waring & Barraket, 2008).

Because online daters are usually expected to create a profile for the purpose of interacting with other users, this means that it is possible to screen other daters for desired characteristics. Because most dating sites encourage users to enter this basic personal information into their profiles, if a dater has a specific preference for age range, religious inclination, height, location, etc., they can make use of search functions to find others who meet their personal criteria (Hitsch, Hortaçsu, & Ariely, 2010). Moreover, this is likely to be far easier than screening for desired characteristics in the offline world, as unless there is already access to this information second-hand, there is normally need to make direct requests for information that is not communicated in a physical sense.

Further advantages to connecting with potential partners via online dating services have been noted by Skopek and colleagues (cited in Aretz, Demuth, Schmidt, & Vierlein, 2010). Specifically, they indicate a number of idiosyncratic features of the online dating arena, including the potential to cast one's net wider, increasing the pool of prospective partners and potentially permitting people to meet individuals who they may have been unlikely to encounter in different circumstances. They also note that online dating does not come with an expectation of only talking to one individual at a time, meaning that daters can send messages to numerous people simultaneously, and therefore increase their odds of finding a connection. Finally, they note that daters can choose to represent themselves in the manner that they want to, primarily because the majority of interactions take place with strangers who do not have access to one's offline identity to verify the authenticity of self-presentation.

That online daters can make strategic decisions about how they choose to represent themselves to other daters links to Walther's Hyperpersonal Model of computer-mediated communication (Walther, 1996; 2007). The basic premise of this model is that being online affords individuals with a far greater degree of control over content creation and the pace of interactions. For example, Walther notes that online interactions are characterized by editability. Online daters can, for instance, decide which photographs they think represent them in the most attractive light, and this may even entail taking images specifically for the purpose of online dating and strategically uploading these to the site(s). It could also include uploading photos taken at a younger age, having them taken professionally, or using software to retouch or edit images to make them look more desirable

(Hancock & Toma, 2009). Daters can write, edit, and re-edit their personal descriptions (even taking advice from friends, family, and the Internet on how to best sell themselves) until they feel that it describes them to other daters in the most appealing way. Communication in the online world can also be distinguished by asynchronicity. This means that one-to-one communications usually take place outside of "real" time, because most dating sites allow communications via e-mail type services rather than synchronous chat. Because conversations are not in real time, users can deliberate more deeply and think more strategically about how they want others to perceive them. This is in stark contrast to face-to-face communications, where there is an expectation to keep the flow of communication going and react in the moment.

Considering the increased control over self-presentation in online dating draws on Goffman's (1959) self-presentation theory, which posits that individuals accentuate positive aspects of the self while suppressing more negative aspects in order to win favor with others and achieve a desired outcome. Indeed, in the world of online dating, there is abundant evidence that online daters regularly "stretch the truth" in their online profiles. For example, Hancock, Toma, and Ellison (2007) found that men were more likely to exaggerate their height, whereas women were more likely to understate their weight. Although online daters will undoubtedly have to walk a fine line between creating a desirable yet authentic online self-representation, particularly if the aim is to progress the relationship to the offline space, being able to craft a more attractive image of the self online may be a more liberating experience (Fullwood & Attrill-Smith, 2018), particularly if this self-presentation relates to a "possible" or "ideal" self (Ellison, Hancock, & Toma, 2012). Indeed, although presenting an idealized image of the self may be considered a form of self-enhancement (Swann, 1990), it is also conceivable that making claims about having certain desirable traits and characteristics might motivate some online daters to work towards self-improvement (Ellison, Hancock, & Toma, 2012; Schlenker, 1980). Additionally, drawing on Higgins' (1987) self-discrepancy theory, in narrowing the gap between the "actual" and the "ideal" self, the individual could also conceivably experience improvements to well-being. Although this research implies that online dating should be particularly appealing to those who are shy or socially anxious, research suggests that those with lower self-esteem (Kim, Kwon, & Lee, 2009) and those with higher dating anxiety (Valkenburg & Peter, 2007) are more likely to avoid joining online dating services. This may be because socially anxious people consider the idea of presenting the self to multiple individuals at once a daunting prospect and therefore engage in an avoidance strategy to protect their own self-worth, for example, from potentially experiencing rejection multiple times (Kim, Kwon, & Lee, 2009).

THE NEGATIVE SIDE OF ONLINE DATING

Thus far, the chapter has looked at how relationships are developed and maintained via the Internet, and how people create an online dating self. This section explores what can happen when these relationships don't work out, or are formed with nefarious intent in mind. It is important to note that not all relationships are started with an intention to hurt or harm another person, either physically, emotionally, or psychologically. As in the offline world, online relationships range from mere acquaintances to romantic liaisons and long-term relationships. Equally, they carry with them similar dangers and impacts as offline relationships. Often, crimes or dangers associated with a romantic relationship are not intentional, but develop during the relationship. That does not mean that they are not associated with personality or mental health disorders. It simply means that sometimes, rage, lust, envy, jealousy, hurt, and other human emotions take over and can drive and dictate negative relationship behaviors both online and offline. Anyone who has experienced a relationship breakdown will likely have experienced the psychological processes outlined in Duck's (1998, 1982) relationship dissolution model. Duck suggests that a relationship can break down in a sequential or compounded manner of the *intrapsychic phase* (the person ponders why the relationship isn't working and might vent emotions to a third party, e.g. a hairdresser), *dyadic phase* (dissatisfaction is discussed with the partner), *social phase* (any relationship exists within a social network—the individual begins to involve that network in the break up), and then finally the *gravedressing phase* (the dissolution of the relationship is final and the individual wants to exit it in a positive light, resulting in negativity towards the ex-partner). This is a simplified version of the model, which also suggests that during the first two phases the relationship might be rescued. Especially during the grave-dressing phase, however, the negativity heaped upon the ex-partner could turn into something far more sinister and damaging than ever considered possible. If we take a moment to consider how easily and wide-reaching such negativity can be bred online, it is not surprising that certain types of negative behaviors are becoming more associated with online than with offline relationships. From stalking and harassment to cyberbullying and domestic abuse, the Internet can, if used inappropriately, offer an offender or perpetrator a golden tool of misuse. These behaviors, and many more, fall within the rubric of cybercrime and are therefore covered in the cybercrime section of this volume. This chapter concentrates on a behavior that has become associated with looking for love online—catfishing. Before doing so, however, it considers briefly what happens when people disseminate sexually explicit images or video of an ex-partner via the Internet. An extremely negative behavior, this act has become known as revenge pornography and since 2015 has become illegal in the UK (see https://www.gov.uk/government/publications/revenge-porn for further information). A jilted lover might hold sexually explicit images or video that they obtained with or without consent from their ex-lover. Taking grave-dressing to the extreme, there are many places across the Internet for sharing such material to bring shame and embarrassment on an ex-partner, not to mention the act of texting such content to the ex's friends, family, and other loved ones. There are a number of high-profile cases which have made the headlines worldwide. As a pre-teen, Amanda Todd began chatting to someone online, and during their online exchanges, she was lured into exposing her breasts to the person she was chatting to. What ensued was a situation of bullying and self-harm, and eventually Amanda took her own life (https://www.youtube.com/watch?v=vOHXGNx-E7E&t=4s). As an aside, Amanda was also the first person to post a flash card story to YouTube in 2012 to leave the legacy of her story prior to taking her own life. As sinister as this event is, Amanda never entered into this online communication imagining it would end the way it did. It could also be suggested that this was one of the very first public cases of catfishing, given that she was lured into exposing herself for nothing other than the perpetrator's manipulation and own gratification.

Catfishing

The term *catfishing* was widely popularized through the MTV program of the same name and a *catfish* refers to someone who pretends to be someone else when interacting with one or many others online (Attrill, Fullwood, & Chadwick, 2015). A catfish may have one or more goals in mind, ranging from financial gain to intentionally inflicting psychological or emotional pain and/or revenge on another person. They do so by using a fake identity to lure someone into communication via dating sites and social media, but also through unsolicited emails and texts. The adopted identity could be a clone of another person's dating or social media profile, or it could be based on fake or stolen images along with false personal information. There are hundreds, if not thousands of mass media reports, TV programs, and even films that concern themselves with the topic of online dating scams. Catfishing is, however, quite specific in that it focuses on adopting an altered or fabricated identity. Those who have seen the TV program Catfish may wonder how the victim did not see or know that the person in the photographs was not real, especially after the claims that their phone camera was permanently broken, they could not afford a mobile phone, or that they could only text and never speak on the phone.

Each person believes in their own ability to spot a fake, but generally, people tend to see what they want to see, i.e. someone will often ignore danger signals present in the online situation in order to feel successful in love. Two fundamental features of human relationships are trust and belonging. The need to feel accepted and wanted by another person is often driven by the basic human need to belong (Baumeister & Leary, 1995; Deci & Ryan, 2000). If that need is being met by someone through an online relationship, recognizing and accepting that they are a fraud or fake could damage that sense of belonging.

News reports in 2013 told the story of a British woman being catfished by a prolific Syrian terrorist with the intent of luring her abroad to engage in warfare. Although the mass media used the term "grooming," Kimberley Miners' experience was equally one of being catfished. In many TV and newspaper reports, Kimberley was cited as saying that she felt like she finally belonged, thus illustrating how perpetrators capitalize on this human need when they lure victims into their control.

Once lured, a person may invest a large amount of time in online exchanges with someone, and there may be an element of embarrassment or self-blame upon recognizing that there is no Adonis or Venus at the other end of the message, but someone who is married, or who is seeking financial gain, revenge, self-gratification, or even terrorist activity. After speaking to someone for a number of months, even years, online, the sudden realization they have been lying about who or what they are not only can result in feelings of being cheated, but also naïve for not seeing danger signals within those exchanges or within the person's dating/social media profile. This self-blame could become even more heightened if the person has told friends and family about dating someone online. While most people recognize danger signals, or red flags, they also admit to not acting on them (Attrill, Fullwood, & Chadwick, 2015). Many maintain the belief in the online relationship, despite all evidence pointing to its being a fraud.

Trust is one of the key components in human relationships. Rarely do people enter into a relationship without some level of trust. Offline, we are more readily able to engage in trust verification to gauge whether someone is the person they present themselves to be, e.g. by meeting their friends and family. The online equivalent of this would be adding someone to social media. It is easier to fabricate these social ties online; indeed, in numerous episodes of *Catfish*, the perpetrator had created multiple Facebook profiles, which they then used to post as different people on the catfish's profile, giving the appearance of an extended social circle. Imagine the elaborative exercise involved in replicating this offline, which would require a number of accomplices to continuously act out certain relative or friend roles! The process of dating someone online, without the ease of trust verification, thus carries an element of risk that does not apply in the same way with offline dating. Although, even offline, the person in the pub who gives you their phone number may initially bend the truth—something common in the early days of relationship building in order to garner interest and liking. The exploration of these questions is beyond the scope of this chapter. However, readers interested in the negatives of online relationships are referred to the crime section of this volume, which covers these issues in much more detail.

Up-Dating

Lastly, this chapter revisits the topic of up-dating as outlined earlier. Up-dating refers to the notion that people often believe that they will attract a more attractive person online than offline (Fullwood & Attrill, 2018). Of course, attraction is in the eye of the beholder, and while one person might be overly concerned with a person's physical appearance, for another that attraction might lie in their financial or social status. And, while up-dating might reflect a positive self-esteem boosting behavior, it could also lead to a culture of catalogue shopping for a partner online. In other words, people may become prone to believing that there is always someone better waiting just beyond the next click, and that they just need to find them. In order to do so, they may constantly browse through a steady stream of online profiles. This could lead to a hyper-negativity or dissatisfaction when meeting dates offline, or even within a relationship, to the point of assuming that one's current partner is just not up to scratch. But what if the flaw lies within one's own skewed perceptions that they are presenting a real self online? Recent research indicates that often people believe that they are presenting a true version of their dating self online, but when independent raters were asked how accurately profile photos represented the same daters, they rated them as being a less accurate portrayal of the daters (Hancock & Toma, 2009). This illustrates the importance of maintaining a balanced and realistic view while dating online if a person doesn't want to become a "serial first dater." This may be similar to offline dating, in that a roving eye and belief in deserving better may make people stray from a current relationship offline. Online, however, there is a much larger pool from which to find a new partner, and engaging in secretive, duplicitous behavior is easier now than before the inception of texting, email, and instant messaging. Touching upon the notion of up-dating demonstrates how the exact same behavior can be positive for one online dater, but negative for another. Clearly, there is a role of individual differences and personality factors that may contribute to how a person experiences up-dating that need further research exploration.

Summary

This chapter has provided an overview of what we know in the field of cyberpsychology, to date, about online relationships. It has considered how the Internet is used with both positive and negative intent and consequences, in the forming of new relationships (as in the case of online dating), and in the maintenance and management of existing relationships. There are numerous individual differences in motivations for engaging in online relationships, and the experiences that people have are equally varied. Online dating is becoming as common as offline methods as a way of meeting people, and it will be fascinating to observe, as time goes on, how this development in the basic human behavior of mate seeking impacts upon people's relationship satisfaction and well-being in the long-term.

References

Abramova, O., Baumann, A., Krasnova, H., & Buxmann, P. (2016). Gender differences in online dating: What do we know so far? A systematic literature review. In *(HICSS) 49th Hawaii International Conference on System Sciences* (pp. 3858–3867). 5–8 January, Koloa, HI. Red Hook, NY: Curran Associates.

Aretz, W., Demuth, I., Schmidt, K., & Vierlein, J. (2010). Partner search in the digital age: Psychological characteristics of online-dating-service-users and its contribution to the explanation of different patterns of utilization. *Journal of Business and Media Psychology* 1(1), 8–16.

Attrill, A. (Ed.). (2015). *Cyberpsychology*. New York: Oxford University Press.

Attrill, A., Fullwood, C., & Chadwick, C. (2015). *Catfish: The detection of red flags, dangers and suspicious behaviours in the pursuit of love online*. Paper presented at the Social Networking in Cyberspace Conference. 3–4 September, Wolverhampton, UK.

Baumeister, R. F., & Leary, M. R. (1995). The need to belong: Desire for interpersonal attachments as a fundamental human motivation. *Psychological Bulletin* 117(3), 497–529.

Bergström, M. (2011). Casual dating online: Sexual norms and practices on French heterosexual dating sites. *Zeitschrift für Familienforschung* 23(3), 319–336.

Billedo, C. J., Kerkhof, P., & Finkenauer, C. (2015). The use of social networking sites for relationship maintenance in long-distance and geographically close romantic relationships. *Cyberpsychology, Behavior, and Social Networking 18*(3), 152–157.

Blackwell, C., Birnholtz, J., & Abbott, C. (2015). Seeing and being seen: Co-situation and impression formation using Grindr, a location-aware gay dating app. *New Media & Society 17*(7), 1117–1136.

Brem, M. J., Spiller, L. C., & Vandehey, M. A. (2015). Online mate-retention tactics on Facebook are associated with relationship aggression. *Journal of Interpersonal Violence 30*(16), 2831–2850.

Bryant, K., & Sheldon, P. (2017). Cyber dating in the age of mobile apps: Understanding motives, attitudes, and characteristics of users. *American Communication Journal 19*(2), 1–15.

Cacioppo, J. T., Cacioppo, S., Gonzaga, G. C., Ogburn, E. L., & VanderWeele, T. J. (2013). Marital satisfaction and break-ups differ across on-line and off-line meeting venues. *Proceedings of the National Academy of Sciences 110*(25), 10135–10140.

Chan, M. (2015). Mobile phones and the good life: Examining the relationships among mobile use, social capital and subjective well-being. *New Media & Society 17*(1), 96–113.

Chan, L. S. (2017). Who uses dating apps? Exploring the relationships among trust, sensation-seeking, smartphone use, and the intent to use dating apps based on the Integrative Model. *Computers in Human Behavior 72*, 246–258.

Cooper, A., & Sportolari, L. (1997). Romance in cyberspace: Understanding online attraction. *Journal of Sex Education and Therapy 22*(1), 7–14.

Craft, S., & Garcia, Y. E. (2016). Interpersonal media used by couples in non-proximal romantic relationships: Implications for psychological practice. In S. Y. Tettegah & Y. E. Garcia (Eds.), *Emotions, technology, and health* (pp. 211–224). London, UK: Academic Press.

Crowcroft, J., Wolisz, A., & Sathiaseelan, A. (2015). Towards an affordable Internet access for everyone: The quest for enabling universal service commitment (Dagstuhl seminar 14471). *Dagstuhl Reports 4*(11). doi:10.4230/DagRep.4.11.78

Dahlgreen, W. (2016). A third of under-40s have used Internet dating. Retrieved from https://yougov.co.uk/news/2016/02/16/one-three-under-40s-have-used-internet-dating

Dainton, M., & Stokes, A. (2015). College students' romantic relationships on Facebook: Linking the gratification for maintenance to Facebook maintenance activity and the experience of jealousy. *Communication Quarterly 63*(4), 365–383.

Deci, E. L., & Ryan, R. M. (2000). The "what" and "why" of goal pursuits: Human needs and the self-determination of behaviour. *Psychological Inquiry 11*(4), 227–268.

Desai, N. G., Jha, S., Choudhury, A., & Garg, B. (2018). Internet infidelity: Interface with mental health. In S. P. Sahni & G. Jain (Eds.), *Internet Infidelity* (pp. 147–156). Singapore: Springer.

Duck, S. W. (1982). A topography of relationship disengagement and dissolution. In S. W. Duck & R. Gilmour (Eds.), *Personal Relationships: Dissolving Personal Relationships*, Vol. 4. London, UK: Academic Press.

Duck, S. W. (1998). *Human Relationships*, 3rd ed. Newbury Park, CA: Sage.

Dutton, W., & Blank, G. (2014). Cultures of the Internet: Five clusters of attitudes and beliefs among users in Britain. In L. Robinson, S. R. Cotten, J. Schulz, T. M. Hale, & A. Williams (Eds.), *Communication and Information Technologies Annual* (Studies in Media and Communications Series, Volume 10) (pp. 3–28). Bingley: Emerald Group Publishing Limited.

Ellison, N. B., Hancock, J. T., & Toma, C. L. (2012). Profile as promise: A framework for conceptualizing veracity in online dating self-presentations. *New Media & Society 14*(1), 45–62.

Finkel, E. J., Eastwick, P. W., Karney, B. R., Reis, H. T., & Sprecher, S. (2012). Online dating: A critical analysis from the perspective of psychological science. *Psychological Science in the Public Interest* 13(1), 3–66.

Fox, J., & Warber, K. M. (2014). Social networking sites in romantic relationships: Attachment, uncertainty, and partner surveillance on Facebook. *Cyberpsychology, Behavior, and Social Networking* 17(1), 3–7.

Fullwood, C., & Attrill-Smith, A. (2018). Up-dating: Ratings of perceived dating success are better online than offline. *Cyberpsychology, Behavior, and Social Networking* 21(1), 11–15.

Gatter, K., & Hodkinson, K. (2016). On the differences between Tinder™ versus online dating agencies: Questioning a myth. An exploratory study. *Cogent Psychology* 3(1), 1162414.

Goffman, E. (1959). *The presentation of self in everyday life.* Garden City, NY: Doubleday.

Goodman-Deane, J., Mieczakowski, A., Johnson, D., Goldhaber, T., & Clarkson, P. J. (2016). The impact of communication technologies on life and relationship satisfaction. *Computers in Human Behavior* 57, 219–229.

Hamilton, N. F. (2016). Romantic relationships and online dating. In A. Attrill & C. Fullwood (Eds.), *Applied cyberpsychology* (pp. 144–160). London: Palgrave Macmillan.

Hampton, A. J., Rawlings, J., Treger, S., & Sprecher, S. (2017). Channels of computer-mediated communication and satisfaction in long-distance relationships. *Interpersona* 11(2), 171.

Hance, M. A., Blackhart, G., & Dew, M. (2017). Free to be me: The relationship between the true self, rejection sensitivity, and use of online dating sites. *The Journal of Social Psychology* 158(4), 421–429.

Hancock, J. T., Toma, C., & Ellison, N. (2007, 30 April–3 May). The truth about lying in online dating profiles. In *Proceedings of the SIGCHI conference on Human Factors in Computing Systems* (pp. 449–452). San Jose, California. New York: ACM.

Hancock, J. T., & Toma, J. T. (2009). Putting your best face forward: The accuracy of online dating photographs. *Journal of Communication* 59, 367–386.

Harrison, K. (2017). "Relive the passion, find your affair". Revising the infidelity script online. *Convergence* [online]. doi:10.1177/1354856517725987.

Haupert, M. L., Gesselman, A. N., Moors, A. C., Fisher, H. E., & Garcia, J. R. (2017). Prevalence of experiences with consensual non-monogamous relationships: Findings from two national samples of single Americans. *Journal of Sex & Marital Therapy* 43(5), 424–440.

Heino, R. D., Ellison, N. B., & Gibbs, J. L. (2010). Relationshopping: Investigating the market metaphor in online dating. *Journal of Social and Personal Relationships* 27(4), 427–447.

Henry-Waring, M., & Barraket, J. (2008). Dating & intimacy in the 21st century: The use of online dating sites in Australia. *International Journal of Emerging Technologies & Society* 6(1).

Higgins, E. T. (1987). Self-discrepancy: A theory relating self and affect. *Psychological Review* 94(3), 319.

Hitsch, G. J., Hortaçsu, A., & Ariely, D. (2010). Matching and sorting in online dating. *American Economic Review* 100(1), 130–163.

Huber, G. A., & Malhotra, N. (2017). Political homophily in social relationships: Evidence from online dating behavior. *The Journal of Politics* 79(1), 269–283.

Janning, M., Gao, W., & Snyder, E. (2018). Constructing shared "space": Meaningfulness in long-distance romantic relationship communication formats. *Journal of Family Issues* 39(5), 1281–1303.

Johnson, K., Vilceanu, M. O., & Pontes, M. C. (2017). Use of online dating websites and dating apps: Findings and implications for LGB populations. *Journal of Marketing Development and Competitiveness* 11(3), 60–66.

Jung, J., Bapna, R., Ramaprasad, J., & Umyarov, A. (2018, forthcoming). Love Unshackled: Identifying the Effect of Mobile App Adoption in Online Dating. *MIS Quarterly*.

Khan, K. S., & Chaudhry, S. (2015). An evidence-based approach to an ancient pursuit: Systematic review on converting online contact into a first date. *BMJ Evidence-Based Medicine* 20(2) [online]. Retrieved from https://ebm.bmj.com/content/20/2/48

Kim, M., Kwon, K. N., & Lee, M. (2009). Psychological characteristics of Internet dating service users: The effect of self-esteem, involvement, and sociability on the use of Internet dating services. *Cyberpsychology & Behavior* 12(4), 445–449.

Lapidot-Lefler, N., & Barak, A. (2015). The benign online disinhibition effect: Could situational factors induce self-disclosure and prosocial behaviors? *Cyberpsychology: Journal of Psychosocial Research on Cyberspace* 9(2).

Lemke, R., & Weber, M. (2017). That man behind the curtain: Investigating the sexual online dating behavior of men who have sex with men but hide their same-sex sexual attraction in offline surroundings. *Journal of Homosexuality* 64(11), 1561–1582.

Lever, J., Grov, C., Royce, T. G., & Gillespie, B. J. (2008). Searching for love in all the "write" places: Exploring Internet personals use by sexual orientation, gender, and age. *International Journal of Sexual Health* 20, 233–246.

Li, N. P., Yong, J. C., Tov, W., Sng, O., Fletcher, G. J., Valentine, K. A.,... Balliet, D. (2013). Mate preferences do predict attraction and choices in the early stages of mate selection. *Journal of Personality and Social Psychology* 105(5), 757.

Lomanowska, A. M., & Guitton, M. J. (2016). Online intimacy and well-being in the digital age. *Internet Interventions* 4, 138–144.

Madden, M. and Lenhart, A. (2006). *Online dating: Americans who are seeking romance use the Internet to help them in their search, but there is still widespread public concern about the safety of online dating.* Washington, DC: Pew Internet & American Life Project.

Manning, J., & Bloedel, A. (2017). Exploring polyamory online: Ethics, relationships and understanding. In P. G. Nixon and I. K. Düsterhöft (Eds.), *Sex in the Digital Age* (pp. 158–167). New York, NY: Routledge.

Martins, A., Pereira, M., Andrade, R., Dattilio, F. M., Narciso, I., & Canavarro, M. C. (2016). Infidelity in dating relationships: Gender-specific correlates of face-to-face and online extradyadic involvement. *Archives of Sexual Behavior* 45(1), 193–205.

Mazur, E. (2017). Diverse disabilities and dating online. In M. F. Wrights (Ed.), *Identity, sexuality, and relationships among emerging adults in the digital age* (pp. 150–167). IGI Global.

Murray, C. E., & Campbell, E. C. (2015). The pleasures and perils of technology in intimate relationships. *Journal of Couple & Relationship Therapy* 14(2), 116–140.

Pettigrew, J. (2009). Text messaging and connectedness within close interpersonal relationships. *Marriage & Family Review* 45(6–8), 697–716.

Rabby, M. K. (2007). Relational maintenance and the influence of commitment in online and offline relationships. *Communication Studies* 58(3), 315–337.

Rosenfeld, M. J., & Thomas, R. J. (2012). Searching for a mate: The rise of the Internet as a social intermediary. *American Sociological Review* 77(4), 523–547.

Sahni, S. P., & Jain, G. (2018). An overview: Internet infidelity. In S. P. Sahni & G. Jain (Eds.), *Internet Infidelity* (pp. 1–12). Singapore: Springer.

Schade, L. C., Sandberg, J., Bean, R., Busby, D., & Coyne, S. (2013). Using technology to connect in romantic relationships: Effects on attachment, relationship satisfaction, and stability in emerging adults. *Journal of Couple & Relationship Therapy 12*, 314–338.

Schlenker, B. R. (1980). *Impression management: The self-concept, social identity, and interpersonal relations.* Monterey, CA: Brooks/Cole.

Sevi, B., Aral, T., & Eskenazi, T. (2017). Exploring the hook-up app: Low sexual disgust and high sociosexuality predict motivation to use Tinder for casual sex. *Personality and Individual Differences 33*, 17–20.

Shaughnessy, K., Fudge, M., & Byers, E. S. (2017). An exploration of prevalence, variety, and frequency data to quantify online sexual activity experience. *The Canadian Journal of Human Sexuality 26*(1), 60–75.

Skopek, J., Schulz, F., & Blossfeld, H. P. (2009). Partnersuche im Internet. *KZfSS Kölner Zeitschrift für Soziologie und Sozialpsychologie 61*(2), 183–210.

Skopek, J., Schulz, F., & Blossfeld, H. P. (2010). Who contacts whom? Educational homophily in online mate selection. *European Sociological Review 27*(2), 180–195.

Smith, A. W., & Duggan, M. (2013). *Online Dating & Relationships.* Washington, DC: Pew Research Center.

Stephure, R. J., Boon, S. D., MacKinnon, S. L., & Deveau, V. L. (2009). Internet-initiated relationships: Associations between age and involvement in online dating. *Journal of Computer-Mediated Communication 14*(3), 658–681.

Suler, J. (2004). The online disinhibition effect. *Cyberpsychology & Behavior 7*(3), 321–326.

Sumter, S. R., Vandenbosch, L., & Ligtenberg, L. (2017). Love me Tinder: Untangling emerging adults' motivations for using the dating application Tinder. *Telematics and Informatics 34*(1), 67–78.

Swann, Jr, W. B. (1990). To be adored or to be known? The interplay of self-enhancement and self-verification. In E. T. Higgins & R. M. Sorrentino (Eds.), *Handbook of motivation and cognition: Foundations of social behavior*, Vol. 2 (pp. 408–448). New York, NY: Guilford Press.

Thompson, A. E., & O'Sullivan, L. F. (2016). Drawing the line: The development of a comprehensive assessment of infidelity judgments. *The Journal of Sex Research 53*(8), 910–926.

Timmermans, E., & De Caluwé, E. (2017a). Development and validation of the Tinder Motives Scale (TMS). *Computers in Human Behavior 70*, 341–350.

Timmermans, E., & De Caluwé, E. (2017b). To Tinder or not to Tinder, that's the question: An individual differences perspective to Tinder use and motives. *Personality and Individual Differences 110*, 74–79.

Tong, S. T., Hancock, J. T., and Slatcher, R. B. (2016). Online dating system design and relational decision making: Choice, algorithms, and control. *Personal Relationship 23*(4), 645–662.

Utz, S., & Beukeboom, C. J. (2011). The role of social network sites in romantic relationships: Effects on jealousy and relationship happiness. *Journal of Computer-Mediated Communication 16*(4), 511–527.

Valkenburg, P. M., & Peter, J. (2007). Who visits online dating sites? Exploring some characteristics of online daters. *CyberPsychology & Behavior 10*(6), 849–852.

Vossler, A. (2016). Internet infidelity 10 years on: A critical review of the literature. *The Family Journal 24*(4), 359–366.

Walther, J. B. (1996). Computer-mediated communication: Impersonal, interpersonal, and hyperpersonal interaction. *Communication Research 23*, 3–43.

Walther, J. B. (2007). Selective self-presentation in computer-mediated communication: Hyperpersonal dimensions of technology, language, and cognition. *Computers in Human Behavior 23*(5), 2538–2557.

Weiser, D. A., Niehuis, S., Flora, J., Punyanunt-Carter, N. M., Arias, V. S., & Baird, R. H. (2017). Swiping right: Sociosexuality, intentions to engage in infidelity, and infidelity experiences on Tinder. *Personality and Individual Differences 133*, 29–33.

Whitty, M. (2007). Love Letters. The development of romantic relationships through the ages. In Joinson, A. (Ed.), *Oxford Handbook of Internet Psychology* (pp. 31–42). Oxford, UK: Oxford University Press.

Wu, P.-L., & Chiou, W. B. (2009). More options lead to more searching and worse choices in finding partners for romantic relationships online: An experimental study. *Cyberpsychology, Behavior, and Social Networking 12*, 315–318.

CHAPTER 12

··

THE SOCIAL
CONSEQUENCES OF
ONLINE INTERACTION

··

JENNA L. CLARK AND MELANIE C. GREEN

INTRODUCTION

SOCIAL connection is critical for both mental and physical well-being. A robust body
of research has linked social integration to a variety of positive health outcomes.
Social support is related to better cardiovascular, endocrine, and immune system
activity (Uchino, Cacioppo, & Kiecolt-Glaser, 1996), marital satisfaction is linked to
health (Kiecolt-Glaser & Newton, 2001), and social isolation is even tied to overall
mortality (Holt-Lunstad, Smith, & Layton, 2010; House, Landis, & Umberson, 1988).
These examples, as well as many other similar findings, argue persuasively that social
integration and connection are critical for our well-being.

But many of these foundational studies were conducted at a time when social connection was primarily built through face-to-face social interactions. In today's world, the
methods through which individuals form and build their close relationships are
changing. Technology-mediated communication—text messaging, social networking,
email, instant messages, voice chat, and video chat—is increasingly common in everyday life to the point that statistics on its prevalence are usually outdated by the point
they are published. This chapter considers how online interaction may contribute to or
diminish social connections.

RESEARCH ON THE CONSEQUENCES
OF ONLINE INTERACTION:
A LANDSCAPE OF CONFLICT

Media coverage paints a primarily negative picture of technology-mediated communication; a Google search for "smartphone effect" returns article titles such as "Have Smartphones Destroyed a Generation?" (Twenge, 2017); "The Psychological Toll of the Smartphone" (Sleek, 2014); and "5 Ways Smartphones Are Harming Our Health" (Stokes, 2015). Lay perceptions appear to match the media's tone. Technology-mediated communication is perceived as less useful than face-to-face communication (Schiffrin, Edelman, Falkenstern, & Stewart, 2010), less deep and broad (Peter & Valkenburg, 2006), and less meaningful and intimate (Brown, 2015).

Academic research on the actual effects of technology-mediated communication, however, paints a more nuanced picture. Initial studies that focused on Internet use as a whole, rather than looking specifically at technology-mediated communication, described negative effects of the Internet on its users' social integration and affective well-being (Kraut et al., 1998; Nie, 2001). However, further research soon presented a different picture. A review of relevant studies published between 1995–2000 did not support any overall negative effects of Internet use on social or community integration. (Katz, Rice, & Aspden, 2001).

Debates on the true effect of Internet use continued even as the Internet, and its social uses, evolved from a new phenomenon at the fringe of society to an increasingly central medium for communication. For example, some researchers suggested that lonely individuals were more drawn to online interaction (Amichai-Hamburger & Ben-Artzi, 2003; Morahan-Martin & Schumacher, 2003), while others suggested that online interaction made users lonelier (Moody, 2001). Similar debates emerged about the effect of the Internet on social capital, defined as the interpersonal bonds and levels of trust within communities. Putnam's (2000) book on the decline of social capital highlighted the possible role of television in drawing people away from community engagement and cautioned that the Internet might also take the place of strong in-person ties. However, later research suggested that using political or civic websites can have positive effects (Shah, Cho, Eveland, & Kwak, 2005), and broadly speaking, informational uses of the Internet can be a positive influence on social capital (e.g., Shah, Kwak, & Holbert, 2001; Shah, McLeod, & Yoon, 2001; Shah, Schmierbach, Hawkins, Espino, & Donavan, 2002). Additionally, both strong and weak ties can contribute to well-being (e.g., Wang, Chua, & Stefanone, 2015).

As social network sites entered common use, their effects also became a point of contention. For example, network size on Facebook is linked to perceived social support in some studies (e.g., Manago, Taylor, & Greenfield, 2012), yet not in others (e.g., Kim & Lee, 2011). In a similar vein, one study on temporary discontinuation of Facebook use suggests that it increases life satisfaction and positive emotions (Tromholt, 2016), while another suggests that it decreases sense of belonging and of having a meaningful existence (Tobin, Vanman, Verreynne, & Saeri, 2015).

FACTORS THAT MODERATE THE CONSEQUENCES OF ONLINE INTERACTION

These disagreements, and others observed in the literature, do not necessarily arise from poor scholarship or lack of thought on any side of the issue. Instead, they reflect the natural complexity of attempting to assess the consequences of interactions that can range from casual public chats with near-strangers on social networking sites to intimate, private conversations with best friends over text messaging. Researchers today are increasingly acknowledging this complexity by focusing on the many moderating factors that determine the consequences of online interaction.

More specifically, much of this research has focused on the features and affordances of different online platforms. For example, in the early days of online interaction, popular platforms such as chat rooms were often anonymous. Online anonymity has been linked to both positive and negative consequences. On the one hand, the lack of obvious physical cues allows online interaction to surmount barriers such as physical appearance or race, creating better opportunities for users to be their "true selves" online (Bargh, McKenna, & Fitzsimons, 2002). This freedom also allows users to experiment with their identities, selecting and discarding self-presentations in the search for an authentic mode of expression (Turkle, 1994). However, free expression has its downsides. Online anonymity also allowed for a tendency toward abusive and insulting behavior; the term "online disinhibition effect" was coined to reflect users' willingness to say and do things online that they would consider inappropriate in person (Suler, 2004). Today, many online activities, such as Facebook posts, are linked with users' real names or images. The decline of online anonymity likely limits users' freedom, both for good and ill.

Similarly, online communication in earlier decades was primarily text-based, whereas today's platforms allow for photos, audio, and video messaging. Added channels of communication further decrease perceived anonymity, but their effects on social behavior likely don't stop there. Visual and non-verbal cues are crucial to social interaction. According to media richness theory (Daft & Lengel, 1983, 1986), additional "channels" such as tone of voice, facial expression, and body language allow interactions to carry more information between communications. Modern messaging platforms, then, may be better suited for the discussion of complex or ambiguous topics—though not all theorists agree that text is a truly limited medium (for example, see Walther, 1996).

Additionally, research has examined the effect of synchrony versus asynchrony (whether messages are responded to in real time versus with a delay). AOL Instant

Messenger, or AIM, was one of the first synchronous platforms, which allow for instantaneous back-and-forth conversation—and while it officially shut down in December 2017, newer services such as Facebook Messenger and Google Hangouts offer a very similar experience. Asynchronous services may be even older, as bulletin board systems (BBS) were among the very first methods of communication over the Internet. Modern-day forums such as Reddit are the successors to BBSs, allowing for users to leave comments that others may reply to minutes, hours, or even days later. Research suggests that individuals feel more socially connected to interaction partners in synchronous communication (where a conversation can flow naturally), but that individuals may interpret pauses or breaks in online messaging negatively, as indicating a lack of interest or responsiveness (Kalman, Scissors, Gill, & Gergle, 2013; Nowak, Watt, & Walther, 2005). Additionally, even in asynchronous communication, individuals have expectations about how quickly a response should occur, and may respond negatively to delayed responses (e.g., an instructor or a job candidate who does not reply quickly to an email; e.g., Kalman & Rafaeli, 2011).

While all of these noted features may be important moderators of the effects of online interactions, current work is increasingly extending beyond affordances in favor of investigating the impact of the specific behaviors that users engage in during online interactions. To highlight a few basic examples of this work, passive use of Facebook results in negative consequences for well-being, while active use of Facebook does not (Frison & Eggermont, 2015; Verduyn et al., 2015). Passive use might include "lurking," or simply reading messages posted by others, whereas active use would involve responding to others' posts or posting one's own updates. One-to-one communication on Facebook has stronger effects on social capital and relational closeness than group communication or passive consumption of information (Burke & Kraut, 2014; Burke, Kraut, & Marlow, 2011; Carpenter, Green, & LaFlam, 2018).

These and other studies suggest that behavior may be the most immediate influence on any given online interaction's consequences. However, interactions are inherently dyadic; a single person's behavior cannot be the sole determinant of an interaction's outcome. Additionally, behavioral choices do not occur in a vacuum. The following sections discuss how other factors likely influence consequences indirectly by inducing users to engage in different behaviors.

Partner Choice

Time spent socializing online with existing friends has a positive impact on well-being, while time spent socializing online with strangers does not (Valkenburg & Peter, 2007). In a similar vein, interaction with partners with whom one has close ties (e.g., friends) has a more positive effect than interaction with people who are connected only by weak ties (e.g., acquaintances)—especially when the interaction is targeted and private (Burke & Kraut, 2016).

Social Anxiety

Social anxiety has been a major focus of research on online interaction. Some research suggests that socially anxious individuals benefit more from online social support and interaction than non-anxious individuals (Bonetti, Campbell, & Gilmore, 2010; Indian & Grieve, 2014). In fact, socially anxious individuals often prefer to interact online, reporting that online communication is deeper, broader, more controllable, and more reciprocal (Caplan, 2003; Peter & Valkenburg, 2006). Controllability may be the key: in online contexts, socially anxious individuals can more effectively manage their self-presentation and set the pace of interaction. Despite preferences, however, socially anxious individuals may have lower well-being if they rely on online communication, possibly due to the potential for problematic or excessive Internet use (Caplan, 2003, 2005; Weidman et al., 2012).

Personality

Major personality traits have been linked to differential outcomes of online interaction. Agreeableness, one of Goldberg's Big Five Personality Traits (Goldberg, 1992), reflects a tendency toward warmth, politeness, and amiability—and agreeable individuals show more social support as a result of more leisure Internet use (Swickert, Hittner, Harris, & Herring, 2002). Goal persistence (a subset of the Behavioral Activation System which is concerned with actively pursuing desired goals even when the reward is not immediate; see Corr, 2008) moderates the effect of online social comparison on well-being (Gerson, Plagnol, & Corr, 2016). Specifically, for individuals high in goal persistence, Facebook social comparison was positively associated with well-being. Individuals interested in others' perspectives (high in an individual difference variable called motivation for mindreading) are more likely to use Facebook to supplement existing relationships, while those less interested in perspective-taking are more likely to pursue Facebook-only relationships (Carpenter, Green, & LaFlam, 2011).

Attitudes

An attitude, defined as "a psychological tendency that is expressed by evaluating a particular entity with some degree of favor or disfavor" (Eagly & Chaiken, 1993, p. 1) orients an individual toward their goal and prepares them to achieve it (Ferguson, 2008). As such, a core function of attitude is to drive behavior, primarily through creating specific intentions to act (Ajzen & Fishbein, 1977). Positive attitudes toward online interactions may change the specific behaviors in which users engage which may in turn change the interactions' consequences.

Only a few studies have actively examined the impact of attitudes toward online interaction on behavior. Positive attitudes toward online communication and self-disclosure predict increased Facebook communication with a specific randomly chosen Facebook friend, which in turn predicts increased relational closeness (Ledbetter et al., 2011). Similar results have been observed for attitudes toward Xbox Live relational maintenance and relational closeness (Ledbetter & Kuznekoff, 2012).

Similar research has been conducted on the perceived reality of online interactions (PROI), or the extent to which online interactions are seen as suitable for the maintenance and formation of close relationships (Clark & Green, 2013). Individuals high in PROI view online interactions as similar to face-to-face interactions, whereas individuals low in PROI hold the attitude that online interactions are less "real" or valid than offline contacts. These perceptions might reflect beliefs about the affordances of online interactions ("If I can't see my friend's face when we talk, we can't really communicate"), the value of online interactions ("A friend's support won't help me feel better if it's just words on a screen"), the perceived weight of online interactions ("It's not like I'm having an actual conversation, it's just text"), or simply the appropriateness of online interactions ("Important topics should be discussed face to face"). Attitudes create a type of self-fulfilling prophecy; individuals who are higher in perceived reality have more social support from online sources and are also more willing to self-disclose and offer social support online (Clark & Green, 2017).

THE INTERPERSONAL CONNECTION BEHAVIORS FRAMEWORK

So far, this chapter has touched briefly on specific areas of study represented in the current literature to make a simple claim: a wealth of different factors appears to moderate the consequences of online interaction. These factors may seem scattered and disparate, but our approach unites these explanatory factors together into a larger theory: the interpersonal connection behaviors framework (see Clark, Algoe, & Green, 2017).

The interpersonal connection behaviors framework suggests that the positive consequences of any given online interaction depend on the extent to which that interaction serves a relational purpose. Online interactions that promote connection build relationships and increase well-being via increased relational closeness and quality. Online interactions that do not promote connection are likely to fall prey to the disadvantages caused by "social snacking" (Gardner, Pickett, & Knowles, 2005), or interactions lacking in meaningful content: loneliness and social comparison.

Our perspective draws heavily on established findings in relationship science, such as the interpersonal process model of intimacy. According to this model, relationships grow through small, everyday interactions that allow opportunities for relational partners to demonstrate responsiveness (care for and understanding/validation of each others' needs; Laurenceau, Barrett, & Pietromonaco, 1998; Reis et al., 1988). Many different interactions fit this bill: social support, self-disclosure, gratitude expression, capitalization (the sharing of positive news; Gable, Reis, Impett, & Asher, 2004), and others. What these different relationship-building processes have in common is the generation of responsiveness, which in turn creates deeper, stronger, and higher-quality relationships.

A focus on relationship-building processes integrates in a logical and coherent way the various disparate moderating factors already discussed. For example, active use of Facebook consists of behaviors such as direct messaging, a valuable context for relationship-building processes; passive use of Facebook rules out relationship-building processes, as it involves no actual interaction. Users are far more likely to engage in relationship-building processes with close others, as well as in private settings; we are not likely to share our most intimate secrets on public channels. The research on attitudes toward online interactions has directly linked such attitudes to several of these processes, such as social support and self-disclosure.

This link back to the established science of close relationships does not imply that relationship-building processes must look exactly the same online. The qualities of any given technological medium have the potential for profound impact on the success of online relationship-building processes. For example, the previously discussed research on attitudes toward online interaction suggests that users may be skeptical of the value or meaning of mediated relationship-building processes. This skepticism may impair the demonstration of responsiveness online—or stop the process from ever beginning in the first place.

Beyond internal obstacles, the specific affordances of any given medium may be a problem as well. Technological difficulties can problematize synchronous interactions, such as difficulty with video or voice quality in online calls. Stripped of information such as tone of voice, facial expression, and body language, text-only mediated interaction presents even more opportunities for trouble. For example, emotion perception is difficult in verbal-only online interaction—often more difficult than users even realize (Kruger, Epley, Parker, & Ng, 2005; Laflen & Fiorenza, 2012). Paralinguistic cues such as emoticons may aid understanding, but they do not always help users disambiguate complex messages (Derks, Fischer, & Bos, 2008; Lo, 2008; Thompson & Filik, 2016; Walther & D'Addario, 2001).

POSITIVE CONSEQUENCES OF ONLINE INTERACTIONS: RELATIONSHIP-BUILDING PROCESSES

These issues do not mean that online relationship-building processes are doomed to fail—merely that they pose particular difficulties when compared to face-to-face interaction. The scope and importance of those difficulties, however, is an empirical question. Among the many relationship-building processes identified in the literature, self-disclosure and social support have received extensive study in an online context. Not only do these processes occur over technological media, but they still show promise for the maintenance and formation of close relationships.

Self-Disclosure

Self-disclosure is a critical component of relationship formation and maintenance. It is strongly linked to intimacy, both mechanistically as the heart of the interpersonal process model (Laurenceau et al., 1998) and conceptually—in fact, self-disclosure is the most commonly offered definition for intimacy (Parks & Floyd, 1996). Self-disclosure is also strongly linked to liking; according to a meta-analytic review, increased self-disclosure increases liking, individuals self-disclose more to those they already like, and they like those to whom they have self-disclosed (Collins & Miller, 1994).

Frequency of Online Self-Disclosure

If theorists only focused on self-disclosure when considering the possibility of building relationships online, the evidence suggests there would be little reason to worry about online interaction.

Both anecdotal information and survey results suggesting that individuals disclose more freely online began to appear with some of the earliest work on online social interaction (Parks & Floyd, 1996). Experimental evidence examining spontaneous self-disclosure as coded by observers further supported this idea: more separate occurrences of self-disclosure were observed in a computer-mediated interaction than a face-to-face interaction on the same topic (Joinson, 2001). This could be considered the positive side of the online disinhibition effect (Suler, 2004): the anonymity on the Internet doesn't solely lead to name-calling and other aggressive behavior—it might also help users get to know one another.

However, it is not entirely clear if the online disinhibition effect truly applies in relational self-disclosure. A review of studies comparing online to offline self-disclosure suggested there is actually no systematic difference in frequency, depth, or breadth of self-disclosure across media, albeit without taking a meta-analytic approach to analyzing the data (Nguyen, Bin, & Campbell, 2012). The paper considered fifteen different studies, six experimental and nine survey, and noted: "There were an equal number of findings showing greater online self-disclosure, greater face-to-face disclosure, and no differences between online and offline disclosure" (p. 105). The lack of any difference between mediated and face-to-face disclosure is the major finding reported by this study; however, a more interesting detail surfaces two paragraphs later. Of the six experimental studies, four report greater disclosure online; of the nine survey studies, six report greater disclosure offline. Perhaps participants believe they self-disclose less online, while in truth they are actually self-disclosing more—a finding in line with the importance of users' perceptions of and attitudes toward online interaction.

Consequences of Online Self-Disclosure

The frequency of self-disclosure online is only half of the equation; it is also important to focus on whether or not online self-disclosure is still successful in building relationships. A review of the literature on online self-disclosure in adolescents concluded that its effects were very similar to offline self-disclosure (Desjarlais, Gilmour, Sinclair, Howell, & West, 2015).

But there is reason to think that online self-disclosure may have an even stronger impact on relationships than offline self-disclosure. This prediction arises from the hyperpersonal model (Walther, 1996), which suggests that individuals can use mediated interactions to optimize their self-presentation. The ease of ideal self-presentation may have two different effects that boost the connection between self-disclosure and intimacy. For one, the ability to selectively self-present may make it easier to not only self-disclose more online, but more deeply and earnestly—without concerns about presenting the negative side of the self, self-disclosure may seem less intimidating and more controllable. This is supported by work demonstrating that individuals are more able to access the idea of their true self (via reaction time data) and successfully portray it to others when interacting online (Bargh et al., 2002).

The other pathway through which online self-disclosure might create more intimacy is directly related to the lack of channels in mediated interaction. Given that much of the information usually shared in face-to-face interactions (such as non-verbal behaviors) is absent, a "receiver" perceives only what a "sender" chooses to share—and, in the absence of other information, small clues achieve an outsized importance. Jiang, Bazarova, & Hancock (2013) examined the amplifying nature of this link for perceptions of intimacy in self-disclosure; their research found that confederates' self-disclosures were rated as more intimate if they occurred online as compared to in a face-to-face context, even though they contained the exact same information. The same amount of self-disclosure, therefore, may create a larger sense of intimacy.

Additional insights come from consideration of the attributions individuals make about self-disclosure within mediated interactions (Jiang, Bazarova, & Hancock, 2011). A self-disclosure may be attributed to the nature of the situation ("she's telling me this because we're at a slumber party") or the nature of the relationship ("she's telling me this because we're such good friends"). Given that online interaction does not seem situationally fitting for disclosure, the researchers hypothesized that individuals who receive self-disclosure in mediated contexts are more likely to attribute it to the nature of the relationship. As such, self-disclosure in a mediated context may be seen as a better "signal" of relationship strength than in a face-to-face context, and therefore may reap greater dividends of intimacy. Jiang and colleagues (2013) tested and supported this hypothesis with a stringent experimental design in which participants interacted with confederates either face to face or in a mediated interaction, with a set level of self-disclosure across conditions. As in their other study, identical amounts of self-disclosure on the part of confederates predicted greater perceptions of intimacy on the part of participants in a mediated context—and this effect was mediated by attributions made about the relationship.

Taken together, this body of research seems to suggest that individuals engage more in self-disclosure online and that this increased self-disclosure may have an even stronger effect on relational closeness and intimacy than face-to-face disclosure. If these findings are true, mediated social interaction may be very well-suited to relationship formation processes—arguably even more so than face-to-face social interaction.

Social Support

Social support is another foundational relationship process; it is also a nebulous, multi-dimensional concept defined differently from researcher to researcher. For example, House defines social support as "an interpersonal transaction involving one or more of the following: (1) emotional concern (liking, love, empathy), (2) instrumental aid (goods or services), (3) information (about the environment), and (4) appraisal (information relevant to self-evaluation)" (1981, p. 39). On the less specific end, Wilcox and Vernberg simply define the target of social support research as "the influence the interpersonal environment has on health" (1985, p. 8). For the purpose of unifying a wide literature, this paper views social support through a similarly broad lens: benefits and resources gained through interpersonal interaction and connection.

Whatever definition championed for the term, social support has been established as a highly beneficial and positive resource. It has been linked to decreased mortality (Berkman & Syme, 1979; House et al., 1988) and increased well-being across a wide variety of indicators (Siedlecki, Salthouse, Oishi, & Jeswani, 2013; Turner, 1981). Many of the health benefits of satisfying relationships (Kiecolt-Glaser & Newton, 2001) may, in fact, be a direct result of social support.

However, the specific reason why social support plays such a key role is not entirely clear. The "buffering" theory suggests that social support is useful primarily in helping individuals recover from stressors, while the "main effect" theory suggests that social support is useful in all situations, as a general resource (Cohen & Wills, 1985). Social support may function as more than just a resource, however; it may also serve as a method for building stronger relationships.

Requests for social support typically involve an acknowledgment that the requester needs help—in other words, an admission of difficulty or emotional distress. This suggests that many requests for social support function like emotional self-disclosure, the type of self-disclosure best suited to build intimacy in the interpersonal process model (Laurenceau et al., 1998). This link is strengthened by evidence that social support must be responsive to provide benefits (Maisel & Gable, 2009; Selcuk & Ong, 2013). In other words, some of the benefits of social support may not derive from the support itself, but from the opportunity social support provides to demonstrate responsiveness and strengthen a relationship via intimacy. As such, social support provided online is doubly interesting as a determinant of the consequences of online interaction.

Online Social Support in Support Groups

The question of how social support functions in mediated interactions has received less attention than self-disclosure. Initially, online social support was studied through the lens of online support groups—individuals explicitly seeking support, usually grouped together by dealing with a specific sort of health-related challenge. Even as early as 2001, reviews aimed to synthesize the existing literature on the topic: the conclusion was that online social support could be powerfully beneficial (White & Dorman, 2001). This finding was supported by later work across a wide array of different health topics, much of which supported the idea that online support groups successfully provide social support to at least some of their users (Coulson, 2005; Tichon & Shapiro, 2003).

Moreover, the support that these groups provide dovetails with conventionally recognized forms of support—informational and emotional support are both frequently apparent in textual analysis of the messages shared within online support groups (Ballantine & Stephenson, 2011; Scharer, 2005; Wright, 2002). Some studies suggested that, despite the boundaries of physical distance, even tangible/instrumental support such as lending items or expressing willingness to visit was also provided through online support groups (Braithwaite, Waldron, & Finn, 1999; Coulson, 2005; Coulson, Buchanan, & Aubeeluck, 2007). In other words, social support is not just beneficial online, but recognizable as the same set of processes—at least, in explicit support groups.

Social Support on Social Networking Sites

More modern research has focused on social support through social networking sites, particularly Facebook. While the context is very different from online social support groups, the same ideas hold: social support online looks very much like social support offline.

Social support is clearly exchanged on Facebook, and frequently; one study found a daily mean of 2.24 supportive interactions across a week (Oh, Ozkaya, & LaRose, 2014), although tangible support may be less common (Stefanone, Kwon, & Lackaff, 2012). This social support is not offered randomly, but in appropriate situations: when individuals self-disclose negative feelings, their Facebook connections respond, especially when they are closer friends (Burke & Develin, 2016; Park et al., 2016). This social support is also beneficial online, much as it would be offline. A review of the literature on Facebook social support suggests that perceived support on Facebook mediates a link between various indicators of Facebook use, such as network size and amount of use, and increased well-being (Meng, Martinez, Holmstrom, Chung, & Cox, 2016).

Overall Conclusions

Both social support and self-disclosure occur online—and when they do, they lead to many of the same positive consequences as they would engender offline. These findings cannot provide causal evidence that relationship-building behaviors are responsible for the positive effects of certain online interactions, but they are suggestive, especially when other factors such as partner choice are taken into account.

Many other relationship-building processes, such as gratitude expression and capitalization (e.g., sharing good news) (Gable et al., 2004) likely operate in similar ways as self-disclosure and social support, but have yet to be extensively studied. In one study, the presence of any of these four relational processes in a given text messaging conversation is positively associated with perceived responsiveness (Clark, 2017).

Negative Consequences of Online Interactions: Social Comparison and Loneliness

The interpersonal connection behaviors framework does not only explain positive consequences of online interaction. It also suggests that negative consequences arise out of online interactions that are devoid of relationship-building processes. This does not mean that every online interaction without a relationship-building process will always have negative consequences. Online interactions can serve many other purposes, such as obtaining information or services. Instead, relationship-building processes can be more considered as a buffer: when a successful relationship-building process occurs online, there is a positive outcome that can cushion against some of the drawbacks that might otherwise arise.

These drawbacks are rooted in both negative consequences that are particularly likely to happen online and in negative consequences that could follow from any interaction, mediated or not. The remainder of the chapter touches on one potential drawback in each category.

Risks of Interpersonal Interaction: Social Comparison

Social comparison may be a particularly dangerous consequence of online interactions simply because many technological media are ideally suited to induce it. Social comparisons happen quickly, perhaps automatically, even in situations where we know that a comparison is unnecessary or invalid (Gilbert, Giesler, & Morris, 1995; Mussweiler, Rüter, & Epstude, 2004). The sheer presence of comparison targets may be enough to induce immediate comparison, and social networking sites produce a great number of targets at a casual glance, bombarding their users with countless glimpses into the lives of others. Simply engaging in more comparisons has been linked to negative effects, such as increased depression (White, Langer, Yariv, & Welch, 2006).

Moreover, social networking sites allow for remarkable control over a user's self-presentation; a user can choose to post only information that presents them in a good light, censoring any negative experiences or difficulties. This behavior is not only hypothetically possible, but frequent (boyd & Ellison, 2007; Fox & Vendemia, 2016). Selective self-presentation ensures that someone browsing a social networking site will be comparing their own personal experience to the best possible version of other users' lives—typically, an upward comparison (comparing to someone who is perceived as superior in some way). Upward comparisons can be useful for motivation or aspiration, but for self-evaluations, individuals prefer downward comparisons (comparing to someone who is worse off) as comparisons to a superior other can be emotionally painful (Taylor & Lobel, 1989).

As such, social networking sites present a perfect storm for negative social comparison experiences. Much of the research on negative effects of Facebook use has posited social comparison as an explanation. The more time a user spends on Facebook, the more likely they are to believe that others are happier and have better lives than they do (Chou & Edge, 2012). Negative effects of Facebook use, quantified as logins or as time, on depression are mediated by social comparison (Feinstein et al., 2013; Steers, Wickham, & Acitelli, 2014), while negative effects of passive Facebook use on well-being are mediated by envy (Verduyn et al., 2015). An overall survey of research on the topic suggests that the links between Facebook use, social comparison, and negative consequences are robust, but more work remains to be done to establish causality (Appel, Gerlach, & Crusius, 2016).

More work must also be done to situate this literature clearly within the interpersonal connection behaviors framework. Existing literature on social comparison does provide evidence that it operates differently when an individual compares to close others, such as when individuals "bask in reflected glory" (Tesser, Millar, & Moore, 1988). These findings may provide some initial, indirect evidence that relationship-building behaviors can serve as a buffer against social comparison. The link between passive Facebook use and social comparison established in Verduyn and colleagues (2015) is also suggestive: it implies that active Facebook use does not carry the same risk. We cannot yet know if this means that active Facebook use inhibits social comparison, or if it allows social comparison to happen but provides a buffer against its harm.

Risks of Interpersonal Interaction: Loneliness

Loneliness has been viewed both as an antecedent (Bonetti, Campbell, & Gilmore, 2010; Morahan-Martin & Schumacher, 2003) and a consequence (Kraut, Patterson, Lundmark, Kiesler, Mukopadhyay, & Scherlis, 1998; Moody, 2001) of online social interaction. It has been particularly studied as a cause of problematic Internet use (PIU; Kim, LaRose & Peng, 2009; Caplan, 2007), or Internet use that results in negative psychological and behavioral symptoms. When studying problematic Internet use, the common approach focuses on loneliness creating a preference for mediated interactions, which then in turn creates PIU.

However, the overall relationship between mediated social interaction and loneliness unfortunately remains unclear. A brief glance at recent work underscores this point; while a recent meta-analysis found loneliness to be a cause rather than a result of mediated social interaction (Song, Zmyslinski-Seelig, Kim, Drent, Victor, Omori, & Allen, 2014), a well-done longitudinal study recently found loneliness as both cause and result (Teppers, Luyckx, Klimstra, & Goossens, 2014), and some work on problematic Internet use sees loneliness primarily as an outcome of excessive mediated interaction (e.g., Yao & Zhong, 2014). Other perspectives suggest that the link between loneliness and preference for online interaction is spurious, confounded by a third variable—social anxiety (Caplan, 2007).

Whatever the exact balance of these theories may be, it is likely that loneliness does function as both the cause and result of online interaction to some extent. Considering this question through the lens of the interpersonal connection behaviors framework, lonely individuals may be drawn to online interaction because they rightly think that relationship-building interactions will ameliorate their loneliness, but interactions that fail to help them build lasting relationships may only make the situation worse. This same process is likely true for offline interactions as well, with one exception: lonely individuals are likely to find online interactions more attractive than offline interactions, due to their ease of use.

Lonely individuals do, in fact, self-disclose more online. This self-disclosure increases support, which in turn increases well-being, partially canceling out the negative effect of loneliness (Lee, Noh, & Koo, 2013). However, we would not assume that every online interaction a lonely person engages in online should serve to build relationships. The overall link between loneliness and amount of online interaction should be non-significant as relational and non-relational interactions wash each other out—a finding supported in the literature (Dienlin, Masur, & Trepte, 2017). However, drawing a distinction between interactions that help build relationships and interactions that don't should show the difference between them. In support of this idea, lonely individuals' passive use of Facebook is related to decreased social support, while their active use of Facebook is related to increased social support (Frison & Eggermont, 2015).

Given the difficulty of experimentally inducing loneliness, we may never be able to determine the precise relationship between loneliness and online interaction. However, the existing research is consistent with an explanation that situates loneliness as both a cause of online interaction and a consequence—specifically, a consequence of interactions that fail to build the social resources that would have prevented loneliness in the first place.

CONCLUSION

Online interactions have become a fundamental part of the social fabric in developed nations, and it is a trend that shows no signs of decreasing. Fortunately, research suggests that despite the possibility of negative outcomes, social media and other forms of online interaction can promote healthy relationships and social connection if used appropriately.

Specifically, we advance the Interpersonal Communication Behaviors Framework as a guiding principle for beneficial online interactions. Engaging in important relational processes such as self-disclosure and social support provision allows online interactions to contribute to the growth of stronger intimate relationships. Less relational online communication, on the other hand, may only present the pitfalls of human interaction: loneliness, social comparison, and other negative consequences.

While the Interpersonal Communication Behaviors Framework is consistent with past research, it has yet to be extensively tested empirically. By situating online interactions in the larger context of close relationships, the Framework provides many potential directions for future study. First and foremost, the link between online interaction and well-being can be explicated through experimental studies focusing on online relational processes. Moderators such as the affordances of any given technological medium or the qualities of a pre-existing relationship may also influence how relational processes unfold online and are worthy of further investigation. Individual differences such as social anxiety, loneliness, and attitudes toward online interaction provide a third valuable direction for research: for example, do socially anxious individuals prefer online interaction because they feel more comfortable engaging in relational processes online?

The social consequences of online interaction are complex, nuanced, and variable. Only by viewing every interaction in both the context of its medium and the context of its relationship can researchers begin to grasp the full picture.

References

Ajzen, I., & Fishbein, M. (1977). Attitude-behavior relations: A theoretical analysis and review of empirical research. *Psychological Bulletin*, *84*(5), 888–918. Retrieved from https://doi.org/10.1037/0033-2909.84.5.888.

Amichai-Hamburger, Y., & Ben-Artzi, E. (2003). Loneliness and Internet use. *Computers in Human Behavior*, *19*(1), 71–80. Retrieved from https://doi.org/10.1016/S0747-5632(02)00014-6.

Appel, H., Gerlach, A. L., & Crusius, J. (2016). The interplay between Facebook use, social comparison, envy, and depression. *Current Opinion in Psychology*, *9*, 44–49. Retrieved from https://doi.org/10.1016/j.copsyc.2015.10.006.

Ballantine, P. W., & Stephenson, R. J. (2011). Help me, I'm fat! Social support in online weight loss networks. *Journal of Consumer Behaviour*, *10*(6), 332–337. Retrieved from https://doi.org/10.1002/cb.374.

Bargh, J. A., McKenna, K. Y. A., & Fitzsimons, G. M. (2002). Can you see the real me? Activation and expression of the "true self" on the Internet. *Journal of Social Issues*, *58*(1), 33–48. Retrieved from https://doi.org/10.1111/1540-4560.00247.

Berkman, L. F., & Syme, S. L. (1979). Social networks, host resistance, and mortality: A nine-year follow-up study of Alameda County residents. *American Journal of Epidemiology*, *109*(2), 186–204.

Bonetti, L., Campbell, M. A., & Gilmore, L. (2010). The relationship of loneliness and social anxiety with children's and adolescents' online communication. *Cyberpsychology, Behavior, and Social Networking*, *13*(3), 279–285. Retrieved from https://doi.org/10.1089/cyber.2009.0215.

boyd, d. m., & Ellison, N. B. (2007). Social network sites: Definition, history, and scholarship. *Journal of Computer-Mediated Communication*, *13*(1), 210–230. Retrieved from https://doi.org/10.1111/j.1083-6101.2007.00393.x.

Braithwaite, D. O., Waldron, V. R., & Finn, J. (1999). Communication of social support in computer-mediated groups for people with disabilities. *Health Communication*, *11*(2), 123–151. Retrieved from https://doi.org/10.1207/s15327027hc1102_2.

Brown, E. (2015). *Always connecting but never connected? The subjective experience of young adults and connection to social technology* (PsyD dissertation). The Chicago School of Professional Psychology. Retrieved from https://search-proquest-com.proxy.lib.duke.edu/docview/1660960314/abstract/B16A6AB75C754391PQ/1.

Burke, M., & Develin, M. (2016). Once more with feeling: Supportive responses to social sharing on Facebook. In *Proceedings of the 19th ACM Conference on Computer-Supported Cooperative Work & Social Computing* (pp. 1462–1474). New York, NY: ACM. Retrieved from https://doi.org/10.1145/2818048.2835199.

Burke, M., & Kraut, R. E. (2014). Growing closer on Facebook: Changes in tie strength through social network site use. In *Proceedings of the 32nd Annual ACM Conference on Human Factors in Computing Systems* (pp. 4187–4196). New York, NY: ACM. Retrieved from https://doi.org/10.1145/2556288.2557094.

Burke, M., & Kraut, R. E. (2016). The relationship between Facebook use and well-being depends on communication type and tie strength. *Journal of Computer-Mediated Communication, 21*(4), 265–281. Retrieved from https://doi.org/10.1111/jcc4.12162.

Burke, M., Kraut, R., & Marlow, C. (2011). Social capital on Facebook: Differentiating uses and users. In *Proceedings of the SIGCHI Conference on Human Factors in Computing Systems* (pp. 571–580). New York, NY, USA: ACM. Retrieved from https://doi.org/10.1145/1978942.1979023.

Caplan, S. E. (2003). Preference for online social interaction: A theory of problematic internet use and psychosocial well-being. *Communication Research, 30*(6), 625–648. Retrieved from https://doi.org/10.1177/0093650203257842.

Caplan, S. E. (2005). A social skill account of problematic Internet use. *Journal of Communication, 55*(4), 721–736.

Caplan, S. E. (2007). Relations among loneliness, social anxiety, and problematic Internet use. *CyberPsychology & Behavior, 10*(2), 234–242. Retrieved from https://doi.org/10.1089/cpb.2006.9963.

Carpenter, J. M., Green, M. C., & LaFlam, J. (2011). People or profiles: Individual differences in online social networking use. *Personality and Individual Differences, 50*(5), 538–541. Retrieved from https://doi.org/10.1016/j.paid.2010.11.006.

Carpenter, J. M., Green, M. C., & LaFlam, J. (2018). Just between us: Exclusive communications in online social networks. *Journal of Social Psychology*. Retrieved from https://doi.org/10.1080/00224545.2018.1431603.

Chou, H.-T. G., & Edge, N. (2012). "They are happier and having better lives than I am": The impact of using Facebook on perceptions of others' lives. *Cyberpsychology, Behavior, and Social Networking, 15*(2), 117–121. Retrieved from https://doi.org/10.1089/cyber.2011.0324.

Clark, J. L. (2017). *The role of text messaging in close relationships.* (Doctoral dissertation).

Clark, J. L., Algoe, S. B., & Green, M. C. (2017). Social network sites and well-being: The role of social connection. *Current Directions in Psychological Science, 27*(1), 32–37.

Clark, J. L., & Green, M. C. (2013). Making "real" connections: The perceived reality of online interactions. *International Journal of Interactive Communication Systems and Technologies, 3*(1), 1–19.

Clark, J. L., & Green, M. C. (2017). Self-fulfilling prophecies: Perceived reality of online interaction drives expected outcomes of online communication. *Personality and Individual Differences.* Advanced online publication. Retrieved from http://doi:10.1016/j.paid.2017.08.031.

Cohen, S., & Wills, T. A. (1985). Stress, social support, and the buffering hypothesis. *Psychological Bulletin, 98*(2), 310–357. Retrieved from https://doi.org/10.1037/0033-2909.98.2.310.

Collins, N. L., & Miller, L. C. (1994). Self-disclosure and liking: A meta-analytic review. *Psychological Bulletin*, *116*(3), 457–475. Retrieved from https://doi.org/10.1037/0033-2909.116.3.457.

Corr, P. J. (Ed.). (2008). *The reinforcement sensitivity theory of personality.* Cambridge University Press.

Coulson, N. S. (2005). Receiving social support online: an analysis of a computer-mediated support group for individuals living with irritable bowel syndrome. *CyberPsychology & Behavior*, *8*(6), 580–584. Retrieved from https://doi.org/10.1089/cpb.2005.8.580.

Coulson, N. S., Buchanan, H., & Aubeeluck, A. (2007). Social support in cyberspace: A content analysis of communication within a Huntington's disease online support group. *Patient Education and Counseling*, *68*(2), 173–178. Retrieved from https://doi.org/10.1016/j.pec.2007.06.002.

Daft, R. L., & Lengel, R. H. (1983). *Information richness: A new approach to managerial behavior and organization design.*

Daft, R. L., & Lengel, R. H. (1986). Organizational information requirements, media richness and structural design. *Management Science*, *32*(5), 554–571. Retrieved from https://doi.org/10.2307/2631846.

Derks, D., Fischer, A. H., & Bos, A. E. R. (2008). The role of emotion in computer-mediated communication: A review. *Computers in Human Behavior*, *24*(3), 766–785. Retrieved from https://doi.org/10.1016/j.chb.2007.04.004.

Desjarlais, M., Gilmour, J., Sinclair, J., Howell, K. B., & West, A. (2015). Predictors and social consequences of online interactive self-disclosure: A literature review from 2002 to 2014. *Cyberpsychology, Behavior, and Social Networking*, *18*(12), 718–725. Retrieved from https://doi.org/10.1089/cyber.2015.0109.

Dienlin, T., Masur, P. K., & Trepte, S. (2017). Reinforcement or displacement? The reciprocity of FtF, IM, and SNS communication and their effects on loneliness and life satisfaction. *Journal of Computer-Mediated Communication*, *22*(2), 71–87. Retrieved from https://doi.org/10.1111/jcc4.12183.

Eagly, A. H., & Chaiken, S. (1993). *The psychology of attitudes* (Vol. xxii). Orlando, FL: Harcourt Brace Jovanovich College Publishers.

Feinstein, B. A., Hershenberg, R., Bhatia, V., Latack, J. A., Meuwly, N., & Davila, J. (2013). Negative social comparison on Facebook and depressive symptoms: Rumination as a mechanism. *Psychology of Popular Media Culture*, *2*(3), 161–170. Retrieved from https://doi.org/10.1037/a0033111.

Ferguson, M. J. (2008). On becoming ready to pursue a goal you don't know you have: Effects of nonconscious goals on evaluative readiness. *Journal of Personality and Social Psychology*, *95*(6), 1268–1294. Retrieved from https://doi.org/10.1037/a0013263.

Fox, J., & Vendemia, M. A. (2016). Selective self-presentation and social comparison through photographs on social networking sites. *Cyberpsychology, Behavior, and Social Networking*, *19*(10), 593–600. Retrieved from https://doi.org/10.1089/cyber.2016.0248.

Frison, E., & Eggermont, S. (2015). Toward an integrated and differential approach to the relationships between loneliness, different types of Facebook use, and adolescents' depressed mood. *Communication Research*, 0093650215617506. Retrieved from https://doi.org/10.1177/0093650215617506.

Gable, S. L., Reis, H. T., Impett, E. A., & Asher, E. R. (2004). What do you do when things go right? The intrapersonal and interpersonal benefits of sharing positive events. *Journal of Personality and Social Psychology*, *87*(2), 228–245. Retrieved from https://doi.org/10.1037/0022-3514.87.2.228.

Gardner, W. L., Pickett, C. L., & Knowles, M. (2005). Social snacking and shielding. *The social outcast: Ostracism, social exclusion, rejection, and bullying*, 227–242.

Gerson, J., Plagnol, A. C., & Corr, P. J. (2016). Subjective well-being and social media use: Do personality traits moderate the impact of social comparison on Facebook? *Computers in Human Behavior*, 63, 813–822. Retrieved from https://doi.org/10.1016/j.chb.2016.06.023.

Gilbert, D. T., Giesler, R. B., & Morris, K. A. (1995). When comparisons arise. *Journal of Personality and Social Psychology*, 69(2), 227–236. Retrieved from https://doi.org/10.1037/0022-3514.69.2.227.

Goldberg, L. R. (1992). The development of markers for the Big-Five factor structure. *Psychological Assessment*, 4(1), 26–42. Retrieved from https://doi.org/10.1037/1040-3590.4.1.26.

Holt-Lunstad, J., Smith, T. B., & Layton, J. B. (2010). Social relationships and mortality risk: A meta-analytic review. *PLoS Med*, 7(7), e1000316. Retrieved from https://doi.org/10.1371/journal.pmed.1000316.

House, J. S. (1981). *Work stress and social support*. Retrieved from http://deepblue.lib.umich.edu/handle/2027.42/99210.

House, J. S., Landis, K. R., & Umberson, D. (1988). Social relationships and health. *Science*, 241(4865), 540.

Indian, M., & Grieve, R. (2014). When Facebook is easier than face-to-face: Social support derived from Facebook in socially anxious individuals. *Personality and Individual Differences*, 59, 102–106. Retrieved from https://doi.org/10.1016/j.paid.2013.11.016.

Jiang, L. C., Bazarova, N. N., & Hancock, J. T. (2011). The disclosure–intimacy link in computer-mediated communication: An attributional extension of the hyperpersonal model. *Human Communication Research*, 37(1), 58–77. Retrieved from https://doi.org/10.1111/j.1468-2958.2010.01393.x.

Jiang, L. C., Bazarova, N. N., & Hancock, J. T. (2013). From perception to behavior: Disclosure reciprocity and the intensification of intimacy in computer-mediated communication. *Communication Research*, 40(1), 125–143. Retrieved from https://doi.org/10.1177/0093650211405313.

Joinson, A. N. (2001). Self-disclosure in computer-mediated communication: The role of self-awareness and visual anonymity. *European Journal of Social Psychology*, 31(2), 177–192. Retrieved from https://doi.org/10.1002/ejsp.36.

Kalman, Y. M., & Rafaeli, S. (2011). Online pauses and silence: Chronemic expectancy violations in written computer-mediated communication. *Communication Research*, 38(1), 54–69.

Kalman, Y. M., Scissors, L. E., Gill, A. J., & Gergle, D. (2013). Online chronemics convey social information. *Computers in Human Behavior*, 29(3), 1260–1269.

Katz, J. E., Rice, R. E., & Aspden, P. (2001). The Internet, 1995–2000: Access, civic involvement, and social interaction. *American Behavioral Scientist*, 45(3), 405–419. Retrieved from https://doi.org/10.1177/00027642010450003004.

Kiecolt-Glaser, J. K., & Newton, T. L. (2001). Marriage and health: His and hers. *Psychological Bulletin*, 127(4), 472–503. Retrieved from https://doi.org/10.1037/0033-2909.127.4.472.

Kim, J., LaRose, R., & Peng, W. (2009). Loneliness as the cause and the effect of problematic Internet use: The relationship between Internet use and psychological well-being. *CyberPsychology & Behavior*, 12(4), 451–455.

Kim, J., & Lee, J.-E. R. (2011). The Facebook paths to happiness: Effects of the number of Facebook friends and self-presentation on subjective well-being. *Cyberpsychology, Behavior, and Social Networking*, 14(6), 359–364. Retrieved from https://doi.org/10.1089/cyber.2010.0374.

Kraut, R., Patterson, M., Lundmark, V., Kiesler, S., Mukophadhyay, T., & Scherlis, W. (1998). Internet paradox: A social technology that reduces social involvement and psychological well-being? *American Psychologist*, 53(9), 1017–1031. Retrieved from https://doi.org/10.1037/0003-066X.53.9.1017.

Kruger, J., Epley, N., Parker, J., & Ng, Z.-W. (2005). Egocentrism over e-mail: Can we communicate as well as we think? *Journal of Personality and Social Psychology*, 89(6), 925–936. Retrieved from https://doi.org/10.1037/0022-3514.89.6.925.

Laflen, A., & Fiorenza, B. (2012). "Okay, my rant is over": The language of emotion in computer-mediated communication. *Computers and Composition*, 29(4), 296–308. Retrieved from https://doi.org/10.1016/j.compcom.2012.09.005.

Laurenceau, J.-P., Barrett, L. F., & Pietromonaco, P. R. (1998). Intimacy as an interpersonal process: The importance of self-disclosure, partner disclosure, and perceived partner responsiveness in interpersonal exchanges. *Journal of Personality and Social Psychology*, 74(5), 1238–1251. Retrieved from https://doi.org/10.1037/0022-3514.74.5.1238.

Ledbetter, A. M., & Kuznekoff, J. H. (2012). More than a game: Friendship relational maintenance and attitudes toward Xbox LIVE communication. *Communication Research*, 39(2), 269–290. Retrieved from https://doi.org/10.1177/0093650210397042.

Ledbetter, A. M., Mazer, J. P., DeGroot, J. M., Meyer, K. R., Mao, Y., & Swafford, B. (2011). Attitudes toward online social connection and self-disclosure as predictors of Facebook communication and relational closeness. *Communication Research*, 38(1), 27–53. Retrieved from https://doi.org/10.1177/0093650210365537.

Lee, K.-T., Noh, M.-J., & Koo, D.-M. (2013). Lonely people are no longer lonely on social networking sites: The mediating role of self-disclosure and social support. *Cyberpsychology, Behavior, and Social Networking*, 16(6), 413–418. Retrieved from https://doi.org/10.1089/cyber.2012.0553.

Lo, S.-K. (2008). The nonverbal communication functions of emoticons in computer-mediated communication. *CyberPsychology & Behavior*, 11(5), 595–597. Retrieved from https://doi.org/10.1089/cpb.2007.0132.

Maisel, N. C., & Gable, S. L. (2009). The paradox of received social support: The importance of responsiveness. *Psychological Science*, 20(8), 928–932. Retrieved from https://doi.org/10.1111/j.1467-9280.2009.02388.x.

Manago, A. M., Taylor, T., & Greenfield, P. M. (2012). Me and my 400 friends: The anatomy of college students' Facebook networks, their communication patterns, and well-being. *Developmental Psychology*, 48(2), 369–380. Retrieved from https://doi.org/10.1037/a0026338.

Meng, J., Martinez, L., Holmstrom, A., Chung, M., & Cox, J. (2016). Research on social networking sites and social support from 2004 to 2015: A narrative review and directions for future research. *Cyberpsychology, Behavior, and Social Networking*, 20(1), 44–51. Retrieved from https://doi.org/10.1089/cyber.2016.0325.

Moody, E. J. (2001). Internet use and its relationship to loneliness. *CyberPsychology & Behavior*, 4(3), 393–401. Retrieved from https://doi.org/10.1089/109493101300210303.

Morahan-Martin, J., & Schumacher, P. (2003). Loneliness and social uses of the Internet. *Computers in Human Behavior*, 19(6), 659–671. Retrieved from https://doi.org/10.1016/S0747-5632(03)00040-2.

Mussweiler, T., Rüter, K., & Epstude, K. (2004). The man who wasn't there: Subliminal social comparison standards influence self-evaluation. *Journal of Experimental Social Psychology*, 40(5), 689–696. Retrieved from https://doi.org/10.1016/j.jesp.2004.01.004.

Nowak, K. L., Watt, J., & Walther, J. B. (2005). The influence of synchrony and sensory modality on the person perception process in computer-mediated groups. *Journal of Computer-Mediated Communication, 10*(3). Retrieved from https://doi.org/10.1111/j.1083-6101.2005.tb00251.x.

Nguyen, M., Bin, Y. S., & Campbell, A. (2012). Comparing online and offline self-disclosure: A systematic review. *Cyberpsychology, Behavior, and Social Networking, 15*(2), 103–111. Retrieved from https://doi.org/10.1089/cyber.2011.0277.

Nie, N. H. (2001). Sociability, interpersonal relations, and the Internet: Reconciling conflicting findings. *American Behavioral Scientist, 45*(3), 420–435. Retrieved from https://doi.org/10.1177/00027640121957277.

Oh, H. J., Ozkaya, E., & LaRose, R. (2014). How does online social networking enhance life satisfaction? The relationships among online supportive interaction, affect, perceived social support, sense of community, and life satisfaction. *Computers in Human Behavior, 30*, 69–78. Retrieved from https://doi.org/10.1016/j.chb.2013.07.053.

Park, J., Lee, D. S., Shablack, H., Verduyn, P., Deldin, P., Ybarra, O., ... Kross, E. (2016). When perceptions defy reality: The relationships between depression and actual and perceived Facebook social support. *Journal of Affective Disorders, 200*, 37–44. Retrieved from https://doi.org/10.1016/j.jad.2016.01.048.

Parks, M. R., & Floyd, K. (1996). Making friends in cyberspace. *Journal of Communication, 46*(1), 80–97. Retrieved from https://doi.org/10.1111/j.1460-2466.1996.tb01462.x.

Peter, J., & Valkenburg, P. M. (2006). Research note: Individual differences in perceptions of Internet communication. *European Journal of Communication, 21*(2), 213–226. Retrieved from https://doi.org/10.1177/0267323105064046.

Putnam, R. D. (2000). Bowling alone: America's declining social capital. In *Culture and politics* (pp. 223–234). Palgrave Macmillan, New York.

Reis, H. T., & Shaver, P. (1988). Intimacy as an interpersonal process. In S. Duck (Ed.), *Handbook of Personal Relationships* (pp. 367–389). Chichester: Wiley.

Scharer, K. (2005). Internet social support for parents: The state of science. *Journal of Child and Adolescent Psychiatric Nursing, 18*(1), 26–35. Retrieved from https://doi.org/10.1111/j.1744-6171.2005.00007.x.

Schiffrin, H., Edelman, A., Falkenstern, M., & Stewart, C. (2010). The associations among computer-mediated communication, relationships, and well-being. *Cyberpsychology, Behavior, and Social Networking, 13*(3), 299–306. Retrieved from https://doi.org/10.1089/cyber.2009.0173.

Selcuk, E., & Ong, A. D. (2013). Perceived partner responsiveness moderates the association between received emotional support and all-cause mortality. *Health Psychology, 32*(2), 231–235. Retrieved from https://doi.org/10.1037/a0028276.

Shah, D. V., Cho, J., Eveland, W. P. Jr., & Kwak, N. (2005). Information and expression in a digital age: Modeling Internet effects on civic participation. *Communication Research, 32*(5), 531–565.

Shah, D. V., Kwak, N., & Holbert, R. L. (2001). "Connecting" and "disconnecting" with civic life: Patterns of Internet use and the production of social capital. *Political Communication, 18*(2), 141–162.

Shah, D. V., McLeod, J. M., & Yoon, S. H. (2001). Communication, context, and community: An exploration of print, broadcast, and Internet influences. *Communication Research, 28*(4), 464–506.

Shah, D., Schmierbach, M., Hawkins, J., Espino, R., & Donavan, J. (2002). Nonrecursive models of Internet use and community engagement: Questioning whether time spent online erodes social capital. *Journalism & Mass Communication Quarterly*, *79*(4), 964–987.

Siedlecki, K. L., Salthouse, T. A., Oishi, S., & Jeswani, S. (2013). The relationship between social support and subjective well-being across age. *Social Indicators Research*, *117*(2), 561–576. Retrieved from https://doi.org/10.1007/s11205-013-0361-4.

Sleek, S. (2014). *The psychological toll of the smartphone*. Retrieved from https://www.psychologicalscience.org/observer/the-psychological-toll-of-the-smartphone.

Song, H., Zmyslinski-Seelig, A., Kim, J., Drent, A., Victor, A., Omori, K., & Allen, M. (2014). Does Facebook make you lonely?: A meta analysis. *Computers in Human Behavior*, *36*, 446–452.

Steers, M.-L. N., Wickham, R. E., & Acitelli, L. K. (2014). Seeing everyone else's highlight reels: How Facebook usage is linked to depressive symptoms. *Journal of Social and Clinical Psychology*, *33*(8), 701–731. Retrieved from https://doi.org/10.1521/jscp.2014.33.8.701.

Stefanone, M. A., Kwon, K. H., & Lackaff, D. (2012). Exploring the relationship between perceptions of social capital and enacted support online. *Journal of Computer-Mediated Communication*, *17*, 451–466.

Stokes, N. (January 15, 2015). *5 ways smartphones are harming our health*. Retrieved from https://www.techlicious.com/tip/5-ways-your-smartphone-could-be-harming-your-health/.

Suler, J. (2004). The online disinhibition effect. *CyberPsychology & Behavior*, *7*(3), 321–326. Retrieved from https://doi.org/10.1089/1094931041291295.

Swickert, R. J., Hittner, J. B., Harris, J. L., & Herring, J. A. (2002). Relationships among Internet use, personality, and social support. *Computers in Human Behavior*, *18*(4), 437–451. Retrieved from https://doi.org/10.1016/S0747-5632(01)00054-1.

Taylor, S. E., & Lobel, M. (1989). Social comparison activity under threat: Downward evaluation and upward contacts. *Psychological Review*, *96*(4), 569–575. Retrieved from https://doi.org/10.1037/0033-295X.96.4.569.

Teppers, E., Luyckx, K., Klimstra, T. A., & Goossens, L. (2014). Loneliness and Facebook motives in adolescence: A longitudinal inquiry into directionality of effect. *Journal of Adolescence*, *37*(5), 691–699.

Tesser, A., Millar, M., & Moore, J. (1988). Some affective consequences of social comparison and reflection processes: The pain and pleasure of being close. *Journal of Personality and Social Psychology*, *54*(1), 49–61.

Thompson, D., & Filik, R. (2016). Sarcasm in written communication: Emoticons are efficient markers of intention. *Journal of Computer-Mediated Communication*, *21*(2), 105–120. Retrieved from https://doi.org/10.1111/jcc4.12156.

Tichon, J. G., & Shapiro, M. (2003). The process of sharing social support in cyberspace. *CyberPsychology & Behavior*, *6*(2), 161–170. Retrieved from https://doi.org/10.1089/109493103321640356.

Tobin, S. J., Vanman, E. J., Verreynne, M., & Saeri, A. K. (2015). Threats to belonging on Facebook: Lurking and ostracism. *Social Influence*, *10*(1), 31–42. Retrieved from https://doi.org/10.1080/15534510.2014.893924.

Tromholt, M. (2016). The Facebook experiment: Quitting Facebook leads to higher levels of well-being. *Cyberpsychology, Behavior, and Social Networking*, *19*(11), 661–666. Retrieved from https://doi.org/10.1089/cyber.2016.0259.

Turkle, S. (1994). Constructions and reconstructions of self in virtual reality: Playing in the MUDs. *Mind, Culture, and Activity*, *1*(3), 158–167. Retrieved from https://doi.org/10.1080/10749039409524667.

Turner, R. J. (1981). Social support as a contingency in psychological well-being. *Journal of Health and Social Behavior*, 22(4), 357–367. Retrieved from https://doi.org/10.2307/2136677.

Twenge, J. (September 2017). *Have smartphones destroyed a generation?* Retrieved from https://www.theatlantic.com/magazine/archive/2017/09/has-the-smartphone-destroyed-a-generation/534198/.

Uchino, B. N., Cacioppo, J. T., & Kiecolt-Glaser, J. K. (1996). The relationship between social support and physiological processes: A review with emphasis on underlying mechanisms and implications for health. *Psychological Bulletin*, 119(3), 488–531. Retrieved from https://doi.org/10.1037/0033-2909.119.3.488.

Valkenburg, P. M., & Peter, J. (2007). Online communication and adolescent well-being: Testing the stimulation versus the displacement hypothesis. *Journal of Computer-Mediated Communication*, 12(4), 1169–1182.

Verduyn, P., Lee, D. S., Park, J., Shablack, H., Orvell, A., Bayer, J., ... Kross, E. (2015). Passive Facebook usage undermines affective well-being: Experimental and longitudinal evidence. *Journal of Experimental Psychology: General*, 144(2), 480–488. Retrieved from https://doi.org/10.1037/xge0000057.

Walther, J. B. (1996). Computer-mediated communication: Impersonal, interpersonal, and hyperpersonal interaction. *Communication Research*, 23(1), 3–43. Retrieved from https://doi.org/10.1177/009365096023001001.

Walther, J. B., & D'Addario, K. P. (2001). The impacts of emoticons on message interpretation in computer-mediated communication. *Social Science Computer Review*, 19(3), 324–347. Retrieved from https://doi.org/10.1177/089443930101900307.

Wang, H., Chua, V., & Stefanone, M. A. (2015). Social ties, communication channels, and personal well-being: A study of the networked lives of college students in Singapore. *American Behavioral Scientist*, 59(9), 1189–1202.

Weidman, A. C., Fernandez, K. C., Levinson, C. A., Augustine, A. A., Larsen, R. J., & Rodebaugh, T. L. (2012). Compensatory Internet use among individuals higher in social anxiety and its implications for well-being. *Personality and Individual Differences*, 53(3), 191–195. Retrieved from https://doi.org/10.1016/j.paid.2012.03.003.

White, J. B., Langer, E. J., Yariv, L., & Welch, J. C. (2006). Frequent social comparisons and destructive emotions and behaviors: The dark side of social comparisons. *Journal of Adult Development*, 13(1), 36–44. Retrieved from https://doi.org/10.1007/s10804-006-9005-0.

White, M., & Dorman, S. M. (2001). Receiving social support online: Implications for health education. *Health Education Research*, 16(6), 693–707. Retrieved from https://doi.org/10.1093/her/16.6.693.

Wilcox, B. L., & Vernberg, E. M. (1985). Conceptual and Theoretical Dilemmas Facing Social Support Research. In I. G. Sarason & B. R. Sarason (Eds.), *Social Support: Theory, Research and Applications* (pp. 3–20). Springer: Dordrecht. Retrieved from http://link.springer.com.libproxy.lib.unc.edu/chapter/10.1007/978-94-009-5115-0_1.

Wright, K. (2002). Social support within an on-line cancer community: An assessment of emotional support, perceptions of advantages and disadvantages, and motives for using the community from a communication perspective. *Journal of Applied Communication Research*, 30(3), 195–209.

Yao, M. Z., & Zhong, Z. J. (2014). Loneliness, social contacts and Internet addiction: A cross-lagged panel study. *Computers in Human Behavior*, 30, 164–170.

PART IV

GROUPS AND
COMMUNITIES

CHAPTER 13

ONLINE SUPPORT COMMUNITIES

NEIL S. COULSON

INTRODUCTION AND BACKGROUND

DURING the early years of the Internet, limited interaction existed between individual users and websites and, as a consequence, individuals were mostly restricted to looking for and reading health-related information. While searching for health-related information remains a common online activity, i.e., in 2016, 51 percent searched for health information online in the UK (Office for National Statistics, 2016), more recent technological advances have facilitated the development of various forms of electronic communication which have encouraged participation, collaboration, and information sharing between users (often referred to as "Web 2.0"). One specific way in which this ability to interact with other users has manifested itself is through the evolution of online support communities.

What Are Online Support Communities?

Generally, online communities are "social aggregations that emerge from the Net when enough people carry on those public discussions long enough, with sufficient human feeling, to form webs of personal relationships in cyberspace" (Rheingold, 1993, p. 5). Online communities have often been described variously as virtual communities, web-based communities, online support groups, and e-communities. Online support communities can be underpinned by several different platforms including Listserv, discussion forums, private messaging, chat rooms, social networking sites (e.g., Facebook), blogs, microblogs (e.g., Twitter), and virtual reality environments. Broadly speaking, two main types of online support community exist: synchronous and asynchronous. A synchronous online community offers a dynamic environment where individuals are able to participate in live, real-time interaction and conversation with each other. Common examples include chat rooms, instant messaging, and online virtual reality environments. In contrast, asynchronous communities offer a much more static environment where content is exchanged and evolves over time (i.e., hours, days, weeks, or months).

The most popular type of asynchronous online community is the discussion forum (also known as the bulletin or message board). In a typical asynchronous forum structure, discussions are usually organized into threads where one member creates a new discussion by posting an initial message, which may ask a question, describe a problem, or talk about an experience that they want to share. Other members of the online community may then choose to post a reply to that message. Members might post further messages in response to these replies, thereby building up a hierarchical thread of messages that stem from the original post (Holtz, Kronberger, & Wagner, 2012). Many online support communities host their own websites, whereas others are built on existing social networking services (e.g., Facebook) or are part of larger websites (e.g., HealthUnlocked, PatientsLikeMe).

Online support communities cover a broad spectrum of topics and interests. The most common types of online support communities are dedicated to supporting those affected (e.g., patients, families, caregivers) by health conditions (e.g., prostate cancer, asthma, hearing loss). However, there are also many online support communities covering a range of other health-related topics, including behavior change (e.g., helping people lose weight), parenting (e.g., helping new mothers with breastfeeding), caregiving (e.g., those who provide support to friends, relatives, or neighbors who are ill), and bereavement (e.g., helping individuals adjust to the death of a loved one).

How Popular Are Online Support Communities?

In the past two decades, there has been an exponential increase in the number of online support communities. Similarly, the number of people accessing online support communities has also increased in recent years, not least because of the steadily rising rates of Internet access (e.g. 88 percent of adults in the UK used the Internet at least every week in 2017). Moreover, it is now easy to gain Internet access through mobile phones or smartphones as well as personal computers and handheld devices (Office for National Statistics, 2017). While accurate estimates of the number of individuals accessing online support communities at any point in time are difficult to make, several recent studies demonstrate their popularity. For example, findings from the Pew Internet and American Life Project (Fox, 2011) revealed that approximately twenty percent of Internet users reported using an online community during 2011. Likewise, in a survey undertaken by the National Cancer Institute (2013), approximately seven percent of adults in the United States of America indicated that they had participated in an online forum or support group for people with a similar health or medical issue in 2012. Similarly, in a UK-wide survey of a thousand Internet users, approximately one-quarter (27.8 percent) of all respondents reported participating in online support communities (O'Neill, Ziebland, Valderas, & Lupiáñez-Villanueva, 2014). A number of studies have suggested that engagement with online support communities may be influenced by members' perceptions of the accessibility, convenience, and relative anonymity of the computer-mediated nature of the communication underpinning these communities.

POTENTIAL ADVANTAGES OF
ONLINE SUPPORT COMMUNITIES

As access to an online support community is possible twenty-four hours a day, seven days a week from any computer or Internet-enabled device, members are able to obtain support whenever it is needed (Vilhauer, McClintock & Matthews, 2010). This high level of availability introduces a far greater level of convenience and flexibility, compared to face-to-face support groups, by allowing members to solicit support at times and places that are convenient to them (Idriss, Kvedar, & Watson, 2009). Furthermore, they may be especially helpful to those with work, family, or education commitments (Coulson & Knibb, 2007; Coulson, 2013). In addition, online support communities have been shown to be a valued alternative to face-to-face groups, particularly when there is some type of crisis and traditional support options are not available (Malik & Coulson, 2008; Coulson, Bullock & Rodham, 2017).

Online support communities also confer a degree of anonymity that can be helpful to members (Allen, Vassilev, Kennedy, & Rogers, 2016; Sinclair, Chambers, & Manson, 2017). For example, socio-demographic characteristics such as age, gender, ethnicity, income, or social status are not appreciable (White & Dorman, 2001). In addition, appearance, disability, and vocal characteristics are not detectable (Davison, Pennebaker, & Dickerson, 2000). As a consequence, individual online support community members can choose how much personal or background information they wish to share with other members. Other studies reported that the anonymous nature of online communication can aid in discussing sensitive or difficult issues and help those in need to actively seek support (Powell, McCarthy, & Eysenbach, 2003; Broom, 2005). For example, Classen and colleagues (2012) reported that 57 percent of participants in a professionally moderated online community for patients with gynecological cancer felt more comfortable discussing sexual issues within the online community compared to a face-to-face group.

For some individuals, the attraction of an online support community relates to the asynchronous nature of the communication that takes place, choosing when and where to access the online support community and what to do once online. For example, some individuals may choose to simply read messages (known as "lurking") or be more active and post messages and contribute to or initiate conversation threads. Indeed, when it comes to posting a message to an online support community, the asynchronous nature of the communication platform has been considered helpful as an individual can take their time in considering what to say and drafting the message (Vilhauer, McClintock, & Matthews, 2010). Similarly, an individual can take their time when reading a message and formulating a reply.

Unlike a traditional face-to-face support group, there is potentially no upper limit to the number of people who can access and contribute to an online support community. Thus, online support communities with many thousands of members drawn from several continents and many different countries are common (White & Dorman, 2001). An online support community is, therefore, likely to be more heterogeneous, compared to a face-to-face support group (Wright & Bell, 2003). For an individual community member, there is likely to be greater exposure to a wider and more diverse range of views, opinions, and experiences (Wright & Bell, 2003; Colvin, Chenoweth, Bold, & Harding, 2004); this can increase the likelihood of an individual finding someone who has had a similar experience (White & Dorman, 2001), can help address a specific issue or problem, and increase the chances of coming across new, useful information (Coulson & Knibb, 2007).

POTENTIAL DISADVANTAGES OF ONLINE SUPPORT COMMUNITIES

Online support communities are not without their potential problems. A frequent concern is that these online communities are simply not accessible to specific groups in society, e.g., those who do not access the Internet, as an individual needs access to an Internet-enabled device in order to participate. However, when considering global usage statistics only 54.4 percent are Internet users (Internet World Stats, 2017). While this figure has clearly increased in recent years, half of the world's population have no access to online support communities. That said, the encouraging increase in levels of Internet availability is likely to continue over the coming years.

However, even for those who are able to access online support communities (i.e., they have both Internet access and the necessary digital skills), there may be a number of potential disadvantages.

Characteristics of Online Asynchronous Communication

Within online support communities, social cues like facial expressions, tone of voice, and body language are not evident, which can lead to problems for members (Pfeil, Zaphiris, & Wilson, 2009). For example, in their thematic analysis of 1013 messages posted on four Parkinson's disease asynchronous online support forums, Attard and

Coulson (2012) identified multiple instances where members misunderstood the meaning or intention behind a message, or made incorrect assumptions about other community members, which led to feelings of awkwardness. One strategy used by many online support community members to mitigate against this is to use excessive punctuation in their messages or emoticons as a potential substitute (van Uden-Kraan, Drossaert, Taal, Lebrun et al., 2008).

Additionally, the lack of physical proximity between members can also prevent the expression of some forms of physical affection, such as giving another group member a hug (Malik & Coulson, 2010). This can also limit the ability to form meaningful face-to-face relationships, and some studies have described how community members may feel isolated and alone in their real lives after logging off (e.g., Coulson, 2013).

Another difficulty arising from the asynchronous nature of the communication is the potential delay in receiving a response to a message posted seeking help, advice, or assistance. While an individual can post a message at any time of the day or night, there may be a delay in receiving a response (e.g., a reply message); this delay can be anywhere from a few hours, days, or weeks and in some situations there may be no response at all. A number of studies have noted the problems surrounding delayed or non-response and how this can negatively impact on community members and their experience and satisfaction with online support (Vilhauer, McClintock, & Matthews, 2010; Coulson, 2013). However, in clear cases of distress or need, the evidence suggests that fellow members are able to identify messages lacking a reply and will respond accordingly (Winefield, 2006), typically within 24 hours (van Uden-Kraan, Drossaert, Taal, Lebrun et al., 2008).

Information Quantity and Quality

As online support communities continue to develop, the potential for information overload increases. Evidence suggests that the high volume of messages posted to online communities can reduce the perceived value of those communities, particularly for new members who may be confused or feel overwhelmed while searching for relevant information (Mo & Coulson, 2014). Similarly, the volume of questions and answers posted in community archives may make it difficult for some members to find relevant information (Coulson, 2013). Some members may respond to the challenge of information overload by only replying to simple messages, by posting simple replies, or, in some instances, disengaging from active participation within the online support community (Jones, Ravid, & Rafaeli, 2004).

Lack of Control on the Quality of Information Posted Online

Wright (2000) notes the importance of credibility of information posted to online communities as being an important determinant of member satisfaction as well as levels of participation. However, as a result of the lack of visual cues and the anonymity conferred through online support communities, there are concerns about the quality of medical and/or health-related information available through online support communities (Winzelberg, 1997; Coulson & Knibb, 2007; Pfeil et al., 2009). Indeed, for some individuals facing health challenges (e.g., prostate cancer), these concerns were significant enough to persuade a number of patients that they should not access an online support community for fear that they would be "fed the wrong information" (Broom, 2005, p. 96).

Early studies that examined the accuracy of information posted to online support communities appeared to confirm the view that inaccurate or unconventional content was commonplace. For example, in their assessment of medical information posted by non-medically trained community members, Culver, Gerr, and Frumkin (1997) reported that 35.6 percent was unconventional (i.e., not consistent with generally accepted medical practice). Similarly, Winzelberg (1997) found that 12 percent of information posted to an eating disorder online support community was inaccurate and outside the standards of medical and psychological care (e.g., ineffective, dangerous, or costly). However, more recent studies have suggested that the vast majority of messages posted to online support communities are not misleading, inaccurate, or harmful (Esquivel, Meric-Bernstam, & Bernstam, 2006), and where inaccurate information is evident, it tends to appear in those communities with lower levels of activity (Hwang et al., 2007) or is unlikely to have been acted upon by members (Cole, Watkins, & Kleine, 2016).

Online support communities have also been shown to benefit from a self-correction process, whereby other community members are often quick to identify and challenge or correct any misleading information (Esquivel et al., 2006; Hwang et al., 2007). Furthermore, many online support communities also benefit from experienced moderators who are also able to remove, challenge, or qualify any potentially erroneous or misleading information (Smedley & Coulson, 2017).

Negative Content

As the majority of online support communities are devoted to illness-related topics, there is concern that members may be more likely to post messages during times when their symptoms are particularly challenging. For example, in a survey of 249 members of Inflammatory Bowel Disease online support communities, Coulson (2013) reported that several respondents described how reading "horror stories" was considered unavoidable. As a consequence of reading such negative content, several respondents described a heightened sense of anxiety and concern about what might happen to them in the future. Similarly, Coulson, Bullock, and Rodham (2017) noted the potential risks associated with reading "triggering" content within self-harm online support communities.

Who Engages with Health-related Online Support Communities?

A number of socio-demographic characteristics have been associated with greater engagement with online support communities. For example, greater levels of engagement have been reported by individuals with higher levels of educational attainment and income (Owen et al., 2010; Han & Belcher, 2001). Furthermore, those who engage more regularly with support communities are less likely to be from an ethnic minority group (McTavish, Pingree, Hawkins, & Gustafson, 2003; Im, Lee, & Chee, 2011). Gender differences have also been reported, with females being more likely to use mixed-gender online support communities (Hu et al., 2012; Klaw et al., 2000).

In terms of illness type, greater levels of engagement have also been reported by individuals experiencing certain conditions, including depression, anxiety, diabetes, cancer, stroke, and arthritis (Owen et al., 2010). In addition, individuals with poorer subjective health (Chou, Hunt, Beckjord, Moser, & Hesse, 2009), who experience greater levels of psychological distress (Chou et al., 2009), or who live with a stigmatized condition (Davison et al., 2000) are also more likely to engage with an online support community.

Why do People Use Online Support Communities?

Considerable research has identified and described the various factors that may underpin the decision to engage with online support communities. In a review of the literature, Wright (2016) identifies four broad themes evident across the literature. These include: 1) limited access to adequate support within traditional social network(s); 2) living with health-related stigma; 3) perceived similarity/credibility of support providers; and 4) convenience and other features of computer-mediated communication.

If an individual has limited access to traditional face-to-face support networks or resources, they may decide to engage with an online support community. There may be several reasons for such limited access, which may include people within the individual's social network having limited knowledge or experience with the particular illness or condition; the illness or condition may not be widely understood by health professionals; the illness or condition may be rare. Several studies have described how online support community members perceived little or no informational or emotional support from people in their social networks and/or health professionals (Coulson, 2013) and therefore turned to online support communities as an alternative source of support. Indeed, the benefits of connecting with others (Coulson, Bullock, & Rodham, 2017) who share similar experiences (Coulson, 2013) and engaging in mutual peer support among community members have been widely acknowledged.

A number of studies have illustrated how individuals who may feel stigmatized by their condition or illness have turned to online support communities (Buchanan & Coulson, 2007; Wright & Rains, 2013). For example, Buchanan and Coulson (2007) surveyed 143 individuals who accessed the Dental Fear Central online support community (which supports those affected by dental anxiety or phobia). One key theme emerging from the open-ended responses to the survey questions was the sense of shame and/or embarrassment they felt with regards their "irrational" fears and the inability to discuss or share their concerns with friends or family. In contrast, they felt that engaging with the online support community allowed them to talk more freely about their concerns with others who truly understood how they felt. Indeed, survey respondents noted that their perceived similarity with other community members was particularly helpful. This, together with the convenience and anonymity conferred by the platform, appeared to encourage individuals to engage with the support community (see "Potential Advantages of Online Support Communities").

WHAT DO COMMUNITY MEMBERS
TALK ABOUT ONLINE?

Many studies, across a range of health-related domains, have described what members discuss within their online support community and have identified several recurring themes. The main focus of discussion within online support communities is around the illness experience, including, symptoms, treatment, and side-effects, as well as a range of psycho-social issues, including the impact of living with a long-term condition, impact on activities of daily living, and hopes and concerns about the future (e.g., Hoch, Norris, Lester, & Marcus, 1999; Elwell, Grogan, & Coulson, 2010; Flower, Bishop, & Lewith, 2014). Additionally, several studies describe how community members discuss the benefits of having someone to talk to who understands them and their issues (Attard & Coulson, 2012) and the value of having a safe place to share, vent, and express their views, opinions, and emotions without fear or risk to their face-to-face networks. Discussion of the personal benefits of engagement with online support communities is commonplace, and several studies describe how members use their posted messages to share positive psychosocial consequences of community engagement, such as a perceived reduction in isolation and loneliness, greater confidence in speaking to health professionals, and the development of positive coping strategies (Buchanan, Coulson, & Malik, 2010).

To date, a great deal of attention has been devoted to the analysis of messages posted in online support communities. In so doing, researchers have been able to examine the underlying therapeutic or social support processes that occur within these contexts.

Social Support

An integral component of the peer interaction that takes place within online support communities is the exchange of social support. Social support is the perception or experience that an individual is cared for by others, esteemed and valued, and part of a social network of mutual assistance and obligations (Wills, 1991). Social support is a crucial resource when facing the challenges of illness and it can promote both physical functioning (e.g., Rutledge et al., 2004) as well as psycho-social well-being (e.g., Turner-Cobb et al., 2002). Indeed, there are a growing number of scholars who have examined both the process and outcome of social support exchange between users of online health communities. Unlike traditional face-to-face interactions, online social support is enacted primarily through text and therefore considerable attention and effort has been devoted to the analysis of support messages exchanged between users (e.g., Chen, 2012; Smedley, Coulson, Gavin, Rodham, & Watts, 2015).

The study of social support online has been advanced through the analysis of messages using a categorization approach reflecting the multidimensional nature of social support. While various typologies exist within the literature, the Social Support Behaviour Code (Cutrona & Suhr, 1992) is widely used. In this coding framework, social support is considered in terms of five macro-categories: 1) emotional support (i.e., the expression of physical affection, empathy, and encouragement); 2) informational support (i.e., the provision of facts, guidance, or advice); 3) esteem support (i.e., compliments and expressions of agreement with a support seekers' perspective); 4) network support (i.e., making a support seeker feel part of a wider community); and 5) tangible assistance (i.e., physical or financial assistance). Such a coding framework has allowed researchers to quantify the presence of social support within messages posted across a range of health and illness domains, including HIV/AIDS (Mo & Coulson, 2008), diabetes (Robinson, Turner, Levine, & Tian, 2011), hearing impairments (Shoham & Heber, 2012) and childhood cancer (Coulson & Greenwood, 2011). This body of work has frequently reported emotional and informational support being the most commonly exchanged types of social support within online support communities, although there are inconsistencies across studies as to which of these is most commonly observable.

In order to consider this body of work, Rains, Peterson, and Wright (2015) undertook a meta-analytical review of 41 published studies that examined support exchanges within health-related online support communities using the Social Support Behaviour Code. The results revealed that emotional and informational support were, equally, the most prevalent categories of message exchanged. Similarly, the prevalence of esteem support and network support did not differ from each other, but both were less common than emotional or informational support exchanges. Tangible support was found to be the least common than any of the other four categories of support exchange. In addition to describing the prevalence of various categories of support exchanges, Rains and colleagues (2015) also considered their prevalence in relation to important characteristics of the illness. They found that *nurturant* forms of support (i.e., support that helps individuals cope with the emotional consequences of a stressor and includes emotional, network, and esteem support) were more prevalent in content analyses that considered health problems likely to affect personal relationships as well as analyses that focused on conditions where there is a greater potential for mortality. *Action-facilitating* types of support (i.e., support which can help support behavior which negates a stressor) were more prevalent in content analyses that considered more chronic conditions.

Self-Help Mechanisms

A number of studies have illustrated how online support communities can offer many of the therapeutic exchanges often present in face-to-face self-help and support groups. To illustrate, Finn (1999) considered the degree to which communication within a disability online support group reflected the helping mechanisms reported within traditional self-help groups and the theoretical advantages and disadvantages of online groups described in the literature. The researchers concluded that the online group offered many of the helping techniques used in face-to-face groups.

The term "self-help mechanisms" was coined by Perron (2002), who described aspects of messages that captured the development of supportive or helping relationships between members of a community. This work was originally based on the analysis of communication within an online community for caregivers of people living with mental illness and it identified multiple self-help mechanisms. In particular, the provision of information or advice, and self-disclosure were reported to be crucial elements of many of the messages posted to the online support community. Similar results have been reported in studies exploring self-help mechanisms across a range of online communities, including infertility (Malik & Coulson, 2010), schizophrenia (Haker, Lauber, & Rossler, 2005), bipolar affective disorder (Schielein, Schmid, Dobemeier, & Spiessl, 2008), and inflammatory bowel disease (Malik & Coulson, 2011).

THEORETICAL FRAMEWORKS USED TO STUDY ONLINE SUPPORT COMMUNITIES

To date, there has been considerable interest in online support communities from a range of disciplines (e.g. psychology, nursing, sociology). As a consequence, there have been multiple theoretical frameworks employed in the study of online support communities. This section provides an overview of selected popular theoretical frameworks.

Optimal Matching Theory

The optimal matching theory (Cutrona & Russell, 1990) was developed within the buffering model of social support and argues that matching specific types of social support according to key dimensions of a stressor (e.g., controllability, life domain) will lead to the most positive outcomes. For example, if an online support community member is seeking specific information about a particular health issue and they believe that fellow members have provided the required information, then this could be considered an optimal match. As discussed in the section Social Support, Rains and colleagues (2015) undertook a meta-analytic review of the content of online social support exchanges between members of online support communities. Findings revealed that the most commonly provided types of social support were associated with the specific support needs of community members, thereby suggesting that individuals engage with communities that address their needs, i.e., an optimal match.

Uses and Gratifications Model

According to the uses and gratification model, individuals will use media to gratify their individual needs and desires (Lee & Hawkins, 2010). This particular theory has its roots in the 1920s where early studies explored why people engaged with various media, such as cinema, radio broadcasts, and newspapers. The advent of the Internet was of particular interest to those researchers engaged with this model as it differed from other media in a number of important ways, including 1) interactivity (i.e., the Internet blurs the line between broadcaster and receiver); 2) demassification (i.e., the Internet lets people choose content that is of interest to them); and 3) asynchronicity (i.e., people can access content at a time of their choice). As a consequence, Ruggiero (2000) argues that the Internet provides users with much more control compared with other mass media outlets, and as a consequence a range of new communication behaviors have become the focus of investigation by researchers using the uses and gratifications model.

A number of studies have considered online support communities using the uses and gratifications model. For example, Lee and Hawkins (2010) reported that individuals who had unmet informational needs or emotional support needs spent more time seeking information or emotional support compared to those who had their needs met by existing resources.

Social Comparison Theory

According to Festinger's Social Comparison Theory (1954), individuals are driven to obtain accurate self-evaluations. One way in which this can be achieved is through comparing themselves to others around them. In the context of online support communities, evidence shows that members may try to assess their own health and coping abilities through comparison with other community members (van Uden-Kraan, Drossaert, Taal, Shaw, et al., 2008). However, this process may not always yield beneficial outcomes, as illustrated by Batenburg and Das (2015). In a study of members of a Dutch breast cancer online support community, their findings suggested that pessimistic comparisons may influence the psychological well-being of active members. That is, active users who identified with community members worse off than they (i.e., downward identification), or members who experienced negative effects when reading the experiences from members doing better than they (i.e., upward contrast), reported poor psychological well-being compared to members who did not compare themselves negatively with others.

Empowerment

Empowerment can be described as an active, participatory process through which individuals, organizations, and communities can exert greater control, efficacy, and social justice (Zimmerman, 1995). In recent years, there has been an increasing number of studies that have taken the empowerment framework forward within the online support community context. The results of these studies describe a range of potentially empowering processes linked to engagement with online support communities. For example, Van Uden-Kraan, Drossaert, Taal, Shaw, Seydel, and van de Larr (2008) interviewed 32 participants drawn from a range of online support communities for breast cancer, arthritis, and fibromyalgia. The results revealed a range of "empowering processes" (i.e., processes that occur while engaging with an online support community) and "empowering outcomes" (i.e., changes resulting from a consequence of engagement with an online support community). The study identified multiple processes, including exchanging information, encountering emotional support, finding recognition, sharing experiences, helping others, and amusement. Similarly, multiple outcomes were identified, including being better informed; feeling confident in their relationship with their physician, their treatment, and their social environment; enhanced acceptance of the condition; enhanced optimism and feelings of control, self-esteem, and social well-being; and collective action. Researchers have continued to study online support communities using this framework and have found supporting evidence for all of the aforementioned empowering processes and outcomes, with feeling better informed and experiencing enhanced social well-being being the most commonly occurring outcomes across a range of online support communities (Bartlett & Coulson, 2011).

Affordance Theory

The origins of affordance theory arise from cognitive and perceptual psychology and are based on how individuals perceive the objects in their environment, both what the object is and its potential use (Gibson, 1986). The properties of each object will therefore contribute to its perceived use, as will the varying experiences, beliefs, and goals of an individual. The focus of the theory is on the interaction between the individual and the object, and its subsequent outcomes. Therapeutic affordances can thus be considered as the "actionable possibilities" of the object as perceived by the user. Through examining therapeutic affordances, researchers have been able to consider not only how online support communities are used, but also what impact they have on those who use them.

Through examining the use of social media by patients living with chronic pain, Merolli, Gray, and Martin-Sanchez (2014) identified and described five therapeutic affordances arising from ten different types of social media: self-presentation, connection, exploration, narration, and adaptation. These affordances were then used to develop the SCENA model (i.e., Self-presentation, Connection, Exploration, Narration, and Adaptation). This model has since been validated in a growing number of studies that examine online support communities (Shoebotham & Coulson, 2016; Coulson, Bullock, & Rodham, 2017). For example, in their online survey of users of self-harm online support communities, Coulson, Bullock, and Rodham (2017) reported evidence for all five therapeutic affordances and a range of outcomes. This included: "self-presentation"— the ability to exercise autonomy over the discussion of self-harm and disclosure of personal information and experiences to others within the community; "connection"—the ability to make contact with others who self-harm for the purposes of mutual support and, in so doing, reduce feelings of isolation and perceived loneliness; "exploration"—the ability to learn about self-harm and develop adaptive coping strategies; "narration"—the ability to share experiences, and read about the experiences of others thereby helping individuals understand and make sense of their condition; and "adaptation"—how use of online support communities varies depending on personal circumstances.

PARTICIPATION IN ONLINE SUPPORT COMMUNITIES AND PSYCHOSOCIAL OUTCOMES

There exists a considerable body of evidence suggesting that members of online support communities can benefit from participation through finding information and advice on how to better understand and manage or cope with their particular illness or condition (Coulson & Knibb, 2007). In particular, several studies have reported how online support community members appreciate being able to learn from others' experiences and, as a consequence, feel more informed and supported (Han & Belcher, 2001; Pfeil, Zaphiris, & Wilson, 2009). In addition, online support community members have reported feeling more empowered (Buchanan & Coulson, 2007; Bartlett & Coulson, 2011), a sense of belonging (Høybye, Johansen, & Tjørnhøj-Thomsen, 2005), and more optimistic about coping with their illness or condition (Zrebiec, 2005; Rodgers & Chen, 2005; Mo & Coulson, 2013).

While there exists comparatively less work which has examined the impact of online support community participation and engagement with health services and health professionals, some studies have found that participation has empowered members and helped with their confidence in communicating with health professionals (Bartlett & Coulson, 2011; Holbrey & Coulson, 2013).

To date, the vast majority of work discussing the impact of participation on psychosocial well-being has been qualitative and/or cross-sectional surveys. These studies have illustrated the benefits of engagement as including: reducing perceived loneliness and isolation (Coulson, Bullock, & Rodham, 2017); feelings of uncertainty around prognosis and ambiguous pain-related symptomology (Høybye, Johansen, & Tjørnhøj-Thomsen, 2005); and distress (Rodgers & Chen, 2005). Furthermore, engagement with online support communities has been linked with improvements in mood (Rodgers & Chen, 2005), levels of anxiety (Coulson & Buchanan, 2008), and acceptance of illness-related issues (Letourneau, Stewart, Masuda, Anderson, Cicutto, McGhan, & Watt, 2012).

More recently, there have been a (limited) number of randomized controlled trials (RCT) that have attempted to generate more robust and convincing evidence for the efficacy of online support communities. For example, Griffiths, Mackinnon, Crisp, Christensen, Bennett, and Farrer (2012) randomized volunteers with elevated psychological distress using a community-based screening postal survey into one of four twelve-week conditions: depression Internet support group (ISG), automated depression Internet Training Program (ITP), combination of the two (ITP+ISG), or a control website with delayed access to the ITP. Assessments were conducted at baseline, post-intervention, at six and twelve months. The results revealed no change in depressive symptoms relative to control after three months of exposure to the ISG. However, both the ISG alone and the combined ISG+ITP group reported a significantly greater reduction in depressive symptoms at six and twelve months follow-up compared to the control group.

In considering the impact of participation on psychosocial outcomes, it is clear that the developing literature draws upon a wide range of research designs and methods. There has been a strong focus within the qualitative method to give voice to those who use online support communities and the many quotes included within such papers illustrate how important online support communities can be to those who use them, as well as some of the problems those users experienced. Similarly, the published cross-sectional studies have allowed researchers to measure specific concepts and constructs, which has helped develop theoretical understanding of online support communities. In contrast, the limited number of RCTs have focused on efficacy as measured by a specific primary outcome, but evidence on efficacy is mixed. Considered together, different designs and methods arguably reveal different things about online support communities; while some researchers may consider the RCT to be the gold standard in terms of the generation of evidence, the voice of the actual support community user should not be overlooked. When the latter is considered, it may reveal a richness around the experience of being a community participant.

CONCLUSION

Online communities have become an increasingly popular source of information, advice, and support. They have the potential to draw together large numbers of people for the purpose of mutual peer support, particularly for those affected by long-term conditions. This chapter has considered many of the widely acknowledged benefits of engaging with online support communities, but has also reflected on their potential limitations. For those who chose to engage with online support communities, the growing body of evidence suggests a range of psycho-social benefits despite the general absence of RCTs, particularly in the area of physical health and well-being.

REFERENCES

Allen, C., Vassilev, I., Kennedy, A., & Rogers, A. (2016). Long-term condition self-management in online communities: A meta-synthesis of qualitative papers. *Journal of Medical Internet Research 18*(3), e61.

Attard, A., & Coulson, N. S. (2012). A thematic analysis of patient communication in Parkinson's disease online support group discussion forums. *Computers in Human Behavior 28*, 500–506.

Bartlett, Y. K., & Coulson, N. S. (2011). An investigation into the empowerment effects of using online support groups and how this affects health professional/patient communication. *Patient Education and Counseling 83*, 113–119.

Batenburg, A., & Das, E. (2015). Virtual support communities and psychological well-being: The role of optimistic and pessimistic social comparison strategies. *Journal of Computer-Mediated Communication 20*, 585–600.

Broom, A. (2005). The eMale: Prostate cancer, masculinity and online support as a challenge to medical expertise. *Journal of Sociology 41*(1), 87–104.

Buchanan, H., & Coulson, N. S. (2007). Accessing dental anxiety online support groups: An exploratory qualitative study of motives and experiences. *Patient Education and Counseling 66*, 263–269.

Buchanan, H., Coulson, N. S., & Malik, S. (2010). Health-related internet support groups and dental anxiety: The fearful patient's online journey. *International Journal of Web-Based Communities 6*(4), 362–375.

Chen, A. T. (2012). Exploring online support spaces: Using cluster analysis to examine breast cancer, diabetes and fibromyalgia support groups. *Patient Education and Counseling 87*, 250–257.

Chou, W. Y. S., Hunt, Y. M., Beckjord, E. B., Moser, R. P., & Hesse, B. W. (2009). Social media use in the United States: Implications for health communication. *Journal of Medical Internet Research 11*(4), e48.

Classen, C. C., Chivers, M. L., Urowitz, S., Barbera, L., Wiljer, D., O'Rinn, S., & Ferguson, S. E. (2012). Psychosocial distress in women with gynecologic cancer: A feasibility study of an online support group. *Psycho-Oncology* 22(4), 930–935.

Cole, J., Watkins, C., & Kleine, D. (2016). Health advice from Internet discussion forums: How bad is dangerous? *Journal of Medical Internet Research* 18(1), e4.

Colvin, J., Chenoweth, L., Bold, M., & Harding, C. (2004). Caregivers of older adults: Advantages and disadvantages of internet-based social support. *Family Relations* 53(1), 49–57.

Coulson, N. S. (2013). How do online patient support communities affect the experience of inflammatory bowel disease? An online survey. *JRSM Short Reports* 4(8), 1–8.

Coulson, N. S., & Buchanan, H. (2008). Self-reported efficacy of an online dental anxiety support group: A pilot study. *Community Dentistry & Oral Epidemiology* 36, 43–46.

Coulson, N. S., Bullock, E., & Rodham, K. (2017). Exploring the therapeutic affordances of self-harm online support communities: An online survey of members. *JMIR Mental Health* 4(4), e1.

Coulson, N. S., & Greenwood, N. (2011). Families affected by childhood cancer: An analysis of the provision of social support within online support groups. *Child: Care, Health & Development* 38(6), 870–877.

Coulson, N. S., & Knibb, R. C. (2007). Coping with food allergy: Exploring the role of the online support group. *CyberPsychology & Behavior* 10(1), 145–148.

Culver, J. D., Gerr, F., & Frumkin, H. (1997). Medical information on the Internet: A study of an electronic bulletin board. *Journal of General Internal Medicine* 12, 466–470.

Cutrona, C. E., & Russell, D.W. (1990). Type of social support and specific stress: Toward a theory of optimal matching. In B. R. Sarason, I. G. Sarason, & G. R. Pierce (Eds.), *Social support: An interactional review* (pp. 319–366). Oxford: John Wiley & Sons.

Cutrona, C. E., & Suhr, J. A. (1992). Controllability of stressful events and satisfaction with spouse support behaviors. *Communication Research* 19, 154–174.

Davison, K. P., Pennebaker, J. W., & Dickerson, S. S. (2000). Who talks? The social psychology of illness support groups. *American Psychologist* 55(2), 205–217.

Elwell, L., Grogan, S., & Coulson, N. (2010). Adolescents living with cancer: The role of computer-mediated support groups. *Journal of Health Psychology* 16(2), 236–248.

Esquivel, A., Meric-Bernstam, F., & Bernstam, E. V. (2006). Accuracy and self-correction of information received from an Internet breast cancer list: Content analysis. *British Medical Journal* 332, 939–942.

Festinger, L. (1954). A theory of social comparison processes. *Human Relations, 7,* 117–140.

Finn, J. (1999). An exploration of helping processes in an online self-help group focusing on issues of disability. *Health and Social Work* 24, 220–231.

Flower, A., Bishop, F. L., & Lewith, G. (2014). How women manage recurrent urinary tract infections: An analysis of postings on a popular web forum. *BMC Family Practice* 15, 162.

Fox, S. (2011). Peer-to-peer healthcare. Pew Internet & American Life Project. http://pewinternet.org/Reports/2011/P2PHealthcare.aspx Published February 28, 2011. Accessed August 26, 2017.

Gibson, J. (1986). *The ecological approach to visual perceptions.* Hillsdale, NJ: Lawrence Erlbaum Associates.

Griffiths, K. M., Mackinnon, A. J., Crisp, D. A., Christensen, H., Bennett, K., & Farrer, L. (2012). The effectiveness of an online support group for members of the community with depression: A randomised controlled trial. *PLoS One* 7(12), e53244.

Haker, H., Lauber, C., & Rossler, W. (2005). Internet forums: A self-help approach for individuals with schizophrenia? *Acta Psychiatrica Scandinavica 112*, 474–477.

Han, H., & Belcher, A. E. (2001). Computer-mediated support group use among parents of children with cancer—An exploratory study. *Computers in Nursing 19*(1), 27–33.

Hoch, D. B., Norris, D., Lester, J. E., & Marcus, A. D. (1999). Information exchange within an epilepsy forum on the World Wide Web. *Seizure 8*, 30–34.

Holbrey, S., & Coulson, N. S. (2013). A qualitative investigation of the impact of peer to peer online support for women living with Polycystic Ovary Syndrome. *BMC Women's Health 13*, 51.

Holtz, P., Kronberger, N., & Wagner, W. (2012). Analyzing Internet forums: A practical guide. *Journal of Media Psychology 24*(2), 55–66.

Høybye, M. T., Johansen, C., & Tjørnhøj-Thomsen, T. (2005). Online interaction. Effects of storytelling in an Internet breast cancer support group. *Psycho-Oncology 14*(3), 211–220.

Hu, X., Bell, R. A., Kravitz, R. L., & Orrange, S. (2012). The prepared patient: Information seeking of online support group members before their medical appointments. *Journal of Health Communication 17*(8), 960–978.

Hwang, K. O., Farheen, K., Johnson, C. W., Thomas, E. J., Barnes, A. S., & Bernstam, E. V. (2007). Quality of weight loss advice on internet forums. *American Journal of Medicine 120*(7), 604–609.

Idriss, S. Z., Kvedar, J. C., & Watson, A. J. (2009). The role of online support communities: Benefits of expanded social networks to patients with psoriasis. *Archives of Dermatology 145*(1), 46–51.

Im, E. O., Lee, B., & Chee, W. (2011). The use of Internet cancer support groups by Asian Americans and White Americans living with cancer. *Journal of Transcultural Nursing 22*(4), 386–396.

Internet World Stats (2017). Usage and population statistics. Retrieved from https://www.internetworldstats.com/stats.htm.

Jones, Q., Ravid, G., & Rafaeli, S. (2004). Information overload and the message dynamics of online interaction spaces: A theoretical model and empirical exploration. *Information Systems Research 15*(2), 194–210.

Klaw, E., Huebsch, P. D., & Humphreys, K. (2000). Communication patterns in an online mutual help group for problem drinkers. *Journal of Community Psychology 28*(5), 535–546.

Lee, S. Y., & Hawkins, R. (2010). Why do patients seek an alternative channel? The effects of unmet needs on patients' health-related Internet use. *Journal of Health Communication 15*(2), 152–166.

Letourneau, N., Stewart, M., Masuda, J. R., Anderson, S., Cicutto, L., McGhan, S., & Watt, S. (2012). Impact of online support for youth with asthma and allergies: Pilot study. *Journal of Pediatric Nursing 27*(1), 65–73.

Malik, S., & Coulson, N. S. (2008). Computer-mediated infertility support groups: An exploratory study of online experiences. *Patient Education and Counseling 73*, 105–113.

Malik, S. H., & Coulson, N. S. (2010). Coping with infertility online: An examination of self-help mechanisms in an online infertility support group. *Patient Education and Counseling 81*(2), 315–318.

Malik, S., & Coulson, N. S. (2011). The therapeutic potential of the Internet: Exploring self-help processes in an Internet forum for young people with Inflammatory Bowel Disease. *Gastroenterology Nursing 34*(6), 439–448.

McTavish, F. M., Pingree, S., Hawkins, R., & Gustafson, D. (2003). Cultural differences in use of an electronic discussion group. *Journal of Health Psychology 8*(1), 105–117.

Merolli, M., Gray, K., & Martin-Sanchez, F. (2014). Therapeutic affordances of social media: Emergent themes from a global online survey of people with chronic pain. *Journal of Medical Internet Research 16*(12), e284.

Mo, P. K. H., & Coulson, N. S. (2008). Exploring the communication of social support within virtual communities: A content analysis of messages posted to an online HIV/AIDS support group. *CyberPsychology & Behavior 11*, 371–374.

Mo, P. K. H., & Coulson, N. S. (2013). Online support group use and psychological health for individuals living with HIV/AIDS. *Patient Education and Counseling 93*(3), 426–432.

Mo, P. K. H., & Coulson, N. S. (2014). Are online support groups always beneficial? A qualitative exploration of the empowering and disempowering processes of participation within HIV/AIDS-related online support groups. *International Journal of Nursing Studies 51*(7), 983–993.

National Cancer Institute (2013). Health Information National Trends Survey. Retrieved from http://hints.cancer.gov.

Office for National Statistics (2016). Internet access—household and individuals: 2016. London: Office for National Statistics.

Office for National Statistics (2017). Internet access—households and individuals: 2017. London: Office for National Statistics.

O'Neill, B., Ziebland, S., Valderas, J., & Lupianez-Villanueva, F. (2014). User-generated online health content: A survey of Internet users in the United Kingdom. *Journal of Medical Internet Research 16*(4), e118.

Owen, J. E., Boxley, L., Goldstein, M. S., Lee, J. H., Breen, N., & Rowland, J.H. (2010). Use of health-related online support groups: Population data from the California Health Interview Survey Complementary and Alternative Medicine study. *Journal of Computer-Mediated Communication 15*, 427–446.

Perron, B. (2002). Online support for caregivers of people with mental illness. *Psychiatric Rehabilitation Journal 26*, 70–77.

Powell, J., McCarthy, N., & Eysenbach, G. (2003). Cross-sectional survey of users of Internet depression communities. *BMC Psychiatry 3*, 19.

Pfeil, U., Zaphiris, P., & Wilson, S. (2009). Older adults' perceptions and experiences of online social support. *Interacting with Computers 21*, 159–172.

Rains, S., Peterson, E., & Wright, K. (2015). Communicating social support in computer-mediated contexts: A meta-analytic review of content analyses examining support messages shared online among individuals coping with illness. *Communication Monographs 82*(4), 403–430.

Rheingold, H. (1993). *The virtual community: Homesteading on the electronic frontier*. London: MIT Press.

Robinson, J. D., Turner, J. W., Levine, B., & Tian, Y. (2011). Expanding the walls of the health care encounter: Support and outcomes for patients online. *Health Communication 26*(2), 125–134.

Rodgers, S. & Chen, Q. (2005). Internet community group participation: Psychosocial benefits for women with breast cancer. *Journal of Computer-Mediated Communication 10*(4).

Ruggiero, T. E. (2000). Uses and gratifications theory in the 21st century. *Mass Communication & Society, 3*(1), 3–37.

Rutledge, T., Reis, S., Olson, M. S., Owens, J., Kelsey, S. F., Pepine, C. J.,...Matthews, K. A. (2004). Social networks are associated with lower mortality rates among women with suspected coronary disease: The National Heart, Lung and Blood Institute-sponsored Women's Ischemia Syndrome Evaluation study. *Psychosomatic Medicine 66*, 882–888.

Schielein, T., Schmid, R., Dobemeier, M., & Spiessl, H. (2008). Self-help from the cyberspace? An analysis of self-help forums for patients with bipolar affective disorders. *Psychiatrische Praxis 35*, 28–32.

Shoebotham, A., & Coulson, N. S. (2016). Therapeutic affordance of online support group use in women with endometriosis. *Journal of Medical Internet Research 18*(5), e109.

Shoham, S., & Heber, M. (2012). Characteristics of a virtual community for individuals who are deaf and hard of hearing. *American Annals of the Deaf 157*, 251–263.

Sinclair, J. M. A., Chambers, S. E., & Manson, C. C. (2017). Internet support for dealing with problematic alcohol use: A survey of the *Soberistas* online community. *Alcohol and Alcoholism 52*(2), 220–226.

Smedley, R., Coulson, N., Gavin, J., Rodham, K., & Watts, L. (2015). Online social support for Complex Regional Pain Syndrome: A content analysis of support exchanges within a newly launched discussion forum. *Computers in Human Behavior 51*, 53–63.

Smedley, R. M., & Coulson, N. S. (2017). A thematic analysis of messages posted by moderators within health-related asynchronous online support forums. *Patient Education and Counseling 100*, 1688–1693.

Turner-Cobb, J. M., Gore-Felton, C., Marouf, F., Koopman, C., Kim, P., Israelski, D., & Speigel, D. (2002). Coping, social support, and attachment style as psychosocial correlates of adjustment in men and women with HIV/AIDS. *Journal of Behavioral Medicine 25*, 337–353.

Van Uden-Kraan, C. F., Drossaert, C. H. C., Taal, E., Lebrun, C. E. I., Drossaers Bakker, K. W., Smit, W. M., & van de Laar, M. A. J. F. (2008). Coping with somatic illnesses in online support groups: Do the feared disadvantages actually occur? *Computers in Human Behaviour 24*(2), 309–324.

Van Uden-Kraan, C. F., Drossaert, C. H. C., Taal, E., Shaw, B. R., Seydel, E. R., & van de Larr, M. A. J. F. (2008). Empowering processes and outcomes of participation in online support groups for people with breast cancer, arthritis, or fibromyalgia. *Qualitative Health Research 18*(3), 405–417.

Vilhauer, R. P., McClintock, M. K., & Matthews, A. K. (2010). Online support groups for women with metastatic breast cancer: A feasibility pilot study. *Journal of Psychosocial Oncology 28*, 560–586.

White, M., & Dorman, S. M. (2001). Receiving social support online: implications for health education. *Health Education Research: Theory & Practice 16*(6), 693–707.

Wills, T. A. (1991). Social support and interpersonal relationships. In M. S. Clark (Ed.), *Prosocial behavior* (pp. 265–289). Newbury Park, CA: Sage.

Winefield, H. R. (2006). Support provision and emotional work in an Internet support group for cancer patients. *Patient Education and Counseling 62*(2), 193–197.

Winzelberg, A. (1997). The analysis of an electronic support group for individuals with eating disorders. *Computers in Human Behavior 13*(3), 393–407.

Wright, K. (2000). Perceptions of on-line support providers: An examination of perceived homophily, source credibility, communication and social support within on-line support groups. *Communication Quarterly 48*(1), 44–59.

Wright, K. B. (2016). Communication in health-related online social support groups/communities: a review of research on predictors of participation, applications of social support theory, and health outcomes. *Review of Communication Research 4*, 65–87.

Wright, K. B., & Bell, S. B. (2003). Health-related support groups on the Internet: Linking empirical findings to social support and computer-mediated community theory. *Journal of Health Psychology* 8(1), 39–54.

Wright, K. B., & Rains, S. A. (2013). Weak-tie support network preference, health related stigma, and health outcomes in computer-mediated support groups. *Journal of Applied Communication Research* 41(3), 309–324.

Zimmerman, M. A. (1995). Psychological empowerment: Issues and illustrations. *American Journal of Community Psychology* 23(5), 581–599.

Zrebiec, J. F. (2005). Internet communities: Do they improve coping with diabetes? *The Diabetes Educator* 31(6), 825–836.

CHAPTER 14

DIGITAL INCLUSION FOR PEOPLE WITH AN INTELLECTUAL DISABILITY

DARREN D. CHADWICK, MELANIE CHAPMAN,
AND SUE CATON

The power of the Web is in its universality. Access by everyone regardless of disability is an essential aspect.

Tim Berners-Lee, Inventor of the World Wide Web

INTRODUCTION

THIS chapter describes the current state of knowledge in the area of digital inclusion and psychological knowledge around the online lives of people with intellectual disabilities (ID). Given the relative newness and nature of this area of study, much of the work conducted has been phenomenological and descriptive in nature, relying on interviews with people with ID and other stakeholders and on survey methodologies, with limited experimental empirical work. Similarly, as it is a new field, theorizing is in its infancy and theories have yet to be thoroughly applied and tested; thus far, research has been primarily conducted in the global north. The chapter aims to provide a global overview, but many of the examples given and the policy perspective taken reflects the dominion of the authors (the UK). The chapter is structured into three sections: the first provides the context and background on the use of the Internet and Information Communication Technologies (ICT); the second explores findings regarding benefits to being online, as well as barriers, risks, and support; and the final section summarizes the state of knowledge and highlights areas where more research is needed.

People with ID and Getting Online: Contextual Underpinnings

Definition

Intellectual disability (ID) is a socially constructed term which is both historically and culturally bound. People are labeled as having ID because they differ from a culturally defined idea of "normal" or "typical" intellectual functioning (Manion & Bersani, 1987). Changes in nomenclature have occurred across time, cultures, and geographies, with terminology often co-opted and naturalized within society into terms of derision (e.g. "idiot," "retard"), which serves to stigmatize and devalue this group societally (Goggin & Newell, 2003).

Clinically, definitions of ID have been deficit focused. The World Health Organization (WHO, 1992) has classified intellectual and developmental disabilities within the International Classification of Diseases (ICD-10).[1] Under this definition, ID is described as "a condition of arrested or incomplete development of the mind, which is characterized by impairment of skills manifested during the developmental period, which contributes to the overall level of intelligence, i.e. cognitive, language, motor, and social abilities" (np). Diagnosis involves three criteria: (i) impaired cognitive functioning; (ii) challenges to adaptive functioning in at least two key areas (e.g. communication, self-care, domestic skills, social skills, self-direction, community, academic skills, work, leisure, health, and safety); and (iii) early developmental onset (younger than eighteen years of age). The purpose of identification of these impairments and challenges faced by those with ID is to identify necessary supports, typically provided by paid support staff or family carers, to ensure that people with ID maximize their life chances, participation, and inclusion (van Loon, Claes, Vandevelde, Van Hove, & Schalock, 2010; Shogren, Luckasson, & Schalock, 2014; Thompson et al., 2009). People with ID are extremely heterogeneous as a group, varying greatly in aspects of life such as etiology, support needs, and comorbidities (e.g. health problems, mental health issues, and physical and sensory impairments). In turn, referring to this group as a community is challenging and necessitates individualized approaches to support.

This chapter focuses on both people with ID specifically, and those people with developmental disabilities where ID is often or always a key component (e.g. Rett syndrome, William syndrome, Autistic Spectrum Condition). Excluded are developmental

---

[1] Though ICD-11 is due to be published in 2018 it had not been finalized at the time of writing this chapter.

disabilities where ID is not a principal component (e.g. specific developmental conditions and attention deficit hyperactivity condition).

Theory

Differing philosophical positions have underpinned the research focusing on people with ID, including ICT and being online. These have ranged from more traditional research that has taken a post-positivist stance more closely aligned with a medical, individual, or a biopsychosocial perspective and used quantitative or mixed methods, to more constructivist approaches in tune with interactionist or social models of disability, which have typically utilized qualitative, discursive, participatory, philosophical, methodological, and analytic approaches (see Oliver, 2013; Shakespeare, 2014). In line with these epistemological and methodological distinctions, the work reviewed herein is not exclusively within the purview of psychology but instead spans a number of disciplines, including sociology, education, social care, and information technology.

Policy

In recent decades there has been a move towards an inclusive and human rights perspective, which is less deficit focused and more concerned with promoting the human rights of people with ID. This move has led to numerous policies aiming to enhance the life opportunities, well-being, and participation of people with ID.

The United Nations Convention on the Rights of Persons with Disabilities (UNCRPD, 2006) aims to promote social justice for people with disabilities and has been adopted across numerous countries across the globe. A number of the articles within the convention are germane to accessing and using the online world and developing ICTs. These include articles 9 (Accessibility), 12 (Right to equal recognition before the law), 19 (Right to be included within the community), and 21 (Freedom of expression and opinion) (See Seale & Chadwick, 2017). Article 21 includes the notion of online freedom of expression and self-determination over what to access online.

These articles provide a precedent in countries that have ratified them for the digital inclusion of people with ID. Despite this legislation, digital inclusion is not consistently manifest in the lives of people with ID (Chadwick, Wesson, & Fullwood, 2013) and scholarly exploration of the articles of the convention in relation to the digital world is still in its infancy.

Prevalence of Internet Use and Being Online

The concept of a digital divide developed in the context of the rise in technology, and initially distinguished between those with and without access to both technology and the Internet. However, ideas around a digital divide have developed with increased nuance identified around this issue in the burgeoning literature (e.g. Van Dijk, 2017). A strong relationship between education, age, geography, health status, employment, economic status, and digital (dis)engagement has been confirmed in the literature (e.g. Helsper, 2012; Jaeger, 2015; Selwyn, 2006) and a resulting division between what people use the Internet for has developed. However, despite the increasing use of ICTs by people with ID, inequity in ownership, access, and use still characterizes the experiences of many people with ID.

Although studies of use have typically failed to disaggregate people with ID from other disabled people, evidence suggests that people with ID have lower levels of access and a more restricted breadth of use than both non-disabled people and other groups of disabled people (e.g. Fox, 2011; Guo, Bricout, & Huang, 2005; National Telecommunications & Information Administration and Economic & Statistical Administration, 2013). As examples, in the US in 2005, 41 percent of adults with ID had access to a computer and 25 percent had access to the Internet (in contrast to 68 percent of US total population at that time) (Carey, Friedman, & Bryen, 2005). In Spain in 2010, 53 percent of people with ID did not access the Internet at all, compared to 37 percent of the wider Spanish population (Gutiérrez & Martorell Zargoza, 2011). More recent data shows that usage in the UK has increased compared to these figures (Ofcom, 2015), although this is based on low numbers of respondents with ID. Ofcom reports that 73 percent of people with ID had access to the Internet, compared to 88 percent of non-disabled people; 68 percent had access to a PC/laptop, compared to 79 percent of non-disabled people; 57 percent had access to a smartphone, compared to 66 percent of non-disabled people; and 41 percent had access to a tablet, compared to 42 percent of non-disabled people. Although these figures demonstrate that people with ID have lower levels of Internet use than the non-disabled population (and indeed the more general disabled population), they also show that currently the divide is shrinking. Given the reduced access to ICTs, digital exclusion, and relative novelty of this research area this chapter does not distinguish between different ICTs (e.g. social networking, mobile phone technology use, etc.); instead, it focuses primarily on Internet use and notes the ICT or social media being investigated in studies cited.

There is limited research exploring what people with ID are using the Internet for due to rapid changes in technology and popular uses of the Internet combined with having few researchers working in this area. Earlier work in this area took place when it was less likely that people with ID would have access to their own devices, so researchers looked at how people with ID experienced using ICTs in groups, or projects specifically set up for the research (e.g. Hegarty & Aspinall, 2006; Kydland, Molka-Danielsen, & Balandin, 2012; McClimens & Gordon, 2008, 2009). More recent research suggests that people with ID are using their own devices more, primarily mobile phones and tablets (e.g. Chiner, Gómez-Puerta, & Cardona-Moltó, 2017; Lough & Fisher, 2016b). In a study of 216 young people with ID, Jenaro and colleagues (2017) found that, compared to non-disabled youth, people with ID use Internet-enabled ICTs less frequently but stay connected for longer periods of time. People with ID made more social and recreational, rather than educational, use of ICTs, uploading photos, watching videos, and chatting on online dating sites more frequently than non-disabled youth. Regarding mobile phone use specifically, while non-disabled youth make greater use of their devices in general, people with ID demonstrated higher use of their device playing games online and texting (Jenaro et al., 2017). This is consistent with findings from the UK that suggest that people with ID were significantly more likely than non-disabled people to use the Internet for gaming (Ofcom, 2015). This finding, however, needs to be considered with care as it may reflect the younger age profile of the respondents with ID.

Finally, prevalence research typically only considers those who have taken part in research and those who can access the technology. As an illustration, those with profound ID can use specifically designed technology as a developmental tool to support participation, communication, and choice making (e.g. BIG MAC™ single button technology, which may aid development of intentional understanding). However, given the impact of the impairment for people with profound ID, it would not be possible to use a complex communication device such as a mobile phone. Hence, this group have, by and large, been overlooked in the literature around digital inclusion.

Online Experiences of People with ID: Motivation for Online Inclusion

People across a broad spectrum of impairments and disabilities are motivated to access and engage with ICTs and the online world (Caton & Chapman, 2016). The Uses and Gratifications approach described by Katz, Blumler, and Gurevitch (1974) can be used as an explanatory framework for why people with ID may be motivated to engage with ICTs to satisfy their psychological needs. Ruggerio (2000, 26) classifies these motivations into four types: (i) social utility; (ii) personal identity; (iii) surveillance and accessing information; and (iv) diversion. Evidence exists supporting each of these motivational needs in people with ID (an adapted version, more pertinent to people with ID, is outlined below in Box 1). The social benefits appear to have been most readily supported in participant accounts, with surveillance and informational motivations being the least investigated and reported.

Benefits of Being Online

At an individual level the Internet can provide people with ID with opportunities for personal development, entertainment, making and maintaining relationships, learning, and employment. As a marginalized group within society, the Internet affords people with ID opportunities for social inclusion and to challenge societal stereotypes and discrimination. Chadwick, Quinn, and Fullwood (2017) explored the perceived risks and benefits of going online and demonstrated that members of the general public perceived the benefits of being online for people with ID as greater than the benefits they themselves might accrue. Numerous benefits of being online have also been identified based on empirical accounts from both people with ID and other commentators and stakeholders. These are discussed and summarized in Box 1 below, and are organized using the uses and gratifications framework (Katz et al., 1974; Ruggerio, 2000).

Box 1 The benefits of ICT and Internet use for people with ID organized using the "uses and gratifications" framework

---

Social utility
- Friendships and relationships
  - Maintaining friendships
  - Building friendships and social capital
  - Development of romantic relationships
- Social inclusion

Personal identity
- Self-esteem and well-being
- Social identity
  - Valued social roles
  - Sharing life
  - Online skills and expertise
- Self-determination, choice, and control
  - Digital skills and competence
  - Cyberlanguage
- Self-advocacy and civic engagement

Accessing information
- Learning and education
- Employment

Occupation and enjoyment
- Occupation and enjoyment online
- Entertainment and leisure
  - Music
  - Films
  - Video games

(Sources: Bowker & Tuffin, 2002; Chadwick & Fullwood, 2018; Dowse, 2001; Holmes & O'Loughlin, 2012; Jenaro et al. 2017; Löfgren-Mårtenson, 2008; Seale, 2007; Shpigelman & Gill 2014; Steinfield et al., 2008)

(Model adapted from Katz et al., 1974; Ruggerio, 2000)

Social Utility

People with ID often have limited social or community integration opportunities (Emerson, Mallam, Davies, & Spencer, 2005; Forrester-Jones et al., 2006) and commonly have smaller social networks that are made up primarily of family members and support workers (Emerson & McVilly, 2004; Gravell, 2012; Robertson et al., 2001). One of the possible benefits of the Internet is the potential to reduce social isolation and loneliness. While many existing social opportunities for people with ID involve mixing with peers with ID, the Internet allows interactions with the wider community. Online social networking has been linked to the creation and maintenance of social capital, i.e. the benefits that a person receives from their relationship with other people at an individual and community level. Indeed, social networking may lead to new forms of social capital, as connections are made with individuals who may have useful information or different perspectives (Steinfield, Ellison, & Lampe, 2008).

Drawing on their experiences working in community ID services and from case studies about Facebook use, Holmes and O'Loughlin (2012) found that people with ID reported using social networking sites as an alternative way of forming meaningful relationships. Social networking sites provided interactions to supplement usual face-to-face interactions and enabled socializing with same age peers without physically being in the same place (which may be difficult for people who are reliant on others for arranging or getting to meetings, or for people with social anxiety).

Similarly, some research has shown that online social networks can provide the possibility of a private life away from the control of carers. Löfgren-Mårtenson (2008) found that the primary use of the Internet by young people with mild ID living in Sweden was for social and romantic purposes. Similar findings have been reported with people with ID in Spain (Jenaro et al., 2017) and the UK (Chadwick & Fullwood, 2018).

The Internet can allow people with ID to participate more fully in society. Many services, such as banking and access to health, social care, and welfare systems are increasingly accessed online (Geniets & Eynon, 2012). For people with ID to be full members of society, they need to have access to digital technology. The Internet itself can also be used to challenge the social and digital exclusion experienced by many people with ID, although significant change is likely to require ongoing advocacy and political pressure from people with ID and their allies (e.g. support groups and organizations) (Chadwick et al., 2013; Chadwick & Wesson, 2016).

Personal Identity

Social networking sites provide an opportunity for people with ID to enhance their self-esteem and well-being, consider their social identity, experience self-determination and control, and engage in self-advocacy. There is growing evidence that social networking sites may be associated with a person's sense of self-worth (Steinfield et al., 2008). The number of friends a person has and the reactions to their posts (e.g. messages and comments) provides positive feedback that leads to increased self-esteem and confidence in interacting with others. All of these aspects of social networking have a potentially positive impact on well-being (Holmes & O'Loughlin, 2012). In addition, gaming and virtual worlds can offer safe environments for people with autism to practice skills that may include taking social risks that may be considered too great in the physical world (Stendal & Balandin, 2015).

The ability to be anonymous online allows people with ID the opportunity to reduce the stigma they may experience in other settings (Cromby & Standen, 1999). Interacting with people online can enable people to avoid the label of intellectual disability; they can choose whether to reveal their disability, promote other aspects of their identity, or project a preferred identity (Holmes & O'Loughlin, 2012; Löfgren-Mårtenson, 2008).

Social network sites also provide an opportunity for people to learn how to express themselves and to voice to others their opinion about hobbies and interests (Holmes & O'Loughlin, 2012; Kydland et al., 2012). Shpigelman, Reiter, and Weiss (2008) found that young people with special needs felt that 'the online medium rendered their disabilities invisible and made them feel like "typical teenagers." Conversely, McClimens and Gordon (2008) found that participants in their UK study did not hide their ID status when blogging. Chadwick and Fullwood (2018) similarly found that adults with ID in the UK did not hide, nor dwell on, their disabled identity; instead, the online world allowed them to share with others their lives and who they were with a sense of positivity and pride.

However, Bowker and Tuffin (2002) argue that non-disclosure of disability can mean that differences are denied, thereby endorsing a non-disabled identity, and further silencing those that are already marginalized. Non-disclosure of disability, however, will do little to reduce stigma or increase acceptance of ID in society. Other studies have found that people with ID use their online presence to engage in a wider range of roles, which helps to counter oppression by challenging perceptions of their competencies and the labels they have placed on them by society. It also helps to enhance feelings of self-esteem and self-efficacy as well as to challenge notions of dependency by highlighting interdependence and relatedness (Bowker & Tuffin, 2002; Chadwick & Fullwood, 2018; Dowse, 2001; Seale, 2007).

One way those with ID can feel empowered online is through the way that communication takes place online. Cyberlanguage can be an advantage for people who have difficulties reading and writing (Löfgren-Mårtenson, 2008), and the reduced requirements of online interaction (e.g. less additional non-verbal communication to process during an interaction), as well as use of emoticons and avatars (which could be easier to decode) may help some people with ID and autism to communicate more comfortably (Mazurek, 2013; Hong, Yarosh, Kim, Abowd, & Arriaga, 2013).

The Internet can support the development of self-advocacy skills by having easy-to-read and easily accessible information. Here, people can learn about their human rights and how to use their rights. In addition, through websites and social media, people with ID can find out about local self-advocacy groups.

Access to Information

The benefits of being online also include access to information, learning, and employment. People with ID tend to be socio-economically poorer; ICTs can help people to access information and learning opportunities and enhance employability skills. The Internet offers easy and (sometimes) accessible information (Bowker & Tuffin, 2002) aimed specifically at people with ID. Easy-to-read information and educational films on a range of topics such as health, sex and relationships, voting, and staying safe online are all available on the web.

The Internet can also reduce physical barriers to education and learning. Although Jenaro et al. (2017) found that young people in Spain with ID made less academic use of the Internet than a non-disabled comparison group, their research still demonstrated that 13.4 percent of young people with ID were using the Internet for personal develop-ment and growth (e.g. online courses and Massive Open Online Courses) and 15.3 percent to find information on health and lifestyles. Adults with ID have also discussed how the online world is a route to valued occupational roles and skills and how they share infor-mation about jobs online, use the Internet to access services, and to apply for jobs (Chadwick & Fullwood, 2018).

Occupation and Enjoyment

Historically people with ID are often inadequately supported to occupy themselves meaningfully, be that via work and education or through leisure. The online world offers a space where people with ID can determine for themselves how they spend their time, with less reliance on support to do this (Chadwick & Fullwood, 2018; Löfgren-Mårtenson, 2008). Caton and Chapman (2016) highlight this benefit of being online in their review of social media use, grouping this under the theme of happiness, entertainment, and enjoyment.

In a recent study, Jenaro et al. (2017) found that more young people with ID (37 percent) were using the Internet for recreational and entertainment purposes (i.e. online gaming) than a comparison group of non-disabled young people (9 percent). A similar proportion of participants with ID (50.9 percent) used the Internet to access informa-tion in areas of personal interest (hobbies) compared with non-disabled young people (52.0 percent). Participants in qualitative work have also highlighted enjoying engaging with social media and going online to play games, listen to and share music, and watch movies and other video media (e.g. Chadwick & Fullwood, 2018). Hence, the online world appears to be used in similar ways to the typically developing majority (Chadwick & Fullwood, 2018; Shpigelman & Gill, 2014), offering self-determined opportunities for occupation, enjoyment, and leisure to a group that historically was underserved and reliant on support for these aspects of their lives.

BARRIERS TO PEOPLE WITH
ID GETTING ONLINE

Factors that promote the digital exclusion and act as barriers to using the Internet for people with ID have been reviewed and summarized previously (Caton & Chapman, 2016; Chadwick et al., 2013; Chadwick & Wesson, 2016). However, barriers are always changing in this fast-paced area of social and technological development. As such, this section outlines an updated summary of barriers identified by research and uses, as a way to examine the barriers, Bronfenbrenner's nested ecological model

(Bronfenbrenner, 1979, 1999), which embraces the relationship between the person, the environment, and the interaction between the two. This model has been adapted and used widely to understand how multiple influences affect individuals (see Figure 1).

The different influential settings were divided into "nested systems." Central to the model is the person, with their unique combination of personality, genetic, and biological factors. Bronfenbrenner identified a "micro-system" consisting of influences closest to the individual (e.g. carer, work, school) and a "meso-system" consisting of two or more micro-systems and the links between them (e.g. home-school). Next comes the "exo-system" a setting that doesn't involve the person as an active participant but where events can affect the person (e.g. a parent's place of work). The "macro-system" involves

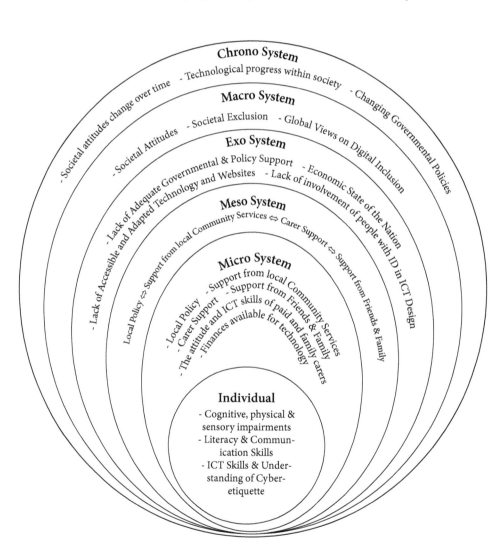

FIGURE 1 Barriers to digital inclusion for people with intellectual disabilities organized using Bronfenbrenner's nested ecological model.

wider cultures or sub-cultures (e.g. current rate of unemployment, societal attitudes). Finally, the "chrono-system" encompasses the dimension of time as it relates to the individual's environments; this can include timing of wider events, or actual physiological changes that occur as we grow older.

Specific barriers may operate both within and across specific systems (e.g. financial barriers may link to governmental funding in the macro system and the family income in the micro system). Within the academic field of cyberpsychology, more research has focused on the individual and micro-systems than the other systems.

Individual

Cognitive impairments and comorbid conditions may impede digital inclusion (see Chadwick et al., 2013). For example, understanding sequencing and processing the order of steps when using ICT may be more challenging for people with ID due to their specific cognitive impairments. Comorbidities, including physical and sensory impairments, are commonly associated with ID (e.g. cerebral palsy, visual and hearing impairments) and may affect the person's ability to interact with ICT (e.g. understanding intricate displays) and may impair co-ordination and the fine motor skills needed to use ICT (e.g. using a mouse, keyboard, selecting icons) (e.g. Johnson & Hegarty, 2003; Wehmeyer, Smith, Palmer, & Davies, 2004).

People with ID commonly have difficulties with reading and writing, and a number of researchers have highlighted how a lack of literacy skills becomes problematic when trying to access the Internet (e.g. Holmes & O'Loughlin, 2012; Keskinen, Heimonen, Turunen, Rajaniemi, & Kauppinen, 2012; Kydland et al., 2012, Löfgren-Mårtenson, 2008; McClimens & Gordon, 2008).

ICT skills and understanding of cyberlanguage and cyberetiquette have also been identified as barriers to social media use (Caton & Chapman, 2016). Challenges with logging in, uploading pictures, and commenting on photos, as well as searching, spelling, word processing, and writing content have also been identified (Kydland et al., 2012; McClimens & Gordon, 2009). Kydland and colleagues (2012) and McClimens and Gordon (2008, 2009) also identified potential difficulties with multiple meaning of words; for example, understanding the implications of the word "friend" offline and on Facebook (Holmes & O'Loughlin, 2012). Navigating cyberetiquette can also be challenging. McClimens and Gordon (2008) identified barriers around navigating the complex combination of pictures and text to invite responses; sometimes this is only achieved by experienced blog users and readers. Keskinen et al. (2012) also found that limitations in the participants' cyberetiquette skills adversely affected their response to incoming communication. Possibly due to a combination of these factors, Löfgren-Mårtenson (2008) found that most participants preferred email rather than chatting, and suggested that this could be due to the impact of cyberetiquette, where subtle codes of Internet chat can be challenging while email can be conducted away from the pressure of "live" chatting and the immediacy of the interaction.

Micro-System

Despite the decreasing costs of some entry-level Internet enabled devices, financial and economic barriers have a direct effect on people with ID in terms of buying devices as well as understanding ongoing costs to service providers (Caton, Chapman, Hynan, & Runswick-Cole, 2013; Watling, 2011).

For those with ID who rely on support, the attitude and skills of paid and family carers who provide this support can also affect online access and activities (Seale & Chadwick, 2017; see "Cybercrime and Online Risk"). The caring role may leave little time for carers to develop and keep pace with ICT and online skills to enable them to effectively support people with ID to get online (Chadwick & Wesson, 2016). Older carers particularly may have little experience of the online world and experience digital exclusion themselves.

Furthermore, lack of support, education, and training for people with ID is a fundamental barrier to digital inclusion. This barrier is linked to the attitudes of carers, society, and government policy (see "Macro System"), which may be underpinned by the belief that people with ID are unable to learn to use ICT (Chadwick et al., 2013).

Meso-System

The meso-system covers the interactions between micro-system influences. For example, support to access social media may vary. Different groups, such as paid and family carers, community services, and professionals may provide differential support and gatekeeping around social media access. Conversely, a more consistently restrictive or supportive approach to social media access may be evident across micro-system influences dependent upon the interactions, communication, and coherence between them.

Differences in availability of technology and support may also vary across settings in the person's environment (e.g. at home, day center, college). Such interactions between these micro-systems may coalesce to promote exclusion but have yet to be explored adequately in the literature.

Exo-System

People with ID may also have difficulties with fine motor skills, sight, physical activity, or hearing, which can mean that accessibility is also a barrier for some people with ID. The design of equipment (Keskinen et al., 2012), websites or apps that are not intuitive (Kydland et al., 2012), and complex security settings can make sites inaccessible (e.g. Watling, 2011), creating or exacerbating digital exclusion. In the UK, three in ten people with ID said their disability limited their use of communication services and devices, and 11 percent reported that they did not use a tablet as their disability, as well as other factors, prevented this (Ofcom, 2015), suggesting that this group may be overlooked at the design stage (Chadwick et al., 2013). Another reason that this barrier exists is the difficulty developing guidelines for web accessibility for people with ID because of the complex diversity of their needs as a heterogeneous group (Kennedy, Evans, & Thomas, 2010).

Lack of government policy can be another barrier to accessibility, and this lack is likely to impact on training and support initiatives to increase digital inclusion. There are various guidelines in circulation, but they often are related to schools or service, and as 80 percent of people with ID are no longer users of these services, they (and their families) may not have access to these guidelines. The wider literature on digital inclusion suggests that, in policy terms, there is still too great a focus on removing the barriers to ICT use and not enough of a focus about what new technologies may actually offer the user or about developing strategies to increase the value of going online for these individuals (Geniets & Eynon, 2012; Verdegem & Verhoest, 2009). Jaeger (2015) posits the need for increased political lobbying and legal change in concert with acknowledgment of digital inclusion as a human rights issue to tackle the fact that, despite rhetoric and research, equality does not yet exist. The barriers still exist at a societal level and, although not empirically investigated, they are likely to affect micro-system supports for digital inclusion.

Macro-System

The social model of disability suggests that it is the wider societal barriers that prevent disabled people from using the Internet as easily as non-disabled people, rather than an individual's impairments (e.g. cognitive, literacy, and communication difficulties). However, adapting Bronfenbrenner's model, the individual-level barriers are "nested" within the micro-level barriers of lack of support and training, which, in turn, are nested within macro-level social exclusion and social attitudes.

Research shows that digital exclusion is closely linked to societal exclusion. This can be for a number of reasons, but Geniets and Eynon (2012) point out the importance of understanding Internet use (or non-use) within the wider context of people's lives; Internet use is influenced and shaped by people's lives, interests, and social networks (Haddon, 2005). These social networks are likely to be influenced by societal perceptions and attitudes, and if people are socially excluded as a result of these attitudes, there subsequently may be less motivation and fewer opportunities to go online (Chadwick et al., 2013).

Societal attitudes and expectations of what people with ID can achieve have been shown to be a barrier to Internet use. Research has shown that among the non-disabled population, the level of support young people receive both in terms of going online in the first place and staying online is important (DiMaggio & Hargittai, 2001). Family members, who reflect societal attitudes to a certain degree, play an important role in introducing Internet use (McMillan & Morrison, 2006) and having "warm experts" around, i.e. people who are a little ahead in terms of Internet experience and skills, can be beneficial for uptake and use of technology (Bakardjieva & Smith, 2001; Chadwick & Fullwood, 2018). These ideas should be considered alongside research involving people with ID where lack of support has been identified as a barrier (Löfgren-Mårtenson, 2008; Parsons, Daniels, Porter, & Robertson, 2008; Watling, 2011). Similarly, global expectations about how accessible technology should be and who technology should be designed for is also an important influence at the macro-level (Chadwick et al., 2013).

Chrono-System

The ever-moving technological progress within society may pose a challenge to digital inclusion. New devices, operating systems, and updates are regularly produced, with the expectation that society will keep abreast of these changes. However, for people with ID, assimilation of new information is likely to be more challenging and require support for changes in devices. Despite this, accessibility is a key consideration within the development of new technology and so applications and devices are likely to become more accessible over time. Additionally, changes to governmental policies and societal attitudes over time should improve the digital inclusion of people with ID (Chadwick & Wesson, 2016).

Cybercrime and Online Risk

In addition to the benefits of Internet and online use, there are also hazards, including cybercrime and engagement or enticement into risky behaviors. Despite offline victimization of people with ID being more common, little research exists to enhance understanding of online victimization and cybercrime (Chadwick & Wesson, 2016; Normand & Sallafranque-St-Louis, 2016). Cybercrime, deviance, and associated online risks are more prescient in societal consciousness that accompanies advances in technology (see Chapter 31 on cybercrime). Cybercrime frameworks developed from research with typically developing young people (e.g. Livingstone & Haddon, 2009) have been adapted for use with people with ID (e.g. Chadwick et al., 2017). The appropriateness of utilizing such a framework with adults and young people with ID is contentious, and some advocate for a framework specific to people with ID (Seale & Chadwick, 2017). Furthermore, the hypothesized negative impact of some behaviors within the online world which have been classified as risky (e.g. watching violent content or pornography) is disputatious and, in some cases, empirically unverified.

Chadwick and colleagues (2017) found that non-disabled people view people with ID as being at greater risk online when compared with themselves. The greatest perceived risks included being threatened, bullied, or harassed online, being vulnerable to online scams, and uninhibited disclosure of personal information. Similarly, academics, carers, and professionals interacting with people with ID have viewed them as having heightened levels of risk online (Bannon, McGlynn, McKenzie, & Quayle, 2015; Holmes & O'Loughlin, 2012; Löfgren-Mårtenson et al., 2015; Lough and Fisher, 2016b;

Molin, Sorbring, & Löfgren-Mårtenson, 2015; Norman & Sallafranque-St-Louis, 2016; Plichta, 2010), with concerns raised due the potential for people with ID to be more sociable and socially isolated, naive and trusting, and unable to detect deception.

A discrepancy exists between perceptions of people with ID and their carers regarding potential benefits and risks of being online (Löfgren-Mårtenson, 2008; Lough & Fisher, 2016a). Such perceptions and concerns about vulnerability and the ability of people with ID to manage online risk may operate as a barrier to digital inclusion, with carers taking a more restrictive gatekeeping role (Seale & Chadwick, 2017). This may offer increased protection for those with ID, but it may also potentially undermine their skill development, self-determination, and digital participation (Bannon et al., 2015; Seale & Chadwick, 2017). Bannon and colleagues (2015) found that restriction varied among the young people interviewed. Some parents put blocks on sites, and implemented supervision and monitoring, although the quality of this monitoring varied. Interestingly, some of the young people indicated that they were more skilled with technology than their parents and could circumvent these gatekeeping strategies.

Despite growing research into perceptions of online risk for people with ID, there remain very few studies exploring experiences of cybercrime, deviance, and online risk among people with ID. Currently, there is inconsistent evidence regarding whether people with ID are at comparatively greater risk of online victimization as when compared with non-disabled people.

Holmes and O'Loughlin (2012) found that people with ID received unwanted messages on Facebook, experienced cyberbullying, and were targeted for sexual and financial exploitation. This is consistent with research involving both people with 22q11 deletion syndrome (Buijs et al., 2017) and with autism (Sallafranque-St-Louis & Normand, 2017). On the other hand, a survey study of the prevalence of mobile phone and Internet cyber-bullying found a reduced likelihood of children with ID being victims of cyberbullying (Didden et al., 2009). A number of hypotheses may explain this discrepancy (cf. Seale & Chadwick, 2017). It may be that digital exclusion through societal and individual routes interacts with gatekeeping to reduce exposure to digital risk. It may be that some people with ID require additional support to manage and avoid more serious online risks. It may also be that digital exclusion and gatekeeping lead to fewer risks being encountered by this group.

Recent quantitative research has explored the prevalence of online risk experience. Adults in Chiner et al.'s (2017) cross-sectional study reported being blocked from online groups or activities (48 percent), insulted (46 percent), threatened (35 percent), receiving unwanted sexual media (35 percent) and others using people's password without consent (36 percent). Caregivers (n=68) were also surveyed, and 39 percent reportedly ignored the problems those they cared for indicated they had encountered online. Though seldom self-reported, people with ID also engaged in anti-social behaviors including being insulting, threatening, or engaging in unwanted flirting.

Mental health issues have been related to experiences of online victimization (Sallafranque-St-Louis & Normand, 2017; Wright, 2017) and problematic cell phone and Internet use (Jenaro et al., 2017) among people with ID. Researchers posit that relationships and leisure activity, and parental mediation of technology could be protective against the negative adjustment consequences associated with cyber victimization (Jenaro, et al., 2017; Wright, 2017). Future research could further explore the experiences of specific risks and cybercrimes amongst distinct groups with particular support arrangements and the factors which mitigate negative outcomes.

Bannon et al. (2015) noted that some individuals who lacked understanding of risks engaged in more risk-taking behavior. Some young people also intentionally took risks. However, despite being perceived as being at greater risk online (compared to non-disabled peers), young people and adults with ID have demonstrated awareness of, and ability to manage, online risk (Bannon et al., 2015; Chadwick, 2018; Löfgren-Mårtenson et al., 2015).

Support for Digital Inclusion

Though influenced by factors within the macro-, exo-, and chrono-systems, support primarily operates within micro-, meso-, and individual-systems (cf. Box 1). An awareness of the numerous barriers has led to work exploring strategies for support. Approaches have varied and occur at several levels, often simultaneously, and include supporting people with ID to learn online skills, overcoming or removing barriers, and managing online risks.

Supporting People with ID to Develop Online Skills

Support can enable greater engagement with care (Kydland, et al., 2012), increase confidence in problem-solving when using the Internet (Holmes & O'Loughlin, 2012), and improve employability (Able to Include, 2017). These benefits, however, can be limited by potential conflicts of interest between the person with ID and the person providing support (e.g. carer, health professional). Where social media may be used to speak up against oppression, the extent to which this would occur could be moderated by the kinds of support the person with ID receives when using the social media tool. Some studies have identified online support needs but these studies were carried out in uncommon settings, i.e., learning social media skills in groups. Therefore, the identified support needs may not reflect the issues that people experience when accessing social media independently (Kydland, et al., 2012; McClimens & Gordon, 2009; Seale, 2007).

Internet training needs to be tailored to meet individual support requirements and impairments (Wong, Chan, Li-Tsang, & Lam, 2009). People with ID may benefit from individual instruction in simple computer skills, such as using a mouse, navigating webpages, and searching (Hoppestad, 2013; Zisimopoulos, Sigafoos, & Koutromanos, 2011). Guided Internet sessions where supporters identified relevant information for people with ID have been used to maintain motivation (Johnson & Hegarty, 2003;

Williamson, Schauder, Stockfield, Wright, & Bow, 2001). The training program developed by Li-Tsang, Lee, Yeung, Siu, and Lam (2007) used a structured environment with appropriate training tools and assistance, where people with ID showed significant improvements in ICT skills (e.g. mouse and keyboard use) in comparison with a control group. Notably, this study represents one of the only intervention studies incorporating a control group to help discern a causative relationship between training and skill improvement.

Strategies to Remove Barriers

Developing more accessible technology can also support people with ID in using the Internet. Examples include developing simpler interfaces, implementing universal design (Wehmeyer et al., 2004), touch screen interfaces, and picture-based instant messenger services (Keskinen et al., 2012). The World Wide Web Consortium (W3C) is an international community where member organizations, W3C staff, and the public work together to develop web standards. W3C has developed Web Content Accessibility Guidelines, and strategies for web designers to make websites accessible for a broader range of disabled people, including people with ID. More recently, developing digital technology applications for the automation of easy-to-read texts may increase the number of texts that are accessible to people with ID (Able to Include, 2017).

A number of specialized social networks have been set up for people with ID (e.g. specialfriends.com, Kaveripiiri.fi) who want to create and maintain online relationships in a more regulated and supported way. Although these sites were introduced with the aim of supporting people with ID to become more digitally included, there is limited evidence of take up, with people often preferring to use mainstream sites (e.g. Able to Include, 2017).

People with ID also reported autonomously accessing peer training and mentorship from their social networks when in need of advice and information about how to use ICT and netiquette (Chadwick & Fullwood, 2018), mirroring findings from the wider literature regarding the utility of mentoring. There are a few examples of this happening; the Healthy Surfers project allowed people with ID to develop and provide training around being online (Speak up Rotherham).

Supporting People to Manage Online Risk

Perceptions of online risk may influence support from carers and family, which could result in digital exclusion. However, there have been calls in the literature for a less risk-averse approach in supporting people with ID using technology and the Internet (see Seale & Chadwick, 2017). Authors have argued for a model of positive risk-taking incorporating creativity, possibility thinking, and resilience when supporting people with ID in accessing technology and the online world (Seale, 2014; Seale et al., 2013;

Seale & Chadwick, 2017); this approach is supported by research demonstrating that risk exposure does not necessarily correlate with greater subsequent harms (Livingstone, Mascheroni, & Staksrud, 2015).

Some guides exist for people with ID about how to stay safe online (e.g. The Foundation for People with Learning Disabilities, 2014). However, there is scant literature detailing the development and effectiveness of these guides in promoting risk awareness and management in either people with ID or those providing support. Studies have urged future practice work to provide training in online risk management (e.g. Kydland et al., 2012; Lough & Fisher, 2016b; McClimens & Gordon, 2008). Bannon et al. (2015) reported in their study that young people with ID sought advice from their social networks around online risk. Given the limited empirical work in this area, more research is needed here.

CONCLUSION

There is currently limited but burgeoning research around the digital inclusion of people with ID. This research has, in the main, been qualitative and small scale. As such, strongly supported theoretical models of the online behavior of people with ID are currently lacking. Future work should endeavor to integrate current understanding into a testable model, and to test this model. Despite these issues, though, by pulling together the literature reviewed in this chapter, a number of tentative conclusions can be drawn.

First, while digital inclusion appears to be improving for people with ID, progress is slow and exclusion persists. People interested in digital technology who are more cognitively able, affluent, and positively supported are more likely to be included. Groups currently excluded from consideration and research include older adults with ID, those living in the global south, and people with profound and multiple ID. Research focusing on the digital inclusion of these people is largely absent from the extant literature.

Second, ICTs and the online world provide people with ID with opportunities for social inclusion, romantic relationships, and social skills; self-determination, choice, and autonomy; digital competences and skills; autonomy in occupation, via leisure activities; accessing employment and educational information; societal inclusion, advocacy, and self-advocacy; increased well-being, self-esteem, and confidence; and promotion and exploration of valued social identities.

Third, barriers to digital exclusion operate at multiple interacting levels within society, which change over time, from the macro-issues of governmental policy and societal attitudes through to the need for user-centered technological design, and digital structure of community services, and current ICT design may not be accessible for people with cognitive, physical and sensory impairments. The factors interact in varying and complex ways to hinder or support digital inclusion; this also requires further investigation.

Fourth, increased digital inclusion brings increased exposure to potential online risks. Current evidence suggests that some predisposing factors might put people with ID at increased risk (e.g. loneliness, difficulty discerning deception online), but this is tempered by digital exclusion. The actual prevalence of risk, therefore, is difficult to discern. Risk-averse approaches are likely to reduce digital inclusion and prevent development of online skills and resilience.

Finally, tentative evidence suggests positive effects of interventions aimed at improving online skills. Findings regarding benefits and support, understandably, tend to be based on small, descriptive, and phenomenological studies and few studies causatively demonstrate the benefits reported. Hence, more well-controlled studies are needed to confirm these benefits and the conditions under which they are most likely to occur. Studies of this nature will enable people with ID to be better supported in accessing the digital world in ways that work for their individual situation and needs.

REFERENCES

Able to Include. (2017, March). Making digital inclusion possible. Retrieved from http://able-to-include.com/wp-content/uploads/2016/06/Able-to-include-Final-newsletter.pdf

Bakardjieva, M., & Smith, R. (2001). The Internet in everyday life: Computer networking from the standpoint of the domestic user. *New Media & Society 3*(1), 67–83.

Bannon, S., McGlynn, T., McKenzie, K., & Quayle, E. (2015). The Internet and young people with Additional Support Needs (ASN): Risk and safety. *Computers in Human Behavior 53*, 495–503.

Bowker, N., & Tuffin, K. (2002). Disability discourses for online identities. *Disability & Society 17*(3), 327–344.

Bronfenbrenner, U. (1979). The ecology of human development: Experiments by design and nature. Cambridge, MA: Harvard University Press.

Bronfenbrenner, U. (1999). Environments in developmental perspective: Theoretical and operational models. In S. L. Friedman & T. D. Wachs (Eds.), *Measuring environment across the life span: Emerging methods and concepts* (pp. 37–43). Washington, DC: APA Publishing.

Buijs, P., Boot, E., Shugar, A., Fung, W. L. A., & Bassett, A. S. (2017). Internet safety issues for adolescents and adults with intellectual disabilities. *Journal of Applied Research in Intellectual Disabilities 30*(2), 416–418.

Carey, A. C., Friedman, M. G., & Bryen, D. N. (2005). Use of electronic technologies by people with intellectual disabilities. *Mental Retardation 43*(5), 322–333.

Caton, S., & Chapman, M. (2016). The use of social media and people with intellectual disability: A systematic review and thematic analysis. *Journal of Intellectual and Developmental Disability 41*(2), 125–139.

Caton, S., Chapman, M., Hynan, A., & Runswick-Cole, K. (2013). *The Use of Digital Technology by People with Learning Disabilities/Difficulties: Report from a Workshop Held on 26th March 2013*. MMU, unpublished.

Chadwick, D. D., (2018). Experiences of People with an Intellectual Disability of Risk, Restriction and Resilience Online. *5th IASSIDD Europe Congress Diversity & Belonging: Celebrating Difference. Athens, Greece,17th – 20th July, 2018.*

Chadwick, D. D., & Fullwood, C. (2018). An online life like any other: Identity, self-determination and social networking among adults with intellectual disabilities. *Cyberpsychology, Behaviour & Social Networking* 21(1), 56–64.

Chadwick, D. D., Quinn, S., & Fullwood, C. (2017). Perceptions of the risks and benefits of Internet access and use by people with intellectual disabilities. *British Journal of Learning Disabilities* 45(1), 21–31.

Chadwick, D. D., & Wesson, C. (2016). Digital inclusion and disability. In A. Attrill & C. Fullwood (Eds.), *Applied Cyberpsychology* (pp. 1–23). Basingstoke: Palgrave Macmillan.

Chadwick, D., Wesson, C., & Fullwood, C. (2013). Internet access by people with intellectual disabilities: Inequalities and opportunities. *Future Internet* 5(3), 376–397.

Chiner, E., Gómez-Puerta, M., & Cardona-Moltó, M. C. (2017). Internet use, risks and online behaviour: The view of Internet users with intellectual disabilities and their caregivers. *British Journal of Learning Disabilities* 45(3), 190–197.

Cromby, J., & Standen, P. (1999). Cyborgs and stigma: technology, disability, subjectivity. In A. J. Gordo-Lopez & I. Parker (Eds.), *Cyberpsychology* (pp. 95–112). New York, NY, USA: Routledge.

Didden, R., Scholte, R. H. J., Korzilius, H., DeMoor, J. M. H., Vermeulen, A., O'Reilly, M.,... Lancioni, G. E. (2009). Cyberbullying along students with intellectual and developmental disability in special education settings. *Developmental Neurorehabilitation* 12, 146–151.

DiMaggio, P., & Hargittai, E. (2001). From the "digital divide" to "digital inequality": Studying Internet use as penetration increases. *Working Paper Series No. 15*. Princeton, NJ: Princeton University Center for Arts and Cultural Policy Studies.

Dowse, L. (2001). Contesting practices, challenging codes: Self-advocacy, disability politics and the social model. *Disability & Society* 16(1), 123–141.

Emerson, E., Mallam, S., Davies, I., & Spencer, K. (2005, September 28). *Adults with learning disabilities in England 2003/4*. Survey Report. Rotherham: NHS Health and Social Care Information Centre/Office for National Statistics.

Emerson, E., & McVilly, K. (2004). Friendship activities of adults with intellectual disabilities in supported accommodation in Northern England. *Journal of Applied Research in Intellectual Disabilities* 17(3), 191–197.

Forrester-Jones, R., Carpenter, J., Coolen-Schrijner, P., Cambridge, P., Tate, A., Beecham, J.,... Wooff, D. (2006). The social networks of people with intellectual disability living in the community 12 years after resettlement from long-stay hospitals. *Journal of Applied Research in Intellectual Disabilities* 19(4), 285–295.

Foundation for People with Learning Disabilities. (2014). *Staying safe on social media and online*. London. Retrieved from https://www.mentalhealth.org.uk/sites/default/files/staying-safe-online.pdf

Fox, S. (2011, January 21). Americans living with disability and their technology profile. Washington, DC: Pew Research Center Internet and American Life Project. Retrieved from http://www.pewinternet.org/2011/01/21/americans-living-with-disability-and-their-technology-profile/

Geniets, A., & Eynon, R. (2012, August 16). *On the Periphery? Understanding Low and Discontinued Internet Use Amongst Young People in Britain*. Oxford Internet Institute, University of Oxford, UK. Retrieved from https://www.oii.ox.ac.uk/archive/downloads/publications/Lapsed_Internet_Users_Report_2012.pdf

Gravell, C. (2012, May 17). *Loneliness and cruelty: People with learning disabilities and their experience of harassment, abuse and related crime in the community*. Report. London: Lemos and Crane.

Goggin, G., & Newell, C. (2003). *Digital Disability: The social construction of disability in new media*. Lanham: Rowman & Littlefield.

Guo, B., Bricout, J. C., & Huang, J. (2005). A common open space or a digital divide? A social model perspective on the online disability community in China. *Disability & Society 20*(1), 49–66.

Gutiérrez, P., & Martorell Zargoza, A. (2011). People with intellectual disability and ICTs. *Revista Comunicar 18*(36), 173–180.

Haddon, L. (2005). Personal information culture: The contribution of research on ICTs in everyday life. UNESCO between two phases of the world summit on the information society. 17–20 May, St. Petersburg, Russia.

Hegarty, J. R., & Aspinall, A. (2006). The use of personal computers with adults who have developmental disability: Outcomes of an organisation-wide initiative. *The British Journal of Development Disabilities 52*(103), 137–154.

Helsper, E. J. (2012). A corresponding fields model for the links between social and digital exclusion. *Communication Theory 22*(4), 403–426.

Holmes, K. M., & O'Loughlin, N. (2012). The experiences of people with learning disabilities on social networking sites. *British Journal of Learning Disabilities 42*(1), 1–7.

Hong, H., Yarosh, S., Kim, J. G., Abowd, G. D., & Arriaga, R. I. (2013). Investigating the use of circles in social networks to support independence of individuals with autism. In *Proceedings of the SIGCHI conference on human factors in computing systems* (pp. 3207–3216). 27 April–2 May, Paris, France. New York: ACM.

Hoppestad, B. S. (2013). Current perspective regarding adults with intellectual and developmental disabilities accessing computer technology. *Disability and Rehabilitation: Assistive Technology 8*(3), 190–194.

Jaeger, P. T. (2015). Disability, human rights, and social justice: The ongoing struggle for online accessibility and equality. *First Monday 20*(9).

Jenaro, C., Flores, N., Cruz, M., Pérez, M. C., Vega, V., & Torres, V. A. (2017). Internet and cell phone usage patterns among young adults with intellectual disabilities. *Journal of Applied Research in Intellectual Disabilities 31*(2), 259–272.

Johnson, R., & Hegarty, J. R. (2003). Websites as educational motivators for adults with learning disability. *British Journal of Educational Technology 34*(4), 479–486.

Katz, E., Blumler, J., & Gurevitch, M. (1974). Utilization of mass communication by the individual. In J. Blumler & E. Katz (Eds.), *The uses of mass communication: Current perspectives on gratifications research* (pp. 19–34). Beverly Hills, CA: Sage.

Kennedy, H., Evans, S., & Thomas, S. (2010). Can the web be made accessible for people with intellectual disabilities? *The Information Society 27*(1), 29–39.

Keskinen, T., Heimonen, T., Turunen, M., Rajaniemi, J. P., & Kauppinen, S. (2012). SymbolChat: A flexible picture-based communication platform for users with intellectual disabilities. *Interacting with Computers 24*(5), 374–386.

Khan, R. F. (1985). Mental retardation and paternalistic control. In R. S. Laura & A. F. Ashman (Eds.), *Moral issues in mental retardation*. London: Croom Helm.

Kydland, F., Molka-Danielsen, J., and Balandin, S. (2012). Examining the use of social media tool "Flickr" for impact on loneliness for people with intellectual disability. In *Proceedings of the 2012 Norsk konferanse for organisasjoners bruk av informasjonsteknologi.* (pp. 253–264). 19–21 November, Bodo, Norway. Trondheim: Akademika forlag.

Li-Tsang, C. W., Lee, M. Y., Yeung, S. S., Siu, A. M., & Lam, C. S. (2007). A 6-month follow-up of the effects of an information and communication technology (ICT) training programme on people with intellectual disabilities. *Research in Developmental Disabilities 28*(6), 559–566.

Livingstone, S., & Haddon, L. (2009). EU kids online. *Zeitschrift Für Psychologie/Journal of Psychology 217*(4), 236.

Livingstone, S., Mascheroni, G., & Staksrud, E. (2015). Developing a framework for researching children's online risks and opportunities in Europe. Retrieved on 28/08/18 from: http://eprints.lse.ac.uk/64470/

Löfgren-Mårtenson, L. (2008). Love in cyberspace: Swedish young people with intellectual disabilities and the Internet 1. *Scandinavian Journal of Disability Research 10*(2), 125–138.

Löfgren-Mårtenson, L., Sorbring, E., & Molin, M. (2015). "T@ngled up in blue": Views of parents and professionals on Internet use for sexual purposes among young people with intellectual disabilities. *Sexuality and Disability 33*(4), 533–544.

Lough, E., & Fisher, M. H. (2016a). Parent and self-report ratings on the perceived levels of social vulnerability of adults with Williams syndrome. *Journal of Autism and Developmental Disorders 46*(11), 3424–3433.

Lough, E., & Fisher, M. H. (2016b). Internet use and online safety in adults with Williams syndrome. *Journal of Intellectual Disability Research 60*(10), 1020–1030.

Manion, M. L., & Bersani, H. A. (1987). Mental retardation as a Western sociological construct: A cross-cultural analysis. *Disability, Handicap & Society 2*(3), 231–245.

Mazurek, M. O. (2013). Social media use among adults with autism spectrum disorders. *Computers in Human Behavior 29*(4), 1709–1714.

McClimens, A., & Gordon, F. (2008). Presentation of self in e-veryday life: How people labeled with intellectual disability manage identity as they engage the blogosphere. *Sociological Research Online 13*(4), 1.

McClimens, A., & Gordon, F. (2009). People with intellectual disabilities as bloggers: What's social capital got to do with it anyway? *Journal of Intellectual Disabilities 13*(1), 19–30.

McMillan, S. J., & Morrison, M. (2006). Coming of age with the Internet: A qualitative exploration of how the Internet has become an integral part of young people's lives. *New Media & Society 8*(1), 73–95.

Molin, M., Sorbring, E., & Löfgren-Mårtenson, L. (2015). Teachers' and parents' views on the Internet and social media usage by pupils with intellectual disabilities. *Journal of Intellectual Disabilities 19*(1), 22–33.

National Telecommunications and Information Administration and Economics and Statistics Administration. (2013). *Exploring the Digital Nation: America's Emerging Online Experience.* Washington, DC: U.S. Department of Commerce. Retrieved from http://www.ntia.doc.gov/report/2013/exploring-digital-nation-americas-emerging-online-experience

Normand, C. L., & Sallafranque-St-Louis, F. (2016). Cybervictimization of young people with an intellectual or developmental disability: Risks specific to sexual solicitation. *Journal of Applied Research in Intellectual Disabilities 29*(2), 99–110.

Ofcom (2015, October 1). *Disabled Consumers' Use of Communication Services.* Report. Retrieved from https://www.ofcom.org.uk/__data/assets/pdf_file/0028/81586/disabled_consumers_use_of_communications_services.pdf

Oliver, M. (2013). The social model of disability: Thirty years on. *Disability & Society 28*(7), 1024–1026.

Parsons, S., Daniels, H., Porter, J., & Robertson, C. (2008). Resources, staff beliefs and organizational culture: Factors in the use of information and communication technology for adults with intellectual disabilities. *Journal of Applied Research in Intellectual Disabilities 21*, 19–33.

Perske, R. (1972). The dignity of risk and the MR. *Mental Retardation 10*(1), 24.

Plichta, P. (2010). Ways of ICT usage among mildly intellectually disabled adolescents: Potential risks and advantages. In E. Dunkels, G-M. Franber, and C. Hallgren (Eds.), *Youth culture and net culture: Online social practices* (pp. 296–315). Hershey, PA: IGI Global.

Robertson, J., Emerson, E., Gregory, N., Hatton, C., Kessissoglou, S., Hallam, A., & Linehan, C. (2001). Social networks of people with mental retardation in residential settings. *Mental Retardation 39*(3), 201–214.

Ruggerio, T. E. (2000). Uses and Gratifications Theory in the 21st Century. *Mass Communication and Society, 3*(1), 3–37.

Sallafranque-St-Louis, F., & Normand, C. L. (2017). From solitude to solicitation: How people with intellectual disability or autism spectrum disorder use the Internet [online]. *Cyberpsychology: Journal of Psychosocial Research on Cyberspace 11*(1), Article 7. http://dx.doi.org/10.5817/CP2017-1-7

Seale, J. K. (2007). Strategies for supporting the online publishing activities of adults with learning difficulties. *Disability & Society 22*(2), 173–186.

Seale, J. (2014). The role of supporters in facilitating the use of technologies by adolescents and adults with learning disabilities: A place for positive risk-taking? *European Journal of Special Needs Education 29*(2), 220–236.

Seale, J., & Chadwick, D. (2017). How does risk mediate the ability of adolescents and adults with intellectual and developmental disabilities to live a normal life by using the Internet? [online] *Cyberpsychology: Journal of Psychosocial Research on Cyberspace, 11*(1), Article 2. https://doi.org/10.5817/CP2017-1-2

Seale, J., Nind, M., & Simmons, B. (2013). Transforming positive risk-taking practices: The possibilities of creativity and resilience in learning disability contexts. *Scandinavian Journal of Disability Research 15*(3), 233–248.

Selwyn, N. (2006). Digital division or digital decision? A study of non-users and low-users of computers. *Poetics 34*(4–5), 273–292.

Shakespeare, T. (2014). *Disability rights and wrongs revisited.* New York: Routledge.

Shogren, K. A., Luckasson, R., & Schalock, R. L. (2014). The definition of "context" and its application in the field of intellectual disability. *Journal of Policy and Practice in Intellectual Disabilities 11*(2), 109–116.

Shpigelman, C. N., Reiter, S., & Weiss, P. L. (2008). E-mentoring for youth with special needs: Preliminary results. *CyberPsychology & Behavior 11*(2), 196–200.

Shpigelman, C. N., & Gill, C. J. (2014). How do adults with intellectual disabilities use Facebook? *Disability & Society 29*(10), 1601–1616.

SpeakUp Rotherham. *Healthy Surfers project.* Retrieved from http://www.speakup.org.uk/?page_id=249

Steinfield, C., Ellison, N. B., & Lampe, C. (2008). Social capital, self-esteem, and use of online social network sites: A longitudinal analysis. *Journal of Applied Developmental Psychology 29*(6), 434–445.

Stendal, K., & Balandin, S. (2015). Virtual worlds for people with autism spectrum disorder: A case study in second life. *Disability and Rehabilitation 37*(17), 1591–1598.

Thompson, J. R., Bradley, V. J., Buntinx, W. H. E., Schalock, R. L., Shogren, K. A., & Snell, M. E. (2009). Conceptualizing supports and the support needs of people with intellectual disability. *Intellectual and Developmental Disabilities 47*(2), 135–146. https://doi.org/10.1352/1934-9556-47.2.135

UN General Assembly. (2006). Convention on the Rights of Persons with Disabilities. Retrieved from: http://www.un.org/disabilities.

Van Dijk, J. A. (2017). Digital Divide: Impact of Access. *The International Encyclopedia of Media Effects*. [online]. Oxford: John Wiley & Sons. Retrieved from https://doi.org/10.1002/9781118783764.wbieme0043

Van Loon, J., Claes, C., Vandevelde, S., Van Hove, G., & Schalock, R. L. (2010). Assessing individual support needs to enhance personal outcomes. *Exceptionality* 18(4), 193–202.

Verdegem, P., & Verhoest, P. (2009). Profiling the non-user: Rethinking policy initiatives stimulating ICT acceptance. *Telecommunications Policy* 33(10), 642–652.

Watling, S. (2011). Digital exclusion: Coming out from behind closed doors. *Disability & Society* 26(4), 491–495.

Wehmeyer, M. L., Smith, S. J., Palmer, S. B., & Davies, D. K. (2004). The effect of student-directed transition planning with a computer-based reading support program on the self-determination of students with disabilities. *Journal of Special Education Technology* 19(4), 7–22.

World Health Organization (1992). *International Classification of Diseases*, 10th Revision. Geneva: WHO.

Williamson, K., Schauder, D., Stockfield, L., Wright, S., & Bow, A. (2001). The role of the Internet for people with disabilities: Issues of access and equity for public libraries. *The Australian Library Journal* 50(2), 157–174.

Wong, A. W., Chan, C. C., Li-Tsang, C. W., & Lam, C. S. (2009). Competence of people with intellectual disabilities on using human–computer interface. *Research in Developmental Disabilities* 30(1), 107–123.

Wright, M. F. (2017). Parental mediation, cyber victimization, adjustment difficulties, and adolescents with autism spectrum disorder. *Cyberpsychology: Journal of Psychosocial Research on Cyberspace* 11(1), Article 6. https://doi.org/10.5817/CP2017-1-6

Zisimopoulos, D., Sigafoos, J., & Koutromanos, G. (2011). Using video prompting and constant time delay to teach an Internet search basic skill to students with intellectual disabilities. *Education and Training in Autism and Developmental Disabilities* 46(2), 238–250.

....

CHAPTER 15

THE PSYCHOLOGY OF ONLINE LURKING

....

MAŠA POPOVAC AND CHRIS FULLWOOD

INTRODUCTION

ANYONE who has visited one of the multifarious online forums dedicated to video games (one of the authors of this chapter has spent countless hours frequenting Fallout 4 forums!) will know that participation levels vary considerably between users. Whereas more "active" members might regularly begin threads bemoaning game bugs and glitches, offer tips and advice to fellow gamers, share achievements or character creations, or ask for help with quests they are stuck on, other members may merely log on to read existing content or observe interactions between members of the community, seemingly without making a tangible contribution. This pattern of behavior is not unique to games forums and indeed all online groups include individuals who do not add content to the community. These individuals have become known as "lurkers". Lurking is thus viewed as a passive behavior linked to observation, invisibility, or bystander behavior (Edelmann, 2013).

In terms definitions, scholars vary in their framing of the phenomenon. Some consider lurking to involve no posting at all (e.g., Neelen & Fetter, 2010; Nonnecke & Preece, 2003), while others consider lurking as some (but minimal) posting (e.g., Golder & Donath, 2004; Ridings, Gefen, & Arinze, 2006). We would contest that the definition of lurking should depend on the social norms associated with specific online groups, which will always constrain and influence how people interact in all online spaces (Van Dijck, 2013). Whereas it might be more common in one community for users to make infrequent contributions, members of other communities may expect their fellow members to actively post. In the latter community, members are likely to perceive lurkers as those who make no or minimal contributions, but in the former those who engage minimally may not be seen as lurking. As discussed by Malinen (2015), it is still unclear how long a user should remain passive before being considered a lurker in an online environment. Nonetheless, for the purposes of this chapter lurkers are considered as individuals who log onto online communities, but who contribute little or no written content, thus spending the majority of their time taking in information created by other members.

Whether in the context of online support groups or video gaming forums, research exploring the determinants and effects of active or passive online behaviors has increased. Two key viewpoints exist with regard to lurking behavior specifically. The first view is that lurking is chiefly a negative behavior as individuals benefit from the content posted by active members and fail to add any real value to a community (Preece, Nonnecke, & Andrews, 2004). Thus, lurkers have been described as "social loafers" or "freeloaders," drawing upon the social capital (the psychological and emotional resources gained through our relationships with others; Coleman, 1988) in communities without providing anything in return (Kollock & Smith, 1996). Following this thinking, one of the principal focal points of early research was on increasing participation of lurkers in order for them to become legitimate members of a group. This is largely due to active and sustained participation being viewed as crucial for making online groups viable and successful (Burke, Marlow, & Lento, 2009; Koh, Kim, Butler, and Bock, 2007).

The alternate view is that lurkers are in fact legitimate members of communities since passive participation can be considered as another form of engagement in online groups. Interestingly, lurkers have been shown to make up the majority of participants, with some studies showing that up to 90 percent of users were lurkers (Mason, 1999; Muller, 2012). However, lurking rates also vary depending on the online environment. For example, lurkers have been shown to make up 45.5 percent of all users in a health support community compared to 82 percent of users in a software support community (Nonnecke & Preece, 2001). Individuals are often also members of multiple online communities or groups simultaneously and engage in varying degrees within these different spaces (Muller, 2012). More specifically, one study found that 84 percent of individuals both lurk and contribute in at least one community (Muller, 2012). Therefore, lurking has been argued to simply be a different form of engagement. The extent of individuals' engagement within online spaces is likely to vary in relation to their personal needs and motivations as well as the characteristics of the online group. Thus, many factors contribute to levels of participation of users and, in order to understand lurking behavior, it is important to consider the determinants of these behaviors as well as the effects of active or passive use.

This chapter discusses the personal and social determinants of lurking in online environments more broadly, before focusing on lurking in the contexts of health (online support groups) and education (e-learning), more specifically, due to the plethora of academic literature exploring these communities.

PERSONAL AND SITUATIONAL DETERMINANTS OF LURKING

Lurking as a Transformatory Process

It has been suggested that participation in online groups or communities is not a fixed behavior. Instead, it can be a transformatory process where individuals move between active and passive participation at various stages of joining a group (Bryant, Forte, & Bruckman, 2005; Malinen, 2015). In the beginning stages of joining an online group, individuals may lurk in order to familiarize themselves with the group dynamics in preparation for becoming active, contributing members (Yeow, Johnson, & Faraj, 2006). Indeed, lurkers stated that the key reason for their passive behavior was the desire to first learn more about the group (Nonnecke & Preece, 2003; Nonnecke, Preece, & Andrews, 2004). Moreover, a quarter of lurkers indicated that telling stories or participating in conversations was their main reason for joining an online community in the first place, and 13 percent reportedly wanted to offer advice and expertise in the online community they had joined (Ridings, Gefen, & Arinze, 2006). Thus, many lurkers join groups with the intention of contributing and can be seen as potential posters.

Upon observation, individuals may choose not to actively participate due to poor usability or technical issues, due to not liking the group dynamics once they had become familiar with it, or not perceiving the group as a good fit for them (Nonnecke et al., 2004; Preece et al., 2004). For example, someone may join a support group in order to find out more about living with a specific health issue but finds that discussions within the group tend to focus more on medical symptoms. Alternatively, the individual may find that members in the group are very negative or aggressive. Therefore, the individual's purpose for joining the group is not fulfilled. Lurking is, thus, not only dependent on the motivations for joining an online group or community but also on a range of situational factors within the group itself. Therefore, lurking is argued to be a more complex and more nuanced activity than previously considered (Yeow et al., 2006), refuting the notion that all lurkers are simply "freeloaders."

Apart from moving between passive and active participation, active members can also become passive over time if they become less enthusiastic or if they become bored with the dynamics of the online group. Additionally, members may appear on the surface to be inactive, but this may be because for all intents and purposes they are no longer a member of the group, but just have not withdrawn their membership status. Thus, consideration of personal and situational determinants is important to understand both active and passive participation at various stages of group membership.

Motivations for Lurking

Sun, Rau, and Ma (2014) established a conceptual framework outlining four factors influencing online participation that could be applied to understand motivations for lurking. The factors include: (i) personal characteristics, (ii) the nature of the online community (iii) commitment to the group and (iv) privacy concerns.

Personal characteristics include the goals individuals aim to achieve by joining an online group. This can include a desire for *information exchange, social interactions* (e.g., friendship in personal interest groups), or *support* (e.g., health or occupational groups) (Ridings & Gefen, 2004). The desire to fulfill informational needs above social needs may lead to different expectations about group participation and, in turn, drives behavior. For example, lurkers indicate that the information they obtain within groups is more important than social interaction as their needs are satisfied from reading content posted by others (Nonnecke & Preece, 2003; Nonnecke et al., 2004).

Lurkers in social networking sites also believed that their social or emotional needs would not be satisfied if they posted (Rau, Gao, & Ding, 2008). In contrast to this, active users tended to be attracted to more extroverted activities that hold social benefits such as professional networking and offering expertise (Nonnecke et al., 2004; Tonteri, Kosonen, Ellonen, & Tarkiainen, 2011), and are more likely to be motivated by altruism and reputation (Horng, 2016). This suggests that, rather than actively deciding not to participate in a group, lurkers may simply be unmotivated to participate as their goals are met through passive use. This may also help to explain variations in lurking behavior across different online contexts, such as the significantly higher prevalence rate of lurking in a software support community compared to a health support community (Nonnecke & Preece, 2001). It is logical to consider that individuals trying to fix a software issue are present in the software support community to find information that would assist in solving the specific problem they are experiencing, while individuals visiting a health community may also desire emotional support and, therefore, richer social exchanges. Furthermore, individuals may also have different sets of needs at different times, which can also help to explain variations in levels of engagement within communities. For example, at the onset of illness people may be more in need of emotional support and may thus be more likely to actively participate in an online group, whereas later on they may be more in need of informational support relating to medication adherence or treatment and may thus be less likely to participate (or "lurk") in an online group (Fullwood, 2016). Therefore, lurking behavior can be attributed to the Uses and Gratifications approach (Blumler & Katz, 1974), as individuals use media to gratify their very unique set of needs; in turn, those needs shape their use of the medium (Orchard & Fullwood, 2010).

Personal characteristics also include the personality traits of users. Research has found that introversion influences participation (Ross et al., 2009) and that extroverts engage in more social online behaviors and are more likely to voice their opinions than introverts (Nov, Arazy, López, & Brusilovsky, 2013). Others have found that agreeableness (associated with co-operation, consideration, and warmth) is linked to the motivation to help others—leading to active use, while conscientiousness (associated with diligence, meticulousness, and attentiveness) is linked to the motivation of finding useful information—leading to passive use (Cullen & Morse, 2011). Those high in neuroticism (associated with moodiness and anxiety) were also found to be less likely to actively engage in online communities (Cullen & Morse, 2011). It may be that neurotic individuals have higher concern for their privacy and may not wish to self-disclose, or they may have a higher concern for how others may respond to their posts.

Another personal characteristic that guides active or passive participation is technological self-efficacy. Self-efficacy relates to an individual's self-confidence and belief about their capabilities of enacting specific behaviors (Bandura, 1977, 1993). Those with higher technological self-efficacy tend to be more confident in engaging in various online spaces, and believe that their posts provide useful information that will be viewed positively by other users (Sun, Rau, & Ma, 2014). Linked to this, a strong positive relationship has been found between lurking and computer anxiety (Osatuyi, 2015). Thus, in addition to gratifying particular needs, individual differences and self-efficacy also contribute to varied participation in online groups.

The second component of the framework suggests that the nature of the online group, such as group identity, reciprocity, and reputation, will influence users' desires to contribute to the group. Zhou (2011) found that the social identity of the group impacts on user participation. The reputation of the group was also an important determinant, as those who wanted to earn respect from others in the group were more likely to contribute to groups with a high reputation (Lakhani & Von Hippel, 2003). Poor quality of messages and low response rates in an online group were also found to impact users' willingness to participate (Wise, Hamman, & Thorson, 2006). Thus, group characteristics and dynamics also influence user willingness to contribute.

Thirdly, user participation in online groups can evolve over time as individuals take on different roles within the community, and as they potentially become more committed to the group (Schneider, Von Krogh, & Jäger, 2013). Commitment to the group can solidify active participation, while lower commitment can lead to reduced contributions over time. Finally, privacy concerns also influence participation. Individuals are more likely to participate if they consider the community to be secure and reliable (Sun et al., 2014), and are more likely to lurk if they are worried about their privacy (Du, 2006; Osatuyi, 2015).

This section highlights that a range of intrinsic (e.g., personal characteristics of the individual) and extrinsic (e.g., the nature of the community) motivations can impact the extent of user participation. This links to self-determination theory (SDT), which posits that individuals are driven by intrinsic and extrinsic sources of motivation related to fulfilling three basic psychological needs: competence, autonomy, and relatedness (for further reading see Deci & Ryan, 2000, 2008, 2011), and the same can explain active and passive online behaviors.

Effects of Lurking

While participation in groups is seen to enhance social capital in offline contexts (e.g., Cullen & Sommer, 2011), research into online communities suggests that these benefits are observed more in active participants than lurkers (Laine, Ercal, & Luo, 2011).

However, other studies have shown that lurkers are as well informed and familiar with group dynamics as active users (Edelmann, 2013). In fact, many lurkers considered themselves community members (Nonnecke et al., 2004) as interaction with the content created by others can make them feel connected to the group (Tonteri et al., 2011). Lurking can also result in vicarious support obtained through the content posted by others without the need for self-disclosure (Walther & Boyd, 2002). This may be particularly attractive to some users, particularly those with higher privacy concerns. However, the effects of lurking are likely to vary depending on the nature of the online community. The following sections consider lurking in more detail in the context of health and education by exploring the motivations and outcomes of lurking behaviors in these domains.

Lurking in Online Support Groups and Health Forums

Online health groups and communities not only provide a wealth of information but they also offer a means of social support to users by connecting individuals who may have similar health concerns (see the chapter "Online Support Communities" by Coulson, this volume). Using online support groups allows individuals to engage in discussions with others through chat rooms, discussion boards, and forums in order to share stories, advice, and offer support. For many users, connecting through shared experiences with others is the key reason for engaging in health-related groups and communities (Oh, Lauckner, Boehmer, Fewins-Bliss, & Li, 2013). Although information-seeking in relation to health is widespread, active use of online support groups through social exchange is less common (Van Uden-Kraan et al., 2009). The following sections outline the predictors of active or passive engagement in the context of online support groups in more detail as well as the outcomes associated with active or passive use.

Predictors of Active or Passive Participation in Online Support Groups

Chung (2014) outlined three key motivations for engagement in online support groups: (i) motivations for social interaction, (ii) motivation for information seeking, and (iii) the need for emotional support. These motivations guide the extent to which individuals engage in online support groups, and the features they use on these sites. For example, those with a strong motivation for social interaction and emotional support were found to be more likely to engage in one-to-one conversations with other users and were more likely to self-disclose, while those with a strong motivation for information seeking were less focused on the social networking features and focused more on discussion board features of online support groups, where information is more likely to be exchanged (Chung, 2014). Thus, motivations for use are crucial in understanding active and passive participation in online health behaviors.

Available offline social support can also impact on the extent to which individuals are motivated to engage in online support groups. Two competing perspectives exist in relation to this: social enhancement and social compensation. Social enhancement relates to the idea that those who already have sufficient social and instrumental support offline may be driven to enhance these resources even further by seeking out online interactions (Kraut et al., 2002). Social compensation, on the other hand, argues that those who have fewer resources available offline may compensate for this by seeking out these resources online (McKenna & Bargh, 1998). Han, Hou, Kim, and Gustafson (2014) considered these models in the context of an online cancer support group and found evidence for both. The findings showed that lurkers were more likely to live alone than active participants in the group, suggesting support for the social enhancement explanation. However, social compensation was also supported as individuals were more likely to engage in online support groups (at least in the short term) if they were depressed, and/or had less knowledge about cancer and lower perceived social support offline (Han et al., 2014). This highlights that participation in online support groups can fulfill different functions depending on social and psychological factors, and that these factors may not be barriers but rather motivators to interact with others (Han et al., 2012).

Outcomes of Active and Passive Participation in Online Support Groups

Engagement in online support groups has been associated with numerous positive outcomes, including social and emotional support and information and advice about illness (Nimrod, 2016). It has also been linked to increased optimism about one's condition (due to learning about positive experiences of others), increased mood and coping, empowerment, higher confidence in relationships with doctors and treatment, as well as self-esteem and well-being (Nimrod, 2016; Van Uden Kraan et al., 2008).

The benefits of online support groups, however, may also differ based on active or passive participation (Tanis, Das, & Fortgens-Sillmann, 2011), although the findings in this area are mixed. Malik and Coulson (2011) found that both active and passive users in an infertility group received benefits from group membership and there was no difference in loneliness, social support, infertility-related stress, or marital satisfaction between them. Similarly, according to Mo and Coulson (2010), there was no difference between lurkers and posters in online support groups in relation to self-care, self-efficacy, loneliness, depression, or optimism. However, this study also found that lurkers reported significantly lower scores on measures of perceived social support and satisfaction with relationships with other group members compared to posters (Mo & Coulson, 2010). Some argue that the process of formulating replies and explaining personal experiences and emotions can be an important contributor to the benefits obtained from using online support groups and working through feelings via self-reflection (Han et al., 2011; Pennebaker, 1997). In addition, offering support to others can also serve to enhance an individual's self-worth, belonging, and sense of purpose (Fullwood, 2016; Taylor & Turner, 2001). Thus, while lurkers may feel equally informed and emotionally supported as more active members through reading messages and learning the perspectives of others (Mo & Coulson, 2010; Van Uden-Kraan et al., 2008), active members are likely to obtain additional benefits (Nimrod, 2016). For example, Barak and Dolev-Cohen (2006) found that the higher an individual's activity level, the lower the level of distress experienced a few months later. Moreover, on a practical level, participation in online support groups was linked to greater adherence to health goals and for a longer period of time than non-participation (Richardson et al., 2010). This could be due to receiving continued encouragement from group members. Thus, while online support groups are beneficial to both active and passive users, it is likely that engagement within these groups or communities may enhance benefits, particularly in the long term.

LURKING IN E-LEARNING ENVIRONMENTS

Internet-based electronic learning (e-learning) systems have revolutionized education, challenging institutions to develop pedagogies and practices which are more student-focused, flexible, and personalized (Wanner & Palmer, 2015). Over the past decade or so, e-learning has radically impacted how students learn at all stages of education (Moller, Foshay, & Huett, 2008). At the most rudimentary level, the Internet creates opportunities to learn in ways which would have been impossible without it and, most importantly, time and location now place far fewer restrictions on access to education (Garrison & Kanuka, 2004).

Evidence supports the notion that universities and other learning establishments are rapidly embracing "blended" or "hybrid" learning, i.e., the integration of online learning with traditional face-to-face methods (Goeman & Van Laer, 2012; Moskal, Dziuban, & Hartman, 2013). Furthermore, this now reflects the learning experiences for the vast majority of students in higher education, at least in more developed and industrialized nations (Johnson, Adams Becker, Estrada, & Freeman, 2015; NMC Horizon Report, 2015). The fact that aspects of a course may be delivered online makes it easier to balance other commitments, such as work and family life, with studying (Deschacht & Goeman, 2015; Vaughan, 2007). A number of factors have been proposed as drivers for the blended learning boom, including a demand for more accessible courses (Johnson, Adams, & Cummins, 2012; NMC Horizon Report, 2015), a more technologically savvy/digitally literate generation who desire to use their own devices during their learning (NMC Horizon Report, 2015), economic constraints, for instance, tighter budgets for universities and rising tuition fees (Allen & Seaman, 2013; Desai, Hart, & Richards, 2008), as well as evolving pedagogical approaches to teaching and learning (Allen & Seaman, 2013).

Advantages and Disadvantages to Blended Learning Approaches

As the vast majority of students' higher education experiences will involve e-learning environments, discussing the merits and drawbacks of this approach may help to elucidate why some learners do not actively participate in online learning environments. One of the most cited disadvantages to online interactions is the paucity of social communication cues. For instance, non-verbal signals such as facial expressions and eye gaze cannot be communicated within the asynchronous, text-only discussion forums regularly found on Virtual Learning Environments (VLEs) like Blackboard or Canvas (Hill, Song, & West, 2009; Mazuro & Rao, 2011). There is abundant evidence that these cues play a significant role in human communication (e.g., see Argyle, 2013). Even online media that provides access to visual information (e.g., videoconferencing services like Skype) are not the same as face-to-face interaction, and there is ample evidence to suggest that non-verbal signals, although present, may be attenuated and therefore do not have the same performative impact (e.g., see Fullwood, 2007; Fullwood & Finn, 2010).

The fact that this important social information is filtered out in computer-mediated communication (CMC) convinced early researchers that online interactions were less friendly, colder, more impersonal, more task-focused, and more business-like in nature (Hiltz, Johnson, & Turoff, 1986; Rice & Love, 1987). More recent theoretical perspectives, however (e.g., Social Information Processing theory, Walther, 2008), argue that the more individuals are highly motivated to manage the impressions of others and develop relationships online, the more they are likely to compensate when certain cues are missing, i.e., gathering and interpreting social information from other cues available online. These cues include language choice, the use of emoticons, or other forms of "textspeak" (Fullwood, Quinn, Chen-Wilson, Chadwick, & Reynolds, 2015). Notwithstanding this perspective, CMC still creates a social distance between the student and his or her lecturers and peers, and may be one reason why drop-out rates tend to be higher on courses which are exclusively or predominantly delivered online. These students are more likely to report feeling isolated and unsupported compared to students who attend in person (e.g., see Deschacht & Goeman, 2015; Diaz, 2000; Frankola, 2001; Levy, 2007). However, it is also important to acknowledge that the backgrounds of students signing up for online courses, or courses which have a higher online component, tend to be quite different, on average, to those who take "traditional" courses. For example, they may be more likely to have disabilities, come from lower socioeconomic backgrounds, be mature, or have dependents (Dekker, Pechenizkiy, & Vleeshouwers, 2009; Diaz, 2000; Rivera & Rice, 2002). Therefore, this must also be factored in to the equation when trying to explain attrition rates.

The educational advantages of blended or online learning approaches are well documented in the academic literature. For instance, via VLEs students can access learning resources at their own convenience (Garrison & Kanuka, 2004; Mazuro & Rao, 2011) so they can learn at a pace that is comfortable for them (Belfi et al., 2015), and develop higher levels of independence (Ginns, Prosser, & Barrie, 2007). E-learning widens participation (Davies & Graff, 2005), and asynchronous discussion forums can promote group learning, collaboration and communication skills (Fåhræus, 2004; Mazuro & Rao, 2011). Additionally, setting online discussion tasks can enable the development of higher order thinking skills because students are permitted time to reflect upon their contributions before making them (Cooner, 2010; Mazuro & Rao, 2011). Furthermore, according to the Online Disinhibition Effect, there is an expectation that online spaces are more egalitarian and socially liberating because cues to status and authority will be minimized (Suler, 2004). Theoretically, then, students who are shy or socially anxious would feel more comfortable contributing here than face to face. Although the research evidence for the impact of blended learning on actual student performance is somewhat mixed, a recent meta-analysis by Liu and colleagues (2016) supports the general perspective that blended learning approaches lead to more effective educational outcomes than non-blended instruction. However, the authors advise caution in interpreting these data given that different institutions will adopt blended learning in quite different ways, including the relative proportion of online versus offline activities and the specific tasks that students perform online between courses, which may be sources of heterogeneity.

Predictors of Active and Passive Participation in e-Learning Environments

There is the argument that delivering learning online allows less independent or less motivated students to hide in the background or refrain from active participation. In the physical classroom, educators can call upon non-participating students to encourage them to join in class discussions, but this may be more difficult to achieve online. In e-learning environments there is considerable variation in terms of the amount (and quality) of contributions students make (Davies & Graff, 2005; Giesbers, Rienties, Tempelaar, & Gijselaers, 2013). One explanation that may account for such a large variation in students' involvement in e-learning environments might lie in the individual differences of learners in their levels of motivation. Some learners are much more autonomous or intrinsically motivated than others, and are likely to engage in learning activities of all types simply because they find learning an enjoyable and challenging experience (Black & Deci, 2000; Giesbers et al., 2013). On the other hand, other learners may be more extrinsically focused and may require larger amounts of support and encouragement to participate, partly because they may feel that they have less control over the learning process (Giesbers et al., 2013).

Referring back to SDT (Deci & Ryan, 2008), three basic needs should be met in order for students to feel sufficiently motivated and happy to engage in the learning process. Students need to feel a level of control over their learning experience, connected to their fellow learners and teachers, and that they have the necessary skills and abilities to perform the learning tasks set for them. Furthermore, the extent to which these needs are satisfied will fluctuate according to contextual factors, for example, deadlines, quality of learning material, support given by teachers, and so on (Giesbers et al., 2013; Ryan & Deci, 2000). Research has found that levels of participation in e-learning environments can be predicted by the extent to which a student is extrinsically or intrinsically motivated (e.g., Fırat, Kılınç, & Yüzer, 2018; Vanslambrouck, Zhu, Lombaerts, Philipsen, & Tondeur, 2018; Waheed, Kaur, Ain, & Hussain, 2016). Lurkers may be more likely to have extrinsically focused motivations, and may feel less autonomous, less included, and that they have less control over their learning (Giesbers et al., 2013; Rienties et al., 2009). Although students will likely differ in their motivation levels, the implication is that through supporting students to become more autonomous, to feel more included, and to feel that they have more control over their learning, lurkers may be transformed into more active participants (Giesbers et al., 2013).

A further theoretical perspective which may help to explain lurking in an educational context is the Technology Acceptance Model (TAM) (Davis, 1989). The basic premise of TAM is that intention to use and actual engagement with any form of technology (including e-learning platforms) can be predicted by two factors: perceived ease of use (i.e., the extent to which a student might find using e-learning systems intuitive and uncomplicated) and perceived usefulness (i.e., the extent to which a learner might feel that engaging with an e-learning system will aid them to learn and improve their educational performance). Evidence in the academic literature supports the notion that TAM is a good predictor of students' intention to engage with e-learning platforms (e.g., Park, 2009) as well as their actual levels of participation (e.g., Van Raaij & Schepers, 2008). However, when applying TAM and SDT to understanding lurking behavior, the implication is that some learners lurk because extrinsic factors (e.g., lack of support) may be inhibiting their participation. However, as mentioned, many lurkers may specifically avoid making direct contributions because they are engaging in goal-directed behavior. In other words, they take what they need from existing contributions without feeling it valuable to them to add to the discourse. In this sense, some lurkers may be taking a more strategic approach to their education and choosing which activities they engage in based on their perceptions of what would most benefit their academic progression and performance (Mazuro & Rao, 2011). This is certainly not surprising in the current education climate where many students will need to balance working and family lives with their education.

Outcomes of Active and Passive Participation on Education Success

Generally, levels of student engagement have been shown to be a strong predictor of academic performance; unsurprisingly, students who put more effort into their studies are likely to achieve better grades (e.g., Hughes, Luo, Kwok, & Loyd, 2008; Ladd & Dinella, 2009). Similarly, there is some evidence to suggest that those who lurk on e-learning platforms receive poorer grades than those who actively post, and that the number of posts that lurkers read is also not related to academic performance (Palmer, Holt, & Bray, 2008). This suggests that even those lurkers who are more actively engaged in their learning are not benefitting substantially from sitting in the background. Although there is the argument that academic ability could be a mediator to this relationship (i.e., better students are just more motivated to engage in all aspects of learning), further evidence from the same study suggests that prior academic ability also predicted a student's final grade on the module, but, crucially, did not correlate with the number of posts made. In other words, both of these variables are significant predictors of academic performance independent of one another.

There is also evidence to support the perspective that lurkers are not at an educational disadvantage compared to active participants. Beaudoin (2002) categorized students into three groups depending on their level of engagement in an online course. High-visibility students were those who logged at least 1,000 words in one of the two one-week online conferences; low-visibility students were those who registered no log ins to one of the online conferences; and no-visibility students were those who did not log in to either of the two conferences. Although the sample size was fairly modest (n=55), the preliminary findings showed that despite a difference in educational outcomes when comparing high-visibility students with no-visibility, there was no difference between the high- and low-visibility students. This suggests that even when students do not actively contribute to discussions, some form of learning is still taking place.

In a much larger study of 513 students using the VLE platform Blackboard, Webb and colleagues (2004) noted that both the number of "accesses" and the number of "posts" made by students significantly and positively related to student grades. The worst-performing students were those who never accessed the VLE and made no contributions at all. Although this might suggest that regularly accessing material and contributing to asynchronous discussions leads to improved academic performance, it is also further evidence to support the notion that "lurking" is still some form of "working" and can have some educational benefits (Mazuro & Rao, 2011). Mazuro and Rao (2011) also argue that non-participation may be characteristic of students who simply fail to engage with their studies generally. In this sense, the contention is that, although students who participate on all levels are likely to benefit most, lurking in e-learning contexts should not be viewed as entirely negative. Furthermore, posting does not necessarily imply that students are getting the most out of their learning experience. For example, Dennen (2008) found that some students focus on posting messages more than reading them because they may be motivated to fulfill course requirements. These students tend to have fewer positive perceptions regarding the impact of e-learning activity on their learning. Prolific posting is one thing, but the quality of the posts is another matter entirely.

RECOMMENDATIONS FOR ENGAGING LURKERS

Even though lurkers may still obtain positive benefits from participating in online communities, they should still be encouraged to participate in a more active sense whenever possible. Indeed, evidence suggests that students who participate on all levels get the most out of their education; this is also true of e-learning aspects (Webb, Jones, Barker, & van Schaik, 2004) and that active participators in online support groups are more likely to adhere to their health goals (Richardson et al., 2010). At the very least, more contributions will always add richness to any online community due to an escalation in the number of ideas, viewpoints, and experiences shared (Fullwood, 2016).

A number of strategies could be considered to encourage active participation from students in e-learning environments. First, educators should consider the relative benefits of engaging students in synchronous (i.e., taking place in real time) versus asynchronous (i.e., taking place outside of real time) discussions and may want to incorporate both into their lesson plans. Although asynchronous communication has the advantage of permitting students time to reflect on their contributions, which has been argued contributes to the development of higher order thinking skills (Cooner, 2010; Mazuro & Rao, 2011), synchronous communication has been shown to increase motivation for learning because students feel less restricted by course content and can more easily work in a collaborative way (Hrastinski, 2008). Referring back to the ideas proposed by Giesbers et al. (2013), synchronous modes of communication (e.g., videoconferencing or instant messaging) in which educators are directly involved may have a positive impact on students' motivation levels, and as feedback is provided instantaneously, this may affect a student's sense of competency. Additionally, particularly in a videoconferencing context, communication should be more personal and may positively affect a student's sense of relatedness. Finally, a student's sense of autonomy may be influenced by peers and educators who provide opportune process-related feedback. Moreover, it might also be more difficult for students to hide from the group in synchronous modes of communication given that lack of participation will be more immediately obvious to other contributors (Carr et al., 2004).

A further recommendation for encouraging participation from lurkers includes using "students as facilitators" in order to entice fellow students into contributing to online discussions. The idea here is that students might feel less intimidated sharing their thoughts with fellow students than with their lecturers. Hew and Cheung (2008) discuss a variety of successful student facilitation techniques, the most fruitful of which involved the student facilitator indicating their stance on a topic when they responded to another post or started a new thread. For example, beginning a reply with "I think that…" or "I'm not sure I agree with this because…" may help to put other potential contributors at ease in knowing that it is acceptable to share personal opinions. Mazuro and Rao (2011) note, however, that this strategy will not always lead to success, particularly if the student feels that his or her opinion is very different from the posters. This may have the effect of discouraging involvement. In order to counteract the potential for hostility that differing viewpoints can sometimes evoke, Mazuro and Rao (2011) discuss the importance of establishing ground rules for appropriate behavior, such as clarifying at the outset that differences in opinion are natural, and that contributors should be respectful of viewpoints that differ from their own. Finally, educators may elicit contributions from quieter students by asking them questions directly, or personally inviting them to post.

In terms of online support groups, non-participation can become problematic when a large proportion of group members do not make any contributions, and individuals do not receive responses to their messages. This not only affects the group dynamics and the level of support offered, but also prevents members from accessing a variety of views and opinions. Encouraging participation in online support groups, therefore, is an important part of ensuring success of the online community. Group moderators can play a significant role here by providing information about the group when new members join and actively encouraging them to post. Moreover, moderators can create an incentive for participation, e.g., posting a list of top contributors to the site (Fullwood, 2016). Ensuring quick responses to new members is also important in motivating engagement. Finally, creating separate groups for newcomers within an online community can encourage participation early on. As individuals may still be learning about the larger group dynamics, participation with other new members can foster commitment to the group and act as a stepping stone to interaction with more experienced group members.

CONCLUSION

Lurking, or passive online participation, has previously been considered a negative online behavior, with individuals drawing upon the social capital in an online environment without providing anything in return. However, current literature exposes the nuances and complexity of this online behavior with both personal and situational factors contributing to active or passive online participation. Indeed, not only do individuals vary with regard to their participation across different groups, but they can also shift between active or passive participation depending on their current goals and motivations. Reasons for joining a group vary from seeking information to social interaction or support, and the extent to which these goals can be gratified through active or passive participation affect the user's engagement. Therefore, it is argued that lurking is a strategic and goal-driven process (Preece et al., 2004; Nonnecke & Preece, 2003). In addition to an individual's goals, their individual differences, self-efficacy, and privacy concerns have also been shown to impact their levels of online participation. Moreover, situational factors such as the group dynamics, reputation, and the user's commitment to the group also influence users' willingness to participate. Thus, myriad factors contribute to active and passive participation in various online spaces and combine to influence individuals' intrinsic and extrinsic motivation to participate. As such, lurking may simply be another form of engagement in online spaces. With regard to the outcomes of active and passive use, studies have shown that both active and passive participation in online communities is associated with benefits to group members, although there is also evidence to suggest that active members obtain additional benefits through their interactions with others. This includes higher social support in the context of health or potentially higher academic performance in the context of e-learning. As such, enhancing participation is recommended, particularly in the context of online support and e-learning.

References

Allen, I. E., & Seaman, J. (2013). *Changing Course: Ten years of tracking online education in the United States*. Oaklandm CA: Babson Survey Research Group and Quahog Research Group. Retrieved from http://files.eric.ed.gov/fulltext/ED541571.pdf

Argyle, M. (2013). *Bodily communication*. New York: Routledge.

Bandura, A. (1977). Self-efficacy: Toward a unifying theory of behavioral change. *Psychological Review 84*(2), 191.

Bandura, A. (1993). Perceived self-efficacy in cognitive development and functioning. *Educational Psychologist 28*(2), 117–148.

Barak, A., & Dolev-Cohen, M. (2006). Does activity level in online support groups for distressed adolescents determine emotional relief. *Counselling and Psychotherapy Research 6*(3), 186–190.

Beaudoin, M. F. (2002). Learning or lurking? Tracking the "invisible" online student. *The Internet and Higher Education 5*(2), 147–155.

Belfi, L. M., Bartolotta, R. J., Giambrone, A. E., Davi, C., & Min, R. J. (2015). "Flipping" the introductory clerkship in radiology: Impact on medical student performance and perceptions. *Academic Radiology 22*(6), 794–801.

Black, A. E., & Deci, E. L. (2000). The effects of instructors' autonomy support and students' autonomous motivation on learning organic chemistry: A self-determination theory perspective. *Science Education 84*(6), 740–756.

Blumler, J. G., & Katz, E. (Eds.) (1974). *The Uses of Mass Communications: Current Perspectives on Gratifications Research. Sage Annual Reviews of Communication Research Volume III*. Beverly Hills, CA: Sage.

Bryant, S. L., Forte, A., & Bruckman, A. (2005). Becoming Wikipedian: Transformation of participation in a collaborative online encyclopedia. In *Proceedings of the 2005 International ACM SIGGROUP conference on Supporting group work* (pp. 1–10) 6–9 November, Sanibel Island, FL. New York: ACM.

Burke, M., Marlow, C., & Lento, T. (2009). Feed me: Motivating newcomer contribution in social network sites. In *Proceedings of the SIGCHI conference on human factors in computing systems* (pp. 945–954), 4–9 April, Boston, MA. New York: ACM.

Carr, T., Cox, L., Eden, N., & Hanslo, M. (2004). From peripheral to full participation in a blended trade bargaining simulation. *British Journal of Educational Technology 35*(2), 197–211.

Chung, J. E. (2014). Social networking in online support groups for health: How online social networking benefits patients. *Journal of Health Communication 19*(6), 639–659.

Coleman, J. S. (1988). Social capital in the creation of human capital. *The American Journal of Sociology 94*, 95–120.

Cooner, T. S. (2010). Creating opportunities for students in large cohorts to reflect in and on practice: Lessons learnt from a formative evaluation of students' experiences of a technology-enhanced blended learning design. *British Journal of Educational Technology 41*(2), 271–286.

Cullen, R., & Morse, S. (2011). Who's contributing: Do personality traits influence the level and type of participation in online communities. In *2011 44th Hawaii International Conference on System Sciences (HICSS)* (pp. 1–11). 4–7 January, Kauai, Hawaii. New York: IEEE.

Cullen, R., & Sommer, L. (2011). Participatory democracy and the value of online community networks: An exploration of online and offline communities engaged in civil society and political activity. *Government Information Quarterly 28*(2), 148–154.

Davies, J., & Graff, M. (2005). Performance in e-learning: Online participation and student grades. *British Journal of Educational Technology 36*(4), 657–663.

Davis, F. D. (1989). Perceived usefulness, perceived ease of use, and user acceptance of information technology. *MIS Quarterly 13*(3), 319–340.

Deci, E. L., & Ryan, R. M. (2000). The "what" and "why" of goal pursuits: Human needs and the self-determination of behavior. *Psychological Inquiry 11*(4), 227–268.

Deci, E. L., & Ryan, R. M. (2008). Self-Determination Theory: A Macrotheory of Human Motivation, Development, and Health. *Canadian Psychology 49*(3): 182–185.

Deci, E. L., & Ryan, R. M. (2011). Self-determination theory. In P. A. M Van Lange, A. W. Kruglanski, and E. T. Higgens (Eds.), *Handbook of Theories of Social Psychology Vol. 1* (pp. 416–433). London: Sage.

Dekker, G., Pechenizkiy, M., & Vleeshouwers, J. (2009). Predicting students drop out: A case study. In *Proceedings of the Second International Conference on Educational Data Mining (EDM)* (pp. 41–50), 1–3 July, Cordoba, Spain. Worcester, MA: IEDMS.

Dennen, V. P. (2008). Pedagogical lurking: Student engagement in non-posting discussion behavior. *Computers in Human Behavior 24*(4), 1624–1633.

Desai, M. S., Hart, J., & Richards, T. C. (2008). E-learning: Paradigm shift in education. *Education 129*(2), 327–335.

Deschacht, N., & Goeman, K. (2015). The effect of blended learning on course persistence and performance of adult learners: A difference-in-differences analysis. *Computers & Education 87*, 83–89.

Diaz, D. P. (2000). *Comparison of student characteristics, and evaluation of student success, in an online health education course* (Unpublished doctoral dissertation) Southeastern University, Fort Lauderdale, Florida.

Du, Y. (2006). Modeling the behavior of lurkers in online communities using intentional agents. In *International Conference on Computational Intelligence for Modelling Control and Automation and International Conference on Intelligent Agents, Web Technologies and Internet Commerce CIMCA '06* (p. 60). 28 November–1 December, Sydney, NSW, Australia. New York: IEEE.

Edelmann, N. (2013). Reviewing the definitions of "lurkers" and some implications for online research. *Cyberpsychology, Behavior & Social Networking 16*(9), 645–649.

Fåhræus, E. R. (2004). Distance education students moving towards collaborative learning-A field study of Australian distance education students and systems. *Journal of Educational Technology & Society 7*(2), 129–140.

Fırat, M., Kılınç, H., & Yüzer, T. V. (2018). Level of intrinsic motivation of distance education students in e-learning environments. *Journal of Computer Assisted Learning 34*(1), 63–70.

Frankola, K. (2001). Why online learners drop out. *Workforce 80*(10), 53–59.

Fullwood, C. (2007). The effect of mediation on impression formation: A comparison of face-to-face & video-mediated conditions. *Applied Ergonomics 38*, 267–273.

Fullwood, C. (2016). Online support groups: Enhancing the user experience with cyberpsychological theory. In A. Attrill & C. Fullwood (Eds.), *Applied Cyberpsychology: Practical applications of cyberpsychological research and theory*. New York: Palgrave Macmillan.

Fullwood, C., & Finn, M. (2010). Video-mediated communication and impression formation: An integrative review. In A. C. Rayler (Ed.), *Videoconferencing: Technology, Impact and Applications* (pp. 35–55). Hauppauge, NY: Nova Science.

Fullwood, C., Quinn, S., Chen-Wilson, J., Chadwick, D., & Reynolds, K. (2015). Put on a smiley face: Textspeak and personality perceptions. *Cyberpsychology, Behavior, and Social Networking 18*(3), 147–151.

Garrison, D. R., & Kanuka, H. (2004). Blended learning: Uncovering its transformative potential in higher education. *The Internet and Higher Education 7*(2), 95–105.

Giesbers, B., Rienties, B., Tempelaar, D., & Gijselaers, W. (2013). Investigating the relations between motivation, tool use, participation, and performance in an e-learning course using web-videoconferencing. *Computers in Human Behavior 29*(1), 285–292.

Ginns, P., Prosser, M., & Barrie, S. (2007). Students' perceptions of teaching quality in higher education: The perspective of currently enrolled students. *Studies in Higher Education 32*(5), 603–615.

Goeman, K., & Van Laer, S. (2012). Blended multicampus education for lifelong learners. In *The future of learning innovations and learning quality. How do they fit together: Proceedings of the European Conference LINQ 2012* (pp. 97–103). 23 October, Brussels, Belgium. Berlin: Gito.

Golder, S. A., & Donath, J. (2004). Social roles in electronic communities. *Internet Research 5*, 19–22.

Han, J. Y., Hou, J., Kim, E., & Gustafson, D. H. (2014). Lurking as an active participation process: A longitudinal investigation of engagement with an online cancer support group. *Health Communication 29*(9), 911–923.

Han, J. Y., Kim, J. H., Yoon, H. J., Shim, M., McTavish, F. M., & Gustafson, D. H. (2012). Social and psychological determinants of levels of engagement with an online breast cancer support group: Posters, lurkers, and nonusers. *Journal of Health Communication 17*(3), 356–371.

Han, J. Y., Shah, D. V., Kim, E., Namkoong, K., Lee, S. Y., Moon, T. J., Cleland, R., Bu, Q. L., McTavish, F. M....& Gustafson, D. H. (2011). Empathic exchanges in online cancer support groups: Distinguishing message expression and reception effects. *Health Communication 26*(2), 185–197.

Hew, K. F., & Cheung, W. S. (2008). Attracting student participation in asynchronous online discussions: A case study of peer facilitation. *Computers & Education 51*(3), 1111–1124.

Hill, J. R., Song, L., & West, R. E. (2009). Social learning theory and web-based learning environments: A review of research and discussion of implications. *The American Journal of Distance Education 23*(2), 88–103.

Hiltz, S. R., Johnson, K., & Turoff, M. (1986). Experiments in group decision making communication process and outcome in face-to-face versus computerized conferences. *Human communication research 13*(2), 225–252.

Horng, S. M. (2016). A study of active and passive user participation in virtual communities. *Journal of Electronic Commerce Research 17*(4).

Hrastinski, S. (2008). The potential of synchronous communication to enhance participation in online discussions: A case study of two e-learning courses. *Information & Management 45*(7), 499–506.

Hughes, J. N., Luo, W., Kwok, O. M., & Loyd, L. K. (2008). Teacher-student support, effortful engagement, and achievement: A 3-year longitudinal study. *Journal of Educational Psychology 100*(1), 1.

Johnson, L., Adams, S., & Cummins, M. (2012). *Technology outlook for Australian Tertiary Education 2012–2017: An NMC horizon report regional analysis*. Austin, Texas: The New Media Consortium. Accessed on 10/08/2017 Retrieve from https://eric.ed.gov/?id=ED532405

Johnson, L., Adams Becker, S., Estrada, V., and Freeman, A. (2015). NMC Horizon Report: 2015 Higher Education Edition. Austin, Texas: The New Media Consortium. Accessed on 10/08/2017 from http://files.eric.ed.gov/fulltext/ED559357.pdf

Koh, J., Kim, Y. G., Butler, B., & Bock, G. W. (2007). Encouraging participation in virtual communities. *Communications of the ACM 50*(2), 68–73.

Kollock, P., & Smith, M. (1996). Managing the virtual commons. In Susan Herring (Ed.), *Computer-mediated communication: Linguistic, Social, and Cross-Cultural Perspectives* (pp. 109–128). Amsterdam: John Benjamins.

Kraut, R., Kiesler, S., Boneva, B., Cummings, J., Helgeson, V., & Crawford, A. (2002). Internet paradox revisited. *Journal of Social Issues 58*(1), 49–74.

Küçük, M. (2010). Lurking in online asynchronous discussion. *Procedia Social and Behavioural Sciences 2*, 2260–2263.

Ladd, G. W., & Dinella, L. M. (2009). Continuity and change in early school engagement: Predictive of children's achievement trajectories from first to eighth grade? *Journal of Educational Psychology 101*(1), 190.

Laine, M. S. S., Ercal, G., & Luo, B. (2011). User groups in social networks: An experimental study on YouTube. In *2011 44th Hawaii International Conference on System Sciences (HICSS)* (pp. 1–10). 4–7 January, Kauai, Hawaii. New York: IEEE.

Lakhani, K. R., & Von Hippel, E. (2003). How open source software works: "Free" user-to-user assistance. *Research Policy 32*(6), 923–943.

Levy, Y. (2007). Comparing dropouts and persistence in e-learning courses. *Computers & Education 48*(2), 185–204.

Liu, Q., Peng, W., Zhang, F., Hu, R., Li, Y., & Yan, W. (2016). The effectiveness of blended learning in health professions: Systematic review and meta-analysis. *Journal of Medical Internet Research 18*(1), e2. doi: 10.2196/jmir.4807

Malik, S. H., & Coulson, N. S. (2011). A comparison of lurkers and posters within infertility online support groups. *CIN: Computers, Informatics, Nursing 29*(10), 564–573.

Malinen, S. (2015). Understanding user participation in online communities: A systematic literature review of empirical studies. *Computers in Human Behavior, 46*, 228–238.

Mason, B. (1999). Issues in virtual ethnography. In K. Buckner (Ed.), Proceedings of Esprit i3 workshop on ethnographic studies in real and virtual environments: *Inhabited information spaces and connected communities* (pp. 61–69), 24–26 January, Edinburgh, Scotland. New York: ACM.

Mazuro, C., & Rao, N. (2011). Online discussion forums in higher education: Is lurking working. *International Journal for Cross-Disciplinary Subjects in Education 2*(2), 364–371.

McKenna, K. Y., & Bargh, J. A. (1998). Coming out in the age of the Internet: Identity "demarginalization" through virtual group participation. *Journal of Personality and Social Psychology 75*(3), 681.

Mo, P. K., & Coulson, N. S. (2010). Empowering processes in online support groups among people living with HIV/AIDS: A comparative analysis of "lurkers" and "posters." *Computers in Human Behavior 26*, 1183–1193.

Moller, L., Foshay, W. R., & Huett, J. (2008). Implications for instructional design on the potential of the web. *TechTrends, 52*(4), 67.

Moskal, P., Dziuban, C., & Hartman, J. (2013). Blended learning: A dangerous idea? *The Internet and Higher Education 18*, 15–23.

Muller, M. (2012). Lurking as a personal trait or situational disposition? Lurking and contributing in enterprise social media. In *Proceedings of the ACM 2012 conference on Computer Supported Cooperative Work CSCW '12* (pp. 253–256), 11–15 February, Seattle, Washington. New York: ACM.

Neelen, M., & Fetter, S. (2010). Lurking: A challenge or a fruitful strategy? A comparison between lurkers and active participants in an online corporate community of practice. *International Journal of Knowledge and Learning* 6(4), 269–284.

Nimrod, G. (2016). Beneficial participation: Lurking vs. posting in online support groups. In R. Ahmed & Bates, B. R. (Eds.), *Health communication and mass media: An integrated approach to policy and practice* (pp. 81–98). New York: Routledge.

Nonnecke, B., & Preece, J. (2001). Why lurkers lurk. *AMCIS 2001 Proceedings*, 294.

Nonnecke, B., & Preece, J. (2003). Silent participants: Getting to know lurkers better. In C. Lueg & D. Fisher (Eds.), *From Usenet to CoWebs: Interacting with social information spaces* (pp. 110–132). London: Springer Verlag.

Nonnecke, B., Preece, J., & Andrews, D. (2004, January). What lurkers and posters think of each other [online community]. In *Proceedings of the 37th Annual Hawaii International Conference on System Sciences, 2004*. New York: IEEE. doi: 10.1109/HICSS.2004.1265462

Nonnecke, B., Andrews, D., & Preece, J. (2006). Non-public and public online community participation: Needs, attitudes and behavior. *Electronic Commerce Research* 6(1), 7–20.

Nov, O., Arazy, O., López, C., & Brusilovsky, P. (2013, April). Exploring personality-targeted UI design in online social participation systems. In *Proceedings of the SIGCHI Conference on Human Factors in Computing Systems* (pp. 361–370). ACM.

Oh, H. J., Lauckner, C., Boehmer, J., Fewins-Bliss, R., & Li, K. (2013). Facebooking for health: An examination into the solicitation and effects of health-related social support on social networking sites. *Computers in Human Behavior* 29(5), 2072–2080.

Orchard, L. J., & Fullwood, C. (2010). Current perspectives on personality and Internet use. *Social Science Computer Review* 28(2), 155–169.

Osatuyi, B. (2015). Is lurking an anxiety-masking strategy on social media sites? The effects of lurking and computer anxiety on explaining information privacy concern on social media platforms. *Computers in Human Behavior* 49, 324–332.

Palmer, S., Holt, D., & Bray, S. (2008). Does the discussion help? The impact of a formally assessed online discussion on final student results. *British Journal of Educational Technology* 39(5), 847–858.

Park, S. Y. (2009). An analysis of the technology acceptance model in understanding university students' behavioral intention to use e-learning. *Journal of Educational Technology & Society* 12(3), 150.

Pennebaker, J. W. (1997). *Opening up: The healing power of emotional expression*. New York: Guilford.

Preece, J., Nonnecke, B., & Andrews, D. (2004). The top 5 reasons for lurking: Improving community experiences for everyone. Special Issue of *Computers in Human Behavior: An Interdisciplinary Perspective* 20(2), 201–223.

Rau, P. L. P., Gao, Q., & Ding, Y. (2008). Relationship between the level of intimacy and lurking in online social network services. *Computers in Human Behavior* 24(6), 2757–2770.

Rice, R. E., & Love, G. (1987). Electronic emotion: Socioemotional content in a computer-mediated communication network. *Communication Research* 14(1), 85–108.

Richardson, C. R., Buis, L. R., Janney, A. W., Goodrich, D. E., Sen, A., Hess, M. L., Mehari, K. S., Fortlage, L. A., Resnick, P. J., Zikmund-Fisher, B. J., Strecher, V. J., . . . & Strecher, V. J. (2010). An online community improves adherence in an Internet-mediated walking program. Part 1: Results of a randomized controlled trial. *Journal of Medical Internet Research* 12(4), e71.

Ridings, C. M., & Gefen, D. (2004). Virtual community attraction: Why people hang out online. *Journal of Computer-Mediated Communication* 10(1). doi: 10.1111/j.1083-6101.2004.tb00229.x

Ridings, C., Gefen, D., & Arinze, B. (2006). Psychological barriers: Lurker and poster motivation and behavior in online communities. *Communications of the Association for Information Systems* 18(1), 16.

Rienties, B., Tempelaar, D., Van den Bossche, P., Gijselaers, W., & Segers, M. (2009). The role of academic motivation in computer-supported collaborative learning. *Computers in Human Behavior* 25(6), 1195–1206.

Rivera, J. C., & Rice, M. L. (2002). A comparison of student outcomes & satisfaction between traditional & web-based course offerings. *Online Journal of Distance Learning Administration* 5(3). Retrieved from https://docplayer.net/10007747-A-comparison-of-student-outcomes-satisfaction-between-traditional-web-based-course-offerings.html

Ross, C., Orr, E. S., Sisic, M., Arseneault, J. M., Simmering, M. G., & Orr, R. R. (2009). Personality and motivations associated with Facebook use. *Computers in Human Behavior* 25(2), 578–586.

Ryan, R. M., & Deci, E. L. (2000). Intrinsic and extrinsic motivations: Classic definitions and new directions. *Contemporary educational psychology* 25(1), 54–67.

Schneider, A., Von Krogh, G., & Jäger, P. (2013). "What's coming next?" Epistemic curiosity and lurking behavior in online communities. *Computers in Human Behavior* 29(1), 293–303.

Suler, J. (2004). The online disinhibition effect. *Cyberpsychology & Behavior* 7(3), 321–326.

Sun, N., Rau, P. P. L., & Ma, L. (2014). Understanding lurkers in online communities: A literature review. *Computers in Human Behavior* 38, 110–117.

Tanis, M., Das, E., & Fortgens-Sillmann, M. (2011). Finding care for the caregiver? Active participation in online health forums attenuates the negative effect of caregiver strain on well-being. *Communications* 36(1), 51–66.

Taylor, J., & Turner, R. J. (2001). A longitudinal study of the role and significance of mattering to others for depressive symptoms. *Journal of Health and Social Behavior* 42(3), 310–325.

Tonteri, L., Kosonen, M., Ellonen, H. K., & Tarkiainen, A. (2011). Antecedents of an experienced sense of virtual community. *Computers in Human Behavior* 27(6), 2215–2223.

Van Dijck, J. (2013). *The culture of connectivity: A critical history of social media*. Oxford: Oxford University Press.

Van Raaij, E. M., & Schepers, J. J. L. (2008). The acceptance and use of a virtual learning environment in China. *Computers and Education* 50, 838–852.

Van Uden-Kraan, C. F., Drossaert, C. H. C., Taal, E., Shaw, B. R., Seydel, E. R., & Van de Laar, M. A. F. J. (2008). Empowering processes and outcomes of participation in online support groups for patients with breast cancer, arthritis, or fibromyalgia. *Qualitative Health Research* 18(3), 405–417.

Van Uden-Kraan, C. F., Drossaert, C. H., Taal, E., Smit, W. M., Moens, H. J. B., Siesling, S., Seydel, E.R., & Van de Laar, M. A. (2009). Health-related Internet use by patients with somatic diseases: Frequency of use and characteristics of users. *Informatics for Health and Social Care* 34(1), 18–29.

Vanslambrouck, S., Zhu, C., Lombaerts, K., Philipsen, B., & Tondeur, J. (2018). Students' motivation and subjective task value of participating in online and blended learning environments. *The Internet and Higher Education* 36, 33–40.

Vaughan, N. (2007). Perspectives on blended learning in higher education. *International Journal on eLearning* 6(1), 81.

Waheed, M., Kaur, K., Ain, N., & Hussain, N. (2016). Perceived learning outcomes from Moodle: An empirical study of intrinsic and extrinsic motivating factors. *Information Development* 32(4), 1001–1013.

Walther, J. B. (2008). The social information processing theory of computer-mediated communication. In L. Baxter & D. O. Braithwaite (Eds.), *Engaging theories in interpersonal communication* (pp. 391–404). Newbury Park, CA: Sage.

Walther, J. B., & Boyd, S. (2002). Attraction to computer-mediated social support. In C. Lin & D. Atkin (Eds.), *Communication technology and society: Audience adoption and uses* (pp. 153–188). Cresswell: Hampton Press.

Wanner, T., & Palmer, E. (2015). Personalising learning: Exploring student and teacher perceptions about flexible learning and assessment in a flipped university course. *Computers & Education* 88, 354–369.

Webb, E., Jones, A., Barker, P., & van Schaik, P. (2004). Using e-learning dialogues in higher education. *Innovations in Education and Teaching International* 41(1), 93–103.

Wise, K., Hamman, B., & Thorson, K. (2006). Moderation, response rate, and message interactivity: Features of online communities and their effects on intent to participate. *Journal of Computer-Mediated Communication* 12(1), 24–41.

Yeow, A., Johnson, S. L., & Faraj, S. (2006). Lurking: Legitimate or Illegitimate Peripheral Participation? In *Proceedings of the International Conference of Information Systems, (ICIS 2006)*, 10–13 December, Milwaukee, WI.

Zhou, T. (2011). Understanding online community user participation: A social influence perspective. *Internet Research* 21(1), 67–81.

CHAPTER 16

....

CONCEPTUALIZING ONLINE GROUPS AS MULTIDIMENSIONAL NETWORKS

....

BEI YAN, YOUNG JI KIM,
ANDREA B. HOLLINGSHEAD,
AND DAVID P. BRANDON

INTRODUCTION

....

OUR collective notions of what constitutes a group have changed radically since the rise of information and communication technologies (ICTs). More "traditional" ICTs (e.g. email, instant messaging, videoconferencing) have allowed groups to move away from the conventional "same time, same place" model of face-to-face groups. Ubiquitous computing, wearable technologies, and intelligent machines (e.g. algorithms, virtual assistants, robots) are blurring the boundary between online and offline, and between people and technology. If the earlier generation of ICTs opened group membership to geographically and culturally distributed participants, the recent wave of technological innovation is completely redefining what it means to be an "online" group. Most individuals are constantly connected with the Internet through portable technologies such as smartphones or smart watches, and can interact with multiple social groups in any place and at any time using a wide range of social media and group communication technologies. The distinctions between online and offline groups, and between people and technology, if they still exist, need to be reconsidered.

THE TRANSFORMING NATURE OF ONLINE GROUPS

Since our chapter in the first edition of this volume (Brandon & Hollingshead, 2007), several significant changes have occurred in the social and technological environment surrounding online groups. First, it has become questionable whether truly "offline" groups still exist, and whether it is still meaningful and possible to dichotomize "online" and "offline" (Rainie & Wellman, 2012). One important driving force for this change is the prevalence of social media, and social network sites in particular. Social network sites (SNSs) (e.g. Facebook, Twitter, Instagram) are web-based services where individuals create a public or semi-public profile and share a connection with a list of other users (boyd & Ellison, 2008). They have made it easy not only to form new connections with strangers but also to maintain existing relationships (Ellison, Steinfield, & Lampe, 2007). Interactions utilizing SNSs often do not reside in the online space exclusively, but simultaneously span online and offline (Reyt & Wiesenfeld, 2015). For example, a family celebrating a holiday in the same living room also exists "online" when they post photos and comments about the celebration on their social media groups (Karapanos, Teixeira, & Gouveia, 2016). In organizations, work teams often use cloud-based group software to manage in-person meetings as well.

Another driving force that pushes groups beyond the online–offline dichotomy is the proliferation of mobile devices, which enable individuals to be connected all the time and everywhere. Technologies are embodied and integrated in our physical living environment or physically embodied in hardware (e.g. cleaning robot, Alexa, smart home). Wearable sensing technologies (e.g. Apple Watch, Fitbit) detect physical signals such as body movement and geo location. Some wearable sensors also measure social signals such as the amount of face-to-face interaction, conversational time, and physical proximity to conversational partners, which can be used to predict the nature of social relationships (Pentland, 2008).

The past decade also witnessed the rise of teaming between humans and intelligent machines (Appenzeller, 2017). While technology in groups was conventionally thought of as a somewhat static tool operated by people to facilitate group goals, non-human agents such as virtual assistants or robots are now capable of performing tasks typically thought as "human work," producing new inputs as well as managing and coordinating human group activities (Geiger, 2011; Geiger & Halfaker, 2013; Harbers, Jonker, & van Riemsdijk, 2014). For example, intelligent agents can create content such as news articles or advertisements (Clerwall, 2014), learn by themselves, and sometimes perform better than human peers on some specialized tasks such as chess and Go (Mozur, 2017). Algorithms also co-ordinate human work by assigning tasks and optimizing workflow as commonly seen in industries where distributed work is managed at a large scale (e.g. Uber, Amazon

Mechanical Turk) (Lee, Kusbit, Metsky, & Dabbish, 2015). Termed "algorithmic management," this phenomenon highlights the emerging role of intelligent agents as potential members or even managers of work groups. These social and technological developments not only break the dichotomy between online and offline, but also challenge the assumption that technologies are merely tools that support human work.

While early conceptualization of online groups almost exclusively focused on interactions within the "online" sphere, these multipronged changes in the social and technological environment have at least two important implications for the study of groups. First, the boundary between online and offline groups is no longer clear. At a given time, groups simultaneously use a mix of communication modes and channels. Gibbs and colleagues summarized this phenomenon aptly, suggesting that "[r]ather than being a new and different breed of team, *all* teams can be characterized on a continuum of virtuality" (Gibbs, Nekrassova, Grushina, & Wahab, 2008, p. 191). Second, the distinction between the roles of people and of technology are being contested. Technology has become intelligent and adaptive, actively contributing and interacting with human members on group tasks. Online groups increasingly include members that are intelligent technologies.

These new developments in the digital age necessitate a new perspective and language to describe and capture the nature of online groups. To that end, this chapter conceptualizes online groups as "embedded" multidimensional networks in which group members are connected with technology through multiple relationships and social processes. Our ideas build directly on the social network framework proposed by Contractor, Monge, and Leonardi (2011), but expands their original proposal to understand emerging phenomena around online groups.

Defining Online Groups

In research on the social psychology of groups, the term "group" has traditionally referred to a relatively small number of people interacting for a common goal. This definition was expanded with the rise of new technologies to support communication and collaboration in the 1980s and 1990s to include a classification for "online" groups, i.e. groups whose members were geographically and/or temporally dispersed and communicated using computer technology (Hollingshead & Contractor, 2006). Later, Web 2.0 technologies and cyber infrastructure made large group (or mass) collaboration on a common task or problem possible. Geographical and/or temporal dispersion is no longer a defining trait of online groups. Even groups that fit the traditional definition of a small group—a small number of members who are co-located working on a common goal with frequent face-to-face interaction—often concurrently use technology to augment their collaboration.

Conceptually, it is useful to define a group and its members as a network of agents assembled in pursuit of a common goal or task, where some agents are humans while others are non-human: databases, "bot," and even "embodied agents"—autonomous virtual humans that collect and disseminates information (Hollingshead & Contractor, 2006; Contractor, Monge, & Leonardi, 2011). This definition probably applies to most groups in modern societies, ranging from chat groups or social networks among families, friends, or coworkers, to human-robot teams (Goodrich et al., 2008), to large-scale open collaboration systems such as Wikipedia (Ren & Yan, 2017), and to massive online crowds (e.g. networked publics participating in political protests using social media hashtags). In this definition, we highlight two things: (a) online groups are composed of both human and non-human agents (e.g. robots, algorithms); (b) the key feature of online groups lies in the technology mediation of interaction between group members, although the level of technology mediation varies both within and across groups. This definition allows us to simultaneously consider multiple types of group members (e.g. people and technologies), multiple types of relations among the members, with the addition of contextual influences.

PRIOR RESEARCH ON ONLINE GROUPS: A BRIEF REVIEW

This section briefly reviews research on online groups conducted by group researchers in the fields of social psychology, communication, management, human-computer interaction, and computer-supported co-operative work since our earlier chapter on this topic (Brandon & Hollingshead, 2007). Although group scholars generally acknowledge that all groups have degrees of virtuality (e.g. Bell & Kozlowski, 2002; Brandon & Hollingshead, 2007; Gibson & Gibbs, 2006; Griffith, Sawyer, & Neale, 2003), the distinction between "online" (i.e. virtual, computer-mediated) and "offline" (i.e. face-to-face) groups still persists.

A great deal of research examines how defining characteristics of "online" groups influence group functioning. Researchers have investigated the effects of geographical and temporal dispersion (Bazarova & Walther, 2009; Boh, Ren, Kiesler, & Bussjaeger, 2007; Bosch-Sijtsema, Fruchter, Vartiainen, & Ruohomäki, 2011; Gibson, Gibbs, Stanko, Tesluk, & Cohen, 2011; Rutkowski, Saunders, Vogel, & van Genuchten, 2007); computer-mediation of interaction (Alberici & Milesi, 2016; Dodgson, Gann, & Phillips, 2013); anonymity/lack of feedback (Kahai, 2009); and cultural or other compositional diversity (Cramton & Hinds, 2014; Han & Beyerlein, 2016; Hardin, Fuller, & Davison, 2007; Köhler, Cramton, & Hinds, 2012; Martins & Shalley, 2011; Peters & Karren, 2009) on group-level outcomes. A common methodology is to experimentally compare "online" groups to "offline" groups (Chattopadhyay, George, & Shulman, 2008; van der Kleij, Maarten Schraagen, Werkhoven, & De Dreu, 2009).

Other studies explored various group processes caused or influenced by these features of online groups, including motivation, contribution, and cooperation (Aristeidou, Scanlon, & Sharples, 2017; Baker & Bulkley, 2014; Nambisan & Baron, 2009); trust (Peters & Karren, 2009); identification (Alberici & Milesi, 2016; Bartel, Wrzesniewski, &

Wiesenfeld, 2011; Jans, Leach, Garcia, & Postmes, 2015; Wilson, Crisp, & Mortensen, 2013); conflict (Martínez-Moreno, Zornoza, González-Navarro, & Thompson, 2012); faultlines/subgroup formation (O'Leary & Mortensen, 2009); learning (Dodgson, Gann, & Phillips, 2013); and attention (Haas, Criscuolo, & George, 2015). Still others looked at how different factors and approaches, such as training (Rentsch, Delise, Mello, & Staniewicz, 2014); governance (O'Mahony & Ferraro, 2007); and leadership (Cogliser, Gardner, Gavin, & Broberg, 2012; Dahlander, Klapper, & Piezunka, 2018; Kahai, Huang, & Jestice, 2012) may help resolve challenges in online groups. Whereas many studied zero-history groups, others examined groups in context, such as online support groups (Wang, Kraut, & Levine, 2012), online classes (de Janasz & Godshalk, 2013), and online games (Kim et al., 2017; Shen, Monge, & Williams, 2014).

Closely related to the dichotomy between online and offline is the assumption that online groups can be understood separately from their "offline" environments. Technology challenges the boundary of groups by redefining who constitutes group members (since group members no longer need to be physically present), and making it easy for people to be in multiple groups simultaneously (Beck, Bourdeaux, DiTunnariello, & Paskewitz, 2016). Although the blurred boundary and abundant external ties have been discussed as defining features of virtual collectives (DeSanctis & Monge, 1999), significantly less attention has been paid to the interdependence between online groups and their environment. Among the limited research that has examined the relation between online groups and their offline contexts, Bosch-Sijtsema and colleagues (2011) found that embedding organizations and workspace environment (physical and virtual) had significant impacts on team co-ordination and communication processes. Several teams they studied reported that long-distance communication was hindered by their organization's ICT policy. Research also shows that offline racial identity moderated the relation between resource competition and social distance among group members in online groups even when members interacted through avatars (Tawa, Negrón, Suyemoto, & Carter, 2015). Participation in social media can have negative impact on users' offline political deliberation as well (Hampton, Shin, & Lu, 2017). The above-mentioned evidence demonstrates the close connection between online groups and their embedding context, both online and offline, and highlights the necessity for more research in this area (Wang, Butler, & Ren, 2012).

Furthermore, most prior research considered groups as only consisting of human members (Baruah & Paulus, 2016; Hardin, Fuller, & Davison, 2007; Martins & Shalley, 2011). While acknowledging technology mediation as the defining feature of online groups, researchers either did not explicitly address the role of technology in online groups (Martins & Shalley, 2011), or considered technology to be a passive tool used by people to assist group functioning and achieve group goals (Erhardt, Gibbs, Martin-Rios, & Sherblom, 2016; Paulus, Kohn, Arditti, & Korde, 2013). These conceptualizations delineate a clear distinction between people and technology. Yet with ubiquitous computing and emergence of artificial intelligence, technology may no longer be considered as a passive tool to human members, but can play an active role in group interaction and task management (Geiger & Halfaker, 2013; Lee et al., 2015).

In addition, the relationships and interaction among group members were largely considered uniplex, as opposed to multiplex. Uniplexity is a term in social network theories to indicate that only one type of relationship exists between the nodes in a network, whereas a multiplex network contains more than one type of relationships among the nodes (Heaney, 2014; Monge & Contractor, 2003). Previous research on online groups tended to focus on only one type of relationship or communication tie. Most took the functional perspective (Hollingshead et al., 2005), followed the input-process-outcome model, and examined how proposed features of online groups impact, or are impacted by, group processes and performance in task-oriented virtual groups (Gibbs et al., 2008; Martins, Gilson, & Maynard, 2004).

Commonly, group interaction serves a particular function (e.g. information processing, conflict management, control) for group goals, and is often reduced to one variable on one side of a regression. As a result, prior research investigating consequences of group interaction often picked one interaction-related variable (e.g. frequency of communication, anonymity in communication), and examined the linear relations between the variable and others (e.g. group cohesion, group performance) (Alberici & Milesi, 2016; Jans et al., 2015; Kahai, 2009; Rentsch et al., 2014; Tanis & Postmes, 2008; Wax, DeChurch, & Contractor, 2017).

Other research went into more detailed content analysis of one particular type of interaction or communication (Black, Welser, Cosley, & DeGroot, 2011; Burke, Kraut, & Joyce, 2010; Köhler, Cramton, & Hinds, 2012; McLeod, 2013; Tirado-Morueta, Maraver-López, & Hernando-Gómez, 2017). Although some studies have applied computational methods such as machine learning and network analysis (Burke, Kraut, & Joyce, 2010; Tirado-Morueta, Maraver-López, & Hernando-Gómez, 2017), they often focus on a singular type of interaction within online groups. However, in intact groups, group members may interact through multiple channels (e.g. face to face, phone, emails, video chat) simultaneously, and develop multiple relationships (e.g. co-workers, friends, competitors) in different contexts.

Taken together, these studies have greatly increased our knowledge of online groups. However, to move research forward and to capture the complex dynamics of people and technology in social systems in the current digital environment, viewing online groups as networks composed of people, technologies, and their multiplex relationships embedded in social contexts can be a beneficial approach.

The Multidimensional Network Framework

Contractor, Monge, and Leonardi (2011) proposed a framework of multidimensional networks based on the social network theories (Katz, Lazer, Arrow, & Contractor, 2004) and the sociomateriality perspective (Callon, 1986; Latour, 2005; Orlikowski, 2007;

Orlikowski & Scott, 2008). A social network is composed of a set of actors (nodes) and their relations (ties) (Wasserman & Faust, 1994). The framework posits that social systems in which people interact with and via technology can be theorized as multidimensional social networks consisting of different types of nodes connected through multiple types of relationships.

These social networks are multidimensional because (a) their nodes include humans with distinctive attributes (e.g. gender, tenure) and/or diverse roles (e.g. manager, salesperson), as well as non-human artifacts/agents such as ICTs (e.g. email, information repository) and artificial intelligence (e.g. robots, algorithms); and (b) the relationships among nodes are multiplex, since the nodes may be connected by different relational ties (e.g. human A is a collaborator to human B, whereas human C is the manager of robot D), and/or multiple connections exist between the same pair of nodes (e.g. human A and B are both collaborators and friends).

Although originally proposed as a framework to understand the relationship between people and technology, the multidimensional network perspective can be useful to guide online group research in the digital age. Building on the sociomateriality perspective (Callon, 1986; Latour, 2005; Orlikowski, 2007; Orlikowski & Scott, 2008), this framework challenges the distinction between people and technology. The sociomateriality perspective breaks the divide between the technological and the social, and argues that social worlds consist of people and materials existing in relation to each other. Taking the sociomateriality perspective means examining materiality as an intrinsic component of social systems. According to this perspective, both social and technological aspects of social systems have their own functioning rules that cannot be determined by each other, yet they are mutually constitutive through their dynamic relations (Leonardi & Barley, 2008). It is therefore sometimes called a post-human perspective, as it displaces human as center of social systems (Latour, 2005).

The multidimensional network perspective also transcends the boundary between online and offline, and offers a viewpoint that incorporates contexts for the study of groups. While prior conceptualization of online groups tends to omit the importance of contexts, the network perspective posits no static boundary between a group's internal and external environment (Katz et al., 2004). It views online groups as open, complex systems that are embedded in contexts. In this regard, online groups are not considered inherently different from offline groups but are instead embedded in (offline) contexts. The context in which groups are embedded can be considered a larger network of connections among people and technology. Its structure can also be measured as the external social ties of online groups. This idea was implicit in the original framework proposed by Contractor, Monge, and Leonardi (2011). We will develop their original conceptualization by adding the embedding social environment as another key component of the framework.

Last but not least, the multidimensional network view of groups conceptualizes groups as dynamic social systems with multiplex relationships among their components. The framework goes beyond the functional perspective and static input-process-output models by considering nodes and relationships as constantly evolving within groups and between groups and their environments (Contractor, Monge, & Leonardi, 2011). As groups develop with time, members come and go, and new technologies may be added while the old ones are replaced. Some members may develop new collaborations with one another while others may no longer interact. In the meantime, groups may develop new relations with other groups.

The network perspective not only acknowledges these internal and external dynamics of groups, but also provides a set of statistical tools to model and analyze the patterns of these dynamics (Katz et al., 2004; Wasserman & Faust, 1994), such as stochastic actor-based models for network analysis (Snijders, van de Bunt, & Steglich, 2010) and relational event modeling (REM) (Butts, 2008). Armed with these methods, researchers can model longitudinal dynamics of relationship formation within groups and test hypotheses regarding what co-variates and past interactions influence future group dynamics. In addition, the multidimensional network perspective allows researchers to conceptualize and investigate multiple relationships simultaneously. For instance, in the automobile manufacturing example provided by Contractor, Monge, and Leonardi (2011), advice-seeking relationships within the company were highly correlated with proximity and friendship among the staff, which in turn affected the status hierarchy and job performance within the collective.

In sum, the multidimensional network framework provides a conceptual framework and analytical tools to break the existing dichotomy between online and offline, and between people and technology, and therefore better captures the characteristics of groups in a time of ubiquitous computing and artificial intelligence.

ONLINE GROUPS AS MULTIDIMENSIONAL NETWORKS

Conceptualizing online groups as multidimensional networks dictates a perspective of groups as open, complex systems composed of different types of nodes connected by various relationships (Contractor, Monge, & Leonardi, 2011; Katz et al., 2004). Human members, along with technologies that they interact with (e.g. ICTs, bots, algorithms), become nodes in the network. The different relationships among human members, among technologies, and between human members and technologies are the multiplex, internal network ties. Group boundaries are fluid, as defined by their external ties (e.g. inter-group collaboration, shared membership) with other entities that constitute the embedding context.

Nodes: People and Technology

As multidimensional networks, groups consist of both people and technologies. Technology plays essential roles in group interaction and functioning. Studies conducted by Sparrow, Liu, and Wegner (2011) have demonstrated that nowadays people are primed to seek help from online search engines when they need to access information, indicating that people develop a transactive memory system with information storage and sorting algorithms as they normally do with their human group members.

Today's intelligent technologies (e.g. algorithms, bots) can learn and perform relatively independently, and collaborate with humans to complete tasks (Lee, Kiesler, Forlizzi, & Rybski, 2012). In Wikipedia, bots not only play a critical role in the community's production by completing laborious editing work that human members would find tedious, but also take part in the community's governance by facilitating the reinforcement of its norms and policies (Geiger, 2011; Geiger & Halfaker, 2013).

Human members may also develop social and psychological attachments to their technological counterparts. Research based on the "computers are social actors" (CASA) paradigm (Lee et al., 2012; Nass & Moon, 2000; Reeves & Nass, 1996) found that humans treat computers as their peers after interacting with them for a while. Researchers have also found that users accept bots' participation in collaborative production like Wikipedia (Clément & Guitton, 2015). Humans also apply gender stereotypes, and exhibit politeness and reciprocity toward computers (Nass & Moon, 2000). In a team setting, humans affiliated with their computer partners as teammates (e.g., had similar perceptions, cooperated with, and conformed to computers) when their outcomes were interdependent (Nass, Fogg, & Moon, 1996).

Ties: Multiplex

The central processes that unite online groups are the relationships and interactions among the nodes. Patterns of interaction are what McGrath and colleagues called the "essence" of groups (McGrath, 1984; Arrow, McGrath, & Berdahl, 2000). Based on the type of nodes they connect, relationships within groups may belong to one of the three categories: people–people relationships, people–technology relationships, and technology–technology relationships. The people–people relationship may include communicative ties (who communicates with whom), friendship (who is friends with whom), collaboration ties (who collaborates with whom), and affective ties (who likes whom).

People–technology relationships may form when a human member utilizes a technology. For instance, a relationship is formed between Bob and the knowledge repository in his group if he reads files in the repository. A people–technology relationship may also form when human members collaborate or communicate with technologies to achieve certain goals. If a human Wikipedia member partners with bots to detect malicious edits in the group, we consider the two as forming a relational tie.

Technological nodes in online groups can also develop relationships with other technologies (technology–technology relationships). For example, cloud servers connected together to support a virtual team's computing needs share relational ties. The three types of relationships are likely to co-exist. For instance, in an online support group, a human participant may engage in conversations with other users and bots for emotional support. The bots may be connected to the group's database that contains users' health and social network information.

Multiple different relationships may also exist between pairs of nodes (i.e. group members). For example, Madeline and Sam are friends (friendship tie) while also working together in the same virtual team (formal organizational tie). These different types of relationships may impact each other. Neff, Fulk, and Yuan (2014) found that affective ties among team members influence advice-seeking ties such that team members are more likely to seek information from peers they like. While multiplexity of relationships seems to be self-evident in groups, little prior research has specifically examined its influence on group processes and outcomes. By viewing online groups as multidimensional networks, all types of relationships between nodes in online groups can be conceptualized and analyzed simultaneously.

Figure 1 visually illustrates groups as a multidimensional network. The network consists of two different types of nodes: human members (triangle) and non-human members (round). Several distinct types of relationships also exist within the network: some human members are friends while others are in collaboration; human member H1 also collaborates with a bot (Bot 1); Database 1 and Database 2 are connected via the Internet; and human members (H2, H3) and the bot (Bot 1) all use the technologies. Two pairs of nodes also have multiple relationships: two human members, H1 and H2, are both friends and collaborators; Bot 1 is connected to Database1 on the Internet while retrieving information from the database.

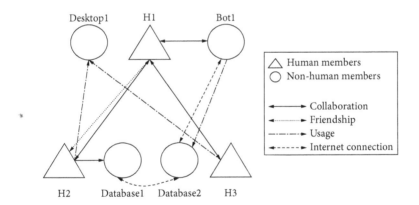

FIGURE 1 Groups as multidimensional networks.

Embedding Context

Multidimensional networks are open, adaptive systems (Arrow, McGrath, & Berdahl, 2000; Katz et al., 2004). They are embedded in and involved in complex exchanges with their environments (Putnam & Stohl, 1996; Stohl & Putnam, 2003; Seibold, Hollingshead, & Yoon, 2014). Our framework adds embedding contexts to Contractor,

Monge, and Leonardi's (2011) original proposal to provide a more comprehensive view of online groups. From the network perspective, there is no fixed boundary between a group and its external environment (Katz et al., 2004). The context in which groups are embedded is simply a larger network of connections among people and technology. Their relations can be captured as the social ties between the focal group and its nodes or collections of nodes outside of the group.

The concept of embeddedness theorizes the relations between groups and their environments. Embeddedness of groups is defined as "overlapping groups interlocked in levels of connectedness" (Putnam, 1989, p. 164). There are three general types of embeddedness: sociological, methodological, and psychological. Sociological embeddedness refers to the relations between online groups and the larger collective. For instance, globally distributed teams usually exist within multinational corporations (MNCs) (Gibson & Gibbs, 2006). Open source software (OSS) communities are likely to emerge from a core group of enthusiastic programmers who already have strong connections (Singh & Phelps, 2013). Facebook groups are embedded in a large web of relationships on the social networking site or in one's existing relationships pre-Facebook (boyd & Ellison, 2008).

The embedding contexts are likely to influence the internal dynamics of online groups. Changes in social contexts often lead to adaptation, readjustment, and realignment for global teams (Bosch-Sijtsema et al., 2011). In a study of groups in virtual worlds, researchers found that the competitive landscape influenced social distance among group members such that the social distance diminished only when competition for resources was absent (Tawa et al., 2015). Research has also shown that in online patient support groups, less offline support predicted higher online participation, and that the integration of online and offline support provided more psychological benefits to patients (Cummings, Sproull, & Kiesler, 2002). The relations between groups and their context, however, are by no means unidirectional. Groups are not just passively shaped by their embedding contexts; they may also generate consequences for their contexts as well. For example, the success of distributed teams can lead to organizational changes to move more routines and activities online.

The second type of embeddedness, methodological embeddedness, focuses on the interactions between different types of groups (Putnam, 1989; Seibold, Hollingshead, & Yoon, 2014). Numerous groups exist in online and offline spheres, and they may interact with each other frequently. The online crowdsourcing community, Kaggle, hosts data-mining competitions to help other communities, such as Yelp, to analyze their community data.[1] Virtual teams in MNCs also need to collaborate with other teams to complete tasks. These interactions also shape the internal dynamics of online groups. For example, the Kaggle community may need to delegate a member to frequently communicate with Yelp. The roles of virtual teams in MNCs are often assigned in accordance with the roles of other teams (Maznevski & Chudoba, 2000). Methodological embeddedness thus captures these interrelations among groups.

Psychological embeddedness is concerned with multiple group memberships. Technology has enabled individuals to belong to a great number of groups at the same

---

[1] Interested readers are referred to https://www.kaggle.com/yelp-dataset/yelp-dataset for more information.

time (Beck et al., 2016). For example, an individual may belong to many groups on Facebook. A Linux programmer is likely to participate in various online Q&A communities, such as Stack Overflow, to seek programming help (Yan & Jian, 2017). Team members in global collaborations often participate in boundary spanning practices with their partner groups (Søderberg & Romani, 2017). Correspondingly, groups may establish interactions with other groups by sharing group members. For example, the online Q&A network Stack Exchange owns a variety of online sub-communities that covers topics from math to cooking. A participant often starts by asking questions in one of its major communities, such as Stack Overflow, for programming-related questions, and subsequently joins other groups, such as cooking groups, for other types of knowledge. Although these sub-groups under Stack Exchange may not directly interact at the group level, they have frequent exchanges between members. Psychological embeddedness differs from the other two types of embeddedness by shifting from a group-centered perspective to a member-centered perspective.

Psychological embeddedness was found to have significant impact on member behavior and within-group dynamics. Mobile, wearable technologies that are almost always "on" keep people simultaneously playing multiple roles in multiple social groups, and have shifted people's way of thinking to be more abstract as they need to adapt to overlapping roles (Reyt & Wiesenfeld, 2015). Meanwhile, the plenitude of groups gives rise to competitions among groups for members. Research suggests that sharing members with other groups may reduce online groups' growth rates, particularly for larger and older groups (Wang, Butler, & Ren, 2012). Membership in multiple groups also has an inverted U-shaped relation with innovation in online communities, and moderates the relation between members' network position and their innovativeness (Dahlander & Frederiksen, 2011). Group membership in ethnic groups also generates impacts on members' social distance in virtual environments (Tawa et al., 2015).

Figure 2 illustrates how online groups are related to its context from the multidimensional network perspective. The embedding context of the groups consists of the offline communities, organizations, and relationships of the group members. Online Group 1,

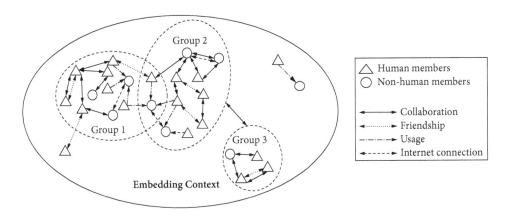

FIGURE 2 Placing groups in context.

2, 3, and a few isolates (unconnected nodes) are embedded in a broader offline community (e.g., MNC) (sociological embeddedness). All the groups consist of both human (triangle) and non-human (round) members. Some of them contain pairs of nodes with multiple types of relationships (e.g. collaborators, friends). Group 1 and Group 2 share two members, one human and one non-human (psychological embeddedness). Group 2 and Group 3 also share a collaboration tie (methodological embeddedness).

Overall, conceptualizing online groups as multidimensional networks characterizes groups as open, adaptive systems in which people and technologies mutually constitute each other through their multiple interactions and relationships within an embedding context. With ubiquitous and intelligent technologies being part of our everyday life, the distinctions between online and offline groups and between human and technological group members are blurred. This framework integrates and expands previous theory and research to encompass the recent development of online groups. It may serve as a starting point for future research to examine the multiplex interpersonal and human-computer interaction in teams, as well as the interplay between internal group dynamics and their embedding environments.

DISCUSSION

The proliferation of ubiquitous and smart computing technologies and social media are redefining the boundaries between online and offline, and between people and technology. The conventional conceptualization, which dichotomizes online groups from their offline counterparts, separates people from technology, and assumes online groups as more or less self-contained entities, can no longer characterize today's online groups. This chapter proposes a framework to characterize online groups as multidimensional networks. The framework emphasizes that (a) online groups consist of both humans and technological artifacts and agents (e.g. databases, algorithms, bots); (b) the essence of groups lies in their multiplex relationships among their components; and (c) groups are embedded in social environments. Groups and their embedding environments are interdependent and mutually constitutive.

This conceptualization places technology as an integral component of groups in digital age. While previous research on groups and technology focused more attention on human interactions with technology support and adoption of new technologies, interaction between human members and intelligent technologies has started to draw research attention from group researchers in more recent years (Kim, Kim, Kim, & Dey, 2016; Murgia, Janssens, Demeyer, & Vasilescu, 2016). We consider the interactional processes between humans and intelligent technologies promising realms for future research, since intelligent technologies are likely to reshape the cognition and behaviors of human members as they become more autonomous and humanlike (Lee et al., 2012). Nevertheless, it remains disputable whether and how intelligent technologies can develop shared mental models with humans and become reliable teammates (Groom & Nass, 2007).

Studies investigating how human members collaborate and build relationships with intelligent bots, and how algorithms shape, and are shaped by, human members would generate interesting insights into sociomateriality and the ethics of utilizing artificial intelligence (Harbers, de Greeff, Kruijff-Korbayová, Neerincx, & Hindriks, 2017).

Besides multiple types of nodes, the framework also highlights the existence of multiple types of relationships among group members. Since research on the multiplexity of relationships within groups has been scarce, future research should investigate how one type of relationship may influence others. Research on transactive memory systems has shown that team members are more likely to engage in information retrieval if they interact in multiple communication channels (Yuan, Carboni, & Ehrlich, 2010). They are also more likely to retrieve information from whom they like (Neff, Fulk, & Yuan, 2014).

Furthermore, the multidimensional network framework stresses embedding contexts as a defining feature of online groups, and calls for more research attention on the interdependence between online groups and their environments. Interdependence is defined not only as the unidirectional influence of environmental factors (e.g. shared membership, competitive landscape) on groups, but also as the environmental consequences engendered by groups. For example, researchers can study how the internal dynamics of a leading online Q&A community (e.g. Stack Overflow) shape the structure and culture of other Q&A communities in the ecological system (e.g. Stack Exchange). Table 1 summarizes key differences between the conventional and network view of groups, and provides sample research questions.

The framework also entails methodologies that can analyze the complex interaction dynamics among group members and between groups and their embedding contexts. This research agenda can be enriched by adapting perspectives and methods from the emerging field of computational social science (Lazer et al., 2009; McGrath, Arrow, & Berdahl, 2000; Pilny & Poole, 2017). To begin with, online digital trace data can provide empirical grounds for the study of group dynamics (Kozlowski, Chao, Chang, & Fernandez, 2015). While prior research on online groups relied heavily on cross-sectional, self-reported data, servers of computer-supported groups have documented massive longitudinal data of detailed group interaction. These datasets, if properly analyzed through computational methods such as natural language processing, can generate new knowledge about the dynamic and emergent processes of online groups. For example, researchers can monitor the longitudinal interaction patterns in online communities to study how leaders or self-governance structures naturally emerge over time (Dahlander, Klapper, & Piezunka, 2018).

Group researchers can also utilize crowd-based online platforms for survey and experimental research. In recent years, various crowdsourcing platforms (e.g. Amazon Mechanical Turk, Prolific Academic) have been developed to recruit research participants, making it faster and less costly for researchers to conduct online studies. Participants recruited on Amazon's Mechanical Turk have been shown to perform with comparable quality as subject pool participants (Goodman & Paolacci, 2017; Hauser & Schwarz, 2016). They are also more diverse than college student populations.

Table 1 Conventional View vs. Network View of Online Groups

	Conventional View	Network View	Research Directions	Sample Research Questions
Group Members	People	People and Technology	Interactional dynamics between human with non-human members in groups.	Does machine personality and human personality affect group dynamics in similar ways (e.g. is having conscientious and agreeable machines beneficial?) Can humans and machines develop team cognition such as team mental models and transactive memory systems?
Internal Relationship	Uniplex	Multiplex	Relations between multiple relationships within groups; influence of multiple types of within-group relationships on group processes and outcomes.	How do collaboration ties among group members influence affective ties within groups, and vice versa? How does the multiplexity of relationships impact group cohesion, creativity, decision making, and learning?
External Relationship	Self-contained	Embedded	The interdependence between groups and their environments (e.g. the effects of external relationships—shared membership, competitive landscape on groups, as well as the consequences that groups generate for their environments).	How does network structure (e.g. small-worldness) of groups' embedded contexts impact groups' innovative practices and outcomes? How do groups influence the norms and culture of other groups through shared members?

A few other platforms have been designed specifically for the study of online groups. For example, the Volunteer Science project (https://volunteerscience.com/) and the Platform for Online Group Studies (pogs.mit.edu) allow researchers to run web-based experiments where groups perform tasks synchronously (Engel, Woolley, Jing, Chabris, & Malone; 2014; Kim et al., 2017). Participants can join an experiment on their own computer wherever they are, making online experiments more scalable.

Much research on online communities and platforms is now being conducted in disciplines such as information systems and computer science. While research in these fields excels at utilizing digital-trace data and computational methods, it runs the risk of reducing online communities to their technological platforms, and neglecting the social processes within online groups (Faraj, von Krogh, Monteiro, & Lakhani, 2016). Group researchers in social science can collaborate with researchers in these fields and complement their research by providing theoretical insights concerning the social and cognitive dynamics in online groups.

In conclusion, the significant advancements in information and communication technologies in the past few decades, as represented by ubiquitous mobile computing, have made it possible to connect with others anytime and everywhere. Artificial intelligence has increasingly become part of work teams across many industries. This revolution challenges the traditional distinction between the online and the offline, raises questions about the relations between people and technology, and provides opportunities to study emergent dynamics of social interaction. It also generates methodological challenges for group researchers, entailing scholarly transformation from the relatively static, functional approach based on self-reported, retrospective data to a more dynamic and holistic perspective using computational modeling and longitudinal analysis. It is difficult to imagine the next generation of human-technology group configurations. However, regardless of what they look like, the multidimensional network approach described in this chapter may be a useful approach to describe, visualize, and study them.

REFERENCES

Alberici, A. I., & Milesi, P. (2016). Online discussion, politicized identity, and collective action. *Group Processes & Intergroup Relations 19*(1), 43–59.

Appenzeller, T. (2017, July 7). The AI revolution in science. *Science*. doi:10.1126/science.aan7064.

Aristeidou, M., Scanlon, E., & Sharples, M. (2017). Profiles of engagement in online communities of citizen science participation. *Computers in Human Behavior 74*, 246–256.

Arrow, H., McGrath, J. E., & Berdahl, J. L. (2000). *Small groups as complex systems: Formation, coordination, development and adaptation*. Thousand Oaks, CA: Sage.

Baker, W. E., & Bulkley, N. (2014). Paying it forward vs. rewarding reputation: Mechanisms of generalized reciprocity. *Organization Science 25*(5), 1493–1510.

Bartel, C. A., Wrzesniewski, A., & Wiesenfeld, B. M. (2011). Knowing where you stand: Physical isolation, perceived respect, and organizational identification among virtual employees. *Organization Science 23*(3), 743–757.

Baruah, J., & Paulus, P. B. (2016). The role of time and category relatedness in electronic brainstorming. *Small Group Research 47*(3), 333–342.

Bazarova, N. N., & Walther, J. B. (2009). Attributions in virtual groups: Distances and behavioral variations in computer-mediated discussions. *Small Group Research 40*(2), 138–162.

Beck, S. J., Bourdeaux, R., DiTunnariello, N., & Paskewitz, E. A. (2016). A review and technological consideration of the bona fide group perspective. *Small Group Research 47*(6), 665–691.

Bell, B. S., & Kozlowski, S. W. (2002). A typology of virtual teams. *Group & Organization Management 27*(1), 14–49.

Black, L. W., Welser, H. T., Cosley, D., & DeGroot, J. M. (2011). Self-governance through group discussion in Wikipedia: Measuring deliberation in online groups. *Small Group Research 42*(5), 595–634.

Boh, W. F., Ren, Y., Kiesler, S., & Bussjaeger, R. (2007). Expertise and collaboration in the geographically dispersed organization. *Organization Science 18*(4), 595–612.

Bosch-Sijtsema, P. M., Fruchter, R., Vartiainen, M., & Ruohomäki, V. (2011). A framework to analyze knowledge work in distributed teams. *Group & Organization Management 36*(3), 275–307.

boyd, d. m., & Ellison, N. B. (2008). Social network sites: Definition, history, and scholarship. *Journal of Computer-Mediated Communication 13*(1), 210–230.

Brandon, D. P., & Hollingshead, A. B. (2007). Categorizing on-line groups. In A. Joinson, K. McKenna, T. Postmes, & U. Reips (Eds.), *The Oxford handbook of Internet psychology* (pp. 105–120). Oxford: Oxford University Press.

Burke, M., Kraut, R., & Joyce, E. (2010). Membership claims and requests: Conversation-level newcomer socialization strategies in online groups. *Small Group Research 41*(1), 4–40.

Butts, C. T. (2008). A relational event framework for social action. *Sociological Methodology 38*, 155–200.

Callon, M. (1986). Some elements of a sociology of translations: Domestication of the scallops and the fishermen in St. Brieuc Bay. In J. Law (Ed.), *Power, action, and belief: A new sociology of knowledge*. London: Routledge.

Chattopadhyay, P., George, E., & Shulman, A. D. (2008). The asymmetrical influence of sex dissimilarity in distributive vs. co-located work groups. *Organization Science 19*(4), 581–593.

Clément, M., & Guitton, M. J. (2015). Interacting with bots online: Users' reactions to actions of automated programs in Wikipedia. *Computers in Human Behavior 50*, 66–75.

Clerwall, C. (2014). Enter the robot journalist. *Journalism Practice 8*(5), 519–531.

Cogliser, C. C., Gardner, W. L., Gavin, M. B., & Broberg, J. C. (2012). Big Five personality factors and leader emergence in virtual teams: Relationships with team trustworthiness, member performance contributions, and team performance. *Group & Organization Management 37*(6), 752–784.

Contractor, N., Monge, P., & Leonardi, P. M. (2011). Multidimensional networks and the dynamics of sociomateriality: Bringing technology inside the network. *International Journal of Communication 5*, 682–720.

Cramton, C. D., & Hinds, P. J. (2014). An embedded model of cultural adaptation in global teams. *Organization Science 25*(4), 1056–1081.

Cummings, J. N., Sproull, L., & Kiesler, S. B. (2002). Beyond hearing: Where the real-world and online support meet. *Group Dynamics: Theory, Research, and Practice 6*(1), 78–88.

Dahlander, L., & Frederiksen, L. (2011). The core and cosmopolitans: A relational view of innovation in user communities. *Organization Science 23*(4), 988–1007.

Dahlander, L., Klapper, H., & Piezunka, H. (2018). You shall (not) pass: Who votes for whom in granting authority in online knowledge production communities? *Academy of Management Global Proceedings, Surrey 2018*, 156.

de Janasz, S. C., & Godshalk, V. M. (2013). The role of E-mentoring in protégés' learning and satisfaction. *Group & Organization Management 38*(6), 743–774.

DeSanctis, G., & Monge, P. (1999). Introduction to the special issue: Communication processes for virtual organizations. *Organization Science 10*(6), 693–703.

Dodgson, M., Gann, D. M., & Phillips, N. (2013). Organizational learning and the technology of foolishness: The case of virtual worlds at IBM. *Organization Science 24*(5), 1358–1376.

Ellison, N. B., Steinfield, C., & Lampe, C. (2007). The benefits of Facebook "friends:" Social capital and college students' use of online social network sites. *Journal of Computer-Mediated Communication 12*(4), 1143–1168.

Engel, D., Woolley, A. W., Jing, L. X., Chabris, C. F., & Malone, T. W. (2014). Reading the mind in the eyes or reading between the lines? Theory of mind predicts collective intelligence equally well online and face-to-face. *PLoS ONE 9*(12), e115212.

Erhardt, N., Gibbs, J., Martin-Rios, C., & Sherblom, J. (2016). Exploring affordances of email for team learning over time. *Small Group Research 47*(3), 243–278.

Faraj, S., von Krogh, G., Monteiro, E., & Lakhani, K. R. (2016). Special section introduction: Online community as space for knowledge flows. *Information Systems Research 27*(4), 668–684.

Geiger, R. S. (2011). The lives of bots. In G. Lovink & N. Tkacz (Eds.), *Critical point of view: A Wikipedia reader* (pp. 78–93). Amsterdam: Institute of Network Cultures.

Geiger, R. S., & Halfaker, A. (2013). When the levee breaks: Without bots, what happens to Wikipedia's quality control processes? In *Proceedings of the 9th International Symposium on Open Collaboration* (p. 6:1–6:6). New York, NY: ACM.

Gibbs, J. L., Nekrassova, D., Grushina, S. V., & Wahab, S. A. (2008). Reconceptualizing virtual teaming from a constitutive perspective review, redirection, and research agenda. *Annals of the International Communication Association 32*(1), 187–229.

Gibson, C. B., & Gibbs, J. L. (2006). Unpacking the concept of virtuality: The effects of geographic dispersion, electronic dependence, dynamic structure, and national diversity on team innovation. *Administrative Science Quarterly 51*(3), 451–495.

Gibson, C. B., Gibbs, J. L., Stanko, T. L., Tesluk, P., & Cohen, S. G. (2011). Including the "I" in virtuality and modern job design: Extending the job characteristics model to include the moderating effect of individual experiences of electronic dependence and copresence. *Organization Science 22*(6), 1481–1499.

Goodman, J. K., & Paolacci, G. (2017). Crowdsourcing consumer research. *Journal of Consumer Research 44*(1), 196–210.

Goodrich, M. A., Morse, B. S., Gerhardt, D., Cooper, J. L., Quigley, M., Adams, J. A., & Humphrey, C. (2008). Supporting wilderness search and rescue using a camera-equipped mini UAV. *Journal of Field Robotics 25*(1–2), 89–110.

Griffith, T. L., Sawyer, J. E., & Neale, M. A. (2003). Virtualness and knowledge in teams: Managing the love triangle of organizations, individuals, and information technology. *MIS Quarterly 27*(2), 265.

Groom, V., & Nass, C. (2007). Can robots be teammates? Benchmarks in human-robot teams. *Interaction Studies 8*(3), 483–500.

Haas, M. R., Criscuolo, P., & George, G. (2015). Which problems to solve? Online knowledge sharing and attention allocation in organizations. *Academy of Management Journal 58*(3), 680–711.

Hampton, K. N., Shin, I., & Lu, W. (2017). Social media and political discussion: When online presence silences offline conversation. *Information, Communication & Society 20*(7), 1090–1107.

Han, S. J., & Beyerlein, M. (2016). Framing the effects of multinational cultural diversity on virtual team processes. *Small Group Research 47*(4), 351–383.

Harbers, M., Greeff, J. de, Kruijff-Korbayová, I., Neerincx, M. A., & Hindriks, K. V. (2017). Exploring the ethical landscape of robot-assisted search and rescue. In M. I. Aldinhas

Ferreira, J. Silva Sequeira, M. O. Tokhi, E. Kadar, & G. S. Virk (Eds.), *A World with robots: International conference on robot ethics: ICRE 2015* (pp. 93–107). Lisbon: Springer.

Harbers, M., Jonker, C. M., & Van Riemsdijk, M. B. (2014). Context-sensitive sharedness criteria for teamwork. In *Proceedings of the 2014 International Conference on Autonomous Agents and Multi-agent Systems* (pp. 1507–1508). Richland, SC: International Foundation for Autonomous Agents and Multiagent Systems.

Hardin, A. M., Fuller, M. A., & Davison, R. M. (2007). I know I can, but can we? Culture and efficacy beliefs in global virtual teams. *Small Group Research 38*(1), 130–155.

Hauser, D. J., & Schwarz, N. (2016). Attentive Turkers: MTurk participants perform better on online attention checks than do subject pool participants. *Behavior Research Methods 48*(1), 400–407.

Heaney, M. T. (2014). Multiplex networks and interest group influence reputation: An exponential random graph model. *Social Network 36*(Suppl C), 66–81.

Hollingshead, A. B., & Contractor, N. S. (2006). New media and small group organizing. In L. Lievrouw and S. Livingstone (Eds.), *Handbook of new media: Student edition*. London, UK: Sage.

Hollingshead, A. B., Wittenbaum, G. M., Paulus, P. B., Hirokawa, R. Y., Ancona, D. G., Peterson, R. S., Jehn, K. A., & Yoon, K. (2005). A look at groups from the functional perspective. In M. S. Poole & A. B. Hollingshead (Eds.), *Theories of small groups: Interdisciplinary perspectives* (pp. 21–62). Thousand Oaks, CA: Sage.

Jans, L., Leach, C. W., Garcia, R. L., & Postmes, T. (2015). The development of group influence on in-group identification: A multilevel approach. *Group Processes & Intergroup Relations 18*(2), 190–209.

Kahai, S. S. (2009). Anonymity and counter-normative arguments in computer-mediated discussions. *Group & Organization Management 34*(4), 449–478.

Kahai, S. S., Huang, R., & Jestice, R. J. (2012). Interaction effect of leadership and communication media on feedback positivity in virtual teams. *Group & Organization Management 37*(6), 716–751.

Karapanos, E., Teixeira, P., & Gouveia, R. (2016). Need fulfillment and experiences on social media: A case on Facebook and WhatsApp. *Computers in Human Behavior 55*, 888–897.

Katz, N., Lazer, D., Arrow, H., & Contractor, N. S. (2004). The network perspective on small groups: Theory and research. In M. S. Poole & A. B. Hollingshead (Eds.), *Theories of small groups: Interdisciplinary perspectives* (pp. 277–312). Thousand Oaks, CA: Sage.

Kim, M. J., Kim, K. J., Kim, S., & Dey, A. K. (2016). Evaluation of StarCraft artificial intelligence competition bots by experienced human players. In *Proceedings of the 2016 CHI conference extended abstracts on human factors in computing systems* (pp. 1915–1921). New York, NY: ACM.

Kim, Y. J., Engel, D., Woolley, A. W., Lin, J. Y.-T., McArthur, N., & Malone, T. W. (2017). What makes a strong team? Using collective intelligence to predict team performance in League of Legends. In *Proceedings of the 2017 ACM conference on computer supported cooperative work and social computing* (pp. 2316–2329). New York, NY: ACM.

Köhler, T., Cramton, C. D., & Hinds, P. J. (2012). The meeting genre across cultures: Insights from three German-American collaborations. *Small Group Research 43*(2), 159–185.

Kozlowski, S. W. J., Chao, G. T., Chang, C. H., & Fernandez, R. (2015). Team dynamics: Using "big data" to advance the science of team effectiveness. In S. Tonidandel, E. King, & J. Cortina (Eds.), *Big data at work: The data science revolution and organizational psychology*. New York, NY: Routledge Academic.

Latour, B. (2005). *Reassembling the social: An introduction to actor–network theory*. Oxford, UK: Oxford University Press.

Lazer, D., Pentland, A., Adamic, L., Aral, S., Barabási, A.-L., Brewer, D., . . . Van Alstyne, M. (2009). Computational social science. *Science 323*(5915), 721–723.

Lee, M. K., Kiesler, S., Forlizzi, J., & Rybski, P. (2012). Ripple effects of an embedded social agent: A field study of a social robot in the workplace. In *Proceedings of the SIGCHI conference on human factors in computing systems* (pp. 695–704). New York, NY: ACM.

Lee, M. K., Kusbit, D., Metsky, E., & Dabbish, L. (2015). Working with machines: The impact of algorithmic and data-driven management on human workers. In *Proceedings of the 33rd Annual ACM conference on human factors in computing systems* (pp. 1603–1612). New York, NY: ACM.

Leonardi, P. M., & Barley, S. R. (2008). Materiality and change: Challenges to building better theory about technology and organizing. *Information and Organization 18*(3), 159–176.

Martínez-Moreno, E., Zornoza, A., González-Navarro, P., & Thompson, L. F. (2012). Investigating face-to-face and virtual teamwork over time: When does early task conflict trigger relationship conflict? *Group Dynamics: Theory, Research, and Practice 16*(3), 159–171.

Martins, L. L., Gilson, L. L., & Maynard, M. T. (2004). Virtual teams: What do we know and where do we go from here? *Journal of Management 30*, 805–835.

Martins, L. L., & Shalley, C. E. (2011). Creativity in virtual work: Effects of demographic differences. *Small Group Research 42*(5), 536–561.

Maznevski, M. L., & Chudoba, K. M. (2000). Bridging space over time: Global virtual team dynamics and effectiveness. *Organization Science 11*(5), 473–492.

McGrath, J. E. (1984). *Groups: Interaction and performance*. Englewood, NJ: Prentice-Hall.

McGrath, J. E., Arrow, H., & Berdahl, J. L. (2000). The study of groups: Past, present, and future. *Personality and Social Psychology Review 4*(1), 95–105.

McLeod, P. L. (2013). Distributed people and distributed information: Vigilant decision-making in virtual teams. *Small Group Research 44*(6), 627–657.

Monge, P. R., & Contractor, N. (2003). *Theories of communication networks*. New York, NY: Oxford University Press.

Mozur, P. (2017, May 23). Google's AlphaGo defeats Chinese Go master in win for A.I. *New York Times*. Retrieved from https://www.nytimes.com/2017/05/23/business/google-deepmind-alphago-go-champion-defeat.html.

Murgia, A., Janssens, D., Demeyer, S., & Vasilescu, B. (2016). Among the machines: Human-bot interaction on social Q&A websites. In *Proceedings of the 2016 CHI conference extended abstracts on human factors in computing systems* (pp. 1272–1279). New York, NY: ACM.

Nambisan, S., & Baron, R. A. (2009). Different roles, different strokes: Organizing virtual customer environments to promote two types of customer contributions. *Organization Science 21*(2), 554–572.

Nass, C., Fogg, B. J., & Moon, Y. (1996). Can computers be teammates? *International Journal of Human-Computer Studies 45*, 669–678.

Nass, C., & Moon, Y. (2000). Machines and mindlessness: Social responses to computers. *Journal of Social Issues 56*, 81–103.

Neff, J. J., Fulk, J., & Yuan, C. Y. (2014). Not in the mood? Affective state and transactive communication. *Journal of Communication 64*(5), 785–805.

O'Leary, M. B., & Mortensen, M. (2009). Go (con)figure: Subgroups, imbalance, and isolates in geographically dispersed teams. *Organization Science 21*(1), 115–131.

O'Mahony, S., & Ferraro, F. (2007). The emergence of governance in an open source community. *The Academy of Management Journal 50*(5), 1079–1106.

Orlikowski, W. J. (2007). Sociomaterial practices: Exploring technology at work. *Organization Studies 28*(9), 1,435–1,448.

Orlikowski, W. J., & Scott, S. V. (2008). Sociomateriality: Challenging the separation of technology, work and organization. *The Academy of Management Annals* 2(1), 433–474.

Paulus, P. B., Kohn, N. W., Arditti, L. E., & Korde, R. M. (2013). Understanding the group size effect in electronic brainstorming. *Small Group Research* 44(3), 332–352.

Pentland, A. (2008). *Honest signals: How they shape our world.* Cambridge, MA: MIT Press.

Peters, L., & Karren, R. J. (2009). An examination of the roles of trust and functional diversity on virtual team performance ratings. *Group & Organization Management* 34(4), 479–504.

Pilny, A., & Poole, M. S. (Eds.). (2017). *Group processes: Data-driven computational approaches.* Cham: Springer International Publishing.

Putnam, L. L. (1989). Perspectives on research on group embeddedness in organizations. In S. S. King (Ed.), *Human communication as a field of study: Selected contemporary views* (pp. 163–181). Albany, NY: State University of New York Press.

Putnam, L. L., & Stohl, C. (1996). Bona fide groups: An alternative perspective for communication and small group decision making. In R. Y. Hirokawa & M. S. Poole (Eds.), *Communication and group decision making* (pp. 147–178). Thousand Oaks, CA: Sage.

Rainie, L., & Wellman, B. (2012). *Networked: The new social operating system.* Cambridge, MA: MIT Press.

Reeves, B., & Nass, C. (1996). *The media equation: How people treat computers, television, and new media like real people and places.* New York, NY: Cambridge University Press.

Ren, R. and Yan, B. (2017). Crowd diversity and performance in Wikipedia: The mediating effects of task conflict and communication. *CHI2017: Proceedings of the ACM conference on human factors in computer systems.* New York, NY: ACM.

Rentsch, J. R., Delise, L. A., Mello, A. L., & Staniewicz, M. J. (2014). The integrative team knowledge building training strategy in distributed problem-solving teams. *Small Group Research* 45(5), 568–591.

Reyt, J. N., & Wiesenfeld, B. M. (2015). Seeing the forest for the trees: Exploratory learning, mobile technology, and knowledge workers' role integration behaviors. *Academy of Management Journal* 58(3), 739–762.

Rutkowski, A.-F., Saunders, C., Vogel, D., & van Genuchten, M. (2007). "Is it already 4 a.m. in your time zone?" Focus immersion and temporal dissociation in virtual teams. *Small Group Research* 38(1), 98–129.

Seibold, D. R., Hollingshead, A. B., & Yoon, K. (2014). Embedded teams and embedding organizations. In L. L. Putnam & D. Mumby (Eds.), *The Sage handbook of organization communication* (pp. 327–349). Thousand Oaks, CA: Sage.

Shen, C., Monge, P., & Williams, D. (2014). Virtual brokerage and closure: Network structure and social capital in a massively multiplayer online game. *Communication Research* 41(4), 459–480.

Singh, P. V., & Phelps, C. (2013). Networks, social influence, and the choice among competing innovations: Insights from open source software licenses. *Information Systems Research* 24(3), 539–560.

Snijders, T. A. B., van de Bunt, G. G., & Steglich, C. E. G. (2010). Introduction to stochastic actor-based models for network dynamics. *Social Networks* 32(1), 44–60.

Søderberg, A.-M., & Romani, L. (2017). Boundary spanners in global partnerships: A case study of an Indian vendor's collaboration with western clients. *Group & Organization Management* 42(2), 237–278.

Sparrow, B., Liu, J., & Wegner, D. M. (2011). Google effects on memory: Cognitive consequences of having information at our fingertips. *Science* 333(6043), 776–778.

Stohl, C., & Putnam, L. L. (2003). Communication in context: Implications for the study of bona fide groups. In L. R. Frey (Ed.), *Group communication in context: Studies of natural groups* (2nd ed.) (pp. 285–292). Hillsdale, NJ: Lawrence Erlbaum.

Tanis, M., & Postmes, T. (2008). Cues to identity in online dyads: Effects of interpersonal versus intragroup perceptions on performance. *Group Dynamics: Theory, Research, and Practice 12*(2), 96–111.

Tawa, J., Negrón, R., Suyemoto, K. L., & Carter, A. S. (2015). The effect of resource competition on Blacks' and Asians' social distance using a virtual world methodology. *Group Processes & Intergroup Relations 18*(6), 761–777.

Tirado-Morueta, R., Maraver-López, P., & Hernando-Gómez, Á. (2017). Patterns of participation and social connections in online discussion forums. *Small Group Research 48*(6), 639–664.

van der Kleij, R., Maarten Schraagen, J., Werkhoven, P., & De Dreu, C. K. W. (2009). How conversations change over time in face-to-face and video-mediated communication. *Small Group Research 40*(4), 355–381.

Wang, X., Butler, B. S., & Ren, Y. (2012). The impact of membership overlap on growth: An ecological competition view of online groups. *Organization Science 24*(2), 414–431.

Wang, Y., Kraut, R., & Levine, J. M. (2012). To stay or leave? The relationship of emotional and informational support to commitment in online health support groups. In *Proceedings of the ACM 2012 conference on computer supported cooperative work* (pp. 833–842). New York, NY: ACM.

Wasserman, S., & Faust, K. (1994). *Social network analysis: Methods and applications.* New York, NY: Cambridge University Press.

Wax, A., DeChurch, L. A., & Contractor, N. S. (2017). Self-organizing into winning teams. Understanding the mechanisms that drive successful collaborations. *Small Group Research 48*(6), 665–718.

Wilson, J., Crisp, C. B., & Mortensen, M. (2013). Extending construal-level theory to distributed groups: Understanding the effects of virtuality. *Organization Science 24*(2), 629–644.

Yan, B., and Jian, L. (2017). Beyond reciprocity: The bystander effect of knowledge response in online knowledge communities. *Computers in Human Behavior 76*, 9–18.

Yuan, Y. C., Carboni, I., & Ehrlich, K. (2010). The impact of awareness and accessibility on expertise retrieval: A multilevel network perspective. *Journal of the American Society for Information Science and Technology 61*(4), 700–714.

PART V

SOCIAL MEDIA

CHAPTER 17

USES AND GRATIFICATIONS OF SOCIAL MEDIA: WHO USES IT AND WHY?

LISA J. ORCHARD

INTRODUCTION

SOCIAL media seems ever present in modern day society—from social meet-ups being organized on Facebook, complaints about poor customer services being played out across Twitter, and social activism and protests being co-ordinated across Reddit sub-groups—social media has become the hub of our Internet use, encapsulating the social, leisure, and informational services that were once used to categorize the Internet as a whole (Orchard, Fullwood, Galbraith, & Morris, 2014). Social plug-ins (small, colorful buttons denoting quick links to specific social media pages) are embedded into web pages across the Internet, inviting content to be shared, liked, and commented on. It is often the first point of call for interacting via the Internet, and for many, ingrained into daily routines. The pull of social media seems inescapable, but what is it that draws people in? What do people get from social media, and why do they continue to use it?

Noticeably, this chapter puts the focus on the user. Indeed, users are those who create, share, and discuss content, and the success of any social media platform is dependent on attracting and retaining users through their continued active participation. However, as users are human, it would be redundant and incorrect to assume all users behave towards social media in the same way. Indeed, people need only to consider their own use of social networks to verify this statement.

Take a minute to think about your own social media usage. How many social media accounts do you hold? How often do you log into social media? How often do you update your social media? Now compare this to other social media behaviors you may have witnessed. Do you have that one Facebook friend that shares a constant barrage of memes followed by a string of laughing emojis; or perhaps you know someone who "Tweets" constant updates about their day? Maybe you have forgotten that you are "Friends" with some of your quieter network connections who lurk in the Facebook shadows, absorbing the content but rarely contributing. Given that social media affords us such diversity in feature use, we should not only question who is using it, but also the reasons why people are so drawn to social media.

Uses and Gratifications

Historically, people have questioned the introduction of new media advances. For instance, the introduction of television spurred a mass of research towards an understanding of its popularity. This provides us with a good theoretical background of research to build upon. When exploring media from a user perspective the Uses and Gratifications (U&G) framework offers an insight into the key motivations behind media use and its resulting benefits.

U&G originated in the 1940s (Papacharissi, 2009) and since its inception has been used to explore media uptake across a range of technological advances. For instance, it has previously been applied to understand the user base of various radio formats, television shows, video games, and the Internet in general. However, unlike alternative media theories, U&G focuses not on the effects of media intake, but rather on the use of media and the motivations for differing media usage (Krcmar, 2017). In other words, it explores the reasons why individuals may choose to use a particular media and why they use specific features within that media. This is vital for understanding the impact of media use. Understanding the motivations behind this use allows better interpretation of the outcome effects of such media. To this end, U&G studies may also explore social or personal antecedents that may predict preferred motives or consequences of such use, in line with chosen motivations (Papacharissi, 2009). In other words, U&G can be expanded to explore the picture as a whole; giving us answers for "why we use social media," as well as providing insight into factors that may predict this use.

The framework of U&G is very positive; it suggests that the user is active in their choices and use of media, as opposed to a more negative view of passively absorbing media. For instance, U&G would suggest that a user selectively decides which media to consume. As an example, an individual can actively choose whether they watch TV, play video games, or indeed use social media, depending on their motivation. Users are thought to be goal-driven and will seek out media that fulfills their individual needs, which can depend on a number of psychological and sociological factors. It is suggested that media use is only maintained if these individual needs can be "gratified" (Rubin, 2009). For instance, someone may have a thirst for knowledge and choose to watch a documentary for informational purposes, but later change the channel if they find they are not learning as much as they had hoped. Thus, choice of media is purposeful. We will only continue to use specific media for as long as we can get something out of it. If a user does not obtain the expected gratification they can become disappointed and eventually disinterested in the media. This will encourage them to seek out other alternative media to fulfill their needs. However, if the media use *does* fulfill the gratifications expected, the user will continue to engage and consume the media in a somewhat predictable fashion (Palmgreen & Rayburn, 1979). Equally, the user will utilize the features of specific media to fulfill their needs in an optimum manner. This may result in individuals valuing different features within a site. For instance, within Facebook some individuals will focus on their own profile and that of their friends (perhaps passively scrolling through their newsfeed and making the occasional status update), while others may be drawn to groups or to commenting on public profiles and posts (perhaps commenting on news articles and talking to those they do not know offline). Thus, individuals will differ in their interaction with social media depending on what they aim to get out of it and the features that best fulfill those needs.

U&G Methodology

To have an appreciation of U&G findings it is important to understand the methodology employed. The framework of U&G is considered both broad and flexible and can be tailored to the needs of a researcher. Despite this, many U&G studies tend to follow a similar pattern of exploration. Generally U&G are studied through the use of self-report scales, although there are many exceptions. For instance, Urista, Dong, and Day (2009) explored U&G of MySpace and Facebook through focus groups by applying a grounded theory approach, while Whiting and Williams (2013) extracted U&G of social media from in-depth interviews. If taking a self-report approach, the creation of such scales is often integral to the process.

Generally, at the start of a U&G study a list of uses (or motivations) are compiled in relation to the explored media. Motivations for media use are fairly consistent across different types of media (Parker & Plank, 2000) and therefore the initial list can often be drawn from previous research. Traditionally, studies build surveys from qualitative data, such as focus groups, but this has not been common practice recently (Sundar & Limperos, 2013), given the wealth of U&G research to draw upon. However, authors do often engage in pilot studies to ensure their list is comprehensive and suitable. Once the list has been finalized, participants are asked to rank each item on a Likert scale (e.g. "How much do you agree with [a specific motivation] on a scale of 1–5?"). This allows for factor analyses to be undertaken, where individual uses are clustered together to form broader motivation factors. These factors provide insight into the reasons people use that particular media and what needs are being gratified through use. As an example, Rubin's (1983) nine key U&G of television use are: relaxation, companionship, habit, to pass time, entertainment, social interaction, information, due to arousal, and/or to escape. Incidentally, these particular motivations are considered fundamental to media usage (Krcmar, 2017).

Although many studies follow a similar methodology, researchers do not always follow a standard theoretical perspective. For instance, some researchers look more specifically at "gratifications sought vs. gratifications obtained." This line of enquiry focuses more on the imbalance between those gratifications that are specifically sought from media usage, and the unintended outcomes that may arise. For instance, one may use a site to seek information, but end up developing a new friendship due to common interests. Indeed, gratifications are not always directly assigned through use, and so clear distinctions between needs and outcomes must be made (Krcmar, 2017). Irrespective of the theoretical stance taken, however, it has been argued that U&G is fundamental to understanding our use of new media, specifically computer-mediated communication (Ruggiero, 2000), upon which social media is built.

WHY DO WE USE SOCIAL MEDIA?

Given past successes of the U&G approach with more traditional media there is a strong rationale for exploring social media through U&G. As such, many researchers have adopted the U&G framework to try and explain why we are drawn to certain sites. Although the flexibility of U&G can be seen as an advantage of an approach, it does have a slight downfall. Many studies use it to their advantage to follow their own research questions, e.g. some will focus on "process" gratifications (derived directly from media usage), while others will incorporate "content" gratifications (derived from specific media content and features) (Rubin, 2009). This can lead to a disorganized broader structure when comparing literature across studies (Kcrmar, 2017). The past decade has seen a huge rise in the number of U&G studies dedicated to social media, and these all vary in their scope and focus. For instance, some studies have focused on the U&G of social media as a whole (e.g. Whiting & Williams, 2013); some have focused on types of social media behaviors, such as content generation (e.g. Leung, 2013; Shao, 2009); and some have focused on U&G of types of social media, such as social networking sites, or comparisons of social media platforms (e.g. Orchard et al., 2014; Quan-Haase & Young, 2010; Urista, Dong, & Day, 2009). Furthermore, many studies are dedicated to the U&G of a specific platform, such as Facebook (e.g. Bumgarner, 2007; Joinson, 2008; Papacharissi & Mendelson, 2010; Sheldon, 2008), YouTube (e.g. Haridakis & Hanson, 2009), Instagram (e.g. Sheldon & Bryant, 2016), and Pinterest (e.g. Mull & Lee, 2014), while others are associated with specific features *within* such platforms (e.g. Smock, Ellison, Lampe, & Wohn, 2011). Regardless of the authors' approach, commonalities can be seen, despite such diversity.

Perhaps, not surprisingly given its title, one of the primary U&G that social media appears to fulfill revolves around social needs. The need to belong and maintain fulfilling relationships is part of Maslow's (1954) classic hierarchy of needs and described as being fundamental to our human nature. Social media allows us to "keep in touch" with our pre-existing (and predominantly offline) social network (Joinson, 2008;

Orchard et al., 2014; Sheldon, 2008; Urista, Dong, & Day, 2009; Whiting & Williams, 2013). Although other technologies have facilitated social communication previously (e.g. the telephone, the introduction of mobile phones, the beginning of computer-mediated communication, such as email and listservs), social media allows us to maintain connections in a novel manner. While comparing Facebook to instant messaging, Quan-Haase and Young (2010) found that the U&G of "social information" was unique to Facebook use. This motivation was associated with being "in the know" and being socially involved. Thus, social media is not only about maintaining individual connections, but also about being a part of a wider social network. Social media allows a user to instantly update their social network through one-to-many communication, such as a "Tweet" or status update. Furthermore, the types of disclosures made on social media tend to be different to the information we would previously disclose via alternative methods. I may consider it a little strange if a distant friend called me up solely to tell me that they were having steak and chips for dinner, yet an Instagram food update may be a welcome and common sight. Thus, by using social media we may feel more connected to the members of our network, and maintain connections that would normally dissipate. This may fuel feelings of belonging. Indeed, Papacharissi and Mendelson (2010) and Sheldon (2008) argue that "companionship" is a U&G of Facebook use.

Social media also provides opportunities to extend our network by initiating communication with those outside of our offline social network and making new connections (Bumgarner, 2007; Haridakis & Hanson, 2009; Joinson, 2008; Orchard et al., 2014; Sheldon, 2008; Quan-Haase & Young, 2010; Urista, Dong, & Day, 2009). Although it is dependent on the aims and features of the platform, such as user control over privacy settings, social media aims to connect individuals who do not know each other through the sharing of content. It is easy to find others with similar interests through the searching of hashtags (e.g. to find similar content on Twitter or Instagram), the joining of groups or subgroups (Facebook, Reddit), or through comments on content (YouTube videos). Thus, social media allows us to discuss common interests and seek out socialization that may not be possible through existing networks. Joinson (2008) also highlights the U&G of "social network surfing," or viewing the profiles of "friends of friends." In their definition of SNSs, boyd and Ellison (2007) argue that making connections with other members and navigating through a visual list of associations were key features of its use. This fits well with the idea that individuals are interested in their wider network and will want to utilize SNSs to view, and potentially interact with, their extended network. Again, this could perhaps increase one's sense of belonging within a large wider structure. It is important to note, however, that such socialization does not have to necessarily be reciprocal to fulfill the social need of an individual. For instance, following a celebrity on Twitter may increase feelings of connection, regardless of whether or not that celebrity follows the user back. Similarly, social media allows us to discretely monitor others, which can facilitate the making of new connections. Urista and colleagues (2009) include the U&G of "curiosity about others" in their analysis, while Joinson (2008) discusses "people watching" as part of a wider U&G of "social investigation." Furthermore, U&G of "surveillance and knowledge about others"

(Sheldon & Bryant, 2016; Whiting & Williams, 2013) and "voyeurism" (Bumgarner, 2007) have also been identified. Thus, it appears that when given the opportunity we may have a natural need to know more about people. The success of reality TV is perhaps founded on such a need. Thus, social media allows us an insight into the lives of others. As an example, snooping on a potential love interest through Facebook may fulfill our need for such curiosity.

Social motivations behind social media are facilitated by U&G of improved practicalities for communication. Some studies have highlighted the use of social media as a social tool. For instance, Whiting and Williams (2013) cite the U&G of "convenience utility" (i.e. convenient and easy access); Bumgarner (2007) cites the U&G of "collection and connection" (i.e. organizing one's social network) and "directory" (i.e. practical uses, such as finding details of a particular individual); while Urista and colleagues (2009) suggest that "efficient communication" (i.e. sharing information quickly) and "convenient communication" (i.e. managing communication, which allows individuals to stay in touch) may be key U&G of social network use. Thus, the ability of social media to facilitate fast communication is also a huge selling point. It allows individuals to socialize with minimal effort and provides tools to visually organize one's social network, which has not been seen within previous media.

Interestingly, social media also appears to indirectly fulfill our social needs by facilitating our offline interactions. Bumgarner (2007) and Whiting and Williams (2013) cite that social media fulfills the U&G of social or communication utility. Despite its firm existence within the technology world, social media still appears to be a buzzword of the times. Sci-fi fans may appreciate an analogy by Orchard, Fullwood, Morris, and Galbraith (2015) suggesting that Facebook communication can be considered akin to Star Trek's "Borg Collective," wherein users cannot escape social media given society's reliance upon it. Indeed, some studies suggest that certain users may be drawn towards social media because everybody else seems to use it (Bumgarner, 2007; Orchard et al. 2014). Thus, social media itself can become the start of a conversational piece to spur offline interactions. This is perhaps enhanced by the break-down of barriers between the "offline" world and our "online" world. By keeping in touch with our offline network in social media we are kept up to date with current news. For instance, a work colleague's Facebook status suggesting they had a late night may become useful water cooler gossip the next morning, while talk of a viral YouTube video may be circulated between friends in a "You've got to see this…" manner.

Moving beyond social needs, research suggests that social media provides a valuable information source. Indeed, Muntinga, Moorman, and Smit (2011) have suggested that surveillance needs (as discussed earlier) may be seen as a subcategory of an information motive. Many studies highlight U&G surrounding both information-seeking and information-sharing behaviors, albeit in differing forms (Haridakis & Hanson, 2009; Mull & Lee, 2014; Orchard et al., 2014; Whiting & Williams, 2013). Social media's reliance on user-generated content allows access to a wealth of information, allowing users to showcase their interests and specialisms to the world. For instance, an amateur handyman may turn towards YouTube for DIY tips and be greeted with a plethora of woodwork tutorials. Furthermore, users may be inclined to turn to their network for recommendations given that our connections leverage a level of trust (leading to the recent introduction of the Facebook recommendations tool). A part of the appeal for information sharing may again be due to the convenience that social media affords. Indeed, Haridakis and Hanson (2009) highlight that YouTube's convenience (i.e. its ease of use, inexpensive and novel nature) feeds into the U&G of information sharing, while Mull and Lee (2014) suggest "organization" (surrounding the collection and browsing of "pins") is a key motivation within Pinterest usage.

Papacharissi and Mendelson (2010) identify the U&G of "expressive information sharing," combining information sharing with self-expression. This makes sense given that the two needs are so entwined. For instance, creating a make-up tutorial video allows users to express their interests, while also fulfilling the aim of sharing information with others. The U&G of self-expression does seem to be particularly important within social media in its own right (Bumgarner, 2007; Orchard et al., 2014; Whiting & Williams, 2013), which is perhaps not surprising given that social media can be tailored to the user. Social media allows us to tell the world what's on our mind; whether it be a highly thought out rant with the aim of going viral, or a mundane moan about a price hike in a local supermarket. Social media provides us with a platform of willing viewers and allows us to fulfill any exhibitionist needs and to get our voices heard. This is exemplified by Joinson's (2008) inclusion of "status updates" as a U&G of Facebook use, and Sheldon and Bryant's (2016) U&G of "documentation" fueling Instagram use.

Many studies draw upon recreational or entertainment based U&G (including Bumgarner, 2007; Leung, 2013; Mull & Lee, 2014; Orchard et al, 2014; Papacharissi & Mendelson, 2010; Sheldon, 2008), suggesting that enjoyment derived *from* use is a key motivation *of* use. Social media is fun, and the element of entertainment may be ingrained in its unique features. For instance, Whiting and Williams (2013) associate entertainment with the use of specific features, such as Facebook games. Alternatively, entertainment may be linked to the fulfillment of other U&G, e.g. users may find it fun due to their social needs being fulfilled ("it's fun because I can snoop on other people"). Also, because it is an entertaining environment, social media use allows us an arena of escapism (Bumgarner, 2007; Orchard et al., 2014; Papacharissi & Mendelson, 2010; Whiting & Williams, 2013) and procrastination from boredom (or a means to pass time) (Orchard et al., 2014; Papacharissi & Mendelson, 2010; Quan-Haase & Young, 2010; Sheldon, 2008; Whiting & Williams, 2013). Again, this is no doubt fueled by its accessibility and ease of use. For example, social media is an entertaining way of passing time on a long bus ride when alternatives are limited.

As expected, given the pattern of U&G literature, many of these U&G directly relate back to those achieved via traditional media. However, it is clear that social media offers us opportunities to fulfill these U&G in a different way. Social media allows users the ability to be more active in their media use than previously seen and it would be unwise to believe that its unique features would not afford us more niche U&G (Sundar & Limperos, 2013). For instance, Papacharissi & Mendelson (2010) suggest that Facebook use may be motivated by the fact that it is a "cool and new trend," while Sheldon (2008),

Sheldon and Bryant (2016), and Quan-Haase and Young (2010) highlight that social media facilitates U&G of "coolness" and "fashion." In other words, users may be drawn to social media to affect their social standing. This relies on social media still being regarded as a new and trendy technology. Urista and colleagues (2009) also tap into the U&G of "popularity," while Leung (2013) draws upon "recognition." These U&G may relate to a need to be noticed. Indeed, social media is often anecdotally associated with attention-seeking behaviors and a push to become "viral." Thus, social media may allow us to feel like others are paying attention to us and that we are important to our network. Other more unique U&G may relate to more content-based gratifications, such as Joinson's (2008) Facebook U&G of "photographs."

Differentiating Between Platforms and Features

It is important that we keep in mind that not everyone will seek all U&G from social media. In line with the theoretical framework, different people will be seeking to fulfill differing U&G, depending on personal needs. Thus, individuals will have their own preferred platforms. Up until this point the chapter has predominantly discussed social media as a singular entity, but the subtleties between platforms are of high importance. As an example, the U&G of keeping in touch can be more easily fulfilled in Facebook (where one can monitor and talk to their social network in a one-to-one or one-to-many capacity) than in Pinterest (which relies on seeking inspiration from others, usually outside of the user's direct social network). As a demonstration of this, Mull and Lee (2014) note that social-based U&G appeared to be less important when specifically exploring motivations of Pinterest. Therefore, the selling point of each platform will lend itself to certain U&G over others. In a comparison between Facebook, forums, and blogs, Leung (2013) explored which platform was better able to fulfill five identified U&G: social and affection needs; venting negative feelings; recognition; entertainment; and cognitive needs. The study found that Facebook and blogs appeared to be better at fulfilling social and affection needs. Blogs also fulfilled the need for recognition, which makes sense given that blogs allow users to become center stage through their writing. Forums were more likely to be used to vent negative feelings, for entertainment needs, and for cognitive needs. The authors argue that the asynchronous nature of forums allows people to vent and this may be further supported by its (usually) anonymous nature. The ability to seek out specific forums to match one's interests or knowledge needs would also contribute to these findings.

Equally, features within platforms promote different U&G and individuals may choose to interact with platforms in different way to optimize their usage of such features. Shao (2009) taps into some of these differences by exploring the U&G of various behaviors within "user-generated media" (e.g. YouTube, MySpace, Wikipedia). Use of such sites was divided into three interconnected categories, and these were found to be associated with differing gratifications. Consuming media (i.e. passive usage, such as watching a YouTube video or reading a Wikipedia page) was associated with the U&G

of information and entertainment. Participating behaviors (i.e. interacting, sharing, and subscribing to content, including commenting) were associated with gratifying social interaction, and community development needs. Finally, producing behaviors (i.e. creation and publication of materials, such as creating a YouTube video or a Wikipedia entry) were associated with self-actualization and self-expression.

U&G can also be associated with specific feature use. For instance, a study by Smock and colleagues (2011) found that predetermined U&G could predict use of various Facebook features. Those motivated by the "habitual pastime" U&G were more likely to make wall posts. Wall posts are often used for mundane messages such as wishing someone a happy birthday; thus, this may reflect the more routine uses of Facebook. The U&G of "expressive information sharing" was associated with making status updates and using groups. The authors state that this is logical given that such features allow one-to-many communication. Those valuing "companionship" were less likely to comment. It may be that more synchronous environments could reduce loneliness, although this was not evident within the other explored features. "Professional advancement" was associated with making wall posts and private messages. The authors argue that individuals using Facebook to fulfill this need will be keen to maintain weak ties in case such a relationship becomes valuable in the future. Furthermore, the use of private messages would make sense given their private nature compared to other avenues. Such individuals may contact others about work opportunities, for instance, and would want to keep such information hidden off their general Facebook. "Social interaction" was associated with all features except status updates. However, the association with groups was negative; that is, those motivated by social interaction did not use groups. This suggests that groups in Facebook do not primarily serve a social function. This makes sense given that social interaction in this instance refers to keeping in touch with existing friends. Facebook groups tend to be used for interacting on Facebook with others around a particular topic, whether such individuals are known to the user or not. "Escapism" and "cool and new trend" were not associated with any specific feature, and therefore may relate to Facebook usage as a whole. The associations highlighted in these studies emphasize the importance of distinguishing between users and exploring factors that may determine differences in social media behaviors.

Who Uses Social Media?

U&G research provides us with a clear overview of *why* individuals may be motivated to use social media. However, we have yet to answer one of our original questions—*who* uses social media. Demographic statistics of social media users provide some insight into differences within the user base. For instance, statistics from the US-based PEW Research Center indicate that out of all age groups, 18- to 29-year-olds have the highest percentage of social media users. Furthermore, the percentage of females who use social media is slightly higher than the percentage of males for most, but not all, platforms

(LinkedIn is an exception) (Greenwood, Perrin, & Duggan, 2016). U&G suggests that individual users will have differing needs and therefore different motivations for engaging with a media. However, demographic data alone does not provide a meaningful connection with such research. This becomes particularly apparent with the growing number of users each year, which may eventually mask any key differences between age groups and sexes. As the digital divide decreases this information becomes somewhat redundant. Therefore, instead of asking *who* uses social media, we should reconceptualize the question to ask "*who* is using social media for *which* reasons?"

One of the key strengths of U&G is the ability to extend the framework to explore potential antecedents of the model, i.e. factors that may impact upon U&G. The importance of exploring such factors dates back to early U&G research. For instance, Rosengren (1974) emphasizes psychological and social characteristics as one of the fundamental principles within U&G research, while Katz, Blumler, and Gurevitch (1974, p. 20), in highlighting the theoretical position of U&G research, suggest that a consideration of the "social and psychological origins of needs" is often an integral stage of U&G research. Thus, antecedents of U&G models are vital for understanding the U&G themselves. It is suggested then that there are a number of factors that could impact upon our individual needs, which will then influence the U&G we seek. In a research sense we can explore this by looking for predictors of specific U&G. One of the key areas of exploration is personality.

Personality as a Predictor of U&G

When considering differences between individual behaviors it is imperative to consider the role of a person's personality. Allport's (1961) classic definition suggests that personality is "a dynamic organization, inside the person, of psychophysical systems that create the person's characteristic patterns of behaviour, thoughts, and feelings" (p. 11). In other words, personality provides us with a consistent typology of how we will react to our environment. Personality can explain our preferences and predispositions, as well as our tendency to react consistently across situations. For instance, personality can give us an insight into one's social preferences. Given that personality can have such a large impact on how we behave offline, it makes sense that these predispositions would drive us towards certain online behaviors. Indeed, research appears to support this, with differing personalities showing preferences towards differing types of online activity (e.g. Amichai-Hamburger, 2007; Orchard & Fullwood, 2010).

Personality has been found to influence general social media uptake. For instance, Correa, Hinsley, and de Zúñiga (2010) found that extraversion and openness to experience were positively associated with social media use, while emotional stability was negatively associated with social media. Thus, social media is used more frequently by extraverts (individuals who are more sociable and socially confident), those scoring higher on openness to experience (those who tend to be more innovative and creative), and those who score low on emotional stability (anxious individuals). The authors argue that this fits in with predicted preferences of such individuals. Lower scorers of extraversion may prefer more anonymous environments, where the focus is on content rather than individuals. The asynchronous nature of communication may be appealing to those low on emotional stability as they are better able to think about and plan out their communication. Furthermore, such an environment may be used to reduce loneliness given previous links with neuroticism. Finally, those high in openness to experience may value the novelty of such sites given that social media is constantly updating. As an aside, it is also worth noting that these results were found to interact with age and sex. Males with high extraversion and low emotional stability tended to use social media more frequently, as did females with high extraversion and openness to experience. Furthermore, extraversion was found to be an important predictor of social media use for younger users; while extraversion, emotional stability (negatively), and openness to experience were all associated to social media use among older users.

This study appears to answer our question, and provides us with a clearer picture of who is using social media. However, it is important to note that frequency of social media use does not necessarily equate to fulfilled need gratification. That is, other personality types may not use social media in such a frequent manner, but do still use it to fulfill the U&G that they personally seek. In line with this rationale some studies have decided to use additional regression analyses to explore whether personality can act as a predictor of certain U&G. In other words, it is expected that personality will impact upon personal needs, which will then determine the U&G sought within social media. U&G research exploring personality appear to support this assertion.

As an example, Orchard and colleagues (2014) used a U&G framework to explore whether personality could predict user motivations for using their preferred SNS. Personality was explored through the inclusion of global traits (i.e. traits that summarize one's whole personality: extraversion, psychoticism, and neuroticism) and two specific traits (sociotropy and autonomy). The study supported the suggestion that personality appears to impact upon the U&G sought from social media, with consistent results across traits. Within the study, extraversion significantly predicted the U&G of "new connections" and "recreation," suggesting that those higher in extraversion are more likely than lower scorers (i.e. those who prefer their own company) to use their preferred SNS to make new friends and because they enjoy the environment. Given that social media is so heavily based upon socializing and networking, it stands to reason that extraverts, rather than introverts, would enjoy such a platform, and would aim to utilize it to extend their existing network. Psychoticism was found to predict "free expression" and "newer connections." People scoring high on this personality tend to fight against societal norms and conformity. Social media, and indeed online communication generally, promotes an arena of disinhibition (Joinson, 2007). It makes sense that these individuals would enjoy using this to their advantage as they might enjoy the freedom of saying what they want. The link to new connections may be due to these individuals finding others similar to themselves (which may be difficult in an offline environment), or may be associated with risk-taking behaviors, which have previously been linked to similar personality traits (e.g. impulsive nonconformity in chat room use;

see Fullwood, Galbraith, & Morris, 2006). Neuroticism was predictive of the motivation "escapism," which suggests that highly anxious individuals may find this environment less anxiety provoking than everyday life; or indeed it may serve as a useful distraction for such anxieties. Sociotropy was predictive of "conformity," "information exchange," and "ritual" U&G. A higher score on sociotropy refers to an individual who has a high dependence on others around them. These individuals tend to conform as they want to be seen as fitting in with everybody else. In terms of information exchange these individuals may feel more confident asking and giving advice online due to the lack of social cues inherent in such an environment. These individuals may worry about how others would react to such information; despite a high need for being sociable. By exchanging the information online, they cannot see the other person's facial response and this may make them feel more at ease. The ritualistic use may be reflective of these individuals highly valuing the medium. After all, such individuals are highly focused on others around them, so SNSs seem a perfect way to fulfill this focus. Autonomy was negatively predicted of the "experimentation" factor, suggesting that those with lower autonomy scores are more motivated to use SNSs due to this factor. High scorers have a high need for control, and may therefore be more cautious of how they present themselves.

Personality has also been found to predict platform preferences for achieving certain U&G. For instance, Hughes, Rowe, Batey, and Lee (2012) studied personality and preferences surrounding social and informational U&G within Facebook and Twitter. Specifically, the authors explored the "big five" (consisting of neuroticism, extraversion, openness to experience, conscientiousness, and agreeableness), sociability, and need for cognition. The study found that personality was associated with differing preferences relating to expected predispositions. Neuroticism was negatively correlated with using Twitter for information purposes, but positively correlated with using Facebook for social and informational purposes. The authors argue that high neuroticism scorers may be drawn to Facebook to avoid loneliness. If this is the case, familiarity of the site may lower anxiety and thus promote use. Extraversion was negatively correlated to using Twitter for informational purposes, but positively related to using Facebook for informational purposes. Extraverts will perhaps enjoy having social discussions based on the information they are seeking, and therefore will value Facebook as their friends will be more involved in the information-seeking process. Openness to experience was correlated to using Twitter to fulfill social needs and Facebook for informational needs. Higher scoring individuals crave novelty and have broad interests. It may be that these individuals value socializing on Twitter as it promotes socialization outside of one's normal social circle more so than Facebook, allowing them to broaden their social perspective. However, Facebook may be valued for informational purposes as it may be easier to follow specific informational sources relating to their interests on their newsfeed. Conscientiousness was positively correlated with using Twitter for informational purposes, and negatively correlated with Twitter for social purposes and also Facebook for informational purposes. Those who are conscientious are thorough and have a strong work ethic. The authors argue that those with high scores value using Twitter for informational purposes as opposed to Facebook, as such information may be more cognitive (e.g. academic or political links) rather than social. It may also reflect Facebook information-seeking as being more heavily associated with procrastination, which would go against the individual needs of this personality. The negative correlation to Twitter for social usage may also be due to such behaviors being viewed as procrastination given that it is so broad compared to Facebook. Sociability was negatively associated with using Twitter for information, yet positively associated to using Twitter for social purposes, and Facebook for social and informational purposes. Highly sociable individuals enjoy social attention and interaction; any avenue to increase socialization would be valued. The preference for Facebook to pursue informational U&G may reflect that information can be gained through socialization, while Twitter is perhaps more solitary. Need for cognition was positively associated with using Twitter for information and negatively related to using Facebook for informational purposes. Individuals scoring high on this measure enjoy cognitive stimulation and finding information. As discussed previously, Facebook information may be viewed as being more subjective and less cognitive than Twitter. Agreeableness was not correlated with any of the U&G across platforms.

Finally, research has found that personality is related to specific feature use, which tends to follow U&G assumptions. Users interact with social media in line with their preferences based on their personal needs. For instance, in an exploration of personality and Facebook interactivity, Amichai-Hamburger and Vinitzky (2010) found that extraversion was related to total number of Facebook friends, which would fit the social needs of extraverts through extending their connections. Personality associations have also been found within more nuanced features. For instance, Eftekhar, Fullwood, and Morris (2014) found that personality was predictive of photo-sharing behaviors. Extraversion, for example, was related to the total number of uploaded photos and total number of cover photos, which the authors argue is a consequence of gratifying self-presentational and communication needs given their exhibitionist nature. Furthermore, personality appears to affect the manner in which we present ourselves online. For example, Seidman (2013) notes that neuroticism was found to be positively associated with general self-disclosures, emotional disclosures, and the expression of actual-, hidden-, and ideal-self aspects on Facebook. This fits in with previous literature and personality expectations. As already noted, social media may be less anxiety provoking for these individuals. This may allow them to feel like they are in a "safe" environment and to disclose more, and portray their actual- and hidden-self. Although the scope of this chapter does not allow for a more in-depth analysis of the literature, similar findings have been extended across other personality traits and across research studies.

Thus, it appears that our personality can influence the U&G we seek from social media. Users are motivated to use social media in a way that fulfills their underlying predispositions. In answer to our original question then (of *who* uses social media), although social media use is preferred by certain personality traits, the diversity of social media appears to allow anyone to use it to their tailored preferences. Our personality influences our personal needs, which then impacts upon the U&G we seek to gratify through social media. This in turn appears to influence our preferred platforms, and determines the features we interact with and the behaviors we undertake.

CRITICISMS AND CAVEATS

U&G is a highly useful and versatile approach, which has been well used to explore usage of social media. Despite this, it is worth emphasizing that the research has not been without its criticisms. A brief overview of such comments is important and may prove useful in informing future research.

The conceptualization of U&G as a whole has been criticized and this can be considered a strong limitation of the approach. For instance, some researchers have argued that the concepts are unclear and the terminology needs clarifying. Sundar and Limperos (2013) argue that the conceptualization of U&G research needs to be particularly reconsidered in light of Web 2.0 technology. They outline two limitations that need to be addressed in future applications of the framework. The authors suggest that the reliance on previous research to draw upon relevant gratifications hinders the findings by masking new gratifications previously unseen in traditional media. This is a particularly valid concern given that U&G studies can only extract the gratifications that they choose to measure. The predominant use of self-report methodology across the field relies on the comprehensiveness of the initial motivation list. Factor analysis will only draw out U&G that have been included at the preliminary stage. Future studies may wish to return to more qualitative methods to capture newer gratifications that may have been previously missed or that were simply not available through previous media. As an aside, this may also help combat criticisms surrounding self-report methodology in general, and the uncertainty around whether someone can accurately rate their own motives on a scale. Additionally, Sundar and Limperos (2013) also suggest that U&G are sometimes conceptualized too broadly. Again, this may mask subtler U&G that would be applicable to newer media. An example of this may be "information-seeking." This motivation may be applied very differently depending on the media platform it refers to, e.g. Twitter information-seeking may be characterized by general news-sourcing behaviors, while within Reddit it may refer to seeking out specific health information. Perhaps taking these two limitations together suggests that U&G research is somewhat flawed, and this may result in valid gratifications of new media being missed or misrepresented. The authors argue that affordances of new media may create unique needs not previously noted. In other words, the media itself may fuel a new need based on the features offered. Examples of these potential new gratifications are listed under four different categories: modality-based (realism, coolness, novelty, being there), agency-based (agency-enhancement, community building, bandwagon, filtering/tailoring, ownness), interactivity-based (interaction, activity, responsiveness, dynamic control), and navigability-based (browsing/variety-seeking, scaffolds/navigation aids, play/fun). Thus, a wider consideration of the "affordances" of new media is necessary.

Given its rapid progression we are always one step behind in cyberpsychology research, and this is particularly true within U&G research. Social media is constantly updating and this impacts upon the way we use it. For instance, Facebook is renowned for its "like" feature, yet this only appeared in 2009, two years after its popularity boom. Equally the "timeline" that now dominates its use was not introduced until 2011. Thus, it is important for U&G to constantly consider such changes and the resulting impact of these. As features change and update, users will react to such changes by reassessing their needs. They may find their needs can be fulfilled in a different and newer manner. Alternatively, they may find that the site no longer gratifies the needs they were expecting it to fulfill. If this is the case, then individuals will be on the lookout for new ways to satisfy them, and may seek alternative media. This falls in line with Niche Theory (Ramirez, Jr., Dimmick, Feaster, & Lin, 2008), which suggests that new media can tempt users by providing novel and unique gratifications that older media do not provide. An example of this may be the uptake of Snapchat, which allows ephemeral communication. The ability to send a photo for a short-lived, predetermined time frame (typically a few seconds) has not been found from previous media, and allows users to fulfill a self-expression gratification in a novel, playful manner (Waddell, 2016). The rapid growth of social media means that updated research is necessary and vital to understand the user base of each site. The user base of a particular platform and the needs that are fulfilled today may be very different if reassessed in the future. The timing of conducting a U&G study is also important. Novelty in itself may be considered a U&G that may fuel short-term use. Along with Niche Theory, this may explain why we have "fads" or trends of specific social media usage.

It has been said that needs and outcomes must be considered independently (Krcmar, 2017). A comprehensive discussion of how needs feed into outcomes is beyond the scope of this chapter. However, an appreciation of such literature is important. Gratifications sought do not always equal gratifications obtained. Although social media can gratify a number of needs to continue use, the outcome of such use is not necessarily positive or negative. For instance, Facebook snooping and monitoring behaviors may fulfill the "voyeurism" need of an individual, but this may also promote upward social comparisons (e.g. perceiving oneself as "worse off" than others), which could lead to negative outcomes. Furthermore, research suggests that Facebook snooping on a partner may incite further monitoring, whereby individuals get caught in a "feedback loop" of needing to find out more information based on the information they have already found (Muise, Christofides, & Desmarais, 2009). Thus, the gratifying of a particular need does not always equate to a positive, or intended, outcome.

Finally, it should be noted that this chapter does not by any means draw upon an exhaustive list of the literature. There are many U&G studies focusing on social media, and many exploring associations between personality and social media interactions. The aim of this chapter is not to provide a full literature review of the topic but rather to highlight similarities between studies and emphasize key findings. It should also be noted that despite the focus of the chapter, social media research does not need to be restricted to a U&G approach. Indeed, McMahon (2015) discusses social media uptake from a range of perspectives. For instance, from a behavioral perspective, the use of platform notifications and the reciprocity of "friending" behaviors reward and reinforce our continued engagement with the site.

CONCLUSION

Despite limitations, U&G is a widely used and highly considered method for exploring the motivations driving social media usage. This chapter started by posing two questions in relation to social media: "*who uses it*" and "*why.*" However, the questions should not be fully considered independently. As we reach a saturation point, it may appear that *everyone* is using a form of social media. In which case, the questions need to be reconceptualized. Social media fulfills a number of purposes, including the gratification of social needs, informational needs, and recreational needs, among others. Although the grouping of research is useful in providing an overview, it is important to consider studies in their own right, given that each platform will have its own unique selling point(s) and distinct available features. Furthermore, not everyone will use social media for all of these reasons. Users differ in regards to the needs they want to gratify through social media use. Among other variables, it is important to consider the impact of one's personality on their social media use given that personality is fundamental in determining our predispositions. Indeed, research has suggested that personality can influence online preferences in terms of the U&G we seek to fulfill and resulting behaviors.

This chapter concludes by asking you to again consider your own social media usage. However, this time, also consider your personality in the offline world. Can you see the connection? Keep this in mind the next time you log on.

REFERENCES

Allport, G. W. (1961). *Pattern & growth in personality*. New York: Holt, Rinehart & Winston.

Amichai-Hamburger, Y. (2007). Personality, individual differences and Internet use. In A. N. Joinson, K. Y. A. McKenna, T. Postmes, & U. D. Reips (Eds.), *Oxford handbook of Internet psychology* (pp. 187–204). Oxford: Oxford University Press.

Amichai-Hamburger, Y., & Vinitzky, G. (2010). Social network use and personality. *Computers in Human Behavior 26*, 1289–1295.

boyd, d. m., & Ellison, N. B. (2007). Social networking sites: Definition, history, and scholarship. *Journal of Computer-Mediated Communication 13*(1), 210–230.

Bumgarner, B. A. (2007). You have been poked: Exploring the uses and gratifications of Facebook among emerging adults. *First Monday 12*(11) [online]. Retrieved from http://firstmonday.org/ojs/index.php/fm/article/view/2026/1897

Correa, T., Hinsley, A. W., & de Zúñiga, H. G. (2010). Who interacts on the Web? The intersection of users' personality and social media use. *Computers in Human Behavior 26*, 247–253.

Eftekhar, A., Fullwood, C., & Morris, N. (2014). Capturing personality from Facebook photos and photo-related activities: How much exposure do you need? *Computers in Human Behavior 37*, 162–170.

Fullwood, C., Galbraith, N. & Morris, N. (2006). Impulsive nonconformity in female chat room users. *CyberPsychology and Behavior* 9(5), 634–637.

Greenwood, S., Perrin, A., & Duggan, M. (2016). *Social media update 2016*. PEW Research Center. Retrieved from http://www.pewinternet.org/2016/11/11/social-media-update-2016/

Haridakis, P. & Hanson, G. (2009). Social interaction and co-viewing with YouTube: Blending mass communication reception and social connection. *Journal of Broadcasting & Electronic Media* 53(2), 317–335.

Hughes, D. J., Rowe, M., Batey, M., & Lee, A. (2012). A tale of two sites: Twitter vs. Facebook and the personality predictors of social media usage. *Computers in Human Behavior* 28, 561–569.

Joinson, A. N. (2007). Disinhibition and the Internet. In J. Gackenbach (Ed.), *Psychology and the Internet: Intrapersonal, interpersonal, and transpersonal implications* (pp. 75–92). London: Elsevier.

Joinson, A. N. (2008). "Looking at," "looking up" or "keeping up with" people? Motives and uses of Facebook. In *Proceedings of the SIGCHI Conference on Human Factors in Computing Systems*. (pp. 1027–1036). 5–10 April, Florence, Italy. New York: ACM.

Katz, E., Blumler, J. G., & Gurevitch, M. (1974). Utilization of mass communication by the individual. In J. G. Blumler & E. Katz (Eds.), *The uses of mass communications: Current perspectives on gratifications research* (pp. 19–32). Beverly Hills, CA: Sage.

Krcmar, M. (2017). Uses and Gratifications: Basic concepts. In P. Rössler, C. A. Hoffner, & L. van Zoonen (Eds.), *The international encyclopaedia of media effects*. Hoboken, NJ: John Wiley & Sons.

Leung, L. (2013). Generational differences in content generation in social media: The roles of the gratifications sought and of narcissism. *Computers in Human Behavior* 29, 997–1006.

Maslow, A. (1954). *Motivation and personality*. New York, NY: Harper.

McMahon, C. (2015). Why do we "like" social media? *The Psychologist* 28, 724–729.

Muise, A., Christofides, E., & Desmarais, S. (2009). More information than you ever wanted: Does Facebook bring out the green-eyed monster of jealousy? *Cyberpsychology & Behavior* 12(4), 441–444.

Mull, I. R., & Lee, S. (2014). "PIN" pointing the motivational dimensions behind Pinterest. *Computers in Human Behavior* 33, 192–200.

Muntinga, D. G., Moorman, M., & Smit, E. G. (2011). Introducing COBRAs: Exploring motivations for brand-related social media use. *International Journal of Advertising* 30(1), 13–46.

Orchard, L. J., & Fullwood, C. (2010). Current perspectives on personality and Internet use. *Social Science Computer Review* 28(2), 155–169.

Orchard, L. J., Fullwood, C., Galbraith, N., & Morris, N. (2014). Individual differences as predictors of social networking. *Journal of Computer-Mediated Communication* 19(3), 388–402.

Orchard, L. J., Fullwood, C., Morris, N., & Galbraith, N. (2015). Investigating the Facebook experience through Q Methodology: Collective investment and a "Borg" mentality. *New Media & Society* 17(9), 1547–1565.

Palmgreen, P., & Rayburn, J. D. (1979). Uses and gratifications and exposure to public television: A discrepancy approach. *Communication Research* 6, 155–180.

Papacharissi, Z. (2009). Uses and Gratifications. In D. W. Stacks & M. B. Salwen (Eds.), *An integrated approach to communication theory and research* (pp. 137–152). Abingdon: Routledge.

Papacharissi, Z., & Mendelson, A. (2010). Toward a new(er) sociability: Uses, gratifications, and social capital on Facebook. In S. Papathanassopoulos (Ed.), *Media perspectives for the 21st century* (pp. 212–230). New York: Routledge.

Parker, B. J., & Plank, R. E. (2000). A Uses and Gratifications perspective on the Internet as a new information source. *American Business Review 18*(2), 43–49.

Quan-Haase, A., & Young, A. L., (2010). Uses and Gratifications of social media: A comparison of Facebook and instant messaging. *Bulletin of Science, Technology & Society 30*(5), 350–361.

Ramirez Jr., A., Dimmick, J., Feaster, J., & Lin, S. (2008). Revisiting interpersonal media competition: The gratification of niches of instant messaging, e-mail, and the telephone. *Communication Research 35*(4), 529–547.

Rosengren, K. E. (1974). Uses and Gratifications: A paradigm outlined. In J. G. Blumler & E. Katz (Eds.), *The uses of mass communications: Current perspectives on gratifications research*, Vol. 3. (pp. 269–286). Beverly Hills, CA: Sage Publications, Inc.

Rubin, A. M. (1983). Television uses and gratifications: The interactions of viewing patterns and motivations. *Journal of Broadcasting & Electronic Media 27*(1), 37–51.

Rubin, A. M. (2009). The uses-and-gratifications perspective on media effects. In J. Bryant & M. B. Oliver (Eds.), *Media effects: Advances in theory and research*, (pp. 165–184). New York: Routledge.

Ruggiero, T. E. (2000). Uses and Gratifications theory in the 21st Century. *Mass Communication & Society 3*(1), 3–37.

Seidman, G. (2013). Self-presentation and belonging on Facebook: How personality influences social media use and motivations. *Personality and Individual Differences 54*, 402–407.

Shao, G. (2009). Understanding the appeal of user-generated media: A Uses and Gratification perspective. *Internet Research 19*(1), 7–25.

Sheldon, P. (2008). Student favourite: Facebook and motives for its use. *Southwestern Mass Communication Journal 23*(2).

Sheldon, P., & Bryant, K. (2016). Instagram: Motives for its use and relationship to narcissism and contextual age. *Computers in Human Behavior 58*, 89–97.

Smock, A. D., Ellison, N. B., Lampe, C., & Wohn, D. Y. (2011). Facebook as a toolkit: A Uses and Gratifications approach to unbundling feature use. *Computers in Human Behavior 27*, 2322–2329.

Sundar, S. S., & Limperos, A. M. (2013). Uses and Grats 2.0: New gratifications for new media. *Journal of Broadcasting & Electronic Media 57*(4), 504–525.

Urista, M. A., Dong, Q., & Day, K. D. (2009). Explaining why young adults use MySpace and Facebook through Uses and Gratifications Theory. *Human Communication 12*(2), 215–229.

Waddell, T. F. (2016). The allure of privacy or the desire for self-expression? Identifying users' gratifications for ephemeral, photograph-based communication. *Cyberpsychology, Behavior, & Social Networking 19*(7), 441–445.

Whiting, A., & Williams, D. (2013). Why people use social media: A Uses and Gratifications approach. *Qualitative Market Research: An International Journal 16*(4), 362–369.

CHAPTER 18

IMAGE SHARING ON SOCIAL NETWORKING SITES: WHO, WHAT, WHY, AND SO WHAT?

MELANIE KEEP, ANNA JANSSEN,
AND KRESTINA L. AMON

INTRODUCTION

WE shared images with each other long before camera phones, and online photo-sharing websites and apps. Photos have been used to construct personal and group memories, to build and maintain relationships, for self-expression and for influencing others' perceptions of oneself for over a century (i.e. self-presentation; van House, Davis, Takhteyev, Ames, & Finn, 2004). Digital photography and online photo-sharing has enabled these social practices to continue, but the affordances of the new image sharing platforms has also facilitated an evolution of such practices.

The evolution of image sharing can be witnessed in the interactions observed on social networking sites (SNSs). In the past, photos were shared with specific audiences, either through printed images shared face-to-face or digital files emailed to particular people. In contrast, SNS users can post an image to a much larger audience. This changes the way stories are constructed and told, and which photos are shared. This chapter focuses on image sharing in SNSs, with particular attention on comparing research into image sharing on Facebook, Instagram, and Snapchat. The ubiquity of these platforms, and the unique pattern of their shared and distinctive functionalities provides a relevant context for understanding the who, what, why, and what for, of image sharing on SNSs.

What Are Facebook, Instagram, and Snapchat?

As SNSs, Facebook, Instagram, and Snapchat allow users to create a profile where they can share updates about almost anything. Other users can access this profile to view the updates, and post their own for the original user to view. On some platforms, the updates are images or videos with accompanying text (e.g. Instagram and Snapchat); on others, the updates can be textual and may or may not include images or videos (Facebook). Additional functionality such as geotagging, privacy limits, types of connections and visibility of connections other users, the temporality of posts, and image enhancements vary between platforms; these are described in more detail below. The different and shared affordances of Facebook, Instagram, and Snapchat enable comparisons that enhance our understanding of the ubiquitous process of online image sharing from intention to behavior to outcome. The sections below provide a brief introduction to each of the platforms. The descriptions of the SNSs are accurate at the time of writing (October 2018).

Facebook

At present, Facebook is the most popular SNS (Greenwood, Perrin, & Duggin, 2016), reporting 1.45 billion daily active users as of June 2018 (Facebook Newsroom, 2018). Facebook users create a profile where they can share information about themselves, such as their current city of residence, workplace, alma mater, sporting affiliations, and relationship status. In addition, users can make regular changes to their profiles through textual, video, or image updates. Via this profile (called a "wall" on Facebook), users can also receive (semi)public messages from other users that they are connected with. A user can control who is able to view different components of their profile by adjusting and personalizing their privacy settings.

Facebook users can interact with each other through direct communication via public posts on walls, privately via a messenger function, or by reacting to a post made by the other user. Facebook has default options so that, with one click, a user can express a range of reactions, including "like," "sad," "anger," and "love." Users can also comment on each other's posts.

The Facebook social network is comprised of "friendships." Users must request to be connected to another user (a "friend" using Facebook nomenclature) and, once connected, each user can access parts of the other user's profile that they've been granted access to. This mutual "friendship" connection is unique to Facebook (when compared to the other two SNSs discussed in this chapter) and may explain why some research findings observed on Facebook might not be applicable on other SNSs (where there may be a power differential between two users and how they connect to each other). Additionally, research suggests that most Facebook friendships are between users who know each other offline (boyd & Ellison, 2007). This prior relationship can also impact on why and how Facebook is used, and what outcomes they derive from the experience.

Instagram

Instagram was designed for users to share real-time moments captured through photo and/or video, with the option to edit using filters. These shared images or videos are represented in a grid on the user's Instagram profile. Unlike other photo-sharing SNSs like Facebook, Flickr, or Pinterest, sharing capabilities are only available on a compatible mobile device and not through a computer web browser.

To build a social network through Instagram, users "follow" other Instagram profiles, which may be profiles of other individuals, organizations, or pets or characters. Instagram profiles show the number of Instagram profiles a user follows and the number of profiles who follow the user (termed "followers" on Instagram), with hyperlinks to those profiles. The ratio of profiles following you and profiles you follow could be used as an indicator of popularity, or power differences.

Photographs can be edited using inbuilt filter options, and users can add a text caption to describe the image or video. To share it with the wider Instagram community, users can post a hashtag/s (#) related to the photograph for other users to find. Users can follow hashtags as they would other users. This allows the top posted pictures of that hashtag to become visible in their feed. Users can "like" a picture by clicking on the heart icon, make a comment on the post (if commenting is made available), direct other users to particular posts by tagging them using their handle through the @ symbol, and privately share posts by direct sharing to individual users or groups. Newly introduced functions include creating picture and short video stories editable using filters and icon stickers that are deleted after 24-hours (similar to Snapchat), and live videos which allows users to share moments with their followers without posting the content directly to their profile (Instagram, 2016a, 2016b).

Snapchat

In contrast to the "permanent" post on Facebook and Instagram, Snapchat posts are automatically erased after a short period of time (Bayer, Ellison, Schoenebeck, & Falk, 2016). Users share "snaps," images or videos, with other users either through direct messaging (where posts can be viewed twice before disappearing, and chat history is deleted once you exit the chat), or on "My Story" (viewable for 24 hours unless manually deleted earlier). Interactions occur through sharing messages (images, video, or text) and there is no equivalent function to the "likes" in Instagram and Facebook. Users can share their snaps to "Our Story" which makes them public to a particular place or event. This enables users not connected to each other on Snapchat to view each other's posts.

Users can manually add each other through phone contacts or sharing usernames. Alternatively, through the Global Positioning System on mobile devices, Snapchat users can search and add other users who are "nearby." Only the user can see who they are following; they cannot, however, see who their followers are. Snapchat users are notified as they are added by others but there is not a permanent list of followers for each profile.

Snapchat functions include the ability to edit using face and location lenses (e.g. adding dog ears and tongue, or sunglasses to selfies), data filters (e.g. including the time, temperature, or speed traveling); color filters to brighten or darken images/videos; changing backdrops; adding stickers, text, doodles, weblinks; cutting and deleting objects from an image, and adding snaps to locations for other users to view (Snapchat, 2017). Snapchat also notifies users when a follower takes a screenshot of their video or image.

Who Shares Images on Social Networking Sites?

With millions of users worldwide it could be easy to think SNSs like Facebook and Snapchat are used by everyone, but that simply isn't the case. The research shows that when it comes to sharing images on SNSs gender and age make all the difference. In the following sections we discuss how these demographic characteristics affect image sharing behaviors on SNSs.

Age

According to a recent survey, 79 percent of American adults reported using Facebook, and 32 percent used Instagram (Greenwood et al., 2016). Although the use of image sharing platforms is widespread, they remain more popular with younger individuals. Recent research shows that 59 percent of Instagram users are young adults aged between 18–29 years (in contrast to 33 percent of users aged between 30–49 years, and 26 percent of users aged 50 years and over; Greenwood, et al., 2016).

Image sharing on SNSs is one of the most popular online activities, and younger adults are more likely to use SNSs that facilitate image sharing than their older counterparts. Specifically, a recent survey found that although Facebook was the most widely used SNS among US adults, 18- to 24-year-olds are more likely to use Snapchat and Instagram than older users (including peers aged between mid- to late twenties; Smith & Anderson, 2018). Similar results have been found in Australia (Sensis, 2017), and the UK (Department for Culture, 2016).

Specific to image sharing, Malik, Hiekkanen, and Nieminen (2016) also found that younger participants were more likely to share photos on Facebook. Younger Facebook users, too, are more likely to trust the platform, and share more images on Facebook than older users but they also report greater levels of concern about the privacy of shared content (Malik, Hiekkanen, & Nieminen, 2016). In addition to trust, there are motivational differences between younger and older adults for using social media. Research has found that older adults prefer to use SNSs to maintain specific relationships and so would (seldomly) post images in a broadcast medium (Brandtzæg, Lüders, & Skjetne, 2010). Young adults (university-aged), in contrast, reported using Facebook to pass the time, and for relaxing entertainment (Papacharissi & Mendelson, 2011). With these goals, it would make sense that younger users would more frequently create content to share and receive feedback about, that is, share images, than older users.

Gender

Early research into image sharing on social media showed no significant gender differences in quantity of images shared on SNSs, or the content of images shared on the platforms (Hum et al., 2011). However, more recent research suggests that the non-significant gender differences observed in earlier research might have been due to the functionalities of SNSs that were researched at the time, such as Facebook, rather than a reflection of gender differences. More contemporary research indicates different genders preference different SNSs, with men more frequently sharing images on Twitter and women more frequently sharing images on Snapchat (Thelwall & Vis, 2017). Aligned with earlier research there appears to be no gender difference in image sharing behaviors on Facebook or Instagram.

Researchers have also explored how privacy concerns about image sharing online are affected by gender. Women have been reported to have significantly greater privacy concerns regarding how their Facebook images could be used and misused by Facebook, third parties, or other users than men (Malik, Hiekkanen, & Nieminen, 2016). However, it has been well documented that there is a disconnect between privacy concerns online and behavior on SNSs. This suggests that even though women may have greater privacy concerns about sharing images online than men, these concerns do not actually reduce the frequency with which female users post images online.

Personality of Users

Personality traits have been shown to play a role in willingness to share images on SNSs, and the types of images shared. The influence of personality on online image sharing is particularly interesting for researchers, due to the way SNSs enable users to showcase various aspects of themselves. In essence, users can curate the personality they present on a SNS. Furthermore, there is growing interest not just in how users showcase their personality on SNSs, but also the flip side of this: how SNSs are shaping us and our personalities. The following sections will discuss some of the research into commonly studied personality traits and their relationship with image sharing on SNSs. These traits are the Big Five (extraversion, neuroticism, agreeableness, conscientiousness, and openness to experience) and narcissism.

Extraversion

Extraverts are commonly perceived as gregarious people, often energetic and outgoing. In contrast, introverts are more quiet, reserved, and prefer not to be the center of attention (John & Srivastava, 1999; McCrae & Costa, 1997). Research into Facebook use more broadly has consistently shown that extraverts perceive social media as an additional tool for gratifying their need to socialize. As such, it is not surprising that research has found that individuals who report high levels of extraversion also post more images on Facebook in general, more selfies, and also upload more cover photos (Eftekhar, Fullwood, & Morris, 2014; Ong et al., 2011; Sorokowska et al., 2016). On Instagram, users who report higher extraversion also report more frequent interaction with others' posts (liking and commenting on Instagram posts, tagging other users in posts), as well as more frequent strategic self-presentation, specifically by posting on particular days at specific times (Keep & Amon, 2017). At present, there is limited understanding of the relationship between personality and Snapchat use, except that extraversion significantly predicts being motivated to use Snapchat for social interactions and impression management (Garnica, 2017). Combined, these findings provide support for the proposal that extraverted individuals use social media to gratify their need for social interactions, and strategically uploading images and engaging with others' posts facilitates these interactions.

In contradiction, some studies have also found no relationship between extraversion and the number of images shared on Facebook (Amichai-Hamburger & Vinitzky, 2010; Ross et al., 2009), and no differences in extraversion between Snapchat users and non-users (Landstrom, 2017). Although further research is needed to clarify these discrepant findings, it is worth noting that research showing a relationship between extraversion and image sharing is more recent, and perhaps the comparison of Snapchat users and non-users could be more nuanced. SNSs are only one method for interacting with others, and perhaps people who are extraverted who are able to satisfy their need for social interaction in other ways are less likely to seek online interactions. This, however, does not necessarily negate the proposal that SNS users who are more extraverted are more likely to engage with social media in ways that promote interaction with others.

Neuroticism

Individuals with a high level of neuroticism are characterized as being temperamental, emotional, easily stressed, and may have low self-esteem (John & Srivastava, 1999; McCrae & Costa, 1997). Conversely, an individual who is low in neuroticism is characterized as emotionally stable, secure, and confident.

Early research into the relationship between neuroticism and image sharing behavior was somewhat conflicted. There was some indication that people with high neuroticism posted fewer photos on SNS, specifically Facebook, than other users (Ross et al., 2009), but other studies showed the opposite (Amichai-Hamburger & Vinitzky, 2010). More recent research suggests that neuroticism positively predicted number of photos uploaded to Facebook, and the average number of photos per Facebook album (Eftekhar, Fullwood, & Morris, 2014).

Research has established that the desire for positive self-presentation on SNS mediates the relationship between neuroticism and self-disclosure (Eftekhar, Fullwood, &

Morris, 2014). In other words, individuals with a high level of neuroticism are balancing a desire to share images on SNS with a desire to control the presentation of themselves to others. Eftekhar and colleagues (2014) suggested that by uploading more images to create particular impressions, highly neurotic users might be trying to control how others perceived them. Furthermore, researchers have shown that participants reporting high neuroticism were also more likely to report using strategic self-presentation strategies. So, one explanation for the mixed findings about the relationship between number of images posted on SNS and neuroticism is individual motivation. Given the importance of the role of motivation in image sharing, this factor is explored further in Motivations for Image Sharing.

Agreeableness

People high in agreeableness are characterized as being cooperative, warm, good team members, and friendly; in contrast, someone low in agreeableness might seem disagreeable, combative, or self-serving (John & Srivastava, 1999; McCrae & Costa, 1997). Unlike other personality traits, researchers have found the relationship between agreeableness and number of images uploaded to SNSs follows a U curve. Specifically, Facebook users high and low in agreeableness post more images than people who scored moderately on agreeableness (Amichai-Hamburger & Vinitzky, 2010). One potential explanation is that people low in agreeableness post more images to promote themselves or assert their individuality. In contrast, people high in agreeableness post more images to connect with their peers. This dichotomy highlights the need for further research into motivations as a key factor to understanding online image sharing.

Researchers have also explored the relationship between agreeableness and other SNS image sharing behaviors. Research exploring personality and Instagram engagement found that participants who scored higher on agreeableness were more likely to like and comment on others' posts, as well as tag people in others' posts (Keep & Amon, 2017). People with a higher level of agreeableness on SNSs also seem to encourage more feedback from their network. Users who score higher on agreeableness are also more likely to be tagged in Facebook photos, perhaps because they are friendly, and so better liked and more likely to be invited to take photos with others (Bachrach, Kosinski, Graepel, Kohli, & Stillwell, 2012). Agreeableness was the only significant predictor of the average number of "likes" received on Facebook profile pictures, again suggesting that since highly agreeable people are more liked, that they would also be receiving more positive feedback on SNSs.

Conscientiousness

Conscientiousness is generally characterized by people who are diligent, hard-working, and disciplined. People low in conscientiousness may be perceived as disorganized, or without a strong sense of purpose (John & Srivastava, 1999; McCrae & Costa, 1997). Given this, it may be difficult to predict how people who are conscientious might engage with SNSs. Some researchers suggest that conscientious individuals may perceive social media to be superfluous or vacuous, and are therefore less likely to engage and share photos at all (Ross et al., 2009). On the other hand, someone who is conscientious may also want to use image sharing platforms to document their experiences and interactions with others, or upload more photos to carefully manage others' impressions of them.

Research into image sharing behaviors of conscientious users of SNS is similarly complex, with mixed findings on the topic. Conscientiousness has been shown to be positively correlated with extensive photo uploading to Facebook (Bachrach et al., 2012), and conscientiousness can also be a predictor of the number of Facebook albums created by users (Eftekhar, Fullwood, & Morris, 2014). Despite this, researchers exploring the relationship between conscientiousness and motivation found it did not have a relationship with participants' intention to use Facebook to disclose personal information or emotions (Seidman, 2013). Unsurprisingly, people who were conscientious were also less likely to use Facebook for attention seeking, or portraying their hidden or ideal selves (Seidman, 2013). On Instagram, Keep and Amon (2017) found that conscientiousness did not predict strategic self-presentation or interactions with others. Together, these studies show the need for further, more nuanced research into the relationships between conscientiousness, motivation, and image sharing on specific (and different) social media platforms.

Openness to Experience

Individuals who demonstrate openness to experience are characterized by being curious, willing to try new things, creativity and being imaginative. Someone low on openness to experience may prefer more routine, structure, and known entities (John & Srivastava, 1999; McCrae & Costa, 1997). Researchers have shown that there is a positive correlation between Instagram users' scores for openness, and the number of images of musical instruments shared on their Instagram profiles (Ferwerda & Tkalcic, 2018). This aligns with the perception that individuals who are high in openness to experience are creative and engaged with the arts. In contrast, studies that consider more broadly the number of videos or images uploaded to Facebook found no relationship between engagement with the arts and openness to experience (Eftekhar, Fullwood, & Morris, 2014). Seidman (2013) also reported no relationship between openness to experience and using Facebook for either belonging or self-presentation.

Openness to experience is quite a broad personality trait and could be manifest in a number of different (and not mutually exclusive) ways in terms of image sharing. As such, the more nuanced research exploring the differences in the content of image posts was able to detect a meaningful (and perhaps sensible) contribution of openness to experience, whereas research into broader image sharing trends found no contribution. Alternatively, it has been suggested that sharing and interacting with others through Facebook photos may no longer be considered a new experience and so this personality trait can't consistently predict its use (Eftekhar, Fullwood, & Morris, 2014). Given the relative recency of Snapchat and the limited research in this area, future studies could compare the relationship between openness to experience and image sharing across different platforms that vary in recency and popularity.

Narcissism

Narcissism is a multidimensional personality trait that can be challenging to comprehensively characterize. The Narcissistic Personality Inventory describes three components (Ackerman et al., 2011). Firstly, leadership/authority (LA): an individual is driven to achieve authority or power over others. Secondly, grandiose exhibitionism (GE): perceived as self-absorbed, vain, attention-seeking, and self-promoting. Finally, entitlement/exploitative (EE): perception that respect is owed and that they should be prioritized and privileged above others usually without clear reasons.

Much of the research into image sharing and narcissism has focused on selfies (images of a person taken by that person and shared on social media). This is due to the perception that selfies are self-indulgent and a way to use physical appearance for social gain, common characteristics of narcissists (Fox & Rooney, 2015). It has also been shown that people with high LA and GE posted selfies more frequently than people reporting lower scores on these dimensions (Weiser, 2015). Narcissism significantly and positively predicted number of selfies posted and frequency of photo editing behaviors, even controlling for age, a factor previously shown to have a positive relationship with narcissism (e.g., Twenge, Konrath, Foster, Campbell, & Bushman, 2008). McCain and colleagues (2016) confirmed, and extended, this research by finding that individuals scoring high on narcissism took more selfies daily, and more selfies of them by themselves. These participants were less likely to take selfies with others, and were more likely to post to Instagram. These findings are also supported in different cultural contexts. For example, university students in Korea who scored high on narcissism posted more selfies to Instagram, updated their profile picture more frequently, and were more likely to rate their own profile pictures as being more physically attractive (Moon, Lee, Lee, Choi, & Sung, 2016).

WHAT TYPES OF IMAGES ARE SHARED?

If someone looked up your Facebook or Instagram profile, what would they see? What experiences are shared through your Snapchat stories? Research analyzing publicly available SNS profiles, and surveys asking SNS users about their image sharing preferences have found that photos and videos shared on social media can portray various aspects of the individual—candid images, risk-taking behaviors, stylized photos, videos of food or landscapes, or self-portraits (Hu, Manikonda, & Kambhampati, 2014). Evidence also suggests that the types of images shared vary according to the platform, motivation, and audience. This section looks at the types of images shared on Facebook, Instagram, and Snapchat, and compares some of the image sharing literature across all three SNSs.

Facebook

According to Mendelson and Papacharissi (2010), images shared on Facebook are much more likely to show people, rather than other subjects such as landscapes or motivational imagery. Perhaps due to the emphasis on "friends" and relationships, individual photos or "selfies" are far less common than images of groups (two or more people) on Facebook (Mendelson & Papacharissi, 2010). The exception to this seems to be profile pictures, which are often of only one person, rather than a group of people, and tend to be posed (Hum et al., 2011).

There also seems to be gender differences in the content of images shared on Facebook. Men post more images of formal events, whereas women are more likely to post images of informal catch ups (Mendelson & Papacharissi 2010). Women seem to be more likely to post profile pictures that contain other people, a trend that has held true for the last ten years (Strano, 2008).

It is also interesting to consider the sorts of images not shared on Facebook. Researchers have observed that landscapes, images of family, images of injuries and embarrassing photos are rare on Facebook (Mendelson & Papacharissi 2010). Candid photos are generally less common than posed ones, and poses are generally inactive rather than demonstrating physical activity (Hum et al., 2011). Facebook users may avoid sharing images with certain types of content because of a focus on controlling the impressions made by their profiles, and a preference for a more conservative image. There is also some suggestion that Facebook users may be aware that potential employers could see their profile, and this may influence the content they post (Hum et al. 2011).

Instagram

Users share a wider range of image types on Instagram than they do on Facebook, possibly because Instagram focuses on image sharing. Researchers, having analyzed 1000 images from public Instagram profiles, identified eight categories of images: friends (pictures with or of friends), food, gadgets (including electronic gadgets, tools, and vehicles), captioned photos (images with text, including memes), pets, activities (e.g. concerts, landmarks), selfies (self-portraits), and fashion (Hu, Manikonda, & Kambhampati, 2014).

Food images, in particular, have received specific attention. In a study on adolescent food image sharing on Instagram, almost 40 percent of the images displayed a brand name (e.g. Coca-Cola, Starbucks) often accompanied by a caption or hashtag of the brand or participating in the brand's promotional activities (Holmberg, Hillman, & Berg, 2016). Additionally, food was presented two ways on Instagram, (i) focusing on the aesthetic features of the food or homemade qualities of food (i.e. food images showing a user's cooking skills), or (ii) focus of the food being part of lifestyle or situation (i.e. the image showing surroundings of the food including people and the location)

(Holmberg, Hillman, & Berg, 2016). It was noted that many of the images were arranged and displayed purposefully and with attention in its presentation, suggesting an intentional approach to impression management.

This idea that Instagram is used to present a curated image of the user is further supported in recent research comparing the content of images shared by users who expected strangers to view their posts and those who did not. Users who expected strangers to view their Instagram images shared more images of their hobbies and memes, while participants who did not expect strangers to view their Instagram posts shared more images about their relationships (Keep, Janssen, & Amon, 2018). Potential reasons include different motivations (those who expected stranger viewers may be motivated by self-presentation whereas those who did not expect stranger viewers may be motivated by relationship maintenance) or privacy concerns (those who did not expect strangers to view their posts felt safer sharing images of family/friends).

Snapchat

As with Instagram and Facebook, the types of images shared on Snapchat are likely influenced by the platform structure itself. A survey of 77 Snapchat users found that the majority of respondents (98.7 percent) posted content on Snapchat that they perceived was funny. Furthermore, 85.7 percent of respondents included videos/images of themselves or provided viewers with information about what they were currently doing. Images/videos of food, events, or other people were shared by approximately 60 percent of participants (Utz, Muscanell, & Khalid, 2015). Building on this, other researchers have found that Snapchat users tended to share posts with individuals, rather than groups or the general public. This suggests that Snapchat is seen by its users more as an instant messaging tool, used with perhaps more awareness of its privacy than other platforms. This is consistent with research finding that young adults use Snapchat to interact with known peers rather than strangers (Vaterlaus, Barnett, Roche, & Young, 2016)

Researchers have also explored the role gender has on type of image shared on Snapchat. Men were more likely to ask for naked Snaps, and that men may use naked Snaps to assess the likelihood of sexual access. The survey found that both men and women were sent the same number of naked Snaps and were equally likely to share them to My Story (Moran, Salerno, & Wade, 2018).

Comparing Across Platforms

There have been few studies comparing the types of content shared across Facebook, Instagram, and Snapchat. Research into sharing alcohol-related images, however, provides insight into how the different affordances of each of these SNSs can affect users' approaches to sharing images of risky behaviors online.

According to recent research, US college students selected Instagram (over Snapchat and Facebook) as the most probable destination for all vignettes and photo posts which glamorized alcohol use (e.g. drinking champagne at a fancy event). Snapchat was found to be most selected as the platform associated with negative consequences associated with alcohol use (e.g. hangovers, sickness). Facebook was selected as the least likely destination for both (Boyle, Earle, LaBrie, & Ballou, 2017). Researchers suggest that the decision to selectively post to different platforms result from the unique affordances of the platform. That is, the editing functions on Instagram allow for the beautifying of images to glamorize behavior, and the ephemeral nature of Snapchat posts may lead students to perceive it to be less risky to share negative images on this platform. Additionally, Instagram and Snapchat have its individual ability to use alternative usernames, and privacy settings, unlike Facebook where real names are recommended by the platform.

MOTIVATIONS FOR IMAGE SHARING

One recurring theme of our discussions so far is how motivation might explain some of the complexity of online image sharing behaviors. Although there is an abundance of research exploring motivations for SNS use (even some comparing motivations for using different platforms; see Alhabash & Ma, 2017), studies specifically investigating why people post photos to SNSs are not as common. This research has grown alongside the (relatively) recent rise in popularity of image-based social media platforms, and is discussed in this section.

Relationship Building and Maintenance

Consistently, research has found that people share images to build and maintain personal relationships, or to create and contribute to a larger community. During disasters such as the December 2004 Indian Ocean tsunami and 2007 London bombings, images were shared online to create a sense of solidarity with the victims, and provide a sense of community among supporters and survivors (Liu, Palen, Sutton, Hughes, & Vieweg, 2008). Members of the Flickr community (an image-sharing site pre-dating Instagram) reported that these shared photo albums provided a means for documenting the events, but also provided support to the communities affected (Liu et al., 2008). These altruistic motivations that suggest a sense of community larger than our traditional network of family, friends, and acquaintances also emerge through research into travel-based image sharing on Facebook. Munar and Jacobsen (2013) found that tourists prefer to share visual content over textual content, and report sharing images on social media to help others make decisions about their own trips, and maintain relationships while they were traveling.

In addition to supporting and sustaining relationships among members of a wider network or community, online photo sharing is used to maintain relationships between personal networks. Utz, Muscanell, and Khalid (2015) found that keeping in touch with family and friends was one of the top three reasons for sharing photos on Facebook and Snapchat, with this motivation being significantly higher for posting images to Facebook than Snapchat. A potential reason is that users tend to use their real names, and connect with people who they already know using these two platforms (in contrast to Instagram), so the focus on these particular relationships is greater. Facebook, as the longer standing SNS, may also be home to more relationships, and Snapchat users tend to only regularly interact with a small group of people, no more than 12 (Piwek & Joinson, 2016). As such, sharing photos on these platforms may be more conducive to maintaining personal relationships.

Recent studies have identified more nuanced motivations regarding relationship maintenance through photo sharing on SNSs. Malik and colleagues (2016) found that among other motivations (personal self-disclosure, sharing information, habit, and social influence, i.e. being perceived as cool), Facebook users shared photos to seek attention and gain affection. So, in terms of relationships, image sharing can be used to increase popularity and garner positive feedback (through likes and comments). This is consistent with research showing that need for popularity significantly predicts frequency of uploading and editing photos for SNSs over and above need for belonging, self-esteem, entitlement, and vanity (Utz, Tanis, & Vermeulen, 2012). Social media users, therefore, have a complex relationship with others online, and are motivated by relationships in so far as they can provide and receive support, but also present particular images of themselves to facilitate these positive relationships.

Self-Expression and Impression Management

Self-presentation and/or impression management have been long identified as motivators for SNS use (Fullwood, 2015). Specific to image sharing, Facebook users choose certain profile pictures to portray themselves as attractive or fun-loving, as popular, or to show their relationship status (Strano, 2008), which aim to create a particular image of the individual and to shape others' impressions of them. Instagram users also report posting images to express themselves or present a particular image to others (Lee, Lee, Moon, & Sung, 2015). In line with this, Facebook users also report untagging themselves from images posted by others if those photos are unattractive or portray them doing something they don't want others to know about (Pempek, Yermolayeva, & Calver, 2009). However, this is not to say that Facebook identities are completely divorced from who the person is offline. Researchers compared self-ratings of individuals' actual personality and their idealized self with ratings made by observers of their Facebook profile (Back et al., 2010). Observer ratings corresponded more closely with actual personality than idealized personality, suggesting that although people can use social media to influence others' perceptions of them, the images presented are not wildly different from their actual selves.

Research into self-presentation on Instagram and personality showed the potential negative consequences of being driven by popularity. Dumas, Maxwell-Smith, Davis, and Giulietti (2017) found that individuals who scored higher on narcissism and lower on peer belonging are more susceptible to using more deceptive, manipulative, and dishonest acts to gain attention and validation on Instagram, thereby increasing their popularity and potentially showcasing their creativity. These researchers also established two unique types of like-seeking behavior that could be further explored in future studies, especially in comparisons between platforms: (i) normative like-seeking behavior, where individuals were more widely accepted and more comfortable admitting to peers of these actions (i.e. using hashtags and filters), and (ii) deceptive like-seeking behavior, where individuals engage in dishonest actions to secure Instagram likes (i.e. buying likes and followers and using software to change appearance).

Documenting, Surveillance/Voyeurism, and Escapism

The need to consider SNSs as distinct is further reinforced by motivations more prevalent in some platforms compared to others. In addition to self-presentation and relationship maintenance, Lee and colleagues (2015), and Sheldon and Bryant (2016) have identified additional motivations through "archiving" and "documenting," that is, using Instagram to store memories as images of past events in the form of virtual photo albums, with ease of identifying the moment or event captured, and ease of returning to the image using hashtags. This could be due to the unique functionality of Instagram, and its focus on creating an image-based identity or profile. This virtual archiving could also serve as shared albums to further reinforce the relationships and communities described earlier.

When considering the use of images on SNSs more broadly—images that are posted, and not just viewed—recent research has seen the emergence of surveillance/voyeurism as reasons for engaging with Facebook and Instagram photos (Lee et al., 2015). As these platforms have become more popular and more content is shared on them, users may view these SNSs as tools for remaining up to date with others, or that checking Facebook/ Instagram/Snapchat has been integrated into modern life. In addition to the relationship and self-presentation motives identified, Facebook and Instagram users indicate that they post images online because it's habitual (i.e. part of ordinary online behavior; Sheldon & Bryant, 2016), or because it is perceived as cool or trendy to do so (Malik, Hiekkanen, & Nieminen, 2016; Piwek & Joinson, 2016; Sheldon & Bryant, 2016). Similarly, Snapchat users are curious about the new SNS and engage with the platform because their friends are doing so (Piwek & Joinson, 2016). Thus, the peer influence and "second nature" aspect of social media in modern life are additional motivations for users to engage with photos on SNSs, if not to post some of their own.

Escapism is another motivator identified in two studies of Facebook and Snapchat use (Lee et al., 2015; Utz, Muscanell, & Khalid, 2015). Participants in both studies reported viewing these platforms as a way of escaping the present, sometimes out of boredom, and sometimes to take them outside where they currently are. With the wealth of travel photos, memes, and advertisements, these platforms enable quick access to entertainment. The Snapchat filters allow users to "play" and share their images of videos as further ways of distracting them from the current situation.

The "So What?" Factor

In addition to exploring the who, what, how, and why of social media use, numerous studies have also examined the "so what?" of interacting on SNSs. Specifically, numerous studies have examined the impact of social media use (usually frequency of logging in or posting) on mental health and well-being (Deters & Mehl, 2013; Tromholt, 2016). This research, however, tends to consider SNS use as a whole rather than considering the impact of using specific functions on mental health. Rocheleau and Shaughnessy (2018) found that different aspects of SNS use (signing up to the platform, populating a profile, and interacting via synchronous direct messaging) has differential impacts on anxiety and privacy concerns. This highlights the need for more nuanced research into the impact of image sharing on mental health in a way that previous studies into overall Facebook use have not been able to articulate. At present, there is limited research on the relationship between photo sharing (and viewing) and well-being, and many studies employ Instagram or Snapchat use (as image-based platforms) as a proxy for studying how sharing, browsing, and interacting with images on SNSs affect well-being. This section focuses particularly on research into depression and image sharing.

Many of the findings about the link between Instagram use and depressive symptoms have been explained with reference to Social Comparison Theory (SCT; Festinger, 1954). According to SCT, a person's perceptions of their own self-worth is formed in part by how they feel they compare to others. SNSs can distort our reference points for this comparison to create a sense that others' lives are superior to ours. This is particularly so as people tend to present positive images of themselves on social media. Thus, where Facebook or Instagram feeds or Snapchat stories are the primary or only source of information about another person (e.g. in the case of strangers or celebrities), browsing images on SNSs may lead to feelings of low self-worth and, relatedly, negative emotional and well-being outcomes. Supporting this, Lup, Trub, and Rosenthal (2015) found that Instagram use was related to increased depressive symptoms among participants who followed more strangers. Similarly, for individuals with a high tendency for social comparison, viewing strangers' positive posts increased negative affect (de Vries, Möller, Wieringa, Eigenraam, & Hamelink, 2018).

It is plausible, though, to consider that viewing and posting images on SNSs both affects and is affected by mood and mental state. Frison and Eggermont (2017) explored the potential bidirectional relationship between Instagram use and depressive mood. They found that frequency of browsing Instagram (but not frequency of posting images or liking others' posts) significantly and positively predicted severity of depressive mood seven months later. The researchers suggested that passive browsing of others' carefully curated images may lead to negative social comparison and explain the well-being outcome. Interestingly, this study also found that depressed mood predicted more frequent image sharing on Instagram (but not browsing or liking posts) seven months later. The researchers proposed that participants may post images to cope with their mood (either as a form of self-expression or distraction), or to strategically present more positive aspects of their own lives in response to the positive aspects of others' lives.

Another way of considering the link between depression and Instagram posts is to see if, by interrogating the images posted, it is possible to distinguish between users with high and low symptoms of depression. Reece and Danforth (2017) used computational machine learning techniques to screen for depression among 43,950 Instagram user posts, and asked participants how happy and sad some of the posts appeared to them. It was found that posts by users who were depressed received more comments (the opposite was true for the number of likes received), were more likely to post photos with faces, tended to be bluer, darker, and grayer, and were less likely to have a filter. When participants who were depressed did use filters, they favored the "Inkwell" filter, which changes the image to black-and-white. This supports the evidence that depression has been linked with a preference for darker, bluer, and monochromatic colors. Participants who were not depressed, on the other hand, favored the "Valencia" filter, which lightens the tints of images. It was also possible for the human participants to distinguish between posts of users who were depressed and those who were not. This lends support to the link between Instagram use and mental health.

Summary

This chapter has discussed current understanding about image sharing on three popular SNSs: Facebook, Instagram, and Snapchat. Sharing images on SNSs is one of the most popular activities on the platforms. This may explain why SNSs more focused on image sharing, such as Instagram, have seen a growth in use over recent years.

User characteristics such as age, gender, and personality have been shown to influence image sharing on SNSs, but not all characteristics have the same effects across the different platforms. Image sharing on SNSs is more common among younger than older adults. This may be due to different motivations for using SNS between the two age groups. Where older users tend to use SNS to maintain specific relationships and seldom post images, and, in contrast, younger users are more likely to uses SNS to pass the time and for relaxing entertainment. Researchers have also shown a relationship between personality traits and image sharing behaviors on SNS. Interestingly, only one personality trait has been shown to predict the number of "likes" received on Facebook: Agreeableness. It seems agreeable people are more liked and so receive more positive feedback on SNSs!

SNS users post different types of images to different platforms based on their functionality. Instagram users share a wider range of images than Facebook users, and Snapchat posts are more likely to portray situations that people don't want associated with them in the long term. Most of the images shared on SNSs focus on highlighting relationships (friendships, family, and romantic relationships).

Motivations for image sharing on SNS are a notable explanation for differences in the type of images shared. Researchers have looked specifically at the role of relationship building and maintenance, self-expression and impression management, archiving/ documenting, or surveillance, and escapism as motivations to share images on SNSs. The motivations seem to differ across platforms (for example, documenting/archiving is more commonly associated with Instagram use), but further research directly comparing reasons for using the different SNSs is needed. The different motivations may also explain the differences in the types of images shared across platforms.

Finally, image sharing on SNSs has also been shown to have an impact on health and well-being outcomes. Specifically, current understanding suggests that passively viewing images is positively related to depressive symptoms, particularly if users tend to compare themselves with others. The relationship between image sharing and depression, however, is bidirectional. Researchers have been able to distinguish between users with high and low symptoms of depression by comparing the types of images posted.

This chapter highlights the interrelationship between personal characteristics, motivations, image sharing (and viewing) behavior, and mental health outcomes. Future research should consider cross-platform comparisons and further exploration of the variables that influence, and are influenced by, image sharing on social media.

References

Ackerman, R. A., Witt, E. A., Donnellan, M. B., Trzesniewski, K. H., Robins, R. W., & Kashy, D. A. (2011). What does the narcissistic personality inventory really measure? *Assessment* 18(1), 67–87. doi:10.1177/1073191110382845

Alhabash, S., & Ma, M. (2017). A tale of four platforms: Motivations and uses of Facebook, Twitter, Instagram, and Snapchat among college students. *Social Media + Society* 3(1). doi:10.1177/2056305117691544

Amichai-Hamburger, Y., & Vinitzky, G. (2010). Social network use and personality. *Computers in Human Behavior* 26(6), 1289–15295. doi:10.1016/j.chb.2010.03.018

Bachrach, Y., Kosinski, M., Graepel, T., Kohli, P., & Stillwell, D. (2012). *Personality patterns of Facebook usage.* Paper presented at the 3rd annual ACM web science conference. 22–24 June, Evanston, IL. New York, NY: ACM.

Back, M. D., Stopfer, J. M., Vazire, S., Gaddis, S., Schmukle, S. C., Egloff, B., & Gosling, S. D. (2010). Facebook profiles reflect actual personality, not self-idealization. *Psychological Science* 21(3), 372–374. doi:10.1177/0956797609360756

Bayer, J. B., Ellison, N. B., Schoenebeck, S. Y., & Falk, E. B. (2016). Sharing the small moments: Ephemeral social interaction on Snapchat. *Information, Communication & Society* 19(7), 956–977. doi:10.1080/1369118X.2015.1084349 boyd, d. m., & Ellison, N. B. (2007). Social network sites: Definition, history, and scholarship. *Journal of Computer-Mediated Communication 13*(1), 210–230. doi:10.1111/j.1083-6101. 2007.00393.x

Boyle, S. C., Earle, A. M., LaBrie, J. W., & Ballou, K. (2017). Facebook dethroned: Revealing the more likely social media destinations for college students' depictions of underage drinking. *Addictive Behaviors 65*, 63–67. doi:10.1016/j.addbeh.2016.10.004

Brandtzæg, P. B., Lüders, M., & Skjetne, J. H. (2010). Too many Facebook "Friends"? Content sharing and sociability versus the need for privacy in social network sites. *International Journal of Human–Computer Interaction 26*(11–12), 1006–1030. doi:10.1080/ 10447318.2010.516719

de Vries, D. A., Möller, A. M., Wieringa, M. S., Eigenraam, A. W., & Hamelink, K. (2018). Social comparison as the thief of joy: Emotional consequences of viewing strangers' Instagram posts. *Media Psychology 21*(2), 222–245. doi:10.1080/15213269.2016.1267647

Department for Culture, Media & Sport (2016). *Taking part focus on: Social media.*London, UK: Gov.uk. Retrieved from https://assets.publishing.service.gov.uk/government/uploads/ system/uploads/attachment_data/file/519678/Social_media_-_FINAL.pdf

Deters, F. G., & Mehl, M. R. (2013). Does posting Facebook status updates increase or decrease loneliness? An online social networking experiment. *Social Psychological and Personality Science, 4*(5). doi:10.1177/1948550612469233

Dumas, T. M., Maxwell-Smith, M., Davis, J. P., & Giulietti, P. A. (2017). Lying or longing for likes? Narcissism, peer belonging, loneliness and normative versus deceptive like-seeking on Instagram in emerging adulthood. *Computers in Human Behavior 71*, 1–10. doi:10.1016/j. chb.2017.01.037

Eftekhar, A., Fullwood, C., & Morris, N. (2014). Capturing personality from Facebook photos and photo-related activities: How much exposure do you need? *Computers in Human Behavior 37*, 162–170. doi:10.1016/j.chb.2014.04.048

Facebook. (2018). Company Info. Retrieved from https://newsroom.fb.com/company-info/

Ferwerda, B., & Tkalcic, M. (2018). *You are what you post: What the content of Instagram pictures tells us about users' personality.* Paper presented at the 2nd Workshop on Theory-Informed User Modeling for Tailoring and Personalizing Interfaces (HUMANIZE). 11 March, Tokyo, Japan.

Festinger, L. (1954). A theory of social comparison processes. *Human Relations 7*(2), 117–140. doi:10.1177/001872675400700202

Fox, J., & Rooney, M. C. (2015). The Dark Triad and trait self-objectification as predictors of men's use and self-presentation behaviors on social networking sites. *Personality and Individual Differences 76*, 161–165. doi:10.1016/j.paid.2014.12.017

Frison, E., & Eggermont, S. (2017). Browsing, posting, and liking on Instagram: The reciprocal relationships between different types of Instagram use and adolescents' depressed mood. *Cyberpsychology, Behavior and Social Networking 20*(10), 603–609. doi:10.1089/cyber.2017.0156

Fullwood, C. (2015). The role of personality in online self-presentation. In A. Attrill (Ed.), *Cyberpsychology.* Oxford: Oxford University Press.

Garnica, T. S. (2017). *A Snapchat marketing perspective: Examining the personality traits and motives that predict attitudes toward and engagement with non-sponsored and sponsored content in Snapchat.* (Master's dissertation). University of Central Florida.

Greenwood, S., Perrin, A., & Duggin, M. (2016). *Social media update 2016.* Retrieved from http://www.pewinternet.org/2016/11/11/social-media-update-2016/

Holmberg, C., J. E. C., Hillman, T., & Berg, C. (2016). Adolescents' presentation of food in social media: An explorative study. *Appetite 99*, 121–129. doi:10.1016/j.appet.2016.01.009

Hu, Y., Manikonda, L., & Kambhampati, S. (2014). *What we Instagram: A first analysis of Instagram photo content and user types*. Paper presented at the Eighth International AAAI Conference on Weblogs and Social Media (pp. 595–598). 1–4 June, Ann Arbor, MI.

Hum, N. J., Chamberlin, P. E., Hambright, B. L., Portwood, A. C., Schat, A. C., & Bevan, J. L. (2011). A picture is worth a thousand words: A content analysis of Facebook profile photographs. *Computers in Human Behavior 27*(5), 1828–1833. doi:10.1016/j.chb.2011.04.003

Instagram. (2016a). Introducing Instagram stories. Retrieved from https://instagram-press.com/blog/2016/08/02/introducing-instagram-stories/

Instagram. (2016b). New ways to share in the moment. Retrieved from http://blog.instagram.com/post/153474421572/161121-launches

John, O. P., & Srivastava, S. (1999). The big-five trait taxonomy: History, measurement, and theoretical perspectives. In L. A. Pervin & O. P. John (Eds.), *Handbook of personality: Theory and research* (Vol. 2) (pp. 102–138). New York: Guilford Press.

Keep, M., & Amon, K. L. (2017). Follow me: Exploring the effect of personality and stranger connections on Instagram use. *International Journal of Virtual Communities and Social Networking 9*(1), 1–16. doi:10.4018/IJVCSN.2017010101

Keep, M., Janssen, A., & Amon, K. L. (2018). *#InstaFollow: Types of Instagram followers affects users' image sharing behaviours*. Paper presented at the 23rd Cyberpsychology, Cybertherapy and Social Networking Conference. 26–28 June, Gatineau, Canada.

Landstrom, I. (2017). *The Power of ephemerality: An explorative study on the influence of personality traits in the use of Snapchat and the potential of the app for the music business* (Master's dissertation). KTH Royal Institute of Technology.

Lee, E., Lee, J.-A., Moon, J. H., & Sung, Y. (2015). Pictures speak louder than words: Motivations for using Instagram. *Cyberpsychology, Behavior and Social Networking 19*(9), 552–556. doi:10.1089/cyber.2015.0157

Liu, S. B., Palen, L., Sutton, J., Hughes, A. L., & Vieweg, S. (2008). *In search of the bigger picture: The emergent role of online photo sharing in times of disaster*. Paper presented at the 5th International ISCRAM Conference. 4–7 May, Washington, DC.

Lup, K., Trub, L., & Rosenthal, L. (2015). Instagram #Instasad? Exploring associations among Instagram use, depressive symptoms, negative social comparison, and strangers followed. *Cyberpsychology, Behavior and Social Networking 15*(5), 247–252. doi:10.1089/cyber.2014.0560

Malik, A., Hiekkanen, K., & Nieminen, M. (2016). Privacy and trust in Facebook photo sharing: Age and gender differences. *Program 50*(4), 462–480. doi:10.1108/PROG-02-2016-0012

McCain, J. L., Borg, Z. G., Rothenberg, A. H., Churillo, K. M., Weiler, P., & Campbell, W. K. (2016). Personality and selfies: Narcissism and the Dark Triad. *Computers in Human Behavior 64*, 126–133. doi:10.1016/j.chb.2016.06.050

McCrae, R. R., & Costa, P. T., Jr. (1997). Personality trait structure as a human universal. *American Psychologist 52*(5), 509–516.

Mendelson, A., & Papacharissi, Z. (2010). Look at us: Collective narcissism in college student Facebook photo galleries. *The Networked Self: Identity, Community and Culture on Social Network Sites 1974*, 1–37.

Moon, J. H., Lee, E., Lee, J.-A., Choi, T. R., & Sung, Y. (2016). The role of narcissism in self-promotion on Instagram. *Personality and Individual Differences 101*. doi:10.1016/j.paid.2016.05.042

Moran, J. B., Salerno, K. J., & Wade, T. J. (2018). Snapchat as a new tool for sexual access: Are there sex differences? *Personality and Individual Differences 129*, 12–16. doi:10.1016/j.paid.2018.02.040

Munar, A. M., & Jacobsen, J. K. S. (2013). Trust and involvement in tourism social media and web-based travel information sources. *Scandinavian Journal of Hospitality and Tourism 13*(1), 1–19. doi:10.1080/15022250.2013.764511

Ong, E. Y. L., Ang, R. P., Ho, J. C. M., Lim, J. C. Y., Goh, D. H., Lee, C. S., & Chua, A. Y. K. (2011). Narcissism, extraversion and adolescents' self-presentation on Facebook. *Personality and Individual Differences 50*(2), 180–185. doi:10.1016/j.paid.2010.09.022

Papacharissi, Z., & Mendelson, A. (2011). Toward a new(er) sociability: Uses, gratifications and social capital on Facebook. *Media Perspectives for the 21st Century 212*, 212–230.

Pempek, T. A., Yermolayeva, Y. A., & Calver, S. L. (2009). College students' social networking experiences on Facebook. *Journal of Applied Developmental Psychology 30*(3), 227–238. doi:10.1016/j.appdev.2008.12.010

Piwek, L., & Joinson, A. (2016). "What do they Snapchat about?" Patterns of use in time-limited instant messaging service. *Computers in Human Behavior 54*, 358–367. doi:10.1016/j.chb.2015.08.026

Reece, A. G., & Danforth, C. M. (2017). Instagram photos reveal predictive markers of depression. *EPJ Data Science 6*(1), 15. doi:10.1140/epjds/s13688-017-0110-z

Rocheleau, J. N., & Shaughnessy, K. (2018). *Context matters: The role of social anxiety and online privacy concern on university students' social networking site experiences.* Paper presented at the 23rd Cyberpsychology, Cybertherapy and Social Networking Conference. 26–28 June, Gatineau, Canada. Retrieved from https://easychair.org/smart-program/CYPSY23/2018-06-28.html#talk:65675

Ross, C., Orr, E. S., Sisic, M., Arseneault, J. M., Simmering, M. G., & Orr, R. R. (2009). Personality and motivations associated with Facebook use. *Computers in Human Behavior 25*, 578–586. doi:10.1016/j.chb.2008.12.024

Seidman, G. (2013). Self-presentation and belonging on Facebook: How personality influences social media use and motivations. *Personality and Individual Differences 54*, 402–407. doi:10.1016/j.paid.2012.10.009

Sensis. (2017, 22 June). Australians and social media. In *Sensis social media report 2017.* Melbourne: Australia. Retrieved from https://irp-cdn.multiscreensite.com/535ef142/files/uploaded/Sensis_Social_Media_Report_2017-Chapter-1.pdf

Sheldon, P., & Bryant, K. (2016). Instagram: Motives for its use and relationship to narcissism and contextual age. *Computers in Human Behavior 58*, 89–97. doi:10.1016/j.chb.2015.12.059

Smith, A., & Anderson, M. (2018). Social Media Use in 2018. Retrieved from http://www.pewinternet.org/2018/03/01/social-media-use-in-2018/

Snapchat. (2017). Snapchat support: Add effects to snaps. Retrieved from https://support.snapchat.com/en-US/article/filters

Sorokowska, A., Oleszkiewicz, A., Frackowiak, T., Pisanski, K., Chmiel, A., & Sorokowski, P. (2016). Selfies and personality: Who posts self-portrait photographs? *Personality and Individual Differences 90*, 119–123. doi:10.1016/j.paid.2015.10.037

Strano, M. M. (2008). User descriptions and interpretations of self-presentation through Facebook profile images. *Cyberpsychology: Journal of Psychosocial Research on Cyberspace 2*(2), article 5.

Thelwall, M., & Vis, F. (2017). Gender and image sharing on Facebook, Twitter, Instagram, Snapchat and WhatsApp in the UK: Hobbying alone or filtering for friends? *Aslib Journal of Information Management 69*(6), 702–720. doi:10.1108/AJIM-04-2017-0098

Tromholt, M. (2016). The Facebook Experiment: Quitting Facebook Leads to Higher Levels of Well-Being. *Cyberpsychology, Behavior, and Social Networking 19*(11), 661–666. doi:10.1089/cyber.2016.0259

Twenge, J. M., Konrath, S., Foster, J. D., Campbell, W. K., & Bushman, B. J. (2008). Egos inflating over time: A cross-temporal meta-analysis of the Narcissistic Personality Inventory. *Journal of Personality 76*(4), 875–902; discussion 903–828. doi:10.1111/j.1467–6494.2008.00507.x

Utz, S., Muscanell, N., & Khalid, C. (2015). Snapchat elicits more jealousy than Facebook: A comparison of Snapchat and Facebook use. *Cyberpsychology, Behavior, and Social Networking 18*(3), 141–146. doi:10.1089/cyber.2014.0479

Utz, S., Tanis, M., & Vermeulen, I. (2012). It is all about being popular: The effects of need for popularity on social network site use. *Cyberpsychology, Behavior, and Social Networking 15*(1), 37–42. doi:10.1089/cyber.2010.0651

van House, N. V., Davis, M., Takhteyev, Y., Ames, M., & Finn, M. (2004). *The social uses of personal photography: Methods for projecting future imaging applications.* Retrieved from http://people.ischool.berkeley.edu/~vanhouse/van_house_et_al_2004b.pdf

Vaterlaus, J. M., Barnett, K., Roche, C., & Young, J. A. (2016). "Snapchat is more personal": An exploratory study on Snapchat behaviors and young adult interpersonal relationships. *Computers in Human Behavior 62*, 594–601. doi:10.1016/j.chb.2016.04.029

Weiser, E. B. (2015). #Me: Narcissism and its facets as predictors of selfie-posting frequency. *Personality and Individual Differences 86*, 477–481. doi:10.1016/j.paid.2015.07.007

CHAPTER 19

··

SOCIAL MEDIA AND CYBERACTIVISM

··

CHRIS STIFF

THE PERSUASIVE POWER OF SOCIAL MEDIA

··

WHEN Barack Obama won the US presidential election in 2008, it was suggested that a sizable contribution to this was his election team's ability to marshal online support for their cause (Eilperin, 2015). That is, they engaged in cyberactivism, utilizing the Internet, and social media in particular, to recruit and co-ordinate disparate individuals to a common cause to bring about social change. The Obama campaign was perhaps one of the first political movements to effectively maneuver these forces, and since then many others have attempt to emulate it, with varying degrees of success. More recently, activism against sexual harassment and exploitation has manifested in the use of the #MeToo hashtag, where individuals post to social media using the label to indicate solidarity with others who have experienced it (Shugerman, 2017).

In our pre-Internet society, engaging in activism required a considerable amount of effort. Advocates would need to physically encounter those they wished to convince, or else contact them via telephone or mailout. Now, those who wish to promote a cause can easily reach an audience of thousands—or even millions—through websites or social media. This chapter explores how this cyberactivism has altered the way societal change is promulgated, and how advocates for a cause may harness the Internet to implement their agendas. It also looks at different kinds of cyberactivism, and how it may be different from more conventional forms of activism. Perhaps most importantly, it examines "slacktivism"—tokenistic support for a cause without any real commitment—and how the ease of engaging in this may have attenuated the effectiveness of online cause promotion (Table 1).

Table 1 Examples of notable cyberactivist causes since 2008

Cause	Year	Details	Legacy
Arab Spring	2010	Revolution in north Africa against dictatorial government regimes, most notably in Tunisia and Egypt.	After gaining some traction, societal change has somewhat halted in this region.
Occupy movement	2011	Protesters camped in high traffic public areas usually associated with wealth, e.g., Wall Street.	Occupiers were eventually evicted from sites, and the campaign has now petered out.
Kony	2012	A video detailing the use of child soldiers by warlord Joseph Kony was released and spread via social media.	Some controversy over the authenticity of the video, combined with questionable behavior by the cause's founder Jason Russell, derailed the campaign.
Black Lives Matter	2013	Following the fatal shooting of a black youth by a police officer in Florida, the Twitter hashtag #blacklivesmatter begins trending (NB other, more traditional forms of activism also occurred).	The campaign has continued to propagate and has recently morphed into the #takeaknee campaign by prominent sports persons.
Ice bucket challenge	2014	To raise money for ALS research, Facebook users are encouraged to donate money, pour a bucket of ice water over themselves, and nominate three friends to do the same (leading to a "viral" phenomenon).	The money raised by the campaign led to a significant breakthrough in ALS research.
Ahmed Mohammed exclusion/arrest	2015	A fourteen-year-old school child was sent home after bringing a homemade clock into school. Social media spread the hashtag #IStandWithAhmed to show solidarity against Islamaphobia.	Ahmed received (mostly) positive media attention, culminating in reinstatement in school, and an invitation to the White House by President Obama.
Harambe the gorilla is killed	2016	A gorilla was shot to protect a four year old boy who fell into his enclosure. Sympathizers voiced their outrage online, and the event spawned many online "memes."	The extent of the blackly humorous jokes made about this incident led to the Cincinnati Zoo requesting they be stopped.
#MeToo hashtag campaign	2017	Following multiple revelations of sexual impropriety by individuals in positions of power in the media and entertainment industries, social media users (both members of the public and celebrities) begin using this hashtag to denote they have been harassed in the past.	Many victims of harassment (and worse) have now felt confident enough to come forward and tell their story. Practices in the film industry that have fostered these deeds in the past are undergoing considerable scrutiny and criminal cases against perpetrators are in motion.

Starting and Propagating Social Media Campaigns

The ubiquity of social media and Internet connectivity in general has allowed activist movements to flourish in a way they never have before. McGarty, Thomas, Lala, Smith, and Bliuc (2014) liken this paradigm shift to the introduction of information dissemination via the printed word in the fifteenth century. Prior to this, information could easily be controlled and censored by the ruling class. When those limitations are removed, the possibilities for linking up with like-minded others are expanded exponentially. The ease with which we can communicate with others online, and can set up sites and other "meeting points" to discuss issues offers myriad opportunities for engagement in activism (Kahn & Kellner, 2004). The power of social media in activism can actually be made visible through the examination of search metrics and network activity that occurs alongside prominent protest movements. Surges of activism-communication are often seen on social media sites like Twitter and Facebook prior to major rallies for causes (Lotan et al., 2011).

Activist movements that wish to gain traction have to contend with the *mobilization problem;* how to get disparate like-minded individuals to coalesce into a group that can achieve a goal. Mobilization consists of four stages (Klandermans & Oegema, 1987; Korolov et al., 2016). First, individuals need to feel sympathetic toward a cause, and have a desire to change the status-quo. Second, they need to encounter others who share this view, either through by recruiting them, or *being* recruited. Third, proto-activists need to be motivated to actually take part in any activist behaviors that are being carried out. Fourth, participants need to actually have the *ability* to participate—for example, a participant could not participate in a blockade of cars if they do not own a vehicle. Access to social media is particularly useful for allowing individuals to encounter, recruit, and be recruited by those who share their view regarding an issue. Depending on how the activism manifests, social media can also be instrumental in providing the capability of participating (see "Distinction between Types of Cyberactivism"). Using social media to build a base for an activist movements has been demonstrated in the recent "Arab spring" (Howard & Hussain, 2011). Second to face-to-face conversation, Facebook was the most prevalent method of learning about protest movements in Egypt, with nearly 50 percent of protesters producing and disseminating photos/videos via this platform (Tufekci & Wilson, 2012). More traditional forms of media—such as the radio and newspapers—accounted for very little in the propagation of activism.

Once mobilization has occurred, cyberactivists then need to continue spreading their message to others in order to gain momentum. The ease of dissemination via the web has led to the cultural phenomena of "viral" photos/videos, wherein content is passed rapidly from one person to the next until it becomes a recognized cultural touchstone (although the permanence of these is sometimes fleeting (Berger & Milkman, 2012; English, Sweetser, & Ancu, 2011; Guadagno, Rempala, Murphy, & Okdie, 2013; Xu, Park,

Kim, & Park, 2016). Many activist causes try and tap into this "virality" to hasten the dissemination and promotion of their cause, but what aspects of a particular message can increase the likelihood of its transition?

The relationship between the sender and receiver of online material seems to be important in this. When a sender transmits information to another person that is intended to be widely disseminated, the strength of ties between those two individuals and the amount of prior communication they have had predicts whether it is passed on (Harvey, Stewart, & Ewing, 2011). This link also influences other reactions by the receiver. Van Noort, Antheunis, and van Reijmersdal (2012) have demonstrated that when a strong tie exists between the individual who sends a campaign message and the one who receives it, it is likely to elicit more powerful emotional responses in the latter. It is also a more potent predictor of subsequent pro-campaign behavior, as the social capital acquired through the close relationship ties reduces the perceived persuasive intent of the message. That is, the receiver is less likely to see the message as a deliberate attempt to change their attitudes and/or behavior, which in return actually reduces their resistance to its persuasiveness.

It is possible that the specificity and uniqueness of the message received regarding a campaign is important. In a study by Coppock, Guess, and Ternovski (2016), Twitter users received a private message from a non-profit organization regarding an online petition. Although they were not intimately familiar with the sender—that is, the strength of their tie was weak—the receipt of an individualized message significantly increased support for that cause. By comparison, a public Tweet from that NPO had little to no effect on engagement. With this, the weak tie between sender and receiver along with the lack of specificity in the message appears to severely dilute its impact. However, individualized messages are not always necessary for a campaign to become viral. The content of a message can affect its propagation. Generally, content that is information-rich is likely to be passed on, as are messages that are controversial and evoke powerful positive or negative emotions (Brown, Bhadury, & Pope, 2010; Eckler & Bolls, 2011; Guadagno et al., 2013). Users may also feel peer pressure from others to pass on the information, and that participating in the propagation of a campaign is an irresistible norm of their peer group (Lee, Ham, & Kim, 2013; Yang & Wang, 2015).

The social validation that a message has received can also moderate reactions to it. Alhabash and colleagues (2013) presented participants with anti-cyberbullying messages which had reportedly received a lot (or few) likes on Facebook, and had been shared many (or few) times through the site. The tone of the message was also manipulated to be positive (e.g., "the world is happier without cyberbullying"), or negative (e.g., "the world is a nasty place with cyberbullying"). More positive messages were more likely to be passed on, as were messages that had already received wide dissemination. Interestingly though, messages that had been received by *fewer* people were evaluated more favorably, indicating again that being part of a more select group when receiving campaign information can be beneficial for the cause. Kim (2015) suggests the relationship between message content and likelihood of transmission is moderate by the *medium* of that transmission. Informational utility and how novel the content was are more important when passing on via email, but the evocativeness of the material—in terms of engagement and emotional reactions—was more significant on social media.

Motives for Using Social Media and Their Relationship with Cyberactivism

Most prominent cyberactivist campaigns utilize social media sites in some way. All social media sites have approximately the same aims: 1) to allow individuals to connect with others to form a network; and 2) to share media to that network. Most platforms also contain a form of private messaging among users which are not broadcast to the rest of the network. What, then, drives the users to participate in social media, and how does this relate to cyberactivism?

Although most social media sites broadly share the same functions, they are obviously not all alike. Some sites, such as Twitter, place more emphasis on short written communication, with posts limited to 280 characters (previously 140 characters). Others, like Instagram, are more concerned with visual images. Luchman, Bergstrom, and Krulikowski (2014) suggests two distinct dimensions which are important in the classification of social media sites. First is *fun-related*; the extent to which the site provides entertainment, updates through the day, and material which may provoke laughter or positive emotions. Second, is *content-specific*, which is the extent to which *information* is shared and sought. The assessment of how a social media site lies on these dimensions give rise to a simple taxonomy; for example, Wikipedia would be considered low fun-related, and high content-specific. Facebook by contrast would be considered high fun-related, and low-content specific.

Examination of motives for using social media by Krishnan and Hunt (2015) suggest four general reasons. The first is termed "*infotainment*," a broad term encompassing using social media to keep in touch with friends and family, for entertainment, and to be kept informed about events and activities. Social media can also be *social tool*, used to find people with similar interests, and new companions. *Passing time* is a further reason for using social media. Users may by trying to alleviate boredom, or to fill gaps between activities. Finally, there is a *conformity motive*. Users may feel excluded if they do not engage in the same social media activities as their friends. As well as these general motives, researchers have also suggested motives for specific social media sites.

Instagram

The popular photo sharing site is more image-orientated and although private messages can be sent, the emphasis for users is on the posting and appreciating of photographs.

Despite this seeming restriction, motives for using the platform are still highly diverse. An exploratory investigation in to users' motives for Instagram use by Lee, Lee, Moon, and Sung (2015) suggested five main reasons. First, the app allows users to interact with others socially through liking others' photos, tagging fellow users, and sending private messages. Second, users can create an *archive* of their own photos—all content posted is saved onto the user's profile, in chronological order. Third, looking at other users' photos—particularly those of affluent celebrities—enables *escapism*. Fourth, Instagram allows users to spy on other people's lives, something the authors' term "peeking." Finally, users find a form of *self-expression*. This aspect is particularly relevant to cyberactivism. Users can choose the media they display to tell a story and convey a message to followers, meaning they can easily inform others of the causes they advocate. Instagram is increasingly becoming the stomping ground for "taste makers" who make posts intending to turn users toward a particular product, with a great deal of success (see De Veirman, Cauberghe, & Hudders, 2017). The number of "likes" accrued by a photo is a proxy for popularity, and users can flaunt their social standing or affluence through their photography on the app (Sheldon & Bryant, 2016). Such posts have been shown to be effective even with products which may carry some stigma, such as smoking (Phua, Jin, & Hahm, 2018). So, posts promoting a particular political position may also inspire a user's followers to rally to that cause.

Facebook

The behaviors available to Facebook users are myriad; they may "update their status" detailing their current activity, post photos and videos, message other users, and—added recently—can broadcast live to their entire friendship retinue. Despite this seeming complexity, Yang and Brown (2013) suggest a simple pair of motives for using the site: users are either *forming* new relationships, or they are *maintaining* existing relationships. The former reason is particularly relevant for individuals who may be suffering from a diminished social circle. These persons may feel severe loneliness and yet—paradoxically—the anxiety of forming new relationships in real life prevents them from addressing this situation. Teppers, Luyckx, Klimstra, and Goossens (2014) suggest that Facebook may remedy this. They found a marked increase in Facebook use among youths who reported high levels of loneliness and inadequacy in social situations. Moreover, over time those individuals' levels of loneliness dropped as they used the more comfortable online environment to secure friendships.

Facebook can therefore be an effective "base" for cyberactivism, as it allows individuals to find new advocates for a cause, and easily keep in touch with those already on board. Facebook groups or pages can disseminate information to those who are interested in a topic. Interestingly though, lack of participation on Facebook can actually galvanize offline activism. Kim (2016) demonstrated that if users perceive Facebook to be a hostile environment to express their views they were less likely to do so *online*, but became more engaged in activist behavior *offline*.

YouTube

Almost all sites allow the viewing of content without providing content in return; for example, images can be viewed on Instagram without logging in or even signing up to the service. However, YouTube has a much sharper delineation between individuals who *create* content, and those that *consume* it compared with other social media sites. As such it is possible to examine the motives of use for those that manufacture videos and post them separately from those that view those videos (although of course they are not mutually exclusive).

The motives for use suggested by Khan (2017) demonstrate this overlap. Users may browse the site hoping the find information for an interest, hobby, or to solve a problem. Complimentary to this, they may be seeking to *provide others* with information in a pedagogical context. Some view YouTube as means of relaxing by consuming entertaining materials. It can also be used to interact with others socially—YouTube offers a "commenting" section under videos where users can indicate their feelings toward a video. YouTube users—both consumers and viewers—may use the site to confer status upon themselves, by demonstrating their knowledge or by looking "cool" through their posts. YouTube therefore can be useful both for individuals attempting to persuade others to their activist cause, and to those seeking further information to feed their own nascent activist tendencies.

Twitter

Twitter is an intriguing platform for analysis as its key feature—and perhaps selling point—is that although users can add multiple pictures to their posts, the text can only be 280 characters. Thus, there is motive to ensure communications are as concise and information rich as possible.

Johnson and Yang (2009) offer a simple dichotomous breakdown of motives for Twitter use. They distinguish between *social* and *information* motives. For the former, individuals use Twitter to keep in touch with others, find out what others are doing, and to be entertained. For the latter, they use Twitter to seek out opinions, answers to questions, or the status of current events.

Other more elaborate dissections of motives have also been posited. Vignoles (2011) has suggested six motives which impact on the way individuals construct their internal identities. Individuals desire to enhance their self-esteem (how positively they think of themselves), continuity (persistency of identity over time), distinctiveness (level of individuality compared to others), meaning (that their life is meaningful), efficacy (that they are competent and capable), and belonging (their need to feel accepted). Selim, Long, and Vignoles (2014) then applied these to a qualitative analysis of why people may use Twitter. They found that each motive was valid for Twitter users, although some were more salient than others. For example, self-esteem can be enhanced if a user is retweeted, continuity by having a consistent theme of one's posts, distinctiveness by posting unique aspects of one's life, meaning by indicating activities and cultural touchstones shared with others (e.g., watching particular television programs), efficacy by using hashtags to promote a cause, and belonging by private messages to interact at an individual level with other users.

Thus, social media provides a compelling set of motives for people to use them. Far from being a frivolous pastime with little consequence, social media in fact allows us to form powerful social ties, discover information, and validate ourselves socially. The need to belong is a powerful one, and has been cited as the motive behind much of our social behavior (Baumeister, 2012; Eshuis, 2013; Pillow, Malone, & Hale, 2015; Tyler, Branch, & Kearns, 2016), such as the strong drive to belong to social groups, or seek out individuals when we are feeling vulnerable or scared. Therefore, it should not be surprising that although social media may seem superficial in nature, it actually fulfills an important psychological function by providing users with a sense of affiliation. In fact, the use of social media can be vital for those individuals who are *lacking* a feeling of belonging because of mental health conditions which may impede "traditional" friendships, or those who are physically isolated. Feelings of social exclusion have been shown to increase the likelihood of participating in activism in those that are particularly sensitive to rejection, and/or have a high need to belong (Bäck et al., 2015). If individuals latch onto a cause online that allows them to feel part of a larger collective, it is likely to lead to activist behaviors.

Kende, van Zomeren, Ujhelyi, and Lantos (2016) highlight the role of social media as a form of *social affirmation*. Individuals can use the information they provide via social media as a way of broadcasting their beliefs, identities, and ideas. Users can accrue credibility in the eyes of others and increase their social "visibility" (or *social capital*) by participating in discussion regarding activist issues and highlighting their standpoint on current events. In their work, users whose motives for social media use included social affirmation tended to have stronger intentions to engage in subsequent activism.

CLASSIC MODELS OF COLLECTIVE ACTION

The *dual pathways* conceptualization (Saab, Tausch, Spears, & Cheung, 2015; Van Zomeren, Spears, Fischer, & Leach, 2004) of collective action points toward two key components that influence individuals' behavior in support of a cause. First is the belief that some kind of injustice or inequality is being perpetrated and needs to be addressed. This belief manifests as emotional reaction, which can then give rise to behaviors intended to address this inequality. *Anger* at the injustice may seem an obvious candidate for such an emotion, and indeed seems to play a role in promoting collective action (Leonard, Moons, Mackie, & Smith, 2011; Miller, Cronin, Garcia, & Branscombe, 2009). However, it may be too diffuse a concept to pin down to predict behaviors precisely. Researchers instead will often pinpoint specific anger components. *Moral outrage* is defined as "anger produced by the perceived violation of a moral standard or principle"

(O'Mara, Jackson, Batson, & Gaertner, 2011, p. 173), and this appears to be more suitable than anger in a more general sense in predicting collective action behaviors (Thomas & McGarty, 2009). As well as emotions reacting to the inequality itself, collective action may also elicit feelings of compassion toward the individuals directly affected by the problem. This emotion—that is, *sympathy*—has also been shown as an emotional reaction that may give rise to collective action (Iyer & Ryan, 2009; Thomas & Louis, 2014; Thomas, Rathmann, & McGarty, 2017).

A second component important in the elicitation of collective action from this perspective is the belief the group can actually accomplish the change they are trying to implement, that is, individuals within the collective must experience sufficient levels of *efficacy*. The precise nature of this efficacy and its parameters has been debated in the literature. A classic perspective would view group efficacy simply as the belief in members of an action that they can succeed, that is, their ability to effect change (Corcoran, Pettinicchio, & Young, 2011). Some theorists (e.g., Hornsey et al., 2006) extend this idea further, highlighting how important the expression of one's values and the tying together of the group in a unified social identity is in collective action. Klein, Spears, and Reicher (2007) have also suggested delineating between general perceptions of effectiveness and *identity consolidation* wherein groups affirm and strengthen their identity against that of other groups.

Other models of collective action point toward the importance of *comparison* between a current state of affairs, and a desired state of affairs. The *relative deprivation* perspective suggests that cognitive appraisals of disparity are the primary motivators for collective action. Smith and Pettigrew, (2014) highlight that these comparisons can occur at an individual level (i.e., a person comparing themselves to other in group or outgroup members), a group level (i.e., comparing their group to another group), or temporal level (comparing themselves/their group presently to their past self/group). Perceptions of a sufficient level of disparity then provoke responses to attempt restitution. Although the model has broadly received support (e.g., Sweeney, McFarlin, & Inderrieden, 1990), there are suggestions in the literature that it may not give a sufficiently detailed explanation. The cultural background of an individual moderates the strength different types of deprivation have. Van den Bos, van Veldhuizen, and Au (2015) argue that whether a culture is *collectivistic* or *individualistic* is an important consideration. In their work, deprivation at a group level was more persuasive in motivating collective action cognitions and behavior in cultures which value group harmony (e.g., among east-Asian participants or more collectivist cultures), whereas the individual level deprivation was more powerful among individualistic cultures (in this case, Dutch participants). This was also true when collectivist, compared to individualist, salience was experimentally primed.

Other moderators have also been proposed in the model. The deservingness of a comparator's resources, feelings of resentment among the perceiver, and manifestation of envy may also factor into the processing of relative deprivation indices (Feather, 2015). When considering changes in deprivation over time, the status of a group is also important. Lower status groups are more sensitive to changes in deprivation compared with those that are higher in status (de la Sablonnière et al., 2015). Finally, Osborne, Sibley, Huo, and Smith (2015) espouse concerns regarding the simplistic taxonomy of the original model. According to the matrix formed by classification of individual and group level deprivation, individuals should fall into one of four categories: 1) individual level deprived, group level not-deprived; 2) individual level not deprived, group level deprived; 3) individual level deprived, group level deprived; and 4) individual level not deprived, group level not deprived. However, in their data participants tended to display much more analogue-esque experiences of data (e.g., feeling "individually somewhat-deprived"), suggesting a simple digital classification may be too simplistic.

ONLINE CONTEXTS FOR COLLECTIVE ACTION—THE SIDE MODEL

Both the dual pathway and relative deprivation models can be integrated quite easily into an online context. Indeed, the introduction of social media can facilitate the necessary conditions for behavior via these models. For example, Alberici and Milesi (2016) have demonstrated that online discussions with other like-minded individuals enhances the feelings of efficacy needed to subsequently engage in activism. The ease with which the Internet can disseminate information via websites and specific social media sites also allows for rapid comparisons of deprivation levels among users, which may instill an impetus for action.

Researchers have now begun to examine specific features of the online context which may be applicable to cyberactivism, with probably the most influential being the Social Identification of Deindividuation Effects (SIDE) model (Postmes, Spears, & Lea, 1998). This model suggests that the anonymity of online interactions leads to a depersonalization of the self, with individuals losing a sense of their own individuality. To retain a semblance of meaning and coherence, individuals then turn to group-level structures; that is, the social identities to which they belong. The increased importance of these causes social identities to strengthen, and group boundaries to become more salient. This in turn leads to greater conformity to group norms, specifically those endorsed by that social identity. Evidence suggests this operates most effectively at a localized group level, where an identity and its norms can be clearly delineated. For example, membership of a university sports club would allow this kind of mechanism to operate. More diffuse identities—such as nationality—are less effective (Lea, Spear, & de Groot, 2001).

The power of online anonymity has considerable implications for the use of social media as a means of marshalling cyberactivists. Individuals who are anonymous online and espouse a particular cause are likely to display high levels of conformity to other members (Sassenberg & Boos, 2003). This allows groups to gain momentum as dissenting viewpoints tend to be minimal. The visual homogeneity of those within a collective action group will also facilitate this. That is, those that support a particular cause tend to indicate this with a visual cue, such as the use of filters on Facebook profiles, or displaying particular Twitter hashtags. According to Lee (2004) individuals are much more likely to conform to the majority's norms if they share a visual representation (and assuming other factors such as anonymity are in place). In their study, participants changed their minds regarding a decision dilemma to bring them in line with an opposition majority more reliably when each person was represented by the same character icon. When each had their own idiosyncratic icon, depersonalization was lessened, and accordingly so was conformity.

The lack of identifiably in an online context may also compromise an individual's critical faculties. When encountering persuasive information, an individual may evaluate the quality of the arguments presented, or they may use simple heuristic cues (such as who is telling them the information) to decide whether they will change their mind (Darke et al., 1998; Jonas, Schulz-Hardt, & Frey, 2005; Petty & Cacioppo, 1979). Online, users seem to be less capable of distinguishing strong and weak arguments when they are depersonalized. That is, they are more easily persuaded by arguments of relatively little merit if they are debating in an anonymous setting, because they can less reliably infer the characteristics of the person making the argument (Lee, 2008).

Thus, social media and online settings are likely to foster cyberactivism if users are anonymous, a social identity is made salient, and group norms are clear. Individuals are likely to conform to these norms and question the veracity of information less. When part of a minority group is pitted against the status-quo, individuals are more likely to voice opinions which are group-normative (and majority-anormative), even if they will be punished for doing so (Spears, Lea, Corneliussen, Postmes, & Haar, 2002). If social media sites are *less* encouraging of users being anonymous, this mechanism may be less effective. For example, Facebook prefers users to go by their real names, and actively shuts down accounts which use pseudonyms or fake names. In these cases, cyberactivism may be attenuated.

DISTINCTION BETWEEN TYPES OF CYBERACTIVISM

Cyberactivism is a somewhat diffuse term, which can be better explicated by applying granularity to the types of activity that are engaged in by cyberactivists. Broadly speaking, cyberactivism can be broken down into categories classified by 1) how much effort is required to do the task; and 2) how much impact they tend to have on individuals who experience them (see also Postmes & Brunsting, 2002 for insight into mapping these types of activism onto *offline* behavior).

Cause Advocation

Cause advocation demonstrates support for a cause by creating a visible indicator that an individual is an advocate for it. For example, Facebook has offered "photo filters" in the past which can be applied to a user's profile picture, either to show support for a cause (e.g., a rainbow flag for gay rights), or to demonstrate unity for an event (e.g., a Tricolor flag overlay following the terrorist attacks in Paris in 2016; see Chapman & Coffé, 2016; Penney, 2015). Twitter hashtags can also be appropriated for this purpose (Bruns, Highfield, & Burgess, 2013; Chiluwa & Ifukor, 2015; Lindgren & Lundström, 2011; Scott, 2015; Veenstra, Iyer, Hossain, & Park, 2014). The individual advocating for the cause may explicitly encourage others to copy their behavior and/or to carry out further behavior in support of the cause (e.g., the donation of money), but this is not a given.

Normative Behavior Demonstration

Here, individuals will post evidence of a behavior supporting a cause and will most likely encourage those viewing that post to do the same. For example, a Facebook user may post that they have donated money to cause, and expound the virtues of doing so (Loss, Lindacher, & Curbach, 2014; Warren, Sulaiman, & Jaafar, 2014). A typical feature of many social media pages is the ability to "tag" another user, so that an alert will appear on their own version of the page/app (Oeldorf-Hirsch & Sundar, 2015) as a gentle form of peer pressure. For example, in the ALS ice-bucket challenge, users were encouraged to dump buckets of freezing water over their own heads, and then tag three Facebook friends who would have to donate money to the fundraising cause, and then perpetuate the challenge (Hrastelj & Robertson, 2016; Ni, Chan, Leung, Lau, & Pang, 2014; Rossolatos, 2015).

Content Creation

A common method of providing comment on hot-button issues is through the creation of media that highlights absurdities, ironies, or flaws with arguments on the opposing side of that issue. Satire has always been a mainstay of social commentary, long before the advent of the Internet; indeed, its repression is a common feature of totalitarian dictatorships (Mascha, 2011). In most modern societies, activists can use the Internet to distribute their lambasting of the opposition on sites such as YouTube or Dailymotion (Vraga, Bode, Wells, Driscoll, & Thorson, 2014). Content creation cyberactivism has a blurred boundary with other content which satirizes contemporary foibles but is not necessarily distributed exclusively online. Many satirical news shows (e.g., *The Daily Show*, *The Colbert Report*) create content which has a somewhat activist bent in that it is advocating (however subtly) a particular political cause or stance (Higgie, 2014).

Brigading

Cyberactivism may be constructive, but it can also be destructive. Brigading is barracking of an opposition advocate's social media content in order to disrupt their endeavors. For example, if a particular cause hosts a Facebook page, opponents of the cause may flood that page with negative comments about the cause or its adopters. This behavior is similar to "trolling" or "griefing" online, where users deliberately attempt to provoke, confuse, or annoy other users (Bishop, 2014; Coyne, Chesney, Logan, & Madden, 2009; March, Grieve, Marrington, & Jonason, 2017; Paul, Bowman, & Banks, 2015). But, whereas the targets of trolling/griefing are usually dictated simply by their availability, brigading is a result of a deliberate choice of recipient.

Vigilantism

Vigilantism is the most extreme element of cyberactivism, and is the deliberate disruption or destruction of online content solely due to the stance of that content (Powell, 2016). A more common term may be "hacking" but the author distinguishes between the two. Where the latter affects online content simply for maliciousness sake, and the former affects it specifically *because* of the content displayed. Vigilantism is distinct from brigading in that it requires actions outside those available to normal users of a website (Woo, Kim, & Dominick, 2004). Posting comments (positive or negative) on a Facebook page can be done by anyone. *Changing* the content on a page through knowledge of administrator passwords or hacking tools requires more specialist knowledge; hence, it is rarer but also usually more damaging.

EFFECTS OF SOCIAL MEDIA—ACTIVISM OR SLACKTIVISM

A key concern when examining the role of social media in activism is whether it truly engenders social change or not. Does an individual who promotes a cause on their Facebook page engage in any additional efforts to further that cause? We could hypothesize two possible consequences from engaging in cyberactivism. First, having promoted a cause online, an individual then continues to enact cause-supporting behavior which allows a cause to gather movement. Individuals generally favor appearing consistent and sincere (Cantarero, Gamian-Wilk, & Dolinski, 2017; Guadagno & Cialdini, 2010; Harmon-Jones, Harmon-Jones, & Levy, 2015; Nolan & Nail, 2014; Rodrigues & Girandola, 2017), and thus they may be motivated to ensure that their subsequent actions are congruent with their online ones. Second, we may postulate that an individual who has engaged in online activism may believe they have done "enough"—with their obligation fulfilled, their subsequent actions to support this cause are actually diminished. The next section examines the literature on this topic to see which of these situations is more likely to arise.

Cyberactivism Predicts Further Social Action/Engagement with Issues

In many cases, the outlook is optimistic. The literature seems to support the idea that participating online in favor of a social cause can indeed predict further participation. For example, Macafee and De Simone (2012) examined participants' usage of four social media outlets—Facebook, YouTube, Twitter, and blogging—as a means of online activism, and their subsequent offline protesting behavior. They found that high levels of protesting online through expressive cause-related posting did indeed predict offline activism. A caveat to this is that simply using social media as a source of information was *not* predictive; users needed to be engaged with the issues online and actively promoting a cause for their behavior to translate into offline activity. This finding is mirrored by Valenzuela (2013), who found that increased levels of social media use predicted offline protest behavior (against changes in education policy in Chile), but the mediator of this relationship was the expression of political opinions via social media. Hwang and Kim (2015) also found that participating regularly in social media activism predicted intentions to engage in social movements. This was most effective in those individuals who had a wide social network online, as these behaviors augmented users' social capital among others.

Social media exposes users to a bombardment of information regarding political and other activist causes. Despite the volume of information, evidence suggests users do not "tune out" this stream. Individuals who encounter these kinds of posts via social media incidentally will often then go on to actively investigate further themselves (Lee & Kim, 2017) and may propagate the messages they find even if their initial encounter was entirely accidental (Valeriani & Vaccari, 2016). Social media also offers users an opportunity to disseminate the causes they support by "sharing" news stories or other cause-related online media. Broadcasting this kind of information leads to increased involvement and interest in the particular cause, especially if others then comment on it (Oeldorf-Hirsch & Sundar, 2015).

Recent successful political and social movements that have leveraged social media demonstrate how cyberactivism and "regular" activism can intertwine to produce meaningful change. At the inception of an activist cause, social media can be used as a method of mobilization. For example, campaigns to reduce campus sexual violence (Linder, Myers, Riggle, & Lacy, 2016) and sexual harassment (Peuchaud, 2014), anti-war protests in the US (Carty & Onyett, 2006), Occupy (i.e., sit-in) movements (Bastos, Mercea, & Charpentier, 2015; Penney & Dadas, 2014), and same-sex marriage support

(Vraga et al., 2014) have all benefited from organization and galvanization via social media. Perceiving online activism to be successful unsurprisingly spurs users on to engage with it for subsequent causes (Velasquez & LaRose, 2015).

Cyberactivism May Undermine Activism—The Problem with Slacktivism

Despite the contribution that cyberactivism can make to social change, some of the concerns regarding cyberactivism have been validated in the literature. Researchers have found that the tokenistic nature of supporting a cause online can then dilute subsequent action. Interviews with those who engage in online activism suggest they believe they are contributing more to their cause that is actually the case (Harlow & Guo, 2014). Experimental evidence supports this idea, too. Schumann and Klein (2015) asked participants to first post a comment in support of a cause they valued on a relevant message board. This was defined by the researchers as "slacktivist" action; a low-cost action which requires little effort and has low risk. Subsequently, those same participants were asked to engage in a panel discussion with other advocates of that cause. Participants were significantly less likely to undertake this task if they had left a supportive comment compared with a no-comment control condition. Interestingly, subsequent analyses suggested that this lack of engagement was *not* due to satisfying personal goals by posting supportive comments. Rather, participants felt they had already made a substantial contribution to the cause with their comment, and so were not obliged to promote their ideals further.

The observable nature of cyberactivism may also undermine its effectiveness. Kristofferson, White, and Peloza (2014) hypothesized that token public support for causes online would contextualize the interaction as an impression-management issue. Thus, engaging in public cyberactivism would not lead to subsequent offline activism. By contrast, *private* token support *would* lead to more meaningful behavior, as actors would feel motivated to maintain their own sense of consistency within themselves. Despite the counterintuitive nature of this idea, support was found for these ideas across their five experiments. Participants who engaged in public "slacktivist" behaviors were much less engaged in real-world activism subsequently compared to those who acted privately. Given that—almost by definition—social media activism is highly conspicuous and public, these findings suggest that using these sites as a platform for a cause may not lead to tangible social change.

Vissers, Hooghe, Stolle, and Maheo (2012) argue that engagement with a cause is platform specific. Individuals advocating a cause online will continue to do so through their social media activity, and those recruited via face-to-face means will also most likely maintain their support of a cause through their behavior (e.g., participating in protest rallies). But, in their work no cross-over between platforms occurred; cyberactivism did not translate into "real" activism.

The visibility of social media activism can also undo the efforts of protest movements precisely because anyone can see them. That is, the organization of activism via social media means that those who are in *opposition* to the activists' cause may be able to see pertinent information, and rally their own troops accordingly (Penney & Dadas, 2014). Thus, the very advantage of using social media also becomes a disadvantage.

The Dangers of Using Social Media to Recruit for a Cause

The rapid dissemination of information via social media does, of course, have its problems. The primary issue with the uncontrolled spread of data is that it is indiscriminate. The veracity of the information individuals post has very little relationship with how well it travels across the Internet. The viral nature of social media has been used to discredit or otherwise slander individuals in the past; for example, by suggesting political opponents are engaged in treasonous activities (Schaffar, 2016).

The sheer volume of information posted online can also cause users to make misattributions regarding how informed they are about a cause. Müller, Schneiders, and Schäfer (2016) asked participants to report their frequency of exposure to news in their Facebook feed, how informed they felt about current affairs, and whether they looked at other news sources. They were also asked how often they read news posts on Facebook, and whether they followed posted links to news sources. Analysis demonstrated that the quantity of news posts on Facebook led users to feel more informed, and to use other sources of information less. However, the level of exposure did not predict actually *reading* the sources presented, or the following of links to detailed accounts of news stories. Among Facebook users the high volume of news stories creates the illusion of being informed, but it does not mean that users will actually investigate further. This demonstrates the potential dangers of social media in promulgating activism.

CONCLUSION—THE FUTURE OF CYBERACTIVISM

Social media is still a relatively new phenomenon to psychology, and cyberpsychology is a nascent—although rapidly growing—discipline. Thus, we are still only beginning to ascertain how cyberactivism operates, and how it will impact on meaningful societal change. It is apparent that the motivations for using social media in any capacity are very strong, and this is unlikely to diminish in the future. Over time, more and more causes will likely contain an online component that will attempt to propagate support via social media elements. Existing models of activism translate fairly well to an online context. Regardless of the medium, potential supports still need to be recruited and mobilized.

In addition, activist behavior is still facilitated more effectively when supporters feel a meaningful sense of cohesion with one another and have a belief that their efforts will be fruitful. Interestingly, in the absence of individual identities (depersonalization), social identity can exert a powerful influence over subsequent behavior.

A key question regarding cyberactivism is if it actually makes any difference. The literature at the moment presents a mixed picture. Some researchers suggest it does, and that initial support online leads to more active participation in other behaviors. But this is not a given, and it seems tokenistic support can sometimes satisfy sufficiently the needs of "slacktivists" with the result that they do not engage any further. As study on this topic grows, the picture will become clearer on this matter. We must also ask at what stage might a saturation point be reached? Offline, many people already feel "donor fatigue" (Gentleman, 2016; Moszynski, 2010)—an aversion to helping others caused by continual requests for time and money by others. Will this trend appear online? It is already easy to screen out adverts from one's web browser; might a similar application for cause appeals be far away? Only time will tell whether cyberactivism will expand its reach and become a force for harnessing like-minded individuals to enact change, or become an online distraction that will simply be filtered out.

References

Alberici, A. I., & Milesi, P. (2016). Online discussion, politicized identity, and collective action. *Group Processes & Intergroup Relations 19*(1), 43–59. https://doi.org/10.1177/1368430215581430

Alhabash, S., McAlister, A. R., Hagerstrom, A., Quilliam, E. T., Rifon, N. J., & Richards, J. I. (2013). Between likes and shares: Effects of emotional appeal and virality on the persuasiveness of anticyberbullying messages on Facebook. *Cyberpsychology, Behavior, and Social Networking 16*(3), 175–182.

Bäck, E. A., Bäck, H., & Knapton, H. M. (2015). Group belongingness and collective action: Effects of need to belong and rejection sensitivity on willingness to participate in protest activities. *Scandinavian Journal of Psychology 56*(5), 537–544. https://doi.org/10.1111/sjop.12225

Bastos, M. T., Mercea, D., & Charpentier, A. (2015). Tents, tweets, and events: The interplay between ongoing protests and social media. *Journal of Communication 65*(2), 320–350. https://doi.org/10.1111/jcom.12145

Baumeister, R. F. (2012). Need-to-belong theory. In Paul A. M. Van Lange, Arie W. Kruglanski, & E. Tory Higgins (Eds.), *Handbook of theories of social psychology, Vol. 2* (pp. 121–140). London: Sage.

Berger, J., & Milkman, K. L. (2012). What makes online content viral? *Journal of Marketing Research 49*(2), 192–205.

Bishop, J. (Ed.). (2014). *Gamification for Human Factors Integration: Social, Education, and Psychological Issues*. Hershey: IGI Global.

Brown, M. R., Bhadury, R. K., & Pope, N. K. L. (2010). The impact of comedic violence on viral advertising effectiveness. *Journal of Advertising 39*(1), 49–66.

Bruns, A., Highfield, T., & Burgess, J. (2013). The Arab Spring and social media audiences: English and Arabic Twitter users and their networks. *American Behavioral Scientist 57*(7), 871–898.

Cantarero, K., Gamian-Wilk, M., & Dolinski, D. (2017). Being inconsistent and compliant: The moderating role of the preference for consistency in the door-in-the-face technique. *Personality and Individual Differences 115*, 54–57.

Carty, V., & Onyett, J. (2006). Protest, cyberactivism and new social movements: The re-emergence of the peace movement post 9/11. *Social Movement Studies 5*(3), 229–249. https://doi.org/10.1080/14742830600991586

Chapman, H., & Coffé, H. (2016). Changing Facebook profile pictures as part of a campaign: Who does it and why? *Journal of Youth Studies 19*(4), 483–500. https://doi.org/10.1080/1367 6261.2015.1083962

Chiluwa, I., & Ifukor, P. (2015). "War against our children": Stance and evaluation in #BringBackOurGirls campaign discourse on Twitter and Facebook. *Discourse & Society 26*(3), 267–296.

Coppock, A., Guess, A., & Ternovski, J. (2016). When treatments are Tweets: A network mobilization experiment over Twitter. *Political Behavior 38*(1), 105–128. https://doi.org/10.1007/s11109-015-9308-6

Corcoran, K. E., Pettinicchio, D., & Young, J. T. N. (2011). The context of control: A cross-national investigation of the link between political institutions, efficacy, and collective action. *British Journal of Social Psychology 50*(4), 575–605. https://doi.org/10.1111/j.2044-8309.2011.02076.x

Coyne, I., Chesney, T., Logan, B., & Madden, N. (2009). Griefing in a virtual community. *Zeitschrift Für Psychologie/Journal of Psychology 217*(4), 214–221. https://doi.org/10.1027/0044-3409.217.4.214

Darke, P. R., Chaiken, S., Bohner, G., Einwiller, S., Erb, H.-P., & Hazlewood, J. D. (1998). Accuracy motivation, consensus information, and the law of large numbers: Effects on attitude judgment in the absence of argumentation. *Personality and Social Psychology Bulletin 24*(11), 1205–1215. https://doi.org/10.1177/01461672982411007

De Veirman, M., Cauberghe, V., & Hudders, L. (2017). Marketing through Instagram influencers: The impact of number of followers and product divergence on brand attitude. *International Journal of Advertising: The Review of Marketing Communications 36*(5), 798–828.

Eckler, P., & Bolls, P. (2011). Spreading the virus: Emotional tone of viral advertising and its effect on forwarding intentions and attitudes. *Journal of Interactive Advertising 11*(2), 1–11.

Eilperin, J. (2015, May 26). Here's how the first president of the social media age has chosen to connect with Americans. *Washington Post*. Retrieved from https://www.washingtonpost.com/news/politics/wp/2015/05/26/heres-how-the-first-president-of-the-social-media-age-has-chosen-to-connect-with-americans/

English, K., Sweetser, K. D., & Ancu, M. (2011). YouTube-ification of political talk: An examination of persuasion appeals in viral video. *American Behavioral Scientist 55*(6), 733–748.

Eshuis, J. (2013). The need to belong. *Theory & Psychology 23*(3), 404–407.

Feather, N. (2015). Analyzing relative deprivation in relation to deservingness, entitlement and resentment. *Social Justice Research 28*(1), 7–26.

Gentleman, A. (2016, September 2). Calais refugee camp running out of food amid donor fatigue. *The Guardian*. Retrieved from https://www.theguardian.com/world/2016/sep/02/calais-refugee-camp-running-out-of-food-as-donor-fatigue-sees-donations-dry-up

Guadagno, R. E., & Cialdini, R. B. (2010). Preference for consistency and social influence: A review of current research findings. *Social Influence 5*(3), 152–163.

Guadagno, R. E., Rempala, D. M., Murphy, S., & Okdie, B. M. (2013). What makes a video go viral? An analysis of emotional contagion and Internet memes. *Computers in Human Behavior 29*(6), 2312–2319. https://doi.org/10.1016/j.chb.2013.04.016

Harlow, S., & Guo, L. (2014). Will the revolution be Tweeted or Facebooked? Using digital communication tools in immigrant activism. *Journal of Computer-Mediated Communication* 19(3), 463–478. https://doi.org/10.1111/jcc4.12062

Harmon-Jones, E., Harmon-Jones, C., & Levy, N. (2015). An action-based model of cognitive-dissonance processes. *Current Directions in Psychological Science* 24(3), 184–189.

Harvey, C. G., Stewart, D. B., & Ewing, M. T. (2011). Forward or delete: What drives peer-to-peer message propagation across social networks? *Journal of Consumer Behaviour* 10(6), 365–372. https://doi.org/10.1002/cb.383

Higgie, R. (2014). Kynical dogs and cynical masters: Contemporary satire, politics and truth-telling. *Humor* 27(2). https://doi.org/10.1515/humor-2014-0016

Hornsey, M. J., Blackwood, L., Louis, W., Fielding, K., Mavor, K., Morton, T.,...White, K. M. (2006). Why do people engage in collective action? Revisiting the role of perceived effectiveness. *Journal of Applied Social Psychology* 36(7), 1701–1722.

Howard, P. N., & Hussain, M. M. (2011). The role of digital media. *Journal of Democracy* 22(3), 35–48.

Hrastelj, J., & Robertson, N. P. (2016). Ice bucket challenge bears fruit for amyotrophic lateral sclerosis. *Journal of Neurology* 263(11), 2355–2357.

Hwang, H., & Kim, K.-O. (2015). Social media as a tool for social movements: The effect of social media use and social capital on intention to participate in social movements. *International Journal of Consumer Studies* 39(5), 478–488. https://doi.org/10.1111/ijcs.12221

Iyer, A., & Ryan, M. K. (2009). Why do men and women challenge gender discrimination in the workplace? The role of group status and in-group identification in predicting pathways to collective action. *Journal of Social Issues* 65(4), 791–814.

Johnson, P. R., & Yang, S. (2009). Uses and gratifications of Twitter: An examination of user motives and satisfaction of Twitter use. Presented at *Communication Technology Division of the Annual Convention of the Association for Education in Journalism and Mass Communication (AEJMC)*. 5–8 August, Boston, MA.

Jonas, E., Schulz-Hardt, S., & Frey, D. (2005). Giving advice or making decisions in someone else's place: The influence of impression, defense, and accuracy motivation on the search for new information. *Personality and Social Psychology Bulletin* 31(7), 977–990.

Kahn, R., & Kellner, D. (2004). New media and Internet activism: From the "Battle of Seattle" to blogging. *New Media & Society* 6(1), 87–95. https://doi.org/10.1177/1461444804039908

Kende, A., van Zomeren, M., Ujhelyi, A., & Lantos, N. A. (2016). The social affirmation use of social media as a motivator of collective action: Social media use and collective action. *Journal of Applied Social Psychology* 46(8), 453–469. https://doi.org/10.1111/jasp.12375

Khan, M. L. (2017). Social media engagement: What motivates user participation and consumption on YouTube? *Computers in Human Behavior* 66, 236–247. https://doi.org/10.1016/j.chb.2016.09.024

Kim, H. S. (2015). Attracting views and going viral: How message features and news-sharing channels affect health news diffusion. *The Journal of Communication* 65(3), 512–534. https://doi.org/10.1111/jcom.12160

Kim, M. (2016). Facebook's spiral of silence and participation: The role of political expression on facebook and partisan strength in political participation. *Cyberpsychology, Behavior and Social Networking* 19(12), 696–702.

Klandermans, B., & Oegema, D. (1987). Potentials, networks, motivations, and barriers: Steps towards participation in social movements. *American Sociological Review* 52(4), 519–531.

Klein, O., Spears, R., & Reicher, S. (2007). Social identity performance: Extending the strategic side of SIDE. *Personality and Social Psychology Review 11*(1), 28–45. https://doi.org/10.1177/1088868306294588

Korolov, R., Lu, D., Wang, J., Zhou, G., Bonial, C., Voss, C.,...Ji, H. (2016). On predicting social unrest using social media. In *Proceedings of the 2016 IEEE/ACM International Conference on Advances in Social Networks Analysis and Mining ASONAM 2016* (pp. 89–95), 18–21 August, San Francisco, CA, Piscataway: IEEE.

Krishnan, A., & Hunt, D. S. (2015). Influence of a multidimensional measure of attitudes on motives to use social networking sites. *Cyberpsychology, Behavior, and Social Networking 18*(3), 165–172. https://doi.org/10.1089/cyber.2014.0423

Kristofferson, K., White, K., & Peloza, J. (2014). The nature of slacktivism: How the social observability of an initial act of token support affects subsequent prosocial action. *Journal of Consumer Research 40*(6), 1149–1166. https://doi.org/10.1086/674137

Lea, M., Spears, R., & de Groot, D. (2001). Knowing me, knowing you: Anonymity effects on social identity processes within groups. *Personality and Social Psychology Bulletin 27*(5), 526–537. https://doi.org/10.1177/0146167201275002

Lee, E., Lee, J.-A., Moon, J. H., & Sung, Y. (2015). Pictures speak louder than words: Motivations for using Instagram. *Cyberpsychology, Behavior, and Social Networking 18*(9), 552–556. https://doi.org/10.1089/cyber.2015.0157

Lee, E.-J. (2004). Effects of visual representation on social influence in computer-mediated communication. *Human Communication Research 30*(2), 234–259. https://doi.org/10.1111/j.1468-2958.2004.tb00732.x

Lee, E.-J. (2008). When are strong arguments stronger than weak arguments: Deindividuation effects on message elaboration in computer mediated communication. *Communication Research 35*(5), 646–665. https://doi.org/10.1177/0093650208321784

Lee, J., Ham, C.-D., & Kim, M. (2013). Why people pass along online video advertising: From the perspectives of the interpersonal communication motives scale and the theory of reasoned action. *Journal of Interactive Advertising 13*(1), 1–13.

Lee, J. K., & Kim, E. (2017). Incidental exposure to news: Predictors in the social media setting and effects on information gain online. *Computers in Human Behavior 75*, 1008–1015.

Leonard, D. J., Moons, W. G., Mackie, D. M., & Smith, E. R. (2011). "We're mad as hell and we're not going to take it anymore": Anger self-stereotyping and collective action. *Group Processes & Intergroup Relations 14*(1), 99–111. https://doi.org/10.1177/1368430210373779

Linder, C., Myers, J. S., Riggle, C., & Lacy, M. (2016). From margins to mainstream: Social media as a tool for campus sexual violence activism. *Journal of Diversity in Higher Education 9*(3), 231–244. https://doi.org/10.1037/dhe0000038

Lindgren, S., & Lundström, R. (2011). Pirate culture and hacktivist mobilization: The cultural and social protocols of #WikiLeaks on Twitter. *New Media & Society 13*(6), 999–1018.

Loss, J., Lindacher, V., & Curbach, J. (2014). Online social networking sites—A novel setting for health promotion? *Health & Place 26*, 161–170.

Lotan, G., Graeff, E., Ananny, M., Gaffney, D., Pearce, I., & boyd, d. (2011). The Arab Spring| the revolutions were tweeted: Information flows during the 2011 Tunisian and Egyptian revolutions. *International Journal of Communication 5*, 31.

Luchman, J. N., Bergstrom, J., & Krulikowski, C. (2014). A motives framework of social media website use: A survey of young Americans. *Computers in Human Behavior 38*, 136–141. https://doi.org/10.1016/j.chb.2014.05.016

Macafee, T., & De Simone, J. J. (2012). Killing the bill online? Pathways to young people's protest engagement via social media. *Cyberpsychology, Behavior, and Social Networking 15*(11), 579–584. https://doi.org/10.1089/cyber.2012.0153

March, E., Grieve, R., Marrington, J., & Jonason, P. K. (2017). Trolling on Tinder˚ (and other dating apps): Examining the role of the Dark Tetrad and impulsivity. *Personality and Individual Differences 110*, 139–143. https://doi.org/10.1016/j.paid.2017.01.025

Mascha, E. (2011). Mocking fascism: Popular culture and political satire. *Studies in Political Humour: In Between Political Critique and Public Entertainment 46*, 191.

McGarty, C., Thomas, E. F., Lala, G., Smith, L. G., & Bliuc, A.-M. (2014). New technologies, new identities, and the growth of mass opposition in the Arab Spring. *Political Psychology 35*(6), 725–740.

Miller, D. A., Cronin, T., Garcia, A. L., & Branscombe, N. R. (2009). The relative impact of anger and efficacy on collective action is affected by feelings of fear. *Group Processes & Intergroup Relations, 12*(4), 445–462. https://doi.org/10.1177/1368430209105046

Moszynski, P. (2010). Donor fatigue is slashing access to AIDS care in Africa, warns charity. *BMJ (Clinical Research Ed.) 340*, c2844–c2844. https://doi.org/10.1136/bmj.c2844

Müller, P., Schneiders, P., & Schäfer, S. (2016). Appetizer or main dish? Explaining the use of Facebook news posts as a substitute for other news sources. *Computers in Human Behavior 65*, 431–441. https://doi.org/10.1016/j.chb.2016.09.003

Ni, M. Y., Chan, B. H. Y., Leung, G. M., Lau, E. H. Y., & Pang, H. (2014). Transmissibility of the Ice Bucket Challenge among globally influential celebrities: Retrospective cohort study. *British Medical Journal 349*. Retrieved from http://search.ebscohost.com/login.aspx?direct=true&db=psyh&AN=2014-57738-001&site=ehost-live

Nolan, J., & Nail, P. (2014). Further evidence that individuals with a high preference for consistency are more susceptible to cognitive dissonance. *Psi Chi Journal of Psychological Research 19*(4), 214–219.

Oeldorf-Hirsch, A., & Sundar, S. S. (2015). Posting, commenting, and tagging: Effects of sharing news stories on Facebook. *Computers in Human Behavior 44*, 240–249. https://doi.org/10.1016/j.chb.2014.11.024

O'Mara, E. M., Jackson, L. E., Batson, C. D., & Gaertner, L. (2011). Will moral outrage stand up? Distinguishing among emotional reactions to a moral violation. *European Journal of Social Psychology 41*(2), 173–179. https://doi.org/10.1002/ejsp.754

Osborne, D., Sibley, C. G., Huo, Y. J., & Smith, H. (2015). Doubling-down on deprivation: Using latent profile analysis to evaluate an age-old assumption in relative deprivation theory. *European Journal of Social Psychology 45*(4), 482–495. https://doi.org/10.1002/ejsp.2099

Paul, H. L., Bowman, N. D., & Banks, J. (2015). The enjoyment of griefing in online games. *Journal of Gaming and Virtual Worlds 7*(3), 243–258. https://doi.org/10.1386/jgvw.7.3.243_1

Penney, J. (2015). Social media and symbolic action: Exploring participation in the Facebook red equal sign profile picture campaign. *Journal of Computer-Mediated Communication 20*(1), 52–66. https://doi.org/10.1111/jcc4.12092

Penney, J., & Dadas, C. (2014). (Re)Tweeting in the service of protest: Digital composition and circulation in the Occupy Wall Street movement. *New Media & Society 16*(1), 74–90. https://doi.org/10.1177/1461444813479593

Petty, R. E., & Cacioppo, J. T. (1979). Issue involvement can increase or decrease persuasion by enhancing message-relevant cognitive responses. *Journal of Personality and Social Psychology 37*(10), 1915–1926.

Peuchaud, S. (2014). Social media activism and Egyptians' use of social media to combat sexual violence: An HiAP case study. *Health Promotion International* 29(Suppl. 1), 113–120. https://doi.org/10.1093/heapro/dau046

Phua, J., Jin, S. V., & Hahm, J. M. (2018). Celebrity-endorsed e-cigarette brand Instagram advertisements: Effects on young adults' attitudes towards e-cigarettes and smoking intentions. *Journal of Health Psychology* 23(4), 550–560.

Pillow, D. R., Malone, G. P., & Hale, W. J. (2015). The need to belong and its association with fully satisfying relationships: A tale of two measures. *Personality and Individual Differences* 74, 259–264.

Postmes, T., & Brunsting, S. (2002). Collective action in the age of the Internet: Mass communication and online mobilization. *Social Science Computer Review* 20(3), 290–301.

Postmes, T., Spears, R., & Lea, M. (1998). Breaching or building social boundaries? SIDE-effects of computer-mediated communication. *Communication Research* 25(6), 689–715. https://doi.org/10.1177/009365098025006006

Powell, A. (2016). Hacking in the public interest: Authority, legitimacy, means, and ends. *New Media & Society* 18(4), 600–616. https://doi.org/10.1177/1461444816629470

Rodrigues, L., & Girandola, F. (2017). Self-prophecies and cognitive dissonance: Habit, norms and justification of past behavior. *North American Journal of Psychology* 19(1), 65–86.

Rossolatos, G. (2015). The ice-bucket challenge: The legitimacy of the memetic mode of cultural reproduction is the message. *Signs and Society* 3(1), 132–152.

Saab, R., Tausch, N., Spears, R., & Cheung, W.-Y. (2015). Acting in solidarity: Testing an extended dual pathway model of collective action by bystander group members. *British Journal of Social Psychology* 54(3), 539–560. https://doi.org/10.1111/bjso.12095

de la Sablonnière, R., Tougas, F., Taylor, D. M., Crush, J., McDonald, D., & Perenlei, O. R. (2015). Social change in Mongolia and South Africa: The impact of relative deprivation trajectory and group status on well-being and adjustment to change. *Social Justice Research* 28(1), 102–122. https://doi.org/10.1007/s11211-015-0236-8

Sassenberg, K., & Boos, M. (2003). Attitude change in computer-mediated communication: Effects of anonymity and category norms. *Group Processes & Intergroup Relations* 6(4), 405–422.

Schaffar, W. (2016). New social media and politics in Thailand: The emergence of fascist vigilante groups on Facebook. *Austrian Journal of South-East Asian Studies* 9(2), 215.

Schumann, S., & Klein, O. (2015). Substitute or stepping stone? Assessing the impact of low-threshold online collective actions on offline participation. *European Journal of Social Psychology* 45(3), 308–322. https://doi.org/10.1002/ejsp.2084

Scott, K. (2015). The pragmatics of hashtags: Inference and conversational style on Twitter. *Journal of Pragmatics* 81, 8–20.

Selim, H. A., Long, K. M., & Vignoles, V. L. (2014). Exploring identity motives in Twitter usage in Saudi Arabia and the UK. *Studies in Health Technology and Informatics* 199, 128–132.

Sheldon, P., & Bryant, K. (2016). Instagram: Motives for its use and relationship to narcissism and contextual age. *Computers in Human Behavior* 58, 89–97. https://doi.org/10.1016/j.chb.2015.12.059

Shugerman, E. (2017, October 17). All you need to know about the MeToo campaign and how it started. *The Independent*. Retrieved from http://www.independent.co.uk/news/world/americas/me-too-facebook-hashtag-why-when-meaning-sexual-harassment-rape-stories-explained-a8005936.html

Smith, H. J., & Pettigrew, T. F. (2014). The subjective interpretation of inequality: A model of the relative deprivation experience. *Social and Personality Psychology Compass 8*(12), 755–765. https://doi.org/10.1111/spc3.12151

Spears, R., Lea, M., Corneliussen, R. A., Postmes, T., & Haar, W. T. (2002). Computer-mediated communication as a channel for social resistance: The strategic side of SIDE. *Small Group Research 33*(5), 555–574. https://doi.org/10.1177/104649602237170

Sweeney, P. D., McFarlin, D. B., & Inderrieden, E. J. (1990). Using relative deprivation theory to explain satisfaction with income and pay level: A multi-study examination. *Academy of Management Journal 33*(2), 423–436.

Teppers, E., Luyckx, K., A. Klimstra, T., & Goossens, L. (2014). Loneliness and Facebook motives in adolescence: A longitudinal inquiry into directionality of effect. *Journal of Adolescence 37*(5), 691–699. https://doi.org/10.1016/j.adolescence.2013.11.003

Thomas, E. F., & Louis, W. R. (2014). When will collective action be effective? Violent and non-violent protests differentially influence perceptions of legitimacy and efficacy among sympathizers. *Personality and Social Psychology Bulletin 40*(2), 263–276. https://doi.org/10.1177/0146167213510525

Thomas, E. F., & McGarty, C. A. (2009). The role of efficacy and moral outrage norms in creating the potential for international development activism through group-based interaction. *British Journal of Social Psychology 48*(1), 115–134.

Thomas, E. F., Rathmann, L., & McGarty, C. (2017). From "I" to "We": Different forms of identity, emotion, and belief predict victim support volunteerism among nominal and active supporters. *Journal of Applied Social Psychology 47*(4), 213–223. https://doi.org/10.1111/jasp.12428

Tufekci, Z., & Wilson, C. (2012). Social media and the decision to participate in political protest: Observations from Tahrir Square. *Journal of Communication 62*(2), 363–379. https://doi.org/10.1111/j.1460-2466.2012.01629.x

Tyler, J. M., Branch, S. E., & Kearns, P. O. (2016). Dispositional need to belong moderates the impact of negative social cues and rejection on self-esteem. *Social Psychology 47*(4), 179–186.

Valenzuela, S. (2013). Unpacking the use of social media for protest behavior: The roles of information, opinion expression, and activism. *American Behavioral Scientist 57*(7), 920–942. https://doi.org/10.1177/0002764213479375

Valeriani, A., & Vaccari, C. (2016). Accidental exposure to politics on social media as online participation equalizer in Germany, Italy, and the United Kingdom. *New Media & Society 18*(9), 1857–1874. https://doi.org/10.1177/1461444815616223

van den Bos, K., van Veldhuizen, T. S., & Au, A. K. (2015). Counter cross-cultural priming and relative deprivation: The role of individualism–collectivism. *Social Justice Research 28*(1), 52–75.

van Noort, G., Antheunis, M. L., & van Reijmersdal, E. A. (2012). Social connections and the persuasiveness of viral campaigns in social network sites: Persuasive intent as the underlying mechanism. *Journal of Marketing Communications, 18*(1), 39–53. https://doi.org/10.1080/13527266.2011.620764

Van Zomeren, M., Spears, R., Fischer, A. H., & Leach, C. W. (2004). Put your money where your mouth is! Explaining collective action tendencies through group-based anger and group efficacy. *Journal of Personality and Social Psychology 87*(5), 649.

Veenstra, A. S., Iyer, N., Hossain, M. D., & Park, J. (2014). Time, place, technology: Twitter as an information source in the Wisconsin labor protests. *Computers in Human Behavior 31*, 65–72.

Velasquez, A., & LaRose, R. (2015). Social media for social change: Social media political efficacy and activism in student activist groups. *Journal of Broadcasting & Electronic Media* 59(3), 456–474. https://doi.org/10.1080/08838151.2015.1054998

Vignoles, V. L. (2011). Identity motives. In Seth J. Schwartz, Koen Luyckx, & Vivian L. Vignoles (Eds.), *Handbook of identity theory and research* (pp. 403–432). New York: Springer.

Vissers, S., Hooghe, M., Stolle, D., & Maheo, V.-A. (2012). The impact of mobilization media on off-line and online participation: Are mobilization effects medium-specific? *Social Science Computer Review 30*(2), 152–169. https://doi.org/10.1177/0894439310396485

Vraga, E. K., Bode, L., Wells, C., Driscoll, K., & Thorson, K. (2014). The rules of engagement: Comparing two social protest movements on YouTube. *Cyberpsychology, Behavior and Social Networking 17*(3), 133–140. https://doi.org/10.1089/cyber.2013.0117

Warren, A. M., Sulaiman, A., & Jaafar, N. I. (2014). Facebook: The enabler of online civic engagement for activists. *Computers in Human Behavior 32*, 284–289.

Woo, H., Kim, Y., & Dominick, J. (2004). Hackers: Militants or merry pranksters? A content analysis of defaced web pages. *Media Psychology 6*(1), 63–82. https://doi.org/10.1207/s1532785xmep0601_3

Xu, W. W., Park, J. Y., Kim, J. Y., & Park, H. W. (2016). Networked cultural diffusion and creation on YouTube: An analysis of YouTube memes. *Journal of Broadcasting & Electronic Media 60*(1), 104–122. https://doi.org/10.1080/08838151.2015.1127241

Yang, C., & Brown, B. B. (2013). Motives for using Facebook, patterns of Facebook activities, and late adolescents' social adjustment to college. *Journal of Youth and Adolescence 42*(3), 403–416. https://doi.org/10.1007/s10964-012-9836-x

Yang, H. C., & Wang, Y. (2015). Social sharing of online videos: Examining American consumers' video sharing attitudes, intent, and behavior. *Psychology & Marketing 32*(9), 907–919. https://doi.org/10.1002/mar.20826

CHAPTER 20

SOCIALLY CONNECTING THROUGH BLOGS AND VLOGS: A SOCIAL CONNECTIONS APPROACH TO BLOGGING AND VLOGGING MOTIVATION

BRADLEY M. OKDIE AND
DANIEL M. REMPALA

INTRODUCTION

MODERN communication technology norms are moving away from anonymity towards increased personalization (for review, see Bargh & McKenna, 2004; McKenna & Bargh, 2000). The Internet is more interactive than traditional forms of mass communication, and the extent to which people are expected to divulge personal information seems to increase with each new technological innovation (Gross & Acquisti, 2005; Statista, 2017). While still possible, maintaining anonymity online has become non-normative. For example, on most media communication platforms there is an expectation for users to provide personal information, such as a profile picture, or to disclose likes and dislikes and to express personal views on a variety of topics (Taraszow, Aristodemou, Shitta, Laouris, & Arsoy, 2010).

The increased personalization of the Internet has increased the extent to which people use it to socially connect, and it provides unique ways to interact with others that were unavailable prior to its advent. Thus, people are no longer using the Internet simply to find information and, instead, are using it as a place to create and maintain social connections (Postmes, Spears, & Lea, 2002). We argue peoples' use of media is often motivated by a desire to socially connect with others. In this chapter, using a social connection lens, we review the literature on the motivations for expressing oneself online through one such vehicle for online social connection: blogging. We examine factors that predict why people blog, what they choose to blog about, and how these motivations may originate through the fundamental human need to belong.

To Be Human is to Seek Belonging

People are driven by a fundamental need to make and keep social connections (Baumeister & Leary, 1995). Alone in the world, humans historically have encountered problems; relatively speaking, humans are slow, weak, have limited ability to defend themselves (e.g., lack claws and fangs), and have terrible night vision. The need to belong originates from the increased survival potential each individual has when in a group compared to being alone. Thus, humans find comfort and meaning in social connections and have adapted physical and cognitive strategies that serve to maintain their presence in groups (Kurzban & Leary, 2001). For instance, being ostracized (excluded and ignored) activates areas of the brain associated with physical pain, such as the dorsal anterior cingulate cortex (Eisenberger, Lieberman, & Williams, 2003). This activation effectively "punishes" isolation and motivates behaviors to build or restore social bonds (Eisenberger et al., 2003). Similarly, the brain has developed cognitive strategies to deal with poor social exchange partners (Kurzban & Leary, 2001). For example, humans have cognitive strategies that detect cheaters (i.e., those who take more than they give; Cosmides, 1989; Cosmides & Tooby, 1992), and those who detect poor social exchange partners (e.g., cheaters) are motivated to exclude them (Wesselmann, Wirth, Pryor, Reeder, & Williams, 2013). Therefore, humans have evolved cognitive and behavioral strategies that drive them to join groups and defend their group status.

In addition to causing emotional pain, ostracism has many negative cognitive and physiological consequences. Ostracized people suffer from a lowered sense of belonging, self-esteem, meaningful existence, and control (Williams, 2009). Moreover, a lack of social connections can lead to profound detrimental consequences across many domains, including negative mood, poor health, and physical discomfort (see Baumeister & Leary, 1995, and Williams, 2009 for discussion). Conversely, having (or perceiving that one has) healthy social networks and attachments has been shown to confer assorted benefits, such as buffering the negative effects of marital stress (Keneski, Neff, & Loving, 2017) and reducing physical pain (Brown, Sheffield, Leary, & Robinson, 2003; Jackson, Iezzi, Chen, Ebnet, & Eglitis, 2005; Master et al., 2009).

Thus, humans are clearly "social animals" and, in order to indulge in the benefits of group membership (e.g., mutual defense, shared resources), have developed cognitive mechanisms that lead them to find social connections rewarding and motivate them to maintain those connections. Conversely, a lack of social connections invites a host of negative consequences, ranging from short-term discomfort to long-term pathologies. Much of the extant research on the benefits of social connection examines traditional face-to-face (FTF) communications; however, the Internet provides novel ways to create and maintain these connections.

Satisfying the Need for Social Connection through Media

Prior to the Internet, barriers such as physical distance limited peoples' ability to create and maintain social connections (see McKenna & Bargh, 2000). Many of these barriers made social interaction with physically distant others difficult, limiting peoples' ability to fulfill their need to belong. The Internet, and the platforms it enables, has eliminated some of these barriers and led to new ways people can satisfy their need to belong (e.g., social networking sites, message boards, online forums, personal web sites, and blogs). For example, people can begin and maintain social connections through social media sites such as Facebook.com (Joinson, 2008); as of 2016, 68 percent of the adult population of the United States maintained a Facebook profile, and 76 percent of that group used the site daily (Pew Research Center, 2017). While the Internet has provided powerful new avenues for creating and maintaining social relationships, it also differs from traditional FTF communication in important ways.

Face-to-Face versus Online Social Connection

Scholars who have discussed the similarities and differences between FTF and online communication have adopted different approaches. Early research took an outcomes-based approach, focusing on the psychological consequences (e.g., anonymity, deindividuation) of using different forms of media (McKenna & Bargh, 2000). More recently, scholars have developed an attribute-based approach to understanding the psychological and behavioral outcomes of media use. Okdie et al. (2014) posit that the psychological effects of both classic and emergent media can be predicted by the extent to which media contain a set of attributes, such as interactivity (the possibility of people to elicit responses from media), fidelity (the degree to which a medium is accurate in its portrayal of information), and privacy (ability of people to hide information from others). The classic outcomes-based approach to understanding similarities and differences among communication types remains useful, although the value in newer approaches (e.g., the attribute approach) is they can account for emergent media by viewing media types on a continuum, rather than as discrete categories of phenomena.

Regardless of theoretical approach, there appears to be a great deal of overlap between contributing factors and consequences of both FTF and computer-mediated communication (CMC), but they also differ in characteristic and reliable ways. For example, research suggests that people will act online similarly to how they act in FTF interactions (Guadagno, Muscanell, Okdie, Burk, & Ward, 2011) and that both FTF (Okdie, Guadagno, Bernieri, Geers, & McLarney-Vesotski, 2011) and CMC (Walther, 1996) can lead to positive impressions of interaction partners. However, FTF interaction (rather than online) leads to more accurate person perception and greater liking of interaction partners, but it also results in a greater difficulty sustaining these interactions (Okdie et al., 2011). As with any new form of communication, interaction through online channels has both positive and negative effects on human psychology and behavior that depend on context (cf. Zettelmeyer, Morton, & Silva-Risso, 2006). Although emerging communication technologies overlap with traditional FTF communication in some areas and differ in others, they are all forms of communication that serve to socially connect people to each other.

CONNECTIONS MADE THROUGH MEDIA ARE MEANINGFUL

While is it clear that people can, and do, maintain social connections though media, these connections are only likely to satisfy an individual's need to belong to the extent that they are meaningful. In support of this position, recent research indicates that belonging needs predict the likelihood of online relationships, social exclusion motivates the formation and maintenance of online relationships, and exposure to online relationships restores thwarted belonging needs (Knowles, Haycock, & Shaikh, 2015). In addition, these consequences are mediated by many of the same factors that are expected to mediate FTF interactions. For example, individuals high in trait rumination (i.e., repetitive thinking that often occurs about negative emotions) suffer maladaptive thoughts and adjustment problems when remaining "friends" with former romantic partners (Tran & Joormann, 2015), while individuals high in social comparison orientation (i.e., a tendency for people to compare themselves with others on social dimensions) showed lower self-esteem after examining profiles on Facebook (Vogel, Rose, Okdie, Eckles, & Franz, 2015).

It even appears that social media platforms play such a pivotal role in the social lives of some users that the platforms themselves have become meaningful—almost talismanic. For example, simply thinking of being disconnected from a social networking site (SNS; i.e., online services enabling users to create and share information to networks of others) has been shown to cause significant distress (Chiou, Lee, & Liao, 2015). Similarly, recent research suggests that viewing social networking symbols (e.g., the Facebook logo) can reduce physical pain by increasing thoughts of others (Ho, Wu, &

Chiou, 2016). So, not only does the presence of social networks alleviate pain (e.g., Brown et al., 2003), but the presence of symbols associated with a social network also helps reduce perceptions of pain. Thus, it is clear that, although online interactions may affect individuals in ways that are unique from traditional FTF communication, interactions that take place online are meaningful and satisfy peoples' need to belong.

THE CURRENT STATE OF BLOGGING

The need to belong is a significant motive for participating in several forms of online communication, including blogging. Blogs (short for weblogs) are personal websites typically maintained by a single author who updates them in reverse chronological order (Herring, Scheidt, Wright, & Bonus, 2005). The collection of blogs on the Internet is often referred to as the Blogosphere. Additionally, blogs often link to other blogs (called a blogroll) and these links have traditionally allowed blog readers to interact with blog authors (e.g., through comments), although this trend appears to be declining.

Creating and maintaining blogs was difficult when blogs first emerged and often required computer coding experience. Not long after the first appearance of blogs, blogging platforms such as "blogger" and "LiveJournal" made blogging easier by providing blog authors with website templates and removing the need for computer coding knowledge. The simplification of blog production ignited extreme growth in the blogosphere. There perhaps were as few as twenty-three blogs on the Internet in 1999, but by 2008, that number had exploded to fifty million (Arnoldzafra, 2008). However, recent reports indicate that blog growth has slowed and that most existing blogs are not regularly updated (Arnoldzafra, 2008). The decline in the number of active blogs can partially be attributed to the emergence of new blog-like media.

The evolution of existing social media sites and the emergence of new forms of online communication make it increasingly difficult to define contemporary blogging. For example, Facebook has added blog-like features, such as the "Notes" feature, that allow users to post material that is the equivalent in length of a typical blog post (Barrett, 2015). Other platforms, such as Tumblr.com, encourage multimedia blog posts. These technologies share features of traditional blogs but are distinct enough to be classified separately. The two main categories of emerging platforms that most closely share the features and functions of traditional blogging are microblogs and vlogs.

Microblogging

Microblogging is a relatively new form of blogging that consists of short blog posts updated more frequently than traditional blogs. The length of microblogs is typically constrained by the media used to create the post. The most widely known microblogging service is Twitter, which has traditionally restricted user's posts to 140 characters but is currently piloting a project that would double that total (Isaac, 2017). Twitter is a popular microblogging site in the United States through which 500 million tweets are posted each day—amounting to 6,000 tweets per second (Twitter, 2017). Sina Weibo (http://weibo.com/) is a similarly popular microblogging platform in China, which recently reported a total of 340 million active monthly users (BBC, 2017).

Microblogging has seen dramatic growth in recent years. The rise in microbloggers and microblogging platforms is likely driven by the proliferation of mobile technology (Smith, 2013; Thomasch, 2007) that allows people to access and update microblogs quickly and conveniently. In 2010, the US Census Bureau reported that 63,718,000 people 18 years or older used mobile devices to access the Internet (US Census, 2010). Mobile devices allow individuals to stay abreast of change and respond quickly to news and current events, but by their nature, mobile devices are smaller (and contain smaller input methods) than stationary devices, making it difficult to compose long-form writing. While microblogging differs from traditional blogs— most notably in length—another emerging blog type distinguishes itself by solely relying on video to convey a message.

Vlogging

Vlogging (or "video blogging") is a relatively new form of blogging that contains some of the characteristics of traditional blogs (e.g., long-form presentations of content and comparable update frequency), but uses video to convey the message, rather than text. The first vlogs appeared in the early 2000s and began as videos embedded in traditional text blogs. In most cases, videos are uploaded to a video hosting service, such as YouTube.com (Sinton, 2010), and are regularly updated, similar to traditional blogging web sites. Most vlogs consist of a single individual speaking to the camera (Frobenius, 2011). Some inherently visual social media platforms, such as Snapchat (i.e., a service that enables the sharing of brief photos and videos), were designed in a manner that was conducive to vlogging, while other already existing services, like Facebook and Instagram (i.e., a picture and video sharing service), have incorporated vlogging features into their platforms. While microblogging and vlogging are unique forms of blogging, they share several key features with traditional blogs (e.g., regularly updated user-generated content, typically created by a single author, wide audience, interactivity), and their creators likely also share similar motivations.

CHARACTERISTICS OF BLOGS AND BLOGGERS

As the definition of blogging becomes increasingly fragmented, tracking the number and content of blogs has become difficult. In fact, little descriptive research on blogging after 2011 exists, and what statistics do exist vary wildly, depending on how the authors operationalize blogging. Despite this fragmentation of the research, a fair amount of demographic information is available about who was blogging, circa 2011. At that time, some researchers distinguished between different types of bloggers, such as hobbyists (who blog for enjoyment rather than for income) and professional bloggers (who blog to supplement their income). The majority of bloggers are hobbyists, male, and located in the United States (Fullwood, Nicholls, & Makichi, 2015; Fullwood, Sheehan, & Nicholls, 2009; Herring et al., 2005; Technorati, 2011). Most bloggers report blogging about personal experiences (Guadagno, Okdie, & Eno, 2008; Lenhart & Fox, 2006; Okdie, Guadagno, Rempala, & Eno, 2011), are identifiable (Guadagno et al., 2008; Herring, et al., 2005; Huffaker & Calvert, 2005; Viegas, 2005), and are between 25 and 44 years old (Technorati, 2011).

Existing research has revealed some common characteristics of blogs. Hobbyists most commonly blog about their life, while professional bloggers mostly write about technology (Technorati, 2011). The majority of bloggers post weekly on their blogs (Crestodina, 2017). Although the general trends suggest that the number of people blogging is declining (Crestodina, 2017; Okdie et al., 2011), the length of individual blog posts increased by nearly hundred words from 2014 to 2015, and now stands at approximately 1,000 words per post. Moreover, most bloggers include at least one image in their posts (Crestodina, 2017).

Although prior to 2011 the typical blogger resided in the United States, recent reports indicate an increase in blogs maintained outside of the United States (Pedersen & Macafee, 2007). However, the behavior of bloggers in *and* outside the United States has been found to be similar (Pedersen & Macafee, 2007), which raises the possibility of a universal set of motivations for blogging.

Gender and Personality

Many studies indicate individual difference factors, such as gender and personality, predict who uses the Internet, and how (see Orchard & Fullwood, 2010 for discussion of the relationship between personality and Internet use). Most research examining the relationship between personality traits and general Internet use, including blogging, has focused on broad dimensions of personality, such as the Five Factor Model of personality (McCrae & Costa, 1997). The Five Factor Model of personality is accepted as the predominant taxonomy of personality traits and posits that personality is composed of and varies on five key traits: extraversion (sociability), neuroticism (emotional reactivity), openness to new experience (imaginativeness; open to new ideas), agreeableness (cooperativeness), and conscientiousness (self-control; John, Naumann, & Soto, 2008). Studies examining personality and general Internet use indicate that people low in extraversion and high in neuroticism report being better able to express their true selves online, which should lead to greater use of online self-expression platforms such as blogging (Amichai-Hamburger, Wainapel, & Fox, 2002; Rice & Markey, 2009).

Researchers have also discovered significant gender differences in Internet use. For example, when comparing blogs of males and females, men's blogs are less likely to focus on their personal lives (Fullwood, Melrose, Morris, & Floyd, 2013). A study of British bloggers found that men were generally less social when blogging and less likely to post creative work, instead choosing to post about opinions, politics, and technical aspects of the Internet (Pedersen & Macafee, 2007).

Perhaps the most compelling findings about individual difference on Internet use come from analyzing the interaction between personality and gender. For example, women high in extraversion and neuroticism are more likely to use the Internet for services that connect them socially with others, allowing them to create and maintain social relationships (Hamburger & Ben-Artzi, 2000). Some researchers suggested that women high in neuroticism may blog for social connectedness (Guadagno et al., 2008). This idea was corroborated by research showing that loneliness mediates the relation between neuroticism and Internet use for women (Amichai-Hamburger & Ben-Artzi, 2003) as well as that women (compared to men) are more likely to blog for social connection (Clarke & van Amerom, 2008; Pedersen & Macafee, 2007). Additionally, women high in neuroticism and openness to new experience are more likely to blog (Guadagno et al., 2008; Okdie et al., 2011). Thus, women who are high in neuroticism and openness to new experience may use the Internet to socially connect with others and are likely to be more open to using new methods to accomplish this goal (such as Blogging).

A different pattern of results emerges when examining the predictors of Internet use among men. For example, men high in extraversion are more likely to use the Internet for leisure and those high in neuroticism are less likely to use the Internet for information services (Hamburger & Ben-Artzi, 2000).

Blogging Motivations

While descriptive data are informative and provide a picture of who is populating the blogosphere, they fail to answer the question of why millions of people spend their limited time and energy on such a labor-intensive activity like blogging. In the early days of researching blogging behavior, most scholars focused their investigations on peoples' motivations for general Internet use (Amichai-Hamburger & Ben-Artzi, 2003; Hamburger & Ben-Artzi, 2000). Those early scholars identified several individual difference factors that predicted an individual's motivation to use the Internet, including the aforementioned personality traits (Amichai-Hamburger, 2002; Yee, Harris, Jabon, & Bailenson, 2011) and gender (see Li & Kirkup, 2007 for discussion), as well as chronic emotional states (e.g., loneliness and anxiety; McKenna & Bargh, 2000) and stigmatized identities (McKenna & Bargh, 1998). However, the Internet continues to evolve at a profound rate, and compared to just a few years ago, it has become more personalized with a greater variety of opportunities for social interaction. So, while these initial investigations provide a baseline for understanding what factors motivate Internet behavior, a more thorough analysis is needed to understand what factors motivate any one type of Internet use. For example, blogging typically involves labor-intensive, solitary personal expression that is much more regimented and regular than casual Internet use. Thus, the expectation is that a particular set of motivations would apply to this particular behavior.

Intrinsic Benefits: Blogging and Mental Health

Roughly one in four bloggers do so with the goal of full-time income (Collamer, 2015), which means that the other three blog for non-monetary reasons. Even if a blogger's primary motivation is income, there are other less precarious methods for making a living than maintaining a blog. This section presents some common intrinsic blogging motivations.

Blogging for the Self

In general, sharing personal experiences facilitates memory retention by allowing for rehearsal and contextualization of the event (Wang, Lee, & Hou, 2017). Social sharing of personal events has additional benefits when the event is distressing (Pennebaker & O'Heeron, 1984). Pennebaker (1997) found that writing in a journal about upsetting events forces the writer to categorize that event, which makes it more manageable and allows for a more beneficial re-categorization later.

Many blogs involve sharing personal events and effectively act as public diaries for the blogger (see Baker & Moore, 2008 for examples of this characterization). To the extent that blogging functions similarly to journaling, the positive effects of journaling should also exist for bloggers, and much research supports this proposition. The social sharing that takes place via personal blogs increases perceptions of subjective well-being and social integration for the blogger (Baker & Moore, 2008; Ko & Kuo, 2009). Moreover, blogging about distressing events (e.g., emotional difficulties) significantly reduces their impact (Boniel-Nissim & Barak, 2013). In many cases, benefits experienced by the blogger appear to be driven by audience participation or awareness (Boniel-Nissim & Barak, 2013; Chen, Liu, Shih, Wu, & Yuan, 2011). Thus, it is likely that blogging provides a positive impact on the self-esteem and well-being of the blogger to the extent that bloggers make or perceive social connections that satisfy their need to belong and provide avenues for social support.

Writing for Social Support

Unlike traditional diaries, most blogs are publicly accessible, making it possible for others to provide social support to the author. Garnering social support is associated with several positive physiological (e.g., increased immune function, decreased blood pressure; Uchino, 2004) and psychological outcomes (Smith, Fernengel, Holcroft, Gerald, & Marien, 1994). Social support for bloggers typically comes in the form of comments from blog readers on individual blog posts, although support via other methods of communication also occurs (Nardi, Schiano, & Gumbrecht, 2004). While negative social feedback from blog readers is possible, it is not the norm (see Herring et al., 2005 for discussion).

Because blogs provide social support, and that social support has meaningful effects on blog author's subjective well-being and health (Rains & Keating, 2011), the social support garnered by blogging may be particularly useful for those suffering from health conditions. Blogging can provide those who suffer from health issues a supportive community in which to self-disclose and vent frustrations, accountability, and validation of their health successes (Sanford, 2010). Similarly, Berry et al. (2017), a recent thematic analysis of mental-health-related tweets, determined that people often discussed mental health issues on Twitter "to express themselves . . . and reflect back on the tweets to recognize their thoughts and feelings over time." Other reasons mentioned include providing a sense of community and a coping mechanism, as well as combatting stereotypes and self-expression.

Blogging for Social Connection

Research suggests blogging (and microblogging) can fulfill thwarted belonging and affiliation needs (Chen, 2011; Knowles et al., 2015). Bloggers often note a desire for social connection as a reason for starting and maintaining their blog (Miura & Yamashita, 2007). For example, bloggers often cite "to share my expertise and feelings with others" and "to meet and connect with like-minded people" as common blogging motivations (Technorati, 2011). Research on blogger motivations supports this self-report data. Fullwood et al. (2009) showed that blogging may fulfill an emotional need, such as validation for one's self-expression. Hollenbaugh (2011) noted seven motives for maintaining a blog, and the majority of these motives related to making social connections. Some research has shown that bloggers (compared to non-bloggers) scored lower on social integration and satisfaction with their number of friends (Baker & Moore, 2008). Additionally, studies report that bloggers are motivated to continue updating their blogs when they are aware others are reading what they have written (Nardi et al., 2004). Thus, motivation for maintaining a blog decreases when there is less chance that bloggers will satisfy their need to belong.

In a similar vein, vlogging has been described as a "participatory culture" (Snelson, 2015), which is characterized by the following (Jenkins, Clinton, Purushotma, Robison, & Weigel, 2006):

1) Low barriers to artistic expression and civic engagement;
2) Strong support for creating and sharing with others;
3) Informal mentorships by which expert knowledge is transmitted to novices;

4) A belief that an individual's contribution matters; and

5) A perceived social connection between members.

In fact, Snelson (2015) identified several vlogger motivations directly related to social connection: "because friends were doing it," to "share information," and to "connect with others" (along with to "alleviate boredom," "for fun," to "build confidence or improve their speaking skills," and to "document their experiences"). Due to the rich personal form of communication that video offers (Warmbrodt, Sheng, Hall, & Cao, 2010), the motivation for social connection may be even stronger among vloggers than among bloggers because of the method used.

The evidence indicates that these efforts to forge a social connection are reciprocated by blog consumers. Blog consumers can seek out topics of interest among the blogs available and further differentiate among the available blogs based on traditional indicators of liking, such as attractiveness and perceived similarity (Lee & Watkins, 2016). They often feel as though they know the blogger and that a "relationship" has been established (Lee & Watkins, 2016); this relationship between a media personality and media users has been described as a "para-social interaction" (e.g., Frederick, Lim, Clavio, & Walsh, 2012). Bloggers also appear responsive when blog readers reciprocate the social connection, as those whose readers communicate with them are more likely to continue blogging (Kawaura, Yamashita, Kawakami, 1999; Liao, Liu, & Pi, 2011), creating and maintaining a cycle of social connectivity.

Self-Presentation

Self-presentation involves the image an individual presents to the public (Goffman, 1978), and the person's goals can dictate the content of the presentation (e.g., economic or social gain, self-esteem, identity maintenance; Leary & Kowalski, 1995).

A blog provides a blogger with a means of publicly stating an opinion on an issue, and thus, provides an opportunity to control one's self-presentation. For instance, such a public stance could have either social-adjustive or self-expressive motivations behind it (DeBono, 2006). A social-adjustive motivation involves the act of "fitting in," the desire to appear socially normal, and to hold a popular opinion for the social rewards that that opinion entails. This motivation is more prominent in individuals who are high self-monitors (i.e., those who spend increased amounts of time reflecting on how their behaviors impact on others; DeBono, Leavitt, & Backus, 2003). Conversely, value-expressive motivation involves authenticity, a desire to show the "true self," and to establish consistency between a public behavior and a privately held opinion (DeBono et al., 2003).

Harnish and Bridges (2016) recently applied this paradigm to so-called "mall haul vlogs," where a YouTube celebrity creates a short video discussing the relative merits of a consumer good (e.g., a cosmetic, a luxury handbag). They found that, compared to low self-monitors, high-self monitors were more likely to create mall haul vlogs, and when they did, they tended to mention fewer products and provide more positive assessments. A similar dynamic would be expected with non-consumer opinion blogs as well (e.g., a political blogger who is a high self-monitor would be unlikely to disparage a candidate admired by the blog's readers).

Twitter also acts as a self-presentation platform (Marwick & Boyd, 2011). However, the nature of tweeting provides an additional complication: tweets are short, which can eliminate much of the context and nuance in a communication (Lasorsa, Lewis, & Holton, 2012). Tweets also have the potential to involve a large, broad audience, so if the presenter's ultimate goal is popularity, the individual is required to manage the presentation so that it appeals to the broadest swath of the audience (the so-called "lowest common denominator"), and, as a result, the posted message can be quite shallow (Marwick & Boyd, 2011).

EXTRINSIC BENEFITS OF BLOGGING: EXPLOITING THE SOCIAL CONNECTION

The major extrinsic motivation for some bloggers is the opportunity to earn a living, working at home, discussing a topic of interest. Approximately 25 percent of bloggers operate their blogs in effort to obtain income equivalent to a full-time job (Collamer, 2015). However, most fail to do so. Although some bloggers can gain employment from established media outlets, obtain consulting work, or receive substantial ad revenue, the majority (57 percent) earned less than $2,500 in 2015, and only 11 percent earn more than $30,000 per year (Collamer, 2015). For popular bloggers, whether it's due to niche, talent, or celebrity status, blogs can be quite lucrative. Even if a blog did not begin as a commercial venture, popular blogs have the potential to evolve into one. By the same token, even commercial blogs contain social elements, such as comments sections, that serve to fill the need to belong.

The social connection between blog consumers and blog owners has a potential for exploitation. One of the "para-social" elements of such a relationship is that many media users will view the relationship as a "friendship" and respond to the advice of the media personality as though it were coming from a friend (Perse & Rubin, 1989). Compared to past forms of media, blogging in its various derivations involves some level of interactivity (or at least, perceived interactivity) between the blogger and his or her audience, and can allow a media personality to expand his or her audience while ultimately still controlling the relationship (Stever & Lawson, 2013). For this reason, so-called "brand managers" have chosen online personalities, such as bloggers and vloggers, to act as "brand ambassadors" for their products and exploit what is perceived as a trust relationship (Lee & Watkins, 2016). As discussed, the "mall haul" YouTube celebrity vloggers extoll the merits of particular brands of consumer products (Harnish & Bridges, 2016); as with any endorsement, the opinion may be inauthentic or legitimately held, but in many cases, the video or the insertion of the product into the video is unlikely to have occurred organically. This appears to be an effective strategy, as consumers appear to trust these types of testimonials more than conventional TV ads (Nielson, 2012).

Thus, even when the motivations behind a blog are commercial in nature, social connection elements persist. They are present for the blogger, who seldom receives an adequate return on investment from a purely economic perspective. They exist for the blog consumer, as well, who feels connected to the blogger enough to trust the blogger above and beyond the blogger's status as a "media personality."

CONCLUSIONS AND IMPLICATIONS

People have a need to maintain positive social connections with others (Baumeister & Leary, 1995), and the Internet has enabled people to fill this need through novel and unique channels, such as blogging. Although there are many blogging motivations, we argue that, to varying degrees, the fundamental need to belong pervades virtually all blogging enterprises. Given this, blogging has the potential to play an important role in the lives of people who feel less able to connect to others via FTF interactions, or who perhaps feel that they are better able to express their "true self" online. The literature reviewed here corroborates this statement by highlighting the many psychological benefits from keeping a blog, such as increasing subjective well-being (Ko & Kuo, 2009), decreasing emotional difficulties (Boniel-Nissim & Barak, 2013), and dealing with stigmatizing identities adaptively (Sanford, 2010). These benefits are driven by interactions with others, either through self-expression or interactions with blog consumers.

While traditional blogging has seen a decrease in recent years (Okdie et al., 2011), it largely has been supplanted by derivations of blogging (e.g., tweeting, vlogging). Economist Paul Krugman, a popular columnist and blogger for the New York Times, recently rationalized tweeting more and blogging less:

> In some ways, it's a step backwards: 140 characters instead of little essays that can run to hundreds or even thousands of words. Some innovations like tweetstorms—a series of linked tweets telling a longer story—are arguably just awkward ways to imperfectly replicate blog posts. But the fact is that a lot more people read a tweetstorm than read a blog post. Also, the logistics turn out to be easier for technical reasons – I can tweet very quickly in response to an event, where blogging, thanks in part to (much needed) Times security features, is a more laborious process.
>
> (Krugman, 2016)

Thus, the same justifications for choosing to communicate via blog in the first place (e.g., convenience, reach) may be driving individuals to find an even more effective and efficient way of communicating. By extension, the same principles that apply to blogging motivations should apply to its derivations, if not to an even greater extent. After all, blogging is, at its heart, a more-or-less authentic personal statement about a particular issue. Making the statement more spontaneous (as with microblogging) or more personal (as with vlogging) would only seem to intensify the essential elements.

While the presence of traditional (lengthy, text-only) posts is shrinking, newer, more immediate forms of online self-expression are emerging and growing rapidly. Empirical studies featuring these newer forms of blogging have produced results that effectively parallel results uncovered by over a decade's worth of blogging research. Both bloggers and neobloggers appear to share the same motivations (e.g., the need to belong) and produce the similar psychological outcomes, making them equally meaningful. Newer forms of blogging, such as microblogging, also bring with them increased accessibility. For example, microblogging platforms are predominantly used on mobile devices that allow constant access to self-expression and receipt of social interaction. The future of blogging appears to be shorter multimedia messages delivered more frequently to a broad audience that expedites the satisfaction of the individual's need to belong.

References

Amichai-Hamburger, Y. (2002). Internet and personality. *Computers in Human Behavior 18*, 1–10.

Amichai-Hamburger, Y., & Ben-Artzi, E. (2003). Loneliness and Internet use. *Computers in Human Behavior 19*, 71–80.

Amichai-Hamburger, Y., Wainapel, G., & Fox, S. (2002). On the Internet no one knows I'm an introvert: Extroversion, neuroticism, and Internet interaction. *Cyberpsychology & Behavior 5*, 125–128. doi:10.1089/109493102752770507

Arnoldzafra (2008, Sept. 23). The State of the Blogosphere According to Technorati. Retrieved from https://www.adweek.com/digital/the-state-of-blogosphere-according-to-technorati/

Baker, J. R., & Moore, S. M. (2008). Distress, coping, and blogging: Comparing new Myspace users by their intention to blog. *CyberPsychology & Behavior 11*, 81–88.

Bargh, J., & McKenna, K. Y. A. (2004). The Internet and social life. *Annual Review of Psychology 55*, 573–590. doi:10.1146/annurev. psych.55.090902.141922.

Barrett, B. (2015, Aug. 17). Remember Facebook notes? It's back with a vengeance. Retrieved from https://www.wired.com/2015/08/facebook-notes-redesign/

Baumeister, R. F., & Leary, M. R. (1995). The need to belong: Desire for interpersonal attachment as a fundamental human motivation. *Psychological Bulletin, 117*, 497–529. doi:10.1037/0033-2909.117.3.497.

BBC (2017, May 17). Twitter user numbers overtaken by China's Sina Weibo. Retrieved from http://www.bbc.com/news/technology-39947442

Berry, N., Lobban, F., Belousov, M., Emsley, R., Nenadic, G., & Bucci, S. (2017). #WhyWeTweetMH: Understanding why people use Twitter to discuss mental health problems. *Journal of Medical Internet Research 19*, 166–178.

Bonds-Raacke, J., & Raacke, J. (2010). MySpace and Facebook: Identifying dimensions of uses and gratifications for friend networking sites. *Individual Differences Research 8*, 27–33.

Boniel-Nissim, M., & Barak, A. (2013). The therapeutic value of adolescents' blogging about social-emotional difficulties. *Psychological Services 10*, 333–341. doi:10.1037/a0026664

Brown, J. L., Sheffield, D., Leary, M. R., & Robinson, M. E. (2003). Social support and experimental pain. *Psychosomatic Medicine 65*, 276–283.

Chen, G. M. (2011). Tweet this: A uses and gratifications perspective on how active Twitter use gratifies a need to connect with others. *Computers in Human Behavior 27*, 755–762.

Chen, Y. L., Liu, E. Z. F., Shih, R. C., Wu, C. T., & Yuan, S. M. (2011). Use of peer feedback to enhance elementary students' writing through blogging. *British Journal of Educational Technology 43*, 1–4. doi:10.1111/j.1467-8535.2010.011139.x.

Chiou, W., Lee, C., & Liao, D. (2015). Facebook effects on social distress: Priming with online social networking thoughts can alter the perceived distress due to social exclusion. *Computers in Human Behavior 49*, 230–236. doi:10.1016/j.chb.2015.02.064.

Clarke, J., & van Amerom, G. (2008). A comparison of blogs by depressed men and women. *Issues in Mental Health and Nursing 29*, 243–264. doi:10.1080/016112840701869403.

Collamer, N. (2015, Aug. 11). How to make money as a blogger. *Forbes*. Retrieved from https://www.forbes.com/sites/nextavenue/2015/08/11/how-to-make-money-as-a-blogger/#7c8a545b1ee9

Cosmides, L. (1989). The logic of social exchange: Has a natural selection shaped how humans reason? Studies with the Watson selection task. *Cognition 31*, 187–276. doi:10.1016/0010-0277(89)90023-1

Cosmides, L., & Tooby, J. (1992). Cognitive adaptions for social exchange. In J. Barkow, L. Cosmides & J. Tooby (Eds.), *The adapted mind: Evolutionary psychology and the generation of culture* (pp. 163–228). New York: Oxford University Press.

Crestodina, A. (2017). Research reveals success tactics of top bloggers: 11 trends. [Blog post]. Retrieved from: https://www.orbitmedia.com/blog/blogger-research/

DeBono, K. G. (2006). Self-monitoring and consumer psychology. *Journal of Personality, 74*, 715–738. doi:10.1111/j.1467-6494.2006.00390.x.

DeBono, K. G., Leavitt, A., & Backus, J. (2003). Product packaging and product evaluation: An individual difference approach. *Journal of Applied Social Psychology, 33*, 513–521. doi:10.1111/j.1559-1816.2003.tb01909.x.

Eisenberger, N. I., Lieberman, M. D., & Williams, K. D. (2003). Does rejection hurt? An FMRI study of social exclusion. *Science, 302*, 290–292. doi:10.1126/science.1089134.

Frederick, E. L., Lim, C. H., Clavio, G., & Walsh, P. (2012). Why we follow: An examination of parasocial interaction and fan motivations for following athlete archetypes on Twitter. *International Journal of Sport Communication 5*, 481–502.

Frobenius, M. (2011). Beginning a monologue: The opening sequence of video blogs. *Journal of Pragmatics 43*, 814–827.

Fullwood, C., Melrose, K., Morris, N., & Floyd, S. (2013). Sex, blogs and baring your soul: Factors influencing UK blogging strategies. *Journal of the American Society for Information Science and Technology 64*, 345–355. doi:10.1002/asi.22736

Fullwood, C., Nicholls, W., & Makichi, R. (2015). We've got something for everyone: How individual differences predict different blogging motivations. *New Media & Society 17*, 1583–1600. doi:10.1177/1461444814530248

Fullwood, C., Sheehan, N., & Nicholls, W. (2009). Blog function revisited: A content analysis of MySpace blogs. *Cyberpsychology & Behavior 12*, 685–689.

Goffman, E. (1978). *The presentation of the self in everyday life*. Harmondsworth: Penguin.

Gross, R., & Acquisti, A. (2005). *Information revelation and privacy in online social networks.* In *Proceedings of the 2005 ACM Workshop on Privacy in the Electronic Society* (pp. 71–80), 7–10 November, Alexandria, VA. New York: ACM.

Guadagno, R. E., Muscanell, N. L., Okdie, B. M., Burk, N. M., & Ward, T. B. (2011). Even in virtual environments women shop and men build: A social role perspective on Second Life. *Computers in Human Behavior 27*, 304–308. doi:10.1016/j.chb.2010.08.008

Guadagno, R. E., Okdie, B. M., & Eno, C. (2008). Why do people blog? Personality predictors of blogging. *Computers in Human Behavior 24*, 1993–2004. doi:10.1016/j.chb.2007.09.001.

Hamburger, Y. A., & Artzi, B. E. (2000). The relationship between extraversion and neuroticism and the different uses of the Internet. *Computers in Human Behavior 16*, 441–449.

Hamburger, Y. A., & Ben-Artzi, E. (2000). Relationship between extraversion and neuroticism and the different uses of the Internet. *Computers in Human Behavior 16*, 441–449.

Harnish, R. J., & Bridges, K. R. (2016). Mall haul videos: Self-presentational motives and the role of self-monitoring. *Psychology & Marketing 33*, 113–124. doi:10.1002/mar.20858

Herring, S. C., Scheidt, L. A., Wright, E., & Bonus, S. (2005). Weblogs as bridging genre. *Information Technology & People 18*, 142–171. doi:10.1108/09593840510601513

Ho, L., Wu, W., & Chiou, W. (2016). Analgesic effect of Facebook: Priming with online social networking may boost felt relatedness. *Personality and Social Psychology 57*, 433–436. doi:10.1111/sjop.12313

Hollenbaugh, E. E. (2011). Motives for maintaining personal journal blogs. *CyberPsychology & Behavior 14*, 13–20. doi:10.1089/cyber.2009.0403

Huffaker, D. A., & Calvert, S. L. (2005). Gender, identity, and language use in teenage blogs. *Journal of Computer-Mediated Communication 10*, 1.

Isaac, M. (2017, Sept. 26). Twitter to test doubling tweet length to 280 characters. *New York Times*, p. B3.

Jackson, T., Iezzi, T., Chen, H., Ebnet, S., & Eglitis, K. (2005). Gender, interpersonal transactions, and the perception of pain: An experimental analysis. *The Journal of Pain 6*, 228–236.

Jenkins, H., Clinton, K., Purushotma, R., Robison, A. J., & Weigel, M. (2006). Confronting the challenges of participatory culture: Media for the 21st Century. Retrieved from https://www.curriculum.org/secretariat/files/Sept30TLConfronting.pdf

John, O. P., Naumann, L. P., & Soto, C. J. (2008). Paradigm shift to the integrative Big Five Trait Taxonomy: History, measurement, and conceptual issues. In O. P. John, R. W. Robins, & L. A. Pervin (Eds.), *Handbook of personality: Theory and research* (pp. 114–158). New York: Guilford Press.

Joinson, A. N. (2008). "Looking at," "looking up", or "keeping up with" people? Motives and uses of Facebook. In *CHI '08: Proceedings of the SIGCHI Conference on Human Factors in Computing Systems* (pp. 1027–1036), 5–10 April, Florence, Italy. New York: ACM.

Kawaura, Y., Yamashita, K., & Kawakami, Y. (1999). What makes people keep writing web diaries? Self-Expression in cyberspace. *Japanese Journal of Social Psychology 14*, 133–143.

Keneski, E., Neff, L. A., & Loving, T. J. (2017). The importance of a few good friends: Perceived network support moderates the association between daily marital conflict and diurnal cortisol. *Social Psychology and Personality Science 1–10*. Online first September 14, 2017). doi:10.1177/1948550617731499

Knowles, M. L., Haycock, N., & Shaikh, I. (2015). Does Facebook magnify or mitigate threats to belonging? *Social Psychology 46*, 313–324. doi:10.1027/1864- 9335/a000246

Ko, H-C., & Kuo, F-Y. (2009). Can blogging enhance subjective well-being through self-disclosure? *CyberPsychology & Behavior 12*, 75–79. doi:10.1089/cpb.2008.0163.

Krugman, P. (2016, Sept. 6). Read me on Twitter! *New York Times*. Retrieved from https://krugman.blogs.nytimes.com/2016/09/06/read-me-on-twitter/

Kurzban, R., & Leary, M. R. (2001). Evolutionary origins of stigmatization: The functions of social exclusion. *Psychological Bulletin 127*, 187–208. doi:10.1037/0033-2909.127.2.187

Liao, H. L., Liu, S. H., & Pi, S. M. (2011). Modeling motivations for blogging: An expectancy theory analysis. *Social Behavior and Personality 39*, 251–264.

Lasorsa, D. L., Lewis, S. C., & Holton, A. E. (2012). Normalizing Twitter: Journalism practice in an emerging communication space. *Journalism Studies 13*, 19–36.

Leary, M. R., & Kowalski, R. M. (1995). *Social anxiety*. New York: Guilford Press.

Lee, J. E., & Watkins, B. (2016). YouTube vloggers' influence on consumer luxury brand perceptions and intentions. *Journal of Business Research 69*, 5753–5760.

Lenhart, A., & Fox, S. (2006). Bloggers: A portrait of the Internet's new storytellers. Pew Trust. Retrieved from http://www.pewtrusts.org/our_work_report_detail.aspx?id=21106

Li, N., & Kirkup, G. (2007). Gender and cultural differences in Internet use: A study of china and the UK. *Computers and Education 48*, 301–317. doi:10.1016/j.compedu.2005.01.007

Marwick, A. E., & Boyd, D. (2011). I tweet honestly, I tweet passionately: Twitter users, context collapse, and the imagined audience. *New Media & Society 13*, 114–133.

Master, S. L., Eisenberger, N. I., Taylor, S. E., Naliboff, B. D., Shirinyan, D., & Lieberman, M. D. (2009). A picture's worth. *Psychological Science 20*, 1316–1318.

McCrae, R. R., & Costa, P. T. (1997). Personality trait structure as a human universal. *American Psychologist 52*, 509–516.

McKenna, K. Y. A., & Bargh, J. A. (1998). Coming out in the age of the Internet: Identity "demarginalization" through virtual group participation. *Journal of Personality and Social Psychology 75*, 681–694.

McKenna, K. Y. A., & Bargh, J. A. (2000). Plan 9 from cyberspace: The implications of the Internet for personality and social psychology. *Personality and Social Psychology Review 4*, 57–75.

Miura, A., & Yamashita, K. (2007). Psychological and social influences on blog writing: An online survey of blog authors in Japan. *Journal of Computer-Mediated Communication 12*, 1452–1471.

Nardi, B. A., Schiano, D. J., & Gumbrecht, M. (2004). Blogging as a social activity, or, would you let 900 million people read your diary? In *Proceedings of the 2004 ACM Conference on Computer Supportive Cooperative Work*. (pp. 222–231), 6–10 November, Chicago, IL. New York: ACM.

Neilson (2012, April 10). Global trust in advertising and brand messages. Retrieved from http://www.nielsen.com/us/en/insights/reports/2012/global-trust-in-advertising-and-brand-messages.html

Okdie, B. M., Ewoldsen, D. R., Muscanell, N. L., Guadagno, R. E., Eno, C. A., Velez, J., Dunn, R. A.,…Smith, R. L. (2014). Missed programs (There is no TiVo for this one): Why psychologists should study the media. *Perspectives on Psychological Science 9*, 180–195. doi:10.1177/1745691614521243

Okdie, B. M., Guadagno, R. E., Bernieri, F. J., Geers, A. L., & McLarney-Vesotski, A. R. (2011). Getting to know you: Face-to-face versus online interactions. *Computers in Human Behavior 27*, 153–159. doi:10.1016/j.chb.2010.07.017

Okdie, B. M., Guadagno, R. E., Rempala, D. M., & Eno, C. A. (2011). Who blogs in 2010? An updated look at individual differences in blogging. *International Journal of Interactive Communication Systems and Technologies 1*, 1–13. doi:10.4018/ijicst.2011070101

Orchard, L. J., & Fullwood, C. (2010). Current perspectives on personality and Internet use. *Social Science Computer Review 28*, 155–169.

Pedersen, S., & Macafee, C. (2007). Gender differences in British blogging. *Journal of Computer-Mediated Communication 12*, 1472–1492. doi:10.1111/j.10836101.2007.00382.x.

Pennebaker, J. W. (1997). Writing about emotional experience as a therapeutic process. *Psychological Science, 8*, 162–166.

Pennebaker, J. W., & O'Heeron, R. C. (1984). Confiding in others and illness rates among spouses of suicide and accidental-death victims. *Journal of Abnormal Psychology 93*, 473–476. doi:10.1037/0021-843X.4.473

Perse, E. M., & Rubin, R. R. (1989). Attribution in social and para-social relationships. *Communication Research 19*, 59–77.

Pew Research Center (2017, Jan. 12). Social media fact sheet. Retrieved from http://www.pewinternet.org/fact-sheet/social-media/

Postmes, T., Spears, R., & Lea, M. (2002). Intergroup differentiation in computer-mediated communication: Effects of depersonalization. *Group Dynamics 6*, 3–15. doi:10.1037/1089-2699.6.1.3

Rains, S. A., & Keating, D. M. (2011). The social dimensions of blogging about health: Health blogging social support and well-being. *Communication Monographs 78*, 511–534.

Rice, L., & Markey, P. M. (2009). The role of extraversion and neuroticism in influencing anxiety following computer-mediated communication. *Personality and Individual Differences 46*, 35–39. doi:10.1016/j.paid.2008.08/022

Sanford, A. A. (2010). "I can air my feelings instead of eating them": Blogging as social support for the morbidly obese. *Communication Studies 61*, 567–584. doi:10.1080/10510974.2010.514676

Sinton, F. (2010, 4 January) State of the vlogosphere 2010. [Blog post]. Retrieved from http://blog.mefeedia.com/vlog-2010. Accessed 29 July 2013.

Smith, A. (2013). Smartphone ownership 2013. Retrieved from http://www.pcwinternet.org/Reports/2013/Smartphone-Ownership-2013.aspx. Accessed October 11, 2017.

Smith, C. E., Fernengel, K., Holcroft, C., Gerald, K., & Marien, L. (1994). Meta-analysis of the associations between social support and health outcomes. *Annals of Behavioral Medicine 16*, 352–362.

Snelson, C. (2015). Vlogging about school on YouTube: An exploratory study. *New Media & Society 17*, 321–339. doi:10.1177/1461444813504271

Statista (2017). *Media use in an Internet minute as of July 2017*. Retrieved from https://www.statista.com/statistics/195140/new-user-generated-content-uploaded-by-users-per-minute/

Stever, G. S., & Lawson, K. (2013). Twitter as a way for celebrities to communicate with fans: Implications for the study of para-social interaction. *North American Journal of Psychology 15*, 339–354.

Taraszow, T., Aristodemou, E., Shitta, G., Laouris, Y., & Arsoy, A. (2010). Disclosure of personal and contact information by young people in social networking sites: An analysis using Facebook profiles as an example. *International Journal of Media and Cultural Politics 6*, 81–102. doi:10.1386/macp.6.1.81/1

Technorati (2011). State of the Blogosphere 2011. Retrieved from http://technorati.com/state-of-the-blogosphere-2011/

Thomasch, P. (2007). *1 in 3 Americans watch TV away from home: Study* [Electronic Version]. Reuters. Retrieved from http://www.reuters.com/article/domesticNews/idUSN0%20437764920070404

Tran, T. B., & Joormann, J. (2015). The role of Facebook use in mediation the relation between rumination and adjustment after a relationship breakup. *Computers in Human Behavior 49*, 56–61. doi:10.1016/j.chb.2015.02.050

Twitter (2017). *Twitter Basics.* Retrieved from https://business.twitter.com/en/basics.html

Uchino, B. N. (2004). *Social support and physical health: Understanding the health consequences of relationships.* New Haven: Yale University Press.

US Census. (2010). *Seven years of media usage* (Statistical abstract). Retrieved from https://www2.census.gov/library/publications/2010/compendia/statab/129ed/tables/infocomm.pdf.

Viegas, F. B. (2005). Bloggers' expectations of privacy and accountability: An initial survey. *Journal of Computer-Mediated Communication 10*, 12.

Vogel, E. A., Rose, J. P., Okdie, B. M., Eckles, K., & Franz, B. (2015). Who compares and despairs? The effects of social comparison orientation on social media use and its outcomes. *Personality and Individual Differences 86*, 249–256. doi:10.1016/j.paid.2015.06.026

Wang, Q., Lee, D., & Hou, Y. (2017). Externalising the autobiographical self: Sharing personal memories online facilitated memory retention. *Memory 25*, 772–776. doi:10.1080/09658211.2016.1221115

Warmbrodt, J., Sheng, H., Hall, R. H., & Cao, J. (2010). Understanding the video bloggers' community. *International Journal of Virtual Communities and Social Networking 2*, 43–59.

Walther, J. B. (1996). Computer-mediated communication: Impersonal, interpersonal, and hyperpersonal interaction. *Communication Research, 23,* 3–43. doi:10.1177/009365096023001001.

Wesselmann, E. D., Wirth, J. H., Pryor, J. B., Reeder, G. D., & Williams, K. D. (2013). When do we ostracize? *Social Psychological and Personality Science 4*, 108–115. doi:10.1177/1948550612443386

Williams, K. D. (2009). Ostracism: A temporal need-threat model. *Advances in Experimental Social Psychology 41*, 275–314. doi:0.1016/S0065-2601(08)00406-1

Yee, N., Harris, H., Jabon, M., & Bailenson, J. N. (2011). The expression of personality in virtual worlds. *Social Psychological and Personality Science 2*, 5–12.

Zettelmeyer, F., Morton, F. S., & Silva-Risso (2006). How the Internet lowers prices: Evidence from matched survey and automobile transaction data. *Journal of Marketing Research 43*, 168–181.

CHAPTER 21

POSITIVE ASPECTS OF SOCIAL MEDIA

SALLY QUINN

INTRODUCTION

AT the turn of the twenty-first century, social media were beginning to emerge, and their use has grown exponentially year on year. Facebook reported 1.28 billion daily active users in the month of March 2017 (Facebook, 2017) and in June of 2016, Twitter reported 328 million active monthly users (Twitter, 2016). The key aims of these sites are to enable people to stay connected, to share experiences, and to keep people informed on topics of interest—Facebook's mission statement is "to give people the power to share and make the world more open and connected" (Facebook, n.d.).

Smartphones have made it even easier to access social media platforms, enabling users to stay connected anytime and anywhere, which has been shown to be related to feelings of connectedness (Quinn & Oldmeadow, 2013). Nevertheless, social media have frequently received bad press in the mainstream media with reports of their use being associated with cyberbullying, stalking, grooming, and poor physical and mental health. Although some of these claims are grounded in good quality research and are real issues experienced by some social media users, there is also a sizable amount of research that suggests some positive associations with social media use. After all, why would billions of people use these sites if there were no benefits?

Before this chapter examines the literature, it offers a definition of social media. Obar and Wildman (2015) discuss the difficulties of defining social media, partly due to the speed at which new platforms emerge, which may not fit with current definitions. Nevertheless, they propose four common characteristics of social media platforms: Social media are: (i) web 2.0 Internet-based platforms where (ii) user-generated content is the central factor to the workings of the platform; (iii) individuals and groups create user profiles specific to each social media platform and that are governed within the boundaries of that platform; (iv) social media platforms facilitate the communication between online social networks by connecting social media profiles with individuals or groups. Given this definition, this chapter focuses on any online platform that allows and encourages social interaction with others and allows users to create content with the intention of sharing with others—it refers to them all as "social media." In looking at these social media platforms, the chapter acknowledges the presence and possibility for negative outcomes associated with their use, but provides a discussion of the literature that focuses on positive associations.

CONNECTING WITH OTHERS

Over the last two decades, the Internet has become more social, offering many different platforms on which to interact with others. In light of this, it is understandable that one of the motivations driving general Internet use is to fulfill social needs (Kaye, 1998; Stafford, Stafford, & Schkade, 2004). Stafford and Gonier (2004) report that people not only use the Internet to stay in touch with others, but also that keeping in contact via the Internet is an enjoyable activity. Further developments in technology (such as the ability to access the Internet on mobile devices) now mean that the opportunities for social interaction via the Internet can take place almost anywhere and at any time.

Social media specifically can offer fulfillment of social or interpersonal needs in ways that face-to-face (FTF) communication or other forms of media cannot. For example, social media can offer social interaction constantly and immediately if the user so desires and individuals will be motivated to use these sites if they think it will fulfill their objective of socializing with others (Urista, Dong, & Day, 2009). Looking at general social media use among adolescents, Barker (2009) found that communicating with friends from the peer group was a central motivation for using these sites. Other motivations included social identity gratification, passing time, social compensation, entertainment, and social learning. Looking at Twitter specifically, Chen (2011) found that the amount of time a user spent on Twitter and the number of Twitter behaviors (e.g., retweeting) correlated highly with the gratification of the need to connect with others on this site. Similar findings have been found among Facebook users who report using this platform to keep in touch with friends (Joinson, 2008) and to feel connected to friends (Bumgarner, 2007). One of the key motivations of using these platforms then is to attempt to satiate the need to keep in touch with and feel connected to others.

However, a key question is whether or not these sites actually satiate this need for interaction and connectedness to others. Sheldon, Abad, and Hinsch (2011) investigated the links between Facebook use and feelings of connection to others, and in a series of studies they concluded that Facebook use increased feelings of connection. Moreover, they found that feelings of disconnection motivated Facebook use, and in an experimental study that deprived people of using Facebook, they found that those who felt more disconnected were more likely to spend a longer period of time on Facebook at the end of the deprivation stage of the experiment. The authors conclude that there is a two-way process involved in Facebook use: feelings of disconnection motivate people to use the site, and feelings of connection increase after using Facebook. There is also evidence to show that the feelings of connectedness felt through social media use is a separate construct from social connectedness felt in FTF settings (Grieve, Indian, Witteveen, Anne Tolan, & Marrington, 2013). Grieve and colleagues asked participants to complete two identical social connectedness scales (one with reference to FTF interactions and the other with reference to Facebook interactions). Subsequent analysis of these two scales showed that both were independent of each other and were therefore not measuring the same construct. Although Grieve and colleagues do not speculate exactly *how* Facebook fulfills feelings of connectedness differently to FTF interactions, they do speculate that Facebook interaction may provide an environment for certain people to gain social connectedness to others that they do not get offline (e.g., those who are socially anxious). This might therefore suggest that Facebook offers different opportunities to that of FTF interactions that help to fulfill feelings of connectedness.

One question to arise from this literature is why does the online world enable people to feel close to others in their social circles? Hyperpersonal Theory addresses this question (Walther, 1995, 1996); the theory is based on the idea that there is a disinhibiting effect when interacting online. Online disinhibition has been described as "any behaviour that is characterised by an apparent reduction in concerns for self-presentation and the judgement of others" (Joinson, 1998, p. 44). As well as providing a "mask" for people to engage in negative behaviors, these feelings of disinhibition have also been found to be linked to positive behaviors (Suler, 2005). The Hyperpersonal Theory proposes that these feelings of disinhibition result in more intimate relationships because of the asynchronous nature of online interactions and the reduction in visual and auditory cues. These two features (reduced cues and asynchronicity) mean that online communicators are able to selectively present themselves, choosing which characteristics they would like to share and having the time to think about how they want to express these characteristics. In the case of social media, this may relate to being able to think about how to respond to someone's post or update, or being able to carefully select a photo of oneself to share on the platform. These reduced cues and asynchronicity lead to users feeling disinhibited, which then results in an increase in self-disclosure (the sharing of intimate, personal information). Self-disclosure is a key factor in developing close relationships (Berndt, 2002) and the positive link between online disinhibition and self-disclosure has been found to be consistent across many studies (e.g. Joinson, 2001; Tidwell & Walther, 2002).

Although there is evidence to support the efficacy of the online environment in supporting self-disclosure, the reduced cues element may be questionable when thinking about the disinhibiting effect on social media. That is, the inclusion of photos and videos on social media could potentially challenge the assumption that these platforms offer complete visual and auditory anonymity. Nevertheless, visual and auditory cues are reduced to some extent in comparison to FTF interactions with others. For example, in the moment of posting a status update on Facebook, users do not need to manage the way they look or sound to people who will read their status. Indeed, there is evidence that supports the idea that users perceive a reduction in visual and auditory cues on social media platforms and that this reduction (along with the asynchronous nature of communication) leads to feelings of disinhibition, which subsequently increases self-disclosure (Green, Wilhelmsen, Wilmots, Dodd, & Quinn, 2016). However, newer social media may challenge this. For example, Snapchat interactions largely consist of photo and video messages, rather than just text, and it is unclear how this difference affects feelings of disinhibition during the interaction itself. In addition, Snapchat allows for control over the length of time the image or video is viewed (up to a maximum of ten seconds), and the ephemerality of the content may add an additional factor which could affect feelings of disinhibition. The present model of the disinhibition effect may need to be updated to consider the more recent characteristics of some social media platforms. Nevertheless, there is evidence that there is a perception of reduced cues and asynchronicity on social media and thus this reduction has been found to be conducive to self-disclosure behaviors.

This ability of social media to provide an environment which helps self-disclosure means these sites can be a useful tool to maintain relationships. Whether people use these sites, and if so, the degree to which they are used, has been of great interest in terms of investigating the links between their use and positive effects on relationships with others. Park, Jin, and Jin (2011) examined different types of self-disclosure on Facebook and how this related to perceived intimacy with Facebook friends. They found that the amount of self-disclosure and the degree of positive self-disclosure (i.e., disclosing positive information about the self) were positively related to feelings of intimacy towards Facebook friends. As most of a user's contacts on Facebook are people known to that user offline (boyd & Ellison, 2007), this study suggests that Facebook could be a useful platform for encouraging intimacy with friends. However, the authors did find that honest and intentional self-disclosure was not related to intimacy; thus, it may be that only certain elements of self-disclosure (e.g., disclosing positive information about the self) on social media has this effect.

Not only is it important to consider the different types of self-disclosure but also the different ways in which people communicate on social media. For example, Bayer, Ellison, Schoenebeck, and Falk (2016) report that Snapchat, a relatively new social media platform, is usually used among close friends to share small moments of day-to-day life, with the content often having some meaning between close friends. In addition, content can be shared for all contacts to see, or it can be targeted at certain individuals. Utz (2015) examined this by asking participants to rate their own Facebook private messages, and their own and friends' status updates (content which is by default shared to all of a user's Facebook contacts). The results showed that private messages were rated as more intimate than status updates, and this intimacy within private messages was found to be the strongest predictor of feelings of connection to the person. These findings may be due to the motivations behind using the different ways of communicating with others on Facebook. For example, Utz also found that the use of private messages was motivated by relationship maintenance, whereas the use of status updates was motivated by wanting to share information and to entertain Facebook contacts. Hence, the different ways of communicating on these sites may serve different functions.

The motivations and subsequent benefits of using social media are strongly linked to connecting with others and using these platforms as a way to maintain relationships with others. Given that these platforms provide social interactions with others, many users find they also offer access to social support from other users.

SOCIAL SUPPORT

Having access to social support can be important in times of need and one motivation of using social media is to receive this support from friends (Kim, Sohn, & Choi, 2011). Moreover, users of Facebook have reported to be satisfied with the support they get through the site (Wright et al., 2013) and perceived emotional support on Facebook has been found to be negatively related to stress among college students (Wright, 2012).

One conceptualization of social support is social capital. Generally, social capital is the degree to which one has access to resources (social, psychological, and physical) through ties and relationships with other people (Coleman, 1988). Having a high degree of social capital gives access to more opportunities for social support. Ellison, Steinfield, and Lampe (2007) investigated links between Facebook use and social capital among university students. They found that high-intensity use of Facebook was associated with high levels of bonding social capital (social capital gained through intimate, close-knit relationships) and with bridging social capital (capital gained through weak ties). Importantly, their findings suggested that this might be particularly useful for people with low levels of self-esteem and life satisfaction because they may find these harder to achieve in their offline lives. Similar findings have been reported for other social media platforms. For example, Piwek and Joinson (2016) found that the intensity of Snapchat use was positively related to both bonding and bridging social capital, with the strongest relationship seen with bonding capital.

However, there is evidence to suggest that only certain uses of social media are related to social capital. In an analysis of Facebook patterns of behaviors, Ellison, Steinfield, and Lampe (2011) found that usage consisted of three forms: initiating friendships with new people, seeking out information on others, and maintaining existing friendships, with the latter being the most common type of usage. Ellison and colleagues examined how these three uses of Facebook were related to both bonding and bridging social capital on this social media platform, and found that information seeking was the only significant predictor of both types of social capital. This may seem counterintuitive, given that one would expect actual interactions (rather than information gathering) to be related to social capital. However, Ellison and colleagues speculate that information seeking on Facebook enables users to learn about potential commonalities (e.g., shared interests, mutual friends) between themselves and other users, which can then act as a catalyst to encourage both online and offline communication, increasing the perception of social capital received through the site. This suggests that people may use Facebook in conjunction with FTF interactions to get to know people. However, this also supports the finding that these sites not only provide support from people with whom users have close relationships, but also from those whom users consider as less close (Rozzell et al., 2014). These weaker ties may be people that are not often seen in FTF settings and thus social media may be facilitating support from a wider array of people than a user could potentially access offline.

Different types of social media may also be perceived as more appropriate platforms on which to seek social support. In their study looking at various social media platforms, Hayes, Carr, and Wohn (2016) report that Facebook, rather than Twitter, was perceived to be more effective in gaining social support, and that Snapchat, Instagram, and LinkedIn were the platforms where participants were least likely to attempt to gain social support from their social media contacts. Moreover, they also found that different platforms might be used for different types of support. Although overall Snapchat was not one of the sites most used to gain social support, it was found to be used for support with self-evaluation (judgments made about one's own performance). One reason given for this was that Snapchat friends are a smaller and more relevant group of friends to a user's own life and the "snaps" (image messages sent through Snapchat) can be targeted towards certain people. On the other hand, Twitter was used mostly for information support (support with solving a problem through providing facts) rather than seeking out emotional support. Hayes and colleagues suggest that social media users may use different social platforms to access different types of social support, implying that the picture may be more complex than all social media platforms offering sources of support.

There is some research backing the idea that support received through social media like Facebook is an extension of the support received offline (Blight, Jagiello, & Ruppel, 2015; Li, Chen, & Popiel, 2015), and so social media does little to increase perceptions of social support (Li et al. 2015). However, these groups of studies as well as those previously discussed do not differentiate between different users, and few examine certain uses of social media, particularly those that are targeted at specific support (e.g., pages or groups set up to support a particular group of people). Those who have unique interests, beliefs, or set of circumstances may be unlikely to find similar others or effective social support in their offline social circles (Stepanikova, Nie, & He, 2010).

Social media offer opportunities for different people who have something in common to connect with and support each other. For example, Facebook pages and groups are often set up to support usual life events such as pregnancy and motherhood, and have been found to be important platforms through which to access support from others (Holtz, Smock, & Reyes-Gastelum, 2015). However, they can also be used in more life-changing circumstances, such as serious illnesses. Chen, Yang, Toso-Salman, Chang, Schear, and McGoldrick (2016) conducted an analysis of a Facebook page set up in Mexico aimed at addressing the stigma around cancer. They found that the site was being used by cancer sufferers and survivors to support one another by sharing stories about their own experiences and how they had coped with the reality of living with cancer. This support was mostly from people unknown to the original poster of the content and consisted predominantly of emotional support, as well as support which gave information about the disease. More importantly, the users shared their feelings of empowerment with each other; having cancer had propelled them into trying to help reduce the stigma in Mexico around cancer.

Groups can also be set up on social media by sufferers themselves, rather than being moderated by an external body. Facebook groups exist for sufferers of certain illnesses and are used to share information with each other as well as to provide support to each other (Greene, Choudhry, Kilabuk, & Shrank, 2011). Greene and colleagues found that on Facebook pages for people with diabetes, sufferers were sharing stories about what it felt like to be diabetic, helping them to create a sense of identity. There were clear examples of advice being given to newly diagnosed diabetics from more "veteran" diabetics. Social support is also found on YouTube. Of the comments found on YouTube videos containing testimonials of people with eating disorders, 75 percent were found to be in support of the person who had made and posted the video (i.e., the individual suffering from the eating disorder; Pereira, Quinn, & Morales, 2016).

Social support is not only visible on pages specifically set up for this purpose. Billions of people use social media, create profiles, add content, interact, and share with others. However, when social media users die, these profiles are often used as a place for friends and family to express their grief and to support each other, generating a feeling of solidarity (Church, 2013). The content of the deceased's profile is a historical record of interaction and conversations with friends and family, and hence is as much a part of the living's life as it was the deceased's (Lingel, 2013). It is understandable how these profiles become a memorial for the dead.

Research that has analyzed social media profiles of the deceased shows that in the early days following the death, posts are made which express disbelief or shock at the death of the person (Brubaker & Hayes, 2011; Church, 2013), but shortly afterwards it becomes an important place to gain information on the funeral (Brubaker & Hayes, 2011), which enables a wider circle of people to publicly grieve "at the graveside" (Lingel, 2013). After these initial days, the comments and messages change and are mostly directed at the deceased. A qualitative analysis of comments left on 1369 MySpace profiles of deceased people found that many of the comments formed a one-sided conversation; some comments suggested a belief that the deceased could see the messages left on the page or profile: "Ashley... you can see already how much you've meant to everyone... there are so many people who cared about u... look at all these comments" (Brubaker & Hayes, 2011, p. 4).

This feeling that the deceased can see the messages was also found by Brubaker, Hayes, and Dourish (2013) who interviewed 16 people about their death-related experiences on social media. These interviews generally indicated that the content left on the deceased's profile was going to the deceased. Brubaker and Hayes (2011) refer to this as "post-mortem social networking" and argue that, in some way, the content left after the death of the profile/page owner is a way in which the deceased are still integrated into the lives of the living through the sharing of memories and telling the deceased about current life events. These sites can create an illusion that the deceased and living are having a two-way conversation (Church, 2013).

The evidence seems to suggest that sites like Facebook can be important platforms to help people cope with the death of a loved one (Lingel, 2013). However, there is no empirical evidence currently to show that engaging in this type of social media use actually aids in the bereavement process, nor is there any information to show whether it is more helpful to certain groups of people. Church (2013) reports that the family of a deceased person take comfort in the messages left by others and Brubaker and colleagues (2013) report that reading others' comments can help other mourners to know the deceased in a better or different way. However, these are qualitative studies that have their own limitations in terms of generalizability. Although the evidence available seems to suggest that bereaved social media users take comfort in this form of social media use, since the majority of studies are qualitative, it cannot be concluded that it is better than or supplements other methods of coping with grief (e.g., offline support networks). Nevertheless, the evidence to date seems to suggest that social media can provide a positive experience for bereaved individuals.

Social media platforms can offer sources of support to many people, from gaining different types of support on different platforms as well as getting support from others who are experiencing similar difficulties. Given this, and that social media can help to maintain friendships and connections with others, there is a body of research that has found links between their use and the well-being of their users.

Social Media and Well-being

Human beings are social creatures and having social connections to and support from others is important for well-being and there is evidence to support the notion that social media use can have positive effects on some aspects of psychological well-being in particular. Liu and Yu (2013) report that Facebook use was an important factor in online social support, which, in turn, had a small but significant direct effect on well-being. Moreover, online social support had an indirect effect on well-being, with general social support being a significant mediator of this relationship. Similar results were found by Nabi, Prestin, and So (2013), who reported that the number of Facebook friends had a positive effect on perceived social support, which was then related to perceptions of reduced stress, and subsequently increases in physical health and psychological well-being. In addition, this pattern seems to be found among adolescents. Valkenburg and Peter (2007a) found that using instant messaging to communicate with friends resulted in better quality of friendships, which, in turn, was positively related to well-being. In addition, there is some evidence which shows that using social media to present the "self" might impact positively on well-being. Kim and Lee (2011) demonstrated that portraying oneself in a positive light (e.g., uploading photographs in which one looks happy) on Facebook was significantly associated with feelings of happiness. They also found that portraying oneself in a more realistic way (e.g., expressing negative emotions) led to higher perceptions of social support, which, in turn, was positively related to feelings of happiness. Social media use may therefore be indirectly related to well-being.

One element of well-being is self-esteem. Self-esteem is a psychological construct that refers to the degree to which a person respects and likes themselves. Having feedback on the self can be an important predictor of self-esteem (Pujazon-Zazik & Park, 2010) and one context in which this can occur is social media. For example, positive comments left on social media profiles can lead to higher levels of self-esteem (Valkenburg, Peter, & Schouten, 2006). However, social media can also provide opportunities for others to leave negative comments, and Valkenburg and colleagues found evidence that those who receive negative comments may be at risk of lower self-esteem. Hence, the ability to leave comments on social media profiles may not be a wholly positive experience for everyone. However, these platforms enable people to feel connected, and these feelings of connectedness have also been found to have a positive effect on self-esteem (Abellera, Ouano, Conway, Camilotes, & Doctor, 2012).

Positive associations have also been found between social media use and other measures of well-being. For example, Grieve and colleagues (2013) found that increased feelings of social connectedness via Facebook was correlated with a reduction in depression and anxiety. Using experimental methods, Deters and Mehl (2012) found that increasing the frequency of posting status updates on Facebook can reduce loneliness. These relationships between social media and well-being may also differ depending on the type of social platform used. Pittman and Reich (2016) examined the relationship between uses of five different social media platforms and well-being. They found that use of the image-based platforms were most strongly related to reduced feelings of loneliness and increased perceptions of happiness and satisfaction with life, suggesting that seeing an image gives a sense of social presence and is therefore more likely to increase feelings of connectedness to others, which in turn increases well-being. Therefore, social media platforms like Snapchat and Instagram (i.e., that are more image based) may be more useful in helping to have a positive effect on well-being.

Thus far, this chapter has outlined several positive aspects related to social media use, including providing connectedness to others, providing sources of social support, and having a positive effect on well-being. However, there are certain groups of people who may benefit from the positive aspects more than other users.

WHO BENEFITS MOST FROM SOCIAL MEDIA USE?

There are two hypotheses regarding who benefits most from general social uses of the Internet. The first is the rich-get-richer (or social enhancement) hypothesis, which states that those who already have a rich offline social life will use social media to further this, widening their social circle and enhancing relationships they already have offline. One key characteristic of this group of people is extraversion, which has been found to be positively related to the frequency of social media use (Correa, Hinsley, & de Zuniga, 2010), the number of friends on social media (Amichai-Hamburger & Vinitzky, 2010; Lönnqvist & große Deters, 2016), and the number of Facebook groups (Ross et al., 2009). This access to more friends may therefore offer more sources of support. In addition, Seidman's (2013) study shows evidence that people high in extraversion are more likely to make emotional self-disclosures via social media. Self-disclosure is conducive to relational development and subsequently helps to increase well-being, and there is evidence to suggest that the relationship between Facebook use and well-being holds more strongly for those high in extraversion (Lönnqvist & große Deters, 2016). These studies therefore suggest that those who are already rich in friendships, social support, and well-being will become socially richer from being on social media.

The second hypothesis is the social compensation hypothesis, which suggests that those who are socially poor offline will benefit from online interactions. As discussed, general Internet communication and social media use can enhance social relationships because the reduced cues and asynchronous nature of the Internet and subsequent feelings of disinhibition can encourage self-disclosure behaviors. Being able to select more intimate communication on social media may be more important to people who may find FTF contact difficult, resulting in them choosing communication via the Internet to fulfill their interpersonal needs (Papacharissi & Rubin, 2000).

Those who experience greater social anxiety typically struggle with FTF interactions as they fear negative evaluations from others (Schlenker & Leary, 1982) and as part of a self-protective strategy may be less likely to self-disclose in FTF situations (Meleshko & Alden, 1993). Additionally, there is evidence to suggest that these people place more importance on the features of online communication (i.e., reduced cues and asynchronicity), which enables them to feel less inhibited (Weidman et al., 2012), leading to more self-disclosure (Schouten, Valkenburg, & Peter, 2007). Green and colleagues (2016) tested this process to see if it held for both private communication on Facebook (i.e., private messages) and public communication on Facebook (e.g., status updates, comments on others' posts). Although those experiencing greater social anxiety valued the controllability and reduced cues of both private and public communication, they only felt disinhibited on private communication which then resulted in higher levels of self-disclosure. Given that Utz (2015) found that private Facebook messages were more intimate than status updates, this suggests that socially anxious people may prefer to self-disclose in more intimate spaces online. These relationships between individual differences and the benefits of communication on social media have also been found for shy people (Baker & Oswald, 2010) and people low in self-esteem (Steinfield, Ellison and Lampe, 2008). Lonely people may also benefit from social media as they have been found to be more likely to use the Internet in general as a source of emotional support and for connecting with others with similar interests, compared to people who are low in loneliness (Morahan-Martin & Schumacher, 2003). This body of research supports the social compensation hypothesis whereby those who are typically socially poor offline will benefit from interacting with others online.

The two hypotheses—the rich-get-richer hypothesis and the social compensation hypothesis—are not necessarily opposing hypotheses since both can co-exist; Zywica and Danowski (2008) found support for both. Some participants showed positive associations between extraversion and self-esteem and being popular online, but some who were less sociable with lower self-esteem used the online environment to try to increase their popularity. The authors argue that self-esteem may play a role in explaining this dual support for the hypotheses. That is, those with lower self-esteem (e.g., those who are socially poor offline) are using the social side of the Internet to attempt to increase their self-esteem by striving to enhance their self-image. Conversely, those with high self-esteem (e.g., those who are socially rich offline) may be using this part of the Internet to protect their self-image as a popular person and to advertise their popularity.

Although social media platforms could offer benefits to all users, the evidence suggests that certain types of users may be more likely to benefit from their use. Another group of social media users are young people (children and adolescents) who are prolific users of sites like Facebook, Snapchat, and Instagram. The following section discusses the positive aspects of social media that are associated with their use among young people.

SOCIAL MEDIA AND YOUNG PEOPLE

There have been various concerns surrounding the use of social media by young people, for example, cyberbullying, exposure to unwanted material, interacting with Internet predators. However, recent evidence suggests this is not the case for all young people. Many see these sites as an important part of their social life (Brennan, 2006) and the key aim of social media use among adolescents is to maintain and strengthen offline relationships (Hew & Cheung, 2012; Reich et al., 2012). Lenhart and colleagues (2015) report that 94 percent of 13- to 17-year-olds spend time with their friends on social media, and 68 percent report having been supported through difficult times by friends on social media platforms. In addition, young people can stay in contact with friends who have moved away or friends who attend a different school (Clarke, 2009). Some young people have also reported that using social media makes them feel as though they are always connected to each other (Markow, 2006); this may be particularly beneficial to children and adolescents who live in rural areas by helping them to feel connected to friends regardless of the geographical challenges of meeting FTF (Valentine & Holloway, 2002).

Due to feelings of disinhibition, early adolescents in particular use social media to share intimate thoughts and feelings (Clarke, 2009), which is one characteristic of friendships at this age, particularly among girls (Maccoby, 2002). One study shows evidence that instant messaging (IM) platforms might be being used as a rehearsal space (particularly by boys) to practise these self-disclosure skills to enable offline intimacy to be carried out more efficiently in the future (Valkenburg, Sumter, & Peter, 2011). Hence, using IM services to contact friends has been found to be related to increased quality of friendships (e.g., increased intimacy, trust, and communication, Blais et al., 2008). In a study with 10–17-year-olds, Valkenburg and Peter (2007b) also found that those who perceived online communication to be conducive to discussing a wider breadth of topics and to discussing topics in more depth were more likely to use the online environment to communicate with others. These perceptions were positively related to actual online communication, which, in turn, was positively related to closeness to friends. Importantly, there is evidence that these positive effects of social media communication are only seen when this communication is with people known offline, and not with people met online (Valkenburg & Peter, 2007a).

Similar effects appear in terms of more recent social media. Mobile use of social media enables more frequent use of social media platforms and has a subsequent relationship with feelings of connectedness to friends (Quinn & Oldmeadow, 2013). Quinn and Oldmeadow (2012) found that among 9–13-year-old boys, social media use, such as Facebook, was positively related to feelings of belonging to their friendship group. In conjunction with Valkenburg and colleagues' (2011) findings that boys in particular are likely to use these kinds of platforms for practising self-disclosure skills, these studies suggest that social media are also important platforms particularly for adolescent boys to practise and create intimacy between friends. This may relate to typical social roles seen offline. For example, girls' friendships during adolescence are characterized by higher levels of intimacy than boys' friendships (Buhrmester, 1996), and this may become an accepted norm (i.e., boys are not expected to self-disclose). However, due to feelings of disinhibition, the constraints of social roles in offline contexts may not hold in online contexts (therefore boys may feel more at ease to self-disclose intimate information online). However, this is only a theory, and future research could investigate the reasons for increased self-disclosure online among boys.

Related to friendship maintenance, children and adolescents also use social media as a space outside school to repair relationships that may have been fractured during the school day. Reich (2010) reports that teens have used social media to help them solve problems with friends. In line with the reduced cues, asynchronicity, and feelings of disinhibition offered by these sites, it may be easier for adolescents to repair these relationships on social media rather than FTF. O'Sullivan (2000) found that people preferred to communicate with others via mediated channels (e.g., email) when sensitive or embarrassing information was being discussed or divulged, as these channels allow people to better control information that may threaten self-presentation. Given this, it is understandable that adolescents may choose social media platforms to make amends for issues that may have occurred during the school day. The ability to maintain and repair relationships is important particularly during adolescence, when belonging to a peer group is extremely important (Brown, 1990), and when friendships are seen as important for cognitive, social, and emotional development (Newcomb & Bagwell, 1996). Social media can therefore offer an alternative way for these friendships to be developed and maintained, but also crucially the idiosyncratic features of social media sites might allow young people to resolve conflicts and ambiguity with greater ease.

Adolescence is also a period of time where children begin to exhibit greater independence, and it is also a time of identity exploration with the reference point for this development of identity shifting to friends rather than family (Kroger, 2000). Greenhow and Robelia (2009) suggest that "adolescence is a time when young people explore the physical, sexual, occupational, and ethnic dimensions of their identity within a larger social context" (p. 123). This exploration also allows the individual to learn how to appropriately socially interact with others and how to manage the impressions people have of them. boyd (2008) asserts that social media are a social context where young people can learn about social interactions, how to behave, and decide how they want others to perceive them through a process of impression management. These platforms are a place where adolescents in particular disclose intimate information about themselves, allowing others to comment on this information (Ahn, 2011). boyd argues that these messages and comments left by others (both positive and negative) are a way for adolescents to experience the process of impression management. Posting content onto their own profile may lead others to leave some sort of feedback, and it is this feedback (positive or negative) that helps the young person to decide whether or not to continue behaving in a certain way. In other words, they are using this process as a way of deciding who they want to be. Manago, Graham, Greenfield, and Salimkhan (2008) support this idea and show that receiving social verification in the form of positive feedback on identity explorations can have a reinforcing effect. Thus, social media platforms provide social spaces where young people can experiment with their identity.

boyd's (2008) work is part of a larger body of research that examines online identity development among adolescents. Valkenburg, Schouten and Peter (2005) found that half of their sample of 9- to 18-year-olds reported that they had used instant messaging platforms or chat rooms for identity exploration. Social media in particular offers users the ability to construct, modify, or completely change their self-presentation (Coyle & Vaughn, 2008; Livingstone, 2008), and it is this flexibility that provides young people with opportunities to explore their identity (Livingstone, 2009; Mitchell & Ybarra, 2009); for example, many sites allow the user to decorate their profile page, add links to external sites, post pictures and video clips, and to update their status. In line with Walther's Hyperpersonal Communication Theory (Walther, 1995, 1996), the asynchronous nature of social media interactions (and to some extent the reduced cues) may provide a safe environment for identity development to those who are less confident, enabling them to express themselves in a more confident way; social media allow the user time to consider their responses and if they do become embarrassed, the emotion is invisible to others (Valentine & Holloway, 2002). Valentine and Holloway also argue that this type of interaction actually provides a higher level of control to the individual over their identity construction, and Greenhow and Robelia (2009) report that young people find construction of identity easier to carry out on social media than they do offline. Another possible reason for this is that it provides a non-adult (and therefore potentially non-judgmental) environment in which to explore identity (Livingstone, 2008).

Although there may be legitimate concerns about the use of social media by young people, this section shows that social media platforms can be a useful place for young people to connect with others, to maintain their relationships, and to explore their identity.

Conclusion

This chapter discussed several positive aspects associated with the use of social media. It is clear that social media are forever changing and the new characteristics of different platforms need to be studied, for example, more recent social media like Snapchat offer the ability to post content that has a very short life span. The impact of ephemerality on aspects like disinhibition and the value this holds to certain groups of people (e.g., the socially anxious) has yet to be studied. While this could potentially encourage negative behaviors, it is also possible that platforms that offer this level of control over content will be particularly attractive to the types of people discussed in Who Benefits Most from Social Media Use (e.g. people who are socially anxious). Research must therefore play "catch up" with this constantly changing landscape.

Despite social media getting bad press in mainstream media, there are many positive outcomes associated with its use. However, it is important to remain cautious about proclaiming that using social media *causes* positive outcomes. As with the literature examining the negative aspects of social media, much of the literature discussed in this chapter includes cross-sectional, non-experimental studies that clearly have their limitations in being able to provide firm conclusions on cause and effect relationships, which should be borne in mind when drawing conclusions. Nevertheless, social media platforms are used by billions of people and are also integrated into many areas of everyday life. It is therefore imperative that research continues to investigate how these platforms can affect relationships, social support, and well-being.

References

Abellera, N., Ouano, J., Conway, G., Camilotes, L., & Doctor, H. (2012). The mediating effect of relatedness on Facebook use and self-esteem. *International Journal of Research Studies in Psychology 1*(3), 59–67.

Ahn, J. (2011). The effect of social network sites on adolescents' social and academic development: Current theories and controversies. *Journal of the American Society for Information Science and Technology 62*(8), 1435–2882.

Amichai-Hamburger, Y., & Vinitzky, G. (2010). Social network use and personality. *Computers in Human Behavior 26*(6), 1289–5632.

Baker, L. R., & Oswald, D. L. (2010). Shyness and online social networking services. *Journal of Social and Personal Relationships 27*(7), 873–4075.

Barker, V. (2009). Older adolescents' motivations for social network site use: The influence of gender, group identity, and collective self-esteem. *Cyberpsychology & Behavior: The Impact of the Internet, Multimedia and Virtual Reality on Behavior and Society 12*(2), 209–213.

Bayer, J. B., Ellison, N. B., Schoenebeck, S. Y., & Falk, E. B. (2016). Sharing the small moments: ephemeral social interaction on Snapchat. *Information, Communication and Society 19*(7), 956–977.

Berndt, T. J. (2002). Friendship quality and social development. *Current Directions in Psychological Science 11*, 7–10.

Blais, J. J., Craig, W. M., Pepler, D., & Connolly, J. (2008). Adolescents online: The importance of Internet activity choices to salient relationships. *Journal of Youth and Adolescence 37*(5), 522–536.

Blight, M. G., Jagiello, K., & Ruppel, E. K. (2015). "Same stuff different day": A mixed-method study of support seeking on Facebook. *Computers in Human Behavior 53*, 366–373.

boyd, d. (2008). Why youth heart social network sites: The role of networked publics. In D. Buckingham (Ed.), *Youth, identity, and digital media* (pp. 119–142). London: MIT Press.

boyd, d., & Ellison, N. B. (2007). Social network sites: Definition, history, and scholarship. *Journal of Computer-Mediated Communication 13*(1), Article 11.

Brennan, M. (2006). *Understanding online social network services and risks to youth.* London: Child Exploitation and Online Protection (CEOP) Centre.

Brown, B. B. (1990). Peer groups and peer culture. In S. S. Feldman & G. R. Elliott (Eds.), *At the threshold: The developing adolescent* (pp. 171–196). Cambridge, MA: Harvard University Press.

Brubaker, J. R., & Hayes, G. R. (2011). We will never forget you [online]: An empirical investigation of post-mortem MySpace comments. In *Proceedings of the ACM 2011 conference on Computer Supported Cooperative Work* (pp. 123–132). New York: ACM.

Brubaker, J. R., Hayes, G. R., & Dourish, P. (2013). Beyond the grave: Facebook as a site for the expansion of death and mourning. *The Information Society 29*(3), 152–163.

Buhrmester, D. (1996). Need fulfillment, interpersonal competence and the developmental contexts of early adolescent friendships. In W. M. Bukowski, A. F. Newcomb, & W. W. Hartup (Eds.), *The company they keep. Friendship in childhood and adolescence* (pp. 158–185). Cambridge: Cambridge University Press.

Bumgarner, B. A. (2007). You have been poked: Exploring the uses and gratifications of Facebook among emerging adults. *First Monday 12*(11). Retrieved from http://www.uic.edu

Chen, G. M. (2011). Tweet this: A uses and gratifications perspective on how active Twitter use gratifies a need to connect with others. *Computers in Human Behavior 27*(2), 755–762.

Chen, X., Yang, L. H, Toso-Salman, J., Chang, Schear R., & McGoldrick, D. (2016). Social support within online communities: Internet reach and content analysis of a cancer anti-stigma Facebook page in Mexico. *Global Media Journal 2016*, S1:1

Church, S. H. (2013). Digital gravescapes: Digital memorializing on Facebook. *The Information Society 29*(3), 184–189.

Clarke, B. (2009). Friends forever: How young adolescents use social-networking sites. *IEEE Intelligent Systems 24*(6), 22–26.

Coleman, J. S. (1988). Social capital in the creation of human capital. *The American Journal of Sociology 94*, S95–S120.

Correa, T., Hinsley, A. W., & de Zuniga, H. G. (2010). Who interacts on the Web?: The intersection of users' personality and social media use. *Computers in Human Behavior 26*(2), 247–253.

Coyle, C. L., & Vaughn, H. (2008). Social networking: Communication revolution or evolution? *Bell Labs Technical Journal 13*(2), 13–17.

Deters, F., & Mehl, M. (2012). Does posting Facebook status updates increase or decrease loneliness? An online social networking experiment. *Social Psychological and Personality Science 4*(5) https://doi.org/10.1177/1948550612469233

Ellison, N. B., Steinfield, C., & Lampe, C. (2007). The benefits of Facebook "friends:" Social capital and college students' use of online social network sites. *Journal of Computer-Mediated Communication 12*(4), 1143–1168.

Ellison, N. B., Steinfield, C., & Lampe, C. (2011). Connection strategies: Social capital implications of Facebook-enabled communication practices. *New Media & Society, 13*(6), 873–892.

Facebook (n.d.). Facebook About. Retrieved July 21, 2017 from https://www.facebook.com/pg/facebook/about/

Facebook (2017). Facebook newsroom statistics. Retrieved July 21, 2017 from https://newsroom.fb.com/company-info/

Green, T., Wilhelmsen, T., Wilmots, E., Dodd, B., & Quinn, S. (2016). Social anxiety, attributes of online communication and self-disclosure across private and public Facebook communication. *Computers in Human Behavior 58*, 206–213.

Greene, J. A., Choudhry, N. K., Kilabuk, E., & Shrank, W. H. (2011). Online social networking by patients with diabetes: a qualitative evaluation of communication with Facebook. *Journal of General Internal Medicine 26*(3), 287–292.

Greenhow, C., & Robelia, B. (2009). Informal learning and identity formation in online social networks. *Learning, Media and Technology 34*(2), 119–140.

Grieve, R., Indian, M., Witteveen, K., Anne Tolan, G., & Marrington, J. (2013). Face-to-face or Facebook: Can social connectedness be derived online? *Computers in Human Behavior 29*(3), 604–609.

Hayes, R. A., Carr, C. T., & Wohn, D. Y. (2016). It's the audience: Differences in social support across social media. *Social Media and Society 2*(4), 1–12.

Hew, K. F., & Cheung, W. S. (2012). Use of Facebook: A case study of Singapore students' experience. *Asia Pacific Journal of Education 32*(2), 181–196.

Holtz, B., Smock, A., & Reyes-Gastelum, D. (2015). Connected motherhood: Social support for moms and moms-to-be on Facebook. *Telemedicine Journal and E-Health 21*(5), 415–421.

Joinson, A. (1998). Causes and implications of disinhibited behavior on the Internet. In J. Gackenbach (Ed.), *Psychology and the Internet: Intrapersonal, interpersonal, and transpersonal implications* (pp. 43–60). San Diego, CA: Academic Press.

Joinson, A. N. (2001). Self-disclosure in computer-mediated communication: The role of self-awareness and visual anonymity. *European Journal of Social Psychology 31*(2), 177–192.

Joinson, A. N. (2008). "Looking at", "looking up", or "keeping up with" people? Motives and uses of Facebook. In *Proceedings of the SIGCHI Conference on Human Factors in Computing Systems CHI 2008* (pp. 1027–1036). Florence, Italy, 5–10 April 2008. New York: ACM.

Kaye, B. K. (1998). Uses and gratifications of the World Wide Web: From couch potato to Web potato. *The New Jersey Journal of Communication 6*(1), 21–40.

Kim, J., & Lee, J.-E. R. (2011). The Facebook paths to happiness: Effects of the number of Facebook friends and self-presentation on subjective well-being. *Cyberpsychology, Behavior and Social Networking 14*(6), 359–364.

Kim, Y., Sohn, D., & Choi, S. M. (2011). Cultural difference in motivations for using social network sites: A comparative study of American and Korean college students. *Computers in Human Behavior 27*(1), 365–372.

Kroger, J. (2000). *Identity development. Adolescence through adulthood.* London: Sage.

Lenhart, A., Smith, A., Anderson, M., Duggan, M., & Perrin, A., "Teens, Technology and Friendships." Pew Research Center, August, 2015. http://www.pewinternet.org/2015/08/06/teens-technology-and-friendships/

Li, X., Chen, W., & Popiel, P. (2015). What happens on Facebook stays on Facebook? The implications of Facebook interaction for perceived, receiving, and giving social support. *Computers in Human Behavior 51*, 106–113.

Lingel, J. (2013). The digital remains: Social media and practices of online grief. *The Information Society 29*(3), 190–195.

Liu, C., & Yu, C. (2013). Can Facebook use induce well-being? *Cyberpsychology, Behavior and Social Networking 16*(9), 674–678.

Livingstone, S. (2008). Taking risky opportunities in youthful content creation: Teenagers' use of social networking sites for intimacy, privacy and self-expression. *New Media & Society 10*(3), 393–411.

Livingstone, S. (2009). *Children and the Internet*. Cambridge: Polity Press.

Lönnqvist, J.-E., & große Deters, F. (2016). Facebook friends, subjective well-being, social support, and personality. *Computers in Human Behavior 55*, 113–120.

Maccoby, E. E. (2002). Gender and group process: A developmental perspective. *Current Directions in Psychological Science 11*, 54–58.

Manago, A. M., Graham, M. B., Greenfield, P. M., & Salimkhan, G. (2008). Self-presentation and gender on MySpace. *Journal of Applied Developmental Psychology 29*(6), 446–458.

Markow, D. (2006). Friendships in the age of social networking websites. *Trends and Tudes*. Harris Interactive.

Meleshko, K. G., & Alden, L. E. (1993). Anxiety and self-disclosure: Toward a motivational model. *Journal of Personality and Social Psychology 64*(6), 1000–1009.

Mitchell, K. J., & Ybarra, M. (2009). Social networking sites finding a balance between their risks and benefits. *Archives of Pediatrics & Adolescent Medicine 163*(1), 87–89.

Morahan-Martin, J., & Schumacher, P. (2003). Loneliness and social uses of the Internet. *Computers in Human Behavior 19*(6), 659–671.

Nabi, R. L., Prestin, A., & So, J. (2013). Facebook friends with (health) benefits? Exploring social network site use and perceptions of social support, stress, and well-being. *Cyberpsychology, Behavior and Social Networking 16*(10), 721–727.

Newcomb, A. F., & Bagwell, C. L. (1996). Developmental significance of friendship. In W. M. Bukowski, A. F. Newcomb, & W. W. Hartup (Eds.), *The Company they keep* (pp. 289–321). Cambridge: Cambridge University Press.

Obar, J., & Wildman, S. (2015). Social media definition and the governance challenge: An introduction to the special issue. *Telecommunications Policy 39*(9), 745–750.

O'Sullivan, B. (2000). What you don't know won't hurt me. *Human Communication Research 26*(3), 403–431.

Papacharissi, Z., & Rubin, A. M. (2000). Predictors of Internet use. *Journal of Broadcasting & Electronic Media 44*(2), 175–196.

Park, N., Jin, B., & Jin, S. A. A. (2011). Effects of self-disclosure on relational intimacy on Facebook. *Computers in Human Behavior 27*(5), 1974–1983.

Pereira, L. M., Quinn, N., & Morales, E. (2016). Breaking news: "I have an eating disorder." Video testimonials on YouTube. *Computers in Human Behavior 63*, 938–942.

Pittman, M., & Reich, B. (2016). Social media and loneliness: Why an Instagram picture may be worth more than a thousand Twitter words. *Computers in Human Behavior 62*, 155–167.

Piwek, L., & Joinson, A. (2016). "What do they snapchat about?" Patterns of use in time-limited instant messaging service. *Computers in Human Behavior 54*, 358–367.

Pujazon-Zazik, M., & Park, M. J. (2010). To tweet, or not to tweet: Gender differences and potential positive and negative health outcomes of adolescents' social Internet use. *American Journal of Men's Health 4*(1), 77–85.

Quinn, S. & Oldmeadow, J. A. (2012). Is the iGeneration a 'we' generation? Social networking use among 9- to 13-year-olds and belonging. *British Journal of Developmental Psychology 31*(1), 136–142.

Quinn, S., & Oldmeadow, J. (2013). The Martini Effect and social networking sites: Early adolescents, mobile social networking and connectedness to friends. *Mobile Media & Communication 1*(2), 237–247.

Reich, S. M. (2010). Adolescents' sense of community on MySpace and Facebook: A mixed-methods approach. *Journal of Community Psychology 38*(6), 688–705.

Reich, S. M., Subrahmanyam, K., & Espinoza, G. (2012). Friending, IMing, and hanging out face-to-face: Overlap in adolescents' online and offline social networks. *Developmental Psychology 48*(2), 356–368.

Ross, C., Orr, E. S., Sisic, M., Arseneault, J. M., Simmering, M. G., & Orr, R. R. (2009). Personality and motivations associated with Facebook use. *Computers in Human Behavior 25*(2), 578–586.

Rozzell, B., Piercy, C. W., Carr, C. T., King, S., Lane, B. L., Tornes, M.,…Wright, K. B. (2014). Notification pending: Online social support from close and nonclose relational ties via Facebook. *Computers in Human Behavior 38*, 272–280.

Schlenker, B. R., & Leary, M. R. (1982). Social anxiety and self-presentation: A conceptualization and model. *Psychological Bulletin 92*(3), 641–669.

Schouten, A. P., Valkenburg, P. M., & Peter, J. (2007). Precursors and underlying processes of adolescents' online self-disclosure: Developing and testing an "Internet-attribute-perception" model. *Media Psychology 10*(2), 292–314.

Seidman, G. (2013). Self-presentation and belonging on Facebook: How personality influences social media use and motivations. *Personality and Individual Differences 54*(3), 402–407.

Sheldon, K. M., Abad, N., & Hinsch, C. (2011). A two-way process view of Facebook use and relatedness need-satisfaction: Disconnection drives use and connection rewards it. *Journal of Personality and Social Psychology 100*(4), 766–775.

Stafford, T. F., & Gonier, D. (2004). What Americans like about being online. *Communications of the ACM 47*(11), 107–112.

Stafford, T. F., Stafford, M. R., & Schkade, L. L. (2004). Determining uses and gratifications for the Internet. *Decision Sciences 35*(2), 259–288.

Steinfield, C., Ellison, N. B., & Lampe, C. (2008). Social capital, self-esteem, and use of online social network sites: A longitudinal analysis. *Journal of Applied Developmental Psychology 29*(6), 434–445.

Stepanikova, I., Nie, N. H., & He, X. (2010). Time on the Internet at home, loneliness, and life satisfaction: Evidence from panel time-diary data. *Computers in Human Behavior 26*(3), 329–338.

Suler, J. (2005). The online disinhibition effect. *International Journal of Applied Psychoanalytic Studies 2*(2), 184–188.

Tidwell, L. C., & Walther, J. B. (2002). Computer-mediated communication effects on disclosure, impressions, and interpersonal evaluations: Getting to know one another a bit at a time. *Human Communication Research 28*(3), 317–348.

Twitter (2016). Company Facts. Retrieved July 21, 2017 from https://about.twitter.com/company

Urista, M. A., Dong, Q., & Day, K. D. (2009). Explaining why young adults use MySpace and Facebook through the uses and gratifications theory. *Human Communication Research 12*(2), 215–229.

Utz, S. (2015). The function of self-disclosure on social network sites: Not only intimate, but also positive and entertaining self-disclosures increase the feeling of connection. *Computers in Human Behavior 45*, 1–10.

Valentine, G., & Holloway, S. L. (2002). Cyberkids? Exploring children's identities and social networks in on-line and off-line worlds. *Annals of the Association of American Geographers* 92(2), 302–319.

Valkenburg, P. M., & Peter, J. (2007a). Online communication and adolescent well-being: Testing the stimulation versus the displacement hypothesis. *Journal of Computer-Mediated Communication* 12(4), Article 2.

Valkenburg, P. M., & Peter, J. (2007b). Preadolescents' and adolescents' online communication and their closeness to friends. *Developmental Psychology* 43(2), 267–277.

Valkenburg, P. M., Peter, J., & Schouten, A. P. (2006). Friend networking sites and their relationship to adolescents' well-being and social self-esteem. *Cyberpsychology & Behavior: The Impact of the Internet, Multimedia and Virtual Reality on Behavior and Society* 9(5), 584–590.

Valkenburg, P. M., Schouten, A. P., & Peter, J. (2005). Adolescents' identity experiments on the Internet. *New Media & Society* 7(3), 383–402.

Valkenburg, P. M., Sumter, S. R., & Peter, J. (2011). Gender differences in online and offline self-disclosure in pre-adolescence and adolescence. *The British Journal of Developmental Psychology* 29(2), 253–269.

Walther, J. B. (1995). Relational aspects of computer-mediated communication—experimental observations over time. *Organization Science* 6(2), 186–203.

Walther, J. B. (1996). Computer-mediated communication: Impersonal, interpersonal, and hyperpersonal interaction. *Communication Research* 23(1), 3–43.

Weidman, A. C., Fernandez, K. C., Levinson, C. A., Augustine, A. A., Larsen, R. J., & Rodebaugh, T. L. (2012). Compensatory Internet use among individuals higher in social anxiety and its implications for well-being. *Personality and Individual Differences* 53(3), 191–195.

Wright, K. B. (2012). Emotional support and perceived stress among college students using Facebook.com: An exploration of the relationship between source perceptions and emotional support. *Communication Research Reports* 29(3), 175–184.

Wright, K. B., Rosenberg, J., Egbert, N., Ploeger, N. A., Bernard, D. R., & King, S. (2013). Communication competence, social support, and depression among college students: a model of Facebook and face-to-face support network influence. *Journal of Health Communication* 18(1), 41–57.

Zywica, J., & Danowski, J. (2008). The faces of Facebookers: Investigating social enhancement and social compensation hypotheses; predicting Facebook and offline popularity from sociability and self-esteem, and mapping the meanings of popularity with semantic networks. *Journal of Computer-Mediated Communication* 14, 1–34.

PART VI

HEALTH AND TECHNOLOGY

CHAPTER 22

....

MANAGING YOUR HEALTH ONLINE: ISSUES IN THE SELECTION, CURATION, AND SHARING OF DIGITAL HEALTH INFORMATION

....

ELIZABETH SILLENCE AND PAM BRIGGS

Introduction

....

RESEARCHERS are now familiar with the idea that the Internet provides a major source of information for people coping with a wide range of health conditions (Fox, Duggan, & Purcell, 2013; Harris, Sillence, & Briggs, 2011). Over the last decade, the number of patients accessing traditional health information providers and sources has decreased, with a comparable increase in traffic to peer-to-peer sharing sites. Here, patients and informal carers themselves are increasingly creating and sharing health resources, and the number of people accessing patient-authored content, in particular those with chronic conditions, has increased (Fox, 2011; O'Neill, Ziebland, Valderas, & Lupiáñez-Villanueva, 2014). Access to user-generated content among surrogate seekers, people looking online for someone else, has also increased (Cutrona et al., 2015). In addition to sharing information, advice, and support, people are collecting, storing, and sharing more quantitative data about themselves through fitness and well-being monitoring and tracking devices (Shih, Han, Poole, Rosson, & Carroll, 2015).

   As people are encouraged to take a more active role in their own health, access to good-quality, appropriate information is vital, and peer-to-peer sharing sites are fast becoming a key resource in this respect. However, the volume and diversity of such sources can be problematic, and the process of managing this information is not straightforward. In fact, managing personal online health information is becoming an increasingly complex and time-consuming process. People have access to more information than ever before, from a wider range of sources, and more opportunities to share, either knowingly or unwittingly, their health information. These increases also prompt questions around how individuals curate their digital information for themselves and their loved ones, both now and in the future.

This chapter focuses on two key issues that arise from the shift towards peer-to-peer health sites. Firstly, as regards sharing and self-disclosure, peer sites are underpinned by active participation, but how do people manage the process of meaningful sharing with others across different platforms? How are multiple identities persevered in the face of context collapse, and how do people manage the issues of anonymity, privacy, and trust in this space? Secondly, what information management strategies are relevant in relation to health information? How do people engage in information curation—keep, manage, and exploit the increasing amount of data they collect, both about themselves and about their health condition more generally? How are different information types and sources integrated and understood, both in relation to personal sense making as well as improved communication with health professionals and family members? This chapter outlines some current thinking associated with these two key concerns and highlights future research directions. It begins by outlining the evolving eHealth landscape as a way of setting the scene for the issues described in this chapter.

The Changing Face of eHealth: Peer-to-Peer Sites

As people are encouraged to take a more pro-active role in their own health (Coulter & Collins, 2011), access to online health resources becomes more important. People search online for health information and advice in order to prepare for meetings with health-care professionals, or to seek support, alternative answers, or reassurance (Rozmovits & Ziebland, 2004; Harris, Sillence, & Briggs, 2011). The shift towards user-generated health content (Ziebland & Wyke, 2012), information, or data created by patients or carers is a noticeable feature of the eHealth landscape. This peer-to-peer resource typically consists of personal experiences of a particular treatment or health condition, and is often in narrative form. Nearly a quarter of people in the UK have accessed and shared personal experiences of health online (O'Neill et al., 2014), and peer resources are now a central tenant of health-related Internet use (Mo & Coulson, 2008; France, Wyke, Ziebland, Entwistle, & Hunt, 2011; Hinton, Kurinczuk, & Ziebland, 2010; Chou, Liu, Post, & Hesse, 2011). Patient experiences offer opportunities for social comparison, helping patients understand how well they are coping with a particular illness (Locock & Brown, 2010). Access to patients' stories is also associated with a sense of feeling supported, of maintaining relationships with others, and, for some people, an ability to visualize the disease (Ziebland & Wyke, 2012). Sharing personal experiences is also useful for those engaged in behavior change, for example, weight loss and smoking cessation (Brindal et al., 2012; Van Mierlo, Voci, Lee, Fournier, & Selby, 2012).

Online support groups or communities are a common and well-researched peer-to-peer health resource (Coulson, 2005; Chou et al., 2011; Meade, Buchanan & Coulson, 2017; Sillence & Bussey, 2017), providing access to social support, shared personal experiences, and offering opportunities for members to form social ties with others in similar circumstances. Social networking sites now also provide a place to seek social support and information, with many Facebook groups dedicated to specific health conditions (Zhang, He, & Sang, 2013). People also share their health information and concerns on Twitter. Researchers have been interested in examining the large data sets that Twitter generates to monitor disease outbreaks and predict flu trends (Culotta, 2010, Ritterman, Osborne, & Klein, 2009) and as a way of understanding public discourse around particular health concerns (McNeill, Harris, & Briggs, 2016).

The increasing volume of information is driven in part by the fact that we are all now health information generators. We are encouraged to monitor and record our "health-related selves" via tracking devices, wearable activity monitors, and apps. Recent studies have examined the adoption of activity trackers (Shih et al., 2015), and although engagement may not always be long lived (Ledger & McCaffrey, 2014; Clawson, Pater, Miller, Mynatt, & Mamykina, 2015), it is often accompanied by a drive to upload and share our data and our personal experiences with other like-minded people. These sharing platforms include photo and video sharing platforms, e.g., Instagram and YouTube, that allow people to share data and visual evidence on a range of health-related issues from mental health to hair loss (Manikonda & De Choudhury, 2017; McNeill & Sillence, 2018). This kind of sharing, however, is not without its problems, as researchers have noted how such platforms may play a role in promoting eating disorder behavior and body image dissatisfaction (Pater, Haimson, Andalibi, & Mynatt, 2016; Deighton-Smith & Bell, 2017).

Where text was once the format of choice for digital health information, videos are becoming an increasingly important part of online health resources (Huh, Liu, Neogi, Inkpen, & Pratt, 2014). Health video blogs (vlogs) have more recently come to the fore as a resource for patient support. Organization-initiated vlogs, e.g., patient interviews about treatment experiences, or health promotion videos, have been shown to improve psychological well-being (Song, Nam, Gould, Sanders, McLaughlin, et al., 2012). User-generated vlogs have also been studied across a number of health topics, including, *inter alia*, vaccination, multiple sclerosis treatment, and organ donation (Briones, Nan, Madden, & Waks, 2012; Mazanderani, O'Neill, & Powell, 2013; Tian, 2010). A few studies have also examined the posters' motivations in creating and uploading these videos, noting journaling, self-reflection, and altruism as key drivers (Huh et al., 2014; Wotanis & McMillan, 2014). Motivations also appear to vary according to health condition. Vloggers (video bloggers) with HIV/AIDS or diabetes report a desire to help others, while MS patients use the videos to document their condition in response to treatment and upload their evidence-based videos as a way of convincing other patients and the wider community of a specific treatment's efficacy (Mazanderani et al., 2013). Such videos can be particularly vivid for those seeking information and support. In a recent laboratory study, informal carers of people with dementia expressed a strong preference for video-based personal experiences of other carers over text-based formats (Sillence & Cooper, 2016). Videos were seen as evocative and provided an instant and strong connection with the authors.

Sharing and Self-disclosure within Digital Health Settings

The volume and availability of peer-sharing sites makes it easy to share health information, but the issues and complexities around sharing and self-disclosure in this context are not straightforward. As previously discussed, sharing has a number of potential benefits for both sharer and reader. Sharing health experiences and information can play an important role in decision-making and lead to greater perceived online support and improved mood (Sillence & Bussey, 2017; Rodgers & Chen, 2005; Nimrod, 2013). Writing about health experiences is known to provide therapeutic benefits for the author (Pennebaker, 1997), and research indicates that, in online health support forums, there is a high level of emotional disclosure (Barak and Gluck-Ofri, 2007).

Trust and privacy play a central role in self-disclosure decisions. Trust in relation to eHealth has been examined from a number of perspectives. Some studies have focused on interpersonal trust within online communities and the process by which people come to trust others and build relationships (Fan, Lederman, Smith, & Chang, 2014; Sillence, 2010). Emotional attachment to an online community affects participation so that those who feel more attached or committed participate more actively in that community and engage in personal health sharing (Bateman, Gray, & Butler, 2011; Kordzadeh & Warren, 2014). There is also a body of research examining the impact of personal dispositions on trust and health information disclosure (Bansal & Gefen, 2010). What is less clear, however, is how people decide to trust the underlying technology or the platform that affords online interpersonal trust to take place. Studies of consumer trust in eHealth websites indicate that both the design of the website and its content are both important in nurturing trust. Health information seekers base their initial trust decisions on the look and feel of the website before undertaking a more considered evaluation of the content itself, evaluating the breadth and depth of the information, and assessing its personal relevance (see Sillence, Briggs, Harris, & Fishwick, 2007 and reviews by Kim, 2016 and Sbaffi & Rowley, 2017). There is less research focusing on peer-to-peer sharing sites specifically, although outside of health, there are a few studies examining how people come to trust social networking sites (SNS). Lankton and McKnight (2008), for example, found that people, in fact, demonstrate aspects of both interpersonal trust and technology trust in relation to their use of SNS. *Functionality* (technology trust) and *competence* (interpersonal trust) strongly correlated with usage intention, suggesting that, in addition to trusting the technology, people bestow some kind of person-like characteristics on the platform and trust it as a "quasi-person."

Within a health context, there is some evidence that funding models for peer-to-peer sites may play a role in fostering trust or mistrust (Sillence, Hardy, & Briggs, 2013), with users having to pass through an initial "trust gate" before they begin to consider the personal experiences contained within the site (Sillence, Hardy, Harris, & Briggs, 2014).

While active sharing in peer-to-peer sharing sites benefits people, some individuals choose to refrain from sharing health information online due to privacy concerns (Frost, Vermeulen, & Beekers, 2014). The increasing diversity of such sites poses new and more complex issues for users around the issue of privacy. Users must make judgments about the type and amount of information disclosure and withholding, weighing up the contextual integrity of their sharing against potential threats to identity and privacy posed by the listeners on the network. Users are faced with the challenge of attempting to balance disclosing and withholding personal information while engaging in peer-to-peer sharing (Stutzman, Gross, & Acquisti, 2013). Typically, people share information if the perceived rewards outweigh the perceived risks Bansal & Gefen, 2010). Within a health-sharing context, this is particularly pertinent, with people recognizing the need to provide at least some personal health information if they are to benefit from relevant guidance and advice. The complexity of privacy threats (see discussion by Li, 2015) is only likely to increase as i) the ownership of different types of peer-led sites increases—peer-led sites can be hosted by large pharmaceutical sites as well as charities, healthcare organizations, and individuals, and as such may have a number of "silent listeners," i.e., third-party applications or indirect advertisements on their networks (Stutzman et al., 2013), and (ii) the increasing diversity of peer-led sites. Interactive online peer-to-peer resources can, for example, include data-centered patient community sites built around the sharing of personal health data as well as those focused on the sharing of richer story-based accounts of health and illness (vlogs, blogs, and discussion boards). Data-driven sites such as https://www.patientslikeme.com/ have been built to support information exchange between patients. These sites enable patients to find others similar to themselves, matched via clinical and demographic characteristics, and to share detailed, computable data about symptoms and treatments in order to improve outcomes (Wicks et al., 2010). These sites, however, may have arrangements to sell user data to pharmaceutical companies, and while the platform will make that clear within their terms and conditions, users often fail to read the conditions carefully and so are sometimes consenting to such data-sharing practices unwittingly and may feel aggrieved when this comes to light (Angwin & Stecklow, 2010). Rich story-based patient communities are more concerned with the sharing of experiences around health and illness. Here, data about health, symptoms, and treatments will also form part of the discussions, but will typically be embedded within a narrative context, for example, concerning the experience of undertaking the treatment, the process of deciding upon the treatment, the outcome of the treatment, or a combination of these (Shaffer & Zikmund-Fisher, 2013, Sillence, 2016). Given the diversity of resources, it is likely that the expectation of privacy by users will depend on the context in which the information exchange takes place. While trust and privacy concerns are important in relation to self-disclosure, a number of other factors have been identified in relation to digital health information sharing, including platform or channel effects, illness phase, and identity and life transition.

Although self-disclosure on social media sites has typically been examined through the lens of impression management (boyd & Ellison, 2007), the self-disclosure goals within online health communities are often quite different, with people having to reveal personal information about themselves in order to receive the health information or the social and emotional support they are seeking. Platforms often comprise a number of different public and private channels, and self-disclosure patterns can vary across these different channels. Yang, Yao, and Kraut (2017) noted that members of online health support groups self-disclosed more in the public channels compared to the private channels offered by the group. Disclosures were often negative in tone as posters were open about the difficulties they faced. While being explicit about health concerns is often a necessary part of gaining help and advice (Wang, Kraut, & Levine, 2015), the tone of the self-disclosure was more positive in the private channels and focused on happier aspects of the posters' lives. These findings resonate with some recent work examining online health communities (Sillence & Bussey, 2017), which observed that private channels were often used to discuss non-health-related aspects of participants' lives. As relationships formed and strengthened on the site, disclosures became more varied and off-topic. Furthermore, the study noted that different platforms were often reserved for different forms of self-disclosure. Choosing to divulge information about family and hobbies did not always feel appropriate for some on a health forum, and likewise, other people found discussing health issues on a more general social media platform, e.g., Facebook, inappropriate—the sense that each platform had a specific role was captured by this participant from our study describing the two platforms she has used in relation to her sleep condition:

> "Well I think the Facebook forum is like any Facebook forum so you get a lot of people posting but you do have to sift through a lot of stuff and some people write as if its (sic) their diary and it can be boring its (sic) like people on your own facebook (sic) page that write every detail of their day do you know what I mean or they write everything about their child or whatever and after a while it can get very boring but on the forum although there's not as many posts not as many recent posts I think it seems more serious really yes on the other forum I think its (sic) more serious."

Engagement with online health communities is not a static process, but one that varies over the course of different life transitions (Massimi, Bender, Witteman, & Ahmed, 2014). Often people engage with an online community during periods when there is an intense need for information, but may leave if there is a lack of continued interest. Pregnancy-related online support communities, for example, may find members join when they discover they are pregnant, but leave once the baby is born as the community discussions no longer support continued interest. People suffering from particular health conditions may also share information with others in support groups in a temporary or intermittent manner, depending on the nature of condition, although in some cases members may remain on the site to help and support others, even though they are no longer dealing with the health condition themselves (Massimi et al., 2014, Sillence & Bussey, 2017). Asking informal carers of people with MS to discuss their engagement with different peer-to-peer sharing sites indicates that the phase of the illness or the relationship is an important factor in their use of peer resources. For informal carers, sharing information online about themselves or the person they are caring for is something that depends very much on the stage of the illness itself, or their relationship with the identity of carer (Hughes, Locock, & Ziebland, 2013). Carers may be keen to engage and share information initially, but then withdraw from such sites, returning, often reluctantly, to peer-to-peer sharing sites as their emotional needs increase (Sillence, Hardy, Briggs, & Harris, 2016). The type of self-disclosure also varies in relation to the stage or phase of the illness or health condition. Eschler, Dehlawi, and Pratt (2015) found that online participants posting immediately after a cancer diagnosis or during treatment typically asked for advice, while those who had successfully completed treatment or were in remission were more likely to share information in the form of personal narratives. Having access to other people's health information and experiences can present patients and their friends and family with an added burden when deciding how to use or disclose that information. Informal carers, for example, have to consider the implied or declared preferences of the person they are caring for when sharing information online or during GP consultations (Mazanderani, Hughes, Hardy, Sillence, & Powell, 2019).

Where social networking sites like Facebook are concerned, periods of engagement may also vary (Baumer et al., 2013). Recent work suggests that managing "digital personhood" can be impacted by illness, resulting in pre- and post-illness personas (Kerrigan & Hart, 2016). Managing our identities across different contexts is often difficult when engaging in social interaction online, a term recognized as "context collapse" (boyd, 2008). Managing self-disclosure practices on Facebook may not be straightforward for individuals during their periods of ill health. People may adopt different strategies, including abstaining from posting on Facebook during particular health episodes, as a form of self-protection and resistance to context collapse.

Van der Velden and El Emam (2013) explored these issues in a group of chronically ill teenage patients. The authors studied teenagers' management of their personal health information on social media and found that they were guarded and very selective about sharing their thoughts and feelings around their health condition on social media, despite being keen Facebook users. Interestingly, the majority of the teenagers did not write status updates in relation to their time in hospital, and applied a variety of techniques to manage how and with whom they communicated. Facebook was seen as a place to be a "regular", rather than an "unwell", teenager, and avoiding context collapse was important for these people.

Likewise, Newman, Lauterbach, Munson, Resnick, and Morris (2011) detail the ways in which people manage their self-disclosure practices between online health communities and Facebook. This involved shortening and reducing the detail of messages on Facebook that related to health issues and not allowing status updates to be shared across the two platforms. The authors noted that the two platforms represented Goffman's (1959) front stage and back stage analogy. In this case, Facebook was the front stage where participants presented the impression of being interesting people who were in control and remained positive, the online community, by contrast, acted as the back stage, and gave people the space to be more open about their difficulties and their need for help. In other cases, this contextual collapse is seen as a natural and welcome aspect of networked lives, as this quote from an interview participant (see Sillence & Bussey, 2017 for details) highlights:

> *"Some people pop in and pop out but there are some regulars that are there all the time and we've also added each other as friends on facebook (sic) so all these different posts about life in general and you sort of share in their successes and their sorrows you know what I mean you don't talk about sleep apnoea any more you talk about their life in general it branches out you do make friends and some people I know have met up from the group things like that you know and also they'll share equipment."*

CURATING DIGITAL HEALTH INFORMATION

People create, store, share, and publish more information than ever before (Jones et al., 2016), and they may need to access and re-use this information in relation to their health condition over a period of months, years, or continually across their lifetime. The process of keeping, managing, and exploiting information as a personal resource is referred to as information curation (Whittaker, 2011). Approaches to information curation are varied, with people adopting a variety of strategies and tools, both technological and non-technological in nature. One tool with a long and distinguished history in the health domain is the diary. Diaries have long been used in relation to health information management, and Mayhew and McArthur (2015) provide a fascinating account of the history of patient diaries from their use in the moribund wards of the Great War to Camp Bastion, the field hospital receiving casualties from the conflict in Afghanistan. In it, they detail how nurses in the First World War recorded all the words and actions of the dying soldiers in their care, passing on the details of those last few hours to family at home. Similarly, soldiers injured in Afghanistan often awake back in the UK confused to be surrounded by family. Diaries kept in the field hospital are transported back to the UK with patients and provide a useful way of filling in missing details for soldiers. Patients in both military and civilian settings are able to review their treatment details and make sense of their experiences by reading clinician and carer notes, and observations and comments by friends and relatives. Such diaries have proved useful for healthcare professionals, their patients, and families across a number of contexts.

Interestingly, a tool designed to be a technological equivalent—the electronic healthcare record, a resource maintained by the patient or to which the patient has access—has suffered from relatively poor uptake. It may be that unlike diaries, electronic healthcare records as yet offer little to patients in terms of sense-making (Faisal, Blandford, & Potts, 2012). Social media, on the other hand, provides numerous opportunities for review and reflection through services such as Facebook's *Timehop* or *Year in Review* features. Recent work investigated how reviewing contributions to social media helps people to make sense of their recent health experiences, and in an interview study with users of online health communities, it was noted that being mindful of all the contributions made to a health group allowed one participant to document her involvement with the community, recall her experiences, and gain perspective on her treatment journey (see Sillence & Bussey, 2017, for study details):

> *"I read [messages on the forum] for quite a while and then sort of started to ask questions and as my learning's improved, I keep a record of all the messages I've posted and I can see to start with I didn't know very much at all and then I can sort of see my learning increase so I'm sort of asking questions now from a different perspective and now I'm really asking questions to get people to think about things as well."*

This finding resonates with the work of Thomas and Briggs (2016), who found that different forms and functions of reminiscence are supported by social media. In a study using the online service *MySocialBook*, they invited participants to curate content from their personal Facebook account to be transformed into a printed book. The book then acted as a prompt to discuss reminiscence in relation to the curated material. The authors noted social media supported both integrative and instrumental reminiscence, allowing participants to review positive experiences as well as reflecting on how past, perhaps more negative, experiences could inform their current coping behaviors. The study also highlighted the role of serendipity in encountering unexpected postings and content and the pleasure that this provided for users.

While focusing on a single health event or reviewing information derived from a single platform provides some indication about the value of information curation, the issues become more complex when considering the large personal health information stores now available. Combining different types of data, for example, activity data with personal experience exchanges and expert medical content, should provide a more integrated picture of one's personal health (Li, Dey, & Forlizzi, 2011), and, as such, allow both reflection and continued monitoring.

For example, in an imaginary scenario, Susan may be experiencing ongoing side-effects from her recent treatment and may decide to exchange messages with people experiencing similar symptoms on a support forum. Additionally, she may read information on a number of different sites provided by a medical expert, digest statistical reports from a published peer-reviewed paper, and monitor and review her own physical state as well as record her mood and her daily experiences of the problem.

This scenario highlights one of the reasons that personal health information management is so difficult, e.g., the large numbers of different data types, each with a different provenance (Garfinkel & Cox, 2009). Jones and colleagues (2016) describe four types of information: (i) information about a person, but under the control of another entity,

(ii) information directed towards a person (email, social media), (iii) information directed outwards from a person (email, blogs, social media profiles), and (iv) information recording or representing a person's activities, experiences, and physical state.

Certainly, information curation can, and should, support people's understanding and sense-making around their illnesses and health conditions, so they can manage them more effectively (Faisal, Blandford, & Potts, 2012). This is particularly relevant in relation to improved communication, shared decision-making, and health monitoring. Towards these ends, a number of researchers have been documenting curation practices and strategies. Sun and Belkin (2015; 2016), for example, have been exploring the information curation strategies of people with diabetes, and Feng and Agosto (2017) have identified problems, e.g., fragmentation of data types around the personal information management of activity data. Others have been exploring ways of integrating and improving technology-based curation tools. Ae Chun and MacKellar (2012), for example, describe a prototype system they developed to link health-related data from across different web communities to integrate information from medical expert content with content written by patients to provide a more linked overview of health information. Other researchers have suggested that improvements to data visualization techniques should consider which elements of health-related lifestyles and experiences could be embedded into a visual representation (Faisal, Blandford, & Potts, 2012), or have advocated better use of metadata in information curation (Whittaker, 2011).

Without effective curation tools, the ongoing accumulation of digital materials is potentially problematic. Managing personal information is not straightforward, and many people lack the time or inclination to engage in any form of systematic approach, citing increasing availability of digital storage (Bergman & Beyth-Marom, 2003). Digital hoarding behaviors—the excessive accumulation of digital materials, are concerning, in part because of their potential to affect everyday functioning (van Bennekom, Blom, Vulink, & Denys, 2015). Finally, all of this curated information has the potential to become a part of an individual's personal legacy. The issue of digital legacy is a growing one, and thinking about how to manage digital health information following the death of the creator is something family and friends will have to consider (alongside digital information in a whole range of contexts). Of course, any discussion of death needs to be handled sensitively, and a literature around "thanosensitive" design considers the appropriate management of data post-mortem (Massimi & Baecker, 2011).

CONCLUSION AND FUTURE DIRECTIONS

Managing our digital health information is an increasingly difficult task and one that challenges researchers and designers to consider how they can best support individuals to effectively use the information to make sense of their health experiences and improve their communication about their health with others. The issue of managing personal digital health information is not new, but the challenges and the data amounts are increasing all the time. Supporting information curation in this domain highlights a number of future research directions. Initially, there is a need to understand not only how people trust one another, but increasingly how they come to trust the technology and the platforms that facilitate information exchange and storage. Secondly, there is a requirement for a strong focus on data integration in support of the "whole person." Huh, Patel, and Pratt (2012) note that many current technological solutions contain disconnects between different types of data, for example, between quantified patient experience (such as symptom logs) and narrative information. Feng and Agosto (2017) refer to a similar concept—that of fragmentation—whereby data collection and recording elements are kept separate and incompatible, limiting any kind of meaningful integration. Linking these different kinds of data would facilitate insights for patients and potentially improve communication with healthcare professionals. West, Giordano, Van Kleek, and Shadbolt (2016) noted a number of different opportunities for the use of self-logged data in relation to diagnosis in clinical decision-making settings, and Bussey and Sillence (2017) have also argued for improving the integration of online health information into discussions with healthcare professionals through better provision of digital curation tools. Providing tools to improve the way patients can search for, select, and curate their own set of relevant health resources has the potential to improve usefulness of the resources available. The tools could expose contradictions in the data, highlight corroboration points and opportunities, and allow easy ways to save and share information relevant to others.

References

Ae Chun, S., & MacKellar, B. (2012, March). Social Health Data Integration Using Semantic Web. In *Proceedings of the 27th Annual ACM Symposium on Applied Computing*. Riva del Garda, Italy (pp. 392–397). New York: ACM.

Angwin, J., & Stecklow, S. (2010, October 12). Scrapers' dig deep for data on web. The *Wall Street Journal*. Retrieved from www.wsj.com/articles/SB10001424052748703358504575544381288117888.

Bansal, G., & Gefen, D. (2010). The impact of personal dispositions on information sensitivity, privacy concern and trust in disclosing health information online. *Decision Support Systems, 49*(2), 138–150.

Barak, A., & Gluck-Ofri, O. (2007). Degree and reciprocity of self-disclosure in online forums. *CyberPsychology & Behavior, 10*(3), 407–417.

Bateman, P. J., Gray, P. H., & Butler, B. S. (2011). Research note—the impact of community commitment on participation in online communities. *Information Systems Research, 22*(4), 841–854.

Baumer, E. P., Adams, P., Khovanskaya, V. D., Liao, T. C., Smith, M. E., Schwanda Sosik, V., & Williams, K. (2013, April). Limiting, leaving, and (re)lapsing: An exploration of Facebook non-use practices and experiences. In *Proceedings of the SIGCHI Conference on Human Factors in Computing Systems*. Paris, France (pp. 3257–3266). New York: ACM.

Bergman, O., & Beyth-Marom, R. (2003). The user-subjective approach to personal information management systems. *Journal of the American Society for Information Science and Technology, 54*(9), 872–878.

boyd, d. (2008). Taken out of context: American teen sociality in networked publics (Doctoral dissertation). University of California, Berkeley.

boyd, d. m., & Ellison, N. B. (2007). Social network sites: Definition, history, and scholarship. *Journal of Computer-Mediated Communication, 13,* 210–230.

Brindal, E., Freyne, J., Saunders, I., Berkovsky, S., Smith, G., & Noakes, M. (2012). Features predicting weight loss in overweight or obese participants in a web-based intervention: Randomized trial. *Journal of Medical Internet Research, 14*(6), e173.

Briones, R., Nan, X., Madden, K., & Waks, L. (2012). When vaccines go viral: An analysis of HPV vaccine coverage on YouTube. *Health Communication, 27*(5), 478–485.

Bussey, L., & Sillence, E. (2017). (How) do people negotiate online information into their decision making with healthcare professionals? In *Proceedings of the 2017 International Conference on Digital Health.* London, UK (pp. 1–5). New York: ACM.

Chou, W. S., Liu, B., Post, S. & Hesse, B. (2011). Health-related internet use among cancer survivors: Data from the Health Information National Trends Survey, 2003–2008. *Journal of Cancer Survivorship, 5*(3), 263–270.

Clawson, J., Pater, J. A., Miller, A. D., Mynatt, E. D., & Mamykina, L. (2015, September). No longer wearing: Investigating the abandonment of personal health-tracking technologies on Craigslist. In *Proceedings of the 2015 ACM International Joint Conference on Pervasive and Ubiquitous Computing.* Osaka, Japan (pp. 647–658). New York: ACM.

Coulson, N. S. (2005). Receiving social support online: An analysis of a computer-mediated support group for individuals living with irritable bowel syndrome. *CyberPsychology & Behavior, 8*(6), 580–584.

Coulter, A., & Collins, A. (2011). Making shared decision-making a reality: No decision about me, without me. London, UK: The King's Fund.

Culotta, A. (2010, July). Towards Detecting Influenza Epidemics by Analyzing Twitter Messages. In P. Melville, J. Leskovec, & F. Provost (Chairs), *Proceedings of the First Workshop on Social Media Analytics.* The 16th ACM SIGKDD International Conference on Knowledge Discovery and Data Mining. Washington, DC (pp. 115–122). New York: ACM.

Cutrona, S. L., Mazor, K. M., Vieux, S. N., Luger, T. M., Volkman, J. E., & Finney Rutten, L. J. (2015). Health information-seeking on behalf of others: Characteristics of "surrogate seekers." *Journal of Cancer Education, 30*(1), 12–19.

Deighton-Smith, N., & Bell, B. T. (2017). Objectifying fitness: a content and thematic analysis of #fitspiration images on social media. *Psychology of Popular Media Culture.* Advance online publication. http://dx.doi.org/10.1037/ppm0000143.

Eschler, J., Dehlawi, Z., & Pratt, W. (2015). Self-characterized illness phase and information needs of participants in an online cancer forum. In D. Quercia & B. Hogan (Eds.), *Proceedings of the 9th International Conference on Web and Social Media, ICWSM 2015* (pp. 101–109). Palo Alto, CA: AAAI Press.

Faisal, S., Blandford, A., & Potts, H. W. (2012). Making sense of personal health information: challenges for information visualization. *Health Informatics Journal, 19*(3), 198–217.

Fan, H., Lederman, R., Smith, S. P., & Chang, S. (2014). How trust is formed in online health communities: a process perspective. *Communications of the Association for Information Systems, 34*(1), Article 28. Available at: http://aisel.aisnet.org/cais/vol34/iss1/28.

Feng, Y., & Agosto, D. E. (2017). A survey on management of personal health information from activity trackers. Paper presented at the iConference 2017 Proceedings (pp. 370–377), Wuhan, China. https://doi.org/10.9776/17208

Fox, S. (2011). The social life of health information. Retrieved from Pew Research Center, Internet & American Life Project website: http://pewinternet.org/~/media/Files/Reports/2011/PIP_Social_Life_of_Health_Info.pdf.

Fox, S., Duggan, M., & Purcell, K. (2013). Family caregivers are wired for health. Pew Internet Report http://www.pewinternet.org/2013/06/20/family-caregivers-are-wired-for-health/.

France, E. F., Wyke, S., Ziebland, S., Entwistle, V. A., & Hunt, K. (2011). How personal experiences feature in women's accounts of use of information for decisions about antenatal diagnostic testing for foetal abnormality. *Social Science and Medicine*, *72*, 755–762.

Frost, J., Vermeulen, I. E., & Beekers, N. (2014). Anonymity versus privacy: Selective information sharing in online cancer communities. *Journal of Medical Internet Research*, *16*(5), e126.

Garfinkel, S. & Cox, D. (2009, February). Finding and archiving the Internet footprint. Invited paper presented at the *First Digital Lives Research Conference: Personal Digital Archives for the 21st Century*, London, UK.

Goffman, E. (1959). *The presentation of self in everyday life*. New York: Anchor Books.

Harris, P. R., Sillence, E., & Briggs, P. (2011). Perceived threat and corroboration: key factors that improve a predictive model of trust in Internet-based health information and advice. *Journal of Medical Internet Research*, *13*(3), e51.

Hinton, L., Kurinczuk, J. J., & Ziebland, S. (2010). Infertility, isolation and the Internet: A qualitative interview study. *Patient Education and Counseling*, *81*(3), 436–441.

Hughes, N., Locock, L., & Ziebland, S. (2013). Personal identity and the role of "carer" among relatives and friends of people with multiple sclerosis. *Social Science and & Medicine*, *96*, 78–85.

Huh, J., Liu, L. S., Neogi, T., Inkpen, K., & Pratt, W. (2014). Health vlogs as social support for chronic illness management. *ACM Transactions on Computer-Human Interaction (TOCHI)*, *21*(4), 23.

Huh, J., Patel, R., & Pratt, W. (2012, May). Tackling dilemmas in supporting "the whole person" in online patient communities. In *Proceedings of the Conference on Human Factors in Computing Systems*. Austin, Texas. (pp. 923–926). New York: ACM.

Jones, W., Bellotti, V., Capra, R., Dinneen, J. D., Mark, G., Marshall, C., Moffatt, K.,...Van Kleek, M. (2016, May). For richer, for poorer, in sickness or in health: The long-term management of personal information. In *Proceedings of the CHI Conference Extended Abstracts on Human Factors in Computing Systems*. San Jose, California (pp. 3508–3515). New York: ACM.

Kerrigan, F., & Hart, A. (2016). Theorising digital personhood: A dramaturgical approach. *Journal of Marketing Management*, *32*(17–18), 1701–1721.

Kim, Y. (2016). Trust in health information websites: A systematic literature review on the antecedents of trust. *Health Informatics Journal*, *22*(2), 355–369.

Kordzadeh, N., & Warren, J. (2014, January). Communicating personal health information in virtual health communities: A theoretical framework. In *System Sciences (HICSS)*, *Hawaii International Conference of System Sciences*. The Big Island, HI: (pp. 636–645). Piscataway, NJ: IEEE.

Lankton, N. K., & McKnight, D. H. (2008, August). Do people trust Facebook as a technology or as a "person"? Distinguishing technology trust from interpersonal trust. In *Proceedings of Americas Conference on Information Systems*, *375*. Available from http://aisel.aisnet.org/amcis2008/375.

Ledger, D., & McCaffrey, D. (2014). Inside wearables: How the science of human behavior change offers the secret to long-term engagement. *Endeavour Partners, LLC*, *93*(1), 36–45.

Li, J. (2015). A privacy preservation model for health-related social networking sites. *Journal of Medical Internet Research, 17*(7), e168.

Li, I., Dey, A. K., & Forlizzi, J. (2011, September). Understanding my data, myself: Supporting self-reflection with Ubicomp technologies. In *Proceedings of the 13th International Conference on Ubiquitous Computing.* Beijing, China (pp. 405–414). New York: ACM.

Locock, L. & Brown, J. B. (2010). "All in the same boat?" Patient and carer attitudes to peer support and social comparison in motor neurone disease (MND). *Social Science and Medicine, 71*(8), 1498–1505.

Manikonda, L., & De Choudhury, M. (2017, May). Modeling and understanding visual attributes of mental health disclosures in social media. In *Proceedings of the 2017 CHI Conference on Human Factors in Computing Systems.* Denver, Colorado. (pp. 170–181). New York: ACM.

Massimi, M., & Baecker, R. (2011, May). Dealing with death in design: Developing systems for the bereaved. *Proceedings of the International Conference on Human Computer Interaction.* Vancouver, Canada. (pp. 1001–1010). New York: ACM.

Massimi, M., Bender, J. L., Witteman, H. O., & Ahmed, O. H. (2014, February). Life transitions and online health communities: Reflecting on adoption, use, and disengagement. In *Proceedings of the 17th ACM Conference on Computer Supported Cooperative Work & Social Computing.* Baltimore, Maryland (pp. 1491–1501). New York: ACM.

Mayhew, E., & McArthur, D. (2015). "A special book kept for the purpose." Writing patient diaries: A century of skill in the silence, from the Great War to Afghanistan and beyond. *Intima: A Journal of Narrative Medicine,* October 2015. Available from: http://www.theintima.org/s/A-Special-Book-Kept-for-the-Purpose.doc.

Mazanderani, F., Hughes, N., Hardy, C., Sillence, E., & Powell, J. (2019). Health information work and the enactment of care in couples and families affected by multiple sclerosis.

Mazanderani, F., O'Neill, B., & Powell, J. (2013). "People power" or "pester power"? YouTube as a forum for the generation of evidence and patient advocacy. *Patient Education and Counseling, 93*(3), 420–425.

McNeill, A., Harris, P. R., & Briggs, P. (2016). Twitter influence on UK vaccination and antiviral uptake during the 2009 H1N1 pandemic. *Frontiers in Public Health, 4*(26). doi: 10.3389/fpubh.2016.00026.

McNeill, A., & Sillence, E. (2018). Motivations and stake management in producing YouTube "Bro-science" videos for baldness treatment. *International Journal of Web Communities, 14*(2), 97–113.

Meade, O., Buchanan, H., & Coulson, N. (2017). The use of an online support group for neuromuscular disorders: A thematic analysis of message postings. *Disability and Rehabilitation,* pp. 1–11. https://doi.org/10.1080/09638288.2017.1334239.

Mo, P. K. H., & Coulson, N. S. (2008). Exploring the communication of social support within virtual communities: A content analysis of messages posted to an online HIV/AIDS support group. *Cyberpsychology & Behavior, 11*(3), 371–374.

Newman, M. W., Lauterbach, D., Munson, S. A., Resnick, P., & Morris, M. E. (2011, March). It's not that I don't have problems, I'm just not putting them on Facebook: Challenges and opportunities in using online social networks for health. In *Proceedings of the ACM 2011 Conference on Computer Supported Cooperative Work.* Hangzhou, China (pp. 341–350). New York: ACM.

Nimrod, G. (2013). Challenging the Internet paradox: Online depression communities and well-being. *International Journal of Internet Science, 8*(1), 30–48.

O'Neill, B., Ziebland, S., Valderas, J., & Lupiáñez-Villanueva, F. (2014). User-generated online health content: A survey of Internet users in the United Kingdom. *Journal of Medical Internet Research*, 16(4), e118, *Sociology of Health and Illness*, 41(2), 395–410.

Pater, J. A., Haimson, O. L., Andalibi, N., & Mynatt, E. D. (2016, February). "Hunger hurts but starving works": Characterizing the presentation of eating disorders online. In *Proceedings of the 19th ACM Conference on Computer-Supported Cooperative Work & Social Computing*. San Francisco, California (pp. 1185–1200). New York: ACM.

Pennebaker, J. W. (1997). Writing about emotional experiences as a therapeutic process. *Psychological Science*, 8(3), 162–166.

Ritterman, J., Osborne, M., & Klein, E. (2009, November). Using prediction markets and Twitter to predict a swine flu pandemic. In *Proceedings of the First International Workshop on Mining Social Media*. Seville, Spain. (pp. 9–17). Madrid: Bubok Publishing.

Rodgers, S., & Chen, Q. (2005). Internet community group participation: Psychosocial benefits for women with breast cancer. *Journal of Computer-Mediated Communication*, 10(4). doi: 10.1111/j.1083-6101.2005.tb00268.x

Rozmovits, L. & Ziebland, S. (2004). What do patients with prostate or breast cancer want from an Internet site? A qualitative study of information needs. *Patient Education and Counseling*, 53, 57–64.

Sbaffi, L., & Rowley, J. (2017). Trust and credibility in web-based health information: A review and agenda for future research. *Journal of Medical Internet Research*, 19(6), e218.

Shaffer, V. A., & Zikmund-Fisher, B. J. (2013). All stories are not alike: A purpose-, content-, and valence-based taxonomy of patient narratives in decision aids. *Medical Decision Making*, 33, 4–13.

Shih, P. C., Han, K., Poole, E. S., Rosson, M. B., & Carroll, J. M. (2015, March). Use and adoption challenges of wearable activity trackers. In iConference Proceedings. Newport Beach, CA. Available from https://www.ideals.illinois.edu/bitstream/handle/2142/73649/164_ready.pdf?sequence=2&isAllowed=y.

Sillence, E. (2010). Seeking out very like-minded others: Exploring trust and advice issues in an online health support group. *International Journal of Web Based Communities*, 6(4), 376–394.

Sillence, E. (2016). Sharing personal experiences and offering advice within online health-based social networks. In G. Riva, B. K. Wiederhold, & P. Cipresso (Eds.), *The Psychology of Social Networking Personal Experience in Online Communities* (Vol. 2), (pp. 104–116). Boston, MA: De Gruyter Open.

Sillence, E., Briggs, P., Harris, P. R., & Fishwick, L. (2007). How do patients evaluate and make use of online health information? *Social Science & Medicine*, 64(9), 1853–1862.

Sillence, E., & Bussey, L. (2017). Changing hospitals, choosing chemotherapy and deciding you've made the right choice: Understanding the role of online support groups in different health decision-making activities. *Patient Education and Counseling*, 100(5), 994–999.

Sillence, E., & Cooper, K. (2016). Evaluating peer-to-peer online resources for carers of people with Alzheimer's disease. Internal report for the Alzheimer's Society.

Sillence, E., Hardy, C., & Briggs, P. (2013, May). Why don't we trust health websites that help us help each other? An analysis of online peer-to-peer healthcare. In *Proceedings of the 5th Annual ACM Web Science Conference*. Paris, France (pp. 396–404). New York: ACM.

Sillence, E., Hardy, C., Briggs, P., & Harris, P. R. (2016). How do carers of people with multiple sclerosis engage with websites containing the personal experiences of other carers and patients? *Health Informatics Journal*, 22(4), 1045–1054.

Sillence, E., Hardy, C., Harris, P. R., & Briggs, P. (2014, April). Modeling patient engagement in peer-to-peer healthcare. In *Proceedings of the 23rd International Conference on World Wide Web*. Seoul, Republic of Korea (pp. 481–486). New York: ACM.

Song, H., Nam, Y., Gould, J., Sanders, W. S., McLaughlin, M., Fulk, J., ... Ruccione, K. S. (2012). Cancer survivor identity shared in a social media intervention. *Journal of Pediatric Oncology Nursing, 29*(2), 80–91.

Stutzman, F., Gross, R., & Acquisti, A. (2013). Silent listeners: The evolution of privacy and disclosure on Facebook. *Journal of Privacy and Confidentiality, 4*(2), 7–41.

Sun, S., & Belkin, N. J. (2015). Managing personal health information in the home: Strategies of diabetes patients in the US and China. *Proceedings of the Association for Information Science and Technology, 52*(1), 1–4.

Sun, S., & Belkin, N. J. (2016). Managing personal information over the long term, or not? Experiences by Type 1 diabetes patients. *Proceedings of the Association for Information Science and Technology, 53*(1), 1–10.

Thomas, L., & Briggs, P. (2016). Reminiscence through the lens of social media. *Frontiers in Psychology, 7*, 870.

Tian, Y. (2010). Organ donation on Web 2.0: Content and audience analysis of organ donation videos on YouTube. *Health Communication, 25*(3), 238–246.

Van Der Velden, M., & El Emam, K. (2013). "Not all my friends need to know": A qualitative study of teenage patients, privacy, and social media. *Journal of the American Medical Informatics, 20*(1), 16–24.

van Bennekom, M. J., Blom, R. M., Vulink, N., & Denys, D. (2015). A case of digital hoarding. *BMJ Case Reports*. Published online October 8, 2015. doi: 10.1136/bcr-2015-210814.

Van Mierlo, T., Voci, S., Lee, S., Fournier, R., & Selby, P. (2012). Superusers in social networks for smoking cessation: Analysis of demographic characteristics and posting behavior from the Canadian Cancer Society's smokers' helpline online and StopSmokingCenter.net. *Journal of Medical Internet Research, 14*(3), e66. doi: 10.2196/jmir.1854.

Wang, Y.-C., Kraut, R. E., & Levine, J. M. (2015). Eliciting and receiving online support: Using computer-aided content analysis to examine the dynamics of online social support. *Journal of Medical Internet Research, 17*(4), e99.

West, P., Giordano, R., Van Kleek, M., & Shadbolt, N. (2016, May). The quantified patient in the doctor's office: Challenges and opportunities. In *Proceedings of the Conference on Human Factors in Computing Systems*. San Jose, California (pp. 3066–3078). New York: ACM.

Whittaker, S. (2011). Personal information management: From information consumption to curation. *Annual Review of Information Science and Technology, 45*(1), 1–62.

Wicks, P., Massagli, M., Frost, J., Brownstein, C., Okun, S., Vaughan, T., ... Heywood, J. (2010). Sharing health data for better outcomes on PatientsLikeMe. *Journal of Medical Internet Research, 12*(2), e19.

Wotanis, L., & McMillan, L. (2014). Performing gender on YouTube: How Jenna Marbles negotiates a hostile online environment. *Feminist Media Studies, 14*(6), 912–928.

Yang, D., Yao, Z., & Kraut, R. E. (2017, May). Self-disclosure and channel difference in online health support groups. In *Proceedings of the International Conference on Web and Social Media*. Montreal, Canada (pp. 704–707). Palo Alto, CA: AAAI Press.

Zhang, Y., He, D., & Sang, Y. (2013). Facebook as a platform for health information and communication: A case study of a diabetes group. *Journal of Medical Systems, 37*(3), 1–12.

Ziebland, S., & Wyke, S. (2012). Health and illness in a connected world: How might sharing experiences on the Internet affect people's health? *The Milbank Quarterly, 90*(2), 219–249.

CHAPTER 23

A PSYCHOLOGICAL OVERVIEW OF GAMING DISORDER

DARIA J. KUSS, HALLEY PONTES,
ORSOLYA KIRÁLY, AND ZSOLT DEMETROVICS

INTRODUCTION

OVER the last decade, the availability of different games has increased rapidly, which coincides with the expeditious development of the gaming industry. The Entertainment Software Association (ESA) quotes its CEO Michael Gallagher as saying "[v]ideo games are the future. From education and business, to art and entertainment, our industry brings together the most innovative and creative minds to create the most engaging, immersive and breathtaking experiences we've ever seen. The brilliant developers, designers and creators behind our games have and will continue to push the envelope, driving unprecedented leaps in technology impacting everyday life for years to come" (ESA, 2015, p. 1). The figures speak for themselves: approximately 63 percent of American households have at least one person who plays video games regularly, i.e., for a minimum of three hours a week, with the average gamer being 35 years old. Video games are most frequently played on personal computers (56%), game consoles (53%), and smartphones (36%). The best-selling computer games in 2015 were strategy (36.4%), casual (25.8%), and role-playing games (18.7%). In 2015, players spent a staggering $23.5 billion on gaming (ESA, 2015), which is more than double the US box office revenue in the same year ($11 billion) (McClintock, 2015).

The appeal of games and a computer-mediated reality can probably best be captured by a quote from the fictional character Cypher from the popular blockbuster *The Matrix* (1999), an alternative reality which has been created by machines to exert control over humans, while their energy is being harvested as a source of power. As he is eating a steak in this simulated reality, Cypher states he thinks the Matrix is more real than his world. He knows the steak does not exist, although his brain is led to believe the steak is juicy and delicious. Cypher says that ignorance is bliss, and that he is tired of the same old things happening every day. Games allow players to step out of their often boring and repetitive everyday lives, allowing them to gain a reputation and become recognized by their gaming community, without having to face the hassles of daily life. Kuss (2013a) outlined this concept in the context of playing *World of Warcraft* and how gameplay in this popular game reflects our participation in popular media culture.

Massively Multiplayer Online Role-Playing Games (MMORPGs), for instance, are games that can be played by thousands or millions of players in great online universes (Massively Multiplayer) over the Internet, with no space or time constraints (Online), and allow players to create online alter egos, their in-game avatars (Role-Playing), which allow them to interact with their fellow gamers and develop their virtual selves (Kuss, Louws, & Wiers, 2012). One of the most popular MMORPGs is Blizzard's *World of Warcraft*, which takes place in the fictional universe of Azeroth, where members of the Horde and the Alliance battle against one another (Kuss, 2013a). *World of Warcraft*'s most recent extension, *Legion*, sold 3.3 million copies on day one alone (McKeand, 2016), allowing the game to boast a total of over ten million subscribers worldwide (Hruska, 2016). The appeal of the game rests in its ability to be very versatile and to tailor to different ages, both genders, and different player motivations and interests (Kuss, 2013b). Gamers enjoy the never-ending gaming opportunities MMORPGs offer, as these games are endless. Once the gamers reach the highest levels in the games, high-end game content is unlocked that enables gamers to participate in large-scale raids, where their gaming groups (or guilds) battle monsters together in complex gaming instances (or dungeons); these require intricate planning and coordination among the group members, and may take many hours to complete (Ducheneaut, Yee, Nickell, & Moore, 2007). Guilds offer social networks for gamers joined by their shared interest: gaming. In addition to this, the social aspect of gaming is a crucial motivator for play as players are encouraged to interact and communicate with one another via various in-game channels (including various messaging functions, chat opportunities, and collaborative quests), often leading to the development of friendships and relationships which may extend beyond the virtual realm (Kuss, 2013a).

Given that online games such as MMORPGs appeal to a broad audience that will spend large amounts of time engaging with these games, it may not come as a surprise that small numbers of highly engaged gamers may develop problems as a consequence of their excessive gaming patterns, which may be tied to particular gaming motivations (Kuss et al., 2012; Pontes, Király, Demetrovics, & Griffiths, 2014; Rho et al., 2016). Assessing nearly 700 primarily male MMORPGs players in their early twenties to early thirties, it was found that the gaming motivations achievement, socializing, and escapism predicted addictive gaming patterns (Zanetta Dauriat et al., 2011). Additional evidence for the interrelation between gaming motivations and addictive gaming comes from a study (Kuss et al., 2012) using nearly 200 MMORPG players in the Netherlands (primarily male, in their late teens to late twenties), suggesting that the motivations escapism, and gaming mechanics were significantly more important predictors of addictive gaming than time spent gaming, which taken together explained nearly 50 percent of the variance in addiction scores using self-reported validated psychometric measures in this study. This finding is important as it indicates that high amounts of time spent gaming by itself cannot account for the development of addiction-related problems (Demetrovics & Király, 2016; Király, Tóth, Urbán, Demetrovics, & Maraz, 2017). It also converges with empirical studies reporting that excessive amounts of time do not necessarily translate into addictive usage (Pontes, Szabo, & Griffiths, 2015; Pontes, Caplan, & Griffiths, 2016).

CURRENT APPROACHES TO CLINICAL AND PSYCHOMETRIC ASSESSMENT

The clinical and psychometric assessment of Gaming Disorder (GD) remains a key area within the field of gaming studies needing further research. A unified assessment approach to GD is needed as substantial differences related to classification within the context of assessment can further generate confusion and render information on the prevalence rates, clinical course, treatment, and biomarkers implicated with GD inconclusive (Kuss, 2013b; Petry & O'Brien, 2013).

Traditionally, researchers investigating GD do not agree on how to approach its assessment in a valid and reliable way that would allow findings across studies to be robustly compared (Griffiths, Király, Pontes, & Demetrovics, 2015; Pontes & Griffiths, 2015b, 2017). This problem was well detailed in a study that reviewed a total of 63 quantitative empirical studies on GD involving 58,415 participants and a set of 18 distinct psychometric assessment tools (King, Haagsma, Delfabbro, Gradisar, & Griffiths, 2013). Accordingly, King et al. (2013) reported a number of problems among the most commonly utilized instruments to assess GD, such as: (i) inconsistency of core addiction indicators between studies, (ii) lack of temporal dimension in the instruments, (iii) inconsistent cut-off scores to determine GD, (iv) insufficient or lack of interrater reliability and predictive validity, and (v) inconsistent and/or untested factor structure. Furthermore, questions regarding the suitability of certain tools for specific settings also emerged, as those used in clinical practice milieus may require a different emphasis than those utilized in epidemiological, experimental, or neurobiological research settings (Griffiths et al., 2015; King et al., 2013; Koronczai et al., 2011). In fact, when the American Psychiatric Association (APA) reviewed the evidence on Internet Gaming Disorder (IGD), the Substance Use Disorder Work-Group (SUD) found that no standard diagnostic criteria were applied consistently across most studies reviewed (Petry & O'Brien, 2013). Furthermore, researchers investigating GD have relied on questionable psychometric tests and criteria that mirrored those from substance use disorder, pathological gambling, a combination of both disorders, and/or other entirely different sets of unstandardized criteria (e.g., time spent playing video games).

In light of the identified heterogeneity issues between most instruments devised for assessing GD and the criticisms previously made, several scholars have called for unification in the assessment of GD following the publication of the nine IGD criteria by the APA (Griffiths, King, & Demetrovics, 2014; King et al., 2013; Petry & O'Brien, 2013; Petry et al., 2014; Pontes, 2016; Pontes & Griffiths, 2014a). They call for commonly agreed-upon assessment criteria or a standardized instrument derived from the need to enhance validity and reliability across GD studies, which in turn may help to advocate appropriate and efficacious prevention and treatments for GD. In this context, Pontes and Griffiths (2014a) contended that the unification in the assessment of GD is equally important if the phenomenon is to be fully recognized by official medical bodies as a bona fide addiction.

The adoption of new assessment tools that adequately reflect the official conceptualization developed by the DSM-5 (American Psychiatric Association, 2013) and the adoption of a standardized and consensual nomenclature (i.e., IGD or GD) should be taken into account by researchers and clinicians researching in this area, as the use of outdated nomenclatures may be stigmatizing to patients struggling with IGD (Kuss, 2013b; Kuss & Griffiths, 2015). Since the publication of the nine IGD criteria in the DSM-5, a total of seven clinical psychometric tools assessing IGD have been developed (Pontes, 2016). Table 1 outlines the most recent tools for assessing IGD.

Based on the assessment issues outlined, and the information presented in Table 1, it is clear that unification in the assessment of IGD is still to be achieved, as several tools for the same construct (i.e., IGD) are still being developed, rendering unification in the assessment a rather far-fetched idea. Additionally, there is a general lack of cross-cultural and clinical validation studies supporting the utility of these assessment tools in other equally important contexts. The cross-cultural evidence in the assessment of IGD in relation to existing tools remains insufficient. More specifically, only the IGD-20 Test, the IGDS9-SF, and the IGDT-10 have been investigated extensively in different cultural settings (e.g., Király, et al., 2017; Pontes, Stavropoulos, & Griffiths, 2017; Stavropoulos et al., 2017), and these tools have been translated and psychometrically validated in a number of countries and languages as presented in Table 1. Emphasizing the importance of the cross-cultural evidence in assessment is a key area of research as "establishing the psychometric properties of instruments assessing these nine [IGD] criteria should begin using a cross-cultural perspective" (Petry et al., 2014, p. 6). It is vital to note, however, that the vast majority of the assessment tools (with the exception of the C-VAT 2.0, see Van Rooij et al., 2015) have not been validated in clinical samples, and that only a clinical interview led by a professional can provide a clear-cut indication of whether or not a full-blown psychopathology is evident which requires treatment (Kuss & Griffiths, 2015; Maraz et al., 2015). Therefore, more research aimed at understanding the context of IGD in both clinical and large representative samples is necessary so a better evidence-based understanding of this disorder and its assessment can be generated.

Several studies and debates (e.g., Griffiths et al., 2015; Griffiths et al., 2016; King et al., 2013; Király, Griffiths, & Demetrovics, 2015; Kuss et al., 2017; Pontes & Griffiths, 2014a; Pontes, Kuss, & Griffiths, 2017) have noted how the use of inconsistent heterogeneous

Table 1 Summary of psychometric and assessment tools for Internet Gaming Disorder (IGD)

Tool	Author	Items	Diagnostic Time-frame	Cutoff	Clinical validity	Cross-cultural validity
IGD-20 Test	Pontes, Király, Demetrovics, & Griffiths (2014)	20	12 months	≥ 71 points	No	**Spanish** (Fuster, Carbonell, Pontes, & Griffiths, 2016) **Arabic** (Hawi & Samaha, 2017)
IGDS9-SF	Pontes & Griffiths (2015a)	9	12 months	≥ 5 criteria	No	**Slovenian** (Pontes, Macur, & Griffiths, 2016b, 2016b) **Portuguese** (Pontes & Griffiths, 2016) **Italian** (Monacis, De Palo, Griffiths, & Sinatra, 2016) **Persian** Wu et al. (2017)
IGDS	Lemmens, Valkenburg, & Gentile (2015)	27	12 months	Not Reported	No	No
IGDS (Short Scales)		9	12 months	≥ 5 criteria	No	No
IGDT-10	Király, Sleczka, et al. (2017)	10	12 months	≥ 5 criteria	No	**Hungarian, Iranian, Norwegian, Czech, Peruvian, French** and **English** (Király, Bőthe, et al., 2017)
C-VAT 2.0	Van Rooij, Schoenmakers, & van de Mheen (2015)	14	12 months	≥ 5 criteria	Yes	No
PIE-9	Pearcy, Roberts, & McEvoy (2016)	9	12 months	≥ 5 criteria	No	No

IGD-20 Test: Internet Gaming Disorder Test; **IGDS9-SF**: Internet Gaming Disorder Scale–Short-Form; **IGDS**: The Internet Gaming Disorder Scale; **IGDT-10**: The Ten-Item Internet Gaming Disorder Test; **C-VAT 2.0**: Clinical Assessment Tool; **PIE-9**: The Personal Internet Gaming Disorder Evaluation.

and non-consensual nomenclatures to describe what appears to be the same phenomenon (i.e., IGD) has influenced the development of a varied number of definitions and frameworks for understanding and assessing IGD inconsistently. Despite being important at some point, these definitions and frameworks largely inspired the development of several psychometric tools assessing IGD, irrespective of their viability (Pontes & Griffiths, 2014a). Moreover, some of the conceptual issues found in the literature regarding the assessment of IGD are important because—as argued by Shaffer, Hall, and Vander Bilt (2000)—without conceptual clarity and empirical support for treatment efficacy, it is also premature to offer efficacious clinical guidelines for the treatment of IGD.

Overall, when assessing the legitimacy of IGD instruments, clinical validation is severely lacking and, therefore, this omission should be fully addressed by future research. In order to overcome some of the problems found across most psychometric instruments used to assess IGD, Koronczai and colleagues (2011) suggested that the measurement instrument should meet six key criteria: (i) comprehensiveness (i.e., examining many and possibly all aspects of IGD), (ii) brevity, so that the tool can be utilized for impulsive individuals and fit time-limited research, (iii) reliability and validity for different data collection techniques, (iv) reliability and validity across different age groups, (v) cross-cultural reliability and validity, and (vi) validation on clinical samples for ascertaining more precise cut-off points based on clinical data.

CONTROVERSIES

The research field of "video gaming addiction" has had its controversies from the very beginning. The inclusion of IGD in Section 3 of the Diagnostic and Statistical Manual of Mental Disorders, 5th edition (DSM-5; American Psychiatric Association, 2013) has further intensified this debate among scholars in multiple areas (Griffiths et al., 2016). Some of the key issues surrounding these controversies relate to (i) whether the IGD definition and criteria proposed in the DSM-5 are appropriate, (ii) what term should be assigned to the disorder, (iii) whether addiction is the best theoretical framework for this problematic behavior, and (iv) whether the acceptance of GD as a formal disorder is timely or not.

The inclusion of IGD in the DSM-5 has been largely decided by the DSM-5 SUD work group (Petry et al., 2014). The nine IGD criteria were chosen and phrased in a way to resemble the substance use and pathological gambling criteria, and were derived in large part from an earlier study by Tao and colleagues (2010) that examined Internet addiction (IA) in a clinical sample in China. In turn, the IA criteria in the Chinese study were based on the authors' clinical experience as well as several previous IA studies. The nine IGD criteria as proposed in the DSM-5 are: (i) preoccupation with video games, (ii) withdrawal symptoms when video gaming is taken away, (iii) tolerance, i.e., spending increasing amounts of time playing video games, (iv) unsuccessful attempts to control participation in video games, (v) loss of interest in previous hobbies and/or entertainment as a result of, and with the exception of, video games, (vi) continued excessive use of video games despite being aware of psychosocial problems, (vii) deception of family members, friends, therapists, or others regarding the amount of gaming, (viii) use of video games to escape or relieve negative feelings, and (ix) jeopardizing or losing a significant relationship, job, or educational or career opportunity because of gaming (American Psychiatric Association, 2013). Among these, the most controversial criteria are arguably withdrawal symptoms (ii), tolerance (iii), preoccupation (i), deception (vii), and escape (viii) (for a thorough review of all the criticisms related to the nine IGD criteria, see Griffiths et al., 2016).

Withdrawal symptoms and tolerance are by far the most debated criteria related to IGD (e.g., Kaptsis, King, Delfabbro, & Gradisar, 2016; King & Delfabbro, 2016). In the case of problematic behaviors (e.g., gaming and gambling), there is no ingestion of any psychoactive substance that is related to physical withdrawal symptoms and tolerance as in the case of substance use disorders. Instead, it refers to what the body produces neurochemically through engaging excessively in the behavior, and therefore the suitability and relevance of these criteria in the case of IGD are questioned (Griffiths et al., 2016). Furthermore, Starcevic (2016) argued that recent definitions of addiction (e.g., American Society of Addiction Medicine, 2011) often do not include withdrawal symptoms and tolerance because these do not always occur in addiction. Similarly, the DSM-5 clearly states that "(n)either tolerance nor withdrawal is necessary for a diagnosis of a substance use disorder." (American Psychiatric Association, 2013, p. 484). Nevertheless, both behavioral addictions (gambling disorder and IGD) include tolerance and withdrawal symptoms among their diagnostic criteria (American Psychiatric Association, 2013), stirring further scholarly debates (Kuss et al., 2017). In addition, tolerance is portrayed in the DSM-5 as the "need to spend increasing amounts of time engaged in Internet games" (American Psychiatric Association, 2013, p. 795). However, increased amounts of time spent with an activity does not necessarily reflect tolerance, as it may be better explained by other reasons that are unproblematic (Billieux, Schimmenti, Khazaal, Maurage, & Heeren, 2015).

Regarding withdrawal symptoms, the importance of the time period has also been emphasized (Griffiths et al., 2016). More specifically, negative feelings related to the sudden interruption of the behavior by an external force (e.g., gaming is stopped by an angry parent) should not be seen as withdrawal symptoms. Similarly, emotions felt days or weeks after the activity has ceased should be considered craving, and not withdrawal symptoms. Genuine withdrawal symptoms should be defined as the unpleasant symptoms experienced a few hours and/or days after a person has stopped playing video games (Griffiths et al., 2016). Consequently, it can be argued that a more precise definition and wording of withdrawal is necessary.

Given that video gaming is a popular leisure time activity, thinking or playing video games excessively (*preoccupation*) may be indicative of high commitment rather than a problematic behavior (Kardefelt-Winther, 2014b). Besides, King and Delfabbro (2014) pointed out that the adaptability of such thoughts is much more important than their frequency, therefore simply assessing the volume of gaming-related thoughts may be misleading. Deception is also a fairly debated criterion because it is highly dependent on players' circumstances, for instance, the personal relationships of the gamer and who he/she lives with (Király, Griffiths, & Demetrovics, 2015). Moreover, if the gamer is a minor, the need for deception may depend to a large extent on their parents' judgment and attitude toward gaming as a hobby (Kardefelt-Winther, 2014b). Finally, playing to escape real-life problems or relieve negative emotions also stirred some debate between scholars. Empirical research suggests that, although escape as a motive for playing video games has been systematically found to be correlated to and predict GD (e.g., Király, Urbán, et al., 2015; Kuss et al., 2012), it is only predictive of GD if the person has low psychosocial well-being (Kardefelt-Winther, 2014c). Therefore, it is likely that many healthy gamers also play video games to escape everyday inconveniences (Griffiths et al., 2016).

Besides the aforementioned controversies related to specific IGD criteria, both the nomenclature and content of IGD are also highly debated. The DSM-5 states that *Internet use disorder, Internet addiction,* or *gaming addiction* are also terms for the same construct ("Internet Gaming Disorder [also commonly referred to as Internet use disorder, Internet addiction, or gaming addiction]) (American Psychiatric Association, 2013, p. 796). As previously argued (Pontes & Griffiths, 2014a), the DSM-5 blends GD with IA, which is highly problematic as it further increases confusion in the field. Empirical studies and theoretical work in the field argued that IA and GD are different nosological entities (Király et al., 2014; Pontes & Griffiths, 2014b; Montag et al., 2014; Rehbein & Mößle, 2013). IA is a more inclusive condition, that also involves, for instance, the problematic use of online pornography or social networking sites (or any activities in which the Internet serves as a communication channel; Kuss & Griffiths, 2017); therefore, applying it to GD is misleading. Unfortunately, numerous studies in the field used the term IA when referring solely to GD, making it difficult, or sometimes even impossible, to know what these studies truly assess (Király, Nagygyörgy, et al., 2015). This issue is mostly notable in neuroimaging studies (see Pontes, Kuss, & Griffiths, 2017). Furthermore, the DSM-5 also states that IGD "most often involves specific Internet games, but it could involve non-Internet computerized games as well" (American Psychiatric Association, 2013, p. 796), making the content of IGD also controversial. If IGD can involve offline games as well, why term it *Internet* gaming disorder (Király, Griffiths, & Demetrovics, 2015)?

Another important debate refers to whether GD should be considered a genuine addiction. For instance, one reason to question the addiction model as the best theoretical framework for this problematic behavior is its apparently transient nature as opposed to substance use disorders that are usually chronic and progressive without treatment (Starcevic, 2017). There is a general lack of longitudinal studies in the field, although the few studies that have examined GD or excessive gaming over time suggest that this problematic behavior is often transient or episodic, appearing in certain life stages and remitting when circumstances change (Konkolÿ Thege, Woodin, Hodgins, & Williams, 2015; Rothmund, Klimmt, & Gollwitzer, 2016). Therefore, it has been argued that formal recognition of GD as a behavioral addiction may be premature as alternative theoretical models may explain this phenomenon better (Aarseth et al., 2016; Starcevic, 2017). For instance, Kardefelt-Winther (2014a, 2017) proposed the model of compensatory Internet use which considers GD a consequence of maladaptive coping or a way of meeting particular needs rather than an addiction, which has been supported by follow-up studies (e.g., Kuss, Dunn, et al., 2017). Conversely, others argue that the framework of behavioral addictions is useful and suitable enough to theorize GD at the moment because gaming, similarly to substance use, is a highly rewarding behavior and as such, is potentially addictive. Moreover, empirical research suggests similarities between GD and substance use disorders in several aspects, including symptomology and underlying neurobiological processes (Griffiths, Kuss, Lopez-Fernandez, & Pontes, 2017; Hellman, Schoenmakers, Nordstrom, & van Holst, 2013; Király & Demetrovics, 2017). Notwithstanding these debates, the majority of the existing evidence on GD is cross-sectional in nature and based on non-probability samples, thus making it methodologically impossible to draw definite conclusions on this matter at the moment.

Finally, the question whether or not the recognition of GD as a formal disorder is timely has been raised more recently during the preparation of the 11th revision of the World Health Organization's (WHO) International Classification of Diseases (ICD-11). The section regarding behavioral addictions has been debated in several WHO meetings before the final version was approved. The ICD-11 proposal for GD clearly reacted to the outlined controversies in two main ways: (i) the definition only contains the more or less consensual IGD criteria (i.e., behavioral salience, losing interest in and reducing other recreational activities, loss of control, continuation of the playing behavior despite negative consequences, and risking/losing relationships and opportunities), (ii) the nomenclature avoids the term "Internet." Still, the fact that GD was proposed as a formal disorder in the ICD-11 further intensified the debate in the field, despite the WHO's efforts to address the controversies discussed earlier.

The main counterarguments and concerns of a large group of researchers regarding a formal diagnosis were conveyed in an open letter that was recently published and addressed to the WHO (Aarseth et al., 2016). These include the arguably (i) low quality of research supporting the proposal, (ii) consideration that the current operationalization of GD derives from the criteria of substance use and gambling disorder, (iii) lack of consensus among scholars regarding the symptomatology and assessment of GD, (iv) possible stigmatization, (v) (possibly compulsory) treatment of engaged but healthy gamers (i.e., the false-positive cases) the formal diagnosis could cause, and (vi) the assumption that a formal diagnosis would hinder exploratory research in the field needed to better understand the phenomenology of GD.

As a response to these concerns, several researchers asserted that, even if consensus is missing in the field, the inclusion and recognition of GD as a disorder has more advantages than disadvantages (e.g., Király & Demetrovics, 2017; Kuss et al., 2017). The main counterargument stated by most researchers was that GD exists and the clinical reality highlights the need for a formal diagnosis (Griffiths et al., 2017; Higuchi et al., 2017; Király & Demetrovics, 2017; Lee, Choo, & Lee, 2017; Müller & Wölfling, 2017; Saunders et al., 2017). Furthermore, scholars also argued that a formal diagnosis: (i) would help the unification of the field in terms of assessment (Fuster et al., 2016; Pontes & Griffiths, 2014b, 2015b), (ii) may improve the overall quality of research (Griffiths et al., 2017; Higuchi et al., 2017; Király & Demetrovics, 2017; Lee et al., 2017; Müller & Wölfling, 2017), and (iii) may provide a context facilitating raising public awareness about the problem and promotion of treatment on a governmental level (Billieux et al., 2017; Higuchi et al., 2017; Saunders et al., 2017). The recent debate has also pointed out that the GD proposal for ICD is a rather consensual one; it emphasizes clinically significant functional impairment as a requirement for diagnosis, and it only contains criteria with empirical and theoretical support (Billieux et al., 2017; Király & Demetrovics, 2017;

Saunders et al., 2017). Scholars acknowledged that the addiction framework may not be the only one to appropriately theorize GD; however, they argue that it is a framework useful and suitable enough to describe the phenomenon and address the problem (Griffiths et al., 2017; Király & Demetrovics, 2017; Saunders et al., 2017). Finally, researchers argue that moral panics are mainly driven and exacerbated by the tendency of mainstream media to sensationalize current affairs, like GD, whereas stigmatization derives mostly from misinformation and lack of understanding. Consequently, researchers supporting the GD proposal challenge the notion that a formal diagnosis would amplify the moral panic and stigmatization related to video games. Instead, they argue that it may help raise awareness by viewing GD objectively and with clinical relevance, decreasing the moral panic around it (Billieux et al., 2017; Griffiths et al., 2017; Higuchi et al., 2017; Király & Demetrovics, 2017; Lee et al., 2017; Müller & Wölfling, 2017).

CONCLUSION

Video games are a very popular pastime activity for many gamers, with the entertainment and software industry figures highlighting their mass appeal. However, with possible overuse, a number of problems can emerge for a minority of gamers, which may be related to symptoms traditionally associated with substance-related addictions. The scientific and clinical community have recently begun debating the viability of including IGD or GD in the diagnostic manuals, resulting in the emergence of research investigating the validity of such diagnostic criteria and their clinical and psychometric assessment. Given the nosological ambiguities and inconsistencies in research outlined in this chapter, some argue that agreeing on a specific diagnostic framework is premature, while others argue that, on the contrary, a formal diagnosis at this point has more advantages than disadvantages. Nevertheless, it appears that there is a general agreement among scholars regarding the need for more research to assess the problem in clinical populations, making use of more comprehensive frameworks that are not limited to perspectives used for substance-related addictions and/or gambling disorder. To summarize the far-reaching recent debates in the field, the main question concerning GD and other potential behavioral addictions (e.g., exercise addiction, compulsive buying, and problematic online pornography use) is whether we are overpathologizing everyday behaviors (Billieux et al., 2015) in an attempt to conceptualize, diagnose, and treat the possibly addicted cases. Or, in other words, are we throwing the baby out with the bathwater?

ACKNOWLEDGMENTS

The contribution of OK and ZD was supported by the Hungarian National Research, Development and Innovation Office (Grant numbers: K111938; KKP126835). OK was supported by the New National Excellence Program of the Ministry of Human Capacities.

REFERENCES

Aarseth, E., Bean, A. M., Boonen, H., Colder Carras, M., Coulson, M., Das, D.,...Van Rooij, A. J. (2016). Scholars' open debate paper on the World Health Organization ICD-11 Gaming Disorder proposal. *Journal of Behavioral Addictions, 6*(3). doi:10.1556/2006.5.2016.088

American Psychiatric Association. (2013). *Diagnostic and Statistical Manual of Mental Disorders* (5th ed). Washington DC: American Psychiatric Association.

American Society of Addiction Medicine. (2011). Definition of Addiction. Retrieved 27 January, 2016, from http://www.asam.org/for-thepublic/definition-of-addiction

Billieux, J., King, D. L., Higuchi, S., Achab, S., Bowden-Jones, H., Hao, W.,...Saunders, J. B. (2017). Functional impairment matters in the screening and diagnosis of gaming disorder: Commentary on: Scholars' open debate paper on the World Health Organization ICD-11 Gaming Disorder proposal (Aarseth et al.). *Journal of Behavioral Addictions, 6*(3), 285–289. doi:10.1556/2006.6.2017.036

Billieux, J., Schimmenti, A., Khazaal, Y., Maurage, P., & Heeren, A. (2015). Are we overpathologizing everyday life? A tenable blueprint for behavioral addiction research. *Journal of Behavioral Addictions, 4*(3), 119–123. doi:10.1556/2006.4.2015.009

Demetrovics, Z., & Király, O. (2016). Internet/gaming addiction is more than heavy use over time: Commentary on Baggio and colleagues (2015). *Addiction, 111*(3), 523–524.

Ducheneaut, N., Yee, N., Nickell, E., & Moore, R. J. (2007). *The life and death of online gaming communities: A look at guilds in world of warcraft.* Paper presented at the Proceedings of the SIGCHI Conference on Human Factors in Computing Systems, San Jose, California, USA.

ESA. (2015). Essential facts about the computer and video game industry. Washington, DC: Entertainment Software Association.

Fuster, H., Carbonell, X., Pontes, H. M., & Griffiths, M. D. (2016). Spanish validation of the Internet Gaming Disorder-20 (IGD-20) Test. *Computers in Human Behavior, 56*, 215–224. doi:10.1016/j.chb.2015.11.050

Griffiths, M. D., King, D. L., & Demetrovics, Z. (2014). DSM-5 Internet Gaming Disorder needs a unified approach to assessment. *Neuropsychiatry, 4*(1), 1–4. doi:10.2217/npy.13.82

Griffiths, M. D., Király, O., Pontes, H. M., & Demetrovics, Z. (2015). An overview of problematic gaming. In E. Aboujaoude & V. Starcevic (Eds.), *Mental health in the digital age: Grave dangers, great promise* (pp. 27–45). Oxford: Oxford University Press.

Griffiths, M. D., Kuss, D. J., Lopez-Fernandez, O., & Pontes, H. M. (2017). Problematic gaming exists and is an example of disordered gaming: Commentary on: Scholars' open debate paper on the World Health Organization ICD-11 Gaming Disorder proposal (Aarseth et al.). *Journal of Behavioral Addictions, 6*(3), 285–289. doi:10.1556/2006.6.2017.037

Griffiths, M. D., van Rooij, A. J., Kardefelt-Winther, D., Starcevic, V., Király, O., Pallesen, S.,...Demetrovics, Z. (2016). Working towards an international consensus on criteria for assessing Internet Gaming Disorder: A critical commentary on Petry et al. (2014). *Addiction, 111*(1), 167–175.

Hawi, N. S., & Samaha, M. (2017). Validation of the Arabic Version of the Internet Gaming Disorder-20 Test. *Cyberpsychology, Behavior, and Social Networking, 20*(4), 268–272. doi:10.1089/cyber.2016.0493

Hellman, M., Schoenmakers, T. M., Nordstrom, B. R., & van Holst, R. J. (2013). Is there such a thing as online video game addiction? A cross-disciplinary review. *Addiction Research & Theory, 21*(2), 102–112.

Higuchi, S., Nakayama, H., Mihara, S., Maezono, M., Kitayuguchi, T., & Hashimoto, T. (2017). Inclusion of gaming disorder criteria in ICD-11: A clinical perspective in favor: Commentary on: Scholars' open debate paper on the World Health Organization ICD-11 Gaming Disorder proposal (Aarseth et al.). *Journal of Behavioral Addictions, 6*(3), 293–295. doi: 10.1556/2006.6.2017.049

Hruska, S. (2016). World of Warcraft subscriptions surge thanks to amazing Legion expansion. *ExtremeTech*. Retrieved 01.06.2017, from https://www.extremetech.com/gaming/237034-world-of-warcraft-subscriptions-surge-thanks-to-amazing-legion-expansion

Kaptsis, D., King, D. L., Delfabbro, P. H., & Gradisar, M. (2016). Withdrawal symptoms in Internet Gaming Disorder: A systematic review. *Clinical Psychology Review, 43*, 58–66. doi:10.1016/j.cpr.2015.11.006

Kardefelt-Winther, D. (2014a). A conceptual and methodological critique of internet addiction research: Towards a model of compensatory internet use. *Computers in Human Behavior, 31*, 351–354.

Kardefelt-Winther, D. (2014b). Meeting the unique challenges of assessing internet gaming disorder. *Addiction, 109*(9), 1568–1570.

Kardefelt-Winther, D. (2014c). The moderating role of psychosocial well-being on the relationship between escapism and excessive online gaming. *Computers in Human Behavior, 38*, 68–74.

Kardefelt-Winther, D. (2017). Conceptualizing Internet use disorders: Addiction or coping process? *Psychiatry and Clinical Neurosciences, 71*(7), 459–466.

King, D. L., & Delfabbro, P. H. (2014). The cognitive psychology of Internet gaming disorder. *Clinical Psychology Review, 34*(4), 298–308.

King, D. L., & Delfabbro, P. H. (2016). Defining tolerance in Internet Gaming Disorder: Isn't it time? *Addiction, 111*(11), 2064–2065. doi:10.1111/add.13448

King, D. L., Haagsma, M. C., Delfabbro, P. H., Gradisar, M., & Griffiths, M. D. (2013). Toward a consensus definition of pathological video-gaming: A systematic review of psychometric assessment tools. *Clinical Psychology Review, 33*(3), 331–342. doi:10.1016/j.cpr.2013.01.002

Király, O., Sleczka, P., Pontes, H. M., Urban, R., Griffiths, M. D., & Demetrovics, Z. (2017). Validation of the Ten-Item Internet Gaming Disorder Test (IGDT-10) and evaluation of the nine DSM-5 Internet Gaming Disorder criteria. *Addictive Behaviors, 64*, 253–260.

Király, O., & Demetrovics, Z. (2017). Inclusion of Gaming Disorder in ICD has more advantages than disadvantages: Commentary on: Scholars' open debate paper on the World Health Organization ICD-11 Gaming Disorder proposal (Aarseth et al.). *Journal of Behavioral Addictions, 6*(3), 280–284. doi:10.1556/2006.6.2017.046

Király, O., Griffiths, M. D., & Demetrovics, Z. (2015). Internet gaming disorder and the DSM-5: Conceptualization, debates, and controversies. *Current Addiction Reports, 2*(3), 254–262. doi:10.1007/s40429-015-0066-7

Király, O., Griffiths, M. D., Urbán, R., Farkas, J., Kökönyei, G., Elekes, Z., ... Demetrovics, Z. (2014). Problematic Internet use and problematic online gaming are not the same: Findings from a large nationally representative adolescent sample. *Cyberpsychology, Behavior, and Social Networking, 17*(12), 749–754.

Király, O., Nagygyörgy, K., Koronczai, B., Griffiths, M. D., & Demetrovics, Z. (2015). Assessment of Problematic Internet Use and Online Video Gaming. In E. Aboujaoude & V. Starcevic (Eds.), *Mental health in the digital age: Grave dangers, great promise* (pp. 46–68). Oxford: Oxford University Press.

Király, O., Sleczka, P., Pontes, H. M., Urbán, R., Griffiths, M. D., & Demetrovics, Z. (2017). Validation of the ten-item Internet Gaming Disorder Test (IGDT-10) and evaluation of the nine DSM-5 Internet Gaming Disorder criteria. *Addictive Behaviors, 64,* 253–260. doi:10.1016/j.addbeh.2015.11.005

Király, O., Tóth, D., Urbán, R., Demetrovics, Z., & Maraz, A. (2017). Intense video gaming is not essentially problematic. *Psychology of Addictive Behaviors, 31*(7), 807–817.

Király, O., Urbán, R., Griffiths, M. D., Ágoston, C., Nagygyörgy, K., Kökönyei, G., & Demetrovics, Z. (2015). Psychiatric symptoms and problematic online gaming: The mediating effect of gaming motivation. *Journal of Medical Internet Research, 17*(4), e88. doi:10.2196/jmir.3515

Konkolÿ Thege, B., Woodin, E. M., Hodgins, D. C., & Williams, R. J. (2015). Natural course of behavioral addictions: A 5-year longitudinal study. *BMC Psychiatry, 15*(1), 4.

Koronczai, B., Urbán, R., Kökönyei, G., Paksi, B., Papp, K., Kun, B.,...Demetrovics, Z. (2011). Confirmation of the three-factor model of problematic Internet use on off-line adolescent and adult samples. *Cyberpsychology, Behavior, and Social Networking, 14*(11), 657–664. doi:10.1089/cyber.2010.0345

Kuss, D. J. (2013a). *For the Horde! How playing World of Warcraft reflects our participation in popular media culture.* Saarbrücken: LAP LAMBERT Academic Publishing.

Kuss, D. J. (2013b). Internet gaming addiction: Current perspectives. *Psychology Research and Behavior Management, 6,* 125–137. doi: http://dx.doi.org/10.2147/PRBM.S39476

Kuss, D. J., Dunn, T. J., Wölfling, K., Müller, K. W., Hędzelek, M., & Marcinkowski, J. (2017). Excessive Internet use and psychopathology: The role of coping. *Clinical Neuropsychiatry, 14*(1), 73–81.

Kuss, D. J., & Griffiths, M. D. (2015). *Internet addiction in psychotherapy.* London: Palgrave Macmillan.

Kuss, D. J. & Griffiths, M. D. (2017). Social Networking Sites and Addiction: Ten lessons learned. *International Journal of Environmental Research and Public Health, 14,* 311–327.

Kuss, D. J., Griffiths, M. D., & Pontes, H. M. (2017). DSM-5 diagnosis of Internet Gaming Disorder: Some ways forward in overcoming issues and concerns in the gaming studies field. *Journal of Behavioral Addictions, 6*(2). http://akademiai.com/doi/abs/10.1556/2006.6.2017.032

Kuss, D. J., Louws, J., & Wiers, R. W. (2012). Online gaming addiction? Motives predict addictive play behavior in massively multiplayer online role-playing games. *Cyberpsychology, Behavior, and Social Networking, 15*(9), 480–485.

Lee, S.-Y., Choo, H., & Lee, H. K. (2017). Balancing between prejudice and fact for Gaming Disorder: Does the existence of alcohol use disorder stigmatize healthy drinkers or impede scientific research? Commentary on: Scholars' open debate paper on the World Health Organization ICD-11 Gaming Disorder proposal. *Journal of Behavioral Addictions, 6*(3), 302–305. doi:10.1556/2006.6.2017.047

Lemmens, J. S., Valkenburg, P. M., & Gentile, D. A. (2015). The Internet Gaming Disorder Scale. *Psychological Assessment, 27*(2), 567–582. doi:10.1037/pas0000062

Maraz, A., Király, O., & Demetrovics, Z. (2015). The diagnostic pitfalls of surveys: if you score positive on a test of addiction, you still have a good chance not to be addicted. A response to Billieux et al. 2015. *Journal of Behavioral Addictions, 4*(3), 151–154. doi: 10.1556/2006.4.2015.026

McClintock, P. (2015). Box Office 2015: How revenue (narrowly) hit a record $11b in the U.S. *Hollywood Reporter.* Retrieved 23.05.2017, from http://www.hollywoodreporter.com/news/box-office-2015-how-revenue-851167

McKeand, K. (2016). WoW: Legion sold 3.3 million copies by day one, matching previous records. *PC Games*. Retrieved 01.06.2017, from https://www.pcgamesn.com/world-of-warcraft/wow-legion-player-count

Monacis, L., De Palo, V., Griffiths, M. D., & Sinatra, M. (2016). Validation of the Internet Gaming Disorder Scale—Short-Form (IGDS9-SF) in an Italian-speaking sample. *Journal of Behavioral Addictions, 5*(4), 683–690. doi:10.1556/2006.5.2016.083

Montag, C., Bey, K., Sha, P., Li, M., Chen, Y. F., Liu, W. Y.,…Reuter, M. (2014). Is it meaningful to distinguish between generalized and specific Internet addiction? Evidence from a cross-cultural study from Germany, Sweden, Taiwan and China. *Asia-Pacific Psychiatry, 7*(1), 20–26. doi:10.1111/appy.12122

Müller, K. W., & Wölfling, K. (2017). Both sides of the story: Addiction is not a pastime activity: Commentary on: Scholars' open debate paper on the World Health Organization ICD-11 Gaming Disorder proposal (Aarseth et al.). *Journal of Behavioral Addictions, 6*(2), 118–120. doi:10.1556/2006.6.2017.038

Pearcy, B. T. D., Roberts, L. D., & McEvoy, P. M. (2016). Psychometric testing of the Personal Internet Gaming Disorder Evaluation-9: A new measure designed to assess Internet Gaming Disorder. *Cyberpsychology, Behavior, and Social Networking, 19*(5), 335–341. doi:10.1089/cyber.2015.0534

Petry, N. M., & O'Brien, C. P. (2013). Internet Gaming Disorder and the DSM-5. *Addiction, 108*(7), 1186–1187. doi:10.1111/add.12162

Petry, N. M., Rehbein, F., Gentile, D. A., Lemmens, J. S., Rumpf, H. J., Mossle, T.,…O'Brien, C. P. (2014). An international consensus for assessing internet gaming disorder using the new DSM-5 approach. *Addiction, 109*(9), 1399–1406. doi:10.1111/add.12457

Pontes, H. M. (2016). Current practices in the clinical and psychometric assessment of internet gaming disorder in the era of the DSM-5: A mini review of existing assessment tools. *Mental Health and Addiction Research, 1*(1), 18–19. doi:10.15761/MHAR.1000105

Pontes, H. M., Caplan, S. E., & Griffiths, M. D. (2016). Psychometric validation of the Generalized Problematic Internet Use Scale 2 in a Portuguese sample. *Computers in Human Behavior, 63*, 823–833. doi:10.1016/j.chb.2016.06.015

Pontes, H. M., & Griffiths, M. D. (2014a). Assessment of Internet Gaming Disorder in clinical research: Past and present perspectives. *Clinical Research and Regulatory Affairs, 31*(2–4), 35–48. doi:10.3109/10601333.2014.962748

Pontes, H. M., & Griffiths, M. D. (2014b). Internet addiction disorder and Internet Gaming Disorder are not the same. *Journal of Addiction Research & Therapy, 5*(4), e124. doi:10.4172/2155-6105.1000e124

Pontes, H. M., & Griffiths, M. D. (2015a). Measuring DSM-5 Internet Gaming Disorder: Development and validation of a short psychometric scale. *Computers in Human Behavior, 45*, 137–143. doi:10.1016/j.chb.2014.12.006

Pontes, H. M., & Griffiths, M. D. (2015b). New concepts, old known issues: The DSM-5 and Internet Gaming Disorder and its assessment. In J. Bishop (Ed.), *Psychological and social implications surrounding Internet and gaming addiction* (pp. 16–30). Hershey, PA: Information Science Reference.

Pontes, H. M., & Griffiths, M. D. (2016). Portuguese validation of the Internet Gaming Disorder Scale–Short-Form. *CyberPsychology, Behavior & Social Networking, 19*(4), 288–293. doi:10.1089/cyber.2015.0605

Pontes, H. M., & Griffiths, M. D. (2017). New concepts, old known issues: The DSM-5 and Internet Gaming Disorder and its assessment. In Information Resources Management

Association (Ed.), *Gaming and Technology Addiction: Breakthroughs in Research and Practice (Volume 2)* (pp. 883–899). Pennsylvania: IGI Global.

Pontes, H. M., Király, O., Demetrovics, Z., & Griffiths, M. D. (2014). The conceptualisation and measurement of DSM-5 Internet Gaming Disorder: The development of the IGD-20 Test. *PloS ONE*, *9*(10), e110137. doi:10.1371/journal.pone.0110137

Pontes, H. M., Kuss, D. J., & Griffiths, M. D. (2017). Psychometric assessment of Internet Gaming Disorder in neuroimaging studies: A systematic review. In C. Montag & M. Reuter (Eds.), *Internet addiction: Neuroscientific approaches and therapeutical implications including smartphone addiction* (pp. 181–208). Cham, Switzerland: Springer International Publishing.

Pontes, H. M., Macur, M., & Griffiths, M. D. (2016a). Construct validity and preliminary psychometric properties of the Internet Gaming Disorder Scale—Short-Form (IGDS9-SF) among Slovenian youth: A nationally representative study. *Journal of Behavioral Addictions*, *5*(s1), 35. doi:10.1556/JBA.5.2015.Suppl.1

Pontes, H. M., Macur, M., & Griffiths, M. D. (2016b). Internet Gaming Disorder among Slovenian primary schoolchildren: Findings from a nationally representative sample of adolescents. *Journal of Behavioral Addictions*, *5*(2), 304–310. doi:10.1556/2006.5.2016.042

Pontes, H. M., Stavropoulos, V., & Griffiths, M. D. (2017). Measurement Invariance of the Internet Gaming Disorder Scale–Short-Form (IGDS9-SF) between the United States of America, India and the United Kingdom. *Psychiatry Research*, *257*, 472–478. doi:10.1016/j.psychres.2017.08.013

Pontes, H. M., Szabo, A., & Griffiths, M. D. (2015). The impact of Internet-based specific activities on the perceptions of Internet addiction, quality of life, and excessive usage: A cross-sectional study. *Addictive Behaviors Reports*, *1*, 19–25. doi:10.1016/j.abrep.2015.03.002

Rehbein, F., & Mößle, T. (2013). Video game and internet addiction: Is there a need for differentiation? *SUCHT*, *59*(3), 129–142.

Rho, M. J., Jeong, J.-E., Chun, J.-W., Cho, H., Jung, D. J., Choi, I. Y., & Kim, D.-J. (2016). Predictors and patterns of problematic Internet game use using a decision tree model. *Journal of Behavioral Addictions*, *5*(3), 500–509. doi:10.1556/2006.5.2016.051

Rothmund, T., Klimmt, C., & Gollwitzer, M. (2016). Low temporal stability of excessive video game use in German adolescents. *Journal of Media Psychology*. doi:10.1027/1864-1105/a000177

Saunders, J. B., Hao, W., Long, J., King, D. L., Mann, K., Fauth-Buhler, M.,…Poznyak, V. (2017). Gaming disorder: Its delineation as an important condition for diagnosis, management, and prevention. *Journal of Behavioral Addictions*, *6*(3), 271–279. doi:10.1556/2006.6.2017.039

Shaffer, H. J., Hall, M. N., & Vander Bilt, J. (2000). "Computer addiction": A critical consideration. *American Journal of Orthopsychiatry*, *70*(2), 162–168. doi:10.1037/h0087741

Starcevic, V. (2016). Tolerance and withdrawal symptoms may not be helpful to enhance understanding of behavioural addictions. *Addiction*, *111*(7), 1307–1308.

Starcevic, V. (2017). Internet gaming disorder: Inadequate diagnostic criteria wrapped in a constraining conceptual model: Commentary on: Chaos and confusion in DSM-5 diagnosis of Internet Gaming Disorder: Issues, concerns, and recommendations for clarity in the field (Kuss et al.). *Journal of Behavioral Addictions*, *6*(2), 110–113. doi:10.1556/2006.6.2017.012

Stavropoulos, V., Beard, C., Griffiths, M. D., Buleigh, T., Gomez, R., & Pontes, H. M. (2017). Measurement invariance of the Internet Gaming Disorder Scale–Short-Form (IGDS9-SF) between Australia, the USA, and the UK. *International Journal of Mental Health and Addiction*. https://doi.org/10.1007/s11469-017-9786-3

Tao, R., Huang, X. Q., Wang, J., Zhang, H., Zhang, Y., & Li, M. (2010). Proposed diagnostic criteria for internet addiction. *Addiction, 105*(3), 556–564.

Van Rooij, A. J., Schoenmakers, T. M., & van de Mheen, D. (2015). Clinical validation of the C-VAT 2.0 assessment tool for gaming disorder: A sensitivity analysis of the proposed DSM-5 criteria and the clinical characteristics of young patients with "video game addiction." *Addictive Behaviors, 64*, 269–274. doi:10.1016/j.addbeh.2015.10.018

Wu, T. Y., Lin, C.-Y., Årestedt, K., Griffiths, M. D., Broström, A., & Pakpour, A. H. (2017). Psychometric validation of the Persian nine-item Internet Gaming Disorder Scale—Short Form: Does gender and hours spent online gaming affect the interpretations of item descriptions? *Journal of Behavioral Addictions, 6*(2), 256–263. doi:10.1556/2006.6.2017.025

Zanetta Dauriat, F., Zermatten, A., Billieux, J., Thorens, G., Bondolfi, G., Zullino, D., & Khazaal, Y. (2011). Motivations to play specifically predict excessive involvement in Massively Multiplayer Online Role-Playing Games: Evidence from an online survey. *European Addiction Research, 17*(4), 185–189. doi:10.1159/000326070

CHAPTER 24

··

MOURNING AND MEMORIALIZATION ON SOCIAL MEDIA

··

ELAINE KASKET

INTRODUCTION

··

IT is difficult to fathom the extent to which social networking sites (SNSs) have transformed life—and, as this chapter demonstrates, death—over the course of just 10 years. Considering the degree of impact, the timeline seems so short: 2002 saw the launch of one of the earliest SNSs, Friendster, which was quickly usurped by MySpace; in 2006 Facebook became available to the general public and advanced steadily to world dominance, acquiring the photo-sharing site Instagram in 2012 and the mobile-messaging platform WhatsApp in 2015. Now, in 2017, it is a personal-data juggernaut, exerting a tremendous influence on how we present ourselves and engage with others online, to include both public and private verbal communications and the sharing of photographs. If its approximately 2 billion current users (Cohen, 2017) were a country, that nation would be the most populous nation on earth. We simply cannot get enough of creating and sharing our own information and accessing that of other people. Pundits, psychologists, and parents, particularly those who are "digital immigrants" (Prensky, 2001), shake their heads and fret over the impact of these platforms; books about the addictive nature of our devices (e.g., Alter, 2017) fly off the shelves as we struggle to comprehend their hold over us.

Given the spread of digital technologies throughout the world, the huge quantities of personal data that we compulsively store, share, and consume online every day, and the fact that these behaviors show no signs of stopping, there is another notable date to consider—a date in the future, rather than in the past: 2098. That year represents one statistician's estimate of the point in time when dead people on Facebook will come to outnumber live users (Brown, 2016), and other scholars have predicted that over 3 billion users will be dead by century's end, depending on Facebook's rate of growth (Öhman & Watson, 2018). If you are tempted to argue that Facebook may not exist by the end of the twenty-first century, remember that this is only one of many fulcrums we could identify—one possible tipping point for the rapidly aggregating data of the dead online. Indeed, the posthumously persistent traces of our ancestors are already infused widely throughout the Internet, not just on social media sites. The data of particular individuals left online after physical death are termed "digital legacies" (Sofka, Noppe Cupit, & Gilbert, 2012, p. 4), and there are myriad ways in which they may affect us psychologically. First, just as our activity in the online sphere changes how we define and experience personhood in life, it may also change the very definition of death, and in the process affect our awareness of and response to our own physical mortality. Secondly, the existence of digital legacies affects how those left behind mourn, memorialize, and interact with people who no longer physically walk the earth.

This chapter explores this new landscape of death in the digital age, with a focus on the role of Facebook as the most popular and most researched social media site. It begins with an illustration and discussion of the link between our online lives and our digital afterlives to encapsulate how posthumous persistence online opens up new possibilities for the ongoing roles and influence of the physically dead. It then switches focus to bereavement, with an emphasis on the continuing-bonds model of grief and the processes associated with it, after which it outlines some of the characteristics of Facebook that are relevant for continuing bonds.

ONLINE LIFE, DIGITAL AFTERLIFE: THE POSTHUMOUS PERSISTENCE OF DIGITAL SELVES

Contemporary evolutions in the psychology of death, mourning, and memorialization are, of course, intimately linked via the data and self-representations that we create, co-create, and share online in our lifetimes. That connection, and the stark difference between this and previous generations for the material we leave behind, is illustrated by the following contrasting scenarios.

I have one black-and-white photograph of my great-grandmother, who was born in 1869, before the invention of the telephone. A child of the industrial revolution, she emigrated to the United States in 1901 on one of the transatlantic steamships of that era, and came through Ellis Island, where her arrival was recorded in a paper register. In the photo I have she is standing by a haystack, a farm implement in her hand; I will never know the date of the photo, its location, or the identity of the young girl in dungarees next to her. I cannot triangulate it easily with other data, as my parents, who are the caretakers of the other photographs and physical artifacts of this woman's life, live far away.

Lost to the mists of time are my great-grandmother's personality, her opinions, her passions, the sound of her voice, and the details of how she looked throughout her life. A few stories about her were passed down through my grandmother, but largely she is little more than a name on a family tree.

I have thousands upon thousands of photographs of my 7-year-old daughter, a child of the digital revolution, the information age. Her birth was announced to friends and family on social media; she has been using an iPad since she was less than a year old. To my knowledge, every photo ever taken of her has been digital, and the vast majority have never been committed to paper. Each is drenched in contextualizing information, typically automatically tagged with dates and locations and, often, the identity of the other people in the photos. These images appear on my own Facebook profile with details and explanations, and they are not the only type of data about her that appear there. There are multiple videos, my own narratives about her, and finally, five years' worth of hundreds of precisely transcribed conversations that convey the development and characteristics of her personality. Meeting adults in her mother's circle of Facebook friends for the first time, she is often astonished at the warm familiarity they show her and at their insider knowledge of her life; her reputation has preceded her through her online representation. She affects people who she has never met. I could say that their sense that they "know" her is not inaccurate but, of course, this impression is from my own vantage point as her current biographer, the primary mirror responsible for her digital reflection. She is, however, an increasingly active co-author of her own biography, a co-constructor of her identity online. She makes contributions to her digital footprint through her choices of entertainment on her Netflix and Spotify profiles, through her selfies and other photos that are automatically uploaded to the cloud, and through the emails that she writes to family and friends using her personal account. As this digital native grows up, her online footprint will only grow broader and deeper, more representative of her as a person, and will be co-constructed with multiple others as her networks develop.

I have no coherent sense of my great-grandmother as a person, only sparse, general data points along the broad arc of her life: birth date, name, place of origin, date of arrival in the United States. While I am able to access her immigration information on the Ellis Island website, the online world retains very little evidence of her onetime existence on earth. My ignorance, this paucity of data and absence of narrative, precludes any sense of meaningful connection with a woman who died in the pre-digital era. By contrast, if only 25 percent of my daughter's data were to persist online after her death, her own great-grandchildren could easily access a detailed reservoir of information about her, to an extent that could facilitate a sense of personal "knowing," just as the people in my own social circle who have never met my daughter have a keen grasp of what she is like. There is a significant possibility that her digital representation will be inherited in some form by her descendants.

We have long thought of our being as a Cartesian duality, made up of inter-related but distinguishable components of body and mind: the physical being that exists in, connects to, and reaches out to the physical world—*res extensa*—and the internal, intangible being of mind, our intrapsychic world—*res cogitans* (Heidegger, 1962). A being that falls somewhere in the middle of physical being and being of mind has been created by the digital age: the *res digitalis* (Kim, 2001), or digital self. Digital self may reflect physical self—albeit with distortions, edits, and filters—and portable and even wearable technologies merge with or extend our physical bodies, generating continuous data related to our physicality in the world. Meanwhile, billions of people, particularly those of the "Always On" generation (Anderson & Rainie, 2012), are constantly infusing their digital selves with material from their minds through frequent disclosure of their thoughts and feelings on social media. In addition, observations of online behavior may enable others to make inferences about those aspects of our inner worlds that are less conscious, or at least not deliberately or intentionally revealed.

When someone dies, two types of being cease to exist: the sentient, breathing physical being, and the being of that person's mind. If someone has generated a large amount of data and "lived their lives online," however, their hybrid digital being—a being composed of data but nevertheless resonant of both *res extensa* and *res cogitans*—has the potential to persist. Mayer-Schönberger (2011) describes that, throughout most of history, it has been easier to forget than to remember; individuals, communities, and wider societies have an inbuilt tendency to jettison information and memories over time. Now, the seemingly infinite storage capacity of the digital age, combined with devices that helpfully capture everything we do, ensures that information is often saved by default and requires effort to erase.

At the time of writing, there is no automatic or effective mechanism of comprehensively removing the digital beings of deceased persons from various places on the Internet when their physical counterparts die. The data of the dead are everywhere, often spread far from places of original storage or publication. It is often not even clear when you are encountering a "ghost" online, as the dead and the living are mingled in most online places. The useful hotel review on TripAdvisor, the blurb that inspires someone to buy a book on Amazon, or a CV on LinkedIn—we may assume that the person who generated all of these is still alive, but how do we know? The online digital reflections of deceased people are not gathered together into a separate place, a digital cemetery on the outskirts of town. Rather, encountering the dead online is analogous to walking down a busy city street and passing grave markers as you go about your business. Some you will notice and some you will not, sometimes you will stop and honor the person and sometimes you will pass by, but the dead are among us. As the tipping point approaches, we will be increasingly surrounded by the physically dead but socially alive (Walter, Hourizi, Moncur, & Pitsillides, 2016). An old saying goes that we are not dead while our names are still spoken. If technology affords us the possibility to continue in our communities—not just having our names spoken, but also having our voices and images actively accessible—might this change our definitions and perceptions of death, and perhaps even the anxiety we feel about non-being (Steffen & Kasket, 2018)? Will the people of my daughter's generation be somehow "less dead" than my great-grandmother and her peers?

This is a fertile ground for future research, but it is too early to do anything other than speculate about whether changes to our conceptualizations of death or reduced anxiety over our physical mortality will occur because it is now easier to remember than to forget (Mayer-Schönberger, 2011). What we do have is a growing body of research about the psychological impact on mourning of posthumously persistent digital beings. Those who have lost a loved one could be seen as beneficiaries of our systems' tendency to remember everything, but there is a sting in the tail, for, as Kim (2001) says, "digital beings can either endure forever . . . or disappear instantly without a trace. Digital beings have two contradictory possibilities simultaneously: eternal endurance and instant vanishment" (p. 101). Where social media accounts are concerned, each of these possibilities may be a source of comfort or torment, depending on the needs and preferences of individual mourners. Little has changed about the disposition of physical remains, but the importance and significance of digital remains in our experience of mourning and memorialization is profound, for just as we are hyperconnected to one another in life, we have the potential to stay connected with our loved ones after death. The next section looks at bereavement models and processes that are salient for technologically mediated mourning.

Models of Bereavement

For virtually the whole of the twentieth century, the prevailing model of grief was heavily influenced by ideas expressed in Sigmund Freud's essay *Mourning and Melancholia* (1917). Freud presented his view about the experience or process of grief as a commonsense, obvious truth. "I do not think," he said, "there is anything far-fetched in presenting it in the following way" (p. 243). He went on to explain the "work" of mourning in this manner:

> Reality-testing has shown that the loved object no longer exists, and it proceeds to demand that all libido shall be withdrawn from its attachments to that object. This demand arouses understandable opposition . . . its orders cannot be obeyed at once. They are carried out bit by bit, at great expense and cathectic energy, and in the meantime the existence of the lost object is psychically prolonged . . . It is remarkable that this painful unpleasure is taken as a matter of course by us. The fact is, however, when the work of mourning is completed the ego becomes free and uninhibited again.   (Freud, 1917, pp. 243–244)

Freud's theoretical ideas about "grief work"—the supposedly key task of gradual, "piecemeal" letting-go of the "loved object", culminating in resolution and freedom from sorrow associated with the loss—did not actually map onto most people's experience, and indeed not even his own experience of grief (Klass & Steffen, 2017). The necessity of relinquishing one's ties with the dead was, in fact, virtually an entirely new concept, but despite the lack of anecdotal or empirical evidence supporting them, the impact of his published ideas was so strong in psychological thought and practice, and so influential in the canonical narrative, that his vision of "normal" bereavement held sway throughout the West for the rest of the twentieth century. Freud's theory is present in the room when people use phrases like "working through grief" and ultimately, "moving on"; you can also hear its echoes in people's concerns about mourners "not getting over it," "finding it hard to let go," and "being in denial." In Freud's conceptualization, to cherish and pursue some form of psychological, emotional tie with a deceased loved one is to veer into the realm of pathology, to have one's ego trapped in a permanently unhealthy state.

Freud's influence was such that multiple thinkers—academics, researchers, practitioners—followed suit. Half a century after *Mourning and Melancholia*, Elisabeth Kübler-Ross, a Swiss psychiatrist who worked with the terminally ill, proposed a five-stage model of grief (Kübler-Ross, 1969) that is still well known and heavily utilized by laypersons and various types of health practitioners today. The five stages—denial, anger, bargaining, depression, and acceptance—were originally presented as linear, although Kübler-Ross later claimed that she had always intended them to be a more flexible description of the phases that could occur at various points in the grieving process (Kübler-Ross & Kessler, 2007). In many ways the progression of stages resembled the grief work described by Freud, for here too we see the resistance to realizing the loss and relinquishing the person, as well as the ultimate acceptance, with its connotations of resolution, moving on, and making new attachments, having "gotten over" the old ones.

The publication of *Continuing Bonds: New Understandings of Grief* (Klass, Silverman, & Nickman, 1996) marked the point at which the discourse began to turn. The authors argued that the dominant models had "proved inadequate to the data" (Klass & Steffen, 2017, p. 4), that empirical evidence did not support the ideas about healthy griefwork that were espoused by Freud and his successors, and that the necessity of relinquishing attachments to the dead was an (early) twentieth-century idea that did not mirror real-life experience. Ever since Freud's theory had entered the popular discourse, generations of people worried that their mourning experience was pathological, and *Continuing Bonds* offered an alternative, and reassuring, view: that maintaining a connection to the dead, far from being concerning, was normal, adaptive, and, in most cases, positive. The authors in the newest continuing-bonds text edited by Klass and Steffen (2017) confirm the existence of continuing bonds as vital, ongoing, evolving relationships, which show themselves in a variety of ways:

> Phenomena that indicate active continuing bonds are a sense of presence, experiences of the deceased person in any of the senses, belief in the person's continuing active influence on thoughts or events, or a conscious incorporation of the characteristics or virtues of the dead into the self. In individuals a continuing bond includes the part of the self actualized in the bond with the person, characterizations and thematic memories of the deceased person, and the emotional states connected with the characterizations and memories. Living people play roles, often complex,

within the family and psychic system. After they die, roles change, but the dead can still be significant members of families and communities.   (p. 4)

Klass and Steffen emphasize that "continuing bonds" should not be thought of as mere ideas or feelings, but as real relational ties that are active in the world. The concept of continuing bonds also helps explain each person's unique grieving experience, which is downplayed by Freudian and stage models of grief. While all bonds between human beings may have similar themes or characteristics, each relationship is as unique as the individuals that share it. By extension, unique relationships in life are just as special in death, and so every loss is different, too.

Furthermore, as the *Continuing Bonds* authors argue, these bonds are not restricted to one-to-one relationships—the bond of one person with their loved one—but can also describe the place of the dead in systems as small as families and as large as entire communities. Sociologist Tony Walter (1996) argues that the purpose of grief is to construct a "durable biography" of the deceased—one that the community of grievers can connect with and comfortably carry forward. He suggests that this construction takes place through conversations about the deceased, for example, those that occur in the traditional rituals following a death: eulogies, funerals, wakes, and other gatherings. In 1996, his concern was that our mobile, secular society might not be conducive to ongoing conversations among those who knew the deceased, which could threaten the construction of these durable biographies and impede healthy, adaptive grieving. Social networking sites, however, arrived on the scene and removed that danger.

BEFORE FACEBOOK: ONLINE MEMORIALS

Before social networking, memorializations on the Internet primarily took the form of dedicated online cemeteries, the longest surviving of which is the World Wide Cemetery, launched in 1995 (http://www.cemetery.org). Platforms such as these enable friends or family members to create open-access memorials with text and images, which visitors from around the world are able to visit at the click of a mouse. Like the cemeteries in the offline world, they are separate, dedicated spaces for remembrance of the dead, and messages and (virtual) flowers can be left by visitors. Similar facilities are offered by modern funeral homes, which publish obituaries on their websites and afford opportunities to write in an online guestbook, enabling interaction among mourners. Visitors to online obituaries are "participating in the same kinds of bereavement activities that scholars have attributed to private web memorials—sending messages to the dead, expressing emotion, and telling stories" (de Vries & Moldaw, 2012, p. 141).

Each of these online rituals has its offline counterparts, both serving a similar psychological and sociological purpose: the collaborative negotiation and establishment of a durable biography, as part of continuing bonds. Offline, people leave flowers and notes at accident locations and gravesites, also addressing themselves in second person to the deceased themselves, a frequently observed behavior on online memorials. Offline, people attend wakes and funerals and exchange stories, share memories, and show photographs, just as they do in virtual cemeteries and online guestbooks. Offline, mourners compose eulogies, obituaries, and words to appear on grave markers, and unless the deceased was particularly deliberate about their planning and keen to stage-manage their own legacy, this text would have minimal input from the dead person. Analogously, online memorials may contain ample information about the dead person, with contributions from multiple people who knew them, but this material is not part of the dead person's own digital legacy, that is, the data that they generated in life that remains after their death. The community of mourners shapes the deceased's legacy in whatever way they wish, perhaps idealizing the deceased or otherwise selectively presenting the preferred aspects of their history and character in their attempt to arrive at a comfortable legacy with which they can continue a bond (Walter, 1996). The dead person, a non-participant in this process, is unable to challenge or edit the image that emerges. The digital legacy that the person built in life, on the other hand, such as a Facebook profile, arguably provides more affordance for continuing bonds.

Continuing Bonds on Facebook

In considering why Facebook is so important for continuing bonds, it is helpful to understand the handful of characteristics that might have the most impact on Facebook profiles' roles as memorials and archives for the dead and their data. First, in common with all SNSs, a Facebook profile is co-constructed. By definition, social networking does not represent the self in isolation, but rather the self as inextricably intertwined with others. Those others contribute content to one's "own" page, making every profile a co-authored enterprise. The digital archive left behind by a deceased user, therefore, raises complex questions about ownership and right of access to material.

Second, a Facebook profile is a context-collapsed forum (Wesch, 2009). Each person on the friends list, irrespective of the strength, proximity, or nature of their tie to the account holder, tends to share an equal level of access to the material there, unless the user micromanages and limits the audiences for individual posts. In offline life, one may regulate and present oneself differently in the face of the demands or expectations of particular social contexts—at gym, at work, among one's family. On Facebook, the default mode is presentation to the *generalized* other. When a user does not wish a par-ticular other (e.g., a parent) to see the image of self that is presented on Facebook, exclu-sion from the friends list is usually the most efficient option. Certain people that are key in an individual's life may therefore have no access to the data on the profile. This has significant implications for the mourning experience, given the individual nature of grief and variability in individual mourners' needs and preferences.

Third, particularly since the arrival of the Timeline layout in 2011, Facebook situates itself as an autobiographical platform. In a description of the launch of Timeline,

Madrigal (2011) said: "Zuckerberg's talk was littered with references to the importance of story. Facebook's new Timeline feature was 'An important next step to help you tell the story of your life', he said. The new product would allow you to 'highlight and curate all your stories so you can tell who you really are' . . . you get an automatic autobiography.'" The Timeline structure, combined with the increasing synthesis of Facebook with other messaging platforms, encourages users to utilize Facebook as the conduit, and ultimately the archive, for the majority of their online social interactions and communications, enfolded into a life narrative. Aside from the Timeline structure itself, Facebook plays the role of steward to one's history and memories in other ways: among its features are algorithmically curated videos encapsulating the history of particular friendships, or the events of the past year (Look Back), and Timehop regularly presents posts and photos from previous years.

Fourth, Facebook is dominant as a vehicle for communication among certain age groups, particularly when associated platforms such as Messenger, WhatsApp, and Instagram are considered. In late 2016, nearly eight in 10 online Americans were Facebook users, with young adults continuing to use the site at high rates while older adults joined in increasing numbers (Greenwood, Perrin, & Duggin, 2016). The vast majority of online adults in those countries where Facebook dominates, therefore, will have a Facebook digital legacy—or "autobiography"—that may be left behind.

Finally, Facebook profiles are durable by default. In order to effect full deletion (rather than deactivation) of an account, a user must contact Facebook directly. In terms of postmortem durability, Facebook views the profiles of deceased users as being valuable as online memorials, as gathering places for the community of mourners, and as personal archives of people's lives (Brubaker & Callison-Burch, 2016); it will only delete or deactivate a profile upon a user's death if the user has stipulated this in the settings, in a legal will, or (in circumstances where it is legally possible) on request of legal next of kin.

Brubaker and Callison-Burch (2016) comprehensively outline the current state of play with Facebook profile memorialization, which has occurred since 2007, although the design and rules for memorialized accounts have both evolved since that time. Under the current system at time of writing, in place since 2015, Facebook's Community Operations team receives notification of a user's death and, once this is verified, places the person's profile into a memorialized state. In the absence of user instruction to delete upon death, the profile stays visible, with privacy settings retained as the user set them in life, privileging the deceased person's choices: "If we don't know what the deceased person would have wanted, we leave the account exactly as that person left it" (Bickert, 2017). Logging into the account is no longer possible, by anyone, and viewing of private messages within Facebook Messenger is also virtually impossible unless Facebook is summoned by a court of law in the context of a criminal investigation (Edina Harbinja, personal communication, 18 September 2017): "We assume that both people intended the messages to remain private. And even where it feels right to turn over private messages to family members, laws may prevent us from doing so" (Bickert, 2017). There is no advertising on a memorialized profile, and it is also excluded from certain features such as birthday reminders (Brubaker, 2016). If the user named a legacy contact in Facebook's settings premortem, that legacy contact has control over a limited number of things: it can add a pinned post to the top of the profile; can change the profile and/or the banner/cover photo; and can add friends (but cannot remove friends that the user added premortem). Additionally, if the user granted permission, the legacy contact can download an archive of the data (excluding private messages) that can then exist independently from the social networking site context and be more readily transferred to others, in whole or in part, in a variety of formats.

In considering the best way forward for memorialized profiles, Facebook designers report that they have attempted to implement a design that permits more individualized end-of-life choices, respects the (explicit or assumed) privacy wishes of the deceased, and balances these with the needs and preferences of bereaved stakeholders (Brubaker & Callison-Burch, 2016). Chief among the concerns of the bereaved may be the impact of the Facebook profile on their ability to continue bonds, a function that the site has served since its inception. I was able to observe this firsthand during my own first interaction with "repurposed" social media profiles in late 2006, before there was the facility for profile memorialization. At that stage, "in-memory-of" pages created postmortem were a commonly observed phenomenon, and I stumbled across one such memorial for a young woman who had died in an accident, from there linking to the unmemorialized and still actively visited profile that she had created in life, which was also open to the public. As evidenced by the large amount of material on both pages, she and her friends were avid Facebook users.

On both the in-memory-of page and the in-life profile of this woman, the community of grievers clearly demonstrated their individually and communally held continuing bonds. They supported and communicated with one another and left messages and photos on the in-memory-of page; sometimes the mode of address was second person, to the deceased ("you"), and sometimes about the deceased ("she," "her"). The third-person posts were sometimes addressed to the family in traditional "sympathy letter" format, particularly in the occasional contribution from a digital immigrant. There was biography-building activity such as the addition of photos and telling of stories about the deceased's life, developing and negotiating a sense of who she was, and portraying those qualities that the community valued and wished to most remember. On the in-life profile, however, the sense that they were speaking directly to the deceased was more marked, partly because some of the material continued exchanges that had begun when she was alive, via ongoing conversation threads under the photos and verbal posts.

The continuing-bonds observations in that single-case study have been affirmed and lent nuance by much subsequent research (e.g., Carroll & Landry, 2010; Irwin, 2017; Kasket, 2012; Pennington, 2013, 2017; Rossetto, Lannutti, & Strauman, 2015). Although Walter et al. (2016) observe that things change quickly in the digital sphere and that "thanatologists"—scholars of death—must work to keep pace, the themes that emerge in successive studies of Facebook and mourning have been consistent over a seven-year period. Early on, Kasket (2012) studied 1,000 wall posts across five "in-memory-of" pages on Facebook and interviewed administrators of in-memory-of sites who also had access to the deceased's "in-life" profiles; extremely similar findings are echoed five years on in

Irwin's (2017) study of 1,260 wall posts. A powerful sense of continuing bonds—the ongoing sense of relationship with the deceased—was present across the data. People spoke directly to the deceased in the same manner that they always had. There was tremendous comfort in communicating with their dead loved one, strong investment in the maintenance of the bond, a strong sense of presence of the deceased, and a terror of the bonds being broken through profile removal. One reason that the threat of profile removal felt terrifying was that the bereaved tended to experience the profile as a particularly vivid representation of not just the person, but of the relationship that the mourners had with that person. The co-constructed nature of the profile, and its reflection of the deceased's connection to mourners, contributes to the sense that losing it would be a particularly severe wrench—a "second death." This experience of or apprehension about a "second death"—the loss of the digital legacy—is a feature of digital-age bereavement observed across the research (Bassett, 2018).

In addition, for mourners for whom the Facebook profile is important, its loss might mean the disappearance of the most effective way of feeling a sense of contact or communication with the deceased. While they still participated in traditional offline rituals—visiting the gravesite, spending time among the person's possessions, speaking to them out loud—individuals interviewed by Kasket (2012) reported that these activities did not have the tangibility, and the sense of contact, of continuing to write to the dead on Facebook. "It's strange but part of me just feels like he sees it somehow," said one participant, and one author of a wall post said, "Happy late birthday! I did not have computer access yesterday…but I did remember your birthday and thought about you all day!" Whether or not participants subscribed to beliefs in an afterlife where the dead remain sentient of activity on earth, there was an explicit (in the case of the IPA interviews) or implicit (as in the analysis of posts) sense that the deceased person would be more likely to be conscious of the communication if it were written online. While Pennington's (2013) in-depth qualitative study of forty-three people found that looking at photos was the most frequent and helpful activity, many also wrote messages; for these people, the idea that the words reach the deceased is often an article of faith (Irwin, 2017; Kasket, 2012).

This feeling that communications reach the deceased may be particularly strong in digital natives, for whom digital devices are extensions of self and digitally mediated communications are the norm (Anderson & Rainie, 2012), and who have learned from the start of their lives that to send a digital communication into the ether is to have it instantaneously received. Given the dominance of Facebook, Facebook Messenger, WhatsApp, and similar platforms among digital natives, these are the "places" where communications tend to occur. After a friend has died, one employs the same tools, and sends communications via the same routes, as they did when the person was alive; hence, the instinct may be that the dead receive the message, even when logic challenges this idea. While there is generally no expectation that the dead will reply directly on social media, despite the occasionally reported uncanny experience, multiple researchers give examples of beliefs that communications return through other means, via dreams, intercessions (being saved from harm), natural-world phenomena like rainbows, butterflies, or snow, and signs via other technologies, like songs on the radio (e.g., Irwin, 2017; Kasket, 2012).

Crucially, however, many of the studies that investigate mourning on Facebook involve participants who are familiar with social media: digital natives, Facebook aficionados, people who had chosen to create in-memory-of pages and/or who were mourners visiting and leaving messages on memorial pages and memorialized profiles. It is unsurprising that those who have chosen this medium for their mourning would report the site as important for their sense of continuing bonds. For other members of the deceased's circle, however, the digital legacy might not be important at all, and may even constitute a threat to how they want the deceased to be remembered.

Pennington (2017) was able to provide empirical evidence that a digital legacy is not always important for continuing bonds and may even be disruptive or painful. Using a survey methodology to understand what variables might affect whether Facebook is helpful for a particular individual in their grief, she found that, indeed, those who use Facebook frequently found it to be more useful in grieving, whereas those who were unfamiliar with it or used it less regularly considered it to be harmful in their process. She notes, "For as many users can go to the page to gain support from fellow friends and family, others still remain conflicted as to whether the page should even remain on the site once their loved one has passed" (pp. 19–20). This is the "coping paradox" observed in Rossetto, Lannutti, and Strauman (2015), wherein Facebook facilitated mourning for some and impeded mourning for others, in the latter case sometimes causing significant pain and complicated grief. The existence of this paradox is intimately connected to an emergent significant feature of digital-age bereavement: the element of *control*.

At one time, the people that would have had the most access to the deceased—to their physical remains, physical mementoes, photographs, and writings—would have been close associates and/or primarily family members. Recall the anecdote at the start of this chapter, in which my parents are the owners and gatekeepers of virtually all the remaining traces of my great-grandmother's life; this was the typical scenario in the pre-digital period. As people with the most access, the family would have controlled who *else* had access. They would have had the most significant contribution in shaping the enduring legacy—the durable biography—of the deceased person. On the margins of access and control were friends who would have had their own bonds with the deceased, but who were at risk of disenfranchised grief: the existence or significance of their relationships unrecognized, and their grief unseen (Parkes & Prigerson, 2010).

In a very short space of time, the balance of power has flipped. Virtually all of the photographs that exist of a digital native may be housed on a Facebook page, and if the deceased had not been comfortable with parents seeing what was on the profile page, mom and dad might well be excluded from this archive, as well as other meaningful memorialization activity. Bassett (2018) details one example of a mother, not on Facebook, wondering why she had received virtually no letters of condolence or remembrance from his friends—"All I have is an empty mantel[piece]," she said. "I felt left out and I don't know what to do about it" (p. 6). It is now parents, former members of the inner circle, who can easily find themselves marginalized and powerless to control, or even access, their loved one's legacy. This can be experienced as especially distressing when there is the perception that the "chief mourners" are people who had weaker ties to the deceased, the "outer circle" in offline life who may be the "inner circle" in the social networking context. Pennington (2017) describes the understandable dilemma that family members feel in such instances: "those who were closest to the deceased see value in going to the page for support, but also want it gone because they do not want to share that grief with the outer circle" (p. 20). This may have been the case for one mother in Brazil, who petitioned the courts to have her deceased daughter's Facebook page deleted:

> The page was left as a memorial wall only available to friends, who could continue to post tributes…Late last year [her mother] decided she had had enough. "This 'wailing wall' just makes me suffer too much," she told the BBC. "On Christmas Eve many of her 200 friends posted pictures they had taken with her and recalled their memories. She was very charismatic, very popular. I cried for days," she said.
> (Puff, 2013)

The desire to influence a deceased loved one's legacy, in the effort to achieve a comfortable durable biography, may be another reason that family may find the continuing existence of a Facebook profile distressing. In the 2006 chance encounter with a posthumously persistent profile example given earlier in this chapter, the deceased had clearly enjoyed parties and drinking; she often wore clothing that was revealing, and chose to present herself in a sexual way. This content would not have been controllable or editable by anyone who did not have the login details for the profile, and so the deceased's preferences for self-presentation continued to make themselves known, framing how she would be remembered. Interestingly, even her peers on the in-life profile seemed to be engaged in an idealization process, in an apparent attempt to address some of the potentially trickier aspects of the lasting digital legacy. After her death, under some of the more risqué photos, the community of mourners made comments about how "sweet," "angelic," and "innocent" she was. These comments about innocence juxtaposed with the overtly sexual photographs were clearly incongruous, but still her friends attempted to establish a durable biography of the deceased as an innocent angel despite considerable challenge from the deceased's own contribution to the narrative of her life.

In this example, there was no evidence of anyone much over the age of twenty on the deceased's friends list. Facebook was in its early days, and her next of kin may only have been dimly aware of her profile. Had they seen it, however, it is indeed possible that they could have had negative or complex feelings about the tone of their daughter's visible legacy. If they exercised their influence as next of kin to have the profile removed, it could have had a considerable impact on the mourners to whom the profile was important for grieving. Many qualitative researchers (e.g., Bassett, 2018; Irwin, 2017; Kasket, 2012) have presented heart-rending raw data describing mourners' fears about "second death," expressing that profile removal would be tantamount to "losing the person all over again." This fear is particularly expressed by non-family, who may assume that Facebook will delete an "inactive" profile or that the family will remove it, and that this may occur without warning. This insecurity about the potential disruption of the bond may add additional layers of complexity and anxiety to an already-painful grieving process. Most people are at least intuitively aware of the dual nature of digital beings described by Kim (2001)—either enduring forever or vanishing in the blink of an eye.

The more unexpected and novel battleground for control, however, comes from a different juxtaposition—family versus Facebook. Because Facebook's terms and conditions privilege the privacy of the account holder and have a policy of maintaining the profile as it was in life, reports of tense conflicts with mourning families are becoming increasingly commonplace, and some are being taken to the courts. In the Hollie Gazzard case, for example, a bereaved family in the United Kingdom wanted her profile to be memorialized, but asked Facebook to selectively remove many photographs of Hollie with her killer, who was her ex-boyfriend (BBC, 2015). Facebook refused, and the family eventually needed independent assistance to get them removed (Nick Gazzard, personal communication, 18 December 2017). When a 15-year-old girl in Germany fell under a train in 2012, her parents appealed to Facebook to allow them access to her private messages, hoping that these communications would cast light on whether their daughter's death was a suicide. Citing user privacy, Facebook refused, and the parents took them to court. The German courts initially supported Facebook's refusal, citing "telecommunications secrecy law, which precludes heirs from viewing the communications of a deceased relative with a third party" (Connolly, 2017). Ultimately, however, the highest court in the land found in favor of the parents and ordered that they be given access to their daughter's Messenger history—a judgment that could prove controversial (AFP/DPA/The Local, 2018).

Other familial conflicts with Facebook have been tried not in the courts, but in the media (Harris, 2015). In the Amy Duffield case, also in the UK, Amy's bereaved mother was highly distressed that Amy's profile had been memorialized "without [her] consent," perhaps not having realized that she would trigger the memorialization when she contacted Facebook to beg for access to Amy's private messages, a request that was categorically denied on grounds of privacy. Sharon described several aspects of her interaction with Facebook that she found painful: the automatic memorialization, which felt out of her control, and which resulted in her no longer receiving the birthday reminders that she wished for; her inability to access private messages, which felt wrong to her as a mother with unresolved wonderings about the time leading up to her daughter's sudden death; and the impersonal way she felt she had been treated, which she characterized as psychologically damaging. Most recently, however, Amy had disappeared from Sharon's own list of friends, a situation that was unresolved until the BBC did a news story on it (Sharon Duffield, personal communication, 18 September 2017).

In another instance, a grieving father, having been unsuccessful in petitioning Facebook to get a "Look Back" video for his deceased son, finally resorted to a beseeching video on YouTube:

My son passed away January 28, 2012. And we can't access his Facebook account. I've tried emailing and different things, but it ain't working. All we want to do is see his movie. That's it. I don't even need to get on his account. If you guys could, if you guys could just do it yourself, I don't care. But regardless, everybody does these [YouTube] videos and things and they go viral. That's all I'm trying to do. So I'm asking my friends to share this video, and your friends to share it and so on and so forth, and maybe, maybe someone will see it that counts. I know it's a shot in the dark, but I don't care. I want to see my son's video. His name's Jesse Berlin. So please help me.

(Berlin, 2014)

As John Berlin had hoped, the video did "go viral," and it took roughly a fortnight for Facebook to change its policies. "We had not initially made the videos for memorialized accounts, but John's request touched the hearts of everyone who heard it, including ours. Since then, many others have asked us to share the Look Back videos of their loved ones, too, and we're now glad to be able to fulfill those requests" (Price & DiSclafani, 2014).

Representatives at Facebook, some of whom have characterized themselves as "stewards" of the digital legacies on the site (Brubaker & Callison-Burch, 2016), repeatedly aver their intention to respect the laws and moral principles of dead users' privacy (Bickert, 2017), while also recognizing the need to continually attend to how they can improve the experience of bereaved family and friends. In one press release, which detailed the change to Look Back video policy as well as the move to retaining privacy settings as they were, the Community Operations team detailed the reflections that had driven these alterations: "How might people feel? Are we honoring the wishes and legacy of the person who passed away? Are we serving people who are grieving the loss of a loved one as best we can?" (Price & DiSclafani, 2014). Unfortunately, given the individuality of mourners' processes and needs, and the context-collapsed nature of a Facebook profile, the answers to the first and last questions are always likely to be "it depends." Just as the Facebook designers had intended, posthumously persistent profiles are perhaps the most coherently autobiographical element of most people's digital legacy; as such, this particular digital remain may be a hugely significant artifact for mourners. When memorialized profiles are beneficial for some but harmful to others, we confront an ethical landscape full of crevasses. These challenges may be better met as time marches on and *all* generations eventually become digital natives, born and raised in highly networked environments. Design improvements will occur. Laws and policies more suitable to the online context will be developed and applied. In the short term, however, psychological practitioners and researchers will likely see many instances of people who have been consoled and supported by the surviving digital reflections of the dead, while also encountering many who suffer complicated grief related to issues of access to, and control over, digital legacies.

Conclusion

In death, as in life, the digital revolution changes everything, but in an ironic twist, where death is concerned, modern technologies have prompted a reversion to a situation we have not witnessed since before the industrial revolution. Before the population explosions, migrations, and technological innovations of that era, the dying were cared for at home and the dead buried within the community—for example, within the churchyard of the local parish, or on private land in close proximity to the surviving members of the family. As the nineteenth century progressed, the sick and dying were gradually shuffled into nursing homes and hospitals, and the dead into cemeteries situated well apart from the living. Now, the dead are rejoining their communities—or, more accurately, persisting in them, in some form. The psychological and sociological impact of this desegregation is yet to be fully felt, and future researchers will have much to investigate in this realm. In the meantime, we continue to make progress on understanding bereavement in the digital age, although there are currently no easy solutions to the paradoxical way in which the Internet both facilitates and disrupts continuing bonds. Much power and responsibility lie with the designers of social networking sites and other online platforms: they have a moral imperative to consider how they can better facilitate individual choice and control over both our own digital legacies, and our interaction with the digital legacies of those we have loved and lost.

References

AFP/DPA/The Local. (2018, 12 July) 'Update: Parents can access dead daughter's Facebook, German court rules,' *The Local DE*. Retrieved from: https://www.thelocal.de/20180712/german-court-to-rule-on-parents-access-to-dead-daughters-facebook

Alter, A. (2017). *Irresistible: Why we can't stop checking, clicking, scrolling and watching*. London: Bodley Head.

Anderson, J., & Rainie, L. (2012). Millennials will benefit *and* suffer due to their hyperconnected lives (Pew Internet & American Life Project). Retrieved from: http://www.pewinternet.org/2012/02/29/millennials-will-benefit-and-suffer-due-to-their-hyperconnected-lives/

Bassett, D. (2018). Ctrl-Alt-Delete: From digital immortality to digital endurance and the fear of second loss. *Current Psychology* [online]. doi:10.1007/s12144-018-0006-5

Berlin, J. (2014, 5 February). My appeal to Facebook [Video File]. Retrieved from: https://www.youtube.com/watch?v=vPT28MGhprY

Bickert, M. (2017, 18 August). Hard questions: What should happen to people's online identity when they die? *Facebook Newsroom*. Retrieved from: https://newsroom.fb.com/news/2017/08/what-should-happen-to-online-identity/

British Broadcasting Corporation (BBC) (2015, 11 November). Facebook removes Hollie Gazzard photos with her killer. *BBC Online*. Retrieved from: http://www.bbc.co.uk/news/uk-england-gloucestershire-34781905

Brown, K. V. (2016, March 4). We calculated the year dead people on Facebook will outnumber the living. *Fusion*. Retrieved from: http://fusion.net/story/276237/the-number-of-dead-people-on-facebook-will-soon-outnumber-the-living/

Brubaker, J. R., & Callison-Burch, V. (2016). Legacy contact: Designing and implementing post-mortem stewardship at Facebook. In *Proceedings of the 2016 CHI Conference on Human Factors in Computing Systems—CHI '16* (pp. 2908–2919). New York: ACM. doi:10.1145/2858036.2858254

Carroll, B., & Landry, K. (2010). Logging on and letting out: Using online social networks to grieve and to mourn. *Bulletin of Science, Technology & Society, 30*(5), 341–349. doi:10.1177/0270467610380006

Cohen, D. (2017, 27 July). Stats and milestones from Facebook's Q2 2017 financial results. *AdWeek*. Retrieved from http://www.adweek.com/digital/facebook-q2-2017/

Connolly, K. (2017, 31 May). Parents lose appeal over access to dead girl's Facebook account. *The Guardian*. Retrieved from: https://www.theguardian.com/technology/2017/may/31/parents-lose-appeal-access-dead-girl-facebook-account-berlin

Freud, S. (1917). Mourning and melancholia. In *The Standard edition of the complete psychological works of Sigmund Freud, Volume XIV (1914–1916): On the history of the psycho-analytic movement, papers on metapsychology and other works* (J. Strachey, Trans.) (pp. 237–258). London: Hogarth Press. Retrieved from: http://www.arch.mcgill.ca/prof/bressani/arch653/winter2010/Freud_Mourningandmelancholia.pdf

Greenwood, S., Perrin, A., & Duggin, M. (2016, 11 November). Social media update 2016: Facebook usage and engagement is on the rise, while adoption of other platforms holds steady. *Pew Research Center*. Retrieved from: http://www.pewinternet.org/2016/11/11/social-media-update-2016/

Harris, A. (Reporter) (2015). Digital legacy report [Television Broadcast]. BBC: East Midlands Today. Retrieved from: https://www.youtube.com/watch?v=8pi72oizNeU

Heidegger, M. (1962). *Being and time*. New York: Harper & Row.

Irwin, M. D. (2017). Mourning 2.0: Continuing bonds between the living and the dead on Facebook: Continuing bonds in cyberspace. In D. Klass & E. Steffen (Eds.), *Continuing bonds in bereavement: New directions for research and practice* (pp. 317–329). New York: Routledge.

Kasket, E. (2012). Continuing bonds in the age of social networking. *Bereavement Care 31*(2), 62–69. doi:10.1080/02682621.2012.710493

Kim, J. (2001). Phenomenology of digital-being. *Human Studies 24*, 87–111. doi:10.1023/A:1010763028785

Klass, D., Silverman, P. R., & Nickman, S. L. (Eds.). (1996). *Continuing bonds: New understandings of grief*. London: Taylor & Francis.

Klass, D., & Steffen, E. (2017). *Continuing bonds in bereavement: New directions for research and practice*. New York: Routledge.

Kübler-Ross, E. (1969). *On death and dying*. New York: Macmillan.

Kübler-Ross, E., & Kessler, D. (2007). *On grief and grieving: Finding the meaning of grief through the five stages of loss*. New York: Scribner Book Company.

Madrigal, A. C. (2011, 22 September). Facebook Timeline: Putting the auto in autobiography. *The Atlantic*. Retrieved from: https://www.theatlantic.com/technology/archive/2011/09/facebook-timeline-putting-the-auto-in-autobiography/245533/

Mayer-Schönberger, V. (2011). *Delete: The virtue of forgetting in the digital age*. Cambridge, MA: Princeton University Press.

Öhman, C., & Watson, D. (2018). Are the dead taking over Facebook: A big data approach to the future of death online. Retrieved from: https://arxiv.org/abs/1811.03416

Parkes, C. M., & Prigerson, H. G. (2010). *Bereavement: Studies of grief in adult life* (4th revised ed.). London: Penguin.

Pennington, N. (2013). You don't defriend the dead: An analysis of grief communication by college students through Facebook profiles. *Death Studies 37*(7), 617–635. doi:10.1080/07481187.2012.673536

Pennington, N. (2017). Tie strength and time: Mourning on social networking sites. *Journal of Broadcasting & Electronic Media 61*(1), 11–23. doi:10.1080/08838151.2016.1273928

Prensky, M. (2001). Digital natives, digital immigrants. *On the Horizon 9*(5), 1–6. doi:10.1108/10748120110424816

Price, C., & DiSclafani, A. (2014, 21 February). Remembering our loved ones. *Facebook Newsroom*. Retrieved from: https://newsroom.fb.com/news/2014/02/remembering-our-loved-ones/

Puff, J. (2013, 24 April). Brazil judge orders Facebook memorial page removed. *BBC News*. Retrieved from: http://www.bbc.co.uk/news/world-latin-america-22286569

Rossetto, K. R., Lannutti, P. J., & Strauman, E. C. (2015). Death on Facebook: Examining the roles of social media communication for the bereaved. *Journal of Social & Personal Relationships 32*, 974–994. doi:10.1177/0265407514555272

Sofka, C. J., Noppe Cupit, I., & Gilbert, K. (2012). Thanatechnology as a conduit for living, dying, and grieving in a contemporary society. In K. Sofka, I. Noppe Cupit, & K. R. Gilbert (Eds.), *Dying, death and grief in an online universe: For counsellors and educators* (pp. 3–15). New York: Springer Publications.

Steffen, E., & Kasket, E. (2018). Continuing bonds between the living and the dead in contemporary Western societies: Implications for our understandings of death and the experience of death anxiety. In R. E. Menzies, R. G. Menzies, & L. Iverach (Eds.), *Curing the dread of death: Theory, research and practice.* (pp. 203–218). Samford Valley QLD: Australian Academic Press.

de Vries, B., & Moldaw, S. (2012). Virtual memorials and cyber funerals: Contemporary expressions of ageless experiences. In K. Sofka, I. Noppe Cupit, & K. R. Gilbert (Eds.), *Dying, death and grief in an online universe: For counsellors and educators* (pp. 135–148). New York: Springer Publications.

Walter, T. (1996). A new model of grief: Bereavement and biography. *Mortality I*(1), 7–25.

Walter, T., Hourizi, R., Moncur, W., & Pitsillides, S. (2016). Does the Internet change how we die and mourn? Overview and analysis. *Omega: Journal of Death and Dying 64*(4), 275–302.

Wesch, M. (2009). YouTube and you: Experiences of self-awareness in the context collapse of the recording webcam. *Explorations in Media Ecology 8*(2), 19–34.

CHAPTER 25

THE THERAPEUTIC AND HEALTH BENEFITS OF PLAYING VIDEO GAMES

MARK D. GRIFFITHS

Introduction

RESEARCH dating back to the early 1980s has consistently shown that playing computer games (irrespective of genre) can have positive effects including increases in reaction times, improved hand–eye co-ordination, increases spatial visualization, and raises players' self-esteem (Griffiths, Kuss, & Ortiz de Gortari, 2017). Furthermore, curiosity, fun and the nature of the challenge also appear to add to a game's therapeutic potential (Griffiths, Kuss, & Ortiz de Gortari, 2017). Such features have also been shown to be of educational benefit (Griffiths, 2010), In a therapeutic context, video games allow participants to experience novelty and challenge when engaging in fictional activities without real life consequences (Washburn & Gulledge, 1995). Video games developed specifically for therapeutic interventions or healthcare (often referred to as "good games" or "serious games") have been used therapeutically. Furthermore, some commercial video games have also been adapted and used for therapeutic purposes (Colder Carras et al., 2018).

Recently, Lu and Kharrazi (2018) carried out a comprehensive systematic content analysis of 1,743 health video games released between 1983 and 2016 across twenty-three different countries. The data were extracted from nine international English health video game directories and databases. The majority of the games were developed in the United States (67 percent) and France (18.5 percent), with 79 percent of games available at no cost. The free video games (n = 1553) were content analyzed and results showed that in-game topics included cognitive training (37 percent), indirect health education (13 percent), and medical care provision (10 percent). Three-quarters of the video games could be completed within one hour. The usability of the video games was also assessed and the main problems identified comprised non-skippable content, a lack of customization, and a lack of instruction and feedback to those playing the games.

In the past two decades, there has been much research on both the positive and negative effects of playing video games. Most of the research on the negative effects tends to focus on the small minority of individuals who have gaming disorder and who are often said to be addicted to the playing of video games (Griffiths, Kuss, & Pontes, 2016). However, there is much research on the positive benefits to playing video games which focuses on the vast majority of players who play moderately and without any negative detriments. This dichotomy was recently highlighted by two systematic reviews that examined the effect of video game playing on cognitive skills. These reviews showed that moderate video game playing has a positive effect on cognitive skills (Nuyens, Kuss, Lopez-Fernandez, & Griffiths, 2018) whereas problematic video game playing has a negative effect on cognitive skills (Nuyens, Kuss, Lopez-Fernandez, & Griffiths, 2017). More specifically, problematic video game playing is associated with poorer multi-second time perception, inhibition, and decision-making (Nuyens et al., 2017). On the other hand, non-problematic video game players (compared to non-video game players) tend to be better at task-switching, top-down attentional control, and sub-second time perception (Nuyens et al., 2017).

Video Games and Cognitive Remediation

It has long been argued that video games have been used to aid cognitive remediation (Fisher, 1986). Areas that can be helped include perceptual disorders, conceptual thinking, attention, concentration, memory, spatial cognition, mental rotation, creativity computation, visual plasticity, executive functioning, processing speed, attention, fluid intelligence, subjective cognitive performance, and difficulties with language (Achtman, Green, & Bavelier, 2008; Chandrasekharan, Mazalek, Nitsche, Chen, & Ranjan, 2010; Eow, Ali, Mahmud, & Baki, 2010; Leng, Ali, Mahmud, & Baki, 2010; Miller & Robertson, 2010; Reijnders, van Heugten, & van Boxtel, 2013).

Other studies have successfully used video games in rehabilitation programs to improve sustained attention in patients with impulsive and attentional difficulties (Clarke & Schoech, 1994; Kappes & Thompson, 1985; Lim et al., 2010; Weerdmeester et al., 2016), Down's syndrome (Joei Mioto & Goncalves Ribas, 2014), craniocerebral trauma (Funk, Germann, & Buchman, 1997; Lawrence, 1986; Skilbeck, 1991), and as a training and rehabilitation aid to cognitive and perceptual-motor disorders in stroke patients (Broeren, Claesson, Goude, Rydmark, & Sunnerhagen, 2008; Joo et al., 2010; Lauterbach, Foreman, & Engsberg, 2013; Lee, Huang, Ho, & Sung, 2017; Yavuzer, Senel, Atay, & Stam, 2008) and other motor deficits (Cameirao, Bermúdez i Badia, Duarte Oller, Zimmerli, & Verschure, 2007). Swanson and Whittinghill (2015) carried out a systematic review on the efficacy of video game-based rehabilitation interventions in motivating stroke survivors. A total of 18 studies were identified and results demonstrated that video games improved the function and health outcomes among stroke patients including energy expenditure, muscle strength, recovery times, and motor functioning. The authors concluded that video game-based interventions were promising tools in motivating the engagement of stroke patients' in effective rehabilitation activities.

There are also a number of studies showing that video games may have beneficial therapeutic effects for the elderly. Given that video game playing involves concentration, attention, hand–eye co-ordination, memory, decision-making, and speed reactions, the activity may be of great benefit to this particular cohort. Researchers working in this area have postulated that the intellectual decline which is part of the natural aging process may be slowed (and perhaps counteracted) by getting the elderly involved as active users of technology (Farris, Bates, Resnick, & Stabler, 1994). Technology with the aged can therefore foster greater independence and can be put to therapeutic use. Dustman, Emmerson, Laurel, and Shearer (1992) showed that video games could increase reaction times among the elderly after an eleven-week period of video game playing. Other studies among the elderly have shown that playing video games can improve self-esteem, well-being and mental functioning (Farris et al., 1994; Goldstein, et al., 1997; Hollander & Plummer, 1986; McGuire, 1984, 1986; Riddick, Spector, & Drogin, 1986; Ryan, 1994; Schueren, 1986; Weisman, 1983, 1994). In addition to this, video games have been found useful regarding home-based step training for older people in terms of choice stepping reaction time (and consequent decreased risk of falling down), better physical assessment scores, and postural sway compared to controls (Schoene et al., 2013).

VIDEO GAMES AS DISTRACTORS IN THE ROLE OF PAIN MANAGEMENT

Studies have shown that cognitive/attentional distraction may block the perception of pain (Wohlheiter & Dahlquist, 2012). The reasoning is that distractor tasks consume some degree of the attentional capacity that would otherwise be devoted to pain perception. Video game playing offers an ideal way to analyze the role of distraction in symptom control in pediatric patients. Redd and colleagues (1987) argued that the main reasons for this are that video games (i) are likely to engage much of a person's individual active attention because of the cognitive and motor activity required; (ii) allow the possibility to achieve sustained achievement because of the level of difficulty (i.e. challenge) of most games during extended play; and (iii) appear to appeal most to adolescents.

Video games have also been used in a number of studies as "distractor tasks." For instance, one early study (Phillips, 1991) reported the case of using a handheld video game (*Nintendo Game Boy*) to stop an eight-year-old boy picking at his face. The child had neurodermatitis and scarring due to continual picking at his upper lip. Previous treatments (e.g. behavior modification program with food rewards for periods free of picking and the application of a bitter tasting product to the child's fingers) had failed so a handheld video game was used to keep the boy's hands occupied. After two weeks the affected area had healed. This pain management technique utilizing video games has also been applied successfully to children undergoing treatment for sickle cell disease (Pegelow, 1992).

There are also a number of studies (e.g. Cole, Yoo, & Knutson, 2012; Comello, Francis, Marshall, & Puglia, 2016; Francis, Comello, & Marshall, 2016; Kato, Cole, Bradlyn, & Pollock, 2008; Kolko & Rickard-Figueroa, 1985; Redd et al., 1987; Reichlin et al., 2011; Vasterling, Jenkins, Tope, & Burish, 1993) that have demonstrated that video games can provide cognitive distraction during cancer chemotherapy in children, adolescents, and adults. All these studies have reported that distracted patients report less nausea prior to chemotherapy and lower systolic pressure after treatment (when compared with controls). Such distraction tasks also reduce the amounts of painkillers needed. There are many practical advantages for using video game therapy for patients during chemotherapy treatment. Redd and colleagues (1987) argue that video games (i) can be easily integrated with most chemotherapy administration procedures; (ii) can be played without medical supervision; and (iii) represent a more cost-effective intervention than many traditional behavioral procedures such as hypnosis and relaxation.

Govender and colleagues (2015) reviewed the clinical and neurobiological perspectives of empowering child cancer patients using video games. Children often experience physical and mental fatigue following chemotherapy. The authors noted that "patient empowerment" reflects an individual's ability to positively affect their own health behavior and that empowerment interventions can enhance patients' resilience, coping skills, internal locus of control, and self-management of symptoms related to their health issues. Govender and colleagues' review summarized clinical strategies for empowering child cancer patients via video games to help develop a "fighting spirit" in mental and physical health. The authors concluded that video games (and accompanying mobile health applications) present translational research opportunities in developing and delivering empowerment interventions to child cancer patients and those with other chronic diseases. To date, there has been no long-term follow-up to such interventions and it is unclear whether patients eventually tire of such games. Therefore, factors need to be explored such as novelty, game preference, and relative level of challenge.

VIDEO GAMES AS PHYSIOTHERAPY AND OCCUPATIONAL THERAPY

Video games have been used as a form of physiotherapy and/or occupational therapy. Much has been written about how boring and repetitive exercises are if someone is attempting to recover from or cope with a physical problem. The introduction of video games into this context can be of huge therapeutic benefit. For instance, video games have been used innovatively as a form of physiotherapy for finger and hand function (Szturm, Peters, Otto, Kapadia, & Desai, 2008), increasing hand strength (King, 1993), arm injuries (Szer, 1983), shoulder injuries (Dahl-Popolizio, Loman, & Cordes, 2014), lower back pain (Butler, 1985), back and neck pain (Jansen-Kosterink et al., 2013), rheumatology (McCormack et al., 2009), chronic severe hemiparesis (Housman, Scott, & Reinkensmeyer, 2009), postural stability and balance (Fitzgerald, Trakarnratanakul, Smyth, & Caulfield, 2010; Sato, Kuroki, Saiki, & Nagatomi, 2015), training movements in Erb's palsy (Krichevets, Sirotkina, Yevsevicheva, & Zeldin, 1994), and cerebral palsy (Huber et al., 2010; Hurkmans, van den Berg-Emons, & Stam, 2010; Jannink et al., 2008; Weightman et al., 2010). Additionally, interactive games have been successfully used to improve balance, mobility, and gait after brain injury (Lange, Flynn, Proffitt, Chang, & Rizzo, 2010). Therapeutic benefits have also been reported for wheelchair users (Synofzik et al., 2013), burns victims (Sharar et al., 2008). Additionally, video games were also used as a respiratory muscle training aid for young patients with Duchenne Muscular Dystrophy (Vilozni, Bar-Yishay, Shapira, Meyer, & Godfrey, 1994).

For instance, some wheelchair users find regular exercise programs too difficult physically or psychologically, and many find that using standard arm crank or roller systems is monotonous. O'Connor and colleagues (2000) looked for ways that individuals with spinal cord injuries would be motivated to exercise on a regular basis. As a consequence, they developed an interactive video game system (*Gamewheels*) that provided an interface between a portable roller system and a computer. This system enabled wheelchair users to play commercially available video games and their results demonstrated improved physical fitness in a sample of people with spinal cord injuries, spinal cord diseases, amputations, nerve diseases, and multiple sclerosis. Most of their participants (86 percent) reported that they would like a *Gamewheels* system for their home.

Adriaenssens, Eggermont, Pyck, Boeckx, and Gilles (1988) reported the use of video game playing as an exercise program to facilitate the rehabilitation of upper-limb burn victims (using a variety of large to smaller joysticks). This technique not only helped overcome initial therapy resistance but also encouraged and shaped movement of the hand, wrist, and elbow by providing feedback for the desired performance while also offering a distraction from pain. Moreover, Fung So and colleagues (2010) found that occupational therapists and physiotherapists advocated the use of video game systems for burn- and non-burn patients for similar reasons. The use of video games in almost all these differing contexts capitalizes on a number of inter-related factors; one of the most important is the person's motivation to succeed. Furthermore, video games have advantages over traditional therapeutic methods that rely on passive, repetitive movements and painful limb manipulation (i.e., they focus attention away from potential discomfort).

VIDEO GAMES AND THE DEVELOPMENT OF SOCIAL AND COMMUNICATION SKILLS AMONG THE LEARNING DISABLED

Video games have also been used in comprehensive programs to help develop social skills in children and adolescents who have learning disabilities, such as dyslexia (Bavelier, Green, & Seidenberg, 2013), who are severely retarded, or who have severe developmental problems like autism (Gaylord-Ross, Haring, Breen, & Pitts-Conway, 1984; Sedlak, Doyle, & Schloss, 1982; Tanaka et al., 2010). Horn, Jones, and Hamlett (1991) used video games to train three children with multiple handicaps (e.g. severely limited vocal speech acquisition) to make scan and selection responses. These skills were later transferred to a communication device. Other researchers have used video games to help learning disabled children in their development of spatial abilities (Masendorf, 1993), problem-solving exercises (Hollingsworth & Woodward, 1993) and mathematical ability (Okolo, 1992a), as well improving achievement and enhancing motivation among the learning disabled (e.g. Blechman, Rabin, & McEnroe, 1986; Okolo, 1992b).

VIDEO GAMES IN PSYCHOTHERAPEUTIC SETTINGS

The playing of video games has also been used to establish an effective patient-therapist relationship, particularly with young people (Ceranoglu, 2010a; Favelle, 1994; Franco, 2016; Horne-Moyer, Moyer, Messer, & Messer, 2014; Matthews et al., 1987; Rico-Olarte et al., 2017). Furthermore, psychotherapy has been conducted exclusively in video game settings (Coyle, Matthews, Sharry, Nisbet, & Doherty, 2005). Therapists working with children have long used games in therapy and games for therapy in sessions with their young patients (Ceranoglu, 2010a, 2010b; Gardner, 1991). The recent technological explosion has brought a proliferation of new games, which some therapists claim to be an excellent ice-breaker and rapport builder with children in therapy and behavior management (Gardner, 1991; Spence, 1988).

Gardner (1991) claimed that the use of video games in his psychotherapy sessions provided common ground between himself and his child clients, and provided excellent behavioral observation opportunities. According to Gardner, such observations allowed him to observe (among other things): (i) the child's repertoire of problem-solving strategies; (ii) the child's ability to perceive and recall subtle cues as well as foresee consequences of behavior and act on past consequences; (iii) the release of aggression and control; (iv) the ability to deal with appropriate methods of dealing with the joys of victory and frustrations of defeat in a more sports-oriented arena; (vi) the satisfaction of cognitive activity in the involvement of the recall of bits of basic information; and (vii) the enjoyment of mutually co-ordinating one's activities with another in the spirit of co-operation

Gardner went on to describe four particular case studies where video games were used to support psychotherapy. Although other techniques were used as an adjunct in therapy (e.g. storytelling, drawing, other games), Gardner claimed it was the video games that were the most useful factors in the improvement during therapy. It is Gardner's contention that clinical techniques tend to change as a function of the trends of the times, although the goals remain the same. Slower paced and more traditional activities like those outlined above may lengthen the time it takes to form a therapeutic relationship as the child may perceive the therapist not to be "cool" or "with it."

Similar techniques have also been advocated for behavioral management of exceptional children (Buckalew & Buckalew, 1983). Brezinka (2008) has argued that therapeutic games can help therapists to structure therapy sessions and reports that psychotherapeutic computer games translated into foreign languages can form a useful tool in the treatment of migrant children. For instance, *Treasure Hunt*, a game based on principles of cognitive behavior modification, was developed for eight- to twelve-year-old children who are in cognitive-behavioral treatment for various disorders. Brezinka claimed reactions of children and therapists to experimental versions of the game are positive and that serious games might prove a useful tool to support psychotherapeutic treatment of children.

Eichenberg and Schott (2017) carried out a systematic review of empirical studies examining the use of serious video games in psychotherapy and psychosomatic rehabilitation using the terms "serious game," "computer game," "psychotherapy," "rehabilitation," "intervention," and "mental disorders" in two databases. A total of fifteen studies met the inclusion criteria. Most of the studies primarily used cognitive-behavioral techniques across a range of mental disorders. The authors concluded that video games were shown to be an effective therapeutic component as both part of psychotherapy as well as a stand-alone intervention.

VIDEO GAMES AND HEALTH COMPLIANCE

Video games have been used in order to change the players' behavior regarding health in a positive way (Baranowski et al., 2016). A meta-analysis (DeSmet et al., 2014) using research on sixty-four different video games targeting improvements in lifestyle indicated that using games had beneficial consequences for health. These beneficial outcomes include effects on diabetes (DeShazo, Harris, & Pratt, 2010), obesity prevention (Lu, Kharrazi, Gharghabi, & Thompson, 2013), visual impairments (Gasperetti, Foley, Yang, Columna, & Lieberman, 2018), as well as health and safety behaviors in young individuals aged eighteen years and under (Hieftje, Edelman, Camenga, & Fiellin, 2013).

In randomized clinical trials, it has been reported that children and adolescents improved their self-care and significantly reduced their use of emergency clinical services after playing health education and disease management video games (Brown et al., 1997; Lieberman, 2001). Three games have been investigated: *Bronkie the Bronchiasaurus* for asthma self-management; *Packy & Marlon* for diabetes self-management; and *Rex Ronan* for smoking prevention. In these interactive video games, children and adolescents assume the role of a main character who also has their chronic condition or is battling the effects of smoking and nicotine addiction. Children who used them for one week (smoking prevention) to six months (diabetes self-care) increased their resolve not to smoke, markedly improved their ability to manage their asthma or diabetes, and reduced by as much as 77 percent, on average, their urgent or emergency care visits related to their illness. More recent research on using video games to promote a smoking-free lifestyle has also found similar findings (Parisod et al., 2017).

Theng, Lee, Patinadan, and Foo (2015) carried out a systematic review concerning the use of video games, virtual environments, and gamification in the self-management of diabetes. A total of ten studies met the inclusion criteria and most of the studies identified had small sample sizes with short intervention duration. All of the interventions examined the (i) reduction of diabetes-related risk and (ii) promotion of healthy behavior. The authors concluded that video games appeared to be helpful tools in educating individuals, whereas gamification and virtual environments provided positive reinforcement and increased extrinsic motivation among participants.

Electronic games have also been used to enhance adolescents' perceived self-efficacy in HIV/AIDS prevention programs (Cahill, 1994; Thomas, Cahill, & Santilli, 1997). Using a time travel adventure video game format, information and opportunities to discuss prevention practices were provided to high-risk adolescents. Video game playing resulted in significant gains in factual information about safe-sex practices, and in the participants' perceptions of their ability to successfully negotiate and implement such practices with a potential partner.

DeSmet and colleagues (2015) carried out a systematic review and meta-analysis of serious video game interventions for sexual health promotion. A total of seven studies were identified that included a control group, allowing the calculation of an effect size (using Hedges' g). The studies identified showed positive effects on determinants (g = 0.242; 95 percent confidence interval) but with a small effect size. Behavioral effects were only assessed in two studies and neither were significant (g = 0.456; 95 percent confidence interval). The authors noted that most video games used strongly relied on pure gamification features (e.g. rewards, feedback). It was concluded there is a need for more rigorous evaluation studies of video game effectiveness, with longer-term follow-ups, and using measures of behavior rather than merely their determinants.

Video games and simulations have been used extensively in a comprehensive health promotion for adolescents. For instance, Bosworth (1994) used these strategies to attract adolescents to BARN (Body Awareness Resource Network), as well as helping to hold interest. In each of the six topic areas (AIDS, Alcohol and Other Drugs, Body Management, Human Sexuality, Smoking, and Stress Management) video game quizzes challenged users to test their knowledge on a topic. Simulations challenged users to apply health information in hypothetical situations. Video games were a more important factor in the selection of BARN for younger users than for older users. BARN game users were not more likely than non-game users to be users of other computer or video games, nor did game users engage in more risk-taking behaviors (e.g. alcohol, other drugs) than non-game users. Similar types of health promotion video games have been used successfully for cystic fibrosis (Davis, Quittner, Stack, & Young, 2004), drug use (Oakley, 1994), alcohol use (Resnick, 1994a), marijuana use

(Henningson, Gold, & Duncan, 1986), depression (Russoniello, Fish, & O'Brien, 2013), sexual behavior (Brüll, Ruiter, Wiers, & Kok, 2016; Chu et al., 2015; Starn & Paperny, 1990), life choices (Thomas, 1994), and anti-social behavior (Resnick, 1994b). One of the major problems with this area is that reported positive effects from video games in a health promotion context is that almost all of the video games evaluated were specially designed rather than those that were already commercially available. This does raise questions about the utility of generally commercial games in helping health promotion activities.

VIDEO GAMES, STRESS, ANXIETY, AND EMOTIONAL REGULATION

Reinecke (2009) demonstrated that the playing of video games can help in recuperation from stress and strain. In fact, therapeutic uses of video games to reduce stress, anxiety, and specific anxiety disorders have taken place in different ways (Fish, Russoniello, & O'Brien, 2014). Potential benefits of video game playing have been reported as a way of reducing preoperative anxiety among children (Patel et al., 2006). There is also evidence that suggests playing puzzle games, specifically the game *Tetris*, can mitigate flashbacks of traumatic experiences (Holmes, James, Coode-Bate, & Deeprose, 2009; James et al., 2015). There is also evidence suggesting that video game playing by military personnel has a protective mechanism versus nightmares (Gackenbach, Ellerman, & Hall, 2011) and in developing their coping skills (Procci, Bowers, Wong, & Andrews, 2013). Video games have also been used not only in a palliative context but also as a more structured form of therapy via the use of simulation video games for the treatment of clinical disorders. Specifically, virtual reality exposure therapy (VRET) has been applied to target anxiety disorders. It has been efficiently used in the treatment of acrophobia (Krijn et al., 2004), claustrophobia (Botella, Banos, Villa, Perpina, & Garcia-Palacios, 2000), panic disorder with agoraphobia (Vincelli et al., 2003), fear of flying (Rothbaum, Hodges, Smith, Lee, & Price, 2000), driving phobia (Wald & Taylor, 2000), spider phobia (Garcia-Palacios, Hoffman, Carlin, Furness, & Botella, 2002), and post-traumatic stress disorder (Holmes et al., 2009; James et al., 2015; Rothbaum, Hodges, Ready, Graap, & Alarcon, 2001; Wiederhold & Wiederhold, 2010). A meta-analysis of VRETs for anxiety disorders conducted by Powers and Emmelkamp (2008) evaluated thirteen studies and reported highly positive results with regards to the efficacy and efficiency of VRET for treating anxiety disorders.

Villani and colleagues (2018) carried out a systematic review assessing empirical studies that had investigated the effects and modalities of using video games in managing affective states (i.e., emotional regulation which is known to promote mental health and well-being). A total of twenty-three studies met the inclusion criteria and were classed as (i) qualitative and cross-sectional studies, (ii) experimental studies, and (iii) emotional regulation (ER) intervention studies (with serious games rather than commercial video games). The findings showed that improvements in ER were found most with commercial games (related to enjoyment and gameplay). However, these studies did not use clinical populations so the health benefits needed to be interpreted cautiously.

VIDEO GAMES AS PHYSICAL ACTIVITY USING "EXERGAMES"

Active video games have also used in the context of "exergaming"—using games as physical exercise (Baranowski et al., 2016; Christison et al., 2016). Research regarding exergaming is mixed, with some naturalistic research (Baranowski et al., 2012) suggesting little effects on physical activity intensity and duration, whereas other research shows that exergaming can decrease body mass index (BMI) and weight (Trost, Sundal, Foster, Lent, & Vojta, 2014). There have been a number of systematic reviews examining the efficacy of exergames. Tabak, Dekker-van Weering, van Dijk, and Vollenbroek-Hutten (2015) carried out a systematic review on the promotion of daily physical activity via mobile video gaming. More specifically, they examined studies utilizing a mobile game that required players to perform physical activity in daily life and where the game included specific goals, rules, and feedback mechanisms (therefore excluding non-mobile "exergames"). A total of eleven studies met the inclusion criteria. The results showed that most studies used goal setting as the motivation strategy for gaming engagement. The majority of the studies used avatars or metaphors to visualize activity, whereas feedback was typically provided in relation to the goal. The most commonly incorporated game elements were competition and rewards. Clinical evidence of efficacy of such games was lacking because only two randomized controlled studies were identified. Most study evaluations simply focused on the feasibility of using such games.

Liang and Lau (2014) systematically reviewed the effects of active video games on physical activity and related outcomes among healthy children. They identified fifty-four studies, of which thirty-two examined the immediate physical activity effects (i.e. energy expenditure and physical activity levels) during the playing of active video games. The remaining studies mainly comprised intervention studies (n = 21) aimed at promoting physical activity. The authors reported that energy expenditure was light to moderate in the studies examining immediate physical activity outcomes. Children playing action video games at home had no effect on physical activity. However, some studies suggested that structured video game play could improve physical activity.

Parisod and colleagues (2014) carried out a systematic review of other systematic reviews concerning the promotion of children's health using video games. A total of fifteen systematic reviews met the inclusion criteria. Results showed that the playing of active video games using both upper and lower body movements can lead to light to moderate levels of physical activity and energy expenditure. In sedentary games the findings showed there was potential to facilitate children's health education, especially dietary habits and in diabetes- and asthma-related behavior.

Murphy and colleagues (2009) reported that music and rhythm video games used with overweight children have a positive effect. *Dance Dance Revolution* (DDR), a game that requires players to move their feet in co-ordination with arrows scrolling across the screen was used in the study with thirty-five overweight children. The results showed that after twelve weeks of playing, the children improved their flow-mediated dilation, aerobics fitness, and mean arterial pressure without changes in inflammatory markers or nitric oxide production. However, a review by Daley (2009) stressed caution on this topic and asserted that active gaming was no substitute for real sports and activities. She also stressed the need for high-quality, randomized, controlled trials to evaluate the effectiveness and sustainability of active gaming.

Lu and colleagues (2013) carried out a systematic review of the efficacy of health video games on childhood obesity prevention and intervention. They identified fourteen papers examining twenty-eight different health video games published between 2005 and 2013. Most of the video games identified were commercially available. Most studies were of short duration and involved both boys and girls who typically played video games at home. They reported that positive outcomes related to obesity were observed in approximately 40 percent of the studies, all of which targeted overweight or obese participants.

It has been suggested that the playing of exergames are an innovative approach in enhancing physical activity among the elderly. Larsen, Schou, Lund, and Langberg (2013) carried out a systematic review to determine the efficacy of exergames in healthy elderly individuals using validated quantitative physical outcomes. The authors identified forty-five studies that met the initial inclusion criteria. However, only seven studies using randomized controlled trials with low-to-moderate methodological quality were reviewed for the final review. The seven studies comprised 311 participants in total, and six of the studies reported a positive effect of exergaming on the health of the elderly. The authors concluded that exergames have potential in improving elderly physical health but that better-designed studies are needed to assess the effectiveness and long-term adherence in this age group.

Staiano and Flynn (2014) carried out a systematic review concerning therapeutic uses of active video games. The authors identified sixty-four studies that evaluated the health outcomes of active video games. The papers included the use of video games used to rehabilitate (in alphabetical order) balance, burn treatment, cancer, cerebral palsy, Down's syndrome, extremity dysfunction or amputation, hospitalization, lupus, Parkinson's disease, spinal injury, or stroke. Results indicated that the majority of studies demonstrated positive results for improved health outcomes of video game interventions compared to usual care. However, the authors also noted that many of the studies were pilot studies with small samples, and that many studies lacked a suitable comparison or control group, with little or no follow-up to test for sustainability. It is also worth noting that some commercial games that are not exergames (such as *Pokémon Go*) have also been shown to foster physical activity in children and adolescents, although such effects have not been rigorously evaluated (Althoff, White, & Horvitz, 2016).

Conclusions

Many of the studies outlined in this chapter used serious video games rather than those that are commercially available. The use of commercial video games in therapy may be controversial since these games have not been created for therapeutic purposes and lack the carefully standardized conditions of therapeutic games. However, it appears important to investigate their uses in therapy as some current video games allow the personalization of the video game settings and content, e.g. modifying the character appearance, integration of real-life elements into the game. This may provide new avenues for clinicians to explore the therapeutic use of video games at a low cost compared to specialized and expensive video games platforms. The recent commercialization of virtual reality headsets, which enhance the sense of presence in the virtual world making gaming a more realistic experience, has opened a world of opportunities for therapy (Griffiths, 2017). Moreover, the advance in artificial intelligence (through the use of more receptive video game characters that simulate understanding and that respond to players' behaviors) may facilitate the use of video game characters as companions. This may be of therapeutic help to specific sub-groups (e.g. autistic children, those with learning difficulties).

It is clear from the studies outlined that, in the right context, video games can have a positive therapeutic benefit to a large range of different sub-groups. Video games have been shown to help children undergoing chemotherapy, children undergoing psychotherapy, children with particular emotional and behavioral problems (attention deficit disorder, impulsivity, autism), individuals with medical and health problems (Erb's palsy, muscular dystrophy, burns, strokes, movement impairment), patients suffering from a variety of anxiety disorders, groups such as the elderly, and individuals looking to overcome real-life challenges (including symptoms of depression) and boost their well-being (including increasing life satisfaction, self-efficacy, and social support). In terms of video games being distractor tasks, it seems likely that the effects can be attributed to most commercially available video games. However, as with the literature on video games aiding health promotion, one of the major problems is that reported positive effects in some of these other instances were from specially designed video games rather than those that were already commercially available. It is therefore hard to evaluate the therapeutic value of video games as a whole. As with research into the more negative effects, it may well be the case that some video games are particularly beneficial, whereas others have little or no therapeutic benefit whatsoever. What is clear from the empirical literature is that the negative consequences of video game playing almost always involve people who are excessive users. It is probably fair to say that therapeutic benefits (including such things as self-esteem) can be gained from moderate video game playing (Nuyens et al., 2018). Video games appear to have great positive therapeutic potential in addition to their entertainment value. Many positive applications in healthcare have been developed. There has been considerable success when games are specifically designed to address a specific problem or to teach a certain skill. However, generalizability outside the game-playing situation remains an important consideration.

REFERENCES

Achtman, R. L., Green, C. S., & Bavelier, D. (2008). Video games as a tool to train visual skills. *Restorative Neurology and Neuroscience 26*(4–5), 435–446.

Adriaenssens, E. E., Eggermont, E., Pyck, K., Boeckx, W., & Gilles, B. (1988). The video invasion of rehabilitation. *Burns 14*, 417–419.

Althoff, T., White, R. W., & Horvitz, E. (2016). Influence of *Pokémon Go* on physical activity: Study and implications. *Journal of Medical Internet Research 18*(12), e315.

Baranowski, T., Abdelsamad, D., Baranowski, J., O'Connor, T. M., Thompson, D., Barnett, A.,... Chen, T.-A. (2012). Impact of an active video game on healthy children's physical activity. *Pediatrics 129*, e636–e642.

Baranowski, T., Blumberg, F., Buday, R., DeSmet, A., Fiellin, L. E., Green, C. S.,...Young, K. (2016). Games for health for children—Current status and needed research. *Games for Health Journal 5*(1), 1–12.

Bavelier, D., Green, C. S., & Seidenberg, M. S. (2013). Cognitive development: Gaming your way out of dyslexia? *Current Biology 23*(7), R282–R283.

Blechman, E. A., Rabin, C., & McEnroe, M. J. (1986). Family communication and problem solving with boardgames and computer games. In C. E. Schaefer & S. E. Reid (Eds.), *Game play: Therapeutic use of childhood games* (pp. 129–145). New York: John Wiley & Sons.

Bosworth, K. (1994). Computer games as tools to reach and engage adolescents in health promotion activities. *Computers in Human Services 11*, 109–119.

Botella, C., Banos, R. M., Villa, H., Perpina, C., & Garcia-Palacios, A. (2000). Virtual reality in the treatment of claustrophobic fear: A controlled, multiple-baseline design. *Behavior Therapy 31*(3), 583–595.

Brezinka, V. (2008). *Treasure Hunt*—A serious game to support psychotherapeutic treatment of children. In S. K. Anderson (Ed.), *eHealth beyond the horizon* (pp. 71–76). Amsterdam: IOS Press.

Broeren, J., Claesson, L., Goude, D., Rydmark, M., & Sunnerhagen, K. S. (2008). Virtual rehabilitation in an activity centre for community-dwelling persons with stroke: The possibilities of 3-dimensional computer games. *Cerebrovascular Diseases 26*(3), 289–296.

Brown, S. J., Lieberman, D. A., Germeny, B. A., Fan, Y. C., Wilson, D. M., & Pasta, D. J. (1997). Educational video game for juvenile diabetes: Results of a controlled trial. *Medical Informatics 22*, 77–89.

Brüll, P., Ruiter, R. A., Wiers, R. W., & Kok, G. (2016). Gaming for safer sex: Young German and Turkish people report no specific culture-related preferences toward educational games promoting safer sex. *Games for Health Journal 5*(6), 357–365.

Buckalew, L. W., & Buckalew, P. B. (1983). Behavioral management of exceptional children using video games as reward. *Perceptual and Motor Skills 56*, 580.

Butler, C. (1985). Utilizing video games to increase sitting tolerance. *Archives of Physical Medicine and Rehabilitation 66*(8), 527–537.

Cahill, J. M. (1994). Health works: Interactive AIDS education videogames. *Computers in Human Services 11*(1–2), 159–176.

Cameirao, M. S., Bermúdez i Badia, S., Duarte Oller, E., Zimmerli, L., & Verschure, P. F. M. J. (2007). *The rehabilitation gaming system: A virtual reality-based system for the evaluation and rehabilitation of motor deficits.* Paper presented at the Proceedings of Virtual Rehabilitation. 27–29 September, Venice, Italy.

Ceranoglu, T. A. (2010a). Star Wars in psychotherapy: Video games in the office. *Academic Psychiatry 34*(3), 233–236.

Ceranoglu, T. A. (2010b). Video games in psychotherapy. *Review of General Psychology 14*(2), 141–146.

Chandrasekharan, S., Mazalek, A., Nitsche, M., Chen, Y. F., & Ranjan, A. (2010). Ideomotor design using common coding theory to derive novel video game interactions. *Pragmatics & Cognition 18*(2), 313–339.

Chen, H., & Sun, H. (2017). Effects of active videogame and sports, play, and active recreation for kids' physical education on children's health-related fitness and enjoyment. *Games for Health Journal 6*(5), 312–318.

Christison, A. L., Evans, T. A., Bleess, B. B., Wang, H., Aldag, J. C., & Binns, H. J. (2016). Exergaming for health: A randomized study of community-based exergaming curriculum in pediatric weight management. *Games for Health Journal 5*(6), 413–421.

Chu, S. K. W., Kwan, A. C., Reynolds, R., Mellecker, R. R., Tam, F., Lee, G.,...& Leung, C. Y. (2015). Promoting sex education among teenagers through an interactive game: Reasons for success and implications. *Games for Health Journal 4*(3), 168–174.

Clarke, B., & Schoech, D. (1994). A computer-assisted game for adolescents: Initial development and comments. *Computers in Human Services 11*(1–2), 121–140.

Cole, S. W., Yoo, D. J., & Knutson, B. (2012). Interactivity and reward-related neural activation during a serious videogame. *PLoS ONE 7*(3), e33909.

Colder Carras, M., van Rooij, A.J., Spruijt-Metz, D., Kvedar, J., Griffiths, M. D., & Labrique, A. (2018). Therapeutic commercial games: A new research agenda to unlock the clinical potential of a global pastime. *Frontiers in Psychiatry 8*, 300.

Comello, M. L. G., Francis, D. B., Marshall, L. H., & Puglia, D. R. (2016). Cancer survivors who play recreational computer games: Motivations for playing and associations with beneficial psychological outcomes. *Games for Health Journal 5*(4), 286–292.

Coyle, D., Matthews, M., Sharry, J., Nisbet, A., & Doherty, G. (2005). Personal investigator: A therapeutic 3D game for adolescent psychotherapy. *Interactive Technology and Smart Education 2*(2), 73–88.

Dahl-Popolizio, S., Loman, J., & Cordes, C. C. (2014). Comparing outcomes of kinect video-game-based occupational/physical therapy versus usual care. *Games for Health Journal 3*(3), 157–161.

Daley, A. (2009). Can exergaming contribute to improving physical activity levels and health outcomes in children? *Pediatrics 124*, 763–771.

Davis, M. A., Quittner, A. L., Stack, C. M., & Young, M. C. (2004). Controlled evaluation of the STARBRIGHT CDROM program for children and adolescents with Cystic Fibrosis. *Journal of Pediatric Psychology 29*(4), 259–267.

DeShazo, J., Harris, L., & Pratt, W. (2010). Effective intervention or child's play? A review of video games for diabetes education. *Diabetes Technology & Therapeutics 12*(10), 815–822.

DeSmet, A., Shegog, R., Van Ryckeghem, D., Crombez, G., & De Bourdeaudhuij, I. (2015). A systematic review and meta-analysis of interventions for sexual health promotion involving serious digital games. *Games for Health Journal 4*(2), 78–90.

DeSmet, A., Van Ryckeghem, D., Compernolle, S., Baranowski, T., Thompson, D., Crombez, G.,... De Bourdeaudhuij, I. (2014). A meta-analysis of serious digital games for healthy lifestyle promotion. *Preventitive Medicine 69*, 95–107.

Dustman, R. E., Emmerson, R. Y., Steinhaus, L. A., Shearer, D. E., & Dustman, T. J. (1992). The effects of videogame playing on neuropsychological performance of elderly individuals. *Journal of Gerontology* 47(3), 168–171.

Eichenberg, C., & Schott, M. (2017). Serious games for psychotherapy: A systematic review. *Games for Health Journal* 6(3), 127–135.

Eow, Y. L., Ali, W. Z. B., Mahmud, R. B., & Baki, R. (2010). Computer games development and appreciative learning approach in enhancing students' creative perception. *Computers & Education* 54(1), 146–161.

Farris, M., Bates, R., Resnick, H., & Stabler, N. (1994). Evaluation of computer games' impact upon cognitively impaired frail elderly. *Computers in Human Services* 11(1–2), 219–228.

Favelle, G. K. (1994). Therapeutic applications of commercially available computer software. *Computers in Human Services* 11(1–2), 151–158.

Fish, M. T., Russoniello, C. V., & O'Brien, K. (2014). The efficacy of prescribed casual video-game play in reducing symptoms of anxiety: A randomized controlled study. *Games for Health Journal* 3(5), 291–295.

Fisher, S. (1986). Use of computers following brain injury. *Activities, Adaptation & Aging* 8(1), 81–93.

Fitzgerald, D., Trakarnratanakul, N., Smyth, B., & Caulfield, B. (2010). Effects of a wobble board-based therapeutic exergaming system for balance training on dynamic postural stability and intrinsic motivation levels. *Journal of Orthopaedic & Sports Physical Therapy* 40(1), 11–19.

Franco, G. E. (2016). Videogames as a therapeutic tool in the context of narrative therapy. *Frontiers in Psychology* 7, 1657.

Francis, D. B., Comello, M. L. G., & Marshall, L. H. (2016). How does gameplaying support values and psychological well-being among cancer survivors? *Games for Health Journal* 5(2), 128–134.

Fung, V., So, K., Park, E., Ho, A., Shaffer, J., Chan, E., & Gomez, M. (2010). The utility of a video game system in rehabilitation of burn and nonburn patients: A survey among occupational therapy and physiotherapy practitioners. *Journal of Burn Care & Research* 31(5), 768–775.

Funk, J. B., Germann, J. N., & Buchman, D. D. (1997). Children and electronic games in the United States. *Trends in Communication* 2, 111–126.

Gackenbach, J. I., Ellerman, E., & Hall, C. (2011). Video game play as nightmare protection: A preliminary inquiry on military gamers. Unpublished manuscript.

Garcia-Palacios, A., Hoffman, H., Carlin, A., Furness, T. A., & Botella, C. (2002). Virtual reality in the treatment of spider phobia: A controlled study. *Behaviour Research and Therapy* 40(9), 983–993.

Gardner, J. E. (1991). Can the Mario Bros. help? Nintendo games as an adjunct in psychotherapy with children. *Psychotherapy* 28, 667–670.

Gasperetti, B. A., Foley, J. T., Yang, S., Columna, L., & Lieberman, L. J. (2018). Comparison of three interactive video games for youth with visual impairments. *British Journal of Visual Impairment* 36(1), 31–41.

Gaylord-Ross, R. J., Haring, T. G., Breen, C., & Pitts-Conway, V. (1984). The training and generalization of social interaction skills with autistic youth. *Journal of Applied Behaviour Analysis* 17, 229.

Goldstein, J., Cajko, L., Oosterbroek, M., Michielsen, M., van Houten, O., & Salverda, F. (1997). Video games and the elderly. *Social Behavior and Personality* 25, 345–352.

Govender, M., Bowen, R. C., German, M. L., Bulaj, G., & Bruggers, C. S. (2015). Clinical and neurobiological perspectives of empowering pediatric cancer patients using videogames. *Games for Health Journal 4*(5), 362–374.

Griffiths, M. D. (2010). Adolescent video game playing: Issues for the classroom. *Education Today: Quarterly Journal of the College of Teachers 60*(4), 31–34.

Griffiths, M. D. (2017). The psychosocial impact of gambling in virtual reality. *Casino and Gaming International 29*, 51–54.

Griffiths, M. D., Kuss, D. J., & Ortiz de Gortari, A. (2017). Videogames as therapy: An updated selective review of the medical and psychological literature. *International Journal of Privacy and Health Information Management 5*(2), 71–96.

Griffiths, M. D., Kuss, D. J., & Pontes, H. (2016). A brief overview of internet gaming disorder and its treatment. *Australian Clinical Psychologist 2*(1), 20108.

Henningson, K. A., Gold, R. S., & Duncan, D. F. (1986). A computerized marijuana decision maze: Expert opinion regarding its use in health education. *Journal of Drug Education 16*(3), 243–261.

Hieftje, K., Edelman, E. J., Camenga, D. R., & Fiellin, L. E. (2013). Electronic media-based health interventions promoting behavior change in youth: A systematic review. *JAMA Pediatrics 167*(6), 574–580.

Hollander, E. K., & Plummer, H. R. (1986). An innovative therapy and enrichment program for senior adults utilizing the personal computer. *Activities, Adaptation & Aging 8*(1), 59–68.

Hollingsworth, M., & Woodward, J. (1993). Integrated learning: Explicit strategies and their role in problem solving instruction for students with learning disabilities. *Exceptional Children 59*, 444–445.

Holmes, E. A., James, E. L., Coode-Bate, T., & Deeprose, C. (2009). Can playing the computer game "Tetris" reduce the build-up of flashbacks for trauma? A proposal from cognitive science. *PLoS ONE 4*(1), e4153.

Horn, E., Jones, H. A., & Hamlett, C. (1991). An investigation of the feasibility of a video game system for developing scanning and selection skills. *Journal for the Association for People with Severe Handicaps 16*, 108–115.

Horne-Moyer, H. L., Moyer, B. H., Messer, D. C., & Messer, E. S. (2014). The use of electronic games in therapy: A review with clinical implications. *Current Psychiatry Reports 16*(12), 520.

Housman, S. J., Scott, K. M., & Reinkensmeyer, D. J. (2009). A randomized controlled trial of gravity-supported, computer-enhanced arm exercise for individuals with severe hemiparesis. *Neurorehabilitation and Neural Repair 23*(5), 505–514.

Huber, M., Rabin, B., Docan, C., Burdea, G. C., AbdelBaky, M., & Golomb, M. R. (2010). Feasibility of modified remotely monitored in-home gaming technology for improving hand function in adolescents with cerebral palsy. *IEEE Transactions on Information Technology in Biomedicine 14*(2), 526–534.

Hurkmans, H. L., van den Berg-Emons, R. J., & Stam, H. J. (2010). Energy expenditure in adults with cerebral palsy playing Wii Sports. *Archives of Physical Medicine and Rehabilitation 91*(10), 1577–1581.

James, E. L., Bonsall, M. B., Hoppitt, L., Tunbridge, E. M., Geddes, J. R., Milton, A. L., & Holmes, E. A. (2015). Computer game play reduces intrusive memories of experimental trauma via reconsolidation-update mechanisms. *Psychological Science 26*, 1201–1215.

Jannink, M. J. A., Van Der Wilden, G. J., Navis, D. W., Visser, G., Gussinklo, J., & Ijzerman, M. (2008). A low-cost video game applied for training of upper extremity function in children with cerebral palsy: A pilot study. *Cyberpsychology & Behavior 11*(1), 27–32.

Jansen-Kosterink, S. M., Huis in't Veld, R. M., Schönauer, C., Kaufmann, H., Hermens, H. J., & Vollenbroek-Hutten, M. M. (2013). A serious exergame for patients suffering from chronic musculoskeletal back and neck pain: A pilot study. *Games for Health Journal 2*(5), 299–307.

Joei Mioto, B. B., & Goncalves Ribas, C. (2014). The usage of videogames as a psychotherapeutic intervention in individuals with Down syndrome. *Open Access Library Journal 1*, 1–9.

Joo, L. Y., Yin, T. S., Xu, D., Thia, E., Chia, P. F., Kuah, C. W. K., & He, K. K. (2010). A feasibility study using interactive commercial off-the-shelf computer gaming: Gaming in upper limb rehabilitation patients after stroke. *Journal of Rehabilitation Medicine 42*(5), 437–441.

Kappes, B. M., & Thompson, D. L. (1985). Biofeedback vs. video games: Effects on impulsivity, locus of control and self-concept with incarcerated individuals. *Journal of Clinical Psychology 41*, 698–706.

Kato, P. M., Cole, S. W., Bradlyn, A. S., & Pollock, B. H. (2008). A video game improves behavioral outcomes in adolescents and young adults with cancer: A randomized trial. *Pediatrics 122*(2), E305–E317.

King, T. I. (1993). Hand strengthening with a computer for purposeful activity. *American Journal of Occupational Therapy 47*, 635–637.

Kolko, D. J., & Rickard-Figueroa. (1985). Effects of video games on the adverse corollaries of chemotherapy in pediatric oncology patients. *Journal of Consulting & Clinical Psychology 53*, 223–228.

Krichevets, A. N., Sirotkina, E. B., Yevsevicheva, I. V., & Zeldin, L. M. (1994). Computer games as a means of movement rehabilitation. *Disability and Rehabilitation 17*, 100–105.

Krijn, M., Emmelkamp, P. M. G., Biemond, R., de Ligny, C. D., Schuemie, M. J., & van der Mast, C. (2004). Treatment of acrophobia in virtual reality: The role of immersion and presence. *Behaviour Research and Therapy 42*(2), 229–239.

Lange, B., Flynn, S., Proffitt, R., Chang, C. Y., & Rizzo, A. (2010). Development of an interactive game-based rehabilitation tool for dynamic balance training. *Topics in Stroke Rehabilitation 17*(5), 345–352.

Larsen, L. H., Schou, L., Lund, H. H., & Langberg, H. (2013). The physical effect of exergames in healthy elderly: A systematic review. *Games for Health Journal 2*(4), 205–212.

Lauterbach, S. A., Foreman, M. H., & Engsberg, J. R. (2013). Computer games as therapy for persons with stroke. *Games for Health Journal 2*(1), 24–28.

Lawrence, G. H. (1986). Using computers for the treatment of psychological problems. *Computers in Human Behavior 2*, 43–62.

Lee, H. C., Huang, C. L., Ho, S. H., & Sung, W. H. (2017). The effect of a virtual reality game intervention on balance for patients with stroke: A randomized controlled trial. *Games for Health Journal 6*(5), 303–311.

Leng, E. Y., Ali, W., Mahmud, R. B., & Baki, R. (2010). Computer games development experience and appreciative learning approach for creative process enhancement. *Computers & Education 55*(3), 1131–1144.

Liang, Y., & Lau, P. W. (2014). Effects of active videogames on physical activity and related outcomes among healthy children: A systematic review. *Games for Health Journal 3*(3), 122–144.

Lieberman, D. A. (2001). Management of chronic pediatric diseases with interactive health games: Theory and research findings. *Journal of Ambulatory Care Management 24*, 26–38.

Lim, C. G., Lee, T. S., Guan, C. T., Fung, D. S. S., Cheung, Y. B., Teng, S. S. W.,…Krishnan, K. R. (2010). Effectiveness of a brain-computer interface based programme for the treatment of ADHD: A pilot study. *Psychopharmacology Bulletin 43*(1), 73–82.

Lu, A. S., & Kharrazi, H. (2018). A state-of-the-art systematic content analysis of games for health. *Games for Health Journal* 7(1), 1–15. doi:10.1089/g4h.2017.0095

Lu, A. S., Kharrazi, H., Gharghabi, F., & Thompson, D. (2013). A systematic review of health videogames on childhood obesity prevention and intervention. *Games for Health Journal* 2(3), 131–141.

Masendorf, F. (1993). Training of learning disabled children's spatial abilities by computer games. *Zeitschrift für Pädagogische Psychologie* 7, 209–213.

Matthews, T. J., De Santi, S. M., Callahan, D., Koblenz-Sulcov, C. J., & Werden, J. I. (1987). The microcomputer as an agent of intervention with psychiatric patients: Preliminary studies. *Computers in Human Behavior* 3(1), 37–47.

McCormack, K., Fitzgerald, D., Fitzgerald, O., Caulfield, B., O'Huiginn, B., & Smyth, B. (2009). A comparison of a computer game-based exercise system with conventional approaches of exercise therapy in rheumatology patients. *Rheumatology* 48, I29–I29.

McGuire, F. A. (1984). Improving quality of life for residents of long-term care facilities through video games. *Activities, Adaptation & Aging* 6(1), 1–7.

McGuire, F. A. (1986). *Computer technology and the aged: Implications and applications for activity programs*. New York: Haworth.

Miller, D. J., & Robertson, D. P. (2010). Using a games console in the primary classroom: Effects of "Brain Training" programme on computation and self-esteem. *British Journal of Educational Technology* 41(2), 242–255.

Murphy, E.C., Carson, L., Neal, W., Baylis, C., Donley, D., & Yeater, R. (2009). Effects of an exercise intervention using Dance Dance Revolution on endothelial function and other risk factors in overweight children. *International Journal of Pediatric Obesity* 3, 1–10.

Nuyens, F., Kuss, D. J., Lopez-Fernandez, O., & Griffiths, M. D. (2017). The experimental analysis of problematic video gaming and cognitive skills: A systematic review. *Journal of Behavioral and Cognitive Therapy* 27, 110–117.

Nuyens, F., Kuss, D. J., Lopez-Fernandez, O., & Griffiths, M. D. (2018). The empirical analysis of non-problematic video gaming and cognitive skills: A systematic review. *International Journal of Mental Health and Addiction*. Epub ahead of print. doi:10.1007/s11469-018-9946-0

O'Connor, T. J., Cooper, R. A., Fitzgerald, S. G., Dvorznak, M. J., Boninger, M. L., VanSickle, D. P., & Glass, L. (2000). Evaluation of a manual wheelchair interface to computer games. *Neurorehabilitation and Neural Repair* 14(1), 21–31.

Oakley, C. (1994). SMACK: A computer driven game for at-risk teens. *Computers in Human Services* 11(1–2), 97–99.

Okolo, C. (1992a). The effect of computer-assisted instruction format and initial attitude on the arithmetic facts proficiency and continuing motivation of students with learning disabilities. *Exceptionality* 3, 195–211.

Okolo, C. (1992b). Reflections on "The effect of computer-assisted instruction format and initial attitude on the arithmetic facts proficiency and continuing motivation of students with learning disabilities". *Exceptionality* 3, 255–258.

Olsen-Rando, R. A. (1994). Proposal for development of a computerized version of talking, feeling and doing game. *Computers in Human Services* 11(1–2), 69–80.

Parisod, H., Pakarinen, A., Axelin, A., Danielsson-Ojala, R., Smed, J., & Salanterä, S. (2017). Designing a health-game intervention supporting health literacy and a tobacco-free life in early adolescence. *Games for Health Journal* 6(4), 187–199.

Parisod, H., Pakarinen, A., Kauhanen, L., Aromaa, M., Leppänen, V., Liukkonen, T. N.,... & Salanterä, S. (2014). Promoting children's health with digital games: A review of reviews. *Games for Health Journal* 3(3), 145–156.

Patel, A., Schieble, T., Davidson M., Tran, M. C., Schoenberg, C., Delphin, E., & Bennett, H. (2006). Distraction with a hand-held video game reduces pediatric preoperative anxiety. *Pediatric Anesthesia* 16,1019–1027.

Pegelow, C. H. (1992). Survey of pain management therapy provided for children with sickle cell disease. *Clinical Pediatrics* 31, 211–214.

Phillips, W. R. (1991). Video game therapy. *The New England Journal of Medicine* 325, 1056–1057.

Powers, M. B., & Emmelkamp, P. M. G. (2008). Virtual reality exposure therapy for anxiety disorders: A meta-analysis. *Journal of Anxiety Disorders* 22(3), 561–569.

Procci, K., Bowers, C., Wong, C., & Andrews, A. (2013). Minigames for mental health: Improving warfighters' coping skills and awareness of mental health resources. *Games for Health Journal* 2(4), 240–246.

Redd, W. H., Jacobsen, P. B., DieTrill, M., Dermatis, H., McEvoy, M., & Holland, J. C. (1987). Cognitive-attentional distraction in the control of conditioned nausea in pediatric cancer patients receiving chemotherapy. *Journal of Consulting & Clinical Psychology* 55, 391–395.

Reichlin, L., Mani, N., McArthur, K., Harris, A. M., Rajan, N., & Dacso, C. C. (2011). Assessing the acceptability and usability of an interactive serious game in aiding treatment decisions for patients with localized prostate cancer. *Journal of Medical Internet Research* 13(1), 188–201.

Reijnders, J., van Heugten, C., & van Boxtel, M. (2013). Cognitive interventions in healthy older adults and people with mild cognitive impairment: A systematic review. *Ageing Research Reviews* 12(1), 263–275.

Reinecke, L. (2009). Games and recovery: The use of video and computer games to recuperate from stress and strain. *Journal of Media Psychology: Theories, Methods, and Applications* 21(3), 126–142.

Resnick, H. (1994a). Ben's Grille. *Computers in Human Services* 11(1–2), 203–211.

Resnick, H. (1994b). Electronic technology and rehabilitation: A computerised simulation game for youthful offenders. *Computers in Human Services* 11(1–2), 61–67.

Rico-Olarte, C., López, D. M., Narváez, S., Farinango, C. D., & Pharow, P. S. (2017). Haphop-Physio: A computer game to support cognitive therapies in children. *Psychology Research and Behavior Management* 10, 209.

Riddick, C. C., Spector, S. G., & Drogin, E. B. (1986). The effects of videogame play on the emotional states and affiliative behavior of nursing home residents. *Activities, Adaptation & Aging* 8(1), 95–107.

Rothbaum, B. O., Hodges, L., Smith, S., Lee, J. H., & Price, L. (2000). A controlled study of virtual reality exposure therapy for the fear of flying. *Journal of Consulting and Clinical Psychology* 68(6), 1020–1026.

Rothbaum, B. O., Hodges, L. F., Ready, D., Graap, K., & Alarcon, R. D. (2001). Virtual reality exposure therapy for Vietnam veterans with posttraumatic stress disorder. *Journal of Clinical Psychiatry* 62(8), 617–622.

Russoniello, C. V., Fish, M., & O'Brien, K. (2013). The efficacy of casual videogame play in reducing clinical depression: A randomized controlled study. *Games for Health Journal* 2(6), 341–346.

Ryan, E. B. (1994). Memory for Goblins: A computer game for assessing and training working memory skill. *Computers in Human Services* 11(1–2), 213–217.

Sato, K., Kuroki, K., Saiki, S., & Nagatomi, R. (2015). Improving walking, muscle strength, and balance in the elderly with an exergame using Kinect: A randomized controlled trial. *Games for Health Journal* 4(3), 161–167.

Schoene, D., Lord, S. R., Delbaere, K., Severino, C., Davies, T. A., & Smith, S. T. (2013). A randomised controlled pilot study of home-based step training in older people using videogame technology. *PLOS ONE* 8(3), e57734.

Schueren, B. (1986). Video games: An exploration of their potential as recreational activity programs in nursing homes. *Activities, Adaptation & Aging* 8(1), 49–58.

Sedlak, R. A., Doyle, M., & Schloss, P. (1982). Video games—A training and generalization demonstration with severely retarded adolescents. *Education and Training in Mental Retardation and Developmental Disabilities* 17(4), 332–336.

Sharar, S. R., Miller, W., Teeley, A., Soltani, M., Hoffman, H. G., Jensen, M. P., & Patterson, D. R. (2008). Applications of virtual reality for pain management in burn-injured patients. *Expert Review of Neurotherapeutics* 8(11), 1667–1674.

Skilbeck, C. (1991). Microcomputer-based cognitive rehabilitation. In A. Ager (Ed.), *Microcomputers and clinical psychology: Issues, applications and future developments* (pp. 95–118). Chichester: Wiley.

Spence, J. (1988). The use of computer arcade games in behaviour management. *Maladjustment and Therapeutic Education* 6, 64–68.

Staiano, A. E., & Flynn, R. (2014). Therapeutic uses of active videogames: A systematic review. *Games for Health Journal* 3(6), 351–365.

Starn, J., & Paperny, D. M. (1990). Computer games to enhance adolescent sex education. *Journal of Maternal Child Nursing* 15(4), 250–253.

Swanson, L. R., & Whittinghill, D. M. (2015). Intrinsic or extrinsic? Using videogames to motivate stroke survivors: A systematic review. *Games for Health Journal* 4(3), 253–258.

Synofzik, M., Schatton, C., Giese, M., Wolf, J., Schols, L., & Ilg, W. (2013). Videogame-based coordinative training can improve advanced, multisystemic early-onset ataxia. *Journal of Neurology* 260(10), 2656–2658.

Szer, J. (1983). Video games as physiotherapy. *Medical Journal of Australia* 1, 401–402.

Szturm, T., Peters, J. F., Otto, C., Kapadia, N., & Desai, A. (2008). Task-specific rehabilitation of finger-hand function using interactive computer gaming. *Archives of Physical Medicine and Rehabilitation* 89(11), 2213–2217.

Tabak, M., Dekker-van Weering, M., van Dijk, H., & Vollenbroek-Hutten, M. (2015). Promoting daily physical activity by means of mobile gaming: A review of the state of the art. *Games for Health Journal* 4(6), 460–469.

Tanaka, J. W., Wolf, J. M., Klaiman, C., Koenig, K., Cockburn, J., Herlihy, L.,…Schultz, R. T. (2010). Using computerized games to teach face recognition skills to children with autism spectrum disorder: The Let's Face It! program. *Journal of Child Psychology and Psychiatry* 51(8), 944–952.

Theng, Y. L., Lee, J. W., Patinadan, P. V., & Foo, S. S. (2015). The use of videogames, gamification, and virtual environments in the self-management of diabetes: A systematic review of evidence. *Games for Health Journal* 4(5), 352–361.

Thomas, D. L. (1994). Life choices: The program and its users. *Computers in Human Services* 11(1–2), 189–202.

Thomas, R., Cahill, J., & Santilli, L. (1997). Using an interactive computer game to increase skill and self-efficacy regarding safer sex negotiation: Field test results. *Health Education and Behavior* 24, 71–86.

Trost, S. G., Sundal, D., Foster, G. D., Lent, M. R., & Vojta, D. (2014). Effects of a pediatric weight management program with and without active video games: A randomized trial. *JAMA Pediatrics 168*(5), 407–413.

Vasterling, J., Jenkins, R. A., Tope, D. M., & Burish, T. G. (1993). Cognitive distraction and relaxation training for the control of side effects due to cancer chemotherapy. *Journal of Behavioral Medicine 16*, 65–80.

Villani, D., Carissoli, C., Triberti, S., Marchetti, A., Gilli, G., & Riva, G. (2018). Videogames for emotion regulation: A systematic review. *Games for Health Journal 7*(2), 85–99.

Vilozni, D., Bar-Yishay, E., Shapira, Y., Meyer, S., & Godfrey, S. (1994). Computerized respiratory muscle training in children with Duchenne Muscular Dystrophy. *Neuromuscular Disorders 4*, 249–255.

Vincelli, F., Anolli, L., Bouchard, S., Wiederhold, B. K., Zurloni, V., & Riva, G. (2003). Experiential cognitive therapy in the treatment of panic disorders with agoraphobia: A controlled study. *Cyberpsychology & Behavior 6*(3), 321–328.

Wald, J., & Taylor, S. (2000). Efficacy of virtual reality exposure therapy to treat driving phobia: A case report. *Journal of Behavior Therapy and Experimental Psychiatry 31*(3–4), 249–257.

Washburn, D. A., & Gulledge, J. P. (1995). Game-like tasks for comparative research: Leveling the playing field. *Behavior Research Methods, Instruments & Computers 27*(2), 235–238.

Weerdmeester, J., Cima, M., Granic, I., Hashemian, Y., & Gotsis, M. (2016). A feasibility study on the effectiveness of a full-body videogame intervention for decreasing attention deficit hyperactivity disorder symptoms. *Games for Health Journal 5*(4), 258–269.

Weightman, A. P. H., Preston, N., Holt, R., Allsop, M., Levesley, M., & Bhakta, B. (2010). Engaging children in healthcare technology design: Developing rehabilitation technology for children with cerebral palsy. *Journal of Engineering Design 21*(5), 579–600.

Weisman, S. (1983). Computer games for the frail elderly. *The Gerontologist 23*(4), 361–363.

Weisman, S. (1994). Computer games for the frail elderly. *Computers in Human Services, 11*(1–2), 229–234.

Wiederhold, B. K., & Wiederhold, M. D. (2010). Virtual reality treatment of posttraumatic stress disorder due to motor vehicle accident. *Cyberpsychology Behavior and Social Networking 13*(1), 21–27.

Wohlheiter, K. A., & Dahlquist, L. M. (2012). Interactive versus passive distraction for acute pain management in young children: The role of selective attention and development. *Journal of Pediatric Psychology 38*(2), 202–212.

Yavuzer, G., Senel, A., Atay, M. B., & Stam, H. J. (2008). "Playstation eyetoy games" improve upper extremity-related motor functioning in subacute stroke: A randomized controlled clinical trial. *European Journal of Physical and Rehabilitation Medicine 44*(3), 237–244.

PART VII

GAMING

CHAPTER 26

....

VIDEO GAMES AND
BEHAVIOR CHANGE

....

JESSICA McCAIN, KYLE MORRISON,
AND SUN JOO (GRACE) AHN

INTRODUCTION

....

SINCE the beginning of documented human culture, games have provided both individual and social entertainment. With the advent of the Internet, game play has largely moved to digital domains and video games have become a widespread activity. According to the Entertainment Software Association (ESA, 2017), video gaming is considered a "regular" activity in 65 percent of American households, with the video game industry contributing $11.7 billion in value to the gross domestic product of the United States. In the recent decade, scholars and practitioners have come to recognize that video games may provide more than just a traditional form of entertainment, and that gaming experiences may yield sustained effects that carry over into the physical world, impacting both attitudes and behavior. Behavioral changes may occur in both positive and negative directions, including health behavior changes and changes in prosocial and antisocial behavior (see chapter "The Social Consequences of Online Interaction" by Clark & Green, this volume). The idea that people can modify physical world behaviors by "just playing games" warrants investigation in what has traditionally been considered a casual pastime.

Through video games designed to create specific, controlled situations, unprecedented opportunities exist to shape individuals' behaviors for the purposes of education, health rehabilitation, training, and more, resulting in the Serious Games movement (Michael & Chen, 2005), or games designed for a purpose other than entertainment; the design of Games With A Purpose (GWAPs; e.g., Von Ahn & Dabbish, 2008); and in the practice of "gamification," or adding elements of games to non-gaming situations to benefit from the effects that gaming has on motivation and behavior (Deterding, Dixon, Khaled, & Nacke, 2011). Social psychologists have generated a substantial body of research demonstrating that behavior change is a product of both the characteristics of individuals and their situations (e.g., Bandura, 2001; Fleeson, 2001; Mischel & Shoda, 1995). Therefore, in addition to investigating contextual elements that yield behavior change, studying the psychosocial mechanisms that drive behavior change is critical to answer the question of why humans are motivated to change their behaviors following game play.

This chapter discusses how video games create virtual situations that are perceived differently from those naturally occurring in reality, allowing the possibility of changing behavior through contextual cues in the environment. It then discusses several known pathways (both cognitive and affective) through which video games can impact behavior change both intentionally and inadvertently. Finally, to illustrate concrete applications, it covers the use of games to extract purposeful behavior change in the field of healthcare.

How Video Games Differ from Traditional Media: Situational Affordances

Most games are comprised of a set of rules, or arbitrary restrictions on individual behaviors, and some element of challenge wherein players must compete against themselves, other players, or an environment within the boundaries of the rules to achieve a certain goal (Hogle, 1996). Through high-definition graphics, interactive controls, and complex narratives, video games can create a convincing virtual world that can influence players' behaviors. Rules can be strictly and precisely enforced with the computational power of consoles or computers. As games gain greater technological sophistication to produce ever more realistic, pleasurable, and challenging experiences, unprecedented situations are created that influence players' behavior in both intentional and unintentional ways.

Virtual worlds like those found in video games have been studied extensively by psychologists, engineers, computer scientists, and communication researchers, among others. Much of the earlier research on virtual worlds has focused either exclusively on the structural features and properties of the virtual world or the properties of individuals using the virtual world. More recently, however, researchers from multiple fields (e.g., Evans, Pearce, Vitak, & Treem, 2017; Treem & Leonardi, 2013) have begun to focus on the dynamic relationship that arises when a unique individual interacts with a given technology, which can be described as "situational affordance."

Gibson (1986) first presented the concept of affordances in the framework of ecological psychology to describe how individuals perceive objects in their environment. Gibson argued that, rather than perceiving only the physical aspects of an object, animals (including people) perceive an object in part by what uses it provides or "affords" to them to fulfill their needs. The perceived affordances differ based on both the individual and the object. To illustrate, consider an example of a rock. To a human, the rock potentially serves as a weapon. However, the same rock may be viewed differently by a snake as a potential place to hide.

Over time, Gibson's concept has been refined and clarified as referring to a unique and dynamic relationship that arises between the individual and the object during interactions (see, e.g., Norman, 1999). In this view, an affordance is neither inherent to the object nor to the individual, but is instead a combination of the object's properties, the individual's present needs, and the individual's ability to perceive that the object could meet his or her needs. Evans et al., (2017) described this relationship between individual agency and an object's properties (e.g., searchability) as a link between the static features of an object (e.g., profile pictures on a social media site) and an outcome (e.g., finding a picture of a specific person). Because interpretations of the term "affordance" still differ within and across fields (Evans et al., 2017), this chapter uses the term "situational affordances" to refer to this interpretation.

Fantasy Migration

Researchers have begun to describe gaming in virtual worlds in terms of novel situational affordances that distinguish them from traditional media. For example, McCain, Gentile, and Campbell (2015) posed the Great Fantasy Migration hypothesis to describe the motivation behind participation in geek culture, including gaming culture. They proposed that, due to increasing trends in cultural narcissism (i.e., the expectation that everyone should be "special") in the United States (Twenge, Konrath, Foster, Campbell, & Bushman, 2008), individuals have greater needs for the admiration, power, and fame needed to support a narcissistic sense of self. Faced with a decreased availability of this "narcissistic supply" in the physical world, individuals high in narcissism may migrate to virtual environments that afford greater opportunities to fulfill their needs. With the opportunity to play grandiose characters, accomplish powerful feats, and even customize appearances, digital games afford the maintenance of a narcissistic self to these individuals (e.g., Campbell & Foster, 2007; Morf & Rhodewalt, 2001). When an aspect of the game that differs from the physical world (e.g., the ability to roleplay a powerful hero) is perceived by an individual to be useful in obtaining his or her needs (e.g., narcissistic supply), this affordance can enable or motivate behavior that otherwise would not occur (e.g., increased time playing a Massively Multiplayer Online Role-Playing Game [MMORPG]).

Presence

Presence can be best defined as the perception of "being there" in the virtual world during the gaming experience (Biocca, 1997) or temporarily forgetting that technological mediation is taking place due to perceived authenticity of the experience (Lombard & Ditton, 1997). Greater levels of perceived presence are associated with higher levels of interactivity, richness, and immersion; thus, more technologically sophisticated virtual environments may be able to produce more presence (Lee, 2004). However, technological features alone are not sufficient to induce feelings of presence. The perception of presence is fundamentally a subjectively evaluated component of a simulated experience, and thus is contingent upon differences between individual traits and capabilities (Sacau, Laarni, & Hartmann, 2008).

Although researchers are inconsistent in their conceptualizations of presence (conflating it, e.g., with immersion or embodiment), there is some consensus that there are three dimensions of presence: self, social, and spatial. Self-presence refers to a perceived congruency between the real self and the virtual self, the feeling that the gamer's actual self is the one experiencing the virtual environment (Biocca, 1997; Lee, 2004). Self-presence can be enhanced by using a first-person perspective (Tamborini & Skalski, 2006), or by increasing body transfer with an avatar (Sanchez-Vives, Spanlang, Frisoli, Bergamasco, & Slater, 2010). Body transfer is an illusion of physically embodying an avatar, which can be induced when an individual feels a body part being touched as he or she watches the avatar also being touched (Botvinick & Cohen, 1998). Sufficient body transfer can lead people to experience real sensations when the avatars are stimulated (Sanchez-Vives et al., 2010).

Social presence refers to feeling as if the individual is present and interacting with another individual or entity in the virtual world, whether that being is an avatar (a representation of another human being) or an agent (a computer-controlled character). Biocca, Inoue, Lee, Polinsky, and Tang (2002) define three dimensions of social presence. "Copresence" is defined as merely mutual awareness between the player and a character and can be facilitated by having characters behave as if they are aware of the player (e.g., pursuit, acknowledgment). "Psychological involvement" requires that the character appears to demonstrate intelligence, which can be heightened by equipping agents with more convincing artificial intelligences (AIs). "Behavioral engagement" depends on the level of synchronistic interaction that is possible with a character, and can be facilitated with appropriate body language (nonverbal mirroring, eye contact) and conversational behavior (turn-taking, small talk). Social presence between co-players can be increased by facilitating all three dimensions through responsive avatars and real-time communication.

Finally, spatial presence refers to a feeling that the virtual world and the objects in it are real (Biocca, 1997; Hartmann et al., 2015). Slater (2009) also proposes a fourth dimension of presence, "plausibility illusion," which refers to the feeling that events in the virtual world are actually happening. In the context of video games, Tamborini and Bowman (2010) argue that game features that support the affordance of interactivity (see Interactivity) are important to spatial presence. Game controls that allow "natural mapping," or the extent to which player actions map onto changes in the game environment in an intuitive and predictable manner (Steuer, 1992), may directly correspond to perceived presence (Tamborini & Skalski, 2006). Basic natural mapping (such as pressing an up button to go up on the screen) is associated with lower levels of presence than using naturalistic movements, á la the Microsoft Kinect or the Nintendo Wii (Skalski, Tamborini, Lange, & Shelton, 2007). Tamborini and Bowman (2010) argue that natural mapping aids in creating more complete and accurate mental models during game play, which in turn results in higher spatial presence.

Interactivity

Interactivity refers to the extent to which a player can and does influence the content he or she experiences in the virtual world (Heeter, 2000; Lombard & Ditton, 1997), including a game's responsiveness to the player's actions (Leiner & Quiring, 2008; Steuer, 1992). Salen and Zimmerman (2004) identify four levels of interactivity: cognitive, functional, explicit, and cultural. Cognitive interactivity refers to the psychological interaction between the person and the game, which is largely driven by the individual's imagination and motivation. Functional interactivity, which is the sense in which the term "interactivity" is most often used, refers to how responsive the interface of the game is to the player's actions. Explicit interactivity adds the layer of player choice, so that the player can make in-game choices that affect the narrative and later outcomes. Finally, cultural interactivity refers to any potential interactions outside of the game itself. This typically takes place in the form of fan behaviors such as role-playing and cosplay (i.e., dressing in detailed self-made costumes of one's favorite characters; see McCain et al., 2015), but external leaderboards, badges, and game communities such as forums also count as cultural interactivity. Explicit interactivity can be especially important to meaningful gameplay (Salen & Zimmerman, 2005), and the inclusion of choice can support fulfillment of autonomy needs (Deci & Ryan, 2000), thus increasing intrinsic motivation to play the game (Gagne & Deci, 2005).

Ideally, interactivity takes place in real-time (Rice & Williams, 1984; e.g., a console game that responds immediately to player actions versus a mobile game that requires time to update) and can respond in ways personalized to the player (called "game intelligence," see Ritterfeld and Weber, 2006). Higher interactivity can lead to greater presence (Ahn et al., 2016; Fortin & Dholakia, 2005) and better engage the player in the narrative, goals, and controls of the virtual world. However, interactive elements of games also increase cognitive load, or the amount of information the player has to process and respond to in real time. This can interfere with processing of pertinent material in educational games (Ritterfeld & Weber, 2006) or distract players from the central message (Moreno & Mayer, 2007). Thus, a balance between realistic interactivity and curation of the player's experience may be sought depending on the purpose of the game.

Anonymity/Identity Multiplicity

Akin to social media, video games afford varying levels of anonymity through features like avatars, pseudonyms, and having players inhabit a generic character. Anonymity can lead to both positive and negative outcomes (see SIDE model; Reicher, Spears, & Postmes, 1995), such as group cohesion or increased hostility toward others. However, in video games, the affordance of anonymity is taken a step further, as players can take on one or many alternate identities during game play, reaping the social and psychological benefits of each identity. This can range from players embodying a named and defined protagonist, to players being able to create and customize their own character's appearance, abilities, and backstory (Ahn, 2018; Yee, 2014). Players can even create multiple game accounts, playing the game as different characters at different times. Thus, identity multiplicity (Jiow & Lim, 2012) may aid players in achieving identity exploration or self-expansion.

Sociability/Collaboration

Also similar to social media, video games offer varying levels of collaboration, from solo missions to intricately planned group missions called "raids" (Yee, 2014). However, beyond collaboration, video games also offer a unique opportunity for sociability (Jiow & Lim, 2012), and many friendships and relationships are formed in games such as MMORPGs. Video game technology increasingly provides features encouraging both colocated (e.g., "couch co-op" games) and non-colocated social interaction (e.g., MMORPGs). A large number of players report gaming specifically for the goals of interacting with or making new friends (Yee, 2014), and thus sociability can be defined as the affordance linking cooperative game features and social outcomes.

Perpetuity/Portability

Recent video games have been trending toward greater perpetuity (Jiow & Lim, 2012), or the ability to play the game ad-infinitum without a clear end-state. For example, MMORPGs such as *World of Warcraft* exist in virtual game worlds that do not disappear when the player logs off, and which offer players a variety of continuous activities (e.g., farming resources) as well as a seemingly infinite number of quests (repeatedly extended by downloadable content (DLCs), game upgrades, and sequels). Also, video games can increasingly be accessed at any time and place via a variety of digital platforms (e.g., console, tablet, smartphone, PC). Thus, the actions taken in game on a computer may be continued via a mobile device even as a player is commuting or away from home. The perpetuity of being able to play endlessly and the portability of content between digital devices (Jiow & Lim, 2012) can lead to increased playtime as well as increasing accessibility[1] for a wider range of individuals (e.g., children) to play and enjoy video games. At the same time, these affordances may also lead to more troubling, and unintended outcomes, such as game addiction (Mentzoni et al., 2011).

---

[1] Although Jiow and Lim (2012) identify accessibility as an affordance, we believe this definition of accessibility qualifies as an outcome, not an affordance, as per the criteria set by Evans et al. (2017).

Restoration

Evans et al. (2017) defined persistence (i.e., the ability to have information and interactions continue to exist permanently online) as an affordance of social media. However, video games to varying degrees offer the opposite of persistence, in that players can go back in time and undo their actions. In many games, storylines and characters can be restarted at will, actions can be undone by simply loading a saved game, and most importantly, character death is impermanent (and in some games, completely inconsequential to a player's progress). The ability to immediately resurrect a character has consequences on social behavior; for example, games in which resurrection is not easy or is impossible tend to encourage more helpful behavior among players, whereas players of games with easy resurrection have an expectation of independence among their peers and may even shame asking for help (Yee, 2014). Easy resurrection further removes the consequences of actions that take place in the game and yields disinhibition and risk-taking not possible in other situations. For example, players of *Grand Theft Auto (GTA)* may engage in reckless in-game behaviors such as destructive driving or direct assaults upon police officers that are not called for by the game's tasks, because going to jail (this game's consequence for such behavior) is a temporary and minor setback. Thus, restoration can be defined as an affordance linking features such as respawning with outcomes such as higher risk-taking behaviors in the game.

SIMULATED EXPERIENCES IN VIDEO GAMES

Although individuals can learn from hearing about or observing others' experiences (e.g., Bandura, 2001), direct experiences have been shown to have a greater impact on behavior change than indirect and observed experiences (Hertwig, Barron, Weber, & Erev, 2004; Rajecki, 1982). The concept of embodied cognition (Wilson, 2002) posits that language, memories, simulations, and other thought processes are at least in part symbolically encoded in sensory information. Engaging the senses in a realistic simulated experience can influence the unconscious mental models of situations, known as schemas (Bandura, 2001) in a way similar to experiences in the physical world. These changes to schemata affect how the individual mentally simulates and predicts the outcome of similar future situations, which in turn affects behavior (Barsalou, 2009). Thus, the simulated experiences that are provided by high-end graphics, interactive feedback, and immersive virtual environments (commonly referred to as virtual reality, or VR) may be sufficiently realistic to affect attitudes and behavior at a deeper level than traditional media (e.g., Ahn, 2015; Ahn, Bailenson, & Park, 2014). In addition to the affordances of presence and interactivity discussed, there are also some features of video games that aid in the construction of simulated virtual experiences that mimic the richly detailed experiences of the physical world.

Richness/Vividness

Vividness refers to how much the player perceives a sensorially rich experience (Steuer, 1992). It is most closely tied to image resolution and clarity but is not necessarily dependent on technology. For example, a console game consisting of a series of high resolution images may be more vivid than a fully interactive and immersive VR game with more dull or simplistic imagery. According to Steuer (1992), the former scenario offers depth of sensory information and the latter offers breadth of sensory information. Thus, vividness is determined by the strength of the sensory impression made on the individual. Higher levels of vividness in a game may amplify its effects on behavior change by producing more vivid mental simulations and changes to schemata.

Media richness is related to vividness, and is the extent that media supports multiple simultaneous cue systems that provide information to the player. Richness refers to how well multiple senses and channels of communication are engaged, while vividness refers to the individual's perception of a rich experience (Steuer, 1992). Greater richness ideally comes from: 1) number of simultaneous cue systems supported, 2) bidirectional synchronicity of feedback provided by the medium, 3) the potential for spontaneous behavior as opposed to formalized interactions, and 4) personalization (Daft & Lengel, 1986).

It was originally thought that rich media should lead to enjoyment of the media consumption experience by increasing presence. However, this was based on the hypothesis that the abundance of communication cues will allow people to communicate faster and more effectively (Daft & Lengel, 1986). In the context of video games, despite being a richer media platform, the communication efficiency during game play does not necessarily indicate enjoyment of the experience. Furthermore, because presence depends on both the media and the individual playing, the functional richness and vividness of the medium does not directly predict perceived presence. Also, depending on the platform, video games are not equally rich; some games are played online using a PC, some are played in VR, and yet others are played through smartphones. As Walther and Parks (2002) point out, some media platforms fail to fit neatly into the four subdimensions of media richness. For instance, a video game played on smartphones might provide fewer sensorial cues than one played on a VR platform but may offer more potential for social interactions. Thus, it is difficult to determine the exact degree of richness based on the subdimensions, and the degree of richness may not predict game engagement or enjoyment.

Although it is not directly predictive, Tamborini and Skalski (2006) consider the richness and vividness provided by a game's technology to be positively predictive of presence. Technology capable of providing more vivid sensory experiences (e.g., VR head-mounted displays that offer stereoscopic vision and head-tracking) can increase presence (Heeter, 1992). Graphics and sounds that provide more sensory information would also increase presence (Tamborini & Skalski, 2006). In addition to the typical visual input, adding cross-sensory stimulation simultaneously through stereo sound and orienting and haptic systems can increase presence (Biocca et al., 2002). Thus, playing a game in high-fidelity VR with a stereoscopic display, head-tracking, stereo sound effects, and vibrations giving haptic feedback through a controller should in most cases provide a strong sense of presence.

Immersion

Immersion refers to the extent to which a virtual world's technological interface can provide a realistic and comprehensive simulated experience. If vividness is considered the depth of sensory information provided by a simulated environment, immersion refers to the breadth of sensory information in terms of the number of layers enveloping the player. Often, this is interpreted as the extent to which the virtual environment can block out or replace the player's experience of his or her physical environment by providing multiple layers of sensory information that allows them to see, hear, and feel as they would in the physical world (Lombard & Ditton, 1997). Thus, this feature can be relatively objectively measured as the capabilities of the technology used. Greater levels of immersion provided by stereoscopic interfaces (as opposed to 2D interfaces, such as the typical computer screen) have repeatedly been shown to improve task performance (Hubona, Wheeler, Shirah, & Brandt, 1999; Teather & Stuerzlinger, 2007), especially when head tracking is added (Arthur, Booth, & Ware, 1993).

Greater immersion may translate to greater presence (Cummings & Bailenson, 2016). Successful cases of behavior change resulting from VR environments (e.g., phobia treatment, military training) have been attributed to the immersion and subsequent increase in presence provided by these environments (Bowman & McMahan, 2007). Thus, the extent to which the graphics, controls, game mechanics, and sound can produce a convincing virtual experience separate from the physical world determines the upper bound for how strongly presence and behavior change can be created.

PSYCHOSOCIAL PATHWAYS FOR VIDEO GAMES TO CHANGE BEHAVIOR

Investigations from multiple disciplines have identified several pathways through which games can produce changes in behavior and learning, at times, over and above other interventions. Below, we will discuss four major pathways prominent in the literature. The first three pathways come from the Entertainment-Education Paradigm (Ritterfeld & Weber, 2006) and from health psychology (Baranowski, Thompson, Buday, Lu, & Baranowski, 2010). They focus on the more rule-based aspects common in games (i.e., the presence of a desirable goal, incremental reinforcement of certain behaviors) as well as the aspects that make games inherently appealing activities. The fourth pathway stems from the social aspects of gaming, both with other players and with non-player characters (e.g., agents). Video games may use one or more of these pathways to influence behavior both during and after game play.

Motivation

Games in general are perceived to be primarily entertainment media because the act of gaming is seen as intrinsically motivated (i.e., for fun). Self-determination theory (SDT; Ryan & Deci, 2000), the predominant theory of human motivation, differentiates intrinsic motivation, which derives from internal wants and needs, from extrinsic motivation, or motivation driven by external rewards and punishments. Intrinsic motivation has been shown to produce greater and more sustained behavior change than extrinsic motivation (Ryan, Connell, & Deci, 1985). SDT identifies three primary psychological needs that drive most behaviors: (1) the need for competence, or a feeling of effectiveness at completing tasks; (2) the need for autonomy, or the sense of freedom to choose one's own behavior; and (3) the need for relatedness, or of feeling tied to others through relationships and shared values. These basic and universal needs tend to motivate behavior in an individual, independent of extrinsic rewards. Several studies (Przybylski, Rigby, & Ryan, 2010; Ryan, Rigby, & Przybylski, 2006; Tamborini et al., 2011) have found that playing games can provide basic need satisfaction, and that this can predict enjoyment or motivation to play games. Thus, depending on their design, video games appear to afford opportunities to fulfill basic needs (see Recommendations for Game Design to Produce Behavior Change) and thus produce intrinsic motivation in players to complete the game. This motivation can be repurposed toward changing behavior by building the desired behavior into the game. Direct practice and improvement of skills can be built into the mechanics of the game, using challenge to motivate skill development.

Reinforcement

In contrast to intrinsic motivation, video games can also use extrinsic rewards to reinforce desired behaviors. This strategy has most extensively been explored in the academic and industry work on gamification (Seaborn & Fels, 2015). Gamification is the addition of game elements (such as points systems, leader boards, and narrative objectives) to non-game contexts in order to motivate and shape behavior (Deterding et al., 2011). Early attempts at gamification were based on behaviorist theory (Skinner, 1953) with the assumption that providing rewards for a desired behavior would lead to an increase in that behavior. This approach led to limited success (Johnson et al., 2016), with particular difficulty getting the desired behavior to continue once the rewards stopped coming.

More informed attempts at gamification now use SDT as a guide as to how to use rewards wisely. External motivators such as rewards and evaluations tend to threaten autonomy needs, which undermines intrinsic motivation (Gagne & Deci, 2005). Thus, rather than increasing motivation to engage in the desired behavior, rewarding a behavior with an extrinsic reward may cause a person to feel manipulated, and thus actually reduce intrinsic motivation. Instead, the goal is to create a personal identification with the behavior so that it becomes an internalized, or self-motivated, behavior. According to SDT, this change can be accomplished by degrees with judicious use of specific external motivators.

Although a wide variety of game elements (for a review, see Hamari, Koivisto, & Sarsa, 2014) are available to use for gamification, those that are supportive of basic needs should be used when attempting to induce behavior change. A review by Lewis, Swartz, and Lyons (2016) recommends verbal rewards, task-noncontingent rewards, and rewards of glory. Verbal rewards consist of kudos, likes, etc., that can be provided by other players of the game, and can promote feelings of relatedness as well as autonomy because they are from other players and thus do not feel controlling. Rewards of glory consist of points, achievements, badges, or animations, and can support competence needs by providing feedback, or support relatedness needs by providing bragging rights. Task non-contingent rewards provided at random or unpredictably also reduce feelings of being manipulated. Tangible rewards and task-contingent rewards should be avoided, as these tend to undermine autonomy needs.

Personalization

A third way in which games can change behavior is by making the desired behavior change personally relevant to the player. Individuals are more likely to devote cognitive effort and attention to a message that they perceive to be personally relevant, and these messages are more likely to change future behavior (Petty & Cacioppo, 1986). By tailoring the narrative of the game to engage the player's emotions and values, game designers can persuade players in a way other forms of persuasion may not (Orji, Mandryk, Vassileva, & Gerling, 2013). This may be done by creating game characters with which the player identifies (De Graaf, Hoeken, Sanders, & Beentjes, 2012) or by casting the player himself as the main character, such as in first person games and "pedagogical dramas" (Marsella, Johnson, & LaBore, 2000). Games with greater "intelligence" (Ritterfeld & Weber, 2006) can further customize the game experience by inserting the player's name, likeness, and even changing the course of the narrative in response to their choices or personal information (e.g., a binge-drinking intervention game that tailors gameplay to the player's reported drinking habits; Jander, Crutzen, Mercken, & De Vries, 2014). In addition to persuasion, having the player adopt desired goals as part of the game narrative can play a significant role in behavior change. There is extensive literature supporting the importance of goal-setting to behavior change (Bandura, 1977), and through role-playing or identifying with a character, players may adopt goals that lead to lasting behavior change.

Proteus Effect

The experience of embodying an avatar in a virtual environment affects multiple aspects of cognition and behavior of the player. Embodying an attractive avatar encouraged friendliness in a user's interaction with a confederate (Yee & Bailenson, 2007; Yee, Bailenson, & Ducheneaut, 2009), whereas embodying an unattractive avatar encouraged social compensation behaviors in dyadic interaction (Van Der Heide, Schumaker, Peterson, & Jones, 2013). Many of these effects have been shown to persist both online and later after the virtual experience has ended.

Video games allow for identity multiplicity wherein players can create and control multiple avatars across different games or even with the same game. If embodying these different avatars yields a collective influence on the player's attitude and behavior, an interesting question may arise when a player's own avatars may be at odds with each other (e.g., an elderly versus a youthful avatar). Also, little empirical evidence is available on how the Proteus Effect may change with avatars who may represent negative traits (c.f. Fox, Bailenson, & Tricase, 2013). It is unclear whether players will be just as willing to accept traits that are viewed negatively into their self-concepts as most of the earlier work on the Proteus Effect has focused on positive or value-neutral traits, such as height or attractiveness. More research is necessary to determine the boundaries and contingencies of the Proteus Effect in video games.

RECOMMENDATIONS FOR GAME DESIGN TO PRODUCE BEHAVIOR CHANGE

In order for a game to provide behavior change, the player must be motivated to first play the game, and then to continue playing the game long enough for it to take effect. The best way to do this is to afford opportunities to fulfill intrinsic needs through the game. The three basic needs of SDT are believed to underlie the behavior of potential players, and thus are rich sources of motivation to draw from. The following game elements have been recommended in the literature to afford each need.

Competence

Humans have an innate need to feel competent and in control of situations. In game design, this can be supported by providing tasks that challenge the player but that can still be reasonably accomplished. At the basic level, game controls that are intuitive and easily learned, such as those using natural mapping (McGloin, Farrar, & Krcmar, 2011), can provide a sense that the player has a reliable effect upon the game world and can accomplish game tasks. In order to account for differences in player ability, designing varying difficulty levels (such as beginner versus advanced modes) as well as increasing the difficulty as the player improves in skill can support a feeling of competence and achievement. Finally, acknowledging player achievements through feedback, such as points systems and performance ratings, and "rewards of glory" (Lewis et al., 2016), such as badges, leaderboards, and unlocked animations, can incentivize the player to continue playing in order to improve his or her performance while feeling competent with what they have already mastered.

Autonomy

Although rewards may support competence needs, they should be used judiciously so as not to undermine autonomy needs. In settings where the player has not autonomously chosen to play the game (e.g., gamification, serious games used as interventions), overuse of performance-contingent rewards and the provision of tangible rewards (such as paying the player) can create feelings of being manipulated (Lewis et al., 2016). Performance-contingent rewards can also lead the player to attribute his or her play behavior to the reward rather than valuing the game (Lepper, Greene, & Nisbett, 1973), which could interfere with internalization of game values. Thus, non-performance-contingent rewards (such as rewards simply for finishing a task, regardless of performance on that task) can support autonomy and reduce feelings of manipulation. Providing choice and customization to the player, whether in the form of avatar customization, freedom to explore, or the ability to affect the course of the narrative (e.g., nonlinearity, multiple endings) may also be effective practical approaches to maintaining the perception of autonomy. Personalization of the game's different elements can also provide added benefits of increasing presence, which will make the player less aware that they are being influenced by a mediating technology (Bailey, Wise, & Bolis, 2009). Games emphasizing player choice (e.g., *Life is Strange, Until Dawn*) and open-world games (i.e., games containing a world in which players can participate at will without the confines of a linear storyline, e.g., *World of Warcraft* or *Minecraft*) allow the player to choose when, where, and how they accomplish goals within the game, and give them the possibility of achieving different endings depending on their actions. Personalization features that allow players to make their own choices would theoretically produce more autonomy than more traditional, linear games.

Relatedness

By nature, humans are social animals, and a fundamental human psychological need is the desire to feel connected, included, and cared for by others—a sense of relatedness (Ryan & Deci, 2000). One of the biggest motivations for gaming reported by players is social interaction (Yee, 2014). Any features supporting collaboration and socialization within games (e.g., remote or co-located cooperative play, in-game chat or voice) will afford a greater chance to meet relatedness needs. MMORPGs such as *World of Warcraft* have resulted in the formation of countless friendships and relationships (Yee, 2014), since cooperative play is emphasized in higher levels and players have plenty of freedom to interact in the game world independently of its story.

Rewards of glory (e.g., badges, points) that are visible to other players, as well as opportunities for players to praise one another (e.g., kudos, likes) can increase one's perceived visibility and acceptance in the eyes of other players. Finally, maximizing cultural interactivity, such as guilds, fan-communities, and meta-game activities (like market-places and advice/lore forums) can create a feeling of being part of a community of players that exists, even when not in play. For example, the *Five Nights at Freddy's* franchise, through the use of cryptic clues about the game's backstory, has spawned a giant YouTube community based around discussing and theorizing about the game's lore. With the introduction of novels and merchandise, the possibilities for engagement with other players outside of the game has created a fandom that can feed belongingness needs (McCain et al., 2015).

Optimize Presence

In addition to enhancing player motivation, presence can play an important role in encouraging behavior change. Many serious games, for example, those addressing phobias, require subconscious changes of threat associations. Such conditioning is more likely to take place following a real experience than after an imagined or indirect experience (Rajecki, 1982). Given sufficient presence, a simulated experience can alter underlying mental models or schemata through repetition (Tamborini & Bowman, 2010), which will impact future decision making in similar situations that activate these mental models (Hertwig et al., 2004). Many memories and emotions are encoded in the brain using sensory information. Technological elements that improve interactivity (especially natural mapping; Tamborini & Bowman, 2010), richness, and immersion close the gap between simulated and real experience, providing realistic sensory stimulation that may impact cognition at a basic level (Hertwig et al., 2004). However, a game need not necessarily be the most technologically advanced to produce strong presence. For instance, presence may be created using a strong narrative or sufficiently relatable character. The award-winning serious games *Depression Quest* and *Gone Home* use simplistic text and picture interfaces (respectively) to provide a strong narrative meant to change attitudes about social issues, such as mental illness and LGBT rights.

Make it Personal

According to SDT, extrinsic motivation can only become intrinsic when the values behind the desired behavior are fully integrated into a person's sense of self (Deci & Ryan, 2000). Facilitating a player's sense of self presence and helping them identify with the narrative as well as them having control over the course of the game should then be more persuasive toward behavior change. Customized avatars, or better yet, an avatar of the player him/herself (Ahn & Fox, 2017) can place the player in the game, while "intelligent" games that learn the player's name and remember and acknowledge the player's decisions can allow the person to fully identify with the main character of the story. Many of the same elements supporting autonomy, such as choice and narrative control, can also increase personalization so that the player feels responsible for his or her actions in the game. Rewarding or punishing those actions then encourages the player to identify with the values behind those actions. The popular independent game *Undertale* uses intelligent responses such as changing character friendliness and plot based on player behavior to give the player a sense of ownership over his own actions. In the end, having an emotionally disturbing reaction to what one would consider typical game behavior (i.e., the monsters are terrified and visibly suffer that the player is attacking and killing them) calls on him or her to question their values about violence in games.

APPLICATION OF GAMES IN HEALTH BEHAVIOR CHANGE

Since the turn of the millennium, there has been a surge of efforts to apply games or game elements to elicit desired attitudes and behaviors in a wide range of contexts. In particular, health interventions have seen some of the earliest integrations of game elements in an effort to induce and sustain changes in health attitudes and behaviors (see Limperos, 2017 for a review).

Physical Activity

Due to poor diet and a sedentary lifestyle, childhood obesity has become an epidemic in many developed nations. A number of research efforts have focused on using the entertaining and intrinsically motivating power of video games to promote exercise. In a typical video game designed to promote physical activity, commonly known as "exergames" or "active video games" (AVG), a child must perform physical activity or demonstrate their knowledge of the benefits of physical activity to progress in the game. Because of the game elements, children are likely to think that they are having fun rather than engaging in programmatic physical activity (Ahn et al., 2015; Baranowski et al., 2012; Peng, Crouse, & Lin, 2013; Primack et al., 2012; Rizzo, Lange, Suma, & Bolas, 2011). Recent studies report small to moderate effects of AVGs in increasing overall physical activity in both low and moderate intensity (Gao, Chen, Pasco, & Pope, 2015), and that AVGs do not produce sustainable change (Barnett, Cerin, & Baranowski, 2011).

However, little research has investigated the effect of active video games over time (Chin, Dukes, & Gamson, 2009; Maloney et al., 2008), particularly with a wide range of populations. One important future area to explore may be the effect of novelty on physical activity, when players no longer find the active video game content to be engaging due to habituation. One review of multiple studies found that the results of activity levels were varied considerably and exercises using upper body movements produced much lower physical activity than those using lower body movements (Biddiss & Irwin, 2010). This suggests that the type of exercise used in AVGs may create significant variation in outcomes.

Diet Change

Video games have also been used to positively affect diet in children. Baranowski, Buday, Thompson, & Baranowski (2008) reviewed 27 articles where researchers had introduced children to games that promoted diet change. Much like the studies on physical activity, the diet change varied substantially between the studies. Games that promoted only diet change in a story-driven manner were the most effective. However, studies that focused on both physical activity and diet change showed only partial change in both areas. One study found a strong change in diet of fruits in vegetables when students went through ten sessions of a story-driven game, *Squire's Quest*, which advocated fruit and vegetable consumption (Baranowski et al., 2003). The study determined that the enjoyability of the game appeared to be the main reason for successful diet change.

Health Education

Games like *Squire's Quest* have proven that a game about a healthy diet that is also entertaining can be successful at providing positive health education. Several researchers have taken this principle further by designing games and game environments to provide health education, training, and awareness of health issues.

In terms of training, Persky and McBride (2009) noted the potential of VR to be integrated into medical training and services by having clinicians embody the viewpoint of their patients to experience and evaluate their own counseling technique. In terms of awareness, disabilities such as schizophrenia (Kalyanaraman, Penn, Ivory, & Judge, 2010) and various visual disabilities (Ahn, Le, & Bailenson, 2013) have been accurately reproduced as virtual simulations. Although the technology is far from perfect and even VR with the highest degree of immersion are still unable to completely mimic the real world, these studies show that VR technology can invoke naturalistic responses from participants and promote learning through real experience.

DISCUSSION AND FUTURE DIRECTIONS

Video games are increasingly becoming integrated into everyday life as elements of daily routine—not just for play, but for work, education, exercise, and therapy as well. This chapter discussed the ways that video game environments interact with individual characteristics to afford unique opportunities for behavior change. Affordances such as presence, interactivity, and sociability allow individuals to learn from simulated experience, whereas affordances such as perpetuity, identity multiplicity, and restoration allow individuals to experiment with behaviors without real world consequence, all of which suggest countless applications in the fields mentioned and more. Judicious use of external rewards and incentives while taking advantage of the intrinsic motivations of players to engage in a fun activity like gaming may induce individuals to internalize the values associated with desired behaviors, while helping them fulfill their basic needs. Using these psychological principles, games can be designed to serve as effective interventions for attitude, behavior, or social change.

As games and the technology that supports them continue to evolve, several areas for future research are emerging. Gartner's (2017a) Hype Cycle for Emerging Technologies predicts that augmented reality and VR will be mainstream in 5–10 years from the time of this publication. In addition to the possibilities for simulated experience, these technologies can allow for unforeseen affordances (e.g., the ability to experience non-human bodies and supernumeral body parts; Won, Bailenson, Lee, & Lanier, 2015) whose effects on behavior will need to be examined. Gamification efforts are expanding as well (Gartner, 2017b) in work and design contexts. As gaming elements continue to be implemented outside of their original context (i.e., outside of self-chosen entertainment experiences), systematic evaluations of their efficacy in novel contexts should be implemented. Finally, as technologies and practices become more commonplace, people will continue to change and adapt to these technologies (Biocca, 1997). Research must continue to examine whether the loss of novelty and the increase of familiarity changes the effects game elements and experiences have on behavior. This chapter presents the hope that games continue to fulfill their potential to teach, heal, and improve the lives of those who play them in a motivating and fulfilling way.

References

Ahn, S. J. (2015). Incorporating immersive virtual environments in health promotion campaigns: A construal-level theory approach. *Health Communication, 30*(6), 545–556.

Ahn, S. J. (2018). Face & hair: Looks that change behaviors. In J. Banks (Ed.), *Avatar, assembled: The social and technical anatomy of digital bodies*. New York: Peter Lang.

Ahn, S. J., Bailenson, J. N., & Park, D. (2014). Short-and long-term effects of embodied experiences in immersive virtual environments on environmental locus of control and behavior. *Computers in Human Behavior, 39*, 235–245.

Ahn, S. J., Bostick, J., Ogle, E., Nowak, K., McGillicuddy, K., & Bailenson, J. N. (2016). Experiencing nature: Embodying animals in immersive virtual environments increases inclusion of nature in self and involvement with nature. *Journal of Computer-Mediated Communication, 21*(6), 399–419.

Ahn, S. J., & Fox, J. (2017). Immersive virtual environments, avatars, and agents for health. In R. Parrott (Ed). *Encyclopedia of health and risk message design and processing*. New York: Oxford University Press.

Ahn, S. J., Johnsen, K., Robertson, T., Moore, J., Brown, S., Marable, A., & Basu, A. (2015). Using virtual pets to promote physical activity in children: An application of the youth physical activity promotion model. *Journal of Health Communication, 20*(7), 807–815.

Ahn, S. J., Le, A. M. T., & Bailenson, J. N. (2013). The effect of embodied experiences in self-other merging, attitude, and helping behavior. *Media Psychology, 16*, 7–38.

Arthur, K. W., Booth, K. S., & Ware, C. (1993). Evaluating 3d task performance for fish tank virtual worlds. *ACM Transactions on Information Systems (TOIS), 11*, 239–265.

Bailey, R., Wise, K., & Bolis, P. (2009). How avatar customizability affects children's arousal and subjective presence during junk food-sponsored online video games. *CyberPsychology & Behavior, 12*, 277–283.

Bandura, A. (1977). Self-efficacy: Toward a unifying theory of behavioral change. *Psychological Review, 84*, 191–215.

Bandura, A. (2001). Social cognitive theory: An agentic perspective. *Annual Review of Psychology, 52*, 1–26.

Baranowski, T., Abdelsamad, D., Baranowski, J., O'Connor, T. M., Thompson, D., Barnett, A.,... Chen, T. A. (2012). Impact of an active video game on healthy children's physical activity. *Pediatrics, 129*(3), 636–642.

Baranowski, T., Baranowski, J., Cullen, K. W., Marsh, T., Islam, N., Zakeri, I., & Honess-Morreale, L. (2003). Squire's Quest!: Dietary outcome evaluation of a multimedia game. *American Journal of Preventive Medicine, 24*, 52–61.

Baranowski, T., Buday, R., Thompson, D. I., & Baranowski, J. (2008). Playing for real: Video games and stories for health-related behavior change. *American Journal of Preventive Medicine, 34*, 74–82.

Baranowski, T., Thompson, D., Buday, R., Lu, A. S., & Baranowski, J. (2010). Design of video games for children's diet and physical activity behavior change. *International Journal of Computer Science in Sport, 9*, 3–17.

Bargh, J. A. (2008). Free will is un-natural. In J. Baer, J. C. Kaufman, & R. F. Baumeister (Eds.), *Are We Free? Psychology and free will* (pp. 128–54). New York: Oxford University Press.

Barnett, A., Cerin, E., & Baranowski, T. (2011). Active video games for youth: A systematic review. *Journal of Physical Activity and Health, 8*, 724–737.

Barsalou, L. W. (2009). Simulation, situated conceptualization, and prediction. *Philosophical Transactions of the Royal Society of London B: Biological Sciences, 364*, 1281–1289.

Biddiss, E., & Irwin, J. (2010). Active video games to promote physical activity in children and youth: A systematic review. *Archives of Pediatrics & Adolescent Medicine, 164*, 664–672.

Biocca, F. (1997). The cyborg's dilemma: Progressive embodiment in virtual environments. *Journal of Computer-Mediated Communication, 3*, doi:10.1111/j.1083-6101.1997.tb00070.x.

Biocca, F., Inoue, Y., Lee, A., Polinsky, H., & Tang, A. (2002). Visual cues and virtual touch: Role of visual stimuli and intersensory integration in cross-modal haptic illusions and the sense of presence. *Proceedings of Presence*, 410–428.

Botvinick, M., & Cohen, J. (1998). Rubber hands 'feel' touch that eyes see. *Nature, 391, 756*.

Bowman, D. A., & McMahan, R. P. (2007). Virtual reality: How much immersion is enough? *Computer, 40*, 36–43.

Campbell, W. K., & Foster, J. D. (2007). The narcissistic self: Background, an extended agency model, and ongoing controversies. In C. Sedikides & S. J. Spender (Eds.), *Frontiers of social psychology. The self* (pp. 115–138). New York: Psychology Press.

Chin, J., Dukes, R., & Gamson, W. (2009). Assessment in simulation and gaming: A review of the last 40 years. *Simulation & Gaming, 40*, 553–568.

Craik, K. J. W. (1943). *The Nature of explanation*. Cambridge: Cambridge University Press.

Cummings, J. J., & Bailenson, J. N. (2016). How immersive is enough? A meta-analysis of the effect of immersive technology on user presence. *Media Psychology, 19*, 272–309.

Daft, R. L., & Lengel, R. H. (1986). Organizational information requirements, media richness and structural design. *Management Science, 32*, 554–571.

Deci, E. L., & Ryan, R. M. (1987). The support of autonomy and the control of behavior. *Journal of Personality and Social Psychology, 53*, 1024–1037.

Deci, E. L., & Ryan, R. M. (2000). Intrinsic and extrinsic motivations: Classic definitions and new directions. *Contemporary Education Psychology, 25*, 54–67.

De Graaf, A., Hoeken, H., Sanders, J., & Beentjes, J. W. (2012). Identification as a mechanism of narrative persuasion. *Communication Research, 39*(6), 802–823.

Deterding, S., Dixon, D., Khaled, R., & Nacke, L. (2011). From game design elements to gamefulness: Defining "gamification". In *MindTrek '11: Proceedings of the 15th International Academic MindTrek Conference on Envisioning Future Media Environments* (pp. 9–15), 28–30 September, Tampere, Finland. New York: ACM.

ESA (2017, October 3). Industry Facts. Retrieved from http://www.theesa.com/about-esa/industry-facts/.

Escalas, J. E. (2004). Imagine yourself in the product: Mental simulation, narrative transportation, and persuasion. *Journal of Advertising, 33*, 37–48.

Evans, S. K., Pearce, K. E., Vitak, J., & Treem, J. W. (2017). Explicating affordances: A conceptual framework for understanding affordances in communication research. *Journal of Computer-Mediated Communication 22*, 35–52.

Fleeson, W. (2001). Towards a structure and process integrated view of personality: Traits as density distributions of state. *Journal of Personality and Social Psychology, 80*, 1011–1027.

Fortin, D. R., & Dholakia, R. R. (2005). Interactivity and vividness effects on social presence and involvement with a web-based advertisement. *Journal of Business Research, 58*, 387–396.

Fox, J., Bailenson, J. N., & Tricase, L. (2013). The embodiment of sexualized virtual selves: The Proteus effect and experiences of self-objectification via avatars. *Computers in Human Behavior, 29*, 930–938.

Gagné, M., & Deci, E. L. (2005). Self-determination theory and work motivation. *Journal of Organizational Behavior, 26*, 331–362.

Gao, Z., Chen, S., Pasco, D., & Pope, Z. (2015). A meta-analysis of active video games on health outcomes among children and adolescents. *Obesity Reviews, 16*, 783–794.

Gartner (October 2017a). Top trends in the Gartner hype cycle for emerging technologies, 2017. Retrieved from http://www.gartner.com/smarterwithgartner/top-trends-in-the-gartner-hype-cycle-for-emerging-technologies-2017/

Gartner (October 2017b). The hype is over—gamification is here to stay. Retrieved from https://www.gamified.uk/2015/08/21/the-hype-is-over-gamification-is-here-to-stay/

Gibson, J. J. (1986). *The ecological approach to visual perception*. Hillsdale, NJ: Lawrence Erlbaum.

Hamari, J., Koivisto, J., & Sarsa, H. (2014, January). Does gamification work? A literature review of empirical studies on gamification. In *(HICSS): 2014 47th Hawaii International Conference on System Sciences* (pp. 3025–3034), 6–9 January, Waikoloa, Hawaii. Redhook, NY: Curran Associates.

Hartmann T., Wirth W., Vorderer P., Klimmt C., Schramm H., & Böcking S. (2015). Spatial presence theory: State of the art and challenges ahead. In M. Lombard, F. Biocca, J. Freeman, W. IJsselsteijn, & R. Schaevitz (Eds.) *Immersed in Media*. Cham: Springer International Publishing.

Heeter, C. (1992). Being there: The subjective experience of presence. *Presence: Teleoperators & Virtual Environments, 1*, 262–271.

Heeter, C. (2000). Interactivity in the context of designed experiences. *Journal of Interactive Advertising, 1*, 3–14.

Hertwig, R., Barron, G., Weber, E. U., & Erev, I. (2004). Decisions from experience and the effect of rare events in risky choice. *Psychological Science, 15*, 534–539.

Hogle, J. G. (1996). *Considering games as cognitive tools: In search of effective "edutainment."* Department of Instructional Technology, University of Georgia (ERIC Document Reproduction Service No. ED 425 737).

Hubona, G. S., Wheeler, P. N., Shirah, G. W., & Brandt, M. (1999). The relative contributions of stereo, lighting, and background scenes in promoting 3D depth visualization. *ACM Transactions on Computer-Human Interaction (TOCHI), 6*, 214–242.

Huizinga, J. (1955). 1938. *Homo ludens: A study of the play element in culture.* Abingdon: Routledge.

Jander, A., Crutzen, R., Mercken, L., & De Vries, H. (2014). A web-based computer-tailored game to reduce binge drinking among 16- to 18-year-old Dutch adolescents: Development and study protocol. *BMC Public Health, 14*(1), 1054.

Jiow, H. J., & Lim, S. S. (2012). The evolution of video game affordances and implications for parental mediation. *Bulletin of Science, Technology & Society, 32*, 455–462.

Johnson, D., Deterding, S., Kuhn, K. A., Staneva, A., Stoyanov, S., & Hides, L. (2016). Gamification for health and wellbeing: A systematic review of the literature. *Internet Interventions, 6*, 89–106.

Kalyanaraman, S., Penn, D., Ivory, J., & Judge, A. (2010). The virtual doppelganger: Effects of a virtual reality simulator on perceptions of schizophrenia. *Journal of Nervous and Mental Disorders, 198*, 437–443.

Kim, T., & Biocca, F. (1997). Telepresence via television: Two dimensions of telepresence may have different connections to memory and persuasion. *Journal of Computer-Mediated Communication, 3*, JCMC325. doi:10.1111/j.1083-6101.1997.tb00073.x.

Lee, K. M. (2004). Presence, explicated. *Communication Theory, 14*, 27–50.

Leiner, D. J., & Quiring, O. (2008). What interactivity means to the user essential insights into and a scale for perceived interactivity. *Journal of Computer-Mediated Communication, 14*, 127–155.

Lepper, M. R., Greene, D., & Nisbett, R. E. (1973). Undermining children's intrinsic interest with extrinsic reward: A test of the "overjustification" hypothesis. *Journal of Personality & Social Psychology, 28*, 129–137.

Lewis, Z. H., Swartz, M. C., & Lyons, E. J. (2016). What's the point? A review of reward systems implemented in gamification interventions. *Games for Health Journal, 5*, 93–99.

Limperos, A. M. (2017). Video games and gaming: Reaching audiences with health and risk messages. In R. Parrott (Ed.), *Encyclopedia of health and risk message design and processing.* New York: Oxford University Press.

Lombard, M., & Ditton, T. (1997). At the heart of it all: The concept of presence. *Journal of Computer-Mediated Communication, 3*, JCMC321. doi:10.1111/j.1083-6101.1997.tb00072.x.

Maloney, A. E., Bethea, T. C., Kelsey, K. S., Marks, J. T., Paez, S., Rosenberg, A. M.,…Sikich, L. (2008). A pilot of a video game (DDR) to promote physical activity and decrease sedentary screen time. *Obesity, 16*(9), 2074–2080.

Marsella, S. C., Johnson, W. L., & LaBore, C. (2000). Interactive pedagogical drama. In *Proceedings of the fourth international conference on autonomous agents* (pp. 301–308), 3–7 June, Barcelona, Spain. New York: ACM.

Mentzoni, R. A., Brunborg, G. S., Molde, H., Myrseth, H., Skouverøe, K. J. M., Hetland, J., & Pallesen, S. (2011). Problematic video game use: Estimated prevalence and associations with mental and physical health. *Cyberpsychology, Behavior, and Social Networking, 14*, 591–596.

McCain, J., Gentile, B., & Campbell, W. K. (2015). A psychological exploration of engagement in geek culture. *PLoS One, 10*, 1–39.

McGloin, R., Farrar, K. M., & Krcmar, M. (2011). The impact of controller naturalness on spatial presence, gamer enjoyment, and perceived realism in a tennis simulation video game. *Presence, 20*, 309–324.

Michael, D. R., & Chen, S. L. (2005). *Serious games: Games that educate, train, and inform.* Mason, OH: Cengage Learning.

Mischel, W., & Shoda, Y. (1995). A cognitive-affective system theory of personality: Reconceptualizing situations, dispositions, dynamics, and invariance in personality structure. *Psychological Review, 102*, 246–68.

Moreno, R., & Mayer, R. (2007). Interactive multimodal learning environments. *Educational Psychology Review, 19*(3), 309–326.

Morf, C. C., & Rhodewalt, F. (2001). Unraveling the paradoxes of narcissism: A dynamic self-regulatory processing model. *Psychological Inquiry, 12*, 177–196.

Norman, D. A. (1999). Affordance, conventions, and design. *Interactions, 6*, 38–43.

Orji, R., Mandryk, R. L., Vassileva, J., & Gerling, K. M. (2013). Tailoring persuasive health games to gamer type. In *Proceedings of the SIGCHI Conference on Human Factors in Computing Systems* (pp. 2467–2476), 27 April–2 May, Paris, France. New York: ACM.

Peng, W., Crouse, J. C., & Lin, J. H. (2013). Using active video games for physical activity promotion: A systematic review of the current state of research. *Health Education & Behavior, 40*, 171–192.

Persky, S., & Blascovich, J. (2008). Immersive virtual video game play and presence: Influences on aggressive feelings and behavior. *Presence: Teleoperators and Virtual Environments, 17*, 57–72.

Persky, S., & McBride, C. M. (2009). Immersive virtual environment technology: A promising tool for future social and behavioral genomics research and practice. *Health Communication, 24*, 677–682.

Petty, R. E., & Cacioppo, J. T. (1986). Message elaboration versus peripheral cues. In *Communication and Persuasion* (pp. 141–172). New York: Springer.

Primack, B. A., Carroll, M. V., McNamara, M., Klem, M. L., King, B., Rich, M.,…Nayak, S. (2012). Role of video games in improving health-related outcomes: A systematic review. *American Journal of Preventive Medicine, 42*, 630–638.

Przybylski, A. K., Rigby, C. S., & Ryan, R. M. (2010). A motivational model of video game engagement. *Review of General Psychology, 14*, 154.

Rajecki, D. W. (1982). *Attitudes: Themes and advances.* Sunderland, MA: Sinauer Associates.

Rapp, A. (2017). Designing interactive systems through a game lens: An ethnographic approach. *Computers in Human Behavior, 71*, 455–468.

Reicher, S. D., Spears, R., & Postmes, T. (1995). A social identity model of deindividuation phenomena. *European Review of Social Psychology, 6*, 161–198.

Rice, R. E., & Williams, F. (1984). Theories old and new: The study of new media. In R. E. Rice and Associates (Eds.), *The New Media: Communication, Research, and Technology* (pp. 55–80). Thousand Oaks, CA: Sage.

Ritterfeld, U., & Weber, R. (2006). Video games for entertainment and education. In P. Vorderer & J. Bryant (Eds.), *Playing video games: Motives, Responses, and Consequences* (pp. 399–413). London: Routledge.

Rizzo, A. S., Lange, B., Suma, E. A., & Bolas, M. (2011). Virtual reality and interactive digital game technology: New tools to address obesity and diabetes. *Journal of Diabetes Science and Technology, 5*, 256–264.

Ryan, R. M., Connell, J. P., & Deci, E. L. (1985). A motivational analysis of self-determination and self-regulation in education. In C. Ames & R. Ames (Eds.), *Research on Motivation in Education: The Classroom Milieu* (Vol. 2) (pp. 13–51). New York: Academic Press.

Ryan, R. M., & Deci, E. L. (2000). Self-determination theory and the facilitation of intrinsic motivation, social development, and well-being. *American Psychologist, 55*, 68–78.

Ryan, R. M., Rigby, C. S., & Przybylski, A. (2006). The motivational pull of video games: A self-determination theory approach. *Motivation and Emotion, 30*, 344–360.

Sacau, A., Laarni, J., & Hartmann, T. (2008). Influence of individual factors on presence. *Computers in Human Behavior, 24*, 2255–2273.

Salen, K., & Zimmerman, E. (2004). *Rules of play: Game design fundamentals*. Cambridge, MA: MIT press.

Salen, K., & Zimmerman, E. (2005). Game design and meaningful play. In J. Raessens & J. Goldstein (Eds.), *Handbook of Computer Game Studies* (pp. 59–79). Cambridge, MA: MIT Press.

Sanchez-Vives, M. V., & Slater, M. (2005). From presence to consciousness through virtual reality. *Nature Reviews Neuroscience, 6*, 332–339.

Sanchez-Vives, M. V., Spanlang, B., Frisoli, A., Bergamasco, M., & Slater, M. (2010). Virtual hand illusion induced by visuomotor correlations. *PLoS One 5*, e10381. doi:10.1371/journal.pone.0010381.

Seaborn, K., & Fels, D. I. (2015). Gamification in theory and action: A survey. *International Journal of Human-Computer Studies, 74*, 14–31.

Sherry, J. L. (2004). Flow and media enjoyment. *Communication Theory, 14*, 328–347.

Skalski, P., Tamborini, R., Lange, R., & Shelton, A. (2007). *Mapping the road to fun: Natural video game controllers, presence, and game enjoyment*. Paper presented at the 57th Annual Conference of the International Communication Association, 24–29 May, San Francisco, California.

Skinner, B. F. (1953). *Science and Human Behavior*. New York: Simon and Schuster.

Slater, M. (2009). Place illusion and plausibility can lead to realistic behaviour in immersive virtual environments. *Philosophical Transactions of the Royal Society of London B: Biological Sciences, 364*, 3549–3557.

Steuer, J. (1992). Defining virtual reality: Dimensions determining telepresence. *Journal of Communication, 42*, 73–93.

Tamborini, R. (2000). The experience of telepresence in violent video games. In *86th Annual Convention of the National Communication Association*, Seattle, WA.

Tamborini, R., & Bowman, N. D. (2010). Presence in video games. In C. Campanella Bracken & P. D. Skalski (Eds.), *Immersed in Media: Telepresence in Everyday Life* (pp. 87–109). New York: Routledge.

Tamborini, R., Grizzard, M., David Bowman, N., Reinecke, L., Lewis, R. J., & Eden, A. (2011). Media enjoyment as need satisfaction: The contribution of hedonic and nonhedonic needs. *Journal of Communication, 61*, 1025–1042.

Tamborini, R., & Skalski, P. (2006). The role of presence in the experience of electronic games. In P. Vorderer & J. Bryant (Eds.), *Playing Video Games: Motives, Responses, and Consequences* (pp. 225–240). London: Routledge.

Teather, R. J., & Stuerzlinger, W. (2007). Guidelines for 3D positioning techniques. In *Proceedings of the 2007 Conference on Future Play* (pp. 61–68). New York: ACM.

Treem, J. W., & Leonardi, P. M. (2013). Social media use in organizations: Exploring the affordances of visibility, editability, persistence, and association. *Annals of the International Communication Association, 36*, 143–189.

Twenge, J. M., Konrath, S., Foster, J. D., Campbell, W. K., & Bushman, B. J. (2008). Egos inflating over time: A cross-temporal meta-analysis of the narcissistic personality inventory. *Journal of Personality, 76*, 875–902.

Van Der Heide, B., Schumaker, E. M., Peterson, A. M., & Jones, E. B. (2013). The Proteus effect in dyadic communication: Examining the effect of avatar appearance in computer-mediated dyadic interaction. *Communication Research, 40*, 838–860.

Van Dijk, T. A. (1998). *Ideology: A multidisciplinary approach*. London: Sage.

von Ahn, L., & Dabbish, L. (2008). Designing games with a purpose. *Communications of the ACM, 51*, 57.

Walther, J. B. (2011). Theories of computer-mediated communication and interpersonal relations. In M. L. Knapp & J. A. Daly (Eds.), *The Sage Handbook of interpersonal communication* (4th ed.) (pp. 443–479). Thousand Oaks, CA: Sage.

Walther, J. B., & Parks, M. R. (2002). Cues filtered out, cues filtered in. In M. L. Knapp & J. A. Daly (Eds.), *Handbook of interpersonal communication* (3rd ed.) (pp. 529–563). Thousand Oaks, CA: Sage.

Wilson, M. (2002). Six views of embodied cognition. *Psychonomic Bulletin & Review, 9*, 625–636.

Won, A. S., Bailenson, J., Lee, J., & Lanier, J. (2015). Homuncular flexibility in virtual reality. *Journal of Computer-Mediated Communication, 20*, 241–259.

Yee, N. (2014). *The Proteus paradox: How online games and virtual worlds change us-and how they don't*. New Haven: Yale University Press.

Yee, N., & Bailenson, J. (2007). The Proteus effect: The effect of transformed self-representation on behavior. *Human Communication Research, 33*, 271–290.

Yee, N., & Bailenson, J. N. (2009). The difference between being and seeing: The relative contribution of self-perception and priming to behavioral changes via digital self-representation. *Media Psychology, 12*, 195–209.

Yee, N., Bailenson, J. N., & Ducheneaut, N. (2009). The Proteus effect: Implications of transformed digital self-representation on online and offline behavior. *Communication Research, 36*, 285–312.

Zillmann, D., & Bryant, J. (1985). Affect, mood, and emotion as determinants of selective exposure. In D. Zillmann & J. Bryant (Eds.), *Selective exposure to communication* (pp. 157–190). Hillsdale, NJ: Lawrence Erlbaum.

....

CHAPTER 27

GAME TRANSFER PHENOMENA: ORIGIN, DEVELOPMENT, AND CONTRIBUTIONS TO THE VIDEO GAME RESEARCH FIELD

....

ANGELICA B. ORTIZ DE GORTARI

INTRODUCTION

....

THERE is no need for holograms or digital images in physical contexts. No technological aid is needed; only the most powerful machinery ever invented, the human mind! Suddenly the real environments of gamers appear transformed by colors, textures, auras around objects, menus, power bars and pixelations; somatosensory sensations, sounds, voices and musical permutations as echoes of gamers' virtual experiences.

While we have a free will, a large part of our daily actions occurs automatically; we are easily influenced by environmental stimuli and by emotional and cognitive biases. We are to a certain degree prone to get songs stuck in our head, after-images after seeing a bright light, experiencing segments of thoughts that pop up in our head and slips of the tongue that intrude into our conversations. Involuntary or non-volitional phenomena are part of everyday life; however, these phenomena do not always come to our conscious awareness claiming attention. It is when these phenomena manifest recurrently, with particular content or when becoming elaborated that they can be intrusive and distressful, and in extreme cases lead to serious mental illness.

A good deal of video game research has dichotomized the effects of playing video games into either positive or negative. Much work has focused on understanding the behavioral, affective, cognitive and physiological effects of video games in isolation or restricted to particular video game formats, content, activities, amount of play and mechanics (Gentile, 2011; Parsons, 2017).

Research on Game Transfer Phenomena (GTP) combines the fields of study on the effects of video games and involuntary phenomena. It emerged as a unified approach for understanding the transfer of effects of interactive media, trying to avoid narrow perspectives that polarized the effects of technology into something positive or negative, normal or pathological, moderated or excessive.

GTP manifest as altered sensorial perceptions and automatic mental processes that sometimes lead to changes in behavior and automatic actions. Examples include at least temporary experiences of seeing images, hearing music, sounds, voices, tactile sensations, involuntary movements of limbs, sensations of unreality, illusion of self-body motion, illogical thoughts, verbal outbursts, etc., with video game content.

This chapter encompasses an overview of current research on GTP, conducted with over 6,000 gamers in total, from different samples and cultural backgrounds. The chapter is divided into three main sections: i) *the phenomena* comprises characteristics and the prevalence of GTP; ii) *the gamer* covers the underlying factors associated with GTP, appraisal and consequences of GTP, and iii) *the game* includes structural characteristics associated with GTP.

Background

Transfer of experiences from video games have been examined from a learning perspective by Bigl (2009, 2013), Wesener (2004), and Witting (2007). Fritz (2005) identified ten different types of transfers (e.g. problem-solving transfers such as thinking about problems, emotional transfers such as anxiety, and associative transfers such as the connection between different stimuli). Benjamin Bigl (2009, 2013) conducted research in online forums (n = 1,146) based on Fritz's perspective and found that almost all participants (87 percent) had experienced some type of transfer. The most common were transfers of dreams (31 percent) and knowledge (21 percent).

Others have examined video game transfers of experiences focusing on game-biased perceptions or associations. This approach is, to a certain degree, along the lines of GTP experiences triggered by real-life stimuli that have been simulated in the game. Poels, Ijsselsteijn, and de Kort (2014) surveyed gamers who played the MMORPG *World of Warcraft* (n = 511) in five domains: (i) memories from the game triggered by physical objects, (ii) daydreams, (iii) nightly dreams, (iv) memories from the game triggered by sound and music, and (v) intentionally using words and expressions from the game. They found that increased playing time (i.e. average playing time per day during the last three months) was positively correlated with the five proposed domains, and interest in the narrative of the game was relevant for associations with physical objects, sounds and music, and dreams.

Cultivation is another area of research relatively related to GTP. The cultivation theory posits that media portray an unrealistic picture of the real world that over time influences the individual's perception of the real world (i.e. beliefs about the world, and personal beliefs and attitudes). Studies using this theory have found that cultivation effects of video games only occur directly related to the contents of the game, rather than affecting general perceptions, expectations and beliefs about the world (Chong, Teng, Siew, & Skoric, 2012; Lee, Peng, & Klein, 2010). This appears to be similar to when GTP occurs when affordances in real-life world contexts facilitate the transfers (Ortiz de Gortari, 2015a). For example, when gamers encounter bottle caps in real life and they start picking them up as they have been doing in a game; if no bottle caps are encountered nothing is picked up.

Moreover, case studies have reported mix-ups between reality and virtual worlds. For instance:

- A drunk man mistakenly punched his wife in the face as he thought he was battling a dungeon boss in a *Zelda* game (Fysh & Thompson, 2009).
- A man in preventive detention without previous clinical history was diagnosed with paranoid schizophrenia after becoming obsessed with collecting points by assaulting cars and stealing motor vehicles. The man developed paranoid delusions as he believed someone was trying to kill him. Additionally, he experienced persistent verbal hallucinations by an abusive and pejorative voice (Forsyth, Harland, & Edwards, 2001).
- A man became obsessed about flying an aircraft and hijacking a plane after playing a flight simulator video game (Ichimura, Nakajima, Sadiq, & Juzoji, 2007).

Gamers have for many years referred to seeing images from video games, or continuing thinking and applying the rules from video games in real-life scenarios, as the "Tetris effect". The Tetris effect covers gamers' experiences of altered visual perceptions and automatic mental processes, identified in studies about GTP. The Tetris effect is understood as:

> "It's the 'Tetris Effect.' Many people, after playing Tetris for more than an hour straight, report being plagued by after-images of the game for up to days afterwards, an ability to play the game in their head, and a tendency to identify everything in the world as being made of four squares and attempt to determine 'where it fits in.'"
> (Kidd, G., 1996)

It was not until research on GTP began that transfer of experiences was investigated as a holistic approach that includes sensory perception, cognition and behavior.

Regarding the Tetris effect, Ortiz de Gortari and Griffiths (2012) have argued that the use of the term Tetris effect for conducting research on transfer of experiences is misleading, particularly because the name itself is inspired by the stereotypical tile puzzle game *Tetris*, suggesting that repetition is what triggers the transfer effects, but there are clearly other factors involved in the experiences. Moreover, the term Tetris effect alternatively refers to the impact and popularity of the Tetris game rather than the actual phenomenon. One example of this is the title and contents of Ackerman's (2016) book *The Tetris Effect: The Game that Hypnotized the World*. A recently (2018) released version of the Tetris game is also called Tetris Effect.

The GTP Research Approach

The Origin of GTP

The term "Game Transfer Phenomenon/a" (GTP) was coined by Angelica B. Ortiz de Gortari (2010) in her seminal master's thesis to refer to gamers' experiences as transfers between the virtual and the real world.

In the 1990s, the psychophysiological-related effects of the use of the Internet (voluntary or involuntary movements of fingers as when typing), other than the side effects in the case of the use of virtual simulators (e.g. motion sickness, cybersickness), were included satirically as withdrawal symptoms among a list of Internet addiction criteria proposed by Ivan Goldberg on a bulletin board of PsyCom.Net (Wallis, 1997). In the context of video games, gamers have reported a variety of involuntary movements of fingers or "Tech-induced dyskinesia" (Ortiz de Gortari, 2014) among their GTP experiences. These include involuntary movements of fingers like pushing the gamepads when trying to fall asleep or when wanting to use video game elements in everyday contexts (Ortiz de Gortari, 2015b; Ortiz de Gortari, Aronsson, & Griffiths, 2011; Ortiz de Gortari & Griffiths, 2014a). For instances, some gamers have reported the following:

> I once played Tetris for so long that when I stopped, I could still hear the music in my head for hours and my fingers kept twitching occasionally (Pachis).
> (Ortiz de Gortari, 2015a, p. 154)

> "I used to play Guitar Hero and Rock Band all the time... Now always my fingers dance trying to play the song that is playing. Not sure if it is annoying or anything but I cannot stop doing it." (Sael)   (Ortiz de Gortari, 2015a, p. 188)

It was not until 2010, many years after the author conducted one of the first studies on Internet addiction (Ortiz de Gortari, 2000), that she noticed the importance of the interplay between cognition, perceptions and behaviors in understanding the effects of interactive media.

In 2010, Ortiz de Gortari started paying attention to involuntary phenomena and how environmental stimuli play a role in thoughts and perceptions. The author's personal experience concerning technology helped pave the way for research of GTP. Once, traveling on the subway, an irrational thought popped up: "I can get off at any subway station because independently of where I get off, I'll arrive at my destination".

This spontaneous, irrational assumption was the result of copious searching for articles with the search engine Google. Google completes misspelled words and hyperlinks take you in different directions, sometimes even to websites with more interesting information than initially intended. Later on, conversations with parents revealed their concerns because their children were elaborating fantasies from the game in real-world scenarios. One gamer had violated traffic rules as in a video game; hearing this anecdote triggered the researcher's curiosity to play video games. Finally, the decision to explore GTP further was due to another new personal experience, which happened during a period of intense video game playing. A thought popped up when the author was visiting a local supermarket. When she could not read a label in the distance, she thought: "If I had the scope of the rifle from the game I could read these labels far away!" (Ortiz de Gortari, 2016b).

The GTP Framework and Definition

Game Transfer Phenomena (GTP) is a multimodal and holistic research approach for understanding the effects of playing video games on cognition, sensory perceptions, and behaviors, considering the interplay of video game contents, subjective phenomena while playing (e.g. immersion, trance state, embodiment), the simulation of activities, and the manipulation of hardware and peripherals on the transfer of experiences from the virtual to the physical world.

In research on GTP it is crucial to differentiate inner or endogenous experiences from outer or exogenous experiences (e.g. visualizing images vs. seeing images in front of the eyes or with open eyes), as well as to establish the difference between volitional and non-volitional phenomena (e.g. deliberate use of slang from a video game vs. involuntary verbal outbursts). Findings suggest that the psychological and potential risks of experiencing GTP depend upon the way and the contexts in which GTP manifests. For example, the consequences or implications of seeing images while trying to fall asleep (that in the worst case can lead to sleep deprivation) is rather different from the potential risks of seeing images while driving (Ortiz de Gortari & Griffiths, 2014a, 2014c).

The conceptualization and definition of GTP have undergone many modifications. Initially, GTP included dreams, spontaneous thoughts, sensory perceptions and voluntary and involuntary behaviors that in many cases appeared to be triggered by game-related cues (Ortiz de Gortari et al., 2011). Also, GTP was divided into *automatic GTP*, which occurs involuntarily and without premeditation by the gamers, e.g. sensorial experiences, sensations, spontaneous thoughts, automatic movements, actions or behaviors, and *intentional GTP*, i.e. intentional integration of video game contents into the players' daily interactions, such as using video games as interacting mediums or tools, or modeling game character and game events.

GTP was defined as:

> when videogame elements are associated with real-life elements triggering subsequent thoughts, sensations and/or player actions.   (Ortiz de Gortari et al., 2011, p. 17)

Soon after this it was noticed that the variety of GTP experiences was broader and that not all were triggered by game-related cues (Ortiz de Gortari & Griffiths, 2014a). With the intent of conceptualizing GTP into the framework of well-known phenomena such as auditory music imagery, hallucinations, and intrusive thoughts, GTP was defined as "involuntary phenomena manifesting as altered sensorial perceptions, automatic mental processes, actions and behaviours as a result of the transfer of experiences from [video game content] to the real world" (Ortiz de Gortari, 2016a, p. 12). However, once again it was noticed that restricting GTP to involuntary phenomena limited the understanding of the effects of these experiences. In many cases, once gamers have experienced GTP, they become aware and voluntarily reproduce it, sometimes for amusement.

Due to the pitfalls found in the definitions of GTP proposed so far, the author has opted to define GTP as "the transfer of experiences from the virtual to the physical world that can manifest as altered sensorial perceptions, sensations, automatic mental processes, behaviours and actions with video game content".

The Phenomena

This section describes the different forms of manifestation of GTP, in parallel discussing the gap in research on the effects of video game playing and showing the commonality of GTP and its characteristics.

Forms of Manifestation of GTP

The interplay of physiological, perceptual, and cognitive mechanisms is involved in GTP. The main theory-driven modalities proposed for the manifestation of GTP and confirmed via Confirmatory Factor Analysis on the GTP scale's twenty items (Ortiz de Gortari, Pontes, & Griffiths, 2015) are: (i) altered sensorial perceptions, (ii) automatic mental processes, and (iii) behaviors and actions.

Altered Sensorial Perceptions

Playing video games involves interaction with often colorful, shiny, and moving stimuli, usually for prolonged periods of time, which can lead to altered sensorial perceptions (Ortiz de Gortari & Griffiths, 2014a).

It is well-documented that altered sensorial perceptions can be induced by sensory deprivation (sensory isolation) or by an overload of sensory information (exposure to a monotonous stimulus) (Sacks, 1970). Altered perceptions can also take place when under the influence of substances, or as symptoms of neurological or mental disorders (Ohayon, 2000).

In general, altered sensorial GTP related experiences manifest as: i) distorted perceptions: perception of physical objects, environments, and/or sounds distorted according to video game features, ii) misperceptions: confusion of objects and sounds with something from a video game, iii) perceptions of video game elements without corresponding stimuli present: e.g. visual, aural, kinesthetic, somatosensory, and iv) visual or auditory imagery including mind visualizations.

Altered sensorial perceptions in GTP comprise perceptions or sensations in all sensorial channels, cross-sensory or multisensory.

Altered Visual Perceptions

Altered visual perceptions identified in studies on GTP include i) mind visualizations, ii) hallucinations or pseudohallucinations, including hypnagogic images and after-images, iii) distorted perceptions of objects and environments in color or shape (i.e. visual after-effects), and iv) visual misperceptions (Ortiz de Gortari & Griffiths, 2014a).

The majority of other studies in this area have mostly focused on the effects of visual cues during gameplay, e.g. use of blue or red color associated with game performance, use of blood color (red or blue) on arousal, and subsequent effects of violent video games (Jeong, Biocca, & Bohil, 2012; Wolfson & Case, 2000) rather than on understanding the post-effects of visual cues. However, a wave of research in the 1980s investigated the effects of exposure to visual cues on TV and video games that trigger seizures due to photo-sensitivity (Chuang, 2006).

Reports of perceptual adaptations such as colored after-effects from exposure to digital images for prolonged periods of time date back to 1984, when users of data terminals experienced neural adaptations and reported perceiving white surfaces tinted with pink color. This was due to the screens which used black backgrounds with green characters (Khan, Fitz, Psaltis, & Ide, 1984).

Dyson (2010) discussed motion after-effects as waterfall effects, which happened after playing music or dance games such as *Guitar Hero*. These games contain visual stimuli in constant movement (e.g. images scrolling down). Gamers describe their visual GTP experiences as dizziness and wavy vision and with objects appearing to levitate when looking away from the screen (Ortiz de Gortari et al., 2011; Ortiz de Gortari & Griffiths, 2014a).

Laboratory studies that investigate the consolidation of memories and the continuity between wakefulness and sleep activities have used video game playing as a novel and mental engaging visuomotor activity for inducing hypnagogic hallucinations. Participants have reported seeing images or hearing elements from video games when falling asleep, kinesthetic-related imagery, and a variety of thoughts with game content. These include mnemonic associations integrated into novel contexts (Kusse, Shaffii-Le Bourdiec, Schrouff, Matarazzo, & Maquet, 2012; Stickgold, Malia, Maguire, Roddenberry, & O'Connor, 2000; Wamsley, Perry, Djonlagic, Reaven, & Stickgold, 2010).

Altered Auditory Perceptions

Altered auditory perceptions identified in the research on GTP include: i) involuntary auditory imagery, ii) auditory hallucinations with music, sounds, or voices, iii) distorted perceptions of voices, sounds, or music, vi) misperceptions or confusions of sounds, v) inner speech, and vi) "Gedankenlautwerden" or thought-echo (i.e. hearing voices which anticipate what the individual is about to think) (Ortiz de Gortari & Griffiths, 2014b).

Other studies into auditory perceptions have mainly been interested in understanding the effects of physiological responses, such as arousal, sense of presence, improvement of memory, and aggression related to auditory cues embedded in virtual environments and video games (Anderson & Casey, 1997; Dinh, Walker, Hodges, Song, & Kobayashi, 1999; Hebert, Beland, Dionne-Fournelle, Crete, & Lupien, 2005; Hendrix & Barfield, 1995; Västfjäll, 2003), rather than the after-effects of these responses and the exposure to auditory cues.

Spence (1993) reported one of the few cases in this area; a female who constantly heard the music from the video game *Super Mario Bros.* In general, earworms or music imagery are their own area of research, as they are very common phenomena (Bailes, 2007), but not much attention has been paid to auditory imagery related with the use of technology. With the popularization of mobile phones, researchers have investigated people who have re-experienced the ringtone from mobile phones, and referred to this as "ring-anxiety", "phantom ringing", "ringing syndrome", etc. (Lin, Lin, Li, Huang, & Chen, 2013; Subba et al., 2013).

Altered Body Perceptions and Related Experiences

GTP experiences related to altered corporeal perceptions include: i) tactile sensations such as feeling a gamepad under the fingers when nothing is there, ii) whole body sensations of self-motion, iii) sensations of involuntary movements of limbs, and iv) adaptation to movement in the game (Ortiz de Gortari & Griffiths, 2014a). Some experiences appear to be better explained by sensory discrepancies or disruption in multisensory integration processes (e.g. vestibular, proprioceptive, tactile, visual) that can lead to neural adaptations (Ortiz de Gortari & Griffiths, 2017), while other experiences appear to be related to the embodiment of virtual entities.

Studies in this area have focused on the psychophysiological effects of virtual immersion, mostly in highly immersive environments such as virtual simulators (Champney et al., 2007) and virtual headsets (Stoffregen, Faugloire, Yoshida, Flanagan, & Merhi, 2008). This can lead to motion sickness symptoms (e.g. nausea) and can temporarily affect the individual's ability to walk, drive, or perform tasks that require precision and coordination (Hakkinen, Vuori, & Paakka, 2002). In extreme cases, motion sickness symptoms can be accompanied by postural instability (disequilibrium) (Gray Cobb & Nichols, 1998), proprioceptive errors (Stanney, Kingdon, Graeber, & Kennedy, 2002), lack of motor flexibility (ataxia), uncoordinated and jerky movements, and dyskinesia (Cobb, Nichols, Ramsey, & Wilson, 1999). For instance, a child thrust a cue stick into his eye while playing pool after having used a home virtual environment system (similar to a head-mounted display) for an extended period. A woman tried to drink soda by pouring the drink into her eye after having used a head-mounted display (Stanney, Kennedy, Drexler, & Harm, 1999). Another relevant phenomenon is the *Sickness of Disembarkment* or *Mal de Débarquement Syndrome*, which manifests as imbalance or having a rocking/swaying sensation after exposure to motion (usually associated with sea or air travel) (Ortiz de Gortari & Griffiths, 2014a).

Most research on the effects of body-related phenomena has focused on understanding cognitive, behavioral, and perceptual changes due to embodied virtual entities.

Particularly, the observation of a virtual self-performing behavior has been found to have the potential to change attitudes and behaviors (Blascovich & Bailenson, 2011).

A case related to involuntary movements of limbs reported by gamers (Ortiz de Gortari & Griffiths, 2014a) is that of a man who entered the US Navy's Substance Abuse and Recovery program. He repetitively lifted his hand towards his temple with the intent to control a Google Glass device when he was not wearing it. This was interpreted as a withdrawal symptom after stopping using the device (Yung, Eickhoff, Davis, Klam, & Doan, 2015).

Other Altered Sensorial Perceptions and Sensations of Unreality

Other alterations of sensorial perceptions identified in the studies of GTP include altered chronoceptive perceptions. This phenomenon is experienced as the sensation that events or velocity are happening at a slow pace, sometimes accompanied by lack of body flexibility. It has been reported after playing video games that include traveling at high speed or that include visual effects of slow motion (Ortiz de Gortari & Griffiths, 2014a). This type of GTP should not be confused with playing for escapism, immersion, or losing track of time denoted by getting in the "flow" and immersed when playing video games (Wood, Griffiths, & Parke, 2007).

Dissociations have been mostly investigated in relation to problematic Internet use (Canan, Ataoglu, Ozcetin, & Icmeli, 2012; Lee et al., 2016), but no attention has been paid to episodic disruptions of conscious awareness associated with video game playing in everyday contexts. In research on GTP, gamers have reported sensations of unreality like feeling as if still being in the game (i.e. derealization-like experiences), or feeling as if being a video game character (i.e. depersonalization-like experiences). Increase in dissociation and decrease of sense of presence in objective reality have been found after using VR, particularly in those with dissociative tendencies (Aardema, O'Connor, Côté, & Taillon, 2010).

Automatic Mental Processes

Automatic mental processes comprise thoughts, urges, and automatic mental actions. Experiences include: i) rumination about the game, ii) spontaneous thoughts about the game, iii) cognitive biases (e.g. paying attention towards game-related cues), iv) jumping to conclusions (e.g. expecting that something as in the game would happen in real life), v) source monitoring errors (e.g. mixing up video game events with real ones).

Research on the effects of video games has focused on understanding how playing video games can lead to changes in cognition. This has been done from perspectives that argue the positive effects of playing "serious games" (i.e. those designed with learning or therapeutic purposes) or commercial video games used for rehabilitation, therapy or learning (Griffiths, Kuss, & de Gortari, 2017).

Other perspectives that highlight the negative effects of playing video games on mind processes explore priming, conditioning behaviors, and selective attention towards game-related cues, mostly on video games with controversial content (e.g. violence, stereotypes, sexual content, perception of the world as a dangerous place) (Gentile, Bender, & Anderson, 2017).

Only research using the framework of behavioral addictions has investigated intrusive thoughts related to video games, labeling these as symptoms of Internet Gaming Disorder or gaming addiction: "preoccupation/salience" (King & Delfabbro, 2014). Some attention has also been paid to maladaptive beliefs involved in the development and maintenance of dysfunctional gaming patterns (Davis, 2001; Haagsma, Caplan, Peters, & Pieterse, 2013). These include overevaluating game rewards, social acceptance via gaming, and maladaptive and inflexible gaming rules (King & Delfabbro, 2016).

Moreover, a few studies have investigated daydreams (Dauphin & Heller, 2010; Poels, Ijsselsteijn, & de Kort, 2014) and the incorporation of video games into dreams (Gackenbach, Rosie, Bown, & Sample, 2011; Gackenbach, Ellerman, & Hall, 2011). Only a few researchers have considered daydreaming relevant for understanding gaming disorder (Demetrovics et al., 2012).

Behaviors and Actions

Studies into GTP have made efforts to distinguish between voluntary and involuntary behaviors with video game contents. Behaviors include a broad variety of simple actions to more elaborated behaviors. *Intentional* behaviors include modeling game movements or game characters for amusement, making jokes or using slang to communicate with others, and applying knowledge from video games to real life scenarios. *Automatic* behaviors occur under episodic lapses of lack of awareness usually triggered by game-related cues. Some behaviors or actions that occur spontaneously and without initial awareness of the gamer have been explained as slips of action "when a thought that was not intended to be voiced or performed gets done anyway" due to consolidated habits that are transferred under inappropriate circumstances (Norman, 1981, p. 3).

GTP experiences regarding behaviors and actions include: i) involuntary mental actions when gamers keep replaying the game in real-life contexts such as tracking objects or evaluating real-life environments as those from the game, ii) carrying out automatic actions such as moving as in the game (e.g. strafing as in first-person shooters), moving of limbs towards game-related cues or approaching objects without awareness, mimicking video game characters involuntarily, mixing up game controls or functions with those in the physical world when intending to use video game elements in a real-life context, and verbal outbursts when saying something with game content without intention, iii) behaviors influenced by video games where gamers get inspired to do activities from the game in a conscious manner, or when gamers' behavior is changed due to game experiences, such as avoiding game-related places or objects, and iv) slips when mixing up game controls or functions with those in the physical world when wanting to use video game elements in a real-life context.

Understanding the influence video game playing has on behaviors is one of the areas where much research has been conducted; however, most studies have investigated violent video games via laboratory experiments measuring behaviors in simulated situations or measuring outcomes of indirect behaviors influenced by playing (Gentile, Li, Khoo, Prot, & Anderson, 2014). Other studies have focused on racing or driving games, where the contents from the game were found to be directly related to the change of behavior, including attitudes while driving (Hull, Draghici, & Sargent, 2012).

General Characteristics of GTP

This section describes the characteristics of GTP and the prevalence and severity of GTP found in various studies conducted via qualitative and quantitative methods.

Incubation Period for the Manifestation of GTP

Most gamers have experienced GTP after playing; mainly hours after playing or directly after playing, but also days, weeks, or even later afterwards, although, slightly less than one in five have experienced GTP *while* playing (16 percent). For instance, gamers have reported altered sensorial perceptions while playing (e.g. seeing everything wavy when looking away from the monitor, seeing tags above people's heads, expecting that something will happen as in the game when taking a short break during a game session, feeling like going into another dimension when going to the bathroom) (Ortiz de Gortari & Griffiths, 2014a). Some examples come from gamers who have played location-based AR (Augmented Reality) games such as *Pokémon Go* and *Ingress*; they have made mix-ups and looked for video game elements outside the mobile screen or believed the Pokémon can be affected by physical events (Ortiz de Gortari, 2017a; Sifonis, 2016). It has been speculated that these types of games would lead to more GTP while playing since these games require the gamers to constantly switch between the game screen and the physical world, facilitating mix-ups (Ortiz de Gortari, 2017a).

Duration and Circumstance of the Experiences

The duration of GTP appears to vary depending on the type of modality of manifestation (sensorial or cognitive). In general, GTP has been reported to typically last for a very short time (seconds or minutes), but many gamers have experienced it recurrently or episodically triggered by game-related cues. Some have reported that a full episode lasts for a prolonged period of time, usually between hours and weeks (Ortiz de Gortari & Griffiths, 2016).

GTP has been reported in numerous circumstances, including when gamers were in solitude or social contexts. Most of the gamers have experienced GTP when doing daily activities rather than sleep-related, sometimes when performing automatic activities such as walking, packing, cooking, driving, listening to a lecturer, watching a film, or zoning out (Ortiz de Gortari & Griffiths, 2016). Two types of conditions have been identified when GTP happens:

i) Exposed to no (or limited) external stimulus: When in darkness, or in bed trying to sleep.

ii) Exposed to everyday stimuli: When in daily contexts.

Spontaneous thoughts and behaviors appear to be more likely to occur when triggered by automatic associations between physical objects and video game elements, while altered sensorial perceptions appear to occur more commonly without any external stimuli as trigger. Nocturnal GTP experiences (although not experienced exclusively in this context) include: constantly hearing music or sound from a game, seeing video game images, and sensations of body movement or limbs and tactile sensations.

Physiological states reported when GTP occurs include: stress, anxiety, and fatigue. Most gamers are not under the influence of any substance (medicine, alcohol, or drugs) when they experience GTP (87.2 percent) (Ortiz de Gortari & Griffiths, 2016).

Prevalence and Severity of GTP

Studies have found that the prevalence of GTP is usually above 95 percent when investigating GTP without any particular game in focus (Dindar & Ortiz de Gortari, 2017; Ortiz de Gortari & Griffiths, 2016; Ortiz de Gortari & Larøi, 2018; Sifonis, 2016); an exception is 82 percent, found in a study on gamers of *Pokémon Go* (Ortiz de Gortari, 2017b).

Most gamers have experienced GTP more than once (95 percent) (n = 2,236) (Ortiz de Gortari & Griffiths, 2016) and most experience mild levels of GTP (Ortiz de Gortari, 2017a; Ortiz de Gortari & Griffiths, 2016). Predictors of severity levels of GTP were positive appraisal, distress and dysfunction, and recall of dreams (Ortiz de Gortari, Oldfield, & Griffiths, 2016).

Figure 1 shows the types of GTP more commonly found in three samples (N_1 = 2,362, N_2 = 954 and N_3 = 1,313) and respective examples of gamers' experiences (Dindar & Ortiz de Gortari, 2017; Ortiz de Gortari, 2017a; Ortiz de Gortari & Griffiths, 2016).

THE GAMER: UNDERLYING INDIVIDUAL FACTORS AND PRONENESS TO GTP

The variables that have been investigated concerning individual factors associated with GTP to date are socio-demographic factors, gaming habits, motivations, in-game behaviors, proficiency, psychophysiological factors, gaming addiction, and dream-related variables.

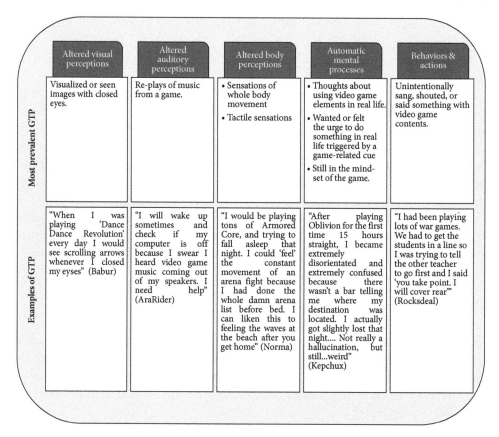

FIGURE 1 GTP modalities, most prevalent GTP types and examples of GTP

Socio-Demographic Factors

No differences have been found regarding gender in three different samples (Dindar & Ortiz de Gortari, 2017), nor when the sample was balanced regarding gender (Ortiz de Gortari, 2017a) However, a study conducted in the location-based AR game *Ingress* found that females were more prone to GTP (Sifonis, 2016).

Young adults, particularly 18- to 22-year-olds and minors (15+), appear to be more susceptible to experiencing GTP (Dindar & Ortiz de Gortari, 2017; Ortiz de Gortari, 2017a; Ortiz de Gortari & Griffiths, 2015; Ortiz de Gortari et al., 2016). However, while minors experience GTP more frequently, a closer look shows that the difference to adults is only significant regarding body-related experiences and automatic mental processes (Dindar & Ortiz de Gortari, 2017).

Gaming Habits

Playing frequency and session length have been found to be associated with GTP severity (i.e. experiencing GTP frequently and many times) (Ortiz de Gortari et al., 2016), although session length appears to be more relevant for GTP (Dindar & Ortiz de

Gortari, 2017; Ortiz de Gortari et al., 2016). However, when examining the GTP sub-scales rather than GTP as a whole it was found that session length was only correlated with automatic actions and behaviors and body-related experiences, but not with visual, auditory, or automatic mental processes (Dindar & Ortiz de Gortari, 2017). GTP with *Pokémon Go* was only associated with hours played per week and number of times played per day (Ortiz de Gortari, 2017a).

Proficiency Level and Experience of Playing Video Games

Research on GTP has mostly been conducted with hardcore gamers. A study found that professional gamers were significantly less likely to experience GTP compare to other gamers (hardcore and beginners) (Ortiz de Gortari & Griffiths, 2015), although this result has not been confirmed (Dindar & Ortiz de Gortari, 2017). Another study found that those with severe GTP were more likely to be professional gamers (Ortiz de Gortari et al., 2016). This may suggest that while there is some evidence that professional gamers are less prone to GTP, if they experience GTP, it is more likely to be severe (Ortiz de Gortari et al., 2016). No differences in experience of playing video games were found between those who have experienced GTP and those who have never experienced it (Dindar & Ortiz de Gortari, 2017).

Psychopathological Factors

The majority who have experienced GTP have no medical conditions nor have consumed drugs (Ortiz de Gortari & Griffiths, 2015; Ortiz de Gortari & Griffiths, 2016; Ortiz de Gortari & Larøi, 2018; Ortiz de Gortari et al., 2016).

Different results have been found regarding the relation between GTP and general medical conditions, mental disorders, and drug use. Some studies suggest that underlying psychopathological factors such as mental disorders make gamers more susceptible to experience GTP (Ortiz de Gortari et al., 2016; Ortiz de Gortari & Larøi, 2018). Moreover, those with mild levels of GTP were significantly less likely to have a psychological condition compared with those with moderate and high levels of GTP. More specifically, those with severe GTP were significantly more likely to have a sleep disorder, and consider themselves as having a problematic gaming addiction (Ortiz de Gortari et al., 2016).

Different results have been found in the relation between GTP and drug use. One study found no association between GTP and drug use or side effects of drug use (i.e. flashbacks) (Ortiz de Gortari & Griffiths, 2015), but another study found significant association (Ortiz de Gortari & Larøi, 2018).

Further analyses to understand the relation between GTP types that have been experienced in high frequency (e.g. hearing music, whole body sensation of self-motion) and underlying psychopathological factors (i.e. drug use, mental disorder, problematic gaming) showed that: i) not all types of GTP were associated with psychopathological factors, but almost all GTP types with high incidence have led to distress and/or dysfunction, ii) some GTP types were associated with psychopathological factor(s) independently if they were experienced very often (e.g. seeing images with open eyes is associated with mental disorder), iii) females seemed to be more likely to experience visual sensory and cognitions-related phenomena, while males seemed to be more likely to show changes in behaviors suggesting failures in control of impulses, iv) those with high incidence of visualized/seen images with closed eyes were significantly more likely to have used drugs, while those who have visual distortions or behaviors (e.g., act different in real-life situations, involuntary movement of fingers toward game-related cues) were significantly less likely to have used drugs, v) those who have visualized/seen images with closed eyes, had visual distortions, illusion of self-motion, heard music, had auditory misperceptions, or experienced verbal outbursts were significantly more likely to have a mental disorder, vi) those who have experienced illusions of self-motion, heard music, and verbal outbursts were significantly more likely to have sleep disorders (Ortiz de Gortari, 2017c).

Gaming Disorder and Problematic Smartphone Use

It has been suggested that profiles of gamers who experienced high levels of GTP (i.e. very frequently and a large variety of GTP types) share profiles with gamers with gaming addiction in terms of playing excessively (i.e. six hours or more), playing for escapism, and experiencing distress and/or dysfunction (Ortiz de Gortari et al., 2016). Considering oneself as having problems with gaming or having addiction has been found to be a predictor of GTP (Ortiz de Gortari et al., 2016). This finding has been confirmed; GTP was moderately correlated with Internet Gaming Disorder/ Gaming Disorder (GD) (n = 678) (Ortiz de Gortari & Larøi, 2018). Moreover, GTP in *Pokémon Go* was correlated with problematic smartphone use (PSPU) (Ortiz de Gortari, 2017c; Ortiz de Gortari, 2018). Binary logistic regression analysis showed that PSPU and dreaming about *Pokémon Go* were predictors of GTP (Ortiz de Gortari, 2017c). The most problematic populations appear to be those with GTP and GD or PSPU. For instance, those with both GTP and GD report higher distress or very negative impact due to GTP in comparasions to those with only GTP or no GTP nor GD (Ortiz de Gortari & Larøi, 2018). Also, those with GTP and PSPU were found significantly higher in gaming-related risks (e.g., accidents, trespassing and in conflicts (e.g., neglect responsibilities, deceive, arguments/fights) than those only prone to GTP or no GTP prone notwith PSPU. The most problematic populations appear to be those with both GTP and GD or both GTP and PSPU. For instance, those with both GTP and GD reported higher distress or very negative impact due to GTP in comparison to those with only GTP or no GTP nor GD (Ortiz de Gortari & Larøi, 2018). Also, those with both GTP and PSPU were more likely to reported gaming-related risks (e.g., accidents, trespassing, conflicts) than those with just GTP or no GTP or no PSPU.

Tendency to Recall Dreams

The tendency to recall dreams has been associated with GTP (Ortiz de Gortari & Griffiths, 2015). When examining the severity of GTP, it was found that those with mild and moderate levels of GTP were less likely to recall dreams. Moreover, the tendency to recall dreams was a predictor of severe levels of GTP (Ortiz de Gortari et al., 2016). Dreaming about Pokémon Go was a predictor of GTP with that game (Ortiz de Gortari, 2017c).

Moreover, another study showed that all the GTP sub-scales were correlated with the sub-scales of the Dream Intensity Scale by (Yu) (2012). Some of the GTP sub-scales were associated with confusion between facts and fantasy and autosuggestion (Gackenbach & Trewin, 2017).

Motivations for Playing and In-Game Behaviors

Studies have showed that socialization-related in-game behaviors or motivations for socialization are not related to GTP (Ortiz de Gortari, 2017b; Ortiz de Gortari & Griffiths, 2015). In fact, even in the game *Pokémon Go* where gamers tend, to a certain degree, to engage in social encounters, related factors such as meeting new people, helping other gamers, or hunting with others were not associated with GTP (Ortiz de Gortari, 2017b). Playing for escapism has been found to be significantly associated with GTP in games in general and in *Pokémon Go* (Ortiz de Gortari, 2017b; Ortiz de Gortari & Griffiths, 2015; Ortiz de Gortari et al., 2016).

Significant relationship has been found between GTP and in-game-related behaviors that suggest focusing on the game world and elements such as exploring and customization, as well as learning about the game mechanics (Ortiz de Gortari & Griffiths, 2015) and role-play in *Pokémon Go* (Ortiz de Gortari, 2017b).

Consequences of Playing

Positive outcomes of playing *Pokémon Go*, such as feeling less anxious to go outside, having fewer negative thoughts, and seeing the world as a nicer place, and negative consequences such as neglecting responsibilities, have all been associated with GTP (Ortiz de Gortari, 2017b).

Appraisal, Consequences, and Implications of GTP

According to a survey conducted with over 2,000 gamers, more than half of the participants were indifferent to their GTP experiences, and more appraised GTP as pleasant, and some even wanted to experience GTP again. However, one in five reported confusion and experienced GTP as unpleasant (Ortiz de Gortari & Griffiths, 2016).

In qualitative studies, gamers have qualified their GTP as positive (e.g. "entertainment", "fun", "creative", "good times", "nerdy", "awesome") or negative (e.g. "annoying", "sign of madness", "scary", "freak me out", "disconcerting"); others qualify GTP as "strange", "crazy", or "trippy" (Ortiz de Gortari & Griffiths, 2014a, 2014b, 2014c).

The consequences described by gamers include surprise, confusion, hyper-vigilant mood states, fright, anxiety, sleep deprivation, lack of concentration, frustration, embarrassment, behaving irrationally, and/or having engaged in risky behaviors. Also, when thoughts and urges to perform controversial acts based on video game contents were aroused, gamers reflected about the influence of video games on their lives and self-boundaries.

Distress and dysfunction have also been reported due to GTP, but only by 20 percent of the participants (Ortiz de Gortari & Griffiths, 2016), although more than half (58 percent) of those who experienced severe GTP (i.e. many types of GTP occurring frequently) reported distress or dysfunction (Ortiz de Gortari et al., 2016). Appraising GTP as pleasant, and experiencing distress or dysfunction in some area of functioning, have been found to be predictors of GTP (Ortiz de Gortari et al., 2016).

Ortiz de Gortari (2015a) argues that the psychosocial implications of GTP depend on:

- The gamers' individual characteristics, e.g. psychological stability, ability to hold back the impulses towards game-related cues.
- Frequency and recurrence of the phenomena, e.g. once, episodically, all the time.
- Duration of the phenomena, e.g. minutes or longer periods of time.
- Internal or external nature of GTP, e.g. outer self-generated phenomena or outer non-self-generated phenomena.
- Circumstances of occurrence, e.g. in compromised situations such as driving or while lying in bed.
- Content of the phenomena, e.g. abstract video game shapes or realistic video game content.
- The gamers' interpretation and reactions to the event, e.g. indifferent or frightened.
- Coping mechanism, e.g. stopping playing the game for a while or developing irrational ideas.
- Looking for support from peers and others by communicating about their GTP or keeping the experience to themselves for fear of being laughed at or perceived as mentally ill (p. 276).

While transfer of effects from passive media such as films, or from engaging in repetitive activities (e.g. working on an assembly line) can take place, the implications are different. The exposure to video game-related cues, but not exposure to film cues, activate brain areas associated with control inhibition, especially motor inhibition (Ahn, Chung, & Kim, 2015), which may require that gamers hold back learned sequences of responses (e.g. jump, hit, move) since events and objects and in-game actions are paired in repetitive fashion (Ortiz de Gortari, 2015a).

THE GAME

This section presents the core elements relevant for GTP related to the video games' structural characteristics, the video game genres associated with GTP, and discusses the relevance of the gaming platform.

Video Game Genres Associated with GTP

GTP has been reported in a broad variety of video games in more than four hundred unique titles (Ortiz de Gortari, 2016a), including games on different platforms such as mobile games and location-based AR games like *Pokémon Go* and *Ingress*. Differences in the severity levels of GTP have been found regarding the type of video game played. Gamers classified with severe levels of GTP compared with those with moderate and mild levels of GTP were more likely to play MMORPGs, simulation games, adventure games, first-person shooter games, puzzle games, music and dance games, and role-playing games. Those with moderate levels of GTP were significantly more likely to play action and racing games. Poels, Ijsselsteijn, and de Kort (2014) found that MMORPG gamers reported game-biased perceptions, which cover some of the GTP experiences triggered by game-related cues.

Relevance of Gaming Platform and Video Game Features

A study conducted on *Pokémon Go* (Ortiz de Gortari, 2017b) showed the importance of the video game features and the game platform for the manifestation of GTP. For example, *Pokémon Go* gamers were more likely to report somatosensory experiences such as tactile sensations associated with the game, rather than proprioceptive experiences such as feeling whole body self-motion, which is the most common GTP type among the bodily-related GTP. Also, playing with sound in *Pokémon Go* appears to be important for the manifestation of several types of GTP, even more than playing using the AR function (Ortiz de Gortari & Griffiths, 2016). Interestingly, while Pokémon Go can be played with or without the Augmented Reality (AR) function (that overlays images in physical context), only visual misperceptions were significantly associated with playing with the AR enabled rather than seeing images with open or closed eyes. This suggest that neuroadaptive mechanisms are necessary to see images with open or closed eyes. These mechanisms are perhaps facilitated by the prolonged exposure to the images, focused attention (which is more likely to be absent in Pokémon Go due to constant shifting the view between the device and the physical world), as well as, perhaps the type and the quality of the images (e.g., brightness) (Ortiz de Gortari, 2017b).

Core In-Game and Structural Characteristics Relevant for GTP

Four core elements from video games related to in-game phenomena and structural characteristics that appear to ease the transfer of effects have been proposed (see Ortiz de Gortari & Griffiths, 2017 for full definitions and sub-categories of GTP related with each one of the factors).

1. Sensory perceptual stimulation—interacting, usually for prolonged periods of time, with repetitive and sometimes stereotypical synthetic sensorial stimuli.
2. High cognitive load—interactive and demanding activity that requires processing a large variety of sensorial stimuli simultaneously during a short period of time, using complex executive functions, perceptual and motor skills.
3. Dissociative states—involvement in normative dissociative phenomena (i.e. a form of non-pathological dissociation that takes place in recreational activities (Butler, 2006), such as losing track of time, state of flow, immersion, sense of presence, and sometimes embodiment.
4. High emotional engagement—rewarding and amusing activity, which tends to lead to mood-modifying states and physiological responses (e.g. arousal) directly related to in-game events and performance in the video game.

CONCLUSIONS, REMARKS, AND DIRECTIONS FOR FUTURE RESEARCH

This chapter provided an overview of the findings on GTP in quantitative and qualitative studies mainly conducted without any specific video games in focus, except for the studies into the location-based AR games *Pokémon Go* and *Ingress*. Most participants in these studies have been adults, although young adults and minors seem to be more prone to GTP.

The GTP framework provides a novel and multidisciplinary approach for investigating the pervasiveness of the effects of video game playing in everyday contexts and increasing the understanding of hallucinatory-like phenomena and automatic thoughts/behaviors not induced by substance use or mental/neurological disorders.

Research on GTP suggests that gaming disorder should be examined beyond the frameworks of addiction (Ortiz de Gortari & Larøi, 2018) or video game content (e.g. violent games). GTP experiences can lead to distress and dysfunction (mimicking symptoms of mental disorders), and in some cases put gamers in compromised situations. Dichotomizing video games (violent vs. pro-social) is not enough for understanding the effects of video games. The transfer of effects does not depend only on the game contents, but also on the affordances found in the real world that facilitate the associations and transfers. Even harmless acts such as jumping can, when taking place in certain contexts and places, be dangerous.

A growing body of literature has emerged from the research on GTP during the last few years. However, it is still an area under development. Future research should try to explain why GTP has been associated with the numerous factors summarized in this chapter (e.g. gaming habits, age) to be able to develop interventions to assist individuals in need. Also, it is important to understand the differences between those who experience GTP and those who do not experience GTP. It is also crucial to understand for which individuals and under what circumstances GTP can posit risks and in what ways GTP and its mechanisms can be applied for therapeutic and learning purposes. Those prone to GTP with GD or PSPU appear to be the population that requires more attention regarding potential risks of GTP (Ortiz de Gortari, 2018; Ortiz de Gortari & Larøi, 2018). Moreover, research on GTP should include experimental designs that allow systematic and controlled assessment of GTP, including longitudinal designs to evaluate the prevalence of GTP over time.

Informing and raising awareness about GTP are believed to contribute to fostering self-control when automatic urges arise triggered by game-related cues, and to demystifying everyday involuntary phenomena that most of the time are erroneously considered pathological, leading to stigma.

ACKNOWLEDGMENTS

The author is a beneficiary of the Marie Curie COFUND fellowship, cofunded by the University of Liège and the European Union.

REFERENCES

Aardema, F., O'Connor, K., Côté, S., & Taillon, A. (2010). Virtual reality induces dissociation and lowers sense of presence in objective reality. *CyberPsychology, Behavior & Social Networking* 13(4), 429–435.

Ackerman, D. (2016). *The Tetris effect: The game that hypnotized the world.* New York, NY: PublicAffairs.

Ahn, H. M., Chung, H. J., & Kim, S. H. (2015). Altered brain reactivity to game cues after gaming experience. *Cyberpsychology, Behavior, and Social Networking* 18(8), 474–479.

Anderson, D. B., & Casey, M. A. (1997). The sound dimension. *Spectrum IEEE* 34(3), 46–50.

Bailes, F. (2007). The prevalence and nature of imagined music in the everyday lives of music students. *Psychology of Music* 35(4), 555–570.

Bigl, B. (2009). *Game over? But what is left over?* Paper presented at the General Online Research. 6–8 April, Vienna, Austria.

Bigl, B. (2013). If the game goes on. Perceived transfer effects from virtual game worlds into everyday life. In B. Bigl & S. Stoppe (Eds.), *Playing with virtuality: Theories and methods of computer game studies* (pp. 135–146). Frankfurt am Main: Peter Lang.

Blascovich, J., & Bailenson, J. (2011). *Infinite reality: Avatars, eternal life, new worlds, and the dawn of the virtual revolution.* New York, NY: William Morrow & Co.

Butler, L. D. (2006). Normative dissociation. *Psychiatric Clinics of North America 29*(1), 45–62.

Canan, F., Ataoglu, A., Ozcetin, A., & Icmeli, C. (2012). The association between Internet addiction and dissociation among Turkish college students. *Comprehensive Psychiatry 53*(5), 422–426.

Champney, R. K., Stanney, K. M., Hash, P. A., Malone, L. C., Kennedy, R. S., & Compton, D. E. (2007). Recovery from virtual environment exposure: Expected time course of symptoms and potential readaptation strategies. *Human Factors 49*(3), 491–506.

Chong, Y. M. G., Teng, K. Z. S., Siew, S. C. A., & Skoric, M. M. (2012). Cultivation effects of video games: A longer-term experimental test of first- and second-order effects. *Journal of Social & Clinical Psychology 31*(9), 952–971.

Chuang, Y.-C. (2006). Massively multiplayer online role-playing game induced seizures: A neglected health problem in Internet addiction. *Cyberpsychology & Behavior 9*(4), 451–456.

Cobb, S. V. G., Nichols, S., Ramsey, A., & Wilson, J. R. (1999). Virtual reality-induced symptoms and effects (VRISE). *Presence: Teleoperators & Virtual Environments 8*(2), 169–186.

Dauphin, B., & Heller, G. (2010). Going to other worlds: The relationships between videogaming, psychological absorption, and daydreaming styles. *Cyberpsychology, Behavior, and Social Networking 13*(2), 169–172.

Davis, R. A. (2001). A cognitive-behavioral model of pathological Internet use. *Computers in Human Behavior 17*(2), 187–195.

Demetrovics, Z., Urbán, R., Nagygyörgy, K., Farkas, J., Griffiths, M. D., Pápay, O.,...Oláh, A. (2012). The development of the Problematic Online Gaming Questionnaire (POGQ). *PLoS ONE 7*(5), e36417.

Dindar, M., & Ortiz de Gortari, A. B. (2017). Turkish validation of the Game Transfer Phenomena Scale (GTPS): Measuring altered perceptions, automatic mental processes and actions and behaviours associated with playing video games. *Telematics and Informatics 34*(8), 1802–1813.

Dinh, H. Q., Walker, N., Hodges, L. F., Song, C., & Kobayashi, A. (1999). *Evaluating the importance of multi-sensory input on memory and the sense of presence in virtual environments.* Paper presented at IEEE Virtual Reality. 13–17 March, Houston, TX. doi:10.1109/VR.1999.756955.

Dyson, B. J. (2010). She's a waterfall: Motion after-effect and perceptual design in video games involving virtual musicianship. *Perception 39*(1), 131–132.

Forsyth, R., Harland, R., & Edwards, T. (2001). Computer game delusions. *Journal of the Royal Society of Medicine 94*(184–185).

Fritz, J. (2005). How virtual worlds affect us: On the structure of transfers from the media world to the real world. In G. Buurman (Ed.), *Total interaction* (pp. 95–121). Basel: Birkhäuser.

Fysh, T., & Thompson, J. (2009). A Wii problem. *Journal of the Royal Society of Medicine 102*(12), 502.

Gackenbach, J., Rosie, M., Bown, J., & Sample, T. (2011). Dream incorporation of video-game play as a function of interactivity and fidelity. *Dreaming 21*(1), 32–50.

Gackenbach, J., & Trewin, C. (2017). *Pokemon Go dreams: Is augmented reality the next stage in gaming associations to dreams?* Paper presented at the 34th Annual Dream Conference. 16–20 June, Anaheim, CA.

Gackenbach, J. I., Ellerman, E., & Hall, C. (2011). Video game play as nightmare protection: A preliminary inquiry in military gamers. *Dreaming 21*(4), 221–245.

Gentile, D. A. (2011). The multiple dimensions of video game effects. *Child Development Perspectives 5*(2), 75–81.

Gentile, D. A., Bender, P. K., & Anderson, C. A. (2017). Violent video game effects on salivary cortisol, arousal, and aggressive thoughts in children. *Computers in Human Behavior 70*, 39–43.

Gentile, D. A., Li, D., Khoo, A., Prot, S., & Anderson, C. A. (2014). Mediators and moderators of long-term effects of violent video games on aggressive behavior: Practice, thinking, and action. *JAMA Pediatrics 168*(5), 450–457.

Gray Cobb, S. V., & Nichols, S. C. (1998). Static posture tests for the assessment of postural instability after virtual environment use. *Brain Research Bulletin 47*(5), 459–464.

Griffiths, M. D., Kuss, D. J., & de Gortari, A. B. O. (2017). Videogames as therapy: An updated selective review of the medical and psychological literature. *International Journal of Privacy and Health Information Management 5*(2), 71–96.

Haagsma, M. C., Caplan, S. E., Peters, O., & Pieterse, M. E. (2013). A cognitive-behavioral model of problematic online gaming in adolescents aged 12–22 years. *Computers in Human Behavior 29*(1), 202–209.

Hakkinen, J., Vuori, T., & Paakka, M. (2002). Postural stability and sickness symptoms after HMD use. *IEEE International Conference on Systems, Man and Cybernetics 1*, 147–152.

Hebert, S., Beland, R., Dionne-Fournelle, O., Crete, M., & Lupien, S. J. (2005). Physiological stress response to video-game playing: The contribution of built-in music. *Life Sciences 76*(20), 2371–2380.

Hendrix, C., & Barfield, W. (1995). Presence in virtual environments as a function of visual and auditory cues. In *Proceedings of the Virtual Reality Annual International Symposium.* (pp. 74–82): Red Hook, NY: Curran and Associates.

Hull, J. G., Draghici, A. M., & Sargent, J. D. (2012). A longitudinal study of risk-glorifying video games and reckless driving. *Psychology of Popular Media Culture 1*(4), 244–253.

Ichimura, A., Nakajima, I., Sadiq, M. A., & Juzoji, H. (2007). Investigation and analysis of a reported incident resulting in an actual airline hijacking due to a fanatical and engrossed VR state. *Cyberpsychology & Behavior 4*(3), 355–363.

Jeong, E. J., Biocca, F. A., & Bohil, C. J. (2012). Sensory realism and mediated aggression in video games. *Computers in Human Behavior 28*(5), 1840–1848.

Khan, J. A., Fitz, J., Psaltis, P., & Ide, C. H. (1984). Prolonged complementary chromatopsia in users of video display terminals. *American Journal of Ophthalmology 98*(6), 756–758.

King, D. L., & Delfabbro, P. H. (2014). Is preoccupation an oversimplification? A call to examine cognitive factors underlying internet gaming disorder. *Addiction 109*(9), 1566–1567.

King, D. L., & Delfabbro, P. H. (2016). The cognitive psychopathology of internet gaming disorder in adolescence. *Journal of Abnormal Child Psychology 44*(8), 1635–1645.

Kusse, C., Shaffii-Le Bourdiec, A., Schrouff, J., Matarazzo, L., & Maquet, P. (2012). Experience-dependent induction of hypnagogic images during daytime naps: A combined behavioural and EEG study. *Journal of Sleep Research 21*(1), 10–20.

Lee, K. M., Peng, W., & Klein, J. (2010). Will the experience of playing a violent role in a video game influence people's judgments of violent crimes? *Computers in Human Behavior 26*(5), 1019–1023.

Lee, T. K., Roh, S., Han, J. H., Park, S. J., Soh, M. A., Han, D. H., & Shaffer, H. J. (2016). The relationship of problematic Internet use with dissociation among South Korean Internet users. *Psychiatry Research 241*(Suppl C), 66–71.

Lin, Y.-H., Lin, S.-H., Li, P., Huang, W.-L., & Chen, C.-Y. (2013). Prevalent hallucinations during medical internships: Phantom vibration and ringing syndromes. *PLoS ONE 8*(6), 1–6.

Norman, D. A. (1981). Categorization of action slips. *Psychological Review 88*, 1–15.

Ohayon, M. M. (2000). Prevalence of hallucinations and their pathological associations in the general population. *Psychiatry Research 97*(2–3), 153–164.

Ortiz de Gortari, A. B. (2000). *Las implicaciones psicosociales del uso del Internet* (Bachelor's dissertation) Universidad de Monterrey.

Ortiz de Gortari, A. B. (2010). *Targeting the Real-life Impact of Virtual interactions: The Game Transfer Phenomenon. 42 video games players' experiences.* (Master's dissertation). Stockholm University.

Ortiz de Gortari, A. B. (2014, October 14). *Google Glasses withdrawal: Tech-induced dyskinesia?* Retrieved from http://gametransferphenomena.com/2014/10/google-glasses-withdrawal-tech-induced-dyskinesia/

Ortiz de Gortari, A. B. (2015a). Exploring Game Transfer Phenomena: A multimodal research approach for investigating video games' effects (Doctoral dissertation). Nottingham Trent University. Retrieved from http://irep.ntu.ac.uk/id/eprint/27888/

Ortiz de Gortari, A. B. (2015b). *The South Korean Ministry of Health and Welfare's campaign based on Game Transfer Phenomena experiences*, February 7. Retrieved from http://gametransferphenomena.com/2015/02/the-south-korean-ministry-of-health-and-welfares-campaign-based-on-game-transfer-phenomena-experiences/

Ortiz de Gortari, A. B. (2016a). The Game Transfer Phenomena framework: Investigating altered perceptions, automatic mental processes and behaviors induced by virtual immersion. *Annual Review of CyberTherapy and Telemedicine 14*, 9–15.

Ortiz de Gortari, A. B. (2016b, October 10). *Game Transfer Phenomena: Echoes of extended gameplay*. Retrieved from http://psychology21c.org/2016/03/game-transfer-phenomena-echoes-of-extended-gameplay/

Ortiz de Gortari, A. B. (2017a). Empirical study on Game Transfer Phenomena in a location-based augmented reality game. *Telematics and Informatics 35*(2), 382–396.

Ortiz de Gortari, A. B. (2017b). *Game transfer phenomena and the augmented reality game Pokémon Go: The prevalence and the relation with benefits, risks, immersion and motivations.* Paper presented at the 22nd Annual CyberPsychology, CyberTherapy & Social Networking. 26–28 June, Wolverhampton, UK.

Ortiz de Gortari, A. B. (2017c). *High incidence of sensory and cognitive intrusions with video-game content: Underlying psychopathological factors.* Paper presented at the 4th International Consortium on Meeting Hallucination Research. 6–8 November, Lille, France.

Ortiz de Gortari, A. B. (2018). *Game Transfer Phenomena and problematic smartphone use in an augmented reality game.* Paper presented at the 18th World Congress of Psychiatry. 27–30 September, Mexico City, Mexico.

Ortiz de Gortari, A. B., Aronsson, K., & Griffiths, M. D. (2011). Game Transfer Phenomena in video game playing: A qualitative interview study. *International Journal of Cyber Behavior, Psychology and Learning 1*(3), 15–33.

Ortiz de Gortari, A. B., & Griffiths, M. D. (2012). An introduction to Game Transfer Phenomena in video game playing. In J. I. Gackenbach (Ed.), *Video game play and consciousness* (pp. 223–250). Hauppauge, NY: Nova Publisher.

Ortiz de Gortari, A. B., & Griffiths, M. D. (2014a). Altered visual perception in Game Transfer Phenomena: An empirical self-report study. *International Journal of Human-Computer Interaction 30*(2), 95–105.

Ortiz de Gortari, A. B., & Griffiths, M. D. (2014b). Auditory experiences in Game Transfer Phenomena: An empirical self-report study. *International Journal of Cyber Behavior, Psychology and Learning 4*(1), 59–75.

Ortiz de Gortari, A. B., & Griffiths, M. D. (2014c). Automatic mental processes, automatic actions and behaviours in Game Transfer Phenomena: An empirical self-report study using online forum data. *International Journal of Mental Health and Addiction 12*(4), 432–452.

Ortiz de Gortari, A. B., & Griffiths, M. D. (2015). Game Transfer Phenomena and its associated factors: An exploratory empirical online survey study. *Computers in Human Behavior 51*(0), 195–202.

Ortiz de Gortari, A. B., & Griffiths, M. D. (2016). Prevalence and characteristics of Game Transfer Phenomena: A descriptive survey study. *International Journal of Human-Computer Interaction 32*(6), 470–480.

Ortiz de Gortari, A. B., & Griffiths, M. D. (2017). Beyond the boundaries of the game: The interplay between in-game phenomena, structural characteristics of video games, and game transfer phenomena. In J. Gackenbach & J. Bown (Eds.), *Boundaries of self and reality online* (pp. 97–121). San Diego, CA: Academic Press.

Ortiz de Gortari, A. B., & Larøi, F. (2018). *Broadening the understanding of the psychopathology of gaming: The relation between involuntary behaviours, sensorial and cognitive intrusions with videogame content and Internet Gaming Disorder.* Paper presented at the 5th International Conference on Behavioural Addictions. 23–25 April, Cologne, Germany.

Ortiz de Gortari, A. B., Oldfield, B., & Griffiths, M. D. (2016). An empirical examination of factors associated with Game Transfer Phenomena severity. *Computers in Human Behavior 64*, 274–284.

Ortiz de Gortari, A. B., Pontes, H., & Griffiths, M. D. (2015). The Game Transfer Phenomena Scale: An instrument for investigating the non-volitional effects of video game playing. *Cyberpsychology, Behavior, and Social Networking 18*(10), 588–594.

Parsons, T. D. (2017). *Cyberpsychology and the brain: The interaction of neuroscience and affective computing.* Cambridge, UK: Cambridge University Press.

Poels, K., Ijsselsteijn, W. A., & de Kort, Y. (2014). *World of Warcraft*, the aftermath: How game elements transfer into perceptions, associations and (day) dreams in the everyday life of massively multiplayer online role-playing game players. *New Media & Society 16*, 1–17.

Sacks, O. W. (1970). *Migraine: The evolution of a common disorder.* Berkeley, CA: University of California Press.

Sifonis, C. (2016). *Game Transfer Phenomena in the Augmented Reality Game, Ingress.* Paper presented at the International Academic Conference on Meaningful Play. 20–22 October, Lansing, Michigan.

Spence, S. A. (1993). Nintendo hallucinations: A new phenomenological entity. *Irish Journal of Psychological Medicine 10*, 98–99.

Stanney, K. M., Kennedy, R. S., Drexler, J. M., & Harm, D. L. (1999). Motion sickness and proprioceptive aftereffects following virtual environment exposure. *Applied Ergonomics 30*(1), 27–38.

Stanney, K. M., Kingdon, K. S., Graeber, D., & Kennedy, R. S. (2002). Human performance in immersive virtual environments: Effects of exposure duration, user control and scene complexity. *Human Performance 15*(4), 339–366.

Stickgold, R., Malia, A., Maguire, D., Roddenberry, D., & O'Connor, M. (2000). Replaying the game: Hypnagogic images in normals and amnesics. *Science 290*(5490), 350–353.

Stoffregen, T. A., Faugloire, E., Yoshida, K., Flanagan, M. B., & Merhi, O. (2008). Motion sickness and postural sway in console video games. *Human Factors 50*(2), 322–331.

Subba, S. H., Mandelia, C., Pathak, V., Reddy, D., Goel, A., Tayal, A.,...Nagaraj, K. (2013). Ringxiety and the mobile phone usage pattern among the students of a medical college in South India. *Journal of Clinical and Diagnostic Research 7*(2), 205.

Tetris Effect. (n.d.). *In Wikipedia, The Free Encyclopedia*. Retrieved 20 February, 2012, from http://en.wikipedia.org/w/index.php?title=Tetris_effect&oldid=478489275

Västfjäll, D. (2003). The subjective sense of presence, emotion recognition and experienced emotions in auditory virtual environments. *Cyberpsychology & Behavior 6*(2), 181–188.

Wamsley, E. J., Perry, K., Djonlagic, I., Reaven, L. B., & Stickgold, R. (2010). Cognitive replay of visuomotor learning at sleep onset: Temporal dynamics and relationship to task performance. *Sleep 1*(33), 59–68.

Wesener, S. (2004). *Spielen in virtuellen Welten: eine Untersuchung von Transferprozessen in Bildschirmspielen*. Wiesbaden: Vs Verlag Fur Sozialwissenschaften.

Witting, T. (2007). *Wie Computerspiele uns beeinflussen: Transferprozesse beim Bildschirmspiel im Erleben der User*. Munich: Kopaed Verlag.

Wolfson, S., & Case, G. (2000). The effects of sound and colour on responses to a computer game. *Interacting with Computers 13*(2), 183–192.

Wood, R. T. A., Griffiths, M. D., & Parke, A. (2007). Experiences of time loss among video-game players: An empirical study. *Cyberpsychology & Behavior 10*, 45–56.

Yung, K., Eickhoff, E., Davis, D. L., Klam, W. P., & Doan, A. P. (2015). Internet addiction disorder and problematic use of Google Glass™ in patients treated at a residential substance abuse treatment program. *Addictive Behaviors 41*, 58–60.

CHAPTER 28

....

PSYCHOSOCIAL EFFECTS
OF GAMING

....

MICHELLE COLDER CARRAS,
RACHEL KOWERT, AND THORSTEN QUANDT

INTRODUCTION

....

FOR the last few decades, video games have been a common leisure activity. Today, 65 percent of households in the United States (US) have at least one person who plays three or more hours of video games a week (Entertainment Software Association, 2017). The popularity of play among adolescents is particularly notable, with 72 percent of US teens (aged 13–17), and 67 percent of young adults (18–29) reporting that they play video games on a computer, handheld device, and/or dedicated gaming console (Duggan, 2015; Lenhart, 2015). It is unsurprising that video games continue to be a popular form of entertainment because—at their core—they are fun, playful activities. While the fun may draw players initially, players continue to enjoy video games because they are intrinsically motivating. That is, they satisfy our needs as humans to feel autonomous (i.e., a sense of freedom), competent (i.e., to be challenged and successfully overcome challenges), and related to others (i.e., to be socially connected; for more on this see Ryan, Rigby, & Przybylski, 2006; Przybylski, Rigby, & Ryan, 2010).

For children and adolescents, the normality of video game play often goes unacknowledged in the scientific literature, as a framework of video game play being somehow abnormal and anti-social remains at the forefront, despite strong evidence to the contrary (Kowert, Festl, & Quandt, 2014; Kowert, Griffiths, & Oldmeadow, 2012). However, as research into the psychosocial outcomes of gaming has progressed, the need to incorporate context, including developmental, individual, social, and societal, has become clearer. People play video games in a variety of contexts and social settings, as well as for a variety of reasons. On top of that, cohort effects due to changes in technology over time have led to new norms for social interactions. As online video games have become wildly popular, they have drawn the same concerns as other Internet-mediated interactions: do these new types of social interactions augment social relationships by providing more opportunities to interact, or do they displace our more "socially valuable" face-to-face relationships?[1]

Alongside the growth of the video game industry has come increased concern as to whether or not engagement with this new medium is psychosocially detrimental. Games are inherently very rewarding to play, so much so that many news articles (and even some scientific articles) describe them as "hijacking" the brain's reward system. In addition, games are another form of media that sometimes have violent content, which may teach players to become aggressive or violent. In both cases, the interactivity of games seems to set them apart from other media in the public discourse. This concern has spread into various areas of scientific inquiry, including their impact on social outcomes (social skills, friendship networks), psychological outcomes (depression, loneliness, social anxiety, empathy, aggression) and learning (moral behavior, desensitization, various knowledge and skills), among others.

However, the motivating properties and the potential for games to teach also suggests that games might be beneficial. They can lead to learning transfer for violence, excessive/problematic play and social, cognitive and mental health benefits such as prosocial behavior, cognitive training, distraction from unpleasant health or mood states, and empowerment to deal with stressful life situations. Although the last few years have seen a greater recognition of the positive sides of gaming, certain areas are still subject to debate and public concern, which have not been resolved within the methodological limitations of studies to date.

Overall, it is clear that the naturally rewarding aspects of games are associated with—and in some cases lead to—psychosocial benefits, as well as potential problems. Understanding the nature of effects requires an in-depth understanding of related theory and how bias has driven public discourse and research approaches.

Concepts and Definitions

Any discussion of research on the psychosocial effects of gaming should first be clear about what is meant by games. Often when people think of video games, they imagine electronic games played on a TV or computer for entertainment. However, technically "video games" are electronic games that use visual feedback. As such, even mobile phone/tablet games and games played on a web browser are considered to be video games. "Digital games" is a broader term that refers to any game that is played on an electronic platform. This term encompasses video games, but in some circles this term is

---

[1] While the inherent value of face-to-face versus mediated relationships remains debated, there is an underlying assumption in the scientific literature that face-to-face relationships are more socially valuable as they are thought to be better able to provide social resources (i.e., physical and psychological support).

used when referring to games used for learning or health, rather than the term video game, which is more often used when talking about games for entertainment.

Video games may be played alone, with others in the same room (co-located play), or online. Online video games are a new game technology that allows people to play video games over the Internet. This technology has vastly expanded video games' multiplayer functionality by allowing players to connect with others in a shared gaming space beyond the boundaries of their geographical location (Kowert, 2014). While gamer communities have been evident since popularization of arcades in the 1970s, these communities have grown substantially alongside the advent of online games. In this context, "gamer" refers to the personal and social identification as a member of the gaming community. The gamer identity is unique as it is both part of virtual (i.e., online gaming guilds or clans) and physical (i.e., being a gamer in your school friendship group) contexts (Grooten & Kowert, 2015). Aside from simply playing games together, gamers connect through applications such as *Steam*, a digital game purchasing platform and *Discord*, a chat service, both of which are accessible even when not gaming. With the rise of interest in gaming, opportunities to watch games being played have developed into sporting events (eSports) and an online streaming service, *Twitch.tv*. All of these online opportunities have changed the ways people interact with games as individuals and in communities.

The effects of games happen within a variety of dimensions and are driven by additional individual factors and social/cultural contexts. Video game effects are driven by amount and content of games (e.g., violent games vs. nonviolent games), the context in which games are played (e.g., solo, social competitive, social-cooperative), and the structure and mechanics of games (Gentile, 2011). The gaming context itself can be broken down further in an integrated ecological model (Elson, Breuer, & Quandt, 2014). In this model, the player is seen as being embedded in a culture/social environment with states and traits that interact with game content and mechanisms. The player's use of games is driven by their states and traits as well as game markets, and it is the interaction between player and their states/traits before, during, and after play that drives both short-term and long-term effects.

Games can have a variety of general psychosocial effects that, in recent years, have been capitalized on for applied effects to health and learning. General psychosocial effects encompass motivations for play as well as individual influences on game play; psychological states (before, during, and after play, and over the long term), social interactions on- and offline related to gaming, and effects on relationships. Applied psychosocial effects are how games are used to change knowledge, behavior and attitudes, or health outcomes. Therefore, understanding the state of research into the psychosocial outcomes of gameplay is not simple. Over the decades of research into the psychosocial effects of video games, debates driven by popular discourse and research methods continue.

This chapter seeks to answer two research questions:

- What are the psychosocial effects of gaming?
- What are the barriers to understanding these effects?

METHOD OF SYSTEMATIC REVIEW AND OVERVIEW OF THE LITERATURE

This chapter deviates from the normal format as it is based not only on the authors' reading and understanding of the literature, but a systematic review. In that sense, it is a very specific reading of the literature, the basis of which needs to be discussed for transparency reasons. In order to fully cover the wide range of literature in psychology, medicine, public health, games studies, communication studies and related disciplines, a thematic synthesis approach (Thomas & Harden, 2008) was used to develop themes and concepts that describe: (i) the scope of literature related to the psychosocial outcomes of gaming, and (ii) the challenges to synthesizing results into evidence for these effects.

To ensure the relevant literature was captured, a pre-planned approach was used to search the most relevant databases (PubMed and PsycInfo) for systematic reviews of associations between gaming and psychosocial predictors or outcomes using a broad search strategy. Inclusion criteria were English-language peer-reviewed systematic reviews of observational and experimental studies in humans, narrative reviews, and reviews that included commentary. The resulting articles were grouped into themes and subthemes based on both emergent concepts (e.g., "other health areas") and existing areas of study in cyberpsychology (e.g., "game addiction"). Although this method resulted in a wide range of reviews, it left out the most recent empirical studies. To supplement this, the authors also considered articles from the current year (2017) that addressed the relevant themes.

Of the 332 articles originally retrieved with the search strategy, 285 articles remained after deduplication, 198 remained after title review, and 155 after abstract review. The 136 articles remaining after full-text review were included in the study. Coding close to the text produced 144 codes, and saturation was determined to be reached after 81 articles. Codes were then combined into 12 primary themes as shown in Table 1 (relevant themes, which were used as subchapters, are indicated in bold text). Some themes resulted from included articles combining discussion of psychosocial outcomes and other excluded topics, such as education.

This chapter discusses the main themes and their findings. Themes that only touch upon aspects of psychosocial effects were incorporated where relevant.

RESULTS

Aggression and Violence

Research on violent content in video games and its effects on—potentially aggressive—behavior is a long-debated topic, not only in scientific journals, but also by the public,

Table 1 Theme and subthemes resulting from systematic review

Violence
Problematic gaming
Psychosocial associations
   Self-efficacy, empowerment, agency
   Social
   Emotional
Theories and frameworks[a]
   Motivational
   Learning-related
   Health behaviors
Clinical mental health
Cognitive effects[b]
   Executive functioning
   Motivation
Other health
Research challenges and gaps[c]
Games and genres
Gamification/serious games
Learning
Play functions and gaming experiences

Note: Themes in bold comprise this chapter's subchapters, while themes in italics are woven into specific subchapters: [a] *incorporated into* Associations Between Gaming and Other Forms of Psychosocial Well-Being, [b] *Incorporated into* Applications: Mental Health and Cognitive Functioning, [c] *incorporated into* Discussion

and it has a comparably long history. Violence in games has been discussed for decades in relation to very early video and computer games, including arcade games and numerous Atari VCS or C64 titles (Kocurek, 2012). Driven by the fear of negative effects on the main users at that time (children and adolescents), many countries installed systems of age ratings and parental control to prevent further harm, and they also restricted access or, in some cases, effectively censored games.

Scientific research on the effects of violent content, primarily on subsequent aggressive behavior (but also related aspects of psychosocial well-being) paralleled and followed the public discussion. Findings were sometimes taken as arguments for heated political debates on regulation of media content, which, in turn, also led to an equally conflicting situation in science. Even today, the field can be characterized by a stark contrast between liberal game supporters and pronounced critics of violent games (Bushman, Gollwitzer, & Cruz, 2015; Greitemeyer & Mügge, 2014; Quandt & Kowert, 2016). Some suspect the human mind to respond to mediated violence in the same (or a very similar) way as real violence and compare the public health impact of mediated violence to lung cancer (Bushman & Huesmann, 2014), or imply that brain changes from violent games or action games (which are said to encourage players to memorize maps so that they can concentrate on responding quickly to game challenges) are similar to those of severe psychiatric disorders (Eiser, 2015; West, Konishi, & Bohbot, 2017). Others do not identify any measurable long-term effects on violent or delinquent behavior (Calvert et al., 2017; Elson & Ferguson, 2014). Overall, evidence reviews conducted by both sides suggest that violent video games have small or very small associations with aggression in correlational, longitudinal, and experimental studies, and that these effects are near zero when other variables such as gender and trait aggression that may influence aggression outcomes are included in the analysis (Ferguson, 2015).

The general situation—not only in relation to aggression, but also other negative effects of gaming—can be described as a "moral panic" (Bowman, 2015; Ferguson, 2008), where societal and scientific reactions reflect an outbreak of deeper moral concerns and fears. In line with this, it has been noted that findings regarding violent media content need to be read with caution, as they are often ideological and transcend the purely scientific (Grimes, Anderson, & Bergen, 2008). As expected, the authors' review revealed conflicting positions, and even systematic reviews seemed to be indicative of the authors' own position, and not fully neutral (Greitemeyer & Mügge, 2014). These issues notwithstanding, there are some general trends in the literature (that should be read in light of the situation sketched here). Empirical studies in the field seem to fall into some main categories, reflecting conceptually and disciplinary differing positions—there are experimental laboratory studies, neuroimaging studies, cross-sectional or longitudinal survey studies, and some studies correlating secondary data sets on a community, country, or multi-country level to get some indication of games' impact on society (especially crime levels/delinquency).

A large part of the studies in the literature follows the pattern of traditional psychological experiments in lab settings. The response to the stimulus (i.e., a violent game) is typically assessed with physiological or neurological measurement during exposure, or via specific questionnaires that indirectly measure aggressive tendencies directly after exposure. For example, one task that purports to measure aggressive cognitions has subjects fill in blanks in a list of words (e.g., EXPLO_E); the responses are then determined to be aggressive (EXPLODE), or not aggressive (EXPLORE). The results of these studies, indeed, indicate short-term effects of violent video games in the expected direction, albeit reported effect sizes vary in strength (and are not necessarily higher than for (non-interactive) television). Thus, games can heighten the level of aggressive tendencies in the answers of respondents, and also seem to have the potential to raise unspecific physiological arousal that is channeled towards aggressive behavior, mirroring the stimulus material of violent games.

However, there is substantial criticism regarding this line of research (Breuer, Vogelgesang, Quandt, & Festl, 2015; Elson & Ferguson, 2014). Critics are worried about a particularly strong publication bias (i.e., just significant results are reported, whereas a potentially larger group of publications with no findings remains unpublished), the ecological validity of artificial lab studies (where people are forced to consume content that does not necessarily fit their own interest and selection principles), and the indirect measurement of aggression via post-test questionnaires. Indeed, scales to measure aggressive behavior cannot directly target the behavior itself, as this cannot be reproduced in lab settings for obvious ethical reasons. Even substitute aggressive behavior (like in Bandura's classic Bobo doll experiments; s. Bandura 1961) is ethically difficult when induced by the experiment, so researchers typically observe behaviors that are supposed to be tied to aggression (like in Bushman's 1995 Competitive Reaction Time Task, and Dewall and colleagues' 2013 voodoo doll task), or questionnaire scales indicative of aggressive tendencies (like in Lieberman, Solomon, Greenberg, & McGregor's 1999 "hot sauce paradigm", or the lexical decision tasks by Krahé et al., 2011), which have been only partially validated (Ferguson & Rueda, 2009; Ritter & Eslea, 2005; Tedeschi & Quigley, 1996). This pattern has also been found in neuroimaging studies. One review study suggests that games arouse the sympathetic nervous system in a way that indicates that the violence "feels real," and that comparisons between the brain responses to playing a violent game in long-term players of violent games vs. those who do not have this experience indicate that long-time players become desensitized to violent content (Brockmyer, 2015). However, this review also points out that similar results have been found for other violent media as well, indicating that these findings are not limited to violent video games. In short, while the lab and neuroimaging studies are indicative of some effects of violent games' content on the users, the interpretation and transfer of these findings to real-life conditions and the actual phenomenon under analysis (aggressive behavior) are difficult.

Thus, many scholars call for additional longitudinal studies on gamers, their personality characteristics, their previous experience with violent game use, and any extremely violent real-world behavior (Calvert et al., 2017; Elson & Ferguson, 2014). Indeed, there are some survey studies following this call, but their number is comparably smaller than cross-sectional studies, they often rely on convenience samples, their findings are mixed, and they do not uniformly support a clear causal effect (Adachi & Willoughby, 2013; Anderson et al., 2008; Breuer et al., 2015; Ferguson, 2011; von Salisch, Vogelgesang, Kristen, & Oppl, 2011). Some scholars argue for an inverse logic, with aggressive tendencies (as traits) preceding the selection and use of violent media content, and some longitudinal studies find evidence for such a "selection effect" (Breuer et al., 2015; von Salisch et al., 2011). Logically, a media effect and a selection effect are not mutually exclusive—it has also been argued that both effects may happen at the same time, amplifying a "downward spiral" (Slater, Henry, Swaim, & Anderson, 2003).

So, despite nearly three decades of research in the field (Elson & Ferguson 2014), the results of research on violent video games and aggression/violence are far from being conclusive. Additionally, the overall impact of violent games on society is difficult to measure. Some researchers use macro-level data on public health, crime, and societal aggression and correlate it with the development and use of (violent) video games. The findings in this chapter contradict the experimental research: it has been noted that Western societies actually became less violent in these three decades, and that there is no indication of a notable (or measurable) "real-life" effect whatsoever (Coulson & Ferguson, 2016; Elson & Ferguson, 2014)—much in contrast to the predicted massive societal and public health effects.

The issues of the research on aggression and violent video games may be linked to the very basic approach that still treats games as fixed stimulus, representing "violent input," and the users as very basic response systems. Even the theoretically more-advanced studies that rely on conceptualizations, like the General Aggression Model (Anderson & Bushman, 2002), primarily improve on the stimulus-response (S-R) logic by differentiating the internal processes in the organism/individual (thus, a stimulus-organism-response, or S-O-R, logic). Environmental and societal aspects are merely regarded as modifiers, but not core to the phenomenon, and alternative compensating factors (for example, on psychosocial well-being) are not taken into account.

In that respect, it can be argued that a reconsideration of basic categories and the general logic in that line of research is needed. Some authors note that, in order to understand the effects of violent content, one also needs to understand the medium and its logic much more. For example, it could be shown that games need to give the user an explanation and justification for violence—without such a "moral disengagement" (Hartmann & Vorderer, 2010)—violent games could not be consumed in a joyful and satisfying way. In addition, the goal of play matters—playing violent games with the intention of "letting off steam" or reducing hostile/aggressive tendencies does seem to produce less aggression, rather than more (Denzler & Förster, 2012). These findings may lead to interesting follow-up questions regarding the psychological and social foundations of violence and aggression, and potentially better explanations. More generally speaking, it may be necessary to think of aggression not only in terms of an undesirable, dysfunctional outcome variable (as it is the case in most of the studies we found), but also as a rather "functional" aspect of human life.

Addiction & Problematic Gaming

Besides aggression/violence, other negative effects of video and computer games on the psychological and social well-being of their users appear frequently in the popular media. For example, there are many concerns about the excessive (and potentially addictive) use of games, especially among adolescent players. Problematic gaming[2] also remains a controversial topic among scholarly communities as the criteria for problematic or "disordered" outcomes of excessive gaming are highly controversial, as there is no standard definition upon which the scientific community agrees (Griffiths et al., 2016, Aarseth et al., 2016). Problematic gaming is, at the time of writing, not identified as a formal disorder in the *Diagnostic and Statistical Manual of Mental Disorders* (DSM-5) by the American Psychiatric Association, but as a condition to be monitored for further study (American Psychiatric Association, 2013). There is also an ongoing discussion to include a similar disorder in the *International Classification of Diseases* by the World Health Organization (WHO) in its 11th edition (World Health Organization, 2017), but this has not yet been formalized either. However, even these steps are regarded to be premature

---

[2] Many terms have been used to refer to problems related to excessive video gaming. As the disorder has yet to be formalized, this chapter primarily uses the term "problematic gaming," as this term does not impose the disease-like state implied by the terms "addiction," "pathological use," and "disorder."

by numerous researchers in the field (Aarseth et al., 2016), as they doubt there is a sufficient consensus of what the aspects of the disorder essentially are. The debate and research, on the one hand, are driven by anecdotal reports on gamers totally losing control of their hobby, including severe conflicts with the social environment and, in the case of minors, with parents (Zastrow, 2017). Ironically, the earliest form of what is now labeled Internet gaming disorder was called Internet addiction, and referred to Internet use more broadly (Young, 1998). Early on, researchers identified parallels between pathological gambling and excessive Internet use, and transferred the criteria for this behavioral disorder to Internet use and then to video and computer games. However, there is no agreement among researchers on whether the behavioral issues with video and computer games can be categorized as "addiction" (Banz, Yip, Yau, & Potenza, 2016), what the diagnostic criteria are, and how to measure them (Griffiths et al., 2016), and how prevalent the problem is (King, Haagsma, Delfabbro, Gradisar, & Griffiths, 2013). Indeed, some warn more generally about the assumption that problematic media use is a behavior that individuals cannot come to grips with on their own (LaRose, Lin, & Eastin, 2003).

Notably, there is some agreement that the time spent on gaming is not a sufficient criterion (Colder Carras et al., 2017; Van Rooij, Schoenmakers, Vermulst, Van den Eijnden, & Van de Mheen, 2011), and indeed, maybe not even a necessary one, despite its prominent status in the public debate. However, the proposed scientific criteria for a diagnosis are very broad, and, primarily analogous to gambling, currently include (but are not limited to): preoccupation with the behavior, withdrawal problems and craving (i.e., a strong urge to return to the behavior), tolerance building (i.c., a diminished reaction to exposure, resulting in an urge to increased use), inability to reduce/stop behavior, impact on other activities, relationship issues, plus continued behavior despite problems, deceit and covering up the behavior, escapism (behavior as an avoidance of other, unpleasant aspects of life), and the severity of the problem (Griffiths, 2005). As noted, researchers disagree on which criteria are more essential, and some researchers question the whole concept of "(Internet) gaming addiction" as ill-defined (Przybylski, Weinstein, & Murayama, 2016; Van Rooij, Van Looy, & Billieux, 2017).

Unsurprisingly, findings on the prevalence rates of problematic gaming vary greatly— from less than a percent to two-digit numbers (Mihara & Higuchi, 2017). The available survey studies rely on different definitions—one recent review found 18 different instruments used to measure problematic gaming in a review of 63 studies (King et al., 2013). As there is no common standard, a wide range of prevalence rates is to be expected. Furthermore, studies focus on different type of games/gaming (online or offline, role-playing games, first person shooters vs. other genres, etc.), varying target populations (adolescents, self-declared gamers, online users, players of a certain game, the overall population, etc.) and different national contexts (see also Müller, Beutel, Egloff, & Wolfling, 2014; Quandt, Chen, & Van Looy, 2014)—so while the numbers are typically cited in the public discussions as a "proof" of the severity of the problem, it is often not exactly clear to which behavior or set of symptoms they refer.

Beyond prevalence rates, surveys can be also helpful in identifying motivations of users, factors that contribute or accompany the phenomenon, and the effects of problematic gaming on psychosocial well-being. A recent review of survey studies in the current analysis points to consistent associations with male sex, problems with grades or school achievement, and lower social skills or feelings of social competence (Mihara & Higuchi, 2017). Impulsivity and neuroticism are personality traits commonly seen to be linked, as well as a host of psychosocial correlates, such as loneliness, low self-esteem, aggression, and low life satisfaction. Problematic gaming is also found in individuals who have other psychiatric disorders like ADHD, depression, and anxiety. Overall, their findings imply the potential for strong effects on a variety of life domains for a relatively small group of affected persons. It has to be noted, though, that most of the survey studies in the field are cross-sectional, and therefore only depict a snapshot in time. Accordingly, as the findings of these studies are correlational, causation cannot be deduced. In other words, these studies suggest that the excessive gaming can be the cause of problems, or it might be the result of them—and as such, it might be an attendant phenomenon to some deeper, underlying issue in the personality or psychological vulnerability, the social environment, stressors, or some other aspect of life.

There are ways to test for causality, like experiments and longitudinal studies. There are comparatively few longitudinal studies on problematic gaming. All in all, their findings are non-conclusive, with no clear patterns emerging and the phenomenon resolving quickly in many cases (Scharkow, Festl, & Quandt, 2014). Some people exhibit problematic behavior at times, but can, and do, stop the behavior without external intervention; fewer people show problematic gaming over long periods (Domahidi & Quandt, 2015; King, Delfabbro, & Griffiths, 2013; Scharkow et al., 2014; Van Rooij et al., 2011). Longitudinal studies may test or report results in a single direction only; for example, rather than measuring whether depression comes before problematic gaming, a study may report only changes in depression after the development of problematic gaming (Gentile et al., 2011). Periodic extreme use is frequently tied to specific game titles, or specific life circumstances, and the opt out of "heavy" gaming is often linked to entering new life phases (Domahidi & Quandt, 2015).

These findings cast some doubts on the classification of a video game "addiction" as analogous to substance dependence. Despite these, the analogy to substance dependence is implied by several experimental studies that try to measure the response to and effect of gaming at a neurological level (Weinstein, Livny, & Weizman, 2017). Typically, they identify brain reactions and mechanisms similar to substance dependence or a comparably problematic behavior, e.g., by showing game "addicts" pictures of game situations and observing that their brains reacted the same way that a person with substance use problems reacts to cues about the substances they crave (Kuss & Griffiths, 2012). Also, brain reactions that are similar to positive behaviors (such as working, eating, helping behavior, or just generally positive mood) are usually not tested in these studies, which may indicate scientific confirmation bias (as the base assumption is already a comparison with something negative). Individuals identified as having problematic gaming seem to have brains that function differently on cognitive or other tasks compared to those without such problems (Banz et al., 2016; Meng, Deng, Wang, Guo, & Li, 2015), usually in ways to reflect greater impulsivity or less ability to control responses (e.g., not saying the wrong word in a test). However, again, selection effects may be at play: it is unclear whether problematic gaming leads to brain changes, or whether it develops because people have problems with impulsivity or other measures of self-control (Kuss & Griffiths, 2012). Finally, and probably most importantly, the fact that video games stimulate the brain's reward pathways may be interpreted as the normal functioning of a brain under the given circumstances, and not as a dysfunctional reaction (Bulaj, 2014; Palaus, Marron, Viejo-Sobera, & Redolar-Ripoll, 2017)—as games manipulate behavior via reward systems by design, it is unsurprising that there should be a correlate in the users' brain reactions (the same is true for comparable studies on the neurological response to violent content in games). All of these factors make it hard to interpret the various studies of neurological outcomes of problematic gaming and suggest yet another area that would benefit from studies designed to tease apart cause and effect.

All in all, the research on problematic gaming and problematic use offers some evidence of such forms of behavior for a small group of users. Conceptually, there is still no consensus on what exactly "defines" such a problem behavior, and even more so, where it comes from—so research on the etiology and logics of excessive gaming is needed.

Associations Between Gaming and Other Forms of Psychosocial Well-Being

Outside of the research and discussion around problematic play, literature on associations between video game play and psychosocial outcomes in general abounds. From a psychological perspective, it is important to understand how interaction with video games can affect thoughts, feelings, and behaviors when used as part of daily life. As a form of technology that provides not only entertainment, but also the opportunity to communicate and interact, video game play has similarities to non-mediated game play (e.g., board games or sports), but also unique features and affordances (Grooten & Kowert, 2015; Kowert, 2014; Kowert & Quandt, 2015).

There are several frameworks for understanding the potential mechanisms behind how games might be associated with psychosocial predictors, correlates, and outcomes. Frameworks such as uses and gratifications theory suggest that individuals choose media to meet certain needs, such as arousal, challenge, or competition (Sherry, Greenberg, Lucas, & Lachlan, 2006) or to manage moods (Zillmann, 1988). The choice is an active one, and having the need satisfied drives further media use. For example, individuals who are bored may choose media that are more arousing/exciting, while individuals who are stressed or anxious might choose media that are relaxing (Bryant & Zillmann, 2009). This may be particularly useful for children, who may choose violent games as a way to regulate emotions and practice making moral decisions in a place where "being the bad guy" will not lead to harm (Agina, 2012; Bergen & Davis, 2011). Self-determination theory (Ryan et al., 2006) addresses motivations as well, suggesting that gaming behavior is intrinsically motivating because it satisfies the basic human needs for competence, autonomy, and relatedness. Enjoyment is then related to how well these needs are satisfied within the game—games that allow greater flexibility in rules are associated with more self-reported competence, while social games produce more feelings of relatedness (Rogers, 2017; Ryan et al., 2006). Stepping outside theories where motivations are closely tied to individual needs, player type theory (Bartle, 1996; Yee, 2006) emphasizes the importance of motivations toward specific types of game activities. In this theory, video game players fall into three separate groupings based on why they play: achievement, socializing, or immersion. A final popular theory concerns the motivational aspects of flow (Csikszentmihalyi, 1990; Weber, Tamborini, Westcott-Baker, & Kantor, 2009), a cognitive state that is said to be inherently motivating. Flow is the experience of being "in the zone," where all focus is on the game, and awareness of self and of time passing fall by the wayside. Flow results from the balance between challenge and skill, and the experience of flow just feels good. It has been hypothesized to represent a qualitatively unique state—a synchronization of attention and reward networks in the brain (Weber et al., 2009). Keeping these frameworks in mind will help put research findings in context as the various associations between psychosocial well-being and gaming are discussed.

Other frameworks focus on the potential negative outcomes of gaming. There is a growing fear that increased video game play, particularly online play, may lead to a displacement of other "real-world" activities that are important for social and psychological development. For example, by dedicating more time to online gaming, players are inevitably dedicating less time to offline socializing, which is important for the development of a range of social skills, such as sending and receiving non-verbal cues (Kowert, 2015). This phenomena, often referred to as the social displacement hypothesis, has gained some empirical support (Cole & Griffiths, 2007; Shen & Williams, 2010; Smyth, 2007; Williams, 2006). For example, Smyth (2007) found that after one month of online game play, participants reported a reduction in the time spent socializing with offline friends than players of offline video games, including arcade and console games. Williams (2006) reported a similar pattern of "cocooning" among online players (i.e., retreating into the seclusion of one's home during leisure time). It should be noted, however, that more recent research has not found evidence of displacement effects among gamers (Domahidi, Breuer, Kowert, Festl, & Quandt, 2016; Kowert, Domahidi, & Quandt, 2014; Kowert, Festl, et al., 2014).

However, it must be noted that it is possible that spending increased time online could also contribute to the acquisition of a different set of social skills, such as the ability to effectively socialize without the use of non-verbal cues. Thus, rather than video games displacing activities to the detriment of its players, they could provide an alternative learning space. Supports of this theory point to the potential for video games be valuable cognitive-social learning grounds (Bandura, 1961, 1977, 1986) as they allow for the observation, rehearsal, and feedback of a wide variety of social strategies from the safety and security of one's own home. For example, players can observe the interactions of other players, try out new social strategies (e.g., various leadership and conversational skills), and receive immediate feedback (e.g., successful or unsuccessful leadership as measured by achieving in-game group goals) with little to no consequence to them in their "offline" lives (Bowman, 2015; Yee, 2008).

Steinkuehler and Williams (2006) have hypothesized that the beneficial social effects could even be much broader, and that online games have the potential to increase an individual's general sociability by expanding his/her world view. By providing the opportunity to interact with a diverse group of other players—young and old, from down the street or across the globe—players are able to engage with a community of others to whom they may not have otherwise been exposed. This broad social immersion could expand and diversify one's worldviews and, in turn, increase one's general sociability.

When contextual factors such as time played or social environment are taken into account, the picture becomes more complex. For instance, when high usage of games is controlled for, some studies have found no association between video games and depression or emotional problems (Kovess-Masfety et al., 2016; Romer, Bagdasarov, & More, 2013). In fact, online game play may be protective against depression. In a study of Korean youth, higher amounts of online video game play were associated with more depression overall, but this situation was reversed for certain groups of youth: in neighborhoods where social support was less available, more online video game play was associated with less depression (Kim & Ahn, 2016). All of these studies point to the likelihood that relationships between video games and psychosocial well-being are very complex. Individuals may be drawn to games and play extensively because of individual factors like depression or low self-esteem. In correlational studies, this may be interpreted as an effect of games, when as we see in the Korean example, it is likely that games are an outcome of poorer well-being. For example, one of our reviews suggests that it is plausible that gaming may increase ADHD symptoms such as inattention, disinhibition, and impulsivity by rewarding players in game play (Weinstein & Weizman, 2012).

It is also possible that rather than video games displacing activities and leading to negative social and psychological outcomes, they are being used as compensatory activities. Proponents of this theory, often referred to as the Social Compensation Hypothesis, argue that the distinctive characteristics of video games (e.g., visual anonymity, communicative flexibility, presence of a shared activity) provide a space that may be uniquely appealing to individuals who are socially unskilled, have an unmet need for socialization in their lives, and/or feel anxious in face-to-face social situations (Chak & Leung, 2004; McKenna & Bargh, 2000; Peters & Malesky, 2008). In support of this hypothesis, researchers have found that more involved video game players have higher rates of loneliness, depression, and social anxiety (Caplan, Williams, & Yee, 2009; Lemmens, Valkenburg, & Peter, 2011; Shen & Williams, 2010), all of which are associated with lower levels of social skills (DiTommaso, Brannen-McNulty, Ross, & Burgess, 2003; Riggio, Throckmorton, & DePaola, 1990; Tse & Bond, 2004; for a more detailed overview of this literature see Kowert, 2015).

The Social Compensation Hypothesis is not without its dissenters, however, as many argue that, while video games may be being used as a socially compensatory space, they do not provide an equivalent learning environment to offline social experiences.

Spending time playing with new online friends or strangers in games does not seem to be related to strong friendships or bonding social capital, but rather to less formal friendships and bridging social capital (Shen & Williams, 2010).

It is also possible that the Social Displacement Hypothesis and the Social Compensation Hypothesis are working together in a "Cycle Model of Use" (Kowert, 2015, 2016). That is, rather than the Social Displacement and Social Compensation models independently underpinning relationships between video game play and psychosocial outcomes, they are intertwined in a model that motivates and perpetuates video game play contributing to both positive and negative outcomes. However, the Cycle Model of Use was developed to primarily address psychological motivations and outcomes for online game players. As such, it is unclear to what extent this model pertains to offline social play.

The enjoyable aspects of gaming clearly lead to positive mood states after play in most players. Experimental studies where game characteristics are manipulated support that most of the variance in reports of enjoyment is actually determined by need satisfaction (Tamborini et al., 2011). This allows for games to be useful to repair unpleasant mood states like boredom or stress, but the balance of difficulty and mood repair has to be just right; games that are too difficult (e.g., very complex controls) do not relieve boredom and stress as well as those that are too simple (Bowman & Tamborini, 2012). These experimental results support the idea that the inherent ability of games to satisfy needs and repair moods may lead to associations with measures of overall well-being among gamers in general.

Survey research on the psychosocial outcomes of gamers in the general population is often split between adults and children/adolescents. Often concerns about the potential negative effects of games drive research, which means that many survey studies come from child and adolescent populations. In our systematic review of reviews, one review of "screen time" behaviors in children and adolescents concluded that high levels of gaming were associated with depression and anxiety compared to no gaming, but no studies examined longitudinal associations between gaming and depression (Hoare, Milton, Foster, & Allender, 2016). A second meta-analysis showed very small but consistent associations between depression and video gaming (Ferguson, 2015). However, other studies show a curvilinear effect where those with low levels of play showed less depression and better well-being than those with high levels or no play (Durkin & Barber, 2002; Przybylski & Weinstein, 2017). Longitudinal studies show no association between video game play and later increases in depressive symptoms (Bickham, Hswen, & Rich, 2015; Etchells, Gage, Rutherford, & Munafò, 2016; Ohannessian, 2009; Primack, Swanier, Georgiopoulos, Land, & Fine, 2009). In fact, the causal relationship may be reversed: higher levels of emotional problems and low self-esteem may lead to more game play over time (Hoare et al., 2016).

Despite concerns about the effects of gaming on psychosocial well-being, studies of real world functioning suggest that any negative effects of time playing games—as compared to problematic gaming—do not extend to measures of functioning. In a systematic review of 30 studies, the two studies that examined associations between video game play and school performance found opposite results: one study showed higher grades among online players, while a second study showed lower grades (Busch et al., 2014; Norris, 2010; Sharif, Wills, & Sargent, 2010). A second review looked at associations between playing massively multiplayer online games (MMOs) and academic performance and found no objective associations between grades and game time in samples of adolescents and adults (Hart et al., 2009; Sublette & Mullan, 2012). In fact, playing sports games was found to lead to improved self-esteem and more involvement with real-life sports (Adachi & Willoughby, 2017), and playing prosocial games (games where characters help one another) was strongly correlated with prosocial behavior (Boyle et al., 2016; Brockmyer, 2015; Greitemeyer & Mügge, 2014). In all, game playing can have many beneficial effects (Boyle 2016).

Two reviews provide some common sense conclusions about the psychosocial outcomes of gaming for children. In one review, the authors recommend that children play non-violent, action-based computer games as well as educational games, that games do not displace social activities but are arranged in a way to foster real-world social engagement, and that they focus on nonviolent, prosocial content (Tran & Subrahmanyam, 2013). A second review suggests that the effects of violent video games on aggression may be small, but that children have other risk factors for aggression as well as protective factors, and that it is the combination of risk and resilience factors that will ultimately determine real-world aggression outcomes (Prot & Gentile, 2014).

One important caveat to studies of psychosocial outcomes of gaming is the likelihood of differential effects by gender. Women are more likely to play socially or to pass the time, so may play less intensively than men (Smyth, 2007). This does not hold true for all gamers, but the pervasiveness of the male gamer stereotype has led female gamers to be marginalized or ignored (Paaßen, Morgenroth, & Stratemeyer, 2017). The "gamer" identity seems to be particularly important for adolescents, as recent research has found that adolescents who play video games and identify as a gamer report increased life satisfaction over time as compared to adult players (Kowert, Vogelgesang, Festl, & Quandt, 2015). Overall, identifying as a gamer and having access to the global community of gamers may offer substantial opportunities for social interaction, but gamers need to make sure to participate in the real world, too.

Applications: Mental Health and Cognitive Functioning

As research into the psychology of commercial games has matured, evidence has mounted for the use of video games in clinical mental health settings to promote flourishing mental health and reduce psychological distress. As a form of play and recreation, games have the traditional mental health benefits of any recreational activity: they provide a break from everyday life and relief from daily stressors, they allow people to get together around shared experiences, and they are just plain fun (Iwasaki, Coyle, & Shank, 2010). Game play can be calming and relaxing or stimulating and exciting. Research into video games and positive psychology suggests that video games enhance the five elements of PERMA that are vital for well-being: They foster Positive emotions such as happiness and satisfaction, they allow their users to be fully Engaged or immersed in an activity, they can improve Relationships, they provide Meaning or a sense of purpose, and they offer many clear opportunities for Accomplishment (Jones, Scholes, Johnson, Katsikitis, & Carras, 2014; Seligman, 2012). With this understanding, several researchers have investigated how games may be useful to relieve symptoms associated with various mental health conditions.

By far, the greatest number of reviews covered the use of games for rehabilitation of cognitive functioning. After years of research on brain training games, it became clear that the effects of these games were strong in the short term, but not applicable to real-world activities—their effects did not transfer, as shown in other areas of this chapter. Two surprising findings came out of that research, however. First, exergames, including *Dance Dance Revolution* and physically active games on the *Nintendo Wii*, were seen to improve not just physical but also cognitive functioning in older adults (Bleakley et al., 2015; Chao, Scherer, & Montgomery, 2015; Ogawa, You, & Leveille, 2016; Stanmore, Stubbs, Vancampfort, de Bruin, & Firth, 2017; Verheijden Klompstra, Jaarsma, & Stromberg, 2014). Older adults (in some studies the average age was almost 80) enjoyed playing the games, felt their mood and depressive symptoms improved, and reported feeling more connected with family members and having a better quality of life (Chao et al., 2015; Verheijden Klompstra et al., 2014). In this case, the social benefits were due mostly to co-located play, which allows people to share fun experiences and accomplishments (Chao et al., 2015). This feeling of connection was especially strong between older adults and those of other generations (Verheijden Klompstra et al., 2014). A review of eight serious games designed to foster intergenerational play showed that they were useful in fostering social interaction, but also pointed out that there were no studies of other types of digital games (e.g., MMOs) that might be helpful in this area (Zhang & Kaufman, 2016a). The same group later found that about half of older adults who played *World of Warcraft* (WoW) felt they could trust their WoW friends, and many felt their relationships in WoW were as important as their real-life friendships (Zhang & Kaufman, 2016b).

Second, the cognitive skills learned in commercial video games were found to transfer to activities outside the game. Action games and 3D platformers are thought to differ in their ability to improve visuospatial skills and task speed because of the different areas of the brain—the hippocampus and the striatum—used while playing them (West et al., 2017). These authors speculated that brain changes in those who play action video games are similar to those with psychiatric disorders such as depression, PTSD, and Alzheimer's, and suggest that game designers consider balancing game features so that they recruit both brain areas equally. Another review of brain imaging studies, however, showed that the cognitive tasks of video games produce brain changes that would be beneficial for people with schizophrenia (Suenderhauf, Walter, Lenz, Lang, & Borgwardt, 2016). Both reviews agree that games are highly motivating and lead to clear changes in the brain, a conclusion that holds for other motivating behaviors, such as sex and eating. This line of reasoning again points to the potential for a public discourse that may be driven by moral panic to suppress the nuances in understanding gamings' effects.

Primack and colleagues (2012) reviewed video games used for psychological support, and the majority of trials showed positive outcomes in relieving mental health conditions. Commercial games were useful for reducing flashbacks in individuals with post-traumatic stress disorder (e.g., Tetris; Holmes, James, Coode-Bate, & Deeprose, 2009) and reducing symptoms of depression (e.g., Bejeweled 2, Bookworm Adventures, Peggle; Russoniello, Fish, & O'Brien, 2013) and stress (Russoniello, 2009), as well as improving overall mood (Russoniello, 2009). Playing a handheld game before surgery was also found to be more effective than a tranquilizer or parental presence for reducing children's preoperative anxiety (Patel et al., 2006). Playing games for an hour or two a day for two months has even been shown to reduce psychotic symptoms in people with schizophrenia (Han et al., 2008). Video games may be the perfect medium for introducing the optimal mood state of flow, as they combine regular feedback with progression in difficulty. Interestingly, advances in brain-computer interfaces show that games may soon have the capability to understand when players are in a flow state, which would allow real-time difficulty balancing, thus optimizing positive mood states.

One area of recent interest is the use of commercial exergames to improve mood. Playing games such as *Wii Fit* and *Dancetown* reduces depressives symptoms, especially in older adults and women (Hall, Chavarria, Maneeratana, Chaney, & Bernhardt, 2012; Li, Theng, & Foo, 2016). This may be related to the potential causes of depression, such as physical isolation and illness, which may affect older adults more (Li et al., 2016). However, games that are more fun to play reduce depression more, which suggests that the inherently rewarding and engaging nature of playing video games is partially responsible for making people feel better.

Video gaming can also be a useful tool in psychotherapy, although here the evidence is not as strong (Horne-Moyer, Moyer, Messer, & Messer, 2014). For example, in one study, researchers worked with three children with autism to help them learn to play *Guitar Hero* (Blum-Dimaya, Reeve, Reeve, & Hoch, 2010). With regular practice, the children were able to learn to stay on task, be persistent, and develop skills in an age-appropriate activity. Other therapists helped children develop self-confidence and responsibility or emotion regulation, just by playing video games during therapy. By playing games with their child patients, therapists can model appropriate behavior and encourage problem solving. Many serious games have shown promise for psychological support as well. Games may decrease depressive symptoms, promote emotional regulation, or improve attention skills (Fleming et al., 2017; Olson, 2016; Primack et al., 2012; Shoemaker, Tully, Niendam, & Peterson, 2015). Finally, therapists and others may find games a useful way to monitor or evaluate psychological traits and states. Simply measuring time spent playing games may be a good indicator of behavioral activation or brain functioning, which could provide information about the severity of disorders like depression and schizophrenia (Suenderhauf et al., 2016; Teo et al., 2016).

Applications: Other Health Behavior Change, Functioning, and Empowerment

The inherently rewarding properties of video games have made them an especially attractive way to engage people in activities designed to improve their health. In fact, most recent reviews from our results focused on using serious games to promote healthy behavior. Although this subject is the focus of the chapter by Griffiths in this volume, here this chapter synthesizes the important topics that result from the current authors' review.

What about video games makes them an effective tool for stimulating behavior change? First, they are inherently exciting and enjoyable because of their combination of challenge, meaningful play, and goal setting, which makes them intrinsically motivating (Swanson & Whittinghill, 2015). Second, they provide extrinsic motivation in the form of feedback mechanisms like encouragement and reports of status, scores, or goal progression (Tabak, Dekker-van Weering, van Dijk, & Vollenbroek-Hutten, 2015). In that review, traditional game elements like immersive stories and attractive avatars were seen to improve health outcomes—making your virtual flower grow worked better than being shown graphs and tables (Lu, Baranowski, Thompson, & Buday, 2012; Tabak et al., 2015). By combining elements of learning (e.g., how to move your arm during physical therapy) and augmented feedback, games may be able to motivate while educating and empowering people to understand and perform the behaviors necessary to support good health outcomes.

The motivating aspects of games have been used outside of mental health and cognitive interventions as well. We found reviews of serious video games used for self-management or prevention of many disorders, including knowledge, skills, and empowerment-focused interventions as described later. Empowerment interventions allow patients to feel more in control, improve coping skills, and make it easier for patients to manage their conditions (Govender, Bowen, German, Bulaj, & Bruggers, 2015). Because games foster a sense of competence and autonomy, they are ideal tools to use in empowerment interventions for health conditions. The current review showed that researchers have developed serious games designed to allow children and adolescents to learn the skills to better self-manage cancer, diabetes, and asthma with promising results (Ghazisaeidi, Safdari, Goodini, Mirzaiee, & Farzi, 2017; Primack et al., 2012). For example, games designed to help children deal with the effects of chemotherapy seek to instill a "fighting spirit" in patients and may be successful at it because they stimulate the brain's reward system while suppressing fear, anxiety, and stress (Govender et al., 2015). Serious games have been used to teach adolescents and young adults to avoid risky substance use, but there is little evidence for their impact beyond increasing knowledge of alcohol and other drugs (Rodriguez, Teesson, & Newton, 2014). Games have been found to be a good distraction from painful procedures (Rahmani & Boren, 2012), probably because their interactive nature allows users to focus attention on the game rather than the painful real world (Trost et al., 2015). In fact, in children, the distraction from playing handheld video games before surgery was better at reducing anxiety than medication (Manyande, Cyna, Yip, Chooi, & Middleton, 2015).

Overall, the positive effects games have in general made them particularly beneficial for changing health behaviors. As games inspire positive emotions and self-efficacy through their inherent motivational nature, they are able to increase performance on tasks and improve the rate at which people learn new skills (Zemankova, Lungu, & Bares, 2016). Ultimately, anything that makes games more fun and supports interaction with health-promoting behaviors has the potential to improve health for populations, not just in the laboratory.

Discussion

Digital games have been a part of daily life for decades now, and the industry continues to grow. Over the years, the debate about the effects of games has hardly slowed. While non-digital games have a long-standing therapeutic role (Schaefer, 2003), digital games have been studied more for their potential harm than their potential good. Although more recent research has had a greater focus on the potential benefits of gaming, scientists are still motivated to find out how, when, and for whom games can help or harm.

As discussed in this chapter, games are motivating to play. They are fun, and as a recreational activity allow people a break from their everyday lives. They also meet a variety of needs that might drive people to use them. Through their clear effects on physiological arousal, they may help people improve players' moods. They can reward players through mechanics like feedback and progression, which promote feelings of competence and satisfy basic psychological needs. Games can be played socially, and by helping people connect, can provide opportunities for social support.

When used as a way to motivate, educate about, or treat health or illness, their level of engagement might prove to promote lasting effects in a way that other interventions cannot. A child with cancer who plays a game about cancer may be in a better position to deal with all the stresses and fear of the condition than a child who gets that information from a healthcare provider. Providing information about safe alcohol use in an online game might allow public health interventions to reach millions of people at once. Therapists might use games to help understand patients or to allow patients to practice social skills, or even to treat PTSD or depression. Gaming communities, as spaces where people can hang out and enjoy shared experiences, might be able to provide members of a gamer culture with social support in an easily accessible and acceptable form. Through these multiple avenues, the potential for positive behavior change is there.

The flip side, however, is that people who have social or emotional vulnerabilities may be drawn to playing games as a way to feel better, and they may develop problems related to play. In this chapter's review of reviews, evidence was found that a small number of individuals may develop life problems related to playing too much. These individuals are more likely to have vulnerabilities, like low self-esteem, impulsivity, and depression, that relate to spending large amounts of time gaming and subsequent problems. For many, however, these gaming-related problems may be short-lived. Although many researchers seem to think that problematic gaming is an addiction-like disorder that may have a significant impact on public health, debate about the best way to define problems related to gaming continues.

A second debate is perhaps starting to slow down: fewer reviews were found in the authors' analysis that focused on links between aggression and video game play. The short-term effects of gaming on aggression—whether violent games or not—is clear, consistent, and small. Many of these studies are experiments that show that subjects may be more likely to identify words that are more related to aggression or choose a louder noise after playing a video game when compared to a control condition. Studies that show longitudinal outcomes of playing games over a long term are few, and do not show clear ties between gaming and real-world violence.

Overall, the study of the psychosocial outcomes of video game play suffers from some serious challenges. The longitudinal studies needed to determine long-term effects of gaming on psychosocial outcomes are far too few to be confident about the potential benefits and problems with gaming for both individuals and society over the long term. Outcomes of studies of violence and aggression range from hot-pepper tests in the lab to hitting, kicking, or stabbing someone in a fight, and scales to measure problematic gaming or Internet gaming disorder continue to proliferate. When studies are heterogeneous like this, drawing conclusions from years of evidence is a challenge. In addition, the approaches used in various disciplines differ: studies in the fields of communications and media psychology are usually theory-driven, while studies of games and other health effects may not always be clear about theory or about the features of games that may drive effects. In contrast, studies in medicine and public health may use longer-term designs and real-world health outcomes to study games, but may not refer to commercial games as such (e.g., using the term "VR technologies" to refer to playing a serious game using a *Microsoft Kinect* controller; Teo et al., 2016). Finally, biases may still be driving research and publishing: since 1980, articles about video games published in psychiatry, psychology, and pediatrics journals tend to have a more negative view of games, while articles in rehabilitation journals and nonmedical journals have become more positive (Segev et al., 2016).

However, many reviews in this analysis provided important suggestions for improving the field in ways that reduce bias and answer the questions about the complex causal relationships between games and psychosocial outcomes. The result is a long list, including (but not limited to):

- Study the long-term impact of games.
- Classify or categorize game titles in a consistent way.
- Use consistent measures of outcomes, exposures, and individual factors.
- Consider individual differences, including selection effect, gender, psychological vulnerabilities.
- Consider developmental context.

- Consider context and content of games and gaming sessions (e.g., solo vs. social).
- Explore complex causal relations by incorporating moderators or mediators of game effects into design and analysis.
- Ensure trials are pre-registered and report all study outcomes.
- Use active control groups.
- Conduct qualitative research to understand mechanisms of effect in serious games and to explore features of problematic gaming.
- Ensure safety of participants in clinical trials and report adverse effects of game-based interventions.
- Report findings in a way that accurately reflects the limits of a study's methods (e.g., do not call outcomes "aggressive thoughts" if they are simply word completion tasks).
- Translate effect sizes into public health importance.
- Test positive and negative effects in the same study.
- Use multiple methods to test the outcomes in a study, e.g., parent report and child report.
- Use random samples for survey research whenever possible.
- Find ways to keep up with new types of games and gaming technologies.

Naturally, our approach to this chapter had some limitations as well. Our systematic review identified several themes, but we included only those we felt were relevant to answer our research questions without overlapping the content of other chapters. A drawback of our review of systematic reviews was that the reviews were not able to capture the most recent studies, but we addressed that by supplementing our findings with additional work from the current year (2017). Again, subsequent overviews and studies can use this as a basis to improve and expand.

Despite these limitations, it became clear that there are some consistent patterns in the literature. In conclusion, researchers found that playing video games is a meaningful and now nearly-ubiquitous recreational activity that has both positive and negative effects. Most of these effects are less striking than initially assumed, which may be disappointing from the perspective of games evangelists, but comforting to know in light of repeated outbreaks of moral panics. That said, the most prominent debates are likely to continue, and as games and gaming technologies change, the ways in which they influence lives for better or worse will likely change as well. As research in various fields progresses, we hope that researchers will find ways to work together to meet the challenges of studying the effects on individuals and societies.

REFERENCES

Aarseth, E., Bean, A. M., Boonen, H., Colder Carras, M., Coulson, M., Das, D.,...Van Rooij, A. J. (2016). Scholars' open debate paper on the World Health Organization ICD-11 Gaming Disorder proposal. *Journal of Behavioral Addictions*, 6(3), 267–270. https://doi.org/10.1556/2006.5.2016.088

Adachi, P. J. C., & Willoughby, T. (2013). More than just fun and games: The longitudinal relationships between strategic video games, self-reported problem-solving skills, and academic grades. *Journal of Youth and Adolescence*, 42(7), 1041–1052. https://doi.org/10.1007/s10964-013-9913-9

Adachi, P. J. C., & Willoughby, T. (2017). The link between playing video games and positive youth outcomes. *Child Development Perspectives*, 11(3), 202–206. https://doi.org/10.1111/cdep.12232

Agina, A. M. (2012). "Who vs. whom and where should we go through?": A reflection towards clarifying the effect of media and entertainment on children's development for future research. *Computers in Human Behavior*, 28(4), 1083–1090. https://doi.org/10.1016/j.chb.2012.01.019

American Psychiatric Association. (2013). *Diagnostic and Statistical Manual of Mental Disorders, Fifth Edition*. Arlington, VA: American Psychiatric Association. Retrieved from dsm.psychiatryonline.org

Anderson, C. A., & Bushman, B. J. (2002). Human aggression. *Annual Review of Psychology*, 53. Retrieved from http://www.annualreviews.org/eprint/wZXD4ZASNg4bU/full/10.1146/annurev.psych.53.100901.135231?siteid=arjournals&keytype=ref

Anderson, C. A., Sakamoto, A., Gentile, D. A., Ihori, N., Shibuya, A., Yukawa, S., ... Kobayashi, K. (2008). Longitudinal effects of violent video games on aggression in Japan and the United States. *Pediatrics*, 122(5), e1067–1072. https://doi.org/10.1542/peds.2008-1425

Bandura, A. (1977). *Social learning theory*. Oxford: Prentice-Hall.

Bandura, A. (1986). *Social foundations of thought and action: A social cognitive theory*. Englewood Cliffs, NJ: Prentice-Hall.

Banz, B. C., Yip, S. W., Yau, Y. H. C., & Potenza, M. N. (2016). Behavioral addictions in addiction medicine: from mechanisms to practical considerations. *Progress in Brain Research*, 223, 311–328. https://doi.org/10.1016/bs.pbr.2015.08.003

Bandura, A., Ross, D., & Ross, S. A. (1961). Transmission of Aggression Through Imitation of Aggressive Models. *Journal of Abnormal and Social Psychology*, 63, 575–582.

Bartle, R. (1996). Hearts, clubs, diamonds, spades: Players who suit MUDs. *Journal of MUD Research*, 1(1), 19.

Bergen, D., & Davis, D. (2011). Influences of technology-related playful activity and thought on moral development. *American Journal of Play*, 4(1), 80–99.

Bickham, D. S., Hswen, Y., & Rich, M. (2015). Media use and depression: Exposure, household rules, and symptoms among young adolescents in the USA. *International Journal of Public Health*, 60(2), 147–155. https://doi.org/10.1007/s00038-014-0647-6

Bleakley, C. M., Charles, D., Porter-Armstrong, A., McNeill, M. D. J., McDonough, S. M., & McCormack, B. (2015). Gaming for health: A systematic review of the physical and cognitive effects of interactive computer games in older adults. *Journal of Applied Gerontology*, 34(3), NP166–189. https://doi.org/10.1177/0733464812470747

Blum-Dimaya, A., Reeve, S. A., Reeve, K. F., & Hoch, H. (2010). Teaching children with autism to play a video game using activity schedules and game-embedded simultaneous video modeling. *Education and Treatment of Children*, 33(3), 351–370.

Bowman, N. (2015). The rise (and refinement) of moral panic. In R. Kowert & T. Quandt (Eds.), *The video game debate: Unraveling the physical, social, and psychological effects of digital games* (pp. 22–38). New York, NY: Routledge.

Bowman, N., & Tamborini, R. (2012). Task demand and mood repair: The intervention potential of computer games. *New Media & Society*, 14(8), 1339–1357. https://doi.org/10.1177/1461444812450426

Boyle, E. A., Hainey, T., Connolly, T. M., Gray, G., Earp, J., Ott, M., ... Pereira, J. (2016). An update to the systematic literature review of empirical evidence of the impacts and outcomes of computer games and serious games. *Computers & Education*, 94, 178–192. https://doi.org/10.1016/j.compedu.2015.11.003

Breuer, J., Vogelgesang, J., Quandt, T., & Festl, R. (2015). Violent video games and physical aggression: Evidence for a selection effect among adolescents. *Psychology of Popular Media Culture*, 4, 305–328.

Brockmyer, J. F. (2015). Playing violent video games and desensitization to violence. *Child and Adolescent Psychiatric Clinics of North America*, 24(1), 65–77. https://doi.org/10.1016/j.chc.2014.08.001

Bryant, J., & Zillmann, D. (2009). Using television to alleviate boredom and stress: Selective exposure as a function of induced excitational states. *Journal of Broadcasting*, 28, 1–20. https://doi.org/10.1080/08838158409386511

Bulaj, G. (2014). Combining non-pharmacological treatments with pharmacotherapies for neurological disorders: A unique interface of the brain, drug-device, and intellectual property. *Frontiers in Neurology*, 5, 126. https://doi.org/10.3389/fneur.2014.00126

Busch, V., Loyen, A., Lodder, M., Schrijvers, A. J. P., van Yperen, T. A., & de Leeuw, J. R. J. (2014). The effects of adolescent health-related behavior on academic performance: A systematic review of the longitudinal evidence. *Review of Educational Research*, 84(2), 245–274. https://doi.org/10.3102/0034654313518441

Bushman, B. J. (1995). *Moderating Role of Trait Aggressiveness in the Effects of Violent Media on Aggression* (Vol. 69, pp. 950–960). Presented at the Annual Convention of the Society for Experimental Social Psychologists, *Journal of Personality and Social Psychology*.

Bushman, B. J., Gollwitzer, M., & Cruz, C. (2015). There is broad consensus: Media researchers agree that violent media increase aggression in children, and pediatricians and parents concur. *Psychology of Popular Media Culture*, 40(3), 200–214.

Bushman, B. J., & Huesmann, L. R. (2014). Twenty-five years of research on violence in digital games and aggression: A reply to Elson & Ferguson (2013). *European Psychologist*, 19, 47–55. https://doi.org/10.1027/1016-9040/a000164

Calvert, S. L., Appelbaum, M., Dodge, K. A., Graham, S., Nagayama Hall, G. C., Hamby, S.,... Hedges, L. V. (2017). The American Psychological Association Task Force assessment of violent video games: Science in the service of public interest. *The American Psychologist*, 72(2), 126–143. https://doi.org/10.1037/a0040413

Caplan, S., Williams, D., & Yee, N. (2009). Problematic internet use and psychosocial well-being among MMO players. *Computers in Human Behavior*, 25(6), 1312–1319. https://doi.org/10.1016/j.chb.2009.06.006

Chak, K., & Leung, L. (2004). Shyness and locus of control as predictors of internet addiction and internet use. *Cyberpsychology & Behavior*, 7(5), 559–570.

Chao, Y.-Y., Scherer, Y. K., & Montgomery, C. A. (2015). Effects of using Nintendo Wii exergames in older adults: A review of the literature. *Journal of Aging and Health*, 27(3), 379–402. https://doi.org/10.1177/0898264314551171

Colder Carras, M., Van Rooij, A. J., Van de Mheen, D., Musci, R., Xue, Q.-L., & Mendelson, T. (2017). Video gaming in a hyperconnected world: A cross-sectional study of heavy gaming, problematic gaming symptoms, and online socializing in adolescents. *Computers in Human Behavior*, 68, 472–479. https://doi.org/10.1016/j.chb.2016.11.060

Cole, H., & Griffiths, M. D. (2007). Social interactions in massively multiplayer online role-playing gamers. *Cyberpsychology & Behavior*, 10(4), 575–583. https://doi.org/10.1089/cpb.2007.9988

Coulson, M., & Ferguson, C. J. (2016). The influence of digital games on aggression and violent crime. In R. Kowert & T. Quandt (Eds.), *The video game debate: Unravelling the physical, social, and psychological effects of digital games* (pp. 54–73). New York, NY: Routledge.

Csikszentmihalyi, M. (1990). *Flow: The psychology of optimal experience*. New York, NY: Harper & Row.

Denzler, M., & Förster, J. (2012). A goal model of catharsis. *European Review of Social Psychology*, 23(1), 107–142. https://doi.org/10.1080/10463283.2012.699358

Dewall, C. N., Finkel, E. J., Lambert, N. M., Slotter, E. B., Bodenhausen, G. V., Pond, R. S.,... Fincham, F. D. (2013). The voodoo doll task: Introducing and validating a novel method for studying aggressive inclinations. *Aggressive Behavior*, 39(6), 419–439. https://doi.org/10.1002/ab.21496

DiTommaso, E., Brannen-McNulty, C., Ross, L., & Burgess, M. (2003). Attachment styles, social skills and loneliness in young adults. *Personality and Individual Differences*, 35(2), 303–312. https://doi.org/10.1016/S0191-8869(02)00190-3

Domahidi, E., Breuer, J., Kowert, R., Festl, R., & Quandt, T. (2016). A longitudinal analysis of gaming-and non-gaming-related friendships and social support among social online game players. *Media Psychology*, [online] 1–20. https://doi.org/10.1080/15213269.2016.1257393

Domahidi, E., & Quandt, T. (2015). "And all of a sudden my life was gone...": A biographical analysis of highly engaged adult gamers. *New Media & Society*, 17(7), 1154–1169. https://doi.org/10.1177/1461444814521791

Duggan, M. (2015, December 15). Gaming and Gamers. Pew Research Center. Retrieved December 30, 2015, from http://www.pewinternet.org/2015/12/15/gaming-and-gamers/

Durkin, K., & Barber, B. (2002). Not so doomed: Computer game play and positive adolescent development. *Journal of Applied Developmental Psychology*, 23(4), 373–392. https://doi.org/10.1016/S0193-3973(02)00124-7

Eiser, A. R. (2015). Postmodern Stress Disorder (PMSD): A possible new disorder. *The American Journal of Medicine*, 128(11), 1178–1181. https://doi.org/10.1016/j.amjmed.2015.04.039

Elson, M., Breuer, J., & Quandt, T. (2014). Know thy player: An integrated model of player experience for digital games research. In M. C. Angelides & H. Agius (Eds.), *Handbook of digital games* (pp. 362–387). Hoboken, NJ: John Wiley & Sons, Inc.

Elson, M., & Ferguson, C. J. (2014). Twenty-five years of research on violence in digital games and aggression: Empirical evidence, perspectives, and a debate gone astray. *European Psychologist*, 19(1), 33–46. https://doi.org/10.1027/1016-9040/a000147

Entertainment Software Association. (2017, April 19). Two-Thirds of American Households Regularly Play Video Games. Retrieved July 22, 2017, from http://www.theesa.com/article/two-thirds-american-households-regularly-play-video-games/

Etchells, P. J., Gage, S. H., Rutherford, A. D., & Munafò, M. R. (2016). Prospective investigation of video game use in children and subsequent conduct disorder and depression using data from the Avon Longitudinal Study of Parents and Children. *PLoS ONE*, 11(1). Retrieved from http://search.ebscohost.com/login.aspx?direct=true&db=psyh&AN=2016-06103-001&site=ehost-live&scope=site

Ferguson, C. J. (2008). The school shooting/violent video game link: Causal relationship or moral panic? *Journal of Investigative Psychology and Offender Profiling*, 5(1–2), 25–37. https://doi.org/10.1002/jip.76

Ferguson, C. J. (2011). Video games and youth violence: a prospective analysis in adolescents. *Journal of Youth and Adolescence*, 40(4), 377–391. https://doi.org/10.1007/s10964-010-9610-x

Ferguson, C. J. (2015). Do angry birds make for angry children? A meta-analysis of video game influences on children's and adolescents' aggression, mental health, prosocial behavior, and academic performance. *Perspectives on Psychological Science, 10*(5), 646–666. https://doi.org/10.1177/1745691615592234

Ferguson, C. J., & Rueda, S. M. (2009). Examining the validity of the modified Taylor competitive reaction time test of aggression. *Journal of Experimental Criminology, 5*(2), 121. https://doi.org/10.1007/s11292-009-9069-5

Fleming, T. M., Bavin, L., Stasiak, K., Hermansson-Webb, E., Merry, S. N., Cheek, C., . . . Hetrick, S. (2017). Serious games and gamification for mental health: Current status and promising directions. *Frontiers in Psychiatry, 7.* https://doi.org/10.3389/fpsyt.2016.00215

Gentile, D. A. (2011). The multiple dimensions of video game effects. *Child Development Perspectives, 5*(2), 75–81. https://doi.org/10.1111/j.1750-8606.2011.00159.x

Gentile, D. A., Choo, H., Liau, A., Sim, T., Li, D., Fung, D., & Khoo, A. (2011). Pathological video game use among youths: A two-year longitudinal study. *Pediatrics, 127*(2), e319–329. https://doi.org/10.1542/peds.2010-1353

Ghazisaeidi, M., Safdari, R., Goodini, A., Mirzaiee, M., & Farzi, J. (2017). Digital games as an effective approach for cancer management: Opportunities and challenges. *Journal of Education and Health Promotion, 6*, 30. https://doi.org/10.4103/jehp.jehp_146_14

Govender, M., Bowen, R. C., German, M. L., Bulaj, G., & Bruggers, C. S. (2015). Clinical and neurobiological perspectives of empowering pediatric cancer patients using video games. *Games for Health, 4*(5), 362–374. https://doi.org/10.1089/g4h.2015.0014

Greitemeyer, T., & Mügge, D. O. (2014). Video games do affect social outcomes: A meta-analytic review of the effects of violent and prosocial video game play. *Personality & Social Psychology Bulletin, 40*(5), 578–589. https://doi.org/10.1177/0146167213520459

Griffiths, M. D. (2005). A "components" model of addiction within a biopsychosocial framework. *Journal of Substance Use, 10*(4), 191–197. https://doi.org/10.1080/14659890500114359

Griffiths, M. D., van Rooij, A. J., Kardefelt-Winther, D., Starcevic, V., Király, O., Pallesen, S., . . . Demetrovics, Z. (2016). Working towards an international consensus on criteria for assessing internet gaming disorder: A critical commentary on Petry et al. (2014). *Addiction, 111*(1), 167–175. https://doi.org/10.1111/add.13057

Grimes, T., Anderson, J. A., & Bergen, L. (2008). *Media violence and aggression: Science and ideology.* Thousand Oaks, CA: Sage.

Grooten, J., & Kowert, R. (2015). Going beyond the game: Development of gamer identities within societal discourse and virtual spaces. *Loading ... The Journal of the Canadian Game Studies Association, 9*(14), 70–87.

Hall, A. K., Chavarria, E., Maneeratana, V., Chaney, B. H., & Bernhardt, J. M. (2012). Health benefits of digital video games for older adults: A systematic review of the literature. *Games for Health, 1*(6), 402–410. https://doi.org/10.1089/g4h.2012.0046

Han, D. H., Renshaw, P. F., Sim, M. E., Kim, J. I., Arenella, L. S., & Lyoo, I. K. (2008). The effect of internet video game play on clinical and extrapyramidal symptoms in patients with schizophrenia. *Schizophrenia Research, 103*(1–3), 338–340. https://doi.org/10.1016/j.schres.2008.01.026

Hart, G. M., Johnson, B., Stamm, B., Angers, N., Robinson, A., Lally, T., & Fagley, W. H. (2009). Effects of video games on adolescents and adults. *Cyberpsychology & Behavior, 12*(1), 63–65. https://doi.org/10.1089/cpb.2008.0117

Hartmann, T., & Vorderer, P. (2010). It's okay to shoot a character: Moral disengagement in violent video games. *Journal of Communication, 60*(1), 94–119. https://doi.org/10.1111/j.1460-2466.2009.01459.x

Hoare, E., Milton, K., Foster, C., & Allender, S. (2016). The associations between sedentary behaviour and mental health among adolescents: A systematic review. *The International Journal of Behavioral Nutrition and Physical Activity*, *13*(1), 108. https://doi.org/10.1186/s12966-016-0432-4

Holmes, E. A., James, E. L., Coode-Bate, T., & Deeprose, C. (2009). Can playing the computer game "Tetris" reduce the build-up of flashbacks for trauma? A proposal from cognitive science. *PloS ONE*, *4*(1). https://doi.org/10.1371/journal.pone.0004153

Horne-Moyer, H. L., Moyer, B. H., Messer, D. C., & Messer, E. S. (2014). The use of electronic games in therapy: A review with clinical implications. *Current Psychiatry Reports*, *16*(12), 520. https://doi.org/10.1007/s11920-014-0520-6

Iwasaki, Y., Coyle, C. P., & Shank, J. W. (2010). Leisure as a context for active living, recovery, health and life quality for persons with mental illness in a global context. *Health Promotion International*, *25*(4), 483–494. https://doi.org/10.1093/heapro/daq037

Jones, C., Scholes, L., Johnson, D., Katsikitis, M., & Carras, M. C. (2014). Gaming well: Links between video games and flourishing mental health. *Developmental Psychology*, *5*, 260. https://doi.org/10.3389/fpsyg.2014.00260

Kim, H. H., & Ahn, S. J. G. (2016). How does neighborhood quality moderate the association between online video game play and depression? A population-level analysis of korean students. *Cyberpsychology, Behavior, and Social Networking*, *19*(10), 628–634. https://doi.org/10.1089/cyber.2016.0155

King, D. L., Delfabbro, P. H., & Griffiths, M. D. (2013). Trajectories of problem video gaming among adult regular gamers: An 18-month longitudinal study. *Cyberpsychology, Behavior, and Social Networking*, *16*(1), 72–76. https://doi.org/10.1089/cyber.2012.0062

King, D. L., Haagsma, M. C., Delfabbro, P. H., Gradisar, M., & Griffiths, M. D. (2013). Toward a consensus definition of pathological video-gaming: A systematic review of psychometric assessment tools. *Clinical Psychology Review*, *33*(3), 331–342. https://doi.org/10.1016/j.cpr.2013.01.002

Kocurek, C. A. (2012). The agony and the exidy: A history of video game violence and the legacy of death race. *Game Studies*, *12*(1). Retrieved from http://gamestudies.org/1201/articles/carly_kocurek

Kovess-Masfety, V., Keyes, K., Hamilton, A., Hanson, G., Bitfoi, A., Golitz, D.,...Pez, O. (2016). Is time spent playing video games associated with mental health, cognitive and social skills in young children? *Social Psychiatry and Psychiatric Epidemiology*, *51*(3), 349–357. https://doi.org/10.1007/s00127-016-1179-6

Kowert, R. (2015). *Video games and social competence*. New York: Routledge.

Kowert, R. (2016). Social outcomes: Online game play, social currency, and social ability. In R. Kowert & T. Quandt (Eds.), *The Video Game Debate: Unravelling the Physical, Social, and Psychological Effects of Digital Games* (pp. 94–115). New York: Routledge.

Kowert, R., Domahidi, E., & Quandt, T. (2014). The relationship between online video game involvement and gaming-related friendships among emotionally sensitive individuals. *Cyberpsychology, Behavior and Social Networking*, *17*(7), 447–453. https://doi.org/10.1089/cyber.2013.0656

Kowert, R., Festl, R., & Quandt, T. (2014). Unpopular, overweight, and socially inept: Reconsidering the stereotype of online gamers. *Cyberpsychology, Behavior, and Social Networking*, *17*(3), 141–146.

Kowert, R., Griffiths, M. D., & Oldmeadow, J. A. (2012). Geek or chic? Emerging stereotypes of online gamers. *Bulletin of Science, Technology & Society*, *32*(6), 471–479. Retrieved from http://journals.sagepub.com/doi/abs/10.1177/0270467612469078

Kowert, R., & Quandt, T. (2015). *The video game debate: Unravelling the physical, social, and psychological effects of video games.* New York: Routledge.

Kowert, R., Vogelgesang, J., Festl, R., & Quandt, T. (2015). Psychosocial causes and consequences of online video game play. *Computers in Human Behavior, 45,* 51–58.

Krahé, B., Möller, I., Huesmann, L. R., Kirwil, L., Felber, J., & Berger, A. (2011). Desensitization to media violence: links with habitual media violence exposure, aggressive cognitions, and aggressive behavior. *Journal of Personality and Social Psychology, 100*(4), 630–646. https://doi.org/10.1037/a0021711

Kuss, D. J., & Griffiths, M. D. (2012). Internet and gaming addiction: A systematic literature review of neuroimaging studies. *Brain Sciences, 2*(3), 347–374.

LaRose, R., Lin, C. A., & Eastin, M. S. (2003). Unregulated internet usage: Addiction, habit, or deficient self-regulation? *Media Psychology, 5*(3), 225–253. https://doi.org/10.1207/S1532785XMEP0503_01

Lemmens, J. S., Valkenburg, P. M., & Peter, J. (2011). Psychosocial causes and consequences of pathological gaming. *Computers in Human Behavior, 27*(1), 144–152.

Lenhart, A. (2015). Teens, social media & technology overview 2015. Retrieved August 14, 2015, from http://www.pewinternet.org/2015/04/09/teens-social-media-technology-2015/

Li, J., Theng, Y.-L., & Foo, S. (2016). Effect of exergames on depression: A systematic review and meta-analysis. *Cyberpsychology, Behavior and Social Networking, 19*(1), 34–42. https://doi.org/10.1089/cyber.2015.0366

Lieberman, J. D., Solomon, S., Greenberg, J., & McGregor, H. A. (1999). A hot new way to measure aggression: Hot sauce allocation. *Aggressive Behavior, 25*(5), 331–348. https://doi.org/10.1002/(SICI)1098-2337(1999)25:5<331::AID-AB2>3.0.CO;2-1

Lu, A. S., Baranowski, T., Thompson, D., & Buday, R. (2012). Story immersion of video games for youth health promotion: A review of literature. *Games for Health, 1*(3), 199–204. https://doi.org/10.1089/g4h.2011.0012

Manyande, A., Cyna, A. M., Yip, P., Chooi, C., & Middleton, P. (2015). Non-pharmacological interventions for assisting the induction of anaesthesia in children. *The Cochrane Database of Systematic Reviews,* (7), CD006447. https://doi.org/10.1002/14651858.CD006447.pub3

McKenna, K. Y. A., & Bargh, J. A. (2000). Plan 9 from cyberspace: The implications of the Internet for personality and social psychology. *Personality and Social Psychology Review, 4*(1), 57–75. https://doi.org/10.1207/S15327957PSPR0401_6

Meng, Y., Deng, W., Wang, H., Guo, W., & Li, T. (2015). The prefrontal dysfunction in individuals with Internet gaming disorder: A meta-analysis of functional magnetic resonance imaging studies. *Addiction Biology, 20*(4), 799–808. https://doi.org/10.1111/adb.12154

Mihara, S., & Higuchi, S. (2017). Cross-sectional and longitudinal epidemiological studies of internet gaming disorder: A systematic review of the literature. *Psychiatry and Clinical Neurosciences, 71*(7), 425–444. https://doi.org/10.1111/pcn.12532

Müller, K. W., Beutel, M. E., Egloff, B., & Wolfling, K. (2014). Investigating risk factors for Internet gaming disorder: A comparison of patients with addictive gaming, pathological gamblers and healthy controls regarding the big five personality traits. *European Addiction Research, 20*(3), 129–136. https://doi.org/10.1159/000355832

Norris, T. L. (2010). *Adolescent academic achievement, bullying behavior, and the frequency of internet use* (Doctoral dissertation). Kent State University.

Ogawa, E. F., You, T., & Leveille, S. G. (2016). Potential benefits of exergaming for cognition and dual-task function in older adults: A systematic review. *Journal of Aging and Physical Activity, 24*(2), 332–336. https://doi.org/10.1123/japa.2014-0267

Ohannessian, C. M. (2009). Media use and adolescent psychological adjustment: An examination of gender differences. *Journal of Child and Family Studies*, 18(5), 582–593. https://doi.org/10.1007/s10826-009-9261-2

Olson, C. K. (2016). Are electronic games health hazards or health promoters? In R. Kowert & T. Quandt (Eds.), *The video game debate: Unravelling the physical, social, and psychological effects of digital games* (pp. 39–53). New York, NY: Routledge.

Paaßen, B., Morgenroth, T., & Stratemeyer, M. (2017). What is a true gamer? The male gamer stereotype and the marginalization of women in video game culture. *Sex Roles*, 76(7–8), 421–435. https://doi.org/10.1007/s11199-016-0678-y

Palaus, M., Marron, E. M., Viejo-Sobera, R., & Redolar-Ripoll, D. (2017). Neural basis of video gaming: A systematic review. *Frontiers in Human Neuroscience*, 11, 248. https://doi.org/10.3389/fnhum.2017.00248

Patel, A., Schieble, T., Davidson, M., Tran, M. C. J., Schoenberg, C., Delphin, E., & Bennett, H. (2006). Distraction with a hand-held video game reduces pediatric preoperative anxiety. *Paediatric Anaesthesia*, 16(10), 1019–1027. https://doi.org/10.1111/j.1460-9592.2006.01914.x

Peters, C. S., & Malesky, A. J. (2008). Problematic usage among highly-engaged players of massively multiplayer online role-playing games. *Cyberpsychology & Behavior*, 11(4), 481–484. https://doi.org/10.1089/cpb.2007.0140

Primack, B. A., Carroll, M. V., McNamara, M., Klem, M. L., King, B., Rich, M., ... Nayak, S. (2012). Role of video games in improving health-related outcomes: A systematic review. *American Journal of Preventive Medicine*, 42(6), 630–638. https://doi.org/10.1016/j.amepre.2012.02.023

Primack, B. A., Swanier, B., Georgiopoulos, A. M., Land, S. R., & Fine, M. J. (2009). Association between media use in adolescence and depression in young adulthood: A longitudinal study. *Archives of General Psychiatry*, 66(2), 181–188. https://doi.org/10.1001/archgenpsychiatry.2008.532

Prot, S., & Gentile, D. A. (2014). Applying risk and resilience models to predicting the effects of media violence on development. *Advances in Child Development and Behavior*, 46, 215–244.

Przybylski, A. K., Rigby, C. S., & Ryan, R. M. (2010). A motivational model of video game engagement. *Review of General Psychology*, 14(2), 154.

Przybylski, A. K., & Weinstein, N. (2017). A large-scale test of the goldilocks hypothesis: Quantifying the relations between digital-screen use and the mental well-being of adolescents. *Psychological Science*, 28(2), 204–215. https://doi.org/10.1177/0956797616678438

Przybylski, A. K., Weinstein, N., & Murayama, K. (2016). Internet Gaming Disorder: Investigating the clinical relevance of a new phenomenon. *American Journal of Psychiatry*, 174(3), 230–236. doi:10.1176/appi.ajp.2016.16020224

Quandt, T., Chen, V., & Van Looy, J. (2014). Gaming around the globe? A comparison of gamer surveys in four countries. In T. Quandt & S. Kröger (Eds.), *Multiplayer. The social aspects of digital gaming* (pp. 23–46). London: Routledge.

Quandt, T., & Kowert, R. (2016). No black and white in video game land! Why we need to move beyond simple explanations in the video game debate. In *The video game debate: Unravelling the physical, social and psychological effects of digital games* (pp. 176–189). New York, NY: Routledge.

Rahmani, E., & Boren, S. A. (2012). Video games and health improvement: A literature review of randomized controlled trials. *Games for Health*, 1(5), 331–340. https://doi.org/10.1089/g4h.2012.0031

Riggio, R. E., Throckmorton, B., & DePaola, S. (1990). Social skills and self-esteem. *Personality and Individual Differences*, *11*(8), 799–804. https://doi.org/10.1016/0191-8869(90)90188-W

Ritter, D., & Eslea, M. (2005). Hot sauce, toy guns, and graffiti: A critical account of current laboratory aggression paradigms. *Aggressive Behavior*, *31*(5), 407–419. https://doi.org/10.1002/ab.20066

Rodriguez, D. M., Teesson, M., & Newton, N. C. (2014). A systematic review of computerised serious educational games about alcohol and other drugs for adolescents. *Drug and Alcohol Review*, *33*(2), 129–135. https://doi.org/10.1111/dar.12102

Rogers, R. (2017). The motivational pull of video game feedback, rules, and social interaction: Another self-determination theory approach. *Computers in Human Behavior*, *73*, 446–450. https://doi.org/10.1016/j.chb.2017.03.048

Romer, D., Bagdasarov, Z., & More, E. (2013). Older versus newer media and the well-being of United States youth: Results from a national longitudinal panel. *The Journal of Adolescent Health*, *52*(5), 613–619. https://doi.org/10.1016/j.jadohealth.2012.11.012

Russoniello, C. V. (2009). The effectiveness of casual video games in improving mood and decreasing stress. *Journal of Cyber Therapy and Rehabilitation*, *2*(1), 53–66.

Russoniello, C. V., Fish, M., & O'Brien, K. (2013). The efficacy of casual videogame play in reducing clinical depression: A randomized controlled study. *Games for Health Journal*, *2*(6), 341–346. https://doi.org/10.1089/g4h.2013.0010

Ryan, R. M., Rigby, C. S., & Przybylski, A. (2006). The motivational pull of video games: A self-determination theory approach. *Motivation and Emotion*, *30*(4), 347–363. https://doi.org/10.1007/s11031-006-9051-8

Schaefer, C. E. (Ed.). (2003). *Foundations of Play Therapy*. Hoboken, NJ, US: Johns Wiley & Sons.

Scharkow, M., Festl, R., & Quandt, T. (2014). Longitudinal patterns of problematic computer game use among adolescents and adults: A 2-year panel study. *Addiction*, *109*(11), 1910–1917. https://doi.org/10.1111/add.12662

Segev, A., Rovner, M., Appel, D. I., Abrams, A. W., Rotem, M., & Bloch, Y. (2016). Possible biases of researchers' attitudes toward video games: Publication trends analysis of the medical literature (1980–2013). *Journal of Medical Internet Research*, *18*(7), 109–118. https://doi.org/10.2196/jmir.5935

Seligman, M. (2012). *Flourish*. New York: Simon & Schuster.

Sharif, I., Wills, T. A., & Sargent, J. D. (2010). Effect of visual media use on school performance: A prospective study. *The Journal of Adolescent Health*, *46*(1), 52–61. https://doi.org/10.1016/j.jadohealth.2009.05.012

Shen, C., & Williams, D. (2010). Unpacking time online: Connecting Internet and massively multiplayer online game use with psychosocial well-being. *Communication Research*, *38*(1), 123–149. https://doi.org/10.1177/0093650210377196

Sherry, J. L., Greenberg, B. S., Lucas, K., & Lachlan, K. (2006). Video game uses and gratifications as predictors of use and game preference. In P. Vorderer & J. Bryant (Eds.), *Playing video games: Motives, responses, and consequences* (pp. 248–262). New York: Routledge.

Shoemaker, E. Z., Tully, L. M., Niendam, T. A., & Peterson, B. S. (2015). The next big thing in child and adolescent psychiatry: Interventions to prevent and intervene early in psychiatric illnesses. *The Psychiatric Clinics of North America*, *38*(3), 475–494. https://doi.org/10.1016/j.psc.2015.05.010

Slater, M. D., Henry, K. L., Swaim, R. C., & Anderson, L. L. (2003). Violent media content and aggressiveness in adolescents: A downward spiral model. *Communication Research*, *30*(6), 713–736. https://doi.org/10.1177/0093650203258281

Smyth, J. M. (2007). Beyond self-selection in video game play: An experimental examination of the consequences of massively multiplayer online role-playing game play. *CyberPsychology & Behavior*, *10*(5), 717–727. https://doi.org/10.1089/cpb.2007.9963

Stanmore, E., Stubbs, B., Vancampfort, D., de Bruin, E. D., & Firth, J. (2017). The effect of active video games on cognitive functioning in clinical and non-clinical populations: A meta-analysis of randomized controlled trials. *Neuroscience and Biobehavioral Reviews*, *78*, 34–43. https://doi.org/10.1016/j.neubiorev.2017.04.011

Steinkuehler, C. A., & Williams, D. (2006). Where everybody knows your (screen) name: Online games as "third places." *Journal of Computer-Mediated Communication*, *11*(4), 885–909. https://doi.org/10.1111/j.1083-6101.2006.00300.x

Sublette, V. A., & Mullan, B. (2012). Consequences of play: A systematic review of the effects of online gaming. *International Journal of Mental Health and Addiction*, *10*(1), 3–23. https://doi.org/10.1007/s11469-010-9304-3

Suenderhauf, C., Walter, A., Lenz, C., Lang, U. E., & Borgwardt, S. (2016). Counter striking psychosis: Commercial video games as potential treatment in schizophrenia? A systematic review of neuroimaging studies. *Neuroscience and Biobehavioral Reviews*, *68*, 20–36. https://doi.org/10.1016/j.neubiorev.2016.03.018

Swanson, L. R., & Whittinghill, D. M. (2015). Intrinsic or extrinsic? Using video games to motivate stroke survivors: A systematic review. *Games for Health Journal*, *4*(3), 253–258. https://doi.org/10.1089/g4h.2014.0074

Tabak, M., Dekker-van Weering, M., van Dijk, H., & Vollenbroek-Hutten, M. (2015). Promoting daily physical activity by means of mobile gaming: A review of the state of the art. *Games for Health Journal*, *4*(6), 460–469. https://doi.org/10.1089/g4h.2015.0010

Tamborini, R., Grizzard, M., David Bowman, N., Reinecke, L., Lewis, R. J., & Eden, A. (2011). Media enjoyment as need satisfaction: The contribution of hedonic and nonhedonic needs. *Journal of Communication*, *61*(6), 1025–1042. https://doi.org/10.1111/j.1460-2466.2011.01593.x

Tedeschi, J. T., & Quigley, B. M. (1996). Limitations of laboratory paradigms for studying aggression. *Aggression and Violent Behavior*, *1*(2), 163–177. https://doi.org/10.1016/1359-1789(95)00014-3

Teo, W.-P., Muthalib, M., Yamin, S., Hendy, A. M., Bramstedt, K., Kotsopoulos, E., ... Ayaz, H. (2016). Does a combination of virtual reality, neuromodulation and neuroimaging provide a comprehensive platform for neurorehabilitation?—A narrative review of the literature. *Frontiers in Human Neuroscience*, *10*, 284. https://doi.org/10.3389/fnhum.2016.00284

Thomas, J., & Harden, A. (2008). Methods for the thematic synthesis of qualitative research in systematic reviews. *BMC Medical Research Methodology*, *8*, 45. https://doi.org/10.1186/1471-2288-8-45

Tran, P., & Subrahmanyam, K. (2013). Evidence-based guidelines for the informal use of computers by children to promote the development of academic, cognitive and social skills. *Ergonomics*, *56*(9), 1349–1362. https://doi.org/10.1080/00140139.2013.820843

Trost, Z., Zielke, M., Guck, A., Nowlin, L., Zakhidov, D., France, C. R., & Keefe, F. (2015). The promise and challenge of virtual gaming technologies for chronic pain: The case of graded exposure for low back pain. *Pain Management*, *5*(3), 197–206. https://doi.org/10.2217/pmt.15.6

Tse, W. S., & Bond, A. J. (2004). The impact of depression on social skills. *The Journal of Nervous and Mental Disease*, *192*(4), 260–268.

Van Rooij, A. J., Schoenmakers, T. M., Vermulst, A. A., Van den Eijnden, R. J. J. M., & Van de Mheen, D. (2011). Online video game addiction: Identification of addicted adolescent gamers. *Addiction*, *106*(1), 205–212. https://doi.org/10.1111/j.1360-0443.2010.03104.x

Van Rooij, A. J., Van Looy, J., & Billieux, J. (2017). Internet Gaming Disorder as a formative construct: Implications for conceptualization and measurement. *Psychiatry and Clinical Neurosciences*, 71(7), 445–458. https://doi.org/10.1111/pcn.12404

Verheijden Klompstra, L., Jaarsma, T., & Stromberg, A. (2014). Exergaming in older adults: A scoping review and implementation potential for patients with heart failure. *European Journal of Cardiovascular Nursing*, 13(5), 388–398. https://doi.org/10.1177/1474515113512203

von Salisch, M., Vogelgesang, J., Kristen, A., & Oppl, C. (2011). Preference for violent electronic games and aggressive behavior among children: The beginning of the downward spiral? *Media Psychology*, 14(3), 233–258. https://doi.org/10.1080/15213269.2011.596468

Weber, R., Tamborini, R., Westcott-Baker, A., & Kantor, B. (2009). Theorizing flow and media enjoyment as cognitive synchronization of attentional and reward networks. *Communication Theory*, 19(4), 397–422. https://doi.org/10.1111/j.1468-2885.2009.01352.x

Weinstein, A., Livny, A., & Weizman, A. (2017). New developments in brain research of internet and gaming disorder. *Neuroscience and Biobehavioral Reviews*, 75, 314–330. https://doi.org/10.1016/j.neubiorev.2017.01.040

Weinstein, A., & Weizman, A. (2012). Emerging association between addictive gaming and attention-deficit/hyperactivity disorder. *Current Psychiatry Reports*, 14(5), 590–597. https://doi.org/10.1007/s11920-012-0311-x

West, G. L., Konishi, K., & Bohbot, V. D. (2017). Video games and hippocampus-dependent learning. *Current Directions in Psychological Science*, 26(2), 152–158. https://doi.org/10.1177/0963721416687342

Williams, D. (2006). Groups and goblins: The social and civic impact of an online game. *Journal of Broadcasting & Electronic Media*, 50(4), 651–670. https://doi.org/10.1207/s15506878jobem5004_5

World Health Organization. (2017, June 17). ICD-11 Beta Draft. Retrieved April 22, 2017, from permalink: https://perma.cc/TZ26-ETGY, original: http://apps.who.int/classifications/icd11/browse/f/en#/http://id.who.int/icd/entity/1448597234

Yee, N. (2006). Motivations for play in online games. *CyberPsychology & Behavior*, 9(6), 772–774. https://doi.org/10.1089/cpb.2006.9.772

Yee, N. (2008). Maps of digital desires: Exploring the topography of gender and play in online games. In *Beyond Barbie and Mortal Kombat: New perspectives on gender and gaming* (pp. 83–96). Cambridge: MIT Press.

Young, K. S. (1998). Internet addiction: The emergence of a new clinical disorder. *CyberPsychology & Behavior*, 1(3), 237–244. https://doi.org/10.1089/cpb.1998.1.237

Zastrow, M. (2017). News feature: Is video game addiction really an addiction? *Proceedings of the National Academy of Sciences of the United States of America*, 114(17), 4268–4272. https://doi.org/10.1073/pnas.1705077114

Zemankova, P., Lungu, O., & Bares, M. (2016). psychosocial modulators of motor learning in Parkinson's Disease. *Frontiers in Human Neuroscience*, 10, 74. https://doi.org/10.3389/fnhum.2016.00074

Zhang, F., & Kaufman, D. (2016a). A review of intergenerational play for facilitating interactions and learning. *Gerontechnology*, 14(3), 127–138. https://doi.org/10.4017/gt.2016.14.3.002.00

Zhang, F., & Kaufman, D. (2016b). Older adults' social interactions in massively multiplayer online role-playing games (MMORPGs). *Games and Culture: A Journal of Interactive Media*, 11(1–2), 150–169. https://doi.org/10.1177/1555412015601757

Zillmann, D. (1988). Mood management through communication choices. *American Behavioral Scientist*, 31(3), 327–340 https://doi.org/10.1177/000276488031003005

....

CHAPTER 29

ENACTING IMMORALITY WITHIN GAMESPACE: WHERE SHOULD WE DRAW THE LINE, AND WHY?

....

GARRY YOUNG

INTRODUCTION

....

THE task of the metaphorical line referred to within the title of this chapter is to demarcate moral from immoral enactments of violent or otherwise taboo activities within gamespace. In other words, what should be permissible from what should not. The agreement must be, it would seem, *where* to draw the line and, by way of a corollary, what justifies this decision. This view is in contrast to the amoralist claim that no such line should exist: for there is no justification for labeling one enactment immoral and another moral.[1] As far as virtual enactments within video games are concerned, anything goes.

While the amoralist's claim elicits sympathy, this does not prevent this chapter from attempting to proffer a normative account of video game morality. An account that is concerned not so much with *where* the line ought to be drawn as it is with delineating what is involved in *agreeing* where the line ought to be drawn (if indeed it should be drawn anywhere). It is the means by which a society arrives at an agreement, in virtue of a shared moral attitude, and the normative strength of this attitude that is of interest in this chapter. Before discussing this and related matters further, however, a clarification of terminology is required.

When using the term *video game*, following Tavinor (2008), it refers to games played by one or more players on personal computers or consoles (such as the *X-Box, PlayStation*, and *Wii*) that are marketed as *games* rather than, say, training devices and

---

[1] Saying this does not negate the possibility that it is possible to *enact* a moral or immoral act.

are *played* in a way that subscribes to certain rules, explicitly or implicitly found within the gameplay. Also, the term "gameplay," means "the pure interactivity of the game" (Juul, 2005, p. 19) which is constitutive of the video game content in terms of the representations found therein and the interactions afforded. These, in turn, are produced through an "interaction between the rules…, the players pursuing a goal, and [their] personal repertoire and preferences" (Juul, 2005, pp. 199–200). The term "gamespace" means simply the virtual environment in which the gameplay is realized.

Video games are, of course, *fictions*, meaning that the narrative is wholly or in part fictional (i.e., it may be set on a fictitious alien world or within some futuristic dystopian society, or be played out against the backdrop of an actual historical event such as the Second World War). They are also *interactive* insofar as the player can to a greater or lesser degree alter the course of the narrative in virtue of actions carried out, including decisions made during the course of the gameplay. Putting all of this together, the following necessary and sufficient conditions apply. *X* is a video game if and only if:

1. It is an artifact in a digital visual medium.
2. It is intended primarily as an object of entertainment.
3. It is intended to provide such entertainment through the employment of one or both of the following modes of engagement: (i) rule-bound gameplay, or (ii) interactive fiction.[2]

When discussing the enactment of immorality within video games, this chapter adopts the term *symbolic taboo activities* (STAs) (Whitty et al., 2011). STAs refer to the virtual enactment of actions that are (typically) both legally and morally proscribed when carried out for real. *Inter alia*, these may involve enacting discrimination, murder, rape, assault (sexual and physical), torture, incest, pedophilia, necrophilia, and bestiality. Following Young (2013b), this chapter refers to these real-world prohibited actions as POTAs (*prohibited offline taboo activities*). It is important to note that POTAs are not homogeneous beyond their shared prohibitive status. Some may consider rape and murder (for example) to be far worse than, say, discrimination; others may disagree. While accepting their lack of homogeneity, POTAs are nevertheless, by definition, *all* worthy of prohibition and so, for this reason, have a status that is at least nominally equivalent. STAs, on the other hand, do not share the same nominal-level prohibitive status; their permissibility within video games varies. The enactment of physical assault and murder, for example, is often considered to be "part of the game" (Hartmann et al., 2010; Young & Whitty, 2011) and is integrated into the gameplays of numerous commercially available "violent" video games (e.g., the *Grand Theft Auto* Series to name one (in) famous example). Enacting child sexual abuse, in contrast, is banned outright in the UK and limited in the US.[3]

---

[2] Adapted from Tavinor (2008).

[3] In the UK, the 2009 *Coroners and Justice Act* made illegal the possession of virtual (or pseudo) images judged to be pedophilic. In the US, in 2003, the PROTECT Act limited the permissibility of virtual representations of child sexuality/abuse to those representations that are not considered to be obscene or "hardcore" based on community standards (Bird, 2011).

Given the discrepancy between the permissibility of STAs (which varies) and the permissibility of POTAs (which typically does not), and given the fact that STAs are, by their very nature, aligned with POTAs (insofar as they are designed to be the virtual representation of POTAs), an inconsistency exists: only *some* STAs are prohibited. And while it is evident that this is the case, what is less apparent, and far more open to conjecture, is why this is.

When considering the normative approach that is possible to take regarding the permissibility of STAs, the following options present themselves:

1. Because all POTAs are prohibited, *all* STAs should be prohibited.
2. Despite the fact that all POTAs are prohibited, *no* STAs should be prohibited.
3. Even though all POTAs are prohibited, only *some* STAs should be prohibited.

Option 1 implies that STAs should be prohibited because of their relationship to POTAs. In other words, underlying option 1 is the view that, in representing the immoral, STAs should be equally prohibited, presumably because such enactments are themselves immoral. Option 2, on the other hand, morally discriminates. It suggests that although STAs represent POTAs, this is not reason enough to prohibit them. The fact that STAs represent POTAs is therefore of no consequence to their morality, and hence their permissibility. Option 3 is compatible with the current state of play (meaning the current situation regarding the permissibility of STAs). It is an expression of *selective prohibition*, and reflects the fact (under the current state of play) that some enactments of immorality are typically permitted (e.g., physical assault, torture, murder, cannibalism) whereas others are not, or their permissibility is considered to be much more contentious (e.g., discrimination, rape, pedophilia).

This chapter presents three attempts to justify the selective prohibition of video game content; that is, three ways of justifying the idea that it is possible to distinguish between what should be permitted and what should not and, in doing so, establish where the aforementioned metaphorical line is to be drawn. It refers respectively to these as the argument from harm, the argument from meaningful expression, and the argument from player motivation. They are not intended to be exhaustive, but do capture popular ways of thinking about the issue of video game violence and the enactment of taboos. It is also worth noting that discussion focuses exclusively on single-player video games in which enactments by the player's avatar are against NPCs (non-player characters). For discussion on the morality of STAs in multi-player gamespace, see Young (2013b), and Young and Whitty (2010, 2012). Finally, it addresses the concern as to whether there are *moral* grounds for prohibiting certain content, not whether this content (*qua* the actions it affords) would make a good game (which is more within the remit of ludology and narratology).

What this chapter intends to show is that none of the aforementioned approaches is able to justify the selective prohibition of STAs. Nevertheless, selective prohibition does occur (as the current state of play attests). How might we explain this? The final section, Immorality as Disapproval and the Construction of an Objectified Moral Norm, briefly presents an account of what it means to state that *x* is immoral, i.e., what is known as *constructive ecumenical expressivism* (Young, 2014, 2015). Based on this account, it proffers an argument for why the current state of play is as it is and what a normative position regarding selective prohibition would look like if one were to endorse constructive ecumenical expressivism.

THE ARGUMENT FROM HARM

...the purpose for which power can be rightfully exercised over any member of a civilized community, against his will, is to prevent harm to others.

Mill ([1859] 2005, p. 9)

A criticism often levelled at violent video game content and the types of engagement it affords (including the enactment of a number of the STAs mentioned in the previous section) is that it increases the likelihood that those who play these games will engage in anti-social behavior when away from the gaming environment and, in doing so, harm others. To understand the shape such a criticism might take, consider the distinction McCormick (2001) makes between:

(i) A *dangerous act*, which is an act that directly increases the risk of harm to self or others (e.g., engaging in a knife-throwing act);

(ii) A *harmful act*, which is an act that results in direct injury or damage to self or others (e.g., hitting one's assistant with a knife or stabbing oneself in the foot with it);

(iii) A *risk-increasing act*, which is an act that increases the person's chances of committing a dangerous or harmful act (e.g., drinking alcohol as a means of encouraging oneself to perform a knife-throwing act).

For McCormick, engaging in video game violence is not a dangerous or a harmful act as defined by (i) and (ii) because one does not physically harm, nor can one run the risk of physically harming directly, either oneself or another as a result of what is done within the game. Engaging in video game violence could, however, be construed as a risk increasing act: although no harm is *directly* incurred through engaging in virtual violence, such activity does (allegedly, or at least potentially) increase the risk of engaging in the sorts of dangerous activities that themselves run the risk of directly causing harm to oneself or others. (This chapter, for the sake of brevity, does not distinguish between harm to self or others; for a detailed discussion on this distinction, see Young, 2013b, and Young & Whitty, 2012).

The premise below (Premise$_{hp}$) is grounded on the *harm principle* formulated by John Stuart Mill (2005 [1859]) which, in essence, asserts that the only justification for a restriction of one's liberty is where one's liberty causes harm to another, such harm being therefore construed as immoral.

Premise$_{hp}$: Any act which is significantly likely to result in harm is immoral.

What evidence is there that STAs result in/are correlated with the sort of indirect harm described previously? By far the most extensive research on the negative consequences of playing violent video games (*qua* indirect harm) has involved their alleged association with increased aggression (e.g., leading to more aggressive interactions outside of gamespace) or other anti-social behavior (e.g., being less responsive to someone believed to be in distress); and, related to this, affective and cognitive changes within the gamer (e.g., changes in feelings and attitudes towards violence). Research has also tended to focus on the effects of enacting *killing* or related violence, characteristic of what Patridge (2013) calls run-of-the-mill first-person shooter games, rather than other STAs (e.g., discrimination, rape, pedophilia).

In support of a link between virtual violence and various "anti-social" factors, Anderson et al. (2010), as a result of their meta-analytic review of work published in 2008, claimed to have found that exposure to video games with violent content is a causal risk factor for increased aggressive behavior, cognition, and affect, and decreases empathy and prosocial behavior (see also Anderson, 2004). More recently, and again based on a meta-analytic review of published findings (this time between 2009–2013), Calvert and colleagues (2017) likewise reported that exposure to violent video games is associated with increased aggressive behavior, cognitions, and affect, as well as increased desensitization, decreased empathy, and increased physiological arousal. They also report similar effect sizes to prior meta-analyses, which they interpret as indicative of stable results across time. In addition, following a six-month longitudinal study, Greitemeyer and Sagioglou (2017) found that repeated exposure to violent video games predicts everyday sadism (i.e., those who derive personal enjoyment from humiliating or otherwise causing harm to others).

While it would be erroneous to ignore such findings (Greitemeyer & Mügge, 2014), Ferguson (2007a, b), based on his meta-analytic review of video game violence, nevertheless warns us to treat many of the results supporting a connection between violent video game content and anti-social behavior with caution, arguing that the measures of aggression used in most studies lack validity and often have effect sizes that are very small (see DeCamp & Ferguson, 2017 for recent findings further supporting the view that exposure to violent video games is not a predictor of youth violence). Ferguson (2007a, b) also suggests that there is a bias in the academic literature in favor of those papers which report statistically significant differences between groups, as opposed to those that do not.[4] Moreover, Markey and colleagues (2015) followed a meta-analytic review of data, including FBI crime statistics and video game sales, yet reported no evidence linking exposure to video game violence to violent crime in the US (see Cunningham et al., 2016, for similar findings).

Putting all of this together, at least in terms of research currently undertaken, there is no consensus on what the effects of playing violent video games are (Ferguson,

[4] By way of additional dissenting voices and further critical discussion on Anderson et al.'s (2010) conclusion, see Bushman et al. (2010); Ferguson and Kilburn (2010); and Huesmann (2010). See also Bensley & Van Eenwyk (2001) and Ferguson (2011).

2013; but also Bushman, Gollwitzer, & Cruz, 2015; Bushman and Huesmann 2014, and Krahé 2014, for a rebuttal of Ferguson's (2013) claims, and therefore as a means of reinforcing the argument for a lack of consensus). Therefore, *a posteriori*, there is no compelling reason (at least where a compelling reason requires a consensus in the empirical findings) to endorse the view that enacting virtual murder (or similar violent killings and/or assaults) is significantly likely to result in harm. Any attempt to posit a direct causal link between video game content and violent (real-world) behavior should therefore be regarded as overly simplistic, largely uncorroborated, and ultimately contentious. Given this, it can be concluded that Premise$_{hp}$ does not apply to violent video games.

In supporting selective prohibition, it is unlikely that the conclusion reached above will be troublesome, and, indeed, it would likely be welcome. While pursuing evidence and argument based on the immorality of harm, and while endorsing selective prohibition, it is possible to apply the following deduction:

a) (Based on Premise$_{hp}$) Any act which is significantly likely to result in harm is immoral;
b) Only *certain* STAs (e.g., virtual rape/pedophilia) are significantly likely to result in harm;
c) Therefore, only *certain* STAs are immoral.

By differentiating between STAs, it is possible that virtual content, akin to more traditional gaming violence (i.e., killing/murder), is not significantly likely to lead to harm—at least, there is no consensus supporting this—while also allowing that other STAs (for reasons yet to be determined) are likely to result in the kind of indirect harm described by McCormick. Is there evidence to support this move?

Currently, there is a paucity of research on the relationship between virtual sexual activity (including violence/abuse) and actual sexual violence/abuse or other harm. Consequently, evidence-based argument examining the merits of premise (b) requires engaging in a degree of extrapolation. To illustrate, in 2008, Bryant and Linz set out to test an assumption made by the US government in defense of the 1996 Child Pornography Protection Act "that virtual child pornography stimulates and whets adults' appetites for sex with children and that such content can result in the sexual abuse or exploitation of minors becoming acceptable to and even preferred by the viewer" (Bryant & Linz, 2008, p. 35). After exposing adults to "barely legal" pornography, Bryant and Linz concluded that, although those who viewed the material were more likely to associate sexual activity to non-sexual images of minors (based on response latency), there was no evidence that exposure caused participants to be more accepting of child pornography or pedophilia. (Barely legal pornography uses models who are over 18 years of age, but who are depicted as being under or just over the legal age of consent.) Imagery of this nature is not "virtual" in the sense applicable to video game content, but it is suggestive of the absence of the connection needed to support premise (b). However, there is the idea that virtual pedophilia could typically afford an interactive element that is absent in most, if not all, barely legal pornography.

In addition, while it remains true that those who are charged with child solicitation (typically via the Internet) and molestation are often caught in possession of child pornography (Kingston et al., 2008; Riegel, 2004), there nevertheless remains a distinct category of offenders who restrict their offending to the voyeuristic pursuit of child abuse images (*sexual voyeurism*) and have no history of molestation or solicitation (Berlin & Sawyer, 2012). Thus, the conclusion is that "some individuals appear to be experiencing compulsive urges to voyeuristically view such images [of child pornography], devoid of any motivation to actually approach a child sexually" (Berlin & Sawyer, 2012, p. 31). Of relevance, here, is the fact that although in 2002 the US Supreme Court (in the case of Ashcroft v. Free Speech Coalition) acknowledged that computer-generated images (virtual child pornography) may lead to actual instances of child molestation, they nevertheless ruled that, at present, there is no evidence to suggest that a causal link between these images and actual abuse is anything other than contingent and indirect (Williams, 2004).

By way of support for this ruling, it is worth noting that, in Japan, *manga* and *anime* illustrative forms are popular across all ages (Norris, 2009; Sabin, 1993; Wilson, 1999) and a certain form—*Hentai*—typically involves an aberration indicative of a sexual perversion or abnormality (Ortega-Brena, 2009). Masuchika (2015, p. 57) alludes to a standard Western view of manga's sexualized imagery when he states: "Japanese manga have an unsavory reputation of containing seemingly pornographic, or even obscene, material. News reporters have written about the proliferation of manga that could be classified as child pornography." Despite the controversy (in the West) over Japanese manga, Diamond and Uchiyama (1999), using official Japanese sex crime statistics, report that the increased availability of pornography (including manga) in Japan since the 1990s was correlated with a decrease in sex crimes.

The discussion above involves a degree of extrapolation. Nevertheless, what is evident is that available evidence does not allow the conclusion that exposure to virtual sexual activity (including violence/abuse) is significantly likely to result in harm.[5] Given this, and the lack of consensus regarding evidence relating to exposure to more traditional gaming violence and anti-social behavior, it is possible to reason thus:

d) (Based on Premise$_{hp}$) Any act which is significantly likely to result in harm is immoral;
e) STAs are not significantly likely to result in harm;
f) STAs are not immoral.

Even if the truth of (d) and (e) is a given, if the conclusion from this is that STAs are not immoral, the conclusion is a result of a deductive fallacy: for the conclusion (f) does not *necessarily* follow from premises (d) and (e). The reason for this is because Premise$_{hp}$,

---

[5] There is even less (if indeed there is any) available evidence indicating a link between other STAs (such as enacting cannibalism, incest, or necrophilia) and harm.

and therefore premise (d), stipulates a *sufficient* condition for immorality, not a necessary one. Premise$_{hp}$ as a sufficient condition can be more explicitly expressed as follows:

Premise$_{hp(s)}$: An act is immoral *if* it is significantly likely to result in harm.

In accordance with Premise$_{hp(s)}$, any STA that is significantly likely to result in harm *is* immoral. Importantly, though, even if a particular STA is not significantly likely to result in harm, as noted, the conclusion presented in (f) does not *necessarily* follow. This is because the STA might satisfy some other (yet to be identified) sufficient condition for a claim to immorality. Moreover, it may be that only certain STAs satisfy this other sufficient condition for immorality. Where this is the case, the selective prohibition of video game content would be justified. What might this other sufficient condition for immorality be, and is there any evidence that some (if any) STAs satisfy it?

The Argument from Meaningful Expression

> I like video games, but they're really violent. I'd like to play a video game where you help the people who were shot in all the other games. It'd be called "Really Busy Hospital".
>
> Demetri Martin, comedian

Brey (2003) argues that it is precisely because virtual reality typically contains representations or simulations of physical and social reality that it warrants moral policing. The manner in which characters or events within a game are represented—the behaviors they simulate and the interactions permitted—should all come under moral scrutiny. What the gamer is communicating, even through the virtual nature of their action, Powers (2003) tells us, is *socially significant expression*. It is therefore morally wrong to engage in STAs, not because they are equivalent to POTAs, but rather because they *represent* them. In other words, the relationship between STAs and POTAs is such that STAs capture what POTAs are assumed to be: in simple terms, morally bad things. Therefore, when scrutinizing the content of video games, it is important to evaluate the meaning of the gameplay in terms of the message it conveys (see Goerger, 2017, Ostritsch, 2017, and Young 2017a, 2017b, for recent discussions).

For some, Powers' (2003) argument may have a certain intuitive appeal. But is it really the case that if I (*qua* my avatar) were to bludgeon to death another avatar with a kitchen utensil (as it is possible to do in *Manhunt 2*), or run them over in a fast car (*Carmageddon*), or set them alight, urinate on them to douse the flames, and then beat them to death with my boot and a shovel (*Postal 2*), I would be promoting actual murder (whether intentionally or inadvertently) by seemingly delighting in the idea of it? (More on player motivation in The Argument from Player Motivation). Perhaps this might be construed as trivializing it. Either way, Pasquinelli (2010) proffers a word of caution when she states that prohibiting such virtual acts risks blurring the boundary between fiction and reality, thereby increasing the confusion over the status of real and imaginary acts. For Pasquinelli, there is a risk that by prohibiting enactments of immorality in gamespace we would be (mistakenly) accrediting these virtual acts with a negative value nominally equivalent to that bestowed on immoral actions (POTAs) committed in the real world.

If there is an argument for the prohibition of all STAs in virtue of the fact that they represent that which is immoral, and therefore that the "wrong message" is being sent if their enactment is permitted within a game, then there seems to be no justifiable basis for selective prohibition. As things stand, either all STAs should be prohibited, or, if the argument is rejected based on socially significant expression, conceding that there is no evidence that they cause harm, permit them all. In other words, what grounds would there be for concluding that the enactment of *this* violent act (say, virtual murder) is not promoting or trivializing actual murder, whereas the enactment of *this* violent act (virtual rape) is promoting or trivializing actual rape?

A possible means of justifying selective prohibition is provided by Patridge (2011). Patridge argues that the meaning of representations, and whether these are or should be deemed offensive and, from this, morally reprehensible, is contingent on whether they have *incorrigible social meaning*. That is, on whether the content reflects an association that has deep-rooted (actual) social meaning to members of a particular society, thereby making it offensive to these members. The representations and virtual enactments targeted by Patridge are those which were once held to be something of a social norm (e.g., institutionalized racism) within the US (for example), but which are no longer viewed in the same way. What she is less concerned with are actual morally/legally prohibited actions that have never been a social norm. Patridge alludes to this with reference to the game *Mafia Wars* when she states: "The fact that we enjoy playing this game seems to say nothing at all by itself about our attitude towards organized crime" (2011, p. 307). This is because organized crime, as far as is known, has never been established as an acceptable social norm in the US. Therefore, if players enjoy playing a game that features organized crime, their enjoyment is not necessarily a sign of approval. The same can presumably be said of the enactment of violent actions like murder, owing to its lack of incorrigible social meaning.

Patridge's (2011) point is that the *epistemic flexibility* humans possess that enables the creation of fictions that may be more or less loosely based on real-life contingent associations (objects/events), and therefore the extent to which players are willing, in the pursuit of these fictions, to suspend their disbelief (by embracing the idea that "it's just a game") must be constrained in relation to their potential incorrigible social meaning. Sometimes, she argues, imaginative and therefore fictional representations should be rejected if they represent associations that still have morally offensive undertones.

For Patridge, then, incorrigible social meaning provides a means of explaining the unease many feel towards the idea of rape games (e.g., *RapeLay, Battle Raper,* or the much older *Custer's Revenge*) or gameplays that contain explicit racism or the enactment of child abuse.[6] She considers virtual rape to have incorrigible social meaning because of the "global history and current reality of women's oppression" (2011, p. 312). What is less clear, however, is how incorrigible social meaning could be used to prohibit virtual pedophilia. While it is true that, historically, cultural attitudes have varied with regard to the permissibility of sex with minors (e.g., the Ancient Greek custom of *paiderastia, boy love*), there is nothing equivalent that can compare to what Patridge reasonably takes to be the history and reality of oppression towards women. Also, and importantly, it is unclear how Patridge's account justifies anything more than a claim of moral insensitivity or poor taste (a metaphorical "up yours" to those offended), rather than immorality per se. What is also unclear, even if incorrigible social meaning could be used to justify the selective prohibition of enacting child abuse, is why the current state of play (at least in the US and UK) permits virtual child murder (e.g., *Fallout 1 & 2, Dying Light* and *No More Room in Hell, Deus Ex* and *Deus Ex: Invisible War*).[7]

By way of a final attempt at justifying selective prohibition, the discussion here turns to an issue that the reader may have been asking themselves since first they were introduced to the possibility of enacting rape or pedophilia, or perhaps other STAs (like bestiality or incest): Why would anyone want to do *that*? The next section examines player motivation. As with the other approaches, it is intended to show why it cannot be relied on to provide a normative account of selective prohibition.

THE ARGUMENT FROM PLAYER MOTIVATION

[W]hether immoral behavior in virtual reality may become acceptable to the offended party may well depend on his or her assessment of the *intentions, values* and *beliefs* of the actor. What may have to be re-established for the offended party is a basic trust that the desire to act immorally in virtual environments does not reflect a fundamental disrespect for the real-life equivalents of the virtual beings or things that are harmed or desecrated in VR [virtual reality].

(Brey, 1999, p. 9; emphasis added)

Young (2013a) presents three motivations for engaging in a virtual act within a game. These motivations are not intended to be exhaustive, nor are they mutually exclusive; although it is Young's contention that each is sufficient. They are intended to help to

---

[6] Patridge (2013) discusses a fictitious game called *Child Sexual Abuse* in which the player engages in virtual pedophilia. Young (2013b) presents a fictitious game called R.A.C.I.S.T. (*Rage Against Community: Intercept, Segregate, Terminate*) in which the object of the game is to hunt and kill members of a particular minority group which the player selects from the drop-down menu.

[7] See Luck (2009) and Young (2016) for a more detailed discussion on this point.

understand what might motivate someone to engage in an STA. The three motivations are:

- $M_{(strategic)}$: S engages in the STA because it benefits S's overall strategy, which is to win the game. As such, S does not desire to engage in the STA because of what it represents but, conversely, neither does S desire not to engage in it for this reason. Ultimately, winning the game is what S desires, and S construes the STA simply as a means of achieving this end.
- $M_{(enjoyment)}$: S engages in the STA because S anticipates that it will be fun/thrilling. S anticipates that it will be fun/thrilling because the virtual act represents something that is taboo. In short, S desires to engage in the STA because the symbolic violation of the real-world taboo (the POTA the STA represents), in virtue of it being the enactment of a *taboo*, is something S anticipates deriving enjoyment from.
- $M_{(substitution)}$: S desires to engage in a particular real-world activity which happens to be taboo (happens to be a POTA). This activity is represented by the STA. S therefore desires to engage in the STA not because it is taboo (as is the case in $M_{(enjoyment)}$) but because it represents the real-world activity S desires to engage in (which happens to be taboo). Enacting the real-world taboo affords S the opportunity to satisfy this desire, vicariously.

The player whose motivation is categorized as $M_{(strategic)}$ is effectively endorsing the amoralist position that it is "just a game." As such, what is being enacted is beyond the realm of moral obligation.[8] There is certainly some truth to this assertion. After all, what is happening within a video game is literally nothing but the manipulation of pixels (Klimmt et al., 2006). In the case of enacting virtual murder, there seems little intuitive appeal in the idea that those who engage in virtual murder do so because they derive some kind of pleasure from the idea of actual murder (and certainly there is no empirical support for this as a trend). If anything, empirically, there is more support for the claim that those who engage in virtual murder or other violence do so for strategic reasons, as captured by $M_{(strategic)}$, out of a sense of competition (Adachi & Willoughby, 2011; Griffiths, Eastin, & Cicchirillo, 2016). Glock and Kneer (2009), for example, when commenting on the findings of a study by Ladas (2003), note how gamers seemed "to focus on competition, success, thrill [indicative of $M_{(enjoyment)}$], and the virtual simulation of power and control rather than damaging other persons" (p. 153). Glock and Kneer consider this way of thinking about the game (notably, *not* in saliently aggressive terms) to be suggestive of the existence of *differentiated knowledge structures* in those with prolonged violent game exposure when compared to novice gamers. It may be, they surmise, that novice players associate violent video games with aggression because of media

---

[8] Saying this does not negate the possibility that a gamer will play in a way that conforms to certain moral principles (Sicart, 2009). In the context under discussion, however, doing so is ultimately for strategic, rather than moral, reasons (e.g., it is possible to benefit from adopting a particular moral approach by not incurring certain penalties that may hinder progression).

coverage to that effect; however, through "repeated exposure to violent digital games, links to game-specific concepts are strengthened, thereby overrunning [media-related] associations to aggression" (Glock and Kneer (2009).

Similarly, with other STAs, gameplays could be contrived where their enactment was of strategic benefit. In the case of virtual pedophilia, for example, Luck (2009) creates a scenario based on a fictitious video game whereby, for reasons in keeping with $M_{(strategic)}$, one might decide to engage in an act of virtual child abuse. In the words of Luck:

> [I]magine you are playing a computer game, the object of which is to steal the Crown Jewels from the Tower of London. One way to achieve this goal is to seduce and sleep with a Beefeater's daughter, who just so happens to be 15. A player who commits this act of virtual paedophilia may do so, not because he enjoys the notion of having sex with a child, but because he wishes to complete the game. (2009, p. 34)

It is possible to likewise contrive an alternate option where the threat to rape the Beefeater's wife will ensure his cooperation in stealing the jewels. If a player's motivation best fits the category $M_{(strategic)}$ then this undermines the assumption that, in the case of virtual pedophilia or rape, to engage in such an act, one *must* find either the idea of the *virtual* act pleasurable (which would accord with $M_{(enjoyment)}$) or delight in the idea of carrying out the act for real (a motivation compatible with $M_{(substitution)}$).[9]

Contrasting virtual murder with, say, virtual pedophilia, in the context of $M_{(strategic)}$, we get:

(a) S engages in virtual murder as a means to an end; it helps them progress through the game.

(b) S engages in virtual pedophilia as a means to an end; it helps them progress through the game.

Statements (a) and (b) provide equivalent motivations for engaging in each respective activity: motivations compatible with $M_{(strategic)}$. Suppose, however, that the gamer admits that the reason they engage in virtual pedophilia is because it is fun/thrilling. Still contrasting with virtual murder, the following possibilities present themselves:

(c) S engages in virtual murder because it is fun/thrilling, irrespective of whether it helps S progress through the game.

(d) S engages in virtual pedophilia because it is fun/thrilling, irrespective of whether it helps S progress through the game.

Is there a sense in which engaging in virtual pedophilia might be deemed pleasurable that does not bolster the assumption that this is because one must derive pleasure from

---

[9] See Ali (2015) for a detailed discussion on the importance of context when judging whether a particular STA should be proscribed.

the idea of actual pedophilia? Before answering this question directly, the question can be re-directed towards other virtual violence, including murder. If there is an argument against the idea that enacting virtual murder because it is fun necessitates that the player derives pleasure from the idea of actual murder, then what would such an argument look like? Moreover, should such an argument be forthcoming, could the same argument be applied to understand better statement (d) and therefore counter the assumption that enjoying virtual pedophilia means the player must enjoy the idea of actual pedophilia?

When considering the appeal of violent video games and why people are drawn to them, Nys (2010) argues that knowing that it is immoral (*qua* represents immorality) is part of the enjoyment. Given Nys' comment, it is not inconceivable that enacting virtual violence holds a certain allure for some people because they enjoy engaging in simulated immorality and identifying with the "bad guy" (Schulzke, 2011; see also Konijn & Hoorn, 2005). In fact, for Hartmann (2011), how gamers' experience STAs may depend on which type of processing—either rational of experiential (Epstein 1994)—is more prominent during a particular virtual interaction. Rational processing may obviate a sense of guilt or help quell one's disgust at the gory spectacle that occurs when dispatching an innocent bystander within the game, because it enables the gamer to understand that what she has just done is not real (see Klimmt et al., 2008, for a discussion on moral management and Hartmann et al., 2014, for a recent review). However, the cognitive effort needed to keep reminding oneself that what one is doing is "just a game"—and so maintain a sense of detachment—may diminish one's enjoyment (Hartmann et al., 2010). Those more prone to experiential processing, on the other hand, may react physiologically to the virtual violence in ways analogous (although no doubt in milder form) to how the gamer might anticipate reacting (and so feeling) if the violence were real (see Whitty et al., 2011).

For Juul (2005), then, video games "are playgrounds where players can experiment with doing things they … would not normally do." Whereas, for Jansz (2005), they act as "private laboratories" (p. 231) within which gamers can engage with different emotions and identities in relative safety—relative to the actual world, that is—and invest in their own form of psychological exploration (see also Konijn, Walma van der Molen, & Hoorn, 2011). Such exploration might occur within a gamespace where social and moral conventions are quite probably violated, and this is likely to add to their enjoyment (Whitaker et al., 2013); conversely, for others, it may elicit disgust, irritation, or guilt. For others still, it might result in them being both disgusted and thrilled by the virtual violence they enact (Rubenking, & Lang, 2014), such that they willingly become what Jansz (2005) calls the *architects of their own disgust*, all of which adds to their enjoyment and motivation to continue.

In essence, under the guidance of $M_{(enjoyment)}$, where the goal is simply to have fun, irrespective of whether the gamer's definition of fun is congruent with facilitating her progression through the game, if "fun" constitutes doing *a, b, c*, she ought to do (in a practical rather than moral sense) *a, b, c*. In the case of $M_{(enjoyment)}$, and with reference to virtual murder (but not exclusively so), the activity has symbolic transcendence insofar as it represents in one space that which is taboo in another. Moreover, the symbolic connection which transcends these two spaces presupposes a different psychological connection to that evident in $M_{(strategic)}$. To explain: Coeckelbergh (2011) argues that players do not tend to treat gaming characters like mere objects—and therefore like chess pieces—but to some extent as a social other, which is why virtually violent actions are potentially of moral concern. The action is psychologically meaningful not only in terms of understanding what it represents, but also as a motivation to engage in the activity in the first place: *because it is fun in virtue of what it represents,* or at least that is what is anticipated. In the case of virtual murder, or indeed the enactment of any real-world taboo, "an inquiry into [its] appeal will reveal that [the] enjoyment *presupposes a moral awareness,* and therefore that morality is included from the start" (Nys, 2010, p. 81; emphasis in original). In accordance with $M_{(enjoyment)}$, then, for some, simulating virtual violence is appealing precisely because it involves enacting taboos and therefore violating an offline moral code.

If enacting STAs does not *necessitate* that a player is motivated by the idea of engaging in what the STA represents (the corresponding POTA), then just as virtual murder (whether done for strategic reasons or because the player enjoys the idea of enacting a *taboo*) does not necessitate a motivation to engage in actual murder (contra $M_{(substitution)}$), so engaging in virtual rape or pedophilia does not necessitate the player's motivation to do either of these for real, or even delight in the *idea* of doing them. It is possible to object, of course, to the reasoning shown here; declaring that it demonstrates only that, in the case of STAs, there is no *logical* connection between representing these acts and promoting or delighting in what these enactments represent. Likewise, there is no logical connection between the enactment itself (and even enjoying the enactment) and being motivated to engage in this activity for real. Therefore, declaring that one event does not necessarily follow from the other does little to obviate the intuition that this must be a motivation in the case of enacting certain taboos (e.g., rape and pedophilia) and therefore that a game involving virtual pedophilia would be a magnet for pedophiles and/or increase the likelihood of actual pedophilic activity in non-pedophiles.

In response: if someone is unconvinced by the a priori argument that enacting pedophilia does not *necessitate* seeking to promote the activity for real and/or delighting in the idea of doing this for real, then the alternative is to draw on empirical evidence. Given this, the reader should recall the discussion in the previous section on the likelihood of harm through engaging in virtual sexual activity (violence/abuse) and how, based on the current paucity in pertinent empirical research, and the fact that extrapolations from what evidence is available proffer little support for harm, any such intuition remains unsubstantiated.

Thus far, there seems little in the way of evidence and argument to support selective prohibition. Moreover, given the lack of evidence of harm, there seems little justification for the prohibition of *all* STAs (option 1, as presented in the Introduction). This leaves option 3: namely, *no* STAs should be prohibited. Certainly there seems to be no moral grounds to dispute this claim, at least based on anything discussed in this chapter (see Young, 2013a, and Young & Whitty, 2010, 2011, 2012 for further detailed discussion and essentially the same conclusion), other than perhaps an argument based on incorrigible social meaning: although this seems to make the case for moral insensitivity in certain contexts rather than immorality. So how might the selective prohibition evidenced by the current state of play be accounted for, and how might this be adopted as a normative position? To address this question, this chapter next introduces constructive ecumenical expressivism (CEE).

Immorality as Disapproval and the Construction of an Objectified Moral Norm

Constructive ecumenical expressivism is a meta-ethical theory that presents as follows:[10]

(CEE) S disapproves of P and believes that x realizes P (thus making anaphoric reference to that of which S disapproves).[11]

Property P can and does amount to different things for different people (subsumed under property P is property p or q or r or s, and so on). For S_1, P may amount to negative utility—the realizing of more displeasure than pleasure in the form of increased harm—while S_2 may hold it to be a violation of God's law, or constitutive of a failure of secular duty to others. S_3, in turn, may characterize P as a vice, rather than a virtue, and so on. What S_1, S_2, and S_3 have in common is that they all *believe* a particular property, although not necessarily the same one, is realized by x.

CEE permits S_1, S_2, S_3, . . . Sn to have a shared negative attitude towards x (murder, in this case), but not necessarily for the same reason. Their different reasons stem from different beliefs about the property x (*qua* murder) realizes, which amount to different tokens of P (p or q or r or s, and so on) and their respective disapproval of these properties. Where a shared moral attitude occurs within a society with regard to some object or event, a social norm is created or *constructed* that then acquires its own objectified moral standard (Prinz, 2007). This view is echoed by McAteer (2016) when drawing on the philosophy of David Hume:

To call something an intersubjective reality is to distinguish it both from objective and subjective reality. Something is *objective* if it is mind-independent, i.e., if it exists independently of all mental representation. Something is *subjective* if it is

---

[10] For a more detailed discussion on constructive ecumenical expressivism, see Young (2014, 2015, 2016).

[11] An anaphoric reference occurs when a word in a text refers to a previous idea in the text for its meaning. In the sentence "Fred always looked unkempt, but this never seemed to bother him," the word "him" refers, and therefore makes anaphoric reference, to Fred. See, also, Ridge (2006) for discussion on ecumenical expressivism: the forerunner to constructive ecumenical expressivism.

individually mind-dependent, i.e., if it exists only in one person's experience and is hence relative to that person's individual point of view. Something is *intersubjective* if is collectively mind-dependent, i.e., if it exists in a group of people's experience such that it is relative to what Hume will call a "common" or "general" point of view. (McAteer, 2016, p. 14)

With the force of social consensus, and the moral norm this creates, adopting a normative position is possible, whereby a particular (agreed) attitude is the one that people *ought* to have, at least with regard to *this* object of moral inquiry. Again, McAteer interprets Hume's common point of view as attesting to this normative standard, whereby intersubjectivity creates:

> …a kind of objectivity in that it is not relative to any individual person's thoughts, feelings, or desires. Moreover, cultural relativity could be explained with reference to various cultures' different ways of specifying the intersubjective standard conditions of moral perception.   (McAteer, 2016, p. 16)

On the occasion when S shares the same moral attitude (an attitudinal rather than experiential common point of view) as her society, she will be commended for doing so. When S does not, society will feel it appropriate to rebuke her for her alternate, some might even say deviant, attitude (given the constructed moral norm's objectified status). This is because both the rebuke and a change of attitude on the part of S are (believed by that society to be) warranted (Nichols, 2008).

When S plays a violent video game in which she enacts the murder of an innocent victim, should she be rebuked for this? In other words, is her action morally problematic? According to CEE, an affirmative answer requires that an objectified moral norm is established against such content/enactments. This author's contention is that such a norm has not been established and, if anything, there is a leaning towards the enactment *not* being considered morally problematic (certainly, there is currently no shared *negative* moral attitude). Young (2015) argues that this is because virtual murder (for example) is ambiguous. People interpret the activity in different ways and so are less likely to believe that x (virtual murder) realizes a property of which they disapprove. Given this, they are less likely to form a negative attitude towards x and so, together, develop a *shared* negative attitude. There will be and indeed are dissenters, of course, but CEE accommodates this.

As far as other STAs are concerned—like enactments of rape and pedophilia—again, the contention is that far more people believe that these enactments realize properties of which they do disapprove, than do not. As such, there are more individuals with a negative attitude towards x (*qua* virtual rape or pedophilia) and therefore more of a shared attitude towards the moral failings of this type of STA than there are not, even if different people have different *reasons* for their shared negative attitude.

To conclude, then, what is important to remember about CEE, is that a negative attitude is based on a *belief*: say, the belief that x realizes p (an increased likelihood of harm), or *q* (that it is a vice rather than a virtue), and so on. Philosophical inquiry and empirical evidence (or the lack thereof) may reveal this belief to be unjustified (as this chapter has attempted to demonstrate through the rebuttal of objections 1–3, above), but this does not negate the fact that someone may hold the *belief* that *x* realizes *p* or *q* (etc.) and therefore form the negative attitude towards (for example) virtual rape or pedophilia (that they are morally repugnant), but not virtual murder. Where enough people share such an attitude, an objectified moral norm, and therefore a *normative* position, at least within that society, is established. Whether the norm can be justified, empirically and philosophically, depends on the extent to which the reasons that contribute to the formation of the norm can themselves be justified (empirically and philosophically). This fact does not stop the norm from forming, however, even in cases where it is not justified; although it may increase the likelihood of it eventually being challenged and replaced. Yet, equally, evidence and/or argument may eventually be found that justifies it.

Where the moral line is drawn for individuals enacting virtual violence will vary. Where it should be drawn, if CEE is anything to go by, is wherever a constructed moral norm based on different reasons for moral attitude positions it.

Acknowledgment

Text extract quoted with permission from Brey, P. (1999). The ethics of representation and action in virtual reality, *Ethics and Information Technology*, *1*(1), pp. 5–14. https://doi.org/10.1023/A:1010069907461, Copyright © Springer Nature.

References

Adachi, P. J. C., & Willoughby, T. (2011). The effect of video game competition and violence on aggressive behavior: Which characteristic has the greatest influence? *Psychology of Violence*, *1*(4), 259–274.

Ali, R. (2015). A new solution to the gamer's dilemma. *Ethics and Information Technology*, *17*(4), 267–274.

Anderson, C. A. (2004). An update on the effects of playing violent video games. *Journal of Adolescence*, *27*, 113–122.

Anderson, C. A., Shibuya, A., Ihori, N., Swing, E. L., Bushman, B. J., Sakamoto, A., . . . Saleem, M. (2010). Violent video game effects on aggression, empathy, and prosocial behavior in eastern and western countries: A meta-analytic review. *Psychological Bulletin*, *136*(2), 151–173.

Bensley, L., & Van Eenwyk, J. (2001). Video games and real-life aggression: Review of the literature. *Journal of Adolescent Health*, *29*, 244–257.

Berlin, F. S., & Sawyer, D. (2012). Potential consequences of accessing child pornography over the internet and who is accessing it. *Sexual Addiction & Compulsivity: The Journal of Treatment & Prevention*, *19*(1–2), 30–40.

Bird, P. (2011). Virtual child pornography and the constraints imposed by the first amendment. *Barry Law Review*, *16*(1), 161–176.

Brey, P. (1999). The ethics of representation and action in virtual reality. *Ethics and Information Technology*, *1*, 5–14.

Brey, P. (2003). The social ontology of virtual environments. *American Journal of Economics and Sociology*, *62*(1), 269–281.

Bryant, P., & Linz, D. G. (2008). The effects of exposure to virtual child pornography on viewer cognition and attitudes toward deviant sexual behavior. *Communication Research*, *35*(1), 3–38.

Bushman, B. J., Gollwitzer, M., & Cruz, C. (2015). There is broad consensus: Media researchers agree that violent media increase aggression in children, and pediatricians and parents concur. *Psychology of Popular Media Culture*, *4*(3), 200–214.

Bushman, B. J., & Huesmann, L. R. (2014). Twenty-five years of research on violence in digital games and aggression revisited: A reply to Elson and Ferguson (2013). *European Psychologist*, *19*(1), 47–55.

Bushman, B. J., Rothstein, H. R., & Anderson, C. A. (2010). Much ado about something: Violent video game effects and a school of red herring: Reply to Ferguson and Kilburn (2010). *Psychological Bulletin*, *136*(2), 182–187.

Calvert, S. L., Appelbaum, M., Dodge, K.A., Graham, S., Nagayama Hall, G.C., Hamby, S....Hedges, L. V. (2017). The American Psychological Association Task Force assessment of violent video games: Science in the service of public interest. *American Psychologist*, *72*(2), 126–143.

Coeckelbergh, M. (2011). Virtue, empathy, and vulnerability: Evaluating violence in digital games. In K. Poels, & S. Malliet (Eds.), *Vice city virtue: Moral issues in digital game play* (pp. 89–105). Leuven: Acco Academic.

Cunningham, S., Engelstätter, B., & Ward, M. R. (2016). Violent video games and violent crime. *Southern Economic Journal*, *82*(4), 1247–1265.

DeCamp, W., & Ferguson, C. J. (2017). The impact of degree of exposure to violent video games, family background, and other factors on youth violence. *Journal of Youth and Adolescence*, *46*, 388–400.

Diamond, M., & Uchiyama, A. (1999). Pornography, rape and sex crimes in Japan. *International Journal of Law and Psychiatry*, *22*(1), 1–22.

Epstein, S. (1994). Integration of the cognitive and psychodynamic unconscious. *American Psychologist*, *49*, 709–724.

Ferguson, C. J. (2007a). Evidence for publication bias in video game violence effects literature: A meta-analytic review. *Aggression and Violent Behavior*, *12*, 470–482.

Ferguson, C. J. (2007b). The good, the bad and the ugly: A meta-analytic review of positive and negative effects of violent video games. *Psychiatric Quarterly*, *78*(4), 309–316.

Ferguson, C. J. (2011). Video games and youth violence: A prospective analysis in adolescents. *Journal of Youth and Adolescence*, *40*, 377–391.

Ferguson, C. J. (2013). Violent video games and the supreme court: Lessons for the scientific community in the wake of *Brown v. Entertainment Merchants Association*. *American Psychologist*, *68*(2), 57–74.

Ferguson, C. J., & Kilburn, J. (2010). Much ado about nothing: The misestimation and overinterpretation of violent video game effects in eastern and western nations: Comment on Anderson et al. (2010). *Psychological Bulletin*, *136*(2), 174–178.

Glock, S., & Kneer, J. (2009). Game over? The impact of knowledge about violent digital games on the activation of aggression-related concepts. *Journal of Media Psychology*, *21*, 151–160.

Goerger, M. (2017). Value, violence, and the ethics of gaming. *Ethics and Information Technology*, *19*(2), 95–105.

Greitemeyer, T., & Mügge, O. (2014). Video games do affect social outcomes: A meta-analytic review of the effects of violent and prosocial video game play. *Personality and Social Psychology Bulletin*, *40*(5), 578–589.

Greitemeyer, T., & Sagioglou, C. (2017). The longitudinal relationship between everyday sadism and the amount of violent video game play. *Personality and Individual Differences*, *104*, 238–242.

Griffiths, R. P., Eastin, M. S., & Cicchirillo, V. (2016). Competitive video game play: An investigation of identification and competition. *Communication Research*, *43*(4), 468–486.

Hartmann, T. (2011). Users' experiential and rational processing of virtual violence. In K. Poels, & S. Malliet (Eds.), *Vice city virtue: Moral issues in digital game play* (pp. 135–150). Leuven: Acco Academic.

Hartmann, T., Krakowiak, K. M., & Tsay-Vogel, M. (2014). How violent video games communicate violence: A literature review and content analysis of moral disengagement factors. *Communication Monographs*, *81*(3), 310–332.

Hartmann, T., Toz, E., & Brandon, M. (2010). Just a game? Unjustified virtual violence produces guilt in empathetic players. *Media Psychology, 13*(4), 339–363.

Huesmann, L. R. (2010). Nailing the coffin shut on doubts that violent video games stimulate aggression: Comment on Anderson et al. (2010). *Psychological Bulletin*, *136*(2), 179–181.

Jansz, J. (2005). The emotional appeal of violent video games for adolescent males. *Communication Theory*, *15*(3), 219–241.

Juul, J. (2005). *Half-real: Video games between real rules and fictional games*. Cambridge, MA: MIT Press.

Kingston, D. A., Fedoroff, P., Firestone, P., Curry, S., & Bradford, J. M. (2008). Pornography use and sexual aggression: The impact of frequency and type of pornography use on recidivism among sexual offenders. *Aggressive Behavior, 34*(4), 341–351.

Klimmt, C., Schmid, H., Nosper, A., Hartmann, T., &. Vorderer, P. (2006). How players manage moral concerns to make video game violence enjoyable. *Communications, 31*, 309–328.

Klimmt, C., Schmid, H., Nosper, A., Hartmann, T., & Vorderer, P. (2008). "Moral management": Dealing with moral concerns to maintain enjoyment of violent video games. In A. Sudmann-Jahn, & R. Stockmann (Eds.), *Computer games as a sociocultural phenomenon: Games without frontiers—wars without tears* (pp. 108–118). Basingstoke: Palgrave.

Konijn, E. A., & Hoorn, J. F. (2005). Some like it bad: Testing a model for perceiving and experiencing fictional characters. *Media Psychology, 7*(2), 107–144.

Konijn, E. A., Walma van der Molen, J. H., & Hoorn J. F. (2011). Babies versus bogeys: In-game manipulation of empathy in violent video games. In K. Poels, & S. Malliet (Eds.), *Vice city virtue: Moral issues in digital game play* (pp. 151–176). Leuven: Acco Academic.

Krahé, B. (2014). Restoring the spirit of fair play in the debate about violent video games: A comment on Elson and Ferguson (2013). *European Psychologist, 19*(1), 56–59.

Ladas, M. (2003). Eine Befragung von 2141 Computerspielern Zuwirkung und Nutzung von Gewalt [A survey of 2,141 computer game players on effect and use of violence]. In F. Rötzer (Ed.), *Virtuelle Welten—Reale Gewalt* [Virtual worlds—real violence] (pp. 26–35). Hannover: Hans Heise Verlag.

Luck, M. (2009). The gamer's dilemma: An analysis of the arguments for the moral distinction between virtual murder and virtual paedophilia. *Ethics and Information Technology, 11*(1), 31–36.

Markey, P. M., Markey, C. N., & French, J. E. (2015). Violent video games and real-world violence: Rhetoric versus data. *Psychology of Popular Media Culture, 4*(4), 277–295.

Masuchika, G. (2015). Japanese cartoons, virtual child pornography, academic libraries, and the law. *Reference and User Services Quarterly, 54*(4), 54–60.

McAteer, J. (2016). How to be a moral taste theorist. *Essays in Philosophy, 17*(1), 5–21.

McCormick, M. (2001). Is it wrong to play violent video games? *Ethics and Information Technology, 3*(4), 277–287.

Mill, J. S. (2005). *On liberty.* New York: Cosimo. (Original work published 1859).

Nichols, S. (2008). Sentimentalism naturalized. In W. Sinnott-Armstrong (Ed.), *Moral psychology: The evolution of morality, Volume 2* (pp. 255–274). Cambridge, MA: MIT Press.

Norris, C. (2009). Manga, anime and visual art culture. In Y. Sugimoto (Ed.), *The Cambridge companion to modern Japanese culture* (pp. 236–260). Cambridge: Cambridge University Press.

Nys, T. (2010). Virtual ethics. *Ethical Perspectives, 17*(1), 79–93.

Ortega-Brena, M. (2009). Peek-a-boo, I see you: Watching Japanese hard-core animation. *Sexuality & Culture, 13*, 17–31.

Ostritsch, S. (2017). The amoralist challenge to gaming and the gamer's moral obligation. *Ethics and Information Technology, 19*(2), 117–128.

Pasquinelli, E. (2010). The illusion of reality: Cognitive aspects and ethical drawbacks. In Wankel, C. & Malleck, S. (Eds.), *Emerging issues in virtual worlds* (pp. 197–215). Charlotte, NC: Information Age.

Patridge, S. (2011). The incorrigible social meaning of video game imagery. *Ethics and Information Technology, 13*(4), 303–312.

Patridge, S. L. (2013). Pornography, ethics, and video games. *Ethics and Information Technology, 15*(1), 25–34.

Powers, T. M. (2003). Real wrongs in virtual communities. *Ethics in Information Technology, 5*, 191–198.

Prinz, J. J. (2007). *The emotional construction of morals.* Oxford: Oxford University Press.

Ridge, M. (2006). Ecumenical expressivism: Finessing Frege. *Ethics, 116*(2), 302–336.

Riegel, D. L. (2004). Effects on boy-attracted pedosexual males of viewing boy erotica. *Archives of Sexual Behavior, 33*(4), 321–323.

Rubenking, B., & Lang, A. (2014). Captivated and grossed out: An examination of processing core and sociomoral disgusts in entertainment media. *Journal of Communication, 64*(3), 543–565.

Sabin, R. (1993). *Adult comics.* London: Routledge.

Schulzke, M. (2011). Reflective play and morality: Video games as thought experiments. In K. Poels, & S. Malliet (Eds.), *Vice city virtue: Moral issues in digital game play* (pp. 51–68). Leuven: Acco Academic.

Sicart, M. (2009). *The ethics of computer games.* Cambridge, MA: MIT Press.

Tavinor, G. (2008). Definition of videogames. *Contemporary Aesthetics, 6*, 1–17.

Whitaker, J. L., Melzer, A., Steffgen, G. & Bushman, B. J. (2013). The allure of the forbidden: Breaking taboos, frustration, and attraction to violent video games. *Psychological Science, 24*(4), 507–513.

Whitty, M. T., Young, G., & Goodings, L. (2011). What I won't do in pixels: Examining the limits of taboo violation in MMORPGs. *Computers in Human Behavior, 27*(1), 268–275.

Williams, K.S. (2004). Child pornography law: Does it protect children? *Journal of Social Welfare and Family Law, 26*(3), 245–261.

Wilson, B. (1999). Becoming Japanese: *Manga*, children's drawings, and the construction of national character. *Visual Arts Research*, 25(2, issue 50), 48–60.

Young, G. (2013a). Enacting taboos as a means to an end; but what end? On the morality of motivations for child murder and paedophilia within gamespace. *Ethics and Information Technology*, 15(1), 13–23.

Young, G. (2013b). *Ethics in the virtual world: The morality and psychology of gaming*. London: Routledge.

Young, G. (2014). A meta-ethical approach to single-player gamespace: Introducing constructive ecumenical expressivism as a means of explaining why moral consensus is not forthcoming. *Ethics and Information Technology*, 16(2), 91–102.

Young, G. (2015). Violent video games and morality: A meta-ethical approach. *Ethics and Information Technology*, 17(4), 311–321.

Young, G. (2016). *Resolving the gamer's dilemma: Examining the moral and psychological differences between virtual murder and virtual paedophilia*. London: Palgrave Pivot.

Young, G. (2017a). Integrating poor taste into the ongoing debate on the morality of violent video games. *The Computer Games Journal*, 6 (4), 227–237. doi: 10.1007/s40869-017-0044-5.

Young, G. (2017b). Objections to Ostritsch's argument in "The amoralist challenge to gaming and the gamer's moral obligation." *Ethics and Information Technology*, 19(3), 209–219.

Young, G. & Whitty, M. T. (2010). Games without frontiers: On the moral and psychological implications of violating taboos within multi-player virtual spaces. *Computers in Human Behavior*, 26(6), 1228–1236.

Young, G. & Whitty, M. T. (2011). Should gamespace be a taboo-free zone? Moral and psychological implications for single-player video games. *Theory and Psychology*, 21(6), 802–820.

Young, G. & Whitty, M. T. (2012). *Transcending taboos: A moral and psychological examination of cyberspace*. London: Routledge.

CHAPTER 30

GAMING CLASSIFICATIONS AND PLAYER DEMOGRAPHICS

LINDA K. KAYE

INTRODUCTION

THROUGH the lens that gaming can comprise four key facets—function, content, platform and context—this chapter outlines player demographics associated with digital games. This definition is important because otherwise, if gaming is considered a generic entity, it is difficult to establish specific nuances to determine a valid account of player demographics. As such, this chapter provides an account of player demographics and how these may vary as a product of these different facets. It also highlights the issues and challenges associated with this endeavor. Finally, it presents a conceptual model that underpins these issues, whereby these facets of gaming may be determined by gaming domains and play formats.

CLASSIFYING DIGITAL GAMES

When classifying digital games, it is first useful to identify, via a number of dimensions, how they correspond to each other. Indeed, this has previously proved to be a useful approach, for example, when theorizing on the benefit of digital games (Granic, Lobel, & Engels, 2014). In particular, it is worth noting how digital games vary in respect of four key facets: function, content (or genre), platform, and context. These four facets form the basis for the structure of this chapter, where each facet is discussed in turn along with an account of the associated player demographics. However, prior to understanding player demographics, it is first important to acknowledge some conceptual issues in the psychological literature and industry figures. This largely refers to the terminology referring to "gamers" and whether this is always a relevant categorization for all players, and is discussed in the next section.

Who is a Gamer?

The simple question of who a gamer is is fraught with conceptual issues. The first common assumption is that a "gamer" is simply someone who plays digital games, but it is becoming increasingly evident that this is by no means a sufficient definition. That is, there are multiple types of games and varying contexts in which games can be played, which appear to have an impact on the extent to which a person identifies as being a gamer. To illustrate, Erica plays online First-Person Shooter games such as *Call of Duty* for an average of five hours per week and regularly chats with her gamer friends while playing. Steven also plays for five hours per week, but plays mobile games during his daily commute. There are qualitative differences here on the extent to which each is likely to identify as a gamer. That is, Steven is less likely to identify as such, primarily as a result of the type of game (casual mobile game) and the context in which it is played. Therefore, simply exploring time spent gaming is not a sufficient metric in itself through which to establish those who fall into a gamer demographic (Grooten & Kowert, 2015). Thus, a distinction should be made between those who are gamers and those who are simply "players," i.e., a gamer will always be a player, but a player will not necessarily be a gamer. Although regular play-time has been found to be associated with those who identify as gamers (De Grove, Courtois, & Van Looy, 2015), it should not be the sole metric to determine this demographic category. For example, as well as play-time, the extent to which individuals play "hardcore" games, or have affiliations or friendships with others who identify as gamers, are both also related to gamer identity (De Grove et al., 2015). Recent data from the Pew Research Center (2015a) found that although 49 percent of American adults ($N = 2001$) have reported playing games, only 10 percent consider themselves gamers. Thus, identity is therefore a key component by which to conceptualize a "gamer" demographic. For the sake of simplicity, the term "players" will be used in the remainder of this chapter, to avoid making assumptions about gamer identity.

To make this conceptualization more complex, there are different sub-domains of digital gaming with which players may identify. These include casual gaming, social gaming, and hardcore gaming, all of which include their own conceptions and associated gaming behaviors. Specifically, casual gaming has been discussed as being equally complex in the various meanings which are afforded to this term. Namely, a "casual gamer" has been assumed both to be someone who plays casual games as well as someone who plays casually (Kuittnen, Kultima, Niemela, & Paavilainen, 2007). In the previous example, this may refer to Steven, who may play games when time is available to do so, whereas hardcore gaming may be assumed to be when players schedule other activities around gaming (Mason, 2013). Overall, it is perhaps best to consider casual gaming as the type of gaming which has been fostered as games and their users have become more diverse, the possibility that they may be "lighter" and easier to play than more hardcore forms of gaming, as well as be more likely to be played in short bursts than longer uninterrupted sessions (Eklund, 2016; Juul, 2010; Kultima, 2009). Additionally, the type of game and console considerations are important here. That is, those who only play only on mobile devices would typically be assumed to be casual gamers compared to those who may primarily play on console or PC devices. Therefore, as well as players' own identification to the domain or sub-domain, there are also additional implications in respect of the gaming context and platform of the activity. Clearly understanding "who gamers are" is a complex issue, and therefore it is best to simply understand "who plays" as a basis for obtaining data on demographic breakdowns.

Perhaps a useful basis from which to understand different types of gaming (hardcore versus casual) is taken from Eklund (2016), who undertook a principal component analysis of game types and their correspondence to player engagement. It was found that those games which appeared to be played less (casual) consisted of game types such as social network, casual puzzle, point-n-click, party, and racing/sports. However, those games with greater engagement (hardcore) included multiplayer online games, strategy, browser, first person shooters, role-playing games, and adventure games. The variations in these sub-types are important to note as they have implications towards the way in which research understands players. That is, this research also found that the time spent playing games in the casual category was relatively equal between genders compared to more hardcore forms of gaming, which have shown more polarized trends (Eklund, 2016).

Therefore, it seems that the advancement and diversity of games technology (mobile devices, variation of types of consoles) as well as increased Internet connectivity (Wi-Fi access, broadband network) is making gaming more accessible to a wider demographic than may have traditionally been the case (Juul, 2010). Traditionally, to engage in gaming activities, an individual may have had to invest financially in buying expensive console equipment or otherwise have had to invest time to visit arcades as a physical place to play. Now, digital gaming can involve playing in "space" (i.e., online communities or through social networking sites) as well as "place," which opens up a range of opportunities for greater participation from a wider demographic who may otherwise not have engaged due to lack of interest in such investment. Establishing player demographics is therefore becoming a challenging task, given the broad means through which gaming can be accessed. Indeed, these diversities have been noted to be the largest change in the gaming landscape (Leaver & Willson, 2016).

Additionally, the advancement of the Internet has wider implications for the digital games market and its increasing popularity. Namely, it is widely acknowledged that network effects are important when understanding the momentum through which goods are utilized (Katz & Shapiro, 1985, 1994). The advancement of online functionality, e.g., online discussion boards and social networks, have meant that network effects may be magnified further and, as a result, digital games are reaching a wider audience than in pre-Internet eras. This may be a further influence behind the changing demographic and audiences of digital gaming.

THE CASE OF THE "SOCIAL GAMER"

Similarly, along with the aforementioned issues, the term "social gamer" is fraught with issues. Typically, these are assumed to be those who play games through social networking sites (e.g., Candy Crush). This definition is used by the Information Solutions Group (ISG), who have previously produced infographics of the demographic breakdown of social gamers. Their most recent figures show that the majority (55%) of social gamers are female (ISG, 2010), which is typically understood to be in contrast to the gender proportionality in other gaming domains. However, this classification is open to interpretation, as "social" is somewhat vague as a concept. The "social" classification in gaming can correspond to a number of different experiences, including direct gameplay (in which players are interacting in real-time with others through cooperative or competitive play). Alternatively, social experiences may also refer to being alone together, a concept by which a player is in an inherently social gaming environment (e.g., an online game), but not necessarily directly interacting or playing with others (Ducheneaut, Yee, Nickell, & Moore, 2006). Beyond this, being social in gaming can also refer to indirect social experiences, such as playing Candy Crush or Angry Birds, and monitoring your leaderboard performance against your friends. These variations are arguably very different gaming experiences and make it difficult to establish what exactly is being referred to by social gaming. Without a clear conceptualization in the literature or industry research, it is ambiguous which gaming behaviors are classified as social, and, thus, it is unclear who exactly these players are, as well as the ability to gather specific data on the demographic breakdown of so-called "social gamers."

PLAYER DEMOGRAPHICS

In respect of the varying four facets previously outlined (function, content, platform, context), this chapter now addresses each one in turn, and provides an overview of the player demographics associated with each. This discussion may help resolve some of the issues in the more typical general assumptions about who players are, which often fails to account for such variations across these dimensions. Digital games themselves are highly multidimensional and diverse, and therefore, specifying some distinctions allows a more nuanced account of these issues.

Function

There are a range of functions of gaming, and while players primarily play for leisure, it should be noted that gaming can also serve alternative functions. It is perhaps best to

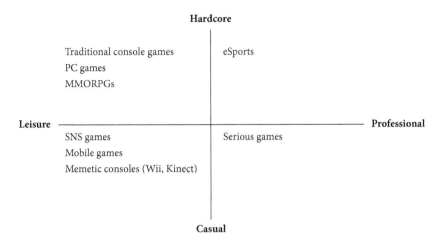

Hardcore

Traditional console games   eSports
PC games
MMORPGs

Leisure ────────────────────────────────────── **Professional**

SNS games   Serious games
Mobile games
Memetic consoles (Wii, Kinect)

Casual

FIGURE 1 Conceptual mapping on two axes for forms of gaming.

conceptualize two key sub-domains here: leisure, and professional (or non-leisure). Figure 1 presents these sub-domains in respect of forms of gaming as hardcore and casual to indicate how certain games and their functionalities may map into playing behaviors and characteristics. Specifically, in respect of gaming for leisure (rather than professionally), most games will function here, but these may vary on a continuum with some being played in more casual formats than others (see Figure 1). In other words, games played on mobile devices or memetic consoles are often played more casually than those played on traditional consoles, which are more likely to be played on a hardcore basis. However, although professional gaming has fewer game types, it can still be mapped between casual and professional forms of gaming. For example, eSports would meet the requirements of being considered hardcore in format, compared to serious games which would typically be played more casually. This conceptual mapping may therefore present a useful framework from which to understand player demographics as a product of function of play (professional versus leisure) and form of gaming (causal versus hardcore play). These will be referred to within the subsequent sections as a conceptual framework to enable a more nuanced account of player demographics.

Gaming for Leisure

Gaming for leisure is the typical conceptualization held towards this activity and correspondingly, who its players are. In this regard, demographics indicate that players are an average of 35 years old (ESA, 2016), although this varies considerably as a result of gender of player (the average age for female players is 44 years of age, and for males, it is 35 years), as well as the platform and type of games being played (discussed in subsequent sections; Platform and Content, respectively). In particular, around three-quarters of these players are adults, with the remaining quarter being under 18 (ESA, 2015, 2016).

In respect of gender, figures reveal a reasonably equal gender divide, with 56–59 percent of these players being men (ESA, 2015, 2016). However, these demographics vary when accounting for game genre, regardless of whether or not the leisurely functions of gaming remains consistent.

One way to establish demographic variations further is from a multiple motivational perspective. For example, a Uses and Gratifications (U&G) perspective suggests a range of motivations for playing different types of digital games, which can vary at different life stages and between genders (Chou & Tsai, 2007; Colwell, 2007; Griffiths, Davies, & Chappell, 2004a and b; Lucas & Sherry, 2004). Namely, men have been found to rate social interaction, as well as fantasy and challenge, as more important motivations for playing compared to women (Jansz, Avis, & Vosmeer, 2010; Lucas & Sherry, 2004; Olson, 2010). This may go some way to explain the observed gender variations in preferences of game genres, discussed in the next main section (see Content).

This area of research has also typically adopted a typology-based approach to model the motivational variations for playing digital games and how this may relate to demographic distinctions. A typically used model is that of Yee's (2006a) 3-factor model of online gaming motivations, which consists of social, immersion, and achievement-oriented motivational factors (Yee, Ducheneaut, & Nelson, 2012). The 3-factor model showed that male players tend to report preferring achievement-related motivations in multiplayer games compared to females, who typically prefer social factors (Yee, 2006b). However, these preferences have been established in Massively Multiplayer Online Role-Playing Games (MMORPGs), and the validity of these distinctions to other types of gaming remains unclear. Other typologies also exist, including the BrainHex (Nacke, Bateman, & Mandryk, 2014), which describes player archetypes based on personality dimensions. These player categories include Seeker, Survivor, Daredevil, Mastermind, Conqueror, Socializer, and Achiever (Nacke et al., 2014). Although this approach is useful for understanding player motivations and play characteristics, it has not yet been widely applied when exploring demographic constitutions. As such, it is difficult to establish how player demographics may vary based on player personality profiles.

Professional Gaming

In contrast to gaming for leisure, it is important to note more professional forms of gaming when considering the demographics of players. This may primarily take two forms: serious games and eSports gaming. eSports (electronic sports) are competitions via the medium of gaming. This often involves competitive team-based multiplayer gaming (e.g., *League of Legends*) whereby professional players undertake tournaments in large arenas, watched my millions of individuals worldwide. This presents an interesting case in the context of gaming, as it is most typically conceptualized as a professional sport, rather than gaming per se (Egliston, 2015; Jenny, Manning, Keiper, & Olrich, 2016), and players are usually referred to as athletes rather than gamers (Jenny et al., 2016). Thus, should eSports should be considered "gaming" at all? Further, gaming itself has such strong connotations with leisure or hobbies (e.g., dominoes, chess, tabletop board games) that it does not necessary serve a useful purpose to take professional player demographics and game classifications under the same framework as gaming for leisure. As such, it is out of the scope of the current chapter to provide this demographic breakdown for professional forms of gaming, such as eSports. The same case could also be made in respect of serious games.

To some extent, serious games can be understood as a form of professional gaming given these are typically not undertaken primarily for leisure-related reasons. In respect of serious games, one key domain relates to educational-based games, which serve the primary function of promoting learning or learning processes (e.g., motivation). As such, these are largely played by a young demographic, as part of formal education, although specific figures on this do not appear to exist in the literature. As such, it is not clear how playing games for educational purposes compares to those played purely for leisure, specifically in relation to the demographics of players. Furthermore, when considering playing games for health- or well-being-related reasons, as a second form of serious gaming, it is even more challenging to obtain a full and accurate account of who players are. That is, digital games can be used for a wide range of health or well-being concerns, including for physiotherapeutic recovery and rehabilitation, as well as for supporting mental well-being or health behaviors (e.g., Baranowski et al., 2016; Betker, Desai, Nett, Kapadia, & Szturm, 2007; Yavuzer, Senel, Atay, & Stam, 2008). In this way, the motivations for play are somewhat distinct. Specifically, in the case of health/well-being purposes, players may not be reflective of the typical gamer, given their motivations are less likely to be driven intrinsically through the love of gaming, and instead are driven by the need to fulfill health-related outcomes. However, previous research has aimed to establish the effectiveness of different persuasive strategies in games for health, based on gamer typology using BrainHex (Orji, Vassileva, & Mandryk, 2014).

Given the aforementioned diverse functions that digital games can offer, issues arise when theorizing on who players are. With this in mind, it is perhaps pertinent to simply understand players as those who play for leisure-related reasons, rather than those who may play to achieve alternative ends, such as in serious or professional forms of gaming. Thus, the remainder of the chapter focuses upon player demographics largely upon the assumption of how the remaining facets are relevant for leisure-based gaming, rather than its other functionalities.

Content (or Game Genre)

One highly cited way digital games differ is in respect of their content, and this is primarily inter-related to their specified genre. These are the most popular game genres on the commercial market:

- Action
- Action-adventure

- Adventure
- MMOs (Massively Multiplayer Online games) and MMORPGs
- Puzzle
- Racing
- Role-playing
- Simulation
- Sport
- Strategy

The content of games provides the criteria upon which they are legally classified for certain players or audiences, and a number of regulatory boards exist worldwide which determine the classification of games based on their content. For example, the United States (US) is regulated by the *Entertainment Software Rating Board* (ESRB), whereas the European Union constitution operates under the *Pan European Game Information* (PEGI) system. Additionally, there are also others, including Russia's *Russian Age Rating System* (RARS), Australia's *Australian Classification Board* (ACB), and Germany's *Unterhaltungssoftware Selbstkontrolle* (USK). These typically follow similar classification systems, although notably the ESRB is the only system which distinguishes between mature (17+ years) and adults only (18+ years), whereby all others do not have a classification stage in between teen/16+ and adult/18+. Furthermore, the ESRB is advisory, rather than restrictive, whereas other systems are stricter in respect of age parameters. The classifications of these systems are typically derived through themes such as extent of sexual content, nudity, profanity, and type of violence (graphic, gore, death, mild threat, and cartoon violence). As such, these legal classifications should provide a loose framework through which to observe player demographics in respect of age, although it is noted that these are not always strictly adhered to by players (Byron, 2008). However, on a more empirical level, it is commonly observed that there are demographic distinctions in the appeal of games in respect of their content; specifically, games that depict violent content are typically more attractive to men (Jansz, 2005; Przybylski, Ryan, & Rigby, 2009), which explains why they are typically played more by men. In addition, men have been found to prefer sports and strategy game genres compared to women (Bonanno & Kommers, 2005; Hartmann & Klimmt, 2006; Scharkow, Festl, Vogelgesang, & Quandt, 2015), where women report puzzle games as the preferred genre (Bonanno & Kommers, 2005). Similarly, other reports suggest that women dominate the player demographic for "Match 3" games (e.g., Jewel Quest) and family games, in which 69 percent of players of these genres are female. Conversely, men out-play women in genres such as tactical shooters and sports, in which only 4 percent and 2 percent, respectively, are female (Quantic Foundry, 2017). For MMOs, specifically, research shows the average player age as approximately 31 years old, with the majority being male (80%) (Griffiths, Davies, & Chappell, 2003, 2004; Williams, Yee, & Caplan, 2008; Yee, 2006). These findings are more or less consistent when exploring the gender proportionality for specific types of MMOs, e.g., *League of Legends* and *Chevaliers' Romance 3* players are 95.9 percent male ($N = 18,627$) and 75 percent male ($N = 18,819$), respectively (Kahn et al., 2015). However, these reports do not necessarily mean that these trends are relevant in all cases. There are millions of women who enjoy playing shooting games and many men who do not enjoy these, and therefore, these findings should not be taken as evidence to exclude players based on gender.

The complexity and diversity of games available on the commercial market makes it challenging to gain full reports of all player demographics, and to track any changes in demographics over time. However, it is noteworthy that, in general, the development of games which are compatible with mobile devices, as well as other "more accessible" games, has been influential in changing the demographics of players, in which a broader age and gender representation is evident.

Platform

The advancement in games technology means that games can be played on a range of different platforms (and by association, different contexts). Platforms can include PCs, mobile devices, handhelds, and consoles, which largely determine the type of game played. Platform itself is a facet which often shows key demographic differences. Recent evidence shows that around 40 percent of US adults own a game console, e.g., *Xbox* or *PlayStation* (Pew Research Center, 2015b), with 42 percent of these being female. However, portable gaming devices, e.g., *PlayStation Portable* (PSP), are less popular, with only 14 percent of adults reporting owning one, of which there are equal rates between men and women (Pew Research Center, 2015b). However, it has been found that women are significantly more likely to play on mobile devices compared to men (Bonanno & Kommers, 2005). Additionally, the development of consoles such as the *Nintendo Wii* and *Microsoft Kinect* have promoted a family-friendly play environment, and thus encouraged play from a much wider age demographic and more equal gender balance (Chambers, 2012). Indeed, commentary suggests that Wii-themed parties have encouraged friends and family to join together for social play (Foster, 2010). It is also important to recognize that individuals may own more than one gaming device, and it is not necessarily uncommon for households to own a gaming device as well as a dedicated game console (ESA, 2016). Within the platform category, it would be intriguing to understand the demographic breakdown of these different uses/formats, and whether there is gender disparity in the ownership of multiple gaming platforms, or whether this is relatively equivalent across demographic groups.

Context

Finally, digital gaming can vary greatly by context. As mentioned previously, the advance of games technology and Internet connectivity are key influential factors that allow digital games to be played in the immediate presence of others (e.g., offline multiplayer, arcade), or online (e.g., solo play, online multiplayer, social networking games).

Context has been the driver for much change in the demographic representation of players, and these platforms afford many more social opportunities than traditional games technology may have previously, and as such, these social openings are attractive to a wider demographic. Specifically, this is represented by the finding that women are often attracted to games due to social-related factors (Yee, 2006), which may explain why inherently social platforms such as the *Nintendo Wii* consists of a higher proportion of female players compared to other platforms. Additionally, Jansz & Martens (2005) noted the importance of social context in gaming, and its variations are attributed to demographic distinctions of players. Further, when exploring online games, additional distinctions appear. Specifically, findings reveal age distinctions across the three types of online game (first person shooter, real-time strategy, and role-playing), and Ghuman & Griffiths (2012) highlight that simply studying online games is not a sufficiently narrow category from which to obtain demographic data. Namely, players of role-playing games (RPGs) have been found to be significantly older than real-time strategy (RTS) players, and RTS games are played by females significantly more than RPGs. Clearly, context is an important facet which reveals some demographic differences, and can, in some cases, underpin whether someone plays or not. Although the aforementioned facets may be more deterministic of playing behavior and the associated demographics, context remains an important aspect of gaming which should not be ignored when theorizing on its characteristics.

Methods of Collecting Demographic Data

Demographical data is typically garnered in one of two ways: through large-scale surveys requesting self-report data, or through commercial purchasing figures. Both methods have their shortcomings. Firstly, large-scale surveys, such as that distributed annually by the ESA, report about gaming and who gamers are in very generic terms (e.g., "There are an average of 1.7 gamers in each game-playing US household"). As previously indicated, this statement has shortcomings in lack of clarity about how people respond to this question; i.e., gamer is a specific form of identity, not a playing behavior, and as such, it is not clear whether the ESA report is reporting on players, or just a sub-sample of those who self-identify as gamers. Likewise, demographics on gender and age of game players as presented by ESA (2016), for example, is equally non-conclusive in this regard; the finding that "59% of game players are male" does not provide any degree of specificity on what type or function of games are referred to here. It is also unclear if this figure is simply referring to games which are primarily serving a leisure function, or those which are educational or health-promoting in nature. As previously discussed, there may be diversity in the demographics of players as a product of the function that games may be serving. As a practical recommendation, it would be beneficial for survey developers to include additional questions within their surveys to garner data on functional usage and explore demographic correlates of these, rather than assuming demographics are equivalent for all types of gaming uses.

In respect of commercial purchasing figures, it is not always possible to determine an overall representation of playing behavior based on who buys games. The ESA (2016) reports that 60 percent of men buy games, and those who are frequent game purchasers are 38 years old. Arguably, it is likely that other people may play the games purchased by these individuals, which raises the question on the utility of purchasing behavior as a means through which to obtain demographic gaming data. Similarly, the availability of online purchasing raises further challenges when establishing player demographics based on buying behavior. There is no specific guarantee that a buyer's online account includes relevant (or even accurate) demographic details. Therefore, questioning the use of purchasing statistics as a useful metric for understanding player demographics.

Conclusion

In summary, collecting data on player demographics is an increasingly challenging task, given the growing provision of games that are available both on the commercial market as well as those available for supporting other functions (professional and serious gaming). Additionally, mobile games and apps that are widely accessible present further issues when monitoring demographic data of players. Arguably, games are played by the majority of the population in some form or other, but the demographic distinctions become more apparent when breaking down the analysis to different facets of games, including function, content, platform, and context. This chapter provides an account of these variations and presents a case for a more nuanced approach to better understand who players are in respect of these distinctions. Data on player demographics appears to typically assume it is relevant in respect of games for leisure, but arguably, responses may be reflective of a wider rhetoric of play functionalities. This somewhat confounds our understanding of player demographics and does not proffer a practically useful set of data. Furthermore, we should remain cautious of using the term "gamer" for all those who report playing games, which presents a rather loaded assumption that gaming behavior equates to identity expression. This is not always the case, and so the term "player" is recommended as a more accurate term to avoid conflating gamer identity into the equation where, in many cases, this is not relevant.

It is recommended that additional data is garnered when collecting demographic data, in respect of these varying facets, which may help to establish a more nuanced account of player demographics (see Appendix 1 for recommended items). Additionally, demographic figures would be best approached by applying the conceptual framework proffered within this chapter (Figure 1) which would better establish gaming functionality as well as playing behaviors, and how there are likely to be demographic distinctions across these quadrants. As such, demographic data can be made more meaningful across the broad spectrum of games on offer in respect of leisure versus professional domains, which has not yet been established in the available data. This conceptual framework may also be pragmatically useful for understanding psychological affordances associated with play across these domains, which is also scant in the existing empirical literature.

APPENDIX 1

RECOMMENDED ADDITIONAL QUESTIONS FOR OBTAINING PLAYER DEMOGRAPHICS

1. Do you play digital games (i.e., any kind of game which is accessed electronically including mobile or social networking games)?

   Yes   No

2. Would you consider yourself to be a "gamer" (i.e., is this part of how you would describe yourself to others)?

   Yes   No   Not sure

3. Please indicate your main reason for gaming

   Leisure
   Work/Profession
   Education
   Physical health or well-being
   Mental well-being
   Other
   None of these

4. Which best describes your playing behavior?

   Hardcore gaming
   Casual gaming
   Other
   Not sure

5. How would you typically play games?

   On a PC.
   On a TV-based console with "traditional" gamepad (e.g., Xbox, PS4).
   On a TV-based console with "user-friendly" controller or body movement function (e.g., Wii, Kinect).
   On a mobile device (e.g., smartphone, tablet).
   On a handheld device (e.g., PSP).
   Other

6. Which of the following best describes your preferred method of playing?

   Solo offline (no connections to others).
   Solo online (solo play but performance is related to others through leaderboards, etc.).
   Multiplayer online.
   Multiplayer offline.

Other
None

7. Which of the following is your preferred genre of game?

Action
Action-adventure
Adventure
MMORPGs
Puzzle
Racing
Role-playing
Side-scroller
Simulation
Sport
Strategy
Other

References

Baranowski, T., Blumberg, F., Buday, R., DeSmet, A., Fiellin, L. E., Green, C. S., Kato, P.,...Young, K. (2016). Games for health for children—current status and needed research. *Games for Health Journal*, *5*(1), 1–12.

Betker, A. L., Desai, A., Nett, C., Kapadia, N., & Szturm, T. (2007). Game-based exercises for dynamic short-sitting balance rehabilitation of people with chronic spinal cord and traumatic brain injuries. *Physical Therapy*, *87*(10), 1389–1398.

Bonanno, P., & Kommers, P. A. M. (2005). Gender differences and styles in the use of digital games, *Educational Psychology*, *25*(1), 13–41. doi: 10.1080/0144341042000294877

Byron, T. (2008). Safer Children in a Digital World: The Report of the Byron Review. Retrieved July 6, 2017, from http://webarchive.nationalarchives.gov.uk/20101101221617/http://publications.education.gov.uk/eOrderingDownload/DCSF-00334-2008.pdf

Chambers, D. (2012). Wii play as a family: The rise in family-centred video gaming. *Leisure Studies*, *31*(1), 69–82.

Chou, C., & Tsai, M.-J. (2007). Gender differences in Taiwan high school students' computer game playing. *Computers in Human Behavior*, *23*, 812–824.

Colwell, J. (2007). Needs met through computer game play among adolescents. *Personality and Individual Differences*, *43*, 2072–2082.

De Grove, F., Courtois, C., & Van Looy, J. (2015). How to be a gamer! Exploring personal and social indicators of gamer identity. *Journal of Computer-Mediated Communication*, *20*(3), 346–361. doi: 10.1111/jcc4.12114

Ducheneaut, N., Yee, N., Nickell, E., & Moore, R. J. (2006, April). *"Alone together?" Exploring the social dynamics of massively multiplayer online games*. Proceedings of the 2006 Conference on Human Factors in Computing Systems, CHI 2006, Montréal, Québec, Canada, 22–27 April 2006.

Egliston, B. (2015). *Playing across media: Exploring transtextuality in competitive games and eSports*. Proceedings of DiGRA 2015: Diversity of play: Games, cultures, identities. Retrieved July 26, 2017, from http://www.digra.org/wp-content/uploads/digital-library/122_Egliston_Playing-Across-Media.pdf

Eklund, L. (2016). Who are the casual gamers? Gender tropes and tokenism in game culture. In T. Leaver & M. Willson (Eds.), *Social, casual and mobile games: The changing gaming landscape* (pp. 15–29). London: Bloomsbury Academic.

ESA (2015). Essential Facts about the computer and video game industry. Entertainment Software Industry. Retrieved January 25, 2017, from http://www.theesa.com/wp-content/uploads/2015/04/ESA-Essential-Facts-2015.pdf

ESA (2016). Essential Facts about the computer and video game industry: 2016 Sales, Demographic and Usage Data. Retrieved June 14, 2017, from http://essentialfacts.theesa.com/Essential-Facts-2016.pdf

Foster, D. (2010). Wii're here for a good time: The sneaky rhetoric of Wii-themed parties. *The Journal of American Culture, 33*(1), 30–39.

Ghuman, D., & Griffiths, M. D. (2012). A cross-genre study of online gaming: Player demographics, motivation for play, and social interactions among players. *International Journal of Cyber Behavior, Psychology and Learning, 2*(1), 13–29.

Granic, I., Lobel, A., & Engels, R. C. M. E. (2014). The benefits of playing video games. *American Psychologist, 69*(1), 66–78. doi: 10.1037/a0034857

Griffiths, M., Davies, M. N., & Chappell, D. (2003). Breaking the stereotype: The case of online gaming. *Cyberpsychology & Behavior, 6*(1), 81–91.

Griffiths, M., D., Davies, M. N., & Chappell, D. (2004a). Demographic factors and playing variables in online computer gaming. *Cyberpsychology and Behavior, 7*(4), 479–487. doi: 10.1089/cpb.2004.7.479

Griffiths, M. D., Davies, M. N. O., & Chappell, D. (2004b). Online computer gaming: A comparison of adolescents and adult gamers. *Adolescence, 27*, 87–96.

Grooten, J. & Kowert, R. (2015). Going Beyond the Game: Development of Gamer Identities Within Societal Discourse and Virtual Spaces. *Loading…The Journal of the Canadian Game Studies Association, 9*(14), 70–87.

Hartmann, T., & Klimmt, C. (2006). Gender and computer games: Exploring females' dislikes. *Journal of Computer-Mediated Communication, 11*(4), 910–931. doi: 10.1111/j.1083-6101.2006.00301.x

Information Solutions Group (2010). *PopCap Social Gaming Research 2010*. Retrieved October 4, 2017, from https://www.slideshare.net/duckofdoom/social-gaming-research-2010

Jansz, J. (2005). The emotional appeal of violent video games for adolescent males. *Communication Theory, 15*(3), 219–241. doi: 10.1111/j.1468-2885-2005-tb00334.x

Jansz, J., Avis, C., & Vosmeer, M. (2010). Playing the Sims2: An exploration of gender differences in players' motivations and patterns of play. *New Media & Society, 12*(2), 235–251.

Jansz, J. & Martens, L. (2005). Gaming at a LAN event: the social context of playing video games. *New Media and Society, 7*, 333–355.

Jenny, S. E., Manning, R. D., Keiper, M. C., & Olrich, T. W. (2016). Virtual(ly) athletes: Where eSports fit within the definition of "sport." *Quest, 69*(1), 1–18.

Juul, J. (2010). *A Casual Revolution: Reinvesting video games and their players*. Cambridge: MIT Press.

Kahn, A. S., Shen, C., Lu, L., Ratan, R. A., Coary, S., Hou, J., Meng, J.,…Williams, D. (2015). The Trojan player typology: A cross-genre, cross-cultural, behaviorally validated scale of video game play motivations. *Computers in Human Behavior, 49*, 354–361. doi: 10.1016/j.chb.2015.03.018

Katz, M. L., & Shapiro, C. (1985). Network externalities, competition, and compatibility. *American Economic Review, 75*(3), 424–440.

Katz, M. L., & Shapiro, C. (1994). Systems competition and network effects. *The Journal of Economic Perspectives, 8*(2), 93–115.

Kuittnen, J., Kultima, A., Niemela, J., & Paavilainen, J. (2007, November). Casual games discussion. Proceedings of 2007 Conference on Future Play (pp. 105–112). 14–17 November, Toronto, Canada. New York: ACM.

Kultima, A. (2009). Casual game design values. In *Proceedings of the 13th Annual International MindTrek Conference: Everyday Life in the Ubiquitous Era* (pp. 58–65). 30 September–2 October, Tampere, Finland. New York: ACM. doi: 10.1145/1621841.1621854

Leaver, T. & Willson, M. (2016). *Social, casual and mobile games: The changing gaming landscape*. London: Bloomsbury Academic.

Lucas, K., & Sherry, J. L. (2004). Sex differences in video game play: A communication-based explanation. *Communication Research*, 31(5), 499–523.

Mason, M. (2013). Demographic breakdown of casual, mid-core and hard-core mobile gamers. *M Dev*. Accessed November 2, 2016, from http://developers.magmic.com/demographic-breakdown-casual-mid-core-hard-core-mobile-gamers/#prettyPhoto

Nacke, L. E., Bateman, C., & Mandryk, R. L. (2014). BrainHex: A neurobiological gamer typology survey. *Entertainment Computing*, 5(1), 55–62.

Olson, C. K. (2010). Children's motivations for video game play in the context of normal development. *Review of General Psychology*, 14(2), 180–187.

Orji, R., Vassileva, J., & Mandryk, R. L. (2014). Modeling the efficacy of persuasive strategies for different gamer types in serious games for health. *User Modeling and User-Adapted Interaction*, 24, 453. doi: 10.1007/s11257-014-9149-8

Pew Research Center (2015a). *Gaming and Gamers*. PewResearch Center: Internet, Science and Tech. Retrieved February 23, 2017, from http://www.pewinternet.org/2015/12/15/gaming-and-gamers/

Pew Research Center (2015b). The demographics of device ownership. Retrieved July 31, 2017, from http://www.pewinternet.org/2015/10/29/the-demographics-of-device-ownership/

Przybylski, A. K., Ryan, R. M., & Rigby, C. S. (2009). The motivating role of violence in video games. *Personality and Social Psychology Bulletin*, 35, 243–259. doi: 10.1177/0146167208327721

Quantic Foundry (2017). *Beyond 50/50: Breaking down the percentage of female gamers by genre*. Retrieved February 7, 2017, from http://quanticfoundry.com/2017/01/19/female-gamers-by-genre/

Scharkow, M., Festl, R., Vogelgesang, J., & Quandt, T. (2015). Beyond the core gamer: Genre preferences and gratification in computer games. *Computers in Human Behavior*, 44, 293–298. doi: 10.1016/j.chb.2014.11.020

Williams, D., Yee, N., & Caplan, S. E. (2008). Who plays, how much and why? Debunking the stereotypical gamer profile. *Journal of Computer-mediated Communication*, 13(4), 993–1018. doi: 10.1111/j.1083 6101.2008.00428.x

Yavuzer, G., Senel, A., Atay, M. B., & Stam, H. J. (2008). "PlayStation eyetoy games" improve upper extremity-related motor functioning in subacute stroke: A randomised controlled clinical trial. *European Journal of Physical and Rehabilitation Medicine*, 44(3), 237–244.

Yee, N. (2006a). Motivations for play in online games. *Cyberpsychology and Behavior*, 9(6), 772–775.

Yee, N. (2006b). The demographics, motivations and derived experiences of users of massively-multiuser online graphical environments. *PRESENCE: Teleoperators and Virtual Environments*, 15, 309–329.

Yee, N., Ducheneaut, N., & Nelson, L. (2012, May). Online Gaming Motivations Scale: Development and Validation. Proceedings of the ACM International Conference on Human Factors in Computing Systems (pp. 2803–2806). 5–10 May, Austin, TX. New York: ACM.

PART VIII

CYBERCRIME AND CYBERSECURITY

CHAPTER 31

THE RISE OF CYBERCRIME

GRAINNE H. KIRWAN

WHAT IS CYBERCRIME?

DESPITE an implicit understanding by many of what cybercrime is, many researchers have lamented the difficulty in explicitly defining cybercrime (see, for example, Gordon & Ford, 2006). This difficulty has extended to legal settings and governance, with suggestions that the Council of Europe's Convention on Cybercrime has a "loose definition of cybercrime," covering many different types of malicious activities online (Hui, Kim, & Wang, 2017). This chapter uses Nurse's (this volume) definition of cybercrime, which is "any crime (traditional or new) that can be conducted or enabled through, or using, digital technologies."

While it is difficult to know for certain how much cybercrime exists, it can be certain that the overall trend is upwards, at least based on a starting point of zero only a few decades ago. Unlike most types of crime, it is possible to say with certainty that before the first networked computers were connected in the early days of the ARPANET (the Advanced Research Projects Agency Network, established in 1969), Internet-based crime did not exist. Nevertheless, it is still difficult to quantify exactly how much cybercrime actually exists. The reasons for this are explored in greater detail later in this chapter, but a key problem is that there is very rarely a crime classification of "cybercrime" or "Internet crime." Frequently, recorded crime statistics include cybercrimes under a variety of different headings; for example, it is unclear how many of the offenses listed under "Abuse of children through prostitution or pornography," as classified in the Recorded Crime Statistics for England and Wales, occurred in online or offline environments (UK Home Office, 2016). Even when specific information regarding cybercrime does exist, this data frequently lacks longitudinal comparisons, and is often focused on specific types of cybercrime. For example, Klahr and colleagues (2017) provide important and detailed information regarding the incidence of cybersecurity breaches and attacks among businesses, identifying that 46 percent of UK businesses had experienced such a breach or attack in the previous twelve months, and that this was more common among large firms and certain sectors, such as information, communications, and utilities.

As well as those texts considering cybercrime and cybersecurity from a technological perspective, many also review the problem from a sociological/criminological (e.g., Clough, 2015; Gillespie, 2016; Holt, Bossler, & Seigfried-Spellar, 2015; Jewkes, 2007; Jewkes & Yar, 2010; Wall, 2001, 2007; Wall & Williams, 2014; Yar, 2013a) or psychological (e.g., Kirwan, 2016; Kirwan & Power, 2012, 2013) perspective.

Types of Cybercrime

As with offline crime, there are many different types of cybercrime. Short descriptions of some of the main categories of cybercrime are presented below (these have been kept concise in the interests of brevity, but further information and psychological research on most of these is presented in Kirwan & Power, 2013).

Online Black Markets

As with offline black markets, these sell goods and services which are difficult or illegal to obtain through traditional methods. Frequently found on the "Dark Net" (an online network which uses advanced security systems to increase anonymity), these have been particularly noted for sales of drugs, malware, and weapons. Several of these online black markets have been shut down by law enforcement in recent years, most famously including "The Silk Road" (BBC News, 2013), "AlphaBay", and "Hansa" (Baraniuk, 2017). Sales conducted via online black markets frequently use cryptocurrencies such as Bitcoin, Ripple, or ZCash.

Child Pornography/Child Exploitation Material (CEM)/Child Abuse Material (CAM)

Researchers, practitioners, and law enforcement opinions vary on the use of terms to describe sexual images of children, with many suggesting that "Child Pornography" is misleading as the term "pornography" implies a consensual act to some people. Regardless, this and the terms "Child Exploitation Material" (CEM) and "Child Abuse Material" (CAM) are widely used in the academic literature. Early dissemination of such material online was limited to still photographs, due to bandwidth capacity. More recently the sharing of videos, and the commissioning of live abuse using webcams, has become more common.

Online Child Predators

The grooming of children for sexual acts using online communication methods is a common fear of parents and caregivers. Children and adolescents may be approached via a range of social media and gaming platforms, including platforms where no record of the communication is kept (such as voice communications during online gaming).

Malware

Any software developed to have malicious impact can be termed "malware." However, there are many subtypes of malware, with varying motives and approaches. Depending on the techniques employed, malware may be given different nomenclature, such as virus, worm, Trojan, logic bomb, and others. Spyware is a specific type of malware which attempts to monitor the user's actions online, thus gaining information such as passwords, bank details, and other data. Recent years have seen an increase in "ransomware," a type of malware which encrypts users' files, and then informs the user that in order to have their files returned to them, they must pay a ransom. As with black markets, ransomware often uses cryptocurrencies for payments. A high-profile ransomware attack was the "WannaCry" infection, which affected computers globally in May 2017 (BBC News, 2017).

Malicious Hacking

Often the term "hacker" is used to describe cybercriminals who engage in unlawful infringements of computer systems, but in truth, not all hackers are cybercriminals, with many focusing on ways of improving technology without illegal activity. However, there are of course, criminal hackers, who infiltrate, damage, and destroy. Various terms have been used to describe sub-types of hackers, including "ethical hackers," who are employed or contracted by organizations to identify vulnerabilities in their systems before malicious (or "black-hat" hackers) do. "White-hat" hackers may or may not be involved in criminal activity, but if they are, it is done without malicious intent (for example, they might be trying to identify similar bugs as ethical hackers do and may advise the organization of these bugs rather than exploit them directly).

Identity Theft

Some of the most desirable content online is that which can be used to conduct identity theft. This includes bank details, credit card details, social security numbers, passwords, and other personally identifiable information. This information is often to be found on the online black markets, but the data itself might be gathered through a variety of means, including offline methods (such as rigged ATM or credit card machines), or online methods (such as a hacked database). It is also possible to collect this information using techniques such as "phishing"—where the potential victim receives an email purporting to be from an authoritative agency (such as a bank, online marketplace, or revenue commissioners) requiring them to click on a link within the email to log in to their account in order to complete a task. The task is often presented with a sense of urgency (e.g., suggesting that a suspected intrusion into their account has taken place), so the victim is motivated to act immediately, and complete the log-in form on the destination page. This provides the criminal with the victim's data, which can then be exploited directly, or sold on to another offender.

Fraud

There are many types of fraud online, disseminated through a variety of means. One of the most common is "Advance Fee Fraud," where the potential victim receives an email indicating that they may be eligible for a large amount of cash, frequently through a foreign inheritance. The fraud occurs as the victim is persuaded into sending some money upfront, often portrayed as an administrative charge. The victim may then be enticed into sending more and more money, while never seeing the promised return. While Advance Fee Fraud is probably the most famous, and the type that most people are likely to be familiar with (as the emails are sent in bulk), there are many other types of online fraud, including the sale of inert or potentially harmful substances which are portrayed as pharmaceutical agents (pharma-fraud), and the online romance scam, where a fraudster utilizes online dating platforms to develop intimacy with potential victims who are later persuaded to send them money to help them in "emergencies" (see, for example, Nurse, this volume; Whitty & Buchanan, 2016).

Copyright Infringement/Digital Piracy

This common type of offending is perpetrated by users who illegally download or stream movies, television programs, music, books, software, and other content. It is likely that this is the cybercrime which people are most likely to commit, rather than experience as a victim.

Cyberbullying

As with offline bullying, cyberbullying is not always criminal in nature. Unless there is a threat of physical harm, or other extreme behavior, it is generally viewed as malicious, but not criminal. In some cases, the perpetrator may not actually intend their actions maliciously, but may believe that the interaction is normal for their peer group. Of course, this does not negate the very harmful effects that cyberbullying can have on those who endure it.

Cyberstalking

Similar to cyberbullying, cyberstalking is not necessarily criminal, nor is there always malicious intent. Again, if there is a threat of physical harm it may be classifiable as a criminal action but repeated undesired messaging on social media is not an offense in itself. As with cyberbullying, the negative impact on the victim can be immense, even if no criminal activity technically takes place.

Cyberharassment

This may form part of cyberbullying or cyberstalking but may also be considered as a separate behavior, depending in particular on the longevity of the interaction and the pre-existing relationship between the perpetrator and victim. Similar to both cyberbullying and cyberstalking, the existence of criminality depends on the specific actions which form the harassment.

Hate Speech

While cyberbullying, cyberharassment, and cyberstalking are typically targeted at a single individual or a small group of related individuals, hate speech may be considerably broader, targeted at entire subgroups of the population (or individuals who are representative of that subgroup). Jurisdiction and the nature of the hate speech can determine the criminality or lack thereof of this behavior. For example, some countries have very strict rules regarding the dissemination of hate speech against certain ethnicities, subcultures, or other groups, while other jurisdictions carefully protect their citizens' rights to free speech, even if that speech is hateful in nature.

Cyberterrorism

There is considerable debate in the academic literature regarding the appropriate definition of the term "cyberterrorism," with many differentiating between the use of technology to carry out an attack which causes terror in a group, and other use of technology by terrorists (see, for example, Conway, 2011; Gordon & Ford, 2002). Many argue that terrorist use of the Internet (e.g., to recruit new members, distribute propaganda, radicalize individuals and groups, plan attacks, buy supplies, and train individuals) should not be defined as cyberterrorism (e.g., Conway, 2011; Denning, 2007). Denning (2007) also suggests that other types of online activity conducted by terrorists, such as website defacements or Distributed Denial of Service (DoS) attacks on websites (where a network of computers is used to make so many requests of a website that it cannot manage the traffic and shuts down), should not necessarily be classified as cyberterrorism. According to such classification systems, only an attack conducted using technology which causes fear or terror in people would be classified as cyberterrorism. This might include remote access or destruction of critical systems, such as safety mechanisms for a nuclear power plant, or taking control of potentially dangerous systems such as air traffic control mechanisms or missile defense technologies.

TYPOLOGIES OF CYBERCRIME

With so many different types of cybercrime in existence, it is understandable that various researchers have attempted to develop typologies of cybercrime in order to classify the mechanisms in place. One of the earliest of these was proposed by David Wall in 2001, who suggested that there were four main types of online harmful activities. The first of these he labeled "(cyber)-trespass," to include hacking activities where the cybercriminal enters computer systems or spaces where they are not supposed to. This category would also include espionage activities online. Wall labeled the second type as "(cyber)-deceptions/thefts," to include offenses such as identity theft and fraud, but also copyright infringement and counterfeit goods. The third category identified by Wall is "(cyber)-pornography/obscenity," which includes both legal and illegal behaviors relating to the generation and distribution of sexually explicit material online. The final category defined by Wall in 2001 was "(cyber)-violence," to include activities such as cyberstalking and hate speech.

Wall (2007) later suggested a different typology with three "criminologies" of cybercrime. The first, "computer integrity crimes," are those which attack network security, including "...hacking and cracking, vandalism, spying, denial of service, the planting and use of viruses and Trojans" (p. 49), thus including mostly hacking and malware. The second was "computer-assisted (or related) crimes," which includes identity theft, phishing, and fraud. The final category was "computer-content crimes," which considers illegal content online, such as hate crime and pornographic materials.

Gordon and Ford (2006) differentiated between "Type I" and "Type II" cybercrime. They indicated that Type I cybercrime is mostly technological in form, characterized by offenses like malware, phishing, hacking, identity theft, and fraud. Type II cybercrime, on the other hand, has a stronger human element, including "cyberstalking and harassment, child predation, extortion, blackmail, stock market manipulation, complex corporate espionage, and planning or carrying out terrorist activities" (pp. 13–14). Gordon and Ford also indicated that Type I cybercrime would usually be a single event, with Type II cybercrime frequently involving repeated events.

Furnell (2001; 2002) suggested another typology that distinguishes between "computer-assisted crimes" (crimes which have an offline equivalent, but can be conducted online, such as fraud and copyright infringement) and "computer-focused crimes" (crimes which have no offline equivalent, and have emerged as technology emerges, such as hacking and malware). A common term used to describe computer-assisted crimes is "old wine in new bottles" (e.g., Grabosky, 2001), i.e., the offense has existed for a long time, but the method of delivery is new. These offenses have historically been easier to categorize and even prosecute—existing laws made it easier for offenders to be charged (once apprehended, of course), and their parallels to offline equivalents gave judicial systems guidance on appropriate penalties to apply. This was less clear for computer-focused crimes, where judicial systems sometimes struggled on how to pursue criminal charges, as the activities were obviously harmful but were not covered under existing legal frameworks. These difficulties can be considered in light of the social construction of crime—societies (and often powerful people within them) determine what is and is not criminal, and this can change over time and across cultural boundaries. For example, at various stages in history slavery was legal in the United States of America, while at other stages the sale and distribution of alcohol was illegal. Similarly, new offense categories had to be developed as motor vehicles were invented, and eventually became widespread. The development of information technologies has resulted in a requirement to create new laws (and adapt existing ones) so that very disruptive online behavior is reflected in society's conceptualization of offending. The implications of this can be seen in historic cybercrime cases. For example, the Filipino students who developed the "ILOVEYOU" or "Lovebug" malware which infected computers in May 2000 were not prosecuted, as the Philippines did not have computer misuse laws at that time (Ward, 2017). Many jurisdictions have amended or created laws to cover such offenses. For example, former student Paras Jha, who plead guilty in a US federal court to, among other related cyber-crimes, helping to create the "Mirai" virus in 2016, faces up to ten years in prison and a fine of USD 250,000 (Heyboer & Sherman, 2017).

Kirwan and Power (2013) provide a final example of cybercrime typology, breaking it down into three types. As well as "Internet-enabled offenses" (similar to Furnell's "computer-assisted crimes") and "Internet-specific offenses" (similar to Furnell's "computer-focused crimes"), they propose a third category—"crimes against the virtual person." This category includes actions against virtual representations of the user online which are not criminal in themselves, but which are conducted against the will of the user, and would be considered criminal should they occur offline (see Kirwan, 2009, for descriptions of such offenses, and the effects that they can have on their victims). This is admittedly a difficult category to clearly define, as many online games include such activities as part of normal gameplay (such as the murder or assault of characters, which is obviously against the desires of the user playing that character). Nevertheless, it is worth considering how such situations should be defined when it is outside of the normal gameplay for the virtual world (for example, a sexual assault conducted on an individual in an online social virtual world).

QUANTIFYING CYBERCRIME

Despite the undeniable increase in cybercrime over the past few decades, it is still extremely difficult to be certain of the actual amount of cybercrime that exists. This is due to a phenomenon noted across criminology called the "dark figure of crime" (not to be confused with the "Dark Net," as the "dark figure" applies to all types of crime, both online and offline). The "dark figure" of crime is the difference between the amount of crime that is recorded in official statistics (such as police reports), and the actual amount of crime that occurs. While there is no exact "dark figure" for any type of crime, it is still possible to estimate the relative sizes of dark figures for each type of crime, based on other available evidence, such as victimization reports. For example, it is suspected that there is a very small dark figure for car theft, as almost everyone has insurance for this because of legal requirements, and the presentation of a police report detailing the theft is normally a requirement to claim this insurance. A much larger dark figure is predicted for vandalism, as many victims may decide that it is not worth the hassle of reporting such a crime. A dark figure of crime may emerge through a variety of factors, which can broadly be categorized into those which were not reported to the police, and those which were not officially recorded by the police.

There are many reasons why a victim may not report a cybercrime to the police (or to other authorities). Part of this may be due to a lack of awareness that a crime has taken place—should a very adept hacker infiltrate the system of an organization, they may cover their tracks sufficiently well so that the organization may never know of the attack. A child who has been the victim of an assault to produce CEM may not know that what they have experienced was a crime or may not have the opportunity to tell anyone. In other cases, a victim may be aware of the cybercrime but may choose not to report it. For example, an organization may have identified a system breach but decide to manage the situation without enlisting the aid of the police as they may fear negative publicity. The relationship between the victim and the police may also affect the likelihood of reporting a cybercriminal incident—the victim may not believe that the police can (or will) do much to help them, and so reporting the crime may be more trouble than it is worth. Finally, some victims may not report the crime as they fear that by doing so they will be identified as having engaged in illegal activity themselves (for example, an individual who illegally downloaded movies from the Internet who later discovers that, via the download, they inadvertently also installed a virus onto their computer).

As well as factors which influence whether or not a cybercrime is reported, it is also possible that an incident which has been reported to the authorities never appears in an official record of crimes. This might occur due to human error on the part of the relevant authority but can also be due to other reasons. For example, a victim of cyber-harassment might report their experiences to the police, but the exact nature of the harassment may mean that it does not fit the criteria of the law, and as such is not technically a criminal event and cannot be recorded as such. Another possibility is that police without specialist training may not be sure of what to do when a cybercrime of this kind is reported, and without a clear plan of investigation, might be tempted to avoid recording the offense completely.

Aside from the problems noted arising from the dark figure of cybercrime, there are other difficulties in determining if the estimates of online crime rates are accurate. For example, there is some debate over the estimates of levels of copyright infringement. One method of determining the cost of illegal downloading has been to estimate the cost in terms of sales lost, presuming that all of those who download would have paid for the content if it had not been available for free. This is not necessarily true, as much downloaded content might not have been sufficiently interesting to the downloader to pay for it, but they downloaded it simply because it was there, and free (and may never actually consume the content at all!). So, while the copyright holder might view each download as a lost sale of a cinema ticket/album/book/DVD, it is very unlikely that all of these sales would have occurred. In other cases, the downloader might have already paid for access to the content via a different means (such as a cable television subscription) but elected to also download the content so that they could use it on a different device (such as viewing it on their laptop if they were traveling away from home). Finally, a single download might appear only once on the records of torrenting websites or the records of an Internet Service Provider (ISP) but might result in many more copies being circulated via offline means such as USB drives. Similar problems in estimates can plague many of the other types of cybercrime described, making this a very difficult problem to quantify.

A further question regarding the rise in cybercrime relates to whether these are new offenses that arose due to the technology, or if at least some are crimes which would have occurred offline and have simply been displaced to online methods. For example, might those who now perpetrate pharmafraud online have displaced their offending to an online context rather than an offline one (there certainly seems to have been a reduction in traveling snake oil salespeople in recent years!). Of course, the potential range and extent of online pharmafraud is far larger than offline equivalents, and it is much easier to manage, so it is possible that some potential offenders who may not have had the means to engage in such offending offline might be drawn to the online equivalent. Again, similar comparisons can be made to many of the Internet-enabled crimes. Internet-specific crimes, on the other hand, came into existence with the relevant technologies, and so it can be more difficult to determine if these are directly the result of displacement of other criminal activities. Nevertheless, many cyber-dependent crimes are conducted with motives similar to offline crimes (for example, use of malware to steal credit card details), and so the displacement argument may still hold for some of these offenses.

A final consideration is whether or not the online nature of cybercrime results in an individual who would not usually commit crime becoming attracted to criminal activity. There are current arguments that violent video games can result in decreased self-control and increased cheating in offline tasks (see, for example, Gabbiadini, Riva, Andrighetto, Volpato, & Bushman, 2014), and the UK National Crime Agency noted in

2017 that some young people may progress to criminal hacking forums from games cheat websites and game modification forums. However, it has yet to be empirically determined if such actions are actually a contributing factor leading to criminal activity online, and the validity of these assertions needs to be tested via peer-reviewed empirical research. It could be argued that almost everyone has engaged in some form of minor criminal act at some stage, be it the taking of office supplies for personal use, the illegal downloading of media, or even minor theft, without going on to more serious offending. It should also be remembered that a relatively high proportion of adolescents are involved in some form of juvenile offending (for example, Loeber and colleagues (2015) found over 27 percent of Caucasian males and over 61 percent of African American males faced charges for delinquency between ten and twenty-one years of age). However, adolescents who offend as juveniles rarely persist into adulthood, and their activities are frequently limited to relatively minor offenses, such as property crimes. However, that is not to say that no users are attracted to criminal behavior online when they would not engage in such offending offline. This may be particularly so for online terrorist activity. An individual might not be willing to move to a foreign country, or to risk physical harm to themselves, in order to pursue their identified cause, but they might be willing to aid from afar, writing code which could be used as part of a malware attack, or contributing to the radicalization of new members via online communication. Aside from the physical aspects, the online terrorist may be able to psychologically distance themselves from their actions—the anonymity and invisibility involved may result in a sense of disengagement from the consequences of their actions, or they may more easily be able to employ a neutralization (a form of justification for their actions, as proposed by Sykes and Matza, 1957) if their contribution to the cause feels less tangible.

PREVENTING CYBERCRIME

Despite the increase in risk from cybercrime, there are still many attempts to both protect victims and potential victims, and to deter offenders and potential offenders. Clarke and Felson (1993) proposed "Routine Activity Theory," which indicates that a crime will take place whenever a motivated offender encounters a suitable target when guardians are absent. This provides a very useful approach to preventing crime in general, and cybercrime in particular. To prevent cybercrime, it is necessary to remove either the offender or target, or to introduce the presence of a capable guardian. As more shopping, banking, and other activities occur in online environments, it is unlikely that we can reduce the number of suitable targets online. However, we can attempt to either remove the offender (perhaps by reducing motivation) or increase guardianship (through policing or more effective guardianship of users of their own data). The next few sections provide a brief overview of some of the potential methods of achieving this.

POLICING

As noted by Wall and Williams (2013), there is limited recent empirical research on the policing of cybercrime. Nevertheless, the potential for law enforcement in the prevention of cybercrime is evident. One frequent suggestion made is that online spaces should be appropriately policed in order to deter cybercrime and immediately apprehend offenders.

In offline crime, it is not possible for the police to be everywhere at all times, with most offenses coming to police attention through reporting by witnesses and victims. Similarly, the Internet is simply too large for police to monitor all interactions, and at least for some, this is not necessarily a bad thing, as it allows some of those in countries with oppressively harsh regimes to interact and make others aware of their cause, as well as providing an opportunity for whistleblowers to bring unethical situations to light. Nevertheless, police can and do use social media in various ways (see, for example, Procter et al., 2013).

Arguments have been made that the policing of online interactions should be distributed to other agencies, such as social media companies and ISPs. Again, similar offline parallels can be made—public venues generally are not responsible if minor crimes (such as pickpocketing) occur on their premises, and car parks frequently display signs indicating that all vehicles are parked at their owner's own risk. There is certainly some expectation of duty of care by online social media companies, and many of these do provide options to report disruptive behaviors when they occur. Nevertheless, this is usually a feature of the more established social media sites and applications, with newer or more transitory equivalents providing this service less frequently.

Policing cybercrime can pose unique problems for law enforcement. Wall (2013) discusses several problems police can face when dealing with identity crimes, such as less visibility, individually minimal in scope, and activities outside of routine policing. Fortune, Rooney, and Kirwan (2018) noted that law enforcement personnel examining child exploitation material as part of their work experience additional stressors to those who are engaged in other activities. Overall, it can be difficult to make firm suggestions regarding policing of cybercrime, partially because of the wide range of offenses within cybercrime. As Yar (2013b) notes, some offenses, such as Internet sex offenses, have a higher perceived seriousness and urgency due to factors such as the level of risk and the vulnerability of potential victims.

DIVERSION AND DETERRENCE

Another method of trying to reduce cybercrime is to prevent the offender from engaging in such activities in the first place, or at least to divert them away from such offending if they do begin. Groups such as the UK National Crime Agency have made some important progress in this area, with their "Pathways into Cyber Crime" document (2017) outlining several methods by which young people might start cybercriminal careers, and identifying several important features of such young offenders, including that key motivations include "completing the challenge, sense of accomplishment, proving oneself to peers" (p. 2), and that deterrence could be achieved via "positive opportunities, role models, mentors" (p. 2). While the report indicates that offenders are not motivated by money, it is possible that the various "bug bounty" programs available might also fulfill the other motivations for such offending. These programs are offered by many of the major software companies, offering rewards for those who identify "bugs" in software and who report them through official channels. It is also possible that the use of positive role models and mentors in programs such as Coder Dojo may divert young people from offending at a very early age, instead encouraging them to invest their programming skills into positive activities.

It is also possible that psychological theories might help in understanding offending behaviors, and possibly change them. Fleming, Watson, Patouris, Bartholomew, and Zizzo (2017) utilized Ajzen's (1985) Theory of Planned Behavior (TPB) to understand the actions of those engaged in copyright infringement. The TPB suggests that a combination of perceived behavioral control, subjective norms, and attitudes all influence intention, which then influences actual behavior. Fleming and colleagues (2017) noted that while not all interactions were significant (or direct), the TPB was still a useful model in predicting various forms of digital piracy. Unfortunately, it takes a massive change in one of the base factors (such as attitude) for a smaller change in intention, for an even smaller change in the actual behavior. And so, while a direct relationship was identified between attitude, intention, and behavior for music piracy, further research is required to determine how to change attitudes sufficiently to influence behavior.

DEVELOPING TARGET RESISTANCE

As mentioned, a potential method of reducing cybercrime is to include the presence of an appropriate guardian, which may be in the form of the potential victim themselves. There are a range of psychological factors which may influence the likelihood of an individual engaging in actions which put their data at risk, many of which are considered in more detail in Kirwan (2015).

Some of those factors relate to cognitive appraisal of stimuli. For example, Vishwanath, Herath, Chen, Wang, and Rao (2011) described the "Integrated Information Processing Model of Phishing Susceptibility," outlining how most phishing emails are peripherally, rather than centrally, processed. The user's perception and focus tend to be on influential cues such as the sense of urgency portrayed and the content, rather than authenticity cues (such as the email address, or the link provided). In essence, some cues are more salient to the user (they appear to "jump out" more)—these could be names of individuals or organizations, logos, and urgency keywords.

Vishwanath, Harrison, and Ng (2016) later developed the "Suspicion, Cognition, and Automaticity Model" (SCAM), which had a similar focus on heuristic, rather than detailed, processing. The SCAM model suggests that when users utilize a more automatic message processing approach, the focus will be on influence techniques, and errors or inconsistencies in the email may be ignored. This has been explored in further detail by researchers such as Williams, Morgan, and Joinson (2017), who used an experimental design to determine that when users were engaged in a demanding task requiring use of memory they were more likely to accept fraudulent messages. It would seem that while users are engaged in difficult tasks they allocate fewer resources to the assessment of messages, and this information is useful if we are to consider approaches to reducing risk of victimization.

Because of effects such as this, cognitive psychology can be particularly helpful in understanding why users may fall victim to cyber-attacks, and what can be done to help potential victims avoid falling into traps. For example, the research by Williams et al. (2017) cited above seems to suggest that users utilize a less thorough form of decision making when under other cognitive demands, and this is similar to Kahneman's (2011) System 1 decision-making, which is fast, based on reflex, and utilizes heuristics, habits, assumptions, emotions, and norms to make quick decisions. People use System 1 frequently in their daily lives—whenever they decide to take a coffee break, or choose which breakfast cereal to buy, they normally employ System 1. The more complex System 2 involves more deliberation when making decisions, where the person tries to avoid bias, gather more information, consider alternatives, and engage logical thinking. People normally use System 2 when making major decisions, such as purchasing a house or a car. Both systems are important—in order to function in society individuals need to be able to make rapid decisions about unimportant elements, and to take longer and be more careful when making important decisions with major consequences.

In effect, it is necessary for one of three things to happen: 1) Users need to be able to identify when System 2 decision-making is required for online security; 2) The system needs to force the user into System 2 decision-making if there is any possibility of a security breach; or 3) System 1 needs to be failsafe—always resulting in the safer decision when employed. Perhaps technological aids could be utilized to compensate for situations involving distractions, which recognize when the user appears to be conducting an already cognitively demanding task and encourages extra caution for any critical decisions to be made at these times. In reality this is very difficult to do—users do not appreciate when systems force particular behaviors on them, particularly if it might result in the loss of a flow state (Csikszentmihalyi, 1990), which is relatively common in many online activities. It is also very difficult to be sure of what the "failsafe" position would be—for example, it is best generally if security updates are installed as soon as possible, and newer versions of software are used rather than older ones (older, unpatched systems are often specifically targeted by cybercriminals, as occurred in the WannaCry ransomware attack). However, many attacks masquerade as security updates, and so using "accept" as the failsafe setting may cause more problems in itself.

Such technological aids should, of course, be used in addition to standard security software, such as anti-malware software and a firewall if appropriate. Ensuring that users install and use such software is not always easy, but psychological theories such as Protection Motivation Theory (PMT; Rogers, 1983) and Social Cognitive Theory (SCT, based on social learning theory by Bandura, 1986) can be helpful in indicating which factors influence users' intentions to engage in protective behaviors. Some of these include social norms (what users believe others in their peer group think or do), perceived self-efficacy, perceived severity, perceived probability, and perceived coping appraisals. Shillair and colleagues (2015) provide a review of how such theories can be utilized to help users to engage in self-protective behaviors. Of course, the Theory of Planned Behavior, discussed in "Diversion and Deterrence", could also be applied to increasing protective behaviors by users.

Personality variables may be a factor in individual susceptibility to cybercrimes. Several studies have indicated that impulsivity may be an indicator of susceptibility to phishing and scams online (see, for example, Kirwan, Fullwood, & Rooney, 2018; Price & Kirwan, 2014). Cybercrime victimization may also have an effect on users (see, for example, Whitty and Buchanan's 2016 paper on the effects of the online dating romance scam on victims). Of interest is that previous victimization may result in increased anxiety for users, but may not necessarily influence precautions taken by them (Reilly & Kirwan, 2014). Why this occurs is unclear, but it might be based in another cognitive bias known as Optimism Bias (Weinstein, 1980); i.e., people tend to believe that negative life experiences are less likely to happen to themselves compared to other members of the population, and that positive life experiences are more likely to happen to them than to others. So, while past victims may be concerned about victimization, optimism bias may result in limited behavioral changes.

It may be that users need to be carefully persuaded to make such behavioral changes. One approach to this may be Fogg's (1997; 1998; 2009) proposed "CAPTology" (Computers As Persuasive Technologies). Computers can be used to persuade users to engage in many different activities, from activism to shopping. It is possible that these same persuasive techniques might be used to encourage safer user behaviors. Various techniques could be used to achieve this, such as presenting the computer as having a somewhat similar personality to the user (Fogg, 2002), although there are of course many ethical considerations with such an approach.

A final method of helping victims and potential victims of cybercrime is through the building of resilience. As mentioned in relation to PMT and SCT, perceived coping appraisals can be important in determining self-protection activities. This may be particularly important for children online—resilience can help with coping with many negative online occurrences, such as grooming by predators and cyberbullying (see, for example, Papatraianou, Levine, & West, 2014; Staksrud & Livingstone, 2009; Tobias & Chapanar, 2016; Vandoninck, d'Haenens, & Segers, 2012). Of course, this does not mean that children are intentionally placed in harm's way online, nor that they are exposed to inappropriate material in order to "inoculate" them. But it is suggested that parents and caregivers discuss the potential dangers in online environments with children in a way appropriate to the child's age and maturity, in a similar manner to how children are informed about other dangers in life. Having discussions like these, along with developing agreements about how such situations would be managed if they occur, could be extremely helpful in encouraging open communication between children and their caregivers about online safety, and increasing resilience should something go wrong.

CONCLUSION

Cybercrime has certainly risen in recent decades, but it remains very difficult to determine exactly how much of it exists. It is also unclear how much of current cybercrime is a displacement of offline crime into online environments, or if similar diversion and deterrence programs will work for online and offline offenders. The possibility exists that cybercriminals are psychologically different to offline offenders, although it may be simply that criminals have moved to using the easiest method to achieve their goals, which currently happens to be online for many individuals. Nevertheless, there are many approaches that users, law enforcement, and software companies can take to reduce cybercrime victimization, and careful empirical investigations are required to identify which of these is effective and acceptable to the relevant populations.

REFERENCES

Ajzen, I. (1985). From intentions to actions: A theory of planned behavior. In J. Kuhl & J. Beckmann (Eds.), *Action control* (pp. 11–39). Berlin: Springer.

Bandura, A. (1986). *Social foundations of thought and action*. Englewood Cliffs, NJ: Prentice-Hall.

Baraniuk, C. (2017, 20 July). AlphaBay and Hansa dark web markets shut down. *BBC News—Technology*. Retrieved from http://www.bbc.com/news/technology-40670010

BBC News—Technology (2013, 2 October). FBI arrests Silk Road drugs site suspect. Retrieved from http://www.bbc.com/news/technology-24373759

BBC News—Technology (2017, 13 May). Massive ransomware infection hits computers in 99 countries. Retrieved from http://www.bbc.com/news/technology-39901382

Clarke, R. V. G., & Felson, M. (Eds.). (1993). *Routine activity and rational choice* (Vol. 5). New Brunswick, NJ: Transaction publishers.

Clough, J. (2015). *Principles of Cybercrime* (2nd ed.). Cambridge: Cambridge University Press.

Conway, M. (2011). Against cyberterrorism. *Communications of the ACM* 54(2), 26–28.

Csikszentmihalyi, M. (1990). *Flow: The psychology of optimal performance*. New York, NY: Harper and Row.

Denning, D. (2007). Cyberterrorism: Testimony Before the Special Oversight Panel on Terrorism, Committee on Armed Services, U.S. House of Representatives. In E.V. Linden's (Ed.) *Focus on Terrorism*, Vol. 9 (pp. 71–76). New York, NY: Nova Science Publishers, Inc.

Fleming, P., Watson, S. J., Patouris, E., Bartholomew, K. J., & Zizzo, D. J. (2017). Why do people file share unlawfully? A systematic review, meta-analysis and panel study. *Computers in Human Behavior 72*, 535–548.

Fogg, B. J. (1997). Captology: The study of computers as persuasive technologies. In CHI'97 Extended Abstracts on Human Factors in Computing Systems (pp. 129–129). New York: ACM.

Fogg, B. J. (1998, January). Persuasive computers: Perspectives and research directions. In *Proceedings of the SIGCHI conference on Human factors in computing systems* (pp. 225–232). New York: ACM.

Fogg, B. J. (2002). *Persuasive technology: Using computers to change what we think and do.* San Francisco, CA: Morgan Kaufmann.

Fogg, B. J. (2009). A behavior model for persuasive design. In *Proceedings of the 4th international Conference on Persuasive Technology* (p. 40). New York: ACM.

Fortune, N., Rooney, B., & Kirwan, G. H. (2018). Supporting law enforcement personnel working with distressing material online. *Cyberpsychology, Behavior, & Social Networking 21,* 138–143.

Furnell, S. M. (2001). The problem of categorising cybercrime and cybercriminals. In W. Hutchinson, M. Warren, & J. Burn (Eds.), *Survival in the e-conomy: 2nd Australian information warfare & security conference 2001* (pp. 29–36). Churchlands: Edith Cowan University. Retrieved from http://ro.ecu.edu.au/cgi/viewcontent.cgi?article=7758&context =ecuworks#page=38

Furnell, S. (2002). *Cybercrime: Vandalising the information society.* London: Addison-Wesley.

Gabbiadini, A., Riva, P., Andrighetto, L., Volpato, C., & Bushman, B. J. (2014). Interactive effect of moral disengagement and violent video games on self-control, cheating, and aggression. *Social Psychological and Personality Science 5*(4), 451–458.

Gillespie, A. A. (2016). *Cybercrime: Key issues and debates.* Abingdon: Routledge.

Gordon, S., & Ford, R. (2002). Cyberterrorism? *Computers & Security 21*(7), 636–647.

Gordon, S., & Ford, R. (2006). On the definition and classification of cybercrime. *Journal in Computer Virology 2*(1), 13–20.

Grabosky, P. (2001). "Virtual Criminality: Old wine in new bottles?" *Social and Legal Studies 10,* 243–249.

Heyboer, K., & Sherman, T. (2017, December 13). Former Rutgers student admits to creating code that crashed Internet. *NJ.com True Jersey.* Retrieved from http://www.nj.com/education/ 2017/12/rutgers_student_charged_in_series_of_cyber_attacks.html

Holt, T. J., Bossler, A. M., & Seigfried-Spellar, K. C. (2015). *Cybercrime and digital forensics: An introduction.* Abingdon: Routledge.

Hui, K. L., Kim, S. H., & Wang, Q. H. (2017). Cybercrime deterrence and international legislation: Evidence from distributed denial of service attacks. *Management Information Systems Quarterly 41*(2), 497–523.

Jewkes, Y. (Ed.) (2007). *Crime online.* Cullompton: Willan Publishing.

Jewkes, Y., & Yar, M. (Eds.) (2010). *Handbook of Internet Crime.* Cullompton: Willan Publishing.

Kahneman, D. (2011). *Thinking, fast and slow.* London: Penguin.

Kirwan, G. (2009). Presence and the victims of crime in online virtual worlds. *Proceedings of Presence 2009: The 12th Annual International Workshop on Presence.* November 11–13, Los Angeles, CA.

Kirwan, G. (2015). Psychology and security: Utilising psychological and communication theories to promote safer cloud security behaviours. In R. Ko & K-K. R. Choo (Eds.) *The cloud security ecosystem: Technical, legal, business and management issues* (pp. 269–281). Waltham, MA: Elsevier.

Kirwan, G. H. (2016). Forensic cyberpsychology. In I. Connolly, M. Palmer, H. Barton, & G. Kirwan (Eds.) *An Introduction to cyberpsychology* (pp. 139–152). New York, NY: Routledge.

Kirwan, G., & Power, A. (2012). *The psychology of cyber crime: Concepts and principles.* Hershey, PA: Information Science Reference.

Kirwan, G., & Power, A. (2013). *Cybercrime: The psychology of online offenders*. Cambridge: Cambridge University Press.

Kirwan, G. H., Fullwood, C., & Rooney, B. (2018). Risk factors for social networking site scam victimisation amongst Malaysian students. *Cyberpsychology, Behavior, and Social Networking 21*, 123–128.

Klahr, R., Navin Shah, J., Sheriffs, P., Rossington, T., Pestell, G., Button, M., & Wang, V. (2017, April). Crime security breaches survey 2017. UK Department for Culture, Media, & Sport. Retrieved from https://www.gov.uk/government/uploads/system/uploads/attachment_data/file/609186/Cyber_Security_Breaches_Survey_2017_main_report_PUBLIC.pdf

Loeber, R., Farrington, D. P., Hipwell, A. E., Stepp, S. D., Pardini, D., & Ahonen, L. (2015). Constancy and change in the prevalence and frequency of offending when based on longitudinal self-reports or official records: Comparisons by gender, race, and crime type. *Journal of Developmental and Life-Course Criminology 1*(2), 150–168.

Nurse, J. R. C. (2018). Cybercrime and you: How criminals attack and the human factors that they seek to exploit. In A. Attrill-Smith, C. Fullwood, M. Keep, & D. Kuss (Eds.) *Oxford handbook of cyberpsychology*. Oxford: Oxford University Press.

Papatraianou, L. H., Levine, D., & West, D. (2014). Resilience in the face of cyberbullying: An ecological perspective on young people's experiences of online adversity. *Pastoral Care in Education 32*(4), 264–283.

Price, K., & Kirwan, G. (2014). Personality caught in the social net: Facebook Phishing. In A. Power and G. Kirwan (Eds.) *Cyberpsychology and new media: A thematic reader* (pp. 126–135). New York: Psychology Press.

Procter, R., Crump, J., Karstedt, S., Voss, A., & Cantijoch, M. (2013). Reading the riots: What were the police doing on Twitter? *Journal of Policing and Society 23*(4), 413–436.

Reilly, K., & Kirwan, G. (2014). Online identity theft: An investigation of the differences between victims and non-victims with regard to anxiety, precautions and uses of the Internet. In A. Power and G. Kirwan (Eds.) *Cyberpsychology and new media: A thematic reader* (pp. 112–125). New York: Psychology Press.

Rogers, R. W. (1983). Cognitive and physiological processes in fear appeals and attitude change: A revised theory of protection motivation. In J. Cacioppo & R. Petty (Eds.), *Social psychophysiology*. New York: Guilford Press.

Shillair, R., Cotten, S. R., Tsai, H. Y. S., Alhabash, S., LaRose, R., & Rifon, N. J. (2015). Online safety begins with you and me: Convincing Internet users to protect themselves. *Computers in Human Behavior 48*, 199–207.

Staksrud, E., & Livingstone, S. (2009). Children and online risk: Powerless victims or resourceful participants? *Information, Communication & Society 12*(3), 364–387.

Sykes, G. M., & Matza, D. (1957). Techniques of neutralization: A theory of delinquency. *American Sociological Review 22*(6), 664–670.

Tobias, S., & Chapanar, T. (2016). Predicting resilience after cyberbully victimization among high school students. *Journal of Psychological and Educational Research 24*(1), 7–25.

UK Home Office (2016). A summary of recorded crime data from year ending Mar 2003 to year ending Mar 2015 (Open Document Spreadsheet). Retrieved from https://www.gov.uk/government/statistics/historical-crime-data

UK National Crime Agency (2017, January 13). Intelligence Assessment—Pathways into Cyber Crime. 0325-CYB V1.0 Retrieved from http://www.nationalcrimeagency.gov.uk/publications/791-pathways-into-cyber-crime/file

Vandoninck, S., d'Haenens, L., & Segers, K. (2012). Coping and resilience: Children's responses to online risks. In S. Livingstone, L. Haddon, & A. Görzig (Eds.), *Children, risk and safety on the Internet: Research and policy challenges in comparative perspective* (pp. 205–218). Bristol: The Policy Press.

Vishwanath, A., Harrison, B., & Ng, Y. J. (2016). Suspicion, cognition, and automaticity model of phishing susceptibility [online]. *Communication Research*. https://doi.org/10.1177/0093650215627483

Vishwanath, A., Herath, T., Chen, R., Wang, J., & Rao, H. R. (2011). Why do people get phished? Testing individual differences in phishing vulnerability within an integrated, information processing model. *Decision Support Systems 51*(3), 576–586.

Wall, D. S. (Ed.) (2001). *Crime and the Internet.* London: Routledge.

Wall, D. S. (2007). *Cybercrime: The transformation of crime in the information age.* Cambridge: Polity Press.

Wall, D. S. (2013). Policing identity crimes. *Journal of Policing and Society 23*(4), 437–460.

Wall, D. S., & Williams, M. L. (2013). Policing cybercrime: Networked and social media technologies and the challenges for policing. *Journal of Policing and Society 23* (4), 409–412.

Wall, D. S., & Williams, M. L. (Eds.) (2014). *Policing cybercrime: Networked and social media technologies and the challenges for policing.* Abingdon: Routledge.

Ward, M. (2017, 16 May). WannaCry and the malware hall of fame. *BBC News—Technology.* Retrieved from http://www.bbc.com/news/technology-39928456

Weinstein, N. D. (1980). Unrealistic optimism about future life events. *Journal of Personality and Social Psychology 39*(5), 806.

Whitty, M. T., & Buchanan, T. (2016). The online dating romance scam: The psychological impact on victims–both financial and non-financial. *Criminology & Criminal Justice 16*(2), 176–194.

Williams, E. J., Morgan, P. L., & Joinson, A. N. (2017). Press accept to update now: Individual differences in susceptibility to malevolent interruptions. *Decision Support Systems, 96,* 119–129.

Yar, M. (2013a). *Cybercrime and Society* (2nd ed.). London: Sage.

Yar, M. (2013b). The policing of Internet sex offences: Pluralised governance versus hierarchies of standing. *Journal of Policing and Society 23*(4), 482–497.

CHAPTER 32

POLICING CYBERCRIME THROUGH LAW ENFORCEMENT AND INDUSTRY MECHANISMS

THOMAS J. HOLT AND JIN REE LEE

INTRODUCTION

THE proliferation of the Internet, digital technology, and mobile computing devices have allowed for human behaviors to transcend traditional boundaries of space and time, rendering instantaneous transnational communications and financial transactions possible (Holt & Bossler, 2016; Newman & Clarke, 2003; Wall, 2001). Given the relative ease with which individuals can access the Internet in most countries, developed or emerging, many people are now dependent on technology and mobile devices (Andress & Winterfield, 2013; Holt & Bossler, 2016; Newman & Clarke, 2003).

Though the benefits of technology are manifest, Internet-enabled devices have also produced unintended consequences such as the opportunity to commit crime and encourage deviant behavior (Holt & Bossler, 2016). Traditional forms of crime that occur in the real world have been enhanced through technology, including prostitution (Cunningham & Kendall, 2010; Holt & Blevins, 2007), fraud (Cross, 2015; Wall, 2004), stalking and harassment (Bocij, 2004; Choi, & Lee, 2017; Choi, Lee, & Lee, 2017), terrorism (Britz, 2010; Weimann, 2005), piracy (Higgins & Marcum, 2011), and child sexual offenses (Jenkins, 2001; Krone, 2004). In addition, new forms of crime have developed as a result of technology, including computer hacking and the dissemination of malicious software (Bossler & Holt, 2009; Jordan & Taylor, 1998) (see also chapters by Kirwan and Nurse, this volume).

The term most commonly used to categorize the expanse of technology-enabled offenses is *cybercrime*, which denotes the use of the Internet and/or Internet-enabled devices to enact criminal and/or deviant behavior (Furnell, 2002; Wall, 2001). Cybercrimes pose unique challenges for law enforcement agencies at all levels of government (i.e. local, state, and federal), as they must cope with constantly changing technologies that require perpetual training to investigate these emerging offenses (Hinduja, 2004; Holt, Burruss, & Bossler, 2015; Senjo, 2004; Stambaugh et al., 2001). The tasks of law enforcement are further complicated by the ability of technology to provide offenders with various levels of anonymity, leaving victims incapable of providing much information on the location or identity of the perpetrator (Hinduja, 2007; Wall, 2001). Moreover, the ubiquity of digital technology makes it possible for aggressors to target individuals transnationally, making it difficult to adjudicate offenders and process cases (Brenner, 2008; Cross, 2015).

Due to the complexities involved in responding to cybercrime, many scholars, police administrators, and legislators have advocated for changes in the criminal justice response to online offenses (Goodman, 1997; Holt, Bossler, & Fitzgerald, 2010; National Institute of Justice, 2008; Stambaugh et al., 2001). Better training and resources for line officers who serve as first responders have been consistently recognized as a primary factor in dire need of reform (Goodman, 1997; Holt & Bossler, 2012; Stambaugh et al., 2001). Furthermore, there is a clear need for improved relations between the public and private sector as they are the primary bodies who own and operate the infrastructure and devices that compose the Internet (PERF, 2014; Stambaugh et al., 2001). Consequently, the private sector has become an essential regulatory arm in the investigation and prevention of certain cyberoffenses (Brenner, 2008; Holt & Bossler, 2016; Wall & Williams, 2013).

Given the intricacies involved in regulating cybercrime, this chapter examines the current state of cybercrime investigation among law enforcement and industry, as well as their perceived benefits and shortcomings. It begins by introducing the range of cybercrimes that occur, as well as the individuals and organizations responsible for policing cybercrime. Then it discusses the efforts and challenges faced by law enforcement and industry bodies. The chapter concludes with a discussion on the challenges, risks, and implications posed by having extralegal efforts in concert with conventional criminal justice procedures in the fight against cybercrime offending and victimization.

DEFINING CYBERCRIMES

The term cybercrime may be somewhat confusing to the general public, as it encompasses a range of offenses affecting both property and persons. This section provides an overview of the various forms of cybercrime that occur, and uses Wall's (2001) four-item typology recognizing: 1) cyber-trespass, 2) cyber-deception/theft, 3) cyber-porn/obscenity, and 4) cyber-violence (see also Kirwan, this volume). Acts of cyber-trespass involve attempts to cross established boundaries of ownership in a networked environment (Wall, 2001).

This category includes computer hacking and the use of malware (i.e., malicious software programs) to penetrate computer systems that perpetrators do not own (Holt & Bossler, 2016). While these actions are often thought to serve similar objectives, it must be noted that computer hackers infiltrate computer systems to secure, compromise, and/or exploit their contents (Schell & Dodge, 2002; Steinmetz, 2015). Malicious software, however, is only disseminated to compromise computer systems to acquire sensitive information, establish backdoor access to systems, or to disrupt network connectivity (Bossler & Holt, 2009; Holt & Kilger, 2012; Schell & Dodge, 2002; Symantec, 2016).

Cyber-deception and theft involves the use of deceit and trickery to acquire information or services (Wall, 2001). This category primarily includes acts of fraud enabled through mass email messaging called spam, which can be used to obtain personal information or steal money from billions of individuals worldwide (Cross, 2015; Edelson, 2003; Holt & Bossler, 2016; Holt & Graves, 2007; Wall, 2004). Some of these crimes may also involve acts of cyber-trespass, such as the use of hacking to acquire sensitive financial information from retailers or corporate databases (Franklin, Paxson, Perrig, & Savage, 2007; Motoyama, McCoy, Levchenko, Savage, & Voelker, 2011). Cyber-deception also includes digital piracy, or the distribution and acquisition of intellectual property without payment to its creator via online sources (Business Software Alliance, 2016; Higgins & Marcum, 2011; Nhan, 2013).

Cyber-porn and obscenity involves the creation and distribution of sexually expressive content or activity through Internet-enabled technology (Wall, 2001). While pornographic content existed before the Internet, its creation led to an explosion in content generated by both amateurs and professionals (Quinn & Forsyth, 2013; Roberts & Hunt, 2012; Yar, 2013). Sex work, particularly prostitution, has thrived as a result of technology by enabling the customers and workers to connect in private channels that reduce the risk of detection by law enforcement (Cunningham & Kendall, 2010; Holt & Blevins, 2007). This category also includes sexual abuse and the exploitation of minors, whether through the distribution of digital images of children engaged in sexual acts (Internet Watch Foundation, 2016), or through real-time child sexual abuse streaming services across a variety of different online mediums (i.e., Snapchat, Skype, FaceTime) (Durkin & Bryant, 1999; GSMA, 2014; Krone, 2004).

The final category includes cyber-violence, where individuals use digital technology to solicit, create, and distribute physically and/or emotionally damaging information to harm individuals (Wall, 2001). The most commonly recognized activities in this category include acts of harassment or stalking enabled by social media, email, or text (i.e., cyber-stalking and harassment) (Bocij, 2004; Hinduja & Patchin, 2014; Reyns, Henson, & Fisher, 2012). There is evidence to suggest that extremist groups and terrorists are increasingly using social media and the Internet as a platform for radicalization to violence, as well as to issue threats to wide audiences based on characteristics such as race, gender, religious affiliation, and/or sexual orientation (Britz, 2010; Yar, 2013).

CYBERCRIME POLICING TYPOLOGY

The diverse threat of cybercrimes and the technologies that enable these offenses create complex landscapes for policing and law enforcement. As with traditional criminality, the local community and traditional policing agencies play significant roles in the notification and investigation of offenses. At the same time, industry and non-governmental organizations play more prominent roles in policing cybercrimes as they may be more prominent targets for offenders, or may inadvertently serve as through-points for evidence to support an investigation. To that end, Wall (2007) identified a seven-category typology of the groups involved in policing online spaces and Internet governance: 1) Internet users and user groups; 2) virtual environment security managers; 3) network infrastructure providers (ISPs); 4) corporate security organizations; 5) non-governmental, non-police organizations; 6) governmental non-police organizations; and 7) public police organizations. Each category is discussed in detail to explore the extent to which they intersect.

INTERNET USERS AND USER GROUPS

Internet users constitute the largest group currently involved in attempts to regulate the Internet by censuring behaviors that disrupt the perceived social order of the online community (Innes, 2004; Wall, 2007, 2010). User populations are pivotal in identifying criminal activity as there are more online spaces and communities than there are law enforcement officers and agencies with a capacity to investigate. Much of this involves self-policing roles in online forums and social media platforms by reporting or blocking users on the basis of behaviors that violate their terms of service and/or user policies. Internet users and user groups may even report illegal activity to formal authorities such as the police, crime reporting websites, or organizations such as the Internet Watch Foundation (Wall, 2010).

In some cases, Internet users also form groups that respond to certain forms of crime that threaten and/or offend their interests and beliefs (Wall, 2007). Some examples of Internet users and user groups include the CyberAngels (i.e. seek to secure children online), Ethical Hackers Against Pedophilia (i.e. combat pedophilia), and The Association of Sites Advocating Child Protection (i.e. elimination of child pornography) (Wall, 2007). Many of these groups explicitly reveal their goals and purposes within their names, rendering transparency and making identification of their mission statements clear (Wall, 2007). Other groups, such as the hacker collective Anonymous, operate with less clear mandates while attempting to investigate wrongdoing or highlight hypocrisy in government and/or religious organizations.

Internet users and user groups have been more engaged in e-commerce governance through vendor rating systems (Wall, 2007). Some of the more prominent examples of this are Amazon and E-bay, both of which maintain an online trading partners profile rating system (i.e., Hayne, Wang, & Wang, 2015; Weiss, Capozzi, & Prusak, 2004). Every prospective seller is given an online profile that documents their customer feedback and sales performance. The objective of this profile is to assist future customers in identifying trustworthy sellers, while shunning less credible operators. Providing feedback scores helps to regulate vendor behavior by dictating a vendor's perceived or real level of trust by participants within the online community (Wall, 2007).

VIRTUAL ENVIRONMENT SECURITY MANAGERS

The next group involved in policing cyberspace are virtual environment security managers who are ostensibly members of the general public who have been given an elevated role in online spaces to aid in the regulation and enforcement of community norms (Wall, 2007). The primary type of security manager exists within forums and other computer-mediated communications platforms, as their goal is to maintain order and prevent disruptive behavior from taking place within their virtual communities (Wall, 2007). Moderators are able to utilize informal social controls to influence participant behavior by banning users, deleting comments, and generally policing encounters between community participants (Wall, 2007). Moderators also aid in the enforcement and regulation of formal legal statutes based on the terms of use provided by the Internet Service Providers (ISP, Wall, 2007). In the event that a community participant engages in behaviors that violate the law, moderators may be expected to report the user to both law enforcement and the ISP to provide further punitive sanctions (Wall, 2007). Security managers' role in policing cyberspace is relatively limited compared to industry and law enforcement.

NETWORK INFRASTRUCTURE PROVIDERS (ISPs)

Network infrastructure/service providers (ISPs) regulate behavior through the contractual agreements they make with their clientele, whether as end users for Internet connectivity or as hosting services (Crawford, 2003; Wall, 2007). This contractual governance is illustrated in the form of terms and conditions arrangements, sometimes called Fair Use Policies (Holt & Bossler, 2016; Wall, 2007). These terms and conditions are typically guided by both legal statutes at the local, state, federal, or national level, and the ISP's own economic interests. For instance, ISP records may be retained for extended periods of time, or provided to law enforcement upon request to support criminal investigations of specific users' activities. Such information must be communicated to end users to ensure transparency to their customer base while at the same time successfully cooperating with law enforcement requirements. Typically, this information is provided in user Terms and Conditions agreements, although evidence suggests that many people neither completely read nor understand the language of these documents (see Holt & Bossler, 2016 for a review).

A unique aspect of ISPs is that, despite being situated in a particular spatial location and jurisdiction, their ability to operate transnationally means that they may have users who live in different nations with unique laws and regulations (Wall, 2010). As a result, ISPs must be compliant with various domestic and foreign legal statutes, as a failure to do so may leave them liable to fines or criminal charges for allowing their services to be used in the furtherance of certain crimes, like the distribution of child pornography (Wall, 2007).

CORPORATE SECURITY ORGANIZATIONS

Similar to network ISPs, corporate security organizations implement contractual agreements with their employees and clientele to 1) govern their own commercial interests, and 2) ensure compliance with all appropriate laws (Wall, 2007). Corporate security organizations commonly enforce software solutions to directly shield themselves from external threats posed by hackers and cybercriminals and identify problematic behavioral patterns in both their systems and among their clientele (Spitzner, 2001; Wall, 2007). The use of programs such as intrusion detection systems (IDS) are essential to identify and terminate malicious activity when it happens within the network, and potentially identify employee misconduct (Holt & Bossler, 2016; Maimon, Wilson, Ren, & Berenblum, 2015). Serious cases may even result in corporate security organizations invoking criminal prosecutions against their employees on the basis of violations to either their contractual agreements or relevant local criminal codes (Wall, 2007).

Corporate security organizations can also play a role in managing the behaviors of their clients and the broader population of Internet users through regulation of their services. For instance, online currency providers can limit the use of their services to pay for certain products. Similarly, Craigslist and Backpage—which serve as online classified ad spaces—limit the kinds of services individuals can advertise, particularly paid sexual encounters (Cunningham & Kendall, 2010). The relatively low public visibility of corporate security interests and their minimalistic contact with law enforcement agencies make it difficult to evaluate their utility in regulating cybercrime (Wall, 2001, 2007).

Non-Governmental, Non-Police Organizations

Non-governmental, non-police organizations are mixtures of both private and public entities that serve as governance figures in cybercrime prevention (Wall, 2007). They frequently serve as clearinghouses for information on cybercrime threats, techniques to reduce victimization, or even operate hotlines to facilitate the reporting of criminal activity to ISPs or police (Holt, Burruss, & Bossler, 2015; Wall, 2007). For instance, the Internet Watch Foundation (IWF) is a charitable organization located in the United Kingdom that is dedicated to removing child pornography and obscene content from the Internet (Internet Watch Foundation, 2017). They operate a hotline to report child pornography and engage in coordinated information sharing with law enforcement and ISPs to facilitate blocking harmful content and investigate child sexual exploitation.

Importantly, a non-governmental, non-police organization has no constitutional role in law enforcement, arrest, or sanctions for offenders—that is, they have no formal accountability in the broader structure of public corporations and traditional police agencies. As a result, their operations tend to focus on streamlined roles that can be facilitated through public functions, like serving as a clearinghouse for information on victimization or attempts to regulate and operate tip-lines for offenses (Wall, 2007).

Governmental Non-Police Organizations

Governmental non-police organizations monitor the Internet and online behaviors through the use of regulations, laws, fines and charges, and threats of prosecution (Wall, 2007). Despite being an informal law enforcement agency, governmental non-police organizations actively participate in the role of investigating, resolving, and adjudicating cases (Wall, 2007). Included in this typology are agencies that govern and oversee cybersecurity policies for Internet protection purposes (Wall, 2007). Governments that use these agencies to control citizens' Internet use and availability of content include Singapore, China, Korea, Vietnam, and Pakistan (Caden & Lucas, 1996). These governmental non-police organizations are also able to set regulatory policies that are responsible for trade and e-commerce (Wall, 2007). In the context of the United Kingdom (UK), this includes the Department of Business, Innovation and Skills (BIS), while in the United States (US), it is the Federal Trade Commission (FTC) (Wall, 2007).

Public Police Organizations

Public police organizations are agents empowered by the government to enforce national law and maintain social order (Wall, 2007). Agents and officers within these organizations have constitutional authority to investigate offenses and arrest suspects. In many Western nations, police organizations are divided into regional forces based on jurisdictions that feed from the local to the federal level. For instance, the US operates on a system where law enforcement agencies serve as the first point of contact for citizens to provide assistance, respond to criminal complaints, investigate crimes, and arrest individuals when necessary. Their jurisdiction is limited to a specific city or county boundary, while state police agencies have the responsibility to investigate crimes which may cross jurisdictions within specific state borders. Federal agencies have the greatest jurisdictional remit, with the ability to investigate crimes that cross state or international boundaries.

Responses to cybercrime vary across local, state, and federal agencies and are dependent in part on their investigative remit, budget, and resources. At the local level, many police and sheriffs' agencies that serve large populations in urban areas tend to have their own cybercrime units, enabling greater investigative capacity (Willits & Nowacki, 2016). Communities that are in rural areas with smaller force sizes tend to partner with neighboring agencies' specialized units to respond to cybercrime calls for service (Willits & Nowacki, 2016). Some also utilize state police cybercrime units due to the potential that offenders and victims reside in different parts of the state.

Generally, police organizations respond to cybercrimes using a mixed approach that combines conventional criminal justice tactics with digital technology and computer investigations (Wall, 2007). Police may even use software programs to proactively monitor and regulate certain priority concerns (Sommer, 2004; Wall, 2007). In the context of child pornography investigations in the US, specialized units called Internet Crimes Against Children (ICAC) task forces are staffed by officers from multiple counties and cities to investigate child sexual exploitation online (Internet Crimes Against Children Task Force, 2017). They utilize torrent tracking software to identify known images of child pornography being shared via peer-to-peer file sharing services (Marcum, Higgins, Freiburger, & Ricketts, 2010). Such information facilitates criminal prosecutions, and may also lead to additional charges in the event officers can demonstrate the individual may have engaged in real-world contact sexual offenses.

The highest levels of law enforcement in most nations are either federal or national police forces which have the ability to respond to serious cybercrimes performed by domestic and international offenders. In the US, the Federal Bureau of Investigation and Secret Service have the greatest remit to investigate computer hacking and fraud cases, with analogous agencies in Canada via the Royal Canadian Mounted Police (RCMP) and the National Crime Agency (NCA) in the UK.

LAW ENFORCEMENT CHALLENGES

Though there are a range of entities involved in policing cyberspace, the majority of formal state-sanctioned powers are consolidated with law enforcement agencies, whether local, state, or federal. However, their abilities to affect cybercrimes are smaller in comparison to their capacities to deal with traditional crimes in the real world. One of the primary challenges lies in the fact that the cross-national nature of cybercrimes—such as hacking and malware—limits the response capability of local and state level law enforcement (Brenner, 2008). It appears that these agencies more often respond to person-based cybercrimes, especially those involving child sexual exploitation and other sex crimes. Not only do these offenses have a greater likelihood that the victim and offender reside within the same jurisdiction, but these offenses also have a greater impact on victims, giving them a higher investigative priority compared to some economic offenses (Brenner, 2008; Holt & Bossler, 2016).

Another significant challenge affecting local and state agencies are their limited budgets for resources, training, and staff. The finite resources of police mean that they must prioritize certain crimes based on their perceived prevalence and harm to the community they service. To that end, rural agencies may place a lower emphasis on cybercrimes compared to urban communities with a younger population. Additionally, the costs to establish a digital forensics unit to investigate cybercrimes can be quite high for a police organization, requiring tens of thousands of dollars in software and hardware, as well as costs for training and staffing (Ferraro & Casey, 2005; Holt et al., 2015). These issues often compound one another, such that a deficiency in one is the result of a shortcoming in another—that is, a lack of resources can contribute to the lack of adequate cybercrime training and/or dearth in staff members (Holt & Bossler, 2012; Holt, Burruss, & Bossler, 2015; Stambaugh et al., 2001; Wall & Williams, 2013). As a result, there is evidence to suggest that local police are increasingly developing specialized units to minimize the need for line officers to respond to calls involving online offenses (Willits & Nowacki, 2016). These conditions may contribute to the perception among local line officers that cybercrimes are not their responsibility, but rather issues that should be investigated by specialized cybercrime units and/or federal agencies (Bossler & Holt, 2012).

Though federal agencies have greater latitude to investigate cybercrime cases, their investigative powers are limited by several factors. Specifically, the lack of extradition arrangements between various nations (i.e. US, China, Russia, Ukraine) and the differences in legal definitions and statutes make it difficult for transnational investigations to lead to an arrest (Brenner, 2011; Holt & Bossler, 2016). These factors diminish the deterrent capacity of federal law enforcement, and create cybercrime safe havens, where perpetrators can target victims in specific nations with impunity. In response to these limitations, nations with favorable extradition treaties have enhanced their information sharing protocols to detect offenders who may be in transit for vacation or short-term stays that may enable arrest while they are abroad (Zetter, 2013).

INDUSTRY MECHANISMS

The constraints in law enforcement responses to cybercrime have led private industry and technology producers to play a prominent role in policing cyberspace. Some of these efforts are a result of collaboration with law enforcement, although a portion also appear to operate without their tacit approval. Such actions present potential challenges to the rule of law and state-power as industrial entities have no formal obligation or mandate to investigate criminal activity beyond misuse or malfeasance stipulated by existing statutes. At the same time, they have legal obligations to support their customer base and protect their intellectual property from harm. As a result, industry responses to cybercrime can be legally justified.

The fact that organizations can operate outside of the bureaucratic structure of government enables their efforts to move with greater speed and latitude than their law enforcement counterparts. Moreover, private industries may have access to unique data sets, technologies, and budgets than what may be available for law enforcement agencies. Finally, different groups responsible for the investigation and policing of cyberspace can band together to increase their response capacity and regulatory power in ways that extend beyond what may be possible by traditional police agencies. In this respect, industry responses may be a more effective mechanism to both investigate and mitigate cybercrimes (Brenner, 2008).

An excellent example of effective industrial coalitions to affect cybercrime is the Financial Coalition Against Child Pornography (FCACP). This group formed in 2006 in response to the recognized problem of individuals using existing financial payment providers' infrastructure to send and receive payments for access to child pornography and sexual exploitation content (National Center for Missing and Exploited Children, 2017). Financial institutions and ISPs banded together with the International Center for Missing and Exploited Children, a leading NGO, to identify child pornography vendors and block their access to financial services (International Center for Missing and Exploited Children, 2017). They also developed standards and screening procedures to proactively keep such vendors from gaining access to merchant services or identify those actors who may have been able to hide their activities (Financial Coalition Against Child Pornography, 2016). Since the FCACP formed, there has been a 93 percent reduction in the number of complaints made regarding commercial child pornography services (Financial Coalition Against Child Pornograpy, 2016). While offenders can still profit from the sale of child pornography via cryptocurrencies, the FCACP has been able to dramatically affect the misuse of legitimate services by illicit vendors.

Similarly co-ordinated responses are evident in the attempts made to disrupt digital piracy distribution channels. For instance, commercial and private ISPs can monitor the traffic of their customer base and identify overt uses of torrent programs and protocols, as well as potential file markers that may reflect the intellectual property being shared.

The ability to monitor this traffic has led ISPs to cooperate with the MPAA and RIAA to send cease and desist letters to customers in violation of the Digital Millennium Copyright Act in the US or other relevant statutes abroad (Nhan, 2013). Cease and desist letters are non-invasive notices sent to active users who illegally download intellectual property to acknowledge that the ISPs can observe their traffic and state that further piracy may lead to punitive sanctions. The letters are intended to serve as a deterrent to further piracy, as they do not stipulate any criminal charges or prosecutorial claims (Nhan, 2013).

Other non-invasive deterrent strategies involving piracy include the use of corrupted files or junk information (i.e. TV Technology, 2007) and compromising underlying mechanisms used in peer-to-peer file sharing software (i.e. Torkington, 2005) to complicate the process of offending. In particular, ISPs and corporations can attempt to introduce false information into file sharing protocols used by BitTorrent and other services to limit individual access to pirated content and cause downloads to fail. The use of these techniques does not produce a substantial decrease in piracy, but instead complicate the process of offending which may lead to a small reduction in attempts to pirate certain content (Holt & Copes, 2010).

The technical capabilities of private industries also enable them access to sensitive information and attack details that may exceed what is initially available to some law enforcement agencies. For instance, anti-virus vendors' products and services are frequently employed not only by consumers, but also within large corporations and government agencies. These technologies serve not only as protective tools, but also provide vendors with nodal points of information about attack attempts. Their technologies can also create errant backdoors into networks that may serve as points of compromise or spying, which recently led the US Department of Homeland Security to ban the use of the Russian security vendor Kaspersky's software (Hatmaker, 2017).

Such capability should not be surprising, as private security vendors are increasingly used to triage high-profile cyberattacks against sensitive targets and develop solutions to mitigate future attacks (Holt & Bossler, 2016). For instance, the firm Crowdstrike is an extremely well-regarded cybersecurity company that provides tailored cybersecurity solutions and has been employed by the Democratic National Committee (DNC) after they were compromised by what was revealed to be Russian state-sponsored hackers (Leopold, 2017). Because of their investigative capabilities and reputation, Crowdstrike has a substantial corporate portfolio that may be targeted by nation-state sponsored hacker groups. Their published insights, especially those intended for public consumption, have consequences for international relations. In 2015, the company published a report on an attack originating from Chinese actors that appeared to violate an agreement between the US and Chinese governments to ban hacks for economic advantage. The company noted that they were "not stating anywhere that the Chinese are violating the agreement" but the information in the report was interpreted as such by the popular press. Similar confusion could easily complicate relationships between nations and place security vendors in geo-political situations that go beyond their remit (Holt & Bossler, 2016).

CHALLENGES WITH EXTRALEGAL EFFORTS
AND INTERVENTIONS

Though there are clear benefits to engaging industry and non-governmental organizations in cybercrime policing efforts, they also face unique challenges that may create unique civil litigation risks or undermine the broader rule of law. For instance, techniques such as sinkholing present many legal and ethical concerns pertaining to the illegal access of victims' personal and sensitive data (Adhikari, 2013). That is, employing such strategies enable industries to observe the privatized data of its users without their consent or permission.

By having no legal or constitutional remit to enforce national laws, many of the industry responses can be seen as being temporary and limiting (Holt & Bossler, 2016; Hutchings & Holt, 2015; Sunshine & Tyler, 2003; Tyler, 2004). Furthermore, some of their responses may be viewed as overstepping their perceived role as private corporations. For instance, the tech giant Microsoft has sued various malicious software operators and ISPs, including the individual creators of malware and the web-hosting services that may be used to host the tools or enable their operations. In 2014, the company filed a civil lawsuit against two men, Naser Al Mutairi from Kuwait and Mohamed Benabdellah from Algeria, claiming that they were responsible for the use of keylogging software that infected millions of computers that featured Microsoft software products (Athow, 2014). The suit also identified a Domain Name Service provider called No-IP, claiming the company did not properly secure its infrastructure from attack which enabled the infections against individual computers.

As a result of the suit, Microsoft seized the domains hosted by No-IP and blocked the infected computers from accessing the Internet. This action not only affected the infected computer users, but also the 1.8 million customers who used the service and were not affected by the malware. Customers were outraged, and No-IP claimed that they were not contacted by Microsoft before this action, even though they could have mitigated the infections in a targeted fashion (Munson, 2014). The suit was eventually settled out of court, making it difficult to understand what else may have occurred or whose claims were truly accurate. Regardless, this incident led to criticism over Microsoft's activities given their status and position as non-law enforcement agents, as well as their overstepping of legal authority to protect the general public. In addition, sensitive information of the No-IP user base was made available to Microsoft, which may constitute a violation of user agreements and individual privacy (Adhikari, 2013).

The increasing dependence on industrial responses may also erode the perceived need for law enforcement agencies at any level of government to respond to cybercrimes. If law enforcement agencies have resources but finite capacity in their regulation abilities, society will most likely lean towards industry mechanisms. Damage to the perceived legitimacy of law enforcement is hazardous to society because it is essential to the social contract and rule of law that the public trusts the authority of law enforcement (Sunshine & Tyler, 2003; Tyler, 2004). If this perception is weakened, the deterrent impact of the criminal justice apparatus may fade and engender higher rates of offending.

While such a situation may seem unlikely, there is already some evidence of an undermining of confidence in federal responses to cybercrime in the US. Over the last year, legislators introduced bills that would enable companies to engage in retaliatory attacks against individuals or groups who attempt to steal intellectual property or sensitive information (Wolff, 2017). One of the individuals supporting the bill, Representative Tom Graves (Rep-Georgia), did so because he feels that government and law enforcement are unable to respond with the same efficiency as organizations who know they have been hacked (Wolff, 2017). Similarly, Stewart Baker, who is a former assistant secretary of homeland security, favors such legislation, having been quoted as saying: "for a company to go to the FBI and say 'I've been hacked, can you find the hacker,' it's like going to a university town's police force and saying, 'Somebody stole my bike'—you're lucky if they don't laugh at you," and that "the government is completely consumed just trying to take care of its own data and tracking its own attackers. It doesn't have the resources to help firms and probably never will" (Wolff, 2017).

Passing legislation that allows companies to actively attack their attackers will be a serious inflection point in the perceived role of law enforcement in combatting cybercrime. While the legislation has language requiring companies to directly coordinate their efforts with law enforcement and increase the transparency of cybercrime reporting, it effectively acknowledges that state-sponsored police agencies have limited power to respond. Efforts to enact such legislation will only continue to degrade confidence in federal law enforcement and challenge their authority to investigate and respond to cybercrimes over the long term.

CONCLUSION

It is imperative that scholars, police administrators, and policy makers examine the effectiveness of cybercrime intervention strategies and devise core mechanisms that regulate cybercrime offenses, but without delegitimizing the authority and trust of law enforcement. In order for this to happen, a greater investment of funds is needed in law enforcement units at all three levels of governance, as well as improvement in transnational bodies of enforcement. That is, there is a need to invest better at both the local and federal levels of law enforcement, while building stronger ties with international bodies. Given the difficulty in forming comprehensive extralegal and transnational relationships, focus needs to be on ascertaining how to make industry more tightly regulated such that we do not give them arrest powers, but abilities nonetheless to enforce misuse effectively.

A response to this dilemma could be to strengthen public and private sector partnerships to encourage greater involvement of the private sector in policing cyberspace.

Given the private sector's undeniable role and ability to combat cybercrime and monitor online spaces, it is imperative for public sectors to forge stronger relationships with private entities so that constant collaboration can be had. Robust public and private partnerships can allow for law enforcement agencies to perform their duties with greater efficiency without having to give private industries arrest powers. Such relationships can also provide the trust and security needed for private industries to support the goals and ambitions of public sector agencies. That is, if public sectors are able to gain access to the resources and techniques that private sectors have at their disposal, efforts towards combatting cybercrime can prove to be more effective and efficient for all the involved entities.

If society is committed to truly involving technology within the policing process, greater support for creative technical solutions are needed. A recent example of a technical solution is Facebook's attempt at preventing revenge porn victimization by having a process of submitting nude photos and creating a repository of content to auto-identify potential reposting. While this particular method has received criticism from wide audiences—and falls short in many aspects—innovative technical solutions to cybercrime should be encouraged and supported if society is truly committed to incorporating specialized solutions. Although complications are bound to arise, if effective cyber-crime policing mechanisms are to be achieved, both greater collaboration between the public and private sectors and innovative technical solutions must be steadily encouraged and implemented by both domestic and international communities alike.

References

Adhikari, R. (2013, December 9). Microsoft's ZeroAccess Botnet Takedown No "Mission Accomplished." *TechNewsWorld* [Online]. Retrieved from http://www.technewsworld. com/story/79586.html

Andress, J., & Winterfeld, S. (2013). *Cyber warfare: Techniques, tactics, and tools for security practitioners* (2nd ed.). Waltham, MA: Syngress.

Athow, D. (2014, July 1). Microsoft seizes 22 No-IP domains in malware crackdown. *TechRadar* [Online] Retrieved from http://www.techradar.com/news/software/security-software/ microsoft-siezes-22-no-ip-domains-in-malware-crackdown-1255625

Bocij, P. (2004). *Cyberstalking: Harassment in the Internet age and how to protect your family.* Westport, CT: Praeger Publishers.

Bossler, A. M., & Holt, T. J. (2009). On-line activities, guardianship, and malware infection: An examination of routine activities theory. *International Journal of Cyber Criminology 3*, 400–420.

Bossler, A. M., & Holt, T. J. (2012). Patrol officers' perceived role in responding to cybercrime. *Policing: An International Journal of Police Strategies & Management 35*, 165–181.

Brenner, S. W. (2008). *Cyberthreats: The emerging fault lines of the nation state.* New York: Oxford University Press.

Brenner, S. W. (2011). Defining cybercrime: A review of federal and state law. In R. D. Clifford (Ed.), *Cybercrime: The investigation, prosecution, and defense of a computer-related crime* (3rd ed.) (pp. 15–104). Raleigh, NC: Carolina Academic Press.

Britz, M. T. (2010). Terrorism and technology: Operationalizing cyberterrorism and identifying concepts. In T. J. Holt (Ed.), *Crime on-line: Correlates, causes, and context* (pp. 193–220). Raleigh, NC: Carolina Academic Press.

Business Software Alliance. (2016). Seizing opportunity through compliance. *Business Software Alliance* [Online]. Retrieved from http://globalstudy.bsa.org/2016/index.html

Caden, M. L., & Lucas, S. E. (1996). Accidents on the information superhighway: On-line liability and regulation. *Richmond Journal of Law & Technology* 2(1), 3.

Choi, K., & Lee, J. R. (2017). Theoretical analysis of cyber-deviance victimization and offending using cyber-routine activities theory. *Computers in Human Behavior 73*, 394–402.

Choi, K., Lee S., & Lee, J. R. (2017). Mobile phone technology and online sexual harassment among juveniles in South Korea: Effects of self-control and social learning. *International Journal of Cyber Criminology 11*(1), 110–127.

Crawford, C. (2003). Cyberplace: Defining a right to Internet access through public accommodation law. *Temple Law Review 76*, 225.

Cross, C. (2015). No laughing matter: Blaming the victim of online fraud. *International Review of Victimology 21*, 187–204.

Cunningham, S., & Kendall, T. (2010). Sex for sale: Online commerce in the world's oldest profession. In T. J. Holt (Ed.), *Crime online: Correlates, causes, and context.* (pp. 114–140). Raleigh, NC: Carolina Academic Press.

Durkin, K. F., & Bryant, C. D. (1999). Propagandizing pederasty: A thematic analysis of the online exculpatory accounts of unrepentant pedophiles. *Deviant Behavior 20*, 103–127.

Edelson, E. (2003). The 419 scam: Information warfare on the spam front and a proposal for local filtering. *Computers and Security 22*(5), 392–401.

Ferraro, M., & Casey, E. (2005). *Investigating child exploitation and pornography: The Internet, the law and forensic science.* New York: Elsevier.

Financial Coalition Against Child Pornography. (2016). *Internet merchant acquisition and monitoring best practices for the prevention and detection of commercial child pornography* [Online]. Retrieved from http://www.missingkids.com/content/dam/ncmec/en_us/internetmerchantacquisitionmay2007.pdf

Franklin, J., Paxson, V., Perrig, A. & Savage, S. (2007). An inquiry into the nature and causes of the wealth of Internet miscreants. In *Proceedings of the ACM Conference on Computer and Communications Security* (pp. 275–288). 29 October–2 November, Alexandria, VA. New York: ACM.

Furnell, S. (2002). *Cybercrime: Vandalizing the information society.* London: Addison-Wesley.

Goodman, M. D. (1997). Why the police don't care about computer crime. *Harvard Journal of Law and Technology 10*, 465–494.

GSMA. (2014). *Preventing mobile payment services from being misused to monetize child sexual abuse content.* Mobile Alliance Against Child Sexual Abuse Content [Online] Available at http://www.gsma.com/publicpolicy/wp-content/uploads/2016/09/GSMA2014_Report_PreventingMobilePaymentServicesFromBeingMisusedToMonetiseChildSexualAbuseContent.pdf

Hatmaker, T. (2017, September 13). *US Government bans Kaspersky software citing fears about Russian intelligence.* TechCrunch [Online]. Available at https://techcrunch.com/2017/09/13/kaspersky-executive-branch-ban-dhs-homeland-security/

Hayne, S. C., Wang, H., & Wang, L. (2015). Modeling reputation as a time-series: Evaluating the risk of purchase decisions on eBay. *Decision Sciences 46*(6), 1077–1107.

Higgins, G. E., & Marcum, C. D. (2011). *Digital piracy: An integrated theoretical approach.* Raleigh, NC: Carolina Academic Press.

Hinduja, S. (2004). Perceptions of local and state law enforcement concerning the role of computer crime investigative teams. *Policing: An International Journal of Police Strategies and Management 3*, 341–357.

Hinduja, S. (2007). Computer crime investigations in the United States: Leveraging knowledge from the past to address the future. *International Journal of Cyber Criminology 1*, 1–26.

Hinduja, S., & Patchin, J. W. (2014). *Bullying beyond the schoolyard: Preventing and responding to cyberbullying.* Thousand Oaks, CA: Corwin Press.

Holt, T. J., & Blevins, K. R. (2007). Examining sex work from the client's perspective: Assessing johns using online data. *Deviant Behavior 28*, 333–354.

Holt, T. J., & Bossler, A. M., Fitzgerald, S. (2010). Examining state and local law enforcement perceptions of computer crime. In T. J. Holt, (Ed.) *Crime on-line: Correlates, causes, and context* (pp. 221–246). Raleigh, NC: Carolina Academic Press.

Holt, T. J., & Bossler, A. M. (2012). Predictors of patrol officer interest in cybercrime training and investigation in selected United States Police Departments. *Cyberpsychology, Behavior, and Social Networking 15*, 464–472.

Holt, T. J., & Bossler, A. M. (2016). *Cybercrime in progress: Theory and prevention of technology-enabled offenses.* Routledge: London.

Holt, T. J., Burruss, G. W., & Bossler, A. M. (2015). *Policing cybercrime and cyberterror.* Raleigh, NC: Carolina Academic Press.

Holt, T. J., & Copes, H. (2010). Transferring subcultural knowledge on-line: Practices and beliefs of persistent digital pirates. *Deviant Behavior 31*(7), 625–654.

Holt, T. J., & Graves, D. C. (2007). A qualitative analysis of advanced fee fraud schemes. *The International Journal of Cyber-Criminology 1*, 137–154.

Holt, T. J., & Kilger, M. (2012). The social dynamics of hacking. *The Honeynet Project* [Online]. Retrieved from https://honeynet.org/papers/socialdynamics

Holt, T. J., Smirnova, O., Chua, Y. T., & Copes, H. (2015). Examining the risk reduction strategies of actors in online criminal markets. *Global Crime 16*(2), 81–103.

Hutchings, A., & Holt, T. J. (2015). A crime script analysis of the online stolen data market. *British Journal of Criminology 55*, 596–614.

Innes, M. (2004). Reinventing tradition? Reassurance, neighbourhood security and policing. *Criminal Justice 4*(2), 151–171.

International Center for Missing and Exploited Children (2017). *Commercial child pornography: A brief snapshot of the Financial Coalition against Child Pornography* [Online]. Retrieved from http://www.icmec.org/wp-content/uploads/2016/09/FCACPTrends.pdf

Internet Crimes Against Children Task Force. (2017). *About* [Online]. Retrieved from https://www.icactaskforce.org/

Internet Watch Foundation. (2016). *Annual Report* [Online]. Retrieved from https://www.iwf.org.uk/sites/default/files/reports/2016-09/IWF%202015%20Annual%20Report%20Final%20for%20web.pdf

Jenkins, P. (2001). *Beyond tolerance: Child pornography on the Internet.* New York: New York University Press.

Jordan, T., & Taylor, P. (1998). A sociology of hackers. *The Sociological Review 46*, 757–780.

Krone, T. (2004). A typology and online child pornography offending. *Trends & Issues in Crime and Criminal Justice 279*, 2–6.

Leopold, J. (2017, November 8). He solved the DNC hack. Now he's telling his story for the first time. *BuzzFeedNews* [Online]. Retrieved from https://www.buzzfeed.com/jasonleopold/

he-solved-the-dnc-hack-now-hes-telling-his-story-for-the?utm_term=.pbJLQlqayY#.xhzbzLd3oD

Maimon, D., Wilson, T., Ren, W., & Berenblum, T. (2015). On the relevance of spatial and temporal dimensions in assessing computer susceptibility to system trespassing incidents. *British Journal of Criminology* 55(3), 615–634.

Marcum, C., Higgins, G. E., Freiburger, T. L., & Ricketts, M. L. (2010). Policing possession of child pornography online: Investigating the training and resources dedicated to the investigation of cybercrime. *International Journal of Police Science & Management* 12, 516–525.

Marks, J. (2017, October 13). *House bill would allow companies to hack back- with limits.* Nextgov Newsletter [Online]. Retrieved from http://www.nextgov.com/cybersecurity/2017/10/house-bill-would-allow-companies-hack-back-limits/141780/

Motoyama, M., McCoy, D., Levchenko, K., Savage, S., & Voelker, G. M. (2011). An analysis of underground forums. In *Proceedings of the 2011 ACM SIGCOMM conference on Internet measurement conference* (pp. 71–79).2–4 November, Berlin, Germany. New York: ACM.

Munson, L. (2014, July 11). *Microsoft and No-IP reach settlement over malware takedown.* Naked Security by Sophos [Online]. Retrieved from https://nakedsecurity.sophos.com/2014/07/11/microsoft-and-no-ip-reach-settlement-over-malware-takedown/

National Center for Missing and Exploited Children. (2017). *Our Partners* [Online] Retrieved from http://www.missingkids.com/supportus/partners/fcacp

National Institute of Justice. (2008). *Electronic Crime Scene Investigations: A Guide for First Responders* (2nd ed.). NCJ 219941. Washington, DC: National Institute of Justice.

Newman, G., & Clarke, R. (2003). *Superhighway robbery: Preventing e-commerce crime.* Cullompton, NJ: Willan Press.

Nhan, J. (2013). The evolution of online piracy: Challenge and response. In T. J. Holt (Ed.), *Crime on-line: Causes, correlates, and context* (pp. 61–80). Raleigh, NC: Carolina Academic Press.

PERF. (2014). The role of local law enforcement agencies in preventing and investigating cybercrime. Washington, DC: Police Executive Research Forum.

Quinn, J. F., & Forsyth, C. J. (2013). Red light districts on blue screens: A typology for understanding the evolution of deviant communities on the Internet. *Deviant Behavior 34,* 579–585.

Reyns, B. W., Henson, B., & Fisher, B. S. (2012). Stalking in the twilight zone: Extent of cyberstalking victimization and offending among college students. *Deviant Behavior 33*(1), 1–25.

Roberts, J. W., & Hunt, S. A. (2012). Social control in a sexually deviant cybercommunity: A cappers' code of conduct. *Deviant Behavior 33,* 757–773.

Schell, B. H., & Dodge, J. L. (2002). *The hacking of America: Who's doing it, why, and how.* Westport, CT: Quorum Books.

Senjo, S. R. (2004). An analysis of computer-related crime: Comparing police officer perceptions with empirical data. *Security Journal 17,* 55–71.

Sommer, P. (2004). The future for the policing of cybercrime. *Computer Fraud & Security 2004*(1), 8–12.

Spitzner, L. (2001). *The value of honeypots, part one: Definitions and values of honeypots.* Symantec [Online] Retrieved from https://www.symantec.com/connect/articles/value-honeypots-part-one-definitions-and-values-honeypots

Stambaugh, H., Beaupre, D.S., Icove, D.J., Baker, R., Cassady, W. & Williams, W.P. (2001), *Electronic crime needs assessment for state and local law enforcement.* NCJ 186276. Washington, DC: National Institute of Justice.

Steinmetz, K. F. (2015). Craft(y)ness: An ethnographic study of hacking. *The British Journal of Criminology 55,* 125–145.

Sunshine, J., & Tyler, T. R. (2003). The role of procedural justice and legitimacy in shaping public support for policing. *Law & Society Review 37*(3), 513–548.

Symantec Corporation. (2016). *Internet security threat report*, Vol. 20 [Online]. Retrieved from http://www.symantec.com/threatreport/

Torkington, N. (2005, October 4). *HBO attacking bittorrent* [Online] Retrieved from http://radar.oreilly.com/2005/10/hbo-attacking-bittorrent.html

TVTechnology. (2007, June 21). *Michael Moore's "Sicko" combats leaks on the Web* [Online]. Retrieved from https://www.tvtechnology.com/news/michael-moores-sicko-combats-leaks-on-the-web

Tyler, T. R. (2004). Enhancing police legitimacy. *The Annals of the American Academy of Political and Social Science 593*(1), 84–99.

Wall, D. S. (2001). Cybercrimes and the Internet. In D. S. Wall (Ed.), *Crime and the Internet.* (pp. 1–17). New York: Routledge.

Wall, D. (2004). Digital realism and the governance of spam as cybercrime. *European Journal on Criminal Policy and Research 10*, 309–335.

Wall, D. (2007). *Cybercrime: The transformation of crime in the information age.* Cambridge, MA: Polity.

Wall, D. (2010). The organization of cybercrime and organized cybercrime. In *Proceedings of current issues in IT security* (pp. 51–66). 12–14 May, Freiberg, Germany. Berlin: Duncker & Humblot.

Wall, D. S., & Williams, M. L. (2013). Policing cybercrime: Networked and social media technologies and the challenges for policing. *Policing and Society 23*, 409–412.

Weimann, G. (2005). How modern terrorism uses the Internet. *The Journal of International Security Affairs 8.*

Weiss, L. M., Capozzi, M. M., & Prusak, L. (2004). Learning from the internet giants. *MIT Sloan Management Review 45*(4), 79.

Willits, D., & Nowacki, J. (2016). The use of specialized cybercrime policing units: An organizational analysis. *Criminal Justice Studies 29*, 105–124.

Wolff, J. (2017, July 14). When companies get hacked, should they be allowed to hack back? The Atlantic [Online] Retrieved from https://www.theatlantic.com/business/archive/2017/07/hacking-back-active-defense/533679/

Yar, M. (2013). *Cybercrime and Society* (2nd ed.). London: Sage Publications.

Zetter, K. (2013, July 1). 9 years after Shadowcrew, Feds get their hands on fugitive cyber-crook. Wired [Online] Retrieved from http://www.wired.com/2013/07/bulgarian-shadowcrew-arrest/

CHAPTER 33

CYBERCRIME AND YOU: HOW CRIMINALS ATTACK AND THE HUMAN FACTORS THAT THEY SEEK TO EXPLOIT

JASON R. C. NURSE

INTRODUCTION

The Internet and Its Significance to Us as Individuals

TECHNOLOGY drives modern day society. It has influenced everything from governments and market economies, to global trade, travel, and communications. Digital technologies have further revolutionized our world, and since the advent of the Internet and the World Wide Web, society has become more efficient and advanced (Graham & Dutton, 2014). There are many benefits of the online world and to such large scales of connectivity. For individual Internet users, instantaneous communication translates into a platform for online purchases (on sites such as Amazon and eBay), online banking and financial management, interaction with friends and family members using messaging apps (e.g., WhatsApp and LINE), and the sharing of information (personal, opinion, or fact) on websites, blogs, and wikis. As the world has progressed technologically, these and many other services (such as Netflix, Uber, and Google services) have been made available to individuals with the aim of streamlining every aspect of our lives.

In a 2017 study of 30 economies including the United Kingdom (UK), United States of America (US), and Australia, it was the citizens of the Philippines that spent the most time online—at eight hours fifty-nine minutes, on average, per day—across PC and mobile devices (We Are Social, 2017). Brazil was second with eight hours fifty-five minutes, followed by Thailand at eight hours forty-nine minutes online. Developed countries such as the US, UK, and Australia posted usage values of between six hours twenty-one minutes and five hours eighteen minutes. This highlights a substantial usage gap compared to some developing states. A key driver of this increased Internet usage is social media, and particularly individuals' use of platforms such as Facebook, Facebook Messenger, WhatsApp, YouTube, and instant messaging service QQ (We Are Social, 2017). Evidence supporting this reality has also been found in other studies, where social networks are more frequently used by Internet users in the emerging world (Poushter, 2016); this type of use is key to understanding the impact of social media in online crime, as will be outlined further later in this chapter.

The Prevalence of Cybercrime

To critically reflect on today's world, while the Internet has various positive uses, it is increasingly being used as a tool to facilitate possibly the most significant challenge facing individuals' use of the Internet: cybercrime. Cybercrime has been defined in several ways but can essentially be regarded as any crime (traditional or new) that can be conducted or enabled through, or using, digital technologies. Such technologies include personal computers (PCs), laptops, mobile phones, and smart devices (e.g., Internet-connected cameras, voice assistants), but the scope is quickly expanding to encompass smart systems and infrastructures (e.g., homes, offices, and buildings driven by the Internet of Things or IoT).

The importance of cybercrime can be seen in its ever-rising prevalence. In the UK, for example, a key finding of an early Crime Survey of England and Wales by the Office for National Statistics (ONS) was that there were 3.8 million reported instances of cybercrime in the twelve months to June 2016 (Scott, 2016). This is generally noteworthy, but even more so, given that the total number of crimes recorded in the other components of the survey (e.g., burglary, theft, violent crimes, but excluding fraud) tallied 6.5 million. The number of cybercrimes, therefore, amounts to more than half of the total crimes. Similar trends can also be found in the 2018 ONS report, with cybercrime and fraud accounting for almost half of crimes (techUK, 2018). This reality becomes more concerning given that these statistics are only based on the reported crimes, and moreover, that such cybercrimes are almost certainly set to increase in the future. Studies from the US also further evidence the extent of cybercrime and identity theft. Research from the 2018 Identity Fraud Study found that $16.8 billion was stolen from 16.7 million US consumers in 2017, which represents an 8% increase in the number of victims from a year earlier (Weber, 2018).

Types of Cybercrime

At its core, there are arguably three types of cybercrime: crimes in the device, crimes using the device, and crimes against the device (Wall, 2007). Crimes in the device relates to situations in which the content on the device may be illegal or otherwise prohibited. Examples include trading and distribution of content that promotes hate crimes or incites violence. The next category, crimes using the device, encompasses crimes where digital systems are used to engage and often, to deceive, victims. An example of this is a criminal pretending to be a legitimate person (or entity) and tricking an individual into releasing their personal details (e.g., account credentials) or transferring funds to other accounts. Wall's final category, crimes against the device, pertains to incidents that compromise the device or system in some way. These crimes directly target the fundamental principles of cybersecurity, i.e., the confidentiality, integrity, and availability (regularly referred to as the *CIA* triad) of systems and data. This typology provides some general insight into the many crimes prevalent online today.

This chapter aims to build on the introduction to cybercrime and security issues online and focus in detail on cybercrimes conducted against individuals. It focuses on many of the crimes being conducted today and offers a topical discourse on how criminals craft these attacks, their motivations, and the key human factors and psychological aspects that make cybercriminals successful. Areas covered include social engineering (e.g., phishing, romance scams, catfishing), online harassment (e.g., cyberbullying, trolling, revenge porn,[1] and hate crimes), identity-related crimes (e.g., identity theft and doxxing), hacking (e.g., malware and account hacking), and denial-of-service (DoS) crimes.

Cybercrimes against Individuals: A Focus on the Core Crimes

The cybercrime landscape is enormous, and so are the varieties of ways in which cybercriminals can seek to attack individuals. This section introduces a taxonomy summarizing the most significant types of online crimes against individuals. These types of cybercrime are defined based on a comprehensive and systematic review of online crimes, case studies, and articles in academic, industry, and government circles. This includes instances and cases of cybercrime across the world (e.g., BBC News, 2016b; Sidek & Rubbi-Clarke, 2017), taxonomies of cybercrime and cyberattacks that have been developed in research (e.g., Gordon & Ford, 2006; Wall, 2007; Wall, 2005/2015), industry reports on prevalent crimes (e.g., CheckPoint, 2017; PwC, 2016), and governmental publications in the space (e.g., NCA, 2017).

The intention is to connect the identified types of cybercrime to real-world situations, but also to maintain a flexible structure as new types of cybercrimes may well emerge. Moreover, the chapter is inclusive in its approach and defines types that are relatable and easily communicated—which has benefits for engagement, especially for those not

---

[1] Or possibly, more appropriately termed, the distribution of sexual images of individuals without their consent.

involved in cybersecurity nor with a technical background or expertise. It is important to note here that many of the types identified here can be seen across prior works. For example, Wall's work (2005/2015) examines crimes against the individual, crimes against the machine, and crimes in the machine, and Gordon and Ford (2006) use some of these types as exemplars of their Type 1 and Type 2 cybercrimes. This taxonomy's value is therefore not in identifying new types of cybercrime, but instead in providing a new perspective on the topic which centers in on the types of cybercrime most prevalent today. The taxonomy is presented in Figure 1.

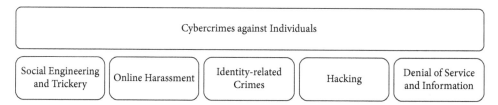

FIGURE 1 Main types of cybercrimes against individuals.

The first type of cybercrime is *Social Engineering and Trickery*, which involves applying deceitful methods to coerce individuals into behaving certain ways or performing some task. Next, *Online Harassment* is similar to its offline counterpart and describes instances where persons online are annoyed/abused and tormented by others. *Identity-related crimes* are those in which an individual's identity is stolen or misused by others for a nefarious or illegitimate purpose (e.g., fraud). *Hacking*, one of the most well publicized cybercrimes both in the news and the entertainment industry (e.g., *Mr. Robot*, *Live Free or Die Hard*, *The Matrix*, *Swordfish*), is the action of compromising computing systems. While traditionally not regarded as a significant personal crime, *Denial of Service* is one of the most used by online criminals, and its popularity is attributed to its simplicity—i.e., it primarily involves blocking legitimate access to information, files, websites, or services—and effectiveness. Finally, *(Denial of) Information* accommodates the new trend of ransomware which is similar in that it denies individuals access to their own information. The next sections analyze the taxonomy and each of its types of crimes in detail.

SOCIAL ENGINEERING AND ONLINE TRICKERY

Trickery, deceit, and scams are examples of some of the oldest means used by adversaries to achieve their goals. In Greek mythology, their army used deceit in the form of a Trojan horse; presented to the Trojans as a gift (or more specifically, an offering to Athena, goddess of war), it was instead a means for the Greek army to enter and destroy the city of Troy. Additionally, in *The Art of War*, fifth-century BCE Chinese military strategist Sun Tzu declares, "Hence, when able to attack, we must seem unable; when using our forces, we must seem inactive; when we are near, we must make the enemy believe we are far away; when far away, we must make him believe we are near" (Tzu/ Giles, 2009). According to this well-known text on war, the intention is to deceive and, ideally, to misdirect, while discretely progressing towards and obtaining the goal—in Tzu's case, winning against the enemy in battle.

Cybercriminals, potentially informed by history itself, have been applying such techniques for decades in *Social Engineering*, i.e., a specific class of cybercrime that uses deception or trickery to manipulate individuals into performing some unauthorized or illegitimate task. It seeks to exploit human psychology and is possibly the most effective means of conducting a crime against an individual.

In one example, a social engineer breaks into an individual's cell-phone provider account in under two minutes.[2] This was achieved by phoning the cell-phone provider's help desk, pretending to be the customer's wife (impersonation is typically a core component of this crime), and using an audio recording of a crying baby (under the guise of it being her baby) to elicit sympathy from the help desk employee. Here, the social engineer used some basic information (i.e., knowing the customer's name), sympathy, and the fact that a help desk is primarily supposed to provide assistance, to manipulate the help desk to grant her unauthorized access to a client account. There are numerous other similar types of attacks, and entire books (e.g., Hadnagy, 2010; Mann, 2008, 2013) and training courses on the topic (e.g., at the well-known hacking conference, BlackHat).

Phishing and Its Variants

Phishing is a specific type of social engineering crime that occurs using electronic communications, such as an email or a website. In it, criminals send an email, or create a website, that appears to be from a legitimate entity with the intention of conning individuals into divulging some sensitive information or performing a particular action. Today there are many different variants of phishing, including spear-phishing, vishing, smishing (or SMSishing), and whaling.

Spear-phishing is a targeted phishing attack on an individual that has been customized based on other key and pertinent information, such as their date of birth, current bank, Internet service provider, or email address. This additional information is used to enhance the appearance of legitimacy and thereby increase the effectiveness of the con. Spear-phishing is held to be the reason for several well-known crimes including "Celebgate," where private photographs of actresses Jennifer Lawrence, Kate Upton, and Scarlett Johansson were stolen and later exposed online. The terms vishing and smishing represent phishing attacks that occur over the phone (i.e., voice), and via text messages (especially SMS, but including WhatsApp, etc.) respectively. These often overlap with traditional phone scams but may also be used in combination with email phishing

---

[2] This is how hackers hack you using simple social engineering. See https://www.youtube.com/watch?v=lc7scxvKQOo

attempts. Whaling is very similar to spear-phishing but targets high-profile individuals (the notion being that a whale is a "big phish") such as company executives, with the goal of a higher payoff for criminals if the attack is successful.

The success of phishing attacks over the last decade has been phenomenal. To take the UK as an example, the City of London Police's National Fraud Intelligence Bureau (NFIB) and the Get Safe Online security awareness campaign estimated that in 2015 alone, phishing scams cost victims £174 million. Moreover, Symantec (2017) estimates that spear-phishing emails as a category in themselves have drained $3 billion from businesses over the last three years. These estimates are likely to increase, as are the various ways in which criminals have targeted individuals.

In one phishing scam, criminals monitored a lady in the process of purchasing a home, and after disguising themselves as her solicitor they requested that she transfer £50,000 into their account (iTV News, 2015). This can be considered as a spear-phishing attack given the amount of information the criminals had on her and her activities, and how they used that information to achieve their goal (similar to the process of reconnaissance). There have also been emails sent to university students where criminals have posed as employees of the university's finance department. They pretend to offer educational grants that can only be redeemed after students provide personal and banking details (BBC News, 2016a). While emails are prominent tools, fake websites also are a popular avenue for phishing crimes. A 2017 study discovered hundreds of fake websites posing as banks, including HSBC, Standard Chartered, Barclays, and Natwest, that targeted the public (McGoogan, 2017). These websites looked identical to official sites and used similar domain names, such as *hsbc-direct.com*, *barclaya.net*, and *lloydstsbs.com* (note the additional letter or slight re-organization of bank name in these addresses).

A key observation about these attacks and those above is that criminals have sought to exploit many human psychological traits. These include a willingness to trust others and to be kind, the impact of anxiety and stress on decision making, personal needs and wants, and in some regards, the naivety in decision making. In the home purchase case, criminals firstly targeted the stressful process of purchasing a home, and then secondly, waited for a specific moment in time where they could impersonate the solicitor to request transfer of funds. While not privy to the email sent, the tone of the email must have emphasized the importance of transferring the funds immediately to secure the purchase. Fear of losing the prospective property, the overall anxiety of house buying, and trust in the (supposed) solicitor are undoubtedly factors that would have led to the transfer of funds. Mann (2008) mentions similar tricks as core to social engineering, and Iuga, Nurse, and Erola (2016) mention these tricks as increasing the susceptibility of individuals to phishing attacks.

In the case of the university students, criminals targeted a prime need of students during their time at university, i.e., financial support to fund their degrees and themselves. By using university logos and other information, they were able to pose as a legitimate entity and thereby not arouse the suspicion of students. This impersonation also occurs within the fake website example. Criminals prey on naïve decision-making abilities, or more specifically, the heuristics (or quick "rules of thumb") that individuals apply to make decisions. Here, they are presenting emails and sites as we expect they should appear, thus deceiving us into accepting them and acting without detailed consideration. This process has previously been described via the psychological heuristic of representativeness by psychologists Tversky and Kahneman during the 1970s. The heuristic posits that humans often make decisions based on how representative an event is grounded on the evidence, rather than what may be probabilistically true (Kahneman & Tversky, 1973). Therefore, because the website or email appears to possess all of the key evidence (a logo, familiar names, etc.), its legitimacy is more likely to be accepted. This is only one example of the ways in which psychology overlaps with cybersecurity; many others can be found in Nurse, Creese, Goldsmith, and Lamberts. (2011a).

Online Scams—Tech Support, Romance, and Catfishing

In addition to phishing, online scams are also worth mentioning. Scams also involve trickery and deceit and typically have financial gain as the prime motive. One prominent example of the now common series of "tech support" scams is that of a global con uncovered in 2017. There, criminals purchased pop-up browser advertisements which appeared on victim's computer screens and locked their browsers (US DoJ, 2017). These pop-ups inaccurately informed individuals that their computers were compromised and that they should call the "tech support" company for assistance. Reports indicate that over 40,000 people across the globe were victimized and defrauded out of more than $25 million USD (US DoJ, 2017). These criminals were using a series of fear tactics to deceive individuals, many of whom were elderly and potentially more vulnerable.

Romance scams are also rampant on the Internet via online dating websites. Here, criminals seek to engage in faked and extensive relationships, again, usually for financial gain. Their technique involves preying on vulnerable individuals seeking romance and love and exploiting them under the guise of a relationship. Research has studied these scams from a variety of perspectives, including understanding their prevalence (e.g., Whitty & Buchanan, 2012) and their impact on victims (e.g., Whitty & Buchanan, 2016). A noteworthy finding for our work on cybercrimes and individuals is that while financial losses may be incurred by victims, it is often the loss of the relationship that was more upsetting and psychologically traumatic. Catfishing is another variant of the common romance scam where fake, online identities and potentially, even social groupings are created to lure individuals into romantic relationships. Similar to traditional scams, the goal may be for financial gain, but notoriety may also be considered as a motive, e.g., American football player Manti Teʹo (Schulman, 2014). Teʹo was famously tricked into believing that he was in a relationship with Stanford University student Lennay Kekua, who, in reality, did not exist: Teʹo was the victim of a year-long girlfriend hoax.

It is also important to consider the reasons behind why people continuously fall for online scams in the face of the large amounts of publicity to educate and warn individuals. Although fear, trickery, and the targeting of vulnerable individuals all play large parts, other research has extended consideration of these issues. Button, Nicholls, Kerr, and Owen (2014) have also identified core motivational factors that include the diversity of scams and frauds (i.e., criminals may find areas where individuals may be less wary of being defrauded), small amounts of money sought by criminals (if small amounts of money are lost, this may worry individuals less), authority and legitimacy displayed by scammers (this touches on the previous point of trickery and impersonation), as well as visceral appeals (i.e., criminals devising scams that appeal to human needs/feelings such as finance, love, sex, and sorrow). These cut across the various scams covered here and provide some insight into the diverse ways criminals use trickery and social engineering to achieve their nefarious goals, and thus why scams continue to be successful.

The Challenge of Online Harassment

Online harassment can broadly be regarded as the targeting of individuals with negative terms or actions. Emphasizing the significance of this crime, a 2016 Data & Society Research Institute study found that 47% of US Internet users have personally experienced online harassment or abuse, and 72% of these users have seen someone harassing someone else online. In terms of types of individuals that have been targeted, the research found that men and women are equally likely to face harassment online, but the latter have experienced a wider diversity of abuse. The individuals that are more likely to experience or witness abuse online include young users, black users, or those that identify as lesbian, gay, and bisexual (LGB). These findings broadly demonstrate an upwards progression from 2014 research by Marie Duggan at the Pew Research Center that also focused specifically on understanding online harassment.

In the UK, statistics collated by the National Society for the Prevention of Cruelty to Children (NSPCC) indicate a similarly worrying situation, especially considering children and online abuse. They note that one in three children have been victims of bullying online and almost one in four young people have come across racist or hate messages online (NSPCC, n.d.). According to the NSPCC, such harassment has led to over 11,000 counseling sessions with young people who talked to ChildLine (a UK help and advice hotline) about online issues between 2015 and 2016.

Cyberbullying

Cyberbullying is one of the various types of online harassment, and one of many that are online manifestations of offline malevolent actions. It affects children, teenagers, and adults alike. It, like bullying, essentially involves repeated aggression (direct or indirect) levied by a group or individual against a victim that is (often) unable to easily defend him/herself. This aggression however, now occurs through modern technological devices such as the Internet or smartphones (Slonje & Smith, 2008). There are countless examples of this crime to be found in the media and, tragically, a number of resulting instances of suicide among youth (e.g., BBC News, 2016b; Turner, 2017). A 2016 BBC report referred to one victim and noted that "His confidence and self-esteem had been eroded over a long period of time by the bullying behavior he experienced in secondary education. People who had never even met [...] were abusing him over social media and he found that he was unable to make and keep friends" (BBC News, 2016b). This example captures the essence of cyberbullying, and also highlights the use of current platforms such as social media as one of its core conduits.

Research also contributes significantly to understanding the problem of cyberbullying. For instance, Whittaker and Kowalski (2015) found that texting and social media are two of the most common venues for cyberbullying in college-age students. More interesting however, is the finding that there may be an overlap in roles between "bully" and "victim" and that despite the significant emotional impact of cyberbullying, many victims do not seek support (Price & Dalgleish, 2010). These factors are important because they suggest a continuation of cyberbullying due to related behavior, and the lack of treatment (which potentially leads to exacerbation). A key factor to point out here, as compared to social engineering, is that perpetrators are usually not conventional criminals. Instead, they tend to be individuals who do not recognize the full extent of the psychologically detrimental impact of their actions. This is especially the case with young people, where there may be a lack of awareness of others' feelings compounded by the inherent immaturity present in this age group. Cyberbullying is, however, also prevalent in adults (e.g., in social media and the workplace (Privitera & Campbell, 2009)) even though the expectation exists for adults to be better informed and more cognitively aware of their actions than are young people.

Internet Trolling and Cyberstalking

Internet trolling and cyberstalking are two other forms of online harassment that both share a few similarities with cyberbullying. Trolling is the action of posting inflammatory messages deliberately with the intention of being disruptive, starting arguments, and upsetting individuals. Bishop (2014) identifies twelve types of "trollers" split into four groups: *Haters* (inflame situations for no benefit to others); *Lolcows* (provoke others to gain attention); *Bzzzters* (chat regardless of accuracy or value of contribution); and *Eyeballs* (wait for the opportune moment to post provocative messages). The motives for such actions have been empirically studied and relate to boredom, attention-seeking and revenge, fun and entertainment, and damage to the community and other people (Shachaf & Hara, 2010). This research provides useful insight into the types of actions that are core to trolling, and the motives of individuals who engage in it.

Real-world examples of trolls can be found in media reports and include people who have used online means such as social media to falsely brand others as pedophiles and witches, and also threatened to harm them (The Guardian, 2014; The Telegraph, 2015). As a result of such online malfeasance, the UK is an example of a country that now has stringent laws regarding this behavior (notably the Malicious Communications Act)[3] and has already sentenced several trolls to jail.

Cyberstalking is the use of electronic means (e.g., Internet, email) by criminals to repeatedly harass, threaten, prey on, or otherwise track an individual. Factors that tend to differentiate cyberstalking from other forms of online harassment include prolonged monitoring (or "keeping tabs") of victims and making victims feel afraid and unsafe. A more interesting distinction to consider, nonetheless, is what separates cyberstalking from offline stalking—which could assist in the understanding of its prevalence. Goodno (2007) defines five peculiarities exclusive to cyberstalking: cyberstalkers use electronic means to instantly harass victims and have opportunities for wide dissemination; they can be physically/geographically far away from their victims; criminals operate under a cloak of (perceived) anonymity online; they can easily impersonate their victims to aggravate situations; and finally, these cybercriminals often encourage third parties in their harassment. These differences are so significant that they have led to cyberstalking overtaking offline physical harassment in the UK as a crime (McVeigh, 2011).

While cyberstalking does affect a cross-section of society, research has shown that some groups and types of individuals are more likely to be targets. In one study for instance, LGB Internet users were found to be almost four times as likely to report experiencing continuous contact which made them feel unsafe (Data & Society Research Institute, 2016). Women are also often targeted, e.g., for one female author, it had a serious impact on her personal and professional life (Gough, 2016), and is one of many examples that illustrate how social media, in particular, can be used to support stalking. Here, the stalker continuously monitored the individual, tracked her movements, gathered personal data (e.g., her address), and contacted her son's school and newly met friends with malicious messages, e.g., from the stalker to a friend via Facebook— "*One of the people around you is author [author's name]. She seems like a nice person at first-but actually she is a toxic person under a silver tongued mask. [Author's name] is a secretly sadistic narcissistic person who tries to get others to commit suicide. STAY AWAY FROM HER... She is a wolf in sheeps' clothing and has no conscience*" (Gough, 2016). This example demonstrates one of the ways in which stalkers can use the Internet to abuse and control their victims, i.e., through targeting friends and family; this is in addition to the more direct forms of harassment (e.g., attempts at ongoing messages or persistent threats).

The challenge here is that the Internet and social media have become so embedded in the modern lifestyle that these technologies and individuals' tendency to overshare provides cyberstalkers and other criminals with copious amounts of personal information they need (Nurse, 2015). Additionally, Cavezza and McEwan (2014) found that, compared to offline stalkers, cyberstalkers may be more likely to be ex-intimate partners. These results are interesting because they provide further insight into the types of people who perform such actions as well as those who are often impacted.

---

[3] http://www.legislation.gov.uk/ukpga/1988/27/introduction

Revenge Porn and Sextortion

Revenge porn and sextortion are two of the newest (in broad terms) forms of online harassment. Within the former, individuals, especially ex-partners, post sexual images of victims online without their permission. Criminals use these photo leaks to embarrass, humiliate, and demean victims. Sextortion is the gathering of sexual images or video (potentially via entrapment), and its use to blackmail individuals for further sexual footage or other favors. Reports indicate the significance of these crimes in cyberspace, with Facebook having to disable more than 14,000 accounts related to this form of crime in a single month alone (Hopkins & Solon, 2017). Examples of these crimes can typically be found in two main scenarios.

The first scenario involves disgruntled ex-partners using private photos, likely shared during a previous sexual relationship, to humiliate their victims—this may occur especially if relationships did not end amicably. This has also become known as revenge porn, or more accurately, non-consensual sharing of private sexual images. Secondly, there are an increasing number of cybercriminal gangs using the guise of attractive young women to trick individuals into sexually explicit actions online (e.g., via webcams or Skype sessions). These actions are recorded and later used to blackmail victims—typically using threats of sharing photos with family and friends unless money is paid (Sawer, 2016).

Cybercriminals have also combined sextortion with phishing and hacked passwords to boost impact. The latest trend has been in emailing individuals claiming to have compromising video of them watching pornography, and recorded via their webcam; the email includes one of the individual's passwords (attained most likely from a prior organizational data breach) to suggest legitimacy. Individuals are asked to pay a certain amount (e.g., via Bitcoin) or risk the video being sent to friends, family and coworkers. A poignant example, taken from the EFF, is as follows: "*Hi, victim. I write you because I put a malware on the web page with porn which you have visited. My virus grabbed all your personal info and turned on your camera which captured the process. . . . Just after that the soft saved your contact list. I will delete the compromising video and info if you pay me 999 USD in bitcoin. . . . I give you 30 hours after you open my message for making the transaction*" (Quintin, 2018).

Similar to the other crimes mentioned, revenge porn and sextortion can have devastating impacts on victims. In possibly one of the largest studies on the topic, Henry, Powell, and Flynn (2017) found that 80% of people who experienced sextortion reported heightened levels of psychological distress, such that it was also consistent with moderate to severe depression and/or anxiety disorder. Furthermore, victims often felt highly fearful for their safety after the ordeal. This response is well-justified as there have been other reports of serious threats (e.g., abuse and threats of rape) to victims of revenge porn (Raven, 2014), and other reports of suicide due to its prolonged effects (BBC News, 2017a). It is worth mentioning that most research up until this point has focused on the legal and criminal aspects of revenge porn and combatting it. Simultaneously, there has been a surge in new laws (e.g., the UK Criminal Justice and Courts Act 2015, the Protecting Canadians from Online Crime Act) and subsequent prosecutions for criminals involved in these types of acts (CPS, 2015).

Hate Crimes

Hate crimes (and hate speech) are another form of offline harassment that have made the transition to online. These are crimes that arise due to prejudice based on race, sexual orientation, gender, religion, ethnicity, or disability (McDevitt, Levin, & Bennett., 2002). In many ways, these crimes overlap with those mentioned, and also extend them in terms of the threats levied. Jacks and Adler (2015) build on earlier work (e.g., McDevitt et al., 2002) to examine the types of users that are engaged in online hate crimes (or with hate materials). They identify four main types: *Browsers* (viewers of hate material); *Commentators* (viewers and those who engage with and post comments); *Activists* (those who add overt hate material and seek to promote their views and engage with others); and *Leaders* (individuals who use the Internet to support, organize, and promote their extremist ideologies). As to be expected, Leaders are typically the smallest group, but as Jacks and Adler (2015) note, they tend to be high repeat offenders.

Social media also plays a central role in hate speech and crimes, particularly those that occur after significant events. For instance, after the Woolwich attack on an off-duty soldier in London in May 2013, there were hundreds of hate messages posted on social media, especially Twitter, targeting Muslims (Awan, 2014). These perpetrators were using the platform of social media, and its wide reach, to openly attack people due to their faith. This issue of hate on social media has become so widespread that London's Met Police have set up an Online Hate Crime Hub unit to address it, and there have been demands for fines on Facebook, Twitter, and YouTube for failing to act swiftly against such content (Fiveash, 2017). It is arguably only via such concerted efforts that progress will be made in tackling the issue of online hate, but also that of online harassment more broadly.

IDENTITY-RELATED CYBERCRIMES

Identity theft and identity fraud are traditional crimes that have flourished due to online systems and the open nature of the Internet. While the theft of identities by criminals is enabled due the amount of information on individuals online, fraud becomes possible when that information is used for monetary gain (e.g., impersonating the individual to purchase an item). In the UK alone, there were just short of 173,000 incidents of identity fraud in 2016, which represents 53.3% of all reported fraud, and more importantly, 88% of this occurred online (BBC News, 2017b). The US market has also witnessed significant rises in identity-related fraud, with a 40% increase in 2016 in "card not present" (i.e., mainly online) fraud (Javelin Strategy & Research, 2017) and in 2017, this type of fraud being 81% more likely than point-of-sale fraud (Weber, 2018). These reports also act to highlight some of the main activities by cybercriminals engaging in identity theft and fraud, e.g., making online purchases, signing up for credit accounts (e.g., credit cards or loans), signing up to paid websites. Depending on the amount of data possessed by these criminals, there are even concerns that they could apply for passports in a victim's name. Other examples of crimes such as unlawful identity delegation and exchange have also been documented in research (Koops, Leenes, Meints, van der Meulen, & Jaquet-Chiffelle, 2009).

Identity theft works by criminals gathering information on individuals and using that as the basis through which to steal their identities. Today, there are two information-gathering techniques preferred by cybercriminals: the monitoring of individuals on social media as they post and interact online, and the gathering and use of personal data from previous online security breaches. The first of these techniques exploits a factor previously mentioned that pertains to phishing, i.e., the nature to overshare, but also the poor management of security and privacy online. A noteworthy study by fraud prevention organization Cifas found that Twitter, Facebook, and LinkedIn are now prime "hunting grounds" used by identity thieves (Samee, 2016); these networks contain an abundance of personal details, from birth dates and family member details to addresses, school histories, and job titles.

Previous research has considered this issue of oversharing and modeled how social media data could be used to place individuals at great risk, both online and offline (Creese, Goldsmith, Nurse, & Phillips, 2012; Nurse, 2015). There are also greater impacts on security and privacy as this data is combined with that from IoT devices such as fitness trackers and smart watches (Aktypi, Nurse, & Goldsmith, 2017). Most recently, people using Strava to track their exercise patterns inadvertently exposed details of military bases when posting their results to the app; such types of exposure can increase the risk to individuals, businesses, and governments (Hern, 2018; Nurse, 2018). In addition to focusing on these risks, other relevant psychological research has sought to understand why individuals tend to disclose more online. This has led to the identification of six factors which explain such behavior and create what has been deemed the "online disinhibition effect": dissociative anonymity (separation of online actions from offline identities); invisibility (opportunity to be physically invisible and unseen); asynchronicity (lack of immediate and real-time reactions); solipsistic introjection (or, merging of minds with other online individuals); dissociative imagination (impression of the online world as make believe and not connected to reality); and minimization of status and authority (based on the perspective that everyone online is equal) (Suler, 2004). These factors, including their interactions, are widely considered to impact online behavior, and thus may also potentially be linked to exposure to risks (such as identity theft and fraud).

The second information gathering technique used by cybercriminals is that of previous online data breaches. Over the last ten years, a significant number of companies have been victims of cyberattacks and subsequently have leaked customer data online.

A few well-known enterprises include Yahoo!, Uber, Target, Sony, Anthem (health insurer), JP Morgan Chase, Ashley Madison, and eHarmony, and the data exposed spans biographic information, medical records, email addresses, family members, social security numbers, card details, and passwords. These customer details have often been available openly on public websites (e.g., *pastebin.com*), or for sale online. Pastebin.com provides an interesting case study given that although it has positive uses, hackers have become increasingly attached to it to publicly share/expose sensitive details (in addition to the above, this includes compromised social media accounts, access credentials to companies, etc.) online. Likely reasons for this preference include the site's lack of requirement for users to register, its lack of proactive moderation of posts, and its ability to handle large text-based files.

The Dark Web is particularly relevant here as it is one of the most well-known places where identity data and banking details can be found and traded by cybercriminals. Because the Web exists on an encrypted network it can only be accessed by tools such as Tor (The Onion Router), and thus offers some level of anonymity. According to the Underground Hacker Marketplace report, credit cards can be purchased for as little as $7 USD, identity packages (including social security number, driver's license, and matching utility bill) for $90 USD, and a dossier of credentials and data (dubbed a Fullz, and containing names, addresses, banking information, and physical counterfeit cards) for $140–$250 USD (Dell SecureWorks, 2016). Such cybercrime marketplaces and ecosystems place individuals at a continued risk of identity theft and fraud, especially considering that much of an individual's most valued identity data (e.g., name, email, social security number, bank accounts) is not easily changed.

Although it is not as significant (at least from a monetary standpoint) as identity theft or fraud, the newer crime of online doxxing (or doxing) is worth a mention here. This attack involves inspecting and researching personal information (e.g., home addresses, emails and phone numbers, preferences) about an individual and then posting that information publicly online. The criminal's intention is generally to infringe on the privacy of that person for malicious reasons such as harassment, or to conduct some form of vigilante justice for an actual or perceived wrong.

HACKING: THE DARK ART

Hacking is one of the most traditional forms of cybercrime and involves activities that result in the compromise of computing systems and/or digital information. By compromise, this chapter refers specifically to the detrimental impact of these actions on the confidentiality and integrity of systems and data. As such, hacking can refer to corporate or personal data (e.g., a person's photo album) being exposed, or accessed by, unintended parties; the unauthorized modification or deletion of that data (with or without the knowledge of the individual); or computer systems being disrupted from functioning as intended.

Malware (Viruses, Worms, Trojans, Spyware, and Cryptojacking)

There is a plethora of crimes that can be labeled as hacking. The most topical threat in this domain however, is arguably that of malware. Malicious software (or malware) describes applications developed and used by criminals to compromise the confidentiality or integrity of systems and information. The cost of managing malware alone for UK organizations in a 2016 study totaled £7.5 billion (Warwick, 2016). This has been matched by an even more drastic increase in the amount of malware applications and variants deployed by criminals. For instance, in 2017, Symantec (2017) reported a three-fold increase in new malware families online, while in 2018 there was a 88% increase in new malware variants (Symantec, 2018). The most popular types of malware that impact individuals are viruses, worms, Trojan horses, and spyware.

Viruses are programs that replicate when executed and spread to other files and systems. They are known for attaching themselves to other programs. The Melissa virus is one of the most famous viruses in history. It was implemented as a Microsoft Word macro virus that once opened by an unwitting individual, automatically distributed itself via email to the first 50 people in that individual's Outlook address book, with the message "*Here is that document you asked for . . . don't show anyone else ;-).*" As these emails were opened and the document was accessed, the virus would spread even further, infecting more computers, and generating thousands of unsolicited emails. A unique characteristic of Melissa (and many of the viruses it has since inspired) was that its success and the continued spread of the virus exploited human psychology. Specifically, it targeted individuals' friendships, i.e., sending to contacts thereby hijacking existing trust relationships, and also used trickery by referencing a document that was supposedly requested and allegedly secretive.

Worms are similar to viruses but they are standalone and do not need to be attached to a file. The prime purpose of worms is to self-replicate especially to other computers on the network (e.g., a home, university, or public network). As a result of its purpose, worms tend to vastly consume system resources (e.g., a computer's CPU and memory, and a network's bandwidth) thus slowing down computers and network speeds. Examples of recorded computer worms include Blaster, which would also cause the user's computer to shut down or restart repeatedly, ILOVEYOU, and the Daprosy worm.

Trojan horses, as the name suggests, are programs that appear legitimate but have another core purpose, which commonly is acting as a back door into computers or systems (most notably, Remote-Access Trojans (RATs)). These malware variants can allow cybercriminals to circumvent security mechanisms to gain unauthorized access into systems. This access may be used to steal files, monitor individuals, or to employ the computer as a proxy for a larger attack. For example, personal information and files (e.g., photo albums, information on finances, private diaries, saved passwords) may be accessed and leaked online, or criminals may remotely turn on web cameras to spy on and take photos of individuals (e.g., Blue, 2016; Korolov, 2016).

The latter of which could lead to sextortion. Furthermore, computers could be used as a platform to launch cyberattacks against other systems. This is similar to the recent case of the DoS attack on DNS provider, Dyn, where IoT devices from within homes and organizations across the world aided in disrupting access to hundreds of popular websites (Krebs, 2016).

Another type of malware targeting individuals online is spyware, which, as the name suggests, spies on and collects information about users, which could span from gathering specific information (e.g., passwords, banking information, search habits, computer-usage information) to storing all of the individual's behavior on the computer or system. The primary goal of spyware is to extract useful information about users that can then be used by the cybercriminal for a financial gain. There are numerous instances of such malware found on computers and smartphones (e.g., CheckPoint, 2017; Lecher, 2016).

While many of the other malware types have been known for some time, a more recent entry in the malware domain is that of cryptojacking typically through coin mining malware. Cryptojacking is the process of using an individual's computing device (PC, laptop, etc.) without their knowledge to 'mine' cryptocurrencies such as Bitcoin. Mining is a computationally expensive problem, and therefore, cybercriminals have sought to use any resources they can find—including hijacking the processing power of unsuspecting user devices—and pool these together to form a remotely linked system for efficient mining. This hijacking typically works by the hacker secretly including mining scripts (pieces of programming code) within webpages or browser extensions which automatically execute when a user visits a website. In early 2018, several government websites in the UK, US, and Australia were compromised by cryptojacking malware (Osborne, 2018), which meant visitors to those sites unwittingly may have participated in mining. Numerous other companies, networks and online sites have also been compromised by this threat, including Tesla, GitHub, a Starbucks Wi-Fi network, and a series of pirate video streaming websites. More worryingly, the problem of cryptojacking is likely to become significantly worse in the future as current reports note that attacks in the UK alone have surged 1200% (Martin, 2018) and over the course of 2017, there was a 34000% increase in coin mining attacks (Symantec, 2018)—the motivation for attackers being new currency or simply, more money.

Having reflected on the several types of malware present, it is also worthwhile to consider the ways in which individuals' technology become infected, and thus what makes such crimes/attacks truly successful. Focusing on viruses and worms first, these are unique as they self-replicate and automatically spread to other systems with little user contact. The computers and users that are initially infected are therefore the key to the prevalence of this computer attack. Trojans horses, spyware, and their variants (e.g., adware and scareware) offer a different challenge to cybercriminals as to how they disseminate their attacks. There is a range of techniques developed to threaten individuals.

Phishing (and spear-phishing) attacks are the most common vector through which criminals transmit malware (Symantec, 2017). These exploit the trust of humans through impersonation and social engineering. Another infection vector is the bundling of malware with legitimate software downloads; this regularly occurs with spyware and third-party browsers or applications such as peer-to-peer file sharing platforms like Kazaa (Moshchuk, Bragin, Gribble, & Levy, 2006). Here, cybercriminals recognize the importance of certain applications and seek to exploit that by pairing installations. In many cases the pairing of additional software may not be known by users, although in some cases it may be and users may still choose to download it. From a psychological perspective, this may occur for multiple reasons. For instance, users may be focused only on their end goal (e.g., watching a film or listening to music) and ignore anything that distracts from that goal, or they may not want to pay for services and so prefer to watch a film online for free. There is also the reality that users often misunderstand the level of risk they are facing and overestimate the capability of protection measures such as anti-virus software (Nurse et al., 2011a). This results in overly risky decisions, and ultimately may lead to the successfulness of a hack.

Watering hole attacks and drive-by downloads are also highly preferred techniques, and these demonstrate how simple it is to compromise individuals. These attacks only require individuals to visit an infected webpage or misclick in a browser window, and the malware will be downloaded automatically for later installation. Watering hole attacks are particularly interesting because they involve the cybercriminal monitoring the types of sites an individual or certain group tends to visit, and then compromising (one or more of) those sites to allow for the injection of malware (in essence, "poisoning the watering hole"). They then wait until the intended targets visit those sites again and thus become infected. This exemplifies one of the many tailored attacks levied by cybercriminals to target individuals. It also demonstrates the research in which cybercriminals often engage and the extent to which they may be willing to monitor human behavior to increase successfulness of their crime. A crucial point worth noting here is that the sites targeted could be regular websites, and there is not necessarily an act, or fault, of the user that makes this attack possible other than visiting the site.

Account and Password Hacking

Beyond malware, the hacking of online accounts (e.g., Facebook, Gmail, Government portals, paid services) and user passwords is a significant challenge faced by individuals. This is due to a variety of techniques being applied by cybercriminals, many of which are now even automated. One popular approach to hacking an individual's account is through the stealing of their username and password credentials. Criminals typically achieve this via shoulder surfing (i.e., looking over someone's shoulder while they are entering their password), and cybercriminals also focus on installing malware on the victim's computer that logs all keys typed (also known as a keylogger) or applying social engineering techniques.

A real-world example of such attacks was the case of a student who installed keyloggers on university computers to steal staff passwords, and then used their accounts to increase his test scores (Vaas, 2015). Keyloggers are particularly dangerous as they can record all keystrokes, from passwords to credit card numbers. It is worth noting, however, that new approaches to stealing passwords are continuously being discovered, as evidenced with PINs deciphered through video recording and tracking the motion/tilt of smartphones (Mehrnezhad, Toreini, Shahandashti, & Hao, 2016; Nurse, Erola, Agrafiotis, Goldsmith, & Creese, 2015). The IoT could pose a real challenge here given the amount of personal information that may be leaked via the usage of smart devices—be they wearables (smart watches, fitness trackers), voice assistants (e.g., Amazon Alexa, Google Home, or Apple HomePod), or smart appliances (e.g., smart TVs, fridges, and ovens). Research has already demonstrated the somewhat irrational behavior of individuals when using the IoT, considering their beliefs regarding privacy versus their inaction to behave privately (i.e., the privacy paradox) (Williams, Nurse, & Creese, 2016, 2017).

Password guessing is another way in which cybercriminals can gain illegitimate access to individuals' accounts. Informed guessing is the most successful technique and is where criminals use prior information to guess account credentials or infer details that would allow them to reset user accounts. Such information can be readily gathered from social media profiles (e.g., hobbies, pets, sports teams, mother's maiden name, family member names, and dates of birth), which is why it is important for individuals to be wary of what they share online. Another avenue used by cybercriminals is that of previously breached passwords. Given the number of data breaches that have occurred over the last few years as discussed earlier and the tendency of individuals to reuse passwords across sites, criminals have the perfect platform to amass sensitive user data and existing credentials. Research has investigated this reality and demonstrated the various ways in which hackers can reuse and guess passwords with some degree of success using this prior knowledge (Das, Bonneau, Caesar, Borisov, & Wang, 2014). Sites such as *haveibeenpwned.com* have since become popular as they allow users to check whether or not their account has been compromised in a breach.

Dictionary attacks, i.e., where words from the dictionary are used to form potential passwords, are also a common password hacking technique. Here, cybercriminals look to exploit poorly created passwords based on dictionary words. One unique aspect of these attacks is that they can be automated using hacking tools such as John the Ripper, Cain and Abel, and LophtCrack. The availability of these tools, and the fact that they require little expertise yet combine several different password crackers into one packaged application, provides cybercriminals with a significant advantage. That is, that upskilling and increasing the scale of attacks is much easier than before and thus less of a barrier to conducting crime.

To exacerbate this issue, there are many common, weak passwords in use by individuals. A study of 10 million passwords sourced from data breaches that occurred in 2016 (Guccione, 2017) highlighted several key points: firstly, the top five common passwords used by individuals were 123456, 123456789, qwerty, 12345678, and 111111; secondly, 17% of users had the password "123456."; thirdly, the list of most frequently used passwords has demonstrated little change over the last few years; and finally, nearly half of the top 15 passwords are six characters or shorter. Fortune Magazine recently reported that many of these same issues occurred again in 2017 (Korosec, 2017). One inference that might be made from these findings is that users prefer to maintain simple and memorable passwords. This is hardly a surprise as security is often known to crumble when placed in conflict with usability (Nurse, Creese, Goldsmith, & Lamberts, 2011b), and after all, humans favor consistency and are known to be creatures of habit. For hackers, however, such weak and common passwords are ideal, and can be guessed extremely quickly, thus placing users at risk of account takeovers.

DENIAL-OF-SERVICE (DoS)
AND RANSOMWARE

A DoS attack involves cybercriminals blocking individuals from accessing legitimate websites and services. This is normally achieved by bombarding the websites/services with an enormous number of fabricated requests (e.g., page visits), which causes legitimate requests to be dropped or the organization's websites/services to crash under the load. This crime is somewhat unique as compared to the others above because it depicts another way that individuals may be impacted by cybercrime, i.e., via attacks on organizations and services that they use. Interestingly, there would be little obvious signs of this to a user other than the website being unavailable. Of course, the unavailability of a website does not necessarily mean a DoS attack has occurred; there are many other reasons that may be behind this, including human errors (BBC News, 2016c).

On Christmas Eve of 2015 a DoS cyberattack inundated BBC services with a substantial number of web requests which eventually forced many offline (Korolov, 2016). While this attack was not unique (and, indeed there have been larger Distributed-DoS (DDoS) attacks, e.g., GitHub (Kottler, 2018) or Dyn in 2016 (Krebs, 2016), there is one very worrying observation about it: the cybercriminals that claimed responsibility, a group named New World Hacking, stated that the attack was only a test and that they had not planned to take the BBC down for multiple hours. This demonstrates the power of cybercriminals today and suggests that, on occasion, they themselves are not fully aware of their capabilities. A compelling reason for this heightened and unknown capability might be the ease at which criminals can procure or rent hacking and botnet[4] services on the Dark Web (Dell SecureWorks, 2016). Often, these services are rented without a proper understanding of their full impact.

In addition to DoS attacks, cybercriminals have also employed other forms of crime to block legitimate access requests by individuals. A popular trend today is using ransomware, which is a form of malware that encrypts individual's information and only allows subsequent access if ransom is paid (typically via the cryptocurrency, Bitcoin). Individuals might become infected by phishing attacks or using infected devices

---

[4] A botnet is a series of Internet-connected computing devices that are infected with malware which allows them to be remotely controlled. These devices are not normally aware they are a part of the botnet.

(e.g., pen-drives). According to Symantec (2017), the growth of ransomware has been phenomenal, especially its use as a profit center for criminals. On average, they note that criminals demand $1,077 USD per victim in each ransomware attack. There are many potential reasons for the growth in this crime, but arguably the most prominent is that criminals have fully recognized that an individual's data, whether it be personal photos and videos, financial spreadsheets, or files, is their most valuable possession. As a result, these attacks are crafted to target that data.

The increasing prevalence of this crime is motivated by its high success rates. For example, 64% of people in the US whose technology was infected were found to be willing to pay the necessary amount to regain access to their data (Symantec, 2017). Similarly, at an organizational level one infected hospital paid $17,000 USD to have its files unencrypted (Wong & Solon, 2017). Psychologically, it is a simple decision of cost versus benefit for individuals and organizations: the cost of paying the ransom is significantly less than the benefit of having access to files, therefore the payment is made. For individuals, this might mean regaining access to precious videos of their child's first steps or photos of a graduation or a selfie with a celebrity. For a hospital, access to the electronic health records database is required to be able to properly treat patients and thereby, to conduct business. Again, therefore, criminals have found a key weakness in these parties and are crafting crimes to carefully exploit them.

To further support their plight, cybercriminals are also making efforts to ensure that the paying of ransoms is as seamless and "painless" as possible. There have been anecdotes of cybercriminals providing ransom payment FAQs, helpdesks, and even offering discounts to individuals who cannot pay the full demands. This demonstrates a level of sophistication by criminals where crime is becoming an industry (see Nurse and Bada, this volume), capable of even offering "customer services". At the same time, there is an increasing amount of ransomware attacks, e.g., the WannaCry attack in 2017, which affected nearly 100 countries and critical services such as the UK's National Health Service (NHS) (Guardian, 2017). These attacks seem to increase due to the combination of reasons and raise a number of interesting questions for us as a society. For example, as these attacks continue to grow, will society simply accept them (and for instance, just pay the ransom)? Will the occasional (e.g., yearly) breach of our data simply be viewed as part of being online? And broadly, will we become desensitized (even further) to online risk? These present interesting avenues for future research in the field.

SUMMARIZING KEY HUMAN FACTORS, AND FUTURE RESEARCH

While the advantages that accompany Internet use and digital technologies are plentiful, there is an abundance of challenges and concerns facing the new, high-tech world. Cybercrime is one of the most prevalent and has the ability to impact people psychologically, financially, and even physically. This chapter reflected on many of the crimes that cybercriminals engage in today and the reasons why these are often quite successful, from social engineering and online harassment to hacking and ransomware attacks. A salient point is that cybercriminals are ready, willing, and have a strong history in exploiting many human psychological needs and weaknesses. Such facets include our innate desire to trust and help each other (e.g., in the case of the mother with the crying baby), the human need for love and affection (e.g., romance scams), the host of biases that affect decision-making on security (Nurse et al., 2011a), and a perfect knowledge of what people consider most important, i.e., the willingness to pay for the return of something valuable (e.g., instances of ransomware). Table 1 summarizes the main types of crimes and the respective human and psychological factors that may be exploited by cybercriminals to lead to their success.

Table 1 Types of cybercrimes and the respective human and psychological factors that are exploited by criminals

Types of cybercriminal attacks	Human and psychological factors that when exploited are likely to increase the crime's success
Social Engineering and Trickery	Individuals' willingness to trust others, willingness to be kind or sympathetic, needs and wants (e.g., visceral appeals or desires for finances or help), suggested urgency or importance of a message (e.g., website or application prompt, email, or call) received (seeking to offset rational decision-making), signs of legitimacy or authority in a message or individual (e.g., branding identical to the official branding of individual or organization, with the aim of cultivating trust), fear as conveyed through a message or individual (meant to offset rational decisions), the targeting of situations that are high stress or where individuals are likely to be highly anxious (as in the case of the house purchase), convenience (where the easier decision may not be the most secure), and heuristics and biases (these overlap with many of the other factors).
Online Harassment	Individuals' tendency to overshare personal details online or trust an online identity too much to the point of exposing themselves (there is the potential for this contributing to specific targeting or harassment). There is also an indirect use of human factors by criminals, i.e., instead of relying on factors held by the victim, they also rely on the guise of their anonymity to launch their harassment (a perception that their real identities are hidden) and that they can encourage others to participate in the harassment. Forms of online harassment, such as sextortion, can also be combined with other crimes including phishing and hacking, to further panic victims and convince them to succumb to the criminal's demands.
Identity-related crimes	Individuals' tendency to overshare personal identity details online, especially on forms of social media, including Facebook, Twitter, LinkedIn (this links human factors closely to the online disinhibition effect), and unfamiliarity with new forms of technology (new technologies such as the IoT may lead to further oversharing of identity data) which open individuals to risk.

(continued)

Table 1 Continued

Types of cybercriminal attacks	Human and psychological factors that when exploited are likely to increase the crime's success
Hacking	Individuals' misunderstanding of how at risk they are (typically an underestimation), misunderstanding of the capability of security and privacy protection measures (often an overestimation), an individual's wants and needs (for instance, bundling spyware with legitimate software), the emphasis on achieving goals potentially at the expense of security, tendency to overshare personal details online (which may lead to password guessing by hackers), selection of weak passwords because they are simple and memorable, and reuse of passwords across websites and applications (passwords which can often be gained from one of the hundreds of data breaches each year).
Denial-of-Service (DoS) and Information	Human and psychological factors in this context primarily relate to ransomware, and include: understanding the real value to an individual of their personal data (thus appreciating that the payment of a ransom is much less in value than that personal data, e.g., photos or financial information), and making the ransom payment process as seamless as possible (e.g., with FAQs, Helpdesks, and discounts)

As the sophistication of cybercriminals has increased, so too must the approaches to prevent, detect, and deter their behaviors. Cyberpsychology research has made significant inroads to the analysis of this problem through the study of criminal behavior and the psychological and social impact on victims. The field of Cybersecurity features a range of new models, systems, and tools that aim to prevent and detect attacks against individuals—these utilize a variety of the latest techniques in machine learning and anomaly detection to boost accuracy and efficiency. Criminology is also a key area, and there are now several laws across the world seeking to deter online crimes and prosecute those who perpetrate them. However, if approaches towards preventing cybercrime are to be truly effective at protecting individuals, a more concerted, cross-disciplinary program is mandatory. It is only in this way that the insight from each field can be properly synthesized and combined to address the issue of online crime.

REFERENCES

Aktypi, A., Nurse, J. R. C., & Goldsmith, M. (2017). Unwinding Ariadne's identity thread: Privacy risks with fitness trackers and online social networks. In *Proceedings of the Multimedia Privacy and Security Workshop at the 24th ACM Conference on Computer and Communications Security (CCS)* (pp. 1–11). 30 October to 3 November, Dallas, Texas. New York: ACM. doi: 10.1145/3137616.3137617

Awan, I. (2014). Islamophobia and Twitter: A typology of online hate against Muslims on social media. *Policy & Internet* 6(2), 133–150. doi: 10.1002/1944-2866.POI364

Aycock, J. (2006). *Computer viruses and malware.* New York: Springer Science & Business Media.

BBC News. (2016a). *Students warned of new "phishing" scam*. Retrieved from http://www.bbc.co.uk/news/education-37408373

BBC News. (2016b). *Felix Alexander death: Worcester mum's open letter against cyberbullying*. Retrieved from http://www.bbc.co.uk/news/uk-england-hereford-worcester-37574528

BBC News. (2016c). *Web host 123-reg deletes sites in clean-up error*. Retrieved from http://www.bbc.co.uk/news/technology-36072240

BBC News. (2017a). *Italy's Tiziana: Tragedy of a woman destroyed by viral sex videos*. Retrieved from http://www.bbc.co.uk/news/world-europe-38848528

BBC News. (2017b). *Identity fraud reached record levels in 2016*. Retrieved from http://www.bbc.co.uk/news/uk-39268542

Bishop, J. (2014). Dealing with Internet trolling in political online communities: Towards the "This Is Why We Can't Have Nice Things" scale. *International Journal of E-Politics (IJEP)* 5(4), 1–20. doi: 10.4018/ijep.2014100101

Blue, V. (2016, 23 September). The FBI recommends you cover your laptop's webcam, for good reason. [blog post]. *Engadget*. Retrieved from https://www.engadget.com/2016/09/23/the-fbi-recommends-you-cover-your-laptops-webcam-good-reasons/

Button, M., Nicholls, C. M., Kerr, J., & Owen, R. (2014). Online frauds: Learning from victims why they fall for these scams. *Australian & New Zealand Journal of Criminology* 47(3), 391–408. doi: 10.1177/0004865814521224

Cavezza, C., & McEwan, T. E. (2014). Cyberstalking versus off-line stalking in a forensic sample. *Psychology, Crime & Law* 20(10), 955–970. doi: 10.1080/1068316X.2014.893334

Check Point Software Technologies Ltd. (2017). Preinstalled malware targeting mobile users. [blog post]. Retrieved from http://blog.checkpoint.com/2017/03/10/preinstalled-malware-targeting-mobile-users/

Creese, S., Goldsmith, M., Nurse, J. R. C., & Phillips, E. (2012). A data-reachability model for elucidating privacy and security risks related to the use of online social networks. *Proceedings of the 11th IEEE International Conference on Trust, Security and Privacy in Computing and Communications (TrustCom)* (pp. 1124–1131). 25–27 June, Liverpool, UK. Red Hook, NY: Curran Associates. doi: 10.1109/TrustCom.2012.22

Crown Prosecution Service (CPS). (2015, 7 August). Prosecutors being advised to learn from revenge porn cases across the country to help them tackle this "humiliating" crime. [blog post]. *CPS News Brief*. Retrieved from http://blog.cps.gov.uk/2015/08/prosecutors-being-advised-to-learn-from-revenge-porn-cases-across-the-country-to-help-them-tackle-th.html

Das, A., Bonneau, J., Caesar, M., Borisov, N., & Wang, X. (2014). The tangled web of password reuse. In *Proceedings of the Network and Distributed System Security Symposium* (pp. 23–26), 23–26 February, San Diego, CA. Reston, VA: Internet Society.

Dell SecureWorks. (2016). *2016 Underground Hacker Marketplace Report*. Retrieved from https://www.secureworks.com/resources/rp-2016-underground-hacker-marketplace-report

Duggan, M. (2014). *Online Harassment*. Washington, DC: Pew Research Center. Retrieved from http://www.pewinternet.org/2014/10/22/online-harassment/

Fiveash, K. (2017). Online hate crime: MPs demand fines for Facebook, Twitter, YouTube. *Ars Technica*. Retrieved from https://arstechnica.co.uk/tech-policy/2017/05/online-hate-crime-fines-facebook-twitter-youtube/

Hadnagy, C. (2010). *Social engineering: The art of human hacking*. Indianapolis: John Wiley & Sons.

Henry, N., Powell, A., & Flynn, A. (2017). *Not Just "Revenge Pornography": Australians' Experiences of Image-Based Abuse*. A Summary Report. Melbourne: RMIT University.

Retrieved from https://www.rmit.edu.au/content/dam/rmit/documents/college-of-design-and-social-context/schools/global-urban-and-social-studies/revenge_porn_report_2017.pdf

Goodno, N. H. (2007). Cyberstalking, a new crime: Evaluating the effectiveness of current state and federal laws. *Missouri Law Review 72*(7). Retrieved from http://scholarship.law.missouri.edu/mlr/vol72/iss1/7

Gordon, S., & Ford, R. (2006). On the definition and classification of cybercrime. *Journal in Computer Virology 2*(1), 13–20. doi: 10.1007/s11416-006-0015-z

Gough, L. (2016, 7 September). What it's like to be cyberstalked: When you can't escape the untraceable threat. *The Guardian*. Retrieved from https://www.theguardian.com/society/2016/sep/07/cyberstalking-online-stalking-email-threats-laurie-gough

Graham, M., & Dutton, W. H. (Eds.). (2014). *Society and the Internet: How networks of information and communication are changing our lives.* Oxford: OUP.

Guccione, D. (2017, January 13). What the most common passwords of 2016 list reveals (Research Study). [blog post]. Retrieved from https://blog.keepersecurity.com/2017/01/13/most-common-passwords-of-2016-research-study/

Hern, A. (2018, 28 January). Fitness tracking app Strava gives away location of secret US army bases. *The Guardian*. Retrieved from https://www.theguardian.com/world/2018/jan/28/fitness-tracking-app-gives-away-location-of-secret-us-army-bases

Hopkins, N., & Solon, O. (2017, 22 May). Facebook flooded with "sextortion" and revenge porn, files reveal. *The Guardian*. Retrieved from https://www.theguardian.com/news/2017/may/22/facebook-flooded-with-sextortion-and-revenge-porn-files-reveal

ITV News. (2015). *Scammed out of £50,000 over email.* Retrieved from http://www.itv.com/goodmorningbritain/news/scammed-out-of-50000-over-email

Iuga, C., Nurse, J. R. C., & Erola, A. (2016). Baiting the hook: Factors impacting susceptibility to phishing attacks. *Human-centric Computing and Information Sciences Journal 6*(1), 1–20. doi: 10.1186/s13673-016-0065-2

Jacks, W., & Adler, J. R. (2015). A proposed typology of online hate crime. *Open Access Journal of Forensic Psychology 7*, 64–89.

Javelin Strategy & Research. (2017). *Identity Fraud Hits Record High with 15.4 Million U.S. Victims in 2016, Up 16 % According to New Javelin Strategy & Research Study.* Retrieved from https://www.javelinstrategy.com/press-release/identity-fraud-hits-record-high-154-million-us-victims-2016-16-percent-according-new

Kahneman, D., & Tversky, A. (1973). On the psychology of prediction. *Psychological Review 80*(4), 237. doi: 10.1037/h0034747

Kochekova, K. (2016, April 28). *Hackers broadcast live footage from hacked webcams on YouTube and trolls are loving it.* Retrieved from https://blog.kaspersky.com/2ch-webcam-hack/11961/

Koops, B. J., Leenes, R., Meints, M., van der Meulen, N., & Jaquet-Chiffelle, D. O. (2009). A typology of identity-related crime: Conceptual, technical, and legal issues. *Information, Communication & Society 12*(1), 1–24. doi: 10.1080/13691180802158516

Korolov, M. (2016, 8 January). DDoS attack on BBC may have been biggest in history. *CSO*. Retrieved from http://www.csoonline.com/article/3020292/cyber-attacks-espionage/ddos-attack-on-bbc-may-have-been-biggest-in-history.html

Korosec, K. (2017, 19 December). The 25 Most Common Passwords of 2017 Include "Star Wars". *Fortune*. Retrieved from http://fortune.com/2017/12/19/the-25-most-used-hackable-passwords-2017-star-wars-freedom/

Kottler, S. (2018, 1 March). February 28th DDoS Incident Report. *GitHub*. Retrieved from https://githubengineering.com/ddos-incident-report/

Krebs, B. (2016). DDoS on Dyn Impacts Twitter, Spotify, Reddit. [blog post]. Krebs on Security. Retrieved from https://krebsonsecurity.com/2016/10/ddos-on-dyn-impacts-twitter-spotify-reddit/

Lecher, C. (2016, 15 November). Budget Android phones are secretly sending users' text messages to China. *The Verge*. Retrieved from https://www.theverge.com/2016/11/15/13636072/budget-android-phones-blu-china-text-messages

Lenhar, A., Ybarra, M., Zickurh, K., & Price-Feeney, M. (2016). *Online Harassment, Digital Abuse, and Cyberstalking in America*. New York: Data & Society Research Institute. Retrieved from https://www.datasociety.net/pubs/oh/Online_Harassment_2016.pdf

Mann, I. (2008). *Hacking the human: Social engineering techniques and security countermeasures*. Aldershot: Gower Publishing, Ltd.

Mann, I. (2013). *Hacking the human II: The adventures of a social engineer*. Whitley Bay: Consilience Media.

Martin, A. J. (2018). *"Cryptojacking" attacks surge 1,200% in UK*. Retrieved from https://news.sky.com/story/cryptojacking-attacks-surge-1200-in-uk-11269594

McDevitt, J., Levin, J., & Bennett, S. (2002). Hate crime offenders: An expanded typology. *Journal of Social Issues 58*(2), 303–317. doi: 10.1111/1540-4560.00262

McGoogan, C. (2017). *Warning over fake bank websites targeting British savers. The Telegraph*. Retrieved from http://www.telegraph.co.uk/technology/2017/05/02/warning-fake-bank-websites-targeting-british-savers/

McVeigh, K. (2011, April 8). Cyberstalking "now more common" than face-to-face stalking *The Guardian*. Retrieved from https://www.theguardian.com/uk/2011/apr/08/cyberstalking-study-victims-men

Mehrnezhad, M., Toreini, E., Shahandashti, S. F., & Hao, F. (2016). Stealing PINs via mobile sensors: Actual risk versus user perception. *International Journal of Information Security 17*(3), 1–23. doi: 10.1007/s10207-017-0369-x

Moshchuk, A., Bragin, T., Gribble, S. D., & Levy, H. M. (2006). A Crawler-based study of spyware in the web. In *13th Annual Proceedings of the Network and Distributed System Security Symposium (NDSS)*. San Diego, CA.

National Crime Agency (NCA). (London, 2017). *Pathways into cybercrime*. Retrieved from http://www.nationalcrimeagency.gov.uk/publications/791-pathways-into-cyber-crime/file

Nurse, J. R. C. (2015). Exploring the risks to identity security and privacy in cyberspace. *XRDS: Crossroads, The ACM Magazine 21*(3), 42–47. doi: 10.1145/2730912

Nurse, J. R. C. (2018). Strava storm: Why everyone should check their smart gear security settings before going for a jog. *The Conversation*. Retrieved from https://theconversation.com/strava-storm-why-everyone-should-check-their-smart-gear-security-settings-before-going-for-a-jog-90880

Nurse, J. R. C., Creese, S., Goldsmith, M., & Lamberts, K. (2011a). Trustworthy and effective communication of cybersecurity risks: A review. *Proceedings of the International Workshop on Socio-Technical Aspects in Security and Trust (STAST)* (pp. 60–68). 8 September, Milan, Italy. Red Hook, NY: Curran Associates. doi: 10.1109/STAST.2011.6059257

Nurse, J. R. C., Creese, S., Goldsmith, M., & Lamberts, K. (2011b). Guidelines for Usable Cybersecurity: Past and Present. *Proceedings of the Third International Workshop on Cyberspace Safety and Security (CSS)* (pp. 21–26). 8 September, Milan, Italy. Red Hook, NY: Curran Associates. doi: 10.1109/CSS.2011.6058566

Nurse, J. R. C., Erola, A., Agrafiotis, I., Goldsmith, M., & Creese, S. (2015). Smart insiders: Exploring the threat from insiders using the Internet-of-Things. In *Proceedings of the International Workshop on Secure Internet of Things (SIoT)* (pp. 5–14). 21–25 September, Vienna, Austria. Los Alamitos, CA: IEEE Computer Society. doi: 10.1109/SIOT.2015.10

Osborne, C. (2018, 12 February). *UK government websites, ICO hijacked by cryptocurrency mining malware.* Retrieved from http://www.zdnet.com/article/uk-government-websites-ico-hijacked-by-cryptocurrency-mining-malware

Peter Nunn jailed for abusive tweets to MP Stella Creasy. (2014, 29 September). [press release]. *The Guardian.* Retrieved from https://www.theguardian.com/uk-news/2014/sep/29/peter-nunn-jailed-abusive-tweets-mp-stella-creasy

Poushter, J. (2016). *Smartphone Ownership and Internet Usage Continues to Climb in Emerging Economies.* Washington, DC: Pew Research Center. Retrieved from http://www.pewglobal.org/files/2016/02/pew_research_center_global_technology_report_final_february_22__2016.pdf

Price, M., & Dalgleish, J. (2010). Cyberbullying: Experiences, impacts and coping strategies as described by Australian young people. *Youth Studies Australia* 29(2), 51.

Privitera, C., & Campbell, M. A. (2009). Cyberbullying: The new face of workplace bullying? *Cyberpsychology & Behavior* 12(4), 395–400. doi: 10.1089/cpb.2009.0025

PwC. (2016). *The Global State of Information Security® Survey 2017.* Retrieved from https://www.pwc.com/gx/en/issues/cyber-security/information-security-survey.html

Quintin, C. (2018). Sextortion Scam: What to Do If You Get the Latest Phishing Spam Demanding Bitcoin. *Electronic Frontier Foundation (EFF).* Retrieved from https://www.eff.org/deeplinks/2018/07/sextortion-scam-what-do-if-you-get-latest-phishing-spam-demanding-bitcoin

Raven, D. (2014, 27 August). "Revenge porn ruined my life": Woman received rape threats after nude leaked pictures online. *The Mirror.* Retrieved from http://www.mirror.co.uk/news/uk-news/revenge-porn-ruined-life-woman-4113969

Samee, S. (2016, 4 July). *Criminals Target UK Youth as Identity Fraud Rises.* [blog post] Retrieved from https://www.cifas.org.uk/newsroom/criminals-target-uk-youth-as-identity-fraud-rises

Sawer, P. (2016, 30 November). *Huge rise in "sextortion" by crime gangs using social media to entrap victims. The Telegraph.* Retrieved from http://www.telegraph.co.uk/news/2016/11/30/huge-rise-sextortion-crime-gangs-using-social-media-entrap-victims/

Schulman, N. (2014). *In real life: Love, lies & identity in the digital age.* London: Hachette UK.

Scott, P. (2016). How much of a problem is cyber-crime in the UK? *The Telegraph.* Retrieved from http://www.telegraph.co.uk/news/2016/11/01/how-much-of-a-problem-is-cyber-crime-in-the-uk/

Shachaf, P., & Hara, N. (2010). Beyond vandalism: Wikipedia trolls. *Journal of Information Science* 36(3), 357–370. doi: 10.1177/0165551510365390

Sidek, F., & Rubbi-Clarke, J. (2017, 11 January). The Top Cyber Security Risks in Asia-Pacific in 2017. *Forbes.* Retrieved from https://www.forbes.com/sites/riskmap/2017/01/11/the-top-cyber-security-risks-in-asia-pacific-in-2017/

Slonje, R., & Smith, P. K. (2008). Cyberbullying: Another main type of bullying? *Scandinavian Journal of Psychology* 49(2), 147–154. doi: 10.1111/j.1467-9450.2007.00611.x

Suler, J. (2004). The online disinhibition effect. *Cyberpsychology & Behavior* 7(3), 321–326. doi: 10.1089/1094931041291295

Symantec. (2017). *2017 Internet Security Threat Report*. Retrieved from https://www.symantec.com/content/dam/symantec/docs/reports/istr-22-2017-en.pdf

Symantec. (2018). *2018 Internet Security Threat Report*. Retrieved from https://www.symantec.com/content/dam/symantec/docs/reports/istr-23-2018-en.pdf

techUK. (2018). *ONS Crime Stats: Fraud & Cyber Crime Still Dominate*. Retrieved from http://www.techuk.org/insights/news/item/13518-ons-crime-stats-fraud-cyber-crime-still-dominate

The National Society for the Prevention of Cruelty to Children (NSPCC). (n.d.). *Online abuse: Facts and statistics*. Retrieved from https://www.nspcc.org.uk/preventing-abuse/child-abuse-and-neglect/online-abuse/facts-statistics/

The Telegraph. (2015, 10 February). *Prolific internet troll who branded victims paedophiles spared jail*. [Agency press release]. Retrieved from http://www.telegraph.co.uk/news/uknews/crime/11404512/Prolific-internet-troll-who-branded-victims-paedophiles-spared-jail.html

Turner, C. (2017, 18 May). *Exclusive: Sayat.me app, that allows cyberbullying, at centre of police investigation into teenager's suicide*. *The Telegraph*. Retrieved from http://www.telegraph.co.uk/education/2017/05/18/exclusive-sayatme-app-allows-cyberbullying-centre-police-investigation/

Tzu, S. (2009). *The Art of War* (L. Giles, Trans.). Pax Librorum.

US Department of Justice (DoJ). (2017, May 12). *Seven Charged in International "Tech Support Scam."* Retrieved from https://www.justice.gov/usao-sdil/pr/seven-charged-international-tech-support-scam

Vaas, L. (2015, April 27). *Student jailed for using keylogger to up his exam marks*. Retrieved from https://nakedsecurity.sophos.com/2015/04/27/student-jailed-for-using-keylogger-to-up-his-exam-marks/

Wall, D. S. (2007). Policing cybercrimes: Situating the public police in networks of security within cyberspace. *Police Practice and Research* 8(2), 183–205. doi: 10.1080/15614260701377729

Wall, D. S. (2005/15). The Internet as a conduit for criminal activity. In A. Pattavina (Ed.), *Information Technology and the Criminal Justice System* (pp. 77–98). Thousand Oaks, CA: Sage.

Warwick, A. (2016, 14 July). Cyber attacks cost UK business more than £34bn a year, study shows. *Computer Weekly*. Retrieved from http://www.computerweekly.com/news/450300330/Cyber-attacks-cost-UK-business-more-than-34bn-a-year-study-shows

We Are Social. (2017). *Digital in 2017 Global Overview: A collection of Internet, Social Media and Mobile Data from around the world*. Retrieved from https://wearesocial.com/blog/2017/01/digital-in-2017-global-overview

Weber, J. (2018). *Identity Fraud Hits All Time High With 16.7 Million U.S. Victims in 2017, According to New Javelin Strategy & Research Study* [press release]. Retrieved from https://www.javelinstrategy.com/press-release/identity-fraud-hits-all-time-high-167-million-us-victims-2017-according-new-javelin

Whittaker, E., & Kowalski, R. M. (2015). Cyberbullying via social media. *Journal of School Violence* 14(1), 11–29. doi: 10.1080/15388220.2014.949377

Whitty, M. T., & Buchanan, T. (2012). The online romance scam: A serious cybercrime. *Cyberpsychology, Behavior and Social Networking* 15(3), 181–183. doi: 10.1089/cyber.2011.0352

Whitty, M. T., & Buchanan, T. (2016). The online dating romance scam: The psychological impact on victims–both financial and non-financial. *Criminology & Criminal Justice* 16(2), 176–194. doi: 10.1177/1748895815603773

Williams, M., Nurse, J. R. C., & Creese, S. (2016). The perfect storm: The privacy paradox and the Internet-of-Things. *Proceedings of the 11th International Conference on Availability, Reliability and Security (ARES)* (pp. 644–652). IEEE. doi: 10.1109/ARES.2016.25

Williams, M., Nurse, J. R. C., & Creese, S. (2017). Privacy is the boring bit: User perceptions and behaviour in the Internet-of-Things. *Proceedings of the 15th International Conference on Privacy, Security and Trust (PST)*. 28–30 August, Calgary, Alberta, Canada. doi: 10.1109/PST.2017.00029

Wong, J. C., & Solon, O. (2017, 12 May). Massive ransomware cyber-attack hits nearly 100 countries around the world. *The Guardian*. Retrieved from https://www.theguardian.com/technology/2017/may/12/global-cyber-attack-ransomware-nsa-uk-nhs

CHAPTER 34

THE GROUP ELEMENT OF CYBERCRIME: TYPES, DYNAMICS, AND CRIMINAL OPERATIONS

JASON R. C. NURSE AND MARIA BADA

INTRODUCTION

THERE are various perspectives through which cybercrime and its association with online groups can be studied, e.g., the groups that are responsible for cyber-attacks and similar acts of online aggression or the groups of individuals that are targeted. Anonymous is one of the most well-known of the hacker groups and has been linked to numerous high-profile online attacks. These include cyber-attacks on the FBI, US Department of Justice, and US Copyright Office (Peckham, 2012), declarations of war on banks and stock exchange markets (Schwartz, 2016), and more recent calls to action against US President Donald Trump (Griffin, 2017). Other popular cybercriminal groups are Lizard Squad, a group that forced the Sony's PlayStation Network offline and caused a flight disruption with a bomb scare (Zorabedian, 2014); and the hacker group, Lulzsec, which stole private data from 24.6 million customers via a hack on Sony's PlayStation Network (Arthur, 2013).

In addition to these hacker groups, traditional organized crime groups are quickly expanding their presence into cyberspace. This is undoubtedly linked to the low barriers of entry, opportunity to vastly expand operations, and the perceived anonymity that the Internet provides. There is also a range of ad hoc groups consisting of members of the public who form online in support of a cause, but whose actions may be regarded as potentially criminal, e.g., the recent call to protest against Trump's January 2017 inauguration with a distributed denial-of-service attack (DDoS) (Metzger, 2017). This protest campaign was publicized online and requested that the public flood the WhiteHouse.gov website with requests to "demonstrate the will of the American people." Though the protest was later canceled because of the potential legal ramifications, it demonstrates the power of group action online.

Research has studied cybercriminal groups to varying extents to better understand their motivations, how they form and organize, and their techniques of attack (Choo & Smith, 2008; Olson, 2013; McGuire, 2012). Traditional organized crime groups, for example, are often driven online by the ability to up-skill quickly (via purchasing cybercrime services and tools) and therefore, to launch high-tech crimes with limited understanding and expertise (European Union Agency for Law Enforcement Co-operation, 2014). Online hacker groups are particularly interesting because unlike traditional groups, they may typically have to self-organize, i.e., as there may not be an agreed leader of the group to direct and co-ordinate operations, the group itself is responsible for these activities. Moreover, their actions are often based on causes, some of which the public may consider to be noble, and thus socially acceptable—the launch of #OpISIS, a cyber-attack campaign against the ISIS terrorist network after the 2015 Paris attacks is one example. In this case, Anonymous even posted a video declaring (cyber) war on the Islamic State group—targeting their websites and social media accounts—in response to attacks such as the Charlie Hebdo massacre in Paris in January 2015 that killed twelve people.

Another perspective in the study of the group element of cybercrime is a focus on groups as the target of crimes. Young Internet users, for instance, are often studied as they represent a particularly vulnerable group online (Kowalski, Giumetti, Schroeder, & Lattanner, 2014). Religion, as one might imagine, is also a topic that has resulted in numerous crimes online, particularly harassment and hate speech. Race is another polarizing subject in online communities, with many online hate groups actively congregating to voice their opinions (Chau & Xu, 2007). Additionally, there are many other groups that are commonly targeted in cybercrimes, e.g., females, the disabled, and lesbian, gay, bisexual, and transgender (LGBT) individuals. Online harassment and threats are two of the common types of aggression against these groups (Lenhart, Ybarra, Zickuhr, & Price-Feeney, 2016).

Having introduced the ways in which to consider the group element to cybercrime, the body of this chapter seeks to critically examine it in further detail. First, it considers the platforms that are used by online groups, including Internet forums and mobile apps. Next, it examines the types of groupings present, including their actions and the factors that motivate crimes and draws heavily on case study examples arising from literature and the news. Then it builds on this foundation to analyze how criminal groups form and operate. This discussion encompasses issues of trust, motives, and means. The aim is to make these discussions pragmatic and provide useful insight into the group component of cybercrime, and issues such as interaction within criminal communities.

Cybercrime and Online Groups

Platforms Used by Online Groups: A Brief Look

Online groups and communities—or simply, people who interact via virtual environments—have existed since the dawn of the Internet. The first widespread groupings could be found on platforms such as Internet Relay Chat (IRC) and in chat-rooms on the once thriving AOL service. Since then, groups have spread to various other online services including social media services such as MySpace, Bebo, and Hi5, over the years. More recent social networks, including Facebook, host a number of groups on a range of diverse topics. The group aspect of Facebook is actually one of its most popular offerings with in excess of 1 billion users, and in December 2016, more than 10 billion comments and 25 billion likes (Frier, 2017). Other networks, such as Twitter and Instagram allow groups to chat, but these are currently via direct messages as opposed to being more openly accessible (to join, use, etc.), as with Facebook. We do note here however, that Facebook does have several closed groups where access is strictly moderated, and may be based on demographics, interest, status, or employer.

Research has explored groups' use of social media and, as alluded to above, they range from the benign to the more disruptive. For instance, groups have been used for teaching and improving writing (Yunus & Salehi, 2012), but also for activist networks, be they associated with contemporary activism or collective action (Gerbaudo, 2012; Vromen, Xenos, & Loader, 2015). One significant challenge for social network platforms in this context has been maintaining the balance between freedom of speech (or excessive censorship) and the public good, particularly when considering those activist groups that may be viewed as extreme. This is a problem that social networks have struggled with for many years, and one that does not appear to be solvable through any simple or individual means.

Forums are another popular venue where groups form and interact. This platform functions analogous to a message board with posts sequentially added by date and/or time to a webpage. Some of the most well-known forums online are Reddit (the self-deemed "Front page of the Internet"), CraigsList (a classified advertisements and discussion website), and 4Chan (an image-board website that allows anonymous posting). Positive uses of forums can be seen in activities such as support groups and those used for health advice (Cole, Watkins, & Kleine, 2016), though negative uses are also abundant. Articles in research have even emphasized that Internet forums often act as an efficient and widely used tool for radical, extremist, and other ideologically "sensitive" groups and organizations to connect and inform on their agendas (Holtz, Kronberger, & Wagner, 2012).

While cybercriminal and terrorist forums can be found on the open web, the most significant and devious are rife on the Dark Web. The Dark Web is the part of the web which exists on an encrypted network and can only be accessed using specific software and networks, such as Tor (or, The Onion Router) and I2P (the Invisible Internet Project). These services provide some level of anonymity hence their attraction to criminals. Dark Web forums and communications have been the focus of researchers for several years as they attempt to better understand how cybercriminals behave and act (TrendMicro Inc., 2016).

To complement online social media and forums, there are an increasing range of applications which allow groups to form and communicate. WhatsApp is one of the most popular of these applications, with around 1 billion users. This platform allows individual and group chat, and boasts secure messaging, a feature which has privacy advantages but is also heavily contested by governments and intelligence communities. Secure messaging in this context refers to WhatsApp's use of full end-to-end encryption, which means that the only persons who can read messages (including photos, videos, files, etc.) are the sender and the intended recipients. As pointed out by WhatsApp, even they cannot see inside the messages (WhatsApp, 2017).

A key reason why there is such heated deliberation around the services of WhatsApp and Telegram (a service similar to WhatsApp which also has end-to-end encrypted messaging) is because they may be seen as a safe space for terrorists and other criminals (Magdy, 2016). There is no shortage of news articles and blogs which suggest this, as can be seen from the following story titles: "Paris terrorists used WhatsApp and Telegram to plot attacks according to investigators" (Billington, 2015), "Inside the app that's become ISIS' biggest propaganda machine" (Engle, 2015), "How Telegram Became The App Of Choice For ISIS" (Robins-Early, 2017), "How terrorists use encrypted messaging apps to plot, recruit and attack" (Hamill, 2017), "WhatsApp accused of giving terrorists 'a secret place to hide' as it refuses to hand over London attacker's messages" (Rayner, 2017), and "Indian Govt May Ban WhatsApp Use In Country, As It Is Terrorist's Favourite App For Messaging" (D'Mello, 2018).

Other apps and instant messaging services that authors (e.g., Magdy, 2016) have found that may be used by activist groups include WeChat (a China-based platform that has over 1 billion monthly active users), SureSpot (an open-source secure mobile messaging app that uses end-to-end encryption) and Kik (a messaging platform originating in Canada that has approximately 300 million users). To add to these, a topical study by TrendMicro of over 2,000 accounts that openly support terrorist groups has also found Wickr (an app that offers secure, ephemeral messaging) and Signal (an open source encrypted communications app) as preferred apps for these groups of individuals (TrendMicro Inc., 2016). As noted by Magdy (2016), this range of apps may be used for different purposes but generally their popularity is driven by the fact that they allow faster, more personalized and secure communication.

Groups as Perpetrators and Victims of Cybercrime

The platforms presented above have supported a range of activities pertaining to the group element of cybercrime. As discussed earlier, at least two approaches that could be explored are groups as the perpetrators and initiators of crime, or groups as the victims thereof, for instance, targeted demographics or minorities. Our aim in this section is to reflect on the group element of cybercrime more critically and identify the set of core group types. These would be beneficial to research and practice in the fields of study in cybercrime, cyberpsychology and criminology.

We begin this analysis with a consideration of the perpetrator's perspective and thus, first look to understand how the public and literature perceive criminal groups. The three descriptions of criminal groupings that form the basis for our discussion are taken from the US Federal Bureau of Investigation, and the research works of Finckenauer and Voronin (2001) and Godson (2003). We focus on organized criminal groups here as these are the most commonly discussed in the literature.

The US Federal Bureau of Investigation (FBI) considers the topic of transnational organized crime and the definition they ascribe to is:

> "Those self-perpetuating associations of individuals who operate transnationally for the purpose of obtaining power, influence, and monetary and/or commercial gains, wholly or in part by illegal means, while protecting their activities through a pattern of corruption and/or violence, or while protecting their illegal activities through a transnational organizational structure and the exploitation of transnational commerce or communication mechanisms."   (FBI, 2016)

From an academic perspective, Finckenauer and Voronin give insight into the group nature of crime through their definition of organized crime.

> "Organized crime is crime committed by criminal organizations whose existence has continuity over time and across crimes, and that use systematic violence and corruption to facilitate their criminal activities. These criminal organizations have varying capacities to inflict economic, physical, psychological, and societal harm. The greater their capacity to harm, the greater the danger they pose to society."
> (Finckenauer and Voronin, 2001, p. 2)

Finally, Godson provides another academic definition on organized crime as he notes:

> "Organized crime refers to individuals and groups with ongoing working relationships who make their living primarily through activities that one or more states deem illegal and criminal. Organized crime can take a variety of institutional or organizational forms. This includes tight vertical hierarchies with lifelong commitments, as well as looser, more ephemeral, nonhierarchical relationships."
> (Godson, 2003, p. 274)

Reflecting on these three definitions, we can begin to see some of the key features of criminal groups. For instance, there is the notion of continuity and group identity in the group (and member relationships) and criminal activities over time. This is particularly evident in the descriptions from the FBI and Finckenauer and Voronin. Motivation is another feature that stands out in the definitions, with influence and financial and commercial gain, acting as common reasons for group formation and crimes. Finckenauer and Voronin extend this point to highlight the generic aims of crimes; that is, inflicting economic, physical, psychological, and societal harms, but also the varying capabilities that criminal groups may possess in achieving such goals.

Godson touches on another important feature in terms of the various organizational forms that groups may take; for instance, they may be tightly bound or ephemeral and non-hierarchical. Group shape will likely depend on their nature and purpose, and the extent to which their activities will interest law enforcement. The FBI description is useful particularly because it emphasizes the transnational nature of criminal groups and their use of global communication channels, many similar to the platforms discussed earlier in this chapter and other chapters (see Nurse, this volume).

The reflection on criminal groups is crucial to the discussion on cybercrime for numerous reasons. In particular, there is almost certain to be many similarities between these groups considering that the Internet may be regarded as just another platform through which crime can occur. The various descriptions above can all be related in some way to cybercriminal groups. The main difference with cybercriminal groups is their focus on technology as a central means for interaction and criminal acts. Unlike traditional crime therefore, physical presence and power (including physical violence) is not as crucial, and technical means and skill tend to be more important. Furthermore, because of technology, cybercriminal groups can become transnational much more easily as they can meet and interact via the various platforms mentioned. Such interactions may be persistent or temporal depending on the nature of the crime. As we will discuss later, there is also the reality that with the Internet, forming groups of like-minded individuals is significantly easier than it is offline. There is less risk to group formation and persistence as well, given the ability online to mask one's identity—these factors often combine to the advantage of criminals. Technology also means a wider availability of hacking platforms and tools, a reality that is predicted to increase in the future via the proliferation of offensive tools (Williams, Axon, Nurse et al., 2016).

Cybercrime groups have been of interest to researchers for some time, and therefore it is not surprising that articles have proposed ways to typify such groups. Possibly one of the most notable pieces of research on the topic is by Choo and Smith (2008). They explore the exploitation of online systems by criminal groups and have defined three categories of such groups. The first category is that of traditional organized criminals who use technology to enhance terrestrial criminal activities. This includes crime syndicates and organized groups that specialize in everything from fraud and forgery to piracy and extortion from online gambling. Their aim is often to apply technology to expand and streamline operations.

Europol has carried out extensive work in the cybercrime space and have highlighted the prevalence of crime-as-a-service business models as a facilitator for traditional groups engaging in cybercrimes (European Union Agency for Law Enforcement Co-operation, 2014). Crime-as-a-service models, which can typically be found on underground Dark Web markets, allow criminals to purchase criminal services including acquiring botnets (or spam networks), launching denial-of-service attacks against specified targets, and customized malware development. As such, criminals can easily and quickly launch sophisticated cyber-attacks on groups or individuals of their choosing.

Organized cybercriminal groups are the second category identified by Choo and Smith and are said to be groups comprised of like-minded individuals working collectively towards a common goal. The Internet is a central enabler to such groups as it is the platform that they meet and plan activities; furthermore, their members may only be known to each other online. These are a few of the factors that distinguish these groups from traditional organized criminals which use technology to enable crimes. One example of such a group is the hacking group Lulzsec, where there are reports that their members never met in person, and were unaware of each other's identities (Arthur, 2013). Another recent example is the Carbanak cybercrime group, named after a piece of malware it used to access banking systems. The head of this group was the mastermind, and also technically talented enough to be able to identify software vulnerabilities and write malware to exploit them (Burgess, 2018). According to reports, the head of the group also worked with three other gang members, who did not know each other and instead chatted online (Burgess, 2018).

The last group category is that of ideologically and politically motivated cyber groups. This spans terrorist organizations and the full range of hacktivist groups. Choo and Smith make an intriguing point in their characterization of this category of groups. That is, that crimes often associated with organized criminal groups (e.g., scam and fraud schemes) are also crimes which terrorist groups engage in to raise funds for their ideological pursuits. A 2015 UK report showed that scamming and ransoms are high on the list of activities undertaken for terrorist financing (HM Treasury and Home Office, 2015). Terrorist groups, e.g., ISIS, are widely known to engage in online activities, but particularly for plotting, recruiting, and claiming responsibility for attacks (Engle, 2015; Hamill, 2017; Nouh, Nurse, & Goldsmith, 2016). Social media continues to be a favored platform for such groups, e.g., the role of Twitter in "Tweeting the Jihad" (Klausen, 2015).

Hacktivists, or politically-motivated hackers, are also an increasingly popular grouping in this cybercriminal category. Such groups are known to carry out activities against governments and large corporations. Anonymous is one of the most well-known of these groups, given its attacks on the FBI and other sites (Peckham, 2012). A key factor that makes Anonymous stand out potentially even more however, is its public-facing nature. There have been a variety of books published on Anonymous including Parmy Olson's *We are Anonymous* (2012) and Gabriella Coleman's *Hacker, Hoaxer, Whistleblower, Spy: The Many Faces of Anonymous* by (2014). Moreover, documentaries have been released on the workings and beliefs of its members—see *We Are Legion: The Story of the Hacktivists* (2012).

Anonymous also maintains a significant presence on social media. At the time of writing, for instance, they appear to possess several Twitter profiles including @AnonyOps, @YourAnonNews, @YourAnonGlobal, @GroupAnon, @AnonPress, and

@AnonyPress; the most popular being @YourAnonNews with more than 1.6 million followers. These various accounts hint to a core value of Anonymous, namely, the lack of central or hierarchical structure (as will be discussed in the third section of this chapter). This is clearly exemplified in the @GroupAnon tweet: *"No, this is not the official #Anonymous account. There is no official account. We have no central leadership. (Other than the FBI/NSA, joke)"* made on 10:39 a.m. 18 Nov 2015.

While the three main groupings highlighted here are undoubtedly the core criminal networks, the authors of this chapter believe that there is another group, whose criminality is much more subjective, emerging in society today—individuals (often not criminals) who use technological means to motivate and organize acts that may be deemed dangerous or illegal. In the Introduction, we presented one of these cases where there was a call to protest against President Trump's January 2017 inauguration using a distributed denial-of-service attack (DDoS) on WhiteHouse.gov (Metzger, 2017). DDoS are regarded as criminal acts by many given that they are commonly used by hacker collectives to force legitimate websites offline.

The case of President Trump is interesting for many reasons. For example, there have been many rallies and protests against President Trump since he began his election campaign, several of which were organized online (CBS News, 2017). While participating in rallies and protests is every citizen's right, the challenge of crime arises when these protests turn violent as they did in Portland, Oregon after the election and in Washington DC at the time of President Trump's inauguration. In DC in particular, demonstrators set cars on fire and smashed shop and car windows (Longbottom, 2017).

Civil action, organized via online networks and platforms, has also been witnessed in many other parts of the world prior to these US instances. In the UK in 2011, thousands rioted following the death of local man Mark Duggan who was shot by the police; these riots led to mass looting and millions of pounds worth of property damage. It is said that the Blackberry Messenger app played a crucial role in the organizing the riots (Fuchs, 2012) in enabling contagion and a group-mob mentality; Reicher (2001) and Stott, Drury and Reicher (2016) provide further insight into the psychology of crowd dynamics broadly, and in the London riots, respectively. Facebook has also been used by activists as a platform for action and engagement with increased online activity found to often correlate with offline group actions (Nouh & Nurse, 2015). In 2010's Arab Spring, Facebook was used to spread the word of the revolution, and many believe that social media contributed to the liberation of those societies (Fuchs, 2012). These are all instances where technology and online interactions have contributed to offline unrest (be it positively or negatively motivated) and, in some instances, crime. There are many group processes at play in these instances, as there are offline. Establishing group identity and common goals plays a crucial role in bringing together individuals to create these groups.

In addition to the work by Choo and Smith (2008), other articles that have sought to identify the types of cybercriminal group include McGuire (2012) and Leukfeldt,

Kleemans, and Stol (2016). McGuire suggests a typology of cybercrime groups with three main types. These are, groups that operate primarily online, those that combine online and offline activities, and groups that are predominantly offline but use online technologies as an enabler for crimes. This typology therefore closely matches up with the categorization of Choo and Smith. The research by Leukfeldt and colleagues adds another dimension to the analysis of cybercrime groups by considering them according to their characteristics. Specifically, they propose technology use (low-tech to high-tech) and the level of offender–victim interaction (no interaction to high interaction), while also noting the extent to which groups have local or international components. The benefit of such an approach is that it allows the correlation of characteristics, and in their case, the discovery of which types of network operate at which levels.

Having reflected on the perpetrator perspective of cybercrime and groups, we now consider the viewpoint of groups as the victims of online crime. While practically any demographic or characteristic can be used to target groups of individuals, some of the most common are those of race, religion, age, gender, and sexual-orientation. It is worth noting that these characteristics are not specially targeted in the online space but happen to be more openly targeted because of the illusion of attacker anonymity online. There are plenty of examples of groups that have formed online to preach hate towards persons of the characteristics highlighted. Chau and Xu (2007) study one such type of hate group of "anti-Blacks" covering 820 bloggers on blog-hosting website, Xanga. A key finding from that research is that hate groups in the blogosphere may not tend to form into centralized organizations. The authors, however, do not eliminate the possibility that such online groups may prepare members for other extremist organizations such as the Ku Klux Klan, for instance.

Beyond race, religion is a significant factor in online victimization. A salient example of this victimization occurred after the Woolwich attack in May 2013 in the UK, where two Islamist terrorists brutally murdered a British soldier. In the days that followed, there were hundreds of messages on social networks containing hate speech directed against the Muslim community (Awan, 2014). Awan found that Muslims were demonized and vilified through negative comments, discrimination, physical threats, and online harassment. Other works have demonstrated this hate towards groups in online message boards as yet another example of how online platforms can be used to target people of certain faiths (Cleland, Anderson, & Aldridge-Deacon, 2017).

While other groups (females, the disabled, and lesbian, gay, bisexual, and transgender (LGBT) individuals) are also the victim of online harassment (Lenhart et al., 2016; Chahal, 2016), youth are a particularly well considered area (by both academia and law enforcement) given their vulnerable nature. Kowalski and colleagues (2014) focus on the crime of cyberbullying among young people to provide a critical review of the existing body of cyberbullying research. Mitchell, Wolak, and Finkelhor (2008) also offer relevant insight that young Internet bloggers also were at an increased risk for online harassment. Furthermore, young individuals who interacted with people that they met online were at a higher likelihood of receiving online sexual solicitations. Population-based studies from other countries, e.g., Oksanen and Keipi (2013), have supported these points and found that young people are generally more likely to be victims of cybercrime. A key novelty of their work is that they consider the risks of victimization that young people face online, to the problems they may face in the offline world.

Drawing on this analysis of the group component of cybercrime, Table 1 presents two main group types of groups: perpetrators and victims of criminal acts. The core subtypes of the former group are largely motivated by the work of Choo and Smith (2008). To this has been added a new group focusing on citizens who use online technological means to mobilize and act. It is important to note that, in most instances, such action is not criminal and only in a few cases results in criminal acts (e.g., offline riots or looting). Furthermore, there may be arguments that this group is already accounted for in the "Organized ideologically and politically motivated cyber groups." It is presented separately here due to its increasing importance in society (with the Arab Spring and the Trump protests arguably only the beginning of what is to come) and the difficulty in categorizing it, given it often borders on criminality.

Table 1 The group element of cybercrime and its main types

Main group types	Group subtypes
Groups as perpetrators	• Traditional organized crime groups that use technology to enable crime. • Organized cybercriminal groups. • Organized ideologically and politically motivated cyber groups. • Citizen groups that use technology to mobilize and act.
Groups as victims	• Race • Age • Disability • Religion/belief • Sex • Sexual orientation

With regards to the category of groups as victims, the subtypes listed have been studied in various articles before. The list included in Table 1 is based heavily on such works and instances of discrimination, victimization, and harassment found online. It is worth noting that these groups align broadly with the protected characteristics of the UK's Equality Act 2010 and similar legislation across the word. This emphasizes their significance in society more widely other than just in cyberspace. Over the next few years, there is expected to be a sharp growth in research into "groups as victims" online, particularly because of the difficulty that platforms such as Facebook and Twitter have in detecting and responding to online abuse and harassment.

How Online Criminal Groups Form and Operate

With the main types of groups identified, this section narrows the focus to "groups as perpetrators." It concentrates specifically on how cybercriminal groups form, engage, and operate.

Group Formation and the Platforms and Networks That Enable It

Case studies suggest that within cybercriminal networks the importance of traditional central actors with the role of "bridge builder" diminishes (Holt & Smirnova, 2014; Motoyama, McCoy, Levchenko, Savage, & Voelker, 2013). However, recent studies also show that such networks still have important social dependency relationships (Leukfeldt et al., 2016; Leukfeldt, Kleemans, & Stol, 2017; Leukfeldt, de Poot, Verhoeven, & Lavorgna, 2017). Research demonstrates that most of the networks have a (more or less) stable group of core members who commit crimes together over an extended period of time. The core members of these networks may know each other from the offline world and recruit only a few specialists through online meeting places. Other studies suggest that cybercriminal networks use offline social ties and, on occasion, online meeting places to come into contact with suitable co-offenders (Leukfeldt et al., 2016, 2017; Odinot, Verhoeven, Pool, & De Poot, 2016). Thus, the reality is that a minority of networks could be labeled as ad hoc networks that were forged in online meeting places to execute one-off cyber-attacks.

Social ties may be strongly clustered and limited to, for example, a region or country. Members of some cybercriminal networks are located in the same offline social cluster—even when executing cybercriminal attacks all over the world (Leukfeldt et al., 2016, 2017; Odinot et al., 2016). Working with trusted acquaintances from the offline world could potentially have many advantages over working with potentially unreliable actors from all over the world who are only known by their online handle (pseudonym).

As with most situations, there are some exceptions to the common case where offenders are distributed across the Internet and not necessarily geographically located in one single place. The hacking group LulzSec is an example of this which is held to have been formed in private online chat rooms of the hacking collective Anonymous. Most notably, LulzSec members never met in the real world (Arthur, 2013). From this example, it can be inferred that cybercrimes and cybercriminals, by their very informational, networked, and global nature, may go against the traditional model of socially and geographically rooted organized crime models. This pertains to the need to gather specialist skills; in particular, such groups tend to have a very detailed division of labor with specific skill sets across individuals. For instance, one person would provide the documents, another would buy credit card details, still another would create identities, and a fourth would provide the drop address (Rodgers, 2007).

Furthermore, not all cybercriminals commit only cybercrimes. Studies suggest that cybercriminals are often also involved in all sorts of offline crimes (Leukfeldt et al., 2016; Van Der Broek, Van der Laan, & Weijters, 2016). Yet, in the online world, distance, location, and time are no longer limiting factors. Compared to the offline world, it is relatively easy for offenders to be part of different criminal networks. For example, newcomers on forums are able to come into contact with existing members quickly and are able to reach a more central position relatively quickly.

To consider enabling platforms for criminal activities, the Internet has several criminal meeting places. Two examples are the forums and chat rooms where criminals meet to exchange information or make plans to carry out attacks. To a certain extent, forums can be regarded as platforms that facilitate the origin and growth of cybercriminal networks. Members of cybercriminal networks spend much of their time in criminal and non-criminal chat rooms and forums, where they meet like-minded people and build relationships. As mentioned, existing offline cultures, communities and social relationships also appear to be important in online forums (Ablon, Libicki, & Golay, 2014).

Additionally, Leukfeldt et al. (2016) found that both social ties and online forums were used by cybercriminal networks to recruit new members. Four types of growth were identified in their work: 1) growth entirely through social contacts; 2) social contacts as a base and forums to recruit specialists; 3) forums as a base and social contacts to recruit local criminals; and 4) growth entirely through forums. Criminals would usually recruit through social ties and less through social contacts and use forums in order to find specialized enablers. An example of such a group is LulzSec. LulzSec's members never met in the real world and were unaware of each other's identities. Some were based in the US, and some in the UK, demonstrating the globalized nature of such groups.

Cybercriminals show a noticeable preference for carding forums. These are websites dedicated to the sharing of stolen credit card information as well as providing discussion boards in which members of the forum may share techniques used in obtaining credit card information. Using interaction data from three prominent carding forums—Shadowcrew, Cardersmarket, and Darkmarket—and drawing on theories from criminology, social psychology, economics, and network science, Yip, Webber, and Shadbolt (2013) identified fundamental socio-economic mechanisms offered by carding forums: formal control and co-ordination, social networking, identity uncertainty mitigation, and quality uncertainty mitigation. Together, these mechanisms give rise to a sophisticated underground market regulatory system that facilitates underground trading over the Internet and thus drives the expansion of the underground crime economy. This demonstrates the robustness of carding forums and alludes to why they are favored by cybercriminals. Moreover, Holt and Lampke (2010) manually analyzed six forums and found that the dynamics of the stolen data markets are governed by key factors, including communications, price, quality, and service. This is intriguingly similar to legitimate markets.

To understand the cyber-threat landscape, it is also important to acknowledge the different ways that cybercriminal groups are organized. First, the cybercrime-as-a-service business model that drives criminal forums on the Dark Web provides the access to tools and services to people with little knowledge of cyber matters. Furthermore, the environment promotes exchange of information as well as "learning kits." This trend is indicative of a growing cyber capability among these criminal groups as their knowledge expands and they exchange expertise. As some terrorist groups are reaching out to recruit in the Western world, they might be able to contact and attract appropriately skilled people for their hacking exploits (European Union Agency for Law Enforcement Co-operation, 2014; National Cyber Security Centre, 2017).

For the most organized and technically advanced groups, however, many of the services are carried out "in-house" as part of their own business model. For smaller groups or individual criminals, these services can be hired in one of many online criminal marketplaces. Most of these services like crime-as-a-service are openly advertised in criminal forums. As Richardson (2007) states, hackers have organized and shifted toward a "professionalization" of computer crimes. A few examples of such criminal forums are Dark Market, Carders Market, Shadowcrew, Carder.su, Darkode, GhostMarket, and the Silk Road.

To analyze the relationships among hackers more generally, it is often common to find a decentralized network structure. Network centralization describes a quality of a group and it indicates the extent to which a network is organized around one or more central points, such as a node or a centroid (Nouh & Nurse, 2015; Wasserman & Faust, 1994). Previous research has shown that the Shadowcrew hackers, for example, were part of a decentralized network, although not everyone in this group had the same type of role or position (Lu, Luo, Polgar, & Cao, 2010). The network structure of this infamous hacker group was established using social network analysis methods. Leaders were identified using actor centrality measures (degree, betweenness, closeness, and eigenvector) and were found to be even more involved in thirteen smaller sub-groups (Lu et al., 2010). Shadowcrew had the three characteristics of a team as defined by Best and Luckenbill (1994): 1) elaborate division of labor; 2) mutual participation; and 3) association. From this observation, the inference is that the members of cybercriminal groups do not necessarily have to be organized around one central point in order to still maintain a hierarchical structure.

In addition, the organization of crime online may often follow a different logic to the organization of crime offline. This is a dis-organized model of organization (Wall, 2007). Existing work identifies a "dis-organized" or distributed model of organization, rather than a hierarchical command and control structure of cybercrime (Wall, 2015). Network technologies and associated social media are creating new forms of networked social relationships that act as the source of new criminal opportunities (Wall, 2007) and crimes such as stalking, bullying, fraud, and sextortion.

Anonymous is an example of a group which does not strictly organize itself and has both swarm and hub characteristics. The fact that Anonymous has no leader makes it difficult to even comprehend its organizational structure (Norton, 2012). The structure of Anonymous has been loosely described as "a series of relationships" with no membership fee or initiation. Anyone who wants to be a part of Anonymous—an Anon—can simply claim allegiance. Many Anonymous members considered themselves crusaders for justice. Publicly, Anonymous persists in claiming to be non-hierarchical (Kushner, 2014).

Apart from collaborating and recruiting their members, it is also interesting to note that organizations operating on the Dark Web seem to also be attacking each other, and trying to prevail over their criminal competitors (Catakoglu, Balduzzi, & Balzarotti, 2017). These attacks could be defacements aimed at subverting the business of another organization in order to promote a competitor website; attempts to spy on communications initiated to, and from, another organization, theft of confidential data from a disguised File Transfer Protocol (FTP) server, or manual attacks against the custom application running the underground forum. These activities demonstrate the tensions between groups as they participate in these various platforms and networks.

Trust as a Factor for Cybercriminal Group Formation

The concept of trust within the human factors domain has focused largely on the user gaining trust as a result of specific website content, attributes, ease of use, and related consumer-centric acceptance models (Corritore, Kracher, & Wiedenbeck, 2003; Nurse, Rahman, Creese, Goldsmith, & Lamberts, 2011). Trust is an enabler of online engagement but also certain levels of trust are required when assessing what is being offered or accessed.

Supporting the growth of the Dark Web, and presumably the trust gained by participants to engage, are anonymity networks like Tor. In fact, it is a mandatory feature of a number of Dark Web forums that participants use Tor and agree to transact only through the use of virtual currencies, such as Bitcoin (Bradbury, 2014) and, increasingly, Monero (a virtual currency with a strong focus on privacy). The users of cybercrime marketplaces must trust that such environments will maintain their anonymity and will also follow through with the service communicated, e.g., provision of information on stolen credit cards. Ironically, the uniqueness of the trust environment for Dark Web participants and hosts appears to distil to the singular issue of preserving anonymity (Lacey & Salmon, 2015). Integrity as a basis for trust in the Dark Web can encapsulate the overall integrity of the marketplace in maintaining anonymity of its users and hosts, which also connects to Mayer, Davis and Schoorman (1995), who observed that anonymity is a binding mutual interest for participants. Trust is dynamic, because it can build, diminish, and be removed at any point.

According to Falcone, Singh, and Tan (2001), various different kinds of trust should be modeled, designed, and implemented when speaking about trust in cyber-societies: 1) trust in the environment and in the infrastructure (the socio-technical system); 2) trust in personal agents and in mediating agents; 3) trust in potential partners; 4) trust in information sources; and 5) trust in warrantors and authorities. Parts of these different kinds of trust have complementary relations with each other. The final kind—trust in a system and/or process—can be the result of various trust attributions to the different components. When an agent has to decide about whether to trust another agent in the perspective of a co-operative relationship, each must weigh the opportunities given by the positive results of a successful trust (benefits of trust) against the risks that the trust might be exploited and betrayed: this problem is known as the trust dilemma. The trust dilemma is the direct consequence of uncertainty—here, the intrinsic social uncertainty (Falcone, Singh, & Tan, 2001), and is similar to the social exchange principle engage in offline relationships to garner trust between one or more people (Thibaut & Kelley, 1959).

For all criminals, a balance must be made between remaining anonymous in order to remain unseen by law enforcement, and retaining certain aspects of identity in order to attract potential criminal collaborators (Lusthaus, 2012). Online identities are the foundation of a cybercriminal's reputation, which provides incentive to maintain that identity or a variation of it. At the same time, there is a competing incentive to change online names regularly in order to create a distance from past crimes. Reputation in some ways may be regarded as the "currency" that cybercriminals trade in on the Dark Web.

Gambetta's (2009) contributions to both criminology and signaling theory expand the understanding of the ways criminals identify themselves to each other and signal trustworthiness in an otherwise untrustworthy environment. Specifically, when there is information asymmetry, it is in a signaler's best interests to signal their trustworthiness, regardless of whether they actually are. Untrustworthy actors attempt to mimic the signals used by their trustworthy counterparts, and it is in the receiver's best interest to differentiate between the two. Legitimate actors use signals that may be too costly for untrustworthy actors to replicate, which provides a potential way for receivers to interpret signals produced. To minimize the risk of harm, forums provide informal mechanisms that encourage trust between participants and sanction less reputable actors (Holt, Smirnova, Chua, & Copes, 2015). Other options also include having required reputation or history to enter closed online forums or to earn the status of "trusted seller" (Yip, Shadbolt, & Webber, 2013; Yip, Webber, & Shadbolt, 2013).

Even with a system such as a carding forum that is capable of providing multiple channels for trust to develop, there is still room for mistrust (McCarthy & Hagan, 2001; Chiles & McMackin, 1996). In cases of mistrust, members of groups can be doxxed, such as the true identities of the members of the LulzSec gang that were made public, which ultimately led to the FBI arresting LulzSec leader Hector "Sabu" Monsegur (Bright, 2012). The interested reader is referred to the previous chapter for further information on doxxing and other common cybercrimes (see Nurse, this volume).

The Darkode forum, which had between 250–300 members, is another interesting case that operated very carefully and was very exclusive. Darkode administrators made sure prospective members were heavily vetted (FBI, 2015). Similar to practices used by the Mafia, a potential candidate for forum membership had to be sponsored by an existing member and sent a formal invitation to join. In response, the candidate had to post an online introduction—a resume—highlighting their past criminal activity, particular cyber skills, and potential contributions to the forum. The forum's active members decided whether to approve applications, which showcases the importance of trust in the formation of cybercriminal groups.

Group Operations, Their Motives and Means

Different organizations such as Anonymous, LulzSec, and the Ghost Security Group each illustrate quite different sets of offender motivations, levels of professionalism, and organization, but they also possess some similarities in terms of their organizing principles (Wall, 2015). There may even be noteworthy patterns and motives across the groups linked to the motive, operating capability and attacks of the cybercriminals (Thornton-Trump, 2018).

A core dynamic of different groups appears to be based upon a reputational economy that binds the group together. As Wall (2015) describes, when looking at the similarities of different groups, it is possible to identify that the key players seek the assistance of a broader group of participants who exist outside the central grouping, but within the idea frame (the crime-motive). These can help in solving problems related to the criminal activity being designed, built, or carried out. There may even be a further layer of individuals linked to the group who are outside the idea frame and who will give advice on specific issues. Sometimes individuals fall out of the information loop, or they are pushed out, or they leave, which makes the structure ephemeral. In most cases, the structure of the group is flat and lacks a hierarchical command and control form.

In brief, cybercriminals display common characteristics in that they often are fairly ephemeral and amorphous in terms of organization, and flex according to the demands and opportunities. They also seem to be self-contained in structure (McGuire, 2012; Yip, Webber, & Shadbolt, 2013). They may regularly be driven by an individual or by a very small group, but not always, because the organizing principle is often like-mindedness with a central common idea or ethic. In Anonymous, for instance, each cell or sub-grouping follows an idea frame (motive). There are not necessarily any relationships or even communications between cells outside the nucleus, just an identification and affiliation with the core idea. The interesting fact here is that this distributed type of organization does possess some similarities with the organization of many offline organized groups. They also reflect the United Nations Office on Drugs and Crime (UNODC) (2002) organized crime group typologies.

One of the most interesting aspects of these communities is that of their characteristics and how they function. For instance, these individuals are likeminded and therefore have some shared culture, at least in the context of their actions. This culture includes values as well as intergroup dynamics. These include own-group perceptions, attitudes, and behaviors, as well as those towards another group. A cybercriminal's social identity may be defined by group membership, as well as the general features that define the group and differentiate it from others (Hogg & Williams, 2000).

The most sophisticated cybercrime organizations are characterized by substantial functional specialization and divisions of labor (Broadhurst, Grabosky, Alazab, &

Chon, 2014). The organization of cybercrime may also occur at a wider level and involve networks of individuals who meet and interact within online discussion forums and chat rooms. Some discussion forums function as "virtual" black markets that advertise, for example, stolen credit card numbers (Holt & Lampke, 2010). A comparison of individual offenders and criminal organizations reveals that both possess impressive skills (Broadhurst, Grabosky, Alazab, & Chon, 2014). Odinot and colleagues (2016) suggest the characteristics of offenders that are important in the offline world, such as age, physical health, and social behavior, are less important within cybercriminal networks. There are new types of offenders not previously found among traditional organized criminal groups: those with an IT background, young offenders, and ill/disabled offenders.

Criminal organizations might also possess a variety of aims, including defiance of authority, freedom of information, sexual gratification of members, and technological challenge. However, the profit motive is more apparent in the organizational cases than with individual offenders, as are the activities undertaken by organizations operating under state auspices, specifically those involving espionage and offensive cyber operations.

While profiling cybercriminals of any type, there are specific common characteristics requiring investigation, such as technical know-how, personal traits, social characteristics, and motivating factors (Nurse et al., 2014). These have been derived from over 100 cases and exclusive reviews of pertinent literature regarding crimes. Often, the prime motivator for the majority of cybercriminals is not only easy profit, but also curiosity (Malenkovich, 2012). Furthermore, in evaluating the motivation of cybercriminals, it is safe to state that some criminal action will be motivated by "need" (Maslow, 1954) or by work and/or environment characteristics (Hunt & Hill, 1969). For example, different groups such as Anonymous, LulzSec, and the Ghost Security Group each illustrate quite different sets of offender motivations, levels of professionalism, and organization, but they also possess some similarities in terms of their organizing principles (Wall, 2015).

In terms of motive, Shinder (2010) lists monetary gain, emotion, political or religious beliefs, sexual impulses, or even boredom or the desire for "a little fun." While these factors are obviously linked to traditional or real-world crime, what is not yet clear is whether cybercrime has the same associations or etiology. Critical in this regard is the understanding of motive: transition from initial motive to sustaining motive, overlapping motives, and the prediction of evolving motives, along with an understanding of primary and secondary gains.

For example, a hacker becoming part of a community of like-minded persons involves a subcultural aspect inherent within creating online relationships that allow a hacker to express themselves (Bossler & Burruss, 2010). This subculture might be characterized by the perception that committing cybercrimes is something normal. Within a group there will exist some resistance to perform immoral activities, while others with a lower moral threshold may opt or enlist to perform them to increase their benefit (Atkinson, 2015). It is of note that cybercriminals will protect the infrastructure rather than destroying it to keep making money from the persons and/or networks that they have compromised (Aiken & McMahon, 2014).

Perry and Olsson (2009) found that the Web created a new common space that fostered a "collective identity" for previously fractured hate groups, strengthening their domestic presence in counties such as the US, Germany, and Sweden. McDevitt, Levin, and Bennett (2002) identified broad categories of hate crime offenders: 1) thrill offenders—those who commit their crimes for the excitement or the thrill; 2) defensive offenders—those who view themselves as defending their "turf"; 3) mission offenders—those whose life's mission is to clear the world of groups they consider evil or inferior; and 4) retaliatory offenders—those who engage in retaliatory violence. Therefore, the motives of these groups define the way they operate.

Models of small group dynamics suggest how conformism, the influence of extremist ideologies on moving people to more extreme attitudes, disinhibition, and the yearning for group acceptance can all conspire to drive a person to commit acts of hate crime (Rieker, 1997). Hate crimes can also be committed due to psychological, social-psychological, historical-cultural, sociological, economic, and political reasons (Green, McFalls, & Smith, 2001).

LulzSec, Anonymous, and the Ghost Security Group offer useful practical examples. In the case of the first, the intention appeared to be gaining attention, embarrassing website owners, and ridiculing security measures (Arthur, 2013). For Anonymous-affiliated activists, perhaps the highest profile was their work under the banner "Operation Isis," or #OpISIS, which consisted largely of finding Twitter feeds that supported the ISIS terrorist group (and were often used to distribute propaganda and share news releases) and reporting them to Twitter so that they could be shut down (Griffin, 2015). Lastly, Ghost Security Group also engaged in similar targeting of jihadists by monitoring suspected ISIS Twitter accounts and infiltrating militant message boards to find information, which they would then pass along to law enforcement (BBC, 2015). These actions could be considered noble and of benefit to society, therefore hinting at the varying motives and values of such groups.

However, there are several instances to the contrary, e.g., under the banner #OpTrump Anonymous targeted Donald Trump before he was elected president. The attack led to temporary shutdowns of Mr. Trump's website and alleged hacks of his voicemail (Griffin, 2017). It is worth reiterating that announcing that their next target would be the Trump campaign set off the most heated debate yet within the movement. Many disavowed the anti-Trump operation as being counter to Anonymous' tradition of not taking sides in political contests (Woolf, 2016). These conflicting aims are not surprising, given the dispersed nature of this cybercrime group. More importantly, it provides a perfect illustration of the context and reality of such online criminal groups and generally issues related to the group element of cybercrime.

CONCLUSION

This chapter reflected on the group element of cybercrime to develop a better understanding of how groups may be perpetrators as well as targets of online crime. It provided an up-to-date analysis of the various online platforms used by cybercriminals as well as examined how these malevolent groups form, how their members develop trust in each other, and the motives that drive a group's success and actions. In addition to elucidating these often-undefined aspects in research, it also presented a characterization of the group element of cybercrime and its main types, including newly emerging group types. The current research forms the basis for a more thorough understanding of online criminal groups, and thereby encourages further discussions on how they might be unraveled and potentially even thwarted.

References

Ablon, L., Libicki, M. C., & Golay, A. A. (2014). *Markets for cybercrime tools and stolen data. Hackers' bazaar.* Santa Monica, CA: RAND Corporation.

Aiken, M. P., & McMahon, C. (2014). *The cyberpsychology of internet facilitated organised crime.* In *The Internet organised crime threat assessment report (iOCTA).* The Hague: EUROPOL.

Arthur, C. (2013, 16 May). LulzSec: What they did, who they were and how they were caught. *The Guardian.* Retrieved from https://www.theguardian.com/technology/2013/may/16/lulzsec-hacking-fbi-jail

Atkinson, S. (2015). *Psychology and the hacker—Psychological Incident Handling.* London: SANS Institute.

Awan, I. (2014). Islamophobia and Twitter: A typology of online hate against Muslims on social media. *Policy & Internet* 6(2), 133–150. doi: 10.1002/1944-2866.POI364

BBC. (2015). *Ghost Security Group: Spying on Islamic State instead of hacking them.* Retrieved February 6, 2018, from http://www.bbc.co.uk/news/blogs-trending-34879990

Best, J., & Luckenbill, D. F. (1994). *Organizing Deviance* (2nd ed.). Upper Saddle River, NJ: Prentice Hall.

Billington, J. (2015, 17 December). *Paris terrorists used WhatsApp and Telegram to plot attacks according to investigators.* International Business Times. Retrieved from http://www.ibtimes.co.uk/paris-terrorists-used-whatsapp-telegram-plot-attacks-according-investigators-1533880

Bossler, A., & Burruss, G. (2010). *The general theory of crime and computer hacking: Low self control hackers?* In T. J. Holt & B. H. Schell (Eds.), *Corporate hacking and technology-driven crime: Social dynamics and implications* (pp. 38–67). Hershey, PA: IGI Global.

Bradbury, D. (2014). Unveiling the dark web. *Network Security* 2014(4), 14–17. doi: 10.1016/S1353-4858(14)70042-X

Bright, P. (2012, 7 March). Doxed: How Sabu was outed by former Anons long before his arrest. *Ars Technica.* Retrieved from https://arstechnica.com/tech-policy/2012/03/doxed-how-sabu-was-outed-by-former-anons-long-before-his-arrest/

Broadhurst, R., Grabosky, P., Alazab, M., & Chon, S. (2014). Organizations and cybercrime: An analysis of the nature of groups engaged in cybercrime. *International Journal of Cyber Criminology* 8(1), 1–20.

Burgess, M. (2018, 4 April). Inside the takedown of the alleged €1bn cyber bank robber. *Wired.* Retrieved from https://www.wired.co.uk/article/carbanak-gang-malware-arrest-cybercrime-bank-robbery-statistics

Catakoglu, O., Balduzzi, M., & Balzarotti, B. (2017). Attacks landscape in the dark side of the web. In *Proceedings of the Symposium on Applied Computing* (pp. 1739–1746). 3–7 April, Marrakech, Morocco. New York: ACM. doi: 10.1145/3019612.3019796

CBS News. (2017). *Behind the online community organizing protests against Trump*. Retrieved from https://www.cbsnews.com/video/behind-the-online-community-organizing-protests-against-trump/

Chahal, K. (2016). *Supporting victims of hate crime: A practitioner guide*. Policy Press.

Chau, M., & Xu, J. (2007). Mining communities and their relationships in blogs: A study of online hate groups. *International Journal of Human-Computer Studies 65*(1), 57–70. doi: 10.1016/j.ijhcs.2006.08.009

Chiles, T. H., & McMackin, J. F., (1996). Integrating variable risk preferences, trust, and transaction cost economics. *The Academy of Management Review 21*(1), 73–99.

Choo, K. K. R., & Smith, R. G. (2008). Criminal exploitation of online systems by organised crime groups. *Asian Journal of Criminology 3*(1), 37–59. doi: 10.1007/s11417-007-9035-y

Cleland, J., Anderson, C., & Aldridge-Deacon, J. (2017). Islamophobia, war and non-Muslims as victims: An analysis of online discourse on an English Defence League message board. *Ethnic and Racial Studies 41*(9), 1–17. doi: 10.1080/01419870.2017.1287927

Cole, J., Watkins, C., & Kleine, D. (2016). Health advice from Internet discussion forums: How bad is dangerous? *Journal of Medical Internet Research 18*(1). doi: 10.2196/jmir.5051

Corritore, C., Kracher, B., & Wiedenbeck, S. (2003). Online trust: Concepts, evolving themes, a model. *International Journal of Human Computer Studies 58*, 737–758. doi: 10.1016/S1071-5819(03)00041-7

D'Mello, G. (2018). *Indian Govt May Ban WhatsApp Use in Country, As It Is Terrorist's Favourite App for Messaging*. Indian Times. Retrieved from https://www.indiatimes.com/technology/news/indian-govt-may-ban-whatsapp-use-in-country-as-it-is-terrorist-s-favourite-app-for-messaging-347251.html

Engle, P. (2015, 21 November). *Inside the app that's become ISIS' biggest propaganda machine*. *Business Insider*. Retrieved from http://uk.businessinsider.com/telegram-isis-app-encrypted-propagandar-2015-11

European Union Agency for Law Enforcement Co-operation. (2014). *Internet Organised Crime Threat Assessment (iOCTA)*.

Falcone, R., Singh, M. P., & Tan, Y. H. (2001). *Trust in cyber-societies: Integrating the human and artificial perspectives*. New York: Springer.

FBI. (2015, 15 July). *Cybercriminal forum taken down, members arrested in 20 countries*. Retrieved from https://www.fbi.gov/news/stories/cyber-criminal-forum-taken-down

FBI. (2016). *Transnational organized crime*. Retrieved from https://www.fbi.gov/investigate/organized-crime.

Finckenauer, J. O., and Voronin, Y. A. (2001). *The threat of Russian organized crime (Vol. 2)*. Washington, DC: US Department of Justice, Office of Justice Programs, National Institute of Justice.

Frier, S. (2017, 27 January). Facebook groups, with 1 billion users, charts path to add more. *Bloomberg*. Retrieved from https://www.bloomberg.com/news/articles/2016-01-27/facebook-groups-with-1-billion-users-charts-path-to-add-more

Fuchs, C. (2012). Social media, riots, and revolutions. *Capital & Class 36*(3), 383–391. doi: 10.1177/0309816812453613

Gambetta, D. (2009). Signalling. In: P. Hedstrom & P. Bearman (Eds.), *The Oxford Handbook of Analytical Sociology* (pp. 168–94). New York: OUP. doi: 10.1093/oxfordhb/9780199215362.013.8

Gerbaudo, P. (2012). *Tweets and the streets: Social media and contemporary activism*. London: Pluto Press.

Glaser, J., Dixit, J., & Green, D. P. (2002). Studying hate crime with the Internet: What makes racists advocate racial violence? *Journal of Social Issues 58*(1), 177–193. doi: 10.1111/1540-4560.00255

Godson, R. (2003). Transnational crime, corruption, and security. In: M. E. Brown (Ed.), *Grave new world: Security challenges in the 21st century* (pp. 259–278). Washington DC: Georgetown University Press.

Green, D. P., McFalls, L. H., & Smith, J. K. (2001). Hate crime: An emergent agenda. *Annual Review of Sociology 27*, 479–504. doi: 10.1146/annurev.soc.27.1.479

Griffin, A. (2015). Paris attack: Anonymous launches biggest operations ever against ISIS. *The Independent*. Retrieved from http://www.independent.co.uk/life-style/gadgets-and-tech/news/paris-attacks-anonymous-launches-its-biggest-operation-ever-against-isis-promises-to-hunt-down-a6735811.html

Griffin, A. (2017). Anonymous tells supporters use tools given by them to attack Donald Trump. *The Independent*. Retrieved from http://www.independent.co.uk/life-style/gadgets-and-tech/news/anonymous-donald-trump-twitter-optrump-opdeatheaters-russia-dossier-information-a7530966.html

Hamill, J. (2017, 28 March). How terrorists use encrypted messaging apps to plot, recruit and attack. *New York Post*. Retrieved from http://nypost.com/2017/03/28/how-terrorists-use-encrypted-messaging-apps-to-plot-recruit-and-attack/

HM Treasury and Home Office. (2015). *UK national risk assessment of money laundering and terrorist financing*. Retrieved from https://www.gov.uk/government/publications/uk-national-risk-assessment-of-money-laundering-and-terrorist-financing

Hogg, M. A., & Williams, K. D. (2000). From I to we: Social identity and the collective self. *Group Dynamics: Theory, Research, and Practice 4*, 81. doi: 10.1037/1089-2699.4.1.81

Holt, T. J., & Lampke, E. (2010). Exploring stolen data markets online: Products and market forces. *Criminal Justice Studies 23*(1), 33–50. doi: 10.1080/14786011003634415

Holt, T. J., & Smirnova, O. (2014). *Examining the structure, organization, and processes of the international market for stolen data*. Washington, DC: US Department of Justice.

Holt, T. J., Smirnova, O., Chua, Y. T., & Copes, H. (2015). Examining the risk reduction strategies of actors in online criminal markets. *Global Crime 16*, 81–103. doi: 10.1080/17440572.2015.1013211

Holtz, P., Kronberger, N., & Wagner, W. (2012). Analyzing internet forums: A practical guide. *Journal of Media Psychology: Theories, Methods, and Applications 24*(2), 55–66. doi: 10.1027/1864-1105/a000062

Hunt, J. G., & Hill, J. W. (1969). The new look in motivation theory for organizational research. *Human Organization 28*(2), 100–109. doi: 10.17730/humo.28.2.98302j32233wptg7

Klausen, J. (2015). Tweeting the Jihad: Social media networks of Western foreign fighters in Syria and Iraq. *Studies in Conflict & Terrorism 38*(1), 1–22. doi: 10.1080/1057610X.2014.974948

Kowalski, R. M., Giumetti, G. W., Schroeder, A. N., & Lattanner, M. R. (2014). Bullying in the digital age: A critical review and meta-analysis of cyberbullying research among youth. *Psychological Bulletin 140*(4), 1073–1137. doi: 10.1037/a0035618

Kushner, D. (2014). The Masked Avengers: How Anonymous incited online vigilantism from Tunisia to Ferguson. *The New Yorker*. Retrieved from http://www.newyorker.com/magazine/2014/09/08/masked-avengers

Lacey, D., Salmon, P. M. (2015). It's dark in there: Using systems analysis to investigate trust and engagement in dark web forums. In: D. Harris (Ed.), *Engineering Psychology and Cognitive Ergonomics*. Cham: Springer. doi: 10.1007/978-3-319-20373-7_12

Lenhart, A., Ybarra, M., Zickuhr K., & Price-Feeney, M. (2016). *Online Harassment, Digital Abuse, and Cyberstalking in America*. New York: Data & Society Research Institute. Retrieved from https://www.datasociety.net/pubs/oh/Online_Harassment_2016.pdf

Leukfeldt, E. R., Kleemans, E. R., & Stol, W. P. (2016). A typology of cybercriminal networks: From low-tech all-rounders to high-tech specialists. *Crime, Law and Social Change 67*(1), 21–37. doi: 10.1007/s10611-016-9662-2

Leukfeldt, E. R., Kleemans, E. R., & Stol, W. P. (2017). Origin, growth, and criminal capabilities of cybercriminal networks. An international empirical analysis. *Crime, Law and Social Change 67*(1), 39–53. doi: 10.1007/s10611-016-9663-1

Leukfeldt, E. R., de Poot, C., Verhoeven, M., & Lavorgna, A. (2017). Cybercriminal networks. In: R. Leukfeldt (Ed.), *Research Agenda: The Human Factor in Cybercrime and Cybersecurity* (pp. 33–42). The Hague: Eleven International.

Longbottom, W. (2017, 21 January). *Protests in Washington after Trump inauguration: Tear gas and stun grenades*. SkyNews. Retrieved from http://news.sky.com/story/anti-trump-protesters-smash-windows-in-tense-scenes-before-inauguration-10735956

Lu, Y., Luo, X., Polgar, M., & Cao, Y. (2010). Social Network Analysis of a Criminal Hacker Community. *Journal of Computer Information Systems 51*(2), 31–41.

Lusthaus, J. (2012). Trust in the World of Cybercrime. *Global Crime 13*(2), 71–94. doi: 10.1080/17440572.2012.674183

Magdy, S. (2016). A safe space for terrorists. *British Journalism Review 27*(4), 23–28. doi: 10.1177/0956474816681736

Malenkovich, S. (2012, 7 December). What Motivates Cybercriminals? Money, Of Course. [blog post]. *Kaspersky Lab*. Retrieved from https://blog.kaspersky.com/what-motivates-cybercriminals-money-of-course/717/

Maslow, A. H. (1954). *Motivation and Personality*. New York: Harper and Row.

Mayer, R. C., Davis, J. H., & Schoorman, F. D. (1995). An integrative model of organizational trust. *Academy of Management Review 20*, 709–734. doi: 10.2307/258792

McCarthy, B., & Hagan, J., (2001). When crime pays: Capital, competence, and criminal success. *Social Forces 79*(3), 1035–1060.

McDevitt, J., Levin, J., & Bennett, S. (2002). Hate crime offenders: An expanded typology. *Journal of Social Issues 58*(2), 303–17. doi: 10.1111/1540-4560.00262

McGuire, M. (2012). *Organized Crime in the Digital Age*. London: John Grieve Centre for Policing and Security.

Metzger, M. (2017, 18 January). Update: Old fashioned DDoS attack planned to protest Trump's inauguration. *SC Media UK*. Retrieved from https://www.scmagazineuk.com/update-old-fashioned-ddos-attack-planned-to-protest-trumps-inauguration/article/632195/

Mitchell, K. J., Wolak, J., & Finkelhor, D. (2008). Are blogs putting youth at risk for online sexual solicitation or harassment? *Child Abuse & Neglect 32*(2), 277–294. doi: 10.1016/j.chiabu.2007.04.015

Motoyama, M., McCoy, D., Levchenko, K., Savage, S., & Voelker, G. M. (2013). An analysis of underground forums. In *Proceedings of the 2011 ACM SIGCOMM Conference on Internet Measurement* (pp. 71–79). 2–4 November, Berlin, Germany. New York: ACM. doi: 10.1145/2068816.2068824

National Cyber Security Centre. (2017). Cyber crime: Understanding the online business model. Retrieved from https://www.ncsc.gov.uk/news/ncsc-publishes-new-report-criminal-online-activity

Norton, Q. (2012, 3 July). How Anonymous Picks Targets, Launches Attacks, and Takes Powerful Organizations Down. *Wired*. Retrieved from https://www.wired.com/2012/07/ff_anonymous/

Nouh, M., & Nurse, J. R. C. (2015). Identifying key-players in online activist groups on the Facebook Social Network. In *Proceedings of the International Conference on Data Mining Workshop (ICDMW)* (pp. 969–978). 14–17 November, Atlantic City, New Jersey. Sandy Hook, NY: Curran Associates. doi: 10.1109/ICDMW.2015.88

Nouh, M., Nurse, J. R. C., & Goldsmith, M. (2016). Towards designing a multipurpose cyber-crime intelligence framework. In *Proceedings of the European Intelligence and Security Informatics Conference (EISIC)* (pp. 60–67). 17–19 August, Uppsala, Sweden. Sandy Hook, NY: Curran Associates. doi: 10.1109/EISIC.2016.018

Nurse, J. R. C., Buckley, O., Legg, P. A., Goldsmith, M., Creese, S., Wright, G. R., & Whitty, M., (2014). Understanding insider threat: A framework for characterising attacks. In *Proceedings of the IEEE Security and Privacy Workshops (SPW)* (pp. 214–228). 17–18 May, San Jose, California. doi: 10.1109/SPW.2014.38

Nurse, J. R. C., Rahman, S. S., Creese, S., Goldsmith, M., & Lamberts, K. (2011). *Information quality and trustworthiness: A topical state-of-the-art review*. In *Proceedings of the International Conference on Computer Applications and Network Security (ICCANS)* (pp. 492–500). 27–29 May, Maldives. Sandy Hook, NY: Curran Associates.

Odinot, G., Verhoeven, M.A., Pool, R. L. D., & De Poot, C. J. (2016). *Cybercrime, organised crime and organised cybercrime in the Netherlands: Empirical findings and implications for law enforcement*. The Hague: WODC.

Oksanen, A., & Keipi, T. (2013). Young people as victims of crime on the internet: A population-based study in Finland. *Vulnerable Children and Youth Studies 8*(4), 298–309. doi: 10.1080/17450128.2012.752119

Olson, P. (2013). *We are Anonymous*. New York: Random House.

Peckham, M. (2012, 20 January). 10 Sites Skewered by Anonymous, Including FBI, DOJ, U.S. Copyright Office. *Time*. Retrieved from http://techland.time.com/2012/01/20/10-sites-skewered-by-anonymous-including-fbi-doj-u-s-copyright-office/

Perry, B., & Olsson, P. (2009). Cyberhate: The globalisation of hate. *Information & Communications Technology Law 18*(2), 185–199. doi: 10.1080/13600830902814984

Rayner, G. (2017). WhatsApp accused of giving terrorists "a secret place to hide" as it refuses to hand over London attacker's messages. *The Telegraph*. Retrieved from http://www.telegraph.co.uk/news/2017/03/26/home-secretary-amber-rudd-whatsapp-gives-terrorists-place-hide/

Reicher, Stephen. (2001). *The Psychology of Crowd Dynamics*. In M. A. Hogg & S. Tindale (Eds.), *Blackwell Handbook of Social Psychology: Group Processes* (pp. 182–208). Malden, MA: Blackwell Publishers.

Richardson, R., (2007). *CSI Survey 2007: The 12th Annual Computer Crime and Security Survey*. San Francisco, CA: Computer Security Institute.

Rieker, P. (1997). *Ethnozentrismus bei jungen Mannern*. Weinheim: Juventa.

Robins-Early, N. (2017, 24 May). How Telegram became the app of choice for ISIS. *The Huffington Post*. Retrieved from http://www.huffingtonpost.co.uk/entry/isis-telegram-app_us_59259254e4b0ec129d3136d5

Rodgers, L. (2007, 20 December). Smashing the criminal's e-bazaar. *BBC News Online*. Retrieved from http://news.bbc.co.uk/1/hi/uk/7084592.stm

Rogers, M. K. (2006). A Two-dimensional circumplex approach to the development of a hacker taxonomy. *Digital Investigations* 3(2), 97–102. doi: 10.1016/j.diin.2006.03.001

Schwartz, M. J. (2016). Anonymous threatens bank DDoS disruptions. [blog post]. Bankinfosecurity.com. Retrieved from http://www.bankinfosecurity.com/anonymous-threatens-bank-ddos-disruptions-a-9085.

Shinder, D. (2010, 19 July). *Profiling and categorizing cybercriminals.* TechRepublic. [blog post]. Retrieved from http://www.techrepublic.com/blog/security/profiling-and-categorizing-cybercriminals/4069

Stott, C., Drury, J., & Reicher, S. (2016). On the role of a social identity analysis in articulating structure and collective action: The 2011 riots in Tottenham and Hackney. *The British Journal of Criminology* 57(4), 964–981. doi: 10.1093/bjc/azw036

Thibaut, J., & Kelley, H. H. (1959). *The Social Psychology of Groups.* New York: Wiley.

Thornton-Trump, I. (2018). Malicious attacks and actors: An examination of the modern cyber criminal. *EDPACS* 57(1), 17–23, doi: 10.1080/07366981.2018.1432180.

TrendMicro Inc. (2016, 3 May). *Dark Motives Online: An Analysis of Overlapping Technologies Used by Cybercriminals and Terrorist Organizations.* Retrieved from https://www.trendmicro.com/vinfo/us/security/news/cybercrime-and-digital-threats/overlapping-technologies-cybercriminals-and-terrorist-organizations

United Nations Office on Drugs and Crime. (2002). *Global Programme Against Transnational Organized Crime.* Vienna, Austria. Retrieved from http://www.unodc.org/pdf/crime/publications/Pilot_survey.pdf

Van Der Broek, T. C., Van der Laan, A. M., & Weijters, G. (2016). Bedreiging via internet: Verschillen in risicofactoren tussen jongeren die online en offline bedreigen. *Panopticon, tijdschrift voor strafrecht, criminologie en forensisch welzijnswerk* 37(2), 90–105.

Vromen, A., Xenos, M. A., & Loader, B. (2015). Young people, social media, and connective action: From organisational maintenance to everyday political talk. *Journal of Youth Studies* 18(1), 80–100. doi: 10.1080/13676261.2014.933198

Wall, D. (2007). *Cybercrime: The transformation of crime in the information age.* Cambridge: Polity.

Wall, D. (2015). Dis-organised crime: Towards a distributed model of the organization of cybercrime. *The European Review of Organised Crime* 2(2), 71–90.

Wasserman, S., & Faust, K. (1994). *Social network analysis: Methods and applications.* Cambridge: CUP.

WhatsApp. (2017). *WhatsApp Encryption Overview.* Retrieve from https://www.whatsapp.com/security/WhatsApp-Security-Whitepaper.pdf.

Williams, M., Axon, L., Nurse, J. R. C., & Creese, S. (2016). Future scenarios and challenges for security and privacy. In *Proceedings of the IEEE 2nd International Forum on Research and Technologies for Society and Industry: Leveraging a better tomorrow (RTSI)* (pp. 1–6). 7–9 September, Bologna, Italy. Red Hook, NY: Curran Associates. doi: 10.1109/RTSI.2016.7740625

Woolf, N. (2016, 24 March). Anti-Trump campaign sparks civil war among Anonymous hackers. *The Guardian.* Retrieved from https://www.theguardian.com/technology/2016/mar/24/anti-donald-trump-campaign-anonymous-hackers-debate-election-2016

Yip, M., Shadbolt, N., & Webber, C. (2013). Why forums? An empirical analysis into the facilitating factors of carding forums. In *Proceedings of the 5th Annual ACM Web Science Conference* (pp. 453–462). 2–4 May, Paris, France. New York: ACM. doi: 10.1145/2464464.2464524

Yip, M., Webber, C., & Shadbolt, N. (2013). Trust among cybercriminals? Carding forums, uncertainty and implications for policing. *Policing & Society* 23(4), 516–539. doi: 10.1080/10439463.2013.780227

Yunus, M. M., & Salehi, H. (2012). The effectiveness of Facebook groups on teaching and improving writing: Students' perceptions. *Journal of Education and Information Technologies* 1(6), 87–96.

Zorabedian, J. (2014, 26 August). "Lizard Squad" hackers force PSN offline and Sony exec from the sky. *NakedSecurity*. Retrieved from https://nakedsecurity.sophos.com/2014/08/26/lizard-squad-hackers-force-psn-offline-and-sony-exec-from-the-sky/

INDEX